HOLT
SOCIAL STUDIES

Creation and Development of North Carolina in United States History

William Deverell
Deborah Gray White

HOLT, RINEHART AND WINSTON
A Harcourt Education Company
Orlando • Austin • New York • San Diego • London

For acknowledgments, see page R141, which is an extension of the copyright page.

Printed in the United States of America

ISBN-13: 978-0-03-094468-0

ISBN 0-03-094468-6

1 2 3 4 5 6 7 8 9 048 10 09 08 07

Authors

William Deverell

William Deverell is Professor of History at the University of Southern California. He is the author of *Railroad Crossing: Californians and the Railroad, 1850-1910* and *Whitewashed Adobe: The Rise of Los Angeles and the Remaking of the Mexican Past.* He is the editor of the *Blackwell Companion to the American West.* With Greg Hise, he co-authored *Eden by Design: The 1930 Olmsted-Bartholomew Plan for the Los Angeles Region* and co-edited *Land of Sunshine: The Environmental History of Metropolitan Los Angeles*. He is the former chairman of the California Council for the Humanities.

Deborah Gray White

Deborah Gray White, a former New York City school teacher, is Distinguished Professor of History at Rutgers University in New Brunswick, New Jersey. A specialist in American history and the history of African Americans, she is the author of several books including: *Ar'n't I A Woman? Female Slaves in the Plantation South; Too Heavy a Load: Black Women in Defense of Themselves, 1894-1994*; and *Let My People Go, African Americans 1804-1860*, Volume 4 in the *Young Oxford History of African Americans*.

Program Consultants

General Editor

Frances Marie Gipson
Secondary Literacy
Los Angeles Unified School District
Los Angeles, California

In her current position, Frances Gipson guides reform work for secondary instruction and supports its implementation. She has designed curriculum at the district, state, and national levels. Her leadership of a coaching collaborative with Subject Matter Projects of the University of California at Los Angeles evolved from her commitment to rigorous instruction and to meeting the needs of diverse learners.

Senior Literature and Writing Specialist

Carol Jago
English Department Chairperson
Santa Monica High School
Santa Monica, California

An English teacher at the middle and high school levels for 26 years, Carol Jago also directs the reading and literature project at UCLA and writes a weekly education column for the Los Angeles Times. She has been published in numerous professional journals and has authored several books, including *Cohesive Writing: Why Concept is Not Enough* (Boynton/Cook, 2002).

Contributing Author

Kylene Beers, Ed.D.
Senior Reading Researcher
School Development Program
Yale University
New Haven, Connecticut

A former middle school teacher, Dr. Beers has turned her commitment to helping struggling readers into the major focus of her research, writing, speaking, and teaching. She is the current editor of the National Council of Teachers of English literacy journal *Voices from the Middle* and the author of *When Kids Can't Read: What Teachers Can Do* (Heinemann, 2002).

North Carolina Program Advisors

Rebecca N. Finger
K-12 Social Studies Curriculum Specialist
Charlotte-Mecklenburg Schools, North Carolina

Susan Hirsch
Social Studies Department Chair
East Wake High School
Wendell, North Carolina

Melissa Hockaday
Grade 7 Team Leader
East Garner Middle School
Garner, North Carolina

Jerri Jeffries
Grade 8 Team Leader
Lufkin Road Middle School
Apex, North Carolina

Karen Kimrey
Grade 8 Team Leader
Social Studies Department Chair
Heritage Middle School
Wake Forest, North Carolina

Scott King-Owen
Instructional Specialist for Social Studies and Foreign Languages, K–12
New Hanover Public Schools
Wilmington, North Carolina

Channing Kirkpatrick
Social Studies Department Chair
Independence High School
Charlotte, North Carolina

Marion O'Quinn
Social Studies Department Chair
Cary High School
Cary, North Carolina

Mary Propes
Social Studies Department Chair
Leesville Road High School
Raleigh, North Carolina

Wyndy Rorie
Social Studies Department Chair
Providence High School
Charlotte, North Carolina

David W. Wiggs
Social Studies Department Chair
Myers Park High School
Charlotte, North Carolina

Consultants

Martha H. Ball, M.A.
Religion Consultant
Utah 3Rs Project Director
Utah State Office of Education
Salt Lake City, Utah

John Ferguson, M.T.S., J.D.
Senior Religion Consultant
Assistant Professor
Political Science/Criminal Justice
Howard Payne University
Brownwood, Texas

J. Frank Malaret
Senior Consultant
Dean, Downtown and West Sacramento Outreach Centers
Sacramento City College
Sacramento, California

Kimberly A. Plummer, M.A.
Senior Consultant
History-Social Science Educator/Advisor
Holt, Rinehart & Winston

Galit Reichlin
Associate Director
Middle Eastern Affairs and International Analysis
Anti-Defamation League
(Reviewed Chapter 30 for Middle East content)

Andrés Reséndez, Ph.D.
Senior Consultant,
Assistant Professor
Department of History
University of California at Davis
Davis, California

Academic Reviewers

Anne C. Bailey, Ph.D.
Spelman College
Atlanta, Georgia

Albert Camarillo, Ph.D.
Department of History
Stanford University

Larry Conyers, Ph.D.
Department of Anthropology
University of Denver

Willard Gatewood, Ph.D.
Emeritus Alumni Distinguished Professor, Department of History
University of Arkansas

Christopher Hendricks, Ph.D.
Department of History
Armstrong Atlantic State University
Savannah, Georgia

Skip Hyser, Ph.D.
Department of History
James Madison University
Harrisonburg, Virginia

Yasuhide Kawashima
Department of History
University of Texas at El Paso

Brenda E. Stevenson, Ph.D.
Department of History
UCLA
Los Angeles, California

David Switzer, Ph.D.
Department of Social Studies
Plymouth State University
Plymouth, New Hampshire

Jessica Wang, Ph.D.
Department of History
UCLA
Los Angeles, California

Nan Woodruff, Ph.D
Department of History
Pennsylvania State University

Craig Yirush, Ph.D.
Department of History
UCLA
Los Angeles, California

Educational Reviewers

Henry Assetto
Twin Valley High School
Elverson, Pennsylvania

Steve Bissette
Middle Creek High School
Apex, North Carolina

Stacy Byrd
Erwin Middle School
Salisbury, North Carolina

Julie Chan, Ed.D.
Director, Literacy Instruction
Newport-Mesa Unified School District
Costa Mesa, California

Kermit Cummings
Cockeysville Middle School
Baltimore County Public Schools
Baltimore, Maryland

Sandra Eades
Ridgely Middle School
Lutherville, Maryland

Ed Felten
Coopersville Public School District
Coopersville, Michigan

Tim Gearhart
Daniel Lewis Middle School
Paso Robles, California

Chris Hollifield
Harris Middle School
Spruce Pine, North Carolina

Joseph P. Macary
Supervisor of Social Studies
Waterbury Public Schools
Waterbury, Connecticut

Carol Eiler Moore
Dundalk Middle School
Dundalk, Maryland

Tina Nelson
Baltimore County Public School District
Baltimore, Maryland

Linda Nore
Carmel Middle School
Charlotte, North Carolina

Anthony Powell
Edmund W. Miles Middle School
Amityville, New York

Linda Prior
Floyd T. Binns Middle School
Culpeper County, Virginia

Wendy Schanberger
Hereford Middle School
Monkton, Maryland

Sue A. Shinn
Culpeper Middle School
Culpeper, Virginia

Kathleen Torquata
Lincoln Middle School
Berwyn, Illinois

Emily Werner
Belmont Middle School
Belmont, North Carolina

Contents

Cherokee mask

Mayan pyramids

Philadelphia's Independence Hall

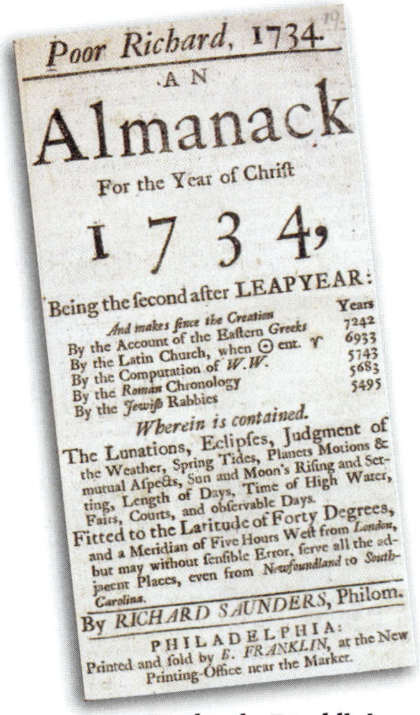

Benjamin Franklin's almanac

Cannon at Fort Niagara, New York

Andrew Jackson

UNIT 4 The Nation Expands (1790–1860) 378

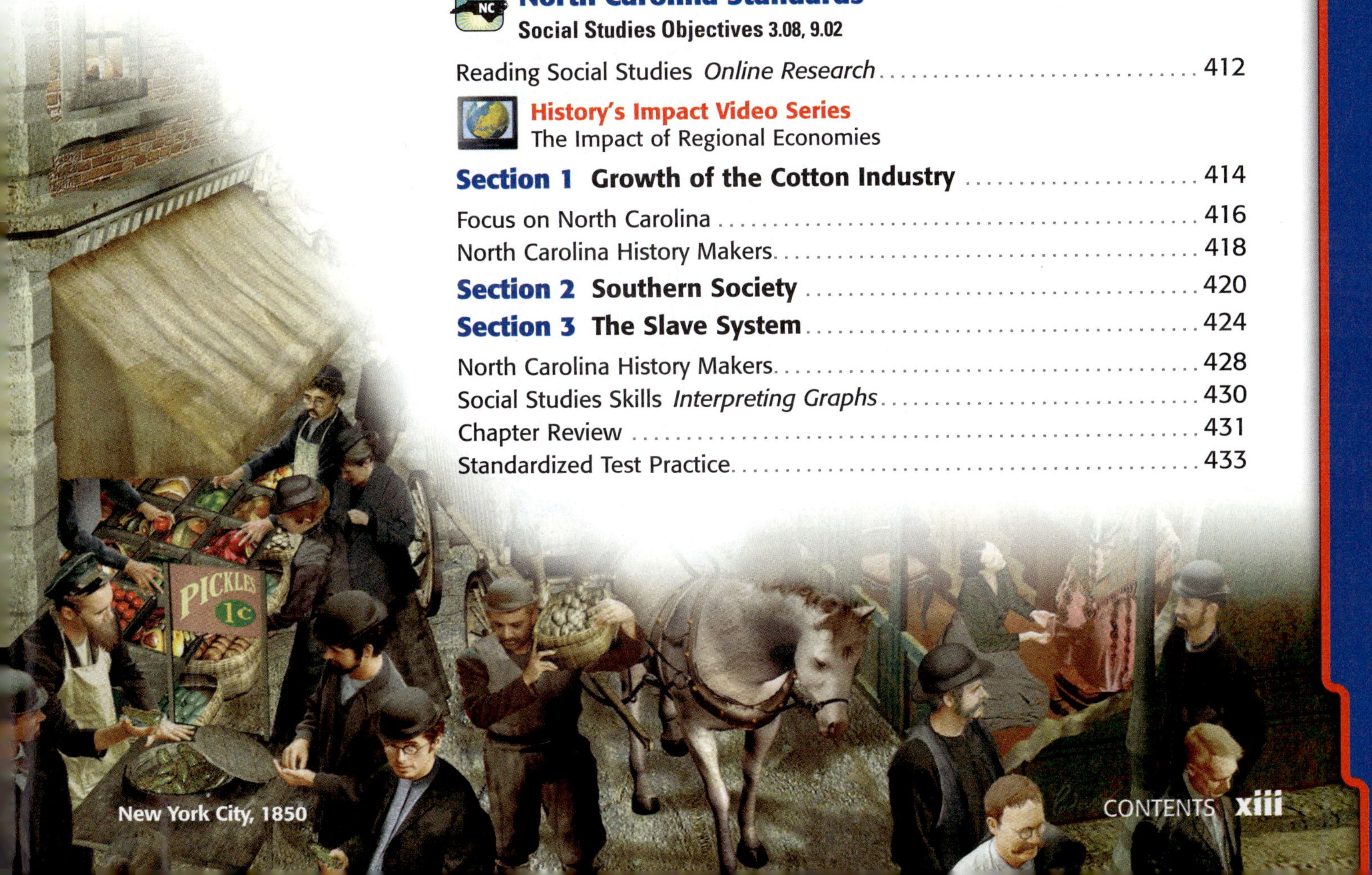

New York City, 1850

Deadwood, South Dakota

Statue of Liberty

UNIT 7 The Beginning of Modern America (1867–1920)

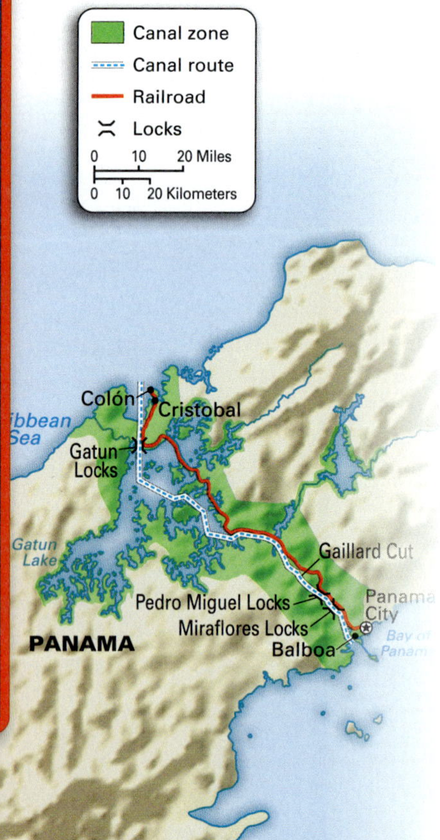

Theodore Roosevelt

We Can Do It!

Ford automobile factory

STOP THE BOMBING
OUT NOW

SUPPORT OUR BOYS IN VIETNAM

March on Washington

CHAPTER 31 America Looks to the Future

Features

History Close-up

See how people lived and how places looked in the past by taking a close-up view of history.

BIOGRAPHIES

Meet the people who have influenced history and learn about their lives.

Eleanor Roosevelt

History and **Geography**

Explore the relationships between history and geography.

The Impact Today

Understand how events from the past have had an impact on our world today.

THE IMPACT TODAY, continued

LINKING TO TODAY

Link people and events from the past to the world you live in today.

QUICK FACTS

Examine key facts and concepts quickly and easily with graphics.

Charts, Graphs, and Tables

Analyze information presented visually to learn more about history.

CHARTS

INFOGRAPHICS

Analyze and interpret information from graphics.

INFOGRAPHICS, continued

TIME LINES

See how key events are related in time.

Points of View

See how different people have interpreted historical issues in different ways.

Historic Documents

Examine key documents that have shaped U.S. history.

Literature in History

Learn about the beliefs and experiences of people who lived in other times and places through literature pieces.

Charlotte bank buildings

Social Studies Skills

Learn, practice, and apply the skills you need to study and analyze history.

Reading Social Studies

Learn and practice skills that will help you read your social studies lesson.

Focus on Writing and Speaking

Use writing to study and reflect on the events and people who made history.

Writing Workshop

Learn to write about history.

Political Cartoons

Interpret political cartoons to learn about U.S. history.

Supreme Court Decisions

Study the impact of Supreme court decisions on U.S. history.

Interdisciplinary Connections

Learn history through connections to other disciplines.

Primary Sources

Read and analyze the exact words of important people and documents as related to the study of U.S. history.

Primary Source

NEWSPAPER ARTICLE

The Boston Massacre

An account of the Boston Massacre appeared in the Boston Gazette and Country Journal *soon after the event.*

"The People were immediately alarmed with the Report of this horrid Massacre, the Bells were set a Ringing, and great Numbers soon assembled at the Place where this tragical Scene had been acted; their Feelings may be better conceived than expressed; and while some were taking Care of the Dead and Wounded, the Rest were in Consultation what to do in these dreadful Circumstances.

But so little intimidated were they [Bostonians], notwithstanding their being within a few Yards of the Main Guard, and seeing the 29th Regiment under Arms, and drawn up in King street; that they kept their Station and appeared, as an Officer of Rank expressed it, ready to run upon the very Muzzles of their Muskets."

—*Boston Gazette and Country Journal,* March 12, 1770

ANALYSIS SKILL **ANALYZING PRIMARY SOURCES**

Why do you think the people described were not intimidated by the soldiers?

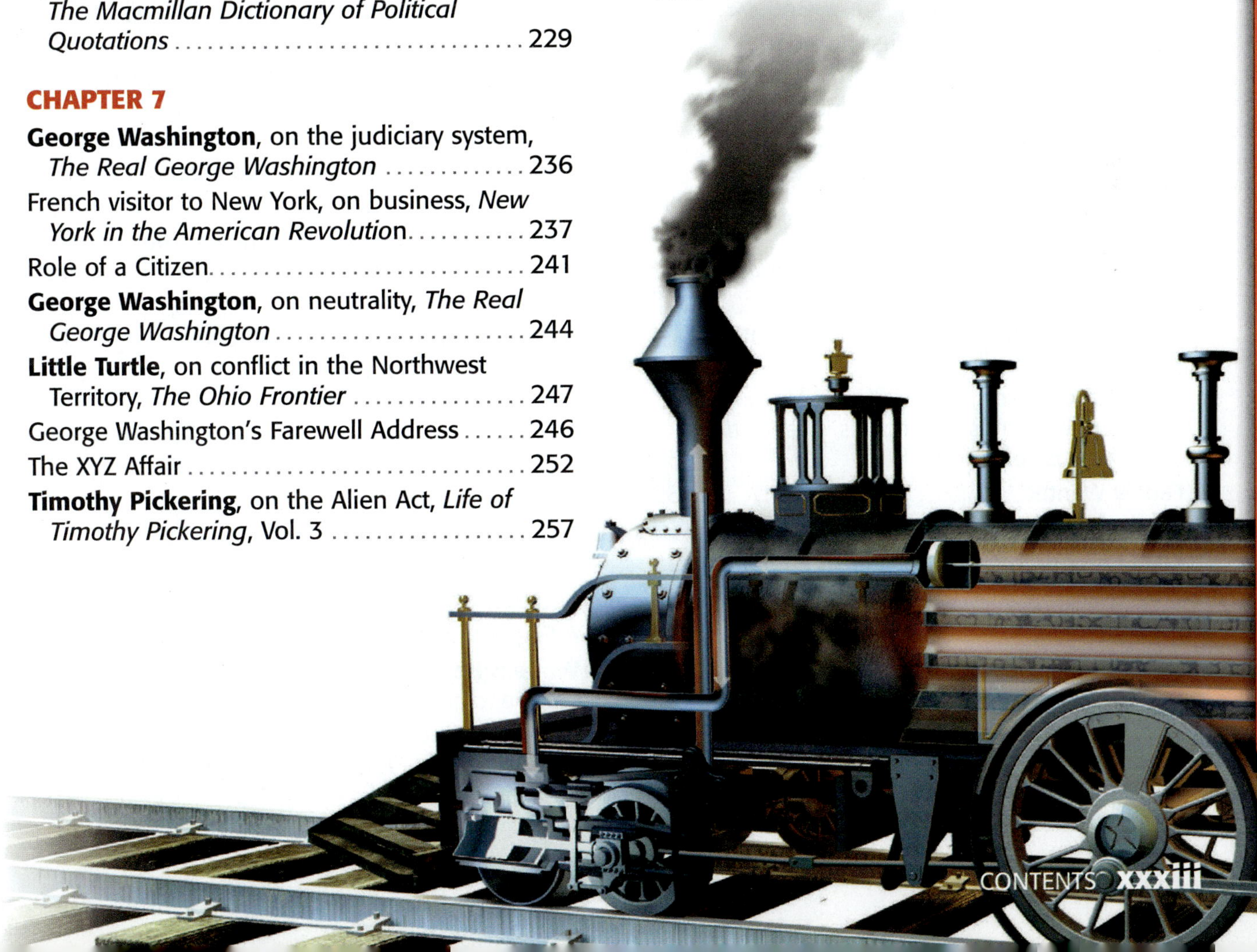

Great Smoky Mountains

CHAPTER 18

CHAPTER 19

CHAPTER 20

CHAPTER 21

CHAPTER 22

CHAPTER 23

CHAPTER 24

CHAPTER 25

Cesar Chavez

Basket weaver on the Qualla Boundary

Maps

Interpret maps to see where important events happened and analyze how geography has influenced history.

Interactive Maps

Program Maps

North Carolina Standard Course of Study: Social Studies

What is the North Carolina Standard Course of Study?

The North Carolina State Board of Education and Department of Public Instruction have organized the teaching of social studies by creating Competency Goals with distinct Objectives, or "standards," that every student should master by the end of eighth grade. The goals and objectives combine content knowledge of United States and North Carolina state history with skills associated with active citizenship. These goals are simply the things you are expected to know, understand, and be able to do as a result of your education.

In this section you will find the Competency Goals that have been approved by the State Board of Education. All public-school students are expected to learn the material covered by these standards. You might notice that some of the subjects in the standards are familiar to you. This course is meant to build on the skills and knowledge you already have. It will also help build a foundation for the more advanced studies you will begin in high school.

How can North Carolina Competency Goals and Objectives help me?

These goals are helpful because they give you a clear picture of what you will be expected to learn. These goals can help you to focus on key material as you work through the school year. You can think of the goals and objectives as a kind of checklist—and you can even check off important subjects and skills as you master them. Another advantage of becoming familiar with the goals is that teachers often base lesson plans and tests on the goals. The standards can give you a preview of what to expect in this course.

Eighth Grade: North Carolina: Creation and Development of the State

Eighth-grade students examine the roles of people, events, and issues in North Carolina history that have contributed to the unique character of the state today. The time frame for this course emphasizes colonial to contemporary history. The organization is primarily chronological, and reference is made to the key national phenomena that impacted North Carolina throughout these periods. Although the value and methods of historical study as a way of learning about people are stressed, key concepts of geography, civics, and economics are incorporated throughout the course for a fuller understanding of the significance of the people, events, and issues. Inherent to the study of North Carolina history is a continuing examination of local, state, and national government structures.

COMPETENCY GOAL 1 The learner will analyze important geographic, political, economic, and social aspects of life in the region prior to the Revolutionary Period.

OBJECTIVES

1.01 Assess the impact of geography on the settlement and developing economy of the Carolina colony.
1.02 Identify and describe American Indians who inhabited the regions that became Carolina and assess their impact on the colony.
1.03 Compare and contrast the relative importance of differing economic, geographic, religious, and political motives for European exploration.
1.04 Evaluate the impact of the Columbian Exchange on the cultures of American Indians, Europeans, and Africans.
1.05 Describe the factors that led to the founding and settlement of the American colonies including religious persecution, economic opportunity, adventure, and forced migration.
1.06 Identify geographic and political reasons for the creation of a distinct North Carolina colony and evaluate the effects on the government and economics of the colony.
1.07 Describe the roles and contributions of diverse groups, such as American Indians, African Americans, European immigrants, landed gentry, tradesmen, and small farmers to everyday life in colonial North Carolina, and compare them to the other colonies.

COMPETENCY GOAL 2 The learner will trace the causes and effects of the Revolutionary War, and assess the impact of major events, problems, and personalities during the Constitutional Period in North Carolina and the new nation.

OBJECTIVES

2.01 Trace the events leading up to the Revolutionary War and evaluate their relative significance in the onset of hostilities.
2.02 Describe the contributions of key North Carolina and national personalities from the Revolutionary War era and assess their influence on the outcome of the war.
2.03 Examine the role of North Carolina in the Revolutionary War.
2.04 Examine the reasons for the colonists' victory over the British, and evaluate the impact of military successes and failures, the role of foreign interventions, and on-going political and economic domestic issues.
2.05 Describe the impact of documents such as the Mecklenburg Resolves, the Halifax Resolves, the Albany Plan of Union, the Declaration of Independence, the State Constitution of 1776, the Articles of Confederation, the United States Constitution, and the Bill of Rights on the formation of the state and national governments.

COMPETENCY GOAL 3 The learner will identify key events and evaluate the impact of reform and expansion in North Carolina during the first half of the 19th century.

OBJECTIVES

3.01 Describe the causes of the War of 1812 and analyze the impact of the war on North Carolina and the nation.
3.02 Investigate the conditions that led to North Carolina's economic, political, and social decline during this period and assess the implications for the future development of the state.
3.03 Identify and evaluate the impact of individual reformers and groups and assess the effectiveness of their programs.
3.04 Describe the development of the institution of slavery in the State and nation, and assess its impact on the economic, social, and political conditions.
3.05 Compare and contrast different perspectives among North Carolinians on the national policy of Removal and Resettlement of American Indian populations.
3.06 Describe and evaluate the geographic, economic, and social implications of the North Carolina Gold Rush.
3.07 Explain the reasons for the creation of a new State Constitution in 1835, and describe its impact on religious groups, African Americans, and American Indians.
3.08 Examine the impact of national events such as the Louisiana Purchase, the Lewis and Clark Expedition, the War with Mexico, the California Gold Rush, and technological advances on North Carolina.

COMPETENCY GOAL 4 The learner will examine the causes, course, and character of the Civil War and Reconstruction, and their impact on North Carolina and the nation.

OBJECTIVES

4.01 Identify and analyze the significance of the causes of secession from the Union, and compare reactions in North Carolina to reactions in other regions of the nation.
4.02 Describe the political and military developments of the Civil War and analyze their effect on the outcome of the war.
4.03 Assess North Carolina's role in the Civil War and analyze the social and economic impact of the war on the state.

4.04 Evaluate the importance of the roles played by individuals at the state and national levels during the Civil War and Reconstruction Period.

4.05 Analyze the political, economic, and social impact of Reconstruction on the state and identify the reasons why Reconstruction came to an end.

COMPETENCY GOAL 5 The learner will evaluate the impact of political, economic, social, and technological changes on life in North Carolina from 1870 to 1930.

OBJECTIVES

5.01 Identify the role played by the agriculture, textile, tobacco, and furniture industries in North Carolina, and analyze their importance in the economic development of the state.

5.02 Examine the changing role of educational, religious, and social institutions in the state and analyze their impact.

5.03 Describe the social, economic, and political impact of migration on North Carolina.

5.04 Identify technological advances, and evaluate their influence on the quality of life in North Carolina.

5.05 Assess the influence of the political, legal, and social movements on the political system and life in North Carolina.

5.06 Describe North Carolina's reaction to the increasing United States involvement in world affairs including participation in World War I, and evaluate the impact on the state's economy.

COMPETENCY GOAL 6 The learner will analyze the immediate and long-term effects of the Great Depression and World War II on North Carolina.

OBJECTIVES

6.01 Identify the causes and effects of the Great Depression and analyze the impact of New Deal policies on Depression Era life in North Carolina.

6.02 Describe the significance of major events and military engagements associated with World War II and evaluate the impact of the war on North Carolina.

6.03 Examine the significance of key ideas and individuals associated with World War II.

6.04 Assess the impact of World War II on the economic, political, social, and military roles of different groups in North Carolina including women and minorities.

COMPETENCY GOAL 7 The learner will analyze changes in North Carolina during the postwar period to the 1970's.

OBJECTIVES

7.01 Analyze the extent and significance of economic changes in North Carolina.

7.02 Evaluate the importance of social changes to different groups in North Carolina.

7.03 Assess the influence of technological advances on economic development and daily life.

7.04 Compare and contrast the various political viewpoints surrounding issues of the post World War II era.

7.05 Evaluate the major changes and events that have affected the roles of local, state, and national governments.

COMPETENCY GOAL 8 The learner will evaluate the impact of demographic, economic, technological, social, and political developments in North Carolina since the 1970's.

OBJECTIVES

8.01 Describe the changing demographics in North Carolina and analyze their significance for North Carolina's society and economy.

8.02 List economic and technological advances occurring in North Carolina since 1970, and assess their influence on North Carolina's role in the nation and the world.

8.03 Describe the impact of state and national issues on the political climate of North Carolina.

8.04 Assess the importance of regional diversity on the development of economic, social, and political institutions in North Carolina.

COMPETENCY GOAL 9 The learner will explore examples of and opportunities for active citizenship, past and present, at the local and state levels.

OBJECTIVES

9.01 Describe contemporary political, economic, and social issues at the state and local levels and evaluate their impact on the community.

9.02 Identify past and present state and local leaders from diverse cultural backgrounds and assess their influence in effecting change.

9.03 Describe opportunities for and benefits of civic participation.

At-Home Goals and Objectives Practice

How does Holt *Creation and Development of North Carolina in United States History* help me practice the state goals and objectives?

Holt *Creation and Development of North Carolina in United States History* provides complete coverage of the North Carolina Goals and Objectives for Eighth Grade Social Studies. To help you use your textbook to learn and practice the standards, use the at-home practice tests for each week.

How can I use the at-home practice tests?

- Each week has a practice test. You will see that each week's test focuses on one of the Competency Goals from the North Carolina Standard Course of Study.
- As you study the book with your class, ask yourself the questions on the practice test.
- There is one question for each day of the week. Each of these questions addresses one of the Objectives that goes with that week's Competency Goal. By the time you finish the week, you will have answered questions related to all Objectives.
- If you have trouble answering the question, look at the reference to the section of the chapter where you can read the answer.
- Check yourself with the Answer Key at the back of this section.

There are 29 weeks of practice questions. Each week has one question for each day of the week.

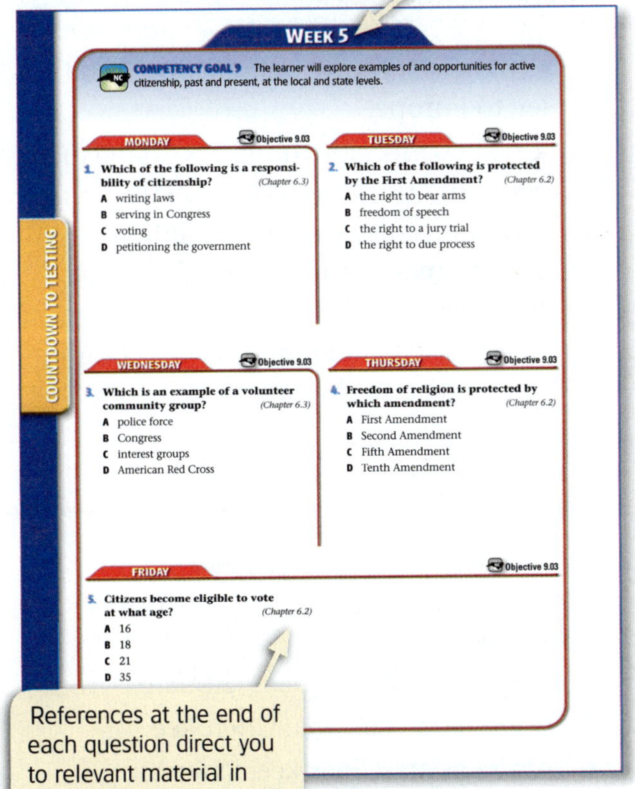
WEEK 5

COMPETENCY GOAL 9 The learner will explore examples of and opportunities for active citizenship, past and present, at the local and state levels.

COUNTDOWN TO TESTING

MONDAY Objective 9.03

1. Which of the following is a responsibility of citizenship? (Chapter 6.3)
A writing laws
B serving in Congress
C voting
D petitioning the government

TUESDAY Objective 9.03

2. Which of the following is protected by the First Amendment? (Chapter 6.2)
A the right to bear arms
B freedom of speech
C the right to a jury trial
D the right to due process

WEDNESDAY Objective 9.03

3. Which is an example of a volunteer community group? (Chapter 6.3)
A police force
B Congress
C interest groups
D American Red Cross

THURSDAY Objective 9.03

4. Freedom of religion is protected by which amendment? (Chapter 6.2)
A First Amendment
B Second Amendment
C Fifth Amendment
D Tenth Amendment

FRIDAY Objective 9.03

5. Citizens become eligible to vote at what age? (Chapter 6.2)
A 16
B 18
C 21
D 35

References at the end of each question direct you to relevant material in your textbook.

WEEK 1

COMPETENCY GOAL 1 The learner will analyze important geographic, political, economic, and social aspects of life in the region prior to the Revolutionary Period.

COUNTDOWN TO TESTING

MONDAY

Objective 1.03

1. Which of the following was a main reason for European exploration? *(Chapter 5.3)*

A to spread democracy
B to find new people
C to find the Americas
D to find new trade routes

TUESDAY

Objective 1.02

2. Which of the following Native American groups made their home in North Carolina? *(Chapter 1.2)*

A Tuscarora
B Seminole
C Iroquois
D Pawnee

WEDNESDAY

Objective 1.04

3. The Columbian Exchange is best described as which of the following? *(Chapter 2.2)*

A Explorers shipped stolen wheat and barley to Europe.
B A successful trade route was established between Europe and the Americas.
C Columbus discovered new animals in the Americas and wrote to Europe about them.
D New plants and animals were brought to Europe and the Americas.

THURSDAY

Objective 1.03

4. Which of the following did Columbus hope to find? *(Chapter 2.2)*

A a sea route to India
B the Americas
C the Northwest Passage
D a sea route around the globe

FRIDAY

Objective 1.04

5. Which three language groups did most North Carolina Native Americans use? *(Chapter 1.2)*

A Iroquoian, Algonquian, Siouan
B Iroquoian, Catawba, Cherokee
C Algonquian, Cherokee, Chowan
D Cherokee, Hatteras, Siouan

WEEK 2

COMPETENCY GOAL 1 The learner will analyze important geographic, political, economic, and social aspects of life in the region prior to the Revolutionary Period.

MONDAY
Objective 1.01

1. Colonial North Carolina's economy was hurt by a lack of which of the following? *(Chapter 3.1)*

A tobacco farms
B slaves
C a deepwater port
D cash crops

TUESDAY
Objective 1.05

2. Maryland was first settled by members of which religion? *(Chapter 3.3)*

A Catholicism
B Protestantism
C Puritanism
D Quakerism

WEDNESDAY
Objective 1.06

3. Which of the following made the Carolina colony difficult to govern? *(Chapter 3.1)*

A Colonists were of different religious groups.
B Settlements were far apart.
C Ships could not land in North Carolina.
D Pirates formed rebellions against the governors.

THURSDAY
Objective 1.07

4. Native Americans helped the colonists in which of the following ways? *(Chapter 3.4)*

A They worked on colonists' plantations.
B They sold their land interests to the Crown.
C They traded with colonists.
D They supported the governors.

FRIDAY
Objective 1.07

5. What did different cultures contribute to life in colonial North Carolina? *(Chapter 3.4)*

A They brought new plants and animals.
B They brought new ideas of democracy.
C They brought a mix of Protestant ideas.
D They brought a mix of art, music, and stories.

WEEK 3

COMPETENCY GOAL 2 The learner will trace the causes and effects of the Revolutionary War, and assess the impact of major events, problems, and personalities during the Constitutional Period in North Carolina and the new nation.

MONDAY

Objective 2.01

1. The Second Continental Congress sent which of the following to King George III? *(Chapter 4.1)*

A the Declaration of Independence
B the Olive Branch Petition
C *Common Sense*
D the Constitution

TUESDAY

Objective 2.02

2. Who was the highest-ranking officer from North Carolina during the Revolutionary War? *(Chapter 4.1)*

A George Washington
B James Iredell
C Joseph Hewes
D Robert Howe

WEDNESDAY

Objective 2.03

3. Which battle led General Cornwallis to abandon the Carolinas? *(Chapter 4.4)*

A Guilford Courthouse
B Yorktown
C Boston
D Moore's Creek Bridge

THURSDAY

Objective 2.04

4. Which foreigner helped train Washington's troops at Valley Forge? *(Chapter 4.3)*

A Lord Cornwallis
B Marquis de Lafayette
C Baron Friedrich von Steuben
D Bernardo de Gálvez

FRIDAY

Objective 2.05

5. What was the first official call for independence in the colonies? *(Chapter 4.2)*

A the Mecklenburg Resolves
B the Declaration of Independence
C the Albany Plan of Union
D the Halifax Resolves

COUNTDOWN TO TESTING

WEEK 4

COMPETENCY GOAL 2 The learner will trace the causes and effects of the Revolutionary War, and assess the impact of major events, problems, and personalities during the Constitutional Period in North Carolina and the new nation.

MONDAY

Objective 2.05

1. Which of the following branches of government was weak in the North Carolina constitution of 1776? *(Chapter 5.1)*

A legislature
B court system
C press
D governor

TUESDAY

Objective 2.05

2. Which of the following was the single branch of the national government under the Articles of Confederation? *(Chapter 5.1)*

A executive
B Senate
C Congress
D court system

WEDNESDAY

Objective 2.05

3. Who proposed the Albany Plan of Union? *(Chapter 5.2)*

A George Washington
B Benjamin Franklin
C Thomas Jefferson
D John Adams

THURSDAY

Objective 2.05

4. People who supported the Constitution were called which of the following? *(Chapter 5.4)*

A Antifederalists
B Federalists
C Patriots
D Loyalists

FRIDAY

Objective 2.05

5. The Bill of Rights helps protect which of the following? *(Chapter 5.4)*

A the rights of citizens
B the rights of slaves
C the rights of government
D the rights of the president

WEEK 5

COMPETENCY GOAL 9 The learner will explore examples of and opportunities for active citizenship, past and present, at the local and state levels.

MONDAY

Objective 9.03

1. Which of the following is a responsibility of citizenship? *(Chapter 6.3)*

A writing laws
B serving in Congress
C voting
D petitioning the government

TUESDAY

Objective 9.03

2. Which of the following is protected by the First Amendment? *(Chapter 6.2)*

A the right to bear arms
B freedom of speech
C the right to a jury trial
D the right to due process

WEDNESDAY

Objective 9.03

3. Which is an example of a volunteer community group? *(Chapter 6.3)*

A police force
B Congress
C interest groups
D American Red Cross

THURSDAY

Objective 9.03

4. Freedom of religion is protected by which amendment? *(Chapter 6.2)*

A First Amendment
B Second Amendment
C Fifth Amendment
D Tenth Amendment

FRIDAY

Objective 9.03

5. Citizens become eligible to vote at what age? *(Chapter 6.2)*

A 16
B 18
C 21
D 35

WEEK 6

COMPETENCY GOAL 3 The learner will identify key events and evaluate the impact of reform and expansion in North Carolina during the first half of the 19th century.

MONDAY

Objective 3.01

1. Which of the following was one effect of the War of 1812 on the United States? *(Chapter 8.4)*

A The United States took control of British Canada.

B Citizens experienced a sense of increased pride and patriotism.

C The United States doubled in size.

D The United States lost control of Lake Erie.

TUESDAY

Objective 3.08

2. Which country sold the Louisiana Purchase to the United States? *(Chapter 8.2)*

A France

B Britain

C Spain

D Russia

WEDNESDAY

Objective 3.01

3. Who was a North Carolina privateer during the War of 1812? *(Chapter 8.4)*

A Richard Warfington

B Dolley Madison

C Otway Burns

D James Iredell

THURSDAY

Objective 3.08

4. Who led the exploration of the Louisiana Purchase? *(Chapter 8.2)*

A Robert R. Livingston and James Monroe

B Meriwether Lewis and William Clark

C James Madison and John Marshall

D Sacagawea and Zebulon Pike

FRIDAY

Objective 3.08

5. How far west did the Lewis and Clark expedition travel? *(Chapter 8.2)*

A to the Missouri River

B to the Mississippi River

C to the Rocky Mountains

D to the Pacific Ocean

WEEK 7

COMPETENCY GOAL 3 The learner will identify key events and evaluate the impact of reform and expansion in North Carolina during the first half of the 19th century.

MONDAY

Objective 3.02

1. Why was North Carolina called the Rip Van Winkle State? *(Chapter 9.2)*

A because of its slow pace of life
B because it had fewer internal improvements than other states
C because it remained loyal to Britain
D because it had fewer slaves than other southern states

TUESDAY

Objective 3.06

2. Who discovered the first gold nugget in the North Carolina gold rush? *(Chapter 9.2)*

A John Reed
B Christopher Bechtler
C Conrad Reed
D an unnamed Charlotte miner

WEDNESDAY

Objective 3.03

3. Which of the following came up with the American System idea? *(Chapter 9.2)*

A Henry Clay
B John Quincy Adams
C Andrew Jackson
D Frances Kemble

THURSDAY

Objective 3.02

4. What did reformers hope to improve in North Carolina during the first half of the 19th century? *(Chapter 9.3)*

A technology and industry
B guns and the military
C education and transportation
D farms and plantations

FRIDAY

Objective 3.06

5. In which year did North Carolina produce the most gold? *(Chapter 9.2)*

A 1824
B 1832
C 1834
D 1836

WEEK 8

COMPETENCY GOAL 3 The learner will identify key events and evaluate the impact of reform and expansion in North Carolina during the first half of the 19th century.

MONDAY

Objective 3.05

1. Andrew Jackson wanted to remove Native Americans from their land for what purpose? *(Chapter 10.3)*

A to save their way of life
B because they were victorious in the Second Seminole War
C to open up more land for settlement
D because the Supreme Court ruled he must

TUESDAY

Objective 3.07

2. Which political party rewrote the North Carolina state constitution in 1835? *(Chapter 10.3)*

A Democrats
B Republicans
C Democratic-Republicans
D Whigs

WEDNESDAY

Objective 3.02

3. What was one effect of the improved education system in North Carolina? *(Chapter 10.1)*

A New books were published.
B William Holden began a newspaper.
C Democrats favored expanded voting rights.
D Roads and canals were destroyed.

THURSDAY

Objective 3.05

4. How did some Cherokee resist Indian Removal? *(Chapter 10.3)*

A They moved to Indian Territory.
B They fought Andrew Jackson's forces.
C They hid in the mountains of North Carolina and Tennessee.
D They marched along the Trail of Tears.

FRIDAY

Objective 3.07

5. Which group(s) lost power and rights in the state constitution of 1835? *(Chapter 10.3)*

A western politicians
B African Americans and Native Americans
C teachers
D landowners

Week 9

COMPETENCY GOAL 3 The learner will identify key events and evaluate the impact of reform and expansion in North Carolina during the first half of the 19th century.

MONDAY

Objective 3.08

1. How did Whig leaders feel about the Mexican-American War? *(Chapter 11.3)*

A They opposed it.

B They supported it

C They agreed with the objectives, but not the methods.

D They did not have an opinion about the war.

TUESDAY

Objective 3.08

2. What led to the decline of Whig power in North Carolina? *(Chapter 11.3)*

A their support of the Mexican-American War

B their education reforms

C their failure to reform government

D their opposition to the Mexican-American War

WEDNESDAY

Objective 3.08

3. What happened in 1848 that affected mining in North Carolina? *(Chapter 11.4)*

A Oil was discovered in West Virginia.

B Silver was discovered in Nevada.

C Gold was discovered in California.

D Coal was discovered in North Carolina.

THURSDAY

Objective 3.08

4. How did the Mexican Cession affect North Carolina? *(Chapter 11.3)*

A Many Mexican citizens moved to the United States, including North Carolina.

B State leaders supported the Mexican Cession.

C Expansion led many settlers from the United States, including those from North Carolina, to move west.

D It did not affect the state.

FRIDAY

Objective 3.08

5. How did most North Carolinians feel about the Mexican-American War? *(Chapter 11.3)*

A They opposed it.

B They supported it.

C They agreed with the objectives but not the methods.

D They did not have an opinion about the war.

WEEK 10

COMPETENCY GOAL 3 The learner will identify key events and evaluate the impact of reform and expansion in North Carolina during the first half of the 19th century.

MONDAY

Objective 3.08

1. Who was the British mechanic who revolutionized textile manufacturing in the United States? *(Chapter 12.1)*

A Moses Brown
B Eli Whitney
C William Almy
D Samuel Slater

TUESDAY

Objective 3.08

2. North Carolina's economy mainly relied on which of the following in the 1840s? *(Chapter 12.1)*

A agriculture
B ironworks
C textile manufacturing
D furniture manufacturing

WEDNESDAY

Objective 3.08

3. North Carolina entrepreneurs began building textile mills during which decade? *(Chapter 12.1)*

A 1820s
B 1830s
C 1840s
D 1850s

THURSDAY

Objective 3.08

4. In which area of North Carolina were many ironworks built? *(Chapter 12.1)*

A Outer Banks
B Coastal Plain
C Piedmont
D Mountains

FRIDAY

Objective 3.08

5. What was the name of the first steamboat in North Carolina? *(Chapter 12.3)*

A *Tom Thumb*
B *Clermont*
C *Lowell Offering*
D *Prometheus*

WEEK 11

COMPETENCY GOAL 3 The learner will identify key events and evaluate the impact of reform and expansion in North Carolina during the first half of the 19th century.

COUNTDOWN TO TESTING

MONDAY

Objective 3.04

1. Compared with other southern states, how many slaves did North Carolina have? *(Chapter 13.1)*

A many more
B about the same
C fewer
D North Carolina did not have any slaves.

TUESDAY

Objective 3.04

2. Which of the following people was a slave in North Carolina who bought his freedom? *(Chapter 12.3)*

A Lunsford Land
B Hinton Rowan Helper
C Toussaint L'Ouverture
D Joseph Anderson

WEDNESDAY

Objective 3.04

3. Slave labor was most often used in which industry? *(Chapter 13.3)*

A textile manufacturing
B skilled trades
C agriculture
D ironworking

THURSDAY

Objective 3.04

4. By 1860 enslaved African Americans accounted for what percentage of North Carolina's population? *(Chapter 13.3)*

A two-thirds
B one-half
C one-third
D one-fourth

FRIDAY

Objective 3.03

5. Who led the violent 1831 slave uprising in Virginia? *(Chapter 13.3)*

A Frederick Douglass
B John Brown
C Denmark Vesey
D Nat Turner

Week 12

COMPETENCY GOAL 3 The learner will identify key events and evaluate the impact of reform and expansion in North Carolina during the first half of the 19th century.

MONDAY

Objective 3.03

1. Which North Carolina reformer published an abolitionist pamphlet? *(Chapter 14.4)*

A Dorothea Dix
B Archibald D. Murphey
C Harriet Jacobs
D David Walker

TUESDAY

Objective 3.03

2. Which North Carolina reformer tried to start a school for slaves? *(Chapter 14.4)*

A Harriet Jacobs
B David Walker
C Levi Coffin
D Archibald D. Murphey

WEDNESDAY

Objective 3.03

3. Which North Carolina reformer published an autobiography? *(Chapter 14.4)*

A Harriet Jacobs
B Dorothea Dix
C David Walker
D Frederick Douglass

THURSDAY

Objective 3.03

4. Which North Carolina reformer was an early leader in education reform? *(Chapter 14.3)*

A Dorothea Dix
B Archibald D. Murphey
C Horace Mann
D David Walker

FRIDAY

Objective 3.03

5. Which reformer visited North Carolina and made recommendations for prison and hospital reform? *(Chapter 14.3)*

A Archibald D. Murphey
B Thomas Gallaudet
C Dorothea Dix
D Harriet Jacobs

WEEK 13

COMPETENCY GOAL 3 The learner will identify key events and evaluate the impact of reform and expansion in North Carolina during the first half of the 19th century.

MONDAY

Objective 3.04

1. Which of the following issues most affected southerners' views of westward expansion? *(Chapter 15.1)*

A tenements
B transcendentalism
C temperance reform
D slavery

TUESDAY

Objective 9.02

2. Who published the abolitionist book *The Impending Crisis of the South*? *(Chapter 15.3)*

A Hinton Rowan Helper
B Lewis Lunsford
C Frederick Douglass
D David Walker

WEDNESDAY

Objective 3.04

3. Southerners who wanted to remain loyal to the United States were called which of the following? *(Chapter 15.4)*

A Secessionists
B Loyalists
C Unionists
D abolitionists

THURSDAY

Objective 3.04

4. The Freeport Doctrine stated which of the following? *(Chapter 15.3)*

A The Supreme Court would uphold slavery.
B Local police regulations would determine whether slavery was legal.
C The Supreme Court would abolish slavery.
D Abraham Lincoln could not legally end slavery in the southern states.

FRIDAY

Objective 3.04

5. Who led the forces opposing John Brown at Harpers Ferry? *(Chapter 15.3)*

A Abraham Lincoln
B Robert E. Lee
C John C. Breckinridge
D John Bell

WEEK 14

COMPETENCY GOAL 4 The learner will examine the causes, course, and character of the Civil War and Reconstruction, and their impact on North Carolina and the nation.

MONDAY

Objective 4.01

1. What action led North Carolina to secede from the Union? *(Chapter 16.1)*

A the election of Abraham Lincoln to the presidency
B the secession of South Carolina
C the firing on Fort Sumter
D Abraham Lincoln's call for troops

TUESDAY

Objective 4.02

2. How did the Union blockade affect life in the South during the Civil War? *(Chapter 16.2)*

A It helped the Confederacy gain needed supplies.
B It prevented the Confederate troops from fighting.
C It prevented needed supplies from reaching southerners.
D It had no effect on the Confederacy.

WEDNESDAY

Objective 4.03

3. What was "the lifeline of the Confederacy?" *(Chapter 16.2)*

A the rail line from Wilmington to Virginia
B the Mississippi River
C the ironclad *Virginia*
D General Robert E. Lee's troops

THURSDAY

Objective 4.04

4. Who was Daniel H. Hill? *(Chapter 16.1)*

A the president of the Confederacy
B the superintendent of the North Carolina Military Institute
C North Carolina's wartime governor
D a ship captain that got needed supplies through the Union blockade

FRIDAY

Objective 9.02

5. Who ran for governor on a peace platform in 1864? *(Chapter 16.4)*

A John Ellis
B D. H. Hill
C John Newland Maffitt
D William W. Holden

WEEK 15

COMPETENCY GOAL 4 The learner will examine the causes, course, and character of the Civil War and Reconstruction, and their impact on North Carolina and the nation.

MONDAY

Objective 4.04

1. Who was appointed governor of North Carolina by President Andrew Johnson? *(Chapter 17.1)*

A Zebulon B. Vance
B John Ellis
C William W. Holden
D Albion Tourgée

TUESDAY

Objective 4.05

2. The rise of which political party signaled the end of Reconstruction in North Carolina? *(Chapter 17.3)*

A Conservatives
B Republicans
C Democrats
D Whigs

WEDNESDAY

Objective 4.04

3. Which group was responsible for violence against African Americans? *(Chapter 17.3)*

A Radical Republicans
B Ku Klux Klan
C scalawags
D Copperheads

THURSDAY

Objective 9.02

4. Which North Carolina governor tried to prevent violence against African Americans? *(Chapter 17.3)*

A William W. Holden
B John Ellis
C Zebulon B. Vance
D Albion Tourgée

FRIDAY

Objective 4.05

5. Which of the following attended the 1868 convention to rewrite the North Carolina constitution? *(Chapter 17.3)*

A Democrats, scalawags, and northerners
B Republicans, northerners, and African Americans
C Democrats, African Americans, and carpetbaggers
D Republicans, Democrats, and northerners

COUNTDOWN TO TESTING

WEEK 16

COMPETENCY GOAL 5 The learner will evaluate the impact of political, economic, social, and technological changes on life in North Carolina from 1870 to 1930.

MONDAY

Objective 9.02

1. Who led the Farmers' Alliance in North Carolina? *(Chapter 18.3)*

A Annie Bidwell
B Oliver Hudson Kelley
C Leonidas K. Polk
D William Jennings Bryan

TUESDAY

Objective 5.03

2. African Americans who moved west to farm were called which of the following? *(Chapter 18.1)*

A Exodusters
B freedpeople
C buffalo soldiers
D Grangers

WEDNESDAY

Objective 5.01

3. By which year had North Carolina agriculture recovered from the Civil War? *(Chapter 18.3)*

A 1870
B 1875
C 1880
D 1885

THURSDAY

Objective 5.02

4. Which group was the main political group for farmers in North Carolina? *(Chapter 18.3)*

A National Grange
B Populist Party
C Fusionists
D Farmers' Alliance

FRIDAY

Objective 5.01

5. Which two crops were most important to North Carolina's economy during the late 1800s? *(Chapter 18.3)*

A corn and wheat
B cotton and corn
C tobacco and wheat
D tobacco and cotton

WEEK 17

COMPETENCY GOAL 5 The learner will evaluate the impact of political, economic, social, and technological changes on life in North Carolina from 1870 to 1930.

MONDAY

Objective 5.04

1. Which North Carolina city installed electric street lights in 1885? *(Chapter 19.1)*

- **A** Wilmington
- **B** Raleigh
- **C** Winston
- **D** Charlotte

TUESDAY

Objective 5.04

2. Which North Carolina city was the first to install electric lights? *(Chapter 19.1)*

- **A** Wilmington
- **B** Winston
- **C** Charlotte
- **D** Raleigh

WEDNESDAY

Objective 5.03

3. Immigrants from which country settled at St. Helena? *(Chapter 20.1)*

- **A** Italy
- **B** Germany
- **C** The Netherlands
- **D** Denmark

THURSDAY

Objective 5.04

4. Which of the following did the Wright brothers invent? *(Chapter 19.1)*

- **A** telephone
- **B** light bulb
- **C** automobile
- **D** gas-powered airplane

FRIDAY

Objective 5.03

5. During the late 1800s many people in North Carolina moved to which of the following? *(Chapter 20.2)*

- **A** other southern states
- **B** northern states
- **C** western states
- **D** rural farms

WEEK 18

COMPETENCY GOAL 5 The learner will evaluate the impact of political, economic, social, and technological changes on life in North Carolina from 1870 to 1930.

MONDAY

Objective 5.05

1. The Fusionist Party was made up of which of the following? *(Chapter 21.1)*

A Republicans and Democrats
B Republicans and Populists
C Democrats and Red Shirts
D Populists and Democrats

TUESDAY

Objective 5.05

2. What was the original "grandfather clause?" *(Chapter 21.1)*

A a law stating that African Americans could vote
B a law stating that illiterate people could not vote
C a law stating that people whose ancestors had voted could vote
D a law stating that poor people could not vote

WEDNESDAY

Objective 5.05

3. In what year were North Carolina's first child labor laws passed? *(Chapter 21.2)*

A 1900
B 1903
C 1917
D 1920

THURSDAY

Objective 5.05

4. Who were the Red Shirts? *(Chapter 21.1)*

A a group of farmers that called for economic reforms
B a group of African Americans who called for voting reforms
C a group of men who threatened African Americans
D a group of Democrats who helped African Americans vote

FRIDAY

Objective 5.05

5. What was the "WCTU No. 2?" *(Chapter 21.3)*

A a men's temperance group
B a state group calling for women's rights
C a national group of female reformers
D an African American women's group

COUNTDOWN TO TESTING

Week 19

COMPETENCY GOAL 5 The learner will evaluate the impact of political, economic, social, and technological changes on life in North Carolina from 1870 to 1930.

MONDAY

Objective 5.06

1. Where did U.S. troops fight during the Spanish-American War? *(Chapter 22.2)*

A Spain, Mexico, and Cuba
B Spain, Cuba, and Puerto Rico
C Cuba, Mexico, and the Philippines
D Cuba, Puerto Rico, and the Philippines

TUESDAY

Objective 5.06

2. Which president oversaw construction of the Panama Canal? *(Chapter 22.3)*

A William McKinley
B Theodore Roosevelt
C William Howard Taft
D Woodrow Wilson

WEDNESDAY

Objective 5.06

3. How did President Taft try to influence foreign affairs? *(Chapter 22.3)*

A through economic incentives
B through military intervention
C through diplomatic assignments
D through isolationism

THURSDAY

Objective 5.06

4. How many North Carolina regiments were raised for the Spanish-American War? *(Chapter 22.2)*

A 0
B 1
C 2
D 3

FRIDAY

Objective 5.06

5. Why were U.S. troops sent into Mexico in 1916? *(Chapter 22.3)*

A because "Pancho" Villa had killed Americans in New Mexico
B because a German ship carrying weapons was headed toward Veracruz
C to aid Porfirio Díaz in the Mexican Revolution
D to promote democracy in Mexico

WEEK 20

COMPETENCY GOAL 5 The learner will evaluate the impact of political, economic, social, and technological changes on life in North Carolina from 1870 to 1930.

MONDAY

Objective 5.06

1. What incident involved the United States in World War I? *(Chapter 23.2)*

A the assassination of Archduke Francis Ferdinand

B Germany's declaration of war on Russia

C the sinking of the *Sussex*

D the discovery of the Zimmermann Note

TUESDAY

Objective 5.06

2. How did women help with the war effort? *(Chapter 23.3)*

A They performed the jobs of absent men.

B They became soldiers.

C They grew more food for the troops.

D They did not help with the war effort.

WEDNESDAY

Objective 5.06

3. How did World War I affect the economy of North Carolina? *(Chapter 23.3)*

A Many large farms and factories were pushed out of business.

B The economy stayed about the same.

C Many small farms and factories were pushed out of business.

D Prices fell during the war.

THURSDAY

Objective 5.06

4. Camp Bragg was first commissioned in which year? *(Chapter 23.2)*

A 1912

B 1916

C 1918

D 1922

FRIDAY

Objective 5.06

5. How did people in the United States help the Allied Powers during World War I? *(Chapter 23.3)*

A They sent food.

B They sent troops and supplies.

C They ran European businesses while soldiers were away.

D They joined European unions.

WEEK 21

COMPETENCY GOAL 5 The learner will evaluate the impact of political, economic, social, and technological changes on life in North Carolina from 1870 to 1930.

MONDAY

Objective 5.02

1. Which of the following changes occurred after World War I? *(Chapter 24.2)*

A Fundamentalism declined in North Carolina.

B The younger generation began challenging social rules.

C Prohibition became illegal.

D Communists became more tolerated.

TUESDAY

Objective 5.02

2. Which religious movement is characterized by the belief in a literal interpretation of the Bible? *(Chapter 24.2)*

A traditionalism

B communism

C fundamentalism

D the Great Migration

WEDNESDAY

Objective 5.02

3. The Twenty-first Amendment made which of the following a national law? *(Chapter 24.2)*

A evolution

B communism

C women's suffrage

D Prohibition

THURSDAY

Objective 5.02

4. Who was a famous author from North Carolina during the 1920s? *(Chapter 24.3)*

A Harriet M. Berry

B Thomas Wolfe

C Langston Hughes

D F. Scott Fitzgerald

FRIDAY

Objective 9.02

5. Who was the first woman to be elected to the North Carolina General Assembly? *(Chapter 24.3)*

A Zora Neale Hurston

B Georgia O'Keefe

C Harriet M. Berry

D Lillian Exum Clement

Week 22

COMPETENCY GOAL 6 The learner will analyze the immediate and long-term effects of the Great Depression and World War II on North Carolina.

MONDAY

Objective 5.01

1. How did the stock market crash lead to bank closures? *(Chapter 25.1)*

A Banks owned all the stock in the stock market.

B People bought more stocks instead of paying back loans.

C Banks had loaned money to buy stocks on margin.

D The stock market could not repay its bank loans.

TUESDAY

Objective 5.01

2. How did the Great Depression affect the furniture industry in North Carolina? *(Chapter 25.1)*

A Production fell by almost half.

B Production stopped.

C Production increased by almost half.

D Production doubled.

WEDNESDAY

Objective 5.01

3. Which New Deal program helped North Carolina farmers more than double their income by 1936? *(Chapter 25.2)*

A Live at Home

B Agriculture Adjustment Act

C Farm Credit Act

D Works Progress Administration

THURSDAY

Objective 5.01

4. Workers from which industry participated in the Great Strike in 1934? *(Chapter 25.3)*

A furniture

B tobacco

C agriculture

D textile

FRIDAY

Objective 5.01

5. In what year was the textile industry's general strike? *(Chapter 25.2)*

A 1928

B 1930

C 1932

D 1934

COUNTDOWN TO TESTING

WEEK 23

COMPETENCY GOAL 6 The learner will analyze the immediate and long-term effects of the Great Depression and World War II on North Carolina.

COUNTDOWN TO TESTING

MONDAY

Objective 6.02

1. The United States entered World War II after which of the following incidents? *(Chapter 26.1)*

A Germany's invasion of Poland

B the Battle of Britain

C Pearl Harbor

D the Normandy invasion

TUESDAY

Objective 6.03

2. Who led the U.S. Pacific Fleet during World War II? *(Chapter 26.4)*

A Chester Nimitz

B Douglas MacArthur

C Dwight D. Eisenhower

D Franklin Roosevelt

WEDNESDAY

Objective 6.02

3. Where was "Torpedo Junction?" *(Chapter 26.2)*

A in the Pacific Ocean

B at Pearl Harbor

C between Italy and North Africa

D off the coast of Cape Hatteras

THURSDAY

Objective 6.03

4. Who became president when Franklin Roosevelt died in office? *(Chapter 26.5)*

A Dwight D. Eisenhower

B Harry Truman

C Douglas MacArthur

D Chester Nimitz

FRIDAY

Objective 6.04

5. How did World War II affect women and minorities? *(Chapter 26.2)*

A They both experienced less social discrimination.

B They both were allowed to become soldiers.

C They both were segregated in the military.

D They both experienced increased economic opportunities.

WEEK 24

COMPETENCY GOAL 7 The learner will analyze changes in North Carolina during the postwar period to the 1970's.

MONDAY

Objective 7.03

1. Why did North Carolina state leaders suggest the idea of Research Triangle Park? *(Chapter 27.1)*

A to increase the importance of agriculture

B to increase the importance of traditional industries

C to decrease dependency on too few industries

D to decrease the state's revenue

TUESDAY

Objective 7.04

2. Leaders from which countries attended the Yalta Conference? *(Chapter 27.1)*

A United States, Soviet Union, Germany

B United States, Germany, Italy

C Germany, Italy, Japan

D United States, Soviet Union, Britain

WEDNESDAY

Objective 7.04

3. What was the original purpose of the United Nations? *(Chapter 27.1)*

A to resolve international conflict

B to provide aid to poorer countries

C to protect the rights of individuals

D to spread democracy and combat communism

THURSDAY

Objective 7.01

4. How did North Carolina's economy change after World War II? *(Chapter 27.3)*

A It became more dependent on agriculture.

B It became more dependent on manufacturing.

C It became weaker.

D It experienced a recession.

FRIDAY

Objective 7.04

5. Which of the following became a growing concern for the United States after World War II? *(Chapter 27.3)*

A providing aid to farmers

B rebuilding the Soviet Union

C contributing troops to the United Nations

D fighting the spread of communism

WEEK 25

COMPETENCY GOAL 7 The learner will analyze changes in North Carolina during the postwar period to the 1970's.

MONDAY

Objective 7.02

1. Where did the first sit-in protest in the South take place? *(Chapter 28.1)*

A Washington, D.C.
B Wilmington, North Carolina
C Raleigh, Virginia
D Greensboro, North Carolina

TUESDAY

Objective 7.02

2. Who was the Equal Rights Amendment designed to help? *(Chapter 28.3)*

A Hispanic Americans
B African Americans
C disabled Americans
D women

WEDNESDAY

Objective 7.05

3. Why did a federal judge order Mecklenburg County to use buses? *(Chapter 28.1)*

A to desegregate its schools
B to desegregate its military bases
C to provide equal protection to women
D to provide equal protection to Hispanic Americans

THURSDAY

Objective 7.03

4. Why did racial minorities fight for equal rights? *(Chapter 28.1)*

A They had no rights under federal law.
B They were often denied their legal rights.
C They refused to integrate with white people.
D They had more rights under state laws than under federal laws.

FRIDAY

Objective 7.05

5. Why were the Freedom Rides discontinued? *(Chapter 28.2)*

A Freedom Riders were breaking the law.
B States agreed to let African Americans use public facilities.
C President Kennedy called for their end.
D Violent protests endangered the lives of the Freedom Riders.

COUNTDOWN TO TESTING

WEEK 26

COMPETENCY GOAL 7 The learner will analyze changes in North Carolina during the postwar period to the 1970's.

MONDAY

Objective 7.04

1. Which of the following began with the Soviet Union placing weapons in Cuba? *(Chapter 29.1)*

A the Bay of Pigs invasion
B the space race
C the Cuban missile crisis
D the Vietnam War

TUESDAY

Objective 7.04

2. Who was the first person to travel into space? *(Chapter 29.1)*

A John Glenn
B Neil Armstrong
C Edwin "Buzz" Aldrin
D Yuri Gagarin

WEDNESDAY

Objective 7.04

3. Why did the United States become involved in the Vietnam War? *(Chapter 29.2)*

A to instate a colonial government
B to help stop the spread of communism
C to install a monarchy
D because South Vietnam attacked American ships

THURSDAY

Objective 7.04

4. The surprise attacks on South Vietnam during a holiday in 1968 was called which of the following? *(Chapter 29.2)*

A Tet Offensive
B Tonkin Gulf Resolution
C search-and-destroy mission
D escalation

FRIDAY

Objective 7.04

5. Some students and young people did which of the following to protest the Vietnam War? *(Chapter 29.3)*

A avoided military service by moving to Canada
B joined construction workers in a march in New York City
C voted for Johnson in the election of 1968
D joined a group called Young Americans for Freedom

COUNTDOWN TO TESTING

WEEK 27

COMPETENCY GOAL 8 The learner will evaluate the impact of demographic, economic, technological, social, and political developments in North Carolina since the 1970's.

COUNTDOWN TO TESTING

MONDAY

Objective 8.03

1. Nixon's New Federalism gave more control of federal funds to which of the following? *(Chapter 30.1)*

- **A** Congress
- **B** the president
- **C** state and local governments
- **D** taxpayers

TUESDAY

Objective 9.02

2. Jesse Helms helped make which of the following movements an important political force? *(Chapter 30.3)*

- **A** the Christian right
- **B** New Federalism
- **C** realpolitik
- **D** détente

WEDNESDAY

Objective 8.03

3. Which of the following was the result of the revision of the state constitution in 1971? *(Chapter 30.1)*

- **A** The governor had more power.
- **B** A new court system was created.
- **C** Religion became an important political force.
- **D** The government was reorganized for efficiency.

THURSDAY

Objective 8.03

4. A new conservative movement helped elect which president? *(Chapter 30.3)*

- **A** Richard Nixon
- **B** Gerald Ford
- **C** Jimmy Carter
- **D** Ronald Reagan

FRIDAY

Objective 8.03

5. "Reaganomics" was an economic policy based on which of the following? *(Chapter 30.3)*

- **A** supply-side economics
- **B** supply and demand economics
- **C** deficit economics
- **D** expansion economics

WEEK 28

COMPETENCY GOAL 8 The learner will evaluate the impact of demographic, economic, technological, social, and political developments in North Carolina since the 1970's.

MONDAY

Objective 8.01

1. Which of the following groups is the second largest in North Carolina's population? *(Chapter 4.1)*

A Hispanic Americans
B African Americans
C Asian Americans
D Native Americans

TUESDAY

Objective 8.04

2. How does outsourcing affect North Carolina? *(Chapter 31.3)*

A It creates more jobs in manufacturing.
B It reduces jobs in service industries.
C It reduces jobs in manufacturing.
D It does not affect North Carolina.

WEDNESDAY

Objective 8.04

3. Which region of North Carolina is home to many high-tech firms? *(Chapter 4.1)*

A Coastal region
B Piedmont region
C Mountain region
D Outer Banks region

THURSDAY

Objective 8.01

4. North Carolina has the fastest-growing population of which of the following? *(Chapter 31.3)*

A elderly Americans
B Asian Americans
C African Americans
D Hispanic Americans

FRIDAY

Objective 9.01

5. Which of the following represents the outcome of diversifying North Carolina's economy? *(Chapter 31.3)*

A Raleigh is one of the nation's fastest-growing areas.
B Charlotte is the second-largest banking center in the nation.
C The western part of the state generally votes for Republicans.
D Preserving the environment is a current challenge for state leaders.

Week 29

COMPETENCY GOAL 9 The learner will explore examples of and opportunities for active citizenship, past and present, at the local and state levels.

MONDAY

Objective 9.01

1. Why did officials move the Cape Hatteras Lighthouse? *(Chapter 31.3)*

- **A** to protect it from vandals
- **B** to protect it from being damaged by coastal erosion
- **C** to make it more accessible to visiting tourists
- **D** to build an office park on the land

TUESDAY

Objective 9.02

2. Who was the first female U.S. senator from North Carolina? *(Chapter 31.2)*

- **A** Lillian Exum Clement
- **B** Jane Simpson McKimmon
- **C** Elizabeth Dole
- **D** Nancy Kassebaum

WEDNESDAY

Objective 9.03

3. What is one example of civic participation? *(Chapter 6.2)*

- **A** voting
- **B** attending church
- **C** abiding by the law
- **D** taking care of your personal finances

THURSDAY

Objective 9.01

4. Which industry does the mountain region of North Carolina rely on heavily? *(Chapter 31.3)*

- **A** furniture building
- **B** tobacco products
- **C** fishing
- **D** tourism

FRIDAY

Objective 9.03

5. Which of the following was one result of civic leaders' creation of Research Triangle Park? *(Chapter 31.3)*

- **A** North Carolina became the fastest-growing state in the nation.
- **B** The North Carolina economy was diversified to include new industries.
- **C** People began a migration away from the Research Triangle.
- **D** Charlotte became the nation's largest center of banking.

COUNTDOWN TO TESTING

Reading like a Historian

Historians use paintings along with many other tools to help understand the past. The famous painting on the next page, *Washington Crossing the Delaware,* captures the determination of Patriot leaders and soldiers to endure brutal conditions in the hope of winning their struggle for liberty. As you study United States history, you too will learn how to use different historical sources to **Read like a Historian.**

To find out more about reading like a historian and the historical sources that follow, visit go.hrw.com More Online KEYWORD: HISTORIAN

By Frances Marie Gipson
Secondary Literacy Coordinator
Los Angeles Unified School District, Los Angeles, California

What Does It Mean to Read like a Historian?

In your history class you will be doing a lot of reading, thinking, and problem-solving. Much of your reading and thinking will center on different types of texts or materials. Since you are in a history class reading all sorts of things, a question to consider is, "What does it mean to think, read, and solve problems like a historian?"

Historians work with different types of sources to understand and learn from history. Two categories of sources are **primary** and **secondary** sources.

Primary Sources are historical documents, written accounts by a firsthand witness, or objects that have survived from the past. A study of primary sources might include letters, government documents, diaries, photographs, art objects, stamps, coins, and even clothing.

Secondary Sources are accounts of past events created by people some time after the events happened. This textbook and other books written about historical events are examples of secondary sources.

As you learn more about your work as a historian, you will begin to ask questions and analyze historical materials. You will be working as a detective, digging into history to create a richer understanding of the mysteries of the past.

How to Analyze Written Sources

Primary Sources

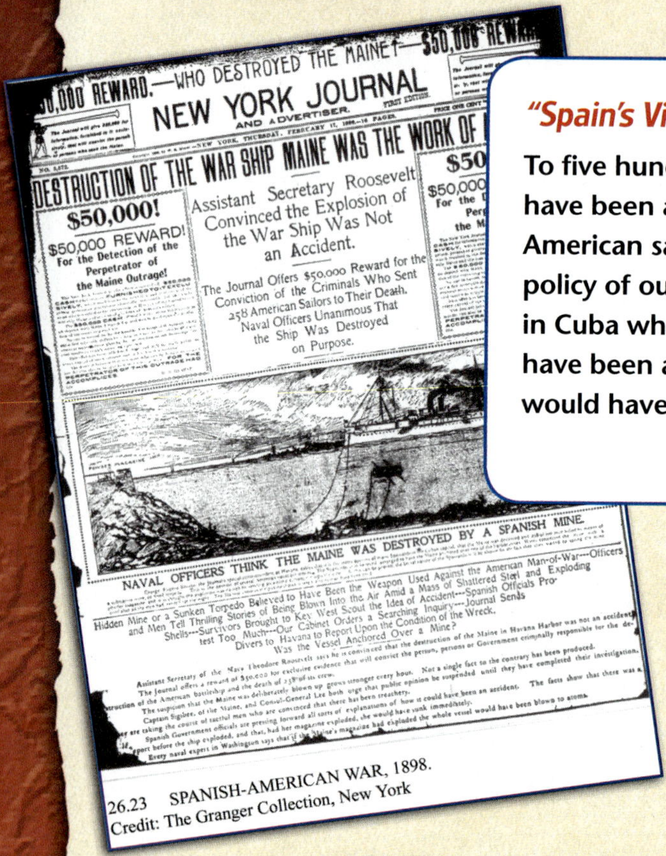
$50,000 REWARD.—WHO DESTROYED THE MAINE?—$50,000 REWARD.

NEW YORK JOURNAL AND ADVERTISER.

DESTRUCTION OF THE WAR SHIP MAINE WAS THE WORK OF

$50,000!

$50,000 REWARD! For the Detection of the Perpetrator of the Maine Outrage!

Assistant Secretary Roosevelt Convinced the Explosion of the War Ship Was Not an Accident.

The Journal Offers $50,000 Reward for the Conviction of the Criminals Who Sent 258 American Sailors to Their Death. Naval Officers Unanimous That the Ship Was Destroyed on Purpose.

NAVAL OFFICERS THINK THE MAINE WAS DESTROYED BY A SPANISH MINE.

Hidden Mine or a Sunken Torpedo Believed to Have Been the Weapon Used Against the American Man-of-War---Officers and Men Tell Thrilling Stories of Being Blown Into the Air Amid a Mass of Shattered Steel and Exploding Shells---Survivors Brought to Key West Scout the Idea of Accident---Spanish Officials Protest Too Much---Our Cabinet Orders a Searching Inquiry---Journal Sends Divers to Havana to Report Upon the Condition of the Wreck. Was the Vessel Anchored Over a Mine?

26.23 SPANISH-AMERICAN WAR, 1898.
Credit: The Granger Collection, New York

"Spain's Victory of Peace"

To five hundred thousand Cubans starved or otherwise murdered have been added an American battleship and three hundred American sailors lost as the direct result of the dilatory [delaying] policy of our government toward Spain. If we had stopped the war in Cuba when duty and policy alike urged us to do the *Maine* would have been afloat today, and three hundred homes, now desolate, would have been unscathed.

–*New York Journal*, February 17, 1898

Asking questions can help you determine the relevance and importance of written primary sources, such as this newspaper editorial about the sinking of an American warship. As you analyze the primary source above and the primary and secondary sources included in this textbook, ask yourself questions like the ones below.

- **Who created the source and why?**
- **Did the writer have firsthand knowledge of the event, or does he report what others saw or heard?**
- **Was the writer a neutral party, or did the author have opinions or interests that might have influenced what was recorded?**
- **Did the writer wish to inform or persuade others?**
- **Was the information recorded during the event, immediately after the event, or after some lapse of time?**

Secondary Sources

The Attack on Lawrence, Kansas

"Sheriff Jones, again at the head of an army of Missourians, marched into Lawrence. In broad daylight, they threw the printing presses of two newspapers into a river. They burned down the Free State Hotel and other buildings. Antislavery Kansans seethed with rage. Here is how one eyewitness described the attack: *Sheriff Jones, after looking at the flames rising from the hotel and saying that it was 'the happiest day of his life,' dismissed the troops and they began their lawless destruction.*"

–John A. Garraty, from *The Story of America*, 1994

When reading secondary sources, such as the description of the attack on Lawrence, Kansas, historians ask additional questions to seek understanding. They try to source the text, build evidence, and interpret the message that is being conveyed. For historians, reading is a quest to find evidence to answer or challenge a historical problem. As you study secondary sources, ask questions like the ones below.

- Who is the author? What do I know about this author?
- Did the author have firsthand information? What is the author's relationship to the event?
- What might be the author's motivation in writing this piece?
- What type of evidence did the author look at?
- Are any assumptions or biases present?
- How does this document fit into the larger context of the events I am studying?
- What kind of source is it?
- Is the source an original?
- Is the content probable or reasonable?
- What does the date tell me about the event?
- What do I already know about this topic that will help me understand more of what I am reading?

How to Analyze an Artifact

Artifacts, such as this phonograph invented by Thomas Edison, take many forms. They might be coins, stone tools, pieces of clothing, or even items found in your backpack. As you study artifacts in this textbook, ask yourself questions like the ones below.

- Why was this object created?
- When and where would it have been used?
- What does the artifact tell me about the technology available at the time it was created?
- What can it tell me about the life and times of the people who used it?
- How does the artifact help to make sense of the time period?

How to Analyze a Historical Map

Maps, such as this one from 1719 of New France, are symbolic representations of places shown in relation to one another. All maps necessarily include some details and leave out others. As you study maps in this textbook, ask questions like the ones below.

- When and where was the map produced?
- What details has the mapmaker chosen to include (or exclude) on this map?
- Why was the map drawn?
- How can I determine if the map is accurate?
- How are maps used to analyze the past, present, and future?

How to Analyze a Photograph

Photographs, like the one above of African American soldiers during the Civil War, are another important source for historians. One way to study a photograph is to write down everything you think is important about it. Then divide the image into four sections and describe the important elements from each section. As you study photographs in this textbook, ask questions like the ones below.

- What is the subject of the photograph?
- What does the image reveal about its subject?
- What is the setting for the photograph?
- What other details can I observe?
- When and where in the past was the photograph created?
- How can I describe the photographer's point of view?

How to Analyze a Political Cartoon

In 1871 Thomas Nast published this cartoon—"Who Stole the People's Money?"—poking fun at corruption in politics. As you study political cartoons in this textbook, use the following helpful tips and questions.

- **List the parts of the political cartoon and the importance of each part.**
- **Describe the focus or significance of the political cartoon.**
- **Do the captions and call-out boxes clarify the political cartoon's purpose?**
- **Does the cartoon help me understand the information that I am studying in my textbook better?**

Become an Active Reader

by Dr. Kylene Beers

Did you ever think you would begin reading your social studies book by reading about reading? Actually, it makes better sense than you might think. You would probably make sure you learned some soccer skills and strategies before playing in a game. Similarly, you need to learn some reading skills and strategies before reading your social studies book. In other words, you need to make sure you know whatever you need to know in order to read this book successfully.

Tip #1
Use the Reading Social Studies Pages

Take advantage of the two pages on reading at the beginning of every chapter. Those pages introduce the chapter themes; explain a reading skill or strategy; and identify key terms, people, and academic vocabulary.

Themes

Why are themes important? They help our minds organize facts and information. For example, when we talk about baseball, we may talk about types of pitches. When we talk about movies, we may discuss animation.

Historians are no different. When they discuss history or social studies, they tend to think about some common themes: Economics, Geography, Religion, Politics, Society and Culture, and Science and Technology.

Reading Skill or Strategy

Good readers use a number of skills and strategies to make sure they understand what they are reading. These lessons will give you the tools you need to read and understand social studies.

Key Terms, People, and Academic Vocabulary

Before you read the chapter, review these words and think about them. Have you heard the word before? What do you already know about the people? Then watch for these words and their meanings as you read the chapter.

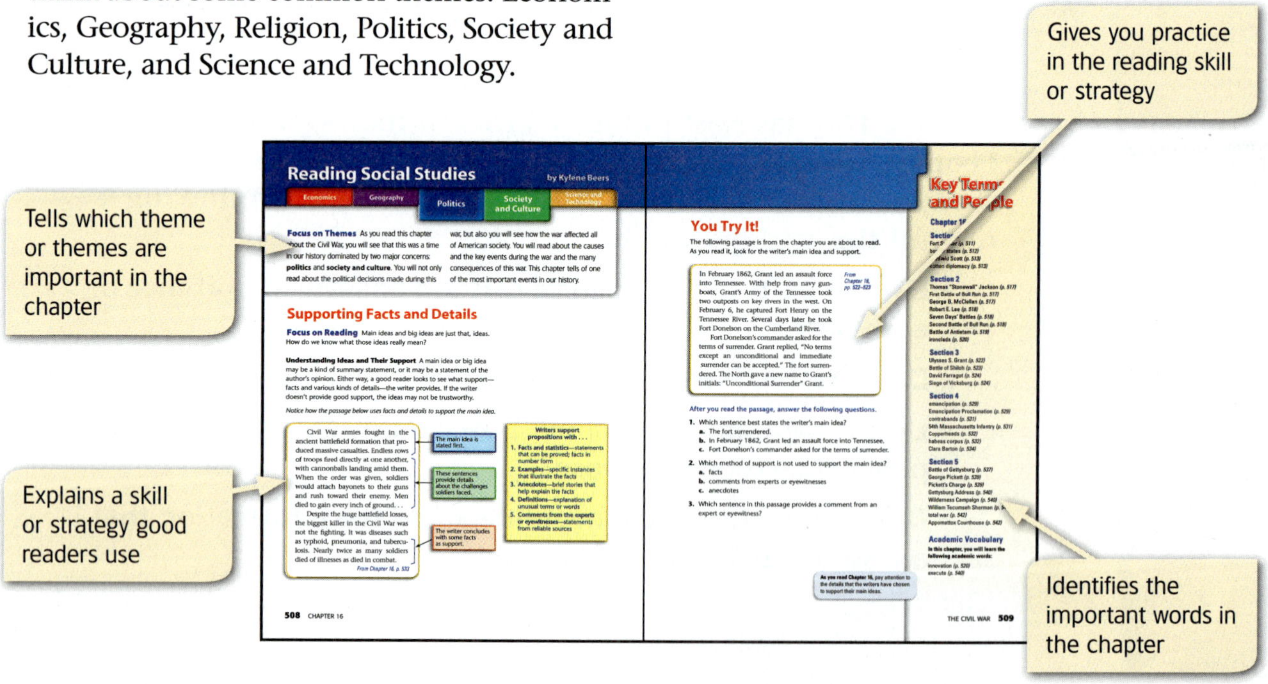

Tip #2

Read like a Skilled Reader

You will never get better at reading your social studies book—or any book for that matter—unless you spend some time thinking about how to be a better reader.

Skilled readers do the following:

- They preview what they are supposed to read before they actually begin reading. They look for vocabulary words, titles of sections, information in the margin, or maps or charts they should study.
- They divide their notebook paper into two columns. They title one column "Notes from the Chapter" and the other column "Questions or Comments I Have."
- They take notes in both columns as they read.
- They read like **active readers**. The Active Reading list below shows you what that means.
- They use clues in the text to help them figure out where the text is going. The best clues are called signal words.

Chronological Order Signal Words: *first, second, third, before, after, later, next, following that, earlier, finally*

Cause and Effect Signal Words: *because of, due to, as a result of, the reason for, therefore, consequently*

Comparison/Contrast Signal Words: *likewise, also, as well as, similarly, on the other hand*

READING SOCIAL STUDIES

Active Reading

Successful readers are **active readers**. These readers know that it is up to them to figure out what the text means. Here are some steps you can take to become an active, and successful, reader.

Predict what will happen next based on what has already happened. When your predictions don't match what happens in the text, reread the confusing parts.

Question what is happening as you read. Constantly ask yourself why things have happened, what things mean, and what caused certain events.

Summarize what you are reading frequently. Do not try to summarize the entire chapter! Read a bit and then summarize it. Then read on.

Connect what is happening in the part you're reading to what you have already read.

Clarify your understanding. Stop occasionally to ask yourself whether you are confused by anything. You may need to reread to clarify, or you may need to read further and collect more information before you can understand.

Visualize what is happening in the text. Try to see the events or places in your mind by drawing maps, making charts, or jotting down notes about what you are reading.

Tip #3

Pay Attention to Vocabulary

It is no fun to read something when you don't know what the words mean, but you can't learn new words if you only use or read the words you already know. In this book, we know we have probably used some words you don't know. But, we have followed a pattern as we have used more difficult words.

Key Terms and People

At the beginning of each section you will find a list of key terms or people that you will need to know. Be on the lookout for those words as you read through the section.

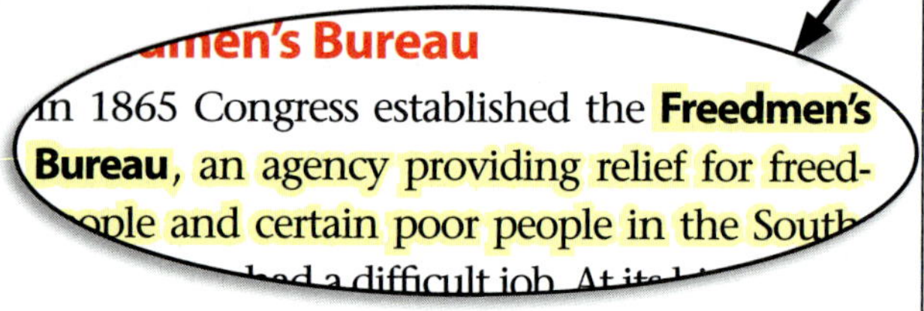

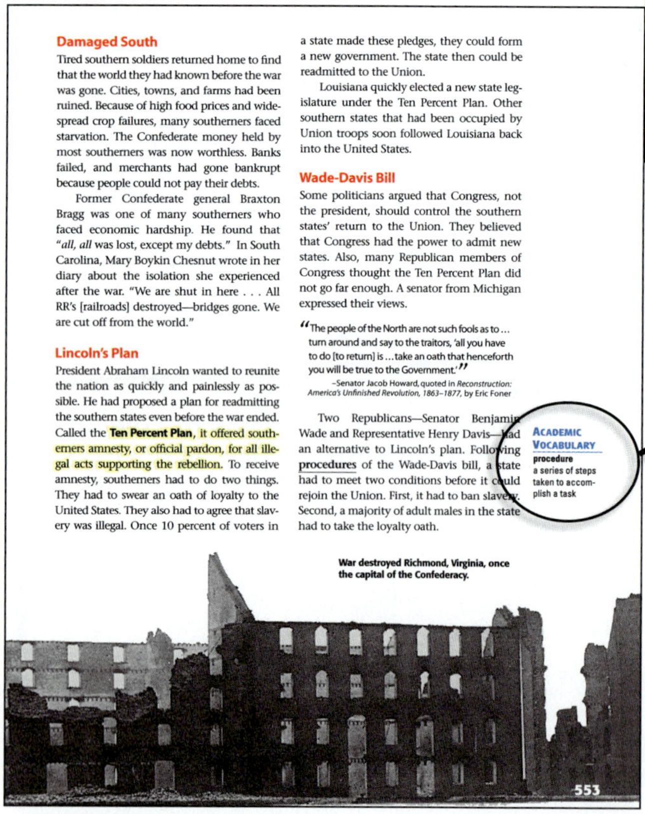

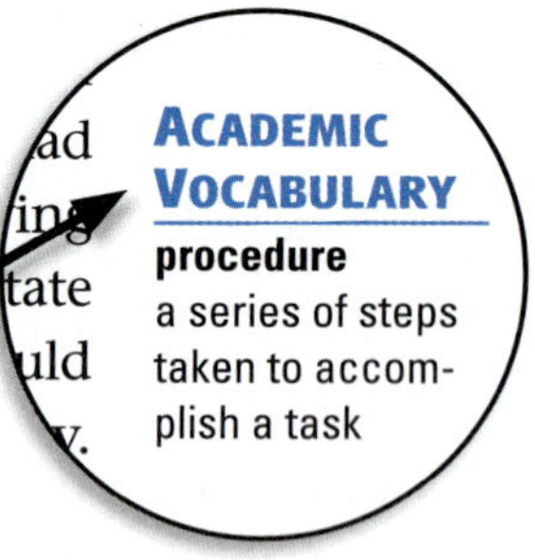

Academic Vocabulary

When we use a word that is important in all classes, not just social studies, we define it in the margin under the heading *Academic Vocabulary.* You will run into these academic words in other textbooks, so you should learn what they mean while reading this book.

Words to Know

As you read this social studies textbook, you will be more successful if you know or learn the meanings of the words on this page. There are two types of words listed here. The first list contains academic words, the words we discussed at the bottom of the previous page. These words are important in all classes, not just social studies. The second list contains words that are special to this particular topic of social studies, U.S. history.

Academic Words

abstract	expressing a quality or idea without reference to an actual thing
acquire	to get
advocate	to plead in favor of
affect	to change or influence
agreement	a decision reached by two or more people or groups
aspects	parts
authority	power, right to rule
cause	the reason something happens
circumstances	surrounding situation
classical	referring to the cultures of ancient Greece or Rome
complex	difficult, not simple
concrete	specific, real
consequences	the effects of a particular event or events
contemporary	existing at the same time
contract	a binding legal agreement
criteria	rules for defining
develop/ development	1. the process of growing or improving 2. Creation
distinct	separate
distribute	to divide among a group of people
effect	the result of an action or decision
efficient/ efficiency	productive and not wasteful
element	part
establish	to set up or create
execute	to perform, carry out
explicit	fully revealed without vagueness
facilitate	to bring about
factor	cause
features	characteristics
function	use or purpose
ideal	ideas or goals that people try to live up to
impact	effect, result
functions	uses or purposes
implement	to put in place
implications	effects of a decision
implicit	understood though not clearly put into words
incentive	something that leads people to follow a certain course of action
influence	change or have an effect on
innovation	a new idea or way of doing something
logic/logical	1. reasoned, well thought out 2. well thought out ideas
method	a way of doing something
motive	a reason for doing something
neutral	unbiased, not favoring either side in a conflict
policy	rule, course of action
primary	main, most important
principle	basic belief, rule, or law
procedure	a series of steps taken to accomplish a task
process	a series of steps by which a task is accomplished
purpose	the reason something is done
reaction	response
rebel	to fight against authority
role	1. a part or function 2. Assigned behavior
strategy	a plan for fighting a battle or war
structure	the way something is set up or organized
traditional	customary, time-honored
values	ideas that people hold dear and try to live by
vary/various	1. To be different 2. of many types

Social Studies Words

AD	refers to dates after Jesus's birth
anthropology	the science of human beings, especially their physical characteristics and cultures
BC	refers to dates before the birth of Jesus
BCE	refers to "Before Common Era," dates before the birth of Jesus
CE	refers to "Common Era," dates after Jesus's birth
century	a period of 100 years
civilization	the culture of a particular time or place
climate	the weather conditions in a certain area over a long period of time
culture	the knowledge, beliefs, customs, and values of a group of people
custom	a repeated practice; tradition
democracy	governmental rule by the people, usually on a majority rule principle
economics	a social science concerned with the production, distribution, and consumption of goods and services
geography	the study of the earth's physical and cultural features
monarchy	governmental rule by one person, a king or queen
political science	the study of government and politics
psychology	the study of mind and behavior
society	a group of people who share common traditions
sociology	the science of society, social institutions, and social relationships

Mapping the Earth

A **globe** is a scale model of the earth. It is useful for showing the entire earth or studying large areas of the earth's surface.

A pattern of lines circles the globe in east-west and north-south directions. It is called a **grid**. The intersection of these imaginary lines helps us find places on the earth.

The east-west lines in the grid are lines of **latitude**. Lines of latitude are called **parallels** because they are always parallel to each other. These imaginary lines measure distance north and south of the **equator**. The equator is an imaginary line that circles the globe halfway between the North and South Poles. Parallels measure distance from the equator in **degrees**. The symbol for degrees is °. Degrees are further divided into **minutes**. The symbol for minutes is ´. There are 60 minutes in a degree. Parallels north of the equator are labeled with an N. Those south of the equator are labeled with an S.

The north-south lines are lines of **longitude**. Lines of longitude are called **meridians**. These imaginary lines pass through the Poles. They measure distance east and west of the **prime meridian**. The prime meridian is an imaginary line that runs through Greenwich, England. It represents 0° longitude.

Lines of latitude range from 0°, for locations on the equator, to 90°N or 90°S, for locations at the Poles. Lines of longitude range from 0° on the prime meridian to 180° on a meridian in the mid-Pacific Ocean. Meridians west of the prime meridian to 180° are labeled with a W. Those east of the prime meridian to 180° are labeled with an E.

Lines of Latitude

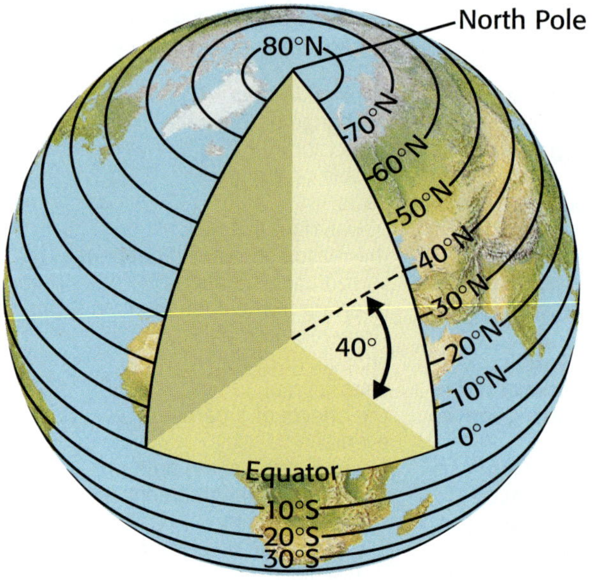

Lines of Longitude

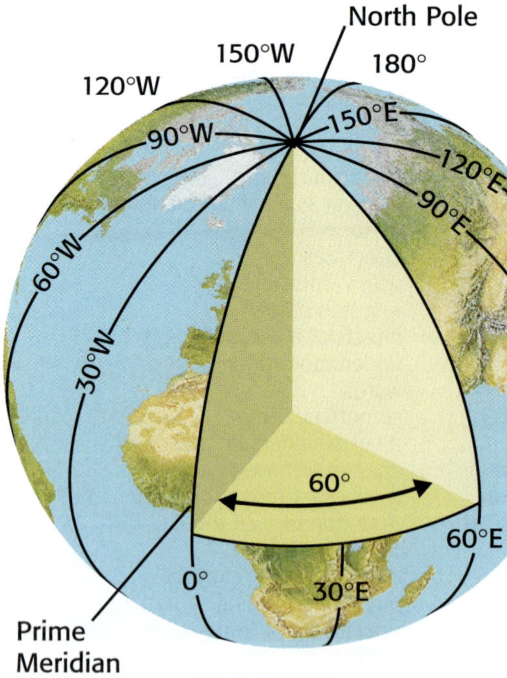

The equator divides the globe into two halves, called **hemispheres**. The half north of the equator is the Northern Hemisphere. The southern half is the Southern Hemisphere. The prime meridian and the 180° meridian divide the world into the Eastern Hemisphere and the Western Hemisphere. However, the prime meridian runs right through Europe and Africa. To avoid dividing these continents between two hemispheres, some mapmakers divide the Eastern and Western hemispheres at 20°W. This places all of Europe and Africa in the Eastern Hemisphere.

Our planet's land surface is divided into seven large landmasses, called **continents**. They are identified in the maps on this page. Landmasses smaller than continents and completely surrounded by water are called **islands**.

Geographers also organize Earth's water surface into parts. The largest is the world ocean. Geographers divide the world ocean into the Pacific Ocean, the Atlantic Ocean, the Indian Ocean, and the Arctic Ocean. Lakes and seas are smaller bodies of water.

Northern Hemisphere

Southern Hemisphere

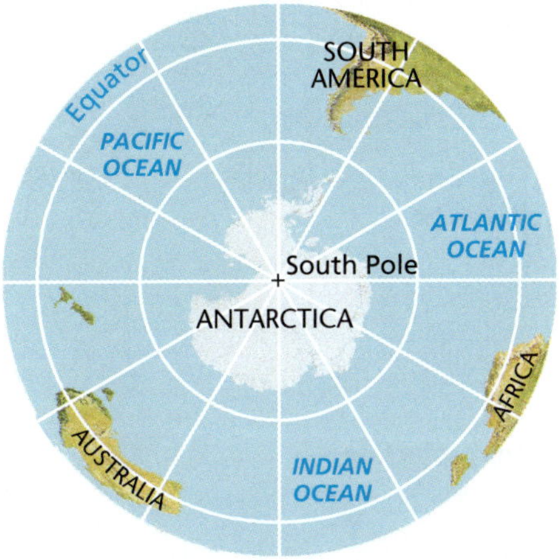

Western Hemisphere

North Pole

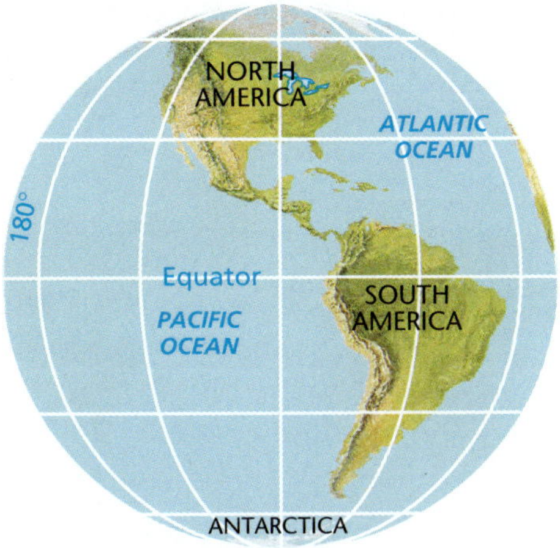

South Pole

Eastern Hemisphere

North Pole

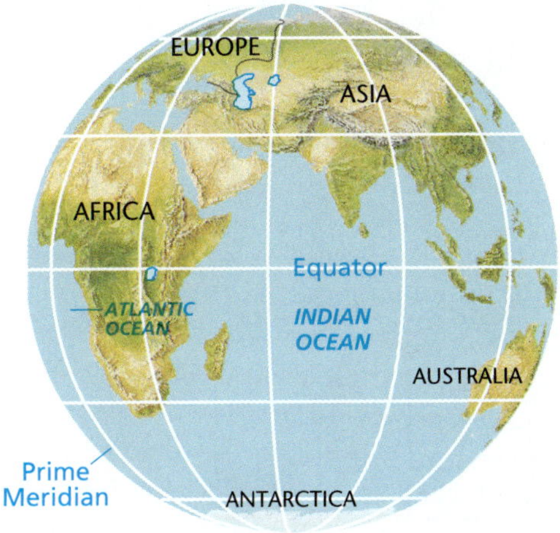

South Pole

GEOGRAPHY AND MAP SKILLS

Mapmaking

A **map** is a flat diagram of all or part of the earth's surface. Mapmakers have created different ways of showing our round planet on flat maps. These different ways are called **map projections**. Because the earth is round, there is no way to show it accurately in a flat map. All flat maps are distorted in some way. Mapmakers must choose the type of map projection that is best for their purposes. Many map projections are one of three kinds: cylindrical, conic, or flat-plane.

Cylindrical Projections

Cylindrical projections are based on a cylinder wrapped around the globe. The cylinder touches the globe only at the equator. The meridians are pulled apart and are parallel to each other instead of meeting at the Poles. This causes landmasses near the Poles to appear larger than they really are. The map below is a Mercator projection, one type of cylindrical projection. The Mercator projection is useful for navigators because it shows true direction and shape. However, it distorts the size of land areas near the Poles.

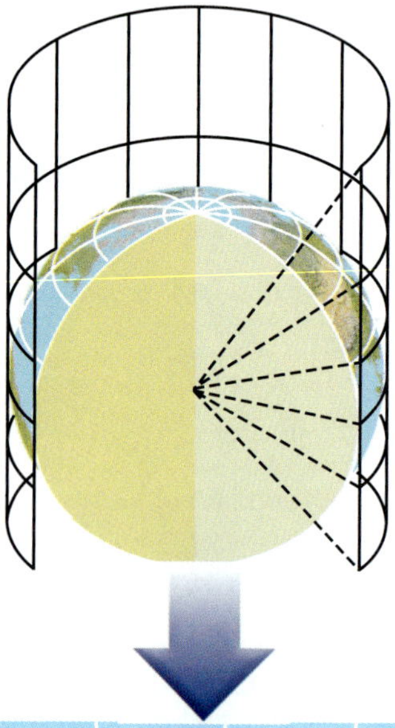

Paper cylinder

Mercator projection

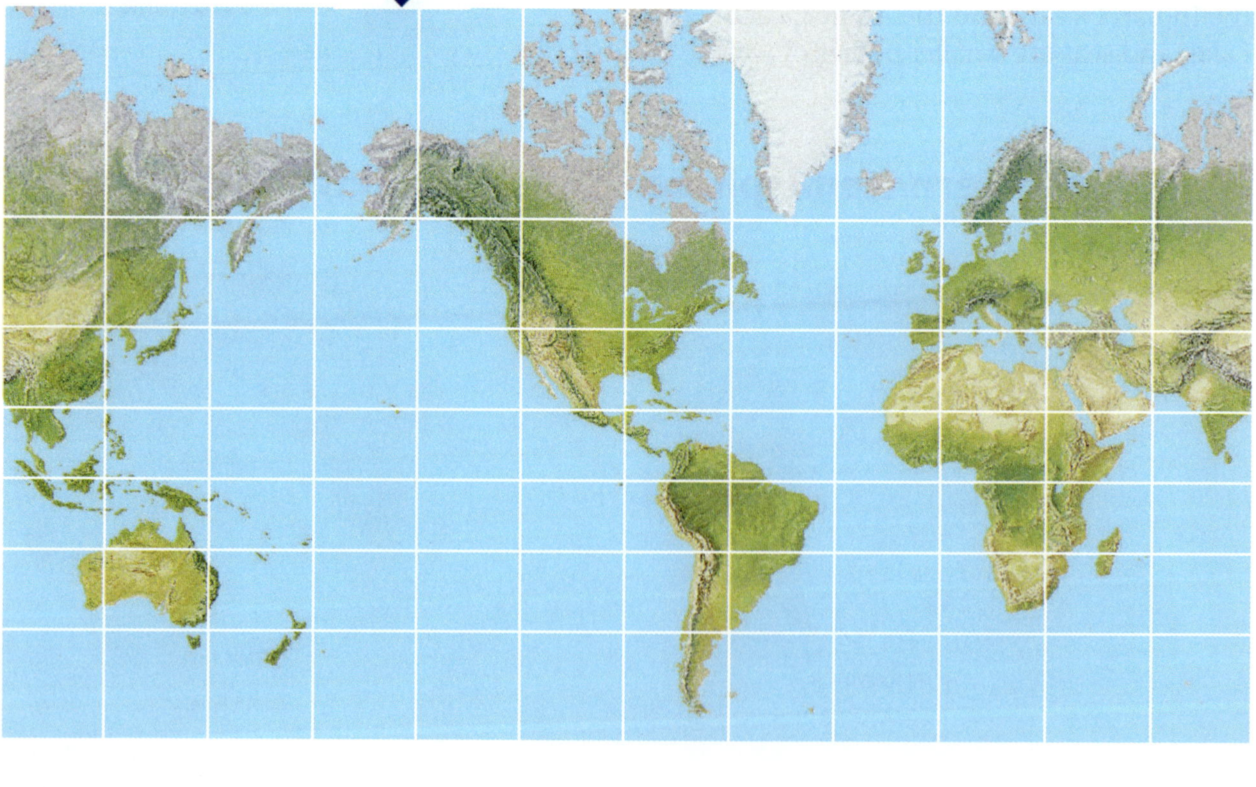

Conic Projections

Conic projections are based on a cone placed over the globe. A conic projection is most accurate along the lines of latitude where it touches the globe. It retains almost true shape and size. Conic projections are most useful for showing areas that have long east-west dimensions, such as the United States.

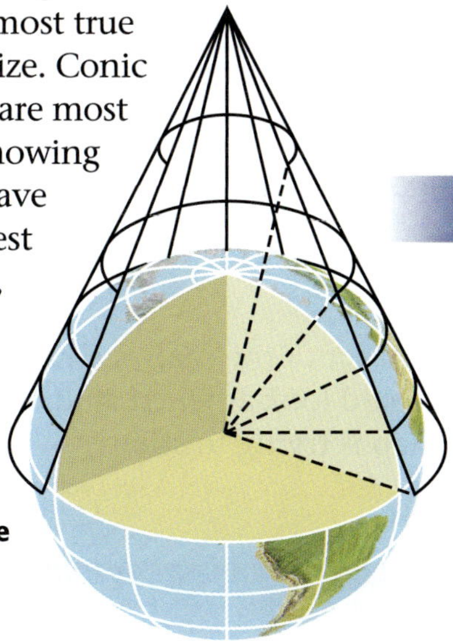

Conic projection

Flat-Plane Projections

Flat-plane projections are based on a plane touching the globe at one point, such as at the North Pole or South Pole. A flat-plane projection is useful for showing true direction for airplane pilots and ship navigators. It also shows true area. However, it distorts the true shapes of land masses.

Flat plane

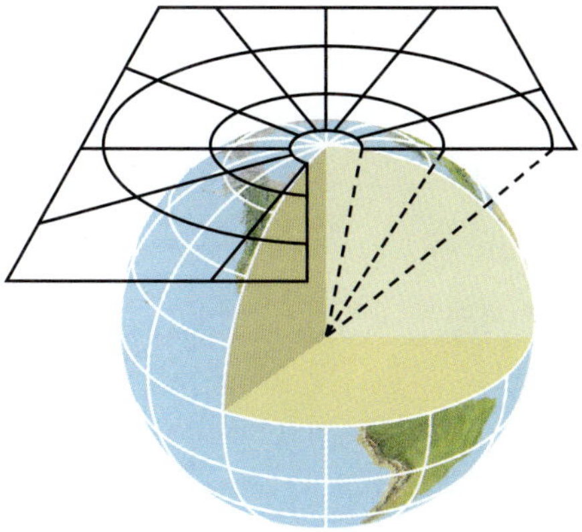

Flat-plane projection

Map Essentials

Maps are like messages sent out in code. Mapmakers provide certain elements that help us translate these codes. These elements help us understand the message they are presenting about a particular part of the world. Of these elements, almost all maps have titles, directional indicators, scales, and legends. The map below has all four of these elements, plus a fifth–a locator map.

1 Title

A map's **title** shows what the subject of the map is. The map title is usually the first thing you should look at when studying a map, because it tells you what the map is trying to show.

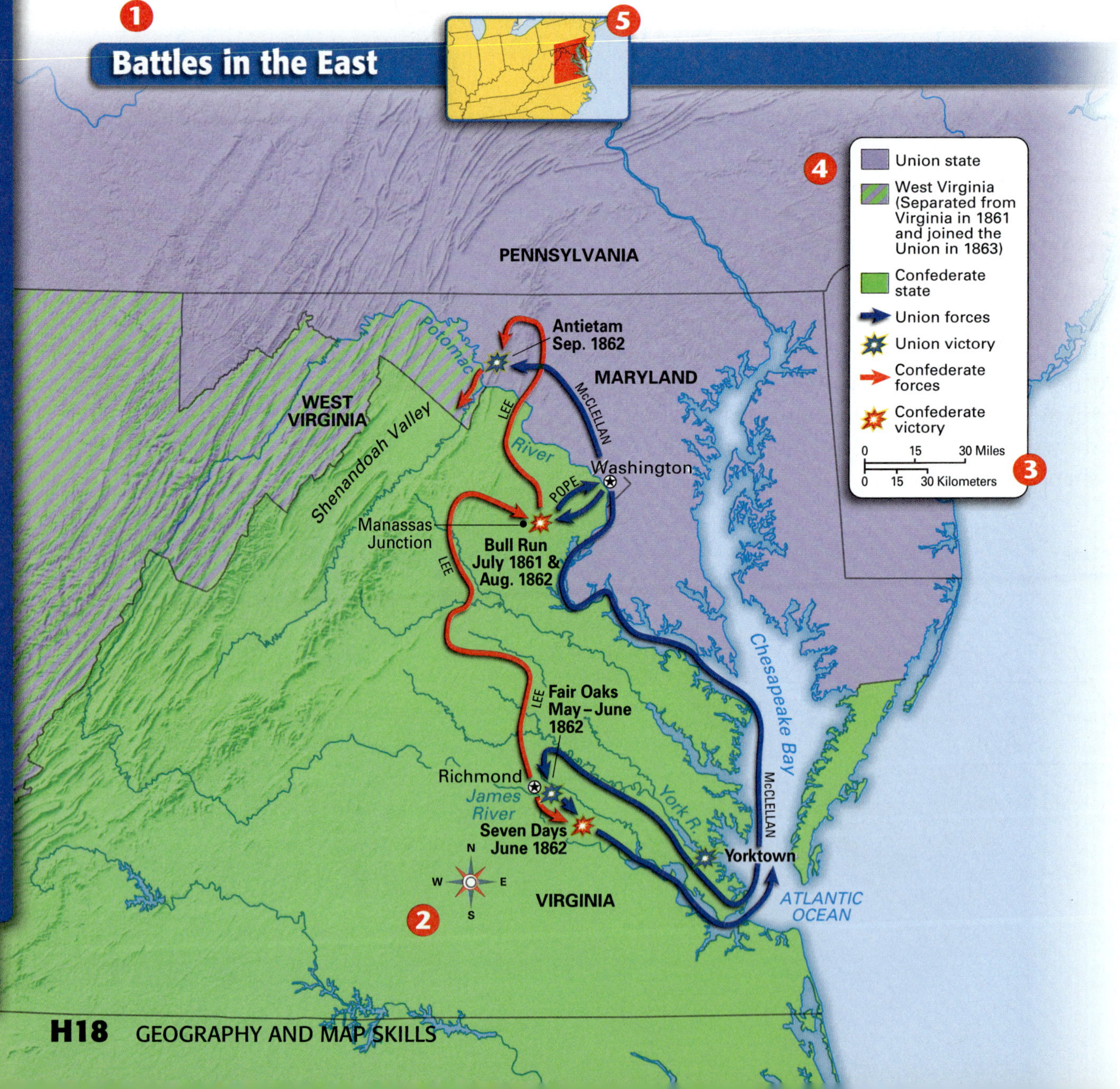

❷ Compass Rose

A directional indicator shows which way north, south, east, and west lie on the map. Some mapmakers use a "north arrow," which points toward the North Pole. Remember, "north" is not always at the top of a map. The way a map is drawn and the location of directions on that map depend on the perspective of the mapmaker. Most maps in this textbook indicate direction by using a compass rose. A **compass rose** has arrows that point to all four principal directions, as shown.

❸ Scale

Mapmakers use scales to show the distances between points on a map. Scales may appear on maps in several different forms. The maps in this textbook provide a bar **scale**. Scales give distances in miles and kilometers.

To find the distance between two points on the map, place a piece of paper so that the edge connects the two points. Mark the location of each point on the paper with a line or dot. Then, compare the distance between the two dots with the map's bar scale. The number on the top of the scale gives the distance in miles. The number on the bottom gives the distance in kilometers. Because the distances are given in large intervals, you may have to approximate the actual distance on the scale.

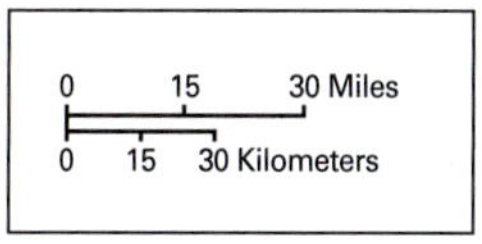

❹ Legend

The **legend**, or key, explains what the symbols on the map represent. Point symbols are used to specify the location of things, such as cities, that do not take up much space on the map. Some legends, such as the one shown here, show colors that represent certain elevations. Other maps might have legends with symbols or colors that represent things such as roads. Legends can also show economic resources, land use, population density, and climate.

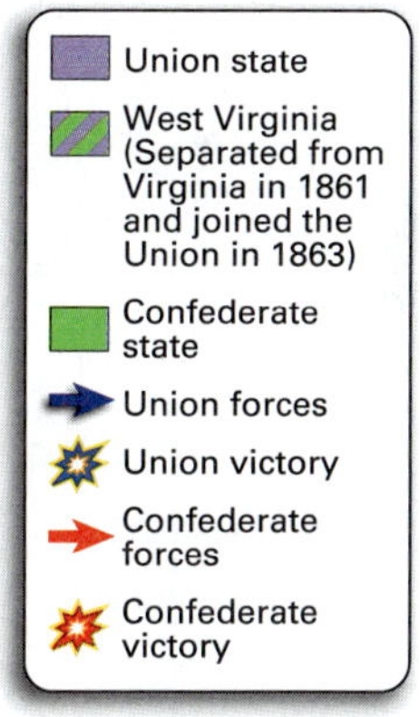

❺ Locator Map

A locator map shows where in the world the area on the map is located. The area shown on the main map is shown in red on the locator map. The locator map also shows surrounding areas so the map reader can see how the information on the map relates to neighboring lands.

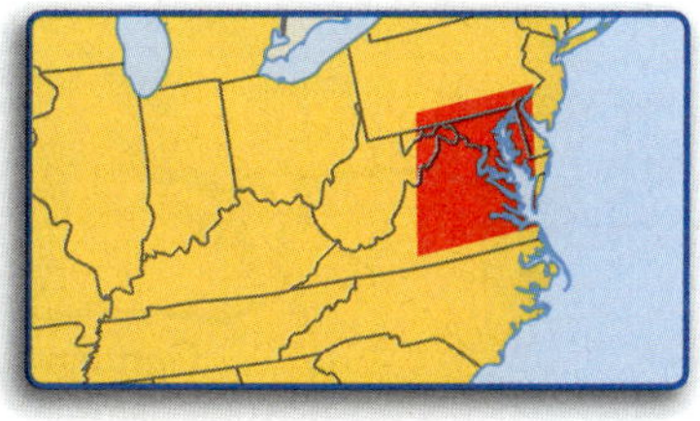

Working with Maps

The Atlas at the back of this textbook includes both physical and political maps. Physical maps, like the one you just saw and the one below, show the major physical features in a region. These features include things like mountain ranges, rivers, islands, and plains. Political maps show the major political features of a region, such as countries and their borders, capitals, and other important cities.

Topographic Maps

Some maps are topographic maps. A topographic map, like this one, shows the shape of the earth's surface using contour lines. Contour lines are imaginary lines connecting points of the same elevation above sea level. The distance between the lines represents the distance between points on the earth's surface. If the lines are close together, the feature is more steep than if the lines are far apart. Symbols on topographic maps represent natural and manmade features such as rivers, mountains, roads, and even buildings. Name five symbols you see on this topographic map.

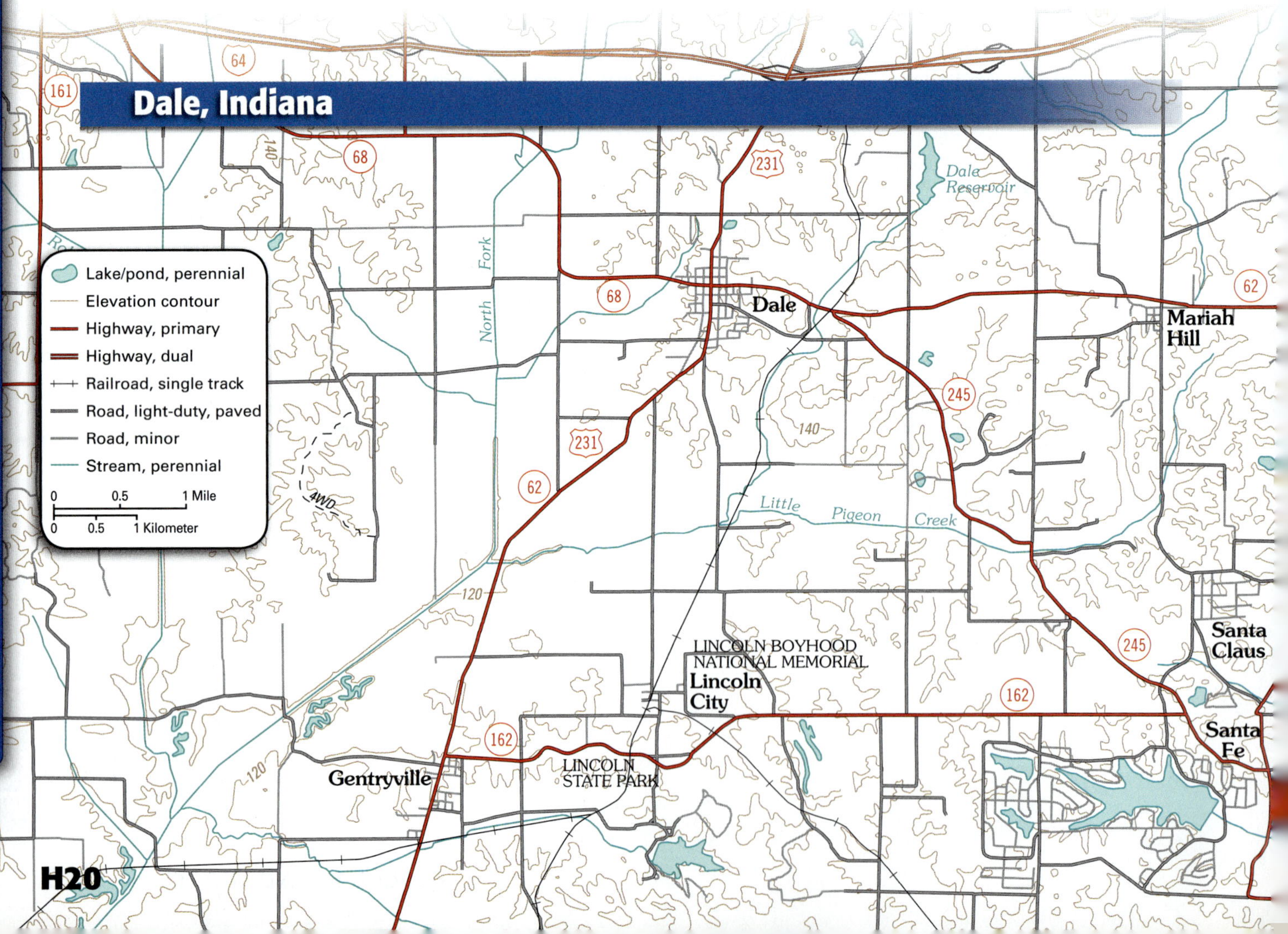

Historical Map

In this textbook, most of the maps you will study are historical maps. Historical maps, such as this one, are maps that show information about the past. This information might be which lands an empire controlled or where a certain group of people lived. Often colors are used to indicate the different things on the map. What does this map show?

Route Map

One special type of historical map is called a route map. A route map, like the one above, shows the route, or path, that someone or something followed. Route maps can show things like trade routes, invasion routes, or the journeys and travels of people. If more than one route is shown, several arrows of different colors may be used. What does this route map show?

The maps in this textbook will help you study and understand history. By working with these maps, you will see where important events happened, where empires rose and fell, and where people moved. In studying these maps, you will learn how geography has influenced history.

Geographic Dictionary

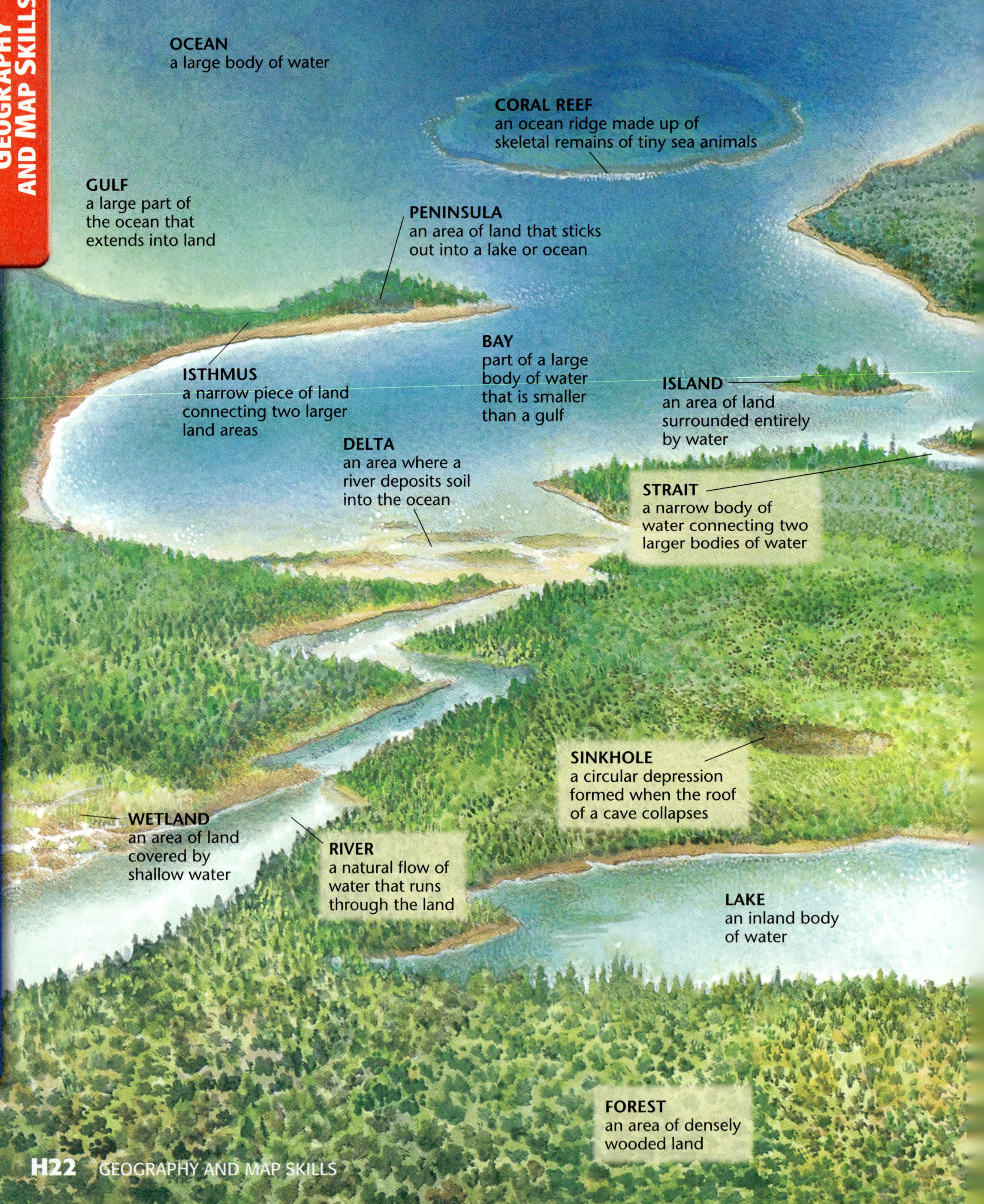

COAST
an area of land near the ocean
MOUNTAIN
an area of rugged land that generally rises higher than 2,000 feet
VALLEY
an area of low land between hills or mountains
VOLCANO
an opening in Earth's crust where lava, ash, and gases erupt
CANYON
a deep, narrow valley with steep walls
GLACIER
a large area of slow-moving ice
HILL
a rounded, elevated area of land smaller than a mountain
PLAIN
a nearly flat area
DUNE
a hill of sand shaped by wind
OASIS
an area in the desert with a water source
DESERT
an extremely dry area with little water and few plants
PLATEAU
a large, flat, elevated area of land

The Five Themes of Geography

Geography is the study of the world's people and places. As you can imagine, studying the entire world is a big job. To make the job easier, geographers have created the Five Themes of Geography. They are: **Location, Place, Human-Environment Interaction, Movement,** and **Region**. You can think of the Five Themes as five windows you can look through to study a place. If you looked at the same place through five different windows, you would have five different perspectives, or viewpoints, of the place. Using the Five Themes in this way will help you better understand the world's people and places.

1 Location The first thing to study about a place is its location. Where is it? Every place has an absolute location—its exact location on Earth. A place also has a relative location—its location in relation to other places. Use the theme of location to ask questions like, "Where is this place located, and how has its location affected it?"

2 Place Every place in the world is unique and has its own personality and character. Some things that can make a place unique include its weather, plants and animals, history, and the people that live there. Use the theme of place to ask questions like, "What are the unique features of this place, and how are they important?"

3 Human-Environment Interaction People interact with their environment in many ways. They use land to grow food and local materials to build houses. At the same time, a place's environment influences how people live. For example, if the weather is cold, people wear warm clothes. Use the theme of human-environment interaction to ask questions like, "What is this place's environment like, and how does it affect the people who live there?"

4 Movement The world is constantly changing, and places are affected by the movement of people, goods, ideas, and physical forces. For example, people come and go, new businesses begin, and rivers change their course. Use the theme of movement to ask questions like, "How is this place changing, and why?"

5 Region A region is an area that has one or more features that make it different from surrounding areas. A desert, a country, and a coastal area are all regions. Geographers use regions to break the world into smaller pieces that are easier to study. Use the theme of region to ask questions like "What common features does this area share, and how is it different from other areas?"

1 LOCATION

The United States is located in the Western Hemisphere. Forty-eight of the states are located between Mexico and Canada. This location has good farmland, many resources, and many different natural environments.

2 PLACE

New York City is one of the most powerful cities in the world. The people of New York also make the city one of the most ethnically diverse places in the world.

3 HUMAN-ENVIRONMENT INTERACTION

People near Las Vegas, Nevada, transform the desert landscape by building new neighborhoods. Americans modify their environment in many other ways—by controlling rivers, building roads, and creating farmland.

5 REGION

The United States is a political region with one government. At the same time, smaller regions can be found inside the country, such as the Badlands in South Dakota.

4 MOVEMENT

People, goods, and ideas are constantly moving to and from places such as Seattle, Washington. As some places grow, others get smaller, but every place is always changing.

How to Make This Book Work for You

Studying U.S. history will be easy for you using this textbook. Take a few minutes to become familiar with the easy-to-use structure and special features of this history book. See how this U.S. history textbook will make history come alive for you!

Unit

Each chapter of this textbook is part of a unit of study focusing on a particular time period. Each unit opener provides an illustration, painting, or photograph that gives you an overview of the exciting topics that you will study in the unit.

Chapter

Each chapter begins with a chapter-opener introduction where the sections of the chapter are listed out, and ends with Chapter Review pages and a Standardized Test Practice page.

Reading Social Studies These chapter-level reading lessons teach you skills and provide opportunities for practice to help you read the textbook more successfully. Within each chapter there is a point-of-reference *Focus on Reading* note in the margin to demonstrate the reading skill for the chapter. There are also questions in the Chapter Review activity to make sure that you understand the reading skill.

Social Studies Skills The Social Studies Skills lessons, which appear at the end of each chapter, give you an opportunity to learn and use a skill that you will most likely use again while in school. You will also be given a chance to make sure that you understand each skill by answering related questions in the Chapter Review activity.

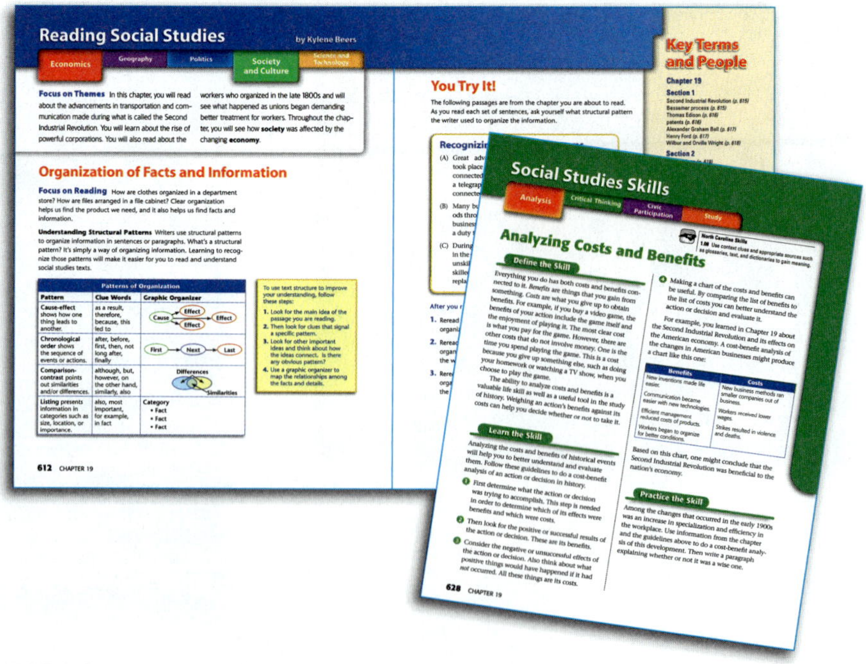

Section

The Section opener pages include: Main Idea statements, an overarching Big Idea statement, and Key Terms and People. In addition, each section includes the following special features.

If You Were There . . . introductions begin each section with a situation for you to respond to, placing you in the time period and in a situation related to the content that you will be studying in the section.

Building Background sections connect what will be covered in this section with what you studied in the previous section.

Short sections of content organize the information in each section into small chunks of text that you should not find too overwhelming.

The **Taking Notes** feature allows you to write down the most important information from the section in a usable format.

Big Business

SECTION 2

If YOU were there...

It is 1895, and your town is home to a large corporation. The company's founder and owner, a wealthy man, lives in a mansion on a hill. He is a fair employer but not especially generous. Many townspeople work in his factory. You and other town leaders feel that he should contribute more to local charities and community organizations.

How could this business leader help the town more?

BUILDING BACKGROUND Advanced technology along with the use of oil and electric power helped American businesses grow. Soon the shape of the American economy changed. Some companies grew so large that they began to dominate entire industries.

Dominance of Big Business

In the late 1800s many entrepreneurs formed their businesses as **corporations**, or businesses that sell portions of ownership called stock shares. The leaders of these corporations were some of the most widely respected members of American society in the late 1800s. Political leaders praised prosperous businesspeople as examples of American hard work, talent, and success.

New sales techniques like those taught by John H. Patterson helped change business practices.

What You Will Learn...

Main Ideas

1. The rise of corporations and powerful business leaders led to the dominance of big business in the United States.
2. People and the government began to question the methods of big business.

The Big Idea

The growth of big business in the late 1800s led to the creation of monopolies.

Key Terms and People

corporations, *p. 619*
Andrew Carnegie, *p. 620*
vertical integration, *p. 620*
John D. Rockefeller, *p. 620*
horizontal integration, *p. 621*
trust, *p. 621*
Leland Stanford, *p. 621*
social Darwinism, *p. 621*
monopoly, *p. 622*
Sherman Antitrust Act, *p. 622*

TAKING NOTES As you read this section, take notes on the new business practices you learn about. Keep them organized in a chart like the one below.

New Business Practice

THE INDUSTRIAL AGE **619**

---

murder if he killed a slave while punishing him. Enslaved Africans, on the other hand, received harsh penalties for minor offenses, such as breaking a tool. Runaways were often tortured and sometimes killed.

The treatment of enslaved Africans varied. Some slaves reported that their masters treated them kindly. To protect their investment, some slaveholders provided adequate food and clothing for their slaves. However, severe treatment was very common. Whippings, brandings, and even worse torture were all part of American slavery.

READING CHECK **Generalizing** How were enslaved Africans treated in the Americas?

Slave Culture in the Americas

Slaves in the Americas came from many different parts of Africa. They spoke different languages and had different cultural backgrounds. But enslaved Africans also shared many customs and viewpoints. They built upon what they had in common to create a new African American culture.

Families were a vital part of slave culture. Families provided a refuge—a place not fully under the slaveholders' control. However, slave families faced many challenges. Families were often broken apart when a family member was sold to another owner. In Latin America, there were many more enslaved males than females. This made it difficult for slaves there to form stable families.

Religion was a second refuge for slaves. It gave enslaved Africans a form of expression that was partially free from their slaveholders' control. Slave religion was primarily Christian, but it included traditional elements from African religions as well. Religion gave slaves a sense of self worth and a hope for salvation in this life and the next. Spirituals were a common form of religious expression among slaves. Slaves also used songs and folktales to tell their stories of sorrow, hope, agony, and joy.

Many slaves expressed themselves through art and dance. Dances were important social events in slave communities. Like most elements of slave culture, art and dance were heavily influenced by African traditions.

READING CHECK **Identifying Points of View** Why was religion important to slaves in the Americas?

SUMMARY AND PREVIEW After disease wiped out much of the Native American population, colonists turned to slave labor. In the next chapter you will learn about English colonies in the Americas.

FOCUS ON NORTH CAROLINA

Slavery began in North Carolina almost as soon as the colony was founded. Some of the Lords Proprietors, or owners, had been planters and slave traders in the West Indies. Although slavery would become an important aspect of life in the state, there were fewer enslaved Africans in North Carolina than in other southern colonies.

Section 5 Assessment

go.hrw.com
Online Quiz
KEYWORD: SC7 HP2

Reviewing Ideas, Terms, and People

1. a. **Recall** Why did so many Native Americans die after coming into contact with Europeans?
   b. **Summarize** Why did plantation owners turn to enslaved Africans as a labor force?
2. a. **Identify** What was the **Middle Passage**?
   b. **Describe** Explain how enslaved Africans were treated after they reached the colonies in the Americas.
3. a. **Explain** What are spirituals?
   b. **Analyze** How did religion and family provide a refuge from the harsh life enslaved Africans were forced to endure?

Critical Thinking

4. **Identifying Cause and Effect** Review your notes on the slave trade. Use a chart like the one below to explain the causes and the effects of the slave trade.

Causes	→	Effects

FOCUS ON WRITING

5. **Writing about Slavery** Add information about the beginnings of slavery in the Americas to your notes. Include notes about slave culture. What refuges did enslaved people have from their suffering?

NEW EMPIRES IN THE AMERICAS **61**

Focus on North Carolina features highlight events in North Carolina state history, while North Carolina History Makers provide information about important North Carolinians.

Reading Check questions end each section of content so that you can test whether or not you understand what you have just studied.

Summary and Preview statements connect what you have just studied in the section to what you will study in the next section.

Section Assessment boxes provide an opportunity for you to make sure that you understand the main ideas of the section. We also provide assessment practice online!

PROLOGUE

A Review of North Carolina History

Building Background Geographers divide the almost 50,000 square miles of North Carolina into three regions based on the features of the land. These three regions are the mountain region in the west, the Piedmont region in the central part of the state, and the coastal plains region in the east. Each of these regions has resources that have influenced settlement and life in the area.

The Blue Ridge Parkway

Early North Carolina

Reading Focus *As you read, think about what life might have been like for a colonial North Carolinian.*

The first Americans came in small groups from Asia over the course of thousands of years. These people spread to the farthest points of North and South America and formed communities along the way. Many similarities and differences arose between Native American groups in different regions of the continents, including what is today North Carolina.

KEY FACTS

- **1524** Giovanni da Verrazano becomes the first European to see North Carolina.
- **1526** Spain begins a settlement south of the Cape Fear River.
- **1584** The Amadas-Barlowe expedition arrives at Roanoke Island.

Native Americans in North Carolina

Native Americans began living in what is today North Carolina perhaps as early as 12,000 years ago. By AD 1000, farmers known as Mississippians were living in the area. Farming provided a stable food supply and led to permanent settlements. Mississipians built large buildings and developed detailed artwork. They also built mounds that served as village centers and places for ceremonies. Several of these mounds are found in North Carolina, including the Town Creek Mound in Montgomery County. The Cherokees, Catawbas, and Tuscaroras were the largest Native American groups living in North Carolina at the time of European contact.

European Exploration

The first European to see North Carolina was Italian explorer Giovanni da Verrazano. In 1524 he sent a glowing description of the area to the king of France, but the king sent no further expeditions. The Spanish began a settlement south of the Cape Fear River in 1526, but it failed.

Later, the English explored North America, including North Carolina. In 1584 the adventurer Walter Raleigh launched the Amadas-Barlowe expedition. Members of the expedition returned with plants from their time on Roanoke Island. They also brought back two Native Americans who lived in the area. Raleigh was knighted, and the area was named Virginia in honor of Queen Elizabeth.

Beginnings to 1584

10,000 BC — AD1500 — 1584

10,000 BC Native Americans settle in North Carolina.

1524 Giovanni da Verrazano becomes the first European to see North Carolina.

1584 Walter Raleigh sends an expedition to explore Roanoke Island.

Hupa jump dance basket

Walter Raleigh

THE GRANGER COLLECTION, NEW YORK

KEY FACTS

- **1587** The "Lost Colony" is established on Roanoke Island.
- **1663** King Charles II grants land to eight Lords Proprietors.
- **1712** The Carolina colony is split into two colonies.
- **1729** North Carolina becomes a royal colony.
- **1771** The Regulator movement ends at the Battle of Alamance.

English Colonization

The English were eager to colonize the area known as Virginia. An expedition landed on Roanoke Island in late 1585, and one of its members, Ralph Lane, established a small colony. Conflict soon broke out between the colonists and Native Americans. When Sir Francis Drake arrived in 1586, most of the colonists returned to England. Another group of colonists arrived at Roanoke Island in 1587. Its inhabitants disappeared, and the colony became known as the "Lost Colony." Members of the colony were never found, but later colonists established themselves in Virginia. In 1655 Nathaniel Batts moved south from Virginia and became the first European to settle permanently in what is now North Carolina.

Settlement continued in 1663 when King Charles II granted a charter to a group of eight men called the Lords Proprietors. The land in the charter included most of the area between Virginia and Spanish Florida west to the Pacific Ocean. The area was named Carolina, from the Latin form of "Charles."

A Proprietary Colony

The Lords Proprietors established three counties and appointed William Drummond the first governor. The governor had the power to appoint council members and other officials, to veto laws, and to call up military forces. The proprietors also established an assembly elected by "freemen," or free, male landowners. Political parties arose in the colony, with one party supporting the rule of the proprietors and governor and another wanting local self-rule.

The colony grew slowly, and the Lords Proprietors changed some of their policies to encourage settlement. Most of their early efforts, however, were unsuccessful. They could not find a good governor for the colony, and Native American attacks threatened the colonists. Pirates like Blackbeard, Stede Bonnet, and Anne Bonny raided ships along the Outer Banks. The large Carolina colony was difficult to govern and protect, and in 1712 the proprietors split the colony into North and South Carolina. Edward Hyde became the first governor of North Carolina.

1585–1771

1585

1587 Virginia Dare becomes the first English child born in the Americas.

1669 The Fundamental Constitutions of Carolina are issued by the eight Lords Proprietors.

1710 New Bern is founded by the Swiss.

1712 Carolina is split into north and south colonies.

Baptism of Virginia Dare

A Royal Colony

In North Carolina as in other colonies in America, settlers and Native Americans sometimes clashed. The Crown decided that a more coordinated colonial empire was necessary to defend against the French and Spanish as well as Native Americans. In 1729 the Crown bought parts of the colony from seven of the eight Lords Proprietors. Only John Carteret, Earl Granville, kept his share. The area he owned—a stretch of land along the border with Virginia—became known as the Granville District. North Carolina became a royal colony, a change that benefited the administration of the colony and made the government more stable.

New Immigrants and New Conflicts

As the government became more stable and land became more crowded in other colonies, people started to migrate to North Carolina. Migrants along the Great Wagon Road, which stretched from Pennsylvania to Georgia, sometimes settled along the road in the Piedmont area of North Carolina. Scots-Irish, Highland Scots, Germans, Moravians, and enslaved Africans made up most of the population explosion between 1730 and 1775.

The increase in new settlers in the colony created political tensions between established communities and newer ones. Older counties and towns had more power in the government, and the newer counties fought for a greater role. A group of western citizens called the Regulators organized to combat what they saw as abuses of power by the colonial government. They rioted and damaged property belonging to government officials. A series of skirmishes were fought between the Regulators and colonial militia. In 1771 Governor William Tryon led a militia force against the Regulators at the Battle of Alamance. The government forces defeated the rebels, and the Regulator movement ended. Six of the men were executed for treason. Tensions between the sections remained, but soon remaining tensions were forgotten as colonists focused more on the growing conflict with Britain.

***Queen Anne's Revenge,* Blackbeard's flagship**

Tryon Palace in New Bern

1718 Raids of the North Carolina coast by Blackbeard and other pirates are at their peak.

1729 North Carolina becomes a royal colony, except the Granville District.

1765 William Tryon becomes governor of North Carolina.

1771 The Battle of Alamance ends the Regulator uprising in the state.

Tryon and the Regulators

THE GRANGER COLLECTION, NEW YORK

KEY FACTS

- **1774** Women of Edenton hold a tea party to protest British taxes.
- **1775** The Mecklenburg Resolves are issued.
- **1776** The Halifax Resolves become the first official call for independence from Britain.
- **1789** North Carolina becomes the twelfth state to ratify the U.S. Constitution.

North Carolina in the Revolution

Tensions between American colonists and the British Parliament grew throughout the 1760s and 1770s. During the French and Indian War, Benjamin Franklin suggested the Albany Plan of Union to unite the colonies in defense. After the war, Britain imposed taxes on the colonies to pay for the war and future defense. Colonists created committees of correspondence to communicate important information about protesting British rule. The North Carolina committee's first action was to issue a statement in support of Boston citizens who were protesting. The women of Edenton, led by Penelope Barker, staged their own protest against British actions by holding the Edenton Tea Party. They declared that they would not drink British tea or buy British goods.

The Beginning of War

Protests soon escalated to violence, and the first shot of the Revolutionary War was fired in 1775. Delegates to the Mecklenburg County Committee of Safety soon issued the Mecklenburg Resolves, a document stating that British laws would no longer be in effect. Colonial officials began organizing Loyalists to fight the Patriots. A Patriot victory at a battle between North Carolinians at Moores Creek Bridge prevented the British from taking over the South at the beginning of the war.

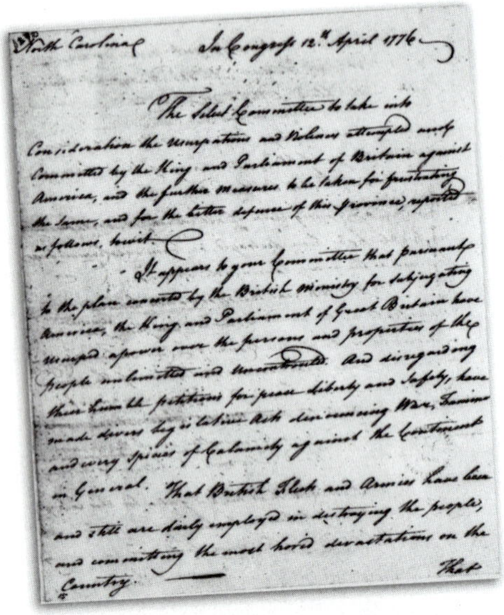

The Halifax Resolves

Independence Is Declared

As the war continued, citizens began meeting to discuss the future of the colonies. The first official call for independence from Great Britain was made by the 83 delegates to North Carolina's Fourth Provincial Congress, which met in Halifax in April 1776. Three months later, a meeting of delegates in Philadelphia approved the Declaration of Independence.

After independence was declared, the states organized regiments of troops to fight the British. Major General Robert Howe led a regiment at battles in Virginia before moving north to join George Washington

1771–1810

1771

1774 Penelope Barker holds the Edenton Tea Party to protest British taxes.

1775 The Mecklenburg Resolves nullify British law in the colony.

1776 The Halifax Resolves call for independence from Britain.

1776 The first state constitution of North Carolina is adopted.

1777 Major General Robert Howe takes command of the Southern Department of the Continental Army.

1778 North Carolina joins the United States by ratifying the Articles of Confederation.

Edenton monument

Robert Howe

in Pennsylvania. Bands of "Over-Mountain men" began fighting the British in the western part of North Carolina.

In the South, Nathanael Greene was placed in charge of the Patriots. He lured British general Charles Cornwallis into a trap at Guilford Courthouse. Unable to defeat Greene's forces in the South, Cornwallis moved his troops to Yorktown. His defeat there by Washington resulted in the end of the war and American independence.

A New State

After the Declaration of Independence, North Carolina's leaders faced the task of organizing a new government. Thomas Burke was elected the first governor of the new state, but his powers were very weak. The legislative assembly, led by Richard Caswell, had more power. In 1776, the assembly adopted a constitution and a declaration of rights.

North Carolina ratified the Articles of Confederation in 1778. The new nation faced a heavy financial burden from the ongoing war. Several states possessed western lands that could be sold to raise money. A debate raged about whether the states should give up these lands to the national government. North Carolina offered its western lands to the government but later withdrew the offer. Inhabitants of the area, however, organized a government in 1784 to seek statehood. They called the area the State of Franklin. The government soon collapsed and the land was returned to North Carolina.

The national government faced other problems, and in 1787 a convention was called to revise the Articles of Confederation. The convention produced a new plan for government, the Constitution. Under the Constitution, the national government would have expanded powers. In North Carolina, James Iredell led the defense of the new plan. North Carolina ratified the Constitution on November 21, 1789, becoming the 12th state to do so.

James Iredell

1784 The State of Franklin is established but soon collapses.

1789 James Iredell supports the U.S. Constitution in North Carolina.

1789 North Carolina becomes the twelfth state to ratify the Constitution.

1799 Gold is first discovered in North Carolina.

1810

Gold nuggets

"The Rip Van Winkle State"

KEY FACTS

- **1812–1815** Otway Burns captains the privateer *Snap Dragon* against the British.
- **1835** State leaders rewrite the North Carolina state constitution.
- **1854** "The Old North State" is published as a poem.

Reading Focus *As you read, notice how life changed for North Carolinians during the early and mid-1800s.*

Not long after the founding of the nation, the United States became involved in another war with Britain, the War of 1812. During the war the young nation relied on privateers, or private ships that raided foreign vessels. Many of these privateers belonged to North Carolinians, including Otway Burns. His ship *Snap Dragon* captured more than a million dollars' worth of goods. When the young nation defeated the British, Americans felt a growing sense of patriotism and turned their efforts to improving their country.

A Slumbering State

Despite a huge movement toward progress in the rest of the nation, North Carolina experienced a time of stagnation. It became known as "The Rip Van Winkle State." (Rip Van Winkle is a fictional character who slept for 20 years.) Some leaders began calling for improvements in government, education, and transportation. Sectional and political divisions kept these plans from being put into action, however.

Eventually, a new political party called the Whigs came to power. They rewrote the state constitution in 1835 and made improvements in transportation and education. A number of social reforms to help less fortunate citizens of the state also occurred under the Whigs. For example, a hospital for people who were mentally disabled opened in 1856.

The Whigs began to decline in North Carolina and national politics with the rise of the Democrats. The Democrats favored expanded voting rights and educational reforms. William W. Holden was a leader of the Democrats in North Carolina. His Raleigh newspaper, the *North-Carolina Standard,* became the most influential in the state.

The improvements and reforms of the Whigs and Democrats changed daily life in North Carolina. One aspect of this change was the literary awakening that was under way by 1835. The change was related to the growth of the educational system. New books about the state were

Otway Burns

1810–1854

1810

1812 Otway Burns begins raiding British ships during the War of 1812.

1818 The *Prometheus* becomes the first steamboat to travel North Carolina rivers.

1835 A new state constitution is written.

The *Prometheus*

published, and North Carolina writers began to produce plays, novels, and poetry. In 1854 "The Old North State" was published as a poem. The poem was written for a musical tune that would become the state song.

The Industrial Revolution

Among the many reforms of the mid-1800s were internal improvements, such as roads and canals, that helped the economy grow. The most important economic activity continued to be agriculture. Cotton and corn were important crops. By 1860 North Carolina produced more ham than any other state. The agricultural economy of the state relied on slavery. Although North Carolina had a smaller percentage of enslaved African Americans than other states in the South, by 1860 slaves accounted for more than one-third of the total population.

Although agriculture remained the main source of income for most North Carolinians, new inventions encouraged some to seek wealth in industry. New steam engines powered cotton and textile mills. Ironworks were established in the Piedmont area to supply the iron products needed for further growth.

The new steam engines also powered steamboats that could navigate the difficult rivers of northeastern North Carolina. The *Prometheus* was the first steamboat in the state. It was built by Otway Burns and traced a route along the Cape Fear River between Fayetteville and Southport. The state also built wooden plank roads. The longest plank road in the country was between Fayetteville and Bethania.

Westward Expansion

Advances in transportation opened up more land to settlers. People began moving farther west. As new territories became part of the United States, Native Americans were pushed off their land. In addition, slavery became an issue in westward expansion. The decision needed to be made whether to allow slavery in the new territories. Debate between abolitionists and people who were pro-slavery occurred in Congress and among voters. The debate caused violence and armed conflict to break out in some places.

Historical marker for plank roads

1843 William W. Holden becomes owner and publisher of the *North-Carolina Standard.*

1852 The Western Plank Road between Fayetteville and Bethania is completed.

1854

1854 William Gaston publishes the poem "The Old North State."

The North-Carolina Standard.
PHILO WHITE,
RALEIGH, N.C: FRIDAY, NOVEMBER 7, 1834.
PROSPECTUS

***North-Carolina Standard* newspaper**

KEY FACTS

- **1857** Hinton Rowan Helper publishes *The Impending Crisis of the South.*
- **1861** North Carolina secedes from the Union.
- **1865** The Civil War ends in North Carolina with the surrender of General Joseph Johnston.

An abolitionist from North Carolina, Hinton Rowan Helper, published a controversial book in 1857. *The Impending Crisis of the South* called for an immediate end to slavery. Northern abolitionists praised the book, but pro-slavery North Carolinians accused Helper of being a traitor to his region and culture.

Secession, War, and Reconstruction

Reading Focus *As you read, draw conclusions about the problems of North Carolina during the Civil War.*

The debate over how to resolve the question of slavery's expansion was the main issue in the presidential election of 1860. After Abraham Lincoln was elected, South Carolina seceded from the Union. Other slave states, including North Carolina, had to decide whether they would secede as well.

Most leaders in North Carolina thought that the division would be settled through diplomacy. When Lincoln called for troops to defend U.S. possessions in the South, however, North Carolinians were outraged. On May 20, 1861, state leaders voted to secede from the Union and to join the Confederate States of America, though many Unionists in the state remained loyal to the United States.

The Civil War

The first troops from North Carolina, led by J. B. Magruder and Daniel Harvey Hill, were victorious at Big Bethel in Virginia. The coast of North Carolina was open to attack, however. The Confederates built forts along the Outer Banks, but Union generals Benjamin Butler and Ambrose Burnside captured these forts and gained control of the coast of North Carolina from Morehead City to the Virginia border.

In addition to capturing much of the coastline, the Union set up a naval blockade. Confederate blockade runners used camouflaged ships to sneak past the Union navy, bringing badly needed supplies to ports for shipment to other parts of the South.

1854–1865

1854

1856 The North Carolina Railroad is completed.

1857 Hinton Rowan Helper publishes the controversial book *The Impending Crisis of the South.*

1861 North Carolina votes to secede from the Union.

1861 The first North Carolinian troops to fight in the Civil War participate in the Confederate victory at Big Bethel, Virginia.

Uniforms of the Confederate troops

In many ways, North Carolina was unique among Confederate states. It provided more troops than any other state in the Confederacy, but it was also the only Confederate state with an outspoken peace movement. After the election of 1862, North Carolina was the only Confederate state led by Unionists. Unionist sentiment was strongest in the western mountain region, and many Confederate army deserters hid there. The state also had conflicts with the Confederate government about resources and policy.

North Carolina was deeply divided about the Civil War, but battles there affected all its citizens. On his march through the South, Union general William Tecumseh Sherman ordered his troops not to raid the private property of the many Unionists in the state. The troops destroyed vast acres of forest, however. Confederate general Robert E. Lee sent General Joseph Johnston to stop Sherman's army, but Johnston surrendered on April 26, 1865. Except for a small skirmish near Waynesville the following month, the war in North Carolina was over. In all, more than 40,000 troops from North Carolina had died in the fighting, more troops than from any other southern state.

Reconstruction in North Carolina

The effects of the Civil War on the South were devastating. President Lincoln had a plan to rebuild the Union, but he was assassinated in 1865. Lincoln's plan was continued by the new president, North Carolinian Andrew Johnson. Johnson appointed William W. Holden provisional governor of North Carolina. Holden appointed more than 3,000 people to political offices across the state. He also called a convention to repeal the Ordinance of Secession. Holden was defeated in the 1865 election for governor, however.

With Holden's defeat, a more conservative government began leading the state. Despite calls for civil rights from black North Carolinians, the state legislature began passing laws called Black Codes that restricted the rights and freedom of freedpeople. Northern newspapers declared North Carolina and other southern states unfit to rejoin the Union.

1862 North Carolinian Mary Jane Patterson becomes the first African American woman to receive a bachelor of arts degree.

Mary Jane Patterson

1865

1865 The last Confederate troops in North Carolina surrender.

Meeting between General Johnston and General Sherman

KEY FACTS

- **1865** Andrew Johnson becomes president.
- **1868** North Carolina is readmitted to the Union.
- **1870** Conservatives gain control of the state legislature.
- **1898** A race riot in Wilmington results in the death of at least 14 African Americans.

The Republican Congress agreed that southern states were not making significant enough changes. Congress took control of Reconstruction, instituted military rule in the South, and appointed Republican leaders to office. White and African American Unionists were encouraged to join the Republicans. A majority of white North Carolinians did not support the Republicans, but their refusal to vote for delegates to an 1867 constitutional convention meant that few Conservatives had a voice in the new state constitution of 1868. With the Republicans leading the state government, North Carolina was readmitted to the Union.

Conservatives felt they had to organize against Republicans and African Americans who were participating in government. Secret political groups like the violent Ku Klux Klan appeared. The Republican state leadership tried to put an end to the Ku Klux Klan's violence by sending troops to two counties, but the Conservatives made gains in the 1870 elections. In 1870 they gained control of the legislature, and by 1877 Reconstruction had ended.

A New Century

Reading Focus *As you read, think about how life changed for North Carolinians after Reconstruction.*

Andrew Johnson

After Reconstruction, the economy of North Carolina continued to depend on agriculture, but the state began expanding its investment in industry as well. As cities grew larger, more railroads were built, which spurred further industrial growth. Tobacco products, textiles, and furniture became important to the state. By 1880 there were 126 tobacco factories in the state, and by the early 1900s North Carolina was on its way to becoming the country's leading producer of fine furniture.

Life in the New South

Along with changes in the South's economy came a change in its social structure. More African American institutions, such as churches, schools, businesses, and social clubs, were established. Instead of a government controlled by plantation owners, businesspeople began to control the

1865–1914

1865

1865 Andrew Johnson becomes president.

1868 North Carolina's first African American state legislators are elected.

1868 North Carolina is readmitted to the Union.

1885 The current state flag is adopted.

1895 Biltmore Mansion is completed.

Biltmore

government. The middle class grew and became more prosperous as industrialization helped create jobs and wealth. Industrialization also led to class divisions between business owners and employees.

The Fusionists

Growing class divisions led to political upheaval. Critics of the state government claimed the Democrats (as the Conservatives had renamed themselves) represented the interests of the wealthy and industrialists over the interests of the common people and farmers. The Republicans joined with the Populists, many of whom were farmers, to create the Fusionists. The Fusionists controlled the state from 1897 to 1899 and began reforms of education and local government.

Democrats regained control of the government after running racist campaigns in 1898 that targeted African Americans. Bands of Democratic supporters known as Red Shirts attacked African American and Fusionist leaders. A riot broke out in Wilmington, and the black mayor fled. After winning the election, the Democrats took steps to eliminate African Americans' right to vote.

Progressivism

At the turn of the 20th century a new political force arose in North Carolina and the nation. Progressivism led to reforms in government and business and to changes that extended some voters' rights. African Americans, however, were still restricted from voting in many places. In North Carolina, improvements were made in education and in prisons.

World War I and the Roaring Twenties

Progressive reform slowed, however, as war broke out in Europe in 1914. By mid-1917 the United States had become involved in World War I, and the nation mobilized for war. Training camps were established in Charlotte and Raleigh, and Camp Bragg was built near Fayetteville. These camps boosted the local economies.

1898 The offices of Alex Manly's newspaper are burned during the Wilmington race riots.

1903 The Wright brothers successfully test their aircraft at Kill Devil Hills near Kitty Hawk, North Carolina.

1914

The Wright brothers take flight.

KEY FACTS

- **1918** Camp Bragg is built near Fayetteville.
- **1929** O. Max Gardner becomes governor of North Carolina.
- **1942** The first airborne units train for duty at Fort Bragg.

After the war's end in 1918 and a brief recession, the nation enjoyed a time of economic prosperity and change. Young people began challenging the rules of society. North Carolina saw a growing fundamentalist Christian movement arise in reaction to the changes. North Carolina was one of the first states to approve Prohibition, or a ban on the sale of alcohol, which became federal law in 1919. State government also changed, with women slowly becoming more involved. In 1920 Lillian Exum Clement became the first woman elected to the North Carolina General Assembly.

The Great Depression

In 1929 the period of prosperity came to an end. A severe drop in the stock market caused a banking crisis. Deflation, the reduction in the value of money, and a loss of jobs seriously weakened the U.S. economy. In North Carolina, the furniture, textile, and tobacco industries were hurt as prices dropped. Between 1930 and 1933 hundreds of banks and savings and loan associations failed.

State Aid

To combat the Great Depression, North Carolina governor O. Max Gardner proposed a plan of limited economic aid. His "Live-at-Home" program encouraged farmers to grow their own food. Home economist Jane Simpson McKimmon helped rural residents preserve this food by pioneering a home-demonstration program that was copied throughout the nation. In a home-demonstration program, experts meet with individuals to show them useful techniques of home economics.

Federal Aid

The election of Franklin Delano Roosevelt as president in 1932 began a new period of federal aid to reduce the hardships caused by the Great Depression. Roosevelt's plan was called the New Deal. Under the Agri-

1915–1946

1915

1918 Camp Bragg is established near Fayetteville.

1920 Lillian Exum Clement becomes the first woman elected to the North Carolina General Assembly.

Lillian Exum Clement

1924 Trinity College is renamed Duke University.

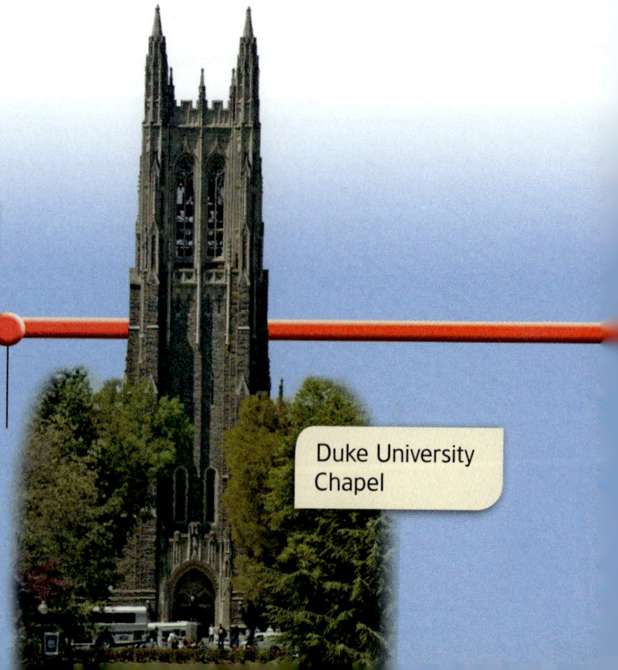

Duke University Chapel

cultural Adjustment Acts of 1933 and 1938, crop prices rose. Reforms in industry gave more rights to workers and provided aid to those who were unemployed. The Works Progress Administration put people to work building public works, such as dams and roads. The Rural Electrification Administration brought electricity to much of rural North Carolina.

World War II in North Carolina

The Great Depression ended as the nation began mobilizing for World War II. The United States entered the war after Japan bombed Pearl Harbor, Hawaii, in 1941. North Carolina, like other states, began manufacturing ships, planes, ammunition, and other supplies for the war effort. The state also supplied crops for food and clothing for the troops. More than 350,000 North Carolinians served in the military during the war, including about 7,000 women.

Government-ordered blackouts—nights when civilians were required to turn off all lights so that the U.S. ships off the coast could not be distinguished as targets—were common in North Carolina during the war. There were so many German submarines in the Atlantic Ocean off Cape Hatteras that the area was known as Torpedo Junction. The submarines targeted oil tankers, and many wounded sailors were treated in local hospitals. At Ocracoke today, there is a British cemetery with the graves of British sailors who died as a result of German attacks.

North Carolina's military bases were also important to the war effort. Camp Bragg was greatly enlarged and became known as Fort Bragg. Camp Lejeune became the second-largest marine base in the country. In addition to training soldiers, the state's camps held prisoners of war. These soldiers often worked on area farms, and some returned after the war to visit the families with whom they had worked. After brutal fighting on three continents, the war ended in 1945.

Army engineers at Fort Bragg

O. Max Gardner

1929 O. Max Gardner becomes governor of the state.

1935 The North Carolina Rural Electrification Authority is established.

1939 North Carolina produces more household wood furnishings than any other state.

1942 The first airborne divisions are trained at camps in the state.

1946

A chair manufacturer in North Carolina

The Postwar World and the Modern Era

Key Facts

- **1960** The first civil rights sit-in in the South takes place in Greensboro.
- **1971** The people adopt a new state constitution.
- **1972** Jesse Helms is elected to the first of six Senate terms.
- **2004** Hurricane Charley hits the coast of North Carolina.

Reading Focus *As you read, identify major issues in North Carolina today.*

Once World War II was over, the United States focused its attention on maintaining a strong economy. In North Carolina, Governor W. Kerr Scott introduced his "Go Forward" program to improve roads, schools, and port facilities. State leaders also began plans for an area between Raleigh, Durham, and Chapel Hill that would become Research Triangle Park, a center for research in the chemical and electronics industries. State business leaders focused on new industries and technologies to help make North Carolina less dependent on its traditional industries.

Social Changes

Rapid economic changes occurred along with dramatic social changes. The issue of civil rights was debated at all levels of society. African Americans and other minorities began calling for change. In 1960 Greensboro, North Carolina, witnessed the first sit-in protest in the South for equal rights for African Americans.

By the 1970s North Carolina leaders focused on reforming state government. They rewrote the state constitution and reorganized the government to be more efficient. Social changes included the rise of a new conservatism. Religion became increasingly influential in political affairs. Republicans like North Carolina senator Jesse Helms made the Christian conservative movement an important political force.

North Carolina Today

During the 1990s North Carolina's economy grew rapidly. Traditional industries are still a crucial part of the economy. In 1999 the state produced about 450 million pounds of tobacco. Textile exports from the state amounted to about $3 billion in 2000. High-tech industries and

1946–Present

1946

1949 The state's first commercial television station opens in Charlotte.

1955 The University of North Carolina admits its first African American freshmen.

1959 Research Triangle Park opens between Raleigh, Durham, and Chapel Hill.

1960 The first lunch counter sit-in protest in the South occurs in Greensboro.

Lunch counter sit-in

electronics manufacturing helped the state during the boom of the 1990s. In recent years Charlotte has become the second-largest banking center in the United States, creating a new source of prosperity for North Carolina. The National Association for Stock Car Auto Racing (NASCAR) and other sports and tourism bring additional revenue to the state.

In spite of growth, many North Carolinians are concerned about creating a diverse economy. The furniture industry has declined as manufacturing jobs have been outsourced, or moved to other countries. North Carolina had the highest rate of jobs lost to outsourcing of any state in the nation in 2006.

Political Divisions

Although state leaders agree that North Carolina's economy is a priority, the question of how best to promote economic development remains a topic of debate. Voting patterns have tended to divide the state into two political regions. The western part of the state generally votes Republican, and the eastern part usually votes Democratic. Highly populated areas have a mix of both parties. In 2006 the majority of state officials and the congressional delegation were Democratic.

North Carolina's Future

Like many other states, North Carolina faces the challenges of a growing population. Charlotte is the thirty-fourth largest city in the nation, and the Raleigh and Wilmington areas are among the country's fastest growing. North Carolina also has one of the fastest-growing Hispanic populations of any state.

One challenge of a growing population is ensuring that all North Carolinians benefit from the state's economic growth. Providing a quality education to all children remains a priority for state leaders. The rapid growth of cities has resulted in the need for new methods of transportation. Additionally, preserving the natural environment of the state and using its resources wisely are important to future generations of state leaders and citizens, who will work together to solve the issues that confront the state and the nation in the coming years.

Elizabeth Dole

1971 A federal court in Charlotte demands busing as a solution to integration.

1972 Jesse Helms is elected to the first of six Senate terms.

1996 Governor Jim Hunt is re-elected to a record fourth term.

2002 Elizabeth Dole becomes the first woman to be elected to the U.S. Senate from North Carolina.

2004 Hurricane Charley hits North Carolina and causes much damage.

2008

Jesse Helms

UNIT 1 BEGINNINGS TO 1783

Our Colonial Heritage

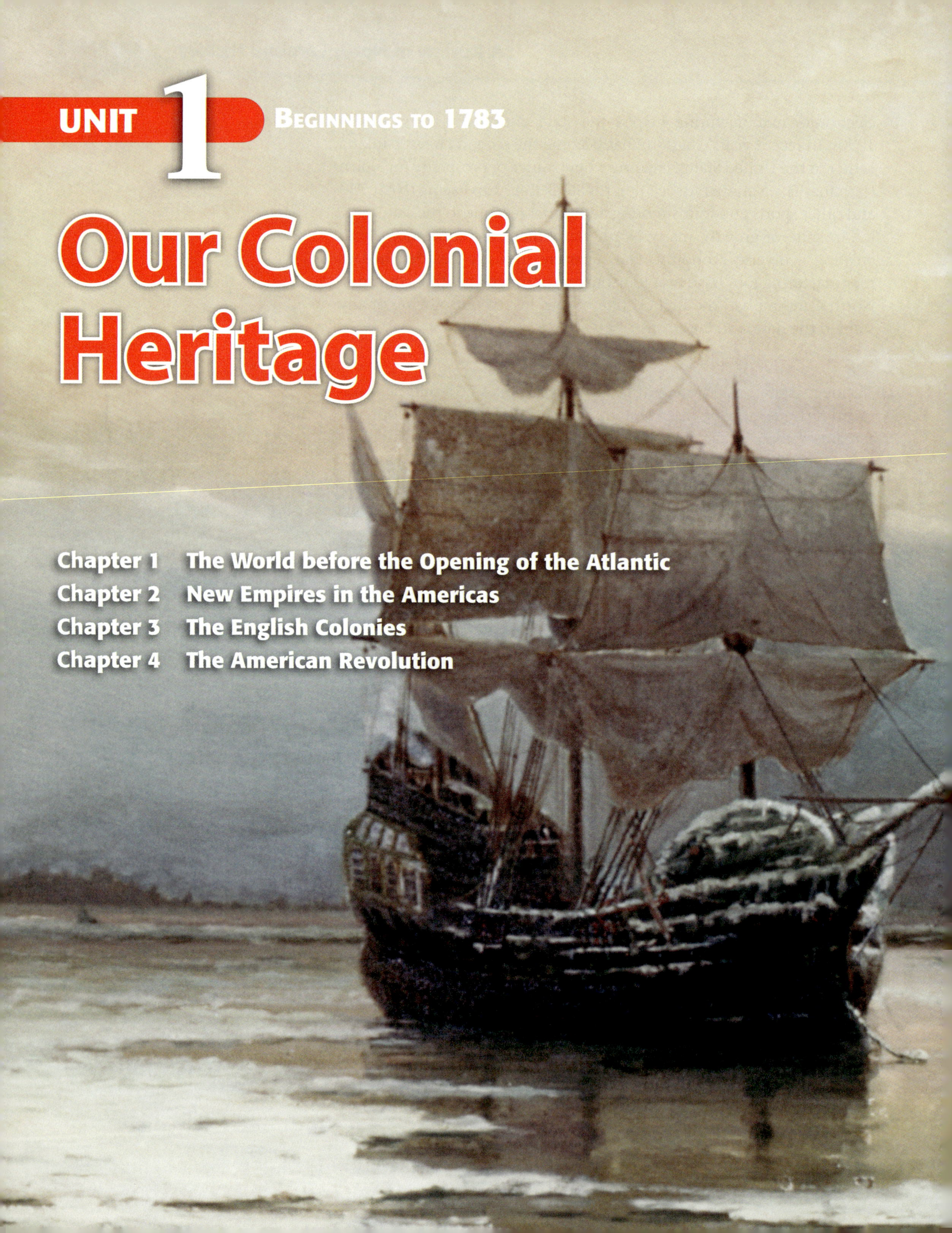

What You Will Learn . . .

North and South America were populated by Native American societies before Europeans arrived and began to colonize them. During the colonial period, Europeans came to the Americas to make new homes and gain wealth. Many people did so using slave labor from Africa.

As England's colonies in North America became more successful, they began to have conflicts with neighboring colonies, Native American people, and the British government. In the first four chapters, you will learn about the world before and after Columbus, and how the American colonies gained their independence.

Explore the Art

This painting by William Halsall shows the *Mayflower*, the ship that brought the Pilgrims to North America, in Plymouth Harbor. What might the Pilgrims have encountered when they first arrived at Plymouth?

CHAPTER 1 BEGINNINGS–1500

The World before the Opening of the Atlantic

North Carolina Standards

Social Studies Objectives

1.02 Identify and describe American Indians who inhabited the regions that became Carolina and assess their impact on the colony.

Language Arts Objectives

2.01 Analyze and evaluate informational materials that are read, heard, and/or viewed by:

- monitoring comprehension for understanding of what is read, heard and/or viewed.
- determining the importance and accuracy of information.
- making connections to related topics/information.

go.hrw.com
North Carolina
KEYWORD: SC7 NC

FOCUS ON WRITING

A Travelogue People who make long trips often write travelogues that describe their journeys. A travelogue allows people who did not make the trip to experience some of the same sights, sounds, and thoughts that the traveler did. In this chapter, you will gather information about different regions of the world and then write a travelogue describing what a place in one of these regions might have been like.

CHAPTER EVENTS

c. 38,000–10,000 BC Paleo-Indians migrate to the Americas.

38,000 BC

WORLD EVENTS

HOLT

History's Impact

▶ **video series**
Watch the video to understand the impact of the global economy.

What You Will Learn...

Buffalo graze on the plains in South Dakota. Millions of these animals used to roam lands from Canada to Texas. In this chapter you will learn about the first peoples in the Americas, some of whom relied on buffalo to survive.

c. 5000 BC Communities in Mexico cultivate corn.

c. 1200 BC Olmec begin their civilization in Mesoamerica.

1492 Christopher Columbus and his crew reach the Americas on October 12.

5000 BC — 1000 BC — AD 1500

c. 2600 BC The Great Pyramid is built at Giza, Egypt, as the tomb for the pharaoh Khufu.

c. 1350 New ideas begin to spread through Europe during the Renaissance.

Reading Social Studies

by Kylene Beers

Economics | Geography | Politics | Society and Culture | Science and Technology

Focus on Themes This chapter explains the early development of Mesoamerica and North America. You will read about early explorers from Europe, learn about early American settlements, and discover why the Spanish, the English, and the French all wanted a part of this new land. As you read the chapter, you will see how **geography** affected exploration and will learn about the **economic** issues that influenced growth and settlement.

Specialized Vocabulary of Social Studies

Focus on Reading If you flipped through the pages of this book, would you expect to see anything about square roots or formulas? How about petri dishes or hypotheses? Of course you wouldn't. Those are terms you'd only see in math and science books.

Specialized Vocabulary Like most subjects, social studies has its own specialized vocabulary. Included in it are words and phrases you will see over and over as you read social studies materials. The charts below list some terms you may encounter as you read this book.

Terms that deal with time	
Decade	a period of 10 years
Century	a period of 100 years
Era	a long period marked by great events, developments, or figures
BC	a term used to identify dates that occurred long ago, before the birth of Jesus Christ, the founder of Christianity; it means "before Christ." BC dates get smaller as time passes, so the larger the number, the earlier the date.
AD	a term used to identify dates that occurred after Jesus's birth; it comes from a Latin phrase that means "in the year of our Lord." Unlike BC dates, AD dates get larger as time passes, so the larger the number, the later the date.
BCE	another way to refer to BC dates; it stands for "before the common era"
CE	another way to refer to AD dates; it stands for "common era"

Terms that deal with government and society	
politics	the art of creating government policies
economics	the study of the creation and use of goods and services
movement	a series of actions that bring about or try to bring about a change in society
campaign	an effort to win a political office, or a series of military actions
colony	a territory settled and controlled by a country

You Try It!

The following passage shows you how some specialized vocabulary is defined in context.

Migration to the Americas

Native Americans in the Pacific Northwest carved images on **totems**—ancestor or animal spirits—on tall, wooden poles. Totem poles held great religious and historical significance for Native Americans of the Northwest. Feasts called potlatches were another unique, or unusual, aspect of these Native Americans' culture.

From Chapter 1, p. 12

Use the clues to understand meaning.

1. Find the word *totems*. The phrase after the **dash** is the definition. Often in this book, specialized vocabulary words are defined after a dash. So be on the lookout for dashes.
2. The word *potlatch* is defined in the third sentence. The clue to finding this definition is the word **called**. Words like **called** and **known as** can indicate that a definition is coming up. In this case, the word *feasts* is a definition of potlatch.
3. In the first sentence, you see a term that is in boldface print. You should recognize that word from seeing it in the section opener. The definition is **highlighted**. Why do you think some specialized vocabulary words are in boldface print, while others are not?
4. The word *unique* is defined in the final sentence. The clue to finding this definition is the **comma** followed by the word **or**. So be on the lookout for commas followed by *or*.

As you read Chapter 1, keep track in your notebook of the specialized vocabulary you learn.

Key Terms and People

Chapter 1

Section 1

Bering Land Bridge *(p. 6)*
Paleo-Indians *(p. 6)*
migration *(p. 6)*
hunter-gatherers *(p. 6)*
environments *(p. 7)*
culture *(p. 7)*

Section 2

pueblos *(p. 11)*
kivas *(p. 11)*
totems *(p. 12)*
teepees *(p. 14)*
matrilineal *(p. 14)*
Iroquois League *(p. 14)*

Section 3

Berbers *(p. 16)*
Mansa Musa *(p. 18)*
hajj *(p. 18)*
mosques *(p. 19)*
Askia the Great *(p. 19)*

Section 4

Socrates *(p. 22)*
Plato *(p. 22)*
Aristotle *(p. 22)*
reason *(p. 22)*
democracy *(p. 23)*
knights *(p. 24)*
Black Death *(p. 25)*
Michelangelo *(p. 26)*
Leonardo da Vinci *(p. 26)*
Johannes Gutenberg *(p. 27)*
joint-stock companies *(p. 27)*

Academic Vocabulary

Success in school is related to knowing academic vocabulary—the words that are frequently used in school assignments and discussions. In this chapter, you will learn the following academic words:

develop *(p. 8)*
classical *(p. 23)*

SECTION 1

The Earliest Americans

What You Will Learn...

Main Ideas

1. Climate changes allowed Paleo-Indians to begin the first migration to the Americas.
2. Early societies existed in Mesoamerica and South America.

The Big Idea

Native American societies developed across Mesoamerica and South America.

Key Terms and People

Bering Land Bridge, *p. 6*
Paleo-Indians, *p. 6*
migration, *p. 6*
hunter-gatherers, *p. 6*
environments, *p. 7*
culture, *p. 7*

TAKING NOTES As you read, take notes on the migrations of early peoples to the Americas as well as their earliest societies and locations.

Early Migrations to the Americas	Early Societies and Their Locations

If YOU were there...

You are living in North America about 10,000 years ago, close to the end of the Ice Age. For weeks, your group has been following a herd of elk across a marshy landscape. This trip has taken you far from your usual hunting grounds. The air is warmer here. There are thick grasses and bushes full of berries. You decide to camp here for the summer and perhaps stay a while.

How would settling here change your way of life?

BUILDING BACKGROUND The first settlers to the Americas probably came in small groups from Asia. Over thousands of years, they moved into nearly every region of North and South America. In the Americas, these people encountered, and adapted to, many different climates and types of land.

First Migration to the Americas

Many scientists believe that the first people arrived in North America during the last Ice Age. At the start of the Ice Age, Earth's climate became intensely cold. Large amounts of water froze into huge, moving sheets of ice called glaciers. As a result, ocean levels dropped more than 300 feet lower than they are today. When the sea level fell, a land bridge between northeastern Asia and present-day Alaska was exposed. Geographers call this strip of land the **Bering Land Bridge**. Although no one knows exactly when or how people crossed into North America, evidence suggests that people called **Paleo-Indians** crossed this bridge into Alaska between 38,000 and 10,000 BC.

This **migration**—a movement of people or animals from one region to another—took place over a long time. It is believed that Paleo-Indians traveled south into Canada, the United States, and Mexico following herds of animals. Over time, their descendants went as far as the southern tip of South America. These people were **hunter-gatherers**, people who hunted animals and gathered wild plants for food.

About 8000 BC, Earth's climate grew warmer, and the Ice Age ended. Rising temperatures melted glaciers. Water levels in the oceans rose, and the Bering Land Bridge was covered with water.

The warmer climate at the end of the Ice Age created new **environments**, climates and landscapes that surround living things. Large herds of animals such as buffalo and deer ate new short grasses that thrived in the warm climate. As the number of these animals grew, Paleo-Indians hunted these animals for survival.

Varied environments influenced the development of different Native American societies, or groups that share a culture. **Culture** is a group's set of common values and traditions, including language, government, and family relationships.

Like all societies, Native American groups changed over time. People planted seeds, and eventually they learned to breed animals, farm, and grow plants. Maize, or corn, was one of their most important early crops. Later, they learned to grow beans and squash. Farming allowed people to stop moving around looking for food and to settle in one place. With adequate food supplies, settlements could support larger populations. As populations grew, more advanced societies began to develop.

READING CHECK **Drawing Conclusions** How did climate change affect early peoples' migrations?

Land Migrations of Early Peoples

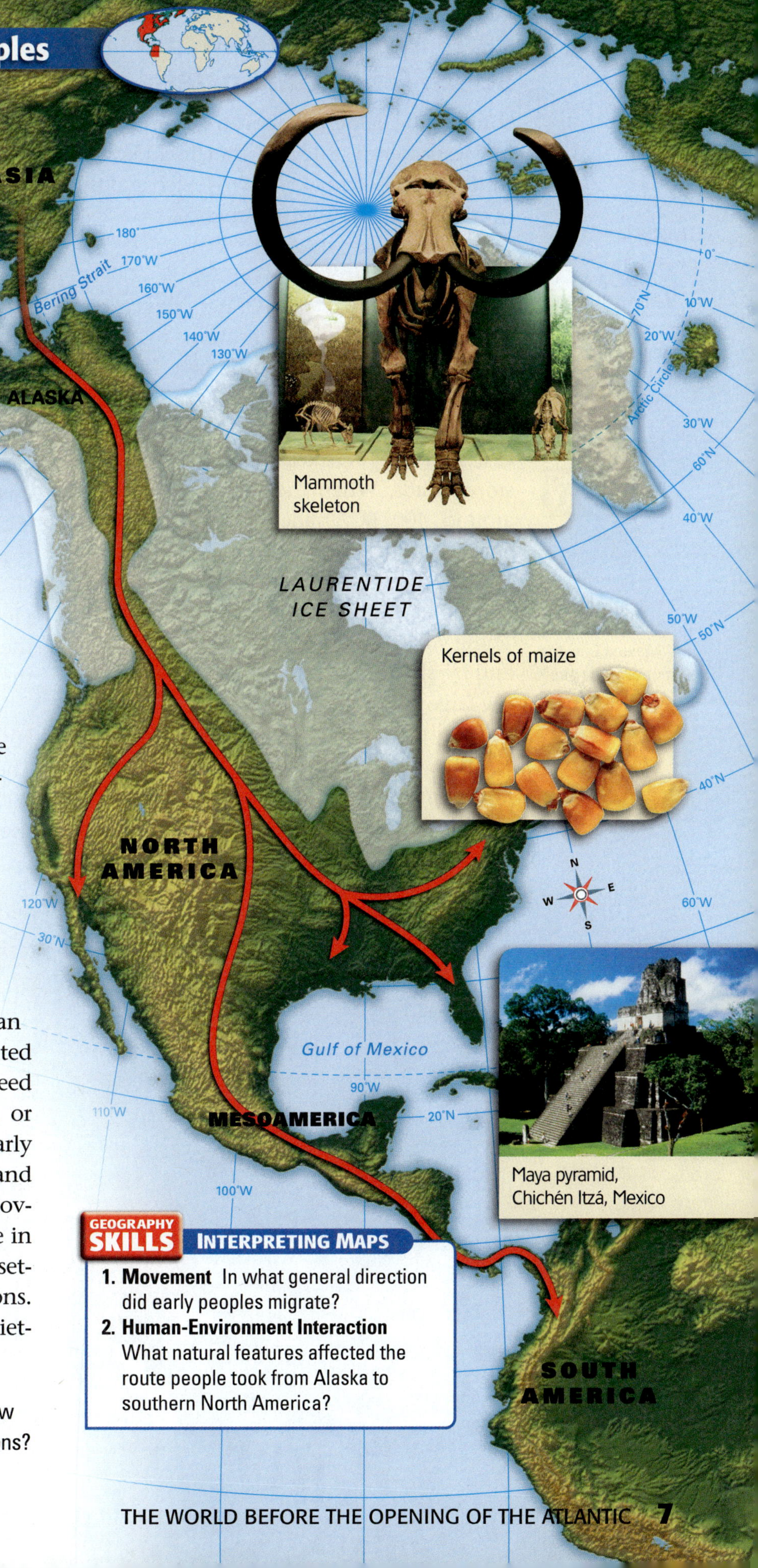

Mammoth skeleton

Kernels of maize

Maya pyramid, Chichén Itzá, Mexico

GEOGRAPHY SKILLS **INTERPRETING MAPS**

1. **Movement** In what general direction did early peoples migrate?
2. **Human-Environment Interaction** What natural features affected the route people took from Alaska to southern North America?

Early Mesoamerican and South American Societies

Some of the earliest American cultures arose in Mesoamerica, a region that includes the southern part of what is now Mexico and the northern parts of Central America.

ACADEMIC VOCABULARY
develop the process of growing or improving

Olmec and Maya

Around 1200 BC the Olmec **developed** the earliest known civilization in Mesoamerica. The Olmec are known for their use of stone in architecture and sculpture. They built the first pyramids in the Americas, and they created sculptures of huge stone heads. When their civilization ended around 400 BC, trade had spread Olmec culture throughout the region.

THE IMPACT TODAY
On the site of the Aztec capital, Tenochtitlán, workers filled the lake to build Mexico City, the modern-day capital of Mexico.

Like the Olmec, the Maya grew maize and other crops and lived in small villages. These villages traded goods with each other, and by about AD 200, the Maya were building large cities.

Maya cities had pyramids, large stone temples, palaces, and bridges. The Maya also paved large plazas for public gatherings and built canals to control the flow of water through the cities.

In the 900s Maya civilization began to collapse. Historians are still not sure what caused this great civilization's decline.

Aztec

The Aztec were fierce warriors, and their superior military ability was key to their success. Around the mid-1100s AD, the Aztec migrated south to central Mexico. They conquered many towns, made alliances to build their empire, and controlled a huge trade network.

In AD 1325, the Aztec founded their capital, Tenochtitlán (tay-nawch-teet-LAHN), on an island in Lake Texcoco. It became the greatest city in the Americas and one of the world's largest cities. The city's island location made travel and trade difficult, so the Aztec built raised roads to connect the island to the shore.

Trade and tribute paid by conquered people in the form of cotton, gold, and food made the Aztec rich. By the early 1500s, they ruled the most powerful state in Mesoamerica.

Inca

The Inca began as a small tribe in the Andes Mountains of South America. They named their capital city Cuzco (KOO-skoh). In the

The ancient Maya city of Palenque was a major power on the border between the Maya highlands and lowlands. Its great temples and plazas were typical of the Classic Age of Maya civilization.

mid-1400s, the Inca began to expand their territory. By the 1500s the empire stretched along the Pacific coast from what is now northern Ecuador to central Chile. In time, the empire was home to about 12 million people. The Inca formed a strong central government with a king as ruler. The official language of the empire was Quechua. Because there was no written language, records were kept on a system of knotted strings called *quipu*.

The Inca are known for building and for art. Massive buildings and forts were made of huge stone blocks. An advanced system of highways ran the length of the empire. Paved roads and rope bridges connected all parts of Inca territory. This enabled the Inca to communicate with and control their large empire.

READING CHECK **Summarizing** What early civilizations existed in Mesoamerica and South America?

SUMMARY AND PREVIEW Early people migrated into North and South America and developed societies. In the next section you will learn about Native American cultures in North America.

GEOGRAPHY SKILLS **INTERPRETING MAPS**

1. **Location** Which early civilization was located in Mesoamerica?
2. **Human-Environment Interaction** Why do you think Peru was settled after Mexico?

Section 1 Assessment

go.hrw.com **Online Quiz** KEYWORD: SC7 HP1

Reviewing Ideas, Terms, and People

1. a. **Recall** What was the Ice Age?
   b. **Summarize** Why were early peoples able to use the **Bering Land Bridge**?
   c. **Predict** Why do you think early peoples in the Americas **migrated** south?
2. a. **Identify** What is the earliest known civilization in the Americas, and where was it located?
   b. **Analyze** How did the Aztec build such a powerful, rich state?
   c. **Draw Conclusions** Which of the four civilizations discussed do you think was the most highly developed?

Critical Thinking

3. **Categorizing** Review your notes on the migration of early peoples and their societies. Then copy the table below and use it to identify the accomplishments of early American civilizations.

	Rise	Significant Accomplishments
Olmec		
Maya		
Aztec		
Inca		

FOCUS ON WRITING

4. **Understanding Ancient Peoples** Use the descriptions of the earliest Americans found in this section to list some similarities and differences between the lives of ancient peoples and your life today.

SECTION 2

Native American Cultures

What You Will Learn...

Main Ideas

1. Several early societies developed in North America long before Europeans explored the continent.
2. Geographic areas influenced Native American cultures.
3. Native American cultures shared beliefs about religion and land ownership.

The Big Idea

Many diverse Native American cultures developed across the different geographic regions of North America.

Key Terms and People

pueblos, *p. 11*
kivas, *p. 11*
totems, *p. 12*
teepees, *p. 14*
matrilineal, *p. 14*
Iroquois League, *p. 14*

TAKING NOTES As you read, take notes on early societies. Write your notes in a chart like the one below.

Early Societies	
Culture Areas	
Beliefs	

If YOU were there...

You live in the North American Southwest about 1,000 years ago. You've been working in the fields for several hours today. The maize crop looks good this summer, and you are hoping for a successful harvest. After finishing your work, you walk home. The opening to your house is in a cliff wall 30 feet above a canyon floor. You must use ladders to get to the opening.

Do you like the location of your home? Why?

BUILDING BACKGROUND After crossing the land bridge from Asia during the Ice Age, hunter-gatherer groups spread into every region of North America. Many diverse cultures formed as Native Americans adapted to their different environments.

Early Societies

The earliest people in North America were hunter-gatherers. After 5000 BC some of these people learned how to farm, and they settled in villages. Although less populated than South America and Mesoamerica, North America had many complex societies long before Europeans reached the continent.

Anasazi

By 1500 BC the people who lived in the North American Southwest, like those who lived in Mesoamerica, were growing maize. One of the early farm cultures in the Southwest was the Anasazi (ah-nuh-SAH-zee). The Anasazi lived in the Four Corners region, where present-day Arizona, Colorado, New Mexico, and Utah meet. Anasazi farmers adapted to their dry environment and grew maize, beans, and squash. Over time, they began to use irrigation to increase food production. By the time the Anasazi settled in the area, they were already skilled basket makers. They wove straw, vines, and yucca to make containers for food and other items, and they eventually became skilled potters as well.

Anasazi Cliff Dwellings

Dwellings like these were built into cliffs for safety. Often, ladders were needed to reach the buildings. The ladders could be removed, keeping invaders from reaching the dwelllings.

The early Anasazi lived in pit houses dug into the ground. After about AD 750 they built **pueblos**, or aboveground houses made of a heavy clay called adobe. The Anasazi built these houses on top of each other, creating large multistoried complexes. Some pueblos had several hundred rooms and could house 1,000 people.

The Anasazi often built their houses in canyon walls and had to use ladders to enter their homes. These cliff dwellings provided a strong defense against enemies. The Anasazi also built **kivas**, underground ceremonial chambers, at the center of each community. Kivas were sacred areas used for religious ceremonies. Some of these rituals focused on the life-giving forces of rain and maize.

The Anasazi thrived for hundreds of years. After AD 1300, however, they began to abandon their villages. Scholars believe that drought, disease, or raids by nomadic tribes from the north may have caused the Anasazi to move away from their pueblos.

Mound Builders

Several farming societies developed in the eastern part of North America after 1000 BC. The Hopewell lived along the Mississippi, Ohio, and lower Missouri river valleys. They supported their large population with agriculture and trade. They built large burial mounds to honor their dead.

The Hopewell culture had declined by AD 700. Another culture, the Mississippian, began to thrive in the same area. Skilled farmers and traders, the Mississippian built large settlements. Their largest city, Cahokia, was located near present-day Saint Louis, Missouri. It had a population of 30,000.

The Mississippian built hundreds of mounds for religious ceremonies. Cahokia alone had more than 100 temple and burial mounds. These mounds had flat tops, and temples were built on top of the mounds. Many of the mounds were gigantic. Monks Mound, near Collinsville, Illinois, for example, was 100 feet high and covered 16 acres.

Several other mound-building cultures thrived in eastern North America. More than 10,000 mounds have been found in the Ohio River valley alone. Some of these mounds are shaped like birds and snakes. The mound-building cultures had declined by the time European explorers reached the Southeast. Their societies no longer existed by the early 1700s.

READING CHECK **Summarizing** Why did some Native American groups build mounds?

Native American Culture Areas

Researchers use culture areas—the geographic locations that influenced societies—to help them describe ancient Native American peoples. North America is divided into several culture areas.

North and Northwest

The far north of North America is divided into the Arctic and Subarctic culture areas. Few plants grow in the Arctic because the ground is always frozen beneath a thin top layer of soil. This harsh environment was home to two groups of people, the Inuit and the Aleut. The Inuit lived in present-day northern Alaska and Canada. Their homes were igloos, hide tents, and huts. The Aleut, whose home was in western and southern Alaska, lived in multifamily houses that were partially underground. The two groups shared many cultural features, including language. Both groups survived by fishing and hunting large mammals. The Aleut and Inuit also depended on dogs for many tasks, such as hunting and pulling sleds.

South of the Arctic lies the Subarctic, home to groups such as the Dogrib and Montagnais peoples. While they followed the seasonal migrations of deer, these peoples lived in shelters made of animal skins. At other times, they lived in villages made up of log houses. Farther south, the Kwakiutl and the Chinook thrived, thanks to the rich supply of game animals, fish, and wild plants that allowed large populations to increase without the need for farming.

Native Americans in the Pacific Northwest carved images of **totems**—ancestor or animal spirits—on tall, wooden poles. Totem poles held great religious and historical significance for Native Americans of the Northwest. Feasts called potlatches were another unique, or unusual, aspect of these Native Americans' culture. At these gatherings, hosts, usually chiefs or wealthy people, gave away most of their belongings as gifts. In this way, the hosts increased their social importance.

Focus on Reading
What is the definition of **totems** according to this sentence?

West and Southwest

Farther south along the Pacific coast was the California region, which included the area between the Pacific and the Sierra Nevada mountain range. Food sources were plentiful, so farming was not necessary. One major plant food was acorns, which were ground into flour. People also fished and hunted deer and other game. Most Native Americans in the California region lived in groups of families of about 50 to 300. Among these groups, including the Hupa, Miwok, and Yokuts, more than 100 languages were spoken.

The area east of the Sierra Nevada Mountains, the Great Basin, received little rain. To survive, Native Americans adapted to the drier climate by gathering seeds, digging roots, and trapping small animals for food. Most groups in this area, including the Paiute, Shoshone, and Ute, spoke the same language.

The Southwest culture region included the present-day states of Arizona and New Mexico, and parts of Colorado and Texas. Pueblo groups, such as the Hopi and Zuni, lived there. Like the Anasazi, these Native Americans also adapted to a dry climate. The Pueblo irrigated the land and grew maize, squash, and beans. These crops were vital to southwestern peoples. The Pueblo religion focused on two key areas of Pueblo life, rain and maize. The Pueblo performed religious rituals hoping to bring rain and a successful maize crop to their peoples.

Pueblo peoples were settled and built multistoried houses out of adobe bricks. Over time their towns grew larger, and some towns had more than 1,000 residents. Pueblo peoples made fine pottery that featured beautifully painted designs.

Native American Culture Areas

Human-hand carving, Great Plains culture area

Beaver-shaped pipe, Northeast culture area

Human figure, Southwest culture area

GEOGRAPHY SKILLS **INTERPRETING MAPS**

1. **Region** Why did some culture areas have fewer groups of people than other culture areas did?
2. **Human-Environment Interaction** What natural features served as boundaries between culture areas?

Iroquois Longhouse

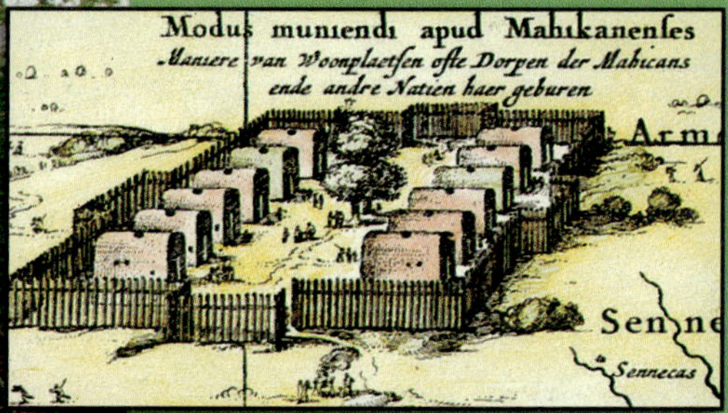

Northeastern Native Americans such as the Iroquois lived in longhouses made of tree bark. The drawing shows the longhouses in one Iroquois village.

Why do you think a fence was placed around the longhouses?

The Apache and Navajo also lived in the Southwest. These groups were nomadic—they moved from place to place hunting small animals and foraging for food. The Apache and Navajo also supported themselves by raiding the villages of the Pueblo and others.

FOCUS ON NORTH CAROLINA

Many Native American groups still live in North Carolina. The state has the largest population of Native Americans east of the Mississippi River. The Eastern Band of Cherokee maintain Oconaluftee Village, a re-creation of a Cherokee village at which visitors can see what life was like for this group in 1750.

Great Plains

The huge Great Plains region stretches south from Canada into Texas. This culture area is bordered by the Mississippi Valley on the east and the Rocky Mountains on the west. The Plains were mainly grassland, home to millions of buffalo. Deer, elk, and other game also thrived there.

Most Great Plains peoples were nomadic hunters. Many groups hunted buffalo using bows and spears. Blackfoot and Arapaho hunters sometimes chased the animals over cliffs, drove them into corrals, or trapped them in a ring of fire. Native Americans used buffalo skins for shields, clothing, and coverings for their **teepees**—cone-shaped shelters.

Some Plains groups were farmers. The Mandan and Pawnee settled in villages and grew corn, beans, and squash. The Pawnee lived in round lodges made of dirt. Like some other Native American groups, Pawnee society was **matrilineal**. This means that people traced their ancestry through their mothers, not their fathers.

Northeast and Southeast

Eastern North America was rich in sources for food and shelter. Animals, plant foods, fish, and wood for housing were plentiful.

Most southeastern groups, including the Cherokee, Creek, and Seminole, lived in farming villages governed by village councils. They also hunted, fished, and gathered plants. In the Northeast, groups like the Algonquian and the Iroquois prospered through trade with other groups. Iroquois groups created the **Iroquois League**. This confederation, or alliance, was established by the Cayuga, Mohawk, Oneida, Onondaga, Seneca, and later the Tuscarora. The league waged war against and made peace with non-Iroquois peoples.

North Carolina was inhabited by groups belonging to three language families. Iroquoian groups like the Cherokee, Tuscarora, and Coree, and Algonquian groups like the Hatteras, Pamlico, and Chowan lived along the coast. The Algonquian groups were the subjects of most historical accounts left by European settlers. Siouan groups like the Cape Fear, Catawba, and Cheraw lived mainly in the Piedmont area of the state. Groups traded among each other for the resources they needed to survive.

READING CHECK **Generalizing** How were the Native American groups of North Carolina related?

Shared Beliefs

Although they were different culturally and geographically, Native American groups of North America shared certain beliefs. The religion of most Native American peoples, for example, was linked to nature. Native Americans believed that spiritual forces were everywhere, dwelling in heavenly bodies and in sacred places on the earth. Spirits even lived within animals and plants. Native Americans tried to honor the spirits in their daily lives.

Ceremonies maintained the group's relationship with Earth and Sky, which were believed to be the sustainers of life. In addition, individuals who wanted help prayed to their spirit protector.

Native Americans also shared beliefs about property. They believed that individual ownership only applied to the crops one grew. The land itself was for the use of everyone in the village, and a person's right to use it was temporary. Native Americans also thought they should preserve the land for future generations. These beliefs contrasted sharply with those of Europeans— a difference that would cause conflict.

Despite their shared beliefs, the diverse culture groups of North America had little interest in joining together into large political units. As a result, Native Americans on the North American continent did not form large empires like the Aztec and Inca of Meso- and South America did.

READING CHECK **Identifying Points of View** What religious beliefs did Native American groups share?

SUMMARY AND PREVIEW People of North America formed many complex societies. In the next section you will read about societies in West Africa.

go.hrw.com
Online Quiz
KEYWORD: SC7 HP1

Section 2 Assessment

Reviewing Ideas, Terms, and People

1. a. **Recall** Why did the Anasazi build **kivas**?
   b. **Summarize** What different types of housing were built by the Anasazi?
   c. **Draw Conclusions** Why do you think that some mounds were built in the shape of birds and snakes?
2. a. **Identify** What are culture areas?
   b. **Contrast** How did food sources for Native Americans of the North and Northwest differ from those of Native Americans living in the West and Southwest?
   c. **Elaborate** Why was the formation of the **Iroquois League** considered to be a significant political development?
3. a. **Recall** How did Native Americans view land ownership?
   b. **Analyze** What role did religion play in the lives of Native Americans?
   c. **Predict** Why do you think most Native American groups did not form large empires like the Aztec and the Inca did?

Critical Thinking

4. **Comparing and Contrasting** Review your notes on early societies and culture areas. Then use a Venn diagram like this one to identify similarities and differences among Native American culture groups.

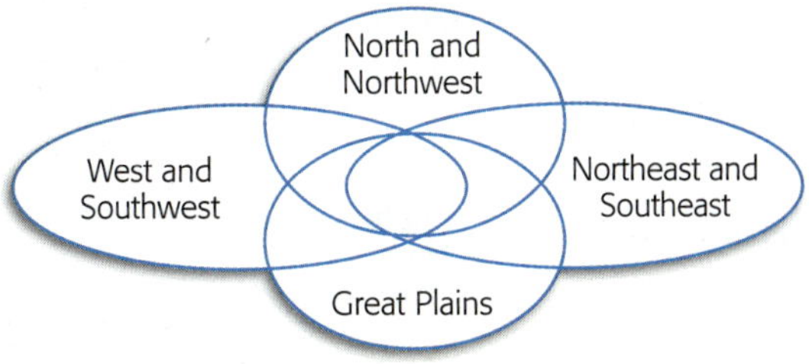

FOCUS ON WRITING

5. **Describing Culture** Look back through this section to discover ways in which a group's beliefs, environment, and practices can be described. Write down phrases that you think are especially useful in understanding Native American cultures.

SECTION 3

Trading Kingdoms of West Africa

What You Will Learn...

Main Ideas

1. West Africa developed three great kingdoms that grew wealthy through their control of trade.
2. Slaves became a valuable trade item in West Africa.

The Big Idea

Using trade to gain wealth, Ghana, Mali, and Songhai were West Africa's most powerful kingdoms.

Key Terms and People

Berbers, *p. 16*
Mansa Musa, *p. 18*
hajj, *p. 18*
mosques, *p. 19*
Askia the Great, *p. 19*

TAKING NOTES As you read, take notes on the rise of early African kingdoms and the role of trade in their development. Use a chart like the one below.

Kingdom	Rise	The Role of Trade
Ghana		
Mali		
Songhai		

If YOU were there...

You are a trader's assistant from the Middle East, traveling in a caravan headed for West Africa. The caravan carries many goods, but the most precious is salt. Your job is to trade the salt for gold and return the gold to your employer immediately. Your boss never meets the traders face to face.

Why is your boss so secretive?

BUILDING BACKGROUND The continent of Africa was luxuriously rich in resources. West Africa had both fertile soils and valuable minerals, especially gold and iron. Ancient trade routes had connected Africa with the Middle East and Asia for hundreds of years. Over time, trade developed between regions with different resources. Trade and abundant resources led to the growth of several great kingdoms in West Africa.

West Africa's Great Kingdoms

For hundreds of years, trade routes crisscrossed West Africa. For most of that time, West Africans did not profit much from the Saharan trade because the routes were run by **Berbers**, a group of people from northern Africa. Eventually, that situation changed. A succession of three great kingdoms came to power as their peoples gained control of valuable trade routes in West Africa. Ghana (GAH-nuh) was the first of these empires, followed by the kingdoms of Mali (MAH-lee) and Songhai (SAWNG-hy).

Kingdom of Ghana

Historians think the first people in Ghana were farmers along the Niger River. Sometime after AD 300 these farmers, the Soninke (soh-NING-kee), were threatened by nomadic herders. The herders wanted to take the farmers' water and pastures. For protection, groups of Soninke families began to band together. This banding together was the beginning of Ghana.

Ghana's rulers grew wealthy by controlling trade in salt and gold. Salt came from the north in large slabs, and gold came from the south.

What does the photo to the left suggest about the amount of salt traded in a market?

Ghana was in an ideal position to become a trading center. To the north lay the vast Sahara, the source of much of the salt. Ghana itself was rich in gold. People wanted gold for its beauty, but they needed salt in their diets to survive. Salt, which could be used to preserve food, also made bland food tasty. These qualities made salt very valuable. In fact, Africans sometimes cut up slabs of salt and used the pieces as money.

As trade in gold and salt increased, Ghana's rulers gained power. Eventually, they built up armies equipped with iron weapons that were superior to the weapons of nearby people. Over time, Ghana took control of trade from merchants. Merchants from the north and south then met to exchange goods in Ghana.

By 800 Ghana was firmly in control of West Africa's trade routes. Nearly all trade between northern and southern Africa passed through Ghana. With so many traders passing through their lands, Ghana's rulers looked for ways to make money from them. One way they raised money was by forcing traders to pay taxes. Every trader who entered Ghana had to pay a special tax on the goods he carried. Then he had to pay another tax on any goods he took with him when he left. Ghana's rulers gained incredible wealth from trade, taxes on traders and on the people of Ghana, and their own personal stores of gold. They used their wealth to build an army and an empire.

Islam in Ghana

Extensive trade routes brought the people of Ghana into contact with people of many different cultures and beliefs. As the kingdom of Ghana extended into the Sahara, increased contact with Arab traders from the east brought the religion of Islam to Ghana.

Islam was founded in the 600s by an Arab named Muhammad. Muslims, followers of Islam, believe that God had spoken to Muhammad through an angel and had made him a prophet, someone who tells of God's messages. After Muhammad's death, his followers wrote down his teachings to form the book known as the Qur'an. Islam spread quickly through the Arabian Peninsula.

In the 1060s, a Muslim group called the Almoravids (al-muh-RAH-vuhdz) attacked Ghana in an effort to force its leaders to

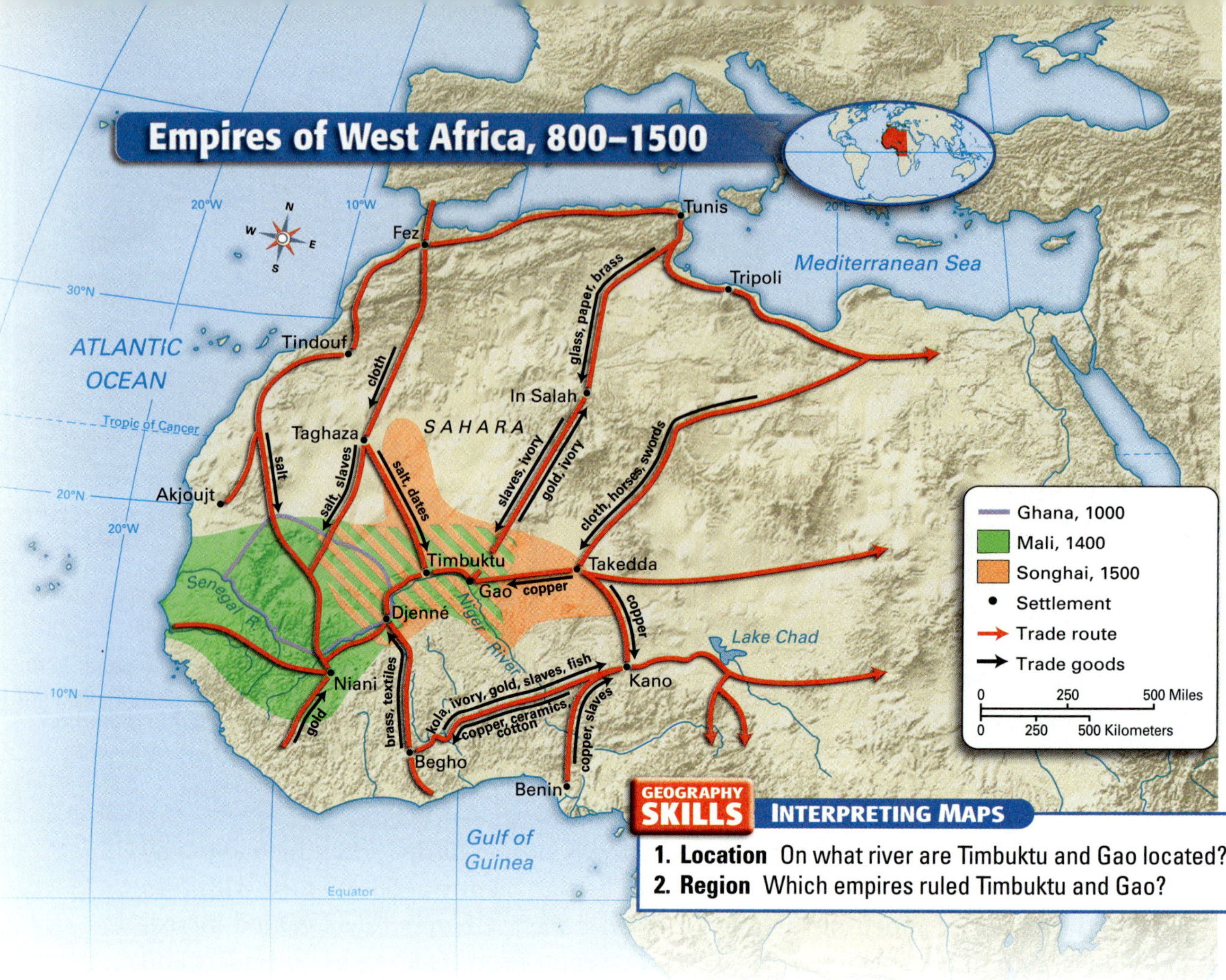

GEOGRAPHY SKILLS **INTERPRETING MAPS**

1. **Location** On what river are Timbuktu and Gao located?
2. **Region** Which empires ruled Timbuktu and Gao?

convert to Islam. The Almoravids weakened Ghana's empire and cut off many trade routes. Without its trade, Ghana could not support its empire, and the empire eventually fell. The influence of Islam, however, remained strong. By the late 1400s Islam would become the most practiced religion in the region.

Kingdom of Mali

Like Ghana, Mali lay along the upper Niger River. This area's fertile soil helped Mali grow. In addition, Mali's location on the Niger allowed its people to control trade on the river. Through this control of trade, the empire grew rich and powerful. According to legend, Mali's rise to power began under a ruler named Sundiata. Sundiata won back his country's independence and conquered nearby kingdoms, including Ghana.

Mali's most famous ruler, however, was a Muslim king named **Mansa Musa** (MAHN-sah moo-SAH). Under his leadership, Mali reached the height of its wealth, power, and fame.

Mansa Musa ruled Mali for about 25 years, from 1312 to 1337. During that time, Mali added many important trade cities, including Timbuktu (tim-buhk-TOO), Djenné (je-NAY), and Gao (GOW), to its empire. Traders came to Timbuktu from the north and the south to trade for salt, gold, metals, shells, and many other goods.

Religion was also very important to Mansa Musa. In 1324 he left Mali on a **hajj**, or pilgrimage to Mecca. Making this journey once in their lives is the spiritual duty of all Muslims. As he traveled to Mecca, Mansa Musa introduced his empire to the world. The stories of Mali's wealth and religion spread far and wide. Because of Mansa Musa's influence, Islam spread through a large part of West Africa.

Mansa Musa wanted all Muslims to be able to read the Qur'an. Therefore, he stressed the importance of learning to read and write the Arabic language. He sent scholars to study in Morocco. These scholars later set up schools in Mali for studying the Qur'an.

To encourage the spread of Islam in West Africa, Mansa Musa brought back artists and architects from other Muslim countries to build **mosques**, or buildings for Muslim prayer, throughout his lands.

The architectural advances in cities like Timbuktu as well as an organized government, an emphasis on education, and expansion of trade all combined to make Mansa Musa Mali's most successful ruler. Much of Mali's success depended on strong leaders. After Mansa Musa died, poor leadership weakened the empire. By 1500 nearly all of the lands the kingdom once ruled were lost. Only a small area of Mali remained.

Songhai Empire

In the 1300s Mansa Musa had conquered a rival kingdom of people called the Songhai, who also lived along the Niger River. As the Mali Empire weakened in the 1400s, the Songhai grew in strength. They took advantage of Mali's decline, regained their independence, and eventually conquered most of Mali.

One of Songhai's greatest rulers was Muhammad Ture, who chose the title *askia,* a title of military rank. He became known as **Askia the Great**. Like Mansa Musa, Askia the Great was a devout Muslim who supported education and learning. Under his rule, the cities of Gao and Timbuktu flourished. They contained great mosques, universities, schools, and libraries. People came from all parts of West Africa to study mathematics, science, medicine, grammar, and law.

Askia understood that an empire needed effective government. He created a professional army, and to improve the government, he set up five provinces within Songhai. He removed local leaders and appointed new governors who were loyal to him. He also created specialized departments to oversee various tasks, much like modern-day government offices do.

THE IMPACT TODAY

Some of the mosques built by Mansa Musa can still be seen in West Africa today.

LINKING TO TODAY

Music from Senegal to Memphis

Did you know that the music you listen to today may have begun with the griots, musicians from West Africa? From the 1600s to the 1800s, many people from West Africa were brought to America as slaves. In America, these slaves continued to sing the way they had in Africa. They also continued to play traditional instruments such as the kora, shown here being played by Senegalese musician Soriba Kouyaté (far right). Over time, this music developed into a style called the blues, made popular by such artists as B. B. King (near right). In turn, the blues shaped other styles of music, including jazz and rock. So, the next time you hear a Memphis blues song or a cool jazz tune, listen for its ancient African roots.

ANALYSIS SKILL **ANALYZING INFORMATION**

How did West African music affect modern American music?

Soon after Askia the Great lost power, the empire of Songhai declined. Songhai was invaded by the Moroccans, the kingdom's northern neighbors. The Moroccans wanted to control the Saharan salt mines. They had superior military power and were able to take over Timbuktu and Gao. Changes in trade patterns completed Songhai's fall.

READING CHECK **Comparing** What did Ghana, Mali, and Songhai have in common?

West African Slave Trade

The practice of slavery had existed in Africa and in many parts of the world for centuries. Traditionally, slavery in West Africa mostly involved only black Africans, who were both slaveholders and slaves. This changed in the 600s when Arab Muslims, and later Europeans, became slave traders. Though Europeans had long traded resources with Africa, they became more interested in the growing slave trade.

People who were captured by warring groups during battle could be sold into slavery. In addition, criminals were sometimes sold as slaves. Other enslaved people were captured during raids on villages, and sometimes even the relatives of people who owed money were sold into slavery as payment for debts. Enslaved Africans were often bought to perform menial labor and domestic chores. In some cultures, having slaves raised the status of the slaveholder.

The market for West African slaves increased as Muslim traders bought or seized black Africans to sell in North Africa. West Africa was also home to many enslaved Africans brought to the Americas.

Over time, the slave trade became even more important to the West African economy. Kings traded slaves for valuable goods, such as horses from the Middle East and textiles and weapons from Europe. The trans-Saharan slave trade contributed to the power of Ghana, Mali, and Songhai.

READING CHECK **Drawing Inferences** Why did the slave trade in West Africa continue to grow?

SUMMARY AND PREVIEW Trade was important to the kingdoms of West Africa. In the next section you will learn about European trade.

Section 3 Assessment

go.hrw.com
Online Quiz
KEYWORD: SC7 HP1

Reviewing Ideas, Terms, and People

1. a. **Identify** How did West African kingdoms grow wealthy through trade?
   b. **Describe** How did **Mansa Musa** introduce his empire to the world?
   c. **Elaborate** Why was trade crucial to the survival of Ghana, Mali, and Songhai?
2. a. **Describe** How did some people become slaves in West Africa?
   b. **Analyze** What role did geography play in the development of the slave trade?
   c. **Judge** Why did the value of slaves as an export increase over time?

Critical Thinking

3. **Comparing and Contrasting** Review your chart on African kingdoms and trade. Then copy the diagram below and use it to show the similarities and differences in the fall of each kingdom.

Fall of Ghana, Mali, and Songhai	Similarities	Differences

FOCUS ON WRITING

4. **Gathering Information on Economies** Make a list of things that were important to the economies of the kingdoms of West Africa. Include your ideas about what seems most important to West Africans and things that you did not know about before reading this section.

BIOGRAPHY

Mansa Musa

How could one man's travels become a historic event?

When did he live? the late 1200s and early 1300s

Where did he live? Mali

What did he do? Mansa Musa, the ruler of Mali, was one of the Muslim kings of West Africa. He became a major figure in African and world history largely because of a pilgrimage he made to the city of Mecca.

Why is he important? Mansa Musa's spectacular journey attracted the attention of the Muslim world and of Europe. For the first time, other people's eyes turned to West Africa. During his travels, Mansa Musa gave out huge amounts of gold. His spending made people eager to find the source of such wealth. Within 200 years, European explorers would arrive on the shores of western Africa.

Identifying Points of View How do you think Mansa Musa changed people's views of West Africa?

KEY FACTS

According to chroniclers of the time, Mansa Musa was accompanied on his journey to Mecca by some 60,000 people. Of those people,

- **12,000** were servants to attend to the king.
- **500** were servants to attend to his wife.
- **14,000** were slaves wearing rich fabrics such as silk.
- **500** carried staffs heavily decorated with gold. Historians have estimated that the gold Mansa Musa gave away on his trip would be worth more than $100 million today.

THE GRANGER COLLECTION, NEW YORK

This Spanish map from 1375 shows Mansa Musa sitting on his throne.

SECTION 4

Europe before Transatlantic Travel

What You Will Learn...

Main Ideas

1. The Greeks and Romans established new forms of government.
2. During the Middle Ages, society eventually changed from a feudal system to a system with a middle class of artisans and merchants.
3. The Renaissance was a time of rebirth in the arts and in learning.

The Big Idea

New ideas and trade changed Europeans' lives.

Key Terms and People

Socrates, *p. 22*
Plato, *p. 22*
Aristotle, *p. 22*
reason, *p. 22*
democracy, *p. 23*
knights, *p. 24*
Black Death, *p. 25*
Michelangelo, *p. 26*
Leonardo da Vinci, *p. 26*
Johannes Gutenberg, *p. 27*
joint-stock companies, *p. 27*

TAKING NOTES As you read, take notes on the changes in society during the periods listed. Write your notes in a chart like this one.

Period of Time	Major Changes
Ancient Greece	
Roman Republic	
Middle Ages	
Renaissance	

If YOU were there...

You are a peasant in the Middle Ages, living on the land of a noble. Although you and your family work very hard from sunrise to sundown, much of the food you grow goes to the noble. Your house is very small and has a dirt floor. Your parents are tired and weak, and you wish you could do something to improve their lives.

Is there any way you could change your life?

BUILDING BACKGROUND Hard work was a constant theme in the lives of peasants in the Middle Ages. Nobles were not free to live as they chose, either. As the Middle Ages ended, the Renaissance brought new ways of thinking, and the growth of cities brought big changes to the way people lived and worked.

Greek and Roman Government

During the Renaissance, European thinkers and artists rediscovered the traditions of Greece and Rome. Ancient Greek and Roman texts were translated, and their ideas began to revolutionize European societies.

Greek Philosophers and Government

Ancient Greeks valued human reason and believed in the power of the human mind to think, explain, and understand life. Three of the greatest Greek thinkers, or philosophers, were **Socrates**, **Plato**, and **Aristotle**. Socrates, a great teacher, wanted to make people think and question their own beliefs. Plato, a philosopher and teacher, wrote a work called *The Republic*. It describes an ideal society based on justice and fairness for everyone. Aristotle taught that people should live lives based on **reason**, or clear and ordered thinking.

Greek scientists and mathematicians also gained fame for their contributions to geometry and for accurately calculating the size of Earth. Doctors studied the human body to understand how it worked. One Greek engineering invention that is still used today is a water screw, which brings water to farm fields.

One of the Greeks' most lasting contributions, however, is their political system. During the time known as the Classical Period, around the fifth and fourth centuries BC, Greece was organized into several hundred independent city-states, which became the foundation for Greek civilization. Athens was the first Greek city-state to establish **democracy**—a form of government in which people rule themselves. All male citizens in Athens had the right to participate in the assembly, a gathering of citizens, to debate and create the city's laws. Because all male citizens in Athens participated directly in government, we call the Greek form of government a direct democracy.

Roman Law and Government

Later, Rome followed Greece's example by establishing a form of democratic government. The Roman Republic was created in 509 BC. Each year Romans elected officials to rule the city. These officials had many powers, but they only stayed in power for one year. This early republic was not a democracy. Later, the Romans changed their government into one with three parts. These three parts were made up of elected representatives who protected the city and its residents.

Roman laws were written and kept on public display so all people could know them. Roman concepts of equality before the law and innocent until proven guilty protected Roman citizens' rights.

The political ideas of Greece and Rome survived to influence governments around the world, including that of the United States. In the U.S. political system, citizens vote for representatives, making the nation a democratic republic.

READING CHECK **Analyzing** How did Roman and Greek governments influence the United States?

QUICK FACTS: Democracy and Republic

Direct democracies and republics are similar forms of government in which the people rule. There are some slight differences, though.

Direct Democracy	Republic
• Every citizen votes on every issue. • Ideas are debated at an assembly of all citizens.	• Citizens elect representatives to vote on issues. • Ideas are debated at an assembly of representatives.

THE IMPACT TODAY

Many of the geometry rules we learn in school today come straight from the Greek mathematician Euclid. Many doctors recite the Hippocratic Oath, named after the Greek doctor Hippocrates.

ACADEMIC VOCABULARY

classical referring to the cultures of ancient Greece or Rome

The Roman Senate played a principal role in the Roman government.

Middle Ages

As the Roman Empire fell, groups from the north and east moved into former Roman lands. By the early 500s Europe was divided into many small kingdoms. This marked the beginning of the Middle Ages, a period that lasted about a thousand years.

Feudalism

In the 480s a powerful group called the Franks conquered Gaul, the region we now call France. The Franks created a huge empire in Europe. When invaders began to attack European settlements in the 800s, the Frankish kings could not defend their empire. Because they could not depend on protection from their kings, nobles had to defend their own lands. As a result, the power of European nobles grew, and kings became less powerful. Although these nobles remained loyal to the king, they ruled their lands as independent territories.

Nobles needed soldiers to defend their lands. Nobles gave **knights**, warriors who fought on horseback, land in exchange for military service. Nobles who gave land to knights so that the knights would defend the land were called lords. A knight who promised to support the noble in battle was called a vassal. This system of promises between lords and vassals is known as feudalism.

Peasants owned no land, so they were not part of the feudal system. They did, however, need to grow food to live. As a result, a new economic system developed. Knights allowed peasants to farm land on their large estates, called manors. In return, the peasants had to give the knights food or other goods as payment.

Because of its structure, feudalism promoted the separation of territories and people. The Catholic Church, however, served as a strong unifying force among the states and people of Europe. During the Middle Ages, nearly everyone in Europe was Christian. Life revolved around the local church with markets, festivals, and religious ceremonies.

The Crusades

In the late 1000s, a long series of wars called the Crusades began between the European Christians and Muslims in Southwest Asia.

Time Line

Key Events in Europe

500 BC

509 BC Rome is established as a republic.

AD 455 The Vandals sack Rome.

600

800

800 Charlemagne is crowned emperor of the Holy Roman Empire.

The Turks had captured Palestine, the Holy Land where Jesus had lived. Christians no longer felt safe to travel there on pilgrimages. Christians were called upon to go to war with the Turks to recapture Palestine.

Although the Crusades failed, they changed Europe forever. Trade between Europe and Asia began to grow, introducing Europeans to new products such as apricots, rice, and cotton cloth, as well as the ideas of Muslim thinkers.

Travel, Trade, and Towns

In the Middle Ages, towns were small. After about 1000, this situation began to change. New technology meant farmers could produce larger harvests. As farmers grew more food, the population increased.

Travel became safer as increased protection from stronger rulers kept larger territories secure. Over time, kingdoms became nation-states—organized political units with central governments. This development provided even more protection to merchants.

The rulers of the Mongols made routes like the Silk Road, a caravan route that started in China and ended at the Mediterranean Sea, safe for travelers and traders. Among these traders was Marco Polo. In 1271 he journeyed from Europe to China along part of the old Silk Road. He spent 20 years living and traveling in Asia. When Marco Polo returned to Europe, he brought back stories of spices, coal, and paper money.

Trade routes spread all across Europe. Merchants brought goods from Asia and Africa to sell in European markets. Their ships also brought back rats infected with the plague. The disease, known as the **Black Death**, spread across Europe, killing an estimated 25 million people. The European economy was dramatically affected by the shortage of workers. Peasants and serfs could now demand payment for their labor. They began to move to cities, which began to grow in size.

In time, the growth of trade led to the decline of feudalism and the manor system. A new middle class of artisans and merchants emerged, and trade cities became commercial centers. Trade associations called guilds became an influential part of European life.

READING CHECK **Drawing Conclusions** How did travel and trade affect the feudal system?

1000

1066 England is conquered by the Norman king William the Conqueror.

1200

1215 Nobles force King John to sign Magna Carta.

1347 The Black Death arrives in Europe, eventually killing millions.

c. 1350 The Renaissance begins.

1400

1436 Johannes Gutenberg perfects his invention of the printing press.

ANALYSIS SKILL **READING TIME LINES**

What two factors on the time line most helped spread literacy in Europe?

Renaissance

The Renaissance period brought new ways of thinking to Europe, weakening the old feudal system even more. The word *Renaissance* means "rebirth" and refers to the period that followed the Middle Ages in Europe. This movement began in Italy and eventually spread to other parts of Europe.

During the Renaissance, European rulers began to increase their power over the nobles in their countries. Fewer invasions from outside forces helped bring a period of order and stability to Europe.

Search for Knowledge

Love of art and education was a key feature of the Renaissance. As Turks conquered much of the Byzantine Empire in the East, scholars fled to Italy. They brought ancient classical writings with them. Some of the works were by Greek thinkers like Plato.

Excited by the discoveries brought by Turkish scholars, European scholars went looking for ancient texts in Latin. They discovered many Latin texts in monasteries, which had preserved works by Roman writers. As Italian scholars read these ancient texts, they rediscovered the glories of Greece and Rome.

The search for knowledge and learning spread to all fields, including art, literature, science, and political thought. The Renaissance emphasized the importance of people rather than focusing on religion. This new focus on human value and the study of humanities was called humanism. People's interest in the humanities led them to respect those who could write, create, or speak well. During the Middle Ages, most people had worked only to glorify God.

Italian artists created some of the most beautiful paintings and sculptures in the world. Their art reflected the basic Renaissance idea—the value of human beings. **Michelangelo** and **Leonardo da Vinci** are two of the greatest Renaissance artists. They are known for their work in painting, sculpture, and architecture. Da Vinci was also an inventor, engineer, and mapmaker.

Italian writers also penned great works of literature. Dante Alighieri was a politician and poet. Before Dante, most authors wrote in Latin, the language of the church. But Dante chose to write in Italian, the common language of the people. This gave ordinary people the opportunity to read Dante's work.

Many texts that Europeans rediscovered in the 1300s dealt with science. After reading these works, Renaissance scholars went on to make their own scientific advances. They also studied ancient math texts and built on the ideas they read about. For example, they created symbols for the square root and for positive and negative numbers. Astronomers discovered that Earth moves around the sun. Other scientists used measurements and made calculations to create better, more accurate maps.

The development of the printing press was a giant step forward in spreading new ideas. In the mid-1400s, a German man, **Johannes Gutenberg** (GOOT-uhn-berk), developed a printing press that used movable type. This allowed an entire page to be printed at once. For the first time in history, thousands of people could read the same books and share ideas about them.

Economic Changes Affect Trade

The growth in trade and services at the beginning of the Renaissance sparked a commercial revolution. This also brought a rise in mercantilism. Mercantilism is an economic system that unifies and increases the power and wealth of a nation.

Four northern Italian cities, Florence, Genoa, Milan, and Venice, developed into important trading centers. These cities played two major roles in trade. They served as ports along the Mediterranean Sea. They also served as manufacturing centers and specialized in certain crafts. This economic activity made some families in these cities very wealthy.

As trade and commerce grew, the need for banks arose. Bankers in Florence, Italy, kept money for merchants from all over Europe. The bankers also made money by charging interest on funds they loaned to merchants. The greatest bankers in Florence were from the Medici family. Although Florence was already wealthy from trade, banking increased that wealth.

During this time, merchants began to create **joint-stock companies**, or businesses in which a group of people invest together. In a joint-stock company, the investors share in the companies' profits and losses. Forming joint-stock companies allowed investors to take fewer risks.

READING CHECK **Drawing Conclusions** How did the Renaissance lead to trade and a commercial revolution?

THE IMPACT TODAY

The demand for more books led to improvements in printing and binding that have made modern books affordable.

SUMMARY AND PREVIEW Greek and Roman traditions provided new ways for people to govern themselves. In the next chapter you will read about how the Renaissance paved the way for exploration of the Americas.

Section 4 Assessment

go.hrw.com
Online Quiz
KEYWORD: SC7 HP1

Reviewing Ideas, Terms, and People

1. a. **Identify** What is the difference between a direct democracy and a republic?
   b. **Elaborate** What is the importance of having a written law code?
2. a. **Describe** What is the relationship between **knights** and nobles?
   b. **Elaborate** How did the Crusades affect the feudal system?
3. a. **Identify** What does the term *Renaissance* mean?
   b. **Analyze** What is the relationship among trade, banking, and **joint-stock companies**?
   c. **Elaborate** What do you think was the greatest accomplishment of the Renaissance?

Critical Thinking

4. **Supporting a Point of View** Review your notes on the major changes that took place in Europe during the periods discussed in the section. In a chart like the one below, identify which period you think was most important, and explain why.

Most Important	Why

FOCUS ON WRITING

5. **Organizing a Chronology** Make a list of important events in Europe during the time discussed in this section. Reorder them from earliest to most recent.

The Black Death

"And they died by the hundreds," wrote one man who saw the horror, "both day and night." The Black Death had arrived. The Black Death was a series of deadly plagues that hit Europe between 1347 and 1351, killing millions. People didn't know what caused the plague. They also didn't know that geography played a key role in its spread—as people traveled to trade, they unknowingly carried the disease with them to new places.

GEOGRAPHY SKILLS **INTERPRETING MAPS**

1. **Movement** How did the Black Death reach Europe from Asia?
2. **Human-Environment Interaction** What helped spread the plague throughout Europe?

Social Studies Skills

Analysis | Critical Thinking | Civil Participation | **Study**

North Carolina Skills
2.01 Use appropriate sources of information.

Interpreting Diagrams

Understand the Skill

Diagrams are drawings that use lines and labels to explain or illustrate something. Different types of diagrams have different purposes. *Pictorial diagrams* show an object in simple form, much like it would look if you were viewing it. *Cutaway diagrams* show the "insides" of an object. *Component diagrams* show how an object is organized by separating it into parts. Such diagrams are sometimes also called *schematic drawings*. The ability to interpret diagrams will help you to better understand a historical object, its function, and how it worked.

Learn the Skill

Use these basic steps to interpret a diagram:

1. Determine what type of diagram it is.
2. Read the diagram's title or caption to find out what the diagram represents.
3. Look for any labels and read them carefully. Most diagrams include text that identifies the object's parts or explains relationships between the parts.
4. If a legend is present, study it to identify and understand any symbols and colors that are used in the diagram.
5. Look for numbers or letters that might indicate a sequence of steps. Also, look for any arrows that might show direction or movement.

An Early Castle

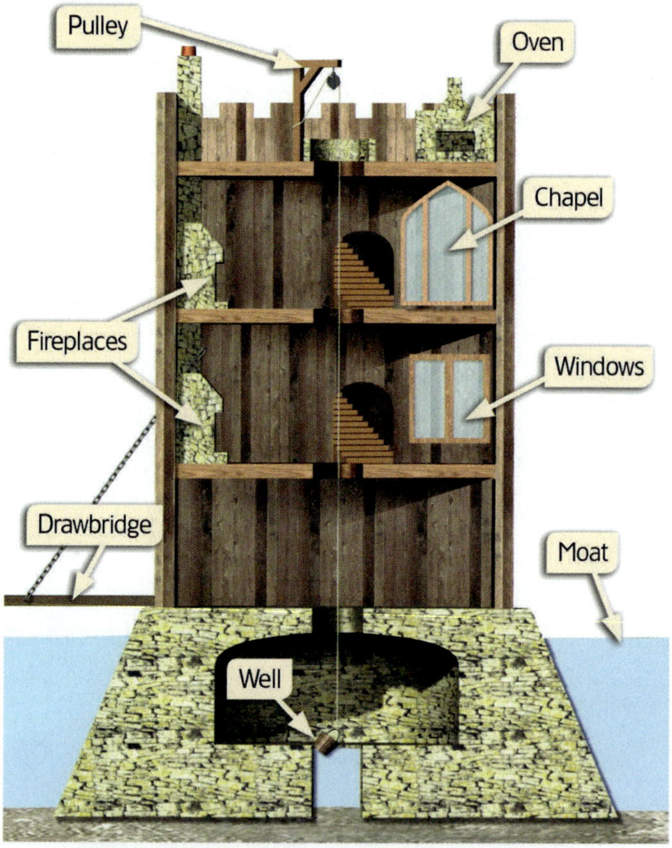

Practice and Apply the Skill

Interpret the diagram of an early castle, and answer the following questions.

1. What type of diagram is this?
2. What labels in the diagram suggest how the castle was heated?
3. What was the purpose of the pulley?
4. Of what materials was the castle made?
5. What features of the castle helped make it secure against attack?

CHAPTER 1 Chapter Review

HOLT

History's Impact

▶ **video series**

Review the video to answer the closing question:

Why do some American exports often depend on imported goods?

Visual Summary

QUICK FACTS

Use the visual summary below to help you review the main ideas of the chapter.

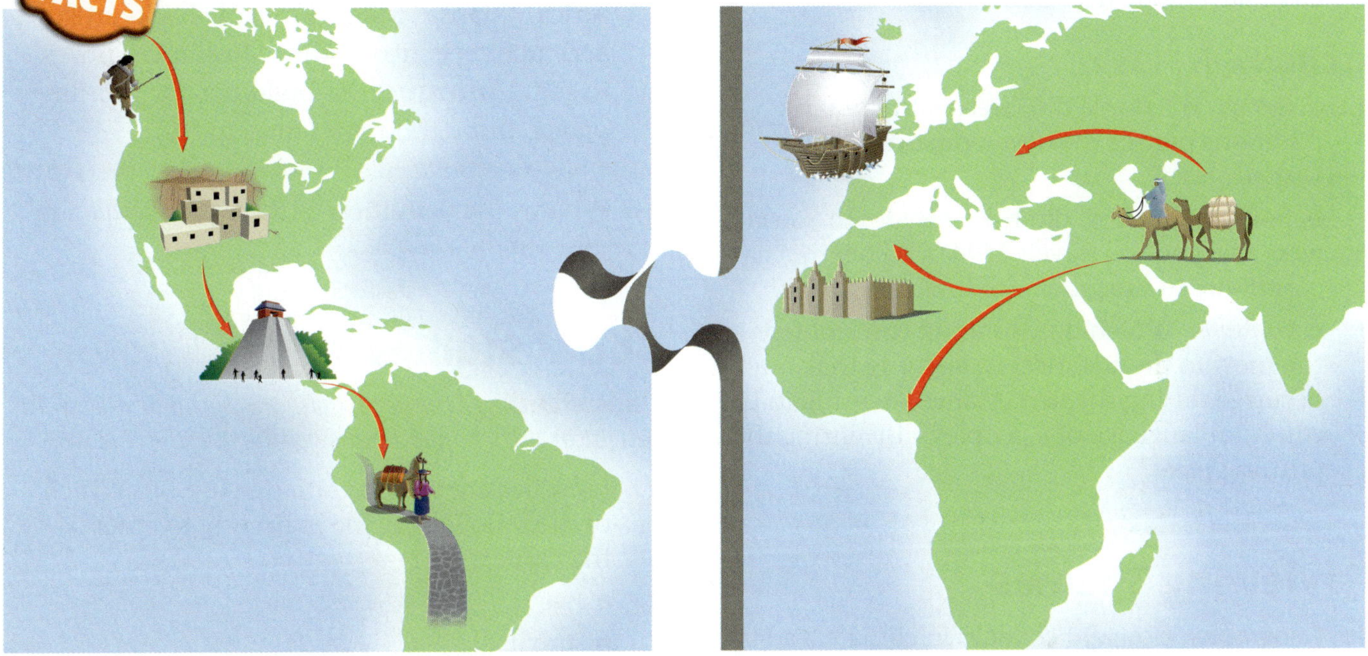

The Americas and the Old World each had complex societies, trade routes, and economies.

Reviewing Vocabulary, Terms, and People

Complete each sentence by filling in the blank with the correct term or person.

1. During the Ice Age, a narrow strip of land called the ____________ was exposed.

2. The ____________ of Paleo-Indians from North to South America took thousands of years.

3. Native Americans living in the Pacific Northwest carved ____________ on tall poles.

4. The first political confederation of Native Americans in North America was the ____________.

5. The most famous ruler of Mali was __________.

6. While Mali's leader was on a ____________, or pilgrimage, to Mecca, he introduced his empire to the world.

7. The most famous ruler of Songhai took the name ____________.

8. ____________ describes an ideal society based on justice in *Republic*.

Comprehension and Critical Thinking

SECTION 1 *(Pages 6–9)*

9. a. Describe How did early peoples in the Americas get their food?

b. Analyze What led to the development of different culture groups in the Americas?

c. Elaborate What features did the early civilizations of Mesoamerica and South America have in common?

SECTION 2 *(Pages 10–15)*

10. a. Identify Which early Native American society built cliff dwellings, and which built mounds?

b. Analyze How did Native Americans' religious beliefs affect their lives in North America?

c. Evaluate Do you think it was easier for Native Americans to live in the dry climates of the Southwest, where rainfall was unpredictable, or in the North, where the cold climate presented a constant challenge?

SECTION 3 *(Pages 16–20)*

11. a. **Describe** How did geography contribute to Ghana's wealth?

    b. **Compare** What characteristics did Mansa Musa and Askia the Great have in common?

    c. **Elaborate** How did West Africa develop a large slave-trade network?

SECTION 4 *(Pages 22–27)*

12. a. **Recall** What role did Greek and Roman traditions play in the development of the United States?

    b. **Summarize** How did the Crusades in Southwest Asia and the travels of Marco Polo in Asia contribute to the growth of trade in Europe?

    c. **Evaluate** Which do you think contributed the most to the advances in learning that occurred during the Renaissance—writing in the common language of a people or inventing the printing press?

Reviewing Themes

13. **Geography** How did changes in climate lead to migration to the Americas?
14. **Economics** Describe the development of the European economy during the Middle Ages.

Using the Internet

go.hrw.com
KEYWORD: SC7 CH1

15. **Activity: Compare and Contrast** What causes large groups of people to migrate? Factors that influence why people migrate can be labeled as "push" and "pull." Poor climate and lack of resources "pushed" Paleo-Indians to North America. This activity will help you understand factors of migration. Enter the activity keyword, then compare and contrast push-pull factors involved in Paleo-Indian migration with the factors influencing immigration to the United States today. Create an illustrated chart to display your research.

Reading Skills

Specialized Vocabulary of Social Studies *Use the Reading Skills taught in this chapter to answer the question about the reading selection below.*

> To encourage the spread of Islam in West Africa, Mansa Musa brought back artists and architects from other Muslim countries to build **mosques**, or buildings for Muslim prayer, throughout his lands. (p. 19)

16. What is the definition of the word *mosques* in the sentence above?

Social Studies Skills

Understanding Diagrams *Use the Social Studies Skills taught in this chapter to answer the question below.*

17. Look back at the diagram on page 30. Which of the following is the main way to enter the castle?

    a. well

    b. moat

    c. drawbridge

    d. windows

FOCUS ON WRITING

18. **Writing Your Travelogue.** You have read about many cultures across a long span of history. Pick one area that you found the most interesting in the chapter. Organize your thoughts about the kinds of people you would have met and the kind of things you would have done if you had traveled there during the time discussed.

    Try to include information about a culture's history, customs, beliefs, practices, economies, political systems, and natural environments. Write a paragraph about what you might have liked or disliked about your trip. Be sure to include a main idea sentence and several sentences that support the main idea with evidence.

CHAPTER 1

Standardized Test Practice

DIRECTIONS: Read each question and write the letter of the best response.

1 The exposure of a land bridge between Asia and present-day Alaska during the last Ice Age resulted in

A the introduction of new plants and animals to Asia and Europe.

B the development of farming in the Americas.

C the migration of people into the Americas.

D the establishment of advanced cultures in North America.

2 Which of the following groups of Native Americans inhabited the area that would become North Carolina?

A Iroquois

B Anasazi

C Navajo

D Cherokee

3 What impact did the slave trade have on the economy of West Africa?

A As a result of the reliance on slave labor, West Africa's economy declined.

B The economy benefited from the increasing demand for slave labor.

C The slave trade did not have a noticeable effect on West Africa's economy.

D Because there was little demand for slave labor, West Africa's economy suffered.

4 Which of the following had the *greatest* impact on the revival of European trade at the end of the Middle Ages?

A an increase in safe travel between Europe and Asia

B Mansa Musa's pilgrimage to Mecca

C the introduction of the slave trade

D the development of democratic governments

5 How did the societies of North America differ from those of Central and South America?

A Societies in North America did not create political units like those in Central and South America.

B North American culture groups lacked the diversity of those in Central and South America.

C North American societies were significantly more advanced than those to the south.

D Culture groups in North America worshipped many gods, while those in Central and South America were monotheistic.

6 Which of the following is an example of the political influence ancient Greece and Rome have had on our world?

A demanding that all traders pay taxes on the goods they carried

B electing officials to run the government

C offering land to individuals in exchange for military service

D appointing local leaders who were loyal to the emperor

7 Examine the following passage by Marco Polo about his travels through China. Then answer the question that follows.

> "Upon leaving Ta-in-fu, we traveled for seven days through a fine county in which there were many cities, where commerce and manufactures [goods] prevailed. We reached a large city named Pi-an-fu, which is very famous. Like Ta-in-fu, this city contains numerous merchants and artisans. Silk is produced here also in great quantity."
>
> —Marco Polo, from the *Travels of Marco Polo: The Venetian*

Document-Based Question What is the main idea of this passage?

CHAPTER 2 1400–1750

New Empires in the Americas

North Carolina Standards

Social Studies Objectives

1.02 Identify and describe American Indians who inhabited the regions that became Carolina and assess their impact on the colony.

1.03 Compare and contrast the relative importance of differing economic, geographic, religious, and political motives for European exploration.

1.04 Evaluate the impact of the Columbian Exchange on the cultures of American Indians, Europeans, and Africans.

1.05 Describe the factors that led to the founding and settlement of the American colonies including religious persecution, economic opportunity, adventure, and forced migration.

3.04 Describe the development of the institution of slavery in the State and nation, and assess its impact on the economic, social, and political conditions.

9.02 Identify past and present state and local leaders from diverse cultural backgrounds and assess their influence in effecting change.

Language Arts Objectives

3.02 Continue to explore and analyze the use of the problem-solution process by:

- recognizing and/or creating an organizing structure appropriate to purpose, audience, and context.

4.03 Use the stance of a critic to:

- consider alternative points of view or reasons.
- remain fair-minded and open to other interpretations.

go.hrw.com
North Carolina
KEYWORD: SC7 NC

Focus on Writing

Writing a Letter Long before telephones and e-mails, most people communicated with friends and family far away by letter. As you read this chapter, you will learn about different groups of people who came to the Americas. You will pretend to be a member of one of these groups and write a letter home to tell your friends and family about the people you meet and the experiences you have in the Americas.

WORLD

1416
Prince Henry the Navigator establishes a center for naval exploration at Sagres, Portugal.

1400

HOLT

History's Impact

▶ **video series**
Watch the video to understand the impact of different cultures.

What You Will Learn...

The ships of explorer Christopher Columbus sail again in the form of these replicas. Columbus discovered land where Europeans did not expect land to be. The news excited Europe and set off the great Age of Exploration. The Americas and Europe—and the world—would never be the same again. In this chapter you will learn more about the Europeans who colonized North America.

1492
Christopher Columbus lands in the Bahamas.

1609
Henry Hudson makes his first voyage to North America.

1619
The first Africans in North America arrive at Jamestown, Virginia.

1500 — 1600 — 1700

1533
Francisco Pizarro and his men kill Inca leader Atahualpa.

1609
Galileo Galilei becomes the first person to use a telescope to view the heavens.

1644
The Qing dynasty begins in China and rules until 1912.

Reading Social Studies

by Kylene Beers

Economics | Geography | Politics | Society and Culture | Science and Technology

Focus on Themes In this chapter you will read about European exploration of the sea and of North and South America. As you read, you will learn about how **politics** encouraged the desire to explore new trade routes and lands. You will also read about how **geography** affected the race for empires in the New World. European nations began exploring the newly discovered continents in an effort to establish colonies.

Outlining and History

Focus on Reading How can you make sense of all the facts and ideas in a chapter? One way is to take notes in the form of an outline.

Outlining a Chapter Here is an example of a partial outline for Section 4 of this chapter. Compare the outline to the information on pages 52–57. Notice how the writer looked at the headings in the chapter to determine the main and supporting ideas.

The writer picked up the first heading in the section (p. 52) as the first main idea. She identified it with Roman numeral I.

The writer identified three facts that supported III.B. She listed them as numbers 1, 2, and 3.

Section 4: The Race for Empires

I. Events in Europe
   A. The Protestant Reformation
   B. Spain and England Go to War
      1. Sea dogs
      2. Spanish Armada
II. Search for a Northwest Passage
III. European Presence in North America
   A. English Presence in the New World
   B. French Presence in the New World
      1. Huguenots
      2. Canada
      3. Explorers
         a. Cartier
         b. Champlain
         c. Jolliet and Marquette
         d. La Salle
   C. Dutch Presence in the New World

The writer saw two smaller headings under the bigger heading on pages 52–53 and listed them as A and B.

The writer decided it was important to note some individual facts under B.3. That's why she added points a. through d.

Outlining a Few Paragraphs When you need to outline only a few paragraphs, you can use the same outline form. Just look for the main idea of each paragraph and give each one a Roman numeral. Supporting ideas within the paragraph can be listed with A, B, and so forth. You can use Arabic numbers for specific details and facts.

You Try It!

Read the following passage from this chapter. Then fill in the blanks to complete the outline below.

Conquest of the Aztec Empire

Moctezuma ruled the Aztec Empire, which was at the height of its power in the early 1500s. Moctezuma's capital, Tenochtitlán, was built in the middle of Lake Texcoco, near the present-day site of Mexico City. Tenochtitlán was a large city with temples, a palace, and buildings that were built on an island in the middle of the lake. The buildings and riches of the city impressed the Spaniards. They saw the Aztec Empire as a good source of gold and silver. They also wanted to convert the Aztec to Christianity.

The Aztec had thousand of warriors. In contrast, Cortés had only 508 soldiers, about 100 sailors, 16 horses, and some guns. Cortés hoped that his superior weapons would bring him victory.

Chapter 2, (p. 46)

Complete this outline based on the passage you just read.

I. Moctezuma and the Aztec Empire were at the height of power in the 1500s.

A. Tenochtitlán was the capital

1. Built in Lake Texcoco

2. ______________________

B. The buildings and riches impressed the conquistadors

1. ___________________________

2. Christianity

II. ________________________________

A. Cortés had fewer soldiers

B. ______________________

Key Terms and People

Chapter 2

Section 1

Leif Eriksson *(p. 38)*
Henry the Navigator *(p. 39)*
astrolabe *(p. 40)*
caravels *(p. 40)*

Section 2

Christopher Columbus *(p. 42)*
Line of Demarcation *(p. 44)*
Treaty of Tordesillas *(p. 44)*
Ferdinand Magellan *(p. 44)*
circumnavigate *(p. 44)*
Columbian Exchange *(p. 45)*

Section 3

conquistadors *(p. 46)*
Hernán Cortés *(p. 46)*
Moctezuma II *(p. 46)*
Francisco Pizarro *(p. 47)*
encomienda system *(p. 50)*
plantations *(p. 50)*
Bartolomé de Las Casas *(p. 51)*

Section 4

Protestant Reformation *(p. 53)*
Protestants *(p. 53)*
Spanish Armada *(p. 53)*
Northwest Passage *(p. 54)*
Jacques Cartier *(p. 54)*
charter *(p. 54)*

Section 5

immune *(p. 58)*
Middle Passage *(p. 59)*
African Diaspora *(p. 60)*

Academic Vocabulary

Success in school is related to knowing academic vocabulary—the words that are frequently used in school assignments and discussions. In this chapter, you will learn the following academic words.

effect *(p. 40)*
structure *(p. 59)*

SECTION 1

Europeans Set Sail

If YOU were there...

You are a sailor living in Portugal in the mid-1400s. Several of your friends are excited about joining an expedition to sail to new lands. Although Portuguese navigators have made improvements to sailing ships and advancements in ocean travel, you have heard about the dangers other sailors have faced on the open seas.

Will you join the expedition or stay behind? Why?

What You Will Learn...

Main Ideas

1. Vikings were skilled sailors, and they were the first Europeans to reach North America.
2. Prince Henry the Navigator established a school for sailors and provided financial support that enabled the Portuguese to start exploring the oceans.
3. Portuguese sailors sailed around Africa and found a sea route to Asia.

The Big Idea

Europeans explored the world, searching for new lands and new trade routes.

Key Terms and People

Leif Eriksson, *p. 38*
Henry the Navigator, *p. 39*
astrolabe, *p. 40*
caravels, *p. 40*

TAKING NOTES As you read, take notes on European exploration. List the countries that explored the world and the places they explored. Write your notes in a chart like the one below.

Countries	Places Explored

BUILDING BACKGROUND Europeans were interested in the goods of Africa and Asia. In order to find new routes to these goods and to find new lands to settle, many European nations sent explorers on voyages.

Viking Sailors Reach North America

The Vikings were the first Europeans to make contact with North America. They came from Scandinavia, a peninsula that includes the present-day countries of Denmark, Norway, and Sweden. The Vikings were skilled sailors who developed a new style of ship, called the longship, that curved up at both ends. Viking vessels traveled the rough North Atlantic seas better than earlier ships because their designs were more stable.

The Vikings raided countries throughout Europe, but they also developed large trading networks. Viking ships sailed to the British Isles and the Mediterranean and Black seas. Eventually, the Vikings sailed west into the North Atlantic. There they founded a settlement on the island of Iceland in about 874. More than 100 years later, Viking Erik the Red left Iceland to settle Greenland.

Leif Eriksson, the son of Erik the Red, shared his father's love of adventure. In the year 1000, he was sailing from west Norway to Greenland when strong winds blew his ship off course and carried his ship all the way to the North American coast.

Eriksson and his crew landed on the Labrador Peninsula in present-day Canada. The Vikings then sailed farther south to the island of Newfoundland, and perhaps to what is now New England. According to their myths, Vikings saw forests, meadows, and rivers that held "larger salmon than they had ever seen."

Eriksson settled in a coastal area he called Vinland, but the Vikings left after only a few years. Attacks by Native Americans posed a constant threat, and the area may have been too far from other Viking settlements to be supported.

After the Vikings left North America, Europeans did not return to the continent for centuries. In the 1400s, however, a growing interest in discovery and exploration spread across Europe.

READING CHECK **Sequencing** List the stages of exploration that led to the Vikings' landing in North America.

Prince Henry the Navigator

In the early 1400s Portugal became a leader in world exploration. One man in particular, Prince **Henry the Navigator**, was responsible for advances that would make exploration more successful. Although he never set out on a voyage himself, Henry greatly advanced Portugal's exploration efforts.

In the early 1400s Prince Henry built an observatory and founded a school of navigation to teach better methods of sailing. He also financed research by mapmakers and shipbuilders. Finally, he paid for expeditions to explore the west coast of Africa.

Riches in Asia

During the 1400s, Europeans had several reasons to explore the world. First, they wanted Asian spices. They hoped to bypass the merchants who had a monopoly on, or economic control of, the Asian products that reached the Mediterranean. If a sea route to Asia could be found, countries could buy spices and other items directly.

Second, religion played a role in exploration. Christians in Europe wanted to convert more people to their faith. Third, many Europeans had become interested in Asian cultures. Explorer Marco Polo's book about his travels throughout Asia remained popular in Europe long after his death in 1324. Many Europeans wanted to learn more about Asia and its cultures.

History Close-up

The Caravel

A special type of ship called the caravel became the workhorse of many European explorers. Though small, caravels were sturdy. They could sail across huge oceans and up small rivers. Caravels featured important advances in sailing technology.

ANALYSIS SKILL **ANALYZING VISUALS**

What features made the caravel an excellent sailing ship?

QUICK FACTS

Causes and Effects of the Discovery of a Sea Route to Asia

Several factors led to the discovery of a sea route from Europe to Asia.

Causes

- Financial backing from Prince Henry the Navigator
- New technology (caravel and mariner's astrolabe)
- Seeking trade with Asia and financial gain
- Converting people to Christianity
- Curiosity

Effects

- Discovery of a sea route to Asia
- Face-to-face contact with traders in distant lands
- Awareness of different cultures and ways of life

ANALYSIS SKILL **ANALYZING INFORMATION**

Why was trade with Asia so important to Europeans?

ACADEMIC VOCABULARY

effect the result of an action or decision

FOCUS ON READING

Make an outline for the heading "A Sea Route to Asia."

Technological Advances

New technology played a major role in advancing world exploration. Sailors began to use tools such as the magnetic compass and the **astrolabe**, a device that enabled navigators to learn their ship's location by charting the position of the stars. Better instruments made it possible for sailors to travel the open seas without landmarks to guide them.

The Portuguese also made advances in shipbuilding. They began designing ships that were smaller, lighter, and easier to steer than the heavy galleons they had used before. These new ships, called **caravels** (ker-uh-velz), used triangular sails that, unlike traditional square sails, allowed ships to sail against the wind. By placing rudders at the back of the ship, the Portuguese also improved the steering of ships.

READING CHECK **Analyzing** How did Henry the Navigator promote exploration?

A Sea Route to Asia

By the 1400s Portugal had several motives, financial support, and the technology necessary for exploration. Portuguese explorers set out to find new lands.

Rounding Africa

Even with new technology, travel on the open seas was dangerous and difficult. One person described the <u>**effect**</u> on sailors of a voyage south from Portugal.

> "Those which survived could hardly be recognized as human. They had lost flesh and hair, the nails had gone from hands and feet . . . They spoke of heat so incredible that it was a marvel that ships and crews were not burnt."
>
> –Sailor, quoted in *World Civilizations*, edited by Edward McNall Burns, et al.

In spite of the dangers, Portuguese explorers continued sailing south, setting up trading posts along the way.

In 1488 Portuguese navigator Bartolomeu Dias led an expedition from Portugal southward along the African coast. A storm blew his ships around the southern tip of Africa. This point became known as the Cape of Good Hope. Dias wanted to continue his voyage, but his men did not. Since supplies were very low, Dias decided to call off the voyage and return to Portugal.

Later, King Manuel of Portugal sent another explorer, Vasco da Gama, on an expedition around the Cape of Good Hope. Da Gama left Lisbon, Portugal, in July 1497 and arrived in southwestern India the next year. Portugal had won the European race for a sea route to Asia.

When da Gama reached the Indian port of Calicut, Muslim traders met him and his men. The Muslims surprised the sailors by speaking to them in Portuguese. Soon da Gama and his crew learned that the people of India had been trading with Muslim and Italian merchants who knew Portuguese. Da Gama made two more trips back to India. He even governed a small colony there.

Results of Exploration

Portugal's explorations would have major results, including the start of the Atlantic slave trade. As Portuguese sailors explored the west coast of Africa, they negotiated for gold, ivory, and slaves. The slave trade devastated African communities. It led to increased warfare among kingdoms and broke up many families. The Portuguese sent many enslaved Africans to Europe and to islands in the Atlantic, where they lived and worked under brutal conditions.

The other nations of Europe watched as new trade routes brought increased wealth and power to Portugal. They soon launched voyages of exploration to find their own water routes to Asia.

READING CHECK **Predicting** How would continued exploration affect Africans?

SUMMARY AND PREVIEW In the 1400s, the Portuguese started a new era of exploration. In the next section you will learn how Europeans reached the American continents.

GEOGRAPHY SKILLS **INTERPRETING MAPS**

1. **Movement** Which explorer was the first to reach the Cape of Good Hope?
2. **Human-Environment Interaction** About how many miles was da Gama's 1497–1499 voyage?

Section 1 Assessment

go.hrw.com
Online Quiz
KEYWORD: SC7 HP2

Reviewing Ideas, Terms, and People

1. a. **Identify** Who was **Leif Eriksson**?
   b. **Summarize** How did the Vikings eventually establish Vinland?
   c. **Draw Inferences** Why do you think the Vikings did not try to colonize the Americas?
2. a. **Identify** Who was Prince **Henry the Navigator**?
   b. **Compare** Why were **caravels** able to sail against the wind while other ships could not?
3. a. **Recall** Who was the first explorer to find a sea route from Europe to Asia?
   b. **Explain** How did Muslims living in India learn Portuguese?
   c. **Draw Conclusions** How did the slave trade affect West Africa?

Critical Thinking

4. **Summarizing** Review your notes on European exploration. Then copy the chart below and use it to explain the reason for the explorations, the technology that made explorations possible, and the results of the explorations.

Reason / Technology	→	Results

FOCUS ON WRITING

5. **Taking Notes on Early Explorers** As you read this section, take notes on groups of explorers. Make sure to note the differences and similarities between the groups, where they traveled, and why.

SECTION 2

Europeans Reach the Americas

What You Will Learn...

Main Ideas

1. Christopher Columbus sailed across the Atlantic Ocean and reached a continent that was previously unknown to him.
2. After Columbus's voyages, other explorers sailed to the Americas.

The Big Idea

Christopher Columbus's voyages led to new exchanges between Europe, Africa, and the Americas.

Key Terms and People

Christopher Columbus, *p. 42*
Line of Demarcation, *p. 44*
Treaty of Tordesillas, *p. 44*
Ferdinand Magellan, *p. 44*
circumnavigate, *p. 44*
Columbian Exchange, *p. 45*

TAKING NOTES As you read, take notes on the explorers, their journeys, and the effects of European voyages to the Americas. Write your notes in a chart like the one below.

Explorer	Sponsored by	Traveled to

Effects of Journeys

If YOU were there...

You are a European explorer who just returned to your homeland from the Americas. While you were gone, you tried new and different foods, including corn, potatoes, and cocoa. You have brought some of these foods back with you. You want your friends and family to sample these items, but they resist.

What will you say about these new foods?

BUILDING BACKGROUND Europeans, Africans, and Asians had traded with each other for centuries using land and sea routes. Native American groups also knew of each other through trade routes. Although sailors often explored new areas, before 1492 the two worlds had no communication with each other.

Columbus Sails across the Atlantic

Stories of fabulous kingdoms and wealth in Asia captured the imagination of **Christopher Columbus**, a sailor from Genoa, Italy. Columbus was convinced that he could reach Asia by sailing west across the Atlantic Ocean.

The Journey Begins

Columbus asked King Ferdinand and Queen Isabella of Spain to pay for an expedition across the Atlantic. He promised them great riches, new territory, and Catholic converts. It took Columbus several years to convince the king and queen, but they finally agreed to help finance the journey. Ferdinand and Isabella ordered Columbus to bring back any items of value and to claim for Spain any lands he explored.

On August 3, 1492, Columbus's three ships set sail. The *Niña* and the *Pinta* were caravels. Columbus sailed in the larger *Santa María*. The ships carried about 90 sailors and a year's worth of supplies. They made a stop in the Canary Islands, and then on September 6, they resumed their journey. Soon, they passed the limits of Columbus's

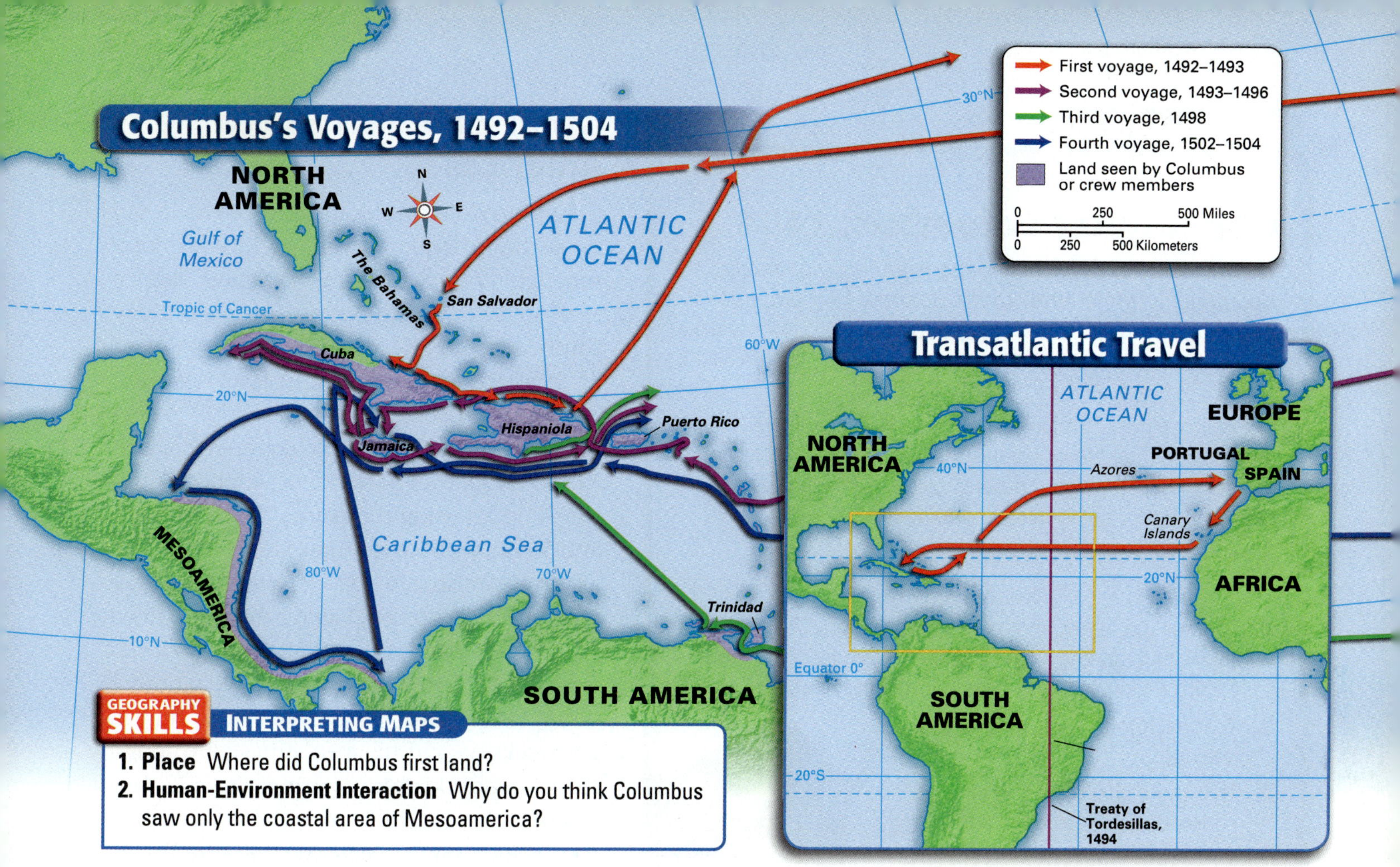

GEOGRAPHY SKILLS **INTERPRETING MAPS**

1. **Place** Where did Columbus first land?
2. **Human-Environment Interaction** Why do you think Columbus saw only the coastal area of Mesoamerica?

maps and sailed into uncharted seas. After more than a month with no sight of land, the crew grew restless.

Soon the crew saw signs of land—birds and floating tree branches. Columbus promised a reward "to him who first sang out that he saw land." On October 12, 1492, a lookout cried, "Land! Land!" ending the long journey from the Canary Islands.

The ships landed on an island in the Bahamas. Columbus thought he had found a new route to Asia. Instead, he had reached another continent that was unknown to him. Columbus called the island San Salvador, which means "Holy Savior." Columbus also visited another island he called Hispaniola. There he met the Taino (TY-noh). At that time Europeans called Asia the Indies, so Columbus, believing he was in Asia, called these Native American people Indians.

The Taino lived in small farming communities. In his journal, Columbus wrote that the Taino were "so generous . . . that no one would believe it who has not seen it." However, Columbus and his crew were not interested in Taino culture, but in gold. After three months of exploring, looking for gold, and collecting exotic plants and animals, Columbus returned to Spain.

Columbus made three more journeys to the Americas during his lifetime. In 1504 he returned to Spain in poor health. Columbus died two years later, still believing that he had reached Asia.

Impact of Columbus's Voyages

The voyages of Columbus changed the way Europeans thought of the world and their place in it. A new era of interaction between Europe and the Americas had begun.

Columbus's discovery also created conflict between European countries. Both Spain and Portugal wanted to add these lands to their growing empires. In 1493, Pope Alexander VI, originally from Spain, issued a decree that drew a new boundary for Spain and Portugal.

Primary Source

LETTER

Christopher Columbus, 1494

Two years after discovering the island of Hispaniola, Columbus wrote a letter to the Spanish king and queen outlining his ideas of its colonization.

Most High and Mighty Sovereigns,

In the first place, as regards the Island of Espanola: Inasmuch as the number of colonists who desire to go thither [there] amounts to two thousand, owing to the land being safer and better for farming and trading . . .

1. That in the said island there shall be founded three or four towns . . .
2. That for the better and more speedy colonization of the said island, no one shall have liberty to collect gold in it except those who have taken out colonists' papers . . .
3. That each town shall have its alcalde [Mayor] . . .
4. That there shall be a church, and parish priests or friars to administer the sacraments, to perform divine worship, and for the conversion of the Indians.

–Christopher Columbus,
letter to the king and queen of Spain, 1494

ANALYSIS SKILL **ANALYZING PRIMARY SOURCES**

What were Columbus's main concerns in founding a colony on Hispaniola?

This imaginary **Line of Demarcation** divided the Atlantic Ocean. Spain could claim all land west of the line.

The Portuguese king believed that this arrangement favored Spain. To prevent war, the leaders of the two nations signed the **Treaty of Tordesillas**, which moved the Line of Demarcation 800 miles further west. This gave Portugal more opportunity to claim lands unexplored by other Europeans.

READING CHECK **Identifying Points of View**
Why did Columbus want to sail across the Atlantic?

Other Explorers Sail to the Americas

Columbus's discoveries inspired others to sail across the Atlantic Ocean. In 1501 explorer Amerigo Vespucci (vuh-SPOO-chee) led a Spanish fleet to the coast of present-day South America. He was convinced the land he reached was not Asia. Instead, Vespucci believed he had found a "new world." A German mapmaker labeled the continents across the ocean *America* in honor of Vespucci. Europeans began using the names North America and South America for these lands.

In a Spanish settlement in present-day Panama, another explorer, Vasco Núñez de Balboa (NOON-yays day bahl-BOH-uh), heard stories from local Native Americans about another ocean farther west. Balboa set out to find it. For weeks he and his men struggled through thick jungle and deadly swamps. In 1513 they reached the top of a mountain. From this spot Balboa saw a great blue sea—the Pacific Ocean—stretching out before him.

In 1519, **Ferdinand Magellan** (muh-JEHL-uhn), a Portuguese navigator, set out with a Spanish fleet to sail down the east coast of South America. After sailing around the southern tip of the continent, Magellan continued into the Pacific even though his ships were dangerously low on food and fresh water.

Magellan's fleet sailed across the Pacific Ocean. In the Philippines, Magellan was killed in a battle with native peoples. Down to three ships, the expedition continued sailing west into the Indian Ocean. In 1522 the voyage's only remaining ship returned to Spain. Only 18 members of Magellan's original crew survived. These sailors were the first people to **circumnavigate**, or go all the way around, the globe. Their entire journey was some 40,000 miles long.

European explorers and settlers took plants and animals with them to the Americas. They also brought back a variety of new plants and animals to Europe, Asia, and Africa.

This transfer became known as the **Columbian Exchange** because it started with Columbus's explorations. The Columbian Exchange dramatically changed the world.

European explorers found many plants in the Americas that were unknown to them, including corn, potatoes, tobacco, and cocoa. They brought these items to Europe, where they were highly valued. The explorers also introduced horses, cattle, and pigs to the Americas. Native Americans came to use these animals for food and transportation. They also started to farm European grains such as wheat and barley.

Without intending to do so, the explorers also introduced deadly new diseases to the Americas. Native Americans had no natural resistance to European diseases and often died as a result of their exposure to them.

Over time, a trading pattern involving the exchange of raw materials, manufactured products, and slaves developed among Europe, Africa, and the Americas. Europeans shipped millions of enslaved Africans to work in the colonies in the New World.

READING CHECK **Evaluating** What were the negative aspects of the Columbian Exchange?

The Columbian Exchange

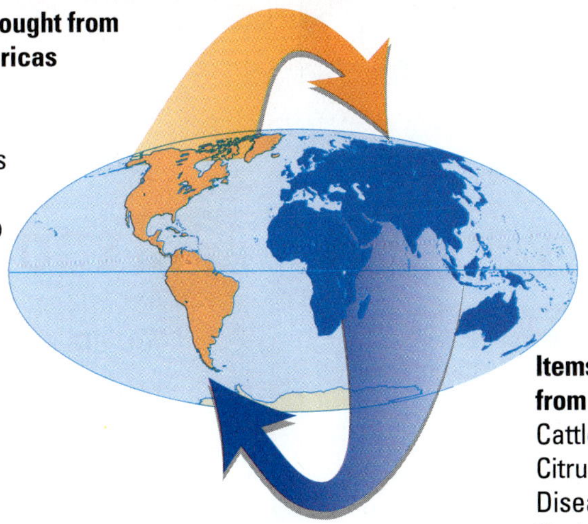

ANALYSIS SKILL

Which side of the Atlantic did cattle come from? Potatoes? Sugarcane?

SUMMARY AND PREVIEW Columbus's voyages to America inspired other Europeans to explore the "New World." This led to new exchanges between both sides of the Atlantic. In the next section you will learn about Spain's empire in the Americas.

Section 2 Assessment

go.hrw.com
Online Quiz
KEYWORD: SC7 HP2

Reviewing Ideas, Terms, and People

1. a. **Recall** What agreement did **Christopher Columbus** make with Queen Isabella and King Ferdinand of Spain?
   b. **Explain** Where did Columbus think he had landed when he reached the Bahamas?
   c. **Evaluate** How did Columbus's voyage lead to a dispute between Spain and Portugal?
2. a. **Identify** Who was the first European explorer to see the Pacific Ocean?
   b. **Summarize** What route did **Ferdinand Magellan**'s ships take to **circumnavigate** the globe?
   c. **Draw Conclusions** How did the **Columbian Exchange** and the slave trade affect the economies and the people of Europe, Africa, and the Americas?

Critical Thinking

3. **Supporting a Point of View** Review your notes on European exploration. Then copy the graphic organizer below and use it to rank, in order, the two most important results of European voyages to the Americas. Explain your choices in the "Why" column.

Most Important	Why

FOCUS ON WRITING

4. **Understanding Christopher Columbus** As you read this section, pay attention to what life might have been like for Columbus and his crew as they sailed across the Atlantic. Note ways in which their voyage changed life for many Europeans.

SECTION 3

Spain Builds an Empire

What You Will Learn...

Main Ideas

1. Spanish conquistadors conquered the Aztec and Inca empires.
2. Spanish explorers traveled through the borderlands of New Spain, claiming more land.
3. Spanish settlers treated Native Americans harshly, forcing them to work on plantations and in mines.

The Big Idea

Spain established a large empire in the Americas.

Key Terms and People

conquistadors, *p. 46*
Hernán Cortés, *p. 46*
Moctezuma II, *p. 46*
Francisco Pizarro, *p. 47*
encomienda system, *p. 50*
plantations, *p. 50*
Bartolomé de Las Casas, *p. 51*

TAKING NOTES Create a chart like the one below. As you read, take notes on Spanish conquest and settlement in the Americas.

Spanish Conquest and Settlement	
Aztec Empire	
Inca Empire	
Borderlands–Southeast	
Borderlands–Southwest	

If YOU were there...

You are an Aztec warrior living in central Mexico in the 1500s. You are proud to serve your ruler, Moctezuma II. One day several hundred foreigners arrive on your shores. They are pale, bearded men, and they have strange animals and equipment.

From where do you think these strangers have come?

BUILDING BACKGROUND Spain sent many expeditions to the Americas. Like explorers from other countries, Spanish explorers claimed the land they found for their country. Much of this land was already filled with Native American communities, however.

Spanish Conquistadors

The Spanish sent **conquistadors** (kahn-kees-tuh-DAWRS), soldiers who led military expeditions in the Americas. Conquistador **Hernán Cortés** left Cuba to sail to present-day Mexico in 1519. Cortés had heard of a wealthy land to the west ruled by a king named **Moctezuma II** (mawk-tay-SOO-mah).

Conquest of the Aztec Empire

Moctezuma ruled the Aztec Empire, which was at the height of its power in the early 1500s. Moctezuma's capital, Tenochtitlán, was built in the middle of Lake Texcoco, near the present-day site of Mexico City. Tenochtitlán was a large city with temples, a palace, and buildings that were built on an island in the middle of the lake. The buildings and riches of the city impressed the Spaniards. They saw the Aztec Empire as a good source of gold and silver. They also wanted to convert the Aztec to Christianity.

The Aztec had thousands of warriors. In contrast, Cortés had only 508 soldiers, about 100 sailors, 16 horses, and some guns. Cortés hoped that his superior weapons would bring him victory. Cortés also sought help from enemies of the Aztec. An Indian woman named Malintzin (mah-LINT-suhn) helped Cortés win allies.

At first Moctezuma believed Cortés to be a god and welcomed him. Cortés then took Moctezuma prisoner and seized control of Tenochtitlán. Eventually, Tenochtitlán was destroyed and Moctezuma was killed. Smallpox and other diseases brought by the Spanish quickened the fall of the Aztec Empire.

Conquest of the Inca Empire

Another conquistador, **Francisco Pizarro** (puh-ZAHR-oh), heard rumors of the Inca cities in the Andes of South America. The Inca ruled a large territory that stretched along the Pacific coast from present-day Chile to northern Ecuador.

Pizarro had fewer than 400 men in his army. But the Inca, like the Aztec, had no weapons to match the conquistadors' swords and guns. Though outnumbered, Pizarro's troops captured the great Inca capital at Cuzco in present-day Peru and killed the Inca leaders. By 1534 Pizarro and his Native American allies had conquered the entire Inca Empire.

In only a few years, the Spanish had conquered two great American empires. During the conquest, the Spanish and their allies killed thousands of Inca and Aztec and looted their settlements. Moreover, possibly more than three-quarters of the Aztec and Inca populations were killed by the diseases the Europeans brought.

Spanish Settlements

The Spanish began to settle their vast empire, which they called New Spain. Spain's government wanted to control migration to the Americas. Most of the emigrants were Spanish, though a few non-Spanish subjects of the king also migrated. Jews, Muslims, and non-Christians were forbidden to settle in New Spain. At first, most emigrants were men. The government then encouraged families to migrate. Eventually, women comprised one-quarter of the total emigration from Spain.

Spain ruled its large American empire through a system of royal officials. At the top was the Council of the Indies, formed in 1524 to govern the Americas from Spain. The Council appointed two viceroys, or royal governors. The Viceroyalty of Peru governed most of South America. The Viceroyalty of New Spain governed all Spanish territories in

LINKING TO TODAY

Armored Warfare

The armor of the Spanish conquistadors helped them defeat the Aztec and Inca. Spanish soldiers and their horses wore armor made of steel. The steel protected the soldiers from enemy weapons but was heavy and hard to wear. Armored weapons of today's soldiers include tanks and other large vehicles. Inside these vehicles, soldiers are safer from enemy gunfire.

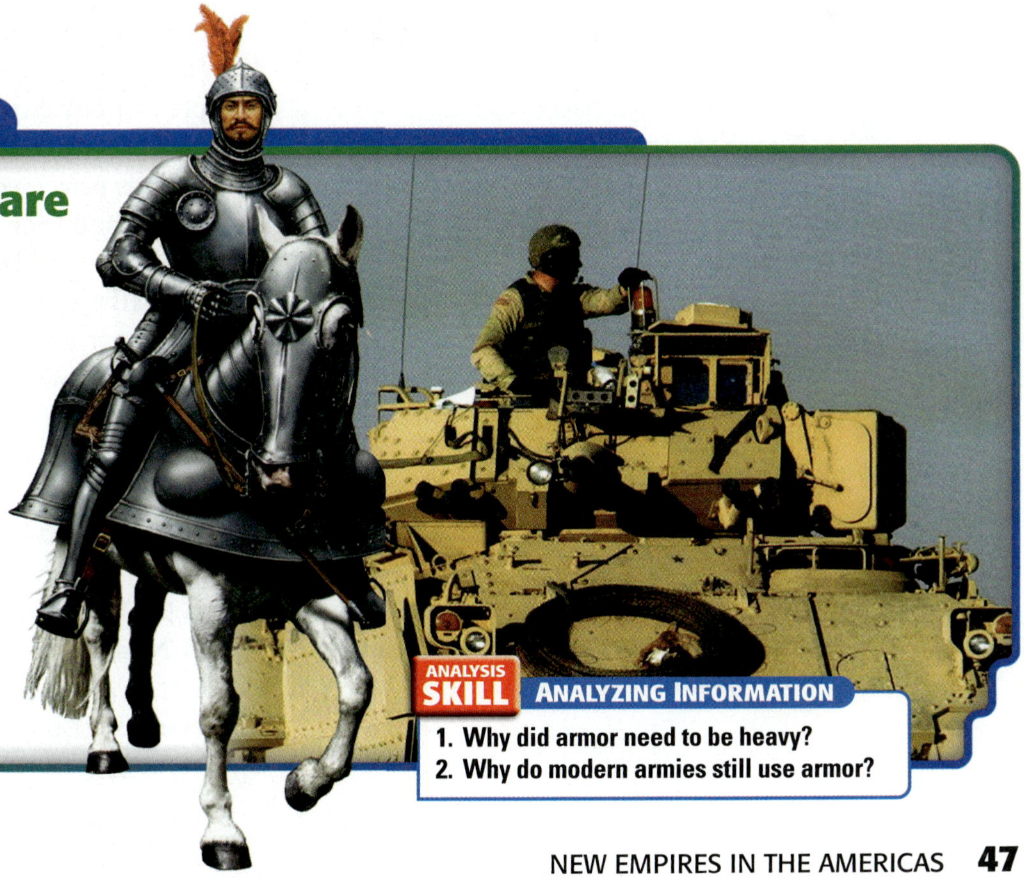

ANALYSIS SKILL ANALYZING INFORMATION

1. Why did armor need to be heavy?
2. Why do modern armies still use armor?

Central America, Mexico, and the southern part of what is now the United States.

The Spanish established three kinds of settlements in New Spain. Pueblos served as trading posts and sometimes as centers of government. Priests started missions where they converted local Native Americans to Catholicism. The Spanish also built presidios, or military bases, to protect towns and missions.

To connect some of the scattered communities of New Spain, Spanish settlers built *El Camino Real*, or "the Royal Road." This network of roads ran for hundreds of miles, from Mexico City to Santa Fe. The roads later stretched to settlements in California.

READING CHECK **Analyzing** How did the Spanish conquer the great Aztec and Inca empires?

QUICK FACTS

Reasons for Spanish Victory

Several advantages helped the Spanish defeat the Aztec and Inca.

Causes of the Aztec and Inca Defeat

- Spanish steel armor and weapons
- Spanish horses
- European diseases
- Spanish alliances with Aztec and Inca enemies

Effects

- Reduced Native American population
- Spanish rule of the Americas
- Columbian Exchange

ANALYSIS SKILL **ANALYZING INFORMATION**

Which cause do you think was most important to the Spanish victory?

Exploring the Borderlands of New Spain

Spain's American empire was not limited to lands taken from the conquered Aztec and Inca empires. Many other Spanish explorers came to North America. They explored the borderlands of New Spain and claimed many new lands for the Spanish crown.

Exploring the Southeast

In 1508 explorer Juan Ponce de León landed on the Caribbean island of Puerto Rico. By 1511 he had conquered the island for Spain and founded the city of San Juan. De León also discovered gold on Puerto Rico. Spanish officials appointed him governor of the colony.

In 1512 de León discovered the coast of present-day Florida. The next year he searched Florida for a mythical Fountain of Youth. Though he never found the fabled fountain, Ponce de León acquired royal permission to colonize Florida. However, he failed in his quest to colonize the area.

Two decades later another explorer traveled through Florida. Royal officials gave Hernando de Soto permission to explore the coastal region of the Gulf of Mexico. In 1539 his expedition landed in an area near the present-day city of Tampa Bay, Florida.

De Soto then led his men north through what is now Georgia and the Carolinas. The expedition then turned west and crossed the Appalachian Mountains. De Soto discovered the Mississippi River in 1541. The explorers then traveled west into present-day Oklahoma. De Soto died in 1542 on this journey.

Exploring the Southwest

The Spanish also explored what is now the southwestern United States. In 1528 explorer Álvar Núñez Cabeza de Vaca joined conquistador Pánfilo de Narváez on an expedition to North America. Their group of 300 men first landed on the Florida coast. They faced many severe problems, including a shortage of food.

The group built boats, which made it possible for them to travel around the Florida panhandle. The explorers continued along the Gulf Coast and eventually reached the Mississippi River. Severe weather hit this group hard, and many members of the expedition died. De Vaca's boat shipwrecked on what is now Galveston Island in Texas. Only de Vaca and three other men survived. One survivor was a Moroccan-born slave named Estevanico. His Spanish slaveholder also survived.

Each of the four survivors was captured and enslaved by Native American groups living in the area. After six years of captivity, the men finally escaped. They journeyed on foot throughout the North American Southwest, receiving help from Native Americans they met along the way. In 1536, after turning south, the group reached Spanish settlements in Mexico.

Soon after their journey ended, Estevanico's slaveholder sold him to a Spanish viceroy. The viceroy assigned Estevanico to serve as a guide for a new expedition he was sending into the Southwest. Native Americans killed the enslaved African in 1539.

De Vaca eventually returned to Spain, where he called for better treatment of Native Americans. De Vaca later wrote about his experiences in the first European book exclusively devoted to North America. De Vaca's book increased Spanish interest in the New World. His writings fueled the rumors that riches could be found in North America.

> "For two thousand leagues did we travel, on land, and by sea in barges, besides ten months more after our rescue from captivity; untiringly did we walk across the land, ... During all that time we crossed from one ocean to the other, ... We heard that on the shores of the South there are pearls and great wealth, and that the richest and best is near there."
>
> –Cabeza de Vaca, *The Journey of Álvar Núñez Cabeza de Vaca*

De Vaca's account inspired other explorers to travel to North America. In 1540 Francisco Vásquez de Coronado set out to explore the North American Southwest. He wanted to find the legendary Seven Cities of Gold that were rumored to exist there. His expedition went through present-day New Mexico and Arizona, where a group of his men discovered the Grand Canyon. Coronado trekked through Texas

Spanish Explorations, 1513–1542

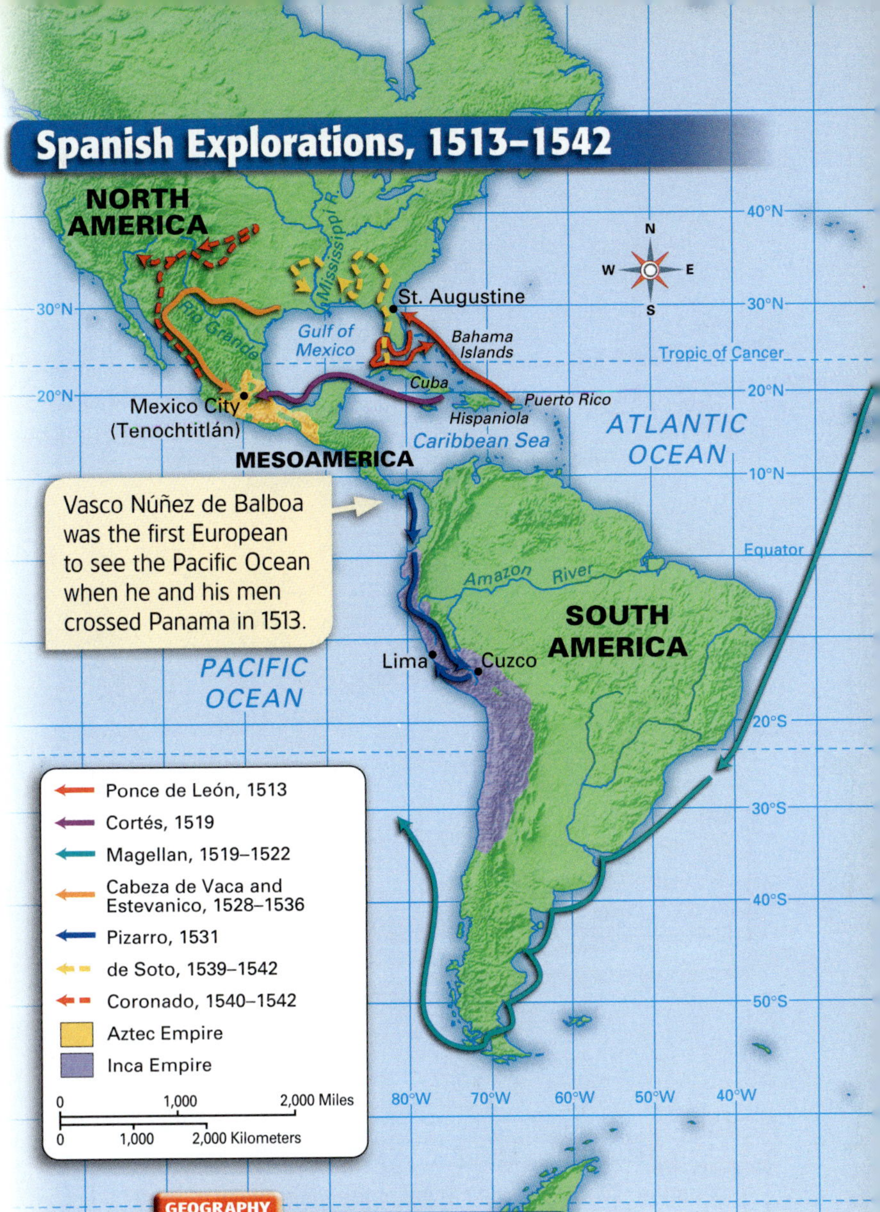

GEOGRAPHY SKILLS **INTERPRETING MAPS**

1. **Movement** Which explorer went the farthest north, according to the map?
2. **Location** What city did Cortés reach in 1519?

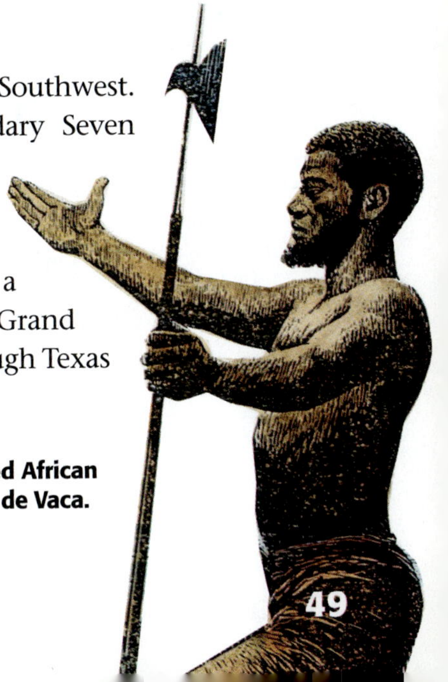

Estevanico was an enslaved African who traveled with Cabeza de Vaca.

Spanish Viceroyalties, c.1650

GEOGRAPHY SKILLS **INTERPRETING MAPS**

1. Location What was the capital of the Viceroyalty of Peru?
2. Place Which viceroyalty included modern-day Mexico?

THE IMPACT TODAY

Roman Catholicism is still the most commonly practiced religion in Latin America. More than 80 percent of the population is Catholic.

and Oklahoma, going as far north as Kansas before turning around. He never found the fabled cities of gold.

READING CHECK **Comparing** How were the expeditions of Ponce de León and Coronado similar?

Spanish Treatment of Native Americans

The journeys of the Spanish explorers allowed Spain to claim a huge empire in the Americas. Spain's American colonies helped make the country very wealthy. From 1503 to 1660, Spanish fleets loaded with treasure carried 200 tons of gold and 18,600 tons of silver from the former Aztec and Inca empires to Spain. Mexico and Peru also grew food to help support Spain's growing empire. However, these gains came with a price for Native Americans. Native peoples suffered greatly at the hands of the Spanish.

Forced Labor

By 1650 the Spanish Empire in the Americas had grown to some 3 to 4 million people. Native Americans made up about 80 percent of the population. The rest were whites, Africans, and people of mixed racial background. Settlers who came from Spain were called *peninsulares* (pay-neen-soo-LAHR-ays) and usually held the highest government positions. To reward settlers for their service to the Crown, Spain established the **encomienda** (en-koh-mee-EN-duh) **system**. It gave settlers the right to tax local Native Americans or to make them work. In exchange, these settlers were supposed to protect the Native American people and convert them to Christianity. Instead, most Spanish treated the Native Americans as slaves. Native Americans were forced to work in terrible conditions. They faced cruelty and desperate situations on a daily basis.

The Spanish operated many **plantations**, large farms that grew just one kind of crop. Plantations throughout the Caribbean colonies made huge profits for their owners. It took many workers to run a plantation, however, so colonists forced thousands of Native Americans to work in the fields. Indians who were taken to work on haciendas, the vast Spanish estates in Central and South America, had to raise and herd livestock. Other Native Americans were forced to endure the backbreaking work of mining gold and silver. The forced labor and harsh treatment killed many native people in New Spain.

The Role of the Catholic Church

The Catholic Church played a major role in the interactions of the Spanish with Native Americans. The Spanish king commanded priests to convert the local people to the Christian faith. Some Native Americans combined Spanish customs with their own. Others rejected Spanish ideas completely.

Some European settlers in the Americas protested the terrible treatment of Native Americans. A priest named **Bartolomé de Las Casas** said that the Spanish should try to convert Native Americans to Christianity by showing them love, gentleness, and kindness. The Spanish monarchs agreed, but the colonists did not always follow their laws.

READING CHECK **Finding Main Ideas** How did the encomienda system strengthen Spanish rule?

SUMMARY AND PREVIEW In the 1500s Spain built a vast empire in the Americas. The Spanish treated the Native Americans harshly in their new empire. In the next section you will learn about other European empires in the Americas.

Primary Source

BOOK

Brief Account of the Devastation of the Indies

Bartolomé de Las Casas, a Catholic priest in New Spain, encouraged better treatment of Native Americans.

"When they [Spaniards] have slain all those who fought for their lives or to escape the tortures they would have to endure, that is to say, when they have slain all the native rulers and young men (since the Spaniards usually spare only the women and children, who are subjected to the hardest and bitterest servitude [slavery] ever suffered by man or beast), they enslave any survivors. With these infernal [devilish] methods of tyranny they debase and weaken countless numbers of those pitiful Indian nations."

–Bartolomé de Las Casas,
from *Brief Account of the Devastation of the Indies*

ANALYSIS SKILL **ANALYZING POINTS OF VIEW**

How did Las Casas's view of the treatment of Native American groups differ from the views of other Spaniards?

Section 3 Assessment

go.hrw.com
Online Quiz
KEYWORD: SC7 HP2

Reviewing Ideas, Terms, and People

1. a. **Identify** Who was **Moctezuma II**?
   b. **Analyze** How was **Hernán Cortés** able to conquer the Aztec Empire?
   c. **Elaborate** What advantages did the Spanish have over Native Americans?
2. a. **Recall** Which Spanish explorer received permission to colonize Florida?
   b. **Analyze** Why do you think Cabeza de Vaca wrote of great riches that could be found in the Americas?
   c. **Evaluate** Why do you think de Vaca called for better treatment of Native Americans after having been held prisoner by them?
3. a. **Identify** What was the **encomienda system**?
   b. **Analyze** Why do you think the king of Spain commanded Catholic priests to teach Native Americans about Christianity?

Critical Thinking

4. **Categorizing** Review your notes on Spanish conquest and settlement in the Americas. Then copy the following graphic organizer and use it to explain the impact Spain had on the Americas.

Spanish America	
government	
religion	
labor	

FOCUS ON WRITING

5. **Taking Notes on the Spanish Empire** Take notes on the Spanish conquest of the Aztec Empire and the founding of the Spanish Empire. How did this empire affect Native Americans?

SECTION 4

The Race for Empires

What You Will Learn...

Main Ideas

1. Events in Europe affected settlement of North America.
2. Several explorers searched for a Northwest Passage to the Pacific Ocean.
3. European nations raced to establish empires in North America.

The Big Idea

Other European nations challenged Spain in the Americas.

Key Terms and People

Protestant Reformation, *p. 53*
Protestants, *p. 53*
Spanish Armada, *p. 53*
Northwest Passage, *p. 54*
Jacques Cartier, *p. 54*
charter, *p. 54*

TAKING NOTES As you read, take notes on the reasons for European voyages to North America, the search for a Northwest Passage, and the development of European empires in North America.

Reasons for Voyages	Explorers' Search for a NW Passage	European Empires

If YOU were there...

The people of your village in France have always belonged to the same church. Now in the 1600s, your village is divided over religious beliefs. You have heard about the Dutch colony of New Netherland in America, where people can practice any religion freely. You would like to leave for America, but your parents are unwilling to leave their home.

How would you persuade your family to emigrate?

BUILDING BACKGROUND During the 1400s, the Catholic Church was one of the most powerful institutions in Europe. Not everyone agreed with all of its teachings, however. Disagreement, and sometimes violence, led some people to search for new places to settle.

Events in Europe

Many significant events took place in Europe in the 1500s. Disagreements about religion threw Europe into turmoil. Some of these disagreements eventually led to wars. At the same time, several European nations began to compete for land and power overseas.

Key Events in European History, 1450–1588

c. 1450
Johannes Gutenberg develops his movable-type printing press.

The Protestant Reformation

In 1517 a German priest named Martin Luther publicly criticized the Roman Catholic Church. Luther charged that the church was too wealthy and that it abused its power. Criticisms like Luther's started the **Protestant Reformation**. This religious movement began in small German towns but quickly spread to most of Europe. It became a part of many political disputes as well. The **Protestants** were reformers who protested some of the Catholic Church's practices. Many Protestants believed God meant for religion to be simple.

The printing press—a machine that produces printed copies using movable type—helped spread the ideas of the Reformation. Protestants printed large numbers of Bibles as well as short essays explaining their ideas. This let more people read and think about the Bible on their own, rather than relying solely on the teachings of a priest.

Conflicts between Catholics and Protestants took place throughout Europe, often leading to civil war. In the late 1500s French Catholics fought French Protestants, known as Huguenots (HYOO-guh-nahts). Many Huguenots eventually emigrated to the Americas in search of religious freedom.

In 1534 King Henry VIII founded the Church of England, or the Anglican Church. By making himself the head of the church, Henry challenged the authority of the pope and angered Catholics. Political issues soon became mixed with the religious struggles.

Spain and England Go to War

In the late 1500s King Philip II used Spain's great wealth to lead a Catholic Reformation against the Protestant movement. He hoped to drive the Protestants out of England. Standing in his way was the Protestant English queen Elizabeth I and her sea dogs. Sea dogs was the name given to English sailors who raided Spanish treasure ships. The most successful and daring was Sir Francis Drake.

Philip was angered by English piracy. He began gathering the **Spanish Armada**, a huge fleet of warships meant to end English plans. The Armada had about 130 ships and some 27,000 sailors and soldiers. This mighty fleet was launched to invade England and overthrow Queen Elizabeth and the Anglican Church. But in July 1588, the smaller, but faster, English fleet defeated the Armada in a huge battle.

The Armada's defeat shocked the Spanish. In addition to the naval defeat, Spain's economy was in trouble. The gold and silver that Spain received from the Americas caused high inflation. Inflation is a rise in the price of goods caused by an increase in the amount of money in use. Economic problems in Spain combined with the defeat of the Spanish Armada led countries such as England, France, and the Netherlands to challenge Spanish power overseas.

READING CHECK **Analyzing** What led to the decline of the Spanish Empire?

1517
Martin Luther nails his ninety-five theses to the door of a church in Wittenberg, Germany.

1588
The English defeat the Spanish Armada. The loss greatly weakens Spain, allowing other European countries to claim land in North America.

History Makers

Sir Walter Raleigh Walter Raleigh financed the first two English colonies in North Carolina.

FOCUS ON NORTH CAROLINA

The mystery of the "lost colony" of Roanoke has inspired many legends. Some historians claim that the Lumbee Indians of North Carolina are descendants of colony survivors who intermarried with Native Americans in the area. There are reports from the 1700s of the Lumbee identifying themselves with names of the colonists, but the claim is disputed.

Search for a Northwest Passage

Europeans wanted to find a **Northwest Passage**, a water route through North America that would allow ships to sail from the Atlantic to the Pacific. The English began sending explorers to find it.

Italian sailor John Cabot knew that the king of England wanted to find such a route. Cabot offered to pay for his own expedition, asking only that the king of England grant him a royal charter to any lands he found. The king agreed, and Cabot made voyages to North America for England in 1497 and 1498.

Cabot sailed to North America, but he left very few records of his journeys. It is believed that he traveled along the coast of present-day Newfoundland in Canada. Although Cabot did not find a passage to the Pacific Ocean, his voyages were successful. They became the basis of England's claim to land in North America.

In 1524 France sent an Italian captain, Giovanni da Verrazano (vayr-raht-SAHN-oh), to seek a Northwest Passage. Verrazano sailed along the coast of North America from present-day North Carolina to Maine. **Jacques Cartier** (kahr-tyay), a French sailor, led France's next major exploration of North America. He made two trips to what is now Canada. Cartier sailed into the Saint Lawrence River and traveled all the way to present-day Montreal, claiming the areas he explored for France.

The Dutch also entered the race. They hired English captain Henry Hudson to find a Northwest Passage. Hudson first sailed to present-day New York in 1609. The following year Hudson returned to North America, sailing under the English flag. He traveled far to the north. Eventually he reached a strait that he hoped would lead to the Pacific Ocean. Instead, it led into a huge bay, later named Hudson Bay.

None of these explorers ever found a Northwest Passage. Their explorations, however, led to increased European interest in North America.

READING CHECK **Finding Main Ideas** Why did European explorers seek a Northwest Passage?

European Presence in North America

The Spanish and the Portuguese were the early leaders in overseas exploration. They dominated the colonization of the New World through the 1500s. However, Spain and Portugal focused on Central America, the Caribbean, and South America. They left much of North America unexplored. The English, French, and Dutch explored North America. These nations then sought to expand their own empires there.

English Presence in the New World

In the late 1500s England decided to set up a permanent settlement in North America. This colony was to establish an English presence in the New World. Sir Walter Raleigh received a **charter**, a document giving him permission to start a colony. In 1584 he sent an expedition that landed in present-day Virginia and North Carolina. Raleigh named the entire area Virginia.

The following year, Raleigh sent another group to found a colony on Roanoke Island, off the coast of North Carolina. The English colonists at Roanoke found life hard. They fought with Native Americans and had trouble finding and growing food. After only a year, the remaining colonists returned to England.

John White, a talented artist, and 150 colonists resettled Roanoke in the spring of 1587. White's granddaughter, Virginia Dare, was the first English colonist born in North America. After a few months, White went back to England to get more supplies. War with Spain prevented White from returning for three years. When he came back, White found the colony deserted. The only clue he found to the fate of the colonists was the word *Croatoan*, the name of a nearby island, carved into a post. Did the colonists try to escape a Native American attack by fleeing to the island? White never found out. To this day, no one is certain what happened to the "lost colony" at Roanoke.

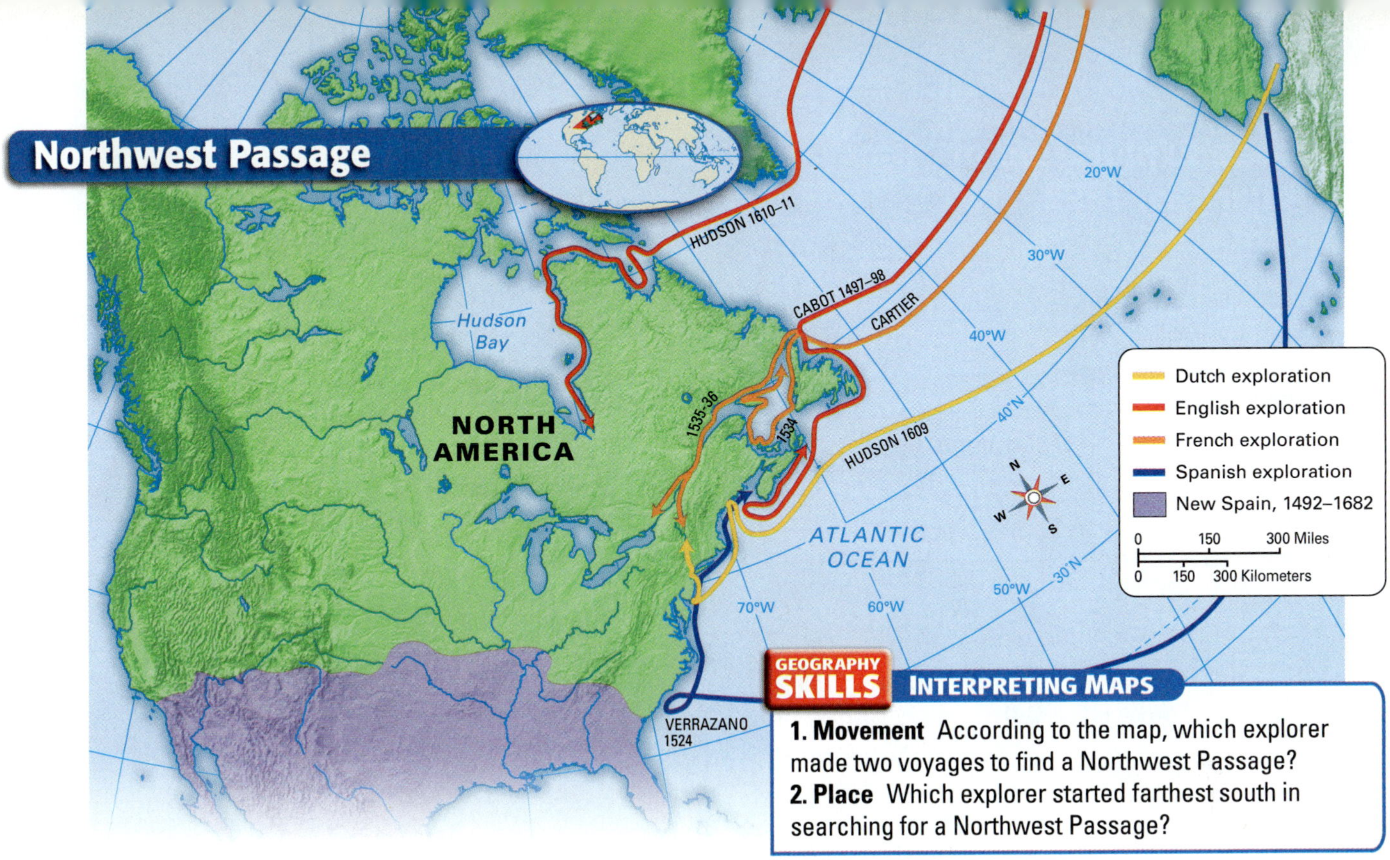

GEOGRAPHY SKILLS **INTERPRETING MAPS**

1. Movement According to the map, which explorer made two voyages to find a Northwest Passage?

2. Place Which explorer started farthest south in searching for a Northwest Passage?

French Presence in the New World

France built its first North American settlement in Florida, when Huguenots started a few small colonies there in 1564. The Spanish soon destroyed these settlements and drove out the French. Religious wars in France slowed further French efforts to colonize North America. When the fighting ended, the French renewed efforts to settle present-day eastern Canada. The explorations of Jacques Cartier and Samuel de Champlain gave France a claim to this region.

Nearly 70 years after Cartier sailed up the Saint Lawrence, French sailor Samuel de Champlain began exploring North America. He recorded his ideas about European exploration in his journal.

> "Through [exploration] we gain knowledge of different countries, regions and kingdoms; through it we attract and bring into our countries all kinds of riches; through it . . . Christianity [is spread] in all parts of the earth."
>
> –Samuel de Champlain, quoted in *The Canadian Frontier, 1534–1760,* by W. J. Eccles

Champlain followed Cartier's old paths. Over the years he made many journeys along the Saint Lawrence River. He also visited the Great Lakes, led by Native American guides.

In 1608 Champlain founded a small colony on the Saint Lawrence River. He named the colony Quebec. This trading post opened fur-trading routes for the French throughout the region. Champlain's explorations became the basis of France's claim to much of Canada.

In the late 1600s the French began spreading out from the Saint Lawrence River. Calling their North American territory New France, French fur traders, explorers, and missionaries were all on the move.

In the 1650s French missionaries told stories about "a beautiful river, large, broad, and deep." In 1673 explorer Louis Jolliet (jahl-ee-ET) and missionary Jacques Marquette set out to find this great river, the Mississippi. (Hernando de Soto was the first European to find the Mississippi River, in 1541.) They reached the river and traveled down it as far as present-day Arkansas.

Nine years later René-Robert de La Salle followed the Mississippi River to the Gulf of

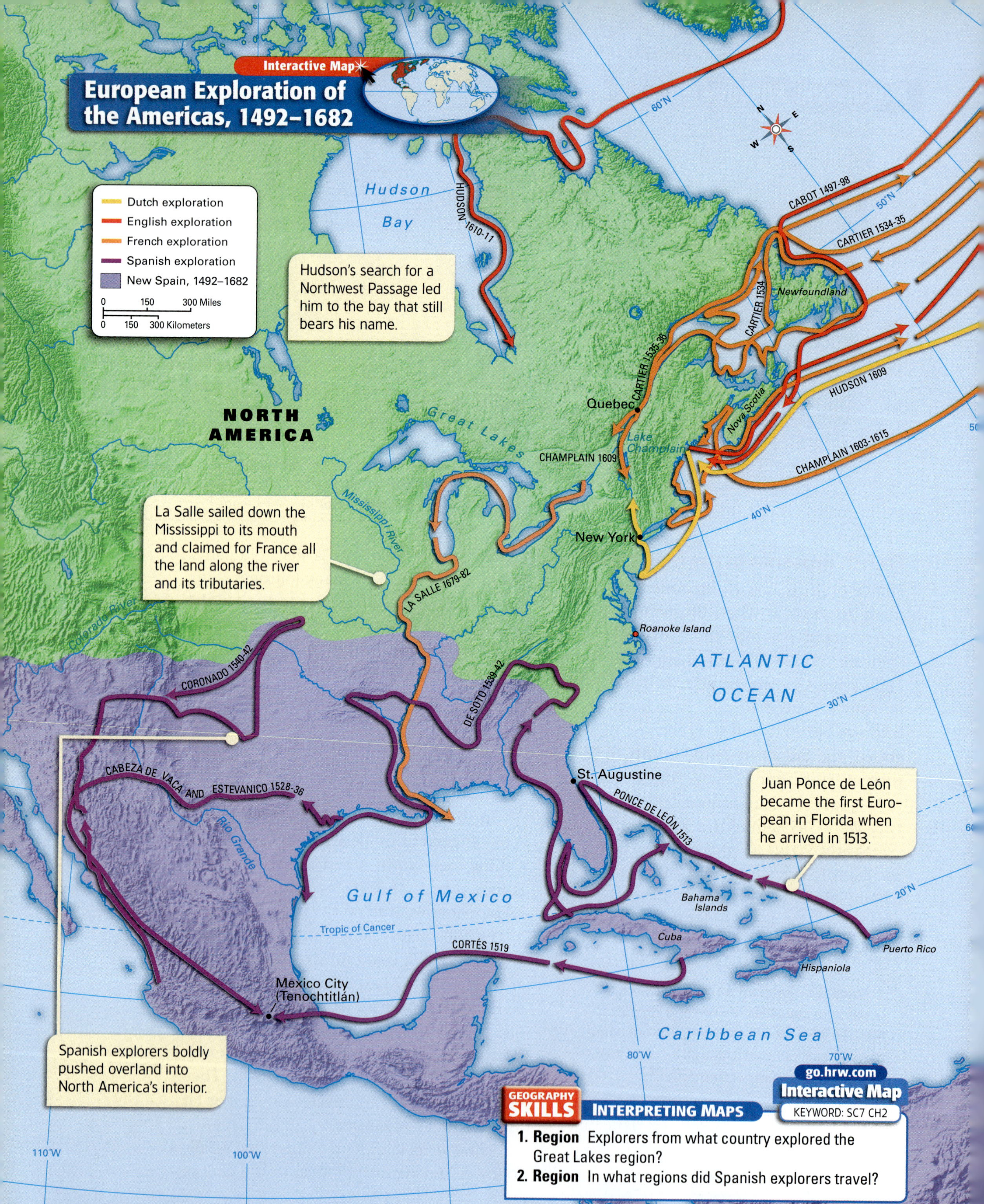

GEOGRAPHY SKILLS **INTERPRETING MAPS**

1. **Region** Explorers from what country explored the Great Lakes region?
2. **Region** In what regions did Spanish explorers travel?

Mexico. He claimed the Mississippi Valley for King Louis XIV of France. To honor the king, La Salle named the region Louisiana.

Starting in the 1700s, the French built new outposts. These included Detroit on the Great Lakes and Saint Louis and New Orleans along the Mississippi River. Most towns in the French territory were small. As late as 1688 there were only about 12,000 French settlers in New France. Its small population and the value of the fur trade led French settlers to ally and trade with local Native American groups.

Because of their close trading relationships, the French treated the Native Americans with more respect than some other European settlers had done. Many French settlers learned Native American languages, and they even adopted their ways of life.

Dutch Presence in the New World

The English and the French were not the only European powers to seek an empire in North America. The Dutch, who had merchant fleets around the world, came in search of trade. They claimed the land between the Delaware and Hudson rivers and called it New Netherland. This area included parts of what is now New York, New Jersey, Connecticut, and Delaware. In 1624 the newly formed Dutch West India Company sent about 30 families to settle in New Netherland. Two years later Peter Minuit bought Manhattan Island from local Native Americans for about $24. Minuit then founded the town of New Amsterdam, today called New York City. To attract colonists, the Dutch allowed members of all religions to settle in their colony.

Minuit also helped Swedish settlers found New Sweden along the Delaware River. The first settlement, Fort Christina, was begun in 1638. The Swedish settlement was small, but the Dutch felt that it threatened Dutch lands and fur trading. The two sides fought a series of battles. Finally, the governor of New Netherland, Peter Stuyvesant (STY-vi-suhnt), conquered New Sweden in 1655. He allowed the Swedes to continue their colony, but he called it the "Swedish Nation."

READING CHECK **Drawing Conclusions** Were the French explorers in North America successful? Explain.

SUMMARY AND PREVIEW The English, French, Dutch, and Swedish explored the North American continent and later established colonies there. In the next section you will learn about the establishment of slavery in the Americas.

Section 4 Assessment

go.hrw.com
Online Quiz
KEYWORD: SC7 HP2

Reviewing Ideas, Terms, and People

1. a. **Identify** What was the **Protestant Reformation**?
   b. **Explain** What role did the printing press play in the Protestant Reformation?
   c. **Summarize** What were Martin Luther's reasons for protesting the Catholic Church?
2. a. **Identify** Who was the first European to search for the **Northwest Passage**?
   b. **Describe** Which French and Dutch explorers tried to find the Northwest Passage?
3. a. **Recall** What happened to the first English settlements in North America?
   b. **Evaluate** Which European empire in North America do you think was most successful? Why?

Critical Thinking

4. **Sequencing** Review your notes on European exploration and settlement. Then create a time line like the one below and place the four events you think were most important to the development of European empires in North America on the time line. Be sure to include the date of the event, as well as a description of it and its significance.

FOCUS ON WRITING

5. **Learning about the French Empire and Other Settlements** Take notes about the French, Dutch, Swedish, and English people who settled in America. Why did they come? What did they want and need in their new home?

SECTION 5

Beginnings of Slavery in the Americas

What You Will Learn...

Main Ideas

1. European diseases wiped out much of the Native American population, causing colonists to look for a new labor force.
2. Europeans enslaved millions of Africans and sent them to work in their colonies.
3. Slaves in the Americas created a distinct culture.

The Big Idea

Europeans forced millions of African slaves to work in their colonies.

Key Terms and People

immune, *p. 58*
Middle Passage, *p. 59*
African Diaspora, *p. 60*

TAKING NOTES As you read, take notes on slavery in the Americas. Use a chart like the one below.

The Slave Trade		
Need for Workers		
Slave Trade		
Slave Culture		

If YOU were there...

You are an enslaved African living in North America. Your family is all that you have. You help each other, and your family provides some relief from the forced labor and harsh life on the plantation. Still, you long for your freedom. A fellow slave has told you of a plan to escape.

Will you stay with your family or try to flee?

BUILDING BACKGROUND European settlers in the Americas relied on support from their home countries to establish trade and provide protection. In return, the colonies were expected to produce money for the home country. Many colonies did this through plantations, mines, and other ventures that required a large labor force.

The Need for a New Labor Force

European diseases had a devastating effect on the Native American population. Measles, smallpox, and typhus were common in Europe. As a result, most adult Europeans were **immune**, or had a natural resistance, to them. Native Americans, however, had never been exposed to such diseases and had no immunity to them. As a result, many Native Americans became terribly sick after their first encounters with Europeans. Millions of them died in the years after Columbus reached the New World.

No one knows exactly how many Native Americans died from European diseases, but the loss of life was staggering. Spanish author Fernández de Oviedo reported in 1548 about the destruction of the Native Americans of Hispaniola. He reported that, of the estimated 1 million Indians who had lived on the island in 1492, "there are not now believed to be at the present time . . . five hundred persons [left]." In North America the Native American population north of Mexico was about 10 million when Columbus arrived. This number would drop to less than a million. The drop in the native population played a major role in the emerging need for an alternative labor force.

Plantation agriculture was a mainstay of the colonial economic **structure**. Spain and Portugal established sugar plantations that relied on large numbers of native laborers. In the 1600s English tobacco farmers in North America also needed workers for their plantations. With a lack of Native American workers, they, too, needed another source of labor. Plantation owners in both North and South America wanted a cheap work force.

Some colonists, including Spanish priest Bartolomé de Las Casas, suggested using enslaved Africans as workers. Africans had already developed immunity to European diseases. The colonists soon agreed that slaves from West Africa could be the solution to their labor needs.

READING CHECK **Analyzing** How did disease contribute to the slave trade?

The Slave Trade

In 1510 the Spanish government legalized the sale of slaves in its colonies. The first full cargo ship of Africans arrived in the Americas eight years later. Over the next century, more than a million enslaved Africans were brought to the Spanish and Portuguese colonies in the New World. The Dutch and English also became active in the slave trade.

ACADEMIC VOCABULARY

structure the way something is set up or organized

Middle Passage

Enslavement was a horrible experience for the slaves. Most enslaved people had been captured in the interior of Africa, often by Africans who profited from selling slaves to Europeans. The captives were chained around the neck and then marched to the coast. This journey could be as long as 1,000 miles.

The **Middle Passage** was the voyage across the Atlantic Ocean that enslaved Africans were forced to endure. Africans were packed like cargo in the lower decks of the slave ships. The slaves were chained together and crammed

Primary Source

LETTER

King Afonso to King Joao III

King Afonso of the African nation of Kongo wrote a letter to the king of Portugal in 1526 asking him to do what he could to stop the practice of taking African slaves.

Sir, Your Highness should know how our Kingdom is being lost in so many ways . . . [M]erchants are taking every day our natives, sons of the land and the sons of our noblemen and vassals and our relatives, because the thieved and men of bad conscience grab them . . . [T]hey grab them and get them to be sold; and so great, Sir, is the corruption and licentiousness [law breaking] that our country is being completely depopulated, and Your Highness should not agree with this nor accept it as in your service. And to avoid it we need from those

(your) Kingdoms no more than some priests and a few people to teach in schools, and no other goods except wine and flour for the holy sacrament [religious service].

–King Afonso of Kongo,
letter to the king of Portugal, 1526

ANALYSIS SKILL **ANALYZING PRIMARY SOURCES**

1. **Why does Afonso ask the Portuguese king to help stop the slave trade?**
2. **What does Afonso request from the king?**

African Diaspora in the United States

The first enslaved Africans to arrive in what is now the United States landed in Jamestown, Virginia, in August 1619. Today, descendants of enslaved Africans and other African Americans live throughout the United States.

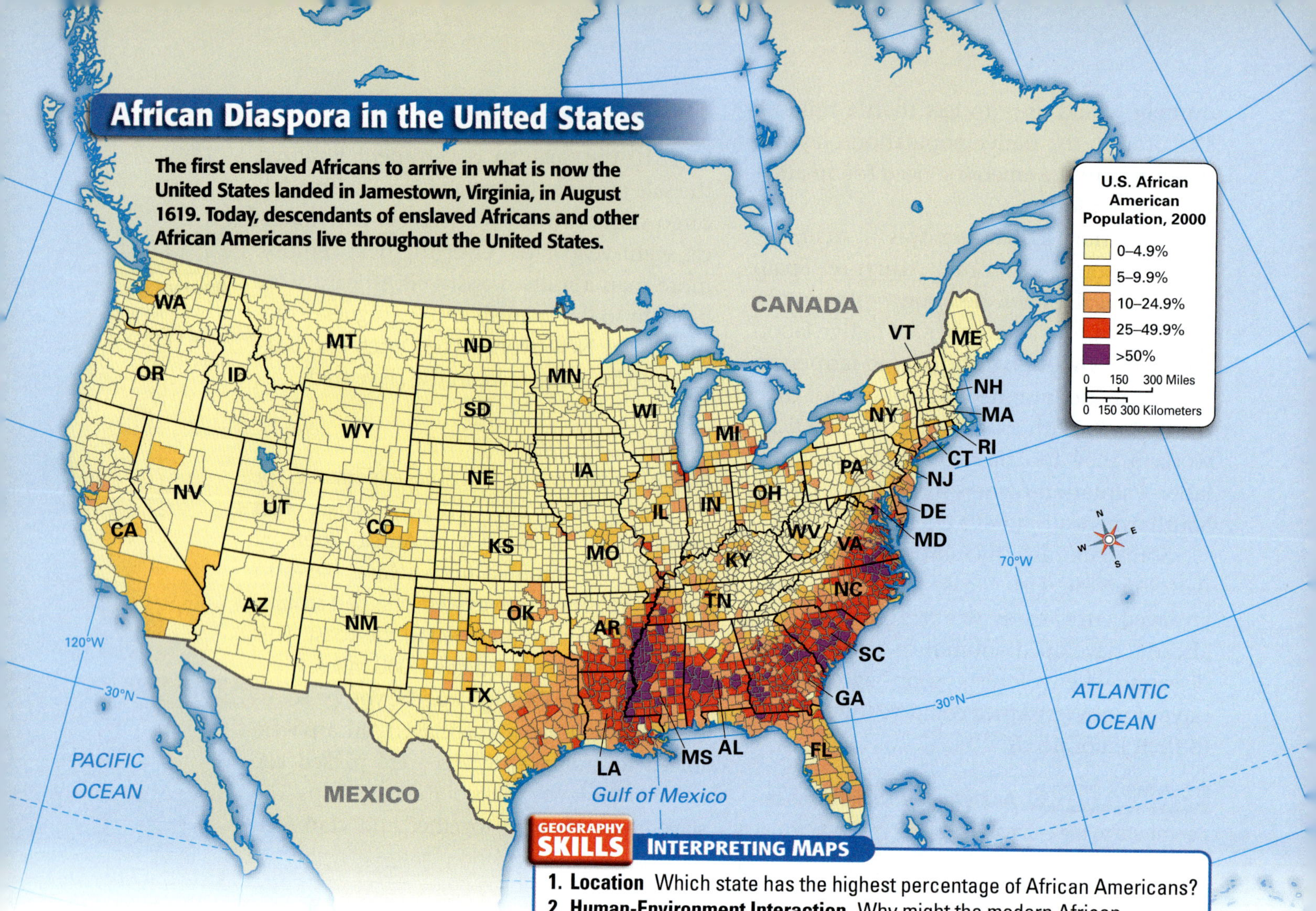

GEOGRAPHY SKILLS **INTERPRETING MAPS**

1. **Location** Which state has the highest percentage of African Americans?
2. **Human-Environment Interaction** Why might the modern African American population be centered in the South?

into spaces about the size of coffins. The height between the decks was sometimes only 18 inches.

In this confinement, disease spread quickly, killing many Africans. Others suffocated or died from malnutrition. Some slaves took their own lives to end their suffering. It is estimated that one out of every six Africans died during the Middle Passage.

THE IMPACT TODAY

Almost half of Brazil's current population is of African descent.

African Diaspora

Between the 1520s and 1860s about 12 million Africans were shipped across the Atlantic as slaves. More than 10 million of these captives survived the voyage and reached the Americas. The slave trade led to the **African Diaspora**. (A diaspora is the scattering of a people.) Enslaved Africans were sent all across the New World.

More than a third of the enslaved Africans, nearly 4 million people, were sent to Brazil. Most of those slaves were forced to work on Portuguese sugar plantations. Nearly 2 million slaves went to the colonies of New Spain. Some worked on plantations in the Caribbean, while others were taken to the mines of Peru and Mexico. Some 3 million slaves worked in British and French colonies in the Caribbean and Latin America. More than 600,000 slaves went to Britain's North American colonies that later became the United States.

Colonial leaders across the Americas developed laws that regulated slave treatment and behavior. Slaves were given few rights in the colonies. The law considered enslaved Africans to be property. In some colonies, a slaveholder was not charged with murder if he killed a slave while punishing him. Enslaved Africans, on the other hand, received harsh penalties for minor offenses, such as breaking a tool. Runaways were often tortured and sometimes killed.

The treatment of enslaved Africans varied. Some slaves reported that their masters treated them kindly. To protect their investment, some slaveholders provided adequate food and clothing for their slaves. However, severe treatment was very common. Whippings, brandings, and even worse torture were all part of American slavery.

READING CHECK **Generalizing** How were enslaved Africans treated in the Americas?

Slave Culture in the Americas

Slaves in the Americas came from many different parts of Africa. They spoke different languages and had different cultural backgrounds. But enslaved Africans also shared many customs and viewpoints. They built upon what they had in common to create a new African American culture.

Families were a vital part of slave culture. Families provided a refuge—a place not fully under the slaveholders' control. However, slave families faced many challenges. Families were often broken apart when a family member was sold to another owner. In Latin America, there were many more enslaved males than females. This made it difficult for slaves there to form stable families.

Religion was a second refuge for slaves. It gave enslaved Africans a form of expression that was partially free from their slaveholders' control. Slave religion was primarily Christian, but it included traditional elements from African religions as well. Religion gave slaves a sense of self worth and a hope for salvation in this life and the next. Spirituals were a common form of religious expression among slaves. Slaves also used songs and folktales to tell their stories of sorrow, hope, agony, and joy.

Many slaves expressed themselves through art and dance. Dances were important social events in slave communities. Like most elements of slave culture, art and dance were heavily influenced by African traditions.

READING CHECK **Identifying Points of View** Why was religion important to slaves in the Americas?

SUMMARY AND PREVIEW After disease wiped out much of the Native American population, colonists turned to slave labor. In the next chapter you will learn about English colonies in the Americas.

FOCUS ON NORTH CAROLINA

Slavery began in North Carolina almost as soon as the colony was founded. Some of the Lords Proprietors, or owners, had been planters and slave traders in the West Indies. Although slavery would become an important aspect of life in the state, there were fewer enslaved Africans in North Carolina than in other southern colonies.

Section 5 Assessment

go.hrw.com
Online Quiz
KEYWORD: SC7 HP2

Reviewing Ideas, Terms, and People

1. a. **Recall** Why did so many Native Americans die after coming into contact with Europeans?
   b. **Summarize** Why did plantation owners turn to enslaved Africans as a labor force?
2. a. **Identify** What was the **Middle Passage**?
   b. **Describe** Explain how enslaved Africans were treated after they reached the colonies in the Americas.
3. a. **Explain** What are spirituals?
   b. **Analyze** How did religion and family provide a refuge from the harsh life enslaved Africans were forced to endure?

Critical Thinking

4. **Identifying Cause and Effect** Review your notes on the slave trade. Use a chart like the one below to explain the causes and the effects of the slave trade.

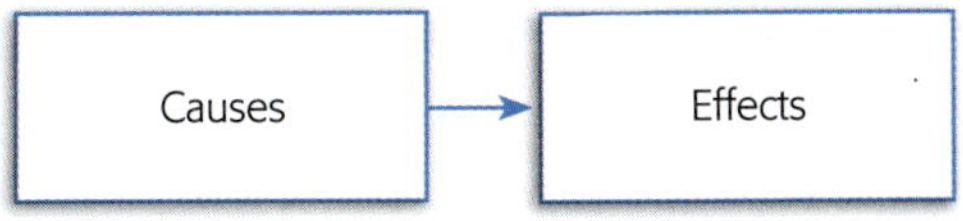

FOCUS ON WRITING

5. **Writing about Slavery** Add information about the beginnings of slavery in the Americas to your notes. Include notes about slave culture. What refuges did enslaved people have from their suffering?

History and Geography

The Atlantic Slave Trade

The slave system that arose in the American colonies was strongly influenced by geographic forces. The climate of the southern colonies was suited to growing certain crops, like cotton, tobacco, and sugarcane. These crops required a great deal of labor to grow and to process. To meet this great demand for labor, the colonists looked to one main source—enslaved Africans.

NORTH AMERICA

Boston

Newport

Charleston

ATLANTIC OCEAN

MIDDLE PASSAGE

WEST INDIES

SOUTH AMERICA

Colonial Slave Ports Slave ships sailed to slave ports, where they unloaded their human cargo. Slave ports like Boston, Newport, and Charleston were located near farming areas and the mouths of rivers.

The West Indies Africans were brought to the West Indies to work on large sugar plantations. Sugarcane thrived in the West Indies, but it required huge amounts of labor to grow.

The Middle Passage The terrifying and deadly voyage across the Atlantic was known as the Middle Passage. Enslaved Africans were chained and crowded together under ships' decks on this long voyage, as this drawing shows.

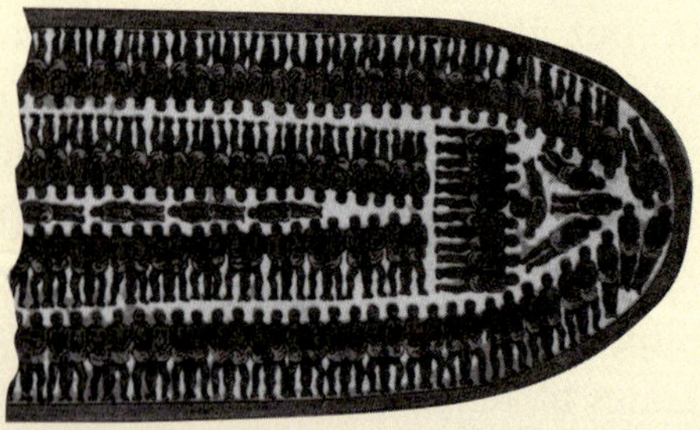

Elmina slave fort, West Africa

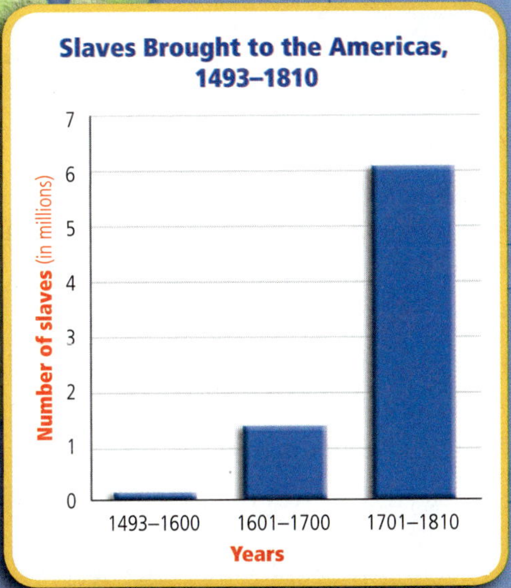

Kidnapped and Taken to a Slave Ship

Mahommah G. Baquaqua was captured and sold into slavery as a young man. In this 1854 account, he recalls being taken to the African coast to board a slave ship.

"I was taken down to the river and placed on board a boat; the river was very large and branched off in two different directions, previous to emptying itself into the sea . . . We were two nights and one day on this river, when we came to a . . . place . . . [where] the slaves were all put into a pen, and placed with our backs to the fire . . . When all were ready to go aboard, we were chained together, and tied with ropes round about our necks, and were thus drawn down to the sea shore."

GEOGRAPHY SKILLS **INTERPRETING MAPS**

1. **Location** Why were slave forts located where they were?
2. **Human-Environment Interaction** What geographic factors influenced the development of the Atlantic slave trade?

Social Studies Skills

Analysis | Critical Thinking | Civic Participation | Study

North Carolina Skills

1.06 Recognize and use social studies terms in written and oral reports.

Framing Historical Questions

Define the Skill

One of the most valuable ways that people gain knowledge is by asking effective questions. An effective question is one that obtains the kind of information the person asking the question desires. The ability to frame, or construct, effective questions is an important life skill as well as a key to gaining a better understanding of history. Asking effective historical questions will aid you in studying history and in conducting historical research.

Learn the Skill

Effective questions are specific, straightforward, and directly related to the topic. When we do not obtain the information we want or need, often it is because we have asked the wrong questions. Asking effective questions is not as easy as it seems. It requires thought and preparation. The following guidelines will help you in framing effective questions about history and other topics as well.

1. Determine exactly what you want to know.
2. Decide what questions to ask and write them down. Having written questions is very important. They will help guide your study or research and keep you focused on your topic and goal.
3. Review each of your questions to make sure it is specific, straightforward, and directly related to your topic.
4. Rewrite any questions that are vague, too broad, or biased.

Questions that are vague or too broad are likely to produce information not directly related to what you want to know. For example, if you wanted to know more about trade and the voyages of exploration that are discussed in Chapter 2, "What were the voyages of exploration?" may not be a good question to ask. This question is too broad. Its answer would not give you the information you want.

Asking "Why was trade the most important cause of the voyages of exploration?" would not be an effective question either. This question is biased because it *assumes* trade was the main reason for the voyages, when that might not have been true. Good historical investigation assumes nothing that is not known to be fact. A more effective question, which would get the information you want, is "Were trade and the voyages of exploration connected, and, if so, in what ways?" Do you see now why wording is so important in asking effective questions and why you should write out and review your questions beforehand?

Practice the Skill

Reread the information about Cortés and the Aztec on pages 46–47, then complete the activities below.

1. Suppose you wanted to learn more about Cortés's defeat of the Aztec. Decide whether each of the following would be an effective question to ask about this topic. Explain why or why not.
   - **a.** What happened when the Aztec and the Spanish met?
   - **b.** Why did other Indians betray the Aztec?
   - **c.** What resources did Cortés have that helped him conquer the Aztec?
2. Frame five questions that would be effective in helping you to learn more about this topic.

Chapter Review

HOLT
History's Impact
▶ **video series**
Review the video to answer the closing question:
How can protesting and demonstrating help people who feel that their ethnic group is not being treated fairly?

Visual Summary

QUICK FACTS

Use the visual summary below to help you review the main ideas of the chapter.

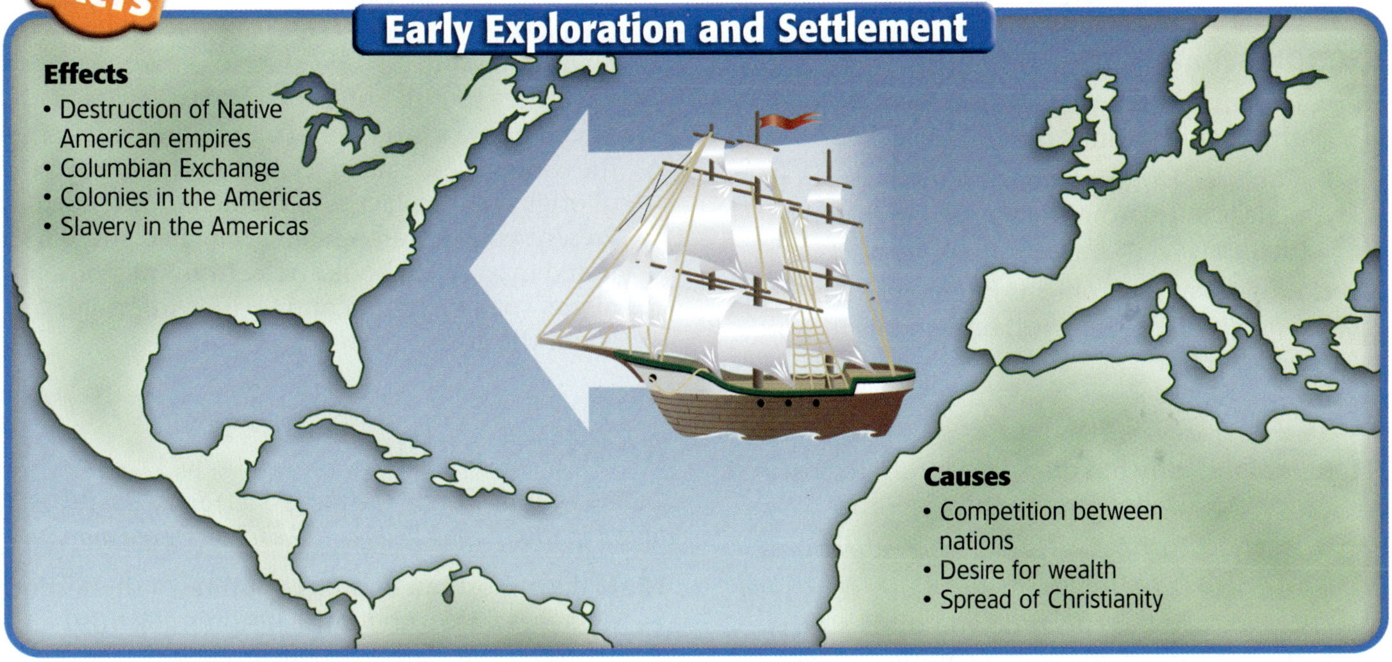

Reviewing Vocabulary, Terms, and People

1. The first Europeans to reach the east coast of North America were the ______________.
2. ______________ established a navigation school and financed expeditions to the west coast of Africa.
3. One of the most important European explorers was ______________, who was the first person to claim lands in the Americas for Spain.
4. The first voyage that sailed completely around the world was headed by ______________.
5. Sir Walter Raleigh founded the colony of Virginia after receiving a ______________, a grant to set up a colony, from the queen of England.
6. Large farms or ______________, that specialize in growing one type of crop for profit, were common in Spanish America.

Comprehension and Critical Thinking

SECTION 1 *(Pages 38–41)*

7. a. Recall On which two islands did the Vikings establish settlements before coming to North America?

b. Analyze What factors led Europeans to begin their voyages of exploration?

c. Evaluate What do you think motivated sailors to sign on for voyages of exploration?

SECTION 2 *(Pages 42–45)*

8. a. Recall Why was Columbus's first voyage important?

b. Summarize Explain the conflict that emerged between Spain and Portugal over their empires in the Americas and how it was resolved.

c. Evaluate Do you think the Columbian Exchange improved life or made life worse in the Americas? Explain your answer.

SECTION 3 *(Pages 46–51)*

9. a. **Identify** What territories in the Americas did Spain control?

   b. **Analyze** What factors enabled the Spanish to defeat the Aztec and the Inca?

   c. **Elaborate** Why was the encomienda system important to Spanish settlers?

SECTION 4 *(Pages 52–57)*

10. a. **Describe** What were the results of the defeat of the Spanish Armada?

    b. **Contrast** How did French settlements in the Americas differ from the English and Spanish settlements?

    c. **Predict** What problems might arise among the different empires with settlements in North America?

SECTION 5 *(Pages 58–61)*

11. a. **Explain** Why did the Spanish turn to enslaved Africans as a labor force in the Americas?

    b. **Analyze** In what ways did enslaved Africans create their own unique culture in the Americas?

    c. **Evaluate** What effects do you think slavery had on the populations and cultures of West African countries?

Reviewing Themes

12. **Geography** What geographic features in North America helped and hindered the exploration and colonization of the continent?

13. **Politics** In what way were the expansions of empires motivated by the politics among European nations?

Using the Internet

go.hrw.com
KEYWORD: SC7 CH2

14. **Activity: Illustrated Map** Columbus's successful return from the New World sparked an interest in exploration that resulted in an explosion of explorers. Each explorer mapped his route and the lands that he explored. Our knowledge of the New World increased quickly as explorers made maps and kept detailed logs to catalog what they found. Enter the activity keyword. Then choose a group of explorers and research the routes these sailors took from the country of origin to the place upon which they landed. Present your research in an annotated and illustrated map or log book. Write from the point of view of an explorer and include information about the areas explored.

Reading Skills

Outlining and History *Use the Reading Social Studies Skill taught in this chapter to answer the following question.*

15. Make a short but complete outline of the section on pages 50–51 under the heading "Spanish Treatment of Native Americans."

Social Studies Skills

Framing Historical Questions *Use the Social Studies Skill taught in this chapter to answer the following question.*

16. Write a historical question for each of the five sections of this chapter.

FOCUS ON WRITING

17. **Writing Your Letter** First, review your notes and decide which group you want to write about. Which details from your notes will your friends and family be most interested in? Which do you find most important? What do you want to tell your family and friends about the Americas?

CHAPTER 2

Standardized Test Practice

DIRECTIONS: Read each question and write the letter of the best response.

1 Which of the following *best* illustrates the process known as the Columbian Exchange?

A Christopher Columbus sailed west to reach Asia and encountered the Americas.

B Corn and tomatoes were introduced to Europe from America.

C Asian goods moved long distances along the Silk Road to reach Europe.

D Advances in technology allowed sailors to better navigate on the open seas.

2 The decimation of the native population of the Americas and the need for plantation labor resulted in the

A encomienda system.

B establishment of religious tolerance.

C transatlantic slave trade.

D Columbian Exchange.

3 Vasco da Gama's discovery of a sea route to India was important because it

A was the first time anyone circumnavigated the globe.

B brought great wealth to Portugal.

C proved that Europeans could reach India by sailing west.

D led to the colonization of the Americas.

4 How did early French colonies in North America differ from those of the English?

A French colonists allied with local Native American groups, while the English often fought with Native Americans.

B The English found vast amounts of gold in their North American colonies, while the French did not.

C English colonies relied heavily on the fur trade, while French colonies depended on agriculture.

D French colonies in North America were located further to the south than English colonies.

5 Which of the following was *most likely* a result of the Columbian Exchange?

A the spread of democratic ideas that led to the creation of the first constitutions

B the introduction of manufacturing to Europe

C an increase in competition for lands in the New World

D the introduction of new foods, changing the diets of Europeans and Americans

6 Slavery was first introduced into North Carolina by

A Sir Walter Raleigh.

B Spanish conquistadors.

C the Lords Proprietors.

D Bartolomé de Las Casas.

7 Examine the following passage from Bernal Díaz del Castillo's account of an Aztec marketplace. Then answer the question below.

> "The bustle and noise caused by this large crowd of people was so great that it could be heard more than four miles away. Some of our men, who had traveled through Italy, said that they never had seen a marketplace that covered so large an area, which was so well regulated, and so crowded with people as this one at Mexico."
>
> —Bernal Díaz del Castillo, adapted from *The Memoirs of the Conquistador Bernal Díaz del Castillo*

Document-Based Question **What is the author's impression of the Aztec marketplace? How can you tell?**

CHAPTER 3 1605–1774

The English Colonies

North Carolina Standards

Social Studies Objectives

1.01 Assess the impact of geography on the settlement and developing economy of the Carolina colony.

1.05 Describe the factors that led to the founding and settlement of the American colonies including religious persecution, economic opportunity, adventure, and forced migration.

1.06 Identify geographic and political reasons for the creation of a distinct North Carolina colony and evaluate the effects on the government and economics of the colony.

1.07 Describe the roles and contributions of diverse groups, such as American Indians, African Americans, European immigrants, landed gentry, tradesmen, and small farmers to everyday life in colonial North Carolina, and compare them to the other colonies.

2.01 Trace the events leading up to the Revolutionary War and evaluate their relative significance in the onset of hostilities.

2.02 Describe the contributions of key North Carolina and national personalities from the Revolutionary War era and assess their influence on the outcome of the war.

2.05 Describe the impact of documents such as the Mecklenburg Resolves, the Halifax Resolves, the Albany Plan of Union, the Declaration of Independence, the State Constitution of 1776, the Articles of Confederation, the United States Constitution, and the Bill of Rights on the formation of the state and national governments.

go.hrw.com
North Carolina
KEYWORD: SC7 NC

FOCUS ON WRITING

Writing an Infomercial What if television had been invented during the time that the English colonies were being founded in North America? Instead of relying on printed flyers and word of mouth to attract settlers, the founders of colonies might have made infomercials. In this chapter you will read about life in the American colonies during different times. You will choose one time period and colony and write an infomercial encouraging English citizens to settle in the colony of your choice.

UNITED STATES

1620
The Pilgrims sign the Mayflower Compact.

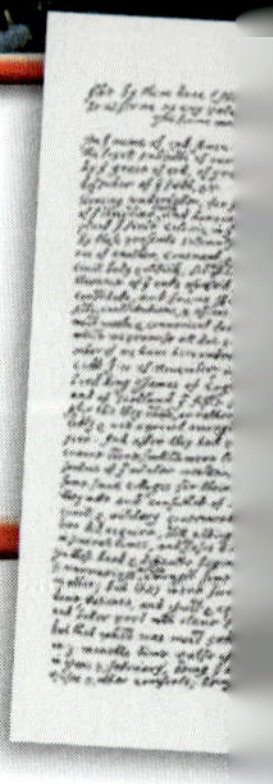

1620

WORLD

1648
Work is finished on India's Taj Mahal.

Mayflower Compact courtesy of the Pilgrim Society, Plymouth, Massachusetts.

HOLT
History's Impact
▶ **video series**
Watch the video to understand the impact of freedom of religion.

What You Will Learn...

Plymouth Colony thrives again in this highly accurate re-creation. The original colonists came to North America in 1620 in search of religious freedom. By 1627, the year this scene re-creates, the colonists were well established. Their success encouraged others. In this chapter you will learn about English settlements that dotted the east coast of North America.

1670

1681 William Penn establishes the colony of Pennsylvania.

1682 Peter the Great becomes czar of Russia.

1720

1763 Pontiac, an American Indian, leads a rebellion on the western frontier.

1768 British explorer James Cook sets sail on his first trip to the South Pacific, meeting people like this Sandwich Islander.

1770

1773 Patriots stage the Boston Tea Party.

Reading Social Studies

by Kylene Beers

Economics | Geography | Politics | Society and Culture | Science and Technology

Focus on Themes In this chapter you will read about the people who settled the early colonies of North America. You will learn about the problems they faced as they felt the tug between their homeland and their new land. You will see how they settled political differences (sometimes peacefully, other times not) and learned how to trade goods and grow crops to establish a thriving economy. You will discover that the **economy** often influenced their **politics**.

Vocabulary Clues

Focus on Reading When you are reading your history textbook, you may often come across a word you do not know. If that word isn't listed as a key term, how do you find out what it means?

Using Context Clues Context means surroundings. Authors often include clues to the meaning of a difficult word in its context. You just have to know how and where to look.

Clue	How It Works	Example	Explanation
Direct Definition	Includes a definition in the same or a nearby sentence	In the late 1600s England, like most western European nations, mercantilism, *a system of creating and maintaining wealth through carefully controlled trade.*	The phrase "a system of creating and maintaining wealth through carefully controlled trade" defines *mercantilism.*
Restatement	Uses different words to say the same thing	The British continued to keep a standing, *or permanent,* army in North America to protect the colonists against Indian attacks.	The word *permanent* is another way to say *standing.*
Comparisons or Contrasts	Compares or contrasts the unfamiliar word with a familiar one	*Unlike legal traders,* smugglers did not have permission to bring goods into the country.	The word *unlike* indicates that smugglers are different from legal traders.

You Try It!

The following sentences are from this chapter. Each uses a definition or restatement clue to explain unfamiliar words. See if you can use the context to figure out the meaning of the words in italics.

Context Clues Up Close

From Chapter 3

1. In 1605 a company of English merchants asked King James I for the right to *found*, or establish, a settlement. *(p. 72)*
2. The majority of workers were *indentured servants*. These servants signed a contract to work four to seven years for those who paid for their journey to America. *(p. 74)*
3. In New England, the center of politics was the *town meeting*. In town meetings people talked about and decided on issues of local interest, such as paying for schools. *(p. 91)*

Answer the questions about the sentences you read.

1. In example 1, what does the word *found* mean? What hints did you find in the sentence to figure that out?
2. In example 2, where do you find the meaning of *indentured servants*? What does this phrase mean?
3. In example 3, you learn the definition of *town meeting* in the second sentence. Can you combine these two sentences into one sentence? Try putting a dash after the word *meeting* and replacing "In town meetings" with "a place where . . ."

As you read Chapter 3, look for context clues that can help you figure out the meanings of unfamiliar words or terms.

Key Terms and People

Chapter 3

Section 1

Jamestown *(p. 72)*
John Smith *(p. 73)*
Pocahontas *(p. 73)*
indentured servants *(p. 74)*
Bacon's Rebellion *(p. 74)*
Toleration Act of 1649 *(p. 75)*
Olaudah Equiano *(p. 77)*
slave codes *(p. 77)*

Section 2

Puritans *(p. 78)*
Pilgrims *(p. 78)*
immigrants *(p. 78)*
Mayflower Compact *(p. 79)*
Squanto *(p. 79)*
John Winthrop *(p. 80)*
Anne Hutchinson *(p. 82)*

Section 3

Peter Stuyvesant *(p. 85)*
Quakers *(p. 86)*
William Penn *(p. 86)*
staple crops *(p. 87)*

Section 4

town meeting *(p. 91)*
English Bill of Rights *(p. 91)*
triangular trade *(p. 93)*
Great Awakening *(p. 94)*
Jonathan Edwards *(p. 94)*
Enlightenment *(p. 95)*
Pontiac *(p. 97)*

Section 5

Samuel Adams *(p. 99)*
Committees of Correspondence *(p. 99)*
Stamp Act of 1765 *(p. 100)*
Boston Massacre *(p. 101)*
Tea Act *(p. 102)*
Boston Tea Party *(p. 102)*
Intolerable Acts *(p. 102)*

Academic Vocabulary

In this chapter, you will learn the following academic words:

authority *(p. 73)*
factors *(p. 74)*

SECTION 1

The Southern Colonies

What You Will Learn...

Main Ideas

1. Jamestown was the first permanent English settlement in America.
2. Daily life in Virginia was challenging to the colonists.
3. Religious freedom and economic opportunities were motives for founding other southern colonies, including Maryland, the Carolinas, and Georgia.
4. Farming and slavery were important to the economies of the southern colonies.

The Big Idea

Despite a difficult beginning, the southern colonies soon flourished.

Key Terms and People

Jamestown, *p. 72*
John Smith, *p. 73*
Pocahontas, *p. 73*
indentured servants, *p. 74*
Bacon's Rebellion, *p. 74*
Toleration Act of 1649, *p. 75*
Olaudah Equiano, *p. 77*
slave codes, *p. 77*

TAKING NOTES As you read, take notes in a chart like the one below on the founding of the southern colonies.

Colony	Year	Why Founded

If YOU were there...

A year ago, in 1609, you moved to the colony of Virginia. Life here has been hard. During the winter many people died of cold or sickness. Food is always scarce. Now it is spring, and a ship has come from England bringing supplies. In a week it will sail home. Some of your neighbors are giving up and returning to England. They ask you to come, too.

Would you take the ship back to England?

BUILDING BACKGROUND Several European nations took part in the race to claim lands in the Americas. Their next step was to establish colonies in the lands that they claimed. The first English colonies were started in the late 1500s but failed. Even in successful colonies, colonists faced hardships and challenges.

Settlement in Jamestown

In 1605 a company of English merchants asked King James I for the right to found, or establish, a settlement. In 1606 the king granted the request of the company to settle in a region called Virginia.

Founding a New Colony

The investors in the new settlement formed a joint-stock company called the London Company. This allowed the group to share the cost and risk of establishing the colony. On April 26, 1607, the first 105 colonists sent by the London Company arrived in America. On May 14, about 40 miles up the James River in Virginia, the colonists founded **Jamestown**, the first permanent English settlement in North America.

A lack of preparation cost a lot of the colonists their lives. Most of the men who came to Jamestown were adventurers with no farming experience or useful skills such as carpentry. Jamestown was surrounded by marshes full of disease-carrying mosquitoes. By the time winter arrived, two-thirds of the original colonists had died.

GEOGRAPHY SKILLS **INTERPRETING MAPS**

1. **Human-Environment Interaction** What were the advantages and disadvantages of locating Jamestown on a river?
2. **Human-Environment Interaction** What do you think would have been a commonly used method of transportation for people in this region?

Powhatan Confederacy

Jamestown fared better under **John Smith,** who took control of the colony and built a fort in 1608. He forced the settlers to work harder and to build better housing by creating rules that rewarded harder workers with food. The colonists received help from the powerful Powhatan Confederacy of Native Americans after Smith made an agreement with them. The Powhatan brought food to help the colonists and taught them how to grow corn.

In 1609 some 400 more settlers arrived in Jamestown. That winter, disease and famine once again hit the colony. The colonists called this period the starving time. By the spring of 1610, only 60 colonists were still alive. Jamestown failed to make a profit until colonist John Rolfe introduced a new type of tobacco that sold well in England.

War in Virginia

John Rolfe married **Pocahontas**, daughter of the Powhatan leader, in 1614. Their marriage helped the colonists form more peaceful relations with the Powhatan. However, Pocahontas died three years later in England, which she was visiting with Rolfe.

In 1622, colonists killed a Powhatan leader. The Powhatan responded by attacking the Virginia settlers later that year. Fighting between the colonists and the Powhatan continued for the next 20 years. Because the London Company could not protect its colonists, the English Crown canceled the company's charter in 1624. Virginia became a royal colony and existed under the **authority** of a governor chosen by the king.

ACADEMIC VOCABULARY
authority power, right to rule

READING CHECK **Finding Main Ideas** What problems did the Jamestown colonists face?

Daily Life in Virginia

In early Virginia, people lived on scattered farms rather than in towns. Tobacco farmers established large farms called plantations. Tobacco was so valuable that it was sometimes used as money.

Headright System

These plantations were made possible in part by the headright system, which was started by the London Company. Under this system, colonists who paid their own way to Virginia received 50 acres of land. A colonist could earn another 50 acres for every additional person brought from England. Rich colonists who brought servants or relatives to Virginia gained large amounts of land.

ACADEMIC VOCABULARY
factors
causes

Primary Source

LETTER

A Note from Virginia

In this 1619 letter, the secretary of the Virginia colony, John Pory, encouraged people to move to Virginia.

"As touching the quality of this country, three things there be, which in few years may bring this colony to perfection; the English plow, vineyards, & cattle . . . All our riches for the present do consist in tobacco, wherein one man by his own labor has in one year, raised to himself to the value of 200 pounds sterling; and another by the means of six servants has cleared at one crop a thousand pound English. These be true, yet indeed rare examples, yet possible to be done by others."

—from *The Power of Words*, edited by T. H. Breen

ANALYSIS SKILL **ANALYZING PRIMARY SOURCES**

How does this letter indicate the importance of tobacco in Virginia?

Labor in Virginia

Colonists in Virginia suffered very high death rates, which led to labor shortages. The majority of workers were **indentured servants**. These servants signed a contract to work for four to seven years for those who paid for their journey to America.

Expansion of Slavery

Not all laborers in Virginia came from Europe. A Dutch ship brought the first Africans to Virginia in 1619. Some Africans were servants; others had been enslaved. Some African servants became successful farmers when their contracts ended.

The demand for workers was soon greater than the supply of people willing to work as indentured servants. Over time, the cost of slaves fell. These **factors** led some colonists to turn to slave labor. By the mid-1600s most Africans in Virginia were being kept in lifelong slavery.

Bacon's Rebellion

As plantations grew, the economy of Jamestown began to expand. Soon, colonial officials began to ask for more taxes. During the mid-1600s poor colonists protested the higher taxes. They were also upset about the governor's policies toward Native Americans. They thought the colony was not well protected against attack. In 1676 a group of former indentured servants led by Nathaniel Bacon attacked some friendly American Indians. Bacon opposed the governor's policies promoting trade with American Indians. He also thought the colonists should be able to take the Indians' land. When the governor tried to stop him, Bacon and his followers attacked and burned Jamestown in an uprising known as **Bacon's Rebellion**.

At one point, Bacon controlled much of the colony. He died of fever, however, and the rebellion soon ended.

READING CHECK **Analyzing** What factors led to the increased use of slave labor in Virginia?

This painting shows life on the North Carolina frontier. Pioneer families relied on Native Americans for trade and information about their environment.

How does this painting show life in colonial North Carolina?

Other Southern Colonies

As Jamestown was developing in Virginia, other colonists began planning their move to America. Many English Catholics came to America to escape religious persecution. English Catholics had long been against England's separation from the Roman Catholic Church, and so they were not allowed by the Church of England to worship freely. English leaders also feared that English Catholics would ally with Catholic countries such as France and Spain in conflicts.

Maryland

In 1632 King Charles I issued a charter to Cecilius Calvert to establish a colony in the Americas for Catholics. Calvert, known as the second Lord Baltimore, named the colony Maryland, in honor of England's queen, Henrietta Maria. The colony was located north of Virginia and was a proprietary colony, meaning that the colony's proprietors, or owners, controlled the government.

In 1634 a group of 200 English Catholics established a colony in Maryland. Protestants began arriving in the 1640s, and soon religious conflicts arose. To reduce tensions, Lord Baltimore presented a bill to the colonial assembly that became known as the **Toleration Act of 1649**. The bill made it a crime to restrict the religious rights of Christians. This was the first law supporting religious tolerance passed in the English colonies.

The Carolinas and Georgia

Colonies were also established south of Virginia. Present-day North Carolina was originally included in the land grant of Virginia. In 1663 the English king, Charles II, named Carolina in his own honor. He gave the territory to eight of his supporters, who became the Lords Proprietors of the Carolina colony.

Virginia began to send explorers to northern Carolina in 1608 in an attempt to find the fate of the "lost colony" on Roanoke Island. In 1653 fur trader Nathaniel Batts was hired to explore the Albemarle Sound region. Batts became the first permanent European settler in the area. Most of the first colonists in northern Carolina had moved from Virginia.

In 1669 the Lords Proprietors issued the Fundamental Constitutions of Caro-

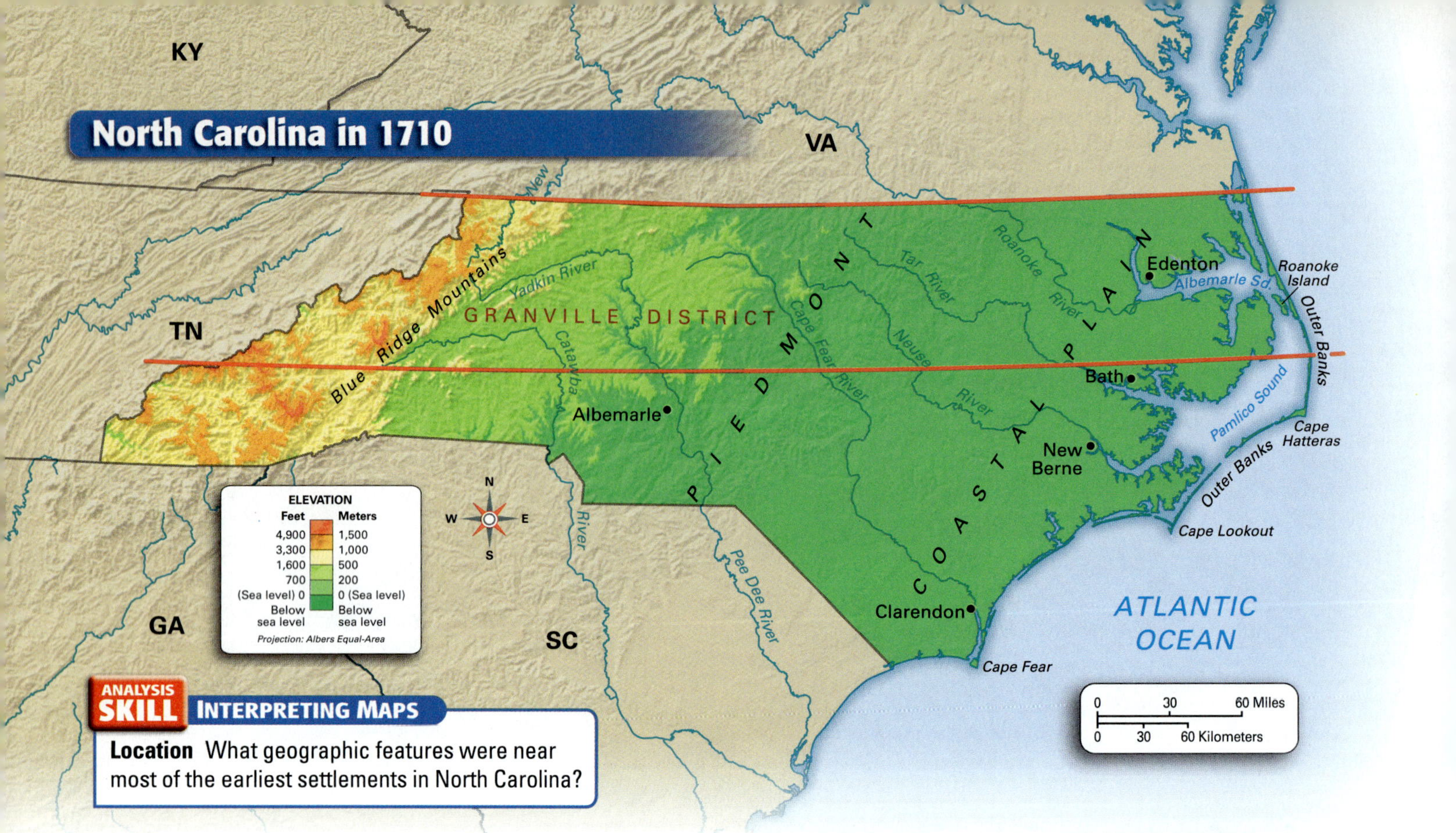

ANALYSIS SKILL INTERPRETING MAPS

Location What geographic features were near most of the earliest settlements in North Carolina?

lina as a design for governing the colony. They appointed several governors, many of whom were unpopular. Some were accused of corruption.

The economy of colonial Carolina was supported by the mix of groups that lived there. European settlers traded with Native Americans for goods, while tradespeople made other products for sale. Agricultural products like tobacco were produced on small farms and on plantations owned by the gentry. The plantations relied on the labor of enslaved Africans for producing crops. Each of these groups contributed to the culture of the colony, bringing different styles of music, stories, and art from around the world.

Political divisions arose between early and later settlers. In 1677 John Culpeper and George Durant led Culpeper's Rebellion against acting governor Thomas Miller. After deposing Miller, Culpeper traveled to England to negotiate with the Lords Proprietors. He was brought to trial when he arrived but was acquitted and returned to northern Carolina.

Settlements in Carolina were far apart, and it was a struggle to govern the colony. The Proprietors faced disputes with Virginia and Native Americans, and piracy off the coast. In 1689 a governor was appointed to the area of North Carolina, and in 1712 the colony of Carolina officially split in two. In 1729 seven of the proprietors sold their interests to the Crown. Only John Carteret, Earl Granville, kept his share. A land area equal to an eighth of the colony became known as the Granville District. Both North and South Carolina became royal colonies.

In 1732 King George II granted a charter to James Oglethorpe and other trustees to found Georgia. Oglethorpe wanted a colony for people who had been jailed in England for their debts. He wanted the colony to be made up of many small farms rather than plantations and outlawed slavery. In 1749 slavery became allowed and soon the British government made Georgia a royal colony. Coastal Georgia was soon filled with large rice plantations worked by thousands of slaves.

READING CHECK **Summarizing** What were some problems in early North Carolina?

FOCUS ON NORTH CAROLINA

Ships sailing in the Outer Banks of North Carolina were frequent victims of piracy. Pirates like Edward Teach, or Blackbeard, and Stede Bonnet raided ships and stripped them of their cargo. Blackbeard was pardoned by North Carolina's governor in 1718 but continued to raid ships until he was killed later that year.

Economies of the Southern Colonies

The economies of the southern colonies depended on agriculture. They also exported materials for building ships, such as wood and tar. Some colonies traded with local Indians for deerskins to sell.

The colonies had many small farms and some large plantations. Many farms grew cash crops that were sold for profit. Tobacco, rice, and indigo—a plant used to make blue dye—were the most important cash crops. North Carolina's shipping industry was hurt by the lack of a deepwater port. Only smaller ships could land in the shallow sounds. This prevented goods from being shipped directly to England. They had to be shipped first to ports in other colonies.

The southern colonies' cash crops required a great deal of difficult work to grow and harvest. This meant a large workforce was needed. By the 1700s enslaved Africans, rather than indentured servants, had become the main source of labor.

Slavery was a viciously brutal condition for many inhabitants of the colonies. One former slave named **Olaudah Equiano** recorded his experiences.

> "Tortures, murder, and every other imaginable barbarity ... are practiced upon the poor slaves with impunity [no punishment]. I hope the slave-trade will be abolished."
>
> —Olaudah Equiano, from *The Interesting Narrative of the Life of Olaudah Equiano, or Gustavus Vassa, the African*

Most of the southern colonies passed **slave codes**, or laws to control slaves. Quakers in North Carolina encouraged slaveholders to treat their slaves well and tried to abolish slavery, but the slave trade continued.

READING CHECK **Summarizing** What role did slavery play in the southern plantation economy? How was it regulated?

SUMMARY AND PREVIEW In this section you read about life in the southern colonies. In the next section you will learn about the New England colonies.

Section 1 Assessment

go.hrw.com
Online Quiz
KEYWORD: SC7 HP3

Reviewing Ideas, Terms, and People

1. a. **Describe** How did **John Smith** improve conditions in **Jamestown**?
   b. **Explain** What events led to a conflict between the Jamestown settlers and the Powhatan Confederacy?
2. a. **Recall** Why were **indentured servants** necessary in Virginia?
   b. **Evaluate** What do you think was the most serious problem faced by settlers in Virginia? Why?
3. a. **Identify** Which colony was the first to promote religious tolerance?
   b. **Analyze** Why did more enslaved Africans live in South Carolina than did white settlers?
   c. **Predict** How might the colony of Georgia have been different if Oglethorpe's plan had succeeded?
4. a. **Recall** What was the purpose of **slave codes**?
   b. **Analyze** Why were slaves in high demand in the southern colonies?

Critical Thinking

5. **Summarizing** Review your notes on the southern colonies. Then add a new column to your chart that summarizes the successes and/or failures of each colony.

Colony	Year	Why Founded	Successes/Failures

FOCUS ON WRITING

6. **Gathering Some Ideas** As you read this section, take notes on the early colonies of Virginia, Maryland, the Carolinas, and Georgia. Be sure to note what advantages they offered to settlers and what difficulties settlers faced. Start to think about the people who would be most likely to settle in the southern colonies.

SECTION 2

The New England Colonies

What You Will Learn...

Main Ideas

1. The Pilgrims and Puritans came to America to avoid religious persecution.
2. Religion and government were closely linked in the New England colonies.
3. The New England economy was based on trade and farming.
4. Education was important in the New England colonies.

The Big Idea

English colonists traveled to New England to gain religious freedom.

Key Terms and People

Puritans, *p. 78*
Pilgrims, *p. 78*
immigrants, *p. 78*
Mayflower Compact, *p. 79*
Squanto, *p. 79*
John Winthrop, *p. 80*
Anne Hutchinson, *p. 82*

TAKING NOTES As you read, identify the reasons English colonists came to New England. Use a chart like the one below for your notes.

Reasons for Coming to New England	
Pilgrims	
Puritans	

If YOU were there...

You live in a town near London in the early 1700s. Some of your neighbors are starting new lives in the American colonies. You would like to go with them, but you cannot afford the cost of the trip. There is one way you can go, though. You can sign a paper promising to work as a servant for five years. Then you would be free—and in a new country!

Would you sign the paper and go to America?

BUILDING BACKGROUND England's first successful colonial settlements were in Virginia. They were started mainly as business ventures. Other colonists in North America had different reasons for leaving their homes. Many, like the Pilgrims and Puritans, came to have freedom to practice their religious beliefs. Others, like the person above, simply wanted a new way of life.

Pilgrims and Puritans

Religious tensions in England remained high after the Protestant Reformation. A Protestant group called the **Puritans** wanted to purify, or reform, the Anglican Church. The Puritans thought that bishops and priests had too much power over church members.

Pilgrims on the Move

The most extreme English Protestants wanted to separate from the Church of England. These Separatists formed their own churches and cut all ties with the Church of England. In response, Anglican leaders began to punish Separatists.

The **Pilgrims** were one Separatist group that left England in the early 1600s to escape persecution. The Pilgrims moved to the Netherlands in 1608. The Pilgrims were **immigrants**—people who have left the country of their birth to live in another country.

The Pilgrims were glad to be able to practice their religion freely. They were not happy, however, that their children were learning the Dutch language and culture. The Pilgrims feared that their children would forget their English traditions. The Pilgrims decided to leave Europe altogether. They formed a joint-stock company with some merchants and then received permission from England to settle in Virginia.

On September 16, 1620, a ship called the *Mayflower* left England with more than 100 men, women, and children aboard. Not all of these colonists were Pilgrims. However, Pilgrim leaders such as William Bradford sailed with the group.

The Mayflower Compact

After two months of rough ocean travel, the Pilgrims sighted land far north of Virginia. The Pilgrims knew that they would thus be outside the authority of Virginia's colonial government when they landed. Their charter would not apply. So, they decided to establish their own basic laws and social rules to govern the colony they would found.

On November 21, 1620, 41 of the male passengers on the ship signed the **Mayflower Compact**, a legal contract in which they agreed to have fair laws to protect the general good. The Compact represents one of the first attempts at self-government in the English colonies.

In late 1620 the Pilgrims landed at Plymouth Rock in present-day Massachusetts. The colonists struggled through the winter to build the Plymouth settlement. Nearly half died during this first winter from sickness and the freezing weather.

Pilgrims and Native Americans

In March 1621 a Native American named Samoset walked boldly into the colonists' settlement. He spoke in broken English. Samoset had learned some English from the crews of English fishing boats. He gave the Pilgrims useful information about the peoples and places of the area. He also introduced them to a Patuxet Indian named **Squanto**. Squanto had at one time lived in Europe and spoke English as well.

Primary Source

HISTORICAL DOCUMENT

The Mayflower Compact

In November 1620, Pilgrim leaders aboard the Mayflower *drafted the Mayflower Compact. This excerpt from the Mayflower Compact describes the principles of the Pilgrim colony's government.*

We whose names are underwritten . . . having undertaken, for the glory of God, and advancement of the Christian faith, and the honour of our King and country, a voyage to plant the first colony in the northern parts of Virginia, do by these presents solemnly and mutually in the presence of God, and one of another, covenant and combine ourselves together into a civil body politic for our better ordering and preservation and furtherance of the ends aforesaid; and by virtue hereof, to enact, constitute, and frame such just and equal laws, ordinances, acts, constitutions, and offices . . . as shall be thought most meet and convenient for the general good of the colony unto which we promise all due . . . obedience.

The Pilgrims describe the reasons they want to form a colony in North America.

The Pilgrims promise to obey laws that help the whole colony.

by these presents: by this document
covenant: promise
civil body politic: group organized to govern
aforesaid: mentioned above
virtue: authority
ordinances: regulations
meet: fitting

ANALYSIS SKILL **ANALYZING PRIMARY SOURCES**

1. **Why do you think the colonists felt the need to establish a government for themselves?**
2. **How do you think the Mayflower Compact influenced later governments in America?**

From Squanto the Pilgrims learned to fertilize the soil with fish remains. Squanto also helped the Pilgrims establish relations with the local Wampanoag Indians. Conditions in the Plymouth colony began to improve.

The Pilgrims invited Wampanoag chief Massasoit and 90 other guests to celebrate their harvest. This feast became known as the first Thanksgiving. For the event, the Pilgrims killed wild turkeys. This event marked the survival of the Pilgrims in the new colony.

Pilgrim Community

Although the Pilgrims overcame many problems, their small settlement still struggled. Most Pilgrims became farmers, but the farmland around their settlement was poor. They had hoped to make money by trading furs and by fishing. Unfortunately, fishing and hunting conditions were not good in the area. Some colonists traded corn with American Indians for beaver furs. The Pilgrims made little money but were able to form a strong community. The colony began to grow stronger in the mid-1620s after new settlers arrived and, as in Jamestown, colonists began to have more rights to farm their own land.

The Pilgrims' settlement was different from Virginia's in that it had many families. The Pilgrims taught their children to read and offered some education to their indentured servants. Families served as centers of religious life, health care, and community well-being.

All family members worked together to survive during the early years of the colony. Women generally cooked, spun and wove wool, and sewed clothing. They also made soap and butter, carried water, dried fruit, and cared for livestock. Men spent most of their time repairing tools and working in the fields. They also chopped wood and built shelters.

Women in the Colony

In Plymouth, women had more legal rights than they did in England. In England women were not allowed to make contracts, to sue, or to own property. In America, Pilgrim women had the right to sign contracts and to bring some cases before local courts. Widows could also own property.

From time to time, local courts recognized the ways women helped the business community. Widow Naomi Silvester received a large share of her husband's estate. The court called her "a frugal [thrifty] and laborious [hardworking] woman."

Puritans Leave England

During the 1620s England's economy suffered. Many people lost their jobs. The English king, Charles I, made the situation worse by raising taxes. This unpopular act led to a political crisis. At the same time, the Church of England began to punish Puritans because they were dissenters, or people who disagree with official opinions. King Charles refused to allow Puritans to criticize church actions.

Great Migration

These economic, political, and religious problems in England led to the Great Migration. Between 1629 and 1640 many thousands of English men, women, and children left England. More than 40,000 of these people moved to English colonies in New England and the Caribbean. In 1629, Charles granted a group of Puritans and merchants a charter to settle in New England. They formed the Massachusetts Bay Company.

In 1630 a fleet of ships carrying Puritan colonists left England for Massachusetts to seek religious freedom. They were led by **John Winthrop**. The Puritans believed that they had made a covenant, or promise, with God to build an ideal Christian community.

A New Colony

The Puritans arrived in New England well prepared to start their colony. They brought large amounts of tools and livestock with them. Like the Pilgrims, the Puritans faced little resistance from local American Indians. Trade with the Plymouth colony helped them too. In addition, the region around Boston had a fairly healthful climate. Thus, few Puritans died from sickness. All of these things helped the Massachusetts Bay Colony do well. By 1691, the Massachusetts Bay Colony had expanded to include the Pilgrims' Plymouth Colony.

READING CHECK **Summarizing** What role did religion play in the establishment of the Massachusetts Bay Colony?

History Close-up

Plymouth Colony

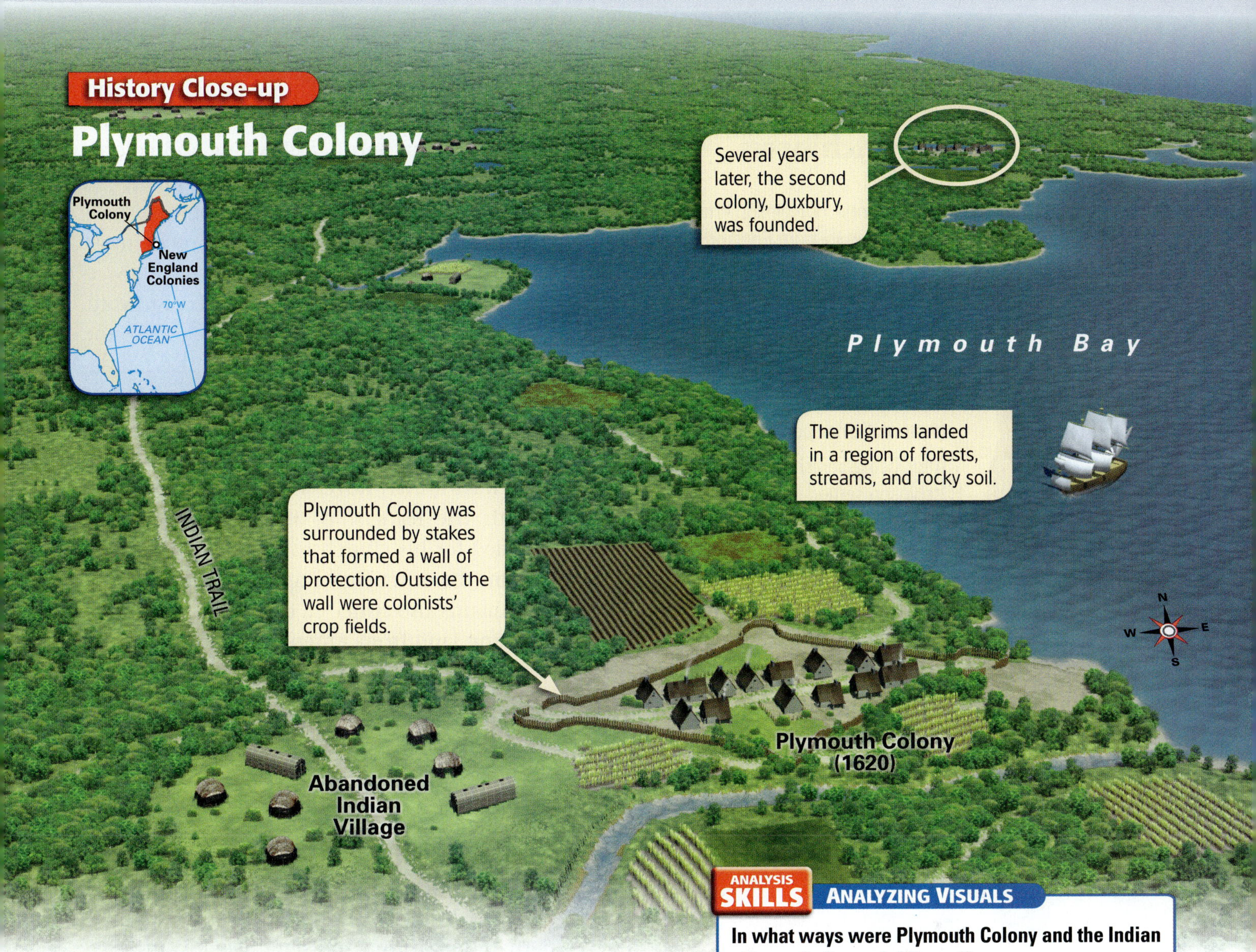

ANALYSIS SKILLS **ANALYZING VISUALS**

In what ways were Plymouth Colony and the Indian village similar and different?

Religion and Government in New England

Massachusetts Bay Colony had to obey English laws. However, its charter provided more independence than did the royal charter of Virginia. For example, it created a General Court to help run the Massachusetts colony.

The Puritan colonists turned this court into a type of self-government to represent the needs of the people. Each town sent two or three delegates to the Court. After John Winthrop served as the colony's first governor, the General Court elected the governor and his assistants. In 1644 the General Court became a two-house, or bicameral, legislature.

Politics and religion were closely linked in Puritan New England. Government leaders were also church members, and ministers often had a great deal of power in Puritan communities. Male church members were the only colonists who could vote. Colonists became full members in the church by becoming what the Puritans called God's "elect," or chosen. Reaching this status was a difficult process. Individuals had to pass a public test to prove that their faith was strong.

BIOGRAPHY

Anne Hutchinson

1591–1643

In 1634 Anne Hutchinson emigrated with her family from England to the Massachusetts Bay Colony. After settling in Boston, she worked as a nurse and midwife. She also hosted a Bible-study class that met in her home. Over time, Hutchinson began to question the teachings of the local ministers. Meanwhile, her popularity grew.

After being banished from the colony, Hutchinson settled in Rhode Island and, later, Long Island. She died in an American Indian attack. Today we remember her as a symbol of the struggle for religious freedom.

Drawing Conclusions Why do you think church leaders disliked Hutchinson's ideas?

Church and State

QUICK FACTS

Religion Affected Government

- Government leaders were church members.
- Ministers had great authority.

Government Affected Religion

- Government leaders outlawed certain religions.
- Government leaders punished dissenters.

In 1636 minister Thomas Hooker and his followers left Massachusetts to help found Connecticut, another New England colony. In 1639 Hooker wrote the Fundamental Orders of Connecticut. This set of principles made Connecticut's government more democratic. For example, the Orders allowed men who were not church members to vote. As a result, some historians call Hooker the father of American democracy. The Fundamental Orders of Connecticut also outlined the powers of the general courts.

Not all Puritans shared the same religious views. Minister Roger Williams did not agree with the leadership of Massachusetts. He called for his church to separate completely from the other New England congregations. Williams also criticized the General Court for taking land from American Indians without paying them.

Puritan leaders worried that Williams's ideas might hurt the unity of the colony. They made him leave Massachusetts. Williams took his supporters to southern New England. They formed a new settlement called Providence. This settlement later developed into the colony of Rhode Island. In Providence, Williams supported the separation of the church from the state. He also believed in religious tolerance for all members of the community.

In Boston, an outspoken woman also angered Puritan church leaders. **Anne Hutchinson** publicly discussed religious ideas that some leaders thought were radical. For example, Hutchinson believed that people's relationship with God did not need guidance from ministers.

Hutchinson's views alarmed Puritans such as John Winthrop. Puritan leaders did not believe that women should be religious leaders. Puritan leaders put Hutchinson on trial for her ideas. The court decided to force her out of the colony. With a group of followers, Hutchinson helped found the new colony of Portsmouth, later a part of the colony of Rhode Island.

Perhaps the worst community conflicts in New England involved the witchcraft trials of the early 1690s. The largest number of trials were held in Salem, Massachusetts. In Salem a group of girls had accused people of casting spells on them. The community formed a special court to judge the witchcraft cases. The court often pressured the suspected witches to confess. Before the trials had ended, the Salem witch trials led to 19 people being put to death.

READING CHECK **Identifying Cause and Effect** What led to religious disagreements among the Puritans, and what was the result?

New England Economy

Connecticut, Massachusetts, New Hampshire, and Rhode Island were very different from the southern colonies. The often harsh climate and rocky soil meant that few New England farms could grow cash crops. Most farming families grew crops and raised animals for their own use. There was thus little demand for farm laborers. Although some people held slaves, slavery did not become as important to this region.

Merchants

Trade was vital to New England's economy. New England merchants traded goods locally, with other colonies, and overseas. Many of them traded local products such as furs, pickled beef, and pork. Many merchants grew in power and wealth, becoming leading members of the New England colonies.

Fishing

Fishing became one of the region's leading industries. The rich waters off New England's coast served as home to many fish, including cod, mackerel, and halibut. Merchants exported dried fish. Colonists also began hunting for whales that swam close to shore. Whales were captured with harpoons, or spears, and dragged to shore. Whaling provided valuable oil for lighting.

Shipbuilding

Shipbuilding became an important industry in New England for several reasons. The area had plenty of forests that provided materials for shipbuilding. As trade—particularly in slaves—in the New England seaports grew, more merchant ships were built. The fishing industry also needed ships. New England shipyards made high-quality, valuable vessels. Ship owners sometimes even told their captains to sell the ship along with the cargo when they reached their destination.

Skilled Craftspeople

The northern economy needed skilled craftspeople. Families often sent younger sons to learn skilled trades such as blacksmithing, weaving, shipbuilding, and printing. The young boys who learned skilled trades were known as apprentices.

Apprentices lived with a master craftsman and learned from him. In exchange, the boys performed simple tasks. Apprentices promised to work for a master craftsman for a set number of years. They learned trades that were essential to the survival of the colonies. Apprentices received food and often clothing from the craftsmen. Gabriel Ginings, for example, was an apprentice in Portsmouth, Rhode Island. He received "sufficient food and raiment [clothing] suitable for such an apprentice," as his 1663 contract stated.

After a certain amount of time had passed, apprentices became journeymen. They usually traveled and learned new skills in their trade. Eventually they would become a master of the trade themselves.

READING CHECK **Categorizing** What types of jobs were common in the New England colonies?

THE IMPACT TODAY

Fishing remains an important industry in New England, earning hundreds of millions of dollars each year.

Education in the Colonies

Education was important in colonial New England. Mothers and fathers wanted their children to be able to read the Bible. The Massachusetts Bay Colony passed some of the first laws requiring parents to provide instruction for their children.

Public Education

To be sure that future generations would have educated ministers, communities established town schools. In 1647 the General Court of Massachusetts issued an order that a school be founded in every township of 50 families.

THE IMPACT TODAY

Public schools remain the primary source of education for most U.S. children. Total enrollment today is around 50 million students.

Schoolchildren often used the *New England Primer,* which had characters and stories from the Bible. They learned to read at the same time that they learned about the community's religious values.

The availability of schooling varied in the colonies. There were more schools in New England than in the other colonies where most children lived far from towns. These children had to be taught by their parents or by private tutors. Most colonial children stopped their education after the elementary grades. Many went to work, either on their family farm or away from home.

Higher Education

Higher education was also important to the colonists. In 1636 John Harvard and the General Court founded Harvard College. Harvard taught ministers and met the colony's need for higher education. The second college founded in the colonies, William and Mary, was established in Virginia in 1693.

By 1700 about 70 percent of men and 45 percent of women in New England could read and write. These figures were much lower in Virginia, where Jamestown was the only major settlement.

READING CHECK **Analyzing** Why was education important to the New England colonies?

SUMMARY AND PREVIEW In this section you learned about the role that religion played in the New England colonies. In the next section you'll learn about New York, New Jersey, and Pennsylvania.

Section 2 Assessment

go.hrw.com
Online Quiz
KEYWORD: SC7 HP3

Reviewing Ideas, Terms, and People

1. a. **Recall** Why did the **Pilgrims** and **Puritans** leave Europe for the Americas?
   b. **Elaborate** Do you think the Pilgrims could have survived without the assistance of **Squanto** and Massasoit? Explain your answer.
2. a. **Describe** What role did the church play in Massachusetts?
   b. **Analyze** Why did some colonists disagree with the leaders of Massachusetts?
3. a. **Identify** Describe the economy in the New England colonies.
   b. **Analyze** Why do you think New England merchants became leading members of society?
4. a. **Describe** What steps did the Massachusetts Bay Colony take to promote education?
   b. **Predict** What are some possible benefits that New England's emphasis on education might bring?

Critical Thinking

5. **Identifying Cause and Effect** Review your notes on the reasons English colonists came to New England. Then copy the diagram below and use it to show how the colonists' experiences caused them to build certain types of colonies.

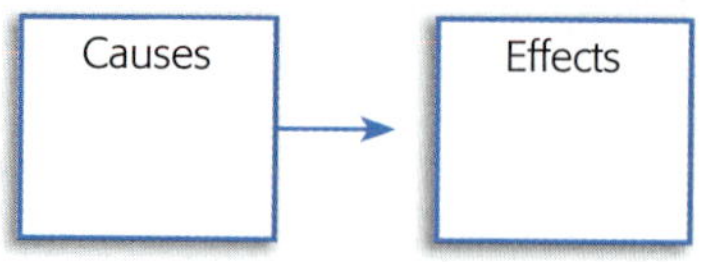

FOCUS ON WRITING

6. **Comparing Colonies** Take notes on the early New England colonies. Be sure to note what advantages they offered to settlers and what difficulties settlers faced. Put a star beside the colony or colonies you might use in your infomercial.

The Middle Colonies

SECTION 3

If YOU were there...

You are a farmer in southern Germany in 1730. Religious wars have torn your country apart for many years. Now you hear stories about a place in America where people of all religions are welcome. But the leaders of the colony—and many of its people—are English. You would not know their language or customs. Still, you would be free to live and worship as you like.

How would you feel about moving to a country full of strangers?

BUILDING BACKGROUND The middle section of the Atlantic coast offered good land and a moderate climate. Several prominent English people established colonies that promised religious freedom. To people like the settler above, these colonies promised a new life.

New York and New Jersey

The Dutch founded New Netherland in 1613 as a trading post for exchanging furs with the Iroquois. The center of the fur trade in New Netherland was the town of New Amsterdam on Manhattan Island. Generous land grants to patroons, or lords, and religious tolerance soon brought Jews, French Huguenots, Puritans, and others to the colony. Director General **Peter Stuyvesant** (STY-vuh-suhnt) led the colony beginning in 1647.

Peter Stuyvesant was forced to surrender New Amsterdam to the English in 1664.

What You Will Learn...

Main Ideas

1. The English created New York and New Jersey from former Dutch territory.
2. William Penn established the colony of Pennsylvania.
3. The economy of the middle colonies was supported by trade and staple crops.

The Big Idea

People from many nations settled in the middle colonies.

Key Terms and People

Peter Stuyvesant, *p. 85*
Quakers, *p. 86*
William Penn, *p. 86*
staple crops, *p. 87*

TAKING NOTES As you read, take notes on which nation founded each of the middle colonies. Record your notes in a chart like the one shown below.

Colony	Founding Nation
New York	
New Jersey	
Pennsylvania	

Characteristics of the Middle Colonies

QUICK FACTS

Social	Economic
• New York: Dutch influence • New Jersey: diverse population • Pennsylvania: founded by Quakers	• successful farming of staple crops • work force of slaves and indentured servants • active trade with Britain and West Indies

In 1664 an English fleet captured the undefended colony of New Amsterdam without firing a single shot. New Netherland was renamed New York, and New Amsterdam became New York City.

THE IMPACT TODAY

Today New York City is the largest city in the United States, with more than 8 million people.

Soon after the English conquest in 1664, the Duke of York made Sir George Carteret and Lord John Berkeley proprietors of New Jersey. This colony occupied lands between the Hudson and Delaware rivers. It had a diverse population, including Dutch, Swedes, Finns, and Scots. The fur trade was important to the economies of New York and New Jersey through the end of the 1600s.

READING CHECK **Comparing** How were New York and New Jersey similar?

BIOGRAPHY

William Penn

1644–1718

William Penn was born in London as the son of a wealthy admiral. Penn joined the Quakers in 1666 and became an active preacher and writer of religious works. He supported toleration of dissenters.

In 1681 he received a charter to establish a new colony called Pennsylvania. There, Penn put his beliefs into practice. He insisted on fair dealings with local American Indians, welcomed immigrants, and promised religious toleration.

Making Generalizations How did Penn's ideas influence the rules of the colony?

Penn's Colony

The Society of Friends, or the **Quakers**, made up one of the largest religious groups in New Jersey. Quakers did not follow formal religious practices and dressed plainly. They believed in the equality of men and women before God. They also supported nonviolence and religious tolerance for all people. At the time, many Quaker beliefs and practices shocked most Christians. As a result, Quakers were persecuted in both England and America.

One proprietor of the New Jersey colony was a Quaker named **William Penn**. Penn wished to found a larger colony under his own control that would provide a safe home for Quakers. In 1681 King Charles II agreed to grant Penn a charter to begin a colony west of New Jersey.

Penn's colony, known as Pennsylvania, grew rapidly. Penn limited his own power and established an elected assembly. He also promised religious freedom to all Christians. His work made Pennsylvania an important example of representative self-government—a government that reflects its citizens' will—in the colonies.

Penn named the capital of his colony Philadelphia, which means "the city of brotherly love." In 1682 the Duke of York sold Penn a region to the south of Pennsylvania. This area, called Delaware, remained part of Pennsylvania until 1776.

READING CHECK **Finding Main Ideas** Why did William Penn establish Pennsylvania, and how did he influence its government?

Economy of the Middle Colonies

The middle colonies combined characteristics of the New England and southern colonies. With a good climate and rich land, farmers there could grow large amounts of **staple crops**—crops that are always needed. These crops included wheat, barley, and oats. Farmers also raised livestock.

Slaves were somewhat more important to the middle colonies than they were to New England. They worked in cities as skilled laborers, such as blacksmiths and carpenters. Other slaves worked on farms, onboard ships, and in the growing shipbuilding industry. However, indentured servants largely filled the middle colonies' growing labor needs. Between 1700 and 1775 about 135,000 indentured servants came to the middle colonies. About half of them moved to Pennsylvania. By 1760 Philadelphia had become the largest British colonial city. Other cities in the middle colonies, such as New York City, also grew quickly.

Trade was important to the economy of the middle colonies. Merchants in Philadelphia and New York City exported colonial goods to markets in Britain and the West Indies. These products included wheat from New York, Pennsylvania, and New Jersey.

Throughout the colonies, women made important contributions to the economy. They ran farms and businesses such as clothing and grocery stores, bakeries, and drugstores. Some women also practiced medicine and worked as nurses and midwives. However, colonial laws and customs limited women's economic opportunities.

Most colonial women worked primarily in the home. Married women managed households and raised children. Sometimes they earned money for their families by selling products like butter. They also provided paid services such as washing clothes.

FOCUS ON READING

You can tell **staple crops** means "crops that are always needed" because of the dash between the vocabulary term and the definition.

READING CHECK **Finding the Main Idea**

On what were the economies of the middle colonies based?

SUMMARY AND PREVIEW In this section you learned about the middle colonies. In the next section you will read about colonial government, the slave trade, and conflicts that arose in the English colonies.

Section 3 Assessment

go.hrw.com
Online Quiz
KEYWORD: SC7 HP3

Reviewing Ideas, Terms, and People

1. a. **Describe** Name the middle colonies. Where were they located?
   b. **Draw Inferences** What led to the diverse populations of New York and New Jersey?
2. a. **Identify** Who are the **Quakers**?
   b. **Analyze** How did **William Penn** attempt to create a colonial government that would be fair to all?
3. a. **Describe** What different types of jobs did slaves in the middle colonies hold?
   b. **Evaluate** In what ways were women essential to the middle colonies?

Critical Thinking

4. **Sequencing** Review your notes about which nation founded each middle colony. Then complete the time line below by listing the event that occurred on each of the dates on the time line.

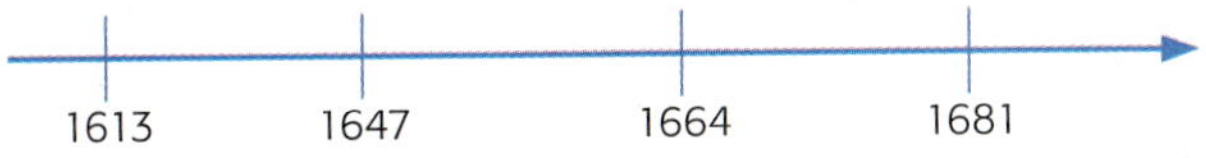

FOCUS ON WRITING

5. **Comparing Colonies** You've just read about early colonies in New York, New Jersey, and Pennsylvania. Think about the advantages they offered to settlers and what difficulties settlers faced. In your notes, put a star beside one of the colonies you might use in your infomercial.

America's Growth 1760

The English colonies in 1760 were located between the Atlantic Ocean and the Appalachian Mountains. The total population of the colonies was around 1.8 million. Soon, however, the colonies began to grow both in size and in population.

In 1763 Great Britain and France signed the Treaty of Paris, giving Britain control over all lands east of the Mississippi River. With the stroke of a pen, the colonies increased enormously in size. The westward expansion of the English colonies—soon to be the United States—had begun.

A Wall of Mountains The 1,500-mile-long Appalachian Mountain range formed a natural barrier to westward expansion. The Appalachians' dense forests and steep terrain made passage on foot or by horse difficult.

America's Population, 1760: 1.8 million

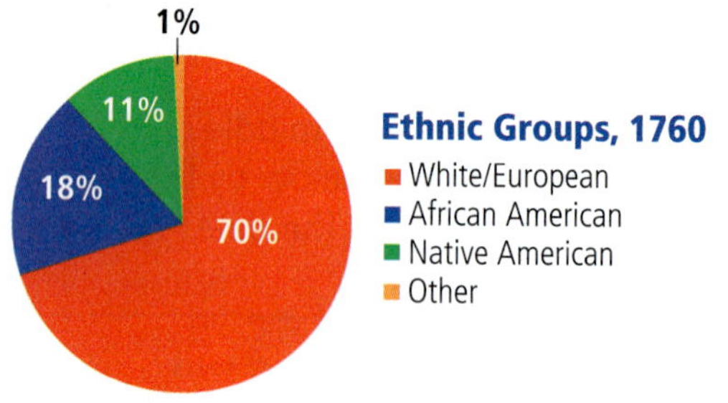

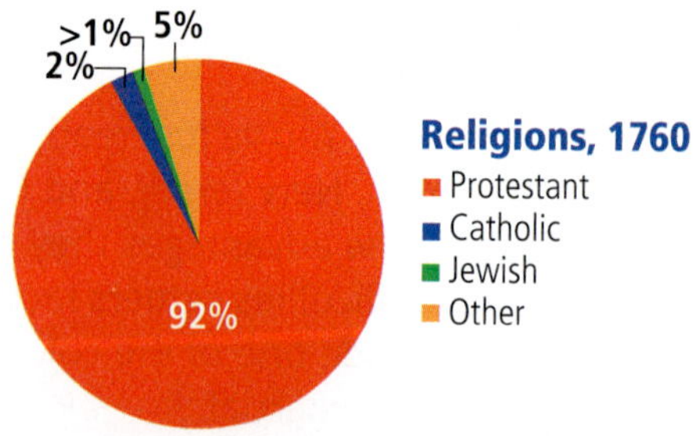

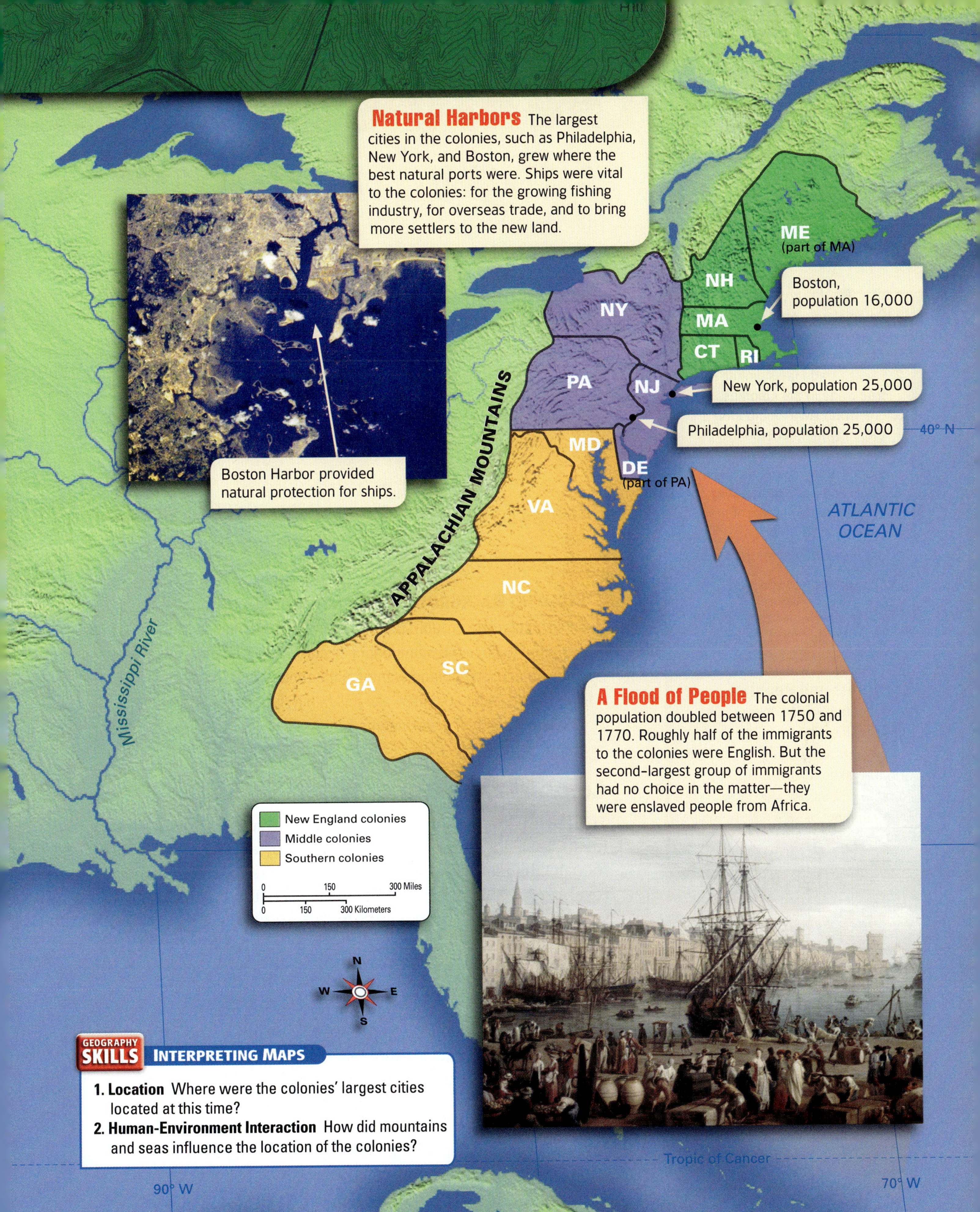

Natural Harbors The largest cities in the colonies, such as Philadelphia, New York, and Boston, grew where the best natural ports were. Ships were vital to the colonies: for the growing fishing industry, for overseas trade, and to bring more settlers to the new land.

Boston Harbor provided natural protection for ships.

A Flood of People The colonial population doubled between 1750 and 1770. Roughly half of the immigrants to the colonies were English. But the second-largest group of immigrants had no choice in the matter—they were enslaved people from Africa.

GEOGRAPHY SKILLS **INTERPRETING MAPS**

1. **Location** Where were the colonies' largest cities located at this time?
2. **Human-Environment Interaction** How did mountains and seas influence the location of the colonies?

SECTION 4

Life in the English Colonies

What You Will Learn...

Main Ideas

1. Colonial governments were influenced by political changes in England.
2. English trade laws limited free trade in the colonies.
3. The Great Awakening and the Enlightenment led to ideas of political equality among many colonists.
4. The French and Indian War gave England control of more land in North America.

The Big Idea

The English colonies continued to grow despite many challenges.

Key Terms and People

town meeting, *p. 91*
English Bill of Rights, *p. 91*
triangular trade, *p. 93*
Great Awakening, *p. 94*
Jonathan Edwards, *p. 94*
Enlightenment, *p. 95*
Pontiac, *p. 97*

TAKING NOTES As you read, take notes on how the following developments affected the growing colonies.

Development	Effects
Establishment of local government	
Political change in England	
Trade laws	
Great Awakening/ Enlightenment	
French and Indian War	

If YOU were there...

Your family migrated to America in the 1700s and started a small farm in western Pennsylvania. Now, more and more people are moving in. You would like to move farther west, into the Ohio River valley. But a new law says you cannot move west of the mountains because it is too dangerous. Still, you are restless and want more land and more freedom.

Why might you decide to break the law and move west?

BUILDING BACKGROUND When they moved to America, the English colonists brought their ideas about government. They expected to have the same rights as citizens in England. However, many officials in England wanted tight control over the colonies. As a result, some colonists, like this family, were unhappy with the policies of colonial governments.

Colonial Governments

The English colonies in North America all had their own governments. Each government was given power by a charter. The English monarch had ultimate authority over all of the colonies. A group of royal advisers called the Privy Council set English colonial policies.

Colonial Governors and Legislatures

Each colony had a governor who served as head of the government. Most governors were assisted by an advisory council. In royal colonies the English king or queen selected the governor and the council members. In proprietary colonies, the proprietors chose all of these officials. In a few colonies, such as Connecticut, the people elected the governor.

In some colonies the people also elected representatives to help make laws and set policy. These officials served on assemblies. Each colonial assembly passed laws that had to be approved first by the advisory council and then by the governor.

Established in 1619, Virginia's assembly was the first colonial legislature in North America. At first it was a single body, but it later split into two houses. One house was known as the Council of State. The governor's advisory council and the London Company selected its members. The House of Burgesses was the assembly's second house. The members were elected by colonists.

In New England the center of politics was the **town meeting**. In town meetings people talked about and decided on issues of local interest, such as paying for schools.

In the southern colonies, people typically lived farther away from one another. Therefore, many decisions were made at the county level. The middle colonies used both county meetings and town meetings to make laws.

North Carolina had a governor and council appointed by Britain and a legislature elected by county voters. Older counties were allowed more representatives. This arrangement eventually caused conflict between the older counties in the east and newly settled areas in the west.

Political Change in England

In 1685 James II became king of England. He was determined to take more control over the English government, both in England and in the colonies. James believed that the colonies were too independent. In 1686 he united the northern colonies under one government called the Dominion of New England and made Sir Edmund Andros the royal governor. The colonists disliked Andros because he used his authority to limit town meetings.

English Bill of Rights

Parliament replaced the unpopular King James and passed the **English Bill of Rights** in 1689. This act reduced the powers of the monarch and increased those of Parliament. Following these changes, the colonies in the Dominion quickly formed new assemblies and charters.

The Thirteen Colonies

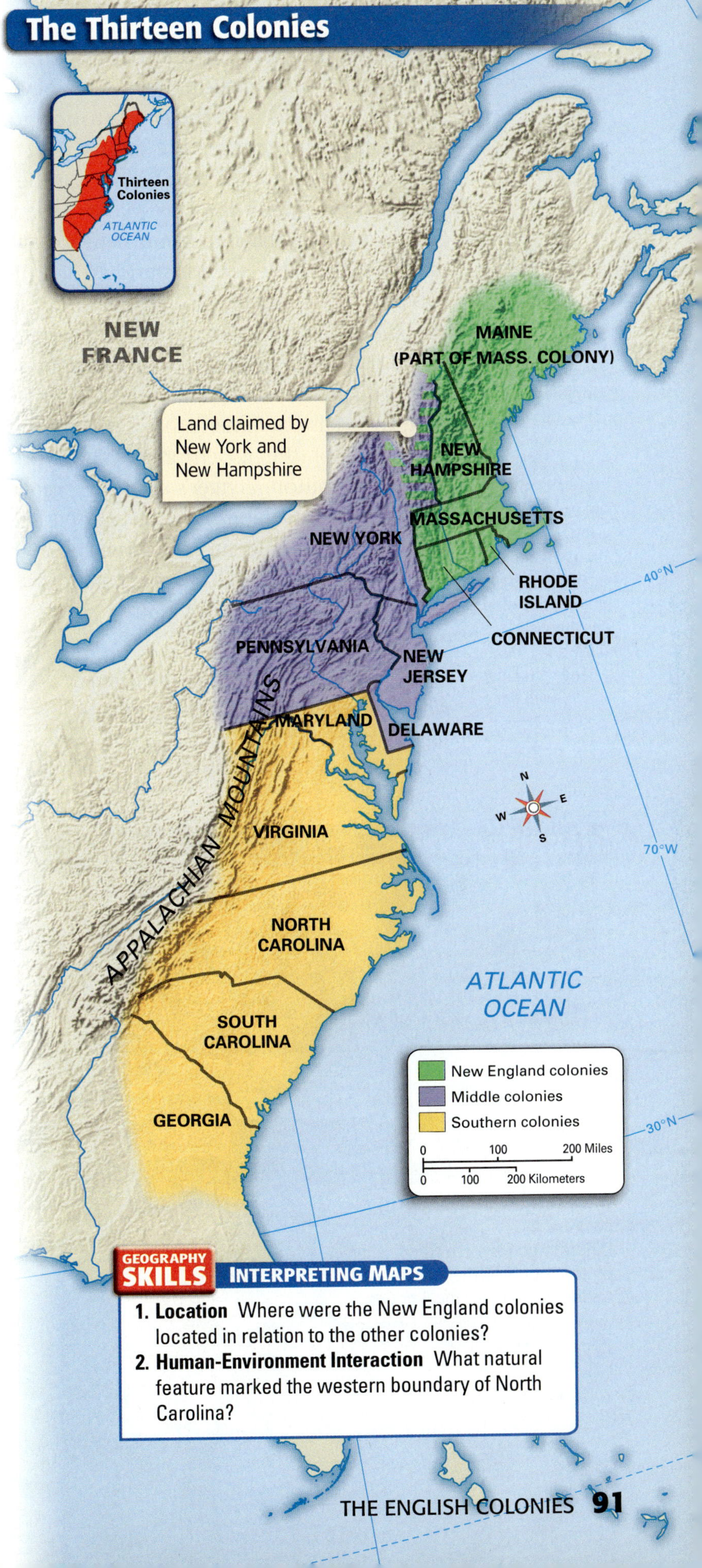

GEOGRAPHY SKILLS INTERPRETING MAPS

1. **Location** Where were the New England colonies located in relation to the other colonies?
2. **Human-Environment Interaction** What natural feature marked the western boundary of North Carolina?

Colonial Courts

Colonial courts made up another important part of colonial governments. Whenever possible, colonists used the courts to control local affairs. In general, the courts reflected the beliefs of their local communities. For example, many laws in Massachusetts enforced the Puritans' religious beliefs. Laws based on the Bible set the standard for the community's conduct.

Sometimes colonial courts also protected individual freedoms. For example, in 1733 officials arrested John Peter Zenger for printing a false statement that damaged the reputation of the governor of New York. Andrew Hamilton, Zenger's attorney, argued that Zenger could publish whatever he wished as long as it was true. Jury members believed that colonists had a right to voice their ideas openly and found him not guilty.

THE IMPACT TODAY

Like the colonies and Great Britain, nations today are economically interdependent. They rely on one another to buy and sell goods and services to keep their economies healthy. Communications technology has increased this interdependence, as huge sums of money can change hands each day with ease.

READING CHECK **Analyzing Information** Why were colonial assemblies and colonial courts created, and what did they do?

English Trade Laws

One of England's main reasons for founding and controlling its American colonies was to earn money from trade. In the late 1600s England, like most western European nations, practiced mercantilism, a system of creating and maintaining wealth through carefully controlled trade. A country gained wealth if it had fewer imports—goods bought from other countries—than exports—goods sold to other countries.

To support this system of mercantilism, between 1650 and 1696 Parliament passed a series of Navigation Acts limiting colonial trade. For example, the Navigation Act of 1660 forbade colonists from trading specific items such as sugar and cotton with any country other than England. The act also required colonists to use English ships to transport goods. Parliament later passed other acts that required all trade goods to pass through English ports, where duties, or import taxes, were added to the items.

Triangular Trade

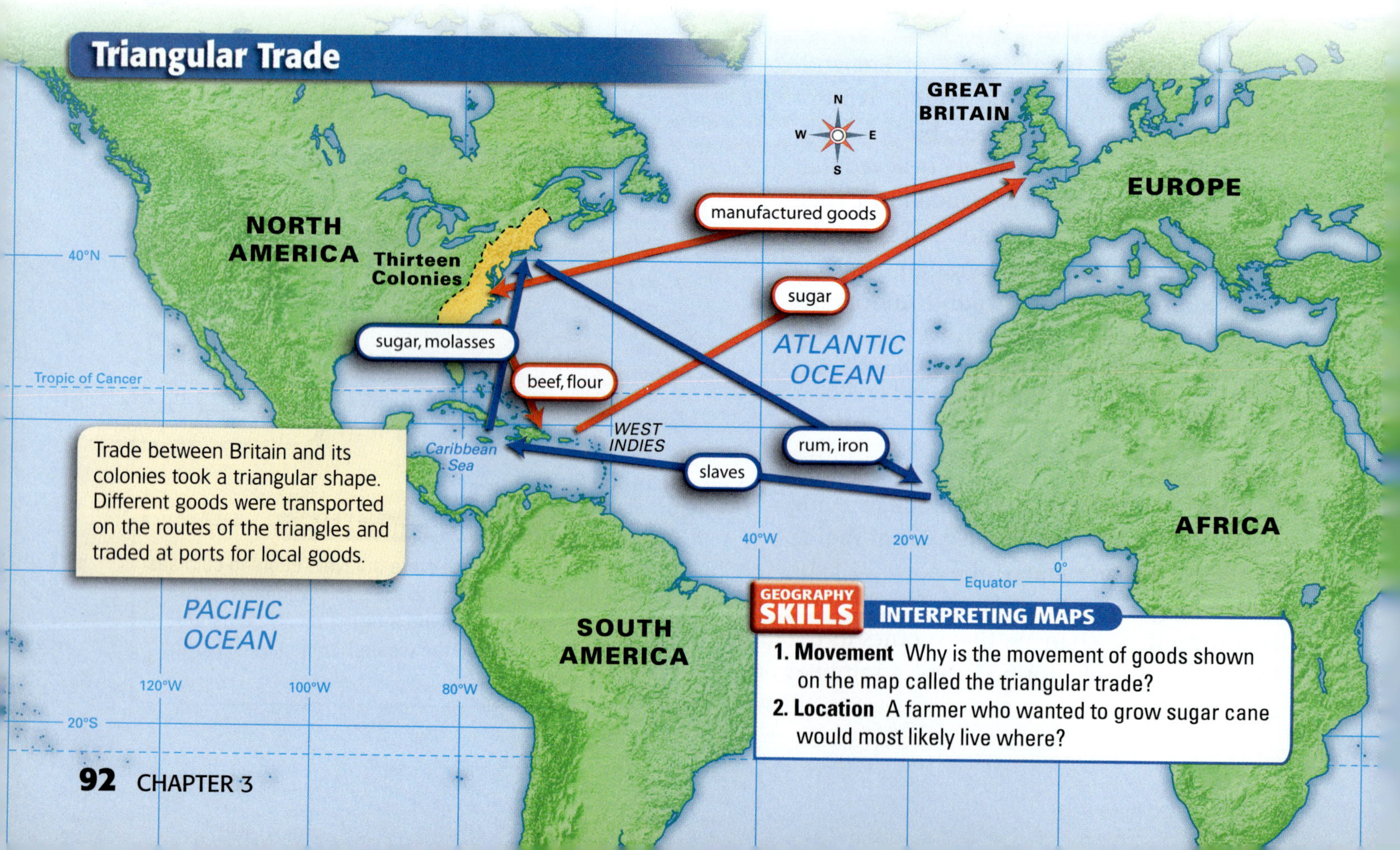

Trade between Britain and its colonies took a triangular shape. Different goods were transported on the routes of the triangles and traded at ports for local goods.

GEOGRAPHY SKILLS **INTERPRETING MAPS**

1. **Movement** Why is the movement of goods shown on the map called the triangular trade?
2. **Location** A farmer who wanted to grow sugar cane would most likely live where?

England claimed that the Navigation Acts were good for the colonies. After all, the colonies had a steady market in England for their goods. But not all colonists agreed. Many colonists wanted more freedom to buy or sell goods wherever they could get the best price. Local demand for colonial goods was small compared to foreign demand.

Despite colonial complaints, the trade restrictions continued into the 1700s. Some traders turned to smuggling, or illegal trading. They often smuggled sugar, molasses, and rum into the colonies from non-English islands in the Caribbean. Parliament responded with the Molasses Act of 1733, which placed duties on these items. British officials, however, rarely carried out this law.

By the early 1700s English merchants were trading around the world. Most American merchants traded directly with Great Britain or the West Indies. By importing and exporting goods such as sugar and tobacco, some American merchants became wealthy.

Triangular Trade

Trade between the American colonies and Great Britain was not direct. Rather, it generally took the form of **triangular trade**—a system in which goods and slaves were traded among the Americas, Britain, and Africa. There were several routes of the triangular trade. In one route colonists exchanged goods like beef and flour with plantation owners in the West Indies for sugar, some of which they shipped to Britain. The sugar was then exchanged for manufactured products to be sold in the colonies. Colonial merchants traveled great distances to find the best markets.

BIOGRAPHY

Olaudah Equiano

1745–1797

Olaudah Equiano was born in Africa in present-day Nigeria. In 1756 he was sold into slavery. Equiano survived the Middle Passage, traveling in a slave ship across the Atlantic. After arriving in the colonies, a Virginia planter purchased him and again sold him to a British naval officer. While working as a sailor, Equiano eventually earned enough money to purchase his own freedom in 1766. Equiano later settled in England and devoted himself to ending slavery.

Analyzing Information How did Equiano gain his freedom?

"I received such a salutation [smell] in my nostrils, as I had never experienced in my life; . . . I became so sick and low that I was not able to eat . . . The groans of the dying, rendered [made] the whole a scene of horror almost inconceivable [unbelievable]."

—Olaudah Equiano, from *The Interesting Narrative of the Life of Olaudah Equiano, or Gustavus Vassa, the African*

The Great Awakening

George Whitefield gives a powerful sermon during the Great Awakening. Ministers like Whitefield emphasized personal religious experiences over official church rules. They also allowed ordinary church members—whatever their race, class, or gender—to play a role in services. The value placed on individuals of all types during the Great Awakening helped shape American political ideas about who should have a say in government.

How do you think religious freedom led to political freedom?

Middle Passage

One version of the triangular trade began with traders exchanging rum for slaves on the West African coast. The traders then sold the enslaved Africans in the West Indies for molasses or brought them to sell in the mainland American colonies.

The slave trade brought millions of Africans across the Atlantic Ocean in a voyage called the Middle Passage. This was a terrifying and deadly journey that could last as long as three months.

Enslaved Africans lived in a space not even three feet high. Slave traders fit as many slaves as possible on board so they could earn greater profits. Thousands of captives died on slave ships during the Middle Passage. In many cases, they died from diseases such as smallpox. As farmers began to use fewer indentured servants, slaves became even more valuable.

READING CHECK **Identifying Cause and Effect** What factors caused the slave trade to grow? How did this affect conditions on the Middle Passage?

Great Awakening and Enlightenment

In the early 1700s revolutions in both religious and nonreligious thought transformed the Western world. These movements began in Europe and affected life in the American colonies.

Great Awakening

After years of population growth, religious leaders wanted to spread religious feeling throughout the colonies. In the late 1730s these ministers began holding revivals, emotional gatherings where people came together to hear sermons.

Many American colonists experienced "a great awakening" in their religious lives. This **Great Awakening**—a religious movement that swept through the colonies in the 1730s and 1740s—changed colonial religion. It also affected social and political life. **Jonathan Edwards** of Massachusetts was one of the most important leaders of the Great Awakening. His dramatic sermons told sinners to seek forgiveness for their sins or face punishment in Hell forever. British minister George Whitefield held revivals from Georgia to New England.

The Great Awakening drew people of different regions, classes, and races. Women, members of minority groups, and poor people often took part in services. Ministers from different colonies met and shared ideas with one another. This represented one of the few exchanges between colonies.

The Great Awakening promoted ideas that may also have affected colonial politics. Sermons about the spiritual equality of all people led some colonists to begin demanding more political equality. Revivals became popular places to talk about political and social issues. People from those colonies with less political freedom were thus introduced to more democratic systems used in other colonies.

Enlightenment

During the 1600s Europeans began to reexamine their world. Scientists began to better understand the basic laws that govern nature. Their new ideas about the universe began the Scientific Revolution. The revolution changed how people thought of the world.

Many colonists were also influenced by the **Enlightenment**. This movement, which took place during the 1700s, spread the idea that reason and logic could improve society. Enlightenment thinkers also formed ideas about how government should work.

Some Enlightenment thinkers believed that there was a social contract between government and citizens. Philosophers such as John Locke thought that people had natural rights such as equality and liberty. Ideas of the Scientific Revolution and the Enlightenment eventually influenced colonial leaders.

READING CHECK **Summarizing** How did the Great Awakening and the Enlightenment influence colonial society?

French and Indian War

By the 1670s tensions had arisen between New England colonists and the Wampanoag. Metacomet, a Wampanoag leader also known as King Philip, opposed the colonists' efforts to take his people's lands. In 1675 these tensions finally erupted in a conflict known as King Philip's War. The colonial militia—civilians serving as soldiers—fought American Indian warriors. Both sides attacked each other's settlements, killing men, women, and children. The fighting finally ended in 1676, but only after about 600 colonists and some 3,000 Indians had been killed, including Metacomet.

Native American Allies

Some Native Americans allied with the colonists to fight against Metacomet and his forces. These Indians had developed trade relations with colonists. They wanted tools, weapons, and other goods that Europeans could provide. In exchange, the colonists wanted furs, which they sold for large profits in Europe. As a result, each side came to depend upon the other.

French colonists traded and allied with the Algonquian and Huron. English colonists traded and allied with the Iroquois League. This powerful group united American Indians from six different groups. Many American Indians trusted the French more than they did the English. The smaller French settlements were less threatening than the rapidly growing English colonies. No matter who their allies were, many Indian leaders took care to protect their people's independence. As one leader said:

> "We are born free. We neither depend upon [the governor of New France] nor [the governor of New York]. We may go where we please … and buy and sell what we please."
>
> —Garangula, quoted in *The World Turned Upside Down*, edited by Colin G. Calloway

FOCUS ON NORTH CAROLINA

While negotiations with Native Americans were taking place, Benjamin Franklin was devising a plan to protect the colonies called the Albany Plan of Union. The plan called for the colonies to unite under a central president-general, appointed by the Crown, and a House of Representatives, chosen by voters in the colonies. North Carolina was to have four representatives in the government. British officials did not encourage the plan out of fear they could not control the united colonies.

Interactive Map

North American Empires before and after the Treaty of Paris

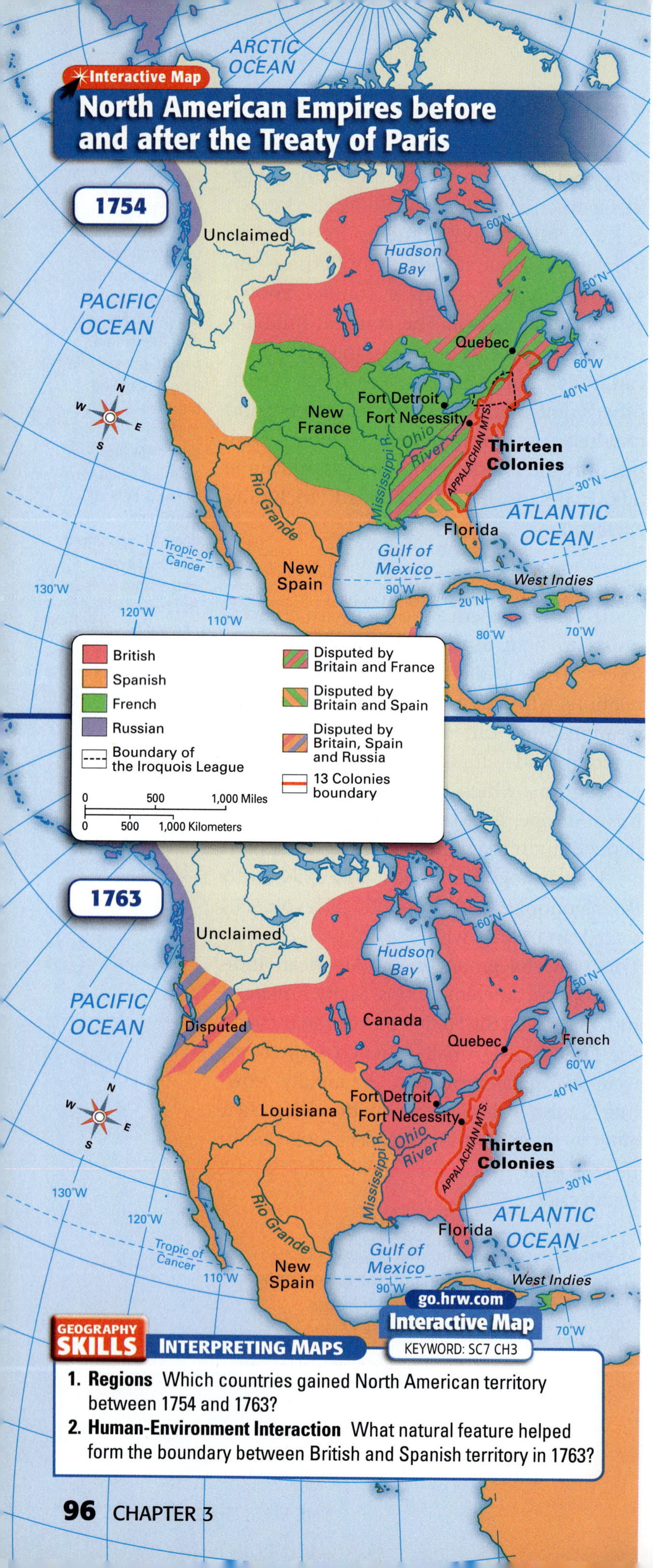

GEOGRAPHY SKILLS **INTERPRETING MAPS**

1. **Regions** Which countries gained North American territory between 1754 and 1763?
2. **Human-Environment Interaction** What natural feature helped form the boundary between British and Spanish territory in 1763?

War Erupts

Until the mid-1700s, France and Great Britain struggled for control of territory in North America. British colonists wanted to settle in the Ohio River valley, where they could take advantage of the valuable fur trade. The French believed this settlement would hurt their fur trade profits. A standoff developed in the Ohio Valley where the French had built three forts. Fighting erupted in 1753 as the British military moved to take over the valley.

When a young Virginian named George Washington arrived with more soldiers, he found the area under French control. Washington and his troops built a small, simple fort that he named Fort Necessity. After his troops suffered many casualties—captured, injured, or killed soldiers—Washington finally surrendered. His defeat in 1754 was the start of the French and Indian War. Leaders from the colonies met to discuss defense. The convention produced a plan for uniting the colonies called the Albany Plan. Meanwhile, in 1756 fighting began in Europe, starting what became known as the Seven Years' War.

Treaty of Paris

The turning point of the war came in 1759. That year British general James Wolfe captured Quebec, gaining the advantage in the war. However, the war dragged on for four more years. Finally, in 1763 Britain and France signed the Treaty of Paris, officially ending the war.

The terms of the treaty gave Canada to Britain. Britain also gained all French lands east of the Mississippi River except the city of New Orleans and two small islands in the Gulf of St. Lawrence. From Spain, which had allied with France in 1762, Britain received Florida. In an earlier treaty, Spain had received Louisiana, the land that France had claimed west of the Mississippi River. The Treaty of Paris changed the balance of power in North America. Soon British settlers began moving west to settle new lands.

Western Frontier

Most colonial settlements were located along the Atlantic coast. Colonial settlers, or pioneers, slowly moved into the Virginia and Carolina backcountry and the Ohio River valley.

Indian leaders like Chief **Pontiac** opposed British settlement of this new land. Pontiac's Rebellion began in May 1763 when his forces attacked British forts on the frontier. Within one month, they had destroyed or captured seven forts. Pontiac then led an attack on Fort Detroit. The British held out for months.

British leaders feared that more fighting would take place on the frontier if colonists kept moving onto American Indian lands. To avoid more conflict, King George III issued the Proclamation of 1763. This law banned British settlement west of the Appalachian Mountains. The law also ordered settlers to leave the upper Ohio River valley.

READING CHECK **Summarizing** Why did George III issue the Proclamation of 1763?

BIOGRAPHY

Pontiac

1720–1769

Pontiac, an Ottawa chief who had fought for France, tried to resist British settlement west of the Appalachians. Calling them "dogs dressed in red who have come to rob us," he attacked the British in the Ohio country in 1763. Pontiac's rebellion was put down, and he surrendered in 1766.

Analyzing Information How did Pontiac try to stop the British?

SUMMARY AND PREVIEW In this section you read about colonial governments, the slave trade, and the conflicts with foreign countries and with Native Americans that the colonies faced as they grew. In the next section you'll learn about the increasing tension between the colonies and Great Britain that led to independence.

Section 4 Assessment

go.hrw.com
Online Quiz
KEYWORD: SC7 HP3

Reviewing Ideas, Terms, and People

1. a. **Describe** How were colonial governments organized?
   b. **Analyze** How did political change in England affect colonial governments?
2. a. **Explain** What is **mercantilism**?
   b. **Analyze** How did the Navigation Acts support the system of mercantilism?
   c. **Evaluate** Did the colonies benefit from mercantilism? Why or why not?
3. a. **Identify** What was the **Great Awakening**?
   b. **Compare** How was the **Enlightenment** similar to the Great Awakening?
4. a. **Explain** What caused the French and Indian War?
   b. **Evaluate** Defend the British decision to ban colonists from settling on the western frontier.

Critical Thinking

5. **Summarizing** Review your notes on the developments in the colonies during the late 1600s to mid-1700s. Then add a box to the bottom of your chart in which you briefly summarize how the colonies grew and changed during the period, as well as the challenges they faced.

Development	Effects
Establishment of local government	
Political change in England	
Trade laws	
Great Awakening/Enlightenment	
French and Indian War	

↓

How the colonies grew and changed and challenges faced

FOCUS ON WRITING

6. **Reviewing the Information** This section focused on what life was like in all the English colonies discussed so far. Does this information give you any new ideas about the colony you'll use in your infomercial?

SECTION 5

Conflict in the Colonies

What You Will Learn...

Main Ideas

1. British efforts to raise taxes on colonists sparked protest.
2. The Boston Massacre caused colonial resentment toward Great Britain.
3. Colonists protested the British tax on tea with the Boston Tea Party.
4. Great Britain responded to colonial actions by passing the Intolerable Acts.

The Big Idea

Tensions developed as the British government placed tax after tax on the colonies.

Key Terms and People

Samuel Adams, *p. 99*
Committees of Correspondence, *p. 99*
Stamp Act of 1765, *p. 100*
Boston Massacre, *p. 101*
Tea Act, *p. 102*
Boston Tea Party, *p. 102*
Intolerable Acts, *p. 102*

TAKING NOTES As you read, take notes in a chart like the one below on each of the new laws passed by the British government.

Law
1.
2.
3.
4.
5.

If YOU were there...

You live in the New England colonies in the 1700s. Recently, British officials have placed new taxes on tea—your favorite beverage. You've never been very interested in politics, but you're beginning to think that people far across the ocean in Britain shouldn't be able to tell you what to do. Some of your friends have joined a group that refuses to buy British tea.

Would you give up your favorite drink to join the boycott?

BUILDING BACKGROUND As the British colonies grew and became prosperous, the colonists got used to running their own lives. Britain began to seem very far away. At the same time, officials in Britain still expected the colonies to obey them and to earn money for Britain. Parliament passed new laws and imposed new taxes. But the colonists found various ways to challenge them.

Great Britain Raises Taxes

Great Britain had won the French and Indian War, but Parliament still had to pay for it. The British continued to keep a standing, or permanent, army in North America to protect the colonists against Indian attacks. To help pay for this army, Prime Minister George Grenville asked Parliament to tax the colonists. In 1764 Parliament passed the Sugar Act, which set duties on molasses and sugar imported by colonists. This was the first act passed specifically to raise money in the colonies.

British officials also tried harder to arrest smugglers. Colonial merchants were required to list all the trade goods they carried aboard their ships. These lists had to be approved before ships could leave colonial ports. This made it difficult for traders to avoid paying duties. The British navy also began to stop and search ships for smuggled goods.

Voice of Protest

Leaders like Patrick Henry made speeches that encouraged colonists to protest the British government. Here, Henry is shown protesting the Crown's control of religion in front of a Virginia court.

Why were public speeches so important to protesting British rule?

Parliament also changed the colonies' legal system by giving greater powers to the vice-admiralty courts. These courts had no juries, and the judges treated suspected smugglers as guilty until proven innocent. In regular British courts, accused persons were treated as innocent until proven guilty.

Taxation without Representation

Parliament's actions upset many colonists who had grown used to being independent. The rising merchant class thought the taxes were unfair and hurt business. Many believed that Great Britain had no right to tax the colonies at all without popular consent.

James Otis argued that the power of the Crown and Parliament was limited. Otis said they could not "take from any man any part of his property, without his consent in person or by representation." Colonial assemblies had little influence on Parliament's decisions. In addition, the colonists had no direct representatives in Parliament. The colonists were subjects of the Crown instead of citizens of England.

At a Boston town meeting in May 1764, local leader **Samuel Adams** agreed with Otis. He believed that Parliament could not tax the colonists without their permission. The ideas of Otis and Adams were summed up in the slogan "No Taxation without Representation," which spread throughout the colonies.

Adams helped found the **Committees of Correspondence**. Each committee got in touch with other towns and colonies. Its members shared ideas and information about the new British laws and ways to challenge them.

A popular method of protest was the boycott, in which people refused to buy British goods. The first colonial boycott started in New York in 1765. It soon spread to other colonies. Colonists hoped that their efforts would hurt the British economy and might convince Parliament to end the new taxes.

FOCUS ON NORTH CAROLINA

Major General Robert Howe was one of the nine North Carolinians on that colony's Committee of Correspondence. Eventually, he would become North Carolina's highest-ranking officer during the American Revolution.

Stamp Act

The British government continued to search for new ways to tax the American colonies, further angering many colonists. For example, Prime Minister Grenville proposed the **Stamp Act of 1765**. This act required colonists to pay for an official stamp, or seal, when they bought paper items. The tax had to be paid on legal documents, licenses, newspapers, pamphlets, and even playing cards. Colonists who refused to buy stamps could be fined or sent to jail.

Grenville did not expect this tax to spark protest. After all, in Britain people already paid similar taxes. But colonists saw it differently. The Stamp Act was Parliament's first attempt to raise money by taxing the colonists directly, rather than by taxing imported goods.

Protests against the Stamp Act began almost immediately. Colonists formed a secret society called the Sons of Liberty. Samuel Adams helped organize the group in Boston. This group sometimes used violence to frighten tax collectors. Many colonial courts shut down because people refused to buy the stamps required for legal documents. Businesses openly ignored the law by refusing to buy stamps.

In May 1765 a Virginia lawyer named Patrick Henry presented a series of resolutions to the Virginia House of Burgesses. These resolutions stated that the Stamp Act violated colonists' rights. In addition to taxation without representation, the Stamp Act denied the accused a trial by jury. Henry's speech in support of the resolutions convinced the assembly to support some of his ideas.

Repealing the Stamp Act

In Boston the members of the Massachusetts legislature called for a Stamp Act Congress. In October 1765, delegates from nine colonies met in New York. They issued a declaration that the Stamp Act was a violation of their rights and liberties.

Pressure on Parliament to repeal, or do away with, the Stamp Act grew quickly. A group of London merchants complained that their trade suffered from the colonial boycott. Parliament repealed the Stamp Act in 1766.

Members of Parliament were upset that colonists had challenged their authority. Thus, Parliament issued the Declaratory Act, which stated that Parliament had the power to make laws for the colonies "in all cases whatsoever." The Declaratory Act further worried the colonists. The act stripped away much of their independence.

Townshend Acts

In June 1767 Parliament passed the Townshend Acts. These acts placed duties on glass, lead, paints, paper, and tea. To enforce the Townshend Acts, British officials used writs of assistance. These allowed tax collectors to search for smuggled goods. Colonists hated the new laws because they took power away from colonial governments.

The colonists responded to the Townshend Acts by once again boycotting many British goods. Women calling themselves the Daughters of Liberty supported the boycott. In February 1768 Samuel Adams wrote a letter arguing that the laws violated the legal rights of the colonists. The Massachusetts legislature sent the letter to other colonies' legislatures, who voted to join the protest.

At the same time, tax collectors in Massachusetts seized the ship *Liberty* on suspicion of smuggling. This action angered the ship's owner and the Sons of Liberty. They attacked the houses of customs officials in protest. In response, the governor broke up the Massachusetts legislature. He also asked troops to restore order. British soldiers arrived in Boston in October 1768.

READING CHECK **Sequencing** What series of events led to the arrival of British troops in Boston in 1768?

Primary Source

NEWSPAPER ARTICLE

The Boston Massacre

An account of the Boston Massacre appeared in the Boston Gazette and Country Journal *soon after the event.*

"The People were immediately alarmed with the Report of this horrid Massacre, the Bells were set a Ringing, and great Numbers soon assembled at the Place where this tragical Scene had been acted; their Feelings may be better conceived than expressed; and while some were taking Care of the Dead and Wounded, the Rest were in Consultation what to do in these dreadful Circumstances.

But so little intimidated were they [Bostonians], notwithstanding their being within a few Yards of the Main Guard, and seeing the 29th Regiment under Arms, and drawn up in King street; that they kept their Station and appeared, as an Officer of Rank expressed it, ready to run upon the very Muzzles of their Muskets."

—*Boston Gazette and Country Journal,* March 12, 1770

ANALYSIS SKILL **ANALYZING PRIMARY SOURCES**

Why do you think the people described were not intimidated by the soldiers?

Boston Massacre

Many Bostonians saw the presence of British troops as a threat by the British government against its critics in Massachusetts. Some colonists agreed with Samuel Adams, who said, "I look upon [British soldiers] as foreign enemies." The soldiers knew that they were not welcome. Both sides resented each other, and name-calling, arguments, and fights between Bostonians and the soldiers were common.

The tension exploded on March 5, 1770. A lone British soldier standing guard had an argument with a colonist and struck him. A crowd gathered around the soldier, throwing snowballs and shouting insults. Soon a small number of troops arrived. The crowd grew louder and angrier by the moment. Some yelled, "Come on you rascals . . . Fire if you dare!" Suddenly, the soldiers fired into the crowd, instantly killing three men, including sailor Crispus Attucks. "Half Indian, half negro, and altogether rowdy," as he was called, Attucks is the best-remembered casualty of the incident. Two others died within a few days.

Samuel Adams and other protesters quickly spread the story of the shootings. They used it as propaganda—a story giving only one side in an argument—against the British. Colonists called the shootings the **Boston Massacre**. Paul Revere created an elaborate color print titled "The Bloody Massacre perpetrated in King Street" (above).

The soldiers and their officer, Thomas Preston, were charged with murder. Two Boston lawyers, Josiah Quincy and John Adams—Samuel Adams's cousin—agreed to defend the soldiers. They argued that the troops had acted in self-defense. The Boston jury agreed, finding Preston and six soldiers not guilty. Two soldiers were convicted of killing people in the crowd by accident. These men were branded on the hand and released. The trial helped calm people down, but many were still angry at the British.

READING CHECK **Analyzing** What was the significance of the Boston Massacre?

The Road to Revolution

QUICK FACTS

Colonists reacted to British laws with anger and violence. Parliament continued to pass tax after tax.

	1764 The Sugar Act	1765 The Stamp Act
British Actions	The Sugar Act is passed to raise money from the colonies for Britain.	The Stamp Act taxes newspapers, licenses, and colonial paper products.
Colonists' Reactions	Samuel Adams founds the Committees of Correspondence to improve communication among the colonies.	A series of resolutions is published stating that the Stamp Act violates the rights of colonists.

FOCUS ON NORTH CAROLINA

The revolutionary sentiment was displayed in North Carolina at the Edenton Tea Party. In October 1774, 51 women gathered and declared they would not drink British tea until the Tea Act was repealed.

NC History Makers

Penelope Barker
Penelope Barker led the women of Edenton in the Edenton Tea Party protest.

The Boston Tea Party

To reduce tensions in the colonies, Parliament repealed almost all of the Townshend Acts. However, it kept the tax on tea. British officials knew that the colonial demand for tea was high despite the boycott. But colonial merchants were smuggling most of this imported tea and paying no duty on it.

The British East India Company offered Parliament a solution. The company had huge amounts of tea but was not allowed to sell it directly to the colonists. If the company could sell directly to the colonists, it could charge low prices and still make money. Cheaper tea might encourage colonists to stop smuggling. Less smuggling would result in more tax money.

Parliament agreed and passed the **Tea Act** in 1773, which allowed the British East India Company to sell tea directly to the colonists. Many colonial merchants and smugglers feared that the British East India Company's cheap tea would put them out of business.

Three ships loaded with tea from the British East India Company arrived in Boston Harbor in 1773. Members of the Sons of Liberty demanded that the ships leave. But the governor of Massachusetts would not let the ships leave without paying the duty. Unsure of what to do, the captains waited in the harbor.

On the night of December 16, 1773, colonists disguised as Indians sneaked onto the three tea-filled ships and dumped over 340 tea chests into Boston Harbor. This event became known as the **Boston Tea Party**. Soon the streets echoed with shouts of "Boston harbour is a teapot tonight!"

READING CHECK **Summarizing** What factors led to the Boston Tea Party?

The Intolerable Acts

Lord North, the new British prime minister, was furious when he heard the news. Parliament decided to punish Boston. In the spring of 1774 it passed the Coercive Acts. Colonists called these laws the **Intolerable Acts**. The acts had several effects.

1. Boston Harbor was closed until Boston paid for the ruined tea.
2. Massachusetts's charter was canceled. The governor decided if and when the legislature could meet.
3. Royal officials accused of crimes were sent to Britain for trial. This let them face a more friendly judge and jury.
4. A new Quartering Act required colonists to house British solders.
5. The Quebec Act gave a large amount of land to the colony of Quebec.

1770 The Boston Massacre

British soldiers fire into a crowd of colonists, killing five men.

Colonists protest and bring the soldiers to trial.

1773 The Boston Tea Party

The Tea Act is passed, making British tea cheaper than colonial tea.

Colonists protest by dumping shipments of British tea into Boston Harbor.

1774 The Intolerable Acts

Boston Harbor is closed, and British troops are quartered.

Colonists' resentment toward Britain builds.

ANALYSIS SKILL ANALYZING VISUALS

In what year did the conflict between Britain and the colonists turn violent?

6. General Thomas Gage became the new governor of Massachusetts.

The British hoped that these steps would bring back order in the colonies. Instead they simply increased people's anger at Britain.

READING CHECK **Analyzing** What was the purpose of the Intolerable Acts?

SUMMARY AND PREVIEW In this section you learned about the increasing dissatisfaction between the colonists and Great Britain. In the next chapter you'll learn about the result of these conflicts—the American Revolution.

Section 5 Assessment

go.hrw.com
Online Quiz
KEYWORD: SC7 HP3

Reviewing Ideas, Terms, and People

1. a. **Explain** Why did Great Britain raise taxes in its American colonies?
   b. **Evaluate** Which method of protesting taxes do you think was most successful for colonists? Why?
2. a. **Describe** What events led to the **Boston Massacre**?
   b. **Elaborate** Why do you think John Adams and Josiah Quincy agreed to defend the British soldiers that were involved in the Boston Massacre?
3. a. **Recall** What was the purpose of the **Tea Act**?
   b. **Draw Conclusions** What message did the **Boston Tea Party** send to the British government?
4. a. **Explain** Why did Parliament pass the **Intolerable Acts**?
   b. **Draw Conclusions** Why do you think the colonists believed that these laws were "intolerable"?

Critical Thinking

5. **Identifying Cause and Effect** Review your notes on the laws passed by the British government. Then add a new column to your chart and identify the laws' results.

Law	Result
1.	
2.	
3.	
4.	
5.	

FOCUS ON WRITING

6. **Gathering Information** Now you have some information about the political situation in Boston in the late 1700s. Why might someone from Britain want to immigrate to Boston at this time? Would you consider the city of Boston, rather than a whole colony, for the subject of your infomercial?

Social Studies Skills

Analysis | Critical Thinking | Civic Participation | Study

North Carolina Skills
1.01 Read for literal meaning.

Interpreting Time Lines

Define the Skill

Knowing the sequence, or order, in which historical events took place is important to understanding these events. Time lines visually display the sequence of events during a particular period of time. They also let you easily see time spans between events, such as how long after one event a related event took place—and what events occurred in between. In addition, comparing time lines for different places makes relationships between distant events easier to identify and understand.

Learn the Skill

Follow these guidelines to read, interpret, and compare time lines.

1. Determine each time line's framework. Note the years it covers and the periods of time into which it is divided. Be aware that a pair of time lines may not have the same framework.
2. Study the order of events on each time line. Note the length of time between events. Compare what was taking place on different time lines around the same time period.
3. Look for relationships between events. Pay particular attention to how an event on one time line might relate to an event on another.

Practice the Skill

Interpret the time lines below to answer the following questions.

1. What is each time line's framework?
2. How long was England without a king?
3. What event in England allowed the colonists to get rid of the Dominion of New England in 1689?
4. Massachusetts's independence had troubled English officials for many years. What do the time lines suggest about why this colony was allowed to remain independent until 1686?

Events in England

- 1642: Civil war breaks out between King Charles I and Parliament.
- 1649: Charles I is executed; Parliament takes power.
- 1660: Monarchy is restored; Charles II becomes king.
- 1688: Parliament overthrows King James II and puts new king on throne.

Events in the Colonies

- 1641: Massachusetts shows independence by passing own code of laws.
- 1659: Virginia pledges loyalty to Charles II as king of England.
- 1686: Massachusetts is united with other colonies in Dominion of New England by King James II.
- 1689: Colonies disband Dominion of New England and re-establish separate governments.

CHAPTER 3 Chapter Review

HOLT

History's Impact

▶ **video series**

Review the video to answer the closing question:

How does the value that Americans place on religious freedom limit government actions?

Visual Summary

QUICK FACTS

Use the visual summary below to help you review the main ideas of the chapter.

Increasing tensions between the colonies and Britain led many colonists to consider cutting ties to Britain.

- Taxation without representation
- Acts of Parliament
- Violence between colonists and British troops

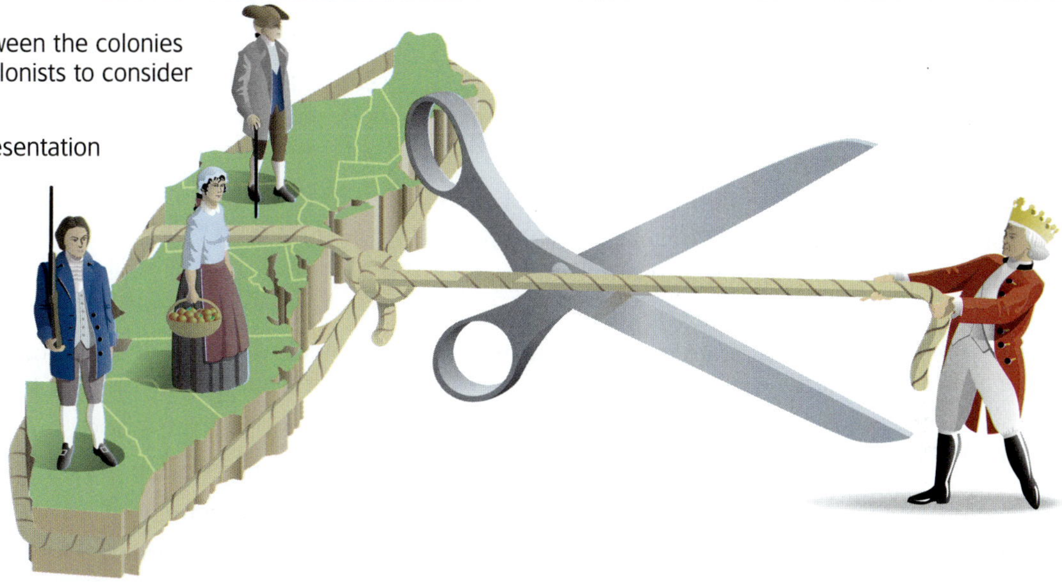

Reviewing Vocabulary, Terms, and People

Match the words in the left column with the correct definition in the right column.

1. Committees of Correspondence
2. Jonathan Edwards
3. mercantilism
4. immigrants
5. indentured servants
6. William Penn
7. Pocahontas
8. Quakers
9. staple crops
10. town meeting

a. colonists who received free passage to North America in exchange for working without pay for a certain number of years
b. created in Massachusetts, these groups helped towns and colonies share information about resisting the new British laws
c. crops that are continuously in demand
d. daughter of Powhatan chief whose marriage to colonist John Rolfe eased tensions between the Powhatan and the colonists
e. one of the leaders of the Great Awakening, he urged sinners to seek forgiveness
f. Protestant sect founded in England that believed salvation was available to all people
g. people who move to another country after leaving their homeland
h. political gathering at which people make decisions on local issues
i. Quaker leader who established a colony with the goal of fair government for all
j. system of creating and maintaining wealth through controlled trade

Comprehension and Critical Thinking

SECTION 1 *(Pages 72–77)*

11. a. Explain What problems did the settlers of Virginia face?

b. Draw Conclusions Why was Maryland's Toleration Act of 1649 important?

c. Predict How might the southern colonies' reliance on slave labor eventually cause problems?

SECTION 2 *(Pages 78–84)*

12. a. Describe On what was the economy of the New England colonies based?

b. Compare and Contrast How were the Pilgrim and Puritan colonies similar and different?

c. Evaluate Explain why you think the close ties between church and state in Massachusetts helped or hurt its government.

SECTION 3 *(Pages 85–87)*

13. a. Identify What types of crops were grown in the middle colonies?

b. Draw Conclusions Why did the middle colonies have a more diverse population than either New England or the South?

c. Elaborate Why would immigrants have chosen to live in the middle colonies?

SECTION 4 *(Pages 90–97)*

14. a. Identify What challenges did the English colonies face?

b. Analyze What effect did the Great Awakening and the Enlightenment have on the colonies?

c. Evaluate Explain which you think had a greater impact on colonial government—the passage of the English Bill of Rights or the Great Awakening.

SECTION 5 *(Pages 98–103)*

15. a. Recall Why did the British believe it was necessary to raise taxes on the American colonists?

b. Draw Conclusions How did the Boston Massacre and the Boston Tea Party affect relations between Great Britain and the colonies?

c. Evaluate Did the British government overreact to colonial protests by issuing the Intolerable Acts? Why or why not?

Reviewing Themes

16. Politics What political influences shaped the governments of the British colonies?

17. Economics How did mercantilism affect the economies of Great Britain and the colonies?

Reading Skills

Vocabulary Clues *Use the Reading Skills taught in this chapter to answer the question about the reading selection below.*

> A popular method of protest was the boycott, in which people refused to buy British goods. *(p. 99)*

18. According to the reading selection above, what is the best definition of *boycott*?

a. a popular method

b. buying British goods

c. people refusing

d. protest in which people refuse to buy goods

Social Studies Skills

Interpreting Time Lines *Use the Social Studies Skills taught in this chapter to answer the questions about the time lines on page 104.*

19. How many years after the English Civil War did Parliament overthrow King James II?

20. How many years did the Dominion of New England last?

a. 41

b. 18

c. 3

d. 6

FOCUS ON WRITING

21. Writing Your Infomercial Choose a colony and time period. Review your list of reasons why English citizens might want to live there. Then write an infomercial with at least four scenes. Each scene should have video and a voice-over telling one of the reasons for immigrating.

CHAPTER 3 Standardized Test Practice

DIRECTIONS: Read each question and write the letter of the best response.

1 **Use the map below to answer the following question.**

The red box on this map indicates which early colonial settlement?

A Plymouth
B Massachusetts Bay
C New Amsterdam
D Jamestown

2 **Which of the following is a similarity between the middle colonies and the New England colonies?**

A Both regions relied heavily on slave labor.
B Colonial governments in both regions supported public education.
C Trade was important to the economies of both regions.
D Both regions were founded by Quakers.

3 **How did Parliament's passage of the English Bill of Rights in 1689 affect England's North American colonies?**

A Colonists became more interested in being governed by representatives they elected.
B Several colonies decided to unite and formed the Dominion of New England.
C The Great Awakening took place.
D A movement to end slavery developed.

4 **What was the central issue in the dispute between Britain and its American colonies?**

A the restrictions Parliament placed on trade
B the presence of British troops in the colonies
C the colonists' right to religious freedom
D the power to tax the colonists

5 **Which of the following statements *best* describes the economy of colonial North Carolina?**

A The lack of a deepwater port prevented the development of an active trade system.
B Manufacturing and shipbuilding were vital to the economy.
C North Carolina's economy benefited greatly from piracy.
D The economy depended only on slave labor.

6 **Examine the following passage from the petition issued by the women of the Edenton Tea Party, and then use it to answer the question below.**

> "The Provincial Deputies of North Carolina, having resolved not to drink any more tea, nor wear any more British cloth, many ladies of this province have determined to give memorable proof of their patriotism, and have accordingly entered into the following honorable and spirited association."
>
> —from the *Edenton Ladies' Agreement*

Document-Based Question **Why did the women of Edenton, North Carolina, call their actions patriotic?**

CHAPTER 4 1774–1783

The American Revolution

North Carolina Standards

Social Studies Objectives

2.01 Trace the events leading up to the Revolutionary War and evaluate their relative significance in the onset of hostilities.

2.02 Describe the contributions of key North Carolina and national personalities from the Revolutionary War era and assess their influence on the outcome of the war.

2.03 Examine the role of North Carolina in the Revolutionary War.

2.04 Examine the reasons for the colonists' victory over the British, and evaluate the impact of military successes and failures, the role of foreign interventions, and on-going political and economic domestic issues.

2.05 Describe the impact of documents such as the Mecklenburg Resolves, the Halifax Resolves, the Albany Plan of Union, the Declaration of Independence, the State Constitution of 1776, the Articles of Confederation, the United States Constitution, and the Bill of Rights on the formation of the state and national governments.

9.02 Identify past and present state and local leaders from diverse cultural backgrounds and assess their influence in effecting change.

Language Arts Objectives

1.04 Reflect on learning experiences by:

- evaluating how personal perspectives are influenced by society, cultural differences, and historical issues.

3.01 Explore and evaluate argumentative works that are read, heard and/or viewed by:

- analyzing the work by identifying the arguments and positions stated or implied and the evidence used to support them.

go.hrw.com
North Carolina
KEYWORD: SC7 NC

FOCUS ON SPEAKING

Giving an Oral Report The Revolutionary War was a very exciting time in our history, a time filled with deeds of courage and daring and ending with an amazing victory for the underdog. As you read this chapter, you will learn about the great events and heroic people of that time. Then you will prepare and give an oral report on the history of the American Revolution.

UNITED STATES

1774 The First Continental Congress meets.

1775 The Revolutionary War begins with the fighting at Lexington and Concord.

1774

WORLD

HOLT

History's Impact

▶ **video series**

Watch the video to understand the impact of being able to choose your own government.

What You Will Learn...

Soldiers fight with single-shot muskets in this re-enactment of the Revolutionary War. The men in the colonial militias did not have regular uniforms like the British soldiers did. They wore their own clothes and often used their own supplies. In this chapter you will learn about the American War for Independence.

1776 On July 4 the thirteen colonies issue the Declaration of Independence and break away from Great Britain.

1781 The British surrender to George Washington at Yorktown.

1783 The Treaty of Paris is signed, ending the war.

1777 — 1780 — 1783

1778 France allies with the Americans and joins the war against Great Britain.

1779 Spain declares war against Great Britain.

1783 Simon Bolívar is born in present-day Venezuela.

Reading Social Studies

by Kylene Beers

Economics | Geography | Politics | Society and Culture | Science and Technology

Focus on Themes In this chapter you will read about the events of the Revolutionary War, the war by which the United States won its independence. You will learn about some of the major battles that occurred between the American colonists and the British army and how **geography** sometimes affected their outcomes. You will also read the Declaration of Independence, one of the most important **political** documents in all of American history.

Main Ideas in Social Studies

Focus on Reading When you are reading, it is not always necessary to remember every tiny detail of the text. Instead, what you want to remember are the main ideas, the most important concepts around which the text is based.

Identifying Main Ideas Most paragraphs in history books include main ideas. Sometimes the main idea is stated clearly in a single sentence. At other times, the main idea is suggested, not stated. However, that idea still shapes the paragraph's content and the meaning of all of the facts and details in it.

News of the work spread throughout the colonies, eventually selling some 500,000 copies. Paine reached a wide audience by writing as a common person speaking to common people. *Common Sense* changed the way many colonists viewed their king. *(p. 118)*

Topic: The paragraph is about the pamphlet *Common Sense* by Thomas Paine.

+

Facts and Details:
- Many people from different colonies read the pamphlet.
- *Common Sense* eventually sold 500,000 copies.
- Thomas Paine's writing style was easy for the common people to read.

Main Idea: The pamphlet *Common Sense* shaped the way some colonists thought about their rulers.

Steps in Identifying Main Ideas

1. Read the paragraph. Ask yourself, "What is this paragraph mostly about?" This will be the topic of the paragraph.
2. List the important facts and details that relate to that topic.
3. Ask yourself, "What seems to be the most important point the writer is making about the topic?" Or ask, "If the writer could say only one thing about this paragraph, what would it be?" This is the **main idea** of the paragraph.

You Try It!

The following passage is from the chapter you are about to read. Read it and then answer the questions below.

The Treaty of Paris

From Chapter 4, p. 139

After Yorktown, only a few small battles took place. Lacking the money to pay for a new army, Great Britain entered into peace talks with America. Benjamin Franklin had an influential role in the negotiations.

Delegates took more than two years to come to a peace agreement. In the Treaty of Paris of 1783, Great Britain recognized the independence of the United States. The treaty also set America's borders. A separate treaty between Britain and Spain returned Florida to the Spanish. British leaders also accepted American rights to settle and trade west of the original thirteen colonies.

After you have read the passage, answer the following questions.

1. The main idea of the second paragraph is stated in a sentence. Which sentence expresses the main idea?

2. What is the first paragraph about? What facts and details are included in the paragraph? Based on your answers to these questions, what is the main idea of the first paragraph?

As you read Chapter 4, identify the main ideas of the paragraphs you are reading.

Key Terms and People

Chapter 4

Section 1

First Continental Congress *(p. 112)*
Patriots *(p. 113)*
minutemen *(p. 114)*
Redcoats *(p. 114)*
Second Continental Congress *(p. 114)*
Continental Army *(p. 114)*
George Washington *(p. 114)*
Battle of Bunker Hill *(p. 115)*

Section 2

Common Sense *(p. 118)*
Thomas Paine *(p. 118)*
Declaration of Independence *(p. 119)*
Thomas Jefferson *(p. 119)*
Loyalists *(p. 119)*

Section 3

mercenaries *(p. 128)*
Battle of Trenton *(p.129)*
Battle of Saratoga *(p. 130)*
Marquis de Lafayette *(p. 131)*
Baron Friedrich von Steuben *(p. 131)*
Bernardo de Gálvez *(p. 131)*
John Paul Jones *(p. 133)*
George Rogers Clark *(p. 133)*

Section 4

Francis Marion *(p. 136)*
Comte de Rochambeau *(p. 137)*
Battle of Yorktown *(p. 137)*
Treaty of Paris of 1783 *(p. 139)*

Academic Vocabulary

Success in school is related to knowing academic vocabulary—the words that are frequently used in school assignments and discussions. In this chapter, you will learn the following academic words:

reaction *(p. 114)*
strategy *(p. 129)*

SECTION 1

The Revolution Begins

What You Will Learn...

Main Ideas

1. The First Continental Congress demanded certain rights from Great Britain.
2. Armed conflict between British soldiers and colonists broke out with the "shot heard 'round the world."
3. The Second Continental Congress created the Continental Army to fight the British.
4. In two early battles, the army lost control of Boston but then regained it.

The Big Idea

The tensions between the colonies and Great Britain led to armed conflict in 1775.

Key Terms and People

First Continental Congress, *p. 112*
Patriots, *p. 113*
minutemen, *p. 114*
Redcoats, *p. 114*
Second Continental Congress, *p. 114*
Continental Army, *p. 114*
George Washington, *p. 114*
Battle of Bunker Hill, *p. 115*

TAKING NOTES As you read, take notes on the events that occurred in the early days of the American Revolution. Write your notes in a graphic organizer like the one below.

First Continental Congress	Battles	Second Continental Congress

If YOU were there...

You are a member of the British Parliament in the 1770s. Some members say that the Americans are defying the king. Others point out that the colonists are British citizens who have certain rights. Now the king must decide to punish the rebellious colonists or listen to their complaints.

What advice would you give the king?

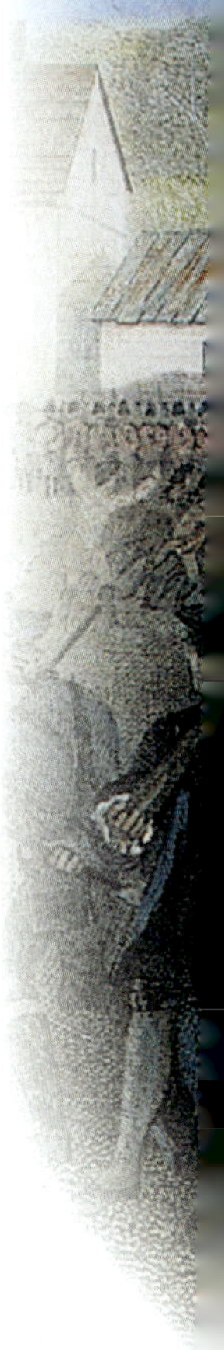

BUILDING BACKGROUND Taxes and harsh new laws led some colonists to protest against the British. In some places, the protests turned violent. The British government refused to listen, ignoring the colonists' demands for more rights. That set the stage for war.

First Continental Congress

To many colonists the closing of Boston Harbor was the final insult. In August 1774 the first anti-British assembly to meet in the colonies was held in New Bern, North Carolina. Two months later, representatives from every colony except Georgia met to discuss the idea of independence. This meeting, known as the **First Continental Congress**, was a gathering of colonial leaders who were deeply troubled about the relationship between Great Britain and its colonies in America. At Carpenters' Hall in Philadelphia, the leaders remained locked in weeks of intense debate. Patrick Henry and others believed that violence was unavoidable. On the other hand, delegates from Pennsylvania and New York had strict orders to seek peace.

Wisely, the delegates compromised. They encouraged colonists to continue boycotting British goods but told colonial militias to prepare for war. Meanwhile, they drafted the Declaration of Rights, a list of 10 resolutions to be presented to King George III. Included was the colonists' right to "life, liberty, and property."

The First Continental Congress did not seek a separation from Britain. Its goal was to state the colonists' concerns and ask the king to correct the problems. But before they left Philadelphia, the delegates agreed to meet in 1775 if the king refused their petition.

Patrick Henry returned from the Congress and reported to his

Battle of Lexington

The Battle of Lexington was the first battle of the Revolutionary War. The map shows the route that Paul Revere used to warn the minutemen of Lexington. He was captured before he could get to Concord. The photo below shows one of the actual candle lanterns used to signal Revere.

fellow Virginians. To encourage them to support the Patriot cause, Henry voiced these famous words:

> "They tell us, Sir, that we are weak; unable to cope with so formidable an adversary. But when will we be stronger? Gentlemen may cry, Peace, Peace—but there is no peace. I know not what course others may take; but as for me, give me liberty or give me death."
>
> —Patrick Henry, quoted in *Eyewitnesses and Others*

In time many colonists came to agree with Henry. They became known as **Patriots**—colonists who chose to fight for independence from Great Britain.

READING CHECK **Identifying Cause and Effect** Why did the delegates attend the First Continental Congress? What were the results?

"Shot Heard 'round the World"

The Continental Congress planned to meet again in 1775. Before it could, the situation in the colonies had changed—for the worse.

The Ride of Paul Revere

British military leaders in the colonies grew uneasy when local militias seemed to be preparing for action. The governor of Massachusetts, Thomas Gage, learned that a stockpile of weapons was stored in Concord, about 20 miles from Boston. In April 1775 he decided to seize the supplies.

Gage thought he had kept his plan a secret. However, Boston was full of spies for the Patriot cause. They noticed the British were preparing for action and quickly informed the Patriots. Unsure of how the British would strike, Sons of Liberty member Paul Revere enlisted the aid of Robert Newman. Newman was to climb into the steeple of the Old North Church and watch for British soldiers. If they advanced across land, Newman would display one lantern from the steeple. If they rowed across the Charles River, Newman would display two lanterns.

When Revere and fellow Patriot William Dawes saw two lights shine, they set off on horseback. Using two different routes out of Boston, they sounded the alert. As the riders advanced, drums and church bells called out the local militia, or **minutemen**—who got their name because they were ready to fight at a minute's notice.

FOCUS ON NORTH CAROLINA

In May 1775 a committee in Charlotte passed the Mecklenburg Resolves, a series of resolutions that declared British laws "null and void" and set up new laws for the colony. Although the document did not declare independence from Britain, it implied it. It was the first such document in the colonies.

Battles at Lexington and Concord

At dawn on April 19, the British troops arrived at the town of Lexington, near Concord, where 70 armed minutemen waited. Patriot captain John Parker yelled to his troops, "Don't fire unless fired upon." Suddenly a shot rang out. To this day, no one knows who fired this "shot heard 'round the world."

The battle at Lexington ended in minutes with only a few volleys fired. When the smoke cleared, 8 of the badly outnumbered minutemen lay dead, and 10 were wounded. The British, with only one soldier wounded, marched on to Concord.

Although Revere had been arrested, the citizens of Concord were warned by another rider, Samuel Prescott. Most of the weapons in Concord had already been hidden, but the few that were left were now concealed. Some of the British troops, frustrated because the stockpile had disappeared, set fire to a few buildings. In reaction the minutemen charged forward.

ACADEMIC VOCABULARY

reaction
response

For the skilled colonial marksmen of Concord, the British soldiers made an easy target. They were wearing the British military uniform with its bright red jacket. For some time the colonists had called the British soldiers **Redcoats** because of these jackets. The British were forced to retreat to Boston, suffering many casualties along the way.

READING CHECK **Drawing Inferences** Why did the Patriots need several riders? Why did they take different routes?

Second Continental Congress

King George III had refused to address the concerns listed in the Declaration of Rights. In May 1775, delegates from 12 colonies met again in Philadelphia for the **Second Continental Congress**. This second group of delegates from the colonies was still far from unified, but represented the first attempt at a Republican government in the colonies.

Some of the delegates called for a war, others for peace. Once again they compromised. Although the Congress did not openly revolt, delegates showed their growing dissatisfaction. They sent word to colonial authorities asking for new state constitutions. States set up conventions to write them. They also authorized the Massachusetts militia to become the **Continental Army**. This force would soon include soldiers from all colonies and would carry out the fight against Britain. Congress named a Virginian, **George Washington**, to command the army.

As Washington prepared for war, the Congress pursued peace. On July 5 the delegates signed the Olive Branch Petition as a final attempt to restore harmony. King George refused to read it. Instead, he looked for new ways to punish the colonies.

READING CHECK **Summarizing** What did the Second Continental Congress accomplish?

Early Battles

While the Congress discussed peace, the Massachusetts militia began to fight. Boston was a key city in the early days of the war. Both Patriots and the British fought to hold it.

Bunker Hill

Desperate for supplies, leaders in Boston sent Benedict Arnold and a force of 400 men to New York State. Their objective was to attack the British at Fort Ticonderoga. In May 1775, Arnold captured the fort and its large supply of weapons.

Meanwhile, the poorly supplied Patriots kept the British pinned down inside Boston. Although British leaders were trying to form a battle plan, they awoke on June 17 to a stunning sight. The colonial forces had quietly dug in at Breed's Hill, a point overlooking north Boston. The Redcoats would have to cross Boston Harbor and fight their way uphill.

As the British force of 2,400 advanced, 1,600 militia members waited. Low on gunpowder, the commander ordered his troops not to fire "until you see the whites of their eyes." As they climbed the exposed hillside with their heavy packs, the British soldiers were cut down. Twice they retreated. Stepping over the dead and wounded, they returned for a third try. The colonists were now out of ammunition, and eventually they had to retreat.

This famous conflict is now known as the **Battle of Bunker Hill**, although it was actually launched from Breed's Hill. While the Patriots lost, they proved they could take on the Redcoats. For the British, the battle was a tragic victory. To win, they had sacrificed about double the number of Patriot soldiers.

NC History Makers

Robert Howe
Robert Howe served as the highest-ranking officer from North Carolina during the Revolutionary War.

GEOGRAPHY SKILLS INTERPRETING MAPS

1. **Place** What geographic advantage did control of Boston provide?
2. **Movement** How did British troops retreat from Boston? How can you tell?

FOCUS ON NORTH CAROLINA

The Battle of Moore's Creek Bridge was the first battle of the Revolution in North Carolina. It occurred in February 1776 and was a Patriot victory against a force of Loyalist Scottish Highlanders.

Dorchester Heights

Shortly after the Battle of Bunker Hill, General Washington arrived in Boston to command the Continental Army. Washington knew that he would need heavier guns to drive the British out of Boston, and he knew where to get them—Fort Ticonderoga. Colonel Henry Knox was assigned to transport the captured cannons from Fort Ticonderoga to Boston. He successfully brought the heavy guns over 300 miles of rough terrain in the middle of winter. When Knox delivered the cannons, Washington was ready to regain control of Boston.

On March 4, 1776, Washington moved his army to Dorchester Heights, an area that overlooked Boston from the south. He stationed the cannons and his troops on Nook's Hill overlooking British general William Howe's position. When Howe awoke the next morning and saw the Patriots' well-positioned artillery, he knew he would have to retreat. "The Rebels have done more in one night than my whole army could do in months," Howe declared. On March 7 Howe retreated from Boston to Canada. The birthplace of the rebellion was now in Patriot hands.

READING CHECK **Drawing Inferences** Why was the geography of the Boston area important in forming a battle plan?

SUMMARY AND PREVIEW Some colonial leaders became convinced that they could not avoid war with Great Britain. In the next section you will read about another step toward war—the writing of the Declaration of Independence.

Section 1 Assessment

go.hrw.com
Online Quiz
KEYWORD: SC7 HP4

Reviewing Ideas, Terms, and People

1. a. **Identify** What was the **First Continental Congress**?
   b. **Make Inferences** Why did the First Continental Congress send the Declaration of Rights to the king?
   c. **Elaborate** Why did King George III refuse to consider the colonists' declaration?
2. a. **Identify** Who warned the colonists of the British advance toward Lexington and Concord?
   b. **Analyze** Why did the British army march on Lexington and Concord?
   c. **Elaborate** What is meant by the expression "shot heard 'round the world"?
3. a. **Describe** What was the purpose of the **Second Continental Congress**?
   b. **Draw Conclusions** Were the delegates to the Second Continental Congress ready to revolt against George III? Explain.
   c. **Evaluate** Defend George III's response to the Declaration of Rights and the Olive Branch Petition.
4. a. **Identify** What leader captured Fort Ticonderoga?
   b. **Draw Conclusions** How was the **Continental Army** able to drive British forces out of Boston?
   c. **Evaluate** How would you evaluate the performance of the Continental Army in the early battles of the war? Explain.

Critical Thinking

5. **Categorizing** Review your notes on the early battles of the Revolution. Then copy the graphic organizer below and use it to categorize events in the early days of the Revolution. Some events will be attempts at peace; others will be movement toward war.

Attempts at Peace	Movement toward War

FOCUS ON SPEAKING

6. **Thinking about the Beginning** You'll have about five minutes for your report and only a minute or two to talk about the beginning of the war. What are the one or two most important things you want to say?

BIOGRAPHY

George Washington

What would you do if you were asked to lead a new country?

When did he live? 1732–1799

Where did he live? George Washington was a true American, born in the Virginia colony. As president, he lived in New York City and Philadelphia, the nation's first two capitals. When he retired, he returned to his plantation at Mount Vernon.

What did he do? Although Washington was a wealthy farmer, he spent most of his life in the military and in politics. Leading the colonial forces to victory in the Revolutionary War, he then helped shape the new government of the United States. On April 30, 1789, he was sworn in as the first president of the United States.

Why is he so important? George Washington inspired Americans and helped to unite them. One of his great accomplishments as president was to keep the peace with Britain and France. Upon leaving the presidency, he urged Americans to avoid becoming politically divided.

Drawing Conclusions How might Washington's leadership in the Revolutionary War have prepared him for his role as president?

KEY EVENTS

- **1775** Serves in Second Continental Congress; selected commander of the Continental Army
- **1789** Inaugurated as president
- **1793** Begins second term as president
- **1796** Publishes his Farewell Address and retires to his plantation at Mount Vernon
- **1799** Dies at Mount Vernon; his will frees his slaves

Mount Vernon was Washington's plantation.

SECTION 2

Declaring Independence

What You Will Learn...

Main Ideas

1. Thomas Paine's *Common Sense* led many colonists to support independence.
2. Colonists had to choose sides when independence was declared.
3. The Declaration of Independence did not address the rights of all colonists.

The Big Idea

The colonies formally declared their independence from Great Britain.

Key Terms and People

Common Sense, *p. 118*
Thomas Paine, *p. 118*
Declaration of Independence, *p. 119*
Thomas Jefferson, *p. 119*
Loyalists, *p. 119*

TAKING NOTES As you read, take notes on the Declaration of Independence. Write your notes in a graphic organizer like the one below.

Influence of *Common Sense* on Declaration	Main Ideas of Declaration	People Not Included

If YOU were there...

You live on a farm in New York in 1776. The conflicts with the British have torn your family apart. Your father is loyal to King George and wants to remain British. But your mother is a fierce Patriot, and your brother wants to join the Continental Army. Your father and others who feel the same way are moving to British-held Canada. Now you must decide what you will do.

Would you go to Canada or support the Patriots?

BUILDING BACKGROUND The outbreak of violence at Lexington, Concord, and Boston took some colonists by surprise. Many, like the father above, opposed independence from Britain. Those who supported freedom began to promote their cause in many ways.

Paine's *Common Sense*

"[There] is something very absurd in supporting a continent to be perpetually [forever] governed by an island." This plainspoken argument against British rule over America appeared in ***Common Sense***, a 47-page pamphlet that was distributed in Philadelphia in January 1776. *Common Sense* was published anonymously—that is, without the author's name. The author, **Thomas Paine**, argued that citizens, not kings and queens, should make laws. At a time when monarchs ruled much of the world, this was a bold idea.

News of the work spread throughout the colonies, eventually selling some 500,000 copies. Paine reached a wide audience by writing as a common person speaking to common people. *Common Sense* changed the way many colonists viewed their king. It made a strong case for economic freedom and for the right to military self-defense. It cried out against tyranny—that is, the abuse of government power. Thomas Paine's words rang out in his time, and they have echoed throughout American history.

READING CHECK **Supporting a Point of View** Would you have agreed with Thomas Paine? Explain.

Independence Is Declared

Many colonial leaders agreed with Paine. In June 1776 the Second Continental Congress formed a committee to write a document declaring the colonies' independence. A committee also created a seal for the new country with the Latin motto "*E pluribus unum*" or "out of many, one." This motto recognized the new union of states.

A New Philosophy of Government

The **Declaration of Independence** formally announced the colonies' break from Great Britain. In doing so, it expressed three main ideas. First, **Thomas Jefferson**, the document's main author, argued that all people possess unalienable rights, including the rights of "life, liberty, and the pursuit of happiness."

Next, Jefferson asserted that King George III had violated the colonists' rights by taxing them without their consent. Jefferson accused the king of passing unfair laws and interfering with colonial governments. He also believed that stationing a large British army within the colonies was a burden.

Third, Jefferson stated that the colonies had the right to break from Britain. Influenced by the Enlightenment ideal of the social contract, he maintained that governments and rulers must protect the rights of citizens. In exchange, the people agree to be governed. Jefferson argued that King George III had broken the social contract.

On July 4, 1776, the Continental Congress approved the Declaration of Independence. This act broke all ties to the British crown. The United States of America was born.

Choosing Sides

The signing of the Declaration made the rebellion a full-scale revolt against Britain. Those who supported it would be considered traitors. Colonists who chose to side with the British were known as **Loyalists**—often called Tories.

NC History Makers

Three North Carolinians, William Hooper, Joseph Hewes, and John Penn, signed the Declaration of Independence.

THE IMPACT TODAY

The Continental Congress voted for independence on July 2. However, because the Declaration was not approved until July 4, the fourth is celebrated today as Independence Day.

Primary Source

HISTORIC DOCUMENT

The Halifax Resolves

On April 12, 1776, North Carolina's Fourth Provincial Congress at Halifax authorized delegates to the Second Continental Congress to vote for independence from Britain. The passing of the Halifax Resolves became the first official action calling for independence in the English colonies.

It appears to your Committee that pursuant to the Plan concerted [put forth] by the British Ministry for subjugating America, the King and Parliament of Great Britain have usurped [taken] a Power over the Persons and Properties of the People unlimited and uncontrouled and disregarding their humble Petitions for Peace, Liberty and safety, have made divers [a variety of] Legislative acts, denouncing War Famine and every Species of Calamity [disaster] daily employed in destroying the People and committing the most horrid devastations on the Country.

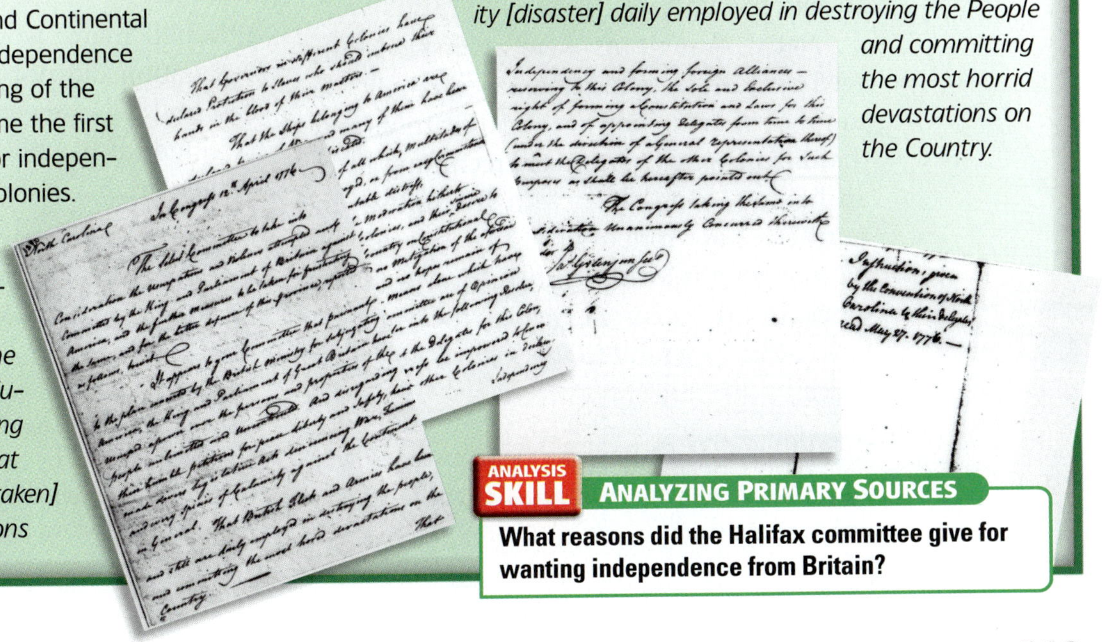

ANALYSIS SKILL ANALYZING PRIMARY SOURCES

What reasons did the Halifax committee give for wanting independence from Britain?

Signing the Declaration of Independence

Historians estimate that 40 to 45 percent of Americans were Patriots, while 20 to 30 percent were Loyalists. The rest were neutral.

Because of persecution by Patriots, more than 50,000 Loyalists fled the colonies during the Revolution. Most went to Canada, where Britain allowed them more self-rule after the Revolution. In doing so, they abandoned their homes and property. Divided allegiances tore apart families and friendships—even Benjamin Franklin became separated from his Loyalist son William.

Native Americans were at first encouraged by both sides to remain neutral. By the summer of 1776, however, both Patriots and the British were aggressively recruiting Indian fighters. Most sided with the British. In northern New York, four of the six Iroquois nations fought for the British. However, the Oneida and Tuscarora helped the Patriots, even delivering food to the soldiers at Valley Forge.

READING CHECK **Drawing Conclusions** Why would Native Americans have lost out no matter who won the war?

Unfinished Business

Today we recognize that the Declaration of Independence excluded many colonists. While it declared that "all men are created equal," the document failed to mention women, enslaved Africans, or Native Americans. The rights of these minorities would be subject to the rule of the majority.

Women

Although many women were Patriots, the Declaration did not address their rights. At least one delegate's wife, Abigail Adams, tried to influence her husband, John, to include women's rights in the Declaration. In a failed effort, she expressed her concerns:

> "Remember the Ladies, and be more generous and favorable to them than your ancestors. Do not put such unlimited power into the hands of the Husbands . . . If particular care and attention is not paid to the Ladies we are and will not hold ourselves bound by Laws in which we have no voice, or Representation."
>
> —Abigail Adams, quoted in *Notable American Women*

The Declaration of Independence was adopted on July 4, 1776. This painting shows 47 of the 56 signers of the document. The man sitting on the right is John Hancock, who was the president of the Second Continental Congress. He is accepting the Declaration from the committee that wrote it.

How realistic do you think this painting is?

African and Native Americans

The Declaration did not recognize the rights of enslaved Africans, either. The authors had compared life under British rule to living as an enslaved people. The obvious question arose: Why did any form of slavery exist in a land that valued personal freedom? Even Thomas Jefferson, the main author of the Declaration, was a slaveholder.

In July 1776 slavery was legal in all the colonies. By the 1780s the New England colonies were taking steps to end slavery. Even so, the conflict over slavery continued long after the Revolutionary War.

The Declaration of Independence also did not address the rights of Native Americans to life, liberty, or property. Despite the Proclamation of 1763, American colonists had been quietly settling on lands that belonged to Native Americans. This tendency to disregard the rights of Native Americans would develop into a pattern after the colonists won their independence from Great Britain.

READING CHECK **Finding Main Ideas** What groups were unrepresented in the Declaration of Independence?

SUMMARY AND PREVIEW In 1776 the colonists declared their independence. To achieve their goal, however, they would have to win a war against the British army. In the next section you will learn about some of the battles of the Revolutionary War. For a time, it seemed as if the British would defeat the colonists.

Section 2 Assessment

go.hrw.com
Online Quiz
KEYWORD: SC7 HP4

Reviewing Ideas, Terms, and People

1. **a. Identify** Who was **Thomas Paine**?
   b. Make Inferences Why do you think Thomas Paine originally published ***Common Sense*** anonymously?
   c. Elaborate Do you think that most colonists would have supported independence from Britain without Thomas Paine's publication of *Common Sense*? Explain.
2. **a. Identify** What two sides emerged in response to the **Declaration of Independence**? What did each side favor?
   b. Explain What arguments did the authors of the Declaration of Independence give for declaring the colonies free from British control?
   c. Predict How might some groups use the Declaration of Independence in the future to gain rights?
3. **a. Identify** Who urged her husband to "remember the ladies"?
   b. Making Inferences Why did the authors of the Declaration of Independence fail to address the rights of women, Native Americans, and African Americans in the document?

Critical Thinking

4. **Analyzing** Review your notes on the Declaration of Independence. Then copy the graphic organizer below and use it to identify three results of the Declaration of Independence.

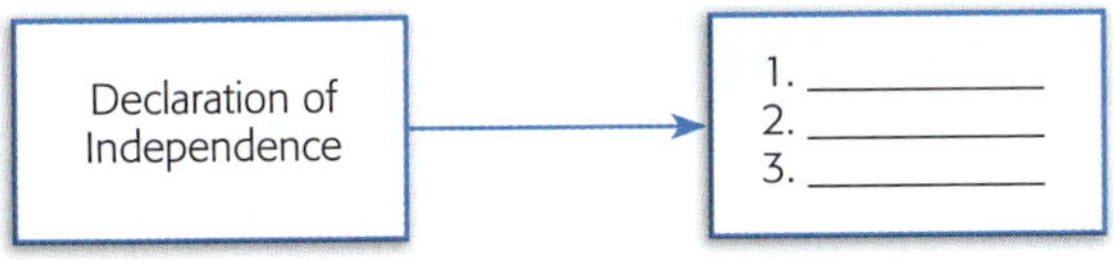

FOCUS ON SPEAKING

5. **Gathering Ideas about the Declaration of Independence** You are living at the time of the American Revolution. What is new and surprising about the colonists' actions? In one or two minutes, what is the most important thing you can say about the colonies' declaring independence?

The Declaration of Independence

EXPLORING THE DOCUMENT Thomas Jefferson wrote the first draft of the Declaration in a little more than two weeks. **How is the Declaration's idea about why governments are formed still important to our country today?**

Vocabulary

impel force

endowed provided

usurpations wrongful seizures of power

evinces clearly displays

despotism unlimited power

tyranny oppressive power exerted by a government or ruler

candid fair

In Congress, July 4, 1776
The unanimous Declaration of the thirteen united States of America,

When in the Course of human events, it becomes necessary for one people to dissolve the political bands which have connected them with another, and to assume among the Powers of the earth, the separate and equal station to which the Laws of Nature and of Nature's God entitle them, a decent respect to the opinions of mankind requires that they should declare the causes which **impel** them to the separation.

We hold these truths to be self-evident, that all men are created equal, that they are **endowed** by their Creator with certain unalienable Rights, that among these are Life, Liberty, and the pursuit of Happiness. That to secure these rights, Governments are instituted among Men, deriving their just powers from the consent of the governed, That whenever any Form of Government becomes destructive of these ends, it is the Right of the People to alter or to abolish it, and to institute new Government, laying its foundation on such principles and organizing its powers in such form, as to them shall seem most likely to effect their Safety and Happiness. Prudence, indeed, will dictate that Governments long established should not be changed for light and transient causes; and accordingly all experience hath shown, that mankind are more disposed to suffer, while evils are sufferable, than to right themselves by abolishing the forms to which they are accustomed. But when a long train of abuses and **usurpations**, pursuing invariably the same Object **evinces** a design to reduce them under absolute **Despotism**, it is their right, it is their duty, to throw off such Government, and to provide new Guards for their future security.—Such has been the patient sufferance of these Colonies; and such is now the necessity which constrains them to alter their former Systems of Government. The history of the present King of Great Britain is a history of repeated injuries and usurpations, all having in direct object the establishment of an absolute **Tyranny** over these States. To prove this, let Facts be submitted to a **candid** world.

EXPLORING THE DOCUMENT Here the Declaration lists the charges that the colonists had against King George III. **How does the language in the list appeal to people's emotions?**

He has refused his Assent to Laws, the most wholesome and necessary for the public good.

He has forbidden his Governors to pass Laws of immediate and pressing importance, unless suspended in their operation till his Assent should be obtained; and when so suspended, he has utterly neglected to attend to them.

He has refused to pass other Laws for the accommodation of large districts of people, unless those people would **relinquish** the right of Representation in the Legislature, a right **inestimable** to them and **formidable** to tyrants only.

He has called together legislative bodies at places unusual, uncomfortable, and distant from the depository of their Public Records, for the sole purpose of fatiguing them into compliance with his measures.

He has dissolved Representative Houses repeatedly, for opposing with manly firmness his invasions on the rights of the people.

He has refused for a long time, after such dissolutions, to cause others to be elected; whereby the Legislative Powers, incapable of **Annihilation**, have returned to the People at large for their exercise; the State remaining in the mean time exposed to all the dangers of invasion from without, and **convulsions** within.

He has endeavored to prevent the population of these States; for that purpose obstructing the Laws of **Naturalization of Foreigners**; refusing to pass others to encourage their migration hither, and raising the conditions of new **Appropriations of Lands**.

He has obstructed the Administration of Justice, by refusing his Assent to Laws for establishing Judiciary Powers.

He has made Judges dependent on his Will alone, for the **tenure** of their offices, and the amount and payment of their salaries.

He has erected **a multitude of** New Offices, and sent hither swarms of Officers to harass our people, and eat out their substance.

He has kept among us, in times of peace, Standing Armies without the Consent of our legislature.

He has affected to render the Military independent of and superior to the Civil Power.

He has combined with others to subject us to a jurisdiction foreign to our constitution, and unacknowledged by our laws; giving his Assent to their Acts of pretended legislation:

For **quartering** large bodies of armed troops among us:

For protecting them, by a mock Trial, from Punishment for any Murders which they should commit on the Inhabitants of these States:

For cutting off our Trade with all parts of the world:

For imposing taxes on us without our Consent:

For depriving us in many cases, of the benefits of Trial by Jury:

Vocabulary

relinquish release, yield
inestimable priceless
formidable causing dread
annihilation destruction
convulsions violent disturbances
naturalization of foreigners the process by which foreign-born persons become citizens
appropriations of lands setting aside land for settlement
tenure term
a multitude of many
quartering lodging, housing

Mum Bett, a Massachusetts slave, believed that the words "all men are created equal" should apply to her and other enslaved Africans. She successfully sued for her freedom in 1781.

For transporting us beyond Seas to be tried for pretended offences:

For abolishing the free System of English Laws in a neighboring Province, establishing therein an **Arbitrary** government, and enlarging its Boundaries so as to **render** it at once an example and fit instrument for introducing the same absolute rule into these Colonies:

For taking away our Charters, abolishing our most valuable Laws, and altering fundamentally the Forms of our Governments:

For suspending our own Legislature, and declaring themselves invested with Power to legislate for us in all cases whatsoever.

He has **abdicated** Government here, by declaring us out of his Protection and waging War against us.

He has plundered our seas, ravaged our Coasts, burnt our towns, and destroyed the lives of our people.

He is at this time transporting large armies of **foreign mercenaries** to complete the works of death, desolation and tyranny, already begun with circumstances of Cruelty & **perfidy** scarcely paralleled in the most barbarous ages, and totally unworthy the Head of a civilized nation.

He has constrained our fellow Citizens taken Captive on the high Seas to bear Arms against their Country, to become the executioners of their friends and Brethren, or to fall themselves by their Hands.

He has excited domestic **insurrections** amongst us, and has endeavored to bring on the inhabitants of our frontiers, the merciless Indian Savages, whose known rule of warfare, is an undistinguished destruction of all ages, sexes and conditions.

In every stage of these Oppressions We have **Petitioned for Redress** in the most humble terms: Our repeated Petitions have been answered only by repeated injury. A Prince, whose character is thus marked by every act which may define a Tyrant, is unfit to be the ruler of a free People.

Nor have We been wanting in attention to our British brethren. We have warned them from time to time of attempts by their legislature to extend an **unwarrantable jurisdiction** over us. We have reminded them of the circumstances of our emigration and settlement here. We have appealed to their native justice and **magnanimity**, and we have **conjured** them by the ties of our common kindred to disavow these usurpations, which, would inevitably interrupt our connections and correspondence. They too have been deaf to the voice of justice and of **consanguinity**. We must, therefore, **acquiesce** in the necessity, which denounces our Separation, and hold them, as we hold the rest of mankind, Enemies in War, in Peace Friends.

Vocabulary

arbitrary not based on law

render make

abdicated given up

foreign mercenaries soldiers hired to fight for a country not their own

perfidy violation of trust

insurrections rebellions

petitioned for redress asked formally for a correction of wrongs

unwarrantable jurisdiction unjustified authority

magnanimity generous spirit

conjured urgently called upon

consanguinity common ancestry

acquiesce consent to

EXPLORING THE DOCUMENT Here the Declaration calls the king a tyrant. **What do you think *tyrant* means in this passage?**

We, therefore, the Representatives of the united States of America, in General Congress, Assembled, appealing to the Supreme Judge of the world for the **rectitude** of our intentions, do, in the Name, and by Authority of the good People of these Colonies, solemnly publish and declare, That these United Colonies are, and of Right ought to be Free and Independent States; that they are Absolved from all Allegiance to the British Crown, and that all political connection between them and the State of Great Britain, is and ought to be totally dissolved; and that as Free and Independent States, they have full Power to levy War, conclude Peace, contract Alliances, establish Commerce, and to do all other Acts and Things which Independent States may of right do. And for the support of this Declaration, with a firm reliance on the Protection of Divine Providence, we mutually pledge to each other our Lives, our Fortunes and our sacred Honor.

John Hancock
Button Gwinnett
Lyman Hall
George Walton
William Hooper
Joseph Hewes
John Penn
Edward Rutledge
Thomas Heyward, Jr.
Thomas Lynch, Jr.
Arthur Middleton
Samuel Chase
William Paca
Thomas Stone
Charles Carroll of Carrollton
George Wythe
Richard Henry Lee
Thomas Jefferson

Benjamin Harrison
Thomas Nelson, Jr.
Francis Lightfoot Lee
Carter Braxton
Robert Morris
Benjamin Rush
Benjamin Franklin
John Morton
George Clymer
James Smith
George Taylor
James Wilson
George Ross
Caesar Rodney
George Read
Thomas McKean
William Floyd
Philip Livingston
Francis Lewis

Lewis Morris
Richard Stockton
John Witherspoon
Francis Hopkinson
John Hart
Abraham Clark
Josiah Bartlett
William Whipple
Samuel Adams
John Adams
Robert Treat Paine
Elbridge Gerry
Stephen Hopkins
William Ellery
Roger Sherman
Samuel Huntington
William Williams
Oliver Wolcott
Matthew Thornton

Vocabulary

rectitude rightness

EXPLORING THE DOCUMENT Here is where the document declares the independence of the colonies. **Whose authority does the Congress use to declare independence?**

EXPLORING THE DOCUMENT The Congress adopted the final draft of the Declaration of Independence on July 4, 1776. A formal copy, written on parchment paper, was signed on August 2, 1776. **From whom did the Declaration's signers receive their authority to declare independence?**

EXPLORING THE DOCUMENT The following is part of a passage that the Congress removed from Jefferson's original draft: "He has waged cruel war against human nature itself, violating its most sacred rights of life and liberty in the persons of a distant people who never offended him, captivating and carrying them into slavery in another hemisphere, or to incur miserable death in their transportation thither." **Why do you think the Congress deleted this passage?**

SECTION 3

The Struggle for Liberty

What You Will Learn...

Main Ideas

1. Many Americans supported the war effort.
2. The Patriots both won and lost battles during the years 1775–1777.
3. France and Spain helped the Patriots fight the British.
4. The winter at Valley Forge tested the strength of Patriot troops.
5. The war continued at sea and in the West.

The Big Idea

Patriot forces faced many obstacles in the war against Britain.

Key Terms and People

mercenaries, *p. 128*
Battle of Trenton, *p. 129*
Battle of Saratoga, *p. 130*
Marquis de Lafayette, *p. 131*
Baron Friedrich von Steuben, *p. 131*
Bernardo de Gálvez, *p. 131*
John Paul Jones, *p. 133*
George Rogers Clark, *p. 133*

TAKING NOTES Create a time line like the one below. As you read, identify and describe the events occurring on each of the dates listed on your time line.

June 1776	Nov. 1776	Dec. 1776	Jan. 1777	Oct. 1777	May 1778	Sept. 1779

If YOU were there...

You are a serving maid at an inn in New York City. British soldiers often stop at the inn for a meal. You sometimes overhear their conversations, though they don't notice you. Now a Patriot leader has asked you to bring him any information you hear. You want to help the Patriot cause but wonder what will happen if you are caught spying.

Would you agree to spy for the Patriots?

BUILDING BACKGROUND Many colonists struggled for the Patriot cause. Men, women, and children all made important contributions. They fought, kept farms and shops running, and provided food and supplies. In spite of their efforts, winning the war was a great challenge.

Supporting the War Effort

George Washington's chief task as the Continental Army's commander in chief was to raise troops. During the war, more than 230,000 soldiers served in the Continental Army, and another 145,000 enlisted in local militias. The typical soldier was young, often under the legal age of 16, and had little money or property. The army offered low pay, harsh conditions, and a big chance of becoming a casualty. Yet the Patriots knew they were fighting for their homes and their freedom.

Finding and keeping dedicated soldiers would be a constant challenge throughout the war. In time, the Continental Congress required states to supply soldiers. Men who could afford it often paid others, such as slaves or apprentices, to fight in their places.

One question facing General Washington was whether to recruit African Americans. Many white southerners opposed the idea, and at first Washington banned African Americans from serving. When the British promised freedom to any slave who fought on their side, however, thousands of African Americans joined the Redcoats.

Interactive Map
Battles in the Middle Colonies, 1776–77

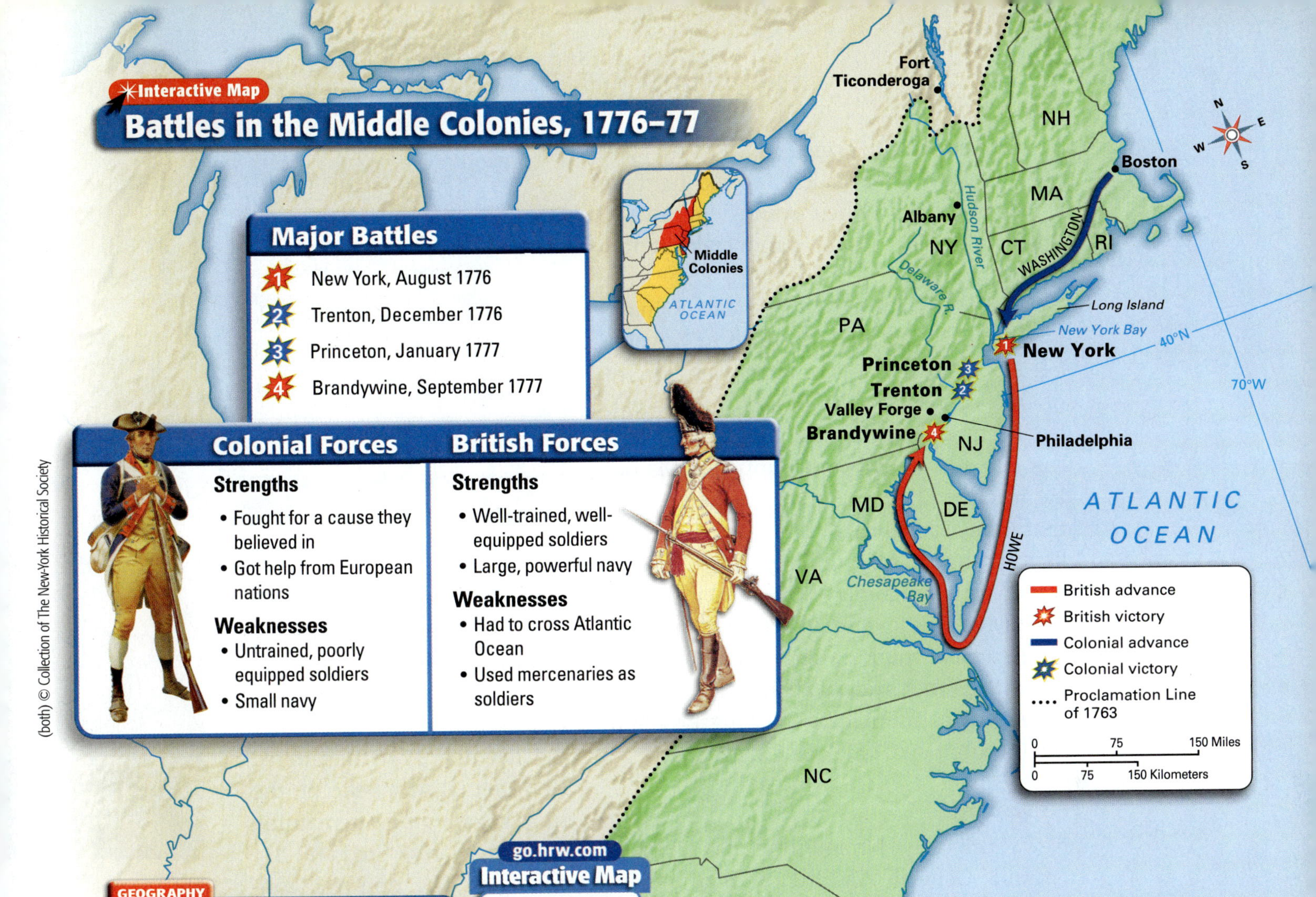

(both) © Collection of The New-York Historical Society

GEOGRAPHY SKILLS **INTERPRETING MAPS**

1. **Movement** About how far was Washington's march from Boston to New York?
2. **Human-Environment Interaction** What line set the western border of North Carolina?

In response, the Continental Army began allowing free African Americans to serve.

While men served as soldiers, many women ran farms and businesses. Others helped the army by raising money for supplies or making clothing. Women served as messengers, nurses, and spies. A Massachusetts man noted:

> "At every house Women and children [are] making Cartridges, running Bullets . . . and at the same time animating [encouraging] their Husbands and Sons to fight."
>
> —Anonymous, quoted in *Born for Liberty*, by Sara M. Evans

Perhaps the best known woman to fight in the war was Mary Ludwig Hays. She was called Molly Pitcher because she brought water to the troops. When her husband was wounded in a 1778 battle, she took his place loading cannons. Another woman, Deborah Sampson, dressed as a man and fought in several battles.

READING CHECK **Summarizing** How did various groups contribute to the war effort?

THE IMPACT TODAY

Women are still banned from ground combat. But in Operation Iraqi Freedom, women operated warships and flew combat jets and helicopters for the first time in a major air-ground conflict.

Defeats and Victories

As the Revolution gathered steam, it became more deadly. At first the Continental Army suffered a number of defeats. In time, though, the Patriots' patience began to pay off.

Canada

In part because the army was short on supplies, many Patriot leaders favored fighting a defensive war. Others wanted to invade British-controlled Canada and make it the "14th colony."

Patriot troops led by General Richard Montgomery captured Montreal in November 1775. The next major target was the city of Quebec. Benedict Arnold, now a general, led his troops north on a remarkable trek through the rough backcountry of Maine. He reached Quebec around the same time that Montreal fell to Montgomery. Since his first attempt to take the city failed, Arnold waited for Montgomery's troops to join his.

Taking an immense chance, the combined armies attacked during a fierce blizzard on New Year's Eve. They were quickly defeated. The Americans had suffered a crushing loss, and the Patriots' hopes of taking Canada faded.

New York

New York City became the next battleground. General Washington had moved his troops to New York, expecting the British arrival. Sure enough, in June 1776, a fleet of British ships approached New York Bay. Led by General William Howe, the British forced the Continental Army off Long Island.

Howe's 32,000 soldiers were much better equipped than Washington's 23,000 men, most of whom were militia. The Patriot general had to use all of his skills just to save his army.

In a series of battles, Howe pounded the Continental Army, forcing it to retreat farther and farther. The Redcoats captured Patriots as well as supplies. Eventually, the British pushed Washington across the Hudson River into New Jersey. Howe's revenge for his defeat at Boston was complete.

Focus on Reading

What is the main idea of the third paragraph under "New York"?

During the New York campaigns, a young Connecticut officer named Nathan Hale went behind British lines to get secret information. Seized by the British with documents hidden in the soles of his shoes, Hale was ordered to be hanged. Before his execution, he is said to have declared, "I regret that I have but one life to lose for my country."

Crossing the Delaware

George Washington and his troops crossed the partially frozen Delaware River on the night of December 25, 1776. This daring act led to a key Patriot victory at the Battle of Trenton. German American artist Emanuel Leutze created this famous painting in 1851. A version of Leutze's *Washington Crossing the Delaware* hangs in the Metropolitan Museum of Art in New York City.

What feelings do you think Leutze wanted to inspire with this painting?

New Jersey

In November 1776 the tattered Continental Army was on the run. Washington's remaining 6,000 men were tired and discouraged. The one-year contract for many of them would end on December 31. Who would re-enlist in this losing army, and who would replace the soldiers who left? Washington's army was in danger of vanishing.

Thinking the rebellion would end soon, Howe left New Jersey in the hands of soldiers from the German state of Hesse. The Hessians were **mercenaries**—foreign soldiers who fought not out of loyalty, but for pay.

On December 7 Washington retreated across the Delaware River into Pennsylvania. Even with 2,000 fresh troops, the Patriots were near the end. "These are the times that try men's souls," wrote Thomas Paine in *The American Crisis*, a series of pamphlets he began publishing in late 1776.

Without a convincing victory, Washington knew he would lose his army. He decided to take a big chance and go on the offensive. The Americans would attack the Hessians at Trenton, New Jersey.

On Christmas night, 1776, with a winter storm lashing about them, Washington and 2,400 soldiers silently rowed across the ice-clogged Delaware River. As morning broke, the men, short on supplies and many with no shoes, marched through the snow to reach the enemy camp.

The Hessians, having celebrated the holiday the night before, were fast asleep when the Patriots sprang upon them. The **Battle of Trenton** was an important Patriot victory. American soldiers took more than 900 prisoners.

British general Charles Cornwallis rushed to stop Washington as he marched northeast to Princeton. On the night of January 2, 1777, the Patriots left their campfires burning, then slipped into the darkness and circled behind the British troops. In the morning, Washington attacked. A local resident witnessed it:

> "The battle was plainly seen from our door . . . and the guns went off so quick and many together that they could not be numbered . . . Almost as soon as the firing was over, our house was filled and surrounded with General Washington's men."
>
> —Anonymous, quoted in *Voices of 1776* by Richard Wheeler

As Washington watched the Redcoats flee Princeton, he cheered, "It is a fine fox chase, my boys!" Now, new soldiers joined the chase. Others re-enlisted. The army—and the Revolution—was saved.

Saratoga

The two quick defeats stung the British. In the spring of 1777, they wanted a victory.

British general John Burgoyne decided to push through New York State and cut off New England from the other colonies. The **strategy** required perfect timing. According

ACADEMIC VOCABULARY

strategy a plan for fighting a battle or war

to the plan, Burgoyne's army would invade from Canada, recapture Fort Ticonderoga, and sweep south to Albany. General Howe, in New York City, would sail up the Hudson River to meet him, strangling New England.

Indeed, Burgoyne took Ticonderoga in early July and headed toward Albany. Here, the timing went wrong for the British. Unknown to Burgoyne, Howe had left New York, sailed up the Chesapeake Bay, and captured Philadelphia. Delegates to the Continental Congress were forced to flee.

Meanwhile, Burgoyne's army bogged down in thick forests. The Patriots had chopped down large trees and dammed rivers to create obstacles. All along the route, the militia swarmed out of nowhere to attack the Redcoats. As Burgoyne neared Saratoga, New York, he found himself surrounded. On October 17, 1777, he was forced to surrender his entire army to General Horatio Gates.

The **Battle of Saratoga** in New York was the turning point of the Revolutionary War. It was the greatest victory yet for the American forces. Morale soared. Patriot James Thacher wrote, "This event will make one of the most brilliant pages of American history."

READING CHECK **Summarizing**
Why was the Battle of Saratoga a turning point in the war?

Help from Europe

The French and Indian War had drastically changed the balance of power in North America. The French and Spanish had lost a large expanse of valuable land to the British. Both countries were delighted to see their powerful rival experiencing trouble in its American colonies.

The victory at Saratoga gave the Patriots something they had been desperately seeking: foreign help. Not surprisingly, it came from Britain's enemies, France and Spain. Even Britain's old ally, Holland, joined the fight on the side of the Patriots.

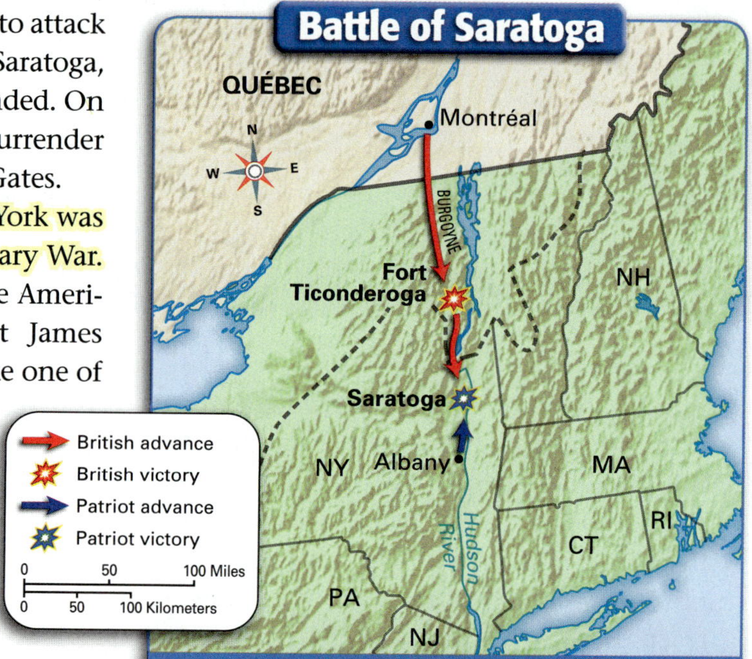

October 17, 1777 British forces under General John Burgoyne marched south, heading for Albany. They were crushed by Patriot forces under General Horatio Gates at Saratoga.

Time Line

The Patriots Gain Ground

1776

December 26, 1776
Patriots win the Battle of Trenton.

1777

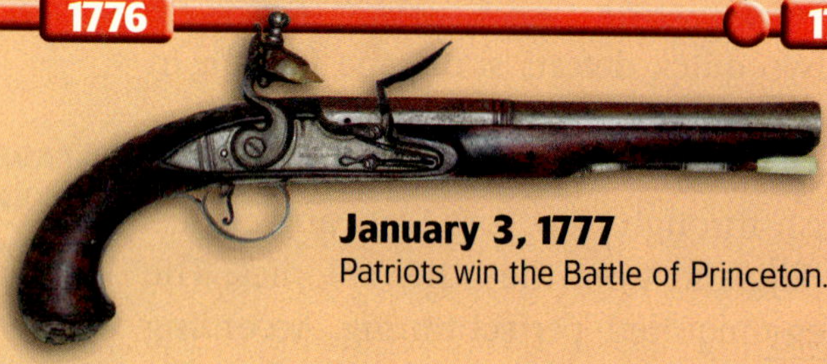

January 3, 1777
Patriots win the Battle of Princeton.

July 27, 1777 Marquis de Lafayette arrives in Philadelphia to offer his assistance to the Patriot cause.

Two Remarkable Europeans

"The welfare of America is closely bound up with the welfare of mankind," declared a wealthy young Frenchman, the **Marquis de Lafayette**. Inspired by the ideas of the Revolution, Lafayette bought his own ship and arrived in America in 1777. He brought with him a group of well-trained soldiers and volunteered to serve in the Continental Army himself without pay.

Lafayette spoke little English and had never seen battle. However, he quickly became a skillful commander, earning the title of major general. Lafayette led 2,000 Patriots to successfully pursue 6,000 Redcoats throughout Virginia during 1780–81. He gave $200,000 of his own money to support the Revolution and wrote many letters home to powerful friends and family asking their aid for the Patriot cause.

In February 1778 another European came to serve heroically under Washington. **Baron Friedrich von Steuben**, an experienced military officer from Prussia, led with a combination of respect and fear. He started training the American troops, focusing on basic military drills. Soon he turned the Continental Army into a finely tuned fighting force. A historian called von Steuben's feat "perhaps the most remarkable achievement in rapid military training in the history of the world."

Help from France

Benjamin Franklin, a skilled and experienced diplomat, had gone to France in 1776 to ask for support from King Louis XVI. Finally, the Battle of Saratoga in 1777 persuaded the French king that the colonists could win the war. Not until then did the king agree to an alliance with the Patriots.

In May 1778 the Continental Congress ratified the treaty of support with France. The French had been helping the Patriots all along with supplies and ammunition. After the treaty became official, the French increased the level of supplies and agreed to provide soldiers and ships. The French naval support would be a key ingredient in defeating the British.

Help from Spain

Spain, also a bitter enemy of Britain, joined the war in 1779. **Bernardo de Gálvez**, the governor of Spanish Louisiana, became a key ally to the Patriots. Gálvez gathered a small army of Spanish soldiers, French Americans, colonists, and Native Americans. Together they made their way east from Louisiana. Gálvez seized British posts all the way to Pensacola, Florida.

READING CHECK **Summarizing** How did France and Spain help the Patriots?

February 1778 Baron Friedrich von Steuben begins training Patriot soldiers.

May 1778 France joins the Patriots in an alliance.

June 21, 1779 Spain declares war against Britain.

March 14, 1780 Bernardo de Gálvez, the governor of Spanish Louisiana, captures the British stronghold of Fort Charlotte at present-day Mobile, Alabama.

1778 | 1779 | 1780

ANALYSIS SKILL **READING TIME LINES**

Which nations joined the Patriot cause?

Primary Source

JOURNAL ENTRY

Valley Forge

A surgeon at Valley Forge, Albigence Waldo kept a journal of what he saw during the winter of 1777–78.

"The Army which has been surprisingly healthy hitherto, now begins to grow sickly from the continued fatigues they have suffered this Campaign. Yet they still show a spirit of Alacrity [cheerful readiness] and Contentment not to be expected from so young Troops. I am Sick—discontented—and out of humour. Poor food—hard lodging—Cold Weather—fatigue—Nasty Cloaths [clothes]—nasty Cookery . . . smoke and Cold—hunger and filthyness—A pox on my bad luck."

—Albigence Waldo, from *Diary of Surgeon Albigence Waldo of the Connecticut Line*

ANALYSIS SKILL **ANALYZING PRIMARY SOURCES**

Why did Waldo seem surprised by the soldiers' attitude?

Winter at Valley Forge

The entry of France and Spain into the war came at a crucial moment. The Continental Army was running very low on food and clothing. In December 1777, Washington settled his 12,000 men at Valley Forge, north of Philadelphia.

To this day, the name of Valley Forge brings to mind suffering—and courage. Yet no battles took place here. The only enemy was the brutal winter of 1777–78.

Washington's men lacked even the most basic protections against shin-deep snows. In spite of the general's repeated requests for supplies, conflicts over funding between state authorities and Congress kept supplies from coming. Washington wrote in a letter:

"To see men without clothes ... without blankets to lie upon, without shoes ... without a house or hut to cover them until those could be built, and submitting without a murmur, is a proof of patience and obedience which, in my opinion, can scarcely be paralleled [matched]."

—George Washington, quoted in *George Washington: A Collection*

As winter roared in, soldiers quickly built crude shelters that offered little protection against the weather. Some soldiers had no shirts. Others had marched the shoes off their feet. At their guard posts, they stood on their hats to keep their feet from touching the freezing ground. One soldier wrote that getting food was the "business that usually employed us."

During that terrible winter, some 2,000 soldiers died of disease and malnutrition. Amazingly, the survivors not only stayed—they drilled and marched to the orders of Baron von Steuben, becoming better soldiers.

While the soldiers suffered through the winter at Valley Forge, the British lived a life of luxury in Philadelphia. Most of the Patriots had fled the city, leaving only Loyalists and British soldiers. Together they enjoyed the city's houses, taverns, and theaters, and held parties and balls.

READING CHECK **Finding Main Ideas** What challenges did the Continental Army face at Valley Forge?

War at Sea and in the West

While some Americans struggled against the British on land in the former colonies, others fought at sea and on the western frontier. Each area posed tough challenges.

War at Sea

The entry of the French navy into the war greatly aided the colonists. Many people had thought that the mighty British navy would crush the much smaller American fleet. However, the British failed to use their powerful navy effectively during the war.

In the fall of 1775, the Continental Congress made plans to build four American warships. Soon afterward the Congress formally established the marines and the Continental Navy. By adapting merchant vessels, the navy had eight fighting ships ready for combat by February 1776.

That month the tiny American navy launched a major offensive to damage the operating ability of the British fleet located off the Carolina coast. Rather than attack the fleet directly, the Patriots went after the British supply base on Nassau, in the Bahamas.

The American troops seized the main supply fort on the island. They then raised the newly created flag of the American Revolution over Nassau. After that campaign, the American navy focused on seizing British supply ships and weakening Britain's naval forces in the West Indies.

John Paul Jones

The Patriots owed much of their success on the seas to naval hero **John Paul Jones**. Jones had once been considered an outlaw. He was born John Paul in Scotland and began working on ships at a young age. After accidentally killing the leader of a mutiny, he fled to America and added Jones to his name.

When the war broke out, Jones volunteered his services to the newly created navy. He quickly established himself as a brave and clever sailor. Considered a pirate by the British, Jones captured many British supply ships. The French greatly admired Jones. When France entered the war in 1778, French leaders presented him with a small fleet of seven vessels to command. He named his flagship *Bonhomme Richard* ("Gentleman Richard") in honor of Benjamin Franklin's *Poor Richard's Almanac.*

One of Jones's most famous victories was the capture of the British warship *Serapis* on September 23, 1779. Early in the battle, the British knocked out the heaviest artillery on the *Bonhomme Richard.* Captain Richard Pearson of the *Serapis* then called out to Jones, "Has your ship struck [surrendered]?" Jones replied, "I have not yet begun to fight!" The battle continued for more than two hours. Finally the Americans wore down the British, who surrendered at 10:30 p.m.

The Continental Navy used fewer than 100 ships over the course of the war. Yet the British lost more than 200 ships to the small but effective American naval force.

War in the West

The lands west of the Appalachian Mountains were controlled by Native American nations. Both the British and the Patriots tried to enlist these groups in their cause.

George Rogers Clark volunteered to lead the western campaign. Clark had been a surveyor along the Ohio and Kentucky rivers. By the time the war broke out, he knew the lands of the Midwest well. Clark created an army from the scattered settlements in the area. One of the best-known groups was the Over Mountain Men, a band of settlers from areas that are now Tennessee and North Carolina.

Determined to weaken British support systems, Clark targeted trading villages. Following the Ohio River to the Tennessee, Clark's force set out on a 120-mile overland trek to Kaskaskia, in present-day Illinois. The village's leaders learned of the attack and surrendered. Other Patriots took Cahokia without a fight.

In February 1779 Clark launched a sur-

GEOGRAPHY SKILLS **INTERPRETING MAPS**

1. **Movement** How far did the Patriots march to get to Vincennes?
2. **Human-Environment Interaction** Why did military forces follow river routes?

prise attack on Fort Sackville near the town of Vincennes. The attack was unexpected because the nearby Wabash River was icy and flooded. Despite overflowing riverbanks, Clark's force of 150 men endured an 18-day march through freezing water. They also managed to bring enough Patriot flags for an army of hundreds. The flags were displayed near the fort, and the skilled pioneers sustained enough musket fire to indicate a much larger army. Falling for the ruse, the commander of Fort Sackville surrendered.

In general the British were more successful at winning over the Native Americans. But Clark's many campaigns undermined British support in the West.

READING CHECK **Finding Main Ideas** How did Jones and Clark help the Patriots' war effort?

SUMMARY AND PREVIEW The Patriots faced hardships as the war continued. In the next section, you will see how they finally achieved their goal of independence.

Section 3 Assessment

go.hrw.com
Online Quiz
KEYWORD: SC7 HP4

Reviewing Ideas, Terms, and People

1. a. **Identify** What groups supported the Patriot war effort? How did each group contribute?
   b. **Analyze** Why was it difficult to find and keep soldiers in the Continental Army?
2. a. **Describe** What early defeats did the Patriots face?
   b. **Elaborate** Was it a mistake for the British to use **mercenaries** to help them fight the war? Why or why not?
3. a. **Elaborate** Why do you think European nations supported the colonists rather than Great Britain?
   b. **Evaluate** Do you think that the Patriots would have won the war without help from France and Spain? Why or why not?
4. a. **Describe** What difficulties did the Patriots face at Valley Forge?
   b. **Elaborate** How might weather conditions affect the outcome of a battle?
5. a. **Identify** Who was **John Paul Jones**?
   b. **Compare** In what ways was Jones's naval strategy like that of the Continental Army?

Critical Thinking

6. **Drawing Conclusions** Review the events on your time line. Copy the chart below and use it to identify the region in which the events took place and how the events reflected the Patriots' successes and failures.

Region	Patriot Problems	Patriot Successes

FOCUS ON SPEAKING

7. **Thinking about the Struggle for Liberty** Why was this period of the war so difficult for the Patriots? How did they struggle through? What are the one or two points that are the most important about this period of the war?

Independence!

SECTION 4

If YOU were there...

You have grown up on a farm in South Carolina. You know every inch of the woods and marshes around your home. You are too young to join the Continental Army, but you have heard stories about a brave group of soldiers who carry out quick raids on the British, then disappear into the woods. These fighters get no pay and live in constant danger.

Would you consider joining the fighters? Why?

BUILDING BACKGROUND As the war moved to the South, American forces encountered new problems. They suffered several major defeats. But American resistance in the southern colonies was strong. Backwoods fighters confused and frustrated the British army.

War in the South

The war across the ocean was not going the way the British government in London had planned. The northern colonies, with their ragged, scrappy fighters, proved to be tough to tame. So the British switched strategies and set their sights on the South.

The British hoped to find support from the large Loyalist populations living in Georgia, the Carolinas, and Virginia. As they moved across the South, the British also planned to free enslaved Africans and enlist them as British soldiers. Under the leadership of a new commander, General Henry Clinton, the strategy paid off—for a while.

Brutal Fighting

The southern war was particularly brutal. Much more than in the North, this phase of the war pitted Americans—Patriots versus Loyalists—against one another in direct combat. The British also destroyed crops, farm animals, and other property as they marched through the South. One British officer, Banastre Tarleton, sowed fear throughout the South by refusing to take prisoners and killing soldiers who tried to surrender.

What You Will Learn...

Main Ideas

1. Patriot forces faced many problems in the war in the South.
2. The American Patriots finally defeated the British at the Battle of Yorktown.
3. The British and the Americans officially ended the war by signing the Treaty of Paris of 1783.

The Big Idea

The war spread to the southern colonies, where the British were finally defeated.

Key Terms and People

Francis Marion, *p. 136*
Comte de Rochambeau, *p. 137*
Battle of Yorktown, *p. 137*
Treaty of Paris of 1783, *p. 139*

TAKING NOTES As you read, take notes on the major events that led to the British defeat. Write your notes in a graphic organizer like the one below.

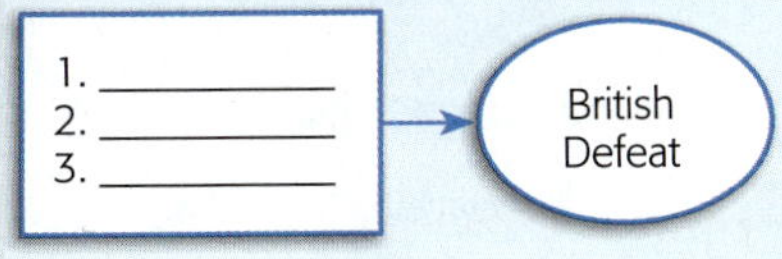

FOCUS ON NORTH CAROLINA

North Carolina's royal governor assured General Cornwallis that he could retake North Carolina because of the many Loyalists there. Cornwallis planned an invasion of North Carolina in 1780 but abandoned the plans when his reinforcements were captured. In 1781 American forces under Nathanael Greene defeated Cornwallis at Guilford Courthouse, forcing the British to abandon the Carolinas.

Georgia, the last colony to join the Revolution, was the first to fall to the British. A force of 3,500 Redcoats easily took Savannah in 1778 and soon put in place a new colonial government.

Britain's next major target was Charleston, South Carolina. In early 1780 General Clinton landed a force of 14,000 troops around the port city. With a minimal cost of about 250 casualties, the British scored one of their biggest victories of the war. The Patriots surrendered Charleston in May, handing over four ships and some 5,400 prisoners.

A Failed Attack

In August 1780, Patriot forces led by Horatio Gates tried to drive the British out of Camden, South Carolina. The attack was poorly executed, however. Gates had only half as many soldiers as he had planned for, and most were tired and hungry. In the heat of battle, many panicked and ran. The Patriot attack quickly fell apart. Of some 4,000 American troops, only about 700 escaped.

General Nathanael Greene arrived to reorganize the army. As he rode through the southern countryside, he was discouraged by the devastation. He later wrote, "I have never witnessed such scenes."

Guerrilla Warfare

The southern Patriots switched to swift hit-and-run attacks known as guerrilla warfare. No Patriot was better at this style of fighting than **Francis Marion**. He organized Marion's Brigade, a group of guerrilla soldiers.

Marion's Brigade used surprise attacks to disrupt British communication and supply lines. Despite their great efforts, the British could not catch Marion and his men. One frustrated general claimed, "As for this . . . old fox, the devil himself could not catch him." From that point on, Marion was known as the Swamp Fox.

READING CHECK **Sequencing** List the events of the war in the South in chronological order.

Battle of Yorktown

In early 1781 the war was going badly for the Patriots. They were low on money to pay soldiers and buy supplies. The help of their foreign allies had not brought the war to a quick end as they had hoped. The British held most of the South, plus Philadelphia and New York City. The Patriots' morale took another blow when Benedict Arnold, one of America's most gifted officers, turned traitor.

Regrouped under Nathanael Greene, the Continental Army began harassing British general Charles Cornwallis in the Carolinas. Hoping to stay in communication with the British naval fleet, Cornwallis moved his force of 7,200 men to Yorktown, Virginia. It was a fatal mistake.

General Washington, in New York, saw a chance to trap Cornwallis at Yorktown. He ordered Lafayette to block Cornwallis's escape by land. Then he combined his 2,500 troops

The Revolution in North Carolina

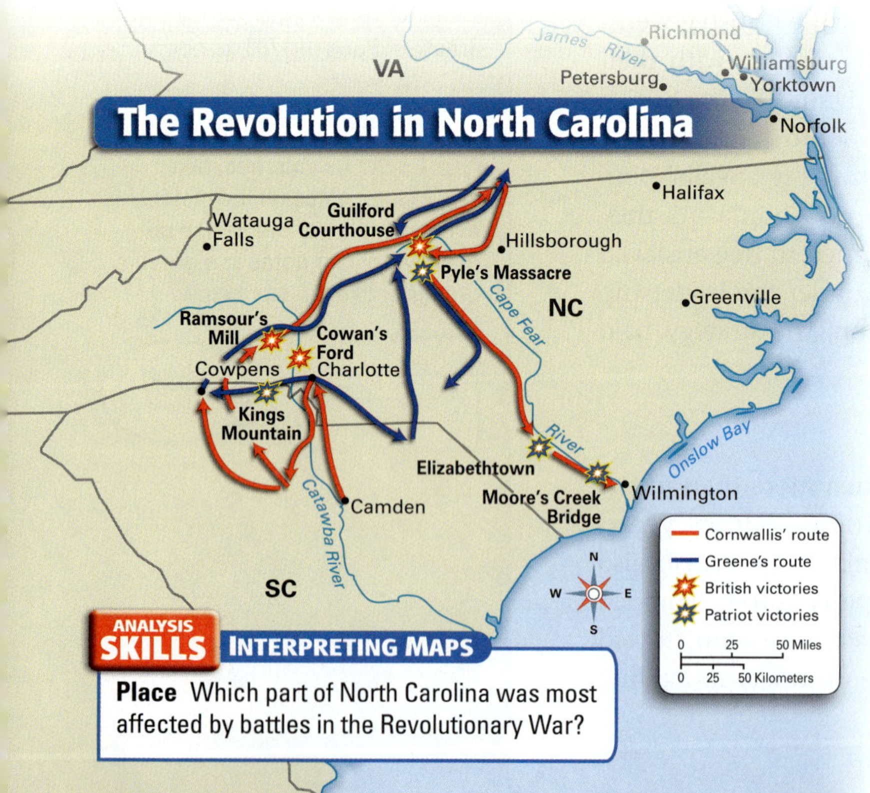

ANALYSIS SKILLS **INTERPRETING MAPS**

Place Which part of North Carolina was most affected by battles in the Revolutionary War?

History Close-up

Battle of Yorktown

In October 1781, American and French troops surrounded British forces and defeated them in the Battle of Yorktown.

ANALYSIS SKILLS **ANALYZING VISUALS**

Human-Environment Interaction How did American and French forces trap the British at Yorktown?

with 4,000 French troops commanded by the **Comte de Rochambeau** (raw-shahn-BOH). Washington led the French-American force on a swift march to Virginia to cut off the other escape routes. The Patriots surrounded Cornwallis with some 16,000 soldiers. Meanwhile, a French naval fleet seized control of the Chesapeake Bay, preventing British ships from rescuing Cornwallis's stranded army.

The siege began. For weeks, the fighting steadily wore down the British defenses. In early October, Washington prepared for a major attack on the weakened British troops.

Facing near-certain defeat, on October 19, 1781, Cornwallis sent a drummer and a soldier with a white flag of surrender to Washington's camp. The Patriots took some 8,000 British prisoners—the largest British army in America.

The **Battle of Yorktown** was the last major battle of the American Revolution. Prime Minister Lord North received word of the Yorktown surrender in November. In shock he declared, "It is all over!"

READING CHECK **Drawing Conclusions** Why did the victory at Yorktown end the fighting?

Primary Source

PAMPHLET

Sentiments of an American Woman

The Continental Army received aid from female Patriots led by Esther DeBerdt Reed and Sarah Franklin Bache, the daughter of Benjamin Franklin. In 1780 these women organized a campaign that raised $300,000 for soldiers' clothing. The following pamphlet, written by the campaign's leaders, announced the campaign. In it, the authors used images of women helping with war efforts of the past to gain support for their cause.

"On the **commencement** of actual war, the Women of America **manifested** a firm resolution to contribute . . . to the deliverance of their country. Animated by the purest patriotism they are sensible of sorrow at this day, in not offering more than barren wishes for the success of so glorious a Revolution. They aspire to **render** themselves more really useful; and this sentiment is universal from the north to the south of the Thirteen United States. Our ambition is kindled by the fame of those heroines of **antiquity**, who . . . have proved to the universe, that . . . if opinion and manners did not forbid us to march to glory by the same paths as the Men, we should at least equal, and sometimes surpass them in our love for the public good. I glory in all that which my sex has done great and **commendable**. I call to mind with enthusiasm and with admiration, all those acts of courage, of constancy and patriotism, which history has transmitted to us . . ."

"So many famous sieges where the Women have been seen . . . building new walls, digging trenches with their feeble hands, furnishing arms to their defenders, they themselves darting the missile weapons of the enemy, resigning the ornaments of their apparel, and their fortune, to fill the public treasury, and to hasten the deliverance of their country; burying themselves under its ruins; throwing themselves into the flames rather than submit to the disgrace of humiliation before a proud enemy."

"Born for liberty, **disdaining** to bear the irons of a **tyrannic** Government, we associate ourselves . . . [with those rulers] who have extended the empire of liberty, and **contented** to reign by sweetness and justice, have broken the chains of slavery, forged by tyrants."

A female spy passes news to a colonial officer.

1. **commencement**: start 2. **manifested**: presented
3. **render**: make 4. **antiquity**: ancient times
5. **commendable**: praiseworthy 6. **disdaining**: refusing
7. **tyrannic**: unjust 8. **contented**: determined

The women declare that they would fight if they were allowed.

The authors list ways in which women have helped fight wars in the past.

In this phrase, the women link themselves to great women rulers of the past.

ANALYSIS SKILL **ANALYZING PRIMARY SOURCES**

1. **What do the writers "call to mind" in asking women to join the Patriots' cause?**
2. **With whom do the writers associate themselves?**

The Treaty of Paris

After Yorktown, only a few small battles took place. Lacking the money to pay for a new army, Great Britain entered into peace talks with America. Benjamin Franklin had a key role in the negotiations.

Delegates took more than two years to come to a peace agreement. In the **Treaty of Paris of 1783**, Great Britain recognized the independence of the United States. The treaty also set America's borders. A separate treaty between Britain and Spain returned Florida to the Spanish. British leaders also accepted American rights to settle and trade west of the original thirteen colonies.

At the war's end, Patriot soldiers returned to their homes and families. The courage of soldiers and civilians had made America's victory possible. As they returned home, George Washington thanked his troops for their devotion. "I . . . wish that your latter days be as prosperous as your former ones have been glorious."

READING CHECK **Summarizing** Explain how the War for Independence finally came to an end.

North America after the Treaty of Paris of 1783

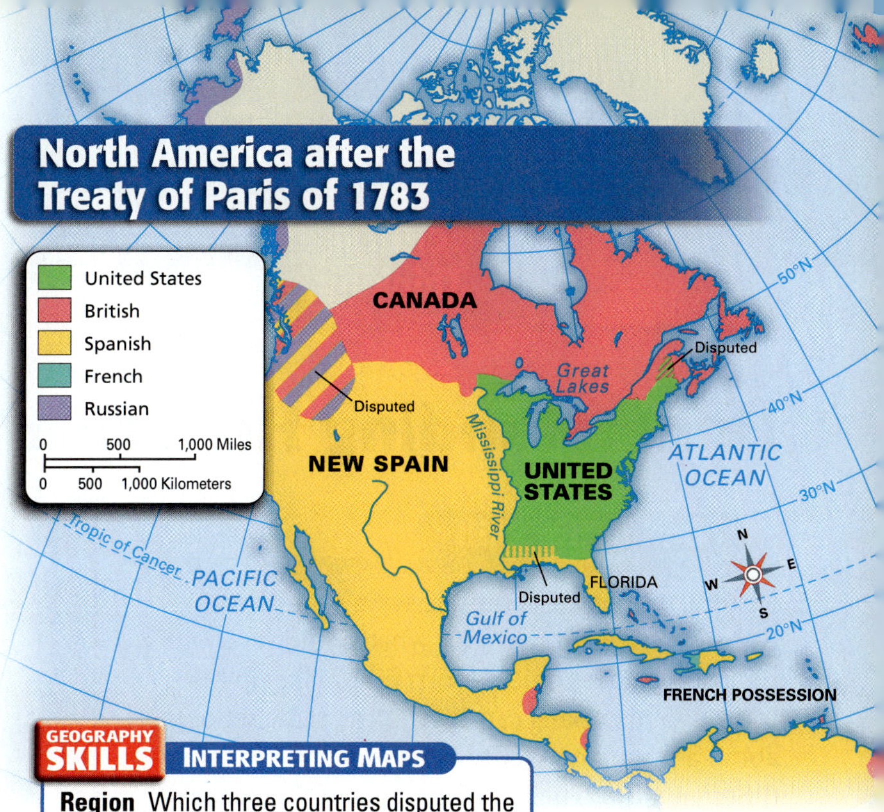

GEOGRAPHY SKILLS **INTERPRETING MAPS**

Region Which three countries disputed the area in the northwest of the continent?

SUMMARY AND PREVIEW Americans won their independence from Great Britain in 1783. In the next chapter you will learn how the new nation formed its first government.

Section 4 Assessment

go.hrw.com
Online Quiz
KEYWORD: SC7 HP4

Reviewing Ideas, Terms, and People

1. a. **Describe** What problems did the Patriots experience in the war in the South?
   b. **Analyze** What advantages did the southern Patriots have over the British in the South?
2. a. **Describe** What was the Patriots' strategy for defeating the British at Yorktown?
   b. **Elaborate** Why do you think General Cornwallis decided to surrender at the **Battle of Yorktown**?
3. a. **Identify** Who helped to negotiate the **Treaty of Paris** for the Americans?
   b. **Predict** How might relations between Great Britain and its former colonies be affected by the war?

Critical Thinking

4. **Evaluating** Review your notes on the events that led to the end of the war. Then copy the graphic organizer below and use it to identify and describe the most important event in turning the war in the Patriots' favor.

Event	Importance to end of war

FOCUS ON SPEAKING

5. **Thinking About the Revolution's End**
After reading this section, you have a picture of the whole war. In your talk, what do you want to say about how the war ended? Were there any moments that were especially trying for the colonists?

Social Studies Skills

Analysis | Critical Thinking | Civic Participation | Study

North Carolina Skills
1.07 Distinguish fact and fiction.

Understanding Historical Interpretation

Define the Skill

Historical interpretations are ways of explaining the past. They are based on what is known about the people, ideas, and actions that make up history. Two historians can look at the same set of facts about a person or event of the past and see things in different ways. Their explanations of the person or event, and the conclusions they reach, can be very different. The ability to recognize, understand, and evaluate historical interpretations is a valuable skill in the study of history.

Learn the Skill

When people study the past, they decide which facts are the most important in explaining why something happened. One person may believe certain facts to be important, while other people may believe other facts are more important. Therefore, their explanation of the topic, and the conclusions they draw about it, may not be the same. In addition, if new facts are uncovered about the topic, still more interpretations of it may result.

Asking the following questions will help you to understand and evaluate historical interpretations.

1. What is the main idea in the way the topic is explained? What conclusions are reached? Be aware that these may not be directly stated but only hinted at in the information provided.
2. On what facts has the writer or speaker relied? Do these facts seem to support his or her explanation and conclusions?
3. Is there important information about the topic that the writer or speaker has dismissed or ignored? If so, you should suspect that the interpretation may be inaccurate or deliberately slanted to prove a particular point of view.

Just because interpretations differ, one is not necessarily "right" and others "wrong." As long as a person considers all the evidence and draws conclusions based on a fair evaluation of that evidence, his or her interpretation is probably acceptable.

Remember, however, that trained historians let the facts *lead* them to conclusions. People who *start* with a conclusion, select only facts that support it, and ignore opposing evidence produce interpretations that have little value for understanding history.

Practice the Skill

Two widely accepted interpretations exist of the causes of the American Revolution. One holds that the Revolution was a struggle by freedom-loving Americans to be free from harsh British rule. In this view the colonists were used to self-government and resisted British efforts to take rights they claimed. The other interpretation is that a clash of economic interests caused the Revolution. In this view, the war resulted from a struggle between British and colonial merchants over control of America's economy.

Review Sections 4 and 5 of Chapter 3 and Sections 1 and 2 of Chapter 4. Then answer the following questions.

1. What facts in the textbook support the economic interpretation of the Revolution? What evidence supports the political interpretation?
2. Which interpretation seems more convincing? Explain why.

CHAPTER 4

Chapter Review

HOLT

History's Impact

▶ **video series**

Review the video to answer the closing question:

Why do you think African Americans, women, and young adults under 21 fought for the vote?

Visual Summary

QUICK FACTS

Use the visual summary below to help you review the main ideas of the chapter.

Speeches and protests ignited revolutionary feelings.

Patriots fought Loyalists in the Revolutionary War.

The American colonies gained independence and became the United States.

Reviewing Vocabulary, Terms, and People

1. What were American colonists who remained loyal to Great Britain called?

a. Whigs
b. Loyalists
c. Royalists
d. Democrats

2. What was the name of the battle in which the Patriots finally defeated the British?

a. Battle of Saratoga
b. Battle of New Jersey
c. Battle of Yorktown
d. Battle of Valley Forge

3. What was the name for the colonial military force created to fight the British?

a. mercenaries
b. Redcoats
c. Hessians
d. Continental Army

4. Who was the French nobleman who helped the Patriots fight the British?

a. Bernardo de Gálvez
b. Marquis de Lafayette
c. Baron von Steuben
d. Lord Dunmore

Comprehension and Critical Thinking

SECTION 1 *(Pages 112–116)*

5. a. Recall What actions did the First and Second Continental Congresses take?

b. Analyze How did the events at Lexington and Concord change the conflict between Great Britain and the colonies?

c. Elaborate Why do you think that control of Boston early in the Revolutionary War was important?

SECTION 2 *(Pages 118–121)*

6. a. Identify Why is July 4, 1776, a significant date?

b. Draw Conclusions What effect did *Common Sense* have on colonial attitudes toward Great Britain?

c. Predict How might the content of the Declaration of Independence lead to questions over the issue of slavery?

SECTION 3 *(Pages 126–134)*

7. a. **Describe** What difficulties did the Patriots experience in the early years of the war?

   b. **Analyze** How did the Patriots turn the tide of the war?

   c. **Elaborate** Could the Patriots have succeeded in the war without foreign help? Explain.

SECTION 4 *(Pages 135–139)*

8. a. **Recall** Why did the British think they might find support in the southern colonies?

   b. **Make Inferences** Why did it take more than two years for the British and the Americans to agree to the terms of the Treaty of Paris?

   c. **Evaluate** In your opinion, what was the most important reason for the Patriots' defeat of the British?

Social Studies Skills

Understanding Historical Interpretation *Use the Social Studies Skills taught in this chapter to answer the questions about the reading selection below.*

> In a series of battles, Howe pounded the Continental Army, forcing it to retreat farther and farther. The Redcoats captured Patriots as well as supplies. Eventually, the British pushed Washington across the Hudson River into New Jersey. Howe's revenge for his defeat at Boston was complete. (p. 128)

9. Which statement from the passage is an interpretation of historical facts?

   a. The Redcoats captured Patriots as well as supplies.

   b. Eventually, the British pushed Washington across the Hudson River into New Jersey.

   c. Howe's revenge for his defeat at Boston was complete.

10. What might a different interpretation of the facts be?

Reviewing Themes

11. **Politics** What are three important rights listed in the Declaration of Independence?

12. **Geography** What role did geography play in the fighting that took place in the West?

Reading Skills

Main Ideas in Social Studies *Use the Reading Skills taught at the beginning of the chapter to answer the question about the reading selection below.*

> (1) Native Americans were at first encouraged by both sides to remain neutral. (2) By the summer of 1776, however, both Patriots and the British were aggressively recruiting Indian fighters. (3) Most sided with the British. (4) In northern New York, four of the six Iroquois nations fought for the British. (p. 120)

13. Which sentence contains the main idea of the paragraph?

   a. Sentence 1

   b. Sentence 2

   c. Sentence 3

   d. Sentence 4

Using the Internet

go.hrw.com
KEYWORD: SC7 CH4

14. **Activity: Researching** The Battle of Saratoga showed the world that the Patriots were capable of defeating the British. This victory gave Benjamin Franklin the chance to use his fame as a scientist and diplomat to convince France to aid the Patriots. Enter the activity keyword and explain how these factors led to a Patriot victory and how the American Revolution affected France.

FOCUS ON SPEAKING

15. **Prepare Your Oral Report** Review your notes and be sure you've identified one or two important ideas, events, or people for each period of the war. Now, start to prepare your oral report by writing a one-sentence introduction to your talk. Then write a sentence or two about each period of the war. Write a concluding sentence that makes a quick connection between the Revolutionary War and our lives today. Practice your talk until you can give it with only a glance or two at your notes.

CHAPTER 4 Standardized Test Practice

DIRECTIONS: Read each question and write the letter of the best response.

1 Which of the following events played the *greatest* role in the outbreak of war between the colonies and Great Britain?

A the ride of Paul Revere

B the meeting of the First Continental Congress

C the march of the British Army on Lexington and Concord

D the Boston massacre

2 In 1775 the Second Continental Congress

A declared war on Great Britain.

B named George Washington commander of the newly formed Continental Army.

C sent the Declaration of Rights to King George III in the hopes that he would address the colonists' grievances.

D decided to invade British-controlled Canada in an effort to make it the "14th colony."

3 Why was the victory at the Battle of Saratoga so important to the Patriot cause?

A It allowed the Declaration of Independence to be issued.

B It forced the British army to retreat from Boston.

C It convinced France to aid the colonies in their fight.

D It caused the British government to give up the war.

4 In the early years of the American Revolution, the Patriot cause struggled as a result of

A a poorly trained and equipped army.

B disagreements between Patriot leaders.

C overwhelming opposition to the war.

D a lack of skilled military leaders.

5 According to the Declaration of Independence, the American colonies had the right to break away from Great Britain because

A British taxes were too high.

B the British government did not protect the colonists' rights.

C the king refused to outlaw slavery.

D the colonists were persecuting Loyalists.

6 Which of the following *best* summarizes the purpose of the Halifax Resolves?

A to outlaw slavery in North Carolina

B to authorize North Carolina representatives to seek peace with Great Britain

C to call up North Carolina military forces for war against Great Britain

D to show North Carolina's support for independence from Great Britain

7 Read the following passage from Thomas Paine's *The Crisis* and use it to answer the question below.

> "These are the times that try men's souls. The summer soldier and the sunshine patriot will, in this crisis, shrink from the service of his country, but he that stands it now, deserves the love and thanks of man and woman. Tyranny . . . is not easily conquered, yet we have this consolation with us, that the harder the conflict, the more glorious the triumph."
>
> —Thomas Paine, *The Crisis,* 1776

Document-Based Question **What point is Paine trying to make in this passage?**

A Biographical Narrative

Assignment

Write a biographical narrative about a person who lived in the early Americas before or during the colonial period.

You have been listening to and telling narratives all your life. A biographical narrative, a form of historical writing, is a true story about an event or brief period in a person's life.

TIP **Asking Questions** Try using the *5W-How?* questions (*Who? What? When? Where? Why? How?*) to help you think of descriptive details. Ask questions such as, **Who** was this person? **What** was he or she doing? Exactly **where** and **when** did the event occur? **How** did the person or other people react to the event?

1. Prewrite

Getting Started

- Think of all the people you read about in this unit. Which ones interested you most?
- What particular events and situations in these people's lives seem most exciting or significant?

Pick one of these events or situations as the subject of your narrative.

Creating an Interesting Narrative

Make your narrative lively and interesting by including

- **Physical descriptions** of people, places, and things, using details that appeal to the five senses (sight, hearing, touch, smell, taste)
- **Specific actions** that relate directly to the story you are telling
- **Dialogue** between the people involved or direct **quotations**
- **Background information** about the place, customs, and setting
- **All relevant details and information** needed to relate the events of the story and how they affected the person (and perhaps history)

Organize the events in your narrative in chronological order, the order in which they occurred.

2. Write

You can use this framework to help you draft your narrative.

A Writer's Framework

Introduction	Body	Conclusion
■ Grab your reader's attention with a striking detail or bit of dialogue. ■ Introduce the historical person and setting, using specific details. ■ Set the scene by telling how the event or situation began.	■ Present actions and details in the order in which they occurred. ■ Connect actions with transition words like *first, then, next,* and *finally.* ■ Provide specific details to make the person and the situation come alive.	■ Wrap up the action of the narrative. ■ Tell how the person was affected by what happened. ■ Explain how the event or situation was important in the person's life and how it affected history.

3. Evaluate and Revise

Evaluating

Read through your completed draft to make sure your narrative is complete, coherent, and clear. Then look for ways to improve it.

Evaluation Questions for a Biographical Narrative

- Does your introduction grab the reader's attention? Do you introduce the historical person and tell how the event or situation began?
- Do you include details to make the person, place, and event seem real?
- Are the actions in the story in the order in which they occurred?
- Have you included all of the actions and details a reader would need to understand what happened?
- Does the conclusion tell how the event or situation affected the person and history?

TIP **Showing Sequence** A clear sense of the sequence of events is important in any narrative. Here is a list of words that show those relationships.

after	next
before	now
finally	soon
first (second, etc.)	still
last	then
later	when
	while

Revising

When you revise your narrative, you may need to add transition words. Transition words help you link ideas between sentences and paragraphs. Notice the words in bold in the following sentences.

After Cabeza de Vaca and the other adventurers left the beach and started inland, they separated into different groups. **Later**, Cabeza de Vaca heard that many of the others had died. **Still**, he never lost faith that he would reach his fellow Spaniards in Mexico.

4. Proofread and Publish

Proofreading

Throughout your narrative, you used transition words to link events. Make sure that you have spelled the words correctly and have not confused them with other words. For example, be sure to use two *l*'s in *finally* and not to mistake the transition word *then* for the comparative word *than*.

Publishing

One good way to share your biographical narrative is to exchange it with one or more classmates who have written about the same person you have. After reading each other's narratives, you can compare and contrast them. How are your stories similar? How do they differ?

5. Practice and Apply

Use the steps and strategies outlined in this workshop to write your biographical narrative.

UNIT 2

1777–1800

A New Nation

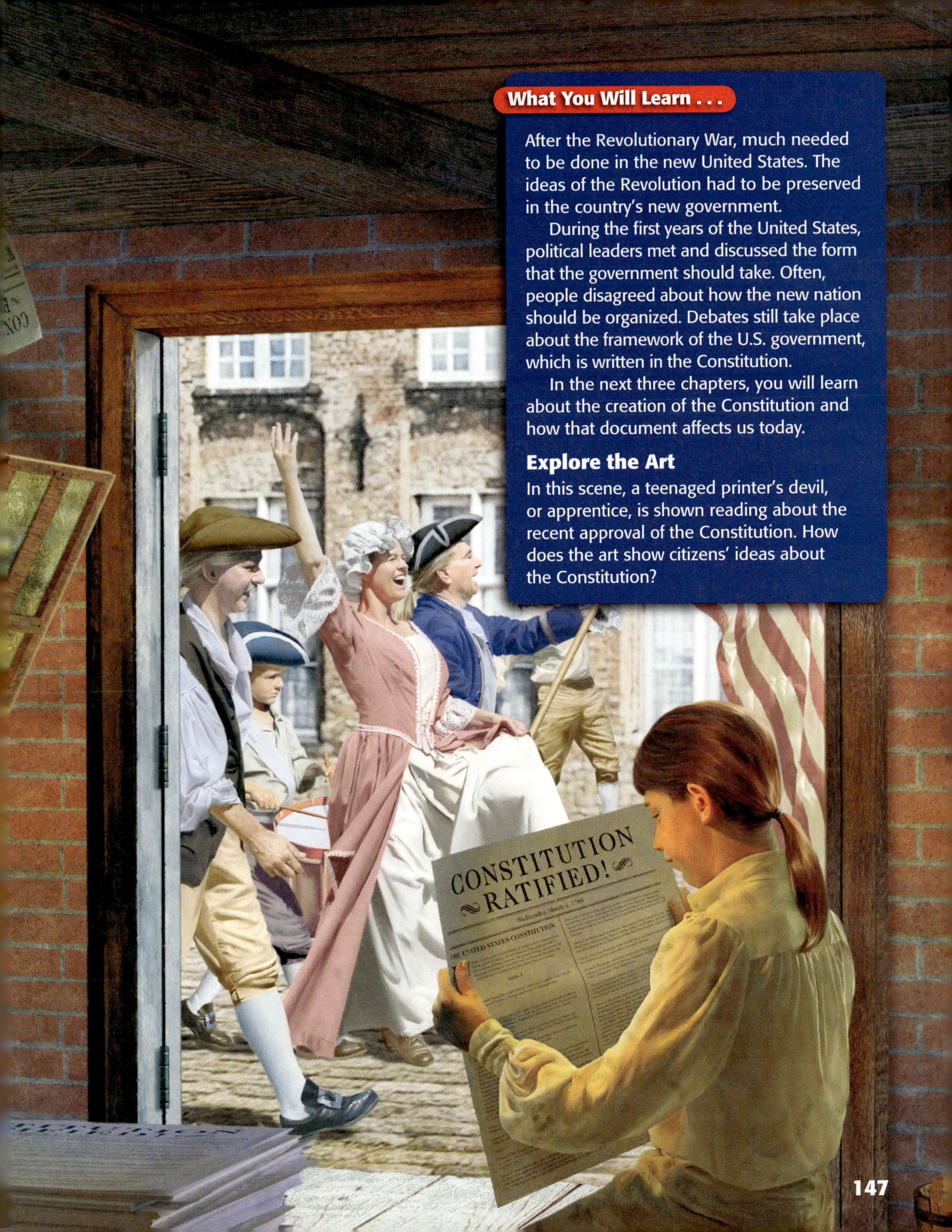

What You Will Learn . . .

After the Revolutionary War, much needed to be done in the new United States. The ideas of the Revolution had to be preserved in the country's new government.

During the first years of the United States, political leaders met and discussed the form that the government should take. Often, people disagreed about how the new nation should be organized. Debates still take place about the framework of the U.S. government, which is written in the Constitution.

In the next three chapters, you will learn about the creation of the Constitution and how that document affects us today.

Explore the Art

In this scene, a teenaged printer's devil, or apprentice, is shown reading about the recent approval of the Constitution. How does the art show citizens' ideas about the Constitution?

CHAPTER 5 1777–1791

Forming a Government

North Carolina Standards

Social Studies Objectives

2.05 Describe the impact of documents such as the Mecklenburg Resolves, the Halifax Resolves, the Albany Plan of Union, the Declaration of Independence, the State Constitution of 1776, the Articles of Confederation, the United States Constitution, and the Bill of Rights on the formation of the state and national governments.

Language Arts Objectives

1.02 Analyze expressive materials that are read, heard, and/or viewed by:

- making connections between works, self and related topics.
- drawing inferences.

3.01 Explore and evaluate argumentative works that are read, heard and/or viewed by:

- identifying the social context of the argument.

4.01 Analyze the purpose of the author or creator and the impact of that purpose by:

- evaluating any bias, apparent or hidden messages, emotional factors, and/or propaganda techniques.
- evaluating the underlying assumptions of the author/creator.

go.hrw.com
North Carolina
KEYWORD: SC7 NC

FOCUS ON WRITING

A Newspaper Editorial It is 1788 and you're writing an editorial for a local newspaper. You want to convince your readers that the new Constitution will be much better than the old Articles of Confederation. In this chapter you'll find the information you need to support your opinion.

UNITED STATES

1777
The Continental Congress approves the Articles of Confederation on November 15.

1775

WORLD

1778
The United States and France become allies.

HOLT

History's Impact

▶ **video series**
Watch the video to understand the impact of adding new states to the United States.

What You Will Learn . . .

This photo shows Speaker of the House Dennis Hastert swearing in the 108th Congress, the legislative branch of the U.S. government. In this chapter, you will learn about the nation's earliest government, the Articles of Confederation, and its failures to achieve national unity. You will also read about the writing of the Constitution and how it attempted to solve the problems of the Articles by creating a new system of government with three branches.

1781
On March 1 the Articles of Confederation go into effect after being ratified by all 13 states.

Collection of the American Numismatic Society, New York

1785
The United States begins using the dollar currency.

1786
Shays's Rebellion breaks out in Massachusetts.

1787
On May 14, state delegates begin to arrive at the Constitutional Convention in Philadelphia.

1791
The Bill of Rights is ratified by the states in December.

1780 — 1785 — 1790

1782
Spain completes its conquest of British Florida.

1787
The Ottoman Empire declares war on Russia.

1791
The *Lady Washington* becomes the first U.S. ship to reach Japan.

Reading Social Studies

by Kylene Beers

Economics | Geography | **Politics** | **Society and Culture** | Science and Technology

Focus on Themes Visualize a row of dominoes, lined up one after the other. Push over the first one, and—one after the other—all eventually fall. In this way, the events in this chapter are like dominoes that cause each other to occur. These events, one after another, finally led to the formation of a new government and a new **society**. If you read closely, you will see that **political** disagreements started the entire process.

Understanding Chronological Order

Focus on Reading Like falling dominoes, historical events can create huge chains of results, often stretching over many years. To understand history and events, therefore, we often need to see how they are related in time.

Understanding Chronological Order The word ***chronological*** means "related to time." Events discussed in this history book are discussed in **sequence**, in the order in which they happened. To understand history better, you can use a sequence chain to take notes about events in the order they happened.

Sequence Chain

1620
The Pilgrims sign the Mayflower Compact.

↓

1639
Connecticut creates the first constitution in the English colonies.

↓

1689
The English Bill of Rights is passed.

↓

1776
The American colonies declare their independence from Great Britain.

Tip: Writers sometimes signal chronological order, or sequence, by using words or phrases like these:

first, before, then, later, soon, after, before long, next, eventually, finally

You Try It!

Read the following passage and answer the questions that follow.

Farmers Rebel

From Chapter 5, p. 161

In August 1786, farmers in three western counties began a revolt. Bands of angry citizens closed down courts in western Massachusetts. Their reasoning was simple—with the courts shut down, no one's property could be taken. In September a poor farmer and Revolutionary War veteran, Daniel Shays, led hundreds of men in a forced shutdown of the Supreme Court in Springfield, Massachusetts. The state government ordered the farmers to stop the revolt under threat of capture and death. These threats only made Shays and his followers more determined. The uprising of farmers to protest high taxes and heavy debt became known as Shays's Rebellion.

Shays's forces were defeated by state troops in January 1787. By February many of the rebels were in prison. During their trials, 14 leaders were sentenced to death. However, the state soon freed most of the rebels, including Shays.

After you have read the passage, answer the following questions.

1. Which happened first—citizens closing courts in western Massachusetts or Shays shutting down the Supreme Court? How can you tell?
2. What happened after Shays's forces were defeated by state troops?
3. Draw a sequence chain that shows the effects of Shays's Rebellion in the order they occurred.

Before you read Chapter 5, look for clues that signal the order in which events occurred.

Key Terms and People

Chapter 5

Section 1

Magna Carta *(p. 152)*
constitution *(p. 153)*
Virginia Statute for Religious Freedom *(p. 153)*
suffrage *(p. 153)*
Articles of Confederation *(p. 154)*
ratification *(p. 154)*
Land Ordinance of 1785 *(p. 155)*
Northwest Ordinance of 1787 *(p. 155)*
Northwest Territory *(p. 155)*

Section 2

tariffs *(p. 159)*
interstate commerce *(p. 160)*
inflation *(p. 161)*
depression *(p. 161)*
Daniel Shays *(p. 161)*
Shays's Rebellion *(p. 161)*

Section 3

Constitutional Convention *(p. 164)*
James Madison *(p. 164)*
Virginia Plan *(p. 164)*
New Jersey Plan *(p. 165)*
Great Compromise *(p. 165)*
Three-Fifths Compromise *(p. 166)*
popular sovereignty *(p. 167)*
federalism *(p. 167)*
legislative branch *(p. 167)*
executive branch *(p. 167)*
judicial branch *(p. 167)*
checks and balances *(p. 167)*

Section 4

Antifederalists *(p. 170)*
George Mason *(p. 170)*
Federalists *(p. 170)*
Federalist Papers (p. 171)
amendments *(p. 173)*
Bill of Rights *(p. 173)*

Academic Vocabulary

In this chapter, you will learn the following academic word:

advocate *(p. 171)*

SECTION 1

The Articles of Confederation

What You Will Learn . . .

Main Ideas

1. The American people examined many ideas about government.
2. The Articles of Confederation laid the base for the first national government of the United States.
3. The Confederation Congress established the Northwest Territory.

The Big Idea

The Articles of Confederation provided a framework for a national government.

Key Terms and People

Magna Carta, *p. 152*
constitution, *p. 153*
Virginia Statute for Religious Freedom, *p. 153*
suffrage, *p. 153*
Articles of Confederation, *p. 154*
ratification, *p. 154*
Land Ordinance of 1785, *p. 155*
Northwest Ordinance of 1787, *p. 155*
Northwest Territory, *p. 155*

TAKING NOTES As you read, take notes on the new American government in a chart like this one.

New American Government	
1. Influences on new government	
2. Structure of the Articles of Confederation	

If YOU were there...

You live in a town in New England during the 1770s. In the town meeting, people are hotly debating about who will have the right to vote. Most think that only men who own property should be able to vote. Some think that all property owners—men and women—should have that right. A few others want all free men to have the vote. Now it is time for the meeting to decide.

How would you have voted on this issue?

BUILDING BACKGROUND At the time of the Revolution, each of the 13 states had its own government. The rights of citizens varied from state to state. In their town meetings, people often argued about exactly what those rights ought to be. Solving such issues was one step in moving toward a national government.

Ideas about Government

The American colonies had taken a bold step in declaring their independence from Great Britain in July 1776. Their next political goal was to form a new government. To do so, the American people drew from a wide range of political ideas.

English Laws and the Enlightenment

One source of inspiration was the rule of law. This rule makes even government officials subject to law. England had limited the power of its kings and queens in two documents. These were Magna Carta and the English Bill of Rights. **Magna Carta**, a document signed by King John in 1215, made the king subject to law. The English Bill of rights, passed in 1689, declared the supremacy of Parliament. It kept the king or queen from changing laws without Parliament's consent. As a result, the people's representatives had a strong voice in England's government.

Many Americans were also influenced by the Enlightenment—a philosophical movement that emphasized the use of reason to examine old ideas and traditions. Philosopher John Locke believed that a social contract existed between political rulers and the people they ruled. Baron de Montesquieu argued that the only way to achieve liberty was through the separation of governmental powers.

American Models of Government

Americans had their own models of self-government to follow, like town meetings, the Virginia House of Burgesses, and the Mayflower Compact. In 1639 the people of Connecticut drew up the English colonies' first written **constitution**. A constitution is a set of basic principles and laws that states the powers and duties of the government. In addition, the Declaration of Independence clearly set forth the beliefs on which Americans thought government should be based.

To keep individual leaders from gaining too much power, the new state constitutions created limited governments, or governments in which all leaders have to obey the laws. Most state constitutions had rules to protect the rights of citizens or those accused of crimes. Some banned slavery. The Massachusetts constitution of 1780 is the oldest state constitution still in effect.

Thomas Jefferson's ideas about religious freedom were included in the **Virginia Statute for Religious Freedom**. This document declared that no person could be forced to attend a particular church or be required to pay for a church with tax money.

Right to Vote

Under British rule, only free, white men that owned land could vote. Many states' constitutions expanded **suffrage**, or the right to vote, by allowing any white man who paid taxes to vote. In every state, however, only landowners could hold public office. Some states originally allowed women and free African Americans to vote, but these rights were soon taken away. Suffrage would not be restored to these groups for decades to come.

READING CHECK **Comparing** What two principles were common to state constitutions written during the Revolutionary War?

FOCUS ON NORTH CAROLINA

North Carolina approved its first constitution in December 1776. The new government included a governor, but the legislature was much more powerful. The document included a bill of rights that protected citizens of the new state.

Women's Suffrage

New Jersey allowed women to vote when it first joined the United States. This right was taken away by 1807.

Why do you think women were not allowed to vote in the early United States?

The Land Ordinances of 1785 and 1787

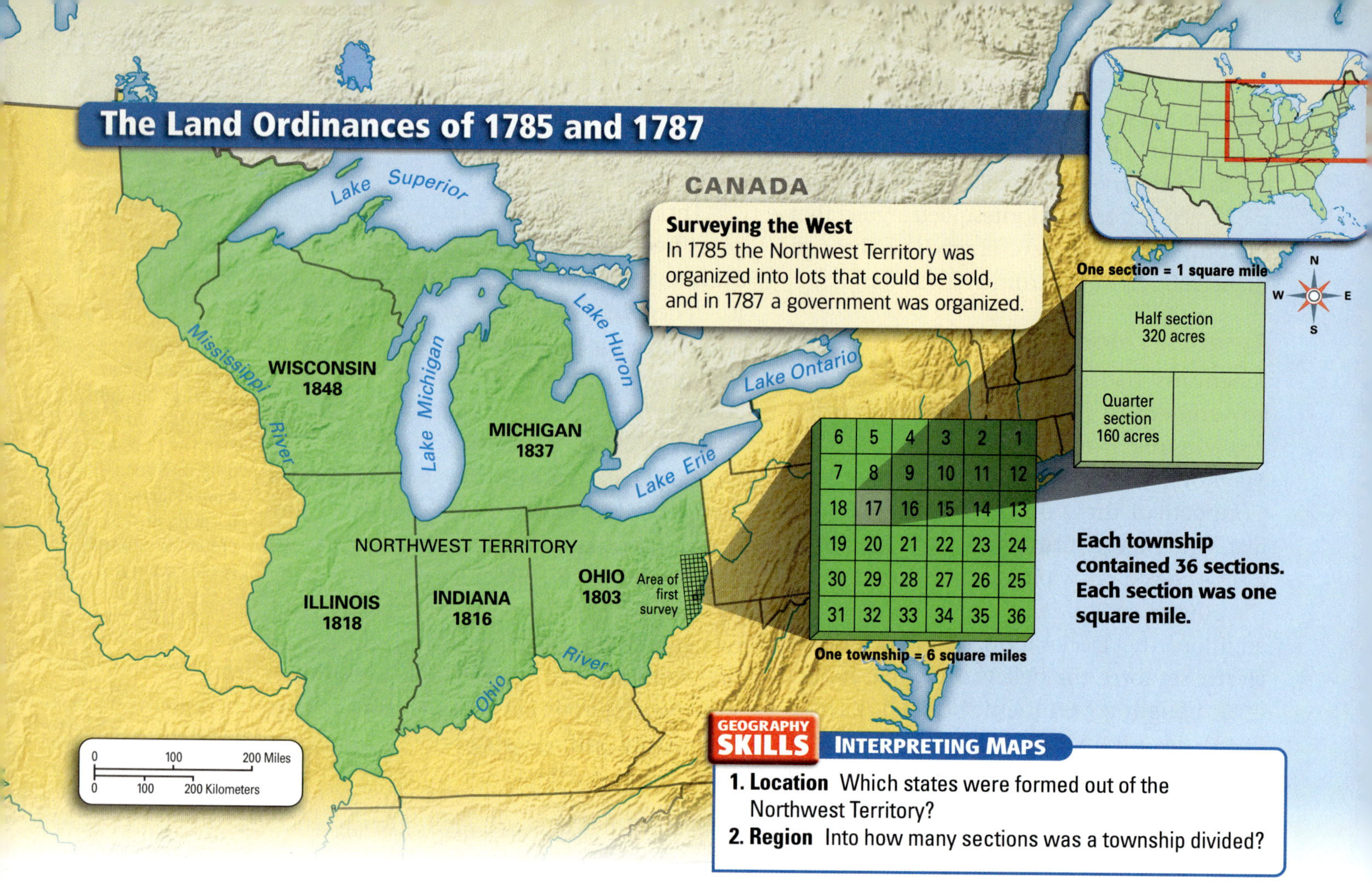

GEOGRAPHY SKILLS **INTERPRETING MAPS**

1. **Location** Which states were formed out of the Northwest Territory?
2. **Region** Into how many sections was a township divided?

Articles of Confederation

The Second Continental Congress was organized to create a national government. The Continental Congress appointed a Committee of Thirteen, with one member from each colony. This group was assigned to discuss and draft the Articles of Confederation, the new national constitution.

Under the **Articles of Confederation**, Congress would become the single branch of the national government, but it would have limited powers in order to protect the liberties of the people. Each state had one vote in the Congress. Congress could settle conflicts among the states, issue coins, borrow money, and make treaties with other countries and with Native Americans. Congress could also ask the states for money and soldiers. However, states had the power to refuse these requests. The government did not have a president or a national court system.

The Second Continental Congress passed the Articles of Confederation on November 15, 1777. Then it sent the Articles to each state legislature for **ratification**, or official approval, before the new national government could take effect.

Conflicts over claims to western lands slowed the process, but by 1779 every state except Maryland had ratified the Articles. Maryland's leaders refused to ratify until other states gave up their western land claims. Thomas Jefferson assured Maryland that western lands would be made into new states, rather than increasing territory for existing states. Satisfied with this condition, in March 1781 Maryland ratified the Articles. This put the first national government of the United States into effect.

READING CHECK **Summarizing** What were two weaknesses of the new national government?

Northwest Territory

Congress had to decide what to do with the western lands now under its control and how to raise money to pay debts. It tried to solve both problems by selling the western lands. Congress passed the **Land Ordinance of 1785**, which set up a system for surveying and dividing western lands. The land was split into townships, which were 36 square miles divided into 36 lots of 640 acres each. One lot was reserved for a public school, and four lots were given to veterans. The remaining lots were sold to the public.

To form a political system for the region, Congress passed the **Northwest Ordinance of 1787**. The ordinance established the **Northwest Territory**, which included areas that are now in Illinois, Indiana, Michigan, Ohio, Minnesota, and Wisconsin. The Northwest Ordinance created a system for bringing new states into the Union. Congress agreed that the Northwest Territory would be divided into several smaller territories with a governor appointed by Congress. When the population of a territory reached 60,000, its settlers could draft their own constitution and ask to join the Union.

In addition, the law protected civil liberties and required that public education be provided. Finally, the ordinance stated that "there shall be neither slavery nor involuntary servitude [forced labor] in the . . . territory." This last condition banned slavery in the Territory and set the standard for future territories. However, slavery would continue to be a controversial issue.

THE IMPACT TODAY

Townships remained the unit of local government after the Northwest Territory was divided into states. Many of these townships still exist today.

READING CHECK **Analyzing Information**

How did the Northwest Ordinance of 1787 affect the United States?

SUMMARY AND PREVIEW The Northwest Ordinance settled the future of the Northwest Territory. In the next section you will read about other challenges the new government faced.

Section 1 Assessment

go.hrw.com
Online Quiz
KEYWORD: SC7 HP5

Reviewing Ideas, Terms, and People

1. a. **Identify** What documents influenced ideas about government in the United States?
   b. **Draw Conclusions** What impact did the **Virginia Statute for Religious Freedom** have on the U.S. government?
   c. **Elaborate** Why is the separation of government powers a requirement for a society to be free?
2. a. **Identify** What was the **Articles of Confederation**?
   b. **Summarize** What powers were granted to Congress by the Articles of Confederation?
   c. **Predict** What are some possible problems that might result from the lack of a national court system?
3. a. **Describe** How were public lands in the West divided by the **Land Ordinance of 1785**?
   b. **Evaluate** In your opinion, what was the most important element of the **Northwest Ordinance of 1787**? Why?
   c. **Elaborate** What does the assignment of township lots reveal about values of Americans at this time?

Critical Thinking

4. **Categorizing** Review your notes on the Articles of Confederation. Copy the chart below and use it to show the strengths and weaknesses of the new government.

Articles of Confederation

Strengths	Weaknesses

FOCUS ON WRITING

5. **Thinking about the Articles of Confederation** Make a list of powers the Articles of Confederation gave the national government. Which ones seem strong? Can you think of any important powers that are missing?

History and Geography

Origins of the Constitution

The U.S. Constitution created a republican form of government based on the consent of the people. The framers of the Constitution blended ideas and examples from both the American colonies and from England to write this lasting document.

THE MAYFLOWER COMPACT, 1620

The *Mayflower*, shown here in an illustration, sailed to America in 1620. Aboard the ship, 41 men signed the Mayflower Compact, the first document in the colonies to establish guidelines for self-government. The signers agreed that they and their families would combine to form a "civil body politic," or community.

COLONIAL ASSEMBLIES

The British Parliament's two-chamber structure also influenced colonial governments. In Article I, Section 1, of the Constitution, the framers continued the practice of a two-chamber legislature.

"All legislative powers . . . shall be vested in a Congress of the United States, which shall consist of a Senate and House of Representatives."
—*Article I, Section 1, U.S. Constitution*

VIRGINIA STATUTE FOR RELIGIOUS FREEDOM, 1786

Classical liberal principles such as the written protection of citizens' personal liberties were reflected in the addition of the Bill of Rights. The First Amendment's freedom of religion clauses were based on Thomas Jefferson's Virginia Statute for Religious Freedom. The document, which was accepted by the Virginia legislature in 1786, ensured the separation of church and state in Virginia.

"Congress shall make no law respecting an establishment of religion, or prohibiting the free exercise thereof . . ."
—*First Amendment, U.S. Constitution*

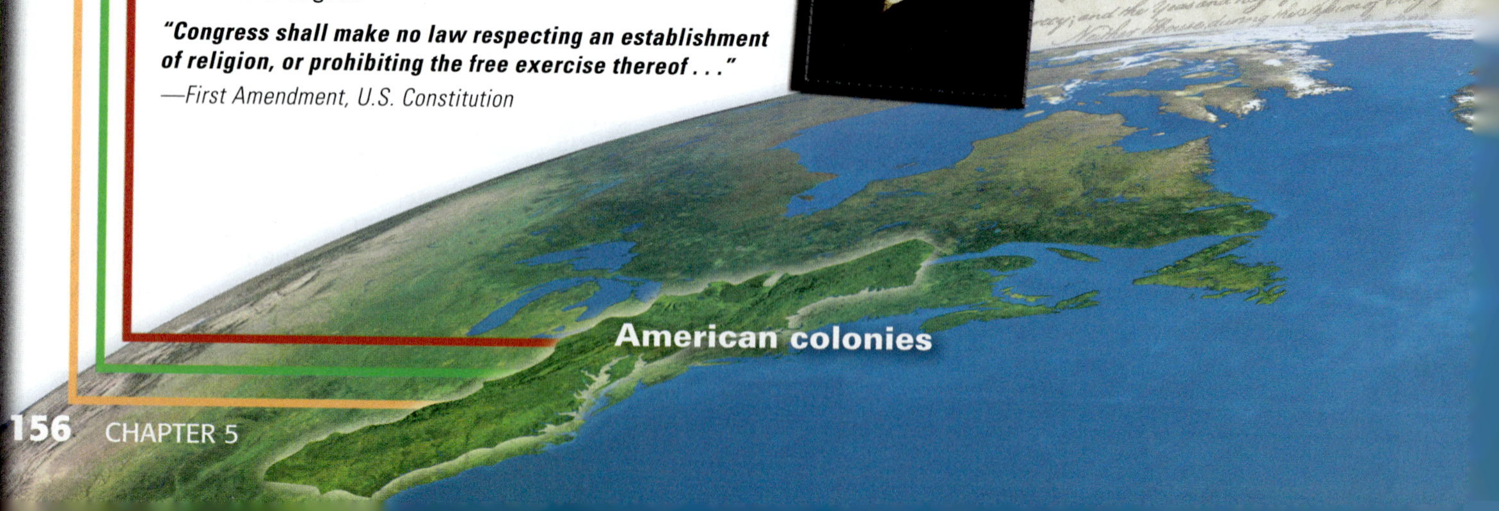

MAGNA CARTA, 1215

In this painting King John of England is signing Magna Carta, or the Great Charter, which established that the king was subject to the law just like everyone else. It also declared that people could not be deprived of their lives, liberty, or property ***"except by the lawful judgment of [their] peers, or by the law of the land."*** Compare this language to that of the Fifth Amendment to the Constitution.

"No person shall be . . . deprived of life, liberty, or property, without due process of law . . ."
—Fifth Amendment, U.S. Constitution

THE ENGLISH BILL OF RIGHTS, 1689

This painting shows King William and Queen Mary of England. Before taking the throne, William and Mary had to accept the English Bill of Rights. The English Bill of Rights took even more power away from the monarch than did Magna Carta. It also protected the rights of English citizens. These ideas would later influence the U.S. Constitution.

"Excessive bail ought not be required, nor excessive fines imposed; nor cruel and unusual punishments inflicted."
—English Bill of Rights

THE ENLIGHTENMENT, 1700s

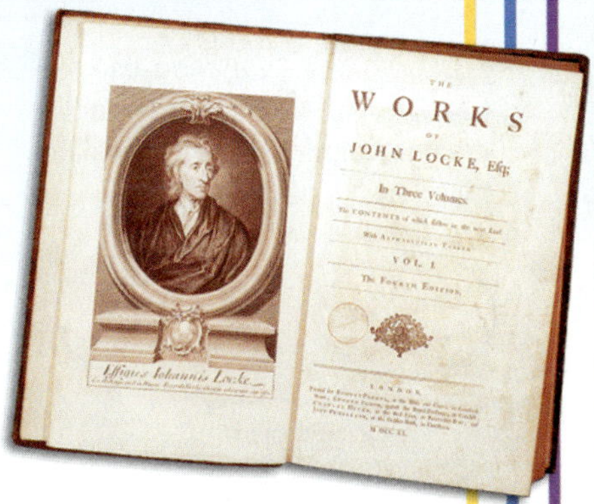

Enlightenment thinkers such as English philosopher John Locke supported the movement toward self-government. Locke argued in his writings that government could exist only with ***"the consent of the governed."*** The framers of the Constitution looked to Locke for inspiration when writing the Constitution, as you can see from its very first words.

"We the people of the United States . . . "
—Preamble, U.S. Constitution

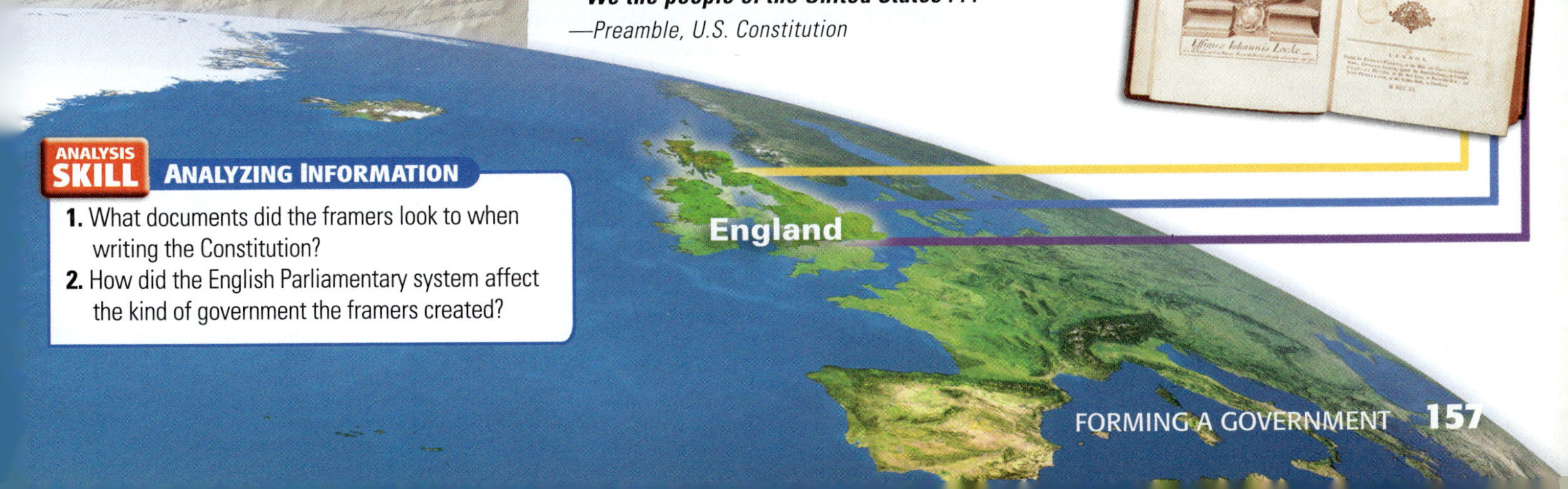

ANALYSIS SKILL **ANALYZING INFORMATION**

1. What documents did the framers look to when writing the Constitution?
2. How did the English Parliamentary system affect the kind of government the framers created?

SECTION 2

The New Nation Faces Challenges

What You Will Learn . . .

Main Ideas

1. The United States had difficulties with other nations.
2. Internal economic problems plagued the new nation.
3. Shays's Rebellion pointed out weaknesses in the Articles of Confederation.
4. Many Americans called for changes in the national government.

The Big Idea

Problems faced by the young nation made it clear that a new constitution was needed.

Key Terms and People

tariffs, *p. 159*
interstate commerce, *p. 160*
inflation, *p. 161*
depression, *p. 161*
Daniel Shays, *p. 161*
Shays's Rebellion, *p. 161*

TAKING NOTES As you read, use a graphic organizer like the one below to identify problems faced by the new nation.

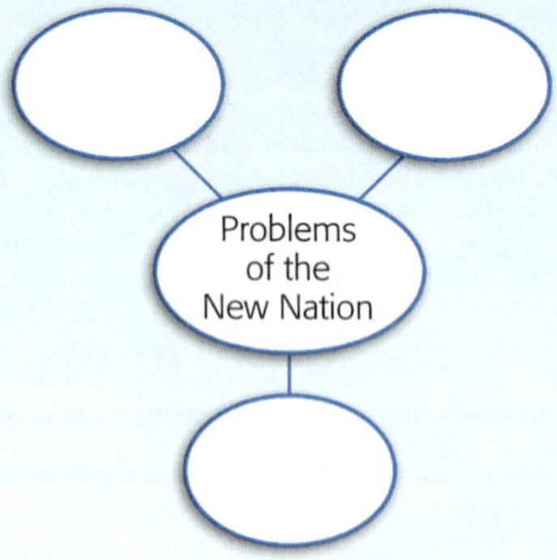

If YOU were there...

You own an orchard in Maryland in the 1780s. When you sell apples and apple pies in the market, people pay you with paper money. But now the tax collector says you must pay your taxes in gold or silver coins, not paper money. You and the other farmers are furious. Is this the liberty you fought a war for?

What would you do to protest these taxes?

BUILDING BACKGROUND Americans surprised the world by winning their independence from Great Britain. But the 13 new states were far from being a strong nation. Internal problems, especially with taxes and the economy, led to protests and rebellion. The government also had trouble with foreign trade and treaties.

Relations with Other Countries

Under the Articles of Confederation, Congress could not force states to provide soldiers for an army. The Continental Army had disbanded, or dissolved, soon after the signing of the Treaty of Paris of 1783. Without an army, the national government found it difficult to protect its citizens against foreign threats.

Trouble with Britain

It was also difficult to enforce international treaties such as the Treaty of Paris of 1783. The United States found it especially hard to force the British to turn over "with all convenient speed" their forts on the American side of the Great Lakes. The United States wanted to gain control of these forts because they protected valuable land and fur-trade routes. Still, Britain was slow to withdraw from the area. A British official warned against the United States trying to seize the forts by force. He said that any attempt to do so would be opposed by the thousands of British soldiers who had settled in Canada after the Revolution "who are ready to fly to arms at a moment's warning."

The United States Faces Trade Barriers

GEOGRAPHY SKILLS INTERPRETING MAPS

1. **Movement** Along what river did trade goods reach the port of New Orleans?
2. **Location** Along what three routes did U.S. trade face foreign barriers?

Trade with Britain

The United States also faced problems trading with Great Britain. After the signing of the Treaty of Paris, Britain closed many of its ports to American ships. Before the Revolutionary War, colonial ships had traded a great deal with the British West Indies and stopped there on their way to other destinations. This travel and trading stopped after 1783.

In addition, Britain forced American merchants to pay high **tariffs**—taxes on imports or exports. The tariffs applied to goods such as rice, tobacco, tar, and oil that were grown or mined in the United States and then sold in Britain. Merchants had to raise prices to cover the tariffs. Ultimately, the costs would be passed on to customers, who had to pay higher prices for the goods. The economic condition of the country was getting worse by the day.

Trade with Spain

In 1784 Spanish officials closed the lower Mississippi River to U.S. shipping. Western farmers and merchants were furious because they used the Mississippi to send goods to eastern and foreign markets. Congress tried to work out an agreement with Spain, but the plan did not receive a majority vote in Congress. The plan could not be passed. As a result, Spain broke off the negotiations.

Many state leaders began to criticize the national government. Rhode Island's representatives wrote, "Our federal government is but a name; a mere shadow without substance [power]." Critics believed that Spain might have continued to negotiate if the United States had possessed a strong military. These leaders believed that the national government needed to be more powerful.

Impact of Closed Markets

The closing of markets in the British West Indies seriously affected the U.S. economy. James Madison of Virginia wrote about the crisis.

> "The Revolution has robbed us of our trade with the West Indies . . . without opening any other channels to compensate [make up for] it. In every point of view, indeed, the trade of this country is in a deplorable [terrible] condition."
>
> —James Madison, quoted in *Independence on Trial* by Frederick W. Marks III

Farmers could no longer export their goods to the British West Indies. They also had to hire British ships to carry their goods to British markets, which was very expensive. American exports dropped while British goods flowed freely into the United States.

This unequal trade caused serious economic problems for the new nation. British merchants could sell manufactured products in the United States at much lower prices than locally made goods. This difference in prices hurt American businesses.

The Confederation Congress could not correct the problem because it did not have the authority either to pass tariffs or to order the states to pass tariffs. The states could offer little help. If one state passed a tariff, the British could simply sell their goods in another state. Most states did not cooperate in trade matters. Instead, states worked only to increase their own trade rather than working to improve the trade situation for the whole country.

In 1785 the situation led a British magazine to call the new nation the Dis-United States. As a result of the trade problems with Britain, American merchants began looking for other markets such as China, France, and the Netherlands. Despite such attempts, Britain remained the most important trading partner of the United States.

READING CHECK **Analyzing** Why was the Confederation Congress unable to solve America's international trade problems?

Economic Problems

In addition to international trade issues, other challenges soon appeared. Trade problems among the states, war debts, and a weak economy plagued the states.

Trade among States

Because the Confederation Congress had no power to regulate **interstate commerce**—trade between two or more states—states followed their own trade interests. As a result, trade laws differed from state to state. This situation made trade difficult for merchants whose businesses crossed state lines.

Inflation

After the Revolutionary War, most states had a hard time paying off war debts and struggled to collect overdue taxes. To ease this hardship, some states began printing large amounts of paper money. The result was inflation. This money had little

A Farmer Leads a Revolt

Daniel Shays, at the top of the steps, stands firm in the face of demands that he leave the courthouse in Springfield, Massachusetts. By shutting down the courts, farmers hoped to stop the government from selling their land.

What was the outcome of Shays's Rebellion?

or no real value, because states did not have gold or silver reserves to back it up. **Inflation** occurs when there are increased prices for goods and services combined with the reduced value of money. Congress had no power to stop states from issuing more paper money and thus stop inflation.

Weak Economy

In Rhode Island the state legislature printed large amounts of paper money worth very little. This made debtors—people who owe money—quite happy. They could pay back their debts with paper money worth less than the coins they had borrowed. However, creditors—people who lend money—were upset. Hundreds of creditors fled Rhode Island to avoid being paid back with worthless money.

The loss of trade with Britain combined with inflation created a **depression**. A depression is a period of low economic activity combined with a rise in unemployment.

READING CHECK **Summarizing** What economic problems did the new nation face?

Shays's Rebellion

Each state handled its economic problems differently. Massachusetts refused to print worthless paper money. It tried to pay its war debts by collecting taxes on land.

Heavy Debts for Farmers

Massachusetts's tax policy hit farmers hard. As landowners, they had to pay the new taxes. However, farmers had trouble paying their debts. The courts began forcing them to sell their property. Some farmers had to serve terms in debtors' prison; others had to sell their labor.

Many government leaders in the state did not care about the problems of poor farmers, however. In some cases, farmers actually owed these leaders money.

Farmers Rebel

In August 1786, farmers in three western counties began a revolt. Bands of angry citizens closed down courts in western Massachusetts. Their reasoning was simple—with the courts shut down, no one's property could be taken. In September a poor farmer and Revolutionary War veteran, **Daniel Shays**, led hundreds of men in a forced shutdown of the Supreme Court in Springfield, Massachusetts. The state government ordered the farmers to stop the revolt under threat of capture and death. These threats only made Shays and his followers more determined. The uprising of farmers to protest high taxes and heavy debt became known as **Shays's Rebellion**.

Shays's Defeat

Shays's forces were defeated by state troops in January 1787. By February many of the rebels were in prison. During their trials, 14 leaders were sentenced to death. However, the state soon freed most of the rebels, including Shays. State officials knew that many citizens of the state agreed with the rebels and their cause.

READING CHECK **Finding Main Ideas** What led to Shays's Rebellion?

Calls for Change

In the end, Shays's Rebellion showed the weakness of the Confederation government. It led some Americans to admit that the Articles of Confederation had failed to protect the ideals of liberty set forth in the Declaration of Independence.

When Massachusetts had asked the national government to help put down Shays's Rebellion, Congress could offer little help. More Americans began calling for a stronger central government. They wanted leaders who would be able to protect the nation in times of crisis.

Weaknesses of the Articles of Confederation (QUICK FACTS)
• Most power held by states
• One branch of government
• Legislative branch has few powers
• No executive branch
• No judicial system
• No system of checks and balances

Earlier in 1786 the Virginia legislature had called for a national conference. It wanted to talk about economic problems and ways to change the Articles of Confederation. The meeting took place in Annapolis, Maryland, in September 1786.

Nine states decided to send delegates to the Annapolis Convention but some of their delegates were late and missed the meeting. Connecticut, Georgia, Maryland, and South Carolina did not respond to the request at all and sent no delegates.

Because of the poor attendance, the participants, including James Madison and Alexander Hamilton, called on all 13 states to send delegates to a Constitutional Convention in Philadelphia in May 1787. They planned to revise the Articles of Confederation to better meet the needs of the nation.

READING CHECK **Finding Main Ideas** Why did some people believe the national government needed to change?

SUMMARY AND PREVIEW Many Americans believed that Shays's Rebellion was final proof that the national government needed to be changed. In the next section you will read about the Constitutional Convention.

Section 2 Assessment

go.hrw.com
Online Quiz
KEYWORD: SC7 HP5

Reviewing Ideas, Terms, and People

1. a. **Summarize** What problems did the United States experience with Spain and Great Britain?
   b. **Predict** What are some possible results of the growing problems between the United States and Great Britain? Why?
2. a. **Describe** What difficulties were involved with **interstate commerce**?
   b. **Analyze** What was the cause of **inflation** in the new nation, and how could it have been prevented?
3. a. **Explain** How did Massachusetts's tax policy affect farmers?
   b. **Evaluate** Defend the actions of **Daniel Shays** and the other rebels.
4. a. **Recall** Why did Madison and Hamilton call for a Constitutional Convention?
   b. **Analyze** How did **Shays's Rebellion** lead to a call for change in the United States?

Critical Thinking

5. **Categorizing** Review your notes on the problems faced by the new nation. Then identify those problems as either domestic or international in a graphic organizer like the one shown below.

Domestic Problems	International Problems

FOCUS ON WRITING

6. **Identifying Problems** In this section you learned about several problems of the young United States. Were any of those problems made worse by the powers that the Articles of Confederation did or did not give the national government?

Creating the Constitution

SECTION 3

If YOU were there...

You are a merchant in Connecticut in 1787. You have been a member of your state legislature for several years. This spring, the legislature is choosing delegates to a convention to revise the Articles of Confederation. Delegates will meet in Philadelphia. It means leaving your business in others' hands for most of the summer. Still, you hope to be chosen.

Why would you want to go to the Constitutional Convention?

BUILDING BACKGROUND It did not take long for people to realize that the Articles of Confederation had many weaknesses. By the mid-1780s most political leaders agreed that changes were needed. To make those changes, they called on people with experience in government.

Constitutional Convention

In February 1787 the Confederation Congress invited each state to send delegates to a convention in Philadelphia. The goal of the meeting was to improve the Articles of Confederation.

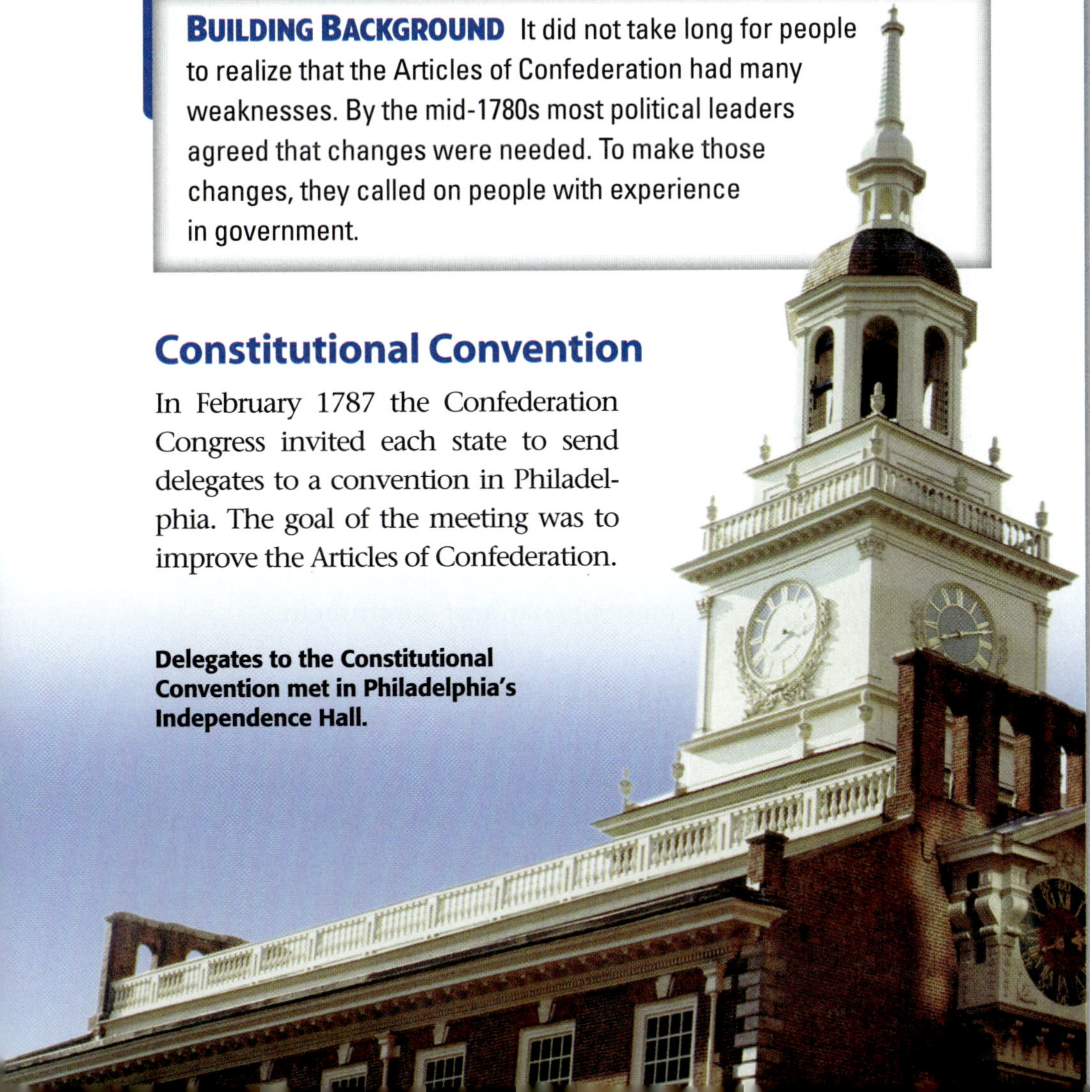

Delegates to the Constitutional Convention met in Philadelphia's Independence Hall.

What You Will Learn . . .

Main Ideas

1. The Constitutional Convention met to improve the government of the United States.
2. The issue of representation led to the Great Compromise.
3. Regional debate over slavery led to the Three-Fifths Compromise.
4. The U.S. Constitution created federalism and a balance of power.

The Big Idea

A new constitution provided a framework for a stronger national government.

Key Terms and People

Constitutional Convention, *p. 164*
James Madison, *p. 164*
Virginia Plan, *p. 164*
New Jersey Plan, *p. 165*
Great Compromise, *p. 165*
Three-Fifths Compromise, *p. 166*
popular sovereignty, *p. 167*
federalism, *p. 167*
legislative branch, *p. 167*
executive branch, *p. 167*
judicial branch, *p. 167*
checks and balances, *p. 167*

TAKING NOTES As you read, take notes on the conflicts that arose during the Constitutional Convention and the compromises reached.

Conflicts → Compromises

Signing of the Constitution

Roger Sherman · James Madison · James Wilson

The **Constitutional Convention** was held in May 1787 in Philadelphia's Independence Hall to improve the Articles of Confederation. However, delegates would leave with an entirely new U.S. Constitution. This decision angered some of the participants.

Most delegates were well educated, and many had served in state legislatures or Congress. Benjamin Franklin and **James Madison** were there. Revolutionary War hero George Washington was elected president of the Convention.

Several important voices were absent. John Adams and Thomas Jefferson could not attend. Patrick Henry chose not to attend because he did not want a stronger central government. Women, African Americans, and Native Americans did not take part because they did not yet have the rights of citizens.

READING CHECK **Summarizing** What was the purpose of the Constitutional Convention?

Great Compromise

Several issues divided the delegates to the Constitutional Convention. Some members wanted only small changes to the Articles of Confederation, while others wanted to rewrite the Articles completely.

Those delegates who wanted major changes to the Articles had different goals. For example, small and large states had different ideas about representation, economic concerns such as tariffs, and slavery. In addition, delegates disagreed over how strong to make the national government.

Virginia Plan

After the delegates had met for four days, Edmund Randolph of Virginia presented the **Virginia Plan**. He proposed a new federal constitution that would give sovereignty, or supreme power, to the central government. The legislature would be bicameral—made

1 Roger Sherman
2 Alexander Hamilton
3 Benjamin Franklin
4 James Madison
5 George Washington
6 James Wilson

This painting shows the signing of the Constitution on September 17, 1787. James Madison, number 4 on the diagram, became known as the "Father of the Constitution" for his ideas about government and his ability to lead the delegates to agreement. ***Which person did the artist choose to make the focus of this painting? Why do you think that is?***

up of two houses, or groups of representatives—and chosen on the basis of state populations. Larger states would thus have more representatives than would smaller states. Delegates from the smaller states believed that it would give too much power to the larger states.

New Jersey Plan

The smaller states came up with a plan to stop the larger states from getting too much power. New Jersey delegate William Paterson presented the small-state or **New Jersey Plan**, which called for a unicameral, or one-house, legislature. The plan gave each state an equal number of votes, and thus an equal voice, in the federal government. The plan gave the federal government the power to tax citizens in all states, and it allowed the government to regulate commerce.

Compromise Is Reached

After a month of debate, the delegates were unable to agree on how states should be represented. The convention reached a deadlock.

Finally, Roger Sherman of Connecticut proposed a compromise plan. The legislative branch would have two houses. Each state, regardless of its size, would have two representatives in the Senate, or upper house. This would give each state an equal voice, pleasing the smaller states. In the House of Representatives, or lower house, the number of representatives for each state would be determined by the state's population. This pleased the larger states. The agreement to create a two-house legislature became known as the **Great Compromise**. James Wilson, a great speaker, saw his dream of a strong national government come true.

THE IMPACT TODAY

All U.S. states but one modeled their legislative branches on the federal one, with a House of Representatives and a Senate. Nebraska has a unicameral legislature.

READING CHECK **Contrasting** How did the Virginia Plan and New Jersey Plan differ?

QUICK FACTS

Virginia Plan
- Gave more power to national government
- Bicameral legislature
- Number in both houses based on population

Great Compromise
- Bicameral legislature
- Number of representatives based on state populations in lower house
- Number of representatives equal from each state in upper house

New Jersey Plan
- Gave more power to state governments
- Unicameral legislature
- Number of representatives equal from each state

Primary Source

POINTS OF VIEW

Compromise and the Slave Trade

The issue of slavery highlighted the growing division between the North and the South. Gouverneur Morris of New York spoke with much emotion against the Three-Fifths Compromise. Also, the idea of banning the foreign slave trade prompted southerners such as John Rutledge of South Carolina to defend the practice.

"If the Convention thinks that North Carolina, South Carolina, and Georgia will ever agree to the plan [to prohibit the slave trade], unless their right to import slaves be untouched, the expectation is vain [useless]."

—John Rutledge,
quoted in *The Atlantic Monthly,* February 1891, by Frank Gaylord Cook

"The admission of slaves into the Representation . . . comes to this: that the inhabitant of [a state] who goes to the coast of Africa and . . . tears away his fellow creatures from their dearest connections and damns them to the most cruel bondage [slavery], shall have more votes in a Government [established] for protection of the rights of mankind."

—Gouverneur Morris,
quoted in *Founding the Republic,* edited by John J. Patrick

ANALYSIS SKILL **ANALYZING PRIMARY SOURCES**

Finding Main Ideas How did these two views of slavery differ?

Three-Fifths Compromise

The debate over representation also involved regional differences. Southern delegates wanted enslaved Africans to be counted as part of their state populations. This way they would have more representatives, and more power, in Congress. Northerners disagreed. They wanted the number of slaves to determine taxes but not representation.

To resolve this problem, some delegates thought of a compromise. They wanted to count three-fifths of the slaves in each state as part of that state's population to decide how many representatives a state would have. After much debate, the delegates voted to accept the proposal, called the **Three-Fifths Compromise**. Under this agreement only three-fifths of a state's slave population would count when determining representation.

Another major issue was the foreign slave trade. Some of the delegates believed slavery was wrong and wanted the federal government to ban the slave trade. Others said that the southern states' economies needed the slave trade. Many southern delegates said they would leave the Union if the Constitution immediately ended the slave trade. Also at issue was Congress's ability to tax imports and exports.

Worried delegates reached another compromise. The Commerce Compromises allowed Congress to levy tariffs on imports, but not exports, and allowed the importation of slaves until the end of 1807. The delegates omitted, or left out, the words *slavery* and *slave* in the Constitution. They referred instead to "free Persons" and "all other Persons."

READING CHECK **Summarizing** What compromise was reached over the issue of the slave trade?

The Living Constitution

Most Convention delegates wanted a strong national government. At the same time, they hoped to protect **popular sovereignty**, the idea that political authority belongs to the people. Americans had boldly declared this idea in the Declaration of Independence.

Federalist Government

The delegates also wanted to balance the power of the central government with the power of the states. Therefore, the delegates created **federalism**. Federalism is the sharing of power between a central government and the states that make up a country. Under the previous confederal system, states were loosely joined together without a strong central government.

Under the Constitution, each state must obey the authority of the federal, or national, government. States have control over government functions not specifically assigned to the federal government. This includes control of local government, education, the chartering of corporations, and the supervision of religious bodies. States also have the power to create and oversee civil and criminal law. States, however, must protect the welfare of their citizens.

Checks and Balances

The Constitution also balances the power among three branches, each responsible for separate tasks. The first is the **legislative branch**, or Congress. Congress is responsible for proposing and passing laws. It is made up of two houses, as created in the Great Compromise. The Senate has two members from each state. In the House of Representatives each state is represented according to its population.

The second branch, the **executive branch**, includes the president and the departments that help run the government. The executive branch makes sure the law is carried out. The third branch is the **judicial branch**. The judicial branch is made up of all the national courts. This branch is responsible for interpreting laws, punishing criminals, and settling disputes between states.

The framers of the Constitution created a system of **checks and balances**, which keeps any branch of government from becoming too powerful. For example, Congress has the power to pass bills into law. The president has the power to veto, or reject, laws that Congress passes. However, Congress can override the president's veto with a two-thirds

LINKING TO TODAY

Legislative Branch

When it first met in 1789, the U.S. House of Representatives had just 65 members. As the nation's population grew, more members were added. Today, the number has been set at 435, to prevent the size of the House from growing unmanageable. Though the numbers of women and minorities in Congress are still unrepresentative of the population as a whole, Congress has become more diverse. Linda and Loretta Sanchez, pictured here, are the first sisters to serve in Congress at the same time.

ANALYSIS SKILL **ANALYZING INFORMATION**

How is the change in makeup of the legislative branch shown through Linda and Loretta Sanchez?

The Constitution Strengthens the National Government

QUICK FACTS

Strengths of the Constitution	Weaknesses of the Articles of Confederation
✔ most power held by national government	• most power held by states
✔ three branches of government	• one branch of government
✔ legislative branch has many powers	• legislative branch has few powers
✔ executive branch led by president	• no executive branch
✔ judicial branch to review the laws	• no judicial system
✔ firm system of checks and balances	• no system of checks and balances

majority vote. The Supreme Court has the power to review laws passed by Congress and strike down any law that violates the Constitution by declaring it *unconstitutional*.

The final draft of the Constitution was completed in September 1787. Only 3 of the 42 delegates who remained refused to sign. The signed Constitution was sent first to Congress and then to the states for ratification. The delegates knew that the Constitution was not a perfect document, but they believed they had protected the ideas of republicanism.

READING CHECK **Comparing and Contrasting** What are the differences between monarchies, federal systems, and confederal systems?

SUMMARY AND PREVIEW The Constitution balanced power among three branches of the federal government but was only written after many compromises. In the next section you will read about Antifederalist and Federalist views of the Constitution, and the struggle to get it approved by the states.

Section 3 Assessment

go.hrw.com
Online Quiz
KEYWORD: SC7 HP5

Reviewing Ideas, Terms, and People

1. a. **Recall** Why did the Confederation Congress call for a **Constitutional Convention**?
   b. **Elaborate** Why do you think it was important that most delegates had served in state legislatures?
2. a. **Identify** What was the **Great Compromise**?
   b. **Draw Conclusions** How did state issues lead to debate over structure of the central government?
3. a. **Explain** What was the debate between North and South over counting slave populations?
   b. **Contrast** How did delegates' views differ on the issue of the foreign slave trade?
4. a. **Recall** Why did the framers of the Constitution create a system of **checks and balances**?
   b. **Evaluate** Did the Constitution resolve the weaknesses in the Articles of Confederation? Explain your answer.

Critical Thinking

5. **Identifying Cause and Effect** Review your notes on the Constitutional Convention compromises. Then copy the graphic organizer below and use it to show how the compromises affected the framework of the new government.

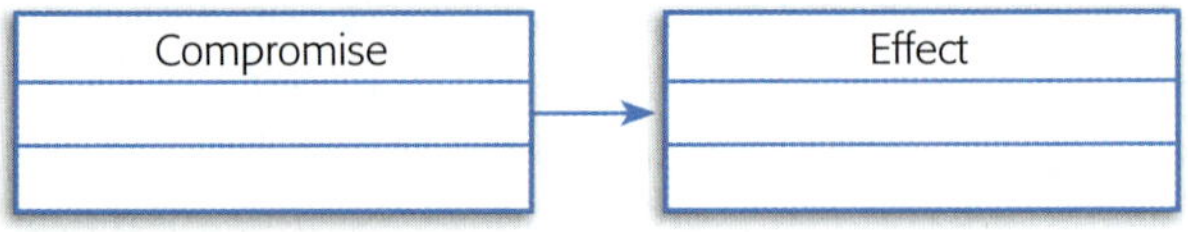

FOCUS ON WRITING

6. **Thinking about the Constitution** Look back through what you've just read and make a list of important features of the Constitution. Be sure to note important compromises.

BIOGRAPHY

Benjamin Franklin

How did one man accomplish so much?

When did he live? 1706–1790

Where did he live? Benjamin Franklin was born in Boston but ran away to Philadelphia at age 17 and made it his home. He also crossed the Atlantic Ocean eight times and visited 10 countries.

What did he do? What *didn't* he do! He was a printer, publisher, creator of the first circulating library, the first president of the University of Pennsylvania, inventor, scientist, philosopher, musician, economist, and the first U.S. Postmaster General. In politics he was a leading revolutionary, signer of the Declaration of Independence, head of an antislavery organization, delegate to the Constitutional Convention, and diplomat.

Why is he important? Benjamin Franklin, son of a candlemaker, became a celebrity in his own time, both in America and in Europe. Few people have mastered so many fields of knowledge and accomplished so much. He invented many useful objects, from bifocal glasses to the lightning rod. One of the oldest founding fathers, Franklin inspired younger revolutionaries such as Thomas Jefferson. Franklin believed strongly that people should volunteer and be in public service.

Finding Main Ideas How did Benjamin Franklin's life reflect his belief in public service?

KEY EVENTS

1729
Becomes owner and publisher of the *Pennsylvania Gazette*

1732–1758
Publishes *Poor Richard: An Almanack*

1752
Performs famous experiment using a kite to show that electricity exists in storm clouds

1775
Submits the Articles of Confederation

1779
Appointed minister to France

1782
Helps negotiate the Treaty of Paris with Britain

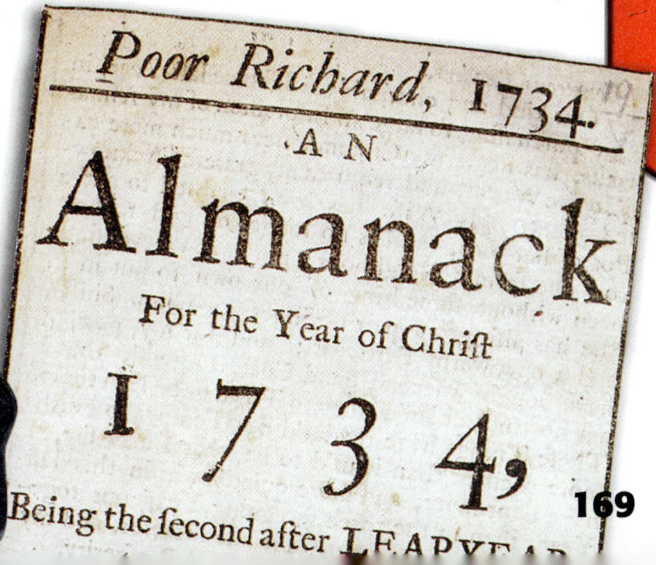
Poor Richard, 1734.
AN
Almanack
For the Year of Chrift
1 7 3 4,
Being the fecond after LEAPYEAR

SECTION 4

Ratifying the Constitution

What You Will Learn . . .

Main Ideas

1. Federalists and Antifederalists engaged in debate over the new Constitution.
2. The *Federalist Papers* played an important role in the fight for ratification of the Constitution.
3. Ten amendments were added to the Constitution to provide a Bill of Rights to protect citizens.

The Big Idea

Americans carried on a vigorous debate before ratifying the Constitution.

Key Terms and People

Antifederalists, *p. 170*
George Mason, *p. 170*
Federalists, *p. 170*
Federalist Papers, *p. 171*
amendments, *p. 173*
Bill of Rights, *p. 173*

TAKING NOTES As you read, take notes on the differing views of the U.S. Constitution.

Federalists		Antifederalists
	vs.	

If YOU were there...

You are a newspaper editor in Philadelphia. During colonial rule, officials sometimes closed down your newspaper because you had criticized the governor. Now you are one of many Americans who want to be sure the new Constitution will guarantee individual rights. You are writing an editorial in your paper explaining what you want.

What rights would you want the Constitution to protect?

BUILDING BACKGROUND The new Constitution did not make everyone happy. Even its framers knew they had not made a perfect document. Many people were afraid a strong national government would become as tyrannical as the British government had been. Before approving the Constitution, they wanted to be sure that their rights would be protected.

Federalists and Antifederalists

When the Constitution was made public, a huge debate began among many Americans. **Antifederalists**—people who opposed the Constitution—thought that the Constitutional Convention should not have created a new government. Others thought the Constitution gave too much power to the central government. For some Antifederalists, the main problem was that the Constitution did not have a section that guaranteed individual rights. Delegate **George Mason** became an Antifederalist for this reason.

Many Antifederalists were small farmers and debtors. Some Patriots were also strong Antifederalists, including Samuel Adams and Patrick Henry. Antifederalists were challenged by those who believed that the United States needed a stronger central government.

Federalists, supporters of the Constitution, included James Madison, George Washington, Benjamin Franklin, and Alexander Hamilton. Most Federalists believed that the Constitution offered a good balance of power between various political views. Many

Federalists vs. Antifederalists

QUICK FACTS

Alexander Hamilton
Federalist

- Supported the Constitution as an excellent plan for government
- Defended his views in the *Federalist Papers*

George Mason
Antifederalist

- Opposed the Constitution
- Believed the Constitution needed a section guaranteeing individual rights

Federalists were wealthy planters, farmers, and lawyers. However, others were workers and craftspeople.

Federalists and Antifederalists debated whether the new Constitution should be approved. They made speeches and printed pamphlets **advocating** their views. Mercy Otis Warren, an ardent Patriot during the war, wrote a pamphlet entitled *Observations on the New Constitution*, in which she criticized the lack of individual rights it provided. The Federalists had to convince people a change in the structure of government was needed. To do this, they had to overcome people's fears that the Constitution would make the government too powerful.

READING CHECK **Comparing and Contrasting** Explain the similarities and differences between the Antifederalists and the Federalists.

Federalist Papers

One of the most important defenses of the Constitution appeared in a series of essays that became known as the ***Federalist Papers***. These essays supporting the Constitution were written anonymously under the name Publius. They were actually written by Hamilton, Madison, and Jay.

The authors of the *Federalist Papers* tried to reassure Americans that the new federal government would not overpower the states. In *Federalist Paper* No. 10, Madison argued that the diversity of the United States would prevent any single group from dominating the government.

The *Federalist Papers* were widely reprinted in newspapers around the country as the debate over the Constitution continued. Finally, they were collected and published in book form in 1788.

FOCUS ON READING

Take notes on the chronological order of this section. Which was written first, the *Federalist Papers* or the Bill of Rights?

ACADEMIC VOCABULARY

advocate to plead in favor of

Primary Source

HISTORIC DOCUMENT

Federalist Paper No. 10

In November 1787, Number 10 in the series called the Federalist Papers *was written in support of the Constitution. In it, James Madison describes the way federalism will overcome disagreements within society.*

"A landed interest, a manufacturing interest, a mercantile [trading] interest, a moneyed interest, with many lesser interests, grow up of necessity in civilized nations, and divide them into different classes, actuated [moved] by different sentiments and views. The regulation of these various and interfering interests [opinions] forms the principal task of modern legislation, and involves the spirit of party and faction [group] in the necessary and ordinary operations of the government . . .

The federal Constitution forms a happy combination . . . the great . . . interests being referred to the national [legislature]; the local and particular to the state legislatures . . . The influence of factious leaders may kindle [start] a flame within their particular states, but will be unable to spread a general conflagration [large fire] through the other states."

—James Madison, quoted in *Living American Documents*, edited by Isidore Starr, et al.

Madison believes that lawmakers are responsible for regulating the many competing concerns that make up society.

The federal government will handle issues affecting the nation as a whole; state and local governments will handle those concerning local issues.

ANALYSIS SKILL **ANALYZING PRIMARY SOURCES**

Why does Madison think federalism will prevent disagreement?

The Constitution needed only 9 states to pass it. However, to establish and preserve national unity, each state needed to ratify it. Every state except Rhode Island held special state conventions that gave citizens the chance to discuss and vote on the Constitution.

Paul Revere served on a committee supporting ratification. He wrote of the Constitution, "The proposed . . . government, is well calculated [planned] to secure the liberties, protect the property, and guard the rights of the citizens of America." Antifederalists also spoke out in state conventions, and wrote articles and pamphlets that became known as the Antifederalist Papers. In New York, one citizen said, "It appears that the government will fall into the hands of the few and the great."

On December 7, 1787, Delaware became the first state to ratify the Constitution. It went into effect in June 1788 after New Hampshire became the ninth state to ratify it.

Political leaders across America knew the new government needed the support of the large states of Virginia and New York, where debate still raged. Finally, Madison and fellow Virginia Federalists convinced Virginia to ratify it in mid-1788. In New York, riots had occurred when the draft of the Constitution was made public. At the state convention in Poughkeepsie to discuss ratification, Hamilton argued convincingly against the Antifederalists led by DeWitt Clinton. When news arrived of Virginia's ratification, New York ratified it as well. Rhode Island was the last state to ratify the Constitution in May 1790.

READING CHECK **Drawing Conclusions** Why were Virginia and New York important to the ratification of the Constitution?

Bill of Rights

Several states ratified the Constitution only after they were promised that a bill protecting individual rights would be added to it. Many Antifederalists did not think that the Constitution would protect personal freedoms.

Some Federalists said that the nation did not need a federal bill of rights because the Constitution itself was a bill of rights. It was, they argued, written to protect the liberty of all U.S. citizens.

James Madison wanted to make a bill of rights one of the new government's first priorities. In Congress's first session, Madison encouraged the legislators to put together a bill of rights. The rights would then be added to the Constitution as **amendments**, or official changes. In Article V of the Constitution, the founders had provided a way to change the document when necessary in order to reflect the will of the people. The process requires that proposed amendments must be approved by a two-thirds majority of both houses of Congress and then ratified by three-fourths of the states before taking effect.

Legislators took ideas from the state ratifying conventions, the Virginia Declaration of Rights, the English Bill of Rights, and the Declaration of Independence to make sure that the abuses listed in the Declaration of Independence would be illegal under the new government. In September 1789 Congress proposed 12 amendments and sent them to the states for ratification. By December 1791 the states had ratified the **Bill of Rights**—10 of the proposed amendments intended to protect citizens' rights.

These 10 amendments set a clear example of how to amend the Constitution to fit the needs of a changing nation. The flexibility of the U.S. Constitution has allowed it to survive for more than 200 years.

READING CHECK **Summarizing** Why is being able to amend the Constitution important?

SUMMARY AND PREVIEW Early disagreements over individual rights resulted in the Bill of Rights. In the next chapter you will learn about the structure of the Constitution.

THE IMPACT TODAY

In 1789, Madison suggested an amendment limiting Congress's power over its own salary. This amendment was not passed until 1992.

go.hrw.com
Online Quiz
KEYWORD: SC7 HP5

Section 4 Assessment

Reviewing Ideas, Terms, and People

1. a. **Identify** Who were the **Federalists** and the **Antifederalists**?
   b. **Draw Conclusions** What was the main argument of the Antifederalists against the Constitution?
   c. **Elaborate** Do you agree with the Antifederalists or the Federalists? Explain your position.
2. a. **Recall** When did the Constitution go into effect?
   b. **Draw Conclusions** Why was it important that all 13 states ratify the Constitution?
   c. **Elaborate** Do you think that the ***Federalist Papers*** played an essential role in the ratification of the Constitution? Explain your answer.
3. a. **Recall** Why did Congress add the **Bill of Rights**?
   b. **Explain** From where did legislators' ideas for the Bill of Rights come?
   c. **Elaborate** Do you think the process for amending the Constitution is too difficult? Explain your position.

Critical Thinking

4. **Analyzing** Review your notes on Federalist and Antifederalist views. Then identify the outcome of the debate in a graphic organizer like the one below. Be sure to mention the Bill of Rights.

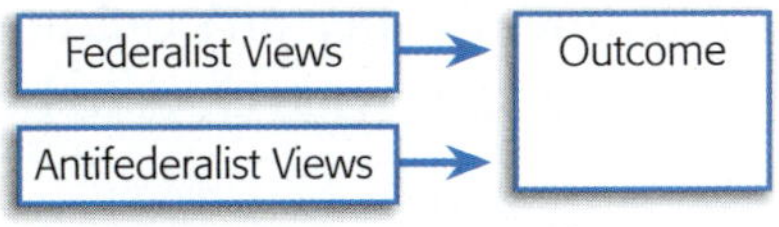

FOCUS ON WRITING

5. **Organizing Your Evidence** In this section you learned how the Bill of Rights was an important addition to the Constitution. You now have all your evidence about the difference between the Articles of Confederation and the Constitution. Choose two or three of the most important points and prepare to defend the Constitution, just like Alexander Hamilton and James Madison did in the *Federalist Papers*.

Social Studies Skills

Analysis | Critical Thinking | Civic Participation | Study

North Carolina Skills
1.05 Recognize bias and propaganda.

Determining Different Points of View

Define the Skill

A *point of view* is a person's outlook or attitude. It is the way that he or she looks at a topic or thing. Each person's point of view is shaped by his or her background. Because people's backgrounds are different, their points of view are too. Since a person's point of view shapes his or her opinions, knowing that point of view helps you understand and evaluate those opinions. Being able to detect differences in point of view is important to understanding differences in people's opinions and actions in history.

Learn the Skill

When you encounter someone's beliefs, opinions, or actions in your study of history, use the following guidelines to determine his or her point of view.

1. Look for information about the person's background.
2. Ask yourself what factors in the person's background might have influenced his or her opinion or action concerning the topic or event.
3. Be aware that sometimes the person's opinions or actions themselves will provide clues to his or her point of view.

Benjamin Lincoln led the troops that put down Shays's Rebellion in Massachusetts. He was also a state politician and a general during the Revolution. Lincoln offered this explanation of Shays's uprising.

> "Among [the main causes] I rank the ease with which … credit was obtained … in the time of [the Revolution] … The moment the day arrived when all discovered that things were fast returning [to normal], … and that the indolent [lazy persons] and improvident [unwise persons] would soon experience the evils of their idleness and sloth, many startled [panicked] … and … complained … of the weight of public taxes … and at the cruelty of … creditors [those to whom money is owed] to call for their just dues [rightful payment] … The disaffected [unhappy people] … attempted … to stop the courts of law, and to suspend the operations of government. This they hoped to do until … an end should thereby be put to public and private debts."

Lincoln's background as a general, state official, and leader against the rebels likely gave him a negative point of view on the revolt. His reference to the rebels as lazy and unwise also provides clues to his attitude. You should weigh such factors when evaluating the accuracy of his statement.

Practice the Skill

The following statement about Shays's Rebellion came from a Massachusetts farmer. Read it and apply the guidelines to answer the questions.

> "I have labored hard … all my days. I have been … obliged to do more than my part in the [Revolution], been loaded with … rates [taxes], … have been … [abused] by sheriffs … and [debt] collectors … I have lost a great deal … [T]he great men are going to get all we have, and I think it is time for us to … put a stop to it."

1. From what point of view is this person commenting on the revolt? What is his opinion of it?
2. How does his view of himself differ from Lincoln's view of people like him?
3. Is this view of the revolt likely to be more accurate than Lincoln's view? Why or why not?

CHAPTER 5 Chapter Review

HOLT

History's Impact

▶ **video series**

Review the video to answer the closing question:

Why would adding more U.S. territory have been appealing in the 1700s and 1800s?

Visual Summary

QUICK FACTS

Use the visual summary below to help you review the main ideas of the chapter.

Reviewing Vocabulary, Terms, and People

Match the numbered person or term with the correct lettered definition.

1. Bill of Rights
2. checks and balances
3. constitution
4. Constitutional Convention
5. *Federalist Papers*
6. inflation
7. Northwest Territory
8. George Mason
9. tariffs
10. Three-Fifths Compromise

a. agreement that stated that each slave would be counted as three-fifths of a person when determining representation

b. delegate to the Constitutional Convention who became an Antifederalist

c. increased prices for goods and services combined with the reduced value of money

d. area including present-day Illinois, Indiana, Michigan, Ohio, Wisconsin, and part of Minnesota

e. meetings held in Philadelphia at which delegates from the states attempted to improve the existing government

f. series of essays in support of the Constitution

g. set of basic principles that determines the powers and duties of a government

h. system that prevents any branch of government from becoming too powerful

i. taxes on imports or exports

j. the first 10 amendments to the Constitution

Comprehension and Critical Thinking

SECTION 1 *(Pages 152–155)*

11. a. Describe What powers did the Articles of Confederation give the national government?

b. Summarize What did the Confederation Congress do to strengthen the United States?

c. Evaluate Which document or institution do you think had the greatest influence on the development of the United States? Why?

SECTION 2 *(Pages 158–162)*

12. a. Recall What was Shays's Rebellion?

b. Draw Conclusions What was the general attitude of foreign nations toward the new government of the United States? Why?

c. Evaluate Of the problems experienced by the Confederation Congress, which do you think was the most harmful? Why?

SECTION 3 *(Pages 163–168)*

13. a. Describe In what ways did the Constitution strengthen the central government?

b. Explain How did the two compromises reached during the Constitutional Convention satisfy competing groups?

c. Elaborate In your opinion were there any weaknesses in the Constitution? Explain your answer.

SECTION 4 *(Pages 170–173)*

14. a. Recall Why was the Bill of Rights added to the Constitution?

b. Draw Conclusions Why were some Americans opposed to the Constitution?

c. Evaluate Would you have supported the Federalists or the Antifederalists? Explain your answer.

Reviewing Themes

15. Politics What political problems resulted from a weak central government under the Articles of Confederation?

16. Politics How did political disagreements lead to important compromises in the creation of the Constitution?

Reading Skills

Understanding Chronological Order *Use the Reading Skills taught in this chapter to answer the question below.*

17. Organize the following events chronologically according to the chapter.

a. The *Federalist Papers* are published.

b. The Constitution is ratified.

c. The Articles of Confederation are ratified.

d. Shays's Rebellion occurs.

e. The Constitutional Convention meets in Philadelphia.

Social Studies Skills

Determining Different Points of View *Use the Social Studies Skills taught in this chapter to answer the question below.*

18. List three differences between the Virginia Plan and the New Jersey Plan.

FOCUS ON WRITING

19. Writing Your Editorial You should start your editorial with a strong statement of your opinion about the Constitution. Then write two sentences about each of your main points of support—a weakness of the Articles of Confederation and/or a strength of the Constitution. End your editorial with a call to action: Ask the delegates to the Constitutional Convention to ratify the Constitution. Remember that you are trying to convince people to make a very important decision for our country—be persuasive.

CHAPTER 5

Standardized Test Practice

DIRECTIONS: Read each question and write the letter of the best response.

1 Which term would *best* describe the newly independent nation in the 1780s?

A strong

B united

C troubled

D confident

2 Under the Articles of Confederation, the greatest amount of power was in the hands of the

A Congress.

B American people.

C national government.

D states.

3 How did North Carolina's Constitution of 1776 affect the rights of citizens?

A It gave more power to the state legislature.

B It included a bill of rights to protect citizens' rights.

C It outlawed slavery.

D It granted women the right to vote.

4 The Articles of Confederation led to conflicts between the United States and foreign countries because the new government

A lacked a bill of rights to protect citizens' rights.

B gave little power to the national government.

C did not grant the Confederation Congress the power to regulate interstate commerce.

D did not establish a judicial system.

5 Which of the following *best* explains why many Antifederalists opposed the Constitution?

A They were upset that the Constitution did not protect individual rights.

B They did not want to outlaw slavery.

C They opposed weakening the power of the federal government.

D They did not support the establishment of three branches of government.

6 Which term is used to describe a situation in which Congress passes a bill and the president vetoes that bill?

A federalism

B popular sovereignty

C ratification

D checks and balances

7 Read the following passage from one of the *Federalist Papers* and use it to answer the question below.

> "The powers delegated by the proposed Constitution to the federal government are few and defined. Those which are to remain in the State governments are numerous and . . . will extend to all objects which . . . concern the lives, liberties, and properties of the people . . . The operations of the federal government will be most extensive and important in times of war and danger; those of the State governments in times of peace and security."
>
> —James Madison, *Federalist Paper* No. 45

Document-Based Question What point was Madison making about the system of government created by the proposed U.S. Constitution?

CHAPTER 6 1787–PRESENT

Citizenship and the Constitution

North Carolina Standards

Social Studies Objectives

9.02 Identify past and present state and local leaders from diverse cultural backgrounds and assess their influence in effecting change.

9.03 Describe opportunities for and benefits of civic participation.

Language Arts Objectives

1.02 Analyze expressive materials that are read, heard, and/or viewed by

- monitoring comprehension for understanding of what is read, heard and/or viewed.

4.01 Analyze the purpose of the author or creator and the impact of that purpose by:

- evaluating the effects of author's craft on the reader/viewer/listener.

4.02 Analyze and develop (with limited assistance) and apply appropriate criteria to evaluate the quality of the communication by:

- using knowledge of language structure and literary or media techniques.

6.01 Model an understanding of conventional written and spoken expression by:

- using a variety of sentence types, punctuating properly, and avoiding fragments and run-ons.
- using subject-verb agreement and verb tense that are appropriate for the meaning of the sentence.

go.hrw.com
North Carolina
KEYWORD: SC7 NC

Focus on Writing

A Pamphlet Everyone in the United States benefits from our Constitution. However, many people don't know the Constitution as well as they should. In this chapter you will read about the Constitution and the rights and responsibilities it grants to citizens. Then you'll create a four-page pamphlet to share this information with your fellow citizens.

UNITED STATES

1788 The Constitution goes into effect after New Hampshire becomes the ninth state to ratify it.

1787 — 1800

1791 The Bill of Rights becomes part of the Constitution on December 15.

HOLT
History's Impact
▶ **video series**
Watch the video to understand the impact of the Bill of Rights.

What You Will Learn...

In this chapter you will learn about the U.S. Constitution, the Bill of Rights, and what it means to be an American citizen. Young citizens like the ones pictured here must be informed in order to fulfill the rights and responsibilities of citizenship.

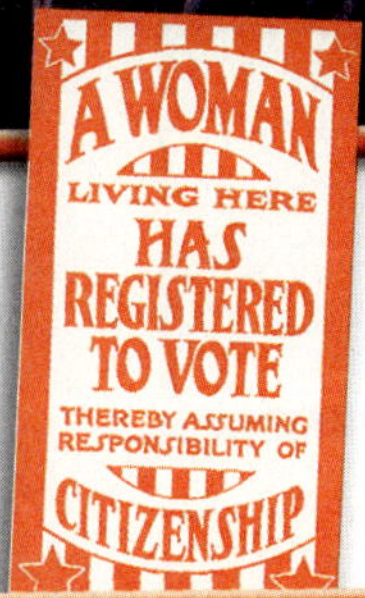

1920 The Nineteenth Amendment gives all American women the right to vote.

1930

1942 The Fair Employment Act bans discrimination in the workplace.

1950

1954 In *Brown* v. *Board of Education*, the Supreme Court declares segregation in public schools to be unconstitutional.

1970

1971 The Twenty-sixth Amendment is ratified, giving the right to vote to all U.S. citizens 18 years or older.

1990

1990 The Americans with Disabilities Act is passed.

Reading Social Studies

by Kylene Beers

Economics | Geography | **Politics** | Society and Culture | Science and Technology

Focus on Themes In this chapter you will read about the three branches of government, the Bill of Rights, and the duties and responsibilities of a United States citizen. As you read about each of these topics, you will see the American **political system** at work—not only in the Bill of Rights, but also through the responsibilities U.S. citizens have as they vote for leaders and work to help their communities and nation.

Summarizing Historical Texts

Focus on Reading History books are full of information. Sometimes the sheer amount of information they contain can make processing what you read difficult. In those cases, it may be helpful to stop for a moment and summarize what you've read.

Writing a Summary A summary is a short restatement of the most important ideas in a text. The example below shows three steps used in writing a summary. First underline important details. Then write a short summary of each paragraph. Finally, combine these paragraph summaries into a short summary of the whole passage.

The Constitution

Article II, Section 1

1. The executive Power shall be vested in a President of the United States of America. He shall hold his Office during the Term of four Years, and, together with the Vice President, chosen for the same Term, be elected, as follows:

2. Each State shall appoint, in such Manner as the Legislature thereof may direct, a Number of Electors, equal to the whole Number of Senators and Representatives to which the State may be entitled in the Congress; but no Senator or Representative, or Person holding an Office of Trust or Profit under the United States, shall be appointed an Elector.

Summary of Paragraph 1
The executive branch is headed by a president and vice president, each elected for four-year terms.

Summary of Paragraph 2
The electors who choose the president and vice president are appointed. Each state has the same number of electors as it has members of Congress.

Combined Summary
The president and vice president who run the executive branch are elected every four years by state-appointed electors.

You Try It!

The following passage is from the U.S. Constitution. As you read it, decide which facts you would include in a summary of the passage.

The Constitution

Article I, Section 2

1. The House of Representatives shall be composed of Members chosen every second Year by the People of the several States, and the Electors in each State shall have the Qualifications requisite for Electors of the most numerous branch of the State Legislature.

2. No person shall be a Representative who shall not have attained to the Age of twenty five years, and been seven Years a Citizen of the United States, and who shall not, when elected, be an Inhabitant of the State in which he shall be chosen.

After you read the passage, answer the following questions.

1. Which of the following statements best summarizes the first paragraph of this passage?

a. Congress has a House of Representatives.

b. Members of the House of Representatives are elected every two years by state electors.

2. Using the steps described on the previous page, write a summary of the second paragraph of this passage.

3. Combine the summary statement you chose in Question 1 with the summary statement you wrote in Question 2 to create a single summary of this entire passage.

As you read Chapter 6, think about what details you would include in a summary of each paragraph.

Key Terms and People

Chapter 6

Section 1

federal system *(p. 182)*
impeach *(p. 184)*
veto *(p. 184)*
executive orders *(p. 185)*
pardons *(p. 185)*
Thurgood Marshall *(p. 186)*
Sandra Day O'Connor *(p. 186)*

Section 2

James Madison *(p. 216)*
majority rule *(p. 216)*
petition *(p. 217)*
search warrant *(p. 218)*
due process *(p. 218)*
indict *(p. 218)*
double jeopardy *(p. 218)*
eminent domain *(p. 218)*

Section 3

naturalized citizens *(p. 222)*
deport *(p. 222)*
draft *(p. 223)*
political action committees *(p. 224)*
interest groups *(p. 224)*

Academic Vocabulary

Success in school is related to knowing academic vocabulary—the words that are frequently used in school assignments and discussions. In this chapter, you will learn the following academic words:

distinct *(p. 183)*
influence *(p. 224)*

SECTION 1

Understanding the Constitution

What You Will Learn...

Main Ideas

1. The framers of the Constitution devised the federal system.
2. The legislative branch makes the nation's laws.
3. The executive branch enforces the nation's laws.
4. The judicial branch determines whether or not laws are constitutional.

The Big Idea

The U.S. Constitution balances the powers of the federal government among the legislative, executive, and judicial branches.

Key Terms and People

federal system, *p. 182*
impeach, *p. 184*
veto, *p. 184*
executive orders, *p. 185*
pardons, *p. 185*
Thurgood Marshall, *p. 186*
Sandra Day O'Connor, *p. 186*

TAKING NOTES As you read, take notes on the structure of each of the branches of government in a chart like the one below.

Branch	Structure
Legislative	
Executive	
Judicial	

If YOU were there...

You have just been elected to the U.S. House of Representatives. You know that committees do much of the work in Congress. They deal with many different fields such as foreign policy, agriculture, national security, science, and education. You would like to ask for a spot on a committee whose work interests you.

Which committee would you ask to serve on?

BUILDING BACKGROUND When the framers of the Constitution met in Philadelphia in 1787, they created a national government with three branches that balance one another's powers.

The Federal System

The framers of the Constitution wanted to create a government powerful enough to protect the rights of citizens and defend the country against its enemies. To do so, they set up a **federal system** of government, a system that divided powers between the states and the federal government.

The Constitution assigns certain powers to the national government. These are called delegated powers. Among them are the rights to coin money and to regulate trade. Reserved powers are those kept by the states. These powers include creating local governments and holding elections. Concurrent powers are those shared by the federal and state governments. They include taxing, borrowing money, and enforcing laws.

Sometimes, Congress has had to stretch its delegated powers to deal with new or unexpected issues. A clause in the Constitution states that Congress may "make all Laws which shall be necessary and proper" for carrying out its duties. This clause, called the elastic clause—because it can be stretched (like elastic)—provides flexibility for the government. The federal government has used this clause to provide public services such as funding for the arts and humanities.

READING CHECK **Summarizing** How is power divided between the federal and state governments?

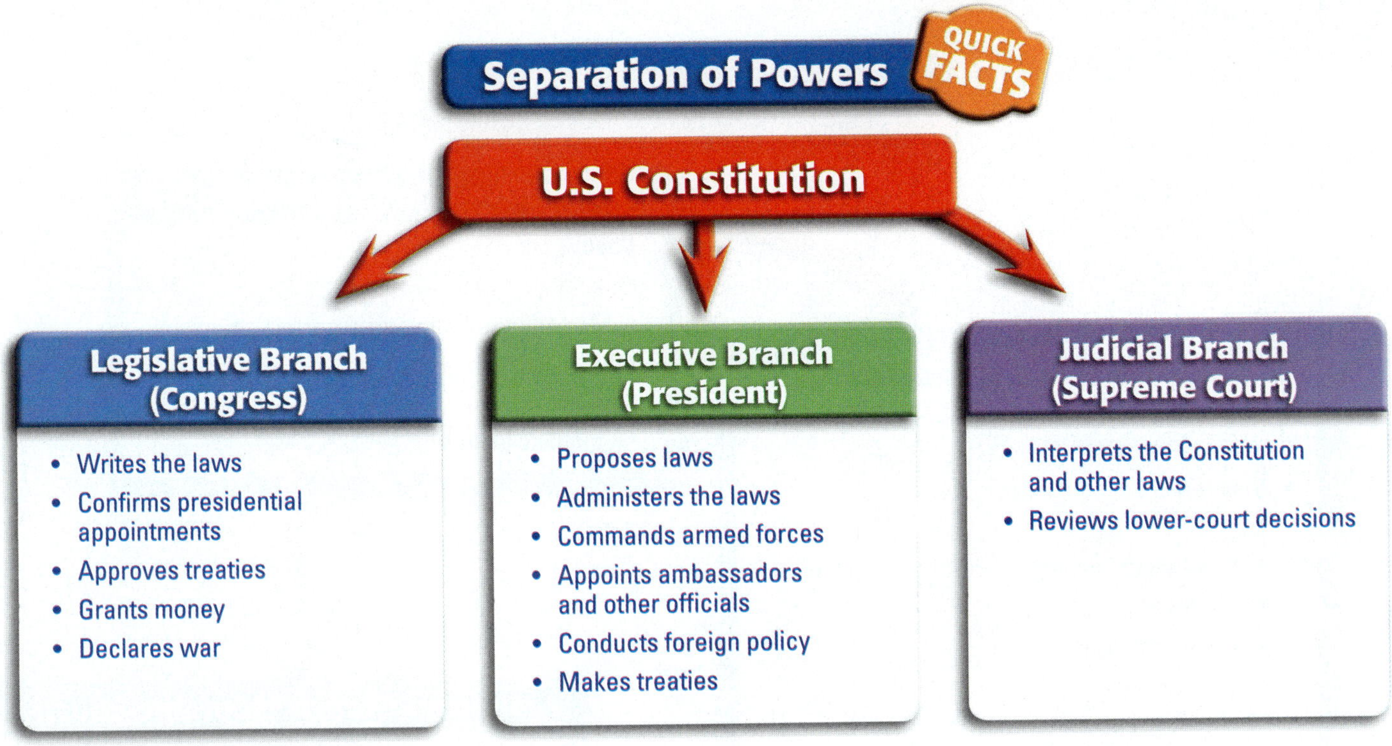

Legislative Branch

The federal government has three branches, each with **distinct** responsibilities and powers. This separation balances the branches and keeps any one of them from growing too powerful. The first branch of government is the legislative branch, or Congress. It makes the nation's laws. Article I of the Constitution divides Congress into the House of Representatives and the Senate.

With 435 members, the House of Representatives is the larger congressional house. The U.S. Census, a population count made every 10 years, determines how many members represent each state. A system called apportionment keeps total membership at 435. If one state gains a member, another state loses one. Members must be at least 25 years old, live in the state where they were elected, and have been U.S. citizens for seven years. They serve two-year terms.

The Senate has two members, or senators, per state. Senators represent the interests of the whole state, not just a district. They must be at least 30 years old, have been U.S. citizens for nine years, and live in the state they represent. They serve six-year terms. The senior senator of a state is the one who has served the longer of the two. Members of Congress can serve an unlimited number of terms in office.

The political party with more members in each house is the majority party. The one with fewer members is the minority party. The leader of the House of Representatives, or Speaker of the House, is elected by House members from the majority party.

The U.S. vice president serves as president of the Senate. He takes no part in Senate debates but can vote to break ties. If he is absent, the president pro tempore (pro tem for short) leads the Senate. There is no law for how the Senate must choose this position, but it traditionally goes to the majority party's senator who has served the longest.

Congress begins sessions, or meetings, each year in the first week of January. Both houses do most of their work in committees. Each committee studies certain types of bills, or suggested laws. For example, all bills about taxes begin in the House Ways and Means Committee.

READING CHECK **Comparing and Contrasting** What are the similarities in requirements for members of the House of Representatives and the Senate? What are the differences?

ACADEMIC VOCABULARY

distinct separate

FOCUS ON NORTH CAROLINA

The state government of North Carolina is made up of branches similar to those of the national government. The governor heads the executive branch, the legislative branch is made up of an upper and lower house, and the Supreme Court of North Carolina has seven justices.

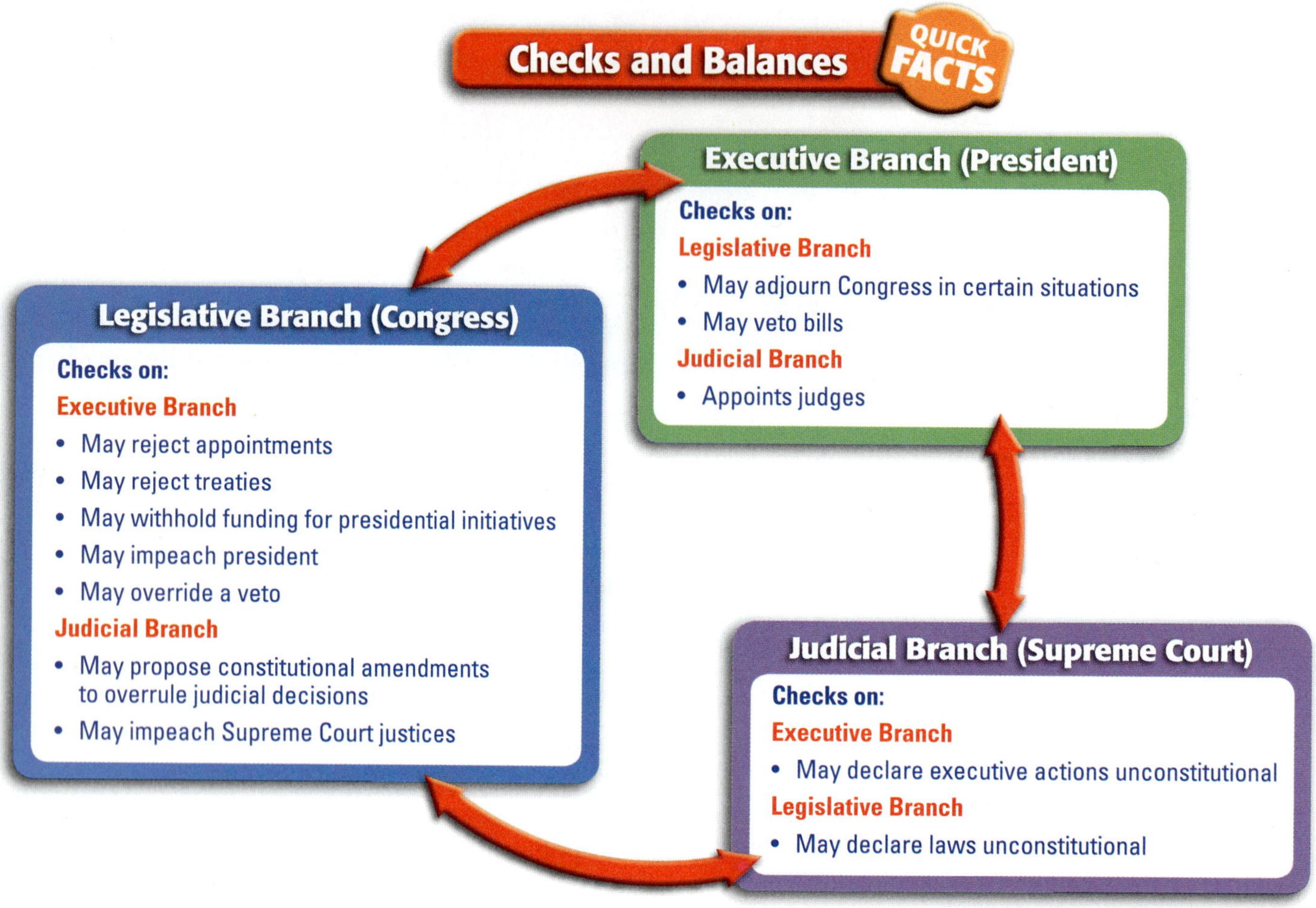

Executive Branch

Article II of the Constitution lists the powers of the executive branch. This branch enforces the laws passed by Congress.

President and Vice President

As head of the executive branch, the president is the most powerful elected leader in the United States. To qualify for the presidency or vice presidency, one must be a native-born U.S. citizen at least 35 years old. The president must also have been a U.S. resident for 14 years.

Americans elect a president and vice president every four years. Franklin D. Roosevelt, who won four times, was the only president to serve more than two terms. Now, the Twenty-second Amendment limits presidents to two terms. If a president dies, resigns, or is removed from office, the vice president becomes president for the rest of the term.

The House of Representatives can **impeach**, or vote to bring charges of serious crimes against, a president. Impeachment cases are tried in the Senate. If a president is found guilty, Congress can remove him from office. In 1868 Andrew Johnson was the first president to be impeached. President Bill Clinton was impeached in 1998. However, the Senate found each man not guilty.

Working with Congress

The president and Congress are often on different sides of an issue. However, they must still work together.

Congress passes laws. The president, however, can ask Congress to pass or reject bills. The president also can **veto**, or cancel, laws Congress has passed. Congress can try to override, or undo, the veto. However, this is difficult since it takes a two-thirds majority vote. To carry out laws affecting the Constitution, treaties, and statutes, the president issues **executive orders**. These commands have the power of law. The president also may grant **pardons**, or freedom from punishment, to persons convicted of federal crimes or facing criminal charges.

The president also commands the armed forces. In emergencies, the president can call on U.S. troops. Only Congress, however, can declare war. Other executive duties include conducting foreign relations and creating treaties. Executive departments do most of the executive branch work. As of 2004 there were 15 such departments. The president chooses department heads, who are called secretaries, and the Senate approves them. The heads make up the cabinet, which advises the president.

READING CHECK **Drawing Conclusions** What is the president's most important power?

Judicial Branch

The third branch of government, the judicial branch, is made up of a system of federal courts headed by the U.S. Supreme Court. The Constitution created the Supreme Court, but the Judiciary Act of 1789 created the system of lower district and circuit courts.

Article III generally outlines the courts' duties. Federal courts can strike down a state or federal law if the court finds a law unconstitutional. Congress can then try to revise the law to make it constitutional.

District Courts

The president makes appointments to federal courts. In an effort to keep federal judges free of party influence, the judges are given life appointments. The lower federal courts are divided according to cases over which they have jurisdiction, or authority. Each state has at least one of the 94 district courts.

NC History Makers

James Iredell
James Iredell helped organize North Carolina's court system and served on the first U.S. Supreme Court.

THE IMPACT TODAY

In 2002 the new Department of Homeland Security was given cabinet-level status to protect against terrorism.

Supreme Court Decisions

Background of the Court

The rest of the Supreme Court decisions you see in this book will highlight important cases of the Court. But in this first one, we'll discuss the history of the Court.

The first Supreme Court met in 1790 at the Royal Exchange in New York City. The ground floor of this building was an open-air market. When the national government moved to Philadelphia, the Court met in basement rooms in Independence Hall. Once in Washington, the Court heard cases in the Capitol building until the present Supreme Court building was completed in 1932.

Circuit Riding

Today the Supreme Court holds court only in Washington, D.C. In the past, however, the justices had to travel through assigned circuits, hearing cases together with a district judge in a practice known as riding circuit.

The justices complained bitterly about the inconvenience of travel, which was often over unpaved roads and in bad weather. This system was not just inconvenient to the justices, however. Some people worried about the fairness of a system that required justices who had heard cases at trial to rule on them again on appeal. Other people, however, thought that the practice helped keep the justices in touch with the needs and feelings of the average citizen. Eventually, circuit riding interfered so much with the increased amount of business of the Supreme Court that Congress passed a law ending the practice in the late 1800s.

Path to the Supreme Court

When a case is decided by a state or federal court, the losing side may have a chance to appeal the decision to a higher court. Under the federal system, this higher court is called the court of appeals. A person who loses in that court may then appeal to the Supreme Court to review the case. But the Supreme Court does not have to accept all appeals. It usually chooses to hear only cases in which there is an important legal principle to be decided or if two federal courts of appeals disagree on how an issue should be decided.

ANALYSIS SKILL **ANALYZING INFORMATION**

1. What are two reasons why the practice of circuit riding ended?
2. Why do you think the Supreme Court does not hear every case that is appealed to it?

Focus on Reading

Jot down a short summary of the appeals process after reading this paragraph.

Courts of Appeals

If someone convicted of a crime believes the trial was unfair, he or she may take the case to the court of appeals. There are 13 courts of appeals. Each has a panel of judges to decide if cases heard in the lower courts were tried appropriately. If the judges uphold, or accept, the original decision, the original outcome stands. Otherwise, the case may be retried in the lower court.

Supreme Court

The Impact Today

Supreme Court rulings can have dramatic effects on the nation, as in *Bush* v. *Gore*, which decided the outcome of the 2000 presidential election.

After a case is decided by the court of appeals, the losing side may appeal the decision to the Supreme Court. Thousands of cases go to the Supreme Court yearly in the hope of a hearing, but the Court has time to hear only about 100. Generally, the cases heard involve important constitutional or public-interest issues. If the Court declines to hear a case, the court of appeals decision is final.

Nine justices sit on the Supreme Court. The chief justice of the United States leads the Court. Unlike the president and members of Congress, there are no specific constitutional requirements for becoming a justice.

In recent decades, the Supreme Court has become more diverse. In 1967 **Thurgood Marshall** became the first African American justice. **Sandra Day O'Connor** became the first female Court justice after her 1981 appointment by President Ronald Reagan.

Reading Check **Summarizing** Describe the structure and responsibilities of the judicial branch.

Summary and Preview In this section you learned about the balance between the different branches of the federal government. In the next section you will learn about the Bill of Rights.

Section 1 Assessment

go.hrw.com
Online Quiz
KEYWORD: SC7 HP6

Reviewing Ideas, Terms, and People

1. a. **Describe** What type of government did the Constitution establish for the United States?
   b. **Contrast** What is the difference between delegated, reserved, and concurrent powers?
2. a. **Recall** What role does the vice president serve in the legislative branch?
   b. **Compare and Contrast** In what ways are the Senate and the House of Representatives similar and different?
   c. **Elaborate** Why do you think the requirements for serving in the Senate are stricter than those for serving in the House of Representatives?
3. a. **Describe** What powers are granted to the president?
   b. **Make Generalizations** Why is it important that the president and Congress work together in resolving governmental issues?
   c. **Evaluate** What do you think is the most important power granted to the president? Why?
4. a. **Explain** What is the main power of the judicial branch?
   b. **Evaluate** Which branch of government do you feel is most important? Explain your answer.

Critical Thinking

5. **Categorizing** Review your notes on the branches of government. Then copy the web diagram below and use it to show two powers of each branch of government.

Focus on Writing

6. **Gathering Information about the Constitution** Look back through what you've just read about the Constitution. Make a list of four or five of the most important features of the Constitution. You'll put that list on the second page of your pamphlet.

BIOGRAPHY

James Madison

What would you do to create a brand-new government?

When did he live? 1751–1836

Where did he live? Like several of the founding fathers, James Madison was a Virginian. He grew up in the town of Montpelier, and he kept a home there for his whole life.

What did he do? Through the persuasive power of his writing, Madison helped create the foundations of the U.S. government.

Why is he important? Madison is known as the Father of the Constitution. A brilliant thinker, he provided many of the basic ideas in the Constitution. He argued tirelessly for a strong national government, for separate branches of government, and for rights such as freedom of religion. He then rallied support for adoption of the Constitution and the Bill of Rights. In 1809 Madison became the fourth president of the United States. As president, he led the country through another war with Britain, the War of 1812. He and his wife, Dolley, were forced to flee Washington temporarily when the British invaded the capital and set fire to the White House.

Summarizing Why is Madison known as the Father of the Constitution?

KEY EVENTS

1780
Madison serves in the Continental Congress.

1787
Madison keeps a written record of the Constitutional Convention.

1787–1788
Madison helps write the *Federalist Papers*, urging support for the Constitution.

1801–1809
Madison serves as secretary of state under President Thomas Jefferson.

1809–1817
Madison serves two terms as president.

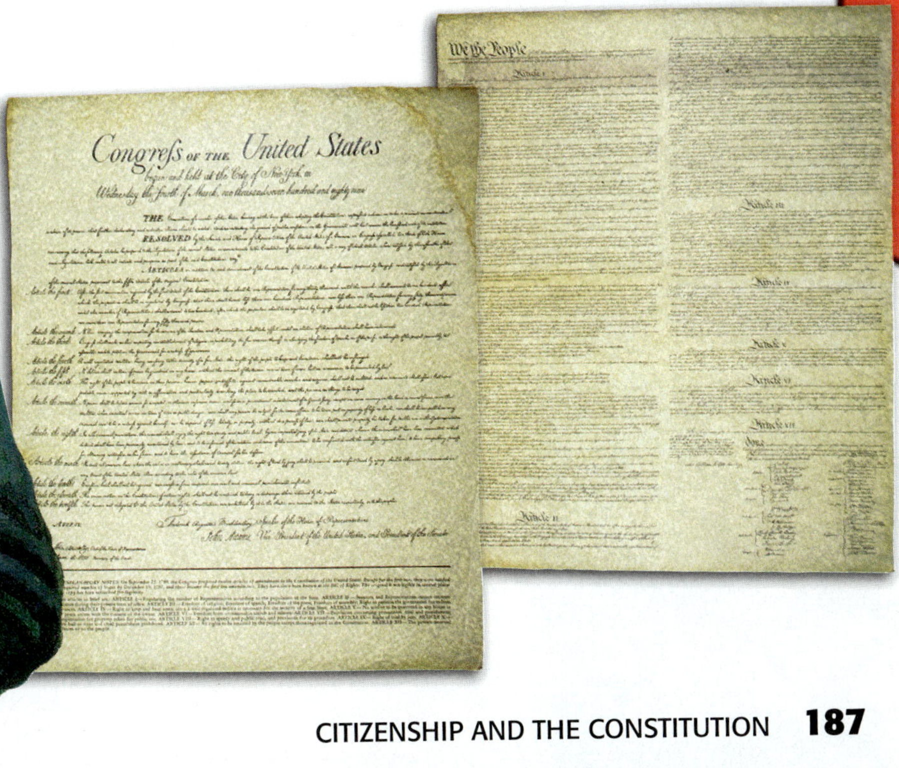

James Madison was an important force in the writing of the Constitution.

The Constitution of the United States

Preamble

The short and dignified preamble explains the goals of the new government under the Constitution.

We the People of the United States, in Order to form a more perfect Union, establish Justice, insure domestic Tranquility, provide for the common defense, promote the general Welfare, and secure the Blessings of Liberty to ourselves and our Posterity, do ordain and establish this Constitution for the United States of America.

Note: The parts of the Constitution that have been lined through are no longer in force or no longer apply because of later amendments. The titles of the sections and articles are added for easier reference.

Article I The Legislature

Section 1. Congress

All legislative Powers herein granted shall be vested in a Congress of the United States, which shall consist of a Senate and House of Representatives.

Section 2. The House of Representatives

1. Elections The House of Representatives shall be composed of Members chosen every second Year by the People of the several States, and the Electors in each State shall have the Qualifications requisite for Electors of the most numerous Branch of the State Legislature.

2. Qualifications No Person shall be a Representative who shall not have attained to the Age of twenty five Years, and been seven Years a Citizen of the United States, and who shall not, when elected, be an Inhabitant of that State in which he shall be chosen.

3. Number of Representatives Representatives and direct Taxes shall be apportioned among the several States which may be included within this Union, according to their respective Numbers~~, which shall be determined by adding to the whole Number of free Persons, including~~ ~~**those bound to Service**~~[1] ~~for a Term of Years, and excluding Indians not taxed, three fifths of~~ ~~**all other Persons**~~.[2] The actual **Enumeration**[3] shall be made within three Years after the first Meeting of the Congress of the United States, and within every subsequent Term of ten Years, in such Manner as they shall by Law direct. The Number of Representatives shall not exceed one for every thirty Thousand, but each State shall have at Least one Representative~~; and until such enumeration shall be made, the State of New Hampshire shall be entitled to choose three, Massachusetts eight, Rhode-Island and Providence Plantations one, Connecticut five, New-York six, New Jersey four, Pennsylvania eight, Delaware one, Maryland six, Virginia ten, North Carolina five, South Carolina five, and Georgia three.~~

4. Vacancies When vacancies happen in the Representation from any State, the Executive Authority thereof shall issue Writs of Election to fill such Vacancies.

5. Officers and Impeachment The House of Representatives shall choose their Speaker and other Officers; and shall have the sole Power of impeachment.

Legislative Branch

Article I explains how the legislative branch, called Congress, is organized. The chief purpose of the legislative branch is to make laws. Congress is made up of the Senate and the House of Representatives.

The House of Representatives

The number of members each state has in the House is based on the population of the individual state. In 1929 Congress permanently fixed the size of the House at 435 members.

Vocabulary

[1] **those bound to Service** indentured servants

[2] **all other Persons** slaves

[3] **Enumeration** census or official population count

Section 3. The Senate

1. Number of Senators The Senate of the United States shall be composed of two Senators from each State, ~~chosen by the Legislature thereof,~~ for six Years; and each Senator shall have one Vote.

2. Classifying Terms Immediately after they shall be assembled in Consequence of the first Election, they shall be divided as equally as may be into three Classes. The Seats of the Senators of the first Class shall be vacated at the Expiration of the second Year, of the second Class at the Expiration of the fourth Year, and of the third Class at the Expiration of the sixth Year, so that one third may be chosen every second Year; ~~and if Vacancies happen by Resignation, or otherwise, during the Recess of the Legislature of any State, the Executive thereof may make temporary Appointments until the next Meeting of the Legislature, which shall then fill such Vacancies.~~

3. Qualifications No Person shall be a Senator who shall not have attained to the Age of thirty Years, and been nine Years a Citizen of the United States, and who shall not, when elected, be an Inhabitant of that State for which he shall be chosen.

4. Role of Vice President The Vice President of the United States shall be President of the Senate, but shall have no Vote, unless they be equally divided.

5. Officers The Senate shall choose their other Officers, and also a President **pro tempore**,[4] in the Absence of the Vice President, or when he shall exercise the Office of President of the United States.

6. Impeachment Trials The Senate shall have the sole Power to try all **Impeachments**.[5] When sitting for that Purpose, they shall be on Oath or Affirmation. When the President of the United States is tried, the Chief Justice shall preside: And no Person shall be convicted without the Concurrence of two thirds of the Members present.

7. Punishment for Impeachment Judgment in Cases of Impeachment shall not extend further than to removal from Office, and disqualification to hold and enjoy any Office of honor, Trust or Profit under the United States: but the Party convicted shall nevertheless be liable and subject to Indictment, Trial, Judgment and Punishment, according to Law.

The Vice President

The only duty that the Constitution assigns to the vice president is to preside over meetings of the Senate. Modern presidents have usually given their vice presidents more responsibilities.

EXPLORING THE DOCUMENT If the House of Representatives charges a government official with wrongdoing, the Senate acts as a court to decide if the official is guilty.
How does the power of impeachment represent part of the system of checks and balances?

Vocabulary

[4] **pro tempore** temporarily

[5] **Impeachments** official accusations of federal wrongdoing

Federal Office Terms and Requirements

QUICK FACTS

Position	Term	Minimum Age	Residency	Citizenship
President	4 years	35	14 years in the U.S.	natural-born
Vice President	4 years	35	14 years in the U.S.	natural-born
Supreme Court Justice	unlimited	none	none	none
Senator	6 years	30	state in which elected	9 years
Representative	2 years	25	state in which elected	7 years

Section 4. Congressional Elections

1. Regulations The Times, Places and Manner of holding Elections for Senators and Representatives, shall be prescribed in each State by the Legislature thereof; but the Congress may at any time by Law make or alter such Regulations, except as to the Places of choosing Senators.

2. Sessions ~~The Congress shall assemble at least once in every Year, and such Meeting shall be on the first Monday in December, unless they shall by Law appoint a different Day.~~

Section 5. Rules/Procedures

1. Quorum Each House shall be the Judge of the Elections, Returns and Qualifications of its own Members, and a Majority of each shall constitute a **Quorum**[6] to do Business; but a smaller Number may **adjourn**[7] from day to day, and may be authorized to compel the Attendance of absent Members, in such Manner, and under such Penalties as each House may provide.

2. Rules and Conduct Each House may determine the Rules of its Proceedings, punish its Members for disorderly Behaviour, and, with the Concurrence of two thirds, expel a Member.

3. Records Each House shall keep a Journal of its Proceedings, and from time to time publish the same, excepting such Parts as may in their Judgment require Secrecy; and the Yeas and Nays of the Members of either House on any question shall, at the Desire of one fifth of those Present, be entered on the Journal.

4. Adjournment Neither House, during the Session of Congress, shall, without the Consent of the other, adjourn for more than three days, nor to any other Place than that in which the two Houses shall be sitting.

Section 6. Payment

1. Salary The Senators and Representatives shall receive a Compensation for their Services, to be ascertained by Law, and paid out of the Treasury of the United States. They shall in all Cases, except Treason, Felony and Breach of the Peace, be privileged from Arrest during their Attendance at the Session of their respective Houses, and in going to and returning from the same; and for any Speech or Debate in either House, they shall not be questioned in any other Place.

2. Restrictions No Senator or Representative shall, during the Time for which he was elected, be appointed to any civil Office under the Authority of the United States, which shall have been created, or the **Emoluments**[8] whereof shall have been increased during such time; and no Person holding any Office under the United States, shall be a Member of either House during his **Continuance**[9] in Office.

Vocabulary

[6] **Quorum** the minimum number of people needed to conduct business

[7] **adjourn** to stop indefinitely

[8] **Emoluments** salary

[9] **Continuance** term

Vocabulary

[10] **Bills** proposed laws

EXPLORING THE DOCUMENT The framers felt that because members of the House are elected every two years, representatives would listen to the public and seek its approval before passing taxes. **How does Section 7 address the colonial demand of "no taxation without representation"?**

Section 7. How a Bill Becomes a Law

1. Tax Bills All **Bills**[10] for raising Revenue shall originate in the House of Representatives; but the Senate may propose or concur with Amendments as on other Bills.

2. Lawmaking Every Bill which shall have passed the House of Representatives and the Senate, shall, before it become a Law, be presented to the President of the United States: If he approve he shall sign it, but if not he shall return it, with his Objections to that House in which it shall have originated, who shall enter the Objections at large on their Journal, and proceed to reconsider it. If after such Reconsideration two thirds of that House shall agree to pass the Bill, it shall be sent, together with the Objections, to the other House, by which it shall likewise be reconsidered, and if approved by two thirds of that House, it shall become a Law. But in all such Cases the Votes of both Houses shall be determined by yeas and Nays, and the Names of the Persons voting for and against the Bill shall be entered on the Journal of each House respectively. If any Bill shall not be returned by the President within ten Days (Sundays excepted) after it shall have been presented to him, the Same shall be a Law, in like Manner as if he had signed it, unless the Congress by their Adjournment prevent its Return, in which Case it shall not be a Law.

EXPLORING THE DOCUMENT The veto power of the president is one of the important checks and balances in the Constitution. **Why do you think the framers included the ability of Congress to override a veto?**

3. Role of the President Every Order, Resolution, or Vote to which the Concurrence of the Senate and House of Representatives may be necessary (except on a question of Adjournment) shall be presented to the President of the United States; and before the Same shall take Effect, shall be approved by him, or being disapproved by him, shall be repassed by two thirds of the Senate and House of Representatives, according to the Rules and Limitations prescribed in the Case of a Bill.

How a Bill Becomes a Law

1. A member of the House or the Senate introduces a bill and refers it to a committee.
2. The House or Senate Committee may approve, rewrite, or kill the bill.

3. The House or the Senate debates and votes on its version of the bill.
4. House and Senate conference committee members work out the differences between the two versions.
5. Both houses of Congress pass the revised bill.

Section 8.
Powers Granted to Congress

1. Taxation The Congress shall have Power To lay and collect Taxes, **Duties**,[11] **Imposts**[12] and **Excises**,[13] to pay the Debts and provide for the common Defense and general Welfare of the United States; but all Duties, Imposts and Excises shall be uniform throughout the United States;

2. Credit To borrow Money on the credit of the United States;

3. Commerce To regulate Commerce with foreign Nations, and among the several States, and with the Indian Tribes;

4. Naturalization and Bankruptcy To establish an uniform **Rule of Naturalization**,[14] and uniform Laws on the subject of Bankruptcies throughout the United States;

5. Money To coin Money, regulate the Value thereof, and of foreign Coin, and fix the Standard of Weights and Measures;

6. Counterfeiting To provide for the Punishment of counterfeiting the **Securities**[15] and current Coin of the United States;

7. Post Office To establish Post Offices and post Roads;

8. Patents and Copyrights To promote the Progress of Science and useful Arts, by securing for limited Times to Authors and Inventors the exclusive Right to their respective Writings and Discoveries;

9. Courts To constitute Tribunals inferior to the supreme Court;

10. International Law To define and punish Piracies and Felonies committed on the high Seas, and Offences against the Law of Nations;

LINKING TO TODAY

Native Americans and the Commerce Clause

The commerce clause gives Congress the power to "regulate Commerce with . . . the Indian Tribes." The clause has been interpreted to mean that the states cannot tax or interfere with businesses on Indian reservations, but that the federal government can. It also allows American Indian nations to develop their own governments and laws. These laws, however, can be challenged in federal court. Although reservation land usually belongs to the government of the Indian group, it is administered by the U.S. government.

Drawing Conclusions How would you describe the status of American Indian nations under the commerce clause?

Vocabulary

[11] **Duties** tariffs

[12] **Imposts** taxes

[13] **Excises** internal taxes on the manufacture, sale, or consumption of a commodity

[14] **Rule of Naturalization** a law by which a foreign-born person becomes a citizen

[15] **Securities** bonds

6 The president signs or vetoes the bill.

7 Two-thirds majority vote of Congress is needed to approve a vetoed bill. Bill becomes a law.

ANALYSIS SKILL **ANALYZING INFORMATION**

Why do you think the framers created this complex system for adopting laws?

Vocabulary

Letters of Marque and Reprisal[16] documents issued by governments allowing merchant ships to arm themselves and attack ships of an enemy nation

11. War To declare War, grant **Letters of Marque and Reprisal**,[16] and make Rules concerning Captures on Land and Water;

12. Army To raise and support Armies, but no Appropriation of Money to that Use shall be for a longer Term than two Years;

13. Navy To provide and maintain a Navy;

14. Regulation of the Military To make Rules for the Government and Regulation of the land and naval Forces;

15. Militia To provide for calling forth the Militia to execute the Laws of the Union, suppress Insurrections and repel Invasions;

16. Regulation of the Militia To provide for organizing, arming, and disciplining, the Militia, and for governing such Part of them as may be employed in the Service of the United States, reserving to the States respectively, the Appointment of the Officers, and the Authority of training the Militia according to the discipline prescribed by Congress;

17. District of Columbia To exercise exclusive Legislation in all Cases whatsoever, over such District (not exceeding ten Miles square) as may, by Cession of particular States, and the Acceptance of Congress, become the Seat of the Government of the United States, and to exercise like Authority over all Places purchased by the Consent of the Legislature of the State in which the Same shall be, for the Erection of Forts, Magazines, Arsenals, dock-Yards, and other needful Buildings;—And

The Elastic Clause

The framers of the Constitution wanted a national government that was strong enough to be effective. This section lists the powers given to Congress. The last portion of Section 8 contains the so-called elastic clause.

18. Necessary and Proper Clause To make all Laws which shall be necessary and proper for carrying into Execution the foregoing Powers, and all other Powers vested by this Constitution in the Government of the United States, or in any Department or Officer thereof.

The Elastic Clause

The elastic clause has been stretched (like elastic) to allow Congress to meet changing circumstances.

Section 9. Powers Denied Congress

1. Slave Trade ~~The Migration or Importation of such Persons as any of the States now existing shall think proper to admit, shall not be prohibited by the Congress prior to the Year one thousand eight hundred and eight, but a Tax or duty may be imposed on such Importation, not exceeding ten dollars for each Person.~~

2. Habeas Corpus The Privilege of the **Writ of Habeas Corpus**[17] shall not be suspended, unless when in Cases of Rebellion or Invasion the public Safety may require it.

3. Illegal Punishment No **Bill of Attainder**[18] or **ex post facto Law**[19] shall be passed.

4. Direct Taxes No **Capitation**,[20] or other direct, Tax shall be laid, unless in Proportion to the Census or enumeration herein before directed to be taken.

5. Export Taxes No Tax or Duty shall be laid on Articles exported from any State.

6. No Favorites No Preference shall be given by any Regulation of Commerce or Revenue to the Ports of one State over those of another; nor shall Vessels bound to, or from, one State, be obliged to enter, clear, or pay Duties in another.

7. Public Money No Money shall be drawn from the Treasury, but in Consequence of Appropriations made by Law; and a regular Statement and Account of the Receipts and Expenditures of all public Money shall be published from time to time.

8. Titles of Nobility No Title of Nobility shall be granted by the United States: And no Person holding any Office of Profit or Trust under them, shall, without the Consent of the Congress, accept of any present, Emolument, Office, or Title, of any kind whatever, from any King, Prince, or foreign State.

Section 10. Powers Denied the States

1. Restrictions No State shall enter into any Treaty, Alliance, or Confederation; grant Letters of Marque and Reprisal; coin Money; emit Bills of Credit; make any Thing but gold and silver Coin a Tender in Payment of Debts; pass any Bill of Attainder, ex post facto Law, or Law impairing the Obligation of Contracts, or grant any Title of Nobility.

2. Import and Export Taxes No State shall, without the Consent of the Congress, lay any Imposts or Duties on Imports or Exports, except what may be absolutely necessary for executing it's inspection Laws: and the net Produce of all Duties and Imposts, laid by any State on Imports or Exports, shall be for the Use of the Treasury of the United States; and all such Laws shall be subject to the Revision and Control of the Congress.

3. Peacetime and War Restraints No State shall, without the Consent of Congress, lay any Duty of Tonnage, keep Troops, or Ships of War in time of Peace, enter into any Agreement or Compact with another State, or with a foreign Power, or engage in War, unless actually invaded, or in such imminent Danger as will not admit of delay.

EXPLORING THE DOCUMENT Although Congress has implied powers, there are also limits to its powers. Section 9 lists powers that are denied to the federal government. Several of the clauses protect the people of the United States from unjust treatment. **In what ways does the Constitution limit the powers of the federal government?**

Vocabulary

[17] **Writ of Habeas Corpus** a court order that requires the government to bring a prisoner to court and explain why he or she is being held

[18] **Bill of Attainder** a law declaring that a person is guilty of a particular crime

[19] **ex post facto Law** a law that is made effective prior to the date that it was passed and therefore punishes people for acts that were not illegal at the time

[20] **Capitation** a direct uniform tax imposed on each head, or person

Executive Branch

The president is the chief of the executive branch. It is the job of the president to enforce the laws. The framers wanted the president's and vice president's terms of office and manner of selection to be different from those of members of Congress. They decided on four-year terms, but they had a difficult time agreeing on how to select the president and vice president. The framers finally set up an electoral system, which varies greatly from our electoral process today.

Presidential Elections

In 1845 Congress set the Tuesday following the first Monday in November of every fourth year as the general election date for selecting presidential electors.

Article II The Executive

Section 1. The Presidency

1. Terms of Office The executive Power shall be vested in a President of the United States of America. He shall hold his Office during the Term of four Years, and, together with the Vice President, chosen for the same Term, be elected, as follows:

2. Electoral College Each State shall appoint, in such Manner as the Legislature thereof may direct, a Number of Electors, equal to the whole Number of Senators and Representatives to which the State may be entitled in the Congress: but no Senator or Representative, or Person holding an Office of Trust or Profit under the United States, shall be appointed an Elector.

3. Former Method of Electing President ~~The Electors shall meet in their respective States, and vote by Ballot for two Persons, of whom one at least shall not be an Inhabitant of the same State with themselves. And they shall make a List of all the Persons voted for, and of the Number of Votes for each; which List they shall sign and certify, and transmit sealed to the Seat of the Government of the United States, directed to the President of the Senate. The President of the Senate shall, in the Presence of the Senate and House of Representatives, open all the Certificates, and the Votes shall~~

The Electoral College

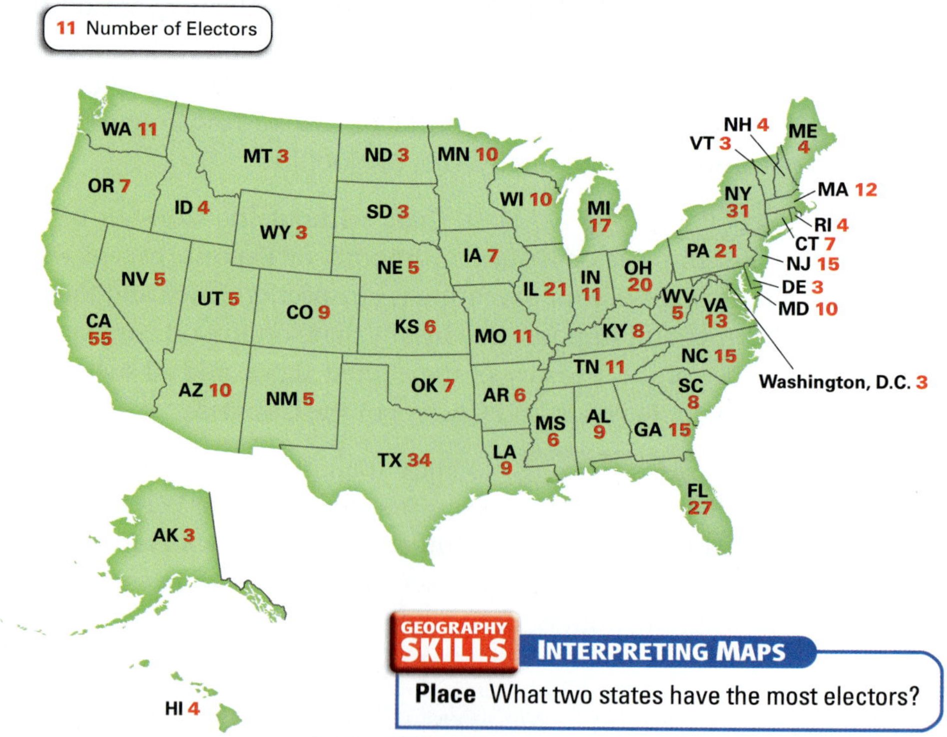

GEOGRAPHY SKILLS **INTERPRETING MAPS**

Place What two states have the most electors?

~~then be counted. The Person having the greatest Number of Votes shall be the President, if such Number be a Majority of the whole Number of Electors appointed; and if there be more than one who have such Majority, and have an equal Number of Votes, then the House of Representatives shall immediately choose by Ballot one of them for President; and if no Person have a Majority, then from the five highest on the List the said House shall in like Manner choose the President. But in choosing the President, the Votes shall be taken by States, the Representation from each State having one Vote; A quorum for this purpose shall consist of a Member or Members from two thirds of the States, and a Majority of all the States shall be necessary to a Choice. In every Case, after the Choice of the President, the Person having the greatest Number of Votes of the Electors shall be the Vice President. But if there should remain two or more who have equal Votes, the Senate shall choose from them by Ballot the Vice President.~~

4. Election Day The Congress may determine the Time of choosing the Electors, and the Day on which they shall give their Votes; which Day shall be the same throughout the United States.

5. Qualifications No Person except a natural born Citizen~~, or a Citizen of the United States, at the time of the Adoption of this Constitution~~, shall be eligible to the Office of President; neither shall any Person be eligible to that Office who shall not have attained to the Age of thirty five Years, and been fourteen Years a Resident within the United States.

6. Succession In Case of the Removal of the President from Office, or of his Death, Resignation, or Inability to discharge the Powers and Duties of the said Office, the Same shall devolve on the Vice President, and the Congress may by Law provide for the Case of Removal, Death, Resignation or Inability, both of the President and Vice President, declaring what Officer shall then act as President, and such Officer shall act accordingly, until the Disability be removed, or a President shall be elected.

7. Salary The President shall, at stated Times, receive for his Services, a Compensation, which shall neither be increased nor diminished during the Period for which he shall have been elected, and he shall not receive within that Period any other Emolument from the United States, or any of them.

8. Oath of Office Before he enter on the Execution of his Office, he shall take the following Oath or Affirmation:—"I do solemnly swear (or affirm) that I will faithfully execute the Office of President of the United States, and will to the best of my Ability, preserve, protect and defend the Constitution of the United States."

EXPLORING THE DOCUMENT The youngest elected president was John F. Kennedy; he was 43 years old when he was inaugurated. (Theodore Roosevelt was 42 when he assumed office after the assassination of McKinley.) **What is the minimum required age for the office of president?**

Presidential Salary

In 1999 Congress voted to set future presidents' salaries at $400,000 per year. The president also receives an annual expense account. The president must pay taxes only on the salary.

Commander in Chief

Today the president is in charge of the army, navy, air force, marines, and coast guard. Only Congress, however, can decide if the United States will declare war.

Appointments

Most of the president's appointments to office must be approved by the Senate.

Vocabulary

[21] **Reprieves** delays of punishment

[22] **Pardons** releases from the legal penalties associated with a crime

The State of the Union

Every year the president presents to Congress a State of the Union message. In this message, the president introduces and explains a legislative plan for the coming year.

Section 2. Powers of Presidency

1. Military Powers The President shall be Commander in Chief of the Army and Navy of the United States, and of the Militia of the several States, when called into the actual Service of the United States; he may require the Opinion, in writing, of the principal Officer in each of the executive Departments, upon any Subject relating to the Duties of their respective Offices, and he shall have Power to grant **Reprieves**[21] and **Pardons**[22] for Offences against the United States, except in Cases of Impeachment.

2. Treaties and Appointments He shall have Power, by and with the Advice and Consent of the Senate, to make Treaties, provided two thirds of the Senators present concur; and he shall nominate, and by and with the Advice and Consent of the Senate, shall appoint Ambassadors, other public Ministers and Consuls, Judges of the supreme Court, and all other Officers of the United States, whose Appointments are not herein otherwise provided for, and which shall be established by Law: but the Congress may by Law vest the Appointment of such inferior Officers, as they think proper, in the President alone, in the Courts of Law, or in the Heads of Departments.

3. Vacancies The President shall have Power to fill up all Vacancies that may happen during the Recess of the Senate, by granting Commissions which shall expire at the End of their next Session.

Section 3. Presidential Duties

He shall from time to time give to the Congress Information of the State of the Union, and recommend to their Consideration such Measures as he shall judge necessary and expedient; he may, on extraordinary Occasions, convene both Houses, or either of them, and in Case of Disagreement between them, with Respect to the Time of Adjournment, he may adjourn them to such Time as he shall think proper; he shall receive Ambassadors and other public Ministers; he shall take Care that the Laws be faithfully executed, and shall Commission all the Officers of the United States.

Section 4. Impeachment

The President, Vice President and all civil Officers of the United States, shall be removed from Office on Impeachment for, and Conviction of, Treason, Bribery, or other high Crimes and Misdemeanors.

Article III The Judiciary

Section 1. Federal Courts and Judges

The judicial Power of the United States shall be vested in one supreme Court, and in such inferior Courts as the Congress may from time to time ordain and establish. The Judges, both of the supreme and inferior Courts, shall hold their Offices during good Behavior, and shall, at stated Times, receive for their Services a Compensation, which shall not be diminished during their Continuance in Office.

Section 2. Authority of the Courts

1. General Authority The judicial Power shall extend to all Cases, in Law and Equity, arising under this Constitution, the Laws of the United States, and Treaties made, or which shall be made, under their Authority;—to all Cases affecting Ambassadors, other public Ministers and Consuls;—to all Cases of admiralty and maritime Jurisdiction;—to Controversies to which the United States shall be a Party;—to Controversies between two or more States ~~—between a State and Citizens of another State;~~ —between Citizens of different States;—between Citizens of the same State claiming Lands under Grants of different States~~, and between a State, or the Citizens thereof, and foreign States, Citizens or Subjects.~~

2. Supreme Authority In all Cases affecting Ambassadors, other public Ministers and Consuls, and those in which a State shall be Party, the supreme Court shall have original Jurisdiction. In all the other Cases before mentioned, the supreme Court shall have appellate Jurisdiction, both as to Law and Fact, with such Exceptions, and under such Regulations as the Congress shall make.

Judicial Branch

The Articles of Confederation did not set up a federal court system. One of the first points that the framers of the Constitution agreed upon was to set up a national judiciary. In the Judiciary Act of 1789, Congress provided for the establishment of lower courts, such as district courts, circuit courts of appeals, and various other federal courts. The judicial system provides a check on the legislative branch: it can declare a law unconstitutional.

3. Trial by Jury The Trial of all Crimes, except in Cases of Impeachment, shall be by Jury; and such Trial shall be held in the State where the said Crimes shall have been committed; but when not committed within any State, the Trial shall be at such Place or Places as the Congress may by Law have directed.

Section 3. Treason

1. Definition Treason against the United States, shall consist only in levying War against them, or in adhering to their Enemies, giving them Aid and Comfort. No Person shall be convicted of Treason unless on the Testimony of two Witnesses to the same overt Act, or on Confession in open Court.

2. Punishment The Congress shall have Power to declare the Punishment of Treason, but no Attainder of Treason shall work **Corruption of Blood**,[23] or Forfeiture except during the Life of the Person attainted.

Vocabulary

[23] **Corruption of Blood** punishing the family of a person convicted of treason

Article IV Relations among States

Section 1. State Acts and Records

Full Faith and Credit shall be given in each State to the public Acts, Records, and judicial Proceedings of every other State. And the Congress may by general Laws prescribe the Manner in which such Acts, Records and Proceedings shall be proved, and the Effect thereof.

The States

States must honor the laws, records, and court decisions of other states. A person cannot escape a legal obligation by moving from one state to another.

Section 2. Rights of Citizens

1. Citizenship The Citizens of each State shall be entitled to all Privileges and Immunities of Citizens in the several States.

2. Extradition A Person charged in any State with Treason, Felony, or other Crime, who shall flee from Justice, and be found in another State, shall on Demand of the executive Authority of the State from which he fled, be delivered up, to be removed to the State having Jurisdiction of the Crime.

3. Fugitive Slaves ~~No Person held to Service or Labour in one State, under the Laws thereof, escaping into another, shall, in Consequence of any Law or Regulation therein, be discharged from such Service or Labour, but shall be delivered up on Claim of the Party to whom such Service or Labour may be due.~~

EXPLORING THE DOCUMENT The framers wanted to ensure that citizens could determine how state governments would operate. **How does the need to respect the laws of each state support the principle of popular sovereignty?**

Federalism QUICK FACTS

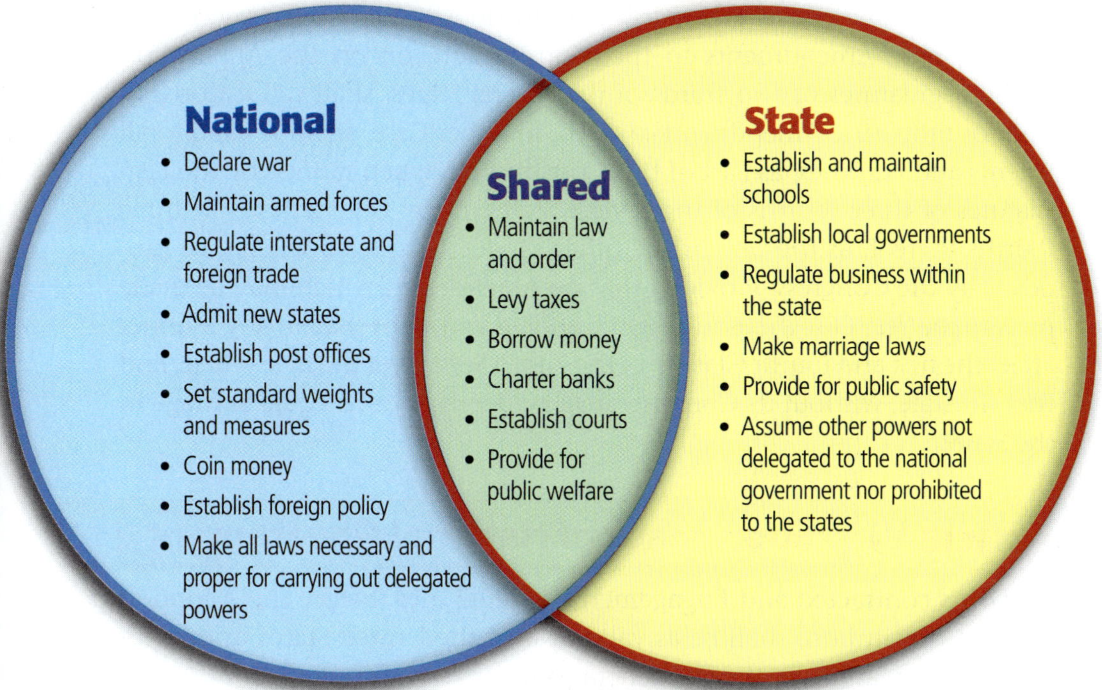

ANALYSIS SKILL — ANALYZING INFORMATION

Why does the power to declare war belong only to the national government?

Section 3. New States

1. Admission New States may be admitted by the Congress into this Union; but no new State shall be formed or erected within the Jurisdiction of any other State; nor any State be formed by the Junction of two or more States, or Parts of States, without the Consent of the Legislatures of the States concerned as well as of the Congress.

2. Congressional Authority The Congress shall have Power to dispose of and make all needful Rules and Regulations respecting the Territory or other Property belonging to the United States; and nothing in this Constitution shall be so construed as to Prejudice any Claims of the United States, or of any particular State.

Section 4. Guarantees to the States

The United States shall guarantee to every State in this Union a Republican Form of Government, and shall protect each of them against Invasion; and on Application of the Legislature, or of the Executive (when the Legislature cannot be convened), against domestic Violence.

EXPLORING THE DOCUMENT In a republic, voters elect representatives to act in their best interest. **How does Article IV protect the practice of republicanism in the United States?**

EXPLORING THE DOCUMENT America's founders may not have realized how long the Constitution would last, but they did set up a system for changing or adding to it. They did not want to make it easy to change the Constitution. **By what methods may the Constitution be amended? Under what sorts of circumstances do you think an amendment might be necessary?**

Article V Amending the Constitution

The Congress, whenever two thirds of both Houses shall deem it necessary, shall propose Amendments to this Constitution, or, on the Application of the Legislatures of two thirds of the several States, shall call a Convention for proposing Amendments, which, in either Case, shall be valid to all Intents and Purposes, as Part of this Constitution, when ratified by the Legislatures of three fourths of the several States, or by Conventions in three fourths thereof, as the one or the other Mode of Ratification may be proposed by the Congress; Provided that ~~no Amendment which may be made prior to the Year One thousand eight hundred and eight shall in any Manner affect the first and fourth Clauses in the Ninth Section of the first Article; and that no State, without its Consent, shall be deprived of its equal Suffrage in the Senate.~~

National Supremacy

One of the biggest problems facing the delegates to the Constitutional Convention was the question of what would happen if a state law and a federal law conflicted. Which law would be followed? Who would decide? The second clause of Article VI answers those questions. When a federal law and a state law disagree, the federal law overrides the state law. The Constitution and other federal laws are the "supreme Law of the Land." This clause is often called the supremacy clause.

Article VI Supremacy of National Government

All Debts contracted and Engagements entered into, before the Adoption of this Constitution, shall be as valid against the United States under this Constitution, as under the Confederation.

This Constitution, and the Laws of the United States which shall be made in Pursuance thereof; and all Treaties made, or which shall be made, under the Authority of the United States, shall be the supreme Law of the Land; and the Judges in every State shall be bound thereby, any Thing in the Constitution or Laws of any State to the Contrary notwithstanding.

The Senators and Representatives before mentioned, and the Members of the several State Legislatures, and all executive and judicial Officers, both of the United States and of the several States, shall be bound by Oath or Affirmation, to support this Constitution; but no religious Test shall ever be required as a Qualification to any Office or public Trust under the United States.

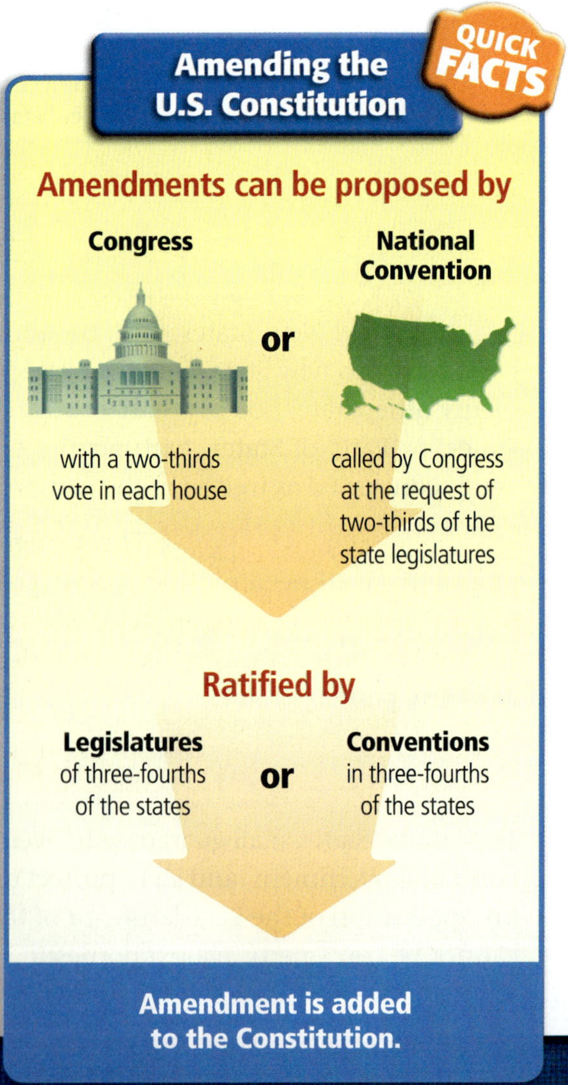

Article VII Ratification

The Ratification of the Conventions of nine States, shall be sufficient for the Establishment of this Constitution between the States so ratifying the Same.

Done in Convention by the Unanimous Consent of the States present the Seventeenth Day of September in the Year of our Lord one thousand seven hundred and Eighty seven and of the Independence of the United States of America the Twelfth In witness whereof We have hereunto subscribed our Names,

George Washington—
President and deputy from Virginia

Delaware
George Read
Gunning Bedford Jr.
John Dickinson
Richard Bassett
Jacob Broom

Maryland
James McHenry
Daniel of St. Thomas Jenifer
Daniel Carroll

Virginia
John Blair
James Madison Jr.

North Carolina
William Blount
Richard Dobbs Spaight
Hugh Williamson

South Carolina
John Rutledge
Charles Cotesworth Pinckney
Charles Pinckney
Pierce Butler

Georgia
William Few
Abraham Baldwin

New Hampshire
John Langdon
Nicholas Gilman

Massachusetts
Nathaniel Gorham
Rufus King

Connecticut
William Samuel Johnson
Roger Sherman

New York
Alexander Hamilton

New Jersey
William Livingston
David Brearley
William Paterson
Jonathan Dayton

Pennsylvania
Benjamin Franklin
Thomas Mifflin
Robert Morris
George Clymer
Thomas FitzSimons
Jared Ingersoll
James Wilson
Gouverneur Morris

Attest:
William Jackson, Secretary

Ratification

The Articles of Confederation called for all 13 states to approve any revision to the Articles. The Constitution required that 9 out of the 13 states would be needed to ratify the Constitution. The first state to ratify was Delaware, on December 7, 1787. Almost two-and-a-half years later, on May 29, 1790, Rhode Island became the last state to ratify the Constitution.

Constitutional Amendments

Note: The first 10 amendments to the Constitution were ratified on December 15, 1791, and form what is known as the Bill of Rights.

Bill of Rights

One of the conditions set by several states for ratifying the Constitution was the inclusion of a bill of rights. Many people feared that a stronger central government might take away basic rights of the people that had been guaranteed in state constitutions.

Amendments 1–10. The Bill of Rights

Amendment I

Congress shall make no law respecting an establishment of religion, or prohibiting the free exercise thereof; or abridging the freedom of speech, or of the press; or the right of the people peaceably to assemble, and to petition the Government for a redress of grievances.

EXPLORING THE DOCUMENT The First Amendment forbids Congress from making any "law respecting an establishment of religion" or restraining the freedom to practice religion as one chooses. **Why is freedom of religion an important right?**

Amendment II

A well regulated Militia, being necessary to the security of a free State, the right of the people to keep and bear Arms, shall not be infringed.

Amendment III

No Soldier shall, in time of peace be **quartered**[24] in any house, without the consent of the Owner, nor in time of war, but in a manner to be prescribed by law.

Amendment IV

The right of the people to be secure in their persons, houses, papers, and effects, against unreasonable searches and seizures, shall not be violated, and no **Warrants**[25] shall issue, but upon probable cause, supported by Oath or affirmation, and particularly describing the place to be searched, and the persons or things to be seized.

Rights of the Accused

The Fifth, Sixth, and Seventh Amendments describe the procedures that courts must follow when trying people accused of crimes.

Amendment V

No person shall be held to answer for a capital, or otherwise **infamous**[26] crime, unless on a presentment or **indictment**[27] of a Grand Jury, except in

Vocabulary

[24] **quartered** housed

[25] **Warrants** written orders authorizing a person to make an arrest, a seizure, or a search

[26] **infamous** disgraceful

[27] **indictment** the act of charging with a crime

Fundamental Liberties

Freedom of Religion

Freedom of Speech

cases arising in the land or naval forces, or in the Militia, when in actual service in time of War or public danger; nor shall any person be subject for the same offence to be twice put in jeopardy of life or limb; nor shall be compelled in any criminal case to be a witness against himself, nor be deprived of life, liberty, or property, without due process of law; nor shall private property be taken for public use, without just compensation.

Amendment VI

In all criminal prosecutions, the accused shall enjoy the right to a speedy and public trial, by an impartial jury of the State and district wherein the crime shall have been committed, which district shall have been previously **ascertained**[28] by law, and to be informed of the nature and cause of the accusation; to be confronted with the witnesses against him; to have compulsory process for obtaining witnesses in his favor, and to have the Assistance of Counsel for his defence.

Amendment VII

In suits at common law, where the value in controversy shall exceed twenty dollars, the right of trial by jury shall be preserved, and no fact tried by a jury, shall be otherwise reexamined in any Court of the United States, than according to the rules of the common law.

Amendment VIII

Excessive bail shall not be required, nor excessive fines imposed, nor cruel and unusual punishments inflicted.

Amendment IX

The enumeration in the Constitution, of certain rights, shall not be construed to deny or disparage others retained by the people.

Amendment X

The powers not delegated to the United States by the Constitution, nor prohibited by it to the States, are reserved to the States respectively, or to the people.

Trials

The Sixth Amendment makes several guarantees, including a prompt trial and a trial by a jury chosen from the state and district in which the crime was committed.

Vocabulary

[28] **ascertained** found out

EXPLORING THE DOCUMENT The Ninth and Tenth Amendments were added because not every right of the people or of the states could be listed in the Constitution. **How do the Ninth and Tenth Amendments limit the power of the federal government?**

Freedom of the Press

Freedom of Assembly

Freedom to Petition the Government

ANALYSIS SKILL **ANALYZING INFORMATION**

Which amendment guarantees these fundamental freedoms?

Amendments to the U.S. Constitution

The Constitution has been amended only 27 times since it was ratified more than 200 years ago. Amendments help the structure of the government change along with the values of the nation's people. Read the time line below to learn how each amendment changed the government.

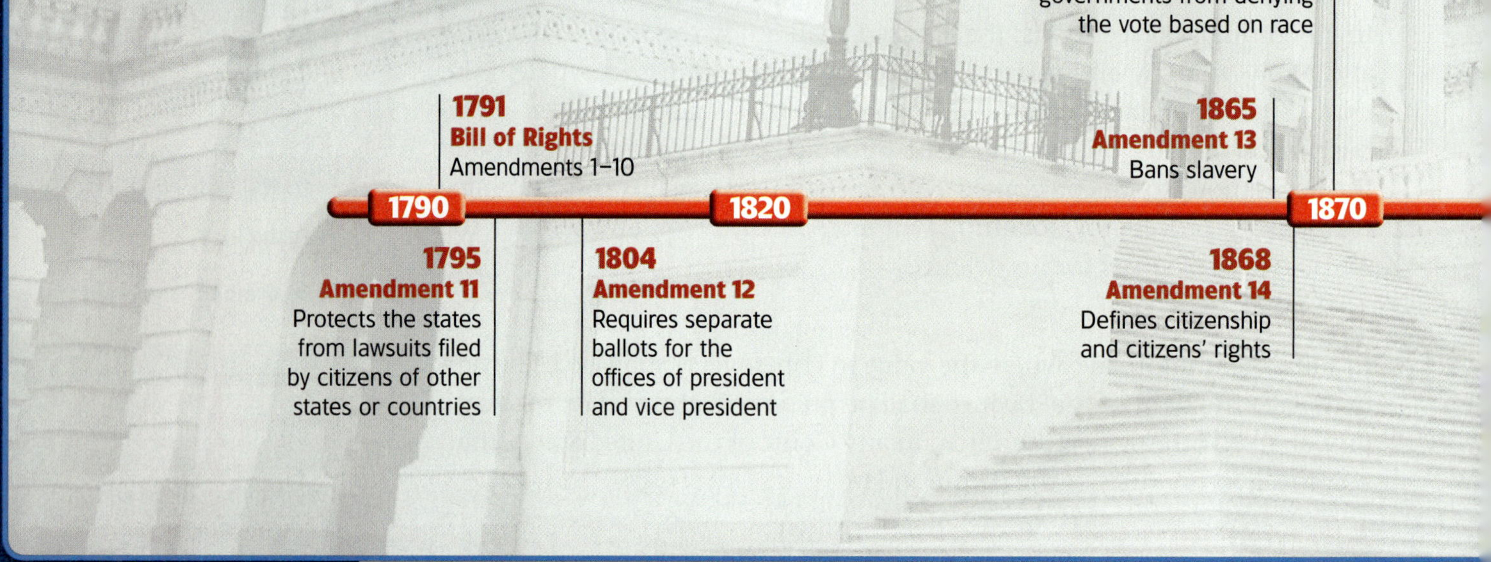

Amendments 11–27

Amendment XI

Passed by Congress March 4, 1794. Ratified February 7, 1795.

The Judicial power of the United States shall not be **construed**[29] to extend to any suit in law or equity, commenced or prosecuted against one of the United States by Citizens of another State, or by Citizens or Subjects of any Foreign State.

Vocabulary

[29] **construed** explained or interpreted

President and Vice President

The Twelfth Amendment changed the election procedure for president and vice president.

Amendment XII

Passed by Congress December 9, 1803. Ratified June 15, 1804.

The Electors shall meet in their respective states and vote by ballot for President and Vice-President, one of whom, at least, shall not be an inhabitant of the same state with themselves; they shall name in their ballots the person voted for as President, and in distinct ballots the person voted for as Vice-President, and they shall make distinct lists of all persons voted for as President, and of all persons voted for as Vice-President, and of the number of votes for each, which lists they shall sign and certify, and transmit sealed to the seat of the government of the United States, directed to the President of the Senate;—the President of the Senate shall, in the presence of the

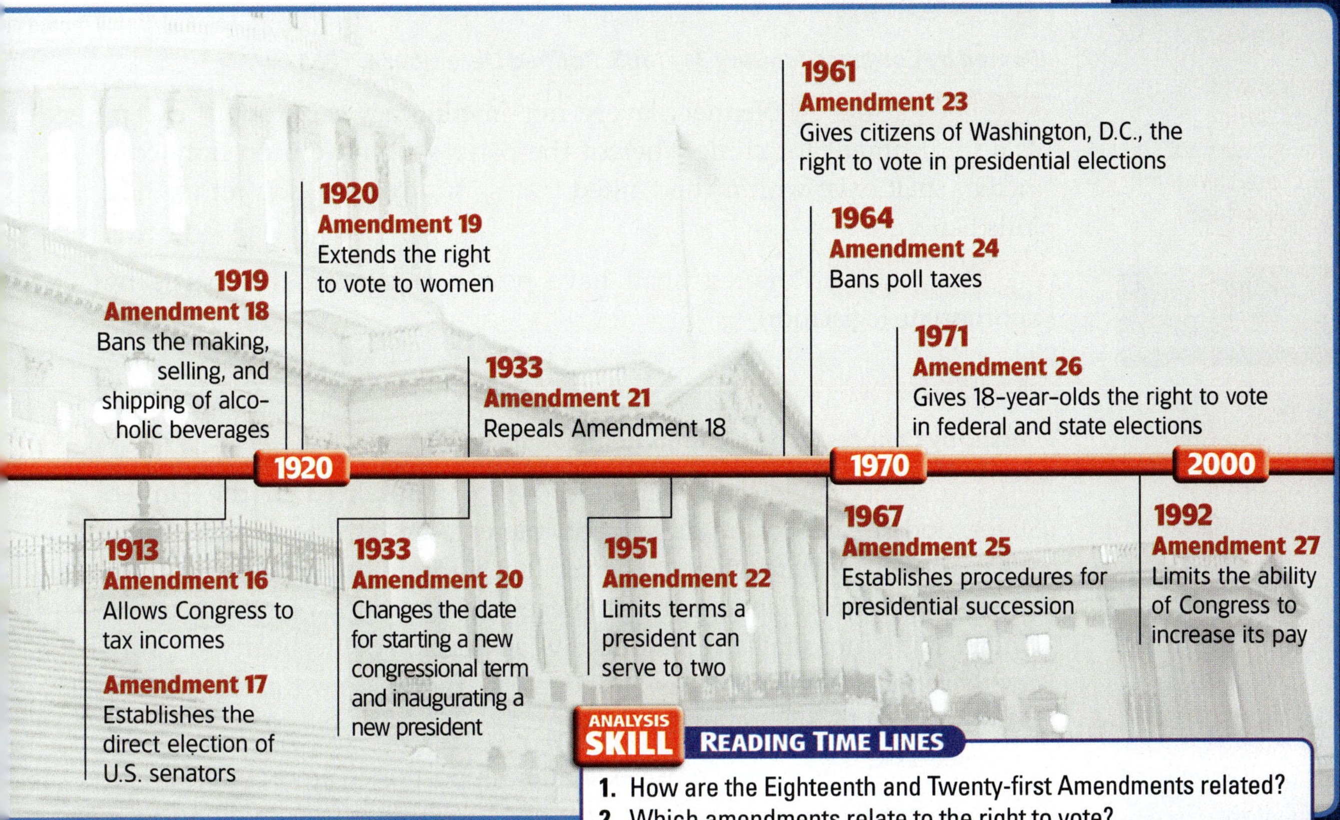

ANALYSIS SKILL **READING TIME LINES**

1. How are the Eighteenth and Twenty-first Amendments related?
2. Which amendments relate to the right to vote?

Senate and House of Representatives, open all the certificates and the votes shall then be counted;—The person having the greatest number of votes for President, shall be the President, if such number be a majority of the whole number of Electors appointed; and if no person have such majority, then from the persons having the highest numbers not exceeding three on the list of those voted for as President, the House of Representatives shall choose immediately, by ballot, the President. But in choosing the President, the votes shall be taken by states, the representation from each state having one vote; a quorum for this purpose shall consist of a member or members from two-thirds of the states, and a majority of all the states shall be necessary to a choice. ~~And if the House of Representatives shall not choose a President whenever the right of choice shall devolve upon them, before the fourth day of March next following, then the Vice-President shall act as President, as in case of the death or other constitutional disability of the President.~~—The person having the greatest number of votes as Vice-President, shall be the Vice-President, if such number be a majority of the whole number of Electors appointed, and if no person have a majority, then from the two highest numbers on the list, the Senate shall choose the Vice-President; a quorum for the purpose shall consist of two-thirds of the whole number of Senators, and a majority of the whole number shall be necessary to a choice. But no person constitutionally ineligible to the office of President shall be eligible to that of Vice-President of the United States.

Amendment XIII

Passed by Congress January 31, 1865. Ratified December 6, 1865.

1. Slavery Banned Neither slavery nor **involuntary servitude**,[30] except as a punishment for crime whereof the party shall have been duly convicted, shall exist within the United States, or any place subject to their jurisdiction.

2. Enforcement Congress shall have power to enforce this article by appropriate legislation.

Abolishing Slavery

Although some slaves had been freed during the Civil War, slavery was not abolished until the Thirteenth Amendment took effect.

Amendment XIV

Passed by Congress June 13, 1866. Ratified July 9, 1868.

1. Citizenship Defined All persons born or naturalized in the United States, and subject to the jurisdiction thereof, are citizens of the United States and of the State wherein they reside. No State shall make or enforce any law which shall abridge the privileges or immunities of citizens of the United States; nor shall any State deprive any person of life, liberty, or property, without due process of law; nor deny to any person within its jurisdiction the equal protection of the laws.

2. Voting Rights Representatives shall be apportioned among the several States according to their respective numbers, counting the whole number of persons in each State, ~~excluding Indians not taxed~~. But when the right to vote at any election for the choice of electors for President and Vice-President of the United States, Representatives in Congress, the Executive and Judicial officers of a State, or the members of the Legislature thereof, is denied to any of the ~~male~~ inhabitants of such State, ~~being twenty-one years of age~~, and citizens of the United States, or in any way abridged, except for participation in rebellion, or other crime, the basis of representation therein shall be reduced in the proportion which the number of such ~~male~~ citizens shall bear to the whole number of ~~male~~ citizens ~~twenty-one years of age~~ in such State.

3. Rebels Banned from Government No person shall be a Senator or Representative in Congress, or elector of President and Vice-President, or hold any office, civil or military, under the United States, or under any State, who, having previously taken an oath, as a member of Congress, or as an officer of the United States, or as a member of any State legislature, or as an executive or judicial officer of any State, to support the Constitution of the United States, shall have engaged in insurrection or rebellion against the same, or given aid or comfort to the enemies thereof. But Congress may by a vote of two-thirds of each House, remove such disability.

4. Payment of Debts The validity of the public debt of the United States, authorized by law, including debts incurred for payment of pensions and

Protecting the Rights of Citizens

In 1833 the Supreme Court ruled that the Bill of Rights limited the federal government but not the state governments. This ruling was interpreted to mean that states were able to keep African Americans from becoming state citizens and keep the Bill of Rights from protecting them. The Fourteenth Amendment defines citizenship and prevents states from interfering in the rights of citizens of the United States.

Vocabulary

[30] **involuntary servitude** being forced to work against one's will

The Reconstruction Amendments

The Thirteenth, Fourteenth, and Fifteenth Amendments are often called the Reconstruction Amendments. This is because they arose during Reconstruction, the period of American history following the Civil War. The country was reconstructing itself after that terrible conflict. A key aspect of Reconstruction was extending the rights of citizenship to former slaves.

The Thirteenth Amendment banned slavery. The Fourteenth Amendment required states to respect the freedoms listed in the Bill of Rights, thus preventing states from denying rights to African Americans. The Fifteenth Amendment gave African American men the right to vote.

African Americans participate in an election.

ANALYSIS SKILL **ANALYZING INFORMATION**

Why was the Thirteenth Amendment needed?

bounties for services in suppressing insurrection or rebellion, shall not be questioned. But neither the United States nor any State shall assume or pay any debt or obligation incurred in aid of insurrection or rebellion against the United States, ~~or any claim for the loss or emancipation of any slave~~; but all such debts, obligations and claims shall be held illegal and void.

5. Enforcement The Congress shall have the power to enforce, by appropriate legislation, the provisions of this article.

Amendment XV

Passed by Congress February 26, 1869. Ratified February 3, 1870.

1. Voting Rights The right of citizens of the United States to vote shall not be denied or abridged by the United States or by any State on account of race, color, or previous condition of servitude.

2. Enforcement The Congress shall have the power to enforce this article by appropriate legislation.

Amendment XVI

Passed by Congress July 2, 1909. Ratified February 3, 1913.

The Congress shall have power to lay and collect taxes on incomes, from whatever source derived, without apportionment among the several States, and without regard to any census or enumeration.

EXPLORING THE DOCUMENT The Seventeenth Amendment requires that senators be elected directly by the people instead of by the state legislatures. **What principle of our government does the Seventeenth Amendment protect?**

Amendment XVII

Passed by Congress May 13, 1912. Ratified April 8, 1913.

1. Senators Elected by Citizens The Senate of the United States shall be composed of two Senators from each State, elected by the people thereof, for six years; and each Senator shall have one vote. The electors in each State shall have the qualifications requisite for electors of the most numerous branch of the State legislatures.

2. Vacancies When vacancies happen in the representation of any State in the Senate, the executive authority of such State shall issue writs of election to fill such vacancies: *Provided,* That the legislature of any State may empower the executive thereof to make temporary appointments until the people fill the vacancies by election as the legislature may direct.

3. Future Elections ~~This amendment shall not be so construed as to affect the election or term of any Senator chosen before it becomes valid as part of the Constitution.~~

Prohibition

Although many people believed that the Eighteenth Amendment was good for the health and welfare of the American people, it was repealed 14 years later.

Amendment XVIII

Passed by Congress December 18, 1917. Ratified January 16, 1919. Repealed by Amendment XXI.

1. Liquor Banned ~~After one year from the ratification of this article the manufacture, sale, or transportation of intoxicating liquors within, the importation thereof into, or the exportation thereof from the United States and all territory subject to the jurisdiction thereof for beverage purposes is hereby prohibited.~~

2. Enforcement ~~The Congress and the several States shall have concurrent power to enforce this article by appropriate legislation.~~

3. Ratification ~~This article shall be inoperative unless it shall have been ratified as an amendment to the Constitution by the legislatures of the several States, as provided in the Constitution, within seven years from the date of the submission hereof to the States by the Congress.~~

Women Fight for the Vote

To become part of the Constitution, a proposed amendment must be ratified by three-fourths of the states. Here, suffragists witness Kentucky governor Edwin P. Morrow signing the Nineteenth Amendment in January 1920. By June of that year, enough states had ratified the amendment to make it part of the Constitution. American women, after generations of struggle, had finally won the right to vote.

ANALYSIS SKILL **ANALYZING INFORMATION**

What right did the Nineteenth Amendment grant?

Amendment XIX

Passed by Congress June 4, 1919. Ratified August 18, 1920.

1. Voting Rights The right of citizens of the United States to vote shall not be denied or abridged by the United States or by any State on account of sex.

2. Enforcement Congress shall have power to enforce this article by appropriate legislation.

Women's Suffrage

Abigail Adams and others were disappointed that the Declaration of Independence and the Constitution did not specifically include women. It took many years and much campaigning before suffrage for women was finally achieved.

Amendment XX

Passed by Congress March 2, 1932. Ratified January 23, 1933.

1. Presidential Terms The terms of the President and the Vice President shall end at noon on the 20th day of January, and the terms of Senators and Representatives at noon on the 3d day of January, of the years in which such terms would have ended if this article had not been ratified; and the terms of their successors shall then begin.

Taking Office

In the original Constitution, a newly elected president and Congress did not take office until March 4, which was four months after the November election. The officials who were leaving office were called lame ducks because they had little influence during those four months. The Twentieth Amendment changed the date that the new president and Congress take office. Members of Congress now take office during the first week of January, and the president takes office on January 20.

2. Meeting of Congress The Congress shall assemble at least once in every year, and such meeting shall begin at noon on the 3d day of January, unless they shall by law appoint a different day.

3. Succession of Vice President If, at the time fixed for the beginning of the term of the President, the President elect shall have died, the Vice President elect shall become President. If a President shall not have been chosen before the time fixed for the beginning of his term, or if the President elect shall have failed to qualify, then the Vice President elect shall act as President until a President shall have qualified; and the Congress may by law provide for the case wherein neither a President elect nor a Vice President shall have qualified, declaring who shall then act as President, or the manner in which one who is to act shall be selected, and such person shall act accordingly until a President or Vice President shall have qualified.

4. Succession by Vote of Congress The Congress may by law provide for the case of the death of any of the persons from whom the House of Representatives may choose a President whenever the right of choice shall have devolved upon them, and for the case of the death of any of the persons from whom the Senate may choose a Vice President whenever the right of choice shall have devolved upon them.

5. Ratification ~~Sections 1 and 2 shall take effect on the 15th day of October following the ratification of this article.~~

6. Ratification ~~This article shall be inoperative unless it shall have been ratified as an amendment to the Constitution by the legislatures of three-fourths of the several States within seven years from the date of its submission.~~

Amendment XXI

Passed by Congress February 20, 1933. Ratified December 5, 1933.

1. 18th Amendment Repealed The eighteenth article of amendment to the Constitution of the United States is hereby repealed.

2. Liquor Allowed by Law The transportation or importation into any State, Territory, or Possession of the United States for delivery or use therein of intoxicating liquors, in violation of the laws thereof, is hereby prohibited.

3. Ratification ~~This article shall be inoperative unless it shall have been ratified as an amendment to the Constitution by conventions in the several States, as provided in the Constitution, within seven years from the date of the submission hereof to the States by the Congress.~~

Amendment XXII

Passed by Congress March 21, 1947. Ratified February 27, 1951.

1. Term Limits No person shall be elected to the office of the President more than twice, and no person who has held the office of President, or acted as President, for more than two years of a term to which some other person was elected President shall be elected to the office of President more than once. ~~But this Article shall not apply to any person holding the office of President when this Article was proposed by Congress, and shall not prevent any person who may be holding the office of President, or acting as President, during the term within which this Article becomes operative from holding the office of President or acting as President during the remainder of such term.~~

2. Ratification ~~This article shall be inoperative unless it shall have been ratified as an amendment to the Constitution by the legislatures of three-fourths of the several States within seven years from the date of its submission to the States by the Congress.~~

EXPLORING THE DOCUMENT From the time of President George Washington's administration, it was a custom for presidents to serve no more than two terms in office. Franklin D. Roosevelt, however, was elected to four terms. The Twenty-second Amendment restricted presidents to no more than two terms in office. **Why do you think citizens chose to limit the power of the president in this way?**

After Franklin D. Roosevelt was elected to four consecutive terms, limits were placed on the number of terms a president could serve.

Amendment XXIII

Passed by Congress June 16, 1960. Ratified March 29, 1961.

1. District of Columbia Represented The District constituting the seat of Government of the United States shall appoint in such manner as Congress may direct:

A number of electors of President and Vice President equal to the whole number of Senators and Representatives in Congress to which the District would be entitled if it were a State, but in no event more than the least populous State; they shall be in addition to those appointed by the States, but they shall be considered, for the purposes of the election of President and Vice President, to be electors appointed by a State; and they shall meet in the District and perform such duties as provided by the twelfth article of amendment.

2. Enforcement The Congress shall have power to enforce this article by appropriate legislation.

Voting Rights

Until the ratification of the Twenty-third Amendment, the people of Washington, D.C., could not vote in presidential elections.

Poll Tax Amendment

Poll taxes were used to deny many poor Americans, including African Americans and Hispanic Americans, their right to vote. These taxes were made unconstitutional by the Twenty-fourth Amendment.

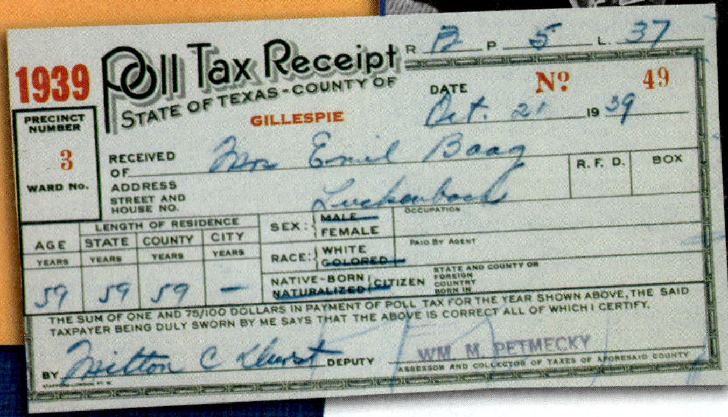
1939 Poll Tax Receipt
STATE OF TEXAS - COUNTY OF GILLESPIE
R B P 5 L 37
Nº 49
DATE Oct. 21 1939
PRECINCT NUMBER 3
WARD No.
RECEIVED OF Mr. Emil Boog
ADDRESS STREET AND HOUSE NO. Luckenbach
R. F. D. BOX
OCCUPATION
AGE YEARS 59 | LENGTH OF RESIDENCE STATE YEARS 59 | COUNTY YEARS 59 | CITY YEARS —
SEX: MALE FEMALE
RACE: WHITE COLORED
NATIVE-BORN NATURALIZED CITIZEN
THE SUM OF ONE AND 75/100 DOLLARS IN PAYMENT OF POLL TAX FOR THE YEAR SHOWN ABOVE, THE SAID TAXPAYER BEING DULY SWORN BY ME SAYS THAT THE ABOVE IS CORRECT ALL OF WHICH I CERTIFY.
BY Milton C. Kurst DEPUTY WM. M. PETMECKY ASSESSOR AND COLLECTOR OF TAXES OF AFORESAID COUNTY

ANALYSIS SKILL **ANALYZING INFORMATION**

How did poll taxes deny poor Americans the opportunity to vote?

Presidential Disability

The illness of President Eisenhower in the 1950s and the assassination of President Kennedy in 1963 were the events behind the Twenty-fifth Amendment. The Constitution did not provide a clear-cut method for a vice president to take over for a disabled president or upon the death of a president. This amendment provides for filling the office of the vice president if a vacancy occurs, and it provides a way for the vice president—or someone else in the line of succession—to take over if the president is unable to perform the duties of that office.

Amendment XXIV

Passed by Congress August 27, 1962. Ratified January 23, 1964.

1. Voting Rights The right of citizens of the United States to vote in any primary or other election for President or Vice President, for electors for President or Vice President, or for Senator or Representative in Congress, shall not be denied or abridged by the United States or any State by reason of failure to pay poll tax or other tax.

2. Enforcement The Congress shall have power to enforce this article by appropriate legislation.

Amendment XXV

Passed by Congress July 6, 1965. Ratified February 10, 1967.

1. Sucession of Vice President In case of the removal of the President from office or of his death or resignation, the Vice President shall become President.

2. Vacancy of Vice President Whenever there is a vacancy in the office of the Vice President, the President shall nominate a Vice President who shall take office upon confirmation by a majority vote of both Houses of Congress.

3. Written Declaration Whenever the President transmits to the President pro tempore of the Senate and the Speaker of the House of Representatives his written declaration that he is unable to discharge the powers and duties of his office, and until he transmits to them a written declaration to the contrary, such powers and duties shall be discharged by the Vice President as Acting President.

4. Removing the President Whenever the Vice President and a majority of either the principal officers of the executive departments or of such other body as Congress may by law provide, transmit to the President pro tempore of the Senate and the Speaker of the House of Representatives their written declaration that the President is unable to discharge the powers and duties of his office, the Vice President shall immediately assume the powers and duties of the office as Acting President.

Thereafter, when the President transmits to the President pro tempore of the Senate and the Speaker of the House of Representatives his written declaration that no inability exists, he shall resume the powers and duties of his office unless the Vice President and a majority of either the principal officers of the executive department or of such other body as Congress may by law provide, transmit within four days to the President pro tempore of the Senate and the Speaker of the House of Representatives their written declaration that the President is unable to discharge the powers and duties of his office. Thereupon Congress shall decide the issue, assembling within forty-eight hours for that purpose if not in session. If the Congress, within twenty-one days after receipt of the latter written declaration, or, if Congress is not in session, within twenty-one days after Congress is required to assemble, determines by two-thirds vote of both Houses that the President is unable to discharge the powers and duties of his office, the Vice President shall continue to discharge the same as Acting President; otherwise, the President shall resume the powers and duties of his office.

Amendment XXVI

Passed by Congress March 23, 1971. Ratified July 1, 1971.

1. Voting Rights The right of citizens of the United States, who are eighteen years of age or older, to vote shall not be denied or abridged by the United States or by any State on account of age.

2. Enforcement The Congress shall have power to enforce this article by appropriate legislation.

Expanded Suffrage

The Voting Rights Act of 1970 tried to set the voting age at 18. However, the Supreme Court ruled that the act set the voting age for national elections only, not for state or local elections. The Twenty-sixth Amendment gave 18-year-old citizens the right to vote in all elections.

Amendment XXVII

Originally proposed September 25, 1789. Ratified May 7, 1992.

No law, varying the compensation for the services of the Senators and Representatives, shall take effect, until an election of representatives shall have intervened.

SECTION 2

The Bill of Rights

What You Will Learn...

Main Ideas

1. The First Amendment guarantees basic freedoms to individuals.
2. Other amendments focus on protecting citizens from certain abuses.
3. The rights of the accused are an important part of the Bill of Rights.
4. The rights of states and citizens are protected by the Bill of Rights.

The Big Idea

The Bill of Rights was added to the Constitution to define clearly the rights and freedoms of citizens.

Key Terms and People

James Madison, *p. 216*
majority rule, *p. 216*
petition, *p. 217*
search warrant, *p. 218*
due process, *p. 218*
indict, *p. 218*
double jeopardy, *p. 218*
eminent domain, *p. 218*

TAKING NOTES As you read, take notes on the freedoms protected by the Bill of Rights and which amendment protects each. The first right has been filled in for you as an example.

Rights/Freedoms	Amendment
1. Freedom of religion	

If YOU were there...

Your father runs a bookshop in colonial Boston in 1770. Your family lives in a very small brick house. You and your sisters must share one small room. One day, a red-coated British officer knocks on your door and strides into the parlor. He says that your family will have to provide a room and meals for two British soldiers. "We're already crowded!" you protest, but he insists.

Would you support the British government's requirement that colonists provide food and shelter for troops? Why?

BUILDING BACKGROUND People in the American colonies resented the British soldiers stationed in their towns. They objected to sudden searches and to soldiers being housed in private homes. They disliked censorship of their newspapers. When the Constitution was written, Americans remembered those wrongs. They insisted on adding a bill of rights to the document.

First Amendment

Federalist **James Madison** promised that a bill of rights would be added to the Constitution. This promise allowed the Constitution to pass. In 1789 Madison began writing down a huge list of proposed amendments. He then presented a shorter list to the House of Representatives. Of those, the House approved 12. The states ratified 10, which took effect December 15, 1791. Those 10 amendments, called the Bill of Rights, protect U.S. citizens' individual liberties.

The protection of individual liberties is important in a representative democracy. Without safeguards, people's rights would not always be protected because of **majority rule**. This is the idea that the greatest number of people in society can make policies for everyone. While this means that most people agree on what the law should be, it also means that smaller groups, or minorities, might lose their rights. The Bill of Rights ensures that the rights of all citizens are protected.

The ideas spelled out in the First Amendment form the most basic rights of all U.S. citizens. These rights include freedom of religion, freedom of the press, freedom of speech, freedom of assembly, and the right to petition.

In the spirit of Thomas Jefferson's Virginia Statute for Religious Freedom, the First Amendment begins, "Congress shall make no law respecting an establishment of religion, or prohibiting the free exercise thereof." In other words, the government cannot support or interfere with the practice of a religion. This amendment keeps the government from favoring one religion over any other or establishing an official religion.

The First Amendment also guarantees freedom of speech and of the press. This means that Americans have the right to express their own ideas and views. They also have the right to hear the ideas and views of others. Former senator Margaret Chase Smith discussed why these freedoms are important. "The key to security," she once said, "is public information."

Freedom of speech does not mean that people can say anything they want to, however. The Constitution does not protect slander—false statements meant to damage someone's reputation. Libel, or intentionally writing a lie that harms another person, is not protected, either. The Supreme Court has also ruled that speech that endangers public safety is not protected. For example, Justice Oliver Wendell Holmes declared in 1919 that falsely shouting "Fire" in a crowded theater is not protected as free speech.

Americans also have freedom of assembly, or of holding meetings. Any group may gather to discuss issues or conduct business. If people gather peacefully and do not engage in illegal activities, the government cannot interfere. The right to **petition**, or make a request of the government, is another right of the American people. Any American can present a petition to a government official. This right lets Americans show dissatisfaction with a law. They can also suggest new laws.

THE IMPACT TODAY

Free-speech protection has also been applied to "symbolic" speech—or nonverbal communication that expresses an idea, such as wearing a protest button.

READING CHECK **Summarizing** What rights does the First Amendment guarantee to Americans?

Amendment I

Congress shall make no law respecting an establishment of religion, or prohibiting the free exercise thereof; or abridging the freedom of speech, or of the press; or the right of the people peaceably to assemble, and to petition the Government for a redress of grievances.

Workers use the right of assembly to protest a proposed budget in New York City.

Amendment II

A well regulated Militia, being necessary to the security of a free State, the right of the people to keep and bear Arms, shall not be infringed.

Amendment III

No Soldier shall, in time of peace be quartered in any house, without the consent of the Owner, nor in time of war, but in a manner to be prescribed by law.

Amendment IV

The right of the people to be secure in their persons, houses, papers, and effects, against unreasonable searches and seizures, shall not be violated, and no Warrants shall issue, but upon probable cause, supported by Oath or affirmation, and particularly describing the place to be searched, and the persons or things to be seized.

Protecting Citizens

The Second, Third, and Fourth Amendments relate to colonial disputes with Britain and reflect many of the ideals outlined in the Declaration of Independence. The Second Amendment deals with state militias and the right to bear arms. Colonial militias played a big role in the Revolutionary War. The framers of the Constitution thought that the states needed their militias for emergencies. Today the National Guard has largely replaced organized state militias.

Supporters of gun-control laws have generally argued that the Second Amendment was intended to protect the collective right of states to maintain well-regulated militia units. Opponents hold that the amendment was meant to protect an individual's right of self-defense. The meaning of the amendment continues to be debated.

The Third Amendment prevents the military from forcing citizens to house soldiers. Before the Revolution, the British pressured colonists to shelter and feed British soldiers. British leaders also forced colonists to submit to having their property searched for illegal goods. Anger over such actions led to the Fourth Amendment rule against "unreasonable searches and seizures." Before a citizen's property can be searched, authorities must now get a **search warrant**. This order gives authorities permission to search someone's property. A judge issues this order only when it seems likely that a search might uncover evidence relating to a crime. In emergencies, however, police can make an emergency search. This may preserve evidence needed to prove possible illegal activity.

READING CHECK **Finding Main Ideas**

Why were the Third and Fourth Amendments matters of great importance to Americans when the Bill of Rights was written?

Rights of the Accused

The Fifth, Sixth, Seventh, and Eighth Amendments provide guidelines for protecting the rights of the accused. According to the Fifth Amendment, the government cannot punish anyone without **due process** of law. This means that the law must be fairly applied. A grand jury decides if there is enough evidence to **indict** (en-DYT), or formally accuse, a person. Without an indictment, the court cannot try anyone for a serious crime. The Fifth Amendment also protects people from having to testify at their own criminal trial. To keep from testifying, a person need only "take the Fifth." In addition, anyone found not guilty in a criminal trial cannot face **double jeopardy**. In other words, he or she cannot be tried again for the same crime.

The final clause of the Fifth Amendment states that no one can have property taken without due process of law. There is one exception: the government's power of **eminent domain**. This is the power to take personal property to benefit the public. One example would be taking private land to build a public road. However, the government must pay the owners a fair price for the property. If the property was gained illegally, then the owners are not paid.

The Sixth Amendment protects the rights of a person who has been indicted. It guarantees that person a speedy public trial. Public trials ensure that laws are being followed by allowing the public to witness the proceedings. Accused people have the right to know the charges against them and can hear and question witnesses testifying against them. Accused people have the right to an attorney. If they cannot pay for legal service, the government must provide it. Sometimes accused persons refuse their Sixth Amendment rights. For example, some defendants refuse the services of an attorney, while others choose to have a trial in front of a judge alone instead of before a jury. In many cases, defendants can forgo trial and agree to a plea bargain. This means that a defendant pleads guilty to a lesser charge and avoids risking conviction for a crime with a greater sentence.

The Seventh Amendment states that juries can decide civil cases. It is possible to harm another person without committing a crime. In such cases, the injured party may sue, or seek justice, in a civil court. Civil cases usually involve disputes over money or property. For example, someone might bring a civil suit against a person who refuses to repay a debt.

Amendment V

No person shall be held to answer for a capital, or otherwise infamous crime, unless on a presentment or indictment of a Grand Jury, except in cases arising in the land or naval forces, or in the Militia, when in actual service in time of War or public danger; nor shall any person be subject for the same offence to be twice put in jeopardy of life or limb; nor shall be compelled in any criminal case to be a witness against himself, nor be deprived of life, liberty, or property, without due process of law; nor shall private property be taken for public use, without just compensation.

Amendment VI

In all criminal prosecutions, the accused shall enjoy the right to a speedy and public trial, by an impartial jury of the State and district wherein the crime shall have been committed, which district shall have been previously ascertained by law, and to be informed of the nature and cause of the accusation; to be confronted with the witnesses against him; to have compulsory process for obtaining witnesses in his favor, and to have the Assistance of Counsel for his defence.

Amendment VII

In suits at common law, where the value in controversy shall exceed twenty dollars, the right of trial by jury shall be preserved, and no fact tried by a jury, shall be otherwise reexamined in any Court of the United States, than according to the rules of the common law.

A judge and jury listen to a witness in a courtroom in Orange County, California.

A Right to Bail

The Eighth Amendment allows for bail. Bail is a set amount of money that defendants promise to pay the court if they fail to appear in court at the proper time.

By posting, or paying, bail, a defendant can avoid staying in jail before and during a trial. If a defendant does not show up in court for trial, the court demands the bail money be paid and issues a warrant for arrest.

The Eighth Amendment keeps courts from setting unfairly high bail. However, in cases of very serious crimes, a judge may refuse to set bail altogether. This can be the case, for example, if the court regards a defendant as being potentially dangerous to the public by being left free. A judge can also deny bail if he or she thinks the defendant will not show up for trial. In such cases the defendant must remain in jail through the trial.

Amendment VIII

Excessive bail shall not be required, nor excessive fines imposed, nor cruel and unusual punishments inflicted.

"Cruel and Unusual Punishments"

The Eighth Amendment also bans "cruel and unusual punishments" against a person convicted of a crime. For many years, Americans have debated the question of what exactly constitutes cruel and unusual punishment. The debate has often centered on the issue of capital punishment. In 1972 the Supreme Court ruled that the way in which most states carried out the death penalty was cruel and unusual. The Court also found that the ways in which many states sentenced people to death were unfair. However, a few years later, the Court ruled that not all executions were in themselves cruel and unusual.

Most states still allow the death penalty. Those that do must follow the Supreme Court's rules. To do so, many states have changed the ways in which they carry out the death penalty.

READING CHECK **Summarizing** What is the purpose of the Eighth Amendment?

Rights of States and Citizens

The final two amendments in the Bill of Rights give a general protection for other rights not addressed by the first eight amendments. These amendments also reserve some governmental powers for the states and the people.

Ninth Amendment

The Ninth Amendment says that the rights listed in the Constitution are not the only rights that citizens have. This amendment has allowed the courts and Congress to decide other basic rights of citizens.

The Constitution does not address the question of education. However, most Americans believe that it is a basic and essential right. This seems especially true in view of the fact that American citizens must be able to vote for the people who represent them in government. "Education is not just another

Amendment IX

The enumeration in the Constitution, of certain rights, shall not be construed to deny or disparage others retained by the people.

Amendment X

The powers not delegated to the United States by the Constitution, nor prohibited by it to the States, are reserved to the States respectively, or to the people.

consumer item. It is the bedrock [foundation] of our democracy," explained educational leader Mary Hatwood Futrell. Today state governments offer free education from elementary to high school—to all citizens.

Tenth Amendment

The Tenth Amendment recognizes that the states and the people have additional powers. These powers are any ones that the Constitution does not specifically give to Congress—the delegated powers. The Tenth Amendment makes it clear that any powers not either delegated to the federal government or prohibited to the states belong to the states and the people. Thus, the last amendment in the Bill of Rights protects citizens' rights and helps keep the balance of power between the federal and state governments.

READING CHECK **Summarizing** How does the Tenth Amendment protect the rights of citizens?

SUMMARY AND PREVIEW In this section you learned about the Bill of Rights. In the next section you will learn about the responsibilities of citizenship.

Students learn about the rights and responsibilities of being a U.S. citizen.

Section 2 Assessment

go.hrw.com
Online Quiz
KEYWORD: SC7 HP6

Reviewing Ideas, Terms, and People

1. a. **Identify** What basic rights are protected by the First Amendment?
   b. **Explain** What does the right to **petition** the government mean?
   c. **Elaborate** Why is freedom of the press an important right?
2. a. **Describe** How are citizens protected under the Third and Fourth Amendments?
   b. **Draw Conclusions** In what ways did British actions before the Revolution lead to the Second, Third, and Fourth Amendments?
3. a. **Identify** What protections does the Eighth Amendment provide for people accused of crimes?
   b. **Elaborate** Why is it important that the Bill of Rights protects people accused of crimes?
4. a. **Recall** What is the purpose of the final two amendments in the Bill of Rights?
   b. **Analyze** How does the Tenth Amendment balance power between national and state governments?

Critical Thinking

5. **Summarizing** Copy the chart below. Use it to summarize the rights guaranteed to citizens by each amendment in the Bill of Rights.

Amendment	Rights
1	
2	
3	
4	
5	
6	
7	
8	
9	
10	

FOCUS ON WRITING

6. **Gathering Information about the Bill of Rights** What freedoms are guaranteed by the Bill of Rights? Make a list of the most important freedoms. You'll list those freedoms on the third page of your pamphlet.

SECTION 3

Rights and Responsibilities of Citizenship

What You Will Learn...

Main Ideas

1. Citizenship in the United States is determined in several ways.
2. Citizens are expected to fulfill a number of important duties.
3. Active citizen involvement in government and the community is encouraged.

The Big Idea

American citizenship involves great privileges and serious responsibilities.

Key Terms

naturalized citizens, *p. 222*
deport, *p. 222*
draft, *p. 223*
political action committees, *p. 224*
interest groups, *p. 224*

TAKING NOTES As you read, look for information on three ways a person can become a U.S. citizen. Take notes in a graphic organizer like the one below.

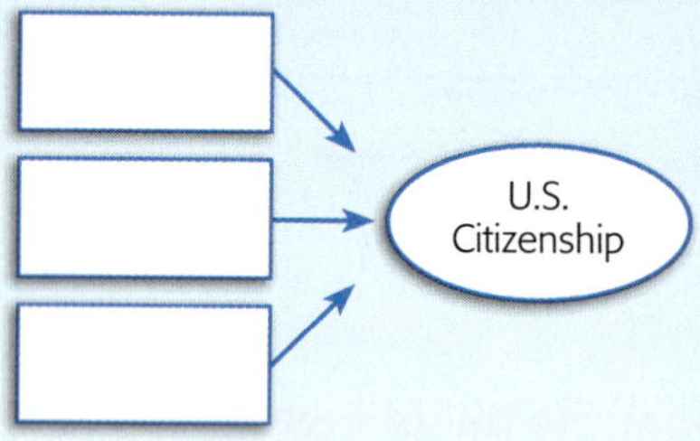

If YOU were there...

Your older brother and his friends have just turned 18. That means they must register with selective service. But it also means that they are old enough to vote in national elections. You are interested in the upcoming elections and think it would be exciting to have a real voice in politics. But your brother and his friends don't even plan to register to vote.

How would you persuade your brother that voting is important?

BUILDING BACKGROUND Whether you are born an American citizen or become one later, citizenship brings many rights and privileges. But it also brings duties and responsibilities. Voting is both a right and a responsibility.

Gaining U.S. Citizenship

People become U.S. citizens in several ways. First, anyone born in the United States or a territory it controls is a citizen. People born in a foreign country are U.S. citizens if at least one parent is a U.S. citizen. Foreign-born people whose parents are not citizens must move to the United States to become **naturalized citizens**. Once in the United States, they go through a long process before applying for citizenship. If they succeed, they become naturalized citizens, giving them most of the rights and responsibilities of other citizens.

In the United States, legal immigrants have many of the rights and responsibilities of citizens but cannot vote or hold public office. The U.S. government can **deport**, or return to the country of origin, immigrants who break the law.

Legal immigrants over age 18 may request naturalization after living in the United States for five years. All legal immigrants have to support themselves financially. If not, someone must assume financial responsibility for them. Immigrants must be law-abiding and support the U.S. Constitution. They must demonstrate understanding of written and spoken English. They also must show basic knowledge of U.S. history and government.

When this is done, candidates go before a naturalization court and take an oath of allegiance to the United States. They then get certificates of naturalization.

Only two differences between naturalized and native-born citizens exist. Naturalized citizens can lose their citizenship, and they cannot become president or vice president. Many famous Americans have been naturalized citizens, including scientist Albert Einstein and former secretary of state Madeleine Albright.

READING CHECK **Drawing Conclusions** Why does U.S. law have such demanding requirements for people to become naturalized citizens?

Becoming a Citizen

For many people around the world, becoming a citizen of the United States is a lifelong dream. The highlight of the naturalization process is the ceremony where candidates promise to "support and defend the Constitution and laws of the United States of America."

Duties of Citizenship

For a representative democracy to work, Americans need to fulfill their civic duties. "The stakes ... are too high for government to be a spectator sport," former Texas congresswoman Barbara Jordan once said.

Citizens elect officials to make laws for them. In turn, citizens must obey those laws and respect the authorities who enforce them. Obeying laws includes knowing what they are and staying informed about any changes to the law. Ignorance of a law will not prevent a person from being punished for breaking it.

Another duty is paying taxes for services such as public roads, police, and public schools. People pay sales taxes, property taxes, and tariffs. Many Americans also pay a tax on their income to the federal, and sometimes state, government.

Citizens have the duty to defend the nation. Men 18 years or older must register with selective service. In the event of a **draft**, or required military service, those able to fight are already registered. Although women do not register, many serve in the armed forces.

Americans have the right to a trial by jury under the Sixth Amendment. To protect this right, citizens should be willing to serve on a jury when they are called. Otherwise, fulfilling each person's Sixth Amendment rights would be difficult.

READING CHECK **Making Inferences** Why does citizenship carry with it certain responsibilities?

Responsibilities of Citizens

For representative democracy to work, citizens must do their part. Each activity pictured here serves an important role in the community.

Jury Duty

Military Service

Citizens and Government

Taking part in the elections process by voting may be a citizen's most vital duty. Through free elections, U.S. citizens choose who will lead their government.

Function of Elections

It is essential for citizens to learn as much as they can about the issues and candidates before voting. Information is available from many sources: the Internet, newspapers, television, and other media. However, voters should also be aware that some material may be propaganda or material that is biased deliberately to help or harm a cause.

In addition to voting, many Americans choose to campaign for candidates or issues. Anyone can help campaign, even if he or she is not eligible to vote. Many people also help campaigns by giving money directly or through **political action committees** (PACs), groups that collect money for candidates who support certain issues.

ACADEMIC VOCABULARY

influence change or have an effect on

Influencing Government

Even after an election, people can **influence** officials. Political participation is part of our nation's identity and tradition. When colonists protested British rule in the 1700s, they formed committees and presented their views to political leaders.

As the new American nation grew, so did political participation. French diplomat Alexis de Tocqueville visited the United States in 1831 to study American democracy. He was amazed at the large number of political groups Americans participated in. He wrote about them:

> "What political power could ever carry on the vast multitude [large number] of lesser undertakings which the American citizens perform every day, with the assistance of the principle of association [joining a group]? Nothing, in my opinion, is more deserving of our attention than the intellectual and moral associations of America."
>
> —Alexis de Tocqueville, *Democracy in America*

U.S. citizens sometimes work with **interest groups**. These groups of people share a common interest that motivates them to take political action. Interest groups organize speeches and rallies to support their cause. However, citizens need not join a group to influence government. They can write letters to leaders of government or attend city council meetings. Active political participation is an important duty for U.S. citizens and immigrants alike.

Helping the Community

Commitment to others moves many Americans to volunteer in community service groups. Some small communities rely on volunteers for services such as fire protection and law enforcement.

Volunteer groups also help government-sponsored agencies. For example, Citizens on

ANALYSIS SKILL **ANALYZING VISUALS**

Which responsibilities can you fulfill now, without waiting until you turn 18 years old?

Patrol and Neighborhood Watch groups ask volunteers to walk their neighborhoods and tell police if they observe possible criminal activity in the area. The American Red Cross helps citizens in times of natural disasters or other emergencies. The Boy Scouts and Girl Scouts plan many projects such as planting trees to improve the environment. Even simple acts such as picking up trash in parks or serving food in shelters help a community.

READING CHECK **Summarizing** In what ways do volunteer groups benefit the community?

SUMMARY AND PREVIEW In this section you learned about citizens' duties toward their nation and their communities. In the next chapter you will learn about the first government formed under the Constitution.

Section 3 Assessment

go.hrw.com
Online Quiz
KEYWORD: SC7 HP6

Reviewing Ideas, Terms, and People

1. a. **Identify** What are the different ways in which a person can become a U.S. citizen?
   b. **Make Inferences** Why do you think the law requires an immigrant to live in the United States at least five years before he or she can apply to become a **naturalized citizen**?
2. a. **Describe** What are three duties expected of U.S. citizens?
   b. **Evaluate** In your opinion, which duty expected of citizens is the most important? Why?
3. a. **Identify** In what ways can citizens participate in the election process?
   b. **Draw Conclusions** Why do you think it is important that citizens participate in the political process?

Critical Thinking

4. **Categorizing** Review your notes on becoming a U.S. citizen. Then add the responsibilities of citizenship to your graphic organizer.

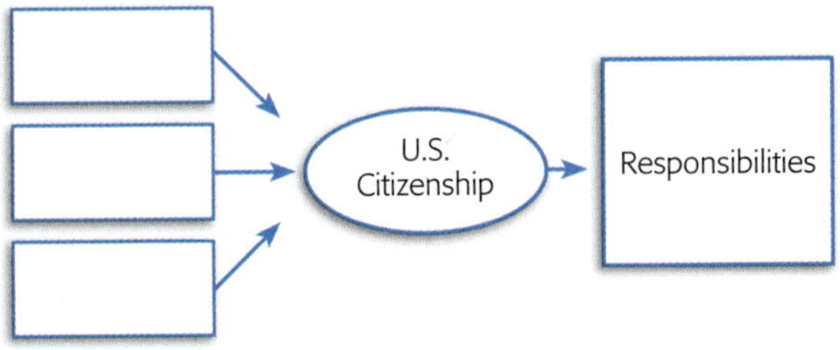

FOCUS ON WRITING

5. **Thinking about Citizenship** The last page of your pamphlet will have two parts—one part on requirements for citizenship and one part on the responsibilities of citizens. Look back through this section and make two lists, one on requirements and one on responsibilities.

Social Studies Skills

Analysis | Critical Thinking | Civic Participation | Study

North Carolina Skills
1.08 Use context clues and appropriate sources such as glossaries, text, and dictionaries to gain meaning.

Determining the Context of Statements

Define the Skill

A *context* is the circumstances under which something happens. *Historical context* includes values, beliefs, conditions, and practices that were common in the past. At times, some of these were quite different from what they are today. To truly understand a historical statement or event, you have to take its context into account. It is not right to judge what people in history did or said based on present-day values alone. To be fair, you must also consider the historical context of the statement or event.

Learn the Skill

To better understand something a historical figure said or wrote, use the following guidelines to determine the context of the statement.

1. Identify the speaker or writer, the date, and the topic and main idea of the statement.
2. Determine the speaker's or writer's attitude and point of view about the topic.
3. Review what you know about beliefs, conditions, or practices related to the topic that were common at the time. Find out more about the times in which the statement was made, if you need to.
4. Decide how well the statement reflects the values, attitudes, and practices of people living at that time. Then, determine how well it reflects values, attitudes, and practices related to the topic today.

Applying these guidelines will give you a better understanding of statements made by the Constitution's framers. You read in Chapter 6 that the Constitution created a representative democracy. However, the original Constitution gave most Americans little voice in choosing their leaders. Only the House of Representatives was elected by the voters. Alexander Hamilton, one of the Constitutional Convention's leaders, told the delegates:

> "The people are turbulent and changing; they seldom judge or determine right. Give therefore to the first [upper] class a distinct, permanent share in government. They will check the unsteadiness of the second [the masses]."

By modern standards, Hamilton's remark is undemocratic. But think about the times in which it was made. Shays's Rebellion had recently occurred. In addition, in those days most Americans had little or no education. Many could not even read or write. When its historical context is considered, the statement seems less harsh and extreme.

Practice the Skill

Read the following statement made by Patrick Henry in 1788. Then answer the questions to determine its context and better understand it.

> "The Constitution is said to have beautiful features, but . . . they appear to me horribly frightful . . . Your dearest rights may be sacrificed by what may be a small minority . . . [that] . . . may continue forever unchangeably this government, although horribly defective."

1. What was Henry's opinion of the Constitution?

2. How might Americans' recent experience in the Revolution have caused him to feel that way?

CHAPTER 6

Chapter Review

HOLT
History's Impact
▶ **video series**
Review the video to answer the closing question:
Why did James Madison think the Tenth Amendment was important for the Bill of Rights?

Visual Summary

QUICK FACTS

Use the visual summary below to help you review the main ideas of the chapter.

- The U.S. Constitution sets up a federal system of government, with powers divided between the federal government and state governments.
- The powers of government are divided among three branches: the legislative, executive, and judicial branches.
- A system of checks and balances prevents any one branch from becoming too powerful.

- The Bill of Rights guarantees important rights and freedoms for American citizens.
- Along with rights, citizens have duties: to obey laws, pay taxes, register for the draft, sit on juries, perform community service, and vote.

Reviewing Vocabulary, Terms, and People

1. Who promised to add a bill of rights to the U.S. Constitution?

a. Benjamin Franklin
b. Thomas Jefferson
c. Alexander Hamilton
d. James Madison

2. What is the term for a person born in another country who becomes a citizen of the United States?

a. immigrant
b. partial citizen
c. naturalized citizen
d. separatist

3. What are powers granted to the states called?

a. reserved powers
b. concurrent powers
c. stately powers
d. delegated powers

4. What is the permission to look for evidence of a crime in a particular location called?

a. petition
b. impeachment
c. indictment
d. search warrant

5. Who was the first female Supreme Court justice?

a. Abigail Adams
b. Susan B. Anthony
c. Barbara Jordan
d. Sandra Day O'Connor

Comprehension and Critical Thinking

SECTION 1 *(Pages 182–186)*

6. a. Describe Name each branch of government and explain the duties of each.

b. Analyze What checks and balances exist between the branches of government?

c. Evaluate Do you think the three branches of government share their power equally? Explain your answer.

SECTION 2 *(Pages 216–221)*

7. a. Identify What is the Bill of Rights, and why was it added to the Constitution?

b. Analyze In what ways does the Bill of Rights protect individuals from the power of government?

c. Elaborate Which of the amendments in the Bill of Rights do you think is the most important? Why?

SECTION 3 *(Pages 222–225)*

8. a. Describe What are the ways in which a person can gain U.S. citizenship?

b. Analyze How are citizens able to influence their government?

c. Predict What might result if individuals failed to fulfill their duties as citizens?

Reading Skills

Summarizing Historical Texts *Use the Reading Skills taught in this chapter to answer the question about the reading selection below.*

> "The judicial power of the United States shall be vested in one supreme Court, and in such inferior Courts as the Congress may from time to time ... establish. The Judges, both of the supreme and inferior Courts, shall hold their Offices during good Behavior, and ... receive for their Services a Compensation..."

9. Which of the following is the best summary of the selection?

a. The U.S. judiciary consists of the Supreme Court and lower courts, and judges are paid.

b. Congress creates lower courts.

Reviewing Themes

10. Politics What important ideas has the U.S. Constitution contributed to government?

11. Politics Why is active political participation an important responsibility for people in the United States?

Social Studies Skills

Determining the Context of Statements *Use the Social Studies Skills taught in this chapter to answer the questions about the quotation below.*

> "What political power could ever carry on the vast multitude [large number] of lesser undertakings which the American citizens perform every day, with the assistance of the principle of association [joining a group]? Nothing, in my opinion, is more deserving of our attention than the intellectual and moral associations of America."
>
> —Alexis de Tocqueville, *Democracy in America*

12. De Tocqueville wrote this about his trip to the United States in 1831. What is his main idea?

a. Governments can fill every need of citizens.

b. American organizations cannot accomplish much.

c. American organizations get too much attention.

d. American organizations fill important needs of citizens that government cannot.

13. Do you think that de Tocqueville's statement accurately describes modern America? Why or why not?

FOCUS ON WRITING

14. Creating a Pamphlet You have gathered information about the Constitution, Bill of Rights, and citizenship. Use that information to create your pamphlet. On the first page, write a title and a phrase that will get your audience's attention. On each of the following pages, you can use this format: (1) a heading and sentence at the top of the page identifying the topic of the page, and (2) the list of the most important points for that topic. Remember that page 2 is on the Constitution, page 3 is on the Bill of Rights, and page 4 is on citizenship.

CHAPTER 6

Standardized Test Practice

DIRECTIONS: Read each question and write the letter of the best response.

1 Which of the following rights is a right protected in the First Amendment?

A the right to bear arms

B the right to public education

C the right to jury trials

D the right to free speech

2 The federal government and the government of North Carolina are *similar* in that both have

A a senate and a house of representatives.

B a legislature made up of only one house.

C an executive branch headed by a president.

D nine Supreme Court justices.

3 Obeying laws, paying taxes, and willingness to serve on a jury are all

A methods of gaining U.S. citizenship.

B duties of U.S. citizens.

C ways in which citizens can influence their government.

D protected by the Second Amendment.

4 The First Amendment would protect

A a reporter that knowingly spreads lies about someone.

B an individual who peacefully protests a government policy.

C an individual who falsely shouts, "Fire" in a crowded theater.

D a hunter who keeps a rifle at home.

5 Which of the following is an example of a check that the executive branch has on the legislative branch?

A The president may declare laws unconstitutional.

B The vice president serves as president of the Senate.

C The president may veto bills passed by Congress.

D The president may appoint members of Congress.

6 Which of the following protects the rights of the accused?

A the guarantee of a speedy trial

B the right to vote regardless of a person's race

C the right to sign a petition

D the right to keep and bear arms

7 Read the following quote from President Lyndon Johnson and use it to answer the question below.

> "What a president says and thinks is not worth five cents unless he has the people and Congress behind him. Without Congress, I'm just a six-feet-four Texan. With Congress, I'm President of the United States in the fullest sense."
>
> — President Lyndon Johnson, quoted in *The Macmillan Dictionary of Political Quotations*

Document-Based Question What point about government was President Johnson making in this remark?

CHAPTER 7 1789–1800

Launching the Nation

North Carolina Standards

Social Studies Objectives

9.02 Identify past and present state and local leaders from diverse cultural backgrounds and assess their influence in effecting change.

Language Arts Objectives

1.01 Narrate a personal account which:

- creates a coherent, organizing structure appropriate to purpose, audience, and context.
- establishes a point of view and sharpens focus.

1.03 Interact in group activities and/or seminars in which the student:

- gives reasons and cites examples from text in support of expressed opinions.

go.hrw.com
North Carolina
KEYWORD: SC7 NC

FOCUS ON WRITING

A Nobel Nomination Every year a few people are nominated for a Nobel Prize for their work to improve the world. In this chapter you will read about four great Americans—Washington, Hamilton, Jefferson, and Adams. Then you'll choose one of these great leaders and write a Nobel Prize nomination for him.

UNITED STATES

1789 George Washington becomes the first president.

1785

1789 The French Revolution begins.

WORLD

HOLT

History's Impact

▶ **video series**

Watch the video to understand the impact of political parties on the new United States.

What You Will Learn...

In this chapter you will learn about the first presidency and how it affected the country. George Washington began many presidential as well as national traditions. He is honored with statues and memorials across the country, including the Washington Monument in Washington, D.C.

1790 — 1795 — 1800

1793
French revolutionaries behead King Louis XVI.

1794
The Whiskey Rebellion begins in Pennsylvania.

1795
Native American leaders sign the Treaty of Greenville.

1796
John Adams is elected president on December 7.

1799
George Washington dies at Mount Vernon, Virginia, on December 14.

1799
The Rosetta Stone is discovered in Egypt. Inscriptions on the stone make it possible for researchers to read Egyptian hieroglyphics.

Reading Social Studies

by Kylene Beers

Economics | Geography | Politics | Society and Culture | Science and Technology

Focus on Themes This chapter, titled "Launching the Nation," describes how the early leaders established this nation's **political** and **economic** systems. You will read about Washington's presidency, Hamilton's plan for financial security for the nation, the establishment of two parties to elect the president, and Jefferson's struggles with both Washington and Hamilton. Throughout the chapter, you will see that disagreement often defined these early days.

Inferences about History

Focus on Reading What's the difference between a good guess and a weak guess? A good guess is an *educated* guess. In other words, the guess is based on some knowledge or information. That's what an **inference** is, an educated guess.

Making Inferences About What You Read To make an inference, combine information from your reading with what you already know, and make an educated guess about what it all means. Once you have made several inferences, you may be able to draw a conclusion that ties them all together.

Question What kind of person was Alexander Hamilton?

Inside the Text

- Hamilton ran a company when he was just a teenager.
- He had a career as a lawyer.
- He became the secretary of the treasury under Washington.

Outside the Text

- Running a company takes intelligence and cleverness.
- Becoming a lawyer takes dedication.
- Washington probably wanted someone clever and capable.

Inference Alexander Hamilton was an intelligent, clever, and dedicated man.

Steps for Making Inferences

1. Ask a question.
2. Note information "Inside the Text."
3. Note information "Outside the Text."
4. **Use both sets of information to make an educated guess, or inference.**

You Try It!

Read the following passage and answer the questions that follow.

Economic Differences

From Chapter 7, p. 240–241

Hamilton wanted new forms of economic growth. He wanted to promote manufacturing and business. He even suggested that the government award a prize to companies that made excellent products.

In addition, Hamilton wanted to pass higher tariffs. Known as protective tariffs, these taxes would raise the prices of foreign products. Hamilton hoped this would cause Americans to buy U.S. goods. As a result, American manufacturing would be protected from foreign competition.

Jefferson worried about depending too much on business and manufacturing. He believed that farmers were the most independent voters . . . Jefferson wanted to help farmers by keeping the costs of the goods they bought low. Lower tariffs would help keep prices low.

After you read the passage, answer the following questions.

1. Which two questions can be answered directly from the text above and which one requires that you make an inference?

- **a.** Who wanted higher tariffs, Hamilton or Jefferson?
- **b.** Why do you think Hamilton and Jefferson had different views on the importance of manufacturing?
- **c.** Which man wanted to help the farmers?

2. To answer question b, it might help to know that Hamilton lived in New York City, and Jefferson was from the more rural area of Virginia. Use that information and information in the passage to explain why one man might have valued manufacturing more than the other.

Key Terms and People

Chapter 7

Section 1

George Washington *(p. 234)*
electoral college *(p. 234)*
Martha Washington *(p. 234)*
precedent *(p. 235)*
Judiciary Act of 1789 *(p. 236)*

Section 2

Alexander Hamilton *(p. 238)*
national debt *(p. 238)*
bonds *(p. 238)*
speculators *(p. 239)*
Thomas Jefferson *(p. 239)*
loose construction *(p. 242)*
strict construction *(p. 242)*
Bank of the United States *(p. 242)*

Section 3

French Revolution *(p. 243)*
Neutrality Proclamation *(p. 244)*
privateers *(p. 244)*
Jay's Treaty *(p. 245)*
Pinckney's Treaty *(p. 245)*
Little Turtle *(p. 246)*
Battle of Fallen Timbers *(p. 247)*
Treaty of Greenville *(p. 247)*
Whiskey Rebellion *(p. 247)*

Section 4

political parties *(p. 250)*
Federalist Party *(p. 250)*
Democratic-Republican Party *(p. 250)*
XYZ affair *(p. 252)*
Alien and Sedition Acts *(p. 253)*
Kentucky and Virginia Resolutions *(p. 253)*

Academic Vocabulary

In this chapter, you will learn the following academic words:

agreement *(p. 237)*
neutral *(p. 244)*

As you read Chapter 7, remember that you need to combine what you already know with the information in the chapter to make inferences.

SECTION 1

Washington Leads a New Nation

What You Will Learn...

Main Ideas

1. In 1789 George Washington became the first president of the United States.
2. Congress and the president organized the executive and judicial branches of government.
3. Americans had high expectations for their new nation.

The Big Idea

President Washington and members of Congress established a new national government.

Key Terms and People

George Washington, *p. 234*
electoral college, *p. 234*
Martha Washington, *p. 234*
precedent, *p. 235*
Judiciary Act of 1789, *p. 236*

TAKING NOTES As you read, take notes in a graphic organizer like the one below on why and how George Washington was chosen as president.

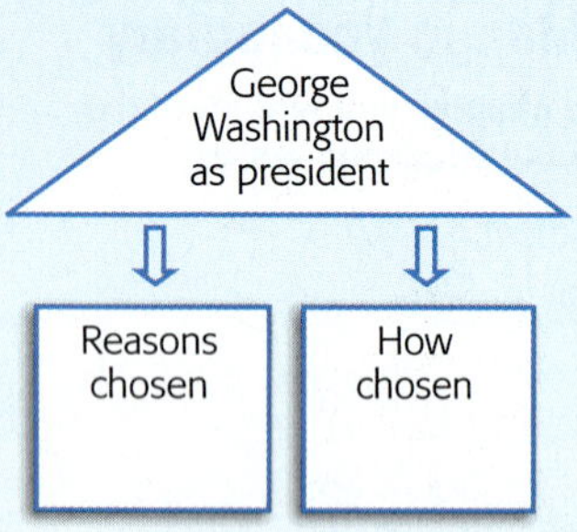

If YOU were there...

You are a seamstress in New York City in 1789. You've joined the excited crowd in the streets for inauguration day. Church bells are ringing, and people are cheering. Even though you were just a young child during the Revolution, Washington is your hero. Now you watch as he takes the oath of office. You are proud to see that he is wearing a suit of American-made cloth.

What do you think America's future will be like under President Washington?

BUILDING BACKGROUND George Washington was more than just a popular war hero. People naturally looked to him as a national leader. He had taken part in the Continental Congresses and in creating the Constitution. He helped establish and strengthen the new national government.

The First President

Americans believed in **George Washington**. They saw him as an honest leader and a hero of the Revolution. Many believed he should be the first U.S. president. Washington had been looking forward to retirement and a quiet life on his Virginia farm. When he hesitated at becoming a candidate for the presidency, his friends convinced him to run. Fellow politician Gouverneur Morris told him, "Should the idea prevail [win] that you would not accept the presidency, it should prove fatal . . . to the new government." Morris concluded confidently, "Of all men, you are the best fitted to fill that office."

In January 1789 each of the 11 states that had passed the Constitution sent electors to choose the first president. These delegates formed a group called the **electoral college**—a body of electors who represent the people's vote in choosing the president. The electoral college selected Washington unanimously, and John Adams became his vice president.

Washington's wife, First Lady **Martha Washington**, entertained guests and attended social events with her husband. She described the scene to her niece: "I have not had one half-hour to myself since the day of my arrival." She ran the presidential household with style.

Other women of the time period, such as author Judith Sargent Murray, believed that women needed to play a greater role in the new nation than Martha Washington did. Murray, Abigail Adams, and others believed in Republican Motherhood, the idea that women played an important role in teaching their children to be good citizens.

Some promoters of Republican Motherhood did not expect women to participate in politics or business. Other people, however, hoped that Republican Motherhood would lead to greater opportunities for women. They hoped more women would receive an education. Only a few families were willing to provide much education for their daughters, and adult women rarely had the time or money to get an education later in life. Most women in the early republic faced long days managing their households and working hard inside or outside the home to support their families.

READING CHECK **Analyzing** Why was Washington selected to be president?

Organizing the Government

Hard work also lay ahead for members of the new government. The new federal government had to create policies and procedures that would determine the future of the country. As President Washington noted in a letter to James Madison, "The first of everything in our situation will serve to establish a precedent." A **precedent** is an action or decision that later serves as an example.

The First Congress created departments in the executive branch for different areas of national policy. Washington met with the department heads, or cabinet members, who advised him.

Today we know that presidents have cabinet meetings with their top advisers. This practice started during Washington's presidency and was common by 1792.

For two of his most important cabinet positions, Washington chose carefully. He picked Alexander Hamilton as secretary of the treasury and Thomas Jefferson as secretary of state. Henry Knox served as secretary of war, and Samuel Osgood was chosen as postmaster general. Hamilton was a gifted

NC History Makers

Nathaniel Macon
Nathaniel Macon served North Carolina as both a member of the U.S. House of Representatives and as a U.S. senator.

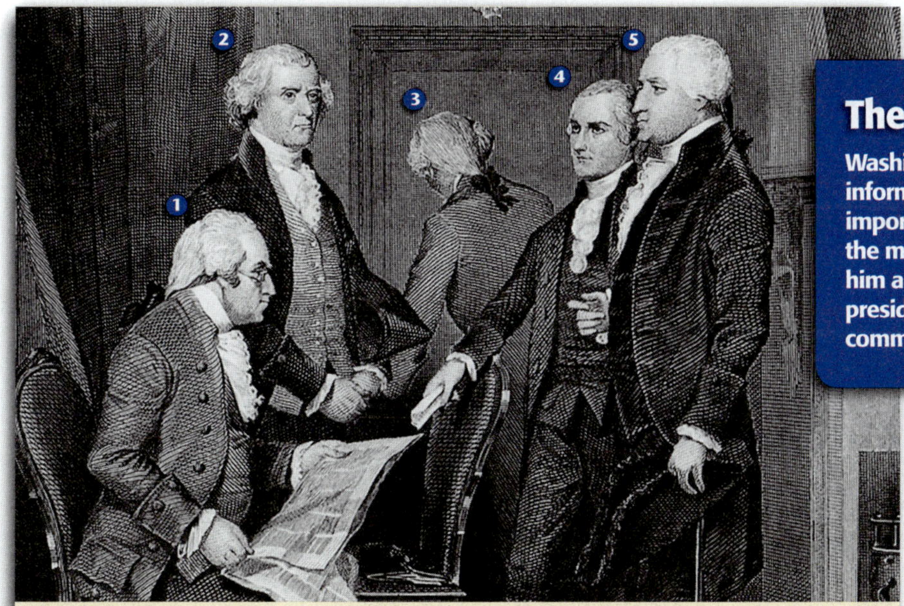

1 Henry Knox, secretary of war
2 Thomas Jefferson, secretary of state
3 Edmund Randolph, attorney general
4 Alexander Hamilton, secretary of the treasury
5 George Washington, president

The First Cabinet

Washington's cabinet members kept him informed on political matters and debated important issues with one another. Each of the men chosen had experience that made him a wise choice to advise the nation's first president. By 1792 cabinet meetings were a common practice.

ANALYSIS SKILL **ANALYZING VISUALS**

How do you think a modern cabinet meeting might look different from the one shown here?

A Rural Nation

FOCUS ON NORTH CAROLINA

In 1790 North Carolina ceded its claims to western lands to the new government. Previously, residents in the western part of the state had seceded from North Carolina to form the State of Franklin. They rejoined North Carolina to obtain protection from Native American attacks. The area eventually became part of Tennessee, which became a state in 1796.

economic planner, and Jefferson had served as ambassador to France. Knox had helped Washington run the Continental Army, and Osgood had government experience.

To set up the federal court system and the courts' location, Congress passed the **Judiciary Act of 1789**. This act created three levels of federal courts and defined their powers and relationship to the state courts. It set up federal district courts and circuit courts of appeals. The president nominated candidates for federal judgeships. Those candidates then had to be approved or rejected by the Senate. Washington wrote about the importance of these duties:

> "I have always been persuaded that the stability and success of the national government ... would depend in a considerable degree on the interpretation and execution of its laws. In my opinion, therefore, it is important that the judiciary system should not only be independent in its operations, but as perfect as possible in its formation."
>
> —George Washington, quoted in *The Real George Washington*, edited by Parry et al.

The basic parts of the federal government were now in place. Leaders began to face the challenges of the new nation. Hard work lay ahead.

READING CHECK **Finding Main Ideas** What two important precedents were established for the federal government?

Americans' Expectations for the Nation

Most Americans had high expectations for the new country. They wanted improved trade, free from too many restrictions. But they also expected the government to protect them and to keep the economy stable. However, the idea of belonging to one united nation was new to them.

In 1790 the United States was home to almost 4 million people. Most Americans lived in the countryside and worked on farms. Farmers wanted fair tax laws and the right to settle western lands. They did not want the government to interfere with their daily lives.

Other Americans worked in towns as craftspeople, laborers, or merchants. These people looked to the government to help their businesses. Most merchants wanted simpler trade laws established. Manufacturers wanted laws to protect them from foreign competitors.

© Collection of The New-York Historical Society

Some Americans lived in growing cities like New York, shown above. However, the new republic was overwhelmingly rural. Most Americans lived and worked on farms.

Why might rural Americans and urban Americans want different things from their new government?

Most cities were small. Only New York City and Philadelphia had populations larger than 25,000. New York City was the first capital of the United States, and it represented the spirit of the new nation. Although badly damaged during the Revolution, the city had already begun to recover. Citizens got rid of many signs of British rule.

New York City had a bustling economy. International trade and business became more active. A French visitor to New York City noted the city's energy.

> "Everything in the city is in motion; everywhere the shops resound [ring out] with the noise of workers . . . one sees vessels arriving from every part of the world."
>
> —A French visitor to New York, quoted in *New York in the American Revolution* by Wilbur Abbott

In 1792 some 24 stockbrokers signed an **agreement** under a buttonwood tree on Wall Street. This agreement was the foundation for what later became the New York Stock Exchange. It cemented Wall Street's image as the economic hub of the United States.

By 1790 the city's population had topped 33,000 and was growing rapidly. To many officials, this vibrant city reflected the potential future of the new nation. It was thus a fitting place for the capital.

ACADEMIC VOCABULARY

agreement a decision reached by two or more people or groups

THE IMPACT TODAY

Today the New York Stock Exchange is the largest market for securities, or stocks, in the world.

READING CHECK **Analyzing** Why was New York City chosen as the first capital of the United States?

SUMMARY AND PREVIEW Americans, led by President George Washington, set up their new government. In the next section you will read about Alexander Hamilton's economic plan.

Section 1 Assessment

go.hrw.com
Online Quiz
KEYWORD: SC7 HP7

Reviewing Ideas, Terms, and People

1. a. **Describe** What role did the electoral college play in **George Washington**'s election to the presidency?
   b. **Summarize** What were some of **Martha Washington**'s duties as First Lady?
2. a. **Describe** What **precedent** did President Washington and Congress establish regarding the executive branch?
   b. **Explain** What was the purpose of the **Judiciary Act of 1789**?
   c. **Evaluate** What do you think was the most important element of the Judiciary Act of 1789? Why?
3. a. **Recall** What city served as the first capital of the United States? Why?
   b. **Draw Conclusions** What expectations did most Americans have for the new nation?
   c. **Make Judgments** Do you think New York City should still be the capital city of the United States? Explain your answer.

Critical Thinking

4. **Comparing** Review your notes on George Washington. Then copy the chart below and use it to compare how Washington and Congress organized the new government.

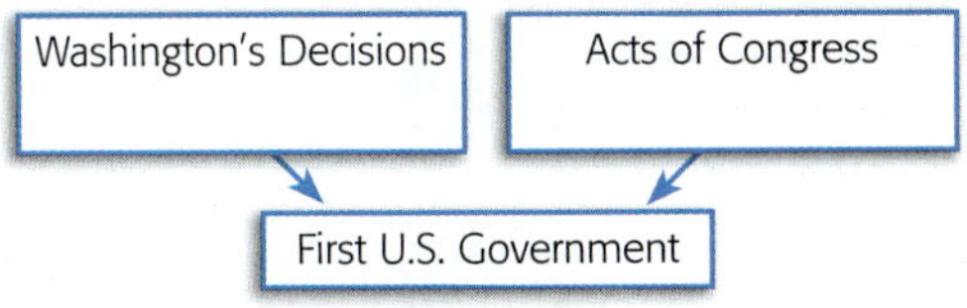

FOCUS ON WRITING

5. **Thinking about Washington's Contributions** In this section you learned some things about George Washington as president. Jot down one or two things you could use to support his nomination for a Nobel Prize.

SECTION 2

Hamilton and National Finances

What You Will Learn...

Main Ideas

1. Hamilton tackled the problem of settling national and state debt.
2. Thomas Jefferson opposed Hamilton's views on government and the economy.
3. Hamilton created a national bank to strengthen the U.S. economy.

The Big Idea

Treasury secretary Alexander Hamilton developed a financial plan for the national government.

Key Terms and People

Alexander Hamilton, *p. 238*
national debt, *p. 238*
bonds, *p. 238*
speculators, *p. 239*
Thomas Jefferson, *p. 239*
loose construction, *p. 242*
strict construction, *p. 242*
Bank of the United States, *p. 242*

TAKING NOTES As you read, take notes on the economic problems facing the nation when Alexander Hamilton became secretary of the treasury, as well as Hamilton's solutions to the problems.

Economic Problems	Solutions
	1. 2. 3. 4. 5. 6.

If YOU were there...

You live on a plantation in North Carolina in the 1790s. You have just heard that the federal government plans to pay most of the northern states' debts from the war. Your neighbors are outraged about this idea. It means more taxes and tariffs! New York and Massachusetts are far away, they say. Why should North Carolina farmers have to pay northern debts?

Would you pay other states' war debts? Why?

BUILDING BACKGROUND Some of the new nation's biggest problems were economic. The national and state governments had run up huge debts during the war. But the proposed solutions to these problems revealed differences in regional viewpoints. Southern planters and northern businesspeople had very different ideas about how the national economy should develop.

Settling the Debt

Alexander Hamilton seemed born with a head for economics. While still in his teens, he helped run a shipping company in his native British West Indies. Family friends then sent him to the American colonies for an education. Hamilton eventually married into a wealthy New York family and began practicing law. He served as Washington's aide and as a delegate to four Continental Congresses.

National Debt

As secretary of the treasury, Hamilton's biggest challenge was paying off the **national debt**—money owed by the United States—from the Revolutionary War. The United States owed about $11.7 million to foreign countries and about $40.4 million to U.S. citizens. During the war the government raised money with bonds. **Bonds** are certificates of debt that carry a promise to buy back the bonds at a higher price. The new government could not afford to keep this promise. Bondholders who needed money sold

Hamilton's Economic Plan

QUICK FACTS

Alexander Hamilton developed a three-point plan to solve the nation's financial problems.

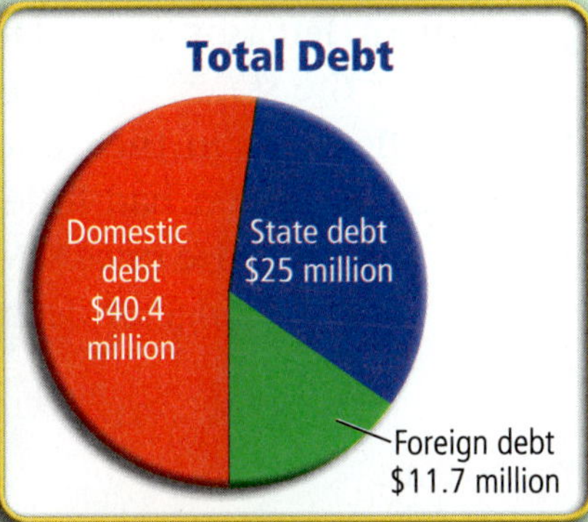

1 Deal with the Debt

- Take on the foreign and domestic debt by replacing creditors' old, low-value bonds with new, interest-bearing bonds — would build investor confidence in the stability of the new nation
- Take over most of the states' $25 million Revolutionary War debts — would free up state money for business and trade

2 Gain Revenue

- Pass a tariff to both bring in money and help American manufacturers

3 Stabilize the Banking System

- Create a national bank
- Create a national mint

their bonds for less than the original value to **speculators**, or people who buy items at low prices in the hope that the value will rise and they can sell the items for a profit.

Hamilton wanted to pay the foreign debt immediately and gradually repay the total value of all bonds. The second part of his plan caused disagreements because paying full value would allow speculators to make a profit. Hamilton thought this was fair. He said, "He [the speculator] paid what the commodity [bond] was worth . . . and took the risks."

Thomas Jefferson disagreed. He thought the idea cheated bondholders who had sold their bonds at low prices. Jefferson wrote, "Immense sums were thus filched [stolen] from the poor and ignorant." But more politicians agreed with Hamilton. In 1790 the government exchanged old bonds for new, more reliable ones that were guaranteed.

States' Debts

The states owed $25 million for Revolutionary War expenses. Hamilton wanted the federal government to pay for $21.5 million of this debt. Hamilton believed that this action would help the federal government. He thought that paying the states' debts would help the national economy. Debtor states would not have to spend so much on repayment and would have money to develop business and trade. Increased business and trade would put more money back into the national economy.

The South, however, did not want to help the federal government pay the debts of other states. States such as Virginia and North Carolina did not have many war debts. They thought Hamilton's idea was unfair. Patrick Henry said he did not believe that the Constitution gave Congress the power to pay state debts. Hamilton knew that he needed the help of southern representatives to get his plan approved.

Moving the Capital

Hamilton also knew that he had something to bargain with. Southern officials wanted to change the location of the nation's capital. Many southerners thought that having the capital in New York gave the northern states too much influence over national policy. Hamilton, Jefferson, and James Madison met in June 1790. Hamilton promised to convince northern members of Congress to move the capital. Jefferson and Madison then agreed to gather support in the South for Hamilton's debt plan.

The compromise worked. The national capital was moved to Philadelphia in 1791 for 10 years. For the capital's permanent location, Washington chose a place on the Potomac River that included part of both Maryland and Virginia. The land was made up of swamps and farms. This site would eventually become the city of Washington, D.C.

THE IMPACT TODAY

Washington, D.C., and the surrounding areas are home to more than 7 million people today. The city is not only the nation's capital but also a major tourist attraction.

READING CHECK **Identifying Points of View**
How did southerners feel about the federal government paying state war debts, and how did Hamilton change their minds?

BIOGRAPHY

Benjamin Banneker (1731–1806)

Benjamin Banneker was born to a free African American family in rural Maryland. He attended a Quaker school but was largely self-educated. He was a skilled mathematician and scientist. His mathematical skills prompted Thomas Jefferson to give him a job surveying the land for the new national capital.

Draw Conclusions How was Benjamin Banneker's life different from most African Americans' of the time?

Jefferson Opposes Hamilton

Hamilton and Jefferson did not cooperate for long. Instead, they began to disagree about how to define the authority of the central government. Hamilton believed in a strong federal government. Jefferson wanted to protect the powers of the states. Their conflict reflected basic differences in their opinions about democracy. Hamilton had little faith in the average individual. He once said that "the people . . . seldom judge or determine [decide] right."

Differing Views

Hamilton wanted a strong central government that balanced power between the "mass of the people" and wealthier citizens. He believed that his approach would protect everyone's liberties while keeping the people from having too much power.

Jefferson disagreed strongly with Hamilton's views of the average citizen's ability to make decisions for the country. He admitted that "the people can not be all, and always, well informed." However, Jefferson believed that it was the right of the people to rule the country.

Economic Differences

Hamilton and Jefferson also fought over how the country's economy should grow. Hamilton wanted new forms of economic growth. He wanted to promote manufacturing and business. He even suggested that the

U.S. Capitol in Washington, D.C.

Primary Source

POINTS OF VIEW

Role of a Citizen

Alexander Hamilton thought that the average citizen had no interest in public affairs.

"We must take man as we find him, and if we expect him to serve the public, [we] must interest his passions in doing so. A reliance on pure patriotism has been the source of many of our errors."

—Alexander Hamilton,
quoted in *Odd Destiny: The Life of Alexander Hamilton* by Marie B. Hecht

Thomas Jefferson believed that each citizen could work to better society.

"It is my principle that the will of the Majority should always prevail [win] . . . Above all things I hope the education of the common people will be attended to; [I am] convinced that on their good sense we may rely with the most security for the preservation of a due degree of liberty."

—Thomas Jefferson,
from *Thomas Jefferson: A Biography in His Own Words*

ANALYSIS SKILL **ANALYZING POINTS OF VIEW**

How did the views of Hamilton and Jefferson differ?

government award a prize to companies that made excellent products.

In addition, Hamilton wanted to pass higher tariffs. Known as protective tariffs, these taxes would raise the prices of foreign products. Hamilton hoped this would cause Americans to buy U.S. goods. As a result, American manufacturing would be protected from foreign competition.

Jefferson worried about depending too much on business and manufacturing. He believed that farmers were the most independent voters. They did not depend on other people's work to make a living.

Jefferson wrote, "Our governments will remain virtuous [pure] for many centuries; as long as they are chiefly agricultural." Jefferson wanted to help farmers by keeping the costs of the goods they bought low. Lower tariffs would help keep prices low.

READING CHECK **Summarizing** What were the main differences between Hamilton and Jefferson concerning the power of the nation's government?

A National Bank

Hamilton's and Jefferson's differences became more and more public in early 1791. The two men had very different opinions about how the government should approach its economic problems.

Hamilton's Plan for a National Bank

Hamilton wanted to start a national bank where the government could safely deposit its money. The bank would also make loans to the government and businesses. Hamilton also thought that the United States should build a national mint, a place to make coins. Then the country could begin issuing its own money.

THE IMPACT TODAY
The U.S. Mint was established in 1792 and now produces between 11 billion and 20 billion coins each year.

Hamilton knew that people who wanted to protect states' rights might have a strong reaction to the idea of a national bank, so he suggested limiting it to a 20-year charter. After that time Congress could decide whether to extend the charter. Hamilton also asked each state to start its own bank so the national bank would not have a monopoly.

Jefferson Opposes the Bank

Both Jefferson and Madison believed that Hamilton's plans for the economy gave too much power to the federal government. They also thought the U.S. Constitution did not give Congress the power to create a bank. But Hamilton quoted the elastic clause, which states that Congress can "make all laws which shall be necessary and proper" to govern the nation.

Hamilton declared that the clause allowed the government to create a national bank. Hamilton believed in loose construction of the Constitution. **Loose construction** means that the federal government can take reasonable actions that the Constitution does not specifically forbid.

Jefferson thought that the elastic clause should be used only in special cases. He wrote to President Washington, "The Constitution allows only the means which are 'necessary,' not those which are merely 'convenient.'"

Jefferson believed in strict construction of the Constitution. People who favor **strict construction** think that the federal government should do only what the Constitution specifically says it can do.

President Washington and Congress agreed with Hamilton. They hoped a bank would offer stability for the U.S. economy. In February 1791 Congress enacted the charter for the **Bank of the United States**—the country's first national bank. The bank played an important role in making the U.S. economy more stable.

READING CHECK **Drawing Conclusions** Why did Congress and the president agree to create a national bank?

SUMMARY AND PREVIEW Washington and Hamilton developed plans for paying the national debt. In the next section you will read about the U.S. neutrality policy.

Section 2 Assessment

go.hrw.com
Online Quiz
KEYWORD: SC7 HP7

Reviewing Ideas, Terms, and People

1. a. **Describe** What economic problems did the new government face?
   b. **Summarize** What compromise did **Alexander Hamilton, Thomas Jefferson**, and James Madison reach regarding repayment of state debts?
2. a. **Identify** What disagreement did Jefferson and Hamilton have over the central government?
   b. **Draw Conclusions** Hamilton was a New Yorker, while Jefferson was from Virginia. How do you think that affected their views on the economy?
   c. **Elaborate** Do you agree with Hamilton or Jefferson regarding the average citizen's ability to make decisions for the country? Explain your answer.
3. a. **Recall** Why did Jefferson oppose the creation of the **Bank of the United States**?
   b. **Contrast** What is the difference between **loose construction** and **strict construction** of the Constitution?
   c. **Elaborate** Defend Alexander Hamilton's stance in favor of the creation of a national bank.

Critical Thinking

4. **Identifying Solutions** Review your notes on U.S. economic problems and Hamilton's solutions. Then copy the chart below and use it to show how Hamilton's views on the economy differed from those of Thomas Jefferson.

	Hamilton	Jefferson
Bonds		
Economy		
Tariffs		
National Bank		

FOCUS ON WRITING

5. **Gathering Information about Hamilton and Jefferson** Both Hamilton and Jefferson were strong leaders who helped shape the government of the young United States. What could you say about either of them to support a nomination for a Nobel Prize?

Challenges for the New Nation

SECTION 3

If YOU were there...

You are the captain of an American merchant ship in the 1790s. Your ship has just picked up cargo in the French West Indies. You are headed back to your home port of Philadelphia. Suddenly, a British warship pulls alongside your ship. Marines swarm aboard. They order you into the nearest harbor and seize your goods.

How would this incident affect your views of Great Britain?

BUILDING BACKGROUND As the new nation tried to get organized, it faced economic problems and internal divisions. Even more difficult challenges came from conflicts in Europe. The United States could not avoid being caught up in fighting between France and Great Britain.

Remaining Neutral

Tensions between France and Britain began to build after the French people rebelled against their king. On July 14, 1789, citizens of Paris attacked and captured the Bastille, a hated fortress and prison that stood as a mighty symbol of royal power.

The storming of the Bastille was one of the first acts of the **French Revolution**—a rebellion of French people against their king in 1789. The French people overthrew their king and created a republican government.

French revolutionaries storm the Bastille.

What You Will Learn...

Main Ideas

1. The United States tried to remain neutral regarding events in Europe.
2. The United States and Native Americans came into conflict in the Northwest Territory.
3. The Whiskey Rebellion tested Washington's administration.
4. In his Farewell Address, Washington advised the nation.

The Big Idea

The United States faced significant foreign and domestic challenges under Washington.

Key Terms and People

French Revolution, *p. 243*
Neutrality Proclamation, *p. 244*
privateers, *p. 244*
Jay's Treaty, *p. 245*
Pinckney's Treaty, *p. 245*
Little Turtle, *p. 246*
Battle of Fallen Timbers, *p. 247*
Treaty of Greenville, *p. 247*
Whiskey Rebellion, *p. 247*

TAKING NOTES As you read, take notes on the challenges faced by the new nation during Washington's administration.

FOCUS ON READING

What can you tell about France before 1793 using this paragraph and what you already know about democracies?

Many French citizens had been inspired to take action by the American Revolution. Many Americans, in turn, supported the French Revolution. They thought that France was creating the same kind of democracy as the United States.

Some Americans worried about the French Revolution's violent riots and attacks on traditional authority. Revolutionaries shocked many Americans by beheading King Louis XVI in January 1793 and Queen Marie-Antoinette later that year.

A few years after the French Revolution started, France and Great Britain went to war. Some Americans supported the French, while others backed the British. Some wanted to remain **neutral**.

ACADEMIC VOCABULARY

neutral unbiased, not favoring either side in a conflict

The Neutrality Proclamation

The debate divided Congress and Washington's cabinet. Washington presented his opinion to Congress on April 22, 1793:

> "The duty and interest of the United States require that they should with sincerity and good faith adopt and pursue a conduct friendly and impartial [unbiased] towards the belligerent [fighting] powers."
>
> —George Washington, quoted in *The Real George Washington* by Parry et al.

This **Neutrality Proclamation** stated that the United States would not take sides with any European countries that were at war. Washington believed his plan was the safest for the long run, but not everyone agreed.

Some members of Congress criticized Washington's ideas. James Madison believed that the president had gone beyond his authority. He questioned Washington's right to issue the proclamation without the approval of Congress.

The French Question

France's new representative to the United States, Edmond Genet (zhuh-NAY), asked American sailors to help France fight England by commanding **privateers**. Privateers were private ships hired by a country to attack its enemies. Washington told Genet that using American privateers violated U.S. neutrality. Jefferson wanted the French revolutionaries to succeed, but even he agreed that allowing France to use American privateers against England was a bad idea.

Jefferson was still upset by U.S. policy toward France. He believed that the United States should back France because France had supported the United States during the Revolutionary War. Hamilton, on the other hand, was pro-British. He hoped to strengthen trading ties with Britain—the most powerful trading nation in the world at the time. Jefferson thought that Hamilton had too much influence on the president's foreign policy and that Hamilton consequently interfered with Jefferson's role as secretary of state. Jefferson decided to resign from Washington's cabinet in 1793.

Time Line

The Struggle for Neutrality

1789

April 1789 George Washington becomes president.

July 1789 French citizens storm the Bastille.

October 1790 British-backed Little Turtle defeats U.S. forces under General Josiah Harmar.

1793

April 1793 President Washington issues the Neutrality Proclamation.

November 1794 Jay's Treaty sparks protest throughout the United States.

Jay's Treaty

There were other threats to U.S. neutrality. In late 1793 the British seized ships carrying food to the French West Indies. Hundreds of the ships were neutral American merchant ships. Also, British officers were helping Native Americans fight settlers.

Washington wanted to prevent another war with the British. He sent Chief Justice John Jay to London to work out a compromise. The British knew the United States lacked a strong navy and that U.S. businesses relied heavily on British trade. However, the British did not want to fight another war in America.

In November 1794 the two sides signed Jay's Treaty. **Jay's Treaty** settled the disputes that had arisen between the United States and Great Britain in the early 1790s. The British would pay damages on seized American ships and abandon their forts on the northwestern frontier. The United States agreed to pay debts it owed the British.

The treaty was unpopular and sparked violent protests. Citizens and congressional leaders thought the treaty hurt trade and did not punish Britain enough for some of its actions. Southerners were especially angry that the treaty did not ask Britain to repay them for slaves that Britain had set free during the Revolutionary War. Washington did not like the treaty but believed it was the most that could be done. At his urging the Senate approved the treaty.

Pinckney's Treaty

American businesses faced problems as well. The Spanish disputed the border between the United States and Florida. Spain closed the port of New Orleans to U.S. trade in 1784. This hurt the American economy because all goods moving down the Mississippi to places in the East or overseas had to pass through New Orleans.

Washington asked Ambassador Thomas Pinckney to meet with Spanish officials to discuss the problem. He asked the Spaniards to reopen New Orleans to U.S. trade. Pinckney also asked for the right of deposit in New Orleans. This right would allow American boats to transfer goods in New Orleans without paying cargo fees.

Spanish minister Manuel de Godoy (goh-THOY) tried to delay reaching an agreement, hoping Pinckney would become desperate and sign a treaty that favored the Spanish. He was worried that the United States and Great Britain might join against Spain after signing Jay's Treaty. Pinckney was patient, however, and his patience was rewarded.

In October 1795, Godoy agreed to **Pinckney's Treaty**, which settled the border and trade disputes with Spain. Under the treaty Spain agreed to recognize the U.S. southern boundary as 31°N latitude. Spain's government also reopened the port at

1795

August 1795 The Treaty of Greenville ends fighting in the Northwest Territory.

October 1795 Pinckney's Treaty reopens the port of New Orleans.

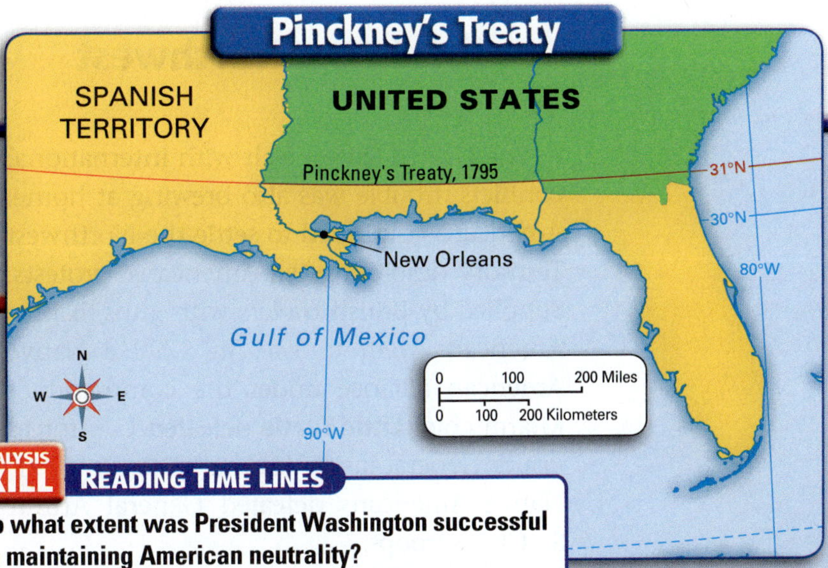

ANALYSIS SKILL **READING TIME LINES**

To what extent was President Washington successful in maintaining American neutrality?

go.hrw.com
Interactive Map
KEYWORD: SC7 CH7

ANALYSIS SKILL **ANALYZING VISUALS**

What types of weapons were used in the fighting in the Northwest Territory?

New Orleans to American ships and gave them the right of deposit. Because it opened the frontier to more expansion, Washington and most other Americans believed that Pinckney's Treaty was a successful compromise.

READING CHECK **Summarizing** Why did President Washington want the United States to remain neutral?

Conflict in the Northwest Territory

As the United States dealt with international conflicts, trouble was also brewing at home. Americans continued to settle the Northwest Territory despite Native Americans' protests. Supplied by British traders with guns, Native Americans went to war. In 1790 a Native American alliance under the command of Miami chief **Little Turtle** defeated U.S. forces under General Josiah Harmar. Then in 1791, Native Americans defeated General Arthur St. Clair's troops.

General Wayne Takes Command

In 1792 President Washington gave command of the army in the West to General Anthony Wayne. Wayne's task was to bring troops to the frontier to fight against the Indians. In 1793 General Wayne arrived in Ohio. Many of his men were ill from smallpox and influenza, so they were unable to fight well.

Wayne's troops moved north and built Fort Greenville, where they remained during the winter. They built additional forts for protection and to have supplies at hand.

As the summer of 1794 neared, several Native American groups led by Little Turtle attacked a supply train near the fort. Wayne and his men responded. They attacked Native American towns and burned crops.

The British no longer aided the Native Americans after this defeat, and Little Turtle realized that he was outmatched. He urged his people to seek peace.

"The trail has been long and bloody; it has no end. The [whites] . . . are many. They are like the leaves of the trees. When the frost comes they fall and are blown away. But when the sunshine comes again they come back more plentiful than ever before."

—Little Turtle, quoted in *The Ohio Frontier* by Douglas Hurt

The End of Conflict

On August 20, 1794, Native Americans fought Wayne's troops in the **Battle of Fallen Timbers** and were defeated. The battle was named for an area where many trees had been destroyed by a tornado. Wayne's forces burned Indians' villages and fields. The strength of Indian forces in the region was broken.

The frontier war soon ended. In August 1795, Native American leaders signed the **Treaty of Greenville**, which gave the United States claim to most Indian lands in the Northwest Territory. The treaty also guaranteed the safety of citizens there. In exchange, Native Americans received $20,000 worth of goods and an acknowledgment of their claim to the lands they still held.

READING CHECK **Finding Main Ideas** What conflicts did the United States face in the late 1700s?

The Whiskey Rebellion

Other conflicts occurred on the frontier. Congress passed a tax on American-made whiskey in March 1791. The tax was part of Hamilton's plan to raise money to help pay the federal debt. He was also testing the power of the federal government to control the states' actions.

Reaction in the West

People in areas such as western Pennsylvania were bitter about the tax. They were already angry with the federal government, which they believed did not protect settlers from Native American attacks and did not allow settlers enough opportunities for trade. The farmers' corn crops were often made into whiskey, which was easier to transport than the corn. Because cash was rare, whiskey became like money in their region. The farmers believed that the tax was aimed specifically at them.

Farmers who produced small amounts of whiskey for trade argued that they could not afford the tax. They believed they should be able to keep the money they had made from a product they created themselves. Protests in 1792 led President Washington to issue a proclamation saying that people had to obey the law.

Westerners also disliked the fact that cases about the law were to be tried in a district court. These courts were usually far away from the people they affected and were a great inconvenience to them.

Whiskey Rebellion Is Crushed

The complaints of western Pennsylvanians were at first expressed peacefully. But by 1794 fighting had broken out. In what became known as the **Whiskey Rebellion**, farmers lashed out against the tax on whiskey. Protesters refused to pay the tax. They even tarred and feathered tax collectors. Some called themselves the new Sons of Liberty.

Incidents of violence spread to other states. President Washington feared that the rebels threatened the federal government's authority. He believed he needed to make people understand that the Constitution gave Congress the right to pass and enforce the tax.

Washington declared that he could "no longer remain a passive [inactive] spectator" in the event. He personally led the army in military action against the rebellion—the first and only time an American president has done so. The army of about 13,000 men approached western Pennsylvania in November 1794. By this time most of the rebels had fled. The Whiskey Rebellion ended without a battle.

READING CHECK **Supporting a Point of View** Defend the viewpoint of the Pennsylvania farmers who did not want to pay the whiskey tax.

Primary Source

HISTORICAL DOCUMENT

Washington's Farewell Address

On September 19, 1796, President George Washington's Farewell Address first appeared in a Philadelphia newspaper. In it, Washington wrote about the nation's economy, political parties, and foreign policy.

While, then, every part of our country . . . feels an immediate and particular interest in union, all the parts combined cannot fail to find in the united mass . . . greater strength, greater resource, proportionally greater security from external danger, [and] a less frequent interruption of their peace by foreign nations; . . .

I have already **intimated**[1] to you the danger of [political] parties in the state, with particular reference to the founding of them on geographical **discriminations**[2]. Let me now take a more **comprehensive**[3] view, and warn you in the most solemn manner against the **baneful**[4] effects of the spirit of party, generally.

If, in the opinion of the people, the distribution or **modification**[5] of the constitutional powers be in any particular wrong, let it be corrected by an amendment . . .

Promote, then, as an object of primary importance, institutions for the general **diffusion**[6] of knowledge . . . As the structure of a government gives force to public opinion, it is essential that public opinion should be enlightened . . .

[Avoid] likewise the accumulation of debt, . . . not ungenerously throwing upon **posterity**[7] the burden, which we ourselves ought to bear . . .

Observe good faith and justice towards all nations; **cultivate**[8] peace and harmony with all . . .

The great rule of conduct for us, in regard to foreign nations, is . . . to have with them as little political connection as possible.

It is our true policy to steer clear of permanent alliances with any portion of the foreign world . . . There can be no greater error than to expect, or **calculate**[9] upon real favors from nation to nation. It is an illusion, which experience must cure, which a just pride ought to discard.

The duty of holding a neutral conduct may be inferred . . . from the obligation which justice and humanity impose on every nation . . . to maintain **inviolate**[10] the relations of peace and **amity**[11] towards other nations.

Washington lists the benefits of uniting the states under one government.

In this phrase, Washington emphasizes his warning against the dangers of political parties.

Washington points out the need for education.

This is Washington's advice to the new nation about foreign policy.

[1] **intimated**: told
[2] **discriminations**: differences
[3] **comprehensive**: complete
[4] **baneful**: destructive
[5] **modification**: change
[6] **diffusion**: spreading
[7] **posterity**: future generations
[8] **cultivate**: seek
[9] **calculate**: plan
[10] **inviolate**: unchanging
[11] **amity**: friendship

ANALYSIS SKILL **ANALYZING PRIMARY SOURCES**

1. What events happened before Washington left office that might have led to his warning against political parties?
2. Why did Washington suggest neutrality as a foreign policy?

Washington Says Farewell

In 1796 Washington decided not to run for a third presidential term. He wrote that he was "tired of public life" and "devoutly [strongly] wished for retirement." He also wanted to remind Americans that the people were the country's true leaders.

With the help of Alexander Hamilton and James Madison, Washington wrote his Farewell Address. In it he spoke about what he believed were the greatest dangers to the American republic. Among these were the dangers of foreign ties and political conflicts at home. Washington warned against forming permanent ties with other countries because choosing sides could draw the United States into war.

He also worried about growing political conflicts within the nation. Washington believed that disagreements between political groups weakened government. Political unity, he said, was a key to national success. Washington left office warning the nation to work out its differences and protect its independence. Washington also warned against too much public debt. He thought the government should try not to borrow money. He wanted future generations to be protected from debt.

He concluded his speech by looking forward to his retirement and praising his country. "I anticipate . . . the sweet enjoyment . . . of good laws under a free government, the ever favorite object of my heart."

READING CHECK **Finding Main Ideas** What issues did Washington believe were most dangerous to the future of the new nation?

SUMMARY AND PREVIEW Americans responded to foreign and domestic conflict during Washington's presidency. In the next section you will read about the formation of political parties in the United States and the presidency of John Adams.

Section 3 Assessment

go.hrw.com
Online Quiz
KEYWORD: SC7 HP7

Reviewing Ideas, Terms, and People

1. a. **Describe** What did Washington's **Neutrality Proclamation** state?
   b. **Compare and Contrast** In what ways were **Jay's Treaty** and **Pinckney's Treaty** similar and different?
2. a. **Identify** Who were the leaders of American Indian and U.S. forces in the conflict in the Northwest Territory?
   b. **Predict** What are some possible consequences of the **Treaty of Greenville** for American Indians in the Northwest Territory?
3. a. **Recall** Why did Congress tax American-made whiskey?
   b. **Explain** How did the tax lead to the **Whiskey Rebellion**?
   c. **Elaborate** Why do you think that President Washington personally led the army against westerners in the Whiskey Rebellion?
4. a. **Describe** What warnings did Washington give the nation in his Farewell Address?
   b. **Draw Conclusions** Why did Washington not run for a third term as president?

Critical Thinking

5. **Categorizing** Review your notes on the challenges the young United States faced. Then categorize those challenges as either foreign or domestic in a graphic organizer like this one.

Challenges	
Foreign	
Domestic	

FOCUS ON WRITING

6. **Thinking about Washington, Hamilton, and Jefferson** In this section you read about the activities of these three men during a difficult time for our country. What did you learn that you could add to a Nobel Prize nomination for any of these leaders?

SECTION 4

John Adams's Presidency

What You Will Learn...

Main Ideas

1. The rise of political parties created competition in the election of 1796.
2. The XYZ affair caused problems for President John Adams.
3. Controversy broke out over the Alien and Sedition Acts.

The Big Idea

The development of political parties in the United States contributed to differing ideas about the role of the federal government.

Key Terms

political parties, *p. 250*
Federalist Party, *p. 250*
Democratic-Republican Party, *p. 250*
XYZ affair, *p. 252*
Alien and Sedition Acts, *p. 253*
Kentucky and Virginia Resolutions, *p. 253*

TAKING NOTES As you read, take notes on the two political parties that emerged during the election of 1796, their views on government, their candidates in the 1796 election, and the outcome of the election. Use a graphic organizer like the one below for your notes.

Election of 1796	
Political Parties	
Views on Government	
Candidates	
Outcome	

If YOU were there...

You are a newspaper editor in Virginia in 1798. You've joined Jefferson's political party, which opposes the new president. In fact, your paper has printed many articles that criticize him, calling him greedy and foolish. You believe that's your right in a free country. But now Congress has passed a law that makes it illegal to criticize the government. You could be arrested for your articles!

Would you stop criticizing the government? Why?

BUILDING BACKGROUND People within the new United States had differing viewpoints on many issues. Personal rivalries among political leaders also created divisions in the new nation. Trying to limit dissent in the country, the federal government passed several unpopular laws.

The Election of 1796

The election of 1796 began a new era in U.S. politics. For the first time, more than one candidate ran for president. **Political parties**, groups that help elect people and shape policies, had begun to form during Washington's presidency. Despite Washington's warnings about political parties, the rivalry between two parties dominated the 1796 election.

Alexander Hamilton helped found the **Federalist Party**, which wanted a strong federal government and supported industry and trade. The Federalists chose John Adams and Thomas Pinckney as candidates. Adams knew he was not well liked in the South or the West, but he hoped people would support him after they thought about his years of loyal public service.

Thomas Jefferson and James Madison founded the **Democratic-Republican Party**. Its members, called Republicans, wanted to limit the federal government's power. (This party is not related to today's Republican Party.) They chose Thomas Jefferson and Aaron Burr as their candidates.

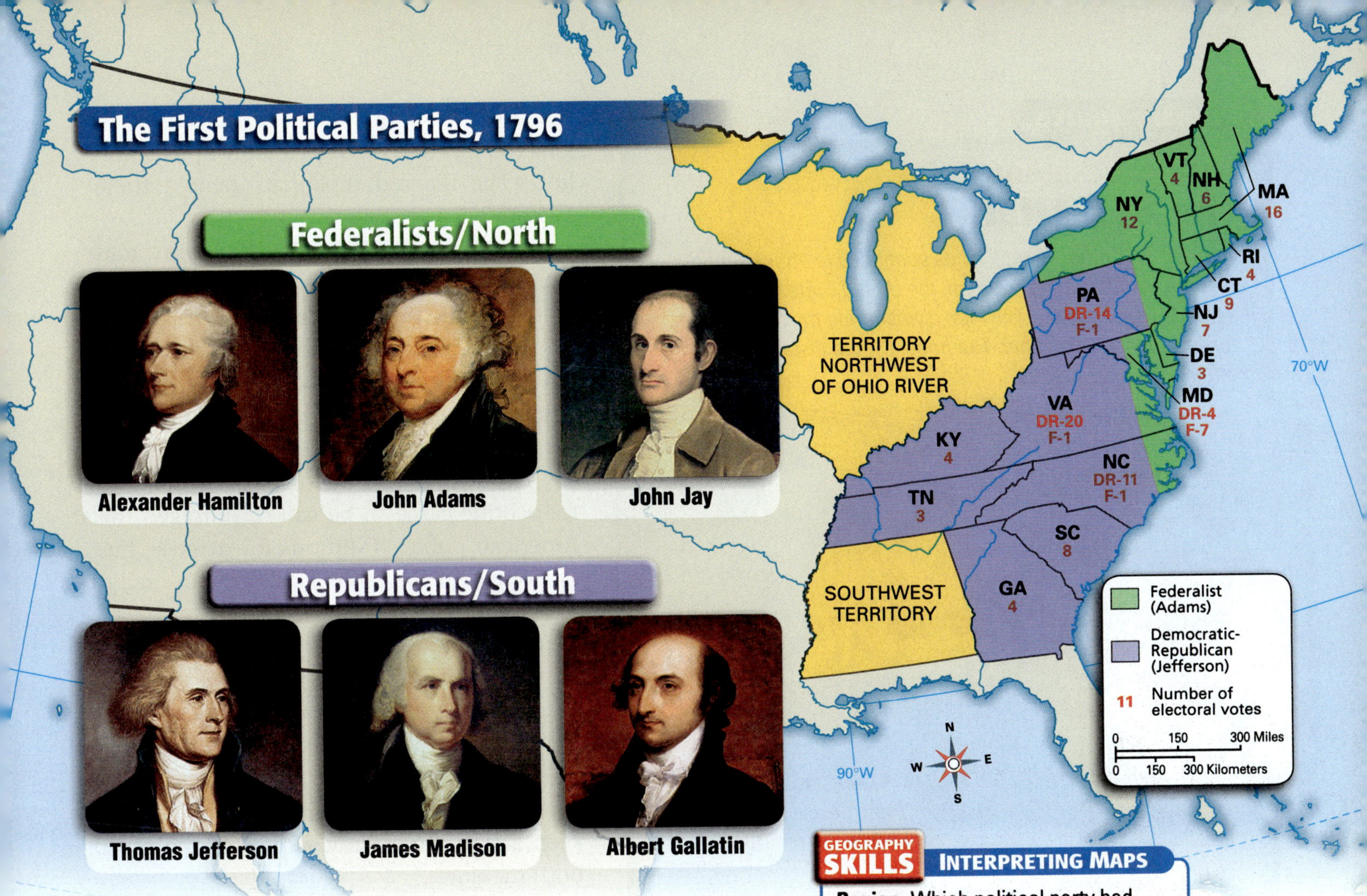

GEOGRAPHY SKILLS **INTERPRETING MAPS**

Region Which political party had more electoral votes in 1796?

Party differences were based partly on where and how people lived. Businesspeople in the cities tended to support the Federalists. Farmers in more isolated areas generally favored the Democratic-Republicans. Both sides attacked each other. Republicans called Adams a royalist—an insult to a man so involved in the Revolution. The Federalists accused the Republicans of favoring the French.

In the end, Adams defeated Jefferson. At the time, the person who came in second in a presidential election became vice president. So, after months of campaigning against one another, Adams and Jefferson took office together.

READING CHECK **Finding Main Ideas**
How did the election of 1796 change the nature of politics in the United States?

President Adams and the XYZ Affair

John Adams had the challenging task of following Washington as president. The people had adored Washington. Adams would have to work hard to win the people's trust.

A New President

At first glance, John Adams did not appear well suited for the presidency. Although Adams had been a leading Patriot during the American Revolution and had later served as a foreign diplomat, he lacked Washington's dignity, and most people saw him as a cold and distant person. Still, many people—even those who opposed him—respected Adams. They recognized his hard work, honesty, and intelligence.

Primary Source

POLITICAL CARTOON
The XYZ Affair

After the XYZ affair, French ships continued to attack American merchant ships. In this cartoon, the United States is represented by the woman. The men, symbolizing the French, are taking valuables from her. The people in the distance are other European nations.

Why do you think this man is encouraging the woman to look away?

These people aren't helping the woman. What do you think the cartoon is suggesting by this?

ANALYSIS SKILL **INTERPRETING POLITICAL CARTOONS**

How does the cartoon show that America is being preyed upon by the French?

The United States and France

One of Adams's first goals as president was to improve the relationship between the United States and France. You may remember that the French had once tried to hire American privateers to help them fight Great Britain, a practice Washington frowned upon. Adams sent U.S. diplomats to Paris to smooth over the conflict and to negotiate a treaty to protect U.S. shipping.

When the diplomats arrived in France, they learned that French foreign minister Talleyrand would not speak to them. Instead, they had a strange and secret visit from three French agents. Shockingly, the agents said that Talleyrand would discuss a treaty only in exchange for a $250,000 bribe. The French government also wanted a loan of $12 million. The amazed diplomats refused these demands.

In March 1798 President Adams told Congress that the peace-seeking mission had failed. He described the French terms, substituting the letters X, Y, and Z for the names of the French agents. Upon hearing the disgraceful news, Federalists in Congress called for war with France.

The **XYZ affair**, as the French demand for a bribe came to be called, outraged the American public. "Millions for defense, but not one cent for tribute!" became the rallying cry of the American people.

Preparations for War

Fearing war, Adams asked Congress to expand the navy to a fleet of more than 30 ships. He thought war with France might be unavoidable. He also decided the United States should keep a peacetime army. Congress approved both measures.

Although Adams had asked Congress for military support, he did not want to go to war with France. He was worried about its cost. So he did not ask Congress to declare war. Instead, he tried to reopen peace talks with France.

Peace Efforts

Adams's decision not to declare war stunned Federalists. Despite intense pressure from members of his own party, Adams refused to change his mind.

American and French ships, however, began fighting each other in the Caribbean. Adams sent a representative to France to engage in talks to try to end the fighting. The United States and France eventually signed a treaty. Adams then forced two members of his cabinet to resign for trying to block his peace efforts.

READING CHECK **Identifying Points of View**
What did Americans mean when they said "Millions for defense, but not one cent for tribute"?

The Alien and Sedition Acts

Many Democratic-Republicans continued to sympathize with France. Federalists, angered by their stand, called them "democrats, mob-ocrats, and all other kinds of rats."

In 1798 the Federalist-controlled Congress passed four laws known together as the **Alien and Sedition Acts**. These laws were said to protect the United States, but the Federalists intended them to crush opposition to war. The most controversial was the Sedition Act, which forbade anyone from publishing or voicing criticism of the federal government. In effect, this cancelled basic protections of freedom of speech and freedom of the press.

The two main Democratic-Republican leaders, Thomas Jefferson and James Madison, viewed these acts as a misuse of the government's power. Attacking the problem at the state level, they wrote resolutions passed by the Kentucky legislature in 1798 and in Virginia in 1799. Known as the **Kentucky and Virginia Resolutions**, these documents argued that the Alien and Sedition Acts were unconstitutional. They stated that the federal government could not pass these acts because they interfered with state government. Madison and Jefferson pressured Congress to repeal the Alien and Sedition Acts. Congress did not, although it allowed the acts to expire within a few years.

The Kentucky and Virginia Resolutions did not have the force of national law, but they supported the idea that states could challenge the federal government. This idea would grow to have a tremendous impact on American history later in the 1800s.

READING CHECK **Analyzing** How did the Kentucky and Virginia Resolutions support the rights of states?

SUMMARY AND PREVIEW Political parties formed to reflect different viewpoints. In the next chapter you will read about Thomas Jefferson's presidency.

Section 4 Assessment

go.hrw.com
Online Quiz
KEYWORD: SC7 HP7

Reviewing Ideas, Terms, and People

1. a. **Recall** What two **political parties** emerged before the election of 1796? Who were the founders of each party?
   b. **Analyze** What effect did political parties have on the election of 1796?
   c. **Elaborate** Do you think it was difficult for Adams and Jefferson to serve together as president and vice president? Explain your answer.
2. a. **Recall** What was one of Adams's first goals as president?
   b. **Make Inferences** Why were Federalists shocked by Adams's decision to resume peace talks with the French?
3. a. **Identify** What did the **Alien and Sedition Acts** state?
   b. **Explain** What idea regarding states' rights did the **Kentucky and Virginia Resolutions** support?
   c. **Elaborate** Would you have supported the Alien and Sedition Acts? Explain your answer.

Critical Thinking

4. **Contrasting** Review your notes on the election of 1796 and the formation of political parties. Then create a chart like this one identifying how each of the terms listed below reflected party disagreements.

XYZ Affair	
Alien and Sedition Acts	
Kentucky and Virginia Resolutions	

FOCUS ON WRITING

5. **Gathering Information about John Adams** Take some notes about John Adams's contributions that would support his nomination for the Nobel Prize. Then begin to compare and contrast all four leaders you have studied in this chapter. Which one will you nominate?

Making Group Decisions

Define the Skill

Democracy is one of the most valued principles of American society. It is based on the idea that the members of society, or representatives they choose, make the decisions that affect society. Decision-making would be much more efficient if just one person decided what to do and how to do it. However, that method is not at all democratic.

Making decisions as a group is a complicated and difficult skill. However, it is an important one at all levels of society—from governing the nation to making group decisions at school, in the community, and with your friends. At every level, the skill is based on the ability of the group's members to interact in effective and cooperative ways.

Learn the Skill

Think about the job the first Congress faced after the Constitution was ratified. The nation was still millions of dollars in debt from the Revolutionary War. Congress had to find a way to pay these debts as well as raise money to run the government.

Leaders like Jefferson and Hamilton had ideas about how to accomplish these goals. However, neither man could act alone. In a democracy the group—in this case Congress—must make the decisions and take action.

This task was complicated by the fact that Jefferson and Hamilton disagreed on what to do. Each man's supporters in Congress pushed his point of view. Fortunately, its members were able to overcome their differences, compromise on goals and actions, and accept group decisions they might not have agreed with personally. Had they not possessed this ability and skill, the nation's early years might have been even more difficult than they were.

Like that first Congress, being part of an effective group requires that you behave in certain ways.

1. **Be an active member.** Take part in setting the group's goals and in making its decisions. Participate in planning and taking group action.
2. **Take a position.** State your views and work to persuade other members to accept them. However, also be open to negotiating and compromising to settle differences within the group.
3. **Be willing to take charge if leadership is needed.** But also be willing to follow the leadership of other members.

Practice the Skill

Suppose that you are a member of the first Congress. With a group of classmates, you must decide what and who should be taxed to raise the money the government needs. Remember that you are an elected official. If you do something to upset the people, you could lose your job. When your group has finished, answer the following questions.

1. Did your group have a plan for completing its task? Did it discuss what taxes to pass? Compared to other members, how much did you take part in those activities?
2. How well did your group work together? What role did you play in that? Was it a positive contribution or a negative one? Explain.
3. Was your group able to make a decision? If not, why? If so, was compromise involved? Do you support the decision? Explain why or why not.

CHAPTER 7

Chapter Review

HOLT
History's Impact
▶ **video series**
Review the video to answer the closing question:
What are the advantages and disadvantages of being a member of a third party?

Visual Summary

QUICK FACTS

Use the visual summary below to help you review the main ideas of the chapter.

Reviewing Vocabulary, Terms, and People

Complete each sentence by filling in the blank with the correct term or person.

1. The ______________ established the structure of the federal court system and its relationship to state courts.
2. Federalists angered many Republicans when they passed the ______________ to protect the United States from traitors.
3. As president, Washington was able to establish several __________, or decisions that serve as examples for later action.
4. Farmers in western Pennsylvania protested taxes in the ____________.
5. The ______________ was created in order to strengthen the U.S. economy.

Comprehension and Critical Thinking

SECTION 1 *(Pages 234–237)*

6. **a. Recall** What precedents did President Washington and Congress establish for the executive and judicial branches?

   b. Draw Conclusions Why did Americans select George Washington as their first president?

   c. Evaluate Do you think the newly established government met the expectations of its citizens? Why or why not?

SECTION 2 *(Pages 238–242)*

7. **a. Identify** What changes did Alexander Hamilton make to the national economy?

   b. Contrast In what ways did Hamilton and Jefferson disagree on the economy?

   c. Evaluate Which of Hamilton's economic plans do you think was the most important to the new nation? Why?

SECTION 3 *(Pages 243–249)*

8. **a. Describe** What challenges did the nation face during Washington's presidency?

   b. Make Inferences Why did Washington believe that it was important for the United States to remain neutral in foreign conflicts?

   c. Evaluate Rate the success of Washington's presidency. Explain the reasons for your rating.

SECTION 4 *(Pages 250–253)*

9. **a. Describe** What role did political parties play in the election of 1796?

   b. Analyze How did the Alien and Sedition Acts create division among some Americans?

   c. Predict How might the political attacks between the Federalist and Democratic-Republican parties lead to problems in the future?

Reviewing Themes

10. **Economics** What economic problems troubled the nation at the beginning of Washington's presidency? How were they solved?

11. **Politics** How did the creation of political parties change politics in the United States?

Using the Internet

go.hrw.com
KEYWORD: SC7 CH7

12. **Activity: Creating a Poster** In 1798 war with France seemed on the horizon. The Federalist-controlled Congress passed a law that made it a crime to criticize the government in print. In 1971 war raged in Vietnam and the president used a court order to stop publication of information critical of the government's actions in Vietnam. What do these events have in common? Enter the activity keyword. Then research the Alien and Sedition Acts and the Pentagon Papers case during the Vietnam War. Create a poster to display your information and to illustrate the connection between a free press and a democratic society.

Reading Skills

Inferences about History *Use the Reading Skills taught in this chapter to answer the question about the reading selection below.*

> Party differences were based partly on where and how people lived. Businesspeople in the cities tended to support the Federalists. Farmers in more isolated areas generally favored the Democratic-Republicans. *(p. 251)*

13. Which of the following statements can be inferred from the selection?

    a. Farmers wanted a large federal government.

    b. Urban Americans were usually Republicans.

    c. Merchants supported John Adams.

    d. People in the cities had different concerns than did the rural population.

Social Studies Skills

Making Group Decisions *Use the Social Studies Skills taught in this chapter to answer the questions below.*

Get together with a group of three or four students and discuss the Alien and Sedition Acts. Answer the following questions individually and as a group.

14. Do you think that limits should have been put on Americans' speeches and printed articles?

15. What other ideas might Congress have considered to resolve the tensions over the issue?

FOCUS ON WRITING

16. **Writing a Nobel Nomination** Now that you've chosen your nominee for the Nobel Prize, you can start to write your nomination. Begin with a sentence that identifies the person you are nominating. Then give at least three reasons for your nomination. Each reason should include a specific achievement or contribution of this person. End your nomination with a sentence that sums up your reasons for nominating this person for the Nobel Prize. Be persuasive. You need to convince the Nobel Prize committee that this person deserves the prize more than anyone else in the world.

CHAPTER 7

Standardized Test Practice

DIRECTIONS: Read each question and write the letter of the best response.

1 In the 1790s most Americans

A lived in the countryside and worked on farms.

B lived in small towns and worked as laborers or craftspeople.

C lived in cities and worked as laborers, craftspeople, or merchants.

D lived west of the Appalachian Mountains and worked as ranchers or trappers.

2 In his Farewell Address, why did President Washington warn of the dangers of forming permanent ties with foreign nations?

A He feared that foreign ties would weaken state governments.

B He feared that favoring one country over another might draw the United States into war.

C He believed that foreign ties might lead to the overthrow of the new government.

D He believed that the Neutrality Proclamation of 1793 was wrong.

3 George Washington demonstrated the power of the president to enforce federal law in his handling of the

A Whiskey Rebellion.

B Alien and Sedition Acts.

C XYZ affair.

D Judiciary Act of 1789.

4 While the Alien and Sedition Acts were said to protect the United States, many people believed they were intended to

A provoke a war with Spain.

B end the Whiskey Rebellion.

C silence opposition to war with France.

D proclaim U.S. neutrality.

5 What was the eventual outcome of political differences between Alexander Hamilton and Thomas Jefferson?

A Hamilton resigned from office due to pressure from Jefferson's supporters.

B Jefferson persuaded Hamilton to abandon his plans for a national bank.

C The two men ran against each other in the presidential election of 1796.

D Two political parties that promoted each of their views were created.

6 Which of the following was a precedent established by President Washington?

A creating cabinet departments within the executive branch

B establishing binding treaties with Native American leaders

C negotiating a settlement between the federal government and rebels

D creating the first U.S. political party

7 Examine the following passage from a description of the Alien Act and then use it to answer the question below.

> "The Alien Law has been bitterly criticized as a direct attack upon our liberties. In fact, it affects only foreigners who are plotting against us, and has nothing to do with American citizens. It gives authority to the President to order out of the country all aliens he judges dangerous to the peace and safety of the United States, or whom he suspects of treason or secret plots against the government."
>
> —Timothy Pickering, adapted from *Life of Timothy Pickering,* Vol. 3

Document-Based Question **What is the author's point of view toward the Alien Law?**

Explaining a Political Process

Assignment

Write a paper explaining how the federal system balances power among the legislative, executive, and judicial branches of government.

How do you register to vote? What is the difference between a civil court and a federal court? When we want to know about a process or system of our government, we often turn to written explanations.

1. Prewrite

Considering Purpose and Audience

In this assignment, you will be writing for an audience of middle school students. You'll need to

- identify questions they might have about the process or system
- identify factors or details that might confuse them

As you plan your paper, keep your audience in mind.

TIP Using a Graphic Organizer

A chart like the following can help you organize the body of your explanation.

Legislative	Executive	Judicial

Collecting and Organizing the Information

The big idea, or thesis, of your explanation will be that the federal system balances the power among the three branches of government. To collect information about each branch and its powers, you can use a chart like the one on the left. Be sure to note the relationships among the parts. Also, note the important characteristics of each part. When you have completed the chart, you will have the basic organization of your paper.

2. Write

You can use this framework to help you write your first draft.

A Writer's Framework

Introduction

- State the big idea of your paper.
- Explain briefly why this topic is important to the reader.

Body

- Identify the important characteristics of each part of the process or system.
- Explain any relationships between or among the parts.
- Define terms your readers might not know.
- Where appropriate, include graphics to illustrate your explanation.

Conclusion

- Restate your big idea in different words.
- Summarize your main points.

3. Evaluate and Revise

Evaluating

Clear, straightforward language is important when explaining how things work. Use the following questions to discover ways to improve your paper.

Evaluation Questions for an Explanation of a Process or System

- Does your big-idea statement accurately reflect your explanation of the process or system?
- Do you discuss each part of the process or system in logical order?
- Do you include details and information to explain each part of the process or system?
- If you used bulleted or numbered lists, are the items parallel—that is, do they have the same grammatical forms or structures?
- Does your conclusion restate your big idea and explain the importance of your topic?

Revising

Sometimes a complex explanation sounds even more complex when you try to explain it in a paragraph. In those cases, a bulleted list of facts or examples may make it easier for your readers to understand the information you are presenting. As you revise your paper, consider whether you have any information you should put in a bulleted list.

4. Proofread and Publish

Proofreading

If you use special formatting in your paper, it is important to make sure that it is consistent. Here are some things to check:

- If you have used boldface or italic type, have you always used it in the same way—for important information, for a heading, for a technical term?
- If you have used a list of items, have you consistently used numbers or bullets?

Publishing

Since you are writing this paper for students, you might find a student in the sixth or seventh grade to read it. Find out whether your explanation seems clear and interesting.

5. Practice and Apply

Use the steps and strategies outlined in this workshop to write your explanation of a process or system.

TIP **Using Bulleted Lists** The items in a bulleted list should be in the **same** grammatical forms or structures.

Not the same:

Duties of the judicial branch include

- interpret laws
- overseeing lower courts

The same:

Duties of the judicial branch include

- interpreting laws
- overseeing lower courts

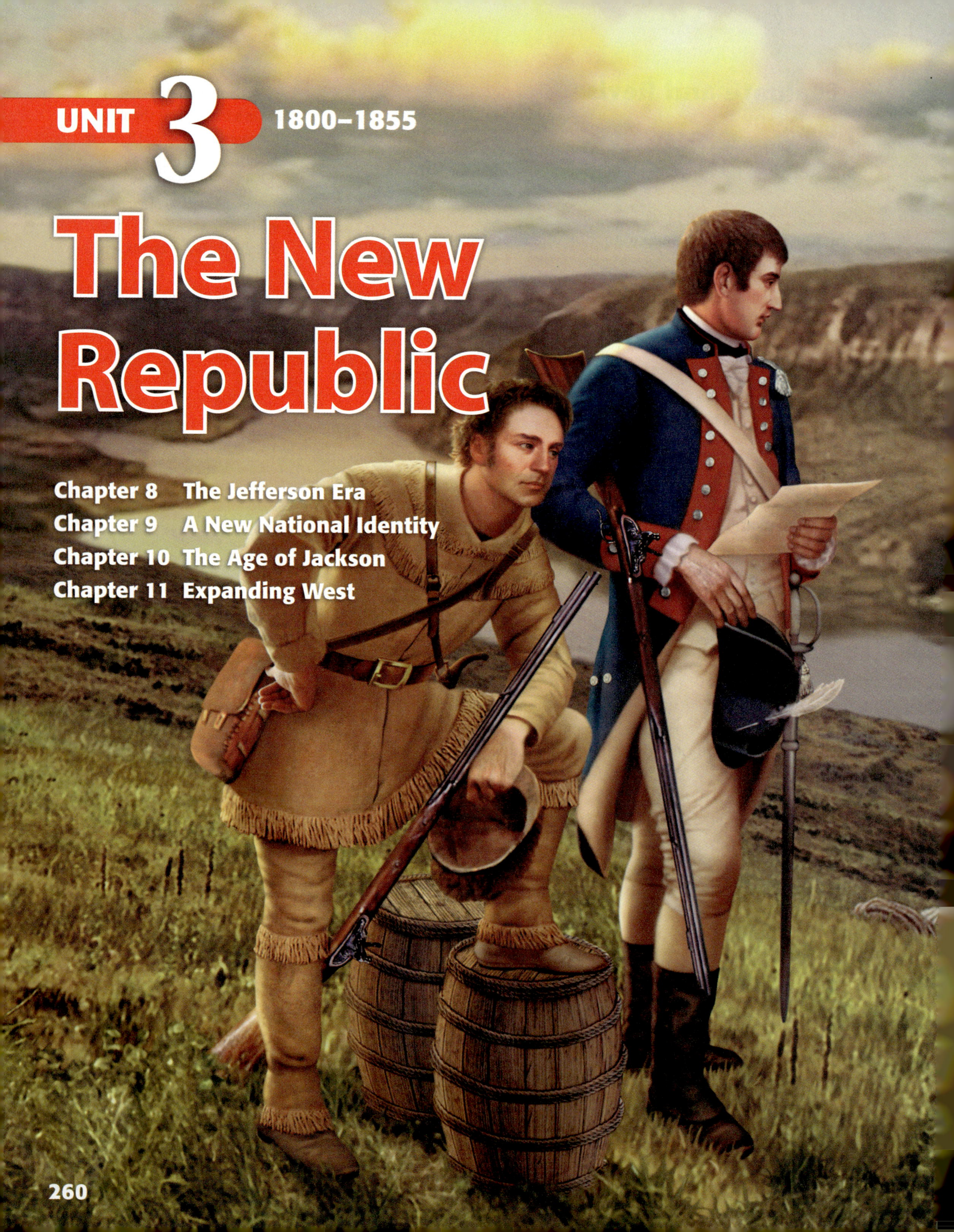

UNIT 3 1800–1855

The New Republic

What You Will Learn…

By the time the country had experienced two presidential terms, people had begun to think of themselves as Americans. A new sense of pride and unity influenced all areas of American society, from politics to art, from economics to religion. Settlers began moving deeper into the continent and the United States began to grow. In the next four chapters, you will learn about the first expansion of the young nation.

Explore the Art

In this picture, Lewis and Clark are shown asking advice from Sacagawea, a teenaged Shoshone Indian who helped them on their exploration of the continent. How does this picture show the challenges facing the explorers?

CHAPTER 8 1800–1815

The Jefferson Era

North Carolina Standards

Social Studies Objectives

3.01 Describe the causes of the War of 1812 and analyze the impact of the war on North Carolina and the nation.

3.02 Investigate the conditions that led to North Carolina's economic, political, and social decline during this period and assess the implications for the future development of the state.

3.08 Examine the impact of national events such as the Louisiana Purchase, the Lewis and Clark Expedition, the War with Mexico, and the California Gold Rush, and technological advances on North Carolina.

Language Arts Objectives

1.01 Narrate a personal account which:

- selects details that best illuminate the topic.
- connects events to self/society.

1.03 Interact in group activities and/or seminars in which the student:

- gives reasons and cites examples from text in support of expressed opinions.

go.hrw.com
North Carolina
KEYWORD: SC7 NC

FOCUS ON WRITING

A Letter of Recommendation Americans love lists—the five best books of the year, the 10 best video games, the three best soccer players. As you read this chapter you will gather some information about Thomas Jefferson. Then you will write a letter to your newspaper telling why Jefferson should be on the newspaper's "Top Ten American Presidents" list.

UNITED STATES

1801 Thomas Jefferson takes office.

1803 U.S. Senate approves the Louisiana Purchase.

1800

WORLD

1802 An army of former slaves led by Toussaint-Louverture defeats a French army in Haiti.

HOLT

History's Impact

▶ **video series**

Watch the video to understand the impact of expanding frontiers on the United States.

What You Will Learn...

In this chapter you will learn about the presidency of Thomas Jefferson. A man of many talents, Jefferson looked back to classical architecture to design his Virginia home, Monticello.

1804 Lewis and Clark begin their westward journey.

1805

1807 Congress passes the Embargo Act.

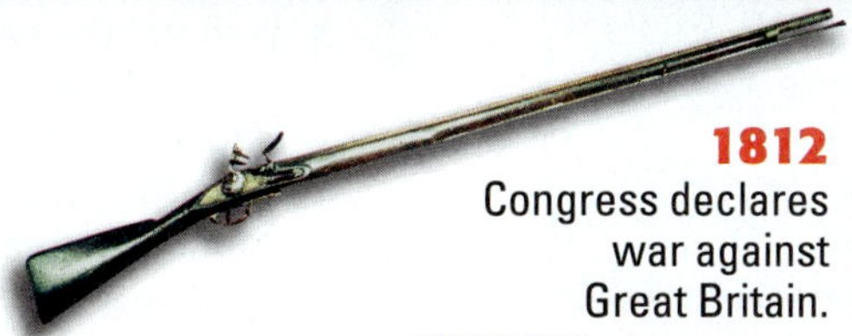

1812 Congress declares war against Great Britain.

1810

1815 The Battle of New Orleans is fought.

1815

1807 The slave trade is abolished in the British Empire.

1814 Kurozumi Munetada founds an influential Shinto religious sect that stresses patriotism in Japan.

Reading Social Studies

by Kylene Beers

Economics | Geography | Politics | Society and Culture | Science and Technology

Focus on Themes In this chapter you will learn about Thomas Jefferson's presidency. You will read what happened when Jefferson's first run to be president ended in a tie. After that, you will learn about his decision to buy Louisiana from the French, see how he encouraged the exploration of the West, and discover why, during his second term, America found itself at war with Great Britain. You will see how America's expanding **geography** and **politics** were intertwined.

Public Documents in History

Focus on Reading Historians use many types of documents to learn about the past. These documents can often be divided into two types—private and public. Private documents are those written for a person's own use, such as letters, journals, or notebooks. Public documents, on the other hand, are available for everyone to read and examine. They include such things as laws, tax codes, and treaties.

Studying Public Documents Studying public documents from the past can tell us a great deal about the politics and society of the time. However, public documents can often be confusing or difficult to understand. When you read such a document, you may want to use a list of questions like the one below to be sure you understand what you're reading.

You can often figure out the topic of a public document from the title and introduction.

Public documents often use unfamiliar words or use familiar words in unfamiliar ways. For example, the document on the next page uses the word *augmented*. Do you know what the word means in this context? If not, you should look it up.

Many public documents deal with several issues and will therefore have several main ideas.

Question Sheet for Public Documents

1. What is the topic of the document?
2. Do I understand what I'm reading?
3. Is there any vocabulary in the document that I do not understand?
4. What parts of the document should I re-read?
5. What are the main ideas and details of the document?
6. What have I learned from reading this document?

You Try It!

The passage below was taken from a Post Office notice from 1815. Read the passage and then answer the questions that follow.

Rates of Postage

Postmasters will take notice, that by an act of Congress, passed on the 23d instant, the several rates of postage are augmented fifty per cent; and that after the first of February next, the Rates of Postage for single Letters will be,

For any distance not exceeding 40 miles, 12 cents

Over 40 miles and not exceeding 90 miles, 15 cents

Over 90 miles and not exceeding 150 miles, 18 1/2 cents

Over 150 miles and not exceeding 300 miles, 25 1/2 cents

Over 300 miles and not exceeding 500 miles, 30 cents

Over 500 miles, 37 1/2 cents

Double letters, or those composed of two pieces of paper, double those rates.

Triple letters, or those composed of three pieces of paper, triple those rates.

Packets, or letters composed of four or more pieces of paper, and weighing one ounce or more, avoirdupois, are to be rated equal to one single letter for each quarter ounce.

After reading the document above, answer the following questions.

1. What is this document about?

2. What was the main idea or ideas of this document? What supporting details were included?

3. Look at the word *packets* in the last paragraph of the document. The word is not used here in the same way we usually use *packets* today. What does the word mean in this case? How can you tell?

4. Are there any other words in this passage with which you are unfamiliar? How might not knowing those words hinder your understanding of the passage?

Key Terms and People

Chapter 8

Section 1

John Adams *(p. 266)*
Thomas Jefferson *(p. 266)*
John Marshall *(p. 270)*
Marbury v. *Madison (p. 270)*
judicial review *(p. 270)*

Section 2

Louisiana Purchase *(p. 274)*
Meriwether Lewis *(p. 275)*
William Clark *(p. 275)*
Lewis and Clark expedition *(p. 275)*
Sacagawea *(p. 276)*
Zebulon Pike *(p. 276)*

Section 3

USS *Constitution (p. 278)*
impressment *(p. 279)*
embargo *(p. 279)*
Embargo Act *(p. 279)*
Non-Intercourse Act *(p. 280)*
Tecumseh *(p. 280)*
Battle of Tippecanoe *(p. 282)*
War Hawks *(p. 282)*
James Madison *(p. 283)*

Section 4

Oliver Hazard Perry *(p. 285)*
Battle of Lake Erie *(p. 285)*
Andrew Jackson *(p. 286)*
Treaty of Fort Jackson *(p. 286)*
Battle of New Orleans *(p. 286)*
Hartford Convention *(p. 287)*
Treaty of Ghent *(p. 287)*

Academic Vocabulary

In this chapter you will learn the following academic words:

functions *(p. 269)*
consequences *(p. 287)*

As you read Chapter 8, look for passages from other public documents. What can these documents teach you about the past?

SECTION 1

Jefferson Becomes President

What You Will Learn...

Main Ideas

1. The election of 1800 marked the first peaceful transition in power from one political party to another.
2. President Jefferson's beliefs about the federal government were reflected in his policies.
3. *Marbury* v. *Madison* increased the power of the judicial branch of government.

The Big Idea

Thomas Jefferson's election began a new era in American government.

Key Terms and People

John Adams, *p. 266*
Thomas Jefferson, *p. 266*
John Marshall, *p. 270*
Marbury v. *Madison*, *p. 270*
judicial review, *p. 270*

TAKING NOTES As you read, take notes in a graphic organizer like this one. List the details of the election of 1800, Jefferson's beliefs and policies, and how the power of the judicial branch changed during his time in office.

Election of 1800	
Jefferson's Beliefs and Policies	
Power of the Judical Branch	

If YOU were there...

You are a Maryland voter from a frontier district—and you are tired! For days, you and your friends have been wrangling over the presidential election. Who shall it be—John Adams or Thomas Jefferson? Your vote depends on your personal judgment.

Which candidate would you choose for president?

BUILDING BACKGROUND John Adams had not been a popular president, but many still admired his ability and high principles. Both he and Thomas Jefferson had played major roles in winning independence and shaping the new government. Now, political differences sharply divided the two men and their supporters. In the election of 1800, voters were also divided.

The Election of 1800

In the presidential election of 1800, Federalists **John Adams** and Charles C. Pinckney ran against Democratic-Republicans **Thomas Jefferson** and Aaron Burr. Each party believed that the American republic's survival depended upon the success of their candidates. With so much at stake, the election was hotly contested.

Unlike today, candidates did not travel around giving speeches. Instead, the candidates' supporters made their arguments in letters and newspaper editorials. Adams's supporters claimed that Jefferson was a pro-French radical. Put Jefferson in office, they warned, and the violence and chaos of the French Revolution would surely follow in the United States. Plus, Federalists argued, Jefferson's interest in science and philosophy proved that he wanted to destroy organized religion.

Democratic-Republican newspapers responded that Adams wanted to crown himself king. What else, they asked, could be the purpose of the Alien and Sedition Acts? Republicans also hinted that Adams would use the newly created permanent army to limit Americans' rights.

When the election results came in, Jefferson and Burr had won 73 electoral votes each to 65 for Adams and 64 for Pinckney. The Democratic-Republicans had won the election, but the tie between Jefferson and Burr caused a problem. Under the Constitution at that time, the two candidates with the most votes became president and vice president. The decision went to the House of Representatives, as called for in the Constitution.

The House, like the electoral college, also deadlocked. Days went by as vote after vote was called, each ending in ties. Exhausted lawmakers put their heads on their desks and slept between votes. Some napped on the floor.

Jefferson finally won on the thirty-sixth vote. The election marked the first time that one party had replaced another in power in the United States.

The problems with the voting system led Congress to propose the Twelfth Amendment. This amendment created a separate ballot for president and vice president.

READING CHECK **Analyzing Information**
What was significant about Jefferson's victory?

Primary Source

SPEECH

Jefferson's Inaugural Address

On March 4, 1801, Thomas Jefferson gave his first inaugural address. In the following excerpt, Jefferson describes his thoughts on the nation's future.

"Let us, then, fellow citizens, unite with one heart and one mind . . . [E]very difference of opinion is not a difference of principle. We have called by different names brethren[1] of the same principle. We are all republicans; we are all federalists."

By using phrases like these, Jefferson tries to reassure his political opponents.

"Still one thing more, fellow citizens, a wise and frugal[2] Government, which shall restrain men from injuring one another, shall leave them otherwise free to regulate their own pursuits of industry and improvement, and shall not take from the mouth of labor the bread it has earned. This is the sum of good government . . ."

Here Jefferson states his opinion of what is essential to good government.

This phrase shows Jefferson's determination to keep government small.

1. **brethren**: brothers 2. **frugal**: thrifty

ANALYSIS SKILL ANALYZING PRIMARY SOURCES

What words and phrases indicate Jefferson's support for a small national government?

Jefferson's Policies

When Jefferson took office, he brought with him a style and political ideas different from those of Adams and Washington. Jefferson was less formal than his predecessors, and he wanted to limit the powers of government.

Jefferson Is Inaugurated

THE IMPACT TODAY

A monument to Thomas Jefferson was completed in 1943 and is one of the most frequently visited sites in Washington, D.C.

Americans looked forward with excitement to Jefferson's first speech as president. People from across the nation gathered in the new capital, Washington, D.C., to hear him. Curious travelers looked with pride at the partially completed Capitol building and at the executive mansion (not yet called the White House). The two buildings dominated the surrounding homes and forests.

Small businesses dotted the landscape. At one of these, a modest boardinghouse, the president-elect was putting the finishing touches on his speech. On the morning of March 4, 1801, he left the boardinghouse and walked to the Capitol. The leader of a republic, Jefferson believed, should not ride in fancy carriages.

Jefferson read his speech in a quiet voice. He wanted to make it clear that he supported the will of the majority. He also stressed the need for a limited government and the protection of civil liberties.

From these humble surroundings in which Jefferson delivered his speech, Washington eventually grew into a large and impressive city. Over the years, the Capitol and the executive mansion were joined by other state buildings and monuments. Jefferson, who had long dreamed of a new national capital that would be independent of the interests of any one state, was pleased to be a part of this process of building a federal city.

Jefferson in Office

President Jefferson faced the task of putting his republican ideas into practice. One of his first actions was to select the members of his cabinet. His choices included James Madison as secretary of state and Albert Gallatin as secretary of the treasury.

Jefferson would also benefit from the Democratic-Republican Party's newly won control of both houses of Congress. At Jefferson's urging, Congress allowed the hated Alien and Sedition Acts to expire. Jefferson lowered military spending and reduced the size of the army. The navy was cut to seven active ships. Jefferson and Gallatin hoped that saving this money would allow the government to repay the national debt. Jefferson also asked Gallatin to find ways to get rid of domestic taxes, like the tax on whiskey. The Democratic-Republican–led Congress passed the laws needed to carry out these policies.

The entire national government in 1801 consisted only of several hundred people. Jefferson preferred to keep it that way. He believed that the primary **functions** of the federal government were to protect the nation from foreign threats, deliver the mail, and collect customs duties.

Jefferson did recognize that some of the Federalist policies—such as the creation of the Bank of the United States—should be kept. Although Jefferson had battled Hamilton over the Bank, as president he agreed to leave it in place.

READING CHECK **Summarizing** What policy changes did Democratic-Republicans introduce, and which Federalist policies did Jefferson keep?

Marbury v. *Madison*

Although Republicans controlled the presidency and Congress, Federalists dominated the federal judiciary. In an effort to continue their control over the judiciary, Federalist legislators passed the Judiciary Act of 1801 shortly before their terms of office ended. This act created 16 new federal judgeships that President Adams filled with Federalists before leaving office. The Republican press called these people midnight judges, arguing that Adams had packed the judiciary with Federalists the night before he left office.

Some of these appointments were made so late that the documents that authorized them had not been delivered by the time Adams left office. This led to controversy once Jefferson took office. William Marbury, named as a justice of the peace by President Adams, did not receive his documents before Adams left office. When Jefferson took office, Marbury demanded the documents. On Jefferson's advice, however, the new secretary of state, James Madison, refused to deliver them. Jefferson argued that the appointment of the midnight judges was not valid.

ACADEMIC VOCABULARY
functions uses or purposes

SUPREME COURT DECISIONS

Marbury v. *Madison* (1803)

Background of the Case Shortly before Thomas Jefferson took office, John Adams had appointed William Marbury to be a justice of the peace. Adams had signed Marbury's commission, but it was never delivered. Marbury sued to force Madison to give him the commission.

The Court's Ruling

The Court ruled that the law Marbury based his claim on was unconstitutional.

The Court's Reasoning

The Judiciary Act of 1789 gave the Supreme Court the authority to hear a wide variety of cases, including those like Marbury's. But the Supreme Court ruled that Congress did not have the power to make such a law. Why? Because the Constitution limits the types of cases the Supreme Court can hear. Thus, the law was in conflict with the Constitution and had to be struck down.

Why It Matters

Marbury v. *Madison* was important for several reasons. It confirmed the Supreme Court's power to declare acts of Congress unconstitutional. By doing so, it established the Court as the final authority on the Constitution. This helped make the judicial branch of government equal to the other two branches. Chief Justice John Marshall and later federal judges would use this power of judicial review as a check on the legislative and executive branches.

ANALYSIS SKILL **ANALYZING INFORMATION**

1. What do you think it means to be the final authority on the Constitution?
2. How did *Marbury* v. *Madison* affect the Constitution's system of checks and balances?

Marbury brought suit, asking the Supreme Court to order Madison to deliver the appointment papers. Marbury claimed that the Judiciary Act of 1789 gave the Supreme Court the power to do so.

John Marshall, a Federalist appointed by John Adams, was the chief justice of the United States. Chief Justice Marshall and President Jefferson disagreed about many political issues. When Marshall agreed to hear Marbury's case, Jefferson protested, saying that the Federalists "have retired into the judiciary as a stronghold." Marshall wrote the Court's opinion in ***Marbury* v. *Madison***, a case that helped establish the Supreme Court's power to check the power of the other branches of government. The Constitution, Chief Justice Marshall noted, gave the Supreme Court authority to hear only certain types of cases. A request like Marbury's was not one of them. The law that Marbury's case depended upon was, therefore, unconstitutional.

John Marshall served as chief justice of the United States for 34 years.

In denying Marbury's request in this way, the Court avoided a direct confrontation with Jefferson's administration. But more importantly, it established the Court's power of **judicial review**, the power to declare an act of Congress unconstitutional. Marshall and later federal judges would use this power of judicial review to make the judiciary a much stronger part of the national government.

READING CHECK **Analyzing Information**
Why was *Marbury* v. *Madison* an important ruling?

SUMMARY AND PREVIEW A peaceful transfer of power took place in Washington after the election of 1800. In the next section you will read about the Louisiana Purchase.

Section 1 Assessment

go.hrw.com
Online Quiz
KEYWORD: SC7 HP8

Reviewing Ideas, Terms, and People

1. a. **Identify** What were the political parties in the election of 1800, and who were their candidates?
   b. **Analyze** Why was the election of 1800 significant?
2. a. **Describe** What ideas for government did **Thomas Jefferson** stress in his inaugural address?
   b. **Compare and Contrast** What similarities and differences did Jefferson's Republican government have with the previous Federalist one?
   c. **Elaborate** Defend Jefferson's preference for keeping the national government small.
3. a. **Identify** Who was **John Marshall**?
   b. **Draw Conclusions** Why is the power of **judicial review** important?
   c. **Predict** How might the ***Marbury* v. *Madison*** ruling affect future actions by Congress?

Critical Thinking

4. **Categorizing** Review your notes on Jefferson's beliefs and policies. Then copy the graphic organizer below and show how Jefferson brought change through his policies.

Jefferson as President

Federalist Policies	Republican Policies

FOCUS ON WRITING

5. **Gathering Ideas about a Person's Accomplishments** Look back through what you have just read to see what you have learned about Jefferson's decisions in office. Make a list of the traits you think each decision shows in Jefferson.

BIOGRAPHY

Thomas Jefferson

How would you inspire people to seek freedom?

When did he live? He was born on April 13, 1743. He died on July 4, 1826, within hours of the death of President John Adams, his rival and friend. The date was also the fiftieth anniversary of the Declaration of Independence.

Where did he live? He was born in Albemarle County, Virginia, where he inherited a large estate from his father. At age 26 he began building his elegant lifetime home, Monticello, which he designed himself. He spent much of his life away from home, in Philadelphia; Washington, D.C.; and Europe. Yet he always longed to return to his peaceful home.

What did he do? Jefferson wanted only three of his accomplishments listed on his tomb: author of the Declaration of American Independence, author of the Virginia Statute for Religious Freedom, and Father of the University of Virginia. What did he *not* mention? Governor of Virginia, lawyer, Revolutionary leader, writer, philosopher, inventor, architect, plant scientist, book collector, musician, astronomer, ambassador, secretary of state—and, of course, president of the United States.

Why is he important? Jefferson's powerful words in the Declaration of Independence have inspired people throughout the world to seek freedom, equality, and self-rule. His most celebrated achievement as president (1801–1809) was the purchase of the Louisiana Territory from France. The Louisiana Purchase of 1803 nearly doubled the size of the United States. Jefferson then sponsored the Lewis and Clark expedition to explore this new territory.

Evaluating Why has Thomas Jefferson been a hero to generations of Americans?

Thomas Jefferson wrote the Declaration of Independence and later served as president of the United States.

KEY EVENTS

- **1767** Begins practicing law in Virginia
- **1769–1776** Serves in Virginia House of Burgesses
- **1776** Drafts the first version of the Declaration of Independence
- **1789** Appointed secretary of state by George Washington
- **1801** Inaugurated as president
- **1803** Authorizes the purchase of Louisiana from France
- **1809** Retires to Monticello

SECTION 2

The Louisiana Purchase

What You Will Learn...

Main Ideas

1. As American settlers moved West, control of the Mississippi River became more important to the United States.
2. The Louisiana Purchase almost doubled the size of the United States.
3. Expeditions led by Lewis, Clark, and Pike increased Americans' understanding of the West.

The Big Idea

Under President Jefferson's leadership, the United States added the Louisiana Territory.

Key Terms and People

Louisiana Purchase, *p. 274*
Meriwether Lewis, *p. 275*
William Clark, *p. 275*
Lewis and Clark expedition, *p. 275*
Sacagawea, *p. 276*
Zebulon Pike, *p. 276*

TAKING NOTES As you read, take notes in a graphic organizer like the one below on the events leading up to the Louisiana Purchase and the exploration that followed.

Events Leading to Louisiana Purchase	Exploration that Followed Louisiana Purchase

If YOU were there...

You and your family live on a small farm in Kentucky in about 1800. Raised on the frontier, you are a skillful hunter and trapper. One day at the trading post, you see a poster calling for volunteers to join the Corps of Discovery. This expedition will explore the vast region west of the Mississippi River. You think it would be exciting—but dangerous. You might never come home.

Would you volunteer to join the Corps of Discovery?

BUILDING BACKGROUND As the 1800s began, the United States was expanding steadily westward. More lands were opened, and settlers moved in to occupy them. Americans were also curious about the vast lands that lay farther West. Adventurous explorers organized expeditions to find out more about those lands.

American Settlers Move West

By the early 1800s, thousands of Americans settled in the area between the Appalachians and the Mississippi River. As the region's population grew, Kentucky, Tennessee, and Ohio were admitted to the Union. Settlers in these states depended upon the Mississippi and Ohio rivers to move their products to eastern markets.

New Orleans, located at the mouth of the Mississippi, was a very important port. Its busy docks were filled with settlers' farm products and valuable furs bought from American Indians. Many of these cargoes were then sent to Europe. At the same time, manufactured goods passed through the port on their way upriver. As American dependence on the river grew, Jefferson began to worry that a foreign power might shut down access to New Orleans.

> "There is on the globe one single spot, the possessor of which is our natural and habitual enemy. It is New Orleans, through which the produce of three-eighths of our territory must pass to market."
>
> —Thomas Jefferson, quoted in *Annals of America, Volume 4, 1797–1820*

Interactive Map

The Louisiana Purchase and Western Expeditions

go.hrw.com
Interactive Map
KEYWORD: SC7 CH8

GEOGRAPHY SKILLS **INTERPRETING MAPS**

1. **Location** What major port city was located at the southern tip of the Louisiana Territory?
2. **Human-Environment Interaction** Why might Lewis and Clark have followed the Missouri River?

Spain controlled both New Orleans and Louisiana. This region stretched west from the mighty Mississippi River to the great Rocky Mountains. Although Spain owned Louisiana, Spanish officials found it impossible to keep Americans out of the territory. "You can't put doors on open country," the foreign minister said in despair.

Years of effort failed to improve Spain's position. Under a secret treaty, Spain agreed to trade Louisiana to France, passing the problem on to someone else. One Spanish officer expressed his relief. "I can hardly wait to leave them [the Americans] behind me," he said.

READING CHECK **Analyzing Information** Why was New Orleans important to settlers in the western regions of the United States?

Louisiana

In 1802, just before handing over Louisiana to France, Spain closed New Orleans to American shipping. Angry farmers worried about what this would do to the economy. President Jefferson asked the U.S. ambassador to France, Robert R. Livingston, to try to buy New Orleans. Jefferson sent James Monroe to help Livingston.

Napoléon and Louisiana

France was led by Napoléon (nuh-POH-lee-uhn) Bonaparte, a powerful ruler who had conquered most of Europe. He wished to rebuild France's empire in North America.

Napoléon's strategy was to use the French colony of Haiti, in the Caribbean, as a supply base. From there he could send troops to Louisiana. However, enslaved Africans had revolted and freed themselves from French rule. Napoléon sent troops to try to regain control of the island, but they were defeated in 1802. This defeat ended his hopes of rebuilding a North American empire.

Jefferson Buys Louisiana

FOCUS ON NORTH CAROLINA

On the whole, North Carolinians supported the Louisiana Purchase. Many residents of the state moved west into the newly acquired land, establishing farms and businesses.

The American ambassador got a surprising offer during his negotiations with French foreign minister Charles Talleyrand. When the Americans tried to buy New Orleans, Talleyrand offered to sell all of Louisiana.

With his hopes for a North American empire dashed, Napoléon had turned his attention back to Europe. France was at war with Great Britain, and Napoléon needed money for military supplies. He also hoped that a larger United States would challenge British power.

Livingston and Monroe knew a bargain when they saw one. They quickly accepted the French offer to sell Louisiana for $15 million.

The news pleased Jefferson. But as a strict constructionist, he was troubled. The Constitution did not mention the purchase of foreign lands. He also did not like spending large amounts of public money. Nevertheless, Jefferson agreed to the purchase in the belief that doing so was best for the country.

On October 20, 1803, the Senate approved the **Louisiana Purchase** agreement, which roughly doubled the size of the United States. With the $15 million in the French treasury, Napoléon boasted, "I have given England a rival who, sooner or later, will humble her pride."

READING CHECK **Making Inferences**
Why was the Louisiana Purchase important to the future of the United States?

The Journey West

The time line and photographs you see here show some of the key events and places of the Lewis and Clark expedition. Read the journal entries to get an idea of what the explorers faced.

A large keelboat and two smaller boats were needed to get the supply-heavy expedition moving west.

Small boats helped the travelers move supplies across the Great Plains.

May 14, 1804
The expedition begins near St. Louis.

August 3, 1804
The first official council between representatives of the United States and Plains Indians is held.

October 1804 – April 1805
The expedition establishes Fort Mandan to spend the winter. There, the explorers meet a French fur trader and his wife, Sacagawea.

April 7, 1805 We are about to penetrate a country at least 2,000 miles in width, on which the foot of civilized man had never trodden (walked upon).
—Meriwether Lewis

Explorers Head West

Americans knew little about western Native Americans or the land they lived on. President Jefferson wanted to learn more about the people and land of the West. He also wanted to see if there was a river route that could be taken to the Pacific Ocean.

Lewis and Clark Expedition

In 1803 the president asked Congress to fund an expedition to explore the West. To lead it, he chose former army captain **Meriwether Lewis**. Lewis then chose his friend Lieutenant **William Clark** to be the co-leader of the expedition.

To prepare for the journey, Lewis spent weeks studying with experts about plants, surveying, and other subjects. This knowledge would allow him to take careful notes on what he saw. With Clark, Lewis carefully selected about 50 skilled frontiersmen to join the Corps of Discovery, as they called their group.

In May 1804 the **Lewis and Clark expedition** began its long journey to explore the Louisiana Purchase. The Corps of Discovery traveled up the Missouri River to the village of St. Charles. Once past this village the men would receive no more letters, fresh supplies, or reinforcements.

Lewis and Clark used the Missouri River as their highway through the unknown lands. As they moved upstream, a lookout on the boats kept a sharp eye out for sandbars and for tree stumps hidden underwater. When darkness fell, the weary explorers would pull their boats ashore. They cooked, wrote in their journals, and slept. Swarms of gnats, flies, and mosquitoes often interrupted their sleep.

FOCUS ON NORTH CAROLINA

North Carolinian Richard Warfington was placed in charge of a group of the Corps of Discovery that returned from the Missouri River. Among the samples the group brought back to President Jefferson was a living prairie dog.

The explorers paddled down the Columbia River toward the Pacific in five canoes.

The expedition relied on 24 horses to cross the Rocky Mountains.

August 12, 1805
Lewis climbs the first ridge to the Continental Divide.

September 1805
The expedition nearly starves. Local peoples help the explorers.

November 7, 1805
The expedition reaches a bay of the Pacific Ocean.

August 23, 1805 *The hills or mountains were not like those I had seen, but like the side of a tree straight up.*
—*William Clark*

ANALYSIS SKILL READING TIME LINES

On what date did the explorers reach the westernmost point of their journey?

Primary Source

JOURNAL ENTRY

September 17, 1804, Great Plains

While traveling across the Great Plains, Meriwether Lewis marveled at the richness of the land.

"The shortness . . . of grass gave the plain the appearance throughout its whole extent of beautiful bowling-green in fine order . . . this scenery, already rich, pleasing, and beautiful was still farther heightened by immense herds of Buffaloe, deer Elk and Antelopes which we saw in every direction feeding on the hills and plains. I do not think I exaggerate when I estimate the number of Buffalo which could be compre[hend]ed at one view to amount to 3000."

—Meriwether Lewis, quoted in *Original Journals of the Lewis and Clark Expedition*, edited by Reuben Bold Theraites

ANALYSIS SKILL **ANALYZING PRIMARY SOURCES**

What did Lewis find so impressive about the Great Plains?

Insects were not the only cause of sleeplessness for the Corps of Discovery. As weeks passed without seeing any Native Americans, the explorers wondered what their first encounter would be like.

Contact with Native Americans

During the summer of 1804 the Corps of Discovery had pushed more than 600 miles upriver without seeing any Native Americans. But when the men spotted huge buffalo herds in the distance, they guessed that Indian groups would be nearby. Many Indian groups depended on the buffalo for food, clothing, and tools.

Lewis used interpreters to talk to the leaders of each of the peoples they met. He told them that the United States now owned the land on which the Native Americans lived. Yet the explorers relied on the goodwill of the people they met. **Sacagawea** (sak-uh-juh-WEE-uh), a Shoshone from the Rocky Mountains, accompanied the group with her husband, a French fur trader who lived with the Mandan Indians and served as a guide and interpreter. Sacagawea helped the expedition by naming plants and by gathering edible fruits and vegetables for the group. At one point, the group met with Sacagawea's brother, who provided horses and a guide to lead the expedition across the mountains.

After crossing the Rocky Mountains, Lewis and Clark followed the Columbia River. Along the way they met the powerful Nez Percé. Like the Shoshone, the Nez Percé provided the expedition with food. At last, in November 1805, Lewis and Clark reached the Pacific Ocean. The explorers stayed in the Pacific Northwest during the rough winter. In March 1806 Lewis and Clark set out on the long trip home.

Lewis and Clark had not found a river route across the West to the Pacific Ocean. But they had learned much about western lands and paths across the Rockies. The explorers also established contact with many Native American groups and collected much valuable information about western plants and animals.

Pike's Exploration

In 1806 a young army officer named **Zebulon Pike** was sent on another mission to the West. He was ordered to find the starting point of the Red River. This was important because the United States considered the Red River to be a part of the Louisiana Territory's western border with New Spain.

Heading into the Rocky Mountains, in present-day Colorado, Pike tried to reach the summit of the mountain now known as Pikes Peak. In 1807 he traveled into Spanish-held lands until Spanish cavalry arrested him. They suspected Pike of being a spy. When he was finally released, he returned to the United States and reported on his trip. Despite his imprisonment, he praised the opportunities for doing business with the Spanish in the Southwest. Pike's

LINKING TO TODAY

The Louisiana Purchase

Lewis and Clark would be surprised to see what has become of the lands they explored. The lands of the Louisiana Purchase are rich with natural resources and support enormous agricultural production.

Natural Resources oil, natural gas, coal, gemstones, copper, iron ore, lead, zinc, silver, limestone, sulphur, diamonds, helium

Major Agricultural and Livestock Production rice, cattle, chicken, hogs, corn, wheat, sugarcane, cotton, dairy products, hay

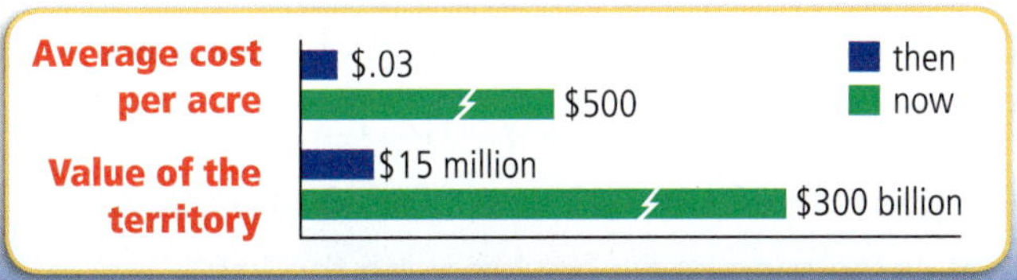

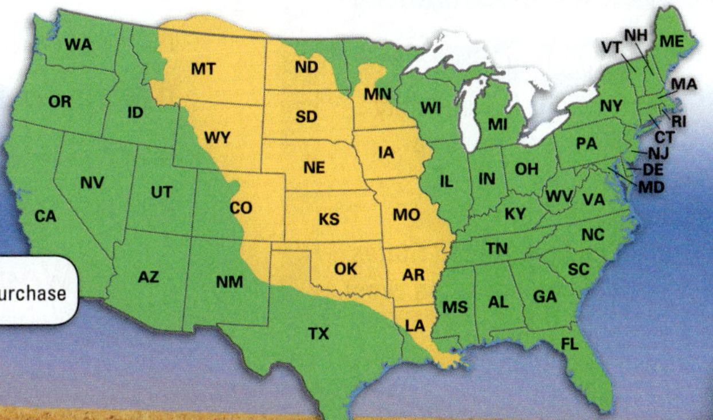

ANALYSIS SKILL — ANALYZING INFORMATION

Other than agricultural goods, what types of valuable resources are found in the former Louisiana Purchase?

report offered many Americans their first description of the Southwest.

READING CHECK **Supporting a Point of View** What would you do if you were Pike and found yourself in Spanish territory?

SUMMARY AND PREVIEW The Louisiana Purchase nearly doubled the size of the United States. In the next section you will learn about increasing tensions between the United States and Great Britain.

Section 2 Assessment

go.hrw.com
Online Quiz
KEYWORD: SC7 HP8

Reviewing Ideas, Terms, and People

1. a. **Identify** What new states were added to the Union by the early 1800s?
   b. **Explain** Why were New Orleans and the Mississippi River important to settlers in the West?
2. a. **Recall** What two reasons did Napoléon have for selling Louisiana to the United States?
   b. **Summarize** Why was the **Louisiana Purchase** important to the United States?
   c. **Predict** What are some possible results of expansion into the Louisiana Purchase?
3. a. **Describe** What areas did the **Lewis and Clark expedition** and the Pike expedition explore?
   b. **Draw Conclusions** Why were **Meriwether Lewis** and **William Clark** chosen to lead the exploration of the Louisiana Purchase?

Critical Thinking

4. **Sequencing** Review your notes on the Louisiana Purchase. Then copy the graphic organizer below and use it to rank the three most important effects of the Louisiana Purchase, from most important to least important, and explain why you chose that order.

Importance	Why
1. 2. 3.	

FOCUS ON WRITING

5. **Gathering Information about a Person's Actions** Make a list of Jefferson's actions—the ones that would put him on that top-ten list. Add any new character traits you have discovered.

SECTION 3

The Coming of War

What You Will Learn...

Main Ideas

1. Violations of U.S. neutrality led Congress to enact a ban on trade.
2. Native Americans, Great Britain, and the United States came into conflict in the West.
3. The War Hawks led a growing call for war with Great Britain.

The Big Idea

Challenges at home and abroad led the United States to declare war on Great Britain.

Key Terms and People

USS *Constitution*, *p. 278*
impressment, *p. 279*
embargo, *p. 279*
Embargo Act, *p. 279*
Non-Intercourse Act, *p. 280*
Tecumseh, *p. 280*
Battle of Tippecanoe, *p. 282*
War Hawks, *p. 282*
James Madison, *p. 283*

TAKING NOTES Create a graphic organizer like the one below. As you read, take notes on the challenges that led the United States to declare war on Great Britain.

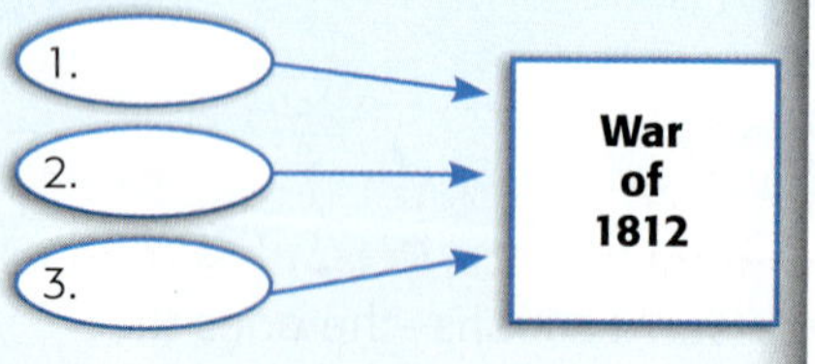

If YOU were there...

You are a tea merchant in Boston in 1807, but right now your business is at a standstill. A new law forbids trading with European nations. Now, Boston Harbor is full of empty ships. It seems to you that the law is hurting American merchants more than European ones! You know that some merchants are breaking the law and smuggling goods, just to stay in business.

Would you obey the law or turn to smuggling?

BUILDING BACKGROUND The United States tried to stay neutral in the conflicts between France and Great Britain, but it was impossible to avoid getting involved. French and British ships interfered with American trade across the Atlantic. The British also caused trouble along the western frontier. Many Americans began to urge war with Great Britain.

Violations of Neutrality

During the late 1700s and early 1800s, American merchant ships fanned out across the oceans. The overseas trade, while profitable, was also risky. Ships had to travel vast distances, often through violent storms. Merchant ships sailing in the Mediterranean risked capture by pirates from the Barbary States of North Africa, who would steal cargo and hold ships' crews for ransom. Attacks continued until the United States sent the **USS *Constitution***, a large warship, and other ships to end them.

The Barbary pirates were a serious problem, but an even larger threat soon loomed. When Great Britain and France went to war in 1803, each country wanted to stop the United States from supplying goods to the other. Each government passed laws designed to prevent American merchants from trading with the other. In addition, the British and French navies captured many American merchant ships searching for war supplies.

The real trouble, however, started when Britain began stopping and searching American ships for sailors who had run away from the British navy, forcing the sailors to return to British ships.

The USS *Constitution*

CONNECT TO SCIENCE AND TECHNOLOGY

In the early years of the republic, foreign trade was critical to the nation's survival. In 1797 Congress decided to create a navy to protect American merchant ships. The powerful warship USS *Constitution* was a key part of the new navy and was undefeated in battle. It is the oldest commissioned warship in the world.

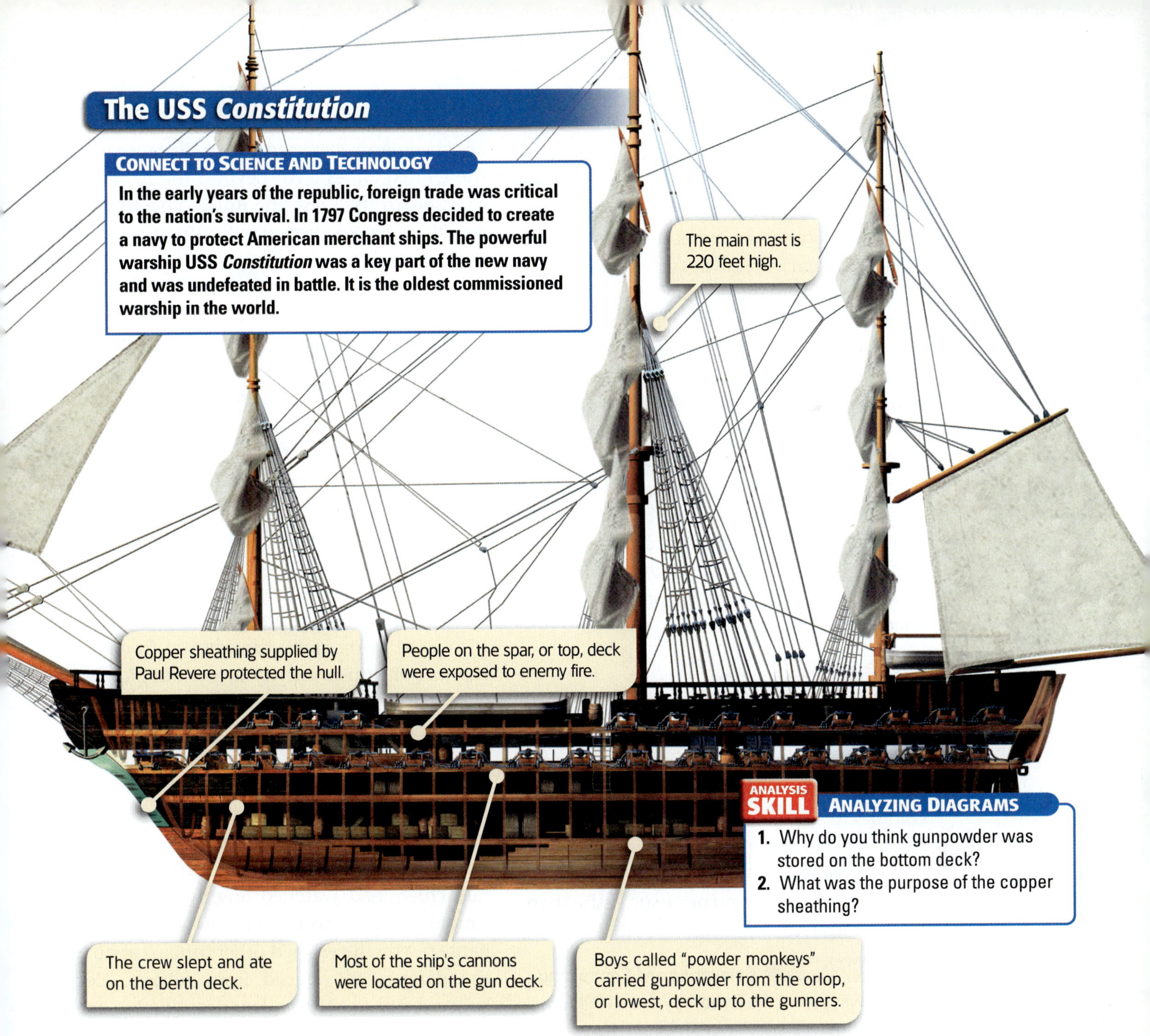

ANALYSIS SKILL **ANALYZING DIAGRAMS**

1. Why do you think gunpowder was stored on the bottom deck?
2. What was the purpose of the copper sheathing?

Sometimes U.S. citizens were captured by accident. This **impressment**, or the practice of forcing people to serve in the army or navy, continued despite American protests.

Soon Britain was even targeting American navy ships. In June 1807, for example, the British ship *Leopard* stopped the U.S. Navy ship *Chesapeake* and tried to remove sailors. When the captain of the *Chesapeake* refused, the British took the sailors by force. The brazen attack on the *Chesapeake* stunned Americans.

The Embargo Act

Great Britain's violations of U.S. neutrality sparked intense debate in America about how to respond. Some people wanted to go to war. Others favored an **embargo**, or the banning of trade, against Britain.

Jefferson, who had easily won re-election in 1804, supported an embargo. At his urging, in late 1807 Congress passed the **Embargo Act**. The law essentially banned trade with all foreign countries. American ships could not sail to foreign ports. American ports were also closed to British ships. Congress hoped that the embargo would punish Britain and France and protect American merchant ships from capture.

The effect of the law was devastating to American merchants. Without foreign trade, they lost enormous amounts of money. Northern states that relied heavily on trade were especially hard hit by the embargo. Congressman Josiah Quincy of Massachusetts, in a speech before Congress, described the situation. "All the business of the nation is in disorder. All the nation's industry is at a standstill," he said.

The embargo damaged Jefferson's popularity and strengthened the Federalist Party. Angry merchants sent Jefferson hundreds of petitions demanding the Embargo Act's repeal. One New Englander said the embargo was like "cutting one's throat to stop the nosebleed." Even worse, the embargo had little effect on Britain and France.

Non-Intercourse Act

In 1809 Congress tried to revive the nation's trade by replacing the unpopular act with the **Non-Intercourse Act**. This new law banned trade only with Britain, France, and their colonies. It also stated that the United States would resume trading with the first side that stopped violating U.S. neutrality. In time, however, the law was no more successful than the Embargo Act.

READING CHECK **Comparing and Contrasting** In what ways were the Embargo Act and the Non-Intercourse Act similar and different?

Conflict in the West

Disagreements between Great Britain and the United States went beyond the neutrality issue. In the West, the British and Native Americans again clashed with American settlers over land.

The Conflict over Land

In the early 1800s, Native Americans in the old Northwest Territory continued to lose land as thousands of settlers poured into the region. The United States had gained this land in the Treaty of Greenville, but Indian leaders who had not agreed to the treaty protested the settlers' arrival. Frustrated Indian groups considered what to do. In the meantime, Britain saw an opportunity to slow America's westward growth. British agents from Canada began to arm Native Americans who were living along the western frontier. Rumors of British activity in the old Northwest Territory quickly spread, filling American settlers with fear and anger.

Tecumseh Resists U.S. Settlers

Soon an Indian leader emerged who seemed more than capable of halting the American settlers. **Tecumseh** (tuh-KUHM-suh), a Shawnee chief, had watched angrily as Native Americans were pushed off their land. A brilliant speaker, he warned other Indians about the dangers they faced from settlers. He believed that the Native Americans had to do what white Americans had done: unite.

Time Line

America's Road to War

1807

June 22, 1807 The British navy takes sailors from the U.S. Navy ship *Chesapeake*.

December 22, 1807 The United States responds to impressment by passing the Embargo Act.

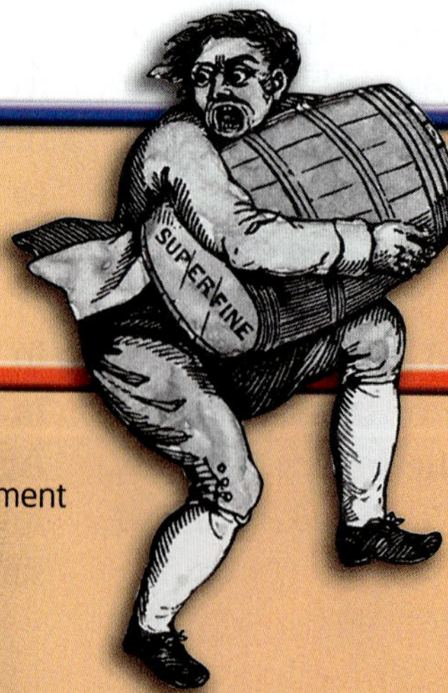

1809

January 9, 1809 Congress passes the Non-Intercourse Act.

Primary Source

POLITICAL CARTOON

The Embargo Act

The unpopularity of the Embargo Act prompted political cartoonists to show visually how the act was hurting American trade.

What do you think the turtle represents?

What is the turtle preventing this man from doing?

What is "ograbme" spelled backward?

ANALYSIS SKILL **ANALYZING PRIMARY SOURCES**

How does the cartoonist emphasize the unpopularity of the Embargo Act?

Tecumseh hoped to unite the Native Americans of the northwestern frontier, the South, and the eastern Mississippi Valley. He was helped by his brother, a religious leader called the Prophet. They founded a village called Prophetstown for their followers near the Wabash and Tippecanoe rivers.

The Battle of Tippecanoe

The governor of the Indiana Territory, William Henry Harrison, watched Tecumseh's activities with alarm. Harrison called him "one of those uncommon geniuses which spring up occasionally to . . . overturn the established order." The governor was convinced that Tecumseh had British backing. If true, Tecumseh could be a serious threat to American power in the West.

In 1810 Tecumseh met face to face with Harrison. The governor urged him to follow the Treaty of Greenville that had been signed in 1795. Tecumseh replied, "The white people have no right to take the land from the Indians, because the Indians had it first." No single chief, he insisted, could sell land belonging to all American Indians who used it. In response, Harrison warned Tecumseh not to resist the power of the United States.

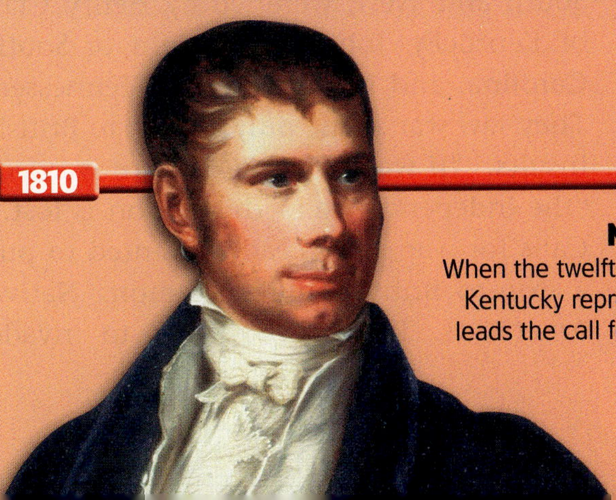

1810

November 4, 1811
When the twelfth Congress convenes, Kentucky representative Henry Clay leads the call for war against Britain.

1812

June 18, 1812
The United States declares war against Britain.

ANALYSIS SKILL **READING TIME LINES**

What events led to war against Great Britain?

Primary Source

POINTS OF VIEW

Views of War

Tecumseh urged Native Americans to unite to oppose what he called the "evil" of white settlement.

"The only way to stop this evil is for all the red men to unite in claiming a common and equal right to the land, as it was at first, and should be yet. Before, the land never was divided, but belonged to all, for the use of each person. No group had a right to sell, not even to each other, much less to strangers who want all and will not do with less."

—Tecumseh

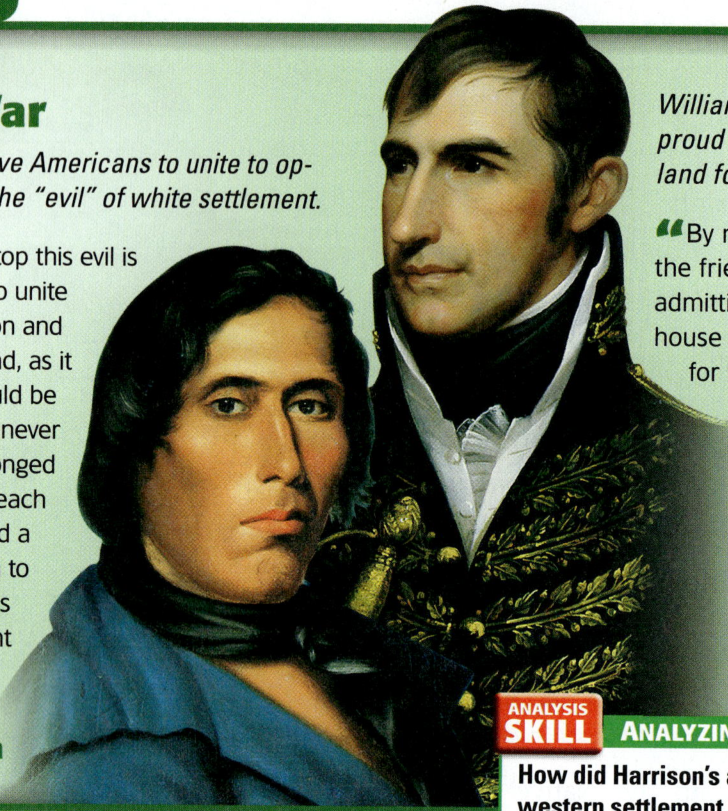

William Henry Harrison was proud of his efforts to obtain land for settlers.

"By my own exertions in securing the friendship of the chiefs . . . by admitting them at all times to my house and table, my propositions for the purchase of their lands were successful beyond my . . . hopes . . . In the course of seven years the Indian title was extinguished to the amount of fifty millions of acres."

—William Henry Harrison

ANALYSIS SKILL **ANALYZING POINTS OF VIEW**

How did Harrison's and Tecumseh's views on western settlement differ?

Tecumseh traveled south to ask the Creek nation to join his forces. In his absence, Harrison attacked. Harrison raised an army and marched his troops close to Prophetstown. Fighting broke out when the Prophet ordered an attack on Harrison's camp on November 7, 1811.

The Indians broke through army lines, but Harrison kept a "calm, cool, and collected" manner, according to one observer. During the all-day battle, Harrison's soldiers forced the Indian warriors to retreat and then destroyed Tecumseh's village. Said Chief Shabbona, "With the smoke of that town and loss of that battle, I lost all hope." Although Tecumseh was safe, U.S. forces defeated Tecumseh and his followers in the **Battle of Tippecanoe**. The defeat destroyed Tecumseh's dream of a great Indian confederation. He fled to Canada.

FOCUS ON READING

What words did Calhoun use that had strong emotions tied to them for Americans? (See "The War Hawks" section.)

READING CHECK **Finding Main Ideas**

Why were U.S. officials worried about Tecumseh's actions?

Call for War

The evidence of British support for Tecumseh further inflamed Americans. A Democratic-Republican newspaper declared, "The war on the Wabash [River] is purely BRITISH." Many Americans felt that Britain had encouraged Tecumseh to attack settlers in the West.

The War Hawks

Several young members of Congress—called **War Hawks** by their opponents—took the lead in calling for war against Britain. These legislators, most of whom were from the South and West, were led by Henry Clay of Kentucky, John C. Calhoun of South Carolina, and Felix Grundy of Tennessee. They saw war as the only answer to British insults. "If we submit," Calhoun warned, "the independence of this nation is lost." Calls for war grew. Leaders wanted to put a stop to British influence among Native Americans. They also wanted to invade

Canada and gain more land for settlement. Others were angered by British trade restrictions that hurt southern planters and western farmers. War Hawks gave emotional speeches urging Americans to stand up to Great Britain.

The Opposition

The strongest opponents of the War Hawks were New England Federalists. British trade restrictions and impressment had hurt New England's economy. People there wanted to renew friendly business ties with Britain instead of fighting another war.

Other politicians argued that war with Great Britain would be foolish. They feared that the United States was not yet ready to fight powerful Britain. America's army and navy were small and poorly equipped compared to Britain's military. In addition, Americans could produce only a fraction of the military supplies Britain could. Senator Obadiah German of New York pleaded with the War Hawks to be patient: "Prior to any declaration of war . . . my plan would be, and my first wish is, to prepare for it—to put the country in complete armor."

Declaring War

Republican **James Madison** was elected president in 1808. He faced the difficulty of continuing an unpopular trade war begun by Jefferson. He also felt growing pressure from the War Hawks. By 1812 he decided that Congress must vote on war. Speaking to Congress, Madison blasted Great Britain's conduct. He asked Congress to decide how the nation should respond.

When Congress voted a few days later, the War Hawks won. For the first time in the nation's brief history, Congress had declared war. Months later, Americans elected Madison to a second term. He would serve as commander in chief during the War of 1812.

READING CHECK **Summarizing** Why did the United States declare war in 1812?

SUMMARY AND PREVIEW Conflicts on the frontier and with Great Britain dominated U.S. foreign policy under Jefferson and Madison. In the next section you will read about the War of 1812.

Section 3 Assessment

go.hrw.com
Online Quiz
KEYWORD: SC7 HP8

Reviewing Ideas, Terms, and People

1. a. **Describe** In what ways did the war between France and Britain cause problems for the United States?
   b. **Make Inferences** What were the reasons for the failure of the **Embargo Act**?
   c. **Elaborate** Why do you think **embargoes** against Britain and France failed?
2. a. **Describe** What was **Tecumseh**'s goal?
   b. **Explain** What role did Great Britain play in the conflict between the United States and American Indians on the western frontier?
3. a. **Identify** Who were the **War Hawks**? Why did they support war with Britain?
   b. **Elaborate** Would you have supported going to war against Great Britain? Explain your answer.

Critical Thinking

4. **Categorizing** Review your notes on the challenges that led to the War of 1812. Were most challenges foreign or domestic? Categorize them in a chart like the one below.

Foreign	Domestic

FOCUS ON WRITING

5. **Taking Notes** Take notes about any of Jefferson's actions and character traits you can identify during the buildup to war with Britain. Save this information for the top-ten list you will create at the end of the chapter.

SECTION 4

The War of 1812

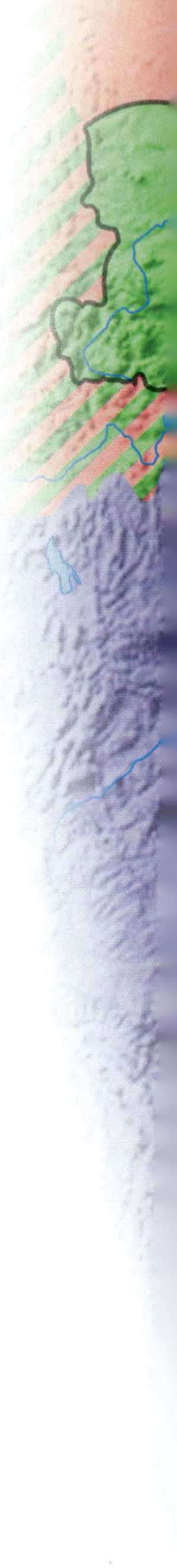

If YOU were there...

It's 1812, and the United States and Great Britain are at war. You are a sailor on an American merchant ship that has been licensed as a privateer. Your ship's mission will be to chase and capture ships of the mighty British navy. Even with the help of merchant ships like yours, the American navy is badly outnumbered. You know you face danger and may not survive.

Do you think your mission will succeed?

BUILDING BACKGROUND Anger against Great Britain's actions finally provoked the United States into the War of 1812. Britain's great navy gave it a clear advantage at sea, but the war was also fought on several other fronts. Victories in major battles along the frontier gave Americans a new sense of unity.

What You Will Learn...

Main Ideas

1. American forces held their own against the British in the early battles of the war.
2. U.S. forces stopped British offensives in the East and South.
3. The effects of the war included prosperity and national pride.

The Big Idea

Great Britain and the United States went to battle in the War of 1812.

Key Terms and People

Oliver Hazard Perry, *p. 285*
Battle of Lake Erie, *p. 285*
Andrew Jackson, *p. 286*
Treaty of Fort Jackson, *p. 286*
Battle of New Orleans, *p. 286*
Hartford Convention, *p. 287*
Treaty of Ghent, *p. 287*

TAKING NOTES Create a graphic organizer like the one below. As you read, take notes on the sequence of events in the War of 1812, from beginning to end.

Sequence of Events
1.
2.
3.
4.
5.
6.
7.

Early Battles

In the summer of 1812 the United States found itself in a war with one of the world's most powerful nations. Despite the claims by the War Hawks, the War of 1812 would not be a quick and easy fight.

War at Sea

When the war began, the British navy had hundreds of ships. In contrast, the U.S. Navy had fewer than 20 ships. None of them was as powerful as the greatest British warships.

Most of the British navy's ships, however, were scattered around the globe. Although small, the U.S. Navy had well-trained sailors and powerful new warships such as the USS *Constitution*. American vessels defeated British ships several times in one-on-one duels. Such victories embarrassed the British and raised American morale. Eventually, the British ships blockaded America's seaports.

Battles Along the Canadian Border

American leaders hoped to follow up victories at sea with an overland invasion of Canada. Three attacks were planned—from Detroit, from Niagara Falls, and from up the Hudson River valley toward Montreal.

GEOGRAPHY SKILLS **INTERPRETING MAPS**

1. **Location** According to the map, what major southern port was affected by the British blockade?
2. **Region** Which battles took place in the Great Lakes region?

The attack from Detroit failed when British soldiers and Indians led by Tecumseh captured Fort Detroit. The other American attacks failed when state militia troops refused to cross the Canadian border, arguing that they did not have to fight in a foreign country.

In 1813 the United States went on the attack again. A key goal was to break Britain's control of Lake Erie. The navy gave the task to Commodore **Oliver Hazard Perry**. After building a small fleet, Perry sailed out to meet the British on September 10, beginning the **Battle of Lake Erie**. The battle ended when the British surrendered. Perry sent a message to General William Henry Harrison: "We have met the enemy and they are ours." Perry's brilliant victory forced the British to withdraw, giving the U.S. Army control of the lake and new hope.

With American control of Lake Erie established, General Harrison marched his army into Canada. At the Battle of the Thames River in October 1813, he defeated a combined force of British troops and Native Americans. Harrison's victory ended British power in the Northwest. Tecumseh's death

FOCUS ON NORTH CAROLINA

The British invaded North Carolina at Ocracoke and Portsmouth in mid-1813. Although they won the initial battle, their plans for further attack were abandoned after an American ship escaped to New Bern with a warning.

THE IMPACT TODAY

Inspired by the Americans' strength at Fort McHenry, Francis Scott Key wrote the national anthem, "The Star-Spangled Banner."

during the fighting also dealt a blow to the British alliance with Native Americans in the region.

The Creek War

Meanwhile, war with American Indians erupted in the South. Creek Indians, angry at American settlers for pushing into their lands, took up arms in 1813. A large force attacked Fort Mims on the Alabama River, destroying the fort and killing close to 250 of its defenders. In response, the commander of the Tennessee militia, **Andrew Jackson**, gathered about 2,000 volunteers to move against the Creek nation.

In the spring of 1814 Jackson attacked the Creek along the Tallapoosa River in Alabama. Jackson's troops won this battle, the Battle of Horseshoe Bend. The **Treaty of Fort Jackson**, signed late in 1814, ended the Creek War and forced the Creek to give up millions of acres of their land.

READING CHECK **Comparing** What advantages did Great Britain and the United States have at the start of the war?

First Lady Saves Washington's Portrait

North Carolinian Dolley Madison refused to leave Washington, D.C., until a famous portrait of the first president was saved from the executive mansion.

Great Britain on the Offensive

Despite U.S. success on the western and southern frontiers, the situation in the East grew worse. After defeating France in April 1814, the British sent more troops to America.

British Attacks in the East

Now reinforced, the British attacked Washington, D.C. President Madison was forced to flee when the British broke through U.S. defenses. The British set fire to the White House, the Capitol, and other government buildings.

The British sailed on to Baltimore, Maryland, which was guarded by Fort McHenry. They shelled the fort for 25 hours. The Americans refused to surrender Fort McHenry. The British chose to retreat instead of continuing to fight.

The Battle of New Orleans

After the attack on Washington, the British moved against New Orleans. British commanders hoped to capture the city and thus take control of the Mississippi River.

Andrew Jackson commanded the U.S. forces around New Orleans. His troops were a mix of regular soldiers, including two battalions of free African Americans, a group of Choctaw Indians, state militia, and pirates led by Jean Lafitte.

The battle began on the morning of January 8, 1815. Some 5,300 British troops attacked Jackson's force of about 4,500. The British began marching toward the U.S. defenses, but they were caught on an open field. The British were cut down with frightening speed. More than 2,000 British soldiers were killed or wounded. The Americans, for their part, had suffered about 70 casualties. The **Battle of New Orleans** made Andrew Jackson a hero and was the last major conflict of the War of 1812.

READING CHECK **Finding Main Ideas** What happened at the Battle of New Orleans?

Effects of the War

Before the battle of New Orleans, a group of New England Federalists gathered secretly at Hartford, Connecticut. At the **Hartford Convention**, Federalists agreed to oppose the war and send delegates to meet with Congress. Before the delegates reached Washington, however, news arrived that the war had ended. Some critics now laughed at the Federalists, and the party lost much of its political power.

Slow communications at the time meant that neither the Federalists nor Jackson knew about the **Treaty of Ghent**. The treaty, which had been signed in Belgium on December 24, 1814, ended the War of 1812.

Though each nation returned the territory it had conquered, the fighting did have several **consequences**. The war produced feelings of patriotism in Americans for having stood up to the mighty British. Some even called it the second war for independence. The war also broke the power of many Native American groups. Finally, a lack of goods caused by the interruption in trade boosted American manufacturing.

ACADEMIC VOCABULARY
consequences the effects of a particular event or events

READING CHECK **Analyzing Information** What were the main effects of the War of 1812?

SUMMARY AND PREVIEW The War of 1812 showed Americans that the nation would survive. In the next chapter you will see how the United States continued to grow.

Section 4 Assessment

go.hrw.com
Online Quiz
KEYWORD: SC7 HP8

Reviewing Ideas, Terms, and People

1. a. **Identify** What losses did American forces face in the early battles of the War of 1812? What victories did they win?
   b. **Make Generalizations** What role did American Indians play in the war?
2. a. **Describe** What attacks did the British lead against American forces?
   b. **Evaluate** What do you think were the two most important battles of the war? Why?
3. a. **Identify** What was the purpose of the **Hartford Convention**?
   b. **Draw Conclusions** How did the United States benefit from the War of 1812?

Critical Thinking

4. **Comparing and Contrasting** Review your notes on the battle dates. Then compare and contrast the details of the major battles during the War of 1812 in a chart like this one.

Battle	Details (Winner, Location, Importance)

FOCUS ON WRITING

5. **Organizing Your Ideas** Reorder the items on your lists from least important to most important.

History and Geography

North Carolina in the Early 1800s

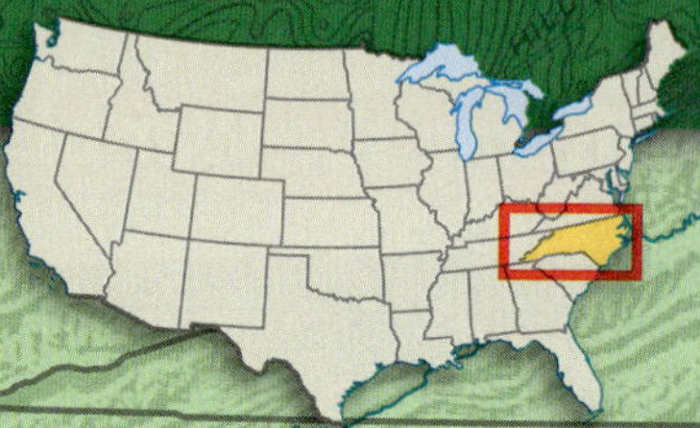

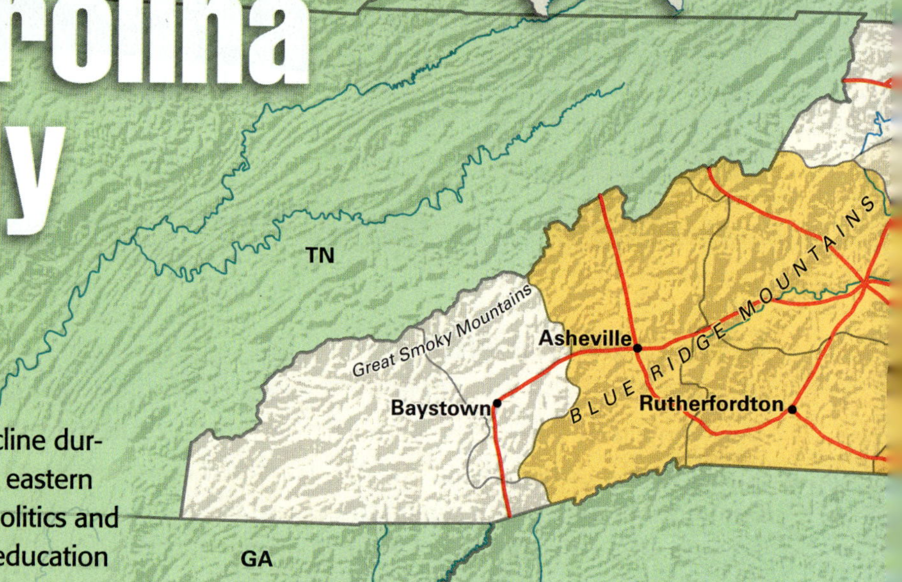

North Carolina experienced a period of decline during the early 1800s. Many leaders from the eastern parts of the state discouraged changes in politics and society, which resulted in little progress in education and transportation. In 1835, residents of the western part of the state finally succeeded in passing several constitutional amendments that helped balance the power between the east and the west. African Americans and Native Americans, however, lost rights in the new constitution, including the right to vote.

Causes and Effects of Stagnation

Causes

- Eastern counties held more power in the legislature, even though western counties had a higher population.
- Many leaders did not want to spend tax money on improvements.
- Free public education was not seen as a necessity.

Effects

- Western counties could not pass laws beneficial to their residents.
- Few roads, railroads, or canals were built, and many of the existing ones had tolls.
- People were unaware of new technologies that could lead to improvements.

Primary Source

"North Carolina is a State without . . . internal communication by rivers, roads, or canals; without a cash market for any article or agricultural product; without manufactures; in short without any object to which native industry and active enterprise could be directed."

—1830 Legislative Report

Indicators of Social Decline

Political Stagnation Eastern counties maintained tight control on the politics of the state, even though more people lived in the west than in the east. The needs of the two regions were different because the east had been settled earlier than the west.

Roads and Population in the Early 1800s

ANALYSIS SKILL **ANALYZING VISUALS**

1. **Place** Why were there fewer roads per capita in the west?
2. **Human-Environment Interaction** How did eastern counties maintain their political power?

Lack of Transportation The state legislature refused to raise taxes to pay for internal improvements such as roads and canals. Most roads and canals were privately owned.

Poor Education Leaders would not spend money on building schools or hiring teachers. Many children were needed to work on family farms, and few attended school for very long.

Social Studies Skills

Analysis | Critical Thinking | **Civic Participation** | Study

North Carolina Skills
4.04 Apply conflict resolutions.

Working in Groups to Solve Issues

Define the Skill

You already know that the decision-making process is more difficult in a group than it is if just one person makes the decisions. However, group decision-making becomes an even greater challenge when controversial issues are involved.

Group members must have additional skills for the group to function effectively when conflict exists within it. These include respect for differing views, the arts of persuasion and negotiation, and an ability to compromise. A group may not be able to find solutions to controversial problems unless its members have these skills.

Learn the Skill

Some of the biggest challenges Congress faced in the early 1800s were related to the war between Great Britain and France. Some Americans supported the British, while others favored the French. Both countries hoped for American help. When the United States would not take sides, they each began interfering with U.S. ships on the open seas.

As you read in this chapter, Congress tried to solve this problem by passing the Embargo Act. That solution was controversial, however. The northern states were hard hit by the law's ban on overseas trade. Their representatives in Congress demanded a less extreme action. The result was the Non-Intercourse Act. This law was a compromise between members who wanted to lift the trade ban and those who wanted to continue it. Congress was able to solve this problem because its members were able to work around their differences.

The skills Congress needed to reach its solution are valuable ones for any group that must make decisions involving controversial issues. They include the following attitudes and behaviors.

1. **Willingness to take a position.** If an issue is controversial, it is likely that group members will have differing opinions about it. You have a right to state your views and try to persuade others that you are correct.
2. **Willingness to listen to differing views.** Every other member has the same right you do. You have a duty to listen to their views, even if you do not agree. Disrespect for those whose views differ from yours makes it more difficult for the group to reach a solution.
3. **Willingness to debate.** Debate is a form of "healthy" argument because it defends and attacks ideas instead of the people who hold them. Debating the group's differences of opinion is an important step in reaching a solution.
4. **Willingness to negotiate and compromise.** If debate does not produce agreement, a compromise may be needed. Often it is better to have a solution that members may not like, but can accept, than to have no agreement at all.

Practice the Skill

Check your understanding of the skill by answering the following questions.

1. Why would refusing to listen to other members make group decision-making more difficult?
2. Why is compromise often a better solution than forcing a decision on members who disagree?

CHAPTER 8 Chapter Review

HOLT

History's Impact

▶ **video series**

Review the video to answer the closing question:

How do the background, value system, and character of the United States reflect its spirit of exploration?

Visual Summary

Use the visual summary below to help you review the main ideas of the chapter.

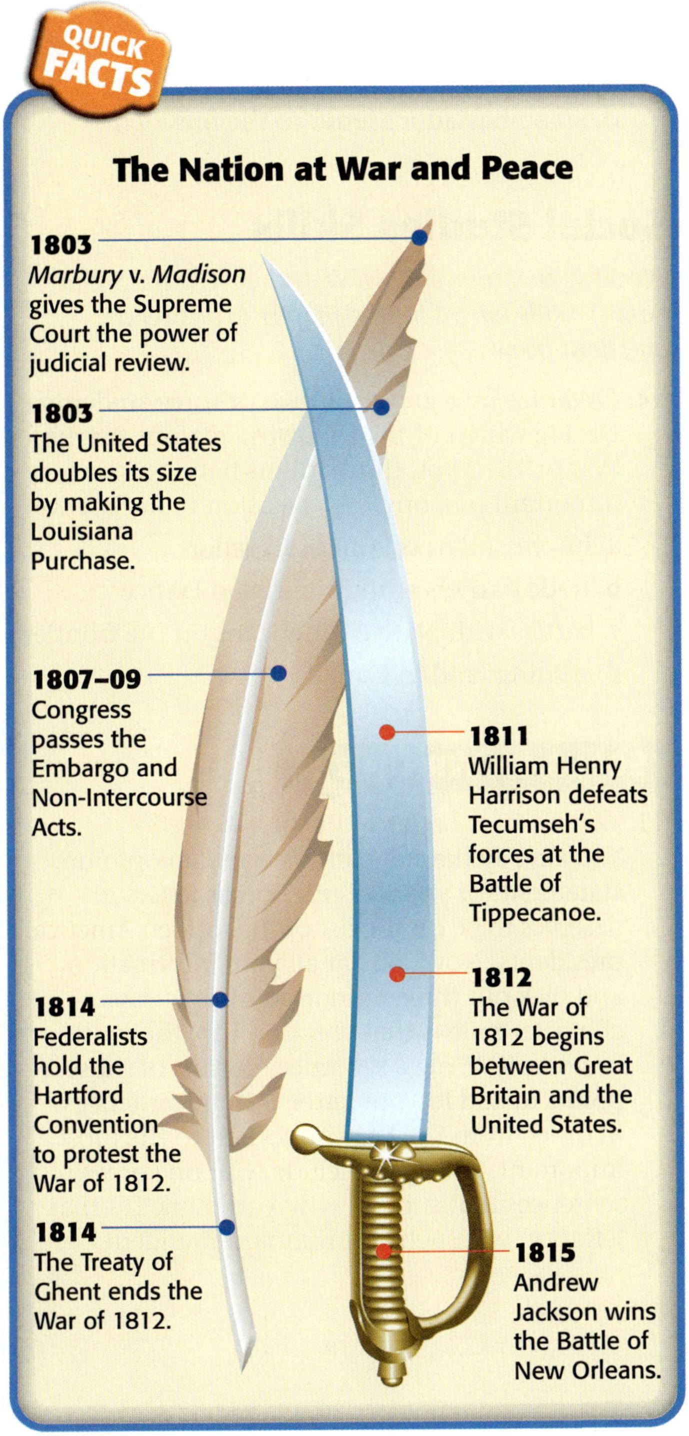

Reviewing Vocabulary, Terms, and People

Complete each sentence by filling in the blank with the correct term or person.

1. The War of 1812 ended soon after the U.S. victory over the British at the ____________.

2. After winning the election of 1800, __________ became the third president of the United States.

3. The power of the Supreme Court to declare acts of Congress unconstitutional is known as ____________.

4. After U.S. neutrality was violated, the United States issued an __________ against trade with foreign nations.

5. In 1803 Congress approved the _________, which added former French territory in the West to the United States.

Comprehension and Critical Thinking

SECTION 1 *(Pages 266–270)*

6. a. Recall What were the key issues in the election of 1800?

b. Analyze In what ways did *Marbury* v. *Madison* affect the power of the judicial branch?

c. Evaluate Which of Jefferson's new policies do you think was most important? Why?

SECTION 2 *(Pages 272–277)*

7. a. Describe What was the purpose of the Lewis and Clark expedition?

b. Draw Conclusions What are three ways in which the United States benefited from the Louisiana Purchase?

c. Evaluate Do you think that Napoléon made a wise decision when he sold Louisiana to the United States? Explain your answer.

SECTION 3 *(Pages 278–283)*

8. a. **Identify** What group led the call for war with Great Britain?

   b. **Contrast** What arguments were given in favor of war with Great Britain? What arguments were given against war with Britain?

   c. **Elaborate** In your opinion, why were the Embargo Act and the Non-Intercourse Act unsuccessful?

SECTION 4 *(Pages 284–287)*

9. a. **Identify** What role did Andrew Jackson play in the War of 1812?

   b. **Make Inferences** Why did the British want to capture the cities of Washington and New Orleans?

   c. **Predict** In what ways might the U.S. victory over Great Britain in the war affect the status of the United States in the world?

Reviewing Themes

10. **Geography** Through what geographic regions did the Lewis and Clark expedition travel?

11. **Politics** What impact did the Hartford Convention have on American politics?

Using the Internet

go.hrw.com
KEYWORD: SC7 CH8

12. **Activity: Journal Entry** Prior to Lewis and Clark's expedition, some thought that woolly mammoths, unicorns, and seven-foot-tall beavers lived in the uncharted West. The Corps of Discovery set off to find out the truth about this uncharted land. Its members also wanted to search for a Northwest Passage that would speed commerce and bring wealth to the young nation. Enter the activity keyword. Research the Web sites and take the point of view of one of the explorers. Write a series of journal entries outlining the thoughts, feelings, discoveries, and events surrounding the journey. Include drawings of what you might have seen in the West in your journal entries.

Reading Skills

Public Documents in History *Use the Reading Skills taught in this chapter to answer the question below.*

13. Which of the following is an example of a public document?

    a. the Constitution

    b. the current president's journal

    c. a tax return

    d. an ambassador's letter to the president

Social Studies Skills

Working in Groups to Solve Issues *Use the Social Studies Skills taught in this chapter to answer the questions below.*

14. Organize into groups of two or three students. Decide which of the following reasons for the War of 1812 you think might have been most important in Congress's decision to declare war.

    a. impressment of American sailors

    b. trade barriers with Britain and France

    c. battles with Native Americans on the frontier

    d. gaining land in Canada

FOCUS ON WRITING

15. **Writing Your Letter of Recommendation** You already have a main idea and an opinion statement for your letter: Thomas Jefferson deserves to be on the list of the top-ten American presidents. Now, look at all your information and pick out three or four points—actions or character traits—that you think are the most important. Write a sentence on each of those points to add to your letter. Put the sentences in order, from the least important to the most important. Finally, conclude with one or two sentences that sum up why you think Thomas Jefferson was such an important president.

CHAPTER 8

Standardized Test Practice

DIRECTIONS: ***Read each question and write the letter of the best response.***

1 The Supreme Court's decision in the 1803 case *Marbury* v. *Madison* is an example of

A checks and balances.

B reserved powers.

C delegated powers.

D dual sovereignty.

2 In the early 1800s North Carolina differed from the rest of the nation in that it

A opposed the annexation of the Louisiana Territory.

B had outlawed slavery.

C opposed the War of 1812.

D was experiencing a period of decline.

3 Why did President Jefferson agree to buy Louisiana from France?

A He wanted to learn more about the lands and peoples east of the Mississippi River.

B He believed that the United States would benefit from the purchase.

C He wanted to end the French threat in North America.

D He hoped to increase the president's constitutional powers.

4 One of the key causes of the War of 1812 was

A British support for Native Americans on the western frontier.

B boycotts of U.S. goods by British merchants.

C British attempts to settle lands in the Louisiana Territory.

D a refusal by the French to obey the Embargo Act.

5 The Lewis and Clark expedition was significant because it

A introduced the United States to valuable raw materials such as coal.

B improved America's knowledge of the West.

C led to U.S. settlement of the Southwest.

D opened trade between the United States and Native Americans in the West.

6 During the War of 1812, trade interruptions resulted in

A the repeal of the Embargo Act.

B a rise in unemployment.

C a decline in cotton production in the South.

D an increase in U.S. manufacturing.

7 Read the following passage from Thomas Jefferson's inaugural address and use it to answer the question below.

> "Though the will of the majority is in all cases to prevail, that will, to be rightful, must be reasonable . . . [T]he minority possess their equal rights, which equal laws must protect . . . Let us then, fellow citizens, unite with one heart and one mind . . . We have been called by different names brethren of the same principle. We are all republicans; we are all federalists."
>
> —President Thomas Jefferson, Inaugural Address, 1801

Document-Based Question **What did Jefferson mean in making this statement?**

CHAPTER 9 1812–1830

A New National Identity

North Carolina Standards

Social Studies Objectives

3.06 Describe and evaluate the geographic, economic, and social implications of the North Carolina Gold Rush.

3.07 Explain the reasons for the creation of a new State Constitution in 1835, and describe its impact on religious groups, African Americans, and American Indians.

Language Arts Objectives

4.02 Analyze and develop (with limited assistance) and apply appropriate criteria to evaluate the quality of the communication by:

- drawing conclusions based on evidence, reasons, or relevant information.

go.hrw.com
North Carolina
KEYWORD: SC7 NC

FOCUS ON WRITING

A Character Sketch Nations, like people, have characters. For example, a nation might be described as peaceful or aggressive, prosperous or struggling. In this chapter you'll read about the United States as a new nation with a new identity, or character. Then you'll write a paragraph describing that character.

UNITED STATES

1816 James Monroe is elected president.

1815

WORLD

1815 Napoléon returns to power in France but is defeated at the Battle of Waterloo.

HOLT

History's Impact

▶ **video series**

Watch the video to understand the impact of the United States on its neighbors.

What You Will Learn...

A modern mule team pulls a packet-boat full of passengers along the Erie Canal. Once the canal was completed, passengers and cargo could travel more easily between the Great Lakes region and the east coast. In this chapter you will learn how Americans built canals and roads to try to unite the rapidly growing young nation.

1820 The Missouri Compromise allows Maine and Missouri to become states.

1823 The Monroe Doctrine is issued.

1824 John Quincy Adams is elected president.

1820 — 1825 — 1830

The Granger Collection, New York

1821 Mexico and Peru gain their independence from Spain.

1824 Liberia is founded by freed American slaves.

1829 The Ottoman Empire recognizes the independence of Greece.

Reading Social Studies

by Kylene Beers

Economics | Geography | **Politics** | **Society and Culture** | Science and Technology

Focus on Themes This chapter is titled "A New National Identity" because it explains how the United States government established relations with European powers and how Americans developed a strong sense of national pride even as they struggled with important state issues. You will learn about the Monroe Doctrine, the Missouri Compromise, the Cumberland Road project, and the rise of American music, literature, and public schools—events that changed the country's **culture** and **politics**.

Bias and Historical Events

Focus on Reading As you read this chapter, you will find that some people supported the idea of using federal dollars to create new and better roads. Others, however, did not think federal dollars should be used that way. People who can only see one side of an issue or situation may become biased, or prejudiced against the opposite view.

Recognizing Bias To understand the events and people in history, you have to be able to recognize a speaker's or writer's bias. Here are some steps you can take to do that.

"The wickedest road, I do think, the hard-heartedest road, that ever [a] wheel rumbled upon."
Frances Anne (Kemble) Butler, Journal

1. The word *wickedest* is full of emotion.

2. She's a British actress—perhaps she didn't like the United States?

3. This information is based on her personal experience, and she is recording it in her own personal journal.

4. Most of this statement is opinion. Where are the facts about the actual condition of the road?

Steps to Recognize Bias

1. **Look at the words and images.** Are they emotionally charged? Do they present only one side or one point of view?
2. **Look at the writer.** What's the writer's background and what does that tell you about the writer's point of view?
3. **Look at the writer's sources.** Where does the writer get his or her information? Does the writer rely on sources who only support one point of view?
4. **Look at the information.** How much is fact and how much is opinion? Remember, facts can be proven. Opinions are personal beliefs—they can easily be biased.

You Try It!

The following passage is from the chapter you are getting ready to read. As you read the passage, think about living during the early to mid-1800s when there were no public schools.

Architecture and Education

From Chapter 9, p. 311

Americans also embraced educational progress. Several early American political leaders expressed a belief that democracy would only succeed in a country of educated and enlightened people. But there was no general agreement on who should provide that education.

Eventually, the idea of a state-funded public school gathered support. In 1837 Massachusetts lawmakers created a state board of education. Other states followed this example, and the number of public schools slowly grew.

After you read the passage, answer the following questions.

1. You are the editor of your town's newspaper in the year 1835. You think schools should be financed by the state government rather than the federal government. You decide to write an editorial to express your opinion. Which of the phrases below would reveal your personal bias to your readers? Why? What words in each statement create bias?

- **a.** Overbearing federal government
- **b.** Protecting state interests
- **c.** Powerful federal government
- **d.** Concerned state citizens

2. If you were going to write the editorial described in question 1, how could you avoid biased statements? How do you think this might affect people's reactions to your writing?

Key Terms and People

Chapter 9

Section 1

Rush-Bagot Agreement *(p. 298)*
Convention of 1818 *(p. 298)*
James Monroe *(p. 299)*
Adams-Onís Treaty *(p. 299)*
Simon Bolívar *(p. 300)*
Monroe Doctrine *(p. 300)*

Section 2

nationalism *(p. 302)*
Henry Clay *(p. 302)*
American System *(p. 302)*
Cumberland Road *(p. 303)*
Erie Canal *(p. 303)*
Era of Good Feelings *(p. 303)*
sectionalism *(p. 304)*
Missouri Compromise *(p. 305)*
John Quincy Adams *(p. 305)*

Section 3

Washington Irving *(p. 308)*
James Fenimore Cooper *(p. 309)*
Hudson River school *(p. 310)*
Thomas Cole *(p. 310)*
George Caleb Bingham *(p. 310)*

Academic Vocabulary

Success in school is related to knowing academic vocabulary—the words that are frequently used in school assignments and discussions. In this chapter, you will learn the following academic words:

circumstances *(p. 300)*
incentive *(p. 303)*

As you read Chapter 9, study the primary source documents carefully. Do you see any examples of bias?

SECTION 1

American Foreign Policy

What You Will Learn...

Main Ideas

1. The United States and Great Britain settled their disputes over boundaries and control of waterways.
2. The United States gained Florida in an agreement with Spain.
3. With the Monroe Doctrine, the United States strengthened its relationship with Latin America.

The Big Idea

The United States peacefully settled disputes with foreign powers.

Key Terms and People

Rush-Bagot Agreement, *p. 298*
Convention of 1818, *p. 298*
James Monroe, *p. 299*
Adams-Onís Treaty, *p. 299*
Simon Bolívar, *p. 300*
Monroe Doctrine, *p. 300*

TAKING NOTES Create a chart like the one below. As you read, take notes on the foreign policy issues the United States had to deal with between 1817 and 1823.

Foreign Policy Issues
•
•
•
•
•
•
•

If YOU were there...

You are a Spanish settler living in West Florida in 1820. Your family has lived in Florida for many years. Only a few years ago, people in Spanish Florida were furious when American soldiers occupied the town of Pensacola. Now you hear that Spain has signed a treaty with the United States—Florida is no longer Spanish territory but rather part of the United States.

How would you feel about living under a new government?

BUILDING BACKGROUND The War of 1812 left the United States stronger and more self-confident. The new nation had remained strong against a great European power. The United States then turned to diplomacy as a way to settle international issues.

Settling Disputes with Great Britain

The Treaty of Ghent had ended the War of 1812, yet there were issues left unresolved. The United States and British Canada both wanted to keep their navies and fishing rights on the Great Lakes. In the spring of 1817, the two sides compromised by establishing the **Rush-Bagot Agreement**, which limited naval power on the Great Lakes for both the United States and British Canada.

Another treaty with Britain gave the United States fishing rights off parts of the Newfoundland and Labrador coasts. This treaty, known as the **Convention of 1818**, also set the border between the United States and Canada at 49°N latitude as far west as the Rocky Mountains. Interest in the valuable fur trade in the Oregon Country was another issue resolved by this treaty. Both countries agreed to occupy the Pacific Northwest together, an agreement that would be tested in the years to come.

READING CHECK **Summarizing** What were the main disputes between the United States and Britain?

U.S. Boundary Changes, 1818–1819

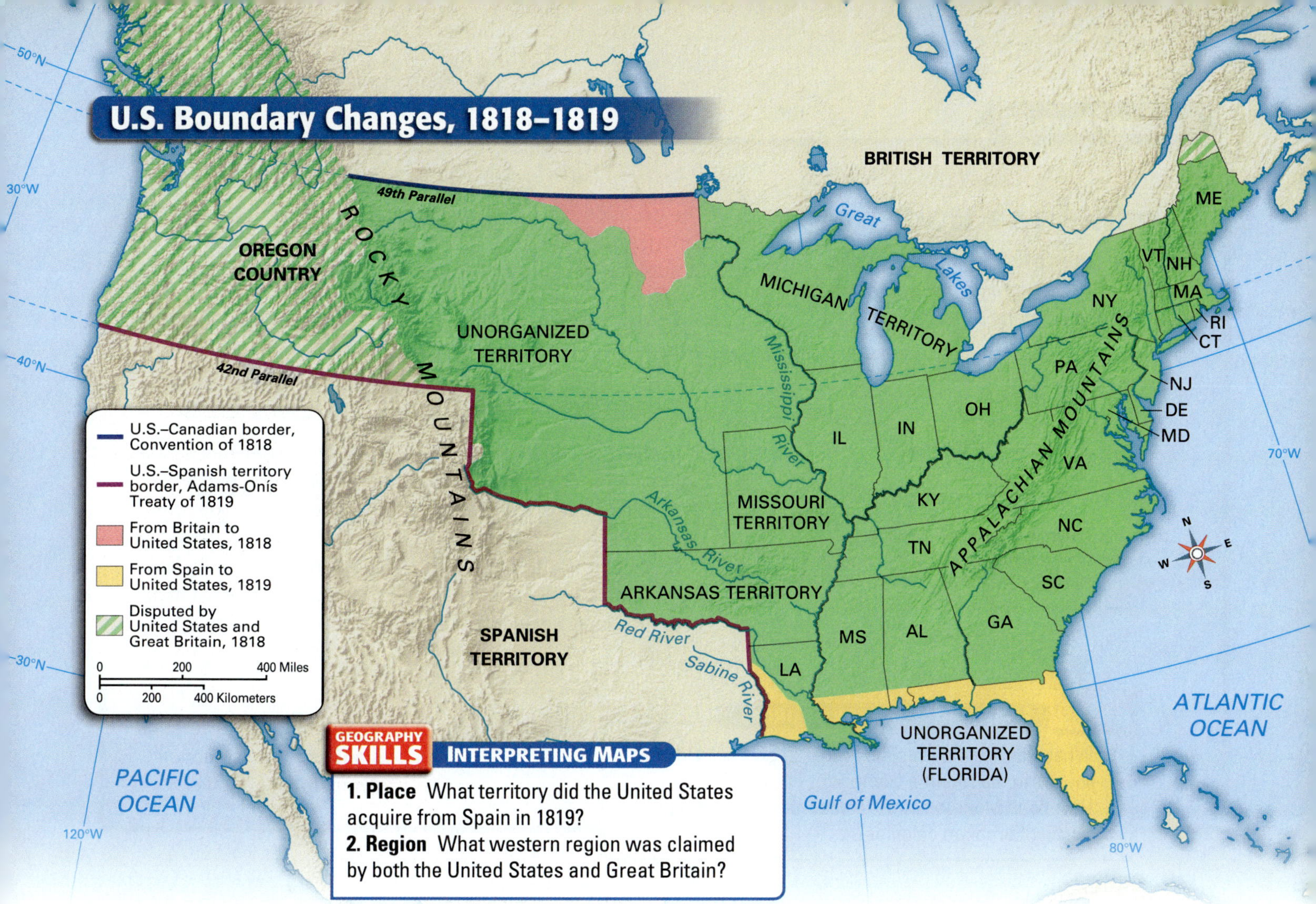

GEOGRAPHY SKILLS **INTERPRETING MAPS**

1. Place What territory did the United States acquire from Spain in 1819?

2. Region What western region was claimed by both the United States and Great Britain?

United States Gains Florida

The United States also had a dispute over its southern border with Spanish Florida. In 1818 Secretary of State John Quincy Adams, son of John and Abigail Adams, held talks with Spanish diplomat Luis de Onís about letting Americans settle in Florida. Meanwhile, President **James Monroe**, elected in 1816, had sent U.S. troops to secure the U.S.–Florida border. General Andrew Jackson led these soldiers.

At the same time, conflicts arose between the United States and the Seminole Indians of Florida. The Seminole often helped runaway slaves and sometimes raided U.S. settlements. In April 1818 Jackson's troops invaded Florida to capture Seminole raiders. This act began the First Seminole War. During the war Jackson took over most of Spain's important military posts. Then he overthrew the governor of Florida. He carried out these acts against Spain without receiving direct orders from President Monroe. Jackson's actions upset Spanish leaders. Most Americans, however, supported Jackson.

Jackson's presence in Florida convinced Spanish leaders to negotiate. In 1819 the two countries signed the **Adams-Onís Treaty**, which settled all border disputes between Spain and the United States. Under this treaty, Spain gave East Florida to the United States. In return, the United States gave up its claims to what is now Texas. U.S. leaders also agreed to pay up to $5 million of U.S. citizens' claims against Spain.

THE IMPACT TODAY

Florida was admitted as a U.S. state in 1845 and is now home to about 16 million people.

READING CHECK **Summarizing** How were the disagreements between the United States and Spanish Florida settled?

Primary Source

HISTORIC DOCUMENT

The Monroe Doctrine

President James Monroe established the foundation for U.S. foreign policy in Latin America in the Monroe Doctrine of 1823.

The occasion has been judged proper for asserting . . . that the American continents . . . are henceforth not to be considered as subjects for future colonization by any European powers . . .

The political system of the allied powers is essentially different . . . from that of America. We . . . declare that we should consider any attempt on their part to extend their system to any portion of this hemisphere as dangerous to our peace and safety . . .

In this phrase, Monroe warns European nations against trying to influence events in the Western Hemisphere.

With the existing colonies . . . we have not interfered and shall not interfere. But with the governments who have declared their independence and maintained it, and whose independence we have . . . acknowledged, we could not view any interposition[1] for the purpose of oppressing them . . . by any European power in any other light than as the manifestation[2] of an unfriendly disposition[3] toward the United States.

Monroe notes here the difference between existing colonies and newly independent countries.

[1] **interposition:** interference
[2] **manifestation:** evidence
[3] **disposition:** attitude

ANALYSIS SKILL **ANALYZING PRIMARY SOURCES**

1. What warning did President Monroe give to European powers in the Monroe Doctrine?
2. How does Monroe say the United States will treat existing European colonies?

Monroe Doctrine

Meanwhile, Spain had other problems. By the early 1820s most of the Spanish colonies in the Americas had declared independence. Revolutionary fighter **Simon Bolívar**, called the Liberator, led many of these struggles for independence. The political circumstances surrounding the revolutions reminded most American leaders of the American Revolution. As a result, they supported these struggles.

ACADEMIC VOCABULARY
circumstances surrounding situation

After Mexico broke free from Spain in 1821, President Monroe grew worried. He feared that rival European powers might try to take control of newly independent Latin American countries. He was also concerned about Russia's interest in the northwest coast of North America.

Secretary of State Adams shared President Monroe's concerns. In a Fourth of July speech before Congress, Adams said that the United States had always been friendly with European powers, and that the country did not want to be involved in wars with them. He implied that he supported the newly independent countries but said the United States would not fight their battles.

Great Britain was also interested in restraining the influence of other European nations in the Americas. This was because Britain had formed close trading ties with most of the independent Latin American countries. Britain wanted to issue a joint statement with the United States to warn the rest of Europe not to interfere in Latin America.

Instead, Secretary of State Adams and President Monroe decided to put together a document protecting American interests. The **Monroe Doctrine** was an exclusive statement of American policy warning European powers not to interfere with the Americas.

The doctrine was issued by the president on December 2, 1823, during his annual message to Congress.

The Monroe Doctrine had four basic points.

1. The United States would not interfere in the affairs of European nations.
2. The United States would recognize, and not interfere with, European colonies that already existed in North and South America.
3. The Western Hemisphere was to be off-limits to future colonization by any foreign power.
4. The United States would consider any European power's attempt to colonize or interfere with nations in the Western Hemisphere to be a hostile act.

Some Europeans strongly criticized the Monroe Doctrine, but few European countries challenged it. The doctrine has remained important to U.S. foreign policy. The United States has continued to consider Latin America within its sphere of influence—the area a nation claims some control over. At times, it has intervened in Latin American affairs when its own interests, such as national security, were at risk.

READING CHECK **Analyzing** What effect did the revolutions in Latin America have on U.S. foreign policy?

SUMMARY AND PREVIEW In this section you learned that U.S. foreign policy was characterized by both compromise and strong leadership in the years following the War of 1812. In the next section you will learn about the rising sense of national pride that developed as the United States grew and expanded.

Section 1 Assessment

go.hrw.com
Online Quiz
KEYWORD: SC7 HP9

Reviewing Ideas, Terms, and People

1. a. **Identify** What issues were settled between the United States and Great Britain in 1817 and 1818?
   b. **Make Inferences** Why would the United States and Britain agree to occupy the Pacific Northwest together?
   c. **Elaborate** Why were the **Rush-Bagot Agreement** and the **Convention of 1818** compromises?
2. a. **Recall** What problems existed between Spain and the United States?
   b. **Analyze** Why was the **Adams-Onís Treaty** important?
   c. **Evaluate** Do you think that Andrew Jackson was right to act without orders? Explain your answer.
3. a. **Describe** What did the **Monroe Doctrine** state?
   b. **Contrast** How did the Monroe Doctrine differ from Adams's Fourth of July Address?
   c. **Elaborate** What do you think the newly independent Latin American countries thought of the Monroe Doctrine?

Critical Thinking

4. **Identifying Cause and Effect** Review your notes regarding U.S. foreign policy issues. Create a new chart and, for each issue, identify the nations involved, the agreement or doctrine, and the effects.

Nations	Agreement/Doctrine	Issue	Effects

FOCUS ON WRITING

5. **Determining Relationships** One of the main ways you can learn about someone's character is by how he or she treats others. As you read this section, start a list of words and phrases that describe how the United States acted in relationships with other nations. For example, lists might include words and phrases like "willing to compromise" and "firm."

SECTION 2

Nationalism and Sectionalism

What You Will Learn...

Main Ideas

1. Growing nationalism led to improvements in the nation's transportation systems.
2. The Missouri Compromise settled an important regional conflict.
3. The outcome of the election of 1824 led to controversy.

The Big Idea

A rising sense of national unity allowed some regional differences to be set aside and national interests to be served.

Key Terms and People

nationalism, *p. 302*
Henry Clay, *p. 302*
American System, *p. 302*
Cumberland Road, *p. 303*
Erie Canal, *p. 303*
Era of Good Feelings, *p. 303*
sectionalism, *p. 304*
Missouri Compromise, *p. 305*
John Quincy Adams, *p. 305*

TAKING NOTES As you read, take notes on how each of the following contributed to national unity.

Roads and canals → National unity
Supreme Court cases → National unity
Missouri Compromise → National unity

If YOU were there...

You live near the western end of the newly completed Erie Canal in New York State in 1831. In fact, your older brothers helped build the canal. Every day you watch as mules pull the canal boats along the still water of the canal. Sometimes the boats carry passengers traveling from city to city. You have never been far from your home, and you are curious about their journey.

What would you like to ask the travelers on the canal boat?

BUILDING BACKGROUND Peace, prosperity, and a growing country gave Americans a sense of national unity. In practical terms, building roads and canals also helped unify the nation. They made travel easier, linking people from different regions of the country. Nevertheless, some regional conflicts continued.

Growing Nationalism

Pleased by successful negotiations with foreign powers, Americans enjoyed a rising sense of nationalism. **Nationalism** is feelings of pride and loyalty to a nation. This new national unity found a strong supporter in U.S. representative **Henry Clay** from Kentucky.

Clay believed that a strong national economy would promote national feeling and reduce regional conflicts. He developed a plan eventually known as the **American System** —a series of measures intended to make the United States economically self-sufficient. To build the economy, he pushed for a national bank that would provide a single currency, making interstate trade easier. Clay wanted the money from a protective tariff to be used to improve roads and canals. These internal improvements would unite the country.

Some members of Congress believed that the Constitution did not permit the federal government to spend money on internal improvements. Clay argued that the possible gains for the country justified federal action.

Roads and Canals

In the early 1800s most roads in the United States were made of dirt, making travel difficult. British actress Frances Kemble described one New York road she had struggled along during a visit in the 1830s.

> "The wickedest road, I do think, the cruellest, hard-heartedest road, that ever [a] wheel rumbled upon."
>
> —Frances Anne (Kemble) Butler, *Journal*

Congress agreed with Clay and, to improve the nation's roads, invested in road building. The **Cumberland Road** was the first road built by the federal government. It ran from Cumberland, Maryland, to Wheeling, a town on the Ohio River in present-day West Virginia. Construction began in 1815. Workers had to cut a 66-foot-wide band, sometimes through forest, to make way for the road. Then they had to use shovels and pickaxes to dig a 12- to 18-inch roadbed, which they filled with crushed stone. All of the work had to be done without the benefit of today's bulldozers and steamrollers.

By 1818 the road reached Wheeling. By 1833 the National Road, as the expansion was called, stretched to Columbus, Ohio. By 1850 it reached all the way to Illinois.

Meanwhile, Americans tried to make water transportation easier by building canals. One of the largest projects was the **Erie Canal**, which ran from Albany to Buffalo, New York.

Construction of the canal began in 1817 and was completed in 1825. Using shovels, British, German, and Irish immigrants dug the entire canal by hand. The canal cost millions of dollars, but it proved to be worth the expense. The Erie Canal allowed goods and people to move between towns on Lake Erie and New York City and the east coast. Its success served as an **incentive** for a canal-building boom across the country.

ACADEMIC VOCABULARY

incentive something that leads people to follow a certain course of action

Era of Good Feelings

From 1815 to 1825 the United States enjoyed the **Era of Good Feelings**, a time of peace, pride, and progress. The phrase was coined

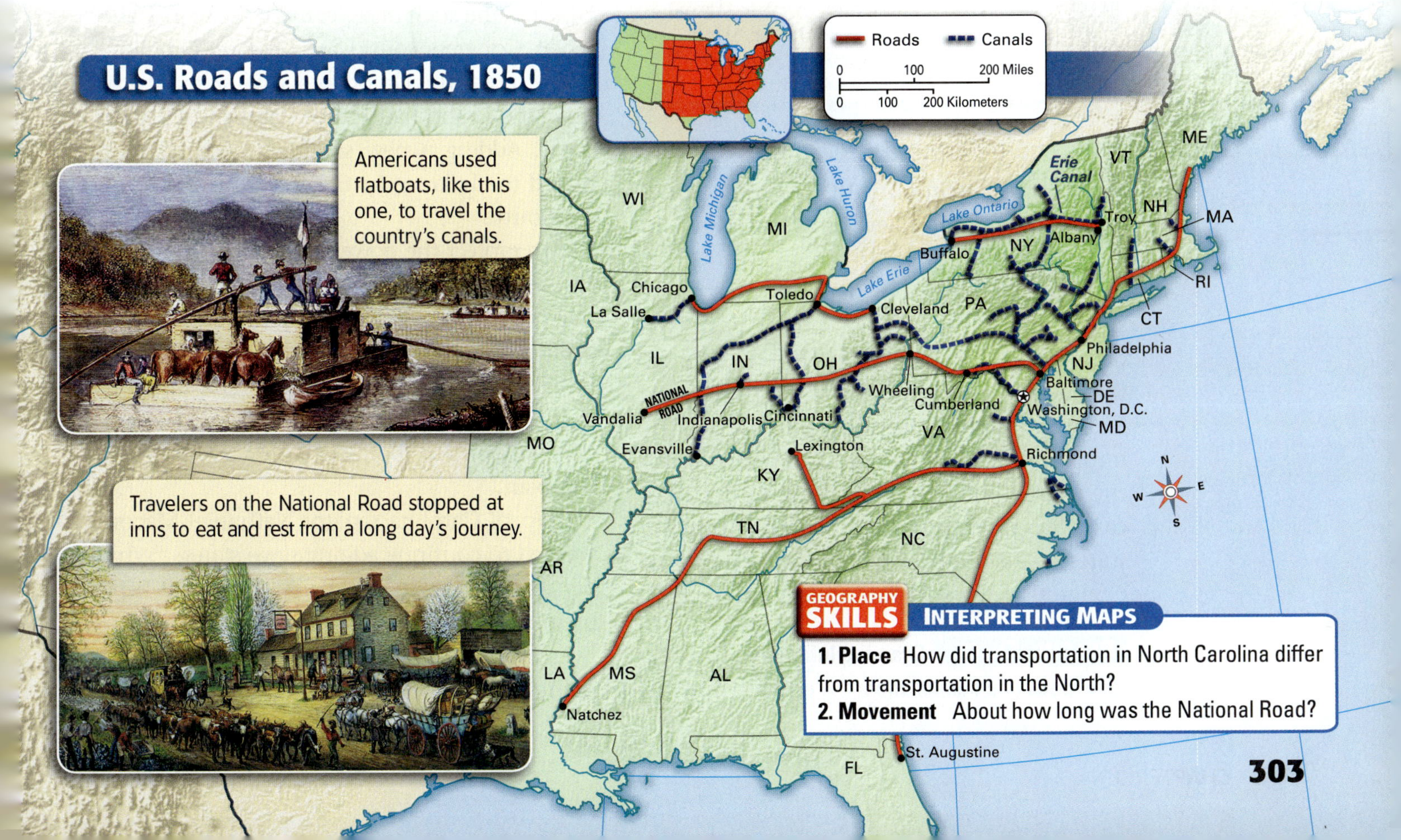

Americans used flatboats, like this one, to travel the country's canals.

Travelers on the National Road stopped at inns to eat and rest from a long day's journey.

GEOGRAPHY SKILLS **INTERPRETING MAPS**

1. **Place** How did transportation in North Carolina differ from transportation in the North?
2. **Movement** About how long was the National Road?

The Missouri Compromise, 1820

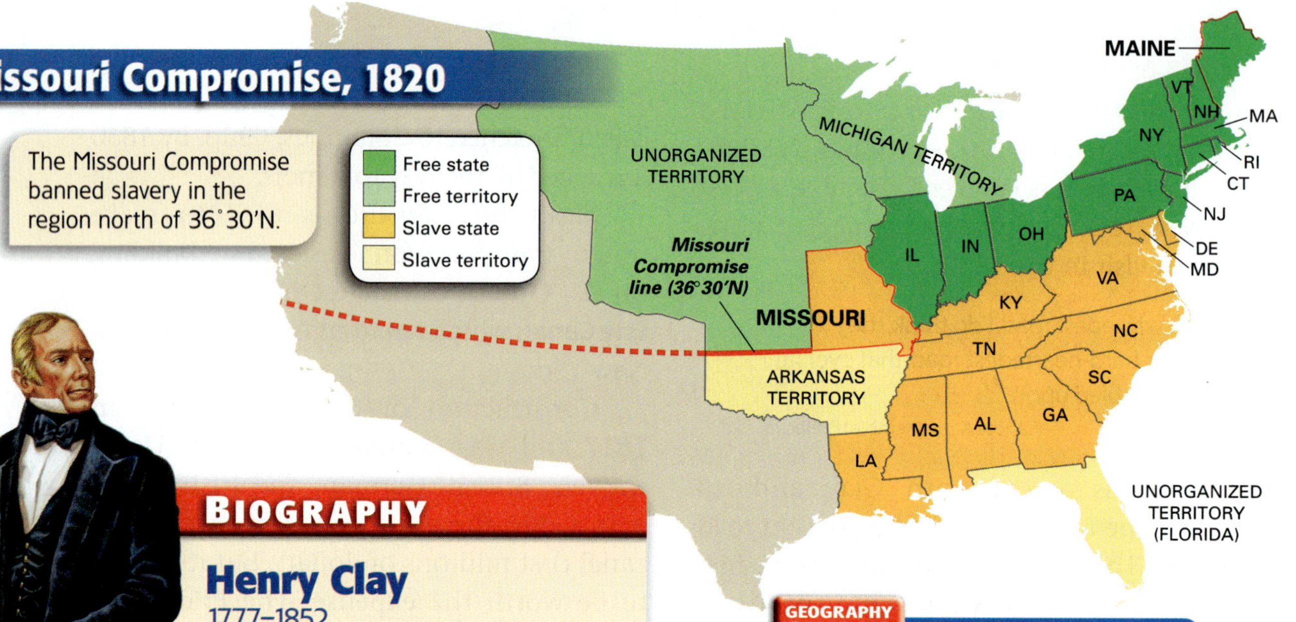

GEOGRAPHY SKILLS INTERPRETING MAPS

1. **Region** In which part of the country was slavery permitted?
2. **Human-Environment Interaction** Why did leaders choose 36° 30′ as the compromise line?

BIOGRAPHY

Henry Clay

1777–1852

Known as the silver-tongued Kentuckian, Henry Clay was a gifted speaker. He became involved in local politics early in his life, and by age 29 he was appointed to the U.S. Senate. Throughout his career in the Senate, he was dedicated to preserving the Union. The Missouri Compromise and a later agreement, the Compromise of 1850, helped to ease sectional tensions, at least temporarily.

Analyzing Why did Henry Clay work for compromises between regions?

by a Boston editor in 1817 during James Monroe's visit to New England early in his presidency.

The emphasis on national unity was strengthened by two Supreme Court case decisions that reinforced the power of the federal government. In the 1819 case *McCulloch* v. *Maryland*, the Court asserted the implied powers of Congress in allowing for the creation of a national bank. In the 1824 case *Gibbons* v. *Ogden*, the Court said that the states could not interfere with the power of Congress to regulate interstate commerce.

READING CHECK **Drawing Inferences** How did new roads and canals affect the economy?

Missouri Compromise

Even during the Era of Good Feelings, disagreements between the different regions—known as **sectionalism**—threatened the Union. One such disagreement arose in 1819 when Congress considered Missouri's application to enter the Union as a slave state. At the time, the Union had 11 free states and 11 slave states. Adding a new slave state would have tipped the balance in the Senate in favor of the South.

To protect the power of the free states, the House passed a special amendment. It declared that the United States would accept Missouri as a slave state, but importing enslaved Africans into Missouri would be illegal. The amendment also set free the children of Missouri slaves. Southern politicians angrily opposed this plan.

North Carolina senator Nathaniel Macon wanted to continue adding slave states. "Why depart from the good old way, which has kept us in quiet, peace, and harmony?" he asked. Eventually, the Senate rejected the amendment. Missouri was still not a state.

Henry Clay convinced Congress to agree to the **Missouri Compromise**, which settled the conflict that had arisen from Missouri's application for statehood. This compromise had three main conditions:

1. Missouri would enter the Union as a slave state.
2. Maine would join the Union as a free state, keeping the number of slave and free states equal.
3. Slavery would be prohibited in any new territories or states formed north of 36°30' latitude—Missouri's southern border.

Congress passed the Missouri Compromise in 1820. Despite the success of the compromise, there were still strong disagreements between the North and South over the expansion of slavery.

READING CHECK **Drawing Conclusions** Why did Henry Clay propose the Missouri Compromise to resolve the issue of Missouri statehood?

The Election of 1824

Soon, a presidential election also brought controversy. Andrew Jackson won the most popular votes in 1824. However, he did not have enough electoral votes to win office. Under the Constitution, the House of Representatives had to choose the winner. When the House chose **John Quincy Adams** as president, Jackson's supporters claimed that Adams had made a **corrupt bargain** with Henry Clay. These accusations grew after Adams chose Clay to be secretary of state. The controversy weakened Adams's support.

READING CHECK **Drawing Inferences** Why did Adams have weak support during his presidency?

SUMMARY AND PREVIEW Strong nationalistic feeling contributed to the development of America's politics and economy. In the next section you will read about the development of a new national culture.

FOCUS ON READING

How is the term **corrupt bargain** an example of semantic slanting?

FOCUS ON NORTH CAROLINA

Andrew Jackson's 1824 run for the presidency was encouraged by the People's Ticket of North Carolina, a group of Jackson's supporters who named him as their candidate.

Section 2 Assessment

go.hrw.com
Online Quiz
KEYWORD: SC7 HP9

Reviewing Ideas, Terms, and People

1. a. **Describe** What was the **Era of Good Feelings?**
   b. **Analyze** Explain the impact the *McCulloch* v. *Maryland* and *Gibbons* v. *Ogden* decisions had on the federal government.
   c. **Predict** How would transportation improvements eventually aid the economy of the United States?
2. a. **Recall** What role did **Henry Clay** play in the debate over Missouri's statehood?
   b. **Explain** What problem did Missouri's request for statehood cause?
   c. **Elaborate** Was the **Missouri Compromise** a good solution to the debate between free states and slave states? Explain your answer.
3. a. **Identify** Who were the candidates in the presidential election of 1824? How was the winner determined?
   b. **Draw Conclusions** Why did **John Quincy Adams** lose popular support following the election of 1824?

Critical Thinking

4. **Evaluating** Review your notes on nationalism during the Era of Good Feelings. Then copy the following graphic organizer, and use it to identify how threats to nationalism were resolved by the Missouri Compromise.

FOCUS ON WRITING

5. **Judging Self-Esteem** Another way you can tell about people's characters is by how they view themselves. Are they self-confident? Do they make healthy choices? As you read this section, think of the United States as a person and jot down notes about the view the United States had of itself. Is the new nation pleased with itself? Does it feel confident or confused?

History and Geography

The North Carolina Gold Rush

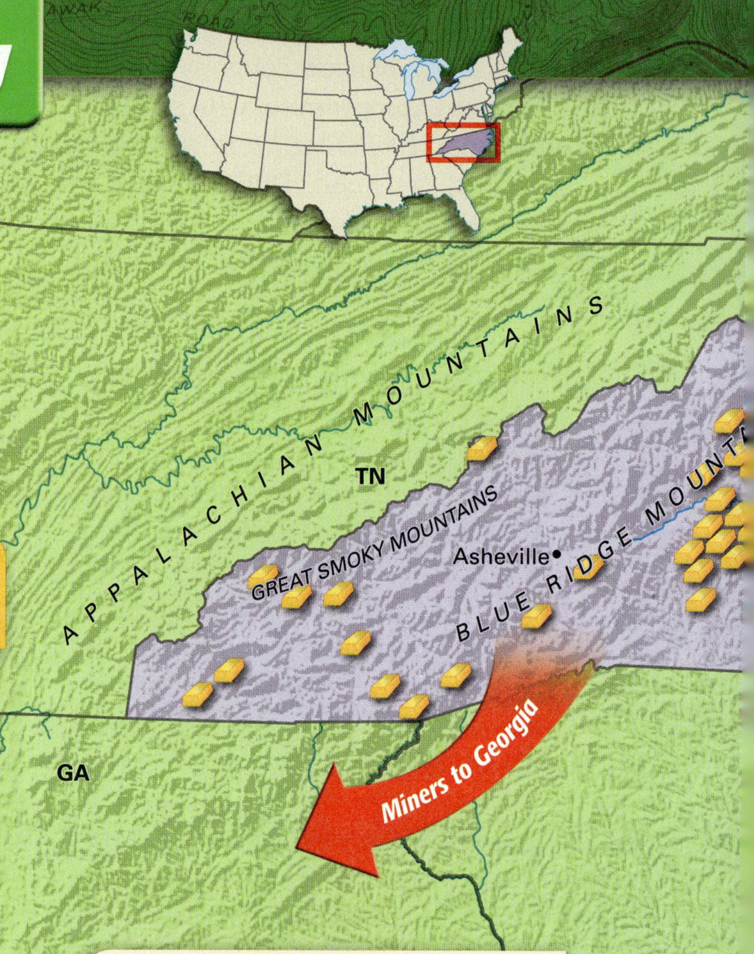

Twelve-year-old Conrad Reed of Cabarrus County helped shape the course of North Carolina history in 1799 when he brought home a large, shiny rock from a nearby creek. Several years later, his discovery led to the nation's first gold rush. The North Carolina gold rush brought many changes to the state. Gold from the state's many mines provided much-needed income. Local farmers turned to mining to support their families. Newcomers flocked to North Carolina, hoping to strike it rich.

End of the Gold Rush

By the late 1830s, many of North Carolina's gold deposits were depleted, forcing many miners to return to farming or to move on to newly discovered gold mines in Georgia.

Gold Mines

1. **In 1803 John Reed, Conrad's father, began digging for gold in the same creek where his son had discovered the valuable nugget. Soon Reed opened North Carolina's first gold mine, the Reed Gold Mine. The opening of gold mines attracted newcomers to North Carolina. Wealthy northerners invested in new mines while thousands of laborers, many from the North and from Europe, came in search of jobs and money.**

Miners dug shafts like this one at the Reed Gold Mine to extract gold deposits deep in the rock.

Gold Mines in North Carolina

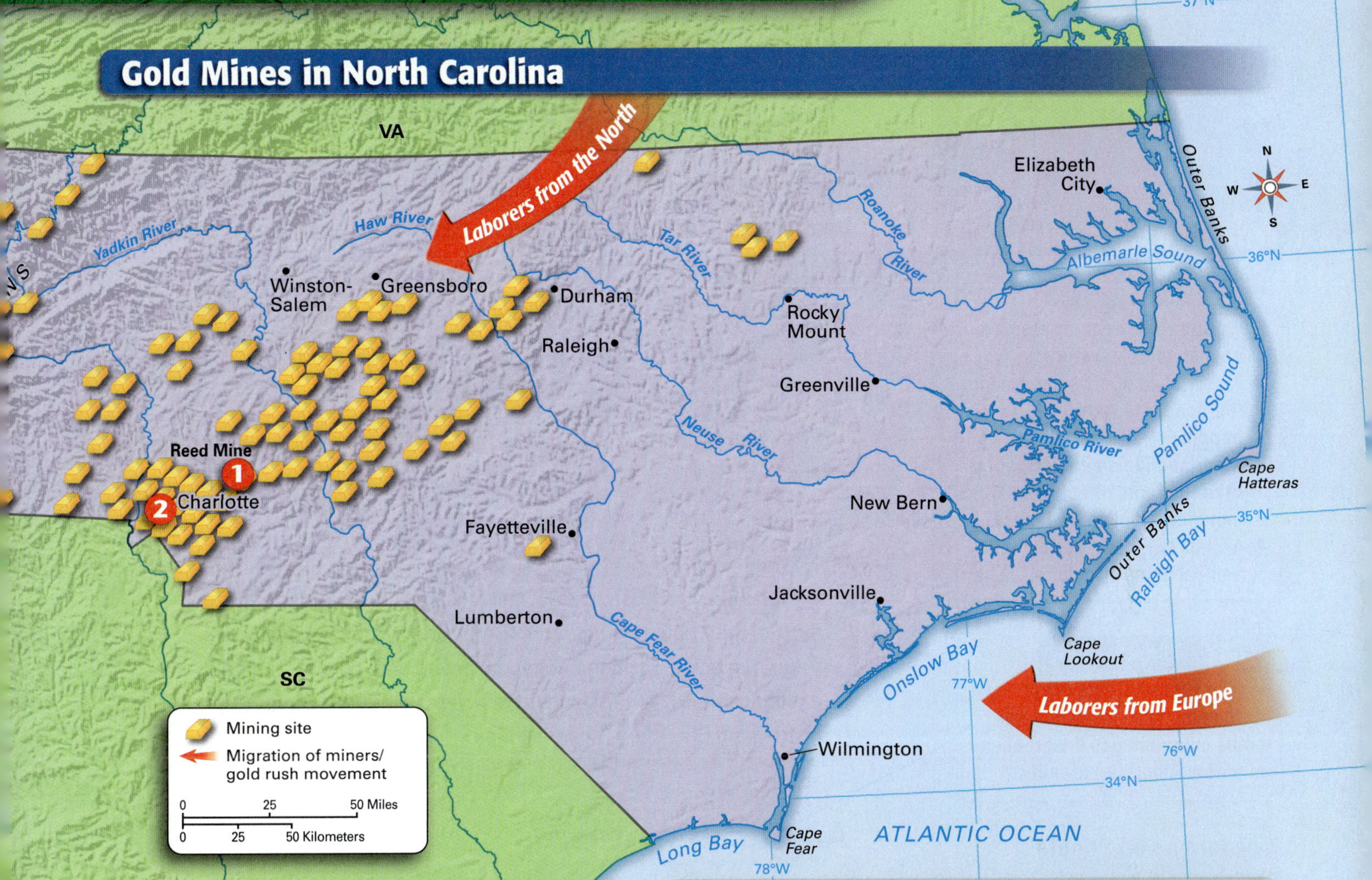

Gold Production, 1824–1837

Year	Number of Ounces	Value in Dollars
1824	242	5,000
1826	968	20,000
1828	2,225	46,000
1830	9,869	204,000
1832	22,158	458,000
1834	18,384	380,000
1836	7,165	148,000

Source: *Gold Mining in North Carolina*

2 Minting Gold In the 1830s two mints opened in North Carolina to coin the newfound gold. Beginning in 1831, Christopher Bechtler minted gold coins like those above at a private mint in Rutherfordton, and a branch of the U.S. Mint operated in Charlotte from 1837 to 1861.

ANALYSIS SKILL **ANALYZING VISUALS**

1. **Location** In what part of the state were most gold mines located?
2. **Movement** How did the North Carolina gold rush affect the movement of people in that state?

SECTION 3

American Culture

What You Will Learn...

Main Ideas

1. American writers created a new style of literature.
2. A new style of art showcased the beauty of America and its people.
3. American ideals influenced other aspects of culture, including religion and music.
4. Architecture and education were affected by cultural ideals.

The Big Idea

As the United States grew, developments in many cultural areas contributed to the creation of a new American identity.

Key Terms and People

Washington Irving, *p. 308*
James Fenimore Cooper, *p. 309*
Hudson River school, *p. 310*
Thomas Cole, *p. 310*
George Caleb Bingham, *p. 310*

TAKING NOTES As you read, take notes on the new developments in American culture in the 1820s and 1830s. Write your notes in a chart like the one below.

	Characteristics
Literature	
Visual arts	
Religious music	
Architecture	
Education	

If YOU were there...

You live in Philadelphia in 1830. Though you've lived in the city all your life, you dream about the West and the frontier. Now you've discovered a wonderful writer whose stories tell about frontier life and events in American history. You can't wait to read his next exciting adventure. You think that perhaps someday you could be a frontier hero, too.

Why would the frontier seem so exciting?

BUILDING BACKGROUND Until the early 1800s, Americans took most of their cultural ideas from Great Britain and Europe. But as American politics and the economy developed, so too did a new national culture. Writers and artists were inspired by American history and the American landscape.

American Writers

Like many people the world over, Americans expressed their thoughts and feelings in literature and art and sought spiritual comfort in religion and music. Developments in education and architecture also reflected the growing national identity.

One of the first American writers to gain international fame was **Washington Irving**. Born in 1783, he was named after George Washington. Irving's works often told about American

American Arts

Early to mid-1800s

American architects are inspired by ancient Greece and Rome.

history. Through a humorous form of writing called satire, Irving warned that Americans should learn from the past and be cautious about the future.

Irving shared this idea in one of his best-known short stories, "Rip Van Winkle." This story describes a man who falls asleep during the time of the American Revolution. He wakes up 20 years later to a society he does not recognize. Irving published this and another well-known tale, "The Legend of Sleepy Hollow," in an 1819–20 collection.

In some of his most popular works, Irving combined European influences with American settings and characters. His work served as a bridge between European literary traditions and a new type of writer who focused on authentically American characters and society.

Perhaps the best known of these new writers was **James Fenimore Cooper**. Cooper was born to a wealthy New Jersey family in 1789. Stories about the West and the Native Americans who lived on the frontier fascinated him. These subjects became the focus of his best-known works.

Cooper's first book was not very successful, but his next novel, *The Spy*, was a huge success. Published in 1821, it was an adventure story set during the American Revolution. It appealed to American readers' patriotism and desire for an exciting, action-filled story.

In 1823 Cooper published *The Pioneers*, the first of five novels featuring the heroic character Natty Bumppo. Cooper's novels told of settling the western frontier and included historical events. For example, his novel *The Last of the Mohicans* takes place during the French and Indian War. By placing fictional characters in a real historical setting, Cooper popularized a type of writing called historical fiction.

Some critics said that Cooper's characters were not interesting. They particularly criticized the women in his stories; one writer labeled them "flat as a prairie." Other authors of historical fiction, such as Catharine Maria Sedgwick, wrote about interesting heroines. Sedgwick's characters were inspired by the people of the Berkshire Hills region of Massachusetts, where she lived. Her works include *A New-England Tale* and *Hope Leslie*.

READING CHECK **Analyzing** How did American writers such as Irving and Cooper help create a new cultural identity in the United States?

A New Style of Art

The writings of Irving and Cooper inspired painters. These artists began to paint landscapes that showed the history of America and the beauty of the land. Earlier American painters had mainly painted portraits. By the

1827

John Audubon begins publishing *The Birds of America*, which is highly admired in England.

1830s the Hudson River school had emerged. The artists of the **Hudson River school** created paintings that reflected national pride and an appreciation of the American landscape. They took their name from the subject of many of their paintings—the Hudson River valley.

Landscape painter **Thomas Cole** was a founder of the Hudson River school. He had moved to the United States from Britain in 1819. He soon recognized the unique qualities of the American landscape. As his work gained fame, he encouraged other American artists to show the beauty of nature. "To walk with nature as a poet is the necessary condition of a perfect artist," Cole once said.

By the 1840s the style of American painting was changing. More artists were trying to combine images of the American landscape with scenes from people's daily lives. Painters like **George Caleb Bingham** and Alfred Jacob Miller travelled west to paint scenes of the American frontier, including trappers, traders, settlers, and Native Americans.

READING CHECK **Finding Main Ideas** How did the style of American art change to reflect the American way of life in the early 1800s?

Religion and Music

Through the early and mid-1800s, several waves of religious revivalism swept the United States. During periods of revivalism, meetings were held for the purpose of reawakening religious faith. These meetings sometimes lasted for days and included large sing-alongs.

At many revival meetings people sang songs called spirituals. Spirituals are a type of folk hymn found in both white and African American folk-music traditions. This type of song developed from the practice of calling out text from the Bible. A leader would call out the text one line at a time, and the congregation would sing the words using a familiar tune. Each singer added his or her own style to the tune. The congregation of singers sang freely as inspiration led them.

While spirituals reflected the religious nature of some Americans, popular folk music of the period reflected the unique views of the growing nation in a different way. One of the most popular songs of the era was "Hunters of Kentucky," which celebrated the Battle of New Orleans. It became an anthem for the spirit of nationalism in the United States and was used successfully in Andrew Jackson's campaign for the presidency in 1828.

READING CHECK **Summarizing** How did music reflect American interests in the early to mid-1800s?

Architecture and Education

American creativity extended to the way in which people designed buildings. Before the American Revolution, most architects followed the style used in Great Britain. After the

American Arts (continued)

1828

Noah Webster publishes his first dictionary of American—not British—English.

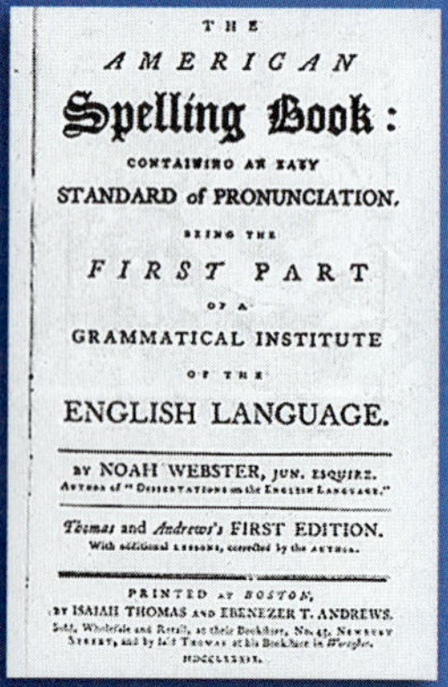
THE AMERICAN Spelling Book: CONTAINING AN EASY STANDARD of PRONUNCIATION. BEING THE FIRST PART OF A GRAMMATICAL INSTITUTE OF THE ENGLISH LANGUAGE.

BY NOAH WEBSTER, JUN. ESQUIRE.

Thomas and Andrews's FIRST EDITION.

PRINTED AT BOSTON, BY ISAIAH THOMAS AND EBENEZER T. ANDREWS.

1830

George Catlin travels widely to paint images of Native American ways of life before they are lost.

1836

Painters of the Hudson River school prove American landscapes are worthy of art. (Thomas Cole's *The Oxbow,* 1836)

Revolution, leaders such as Thomas Jefferson called for Americans to model their architecture after the styles used in ancient Greece and Rome. Many Americans admired the ancient civilization of Greece and the Roman Republic because they contained some of the same democratic and republican ideals as the new American nation did.

As time went by, more architects followed Jefferson's ideas. Growing American cities soon had distinctive new buildings designed in the Greek and Roman styles. These buildings were usually made of marble or other stone and featured large, stately columns.

Americans also embraced educational progress. Several early American political leaders expressed a belief that democracy would only succeed in a country of educated and enlightened people. But there was no general agreement on who should provide that education.

Eventually, the idea of a state-funded public school gathered support. In 1837 Massachusetts lawmakers created a state board of education. Other states followed this example, and the number of public schools slowly grew.

READING CHECK **Identifying Points of View**
Why did some Americans call for new architectural styles and more education after the American Revolution?

ANALYSIS SKILL **ANALYZING INFORMATION**

How do these artistic developments show Americans' increasing sense of identity?

SUMMARY AND PREVIEW As the United States grew, so did a unique national identity. In Chapter 10 you will read about the changing face of American democracy.

Section 3 Assessment

go.hrw.com
Online Quiz
KEYWORD: SC7 HP9

Reviewing Ideas, Terms, and People

1. **a. Describe** What topics interested American writers in the early 1800s?
   b. Draw Conclusions Why is **Washington Irving** considered an important American writer?
2. **a. Identify** What influence did **Thomas Cole** have on American painters?
   b. Describe How did American painting styles change from the early period to the mid-1800s?
3. **a. Describe** What effect did religious revivalism have on American music?
   b. Elaborate Why do you think folk songs like "Hunters of Kentucky" were popular?
4. **a. Identify** On what historical examples did many American architects model their buildings?
   b. Predict What might be some possible results of the growing interest in education in the United States?

Critical Thinking

5. **Categorizing** Review your notes about new developments in American culture. Copy the graphic organizer below and use it to show how these cultural developments reflected a new American identity.

Cultural Development → New Identity
Cultural Development → New Identity
Cultural Development → New Identity
Cultural Development → New Identity
Cultural Development → New Identity

FOCUS ON WRITING

6. **Identifying Values** You can tell much about someone's values by what that person makes. For instance, you could guess that a person who creates a collage of personal mementos for a friend's birthday is creative and values personal relationships. As you read this section, make note of what the United States created and what it valued.

Literature of the American Frontier

from *The Last of the Mohicans*

by James Fenimore Cooper (1789–1851)

About the Reading The Last of the Mohicans *is one of five novels known as the* Leatherstocking Tales. *These novels follow the life and adventures of American pioneer Natty Bumppo (also known as Leatherstocking, Hawkeye, and the Deerslayer). Bumppo is the perfect woodsman: resourceful, honest, kind to both his friends and his enemies, but always a loner at heart.*

AS YOU READ **Try to imagine what Natty Bumppo looks like.**

On that day, two men were lingering on the banks of a small but rapid stream . . . While one of these loiterers showed the red skin and wild accoutrements of a native of the woods, the other exhibited, through the mask of his rude and nearly savage equipments, the brighter though sunburnt and long-faded complexion of one who might claim descent from a European parentage. ❶

The frame of the white man, judging by such parts as were not concealed by his clothes, was like that of one who had known hardships and exertion from his earliest youth. His person, though muscular, was rather attenuated than full; but every nerve and muscle appeared strung and indurated by unremitted exposure and toil. He wore a hunting shirt of forest green, fringed with faded yellow, and a summer cap of skins which had been shorn of their fur. He also bore a knife in a girdle of wampum, ❷ like that which confined the scanty garments of the Indian, but no tomahawk. His moccasins were ornamented after the . . . fashion of the natives, while the only part of his underdress which appeared below the hunting frock was a pair of buckskin leggings that laced at the sides, and which were gartered above the knees with the sinews of a deer. A pouch and horn completed his personal accoutrements, though a rifle of great length, which the theory of the more ingenious whites had taught them was the most dangerous of all firearms, leaned against a neighboring sapling.

GUIDED READING

WORD HELP

accoutrements dress and gear
rude crude, rough
attenuated made thin
indurated hardened
unremitted ongoing
gartered fastened
ingenious clever

❶ ***What do you learn about Natty Bumppo in the first paragraph?***

❷ A "girdle of wampum" is a belt strung with beads. Wampum were used by Native Americans for both money and decoration.

Make a list of the items Bumppo wears and carries. What does each item suggest about him?

from *The Legend of Sleepy Hollow*

by Washington Irving (1783–1859)

About the Reading *"The Legend of Sleepy Hollow" has been called one of the first American short stories. Even though it is based on an old German folktale, its setting, a small village in the Hudson River valley, is American through and through. Irving's knack for capturing the look and the feel of the region made the story instantly popular—as did the tale's eerie central character, a horseman without a head.*

AS YOU READ **Try to picture both the ghost and the setting.**

The dominant spirit, however, that haunts this enchanted region, and seems to be commander in chief of all the powers of the air, is the apparition of a figure on horseback without a head. It is said by some to be the ghost of a Hessian trooper, ❶ whose head had been carried away by a cannon ball, in some nameless battle during the revolutionary war, and who is ever and anon seen by the country folk, hurrying along in the gloom of night, as if on the wings of the wind. His haunts are not confined to the valley, but extend at times to the adjacent roads, and especially to the vicinity of a church at no great distance. Indeed, certain of the most authentic historians of those parts, who have been careful in collecting and collating the floating facts concerning this spectre, allege, that the body of the trooper having been buried in the church yard, the ghost rides forth to the scene of battle in nightly quest of his head, ❷ and that the rushing speed with which he sometimes passes along the hollow, like a midnight blast, is owing to his being belated, and in a hurry to get back to the church yard before day break.

Such is the general purport of this legendary superstition, which has furnished materials for many a wild story in that region of shadows; and the spectre is known, at all the country firesides, by the name of The Headless Horseman of Sleepy Hollow. ❸

GUIDED READING

WORD HELP

dominant prevailing; ruling
apparition a ghostlike form that appears suddenly
collating comparing
spectre ghost
allege to firmly state
purport sense; gist

❶ A Hessian trooper is a German mercenary soldier from the American Revolution.

How and when is the horseman said to have died?

❷ ***Why does the horseman ride forth each night?***

❸ ***What is happening "at all the country firesides"? What does this suggest about how early Americans entertained themselves?***

CONNECTING LITERATURE TO HISTORY

1. **Drawing Inferences** The writing of the period reflects a new national culture and identity. What do these passages suggest about the thoughts, feelings, or lives of early Americans?
2. **Making Predictions** *The Last of the Mohicans* takes place during the French and Indian War. Whose side do you think Natty Bumppo would most likely take—that of the French and Indians, that of the English, or neither? Explain.
3. **Drawing Conclusions** Both of these stories were very popular in their time. Why do you think these stories were so popular? What is it about the stories that makes them entertaining?

North Carolina Skills
1.02 Summarize to select main ideas.

Identifying Central Issues

Define the Skill

The reasons for historical events are often complex and difficult to determine. An accurate understanding of them requires the ability to identify the central issues involved. A *central issue* is the main topic of concern in a discussion or dispute. In history, these issues are usually matters of public debate or concern. They generally involve political, social, moral, economic, or territorial matters.

Being able to identify central issues lets you go beyond what the participants in an event said and gain a more accurate understanding of it. The skill is also useful for understanding issues today, and for evaluating the statements of those involved.

Learn the Skill

In this chapter you learned about the dispute that arose over Missouri's admission to the Union. Yet that was not what this controversy was really about. Recognizing the central issue in this dispute helps you understand why each side fought so hard over just one state.

Use the following steps to identify central issues when you read about historical events.

1. Identify the main subject of the information.
2. Determine the nature and purpose of what you are reading. Is it a primary source or a secondary one? Why has the information been provided?
3. Find the strongest or most forceful phrases or statements in the material. These are often clues to the issues or ideas the speaker or writer thinks most central or important.
4. Determine how the information might be connected to the major events or controversies that were concerning the nation at the time.

Practice the Skill

Soon after the Missouri Compromise passed, Secretary of State John Quincy Adams wrote:

> "The impression produced upon my mind by the progress of this discussion [the dispute over Missouri] is that the bargain between freedom and slavery contained in the Constitution . . . is morally and politically vicious, . . . cruel and oppressive. . . . I have favored this Missouri Compromise, believing it to be all that can be effected [accomplished] under the present Constitution, and from an extreme unwillingness to put the Union at hazard [risk]. But perhaps it would have been a . . . bolder course to have persisted in the restriction upon Missouri till it should have terminated [ended] in a convention of the states to . . . amend the Constitution. This would have produced a new Union of thirteen or fourteen states unpolluted with slavery . . . If the Union must be dissolved, slavery is precisely the question upon which it ought to break. For the present, however, this contest [issue] is laid to sleep."

Apply the steps to identifying central issues to analyze Adams's statement and answer the following questions:

1. About what subject was Adams writing? What was his reason for making these remarks?
2. What did Adams believe was the most important issue in the dispute? What strong language does he use to indicate this?
3. What evidence suggests Adams did not think the breakup of the Union the central issue?

CHAPTER 9

Chapter Review

History's Impact
▶ **video series**
Review the video to answer the closing question:
How did the Roosevelt Corollary change the Monroe Doctrine?

Visual Summary

QUICK FACTS

Use the visual summary below to help you review the main ideas of the chapter.

Reviewing Vocabulary, Terms, and People

Match the word in the left column with the correct definition in the right column.

1. American System
2. George Caleb Bingham
3. Simon Bolívar
4. Henry Clay
5. Erie Canal
6. Hudson River school
7. James Monroe
8. Monroe Doctrine
9. nationalism
10. Rush-Bagot Agreement

a. an agreement that limited naval power on the Great Lakes for both the United States and British Canada
b. American artist known for his focus on the American landscape and people
c. sense of pride and devotion to a nation
d. a group of American artists in the mid-1800s who focused on the American landscape
e. a leader of independence movements in Latin America, known as the Liberator
f. the plan to raise tariffs in order to finance internal improvements such as roads and canals
g. president who promoted the acquisition of Florida, closer ties to Latin America, and presided during the Era of Good Feelings
h. project that connected the Hudson River to Lake Erie and improved trade and transportation
i. representative from Kentucky who promoted improvements in transportation and the Missouri Compromise
j. U.S. declaration that any attempt by a foreign nation to establish colonies in the Americas would be viewed as a hostile act

Comprehension and Critical Thinking

SECTION 1 *(Pages 298–301)*

11. a. Identify What were the four main points of the Monroe Doctrine?

b. Draw Conclusions How did the United States compromise in its disputes with British Canada?

c. Evaluate Which of the issues that the United States faced with foreign nations do you think was most important? Why?

SECTION 2 *(Pages 302–305)*

12. a. Recall What developments helped strengthen national unity in this period?

b. Analyze How was the disagreement over Missouri's statehood an example of sectionalism? How was the disagreement resolved?

c. Predict What effect might the election of 1824 have on national unity? Why?

SECTION 3 *(Pages 308–311)*

13. a. Describe How did popular music show the interests of Americans in the early 1800s?

b. Make Inferences Why do you think new American styles of art and literature emerged?

c. Elaborate Which element of American culture of the early 1800s do you find most appealing? Why?

Reviewing Themes

14. Politics How did the relations of the United States with foreign nations lead to a rise in nationalism?

15. Society and Culture What led to the creation of a uniquely American culture?

Using the Internet

go.hrw.com
KEYWORD: SC7 CH9

16. Activity: Researching In this chapter, you learned about the development of a new, creative spirit in American arts. Artists created works that featured American scenes and characters. Enter the activity keyword and research the development of American culture in art and literature. Then create a visual display.

Reading Skills

Bias and Historical Events *Use the Reading Skills taught in this chapter to answer the question about the reading selection below.*

> When the House chose John Quincy Adams as president, Jackson's supporters claimed that Adams had made a corrupt bargain with Henry Clay. These accusations grew after Adams chose Clay to be secretary of state. *(p. 305)*

17. Which of the following used a biased definition, according to the above selection?

a. Andrew Jackson

b. supporters of Jackson

c. Henry Clay

d. John Quincy Adams

Social Studies Skills

Identifying Central Issues *Use the Social Studies Skills taught in this chapter to answer the question about the reading selection below.*

> [Henry Clay] developed a plan that came to be known as the American System—a series of measures intended to make the United States economically self-sufficient. To build the economy, he pushed for a national bank that would provide a single currency, making interstate trade easier. Clay wanted the money from a protective tariff to be used to improve roads and canals. *(p. 302)*

18. Which of the following is the central issue addressed by the American System?

a. economic unity

b. protective tariff

c. national bank

d. improving roads and canals

FOCUS ON WRITING

19. Writing a Character Sketch Write a paragraph describing your overall impression of the nation's character. Write one sentence describing each of these aspects of the United States: its relationships with others, its feelings about itself, and its values.

CHAPTER 9

Standardized Test Practice

DIRECTIONS: Read each question and write the letter of the best response.

1 Use the map below to answer the following question.

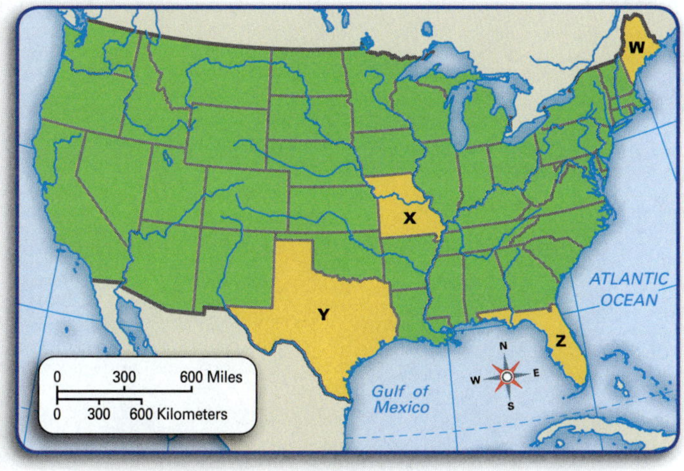

The present-day state that became part of the United States in the Adams-Onís Treaty of 1819 is shown on the map by the letter

A W.

B X.

C Y.

D Z.

2 The principle that European nations could establish no more colonies in North and South America was set forth in the

A Missouri Compromise.

B Rush-Bagot Agreement.

C Monroe Doctrine.

D Convention of 1818.

3 The Missouri Compromise had a significant effect on the United States because it

A established the present border with Canada.

B prohibited slavery north of Missouri's southern border.

C led to the expansion of roads and canals.

D settled conflicts between Native Americans in the West and the federal government.

4 Which of the following *most likely* explains why farmers often became part-time miners during the North Carolina gold rush?

A They hoped to be the first to discover gold in North Carolina.

B There were no valuable crops to grow during much of the year.

C Mining was an easier job than farming.

D They hoped to supplement their farming income with income from gold mining.

5 Which painting would have been typical of an artist of the Hudson River school in the 1830s and 1840s?

A a portrait of a famous American

B a Native American hunting game

C a portrait of an ancient Greek or Roman lawmaker

D a scene showing America's natural beauty

6 Examine the following passage from a letter about American education and then use it to answer the question below.

> "A lady asked me one day, 'What state is Virginia in?' Another asked, 'Is Canada in Kentucky?' Another supposed that 'Joe Graphy [geography] was very hard to learn.' Such is the cause of all our mistakes in religion, morals, and politics. When we are educated we can cast off prejudice and superstition. Education improves our judgments and restrains our passions. In short, it enables us to discover what is best for our welfare."
>
> —Anne Newport Royall, adapted from *Letters from Alabama, 1817-1822*

Document-Based Question Why might Royall and others try to make education available to more Americans? Explain.

CHAPTER 10 1828–1840

The Age of Jackson

North Carolina Standards

Social Studies Objectives

3.05 Compare and contrast different perspectives among North Carolinians on the national policy of Removal and Resettlement of American Indian populations.

3.07 Explain the reasons for the creation of a new State Constitution in 1835, and describe its impact on religious groups, African Americans, and American Indians.

9.02 Identify past and present state and local leaders from diverse cultural backgrounds and assess their influence in effecting change.

Language Arts Objectives

1.02 Interact in group activities and/or seminars in which the student:

- shares personal reactions to questions raised.

3.02 Continue to explore and analyze the use of the problem-solution process by:

- evaluating problems and solutions within various texts and situations.
- utilizing the problem-solution process within various contexts/situations.

go.hrw.com
North Carolina
KEYWORD: SC7 NC

FOCUS ON WRITING

An Interview You are a reporter for a large city newspaper in the year 1837. Andrew Jackson has just left office, and you have been given the assignment of interviewing him about his presidency and his role in American politics. As you read this chapter, you will write interview questions for your interview with Jackson.

UNITED STATES

1828
Andrew Jackson is elected president.

Sequoya finishes a written language for the Cherokee.

1830

WORLD

1829
Louis Braille publishes a reading system for the blind.

HOLT

History's Impact

▶ **video series**

Watch the video to understand the impact of Native American reservations.

What You Will Learn...

In this chapter you will learn about how President Andrew Jackson helped shape the United States. He was so influential that historians refer to his presidency as the Age of Jackson. This statue of Jackson has stood in Washington, D.C., for more than 150 years and captures the drive and spirit of the seventh president of the United States.

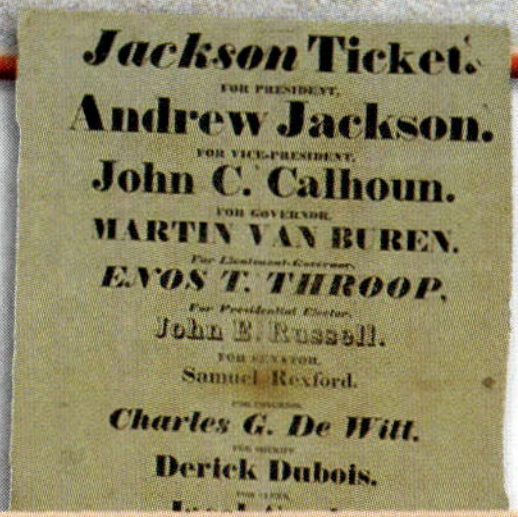

1832 Andrew Jackson vetoes the charter renewal of the national Bank of the United States.

1836 Martin Van Buren is elected president.

1838 The Trail of Tears begins when U.S. troops remove the Cherokee from Georgia.

1835

1832 A British reform bill doubles the number of British men who can vote.

1833 Slavery is abolished in the British Empire.

1838 Dutch colonists known as Boers clash with the Zulu in southern Africa.

1839 The Opium War breaks out between Great Britain and China.

Reading Social Studies

by Kylene Beers

Economics | Geography | Politics | Society and Culture | Science and Technology

Focus on Themes In this chapter you will read about the events that shaped the United States from 1828 to 1838. You will see how **political** and **economic** decisions were intertwined. For instance, you will read about the tensions between southern and northern states over tariff regulations. You will also read about the forced relocation of many Native Americans to the West. Understanding how economic issues led to political decisions will help you understand this time.

Drawing Conclusions about the Past

Focus on Reading Writers don't always tell you everything you need to know about a subject. Sometimes you need to think critically about what they have said and make your own decisions about what you've read.

Drawing Conclusions Earlier in this book, you learned how to make inferences. Sometimes when you read, you will need to make several inferences and put them together. The result is a **conclusion**, an informed judgment that you make by combining information.

Election of 1828

The 1828 campaign focused a great deal on the candidates' personalities. Jackson's campaigners described him as a war hero who had been born poor and rose to success through his own hard work.

Adams was a Harvard graduate whose father had been the second U.S. president. Jackson's supporters described Adams as being out of touch with everyday people . . . When the ballots were counted, Jackson had defeated Adams, winning a record number of popular votes. *(pp. 323–324)*

Inference: Jackson shared many qualities with American voters.

+

Inference: Adams enjoyed many privileges that most Americans did not.

+

Inference: Jackson easily won the election by a huge majority.

↓

Conclusion: In 1828, Americans chose a president to whom they could relate.

You Try It!

The following passage is from the chapter you are getting ready to read. As you read the passage, look for the facts of the situation.

The Election of 1834

In 1834 a new political party formed to oppose Jackson. Its members called themselves Whigs, after an English political party that opposed the monarchy, to make the point that Jackson was using his power like a king. The Whig Party favored the idea of a weak president and a strong Congress. Unable to agree on a presidential candidate, the Whigs nominated four men to run against Vice President Martin Van Buren. With strong backing from Jackson, Van Buren won the election.

From Chapter 10, p. 330

After you read the passage, answer the following questions.

1. From this passage, what can you infer about President Jackson's popularity with the Whig Party?
2. The Whigs could not choose a single presidential candidate, so they nominated four men. Based on what you know about elections from your studies and your past experiences, how do you think this affected the votes each man received?
3. Jackson's backing helped Van Buren win the presidency. From this, what can you infer about Jackson's popularity with the American people as a whole?
4. Using the inferences you made answering questions 1 through 3, draw a conclusion about why Van Buren won the election of 1834.

As you read Chapter 10, use your personal background knowledge and experience to draw conclusions about what you are reading.

Key Terms and People

Chapter 10

Section 1

nominating conventions *(p. 323)*
Jacksonian Democracy *(p. 323)*
Democratic Party *(p. 323)*
John C. Calhoun *(p. 323)*
spoils system *(p. 324)*
Martin Van Buren *(p. 324)*
Kitchen Cabinet *(p. 324)*

Section 2

Tariff of Abominations *(p. 327)*
states' rights doctrine *(p. 328)*
nullification crisis *(p. 328)*
Daniel Webster *(p. 328)*
McCulloch v. *Maryland* *(p. 330)*
Whig Party *(p. 330)*
Panic of 1837 *(p. 331)*
William Henry Harrison *(p. 331)*

Section 3

Indian Removal Act *(p. 332)*
Indian Territory *(p. 332)*
Bureau of Indian Affairs *(p. 332)*
Sequoya *(p. 333)*
Worcester v. *Georgia* *(p. 334)*
Trail of Tears *(p. 334)*
Black Hawk *(p. 335)*
Osceola *(p. 335)*

Academic Vocabulary

Success in school is related to knowing academic vocabulary—the words that are frequently used in school assignments and discussions. In this chapter, you will learn the following academic words:

criteria *(p. 328)*
contemporary *(p. 333)*

SECTION 1

Jacksonian Democracy

What You Will Learn...

Main Ideas

1. Democracy expanded in the 1820s as more Americans held the right to vote.
2. Jackson's victory in the election of 1828 marked a change in American politics.

The Big Idea

The expansion of voting rights and the election of Andrew Jackson signaled the growing power of the American people.

Key Terms and People

nominating conventions, *p. 323*
Jacksonian Democracy, *p. 323*
Democratic Party, *p. 323*
John C. Calhoun, *p. 323*
spoils system, *p. 324*
Martin Van Buren, *p. 324*
Kitchen Cabinet, *p. 324*

TAKING NOTES As you read, take notes on how an expansion of voting rights led to Andrew Jackson's election to the presidency. Write your notes in a flowchart like the one below.

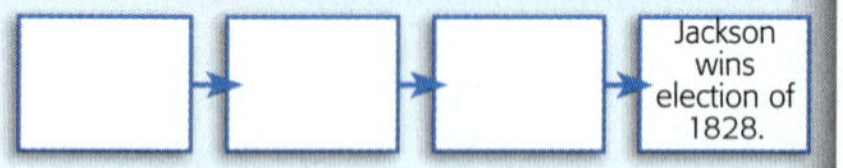

If YOU were there...

It's 1829, and you live in Washington, D.C. You've come with a friend to the party for Andrew Jackson's inauguration as president. Your friend admires Jackson as a man of the people. You are less sure about his ability. Jackson's inauguration soon turns into a rowdy party, as mobs crowd into the White House. They break glasses and overturn the furniture.

How would you feel about having Jackson as your president?

BUILDING BACKGROUND In the early years of the United States, the right to vote belonged mainly to a few—free white men who owned property. As the country grew, more men were given the right to vote. This expansion of democracy led to the election of Andrew Jackson, a war hero. But not everyone approved of Jackson.

Expansion of Democracy

America in the early 1800s was changing fast. In the North, workshops run by the craftspeople who owned them were being replaced by large-scale factories owned by businesspeople and staffed by hired workers. In the South, small family farms began to give way to large cotton plantations, owned by wealthy white people and worked by enslaved African Americans. Wealth seemed to be concentrating into fewer hands. Many ordinary Americans felt left behind.

These same people also began to believe they were losing power in their government. In the late 1700s some Americans thought that government was best managed by wealthy, property-owning men. Government policies seemed targeted to help build the power of these people. The result was a growing belief that the wealthy were tightening their grip on power in the United States.

Hoping for change, small farmers, frontier settlers, and slaveholders rallied behind reform-minded Andrew Jackson, the popular hero of the War of 1812 and presidential candidate in the 1824 election. They believed Jackson would defend the rights of the common

LINKING TO TODAY

Democracy in Action

Democracy spread in the early 1800s as more people became active in politics. Many of these people lived in the new western states. In these mostly rural areas, a political rally could be as simple as neighboring farmers meeting to talk about the issues of the day, as the farmers in the painting on the right are doing.

During the early 1800s democracy and demonstrations blossomed in the United States. The demonstrators of today owe much to the Americans of Andrew Jackson's time. Today, political rallies are a familiar sight in communities all over the country.

ANALYSIS SKILL **ANALYZING INFORMATION**

How are the people in both pictures practicing democracy?

people and the slave states. And they had been bitterly disappointed in the way Jackson had lost the 1824 election because of the decision in the House of Representatives.

During the time of Jackson's popularity, many democratic reforms were made. Some states changed their qualifications for voters to grant more white males suffrage. The revised rules, however, usually excluded free blacks from voting as they had been allowed under original state constitutions. Political parties began holding public **nominating conventions**, where party members choose the party's candidates instead of the party leaders. This period of expanding democracy in the 1820s and 1830s later became known as **Jacksonian Democracy**.

READING CHECK **Finding Main Ideas**
How did voting rights change in the early 1800s?

Election of 1828

Jackson supporters were determined that their candidate would win the 1828 election. They formed the **Democratic Party** to support Jackson's candidacy. Many people who backed President Adams began calling themselves National Republicans.

The 1828 presidential contest was a rematch of the 1824 election. Once again, John Quincy Adams faced Andrew Jackson. Jackson chose **John C. Calhoun** as his vice presidential running mate.

The Campaign

The 1828 campaign focused a great deal on the candidates' personalities. Jackson's campaigners described him as a war hero who had been born poor and rose to success through his own hard work.

THE IMPACT TODAY

Just as they did in the 1820s, presidential campaigns today frequently focus on personal image—strong versus weak or government-insider versus newcomer, for example.

Primary Source

LETTER

People's President

Washington resident Margaret Bayard Smith was surprised by the chaos surrounding Jackson's inauguration.

"What a scene did we witness! . . . a rabble, a mob, of boys, . . . women, children, scrambling, fighting, romping . . . Cut glass and china to the amount of several thousand dollars had been broken . . . But it was the people's day, and the people's President, and the people would rule."

—Margaret Bayard Smith, quoted in *Eyewitness to America*, edited by David Colbert

ANALYSIS SKILL **ANALYZING PRIMARY SOURCES**

How does the author view the people that support Jackson?

Adams was a Harvard graduate whose father had been the second U.S. president. Jackson's supporters described Adams as being out of touch with everyday people. Even a fan of Adams agreed that he was "as cold as a lump of ice." In turn, Adams's supporters said Jackson was hot tempered, crude, and ill-equipped to be president of the United States. When the ballots were counted, Jackson had defeated Adams, winning a record number of popular votes.

Jackson's Inauguration

Jackson's supporters saw his victory as a win for the common people. A crowd cheered outside the Capitol as he took his oath of office. The massive crowd followed Jackson to a huge party on the White House lawn. The few police officers on hand had difficulty controlling the partygoers.

As president, Jackson rewarded some of his supporters with government jobs. This **spoils system**—the practice of giving government jobs to political backers—comes from the saying "to the victor belong the spoils [valued goods] of the enemy."

Secretary of State **Martin Van Buren** was one of Jackson's strongest allies in his official cabinet. President Jackson also relied a great deal on his **Kitchen Cabinet**, an informal group of trusted advisers who sometimes met in the White House kitchen.

READING CHECK **Analyzing** How might the spoils system cause disputes?

SUMMARY AND PREVIEW The expansion of democracy swept Andrew Jackson into office. In the next section you will read about the increasing regional tensions that occurred during Jackson's presidency.

Section 1 Assessment

go.hrw.com **Online Quiz** KEYWORD: SC7 HP10

Reviewing Ideas, Terms, and People

1. a. **Recall** What changes did the new western states make that allowed more people to vote?
   b. **Draw Conclusions** How did **nominating conventions** allow the people more say in politics?
   c. **Predict** How might changes to the voting process brought about by **Jacksonian Democracy** affect politics in the future?
2. a. **Recall** What two new political parties faced off in the election of 1828? Which candidate did each party support?
   b. **Make Inferences** Why did **Andrew Jackson** have more popular support than did Adams?
   c. **Evaluate** Do you think the **spoils system** was an acceptable practice? Explain your answer.

Critical Thinking

3. **Identifying Effect** Review your notes on the election of Andrew Jackson to the presidency. Then use a cause-and-effect chart like this one to show the ways in which Jacksonian Democracy increased Americans' political power.

Jacksonian Democracy	→ increased Americans' political power	

FOCUS ON WRITING

4. **Noting Significance** As you read this section, note things that made Jackson's political campaign and election significant in the history of American politics.

Andrew Jackson

If you were president, how would you use your powers?

When did he live? 1767–1845

Where did he live? Jackson was born in Waxhaw, a region along the border of the North and South Carolina colonies. In 1788 he moved to Nashville, Tennessee, which was still a part of North Carolina. There he built a mansion called the Hermitage. He lived in Washington as president, then retired to the Hermitage, where he died.

What did he do? Jackson had no formal education, but he taught himself law and became a successful lawyer. He became Tennessee's first representative to the U.S. Congress and also served in the Senate. Jackson became a national hero when his forces defeated the Creek and Seminole Indians. He went on to battle the British in the Battle of New Orleans during the War of 1812. Jackson was elected as the nation's seventh president in 1828 and served until 1837.

Why is he so important? Jackson's belief in a strong presidency made him both loved and hated. He vetoed as many bills as the six previous presidents together. Jackson also believed in a strong Union. When South Carolina tried to nullify, or reject, a federal tariff, he threatened to send troops into the state to force it to obey.

Identifying Cause and Effect Why did Jackson gain loyal friends and fierce enemies?

KEY EVENTS

- **1796–1797** Served in the U.S. House of Representatives
- **1797–1798** Served in the U.S. Senate
- **1798–1804** Served on the Tennessee Supreme Court
- **1821** Governor of Florida Territory
- **1823–1825** Served in the U.S. Senate
- **1829–1837** Served as president of the United States
- **1832** Vetoed rechartering the Second Bank of the United States. Threatened to send troops to South Carolina when it tried to nullify a federal tariff

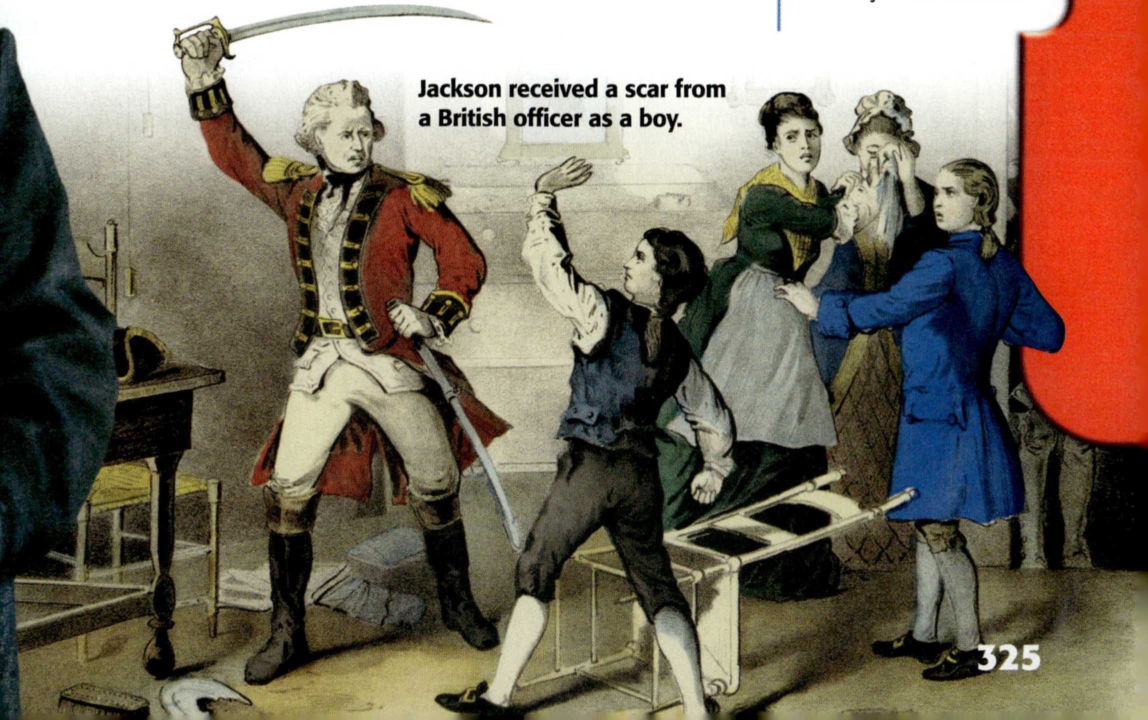

Jackson received a scar from a British officer as a boy.

SECTION 2

Jackson's Administration

What You Will Learn...

Main Ideas

1. Regional differences grew during Jackson's presidency.
2. The rights of the states were debated amid arguments about a national tariff.
3. Jackson's attack on the Bank sparked controversy.
4. Jackson's policies led to the Panic of 1837.

The Big Idea

Andrew Jackson's presidency was marked by political conflicts.

Key Terms and People

Tariff of Abominations, *p. 327*
states' rights doctrine, *p. 328*
nullification crisis, *p. 328*
Daniel Webster, *p. 328*
McCulloch v. *Maryland*, *p. 330*
Whig Party, *p. 330*
Panic of 1837, *p. 331*
William Henry Harrison, *p. 331*

TAKING NOTES As you read, use a diagram like the one below to show the conflicts facing Andrew Jackson during his administration. Add more ovals to your organizer as necessary.

Three distinct regions emerge.
↓
Congress passes Tariff of Abominations.
↓
(blank oval)

If YOU were there...

You live on a small farm in South Carolina in 1829. Your family grows corn and cotton to sell, as well as vegetables for your own table. Although you grow your own food, you also depend on imported wool, flax, iron, and hemp to make ropes. But the government has just put new taxes on these products from Europe. Now they're too expensive for you to buy!

How would you feel about the new taxes on imports?

BUILDING BACKGROUND Even though Americans had a new feeling of national unity, different sections of the country still had very different interests. The industrial North competed with the agricultural South and the western frontier. As Congress favored one section over another, political differences grew.

Sectional Differences Increase

Regional differences had a major effect on Andrew Jackson's presidency. Americans' views of Jackson's policies were based on where they lived and the economy of those regions.

Three Regions Emerge

There were three main U.S. regions in the early 1800s. The North, first of all, had an economy based on trade and on manufacturing. Northerners supported tariffs because tariffs helped them compete with British factories. Northerners also opposed the federal government's sale of public land at cheap prices. Cheap land encouraged potential laborers to move from northern factory towns to the West.

The second region was the South. Its economy was based on farming. Southern farmers raised all types of crops, but the most popular were the cash crops of cotton and tobacco. Southerners sold a large portion of their crops to foreign nations.

Regions of the United States, Early 1800s

QUICK FACTS

NORTH
- Economy based on manufacturing
- Support for tariffs—American goods could be sold at lower prices than could British goods

SOUTH
- Economy based on agriculture
- Opposition to tariffs, which increased the cost of imported goods

WEST
- Emerging economy
- Support for internal improvements and the sale of public lands

Southerners imported their manufactured goods. Tariffs made imported goods more expensive for southern farmers. In addition, high tariffs angered some of the South's European trading partners. These trading partners would likely raise their own tariffs in retaliation. To avoid this situation, southerners called for low tariffs.

Southerners also relied on enslaved African Americans to work the plantations. The issue of slavery would become increasingly controversial between the North and South.

In the third region, the West, the frontier economy was just emerging. Settlers favored policies that boosted their farming economy and encouraged further settlement. Western farmers grew a wide variety of crops. Their biggest priority was cheap land and internal improvements such as better roads and water transportation.

Tariff of Abominations

Tariffs became one of the first issues that President Jackson faced. In 1827, the year before Jackson's election, northern manufacturers began to demand a tariff on imported woolen goods. Northerners wanted the tariff to protect their industries from foreign competition, especially from Great Britain.

British companies were driving American ones out of business with their inexpensive manufactured goods. The tariff northerners supported, however, was so high that importing wool would be impossible. Southerners opposed the tariff, sayng it would hurt their economy.

Before Andrew Jackson took office, Congress placed a high tariff on imports. Angry southerners called it the **Tariff of Abominations**. (An abomination is a hateful thing.) Southern voters were outraged.

President John Quincy Adams signed the tariff legislation, though he did not fully support it. In early U.S. history, presidents tended to reserve veto power for legislation that they believed violated the Constitution. Signing the tariff bill meant Adams would surely be defeated in his re-election bid. The new tariff added fuel to the growing sectional differences plaguing the young nation.

READING CHECK **Summarizing** Describe the sectional economic differences in the United States during the early 1800s.

FOCUS ON NORTH CAROLINA

Prominent North Carolina leaders, including James Iredell Jr. and Nathaniel Macon, opposed the tariff.

States' Rights Debate

When Andrew Jackson took office in 1829, he was forced to respond to the growing conflict over tariffs. At the core of the dispute was the question of an individual state's right to disregard a law that had been passed by the U.S. Congress.

Nullification Crisis

ACADEMIC VOCABULARY
criteria basic requirements

Early in his political career, Vice President John C. Calhoun had supported the **criteria** of a strong central government. But in 1828 when Congress passed the Tariff of Abominations, Calhoun joined his fellow southerners in protest. Economic depression and previous tariffs had severely damaged the economy of his home state, South Carolina. It was only beginning to recover in 1828. Some leaders in the state even spoke of leaving the Union over the issue of tariffs.

FOCUS ON READING
What conclusions can you draw about the importance of the states' rights debate after reading this section?

In response to the tariff, Calhoun drafted the *South Carolina Exposition and Protest*. It said that Congress should not favor one state or region over another. Calhoun used the *Protest* to advance the **states' rights doctrine**, which said that since the states had formed the national government, state power should be greater than federal power. He believed states had the right to nullify, or reject, any federal law they judged to be unconstitutional.

Calhoun's theory was controversial, and it drew some fierce challengers. Many of them were from the northern states that had benefited from increased tariffs. These opponents believed that the American people, not the individual states, made up the Union. Conflict between the supporters and the opponents of nullification deepened. The dispute became known as the **nullification crisis**.

Although he chose not to put his name on his *Exposition and Protest*, Calhoun did resign from the vice presidency. He was then elected to the Senate, where he continued his arguments in favor of nullification. Martin Van Buren replaced Calhoun as vice president when Jackson was re-elected president.

The Hayne-Webster Debate

The debate about states' rights began early in our nation's history. Thomas Jefferson and James Madison supported the states' power to disagree with the federal government in the Virginia and Kentucky Resolutions of 1798–99. Some of the delegates at the Hartford Convention supported states' rights. But Calhoun's theory went further. He believed that states could judge whether a law was or was not constitutional. This position put the power of the Supreme Court in question.

The issue of nullification was intensely debated on the floor of the Senate in 1830. Robert Y. Hayne, senator from South Carolina, defended states' rights. He argued that nullification gave states a way to lawfully protest federal legislation. **Daniel Webster** of Massachusetts argued that the United States was one nation, not a pact among independent states. He believed that the welfare of the nation should override that of individual states.

Jackson Responds

Although deeply opposed to nullification, Jackson was concerned about economic problems in the southern states. In 1832 he urged Congress to pass another tariff that lowered the previous rate. South Carolina thought the slight change was inadequate. The state legislature took a monumental step; it decided to test the doctrine of states' rights.

South Carolina's first action was to pass the Nullification Act, which declared the 1828 and 1832 tariffs "null, void ... [and not] binding upon this State, its officers or citizens." South Carolina threatened to withdraw from the Union if federal troops were used to collect duties. The legislature also voted to form its own army. Jackson was enraged.

The president sternly condemned nullification. Jackson declared that he would enforce the law in South Carolina. At his request, Congress passed the Force Bill, approving use of the army if necessary. In light of Jackson's determined position, no other state chose to support South Carolina.

Early in 1833, Henry Clay of Kentucky had proposed a compromise that would gradually lower the tariff over several years. As Jackson's intentions became clear, both the U.S. Congress and South Carolina moved quickly to approve the compromise. The Congress would decrease the tariff, and South Carolina's leaders would enforce the law.

Despite the compromise, neither side changed its beliefs about states' rights. The argument continued for years, ending in the huge conflict known as the Civil War.

READING CHECK **Summarizing** What led to the nullification crisis, and why was it important?

Jackson Attacks the Bank

President Jackson upheld federal authority in the nullification crisis. He did not, however, always support greater federal power. For example, he opposed the Second Bank of the United States, founded by Congress in 1816.

The Second Bank of the United States was given a 20-year charter. This charter gave it the power to act exclusively as the federal government's financial agent. The Bank held federal deposits, made transfers of federal funds between states, and dealt with any payments or receipts involving the federal government. It also issued bank notes, or paper currency. Some 80 percent of the Bank was privately owned, but its operations were supervised by Congress and the president.

Many states, particularly in the South, had opposed the Bank. Small farmers believed that the Bank only helped wealthy businesspeople. Jackson also questioned the legality of the Bank. He believed it was an unconstitutional extension of the power of Congress. The states, he thought, should have the power to control the banking system.

Some states decided to take action. Maryland tried to pass a tax that would limit the

Primary Source

POINTS OF VIEW

States' Rights vs. the Union

The framers of the Constitution created a document that was remarkable in its scope. But a few issues were unresolved. One of the most controversial was the matter of states' rights versus the authority of the federal government. Daniel Webster insisted that the interests of the Union should prevail. John C. Calhoun believed that the powers of the states were greater.

"While the Union lasts we have high, exciting, gratifying [rewarding] prospects spread out before us, for us and our children. God grant that in my day . . . my eyes shall be turned to behold the gorgeous ensign [flag] of the republic . . . bearing for its motto . . . Liberty and Union, now and forever one and inseparable."

—Daniel Webster

from the Hayne-Webster debate, 1830

"If there be no protective power in the reserved rights of the states, they must in the end be forced to rebel . . ."

—John C. Calhoun

from a letter to Virgil Maxcy, September 11, 1830

ANALYSIS SKILL **ANALYZING PRIMARY SOURCES**

Finding Main Ideas How did the views of Calhoun and Webster differ?

Primary Source

POLITICAL CARTOON

Jackson against the Bank

Andrew Jackson's fight with the Bank was the subject of many political cartoons, like this one.

In this scene, Jackson is shown fighting a hydra that represents the national bank. The hydra is a mythological monster whose heads grow back when cut off. The heads of the hydra are portraits of politicians who opposed Jackson's policies.

Nicholas Biddle is at the center of the hydra. Why?

Andrew Jackson fights the hydra with a cane labeled "veto."

Why do you think the cartoonist chose this monster to represent the Bank?

ANALYSIS SKILL **ANALYZING PRIMARY SOURCES**

How does this image show the difficulty Jackson had politically?

Bank's operations. James McCulloch, cashier of the Bank's branch in Maryland, refused to pay this tax. The state took him to court, and the resulting case went all the way to the U.S. Supreme Court. In ***McCulloch v. Maryland***, the Court ruled that the national bank was constitutional.

Nicholas Biddle, the Bank's director, decided to push for a bill to renew the Bank's charter in 1832. Jackson campaigned for the bill's defeat. "I will kill it," he promised. True to his word, Jackson vetoed the legislation when Congress sent it to him.

Congress could not get the two-thirds majority needed to override Jackson's veto. Jackson also weakened the Bank's power by moving most of its funds to state banks. In many cases, these banks used the funds to offer easy credit terms to people buying land. While this practice helped expansion in the West, it also led to inflation.

In the summer of 1836 Jackson tried to slow this inflation. He ordered Americans to use only gold or silver—instead of paper state-bank notes—to buy government-owned land. This policy did not help the national economy as Jackson had hoped. Jackson did improve the economy by lowering the national debt. However, his policies opened the door for approaching economic troubles.

READING CHECK **Analyzing** Why did critics of the Second Bank of the United States oppose it?

Panic of 1837

Jackson was still very popular with voters in 1836. He chose not to run in 1836, however, and the Democrats nominated Vice President Martin Van Buren.

In 1834 a new political party had formed to oppose Jackson. Its members called themselves Whigs, after an English political party that opposed the monarchy, to make the point that Jackson was using his power like a king. The **Whig Party** favored the idea of a weak president and a strong Congress. Unable to agree on a candidate, the Whigs chose four men to run against Van Buren. Because of this indecision, and with backing from Jackson, Van Buren won the election.

The Supreme Court and Capitalism

CONNECT TO ECONOMICS

During the early 1800s, the Supreme Court made several rulings that helped define federal power over contracts and commerce. These rulings reinforced capitalism as the ruling economic system in the United States.

What effect did the Supreme Court have on economic development?

1810

Fletcher* v. *Peck
State legislatures could not pass laws violating existing contracts.

1819

Dartmouth College* v. *Woodward
State legislatures could not pass laws to change the charters of institutions or businesses.

McCulloch* v. *Maryland
States do not have the power to tax federal institutions.

1824

Gibbons* v. *Ogden
Only the federal government has the power to regulate interstate and foreign commerce.

Shortly after Van Buren took office, the country experienced the **Panic of 1837**, a severe economic depression. Jackson's banking policies and his unsuccessful plan to curb inflation contributed to the panic. But people blamed Van Buren.

In 1840 the Whigs united against the weakened Van Buren to stand behind one candidate, **William Henry Harrison**, an army general. Harrison won in an electoral landslide. The Whigs had achieved their goal of winning the presidency.

READING CHECK **Identifying Cause and Effect** What contributed to the Panic of 1837, and how did it affect the 1840 election?

SUMMARY AND PREVIEW The states' rights debate dominated much of Jackson's presidency. In the next section you will learn about the removal of American Indians from the southeastern United States.

Section 2 Assessment

go.hrw.com
Online Quiz
KEYWORD: SC7 HP10

Reviewing Ideas, Terms, and People

1. a. **Recall** On what were the economies of the northern, southern, and western states based?
   b. **Predict** How might the sectional issues involved in the dispute over the **Tariff of Abominations** lead to future problems between North and South?
2. a. **Describe** What roles did **Daniel Webster** and John C. Calhoun play in the **nullification crisis**?
   b. **Summarize** What idea did supporters of the **states' rights doctrine** promote?
3. a. **Describe** What problems resulted from weakening the Bank?
   b. **Draw Conclusions** Why did Jackson veto the bill to renew the Second Bank of the United States?
4. a. **Recall** What caused the **Panic of 1837**?
   b. **Summarize** How did the **Whig Party** win the election of 1840?
   c. **Elaborate** Why do you think Jackson chose not to run for the presidency in 1836? Do you think he made the right decision? Why?

Critical Thinking

5. **Identifying Cause and Effect** Review your notes on the political conflicts during Jackson's administration. Then use a graphic organizer like the one below to show how some of Jackson's policies dealing with conflicts led to the Panic of 1837.

Jackson's Policies	→	Panic of 1837

FOCUS ON WRITING

6. **Identifying Important Conflicts** Stories about conflict sell newspapers. As you read this section, list important conflicts that occurred during Jackson's presidency and note the role Jackson played in creating or resolving the conflicts.

SECTION 3

Indian Removal

What You Will Learn...

Main Ideas

1. The Indian Removal Act authorized the relocation of Native Americans to the West.
2. Cherokee resistance to removal led to disagreement between Jackson and the Supreme Court.
3. Other Native Americans resisted removal with force.

The Big Idea

President Jackson supported a policy of Indian removal.

Key Terms and People

Indian Removal Act, *p. 332*
Indian Territory, *p. 332*
Bureau of Indian Affairs, *p. 332*
Sequoya, *p. 333*
Worcester v. *Georgia*, *p. 334*
Trail of Tears, *p. 334*
Black Hawk, *p. 335*
Osceola, *p. 335*

TAKING NOTES As you read, use a graphic organizer like the one below to show the steps Andrew Jackson and the U.S. government took toward Indian removal.

Indian removal

If YOU were there...

You belong to the Cherokee nation. Your family has farmed rich lands in Georgia for as long as anyone can remember. You've learned some new ways from white settlers, too. At school you've learned to read both English and Cherokee. But now that doesn't seem important. The U.S. government is sending you and your people far away to unknown places in the West.

How would you feel about being taken away from your home?

BUILDING BACKGROUND President Andrew Jackson had become famous as an American Indian fighter. He had no sympathy with Native Americans' claim to the lands where they had always lived. With public support, he reversed the government's pledge to respect Indian land claims. The result was the brutal removal of the southeastern peoples to empty lands in the West.

Indian Removal Act

Native Americans had long lived in settlements stretching from Georgia to Mississippi. However, President Jackson and other political leaders wanted to open this land to settlement by American farmers. Under pressure from Jackson, Congress passed the **Indian Removal Act** in 1830, authorizing the removal of Native Americans who lived east of the Mississippi River to lands in the West.

Congress then established **Indian Territory**—U.S. land in what is now Oklahoma—and planned to move Native Americans there. Some supporters of this plan, like John C. Calhoun, argued that removal to Indian Territory would protect Indians from further conflicts with American settlers. "One of the greatest evils to which they are subject is that incessant [constant] pressure of our population," he noted. "To guard against this evil . . . there ought to be the strongest . . . assurance that the country given [to] them should be theirs." To manage Indian removal to western lands, Congress approved the creation of a new government agency, the **Bureau of Indian Affairs**.

Indian Removal

During the Trail of Tears, thousands of Cherokee died from disease, starvation, and harsh weather. They were forced to walk hundreds of miles to their new land in the West. Other Native Americans were also moved, with similar results.

What can you see in this painting that indicates this was a difficult journey?

The Choctaw were the first Indians sent to Indian Territory. The Mississippi legislature abolished the Choctaw government and then forced the Choctaw leaders to sign the Treaty of Dancing Rabbit Creek. This treaty gave more than 7.5 million acres of their land to the state. The Choctaw moved to Indian Territory during a disastrous winter trip. Federal officials in charge of the move did not provide enough food or supplies to the Choctaw, most of whom were on foot. About one-fourth of the Choctaw died of cold, disease, or starvation.

News of the Choctaw's hardships caused other Indians to resist removal. When the Creek resisted in 1836, federal troops moved in and captured some 14,500 of them. They led the Creek, many in chains, to Indian Territory. One Creek woman remembered the trip being filled with "the awful silence that showed the heartaches and sorrow at being taken from the homes and even separation from loved ones." The Chickasaw, who lived in upper Mississippi, negotiated a treaty for better supplies on their trip to Indian Territory. Nevertheless, many Chickasaw lives were also lost during removal.

READING CHECK **Finding Main Ideas** What major changes did President Jackson make to U.S. policy regarding Native Americans?

Cherokee Resistance

Many Cherokee had believed that they could prevent conflicts and avoid removal by adopting the **contemporary** culture of white people. In the early 1800s they invited missionaries to set up schools where Cherokee children learned how to read and write in English. The Cherokee developed their own government modeled after the U.S. Constitution with an election system, a bicameral council, and a court system. All of these were headed by a principal chief.

ACADEMIC VOCABULARY
contemporary existing at the same time

A Cherokee named **Sequoya** used 86 characters to represent Cherokee syllables to create a writing system for their own complex language. In 1828 the Cherokee began publishing a newspaper printed in both English and Cherokee.

The adoption of white culture did not protect the Cherokee. After gold was discovered on their land in Georgia, their treaty rights were ignored. Georgia leaders began preparing for the Cherokee's removal. When they refused to move, the Georgia militia began attacking Cherokee towns. In response, the Cherokee sued the state. They said that they were an independent nation and claimed that the government of Georgia had no legal power over their lands.

In 1832 the Supreme Court, under the leadership of Chief Justice John Marshall, agreed. In ***Worcester* v. *Georgia*** the Court ruled that the Cherokee nation was a distinct community in which the laws of Georgia had no force. The Court also stated that only the federal government, not the states, had authority over Native Americans.

THE IMPACT TODAY

Today more than 60,000 Cherokee or Cherokee descendants live in present-day Oklahoma.

Georgia, however, ignored the Court's ruling, and President Jackson took no action to make Georgia follow the ruling. "John Marshall has made his decision; now let him enforce it," Jackson supposedly said. By not enforcing the Court's decision, Jackson violated his presidential oath to uphold the laws of the land. However, most members of Congress and American citizens did not protest the ways Jackson removed Native Americans.

In the spring of 1838, U.S. troops began to remove all Cherokee to Indian Territory. A few were able to escape and hide in the mountains of North Carolina. After the Cherokee were removed, Georgia took their businesses, farms, and property.

The Cherokee's 800-mile forced march became known as the **Trail of Tears**. During the march, the Cherokee suffered from disease, hunger, and harsh weather. Almost one-fourth of the 18,000 Cherokee died on the march.

READING CHECK **Finding Main Ideas**
What was the *Worcester* v. *Georgia* ruling, and what was Jackson's response?

Primary Source

PERSONAL ACCOUNTS

Trail of Tears

The Cherokee knew that they would be forced to march West, but they did not know that so many of their people would die on the way. Here are two accounts of the Trail of Tears, one written before it started and one written after, both by Cherokee who made the trip.

March 10, 1838
Beloved Martha, I have delayed writing to you so long . . . If we Cherokees are to be driven to the west by the cruel hand of oppression to seek a new home in the west, it will be impossible . . . It is thus all our rights are invaded."

—Letter from Jenny, a Cherokee girl, just before her removal

"Long time we travel on way to new land. People feel bad when they leave Old Nation. Women cry and make sad wails, Children cry and many men cry . . . but they say nothing and just put heads down and keep on go towards West. Many days pass and people die very much."

—Recollections of a survivor of the Trail of Tears

ANALYSIS SKILL **ANALYZING POINTS OF VIEW**

1. What is different about the concerns of the Cherokee before and after the Trail of Tears?
2. How do you think the survivors of the Trail of Tears felt when they reached Indian Territory?

Other Native Americans Resist

Other Native Americans decided to fight U.S. troops to avoid removal. Chief **Black Hawk**, a leader of Fox and Sauk Indians, led his people in a struggle to protect their lands in Illinois. By 1832, however, the Sauk forces were running out of food and supplies, and by 1850 they had been forced to leave.

In Florida, Seminole leaders were forced to sign a removal treaty that their followers decided to ignore. A leader named **Osceola** called upon his people to resist with force, and the Second Seminole War began. Osceola was captured and soon died in prison. His followers, however, continued to fight. Some 4,000 Seminole were removed and hundreds of others killed. Eventually, U.S. officials decided to give up the fight. Small groups of Seminole had resisted removal, and their descendants live in Florida today.

READING CHECK **Evaluating** How effective was Native American resistance to removal?

GEOGRAPHY SKILLS **INTERPRETING MAPS**

1. **Location** In what parts of Florida was the Second Seminole War fought?
2. **Place** Where was the last battle of the Second Seminole War fought?

SUMMARY AND PREVIEW President Jackson supported the removal of thousands of Native Americans from their traditional lands to the federal territory in the West. In the next chapter you will learn about the westward growth of the nation as farmers, ranchers, and other settlers moved West.

Section 3 Assessment

go.hrw.com
Online Quiz
KEYWORD: SC7 HP10

Reviewing Ideas, Terms, and People

1. a. **Identify** What Native American groups were affected by the **Indian Removal Act**? Where were they relocated?
   b. **Explain** Why did government officials want to relocate Native Americans to the West?
   c. **Predict** What are some possible effects that the Indian Removal Act might have on Native Americans already living in the West?
2. a. **Identify** What was the **Trail of Tears**?
   b. **Analyze** Why did the state of Georgia want to relocate the Cherokee, and what did the Cherokee do in response?
   c. **Elaborate** What do you think of President Jackson's refusal to enforce the ***Worcester* v. *Georgia*** ruling?
3. a. **Describe** What led to the Second Seminole War?
   b. **Compare and Contrast** How were the Seminole and the Sauk resistance efforts similar and different?

Critical Thinking

4. **Comparing and Contrasting** Review your notes on Indian removal. Then copy the chart below and use it to identify the Native American groups and their responses to removal.

Native American Group	Response to Removal

FOCUS ON WRITING

5. **Understanding Causes and Effects** As you read, identify the causes and effects of the Jackson administration's policy of Indian relocation.

History and Geography

Indian Removal in North Carolina

In 1835, against the will of the majority, a small group of Cherokee negotiated a treaty with the U.S. government that said all Cherokee would leave their lands east of the Mississippi. By 1838, federal troops began forcibly removing 17,000 Cherokee in a march west that became known as the Trail of Tears. About 1,000 Cherokee escaped removal and hid in the mountains of North Carolina and Tennessee. These Cherokee later formed the Eastern Band of Cherokee. Their descendants live in the region today, many within a small region called the Qualla Boundary.

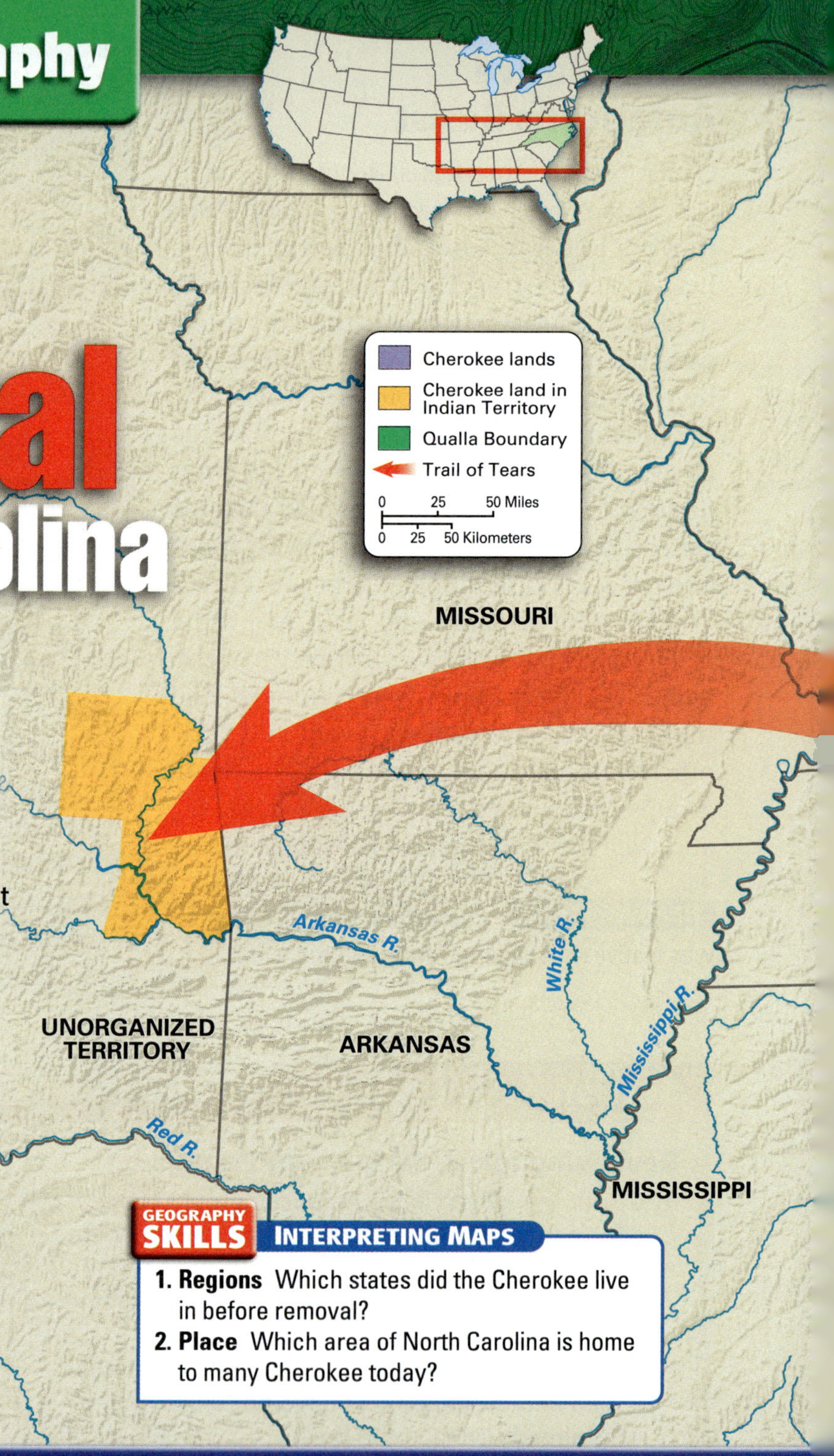

GEOGRAPHY SKILLS INTERPRETING MAPS

1. **Regions** Which states did the Cherokee live in before removal?
2. **Place** Which area of North Carolina is home to many Cherokee today?

Time Line

Native Americans of North Carolina

1000 BC Woodland Mound Builders begin living in permanent settlements.

1540 Spanish explorer Hernando de Soto encounters Native Americans while searching eastern North Carolina for gold.

1650 White settlers begin to move onto Native American lands along the coast and rivers of North Carolina.

1711 The Tuscarora War begins.

1000 BC — 1600 — 1700

Primary Source **POINT OF VIEW**

Trail of Tears

Newspapers published a letter signed by Andrew Jackson in 1835, giving his reasons for approving the removal of the Cherokee.

"Circumstances that cannot be controlled, and which are beyond the reach of human laws, render it impossible that you can flourish in the midst of a civilized community. You have but one remedy within your reach. And that is, to remove to the West and join your countrymen, who are already established there. And the sooner you do this, the sooner you will commence [begin] your career of improvement and prosperity."

—President Andrew Jackson

Most Cherokee wanted to stay on their land. An 1830 newspaper article made this view clear.

"We wish to remain on the land of our fathers . . . The treaties with us, and laws of the United States . . . guaranty our residence and our privileges, and secure us against intruders. Our only request is, that these treaties may be fulfilled, and these laws executed."

—General Council of the Cherokee Nation

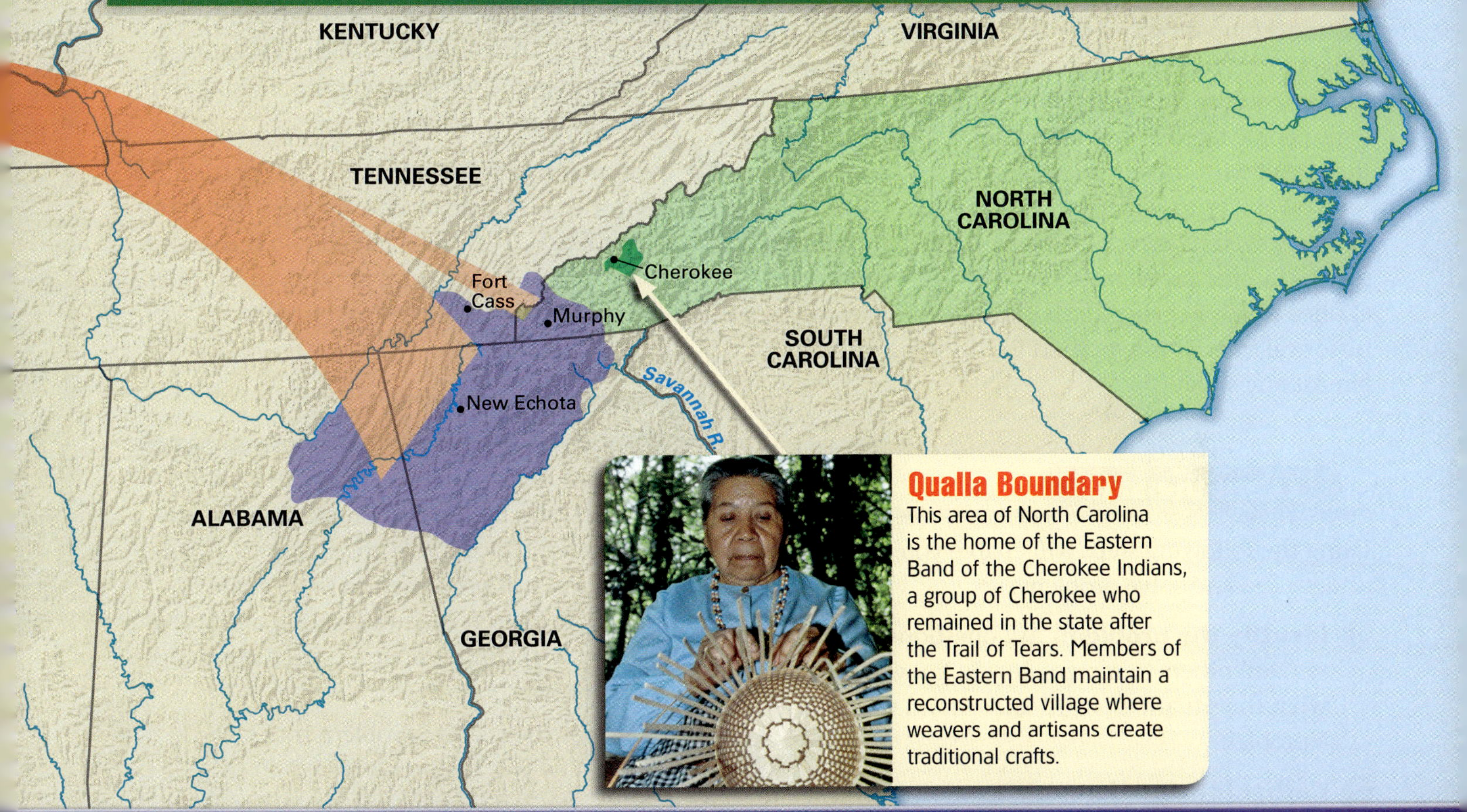

Qualla Boundary
This area of North Carolina is the home of the Eastern Band of the Cherokee Indians, a group of Cherokee who remained in the state after the Trail of Tears. Members of the Eastern Band maintain a reconstructed village where weavers and artisans create traditional crafts.

1763 A proclamation by King George III tries to create a boundary between Native Americans and British settlers.

1828 The *Cherokee Phoenix,* a newspaper written in Cherokee and English, is published for the first time.

1838 Federal troops begin forcing the Cherokee to leave their homes.

1887 A school for Native Americans opens in Pembroke, North Carolina.

1948 The Museum of the Cherokee Indian opens in Cherokee, North Carolina.

1800 1900 2000

Social Studies Skills

Analysis | **Critical Thinking** | Civic Participation | Study

North Carolina Skills
4.01 Use hypothetical reasoning process.

Solving Problems

Define the Skill

Problem solving is a process for finding workable solutions to difficult situations. The process involves asking questions, identifying and evaluating information, comparing and contrasting, and making judgments. Problem solving is useful in studying history because it helps you better understand problems people faced at certain points in time and how they dealt with those difficulties.

The ability to understand and evaluate how people solved problems in the past also can help in solving similar problems today. The skill can also be applied to many other kinds of difficulties besides historical ones. It is a method for thinking through almost any situation.

Learn the Skill

Using the following steps will enable you to better understand and solve problems.

1. **Identify the problem.** Ask questions of yourself and others to make sure you know exactly what the situation is and understand why it is a problem.
2. **Gather information.** Ask questions and conduct research to learn more about the problem, such as its history, what caused it, what contributes to it, and other factors.
3. **List options.** Based on the information you have gathered, identify possible options for solving the problem that you might consider. Be aware that your final solution will probably be better and easier to reach if you have as many options as possible to consider.
4. **Evaluate the options.** Weigh each option you are considering. Think of and list the advantages it has as a solution, as well as its potential disadvantages.
5. **Choose and implement a solution.** After comparing the advantages and disadvantages of each possible solution, choose the one that seems best and apply it.
6. **Evaluate the solution.** Once the solution has been tried, evaluate its effectiveness in solving the problem. This step will tell you if the solution was a good one, or if another of the possible solutions should be tried instead.

Practice the Skill

One of the most challenging situations that President Jackson faced was the nullification crisis. You can use the problem-solving skills to better understand this problem and to evaluate his solution for it. Review the information about the nullification crisis in this chapter. Then answer the questions below.

1. What was the specific problem that Jackson faced? Why was it a problem?
2. What event led to the problem? What earlier circumstances and conditions contributed to it?
3. List possible solutions to the problem that you would have considered if you had been president, along with advantages and disadvantages.
4. Jackson threatened to send troops to South Carolina to enforce federal law. Do you think his solution was the best one? Explain why, or if not, what solution would have been better.

CHAPTER 10

Chapter Review

HOLT

History's Impact

▶ **video series**

Review the video to answer the closing question:

How may the U.S. government's early treatment of Native Americans have contributed to the reservations' current situation?

Visual Summary

QUICK FACTS

Use the visual summary below to help you review the main ideas of the chapter.

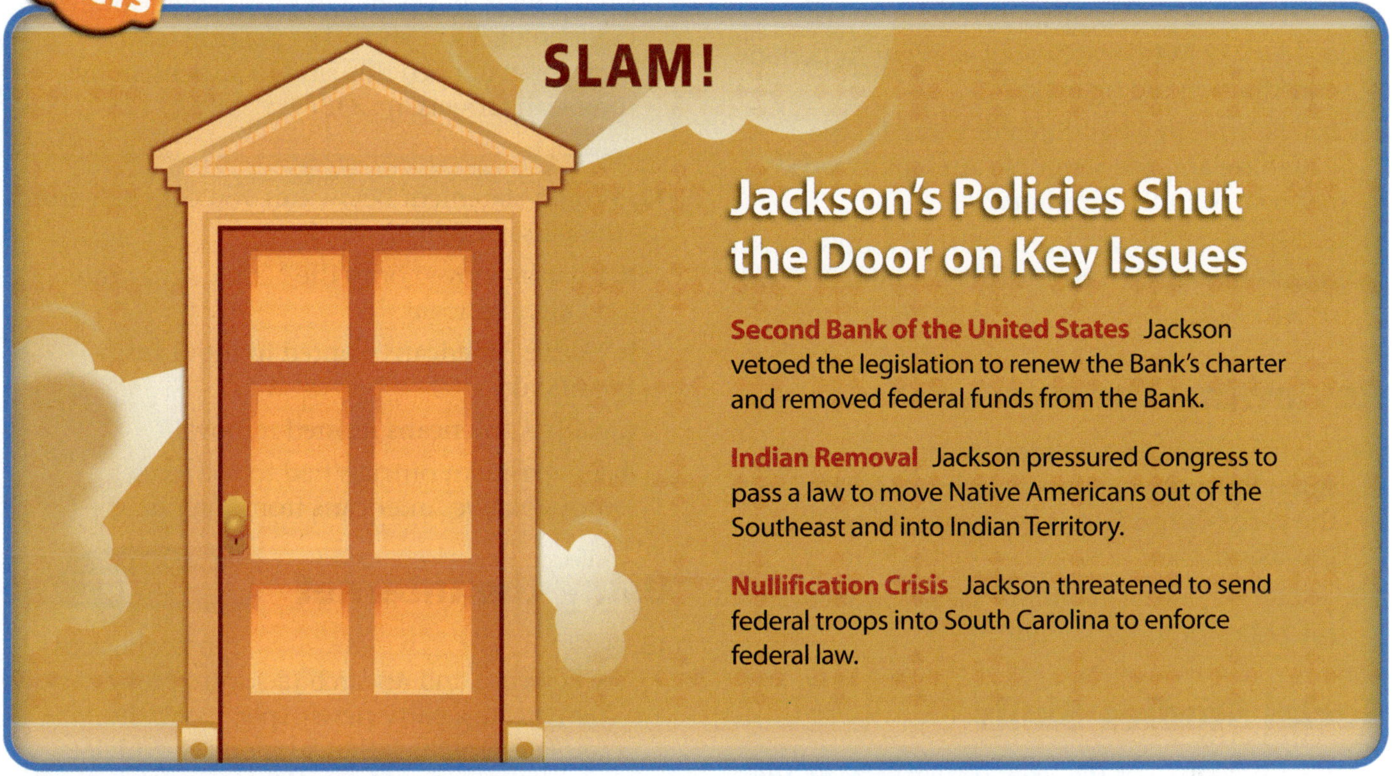

Reviewing Vocabulary, Terms, and People

Complete each sentence by filling in the blank with the correct term or person.

1. In the Supreme Court case of ______________, the Court ruled that the federal government, not the states, had authority over the Cherokee.

2. President Jackson's group of advisers was known as the _____________ because of where its members met in the White House.

3. _____________ served as Andrew Jackson's vice president until he resigned due to the dispute over nullification.

4. The _____________ supported the power of the states over the federal government.

5. The practice of rewarding supporters with positions in government is known as the ______.

Comprehension and Critical Thinking

SECTION 1 *(Pages 322–324)*

6. a. Identify What changes took place in the early 1800s that broadened democracy in the United States?

b. Analyze How was Jackson's victory in the election of 1828 a reflection of a change in American politics?

c. Evaluate Do you think the changes brought about by Jacksonian Democracy went far enough in expanding democracy? Why or why not?

SECTION 2 *(Pages 326–331)*

7. a. Describe What conflicts troubled the Jackson administration?

b. Draw Conclusions What were the results of the conflict over the Second Bank of the United States?

c. Predict How might sectional differences and the debate over states' rights lead to future problems for the United States?

SECTION 3 *(Pages 332–335)*

8. **a. Identify** Who was Sequoya? What important contribution did he make?

   b. Contrast In what different ways did the Cherokee and the Seminole attempt to resist removal to Indian Territory?

   c. Elaborate Do you agree with Jackson's refusal to enforce the *Worcester* v. *Georgia* ruling? Why or why not?

Reviewing Themes

9. **Politics** What new political party rose in opposition to President Andrew Jackson? What was the party's attitude toward the power of the president?

10. **Economics** What economic factors influenced the policy of Indian removal?

Social Studies Skills

Solving Problems *Use the Social Studies Skills taught in this chapter to answer the question about the reading selection below.*

> Northerners wanted the tariff to protect their industries from foreign competition, especially from Great Britain.
>
> British companies were driving American ones out of business because they could manufacture goods more cheaply than American businesses could . . . Southerners opposed the tariff, claiming it would hurt their economy. *(p. 327)*

11. Which of the following might be a reasonable solution to the problem discussed above?

    a. passing a low tariff

    b. passing a high tariff only in the South

    c. Britain passing a tariff

    d. selling northern and British goods for a higher price

Reading Skills

Drawing Conclusions about the Past *Use the Reading Skills taught in this chapter to answer the question about the reading selection below.*

> Native Americans had long lived in settlements stretching from Georgia to Mississippi. However, President Jackson and other political leaders wanted to open this land to settlement by American farmers. *(p. 332)*

12. Which statement below can you conclude from the passage above?

    a. Farmers moved onto the Native Americans' land after removal.

    b. Native Americans wanted to move from their lands.

    c. Native Americans resisted removal.

    d. Government officials had to use force to remove Native Americans from their land.

Using the Internet

go.hrw.com
KEYWORD: SC7 CH10

13. **Activity: Writing a newspaper** Enter the activity keyword and research Jackson's presidency. Then create a party newspaper, using the template provided, that supports or criticizes Jackson's policies. Use evidence to support your articles either in favor of or against his policies. Write from the point of view of a supporter or from the point of view of a political enemy.

FOCUS ON WRITING

14. **Writing Interview Questions** Review the notes you have taken about Jackson's political significance, the conflicts he was involved in, and the causes and effects of his policies toward Indians. Then, based on your notes, begin writing questions for your interview with Jackson. What will the readers of your newspaper want to learn more about? Write at least 10 interview questions that your readers will want answered.

CHAPTER 10 Standardized Test Practice

DIRECTIONS: Read each question and write the letter of the best response.

1 The era surrounding the presidency of Andrew Jackson is *best* known for an expansion in

A freedom of speech.

B religious toleration.

C states' rights.

D voting rights.

2 Southerners opposed the so-called Tariff of Abominations because they

A believed the tariff was unconstitutional.

B feared the tariff would give an unfair advantage to northern states.

C wanted to eliminate competition with the British.

D believed the tariff would hurt their economy.

3 What action did the Cherokee take to resist their removal from Georgia and North Carolina to the West?

A sued the state of Georgia in the courts

B destroyed neighbors' farms and businesses

C went to war against the U.S. government

D staged a protest called the Trail of Tears

4 The debate between John C. Calhoun and Daniel Webster over states' rights was *most like* the debate between

A the Patriots and the Loyalists.

B the Antifederalists and the Federalists.

C England and France during the French and Indian War.

D the large states and the small states during the Constitutional Convention.

5 President Jackson was very vocal in his opposition to the

A federal Indian Removal policy.

B expansion of voting rights.

C Second Bank of the United States.

D Second Seminole War.

6 Despite the U.S. policy to remove Native Americans living east of the Mississippi River, the Eastern Cherokee

A were allowed to remain in the mountains of North Carolina.

B fought a long war against the U.S. Army.

C developed their own government modeled after the U.S. Constitution.

D chose to settle instead in Canada.

7 Read the following quote from the 1835 revision to the North Carolina state constitution and use it to answer the question below.

> "The House of Commons shall be composed of one hundred and twenty representatives, biennially chosen by ballot, to be elected by counties according to their federal population, that is, according to their respective numbers . . . and each county shall have at least one member in the House of Commons, although it may not contain the requisite ratio of population."
>
> — from *Journal of the Convention to Amend the Constitution of the State*

Document-Based Question How did this clause of the constitution expand democracy in North Carolina?

CHAPTER 11 1800–1855

Expanding West

North Carolina Standards

Social Studies Objectives

3.08 Examine the impact of national events such as the Louisiana Purchase, the Lewis and Clark Expedition, the War with Mexico, and the California Gold Rush, and technological advances on North Carolina.

9.02 Identify past and present state and local leaders from diverse cultural backgrounds and assess their influence in effecting change.

Language Arts Objectives

2.02 Analyze and evaluate informational materials that are read, heard, and/or viewed by:

- recognizing the characteristics of informational materials.
- summarizing information.
- determining the importance and accuracy of information.
- making connections to related topics/information.

go.hrw.com
North Carolina
KEYWORD: SC7 NC

Focus on Writing

Outline for a Documentary Film Many documentary films have been made about the history of the United States, but there is always room for one more. In this chapter you will read about the westward expansion of the United States, a period filled with excitement and challenge. Then you will create an outline for a documentary film to be used in middle-school history classes.

United States

1811
John Jacob Astor founds the fur-trading post Astoria on the Columbia River.

1810

World

HOLT

History's Impact

▶ **video series**

Watch the video to understand the impact of the California gold rush on the West.

What You Will Learn...

In this chapter you will learn about how the United States expanded west. The country acquired vast amounts of territory in a short time. Lured by land and gold, hundreds of thousands of Americans followed trails west in search of a better life. However, many Californio families, like the one pictured here, had already lived in California for generations.

1820

1821 Mexico wins its independence from Spain.

1827 The United States and Great Britain agree to continue joint occupation of Oregon Country.

1830

1838 Californios revolt unsuccessfully against the Mexican government.

1840

1842 China gives Great Britain control of the island of Hong Kong.

1846 The United States declares war against Mexico.

1848 Gold is discovered in California on January 24.

1850

1854 Commodore Matthew Perry negotiates a trade treaty with Japan.

Reading Social Studies

by Kylene Beers

Economics | Geography | Politics | Society and Culture | Science and Technology

Focus on Themes In this chapter you will read about the American people as they continued to move west. You will find out about the famous Oregon and Santa Fe trails, Texas's fight for independence from Mexico, and Mexico's war with the United States. Finally, you will read about the California gold rush that brought thousands of people west. As you read each section, you will see how **economic** issues affected the growth of different **geographic** areas.

Vocabulary in Context

Focus on Reading In Chapter 3 you learned how writers sometimes give you clues to a word's meaning in the same or a nearby sentence. Those clues are usually definitions, restatements in different words, or comparisons or contrasts. But what do you do if you do not know the word and the writer doesn't think to give you a direct clue?

Using Broader Context Clues If the writer does not give you one of those direct clues, you have to try to figure out the meaning of the word for yourself.

1. Read the whole paragraph and look for information that will help you figure out the meaning.
2. Look up the word in the dictionary to be sure of its meaning.

Notice how a student used information from the whole paragraph to learn the meaning of two unknown words.

In 1844, the Whig Party passed up Tyler and chose Senator Henry Clay of Kentucky as its presidential candidate. At first opposing *annexation*, Clay changed his mind due to pressure from southern politicians. The Democratic Party chose former Tennessee governor James K. Polk to oppose Clay. Both candidates strongly favored *acquiring* Texas and Oregon. *(p. 355)*

I'm not sure about *annexation*. The southerners convinced Clay to be for it. Maybe I'll understand if I read some more.

Oh, both presidential candidates favored *acquiring* Texas and Oregon. Maybe *annexation* means almost the same thing as *acquiring*. I'll check the dictionary.

Key Terms and People

Chapter 11

Section 1
John Jacob Astor *(p. 346)*
mountain men *(p. 346)*
Oregon Trail *(p. 348)*
Santa Fe Trail *(p. 349)*
Mormons *(p. 349)*
Brigham Young *(p. 349)*

Section 2
Father Miguel Hidalgo y Costilla *(p. 350)*
empresarios *(p. 350)*
Stephen F. Austin *(p. 351)*
Antonio López de Santa Anna *(p. 351)*
Alamo *(p. 352)*
Battle of San Jacinto *(p. 352)*

Section 3
manifest destiny *(p. 354)*
James K. Polk *(p. 355)*
vaqueros (p. 357)
Californios *(p. 357)*
Bear Flag Revolt *(p. 358)*
Treaty of Guadalupe Hidalgo *(p. 361)*
Gadsden Purchase *(p. 361)*

Section 4
John Sutter *(p. 365)*
Donner party *(p. 365)*
forty-niners *(p. 365)*
prospect *(p. 366)*
placer miners *(p. 366)*

Academic Vocabulary

Success in school is related to knowing academic vocabulary—the words that are frequently used in school assignments and discussions. In this chapter, you will learn the following academic words:

explicit *(p. 351)*
element *(p. 357)*

You Try It!

The following passage is from the chapter you are about to read. Read the passage and then answer the questions.

American Settlement in the Mexican Cession

From Chapter 11, p. 361

The war ended after Scott took Mexico City. In February 1848, the United States and Mexico signed the Treaty of Guadalupe Hidalgo, which officially ended the war and forced Mexico to turn over much of its northern territory to the United States. Known as the Mexican Cession, this land included the present-day states of California, Nevada, and Utah . . .

In exchange for this vast territory, the United States agreed to pay Mexico $15 million. In addition, the United States assumed claims of more than $3 million held by American citizens against the Mexican government.

Refer to the passage to answer the following questions.

1. Do you know what the word *cession* means? What clues in the first paragraph can help you figure out what the word might mean? Use those clues to write a definition of *cession*.

2. Look *cession* up in a dictionary. How does your definition compare to the dictionary definition?

3. In your experience, what does the word *assume* usually mean? Do you think that meaning is the one used in the second paragraph? If not, what do you think *assume* means in this case?

4. Look *assume* up in a dictionary. Does one of its meanings match the one you came up with?

As you read Chapter 11, use context clues to figure out the meanings of unfamiliar words. Check yourself by looking the words up in a dictionary.

SECTION 1

Trails to the West

What You Will Learn...

Main Ideas

1. During the early 1800s, Americans moved west of the Rocky Mountains to settle and trade.
2. The Mormons traveled west in search of religious freedom.

The Big Idea

The American West attracted a variety of settlers.

Key Terms and People

John Jacob Astor, *p. 346*
mountain men, *p. 346*
Oregon Trail, *p. 348*
Santa Fe Trail, *p. 349*
Mormons, *p. 349*
Brigham Young, *p. 349*

TAKING NOTES Create a diagram like the one below. As you read, take notes on the different groups that settled in the American West, the trails they took, and their motives for moving West.

Trails	Travelers	Motives

If YOU were there...

You live in Ohio in 1840. A few months ago, you and your family heard stories about a wonderful land in the Northwest, with sparkling rivers and fertile valleys. You all decide to pull up stakes and head West. You travel to Independence, Missouri, planning to join a wagon train on the Oregon Trail. In Missouri, you're surprised to find hundreds of other people planning to make the trip.

What would you expect your journey West to be like?

BUILDING BACKGROUND Many Americans in the Jacksonian Era were restless, curious, and eager to be on the move. The American West drew a variety of settlers. Some looked for wealth and adventure. Others, like this family on its way to the Northwest, dreamed of rich farmland and new homes.

Americans Move West

In the early 1800s, Americans pushed steadily westward, moving even beyond the territory of the United States. They traveled by canoe and flatboat, on horseback, and by wagon train. Some even walked much of the way.

The rush to the West occurred, in part, because of a hat. The "high hat," made of water-repellent beaver fur, was popular in the United States and Europe. While acquiring fur for the hats, French, British, and American companies gradually killed off the beaver population in the East. Companies moved west in search of more beavers. Most of the first non-Native Americans who traveled to the Rocky Mountains and the Pacific Northwest were fur traders and trappers.

American merchant **John Jacob Astor** created one of the largest fur businesses, the American Fur Company. His company bought skins from western fur traders and trappers who became known as **mountain men**. These adventurers were some of the first easterners to explore and map the Rocky Mountains and lands west of them. Mountain men lived lonely and often dangerous lives. They trapped animals on their own, far from towns and settlements. Mountain men such as Jedediah Smith, Manuel Lisa, Jim Bridger, and Jim

Trails Leading West

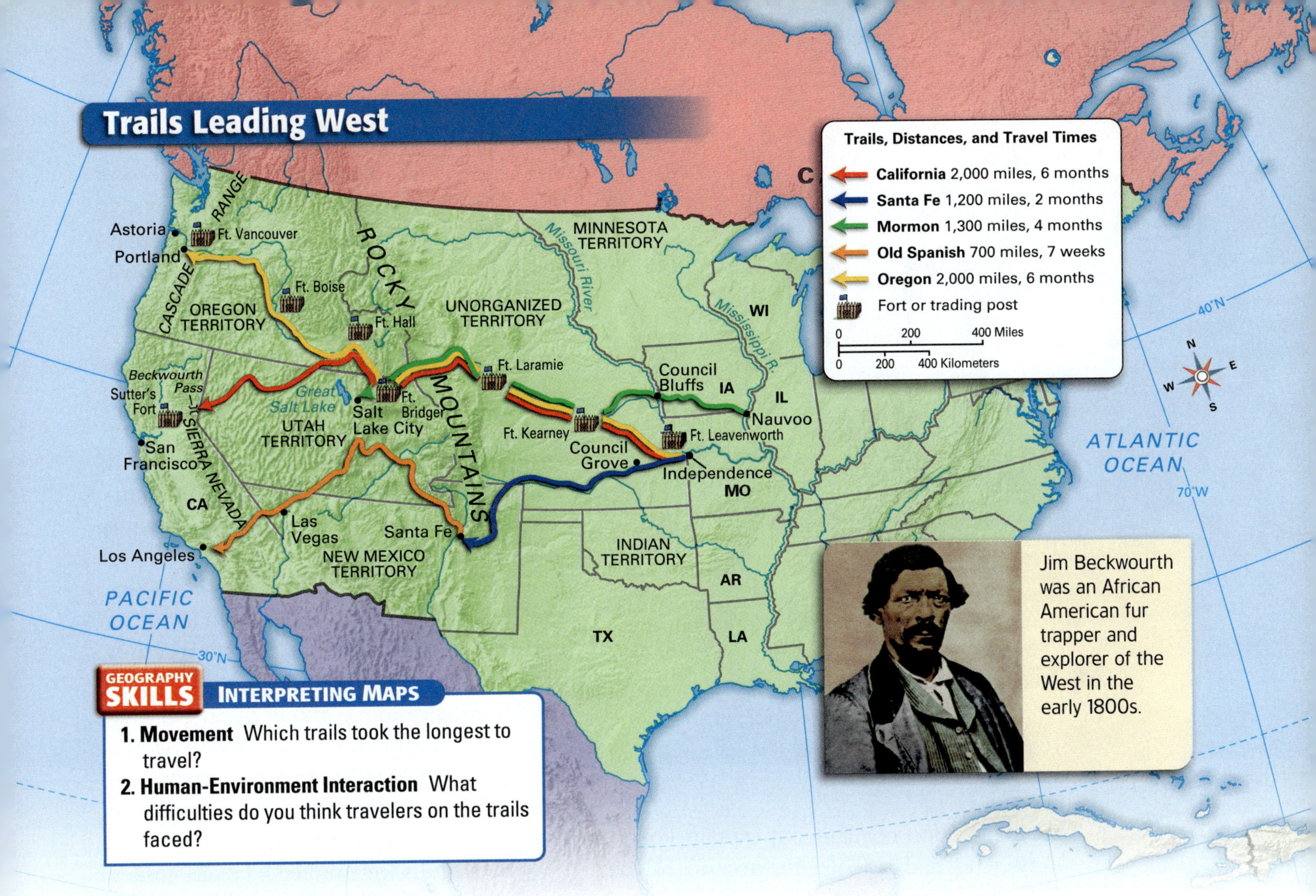

Jim Beckwourth was an African American fur trapper and explorer of the West in the early 1800s.

GEOGRAPHY SKILLS **INTERPRETING MAPS**

1. **Movement** Which trails took the longest to travel?
2. **Human-Environment Interaction** What difficulties do you think travelers on the trails faced?

Beckwourth survived many hardships during their search for wealth and adventure. To survive on the frontier, mountain men adopted Native American customs and clothing. In addition, they often married Native American women. The Indian wives of trappers often worked hard to contribute to their success.

Pioneer William Ashley saw that frequently bringing furs out of the Rocky Mountains was expensive. He asked his traders to stay in the mountains and meet once a year to trade and socialize. This practice helped make the fur trade more profitable. The yearly meeting was known as the rendezvous. At the rendezvous, mountain men and Native American trappers sold their fur to fur-company agents. It was thus important to bring as many furs as possible. One trapper described the people at a typical rendezvous in 1837. He saw Americans, Canadian French, some Europeans, and "Indians, of nearly every tribe in the Rocky Mountains."

The rendezvous was filled with celebrating and storytelling. At the same time, the meeting was also about conducting business. Western artist Alfred Jacob Miller described how trade was begun in the rendezvous camp.

> "The Fur Company's great tent is raised; the Indians erect their picturesque [beautiful] white lodges; the accumulated [collected] furs of the hunting season are brought forth and the Company's tent is a . . . busy place."
>
> —Alfred Jacob Miller, quoted in *The Fur Trade of the American West*, by David J. Wishart

In 1811, John Jacob Astor founded a fur-trading post called Astoria at the mouth of the Columbia River. Astoria was one of the first American settlements in what became known as Oregon Country. American Indians occupied the region, which was rich in forests, rivers, and wildlife. However, Britain, Russia, Spain, and the United States all claimed the land. The United States based its claim on

Mormon Pioneers

This Mormon family left Iowa in 1856 and took the Mormon Trail to Utah. The children walked 1,200 miles on this long and difficult journey.

How many family members can you see in this photo?

the exploration of merchant captain Robert Gray, who had reached the mouth of the Columbia River in 1792.

Recognizing the huge economic value of the Pacific Northwest, the United States made treaties in which Spain and Russia gave up their claims to various areas. The United States also signed treaties with Britain allowing both countries to occupy Oregon Country, the Columbia River, and its surrounding lands.

By the 1840s, the era of American fur trading in the Pacific Northwest was drawing to a close. The demand for beaver furs had fallen because fashions changed. Too much trapping had also greatly reduced the number of beavers. Some mountain men gave up their work and moved back east. Their daring stories, however, along with the treaties made by the U.S. government, inspired other Americans to move West. Lured by rich resources and a mild climate, easterners poured into Oregon Country in the 1840s. These new settlers soon replaced the mountain men on the frontier.

The Oregon Trail

Many settlers moving to Oregon Country and other western areas followed the 2,000-mile-long **Oregon Trail**, which stretched from places such as Independence, Missouri, or Council Bluffs, Iowa, west into Oregon Country. The trail followed the Platte and Sweetwater Rivers over the Plains. After it crossed the Rocky Mountains, the trail forked. The northern branch led to the Willamette Valley in Oregon. The other branch went to California and became known as the California Trail.

Traveling the trail challenged the strength and determination of pioneer families. The journey usually began after the rainy season ended in late spring and lasted about six months. The cost, about $600 for a family of four, was high at a time when a typical worker usually made about $1.50 per day. Young families made up most groups of settlers. They gathered in wagon trains for the trip. There could be as few as 10 wagons or as many as several dozen in a wagon train.

The wagons were pulled by oxen, mules, or horses. Pioneers often walked to save their animals' strength. They kept up a tiring pace, traveling from dawn until dusk. Settler Jesse Applegate recalled the advice he received from one experienced Oregon pioneer: "Travel, *travel*, TRAVEL . . . Nothing is good that causes a moment's delay."

Some pioneers brought small herds of cattle with them on the trail. They faced severe hardships, including shortages of food, supplies, and water. Rough weather and geographic barriers, such as rivers and mountains, sometimes forced large numbers of pioneers to abandon their wagons. In the early days of the Oregon Trail, many Native Americans helped the pioneers, acting as guides and messengers. They also traded goods for food. Although newspapers sometimes reported Native American "massacres" of pioneers, few settlers died from Indian attacks.

The settlers who arrived safely in Oregon and California found generally healthy and pleasant climates. By 1845 some 5,000 settlers occupied the Willamette Valley.

The Santa Fe Trail

The **Santa Fe Trail** was another important path west. It led from Independence, Missouri, to Santa Fe, New Mexico. It followed an ancient trading route first used by Native Americans. American traders loaded their wagon trains with cloth and other manufactured goods to exchange for horses, mules, and silver from Mexican traders in Santa Fe.

The long trip across blazing deserts and rough mountains was dangerous. But the lure of high profits encouraged traders to take to the trail. One trader reported a 2,000 percent profit on his cargo. The U.S. government helped protect traders by sending troops to ensure that Native Americans were not a threat.

READING CHECK **Contrasting** How were the Oregon and Santa Fe trails different?

Mormons Travel West

One large group of settlers traveled to the West in search of religious freedom. In 1830 a young man named Joseph Smith founded the Church of Jesus Christ of Latter-day Saints in western New York. The members of Joseph Smith's church became known as **Mormons**. Smith told his followers that he had found and translated a set of golden tablets containing religious teachings. The writings were called the *Book of Mormon*.

Church membership grew rapidly, but certain beliefs and practices caused Mormons to be persecuted. For example, beginning in the 1850s some Mormon men practiced polygamy—a practice in which one man is married to several women at the same time. This practice was outlawed by the church in 1890.

In the early 1830s Smith and his growing number of converts left New York. They formed new communities, first in Ohio, then in Missouri, and finally in Illinois. All three communities eventually failed, and an anti-Mormon mob murdered Smith in 1844. Following Smith's murder, **Brigham Young** became head of the Mormon Church. Young chose what is now Utah as the group's new home, and thousands of Mormons took the Mormon Trail to the area near the Great Salt Lake, where they prospered. By 1860 there were about 40,000 Mormons in Utah.

READING CHECK **Finding Main Ideas** Why did Mormons move west?

SUMMARY AND PREVIEW Some of the first Americans to move West were fur traders and trappers. Settlers soon followed. In the next section you will learn about the Texas Revolution.

Section 1 Assessment

go.hrw.com
Online Quiz
KEYWORD: SC7 HP11

Reviewing Ideas, Terms, and People

1. a. **Identify** What was the **Oregon Trail**?
   b. **Elaborate** Would you have chosen to leave your home to travel west? Why?
2. a. **Identify** Who are the **Mormons**?
   b. **Summarize** What difficulties led Mormons to move to Utah?

Critical Thinking

3. **Drawing Conclusions** Review your notes on early American settlement in the West. Then copy the chart below and use it to identify challenges of the trip that western travelers faced.

Travelers	Challenges Faced

FOCUS ON WRITING

4. **Describing Trails West** As you read this section, note important topics that you might want to cover in your documentary film. In addition, write down ideas about how you might present information about each topic. For example, will you use a narrator to tell the life story of Joseph Smith, or will you have actors present it dramatically?

SECTION 2

The Texas Revolution

What You Will Learn...

Main Ideas

1. Many American settlers moved to Texas after Mexico achieved independence from Spain.
2. Texans revolted against Mexican rule and established an independent nation.

The Big Idea

In 1836, Texas gained its independence from Mexico.

Key Terms and People

Father Miguel Hidalgo y Costilla, *p. 350*
empresarios, *p. 350*
Stephen F. Austin, *p. 351*
Antonio López de Santa Anna, *p. 351*
Alamo, *p. 352*
Battle of San Jacinto, *p. 352*

TAKING NOTES As you read, take notes on the events that led to the independence of Texas. Write your notes in steps, as shown below.

1. Mexican government hires empresarios.
2. ______
3. ______
4. ______

If YOU were there...

You are the father of a large farm family in Missouri. There is not enough land for everyone, so you're looking for another opportunity. One day, a Mexican government official comes to town. He is looking for people to settle in Texas. The Mexican government is offering generous tracts of land to colonists. However, you have to become a citizen of Mexico and follow Mexican laws.

Would you decide to move your family to Texas? Why?

BUILDING BACKGROUND Spain controlled a vast amount of territory in what would later become the American Southwest. The Spanish built missions and forts in Texas to establish control of that region. But the settlements were far apart, and conflicts with Native Americans discouraged Spanish settlers from moving to Texas. When Mexico became an independent republic, it actively looked for more settlers.

American Settlers Move to Texas

Mexico had a long, unprotected border that stretched from Texas to California. Mexico's Spanish rulers worried constantly about attacks from neighbors. They also were concerned about threats from within Mexico.

Their fears were justified. Mexicans moved to overthrow Spanish rule in the early 1800s. In September 1810 **Father Miguel Hidalgo y Costilla**, a Mexican priest, led a rebellion of about 80,000 poor Indians and mestizos, or people of Indian and Spanish ancestry. They hoped that if Mexico became independent from the Spanish monarchy, their lives would improve.

Hidalgo's revolt failed, but the rebellion he started grew. In 1821 Mexico became independent. In 1824 it adopted a republican constitution that declared rights for all Mexicans. The new Mexican government hired **empresarios**, or agents, to bring settlers to Texas. They paid the agents in land.

Settling Texas

Stephen F. Austin (standing, in black coat) and other settlers were empresarios—they received land from the Mexican government for the purpose of bringing settlers to Texas. Their holdings were guaranteed with a contract like the one below.

Why do you think the Mexican government wanted to attract settlers to Texas?

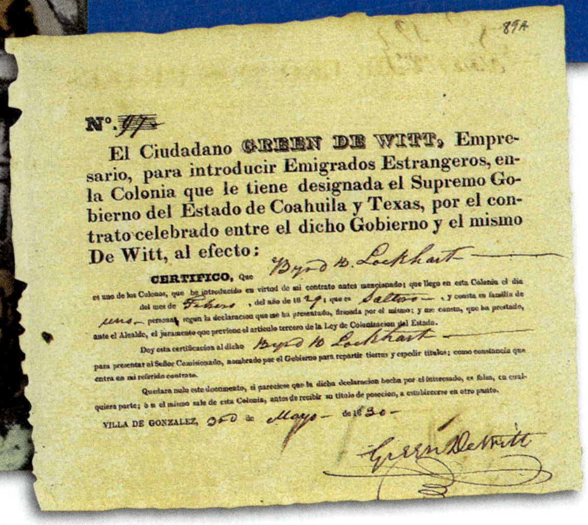

N°. 77

El Ciudadano GREEN DE WITT, Empresario, para introducir Emigrados Estrangeros, en la Colonia que le tiene designada el Supremo Gobierno del Estado de Coahuila y Texas, por el contrato celebrado entre el dicho Gobierno y el mismo De Witt, al efecto:

CERTIFICO, Que Byrd B. Lockhart es uno de los Colonos, que he introducido en virtud de mi contrato antes mencionado; que llegó en esta Colonia el dia del mes de Febrero, del año de 1829; que es Saltero, y consta su familia de una persona, segun la declaracion que me ha presentado, firmada por el mismo; y me consta, que ha prestado, ante el Alcalde, el juramento que previene el articulo tercero de la Ley de Colonizacion del Estado.

Doy esta certificacion al dicho Byrd B. Lockhart para presentar al Señor Comisionado, nombrado por el Gobierno para repartir tierras y espedir titulos; como constancia que entra en mi referido contrato.

Quedará nulo este documento, si pareciese que la dicha declaracion hecha por el interesado, es falsa, en cualquiera parte; ó si el mismo sale de esta Colonia, antes de recibir su titulo de posecion, a establecerse en otro punto.

VILLA DE GONZALEZ, 3 de Mayo de 1830.

Green DeWitt

In 1822 one young agent, **Stephen F. Austin**, started a Texas colony on the lower Colorado River. The first 300 families became known as the Old Three Hundred. Austin's successful colony attracted other agents, and American settlers flocked to the region.

In exchange for free land, settlers had to obey Mexican laws. But some settlers often **explicitly** ignored these laws. For example, despite the ban on slavery, many brought slaves. Concerned that it was losing control of the growing American population, Mexico responded. In 1830, it banned further settlement by Americans. Angry about the new law, many Texans began to think of gaining independence from Mexico.

Meanwhile, Mexico had come under the rule of General **Antonio López de Santa Anna**. He soon suspended Mexico's republican constitution and turned his attention to the growing unrest in Texas.

READING CHECK **Finding Main Ideas** Why did settlers move to Texas?

Texans Revolt against Mexico

In October 1835 the Mexican army tried to remove a cannon from the town of Gonzales, Texas. Rebels stood next to the cannon. Their flag read, "Come and take it." In the following battle, the rebels won. The Texas Revolution, also known as the Texas War for Independence, had begun.

ACADEMIC VOCABULARY

explicit fully revealed without vagueness

Texas Independence

On March 2, 1836, Texans declared their independence from Mexico. The new Republic of Texas was born. Both the declaration and the constitution that shortly followed were modeled after the U.S. documents. The Texas constitution, however, made slavery legal.

Delegates to the new Texas government chose politician David Burnet as president and Lorenzo de Zavala as vice president. Another revolutionary, Sam Houston, was named to head the Texas army. Austin went to the United States to seek money and troops.

Battle at the Alamo

FOCUS ON READING
Use this section to summarize the events of the battle at the Alamo.

The Texans' actions angered Santa Anna. He began assembling a force of thousands to stop the rebellion.

A hastily created army of Texas volunteers had been clashing with Mexican troops for months. Under Colonel William Travis, a small force took the town of San Antonio. It then occupied the **Alamo**, an abandoned mission near San Antonio that became an important battle site in the Texas Revolution. Volunteers from the United States, including frontiersman Davy Crockett and Colonel Jim Bowie, joined the Alamo's defense.

The rebels, numbering fewer than 200, hoped to stall the huge Mexican force while a larger Texas army assembled. For almost two weeks, from February 23 to March 6, 1836, the Texans held out. Travis managed to get a message to other Texans through enemy lines:

> "I call on you in the name of Liberty, of patriotism, and everything dear to the American character, to come to our aid with all dispatch [speed] ... VICTORY OR DEATH."
>
> —William Travis, from a letter written at the Alamo, 1836

Before dawn on March 6, the Mexican army attacked. Despite heavy losses, the army overcame the Texans. All the defenders of the Alamo were killed, though some civilians survived. Following a later battle, at Goliad, Santa Anna ordered the execution of 350 prisoners who had surrendered. Texans were enraged by the massacres.

Battle of San Jacinto

Santa Anna now chased the untrained forces of Sam Houston. Outnumbered, the Texans fled east. Finally, they reorganized at the San Jacinto River, near Galveston Bay. There, the Texans took a stand.

Santa Anna was confident of victory, but he was careless in choosing the site for his camp. On the afternoon of April 21, 1836, while Mexican troops were resting, Houston's forces swarmed the camp, shouting, "Remember the Alamo! Remember Goliad!"

The fighting ended swiftly. Santa Anna's army was destroyed. In the **Battle of San Jacinto**, the Texans captured Santa Anna and forced him to sign a treaty giving Texas its independence.

An Independent Nation

Sam Houston was the hero of the new independent nation of Texas. The republic created a new town named Houston and made it the capital. Voters elected Sam Houston as president. Stephen F. Austin became secretary of state.

To increase the population, Texas offered land grants. American settlers came from nearby southern states, often bringing slaves with them to help grow and harvest cotton.

Most Texans hoped that the United States would annex, or take control of, Texas, making it a state. The U.S. Congress also wanted to annex Texas. But President Andrew Jackson refused. He was concerned that admitting Texas as a slave state would upset the fragile balance of free and slave states. The president also did not want to have a war with Mexico over Texas.

Finally, Jackson did recognize Texas as an independent nation. France did so in 1839. Britain, which wanted to halt U.S. expansion, recognized Texas in 1840.

The Mexican government, however, did not recognize Santa Anna's forced handover of Texas. For this reason, in 1837 the republic organized the Texas Rangers to guard its long frontier from Mexican and Native American attacks. Finally, in 1844 Texas and Mexico signed a peace treaty.

On March 6, 1836, Texans fought and lost the Battle of the Alamo. A rallying cry for the Texans at the Battle of San Jacinto was "Remember the Alamo!" The single star of the flag represents the Republic of Texas, also called the Lone Star Republic.

Why do you think "Remember the Alamo!" was a rallying cry for Texas troops at San Jacinto?

READING CHECK **Finding Main Ideas** What issues did the new nation of Texas face?

SUMMARY AND PREVIEW American settlers in Texas challenged the Mexican government and won their independence. In the next section you will learn about the war between Mexico and the United States.

Section 2 Assessment

go.hrw.com
Online Quiz
KEYWORD: SC7 HP11

Reviewing Ideas, Terms, and People

1. a. **Identify** What role did **Stephen F. Austin** play in the settlement of Texas?
   b. **Make Inferences** Why did Mexican officials want to bring more settlers to Texas?
   c. **Evaluate** Do you think Mexico's requirements for foreign immigrants were reasonable or unreasonable? Explain.
2. a. **Describe** What were the important battles in the War for Texas Independence? Why was each important?
   b. **Make Inferences** Why did Texas offer land grants to settlers?
   c. **Predict** What problems might the Republic of Texas face?

Critical Thinking

3. **Sequencing** Review your notes on American settlement in Texas. Then copy the graphic organizer below and use it to show the significant events in the history of the Republic of Texas.

Significant Events
1. Houston is founded and made the capital.
2.
3.
4.
5.
6.
7.

FOCUS ON WRITING

4. **Explaining the Texas Revolution** As you read this section, make note of the most important players and events in the story of how Texas gained independence from Mexico. Consider also how you will present information about these people and events to your film's audience. What words, images, and sounds will make the story of the revolution come alive for the audience?

SECTION 3

The Mexican-American War

What You Will Learn...

Main Ideas

1. Many Americans believed that the nation had a manifest destiny to claim new lands in the West.
2. As a result of the Mexican-American War, the United States added territory in the Southwest.
3. American settlement in the Mexican Cession produced conflict and a blending of cultures.

The Big Idea

The ideals of manifest destiny and the outcome of the Mexican-American War led to U.S. expansion to the Pacific Ocean.

Key Terms and People

manifest destiny, *p. 354*
James K. Polk, *p. 355*
vaqueros, *p. 357*
Californios, *p. 357*
Bear Flag Revolt, *p. 358*
Treaty of Guadalupe Hidalgo, *p. 361*
Gadsden Purchase, *p. 361*

TAKING NOTES Create a graphic organizer like the one below. Use it to define *manifest destiny* and then list the events in the expansion of the United States.

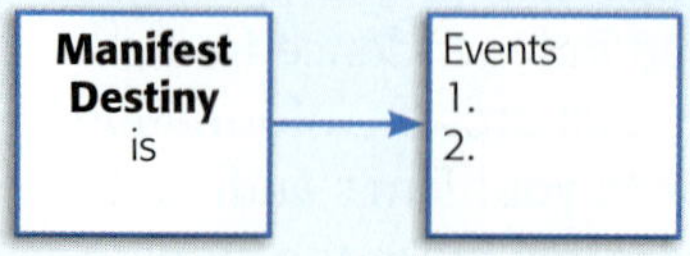

If YOU were there...

Your family are Californios, Spanish settlers who have lived in California for many years. You raise horses on your ranch. So far, you have gotten along with American settlers. But it has become clear that the American government wants to take over California. You hear that fighting has already started between American and Mexican troops.

How might life change under American rule?

BUILDING BACKGROUND Mexican independence set the stage for conflict and change in the West and Southwest. At the same time, American settlers continued to move westward, settling in the Mexican territories of Texas and California. American ambitions led to clashes with Mexico and the people who already lived in Mexico's territories.

Manifest Destiny

"We have it in our power to start the world over again."

—Thomas Paine, from his pamphlet *Common Sense*

Americans had always believed they could build a new, better society founded on democratic principles. In 1839 writer John O'Sullivan noted, "We are the nation of human progress, and who will, what can, set limits to our onward march?"

Actually, there was one limit: land. By the 1840s the United States had a booming economy and population. Barely 70 years old, the nation already needed more room for farms, ranches, businesses, and ever-growing families. Americans looked West to what they saw as a vast wilderness, ready to be taken.

Some people believed it was America's **manifest destiny**, or obvious fate, to settle land all the way to the Pacific Ocean in order to spread democracy. O'Sullivan coined the term in 1845. He wrote that it was America's "manifest destiny to overspread and to possess the whole continent which Providence [God] has given us for the development of the great experiment of liberty . . . "

Manifest Destiny

John Gast's 1872 painting *American Progress* shows the spirit of manifest destiny leading settlers westward.

What in this painting shows how settlers traveled west?

In the 1840s and 1850s, manifest destiny was tied up with the slavery issue. If America expanded, would slavery be allowed in the new territories? Several presidents became involved in the difficult issue. Among them was President John Tyler. A pro-slavery Whig, Tyler wanted to increase the power of the southern slave states by annexing Texas. His fellow Whigs disagreed.

In 1844, the Whig Party passed up Tyler and chose Senator Henry Clay of Kentucky as its presidential candidate. At first opposing annexation, Clay changed his mind due to pressure from southern politicians. The Democratic Party chose former Tennessee governor **James K. Polk** to oppose Clay. Both candidates strongly favored acquiring Texas and Oregon.

Southerners feared the loss of Texas, a possible new slave state. Others worried that Texas might become an ally of Britain. These concerns helped Polk narrowly defeat Clay.

Acquiring New Territory

President Polk quickly set out to fulfill his campaign promise to annex Oregon and Texas. By the 1820s, Russia and Spain had given up their claims to Oregon Country. Britain and the United States had agreed to occupy the territory together.

As more Americans settled there, they began to ask that Oregon become part of the United States. Polk wanted to protect these settlers' interests. Some politicians noted that Oregon Country would provide a Pacific port for the growing U.S. trade with China.

Meanwhile, Britain and the United States disagreed over how to draw the United States–Canadian border. American expansionists cried, "Fifty-four forty or fight!" This slogan referred to 54°40' north latitude, the line to which Americans wanted their northern territory to extend.

Neither side really wanted a war, though. In 1846 Great Britain and the United States signed a treaty that gave the United States all Oregon land south of the forty-ninth parallel. This treaty drew the border that still exists today. Oregon became an organized U.S. territory in February 1848.

Texas came next. By March 1845, Congress had approved annexation and

NC **History Makers**

James K. Polk
North Carolinian James Polk was president of the United States during key events of the country's westward expansion.

needed only the support of the Republic of Texas. Americans continued to pour into Texas. Texas politicians hoped that joining the United States would help solve the republic's financial and military problems. The Texas Congress approved annexation in June 1845. Texas became part of the United States in December. This action angered the Mexican government, which considered Texas to be a "stolen province."

California under Mexico

Though it had lost Texas, Mexico still had settlements in other areas of the present-day Southwest to govern. New Mexico was the oldest settled area, with its capital at Santa Fe. Mexico also controlled present-day Arizona, Nevada, and California.

During early Spanish rule, the mission system had dominated much of the present-day Southwest. Over time, it had become less important there, especially in New Mexico, where settlers lived in small villages. In California, however, missions remained the focus of everyday life. Missions under later Spanish rule carried out huge farming and ranching operations using the labor of Native Americans. Some of the Indians came willingly to the missions. Others were brought by force. Usually, they were not allowed to leave the mission once they had arrived. They had to adopt the clothing, food, and religion of the Spanish priests.

Missions often sold their goods to local pueblos, or towns, that arose near the missions and presidios. One wealthy California settler, Mariano Guadalupe Vallejo, remembered the early days.

> "We were the pioneers of the Pacific coast, building towns and missions while General [George] Washington was carrying on the war of the Revolution."
>
> —Mariano Guadalupe Vallejo, quoted in *Eyewitnesses and Others*

After winning independence from Spain in 1821, Mexico began to change old Spanish

History Close-up

Ranch Life

Spanish and Mexican *vaqueros*, or cowboys, were expert horse riders. They used their horses to herd cattle on the ranches of the Spanish Southwest.

ANALYSIS SKILL **ANALYZING VISUALS**

What features of the *vaqueros'* life are shown in this painting?

policies toward California and Texas. In 1833, for example, Mexico ended the mission system in California. Mission lands were broken up, and huge grants were given to some of the wealthiest California settlers, including Vallejo. They created vast ranchos, or ranches, with tens of thousands of acres of land. ***Vaqueros***, or cowboys, managed the large herds of cattle and sheep. Cowhides were so valuable that they were called "California banknotes." Hides were traded for household items and luxury goods with ship captains from the eastern United States. Some settlers also made wine and grew citrus fruits.

Although they had been freed from the missions, for most California Indians the elements of life changed very little. They continued to herd animals and do much of the hard physical labor on ranches and farms. Some, however, ran away into the wilderness or to the nearby towns of San Diego and Los Angeles.

The Californios

Because of the great distance between California and the center of Mexico's government, by the early 1820s California had only around 3,200 colonists. These early California settlers, called **Californios**, felt little connection to their faraway government.

Californios developed a lasting reputation for hospitality and skilled horse riding. In *Two Years Before the Mast*, American novelist Richard Henry Dana Jr. wrote about his encounters with Californio culture. He described, for example, what happened after a Californio served a feast to Dana and a friend.

> "We took out some money and asked him how much we were to pay. He shook his head and crossed himself, saying that it was charity—that the Lord gave it to us."
>
> —Richard Henry Dana Jr., from *Two Years Before the Mast*

In addition to traders and travelers, a small number of settlers also arrived from the United States. They were called Anglos by the Californios. Although there were few Anglo settlers in California, their calls for independence increased tensions between Mexico and the United States.

BIOGRAPHY

Mariano Guadalupe Vallejo
1808–1890

Mariano Guadalupe Vallejo was born to an influential Californio family in Monterey. He joined the Mexican army shortly after Mexico's independence from Spain. He was soon put in charge of Mexico's efforts to increase settlement in northern California. Vallejo eventually became the richest man in California, owning enormous amounts of land and livestock. He welcomed American rule of California, believing it would result in self-government for Californios. Vallejo served at the state constitutional convention as well as in the first state senate.

Analyzing Why did Vallejo encourage American rule of California?

READING CHECK **Drawing Inferences** How did manifest destiny affect Spanish and Mexican rule in California?

ACADEMIC VOCABULARY
element a basic part of an individual's surroundings

Mexican-American War

Diplomatic relations between Mexico and the United States became increasingly strained. U.S. involvement in California and Texas contributed to this tension.

Conflict Breaks Out

Mexico had long insisted that its northern border lay along the Nueces River. The United States said the border was farther south, along the Rio Grande. In June 1845 President Polk ordered General Zachary Taylor to lead an army into the disputed region.

Polk sent diplomat John Slidell to Mexico City to try to settle the border dispute. Slidell came with an offer to buy New Mexico and California for $30 million. Mexican officials refused to speak to him.

In March 1846, General Taylor led his troops to the Rio Grande. He camped across from Mexican forces stationed near the town of Matamoros, Mexico. In April, the Mexican commander told Taylor to withdraw from Mexican territory. Taylor refused. The two sides clashed, and several U.S. soldiers were killed.

In response, President Polk said to Congress:

> "Mexico has passed the boundary of the United States, has invaded our territory, and shed American blood upon the American soil ... The two nations are now at war."
>
> —James K. Polk, from his address to Congress, May 11, 1846

Polk's war message was persuasive. Two days later, Congress declared war on Mexico.

War Begins

At the beginning of the war with Mexico, the U.S. Army had better weapons and equipment. Yet it was greatly outnumbered and poorly prepared. The government put out a call for 50,000 volunteers. About 200,000 responded. Many were young men who thought the war would be a grand adventure in a foreign land.

On the home front, many Americans supported the war. However, many Whigs thought the war was unjustified and avoidable. Northern abolitionists also opposed the conflict. They feared the spread of slavery into southwestern lands.

While Americans debated the war, fighting proceeded. General Taylor's soldiers won battles south of the Nueces River. Taylor then crossed the Rio Grande and occupied Matamoros, Mexico. While Taylor waited for more men, Polk ordered General Stephen Kearny to attack New Mexico. On August 18, 1846, Kearny took Santa Fe, the capital city, without a fight. He claimed the entire province of New Mexico for the United States and marched west to California, where another conflict with Mexico was already under way.

The Bear Flag Revolt

In 1846, only about 500 Americans lived in the huge province of California, in contrast to about 12,000 Californios. Yet, in the spirit of manifest destiny, a small group of American settlers seized the town of Sonoma, north of San Francisco, on June 14. Hostilities began between the two sides when the Americans took some horses that were intended for the Mexican militia. In what became known as the **Bear Flag Revolt**, the Americans declared California to be an independent nation. Above the town, the rebels hoisted a hastily made flag of a grizzly bear facing a red star. Californios laughed at the roughly-made bear, thinking it "looked more like a pig than a bear."

John C. Frémont, a U.S. Army captain, was leading a mapping expedition across the Sierra Nevada when he heard of the possible war with Mexico. Frémont went to Sonoma and quickly joined the American settlers in their revolt against the Californios. Because war had already broken out between the United States and Mexico, Frémont's actions were seen as beneficial to the American cause in the region. His stated goal, however, was Californian independence, not to annex California to the United States. During the revolt, several important Californios were taken prisoner, including Mariano Vallejo. Vallejo and his brother were held at an Anglo settlement for two months without any formal charges being brought against them. Long after his release, Vallejo wrote a history of California that included an account of his time as a bear flag prisoner.

But the bear flag was quick to fall. In July, U.S. naval forces came ashore in California and raised the stars and stripes. Kearny's army arrived from the East. The towns of San Diego, Los Angeles, and San Francisco fell rapidly. In August, U.S. Navy commodore Robert Stockton claimed California for the United States. Some Californios continued to resist until early 1847, when they surrendered.

Interactive Map

Mexican-American War, 1846–1847

The Bear Flag Revolt

American settlers took over Sonoma, the regional headquarters of the Mexican army. They captured Mexican general Mariano Vallejo and declared California a new country: the California Republic.

End of the War

General Winfield Scott landed at Veracruz and defeated troops in the Mexican fortress there. He then marched inland, toward Mexico City. Scott's capture of the Mexican capital led to the end of the war.

go.hrw.com
Interactive Map
KEYWORD: SC7 CH11

GEOGRAPHY SKILLS INTERPRETING MAPS

1. **Location** What Mexican city did Scott's forces attack in March 1847?
2. **Movement** Which U.S. commander led forces from Santa Fe to San Diego?

American soldier

War's End

In Mexico General Taylor finally got the reinforcements he needed. He drove his forces deep into enemy lands. Santa Anna, thrown from office after losing Texas, returned to power in Mexico in September 1846. He quickly came after Taylor.

The two armies clashed at Buena Vista in February 1847. After a close battle with heavy casualties on both sides, the Mexican Army retreated. The next morning, the cry went up: "The enemy has fled! The field is ours!"

Taylor's success made him a war hero back home. The general's popularity troubled President Polk, and when Taylor's progress stalled, Polk gave the command to General Winfield Scott. A beloved leader, he was known by his troops as "Old Fuss and Feathers" because of his strict military discipline.

Scott sailed to the port of Veracruz, the strongest fortress in Mexico. On March 29, after an 88-hour artillery attack, Veracruz fell. Scott moved on to the final goal, Mexico City, the capital. Taking a route similar to one followed by Spanish conquistador Hernán Cortés in 1519, the Americans pushed 200 or so miles inland. Santa Anna tried to stop the U.S. forces at Cerro Gordo in mid-April, but failed. By August 1847, U.S. troops were at the edge of Mexico City.

After a truce failed, Scott ordered a massive attack on Mexico City. Mexican soldiers and civilians fought fierce battles in and around the capital. At a military school atop the steep, fortified hill of Chapultepec, young Mexican cadets bravely defended their hopeless position. At least one soldier jumped to his death rather than surrender to the invading forces. Finally, on September 14, 1847, Mexico City fell. Santa Anna soon fled the country.

READING CHECK **Sequencing** In chronological order, list the key battles of the Mexican-American War.

FOCUS ON NORTH CAROLINA

Two North Carolinians played important roles in the Mexican-American War. James Knox Polk served as president and Braxton Bragg rose through the ranks of the army to become a prominent officer. Today a memorial in Pineville commemorates Polk's time in office, and Fort Bragg continues Bragg's legacy of military discipline.

Battle of Buena Vista

After the two-day Battle of Buena Vista, the American army gained control of northern Mexico. At the beginning of the battle, Mexican forces outnumbered the Americans. But the Mexicans suffered more than twice as many casualties.

Why was the Battle of Buena Vista a turning point in the Mexican-American War?

Mexican soldier

American Settlement in the Mexican Cession

The war ended after Scott took Mexico City. In February 1848, the United States and Mexico signed the **Treaty of Guadalupe Hidalgo**, which officially ended the war and forced Mexico to turn over much of its northern territory to the United States. Known as the Mexican Cession, this land included the present-day states of California, Nevada, and Utah. In addition, it included most of Arizona and New Mexico and parts of Colorado and Wyoming. The United States also won the area claimed by Texas north of the Rio Grande. The Mexican Cession totaled more than 500,000 square miles and increased the size of the United States by almost 25 percent.

Agreements and Payments

In exchange for this vast territory, the United States agreed to pay Mexico $15 million. In addition, the United States assumed claims of more than $3 million held by American citizens against the Mexican government. The treaty also addressed the status of Mexicans in the Mexican Cession. The treaty provided that they would be "protected in the free enjoyment of their liberty and property, and secured in the free exercise of their religion." The Senate passed the treaty in March 1848.

After the war with Mexico, some Americans wanted to guarantee that any southern railroad to California would be built completely on American soil. James Gadsden, U.S. minister to Mexico, negotiated an important agreement with Mexico in December 1853. Under the terms of the **Gadsden Purchase**, the U.S. government paid Mexico $10 million. In exchange, the United States received the southern parts of what are now Arizona and New Mexico. With this purchase, the existing boundary with Mexico was finally fixed.

Surge of American Settlers

After the Mexican-American War, a flood of Americans moved to the Southwest. American newcomers struggled against longtime residents to control the land and other valuable resources, such as water and minerals. Most Mexicans, Mexican Americans, and Native Americans faced legal, economic, and social discrimination. As a result, they found it difficult to protect their rights.

The Treaty of Guadalupe Hidalgo promised to protect Mexican American residents' property rights. Yet differences between Mexican and U.S. land laws led to great confusion. The U.S. government often made Mexican American landowners go to court to prove that they had titles to their land. Landowners had to pay their own travel costs as well as those of witnesses and interpreters. They also had to pay attorneys' and interpreters' fees. These legal battles often bankrupted landowners. New settlers also tended to ignore Mexican legal concepts, such as community property or community water rights.

LINKING TO TODAY

Mexican Americans Today

Today Mexican Americans are about 8 percent of the U.S. population. More than 20 million Mexican Americans live in all 50 states. Many who live in the West are descended from people who lived there long before the region became part of the United States.

GEOGRAPHY SKILLS **INTERPRETING MAPS**

1. **Region** In what region does the largest percentage of Mexican Americans live?
2. **Place** Which two states have the highest concentrations of Mexican Americans?

White settlers also battled with American Indians over property rights. In some areas, for example, new white settlers soon outnumbered southwestern Native Americans. The Anglo settlers often tried to take control of valuable water resources and grazing lands. In addition, settlers rarely respected Indian holy places. Native American peoples such as the Navajo and the Apache tried to protect their land and livestock from the settlers. Indians and settlers alike attacked one another to protect their interests.

THE IMPACT TODAY

Mexican holidays like Cinco de Mayo and Día de los Muertos are still popular holidays in the Southwest.

Cultural Encounters

Despite conflicts, different cultures shaped one another in the Southwest. In settlements with large Mexican populations, laws were often printed in both English and Spanish. Names of places—such as San Antonio, San Diego, and Santa Barbara—show Hispanic heritage. Other place-names, such as Taos and Tesuque, are derived from Native American words. Communities throughout the Southwest regularly celebrated both Mexican and American holidays.

Mexican and Native American knowledge and traditions also shaped many local economies. Mexican Americans taught Anglo settlers about mining in the mountains. Many ranching communities were first started by Mexican settlers. In addition, Mexican Americans introduced new types of saddles and other equipment to American ranchers. Adobe, developed by the Anasazi Indians, was adopted from the Pueblo people by the Spanish. It is still commonly used by American residents in New Mexico, Arizona, and California.

Trade also changed the Southwest. For example, the Navajo created handwoven woolen blankets to sell to Americans. Americans in turn brought manufactured goods and money to the Southwest. Due to exchanges like these, the economies of many Mexican American and Native American communities in the Southwest began to change.

Water Rights

Eastern water-use laws commonly required owners whose land bordered streams or rivers to maintain a free flow of water. These restrictions generally prevented landowners from constructing dams because doing so would infringe upon the water rights of neighbors downstream.

In the typically dry climate of the West, large-scale agriculture was not possible without irrigation. Dams and canals were required to direct scarce water to fields. This need conflicted with the accepted eastern tradition of equal access to water.

Brigham Young established a strict code regulating water rights for the Mormon community. In any dispute over water use, the good of the community would outweigh the interests of individuals. Young's approach stood as an example for modern water laws throughout the West.

READING CHECK **Summarizing** What were some of the early important agreements between the United States and Mexico, and why were they significant?

SUMMARY AND PREVIEW America's westward expansion continued rapidly after the Mexican-American War. In the next section you will learn about the California gold rush.

Section 3 Assessment

go.hrw.com
Online Quiz
KEYWORD: SC7 HP11

Reviewing Ideas, Terms, and People

1. a. **Define** What was **manifest destiny**?
   b. **Make Inferences** Why was westward expansion such an important issue in the election of 1844?
   c. **Evaluate** Do you think California benefited from Mexican independence? Why or why not?
2. a. **Recall** Why did the United States declare war on Mexico?
   b. **Summarize** What was General Winfield Scott's strategy for winning the war with Mexico?
   c. **Elaborate** Would you have sided with those who opposed the war with Mexico or with those who supported it? Why?
3. a. **Describe** What conflicts did American settlers, Native Americans, and Mexican Americans in the Mexican Cession experience?
   b. **Draw Conclusions** Why were water rights so important in the American Southwest?
   c. **Evaluate** In your opinion, what was the most important effect of the annexation of the Mexican Cession?

Critical Thinking

4. **Identifying Cause and Effect** Review your notes on manifest destiny and U.S. territorial expansion. Then use the graphic organizer below to show how Americans' expansion into California caused war, as well as the effects of the war.

FOCUS ON WRITING

5. **Explaining the Mexican-American War** How will you convey ideas, such as manifest destiny, in a film? How will you explain to your audience the Mexican-American War's role in expansion of the United States? Consider these questions as you read this section.

SECTION 4

The California Gold Rush

What You Will Learn...

Main Ideas

1. The discovery of gold brought settlers to California.
2. The gold rush had a lasting impact on California's population and economy.

The Big Idea

The California gold rush changed the future of the West.

Key Terms and People

John Sutter, *p. 365*
Donner party, *p. 365*
forty-niners, *p. 365*
prospect, *p. 366*
placer miners, *p. 366*

TAKING NOTES As you read, take notes on the California gold rush in a chart like the one below.

Gold Rush	
How was gold first discovered?	
How was a stake claimed?	
What was life like in camps?	
Who came to California for gold?	

If YOU were there...

You are a low-paid bank clerk in New England in early 1849. Local newspaper headlines are shouting exciting news: "Gold Is Discovered in California! Thousands Are on Their Way West." You enjoy having a steady job. However, some of your friends are planning to go west, and you are being influenced by their excitement. Your friends are even buying pickaxes and other mining equipment. They urge you to go west with them.

Would you go west to seek your fortune in California? Why?

BUILDING BACKGROUND At the end of the Mexican-American War, the United States gained control of Mexican territories in the West, including all of the present-day state of California. American settlements in California increased slowly at first. Then, the discovery of gold brought quick population growth and an economic boom.

Discovery of Gold Brings Settlers

In the 1830s and 1840s, Americans who wanted to move to California started up the Oregon Trail. At the Snake River in present-day Idaho, the trail split. People bound for California took the southern route, which became known as the California Trail. This path ran through the Sierra Nevada mountain range. American emigrants and traders on the California Trail tried to cross these mountains before the season's first snows.

Although many Americans traveled along the California Trail, few actually settled in California. American merchants were usually more interested in trading goods made in factories than in establishing settlements. They traded for gold and silver coins, hides, and tallow (animal fat used to make soap and candles) from Mexico. California became a meeting ground for traders from Mexico and the United States.

Before the Mexican-American War, California's population consisted mostly of Mexicans and Native Americans. When Mexico controlled California, Mexican officials did not want many Americans to settle there. However, in 1839 they did give Swiss immigrant **John Sutter** permission to start a colony. Sutter's Fort, located near the Sacramento River, soon became a popular rest stop for many American emigrants. These new arrivals praised Sutter's hospitality and helpfulness. By the mid-1840s some Anglo Californians were publishing newspaper advertisements and guidebooks encouraging other settlers to move West.

The **Donner party** was a group of western travelers who went to California but were stranded in the Sierra Nevada Mountains during winter. The party began its journey West in the spring of 1846. Trying to find a shortcut, the group left the main trail and got lost. When the Donner party reached the Sierra Nevada Mountains, they became trapped by heavy snows. They were stuck and had almost no food.

A rescue party found the starving and freezing group in February 1847. Of the original 87 travelers, 42 had died.

Gold in California

In January 1848, Sutter sent a carpenter named James Marshall to build a sawmill beside a nearby river. While working near Sutter's Mill, Marshall glanced at the ground. "I reached my hand down and picked it up; it made my heart thump, for I was certain it was gold."

Sutter and Marshall agreed to keep the discovery a secret. However, when they examined the work site the next day, they met a Spanish-speaking Native American worker holding a nugget and shouting, "Oro [gold]! Oro! Oro!"

Sutter's workers soon quit to search for gold. Stories of the discovery rapidly spread across the country. President Polk added to the national excitement by confirming the California gold strike in his farewell message to Congress in December 1848. In 1849 about 80,000 gold-seekers came to California, hoping to strike it rich. These gold-seeking migrants to California were called **forty-niners**. As one Iowa woman who

"Gold Fever"

"Gold fever" brought 80,000 people, like this miner, to California in 1849 alone. One California newspaper captured the excitement: "The whole country, from San Francisco to Los Angeles, and from the sea shore to the base of the Sierra Nevadas, resounds with the cry of 'gold, GOLD, GOLD!' while the field is left half planted, the house half built, and everything neglected but the manufacture of shovels and pickaxes." Below is a piece of jewelry made from nuggets found in California.

Why was everything neglected except for "the manufacture of shovels and pickaxes"?

California State Library

left to find gold recalled, "At that time the 'gold fever' was contagious, and few, old or young, escaped the malady [sickness]." Nearly 80 percent of the forty-niners were Americans, while the rest came from all over the world.

Most forty-niners braved long and often dangerous journeys to reach California. Many easterners and Europeans arrived via sea routes. Midwestern gold-seekers usually traveled West in wagon trains. Most forty-niners first arrived in San Francisco. This port town became a convenient trade center and stopping point for travelers. As a result, its population increased from around 800 in March 1848 to more than 25,000 by 1850.

Staking a Claim

Few of the forty-niners had any previous gold-mining experience. The work was difficult and time-consuming. The forty-niners would **prospect**, or search for gold, along the banks of streams or in shallow surface mines. The early forty-niners worked an area that ran for 70 miles along rivers in northern California.

The first person to arrive at a site would "stake a claim." Early miners frequently banded together to prospect for gold. The miners agreed that each would keep a share of whatever gold was discovered. When one group abandoned a claim, more recent arrivals often took it over, hoping for success. Sometimes, two or more groups arrived in an area at the same time. In the early gold-rush days, before courts were established, this competition often led to conflict. Occasionally, violent disputes arose over competing claims.

Mining methods varied according to the location. The most popular method, placer (PLA-suhr) mining, was done along rivers and streams. **Placer miners** used pans or other devices to wash gold nuggets out of loose rock and gravel. To reach gold deposits buried in

Miners came to California from around the world to make their fortune. In the photo on the left, Anglo and Chinese miners work together in Auburn Ravine in 1852. Above, a woman joins men to look for gold. Fewer women than men moved west to search for gold, but the ones that did often found greater social and economic opportunity than they had in the east.

Why might people leave their homes and travel long distances in search of gold?

the hills, miners had to dig shafts and tunnels. These tasks were usually pursued by mining companies, rather than by individuals.

In 1853 California's yearly gold production peaked at more than $60 million. Individual success stories inspired many miners. One lucky man found two and a half pounds of gold after only 15 minutes of work. Two African American miners found a rich gold deposit that became known as Negro Hill in honor of their discovery. The vast majority of miners, however, did not become rich. Forty-niner Alonzo Delano commented that the "lean, meager [thin], worn-out and woebegone [sorrowful] miner . . . might daily be seen at almost every point in the upper mines."

Life in the Mining Camps

Mining camps sprang up wherever enough people gathered to look for gold. These camps had colorful names, such as Hangtown or Poker Flat.

Miners in the camps came from many cultures and backgrounds. Most miners were young, unmarried men in search of adventure. Only around 5 percent of gold-rush immigrants were women or children. The hardworking women generally made good money by cooking meals, washing clothes, and operating boardinghouses. One such woman, Catherine Haun, recalled her first home in California.

> "We were glad to settle down and go housekeeping in a shed that was built in a day of lumber purchased with the first fee . . . For neighbors, we had a real live saloon. I never have received more respectful attention than I did from these neighbors."
>
> —Catherine Haun, quoted in *Ordinary Americans,* edited by Linda R. Monk

Haun's husband was a lawyer. He concluded that he could make more money practicing law than he could panning for gold. He was one of many people who made a good living supplying miners with food, clothing, equipment, and other services. Miners paid high prices for basic necessities because the large amounts of gold in circulation caused severe inflation in California. A loaf of bread, for example, might cost 5 cents in the East, but it would sell for 50 to 75 cents in San Francisco. Eggs sometimes sold for $1 apiece.

Some settlers took full advantage of these conditions for free enterprise. Biddy Mason and her family, for instance, had arrived in California as slaves. A Georgia slaveholder had brought them during the gold-rush years. Mason quickly discovered that most Californians opposed slavery, particularly in the gold mines. She and her family gained their freedom and moved to the small village of Los Angeles. There she saved money until she could purchase some land. Over time, Mason's property increased in value from $250 to $200,000. She became one of the wealthiest landowners in California, a community leader, and a well-known supporter of charities.

FOCUS ON NORTH CAROLINA

Many miners who had lived in North Carolina during its gold rush moved to California looking for gold. Before gold was discovered in California, North Carolina and Georgia provided most of the country's gold for coins.

Westward Movement in the United States

QUICK FACTS

Causes

- Americans believe in the idea of manifest destiny.
- The United States acquires vast new lands in the West.
- Pathfinders open trails to new territories.
- Gold is discovered in California.

Effects

- Native Americans are forced off lands.
- Americans travel west to settle new areas.
- The United States stretches to the Pacific Ocean.
- California experiences a population boom.

Immigrants to California

The lure of gold in California attracted miners from around the world. Many were from countries that had seen few immigrants to the United States in the past. They were drawn to California by the lure of wealth. For example, famine and economic hardship in southeastern China caused many Chinese men to leave China for America. Most hoped to find great wealth, and then return home to China. These immigrants were known in Chinese as *gam saan haak*, or "travelers to Gold Mountain." Between 1849 and 1853 about 24,000 Chinese men moved to California. "From far and near we came and were pleased," wrote merchant Lai Chun-chuen in 1855.

THE IMPACT TODAY

Today California is the nation's most populous state.

Chinese immigrants soon discovered that many Americans did not welcome them, however. In 1852, California placed a high monthly tax on all foreign miners. Chinese miners had no choice but to pay this tax if they wanted to prospect for gold in California. Some Chinese workers were the targets of violent attacks. If the Chinese miners dared to protest the attacks, the legal system favored Americans over immigrants.

Despite such treatment, many Chinese immigrants still worked in the gold mines. Some looked for other jobs. Others opened their own businesses. A newspaper reported Chinese working as "ploughmen, laundrymen, placer miners, woolen spinners and weavers, domestic servants, cigar makers, [and] shoemakers."

In 1849 alone, about 20,000 immigrants arrived in California not only from China but also from Europe, Mexico, and South America. Like most Americans who sought gold, these new arrivals intended to return home after they had made their fortunes. However, many decided to stay. Some began businesses. For example, Levi Strauss, a German immigrant, earned a fortune by making tough denim pants for miners.

READING CHECK **Categorizing** What types of people came to California hoping to benefit from the gold rush?

Impact on California

During the Spanish and Mexican periods of settlement, California's population grew slowly. The arrival of the forty-niners changed this dramatically.

Population Boom

California's population explosion made it eligible for statehood only two years after being acquired by the United States. In 1850 California became the 31st state.

However, fast population growth had negative consequences for many Californios and California Native Americans. One early observer of the gold rush described why.

> "The Yankee regarded every man but [his own kind] as an interloper [trespasser], who had no right to come to California and pick up the gold of 'free and enlightened citizens.'"
>
> —W. Kelly, quoted in *The Other Californians,* by Robert F. Heizer and Alan F. Almquist

San Francisco Grows

San Francisco boomed in the early years of the gold rush.

What factors led to San Francisco's population growth?

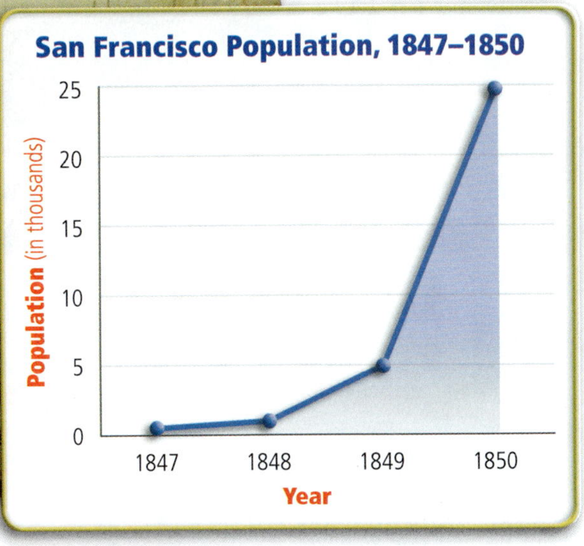

Economic Growth

In addition to rapid population growth, a flood of new businesses and industries transformed California's economy. Gold mining remained an important part of the state's early economy. But Californians soon discovered other ways to make a living. Farming and ranching, for example, became industries for those willing to do the necessary hard labor.

California faced an obstacle to growth, though. The state was isolated from the rest of the country. It was difficult to bring in and ship out goods. The answer to the isolation problem was to bring the railroad all the way to California. Californians would have to wait almost 20 years for that. Completion of the transcontinental railroad in 1869 at last gave Californians the means to grow a stronger economy.

READING CHECK **Analyzing Information** What political effect resulted from California's rapid population growth?

SUMMARY AND PREVIEW Americans moved west to create new lives and seize new opportunities. In the next chapter you will learn about the Industrial Revolution in America.

Section 4 Assessment

go.hrw.com
Online Quiz
KEYWORD: SC7 HP11

Reviewing Ideas, Terms, and People

1. a. **Recall** Why was Sutter's Mill important?
   b. **Summarize** What types of people participated in the California gold rush, and how did they take part in it?
   c. **Elaborate** What are some possible problems caused by the arrival of so many new settlers to California?
2. a. **Describe** How did some people hope to solve the problem of California's isolation from the rest of the country?
   b. **Draw Inferences** What effect did California's rapid population growth have on Californios and Native Americans?
   c. **Evaluate** Overall, do you think that the gold rush had a positive or negative effect on California? Explain.

Critical Thinking

3. **Evaluating** Review your notes on the gold rush. Then copy the graphic organizer below. Use it to show how the discovery of gold changed California.

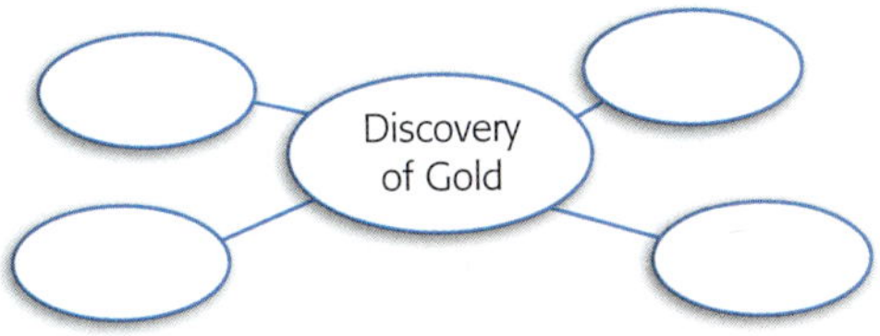

FOCUS ON WRITING

4. **Describing the California Gold Rush** As you read this section, take note of significant events and effects of the gold rush. Consider also how your film can convey the excitement of that time in American history.

History and Geography

America's Growth 1850

In the 1830s, a new dream began to shape the American mind—manifest destiny. Manifest destiny was the belief that the United States should extend all the way to the Pacific Ocean. By 1850, that dream had become a reality. In 1845, the United States annexed Texas. In 1848, it acquired Oregon and the huge Mexican Cession. By 1853, with the Gadsden Purchase, the United States had taken the basic shape it still has today.

America's Population, 1850: 23.6 million

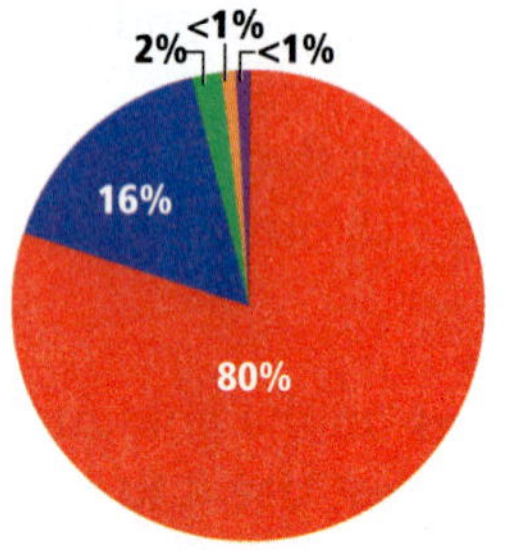

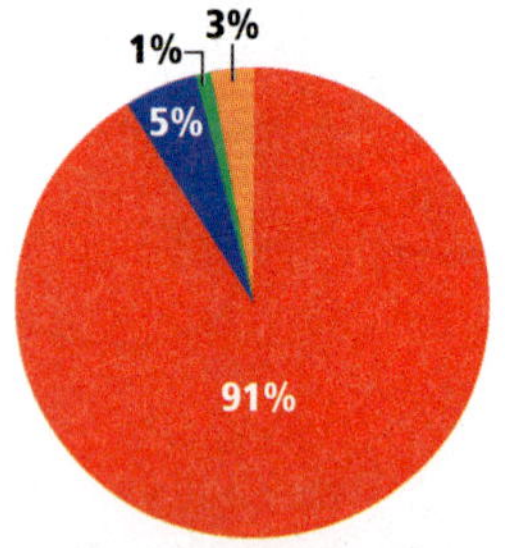

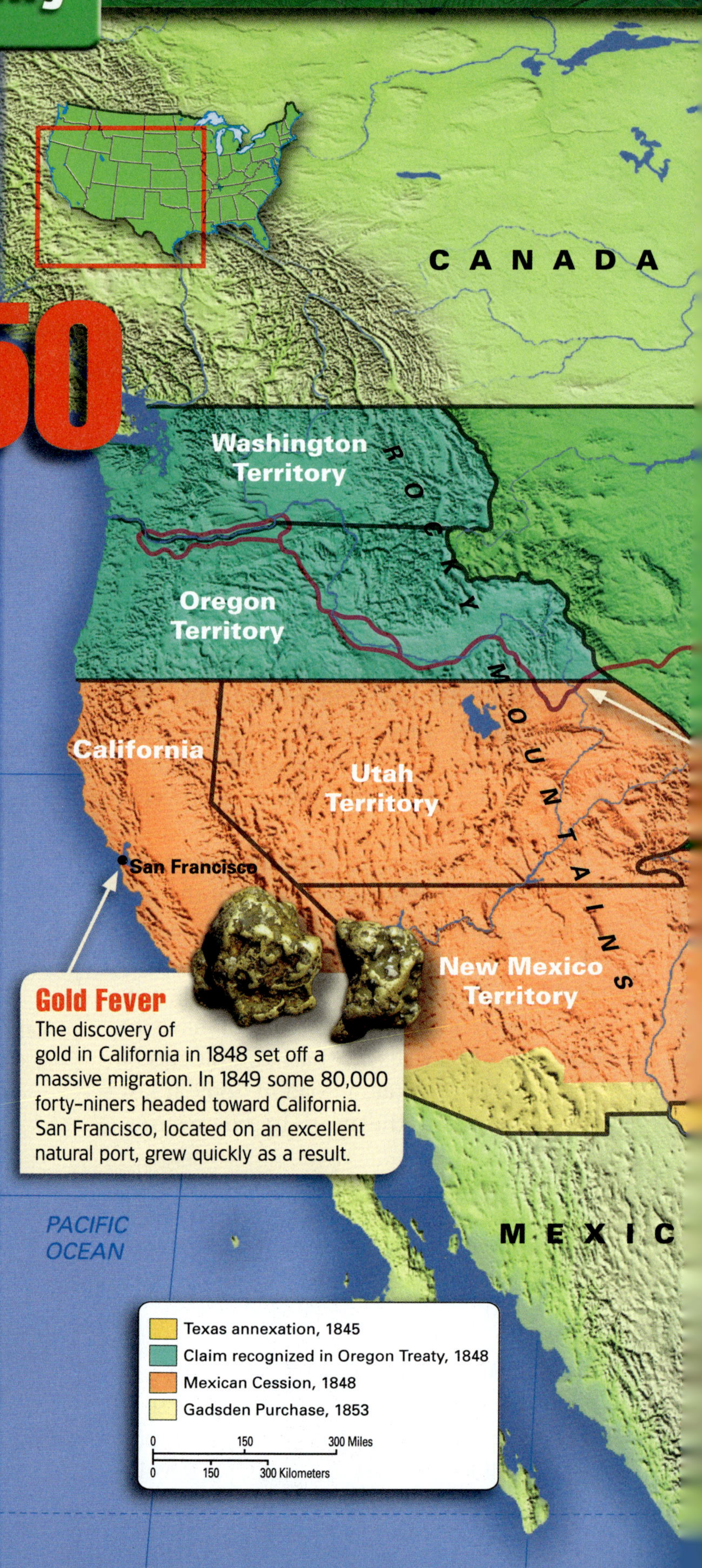

Gold Fever
The discovery of gold in California in 1848 set off a massive migration. In 1849 some 80,000 forty-niners headed toward California. San Francisco, located on an excellent natural port, grew quickly as a result.

Water Rights Water was critical in the dry West. Bitter disputes arose over who had the water rights to streams. Gold rush miners developed a simple system: whoever used the water first owned the rights to it. In other parts of the West, the community as a whole had a right to use the water source.

Manifest Destiny Supporters of manifest destiny believed it was God's will that the United States should expand and spread democracy across North America. Huge numbers of settlers headed West to tame new lands.

The Rocky Mountains The Rocky Mountains were a gigantic obstacle to settlers on their way West. Pathfinders like Lt. John C. Frémont traveled widely in the region, making maps and noting possible trails. The South Pass, through which the Oregon Trail ran, was one of the few easy ways through the great chain of mountains.

GEOGRAPHY SKILLS **INTERPRETING MAPS**

1. **Movement** Why did San Francisco grow so rapidly?
2. **Human-Environment Interaction** Which two mountain ranges woud someone from North Carolina have to cross to reach Oregon Territory?

Social Studies Skills

Analysis | Critical Thinking | Civic Participation | **Study**

North Carolina Skills
2.02 Explore print and non-print materials.

Interpreting Maps: Expansion

Define the Skill

Maps show features on Earth's surface. These can be physical features, such as mountains and rivers, or human features, such as roads and settlements. Historical maps show an area as it was in the past. Some show how a nation's boundaries changed over time. Interpreting maps can answer questions about history as well as geography.

Learn the Skill

Follow these steps to gain information from a map.

1. Read the title to determine what the map is about and the time period it covers.
2. Study the legend or key to understand what the colors or symbols on the map mean. Note the map scale, which is used to measure distances.
3. Note the map's other features. Maps often contain labels and other information in addition to what is explained in the legend or key.

Practice the Skill

Interpret the map below to answer the following questions about the expansion of the United States.

1. The addition of which territory almost doubled the size of the United States?
2. What was the smallest expansion of U.S. borders, and when did it take place?
3. According to the map, when did California become part of the United States?
4. What choice of overland routes did a traveler have for getting to California?
5. What physical obstacles does the map show such a traveler would face?

CHAPTER 11 Chapter Review

HOLT
History's Impact
▶ **video series**
Review the video to answer the closing question:
What does the modern success of Silicon Valley have in common with the California gold rush? How is it different?

Visual Summary

Use the visual summary below to help you review the main ideas of the chapter.

QUICK FACTS

U.S. Expansion

1839 Sutter's Fort established.

1840 Pioneers begin traveling West on the Oregon Trail.

1845 United States annexes Texas.

1846 Mexican War begins.

1848 United States wins the Mexican War and gains the Mexican Cession. Oregon becomes a U.S. territory.

1849 California gold rush begins.

1853 Gadsden Purchase establishes the southwestern U.S. border.

Reviewing Vocabulary, Terms, and People

Identify the correct term or person from the chapter that best fits each of the following descriptions.

1. Mexican priest who led a rebellion for independence from Spain
2. Spanish cowboys in California
3. A group of pioneers who were stranded in the Sierra Nevada Mountains and struggled to survive the winter
4. Agents hired by the Mexican government to attract settlers to Texas
5. The belief that the United States was meant to expand across the continent to the Pacific Ocean
6. Members of the Church of Jesus Christ of Latter-day Saints
7. Fur traders and trappers who lived west of the Rocky Mountains and in the Pacific Northwest
8. Mexican ruler who fought to keep Texas from gaining independence
9. Swiss immigrant who received permission from Mexico to start a colony in California
10. Western trail from Missouri to New Mexico that was an important route for trade between American and Mexican merchants

Comprehension and Critical Thinking

SECTION 1 *(Pages 346–349)*

11. a. Identify What different groups of people traveled West?

b. Draw Conclusions Why did Brigham Young move the Mormon community to Utah?

c. Predict What are some possible problems that might result from American settlement in the West?

SECTION 2 *(Pages 350–353)*

12. a. Identify Who were Stephen F. Austin and Antonio López de Santa Anna?

b. Draw Conclusions Why did settlers in Texas rebel against Mexican rule?

c. Elaborate In what ways was the Texas struggle for independence similar to that of the United States?

SECTION 3 *(Pages 354–363)*

13. a. Recall Why were some Americans opposed to the annexation of new territories?

b. Draw Conclusions What economic and cultural influences did Native Americans and Mexican Americans have on American settlers in the Mexican Cession?

c. Predict What are some possible problems the acquisition of so much territory might cause the United States?

SECTION 4 *(Pages 364–369)*

14. a. Identify What roles did women and immigrants play in the California gold rush?

b. Make Inferences Why were most gold-rush settlers young, unmarried men?

c. Predict What long-term effects might the gold rush have on California's future?

Reviewing Themes

15. Economics What role did economics play in the desire of Americans to go west?

16. Geography What were the main trails to the West, and what areas did they pass through?

Reading Skills

Vocabulary in Context *Use the Reading Skills taught in this chapter to answer the question about the reading selection below.*

> Texas politicians hoped that joining the United States would help solve the republic's financial and military problems. The Texas Congress approved annexation in June 1845. Texas became part of the United States in December. *(p. 356)*

17. Determine the definition of *annexation* using context clues.

Social Studies Skills

Interpreting Maps: Expansion *Use the Social Studies Skills taught in this chapter to answer the question about the map below.*

18. Place the expansions in the order in which they were acquired by the United States, according to the map.

Focus on Writing

19. Writing an Outline for a Documentary Film Look back through all your notes, and choose one topic from this chapter that you think would make a good 10-minute documentary. Your outline should be organized by scene (no more than 3 scenes), in chronological order. For each scene, give the following information: main idea of scene, costumes and images to be used, audio to be used, and length of scene. As you plan, remember that the audience will be students your own age.

Standardized Test Practice

DIRECTIONS: Read each question and write the letter of the best response.

1 ***Use the map below to answer the following question.***

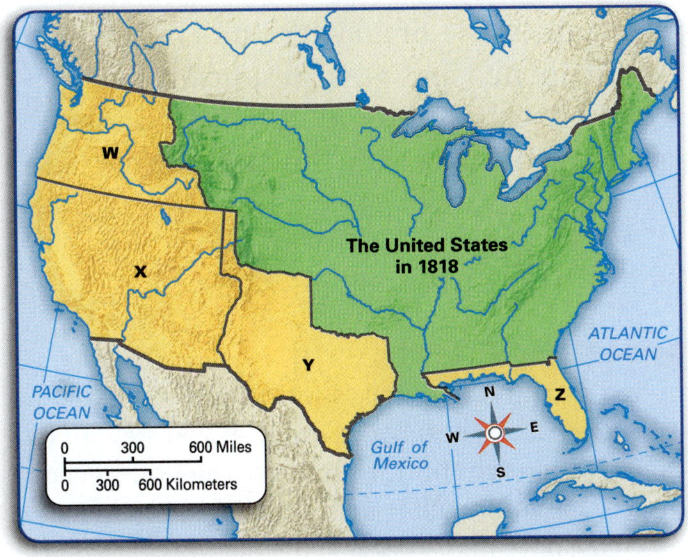

The part of the present-day United States that was once claimed by Britain, Spain, and Russia is shown on the map by which letter?

A W

B X

C Y

D Z

2 **Which statement *best* explains why Whigs fell from power in North Carolina?**

A Most Whigs supported the annexation of Texas.

B Whig leaders opposed the Mexican War and the Mexican Cession.

C The Whig-led state government refused to allow the sale of lands to foreigners.

D Whigs supported the North Carolina gold rush.

3 **The *main* attraction of Texas for many Americans in the 1820s and 1830s was the**

A freedom to practice the Catholic faith.

B availability of cheap or free land.

C desire to become citizens of Mexico.

D Mexican rebellion against Spain.

4 **Which of the following is an example of the concept of manifest destiny?**

A the creation of laws governing water rights

B the annexation of Oregon Territory

C the discovery of gold in California

D the establishment of trade relations with Native American fur trappers

5 **The California gold rush differed from the North Carolina gold rush in that**

A foreign immigrants were not allowed to mine for gold in California.

B the California economy struggled for many years after the gold rush.

C the California gold rush led to a population explosion for that state.

D very few citizens of California took part in the search for gold.

6 **Examine the following flier about cheap land available in the Dakota Territory and then use it to answer the question below.**

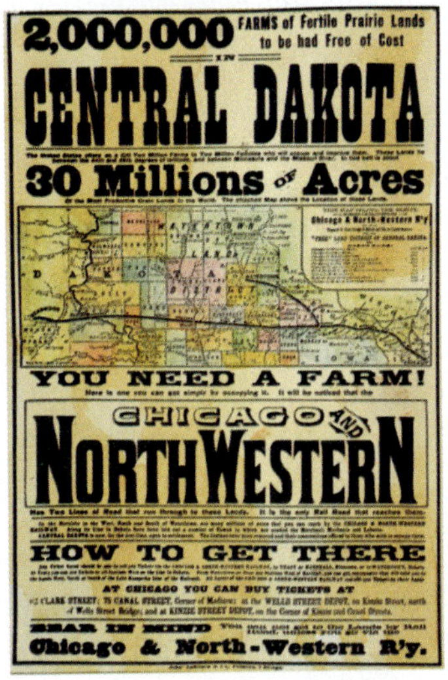

Document-Based Question **Who might have been attracted by this description of Dakota? Why?**

Assignment

Write a paper explaining the causes or the effects of the War of 1812.

Cause and Effect in History

Historians try to make sense of an event by considering why the event happened and what resulted from it. Exploring causes and effects can provide a deeper understanding of historical events and how they are connected to one another.

1. Prewrite

Identifying Causes and Effects

A **cause** is an action or a situation that makes something else happen. What happens is called an **effect**. For example, if you stay up too late watching TV (cause), you might find yourself nodding off in class (effect). Often an event or situation will have several causes as well as several effects. In those cases, we may look at the order in which the causes or effects occurred, or we may look at their relative importance.

Researching and Organizing

For this paper, you will write about the causes or the effects of the event —the War of 1812. Gather information from the chapter in this textbook, an encyclopedia, or another source recommended by your teacher.

- Look for two or three reasons (causes) why the War of 1812 (the event or situation) occurred.
- At the same time, consider the war as a cause. Look for two or three effects of the war.

Then choose whether to write about the causes or the effects.

TIP Using a Graphic Organizer

Use a graphic organizer like this to organize your research.

Cause 1
↓
Cause 2
↓
Event or Situation
↓
Effect
↓
Effect

2. Write

You can use this framework to help you write your first draft.

A Writer's Framework

Introduction	Body	Conclusion
■ Begin with a quote or interesting fact about the event. ■ Identify the event you will discuss. [The War of 1812] ■ Identify whether you will be discussing the causes or the effects.	■ Present the causes or effects in chronological (time) order or order of importance. ■ Explain each cause or effect in its own paragraph, providing support with facts and examples.	■ Summarize your ideas about the causes or the effects of the event [the war].

3. Evaluate and Revise

Evaluating

Drawing clear, logical connections is the key to writing about causes and effects. Use these questions to evaluate and revise your paper.

Evaluation Questions for an Explanation of Causes or Effects

- Does the introduction begin with an interesting quotation or fact?
- Does the introduction identify the event [the war] and the causes or events to be discussed?
- Is each cause or effect explained in its own paragraph?
- Do facts and examples help to explain each cause or effect and connect it to the event [the war]?
- Are the causes or effects organized clearly—by chronological order or order of importance?
- Does the conclusion summarize the causes or effects and their importance?

Revising

Make sure the connections between the war and its causes or effects are clear by sharing your paper with a classmate. If your classmate is confused, add background information. If he or she disagrees with your conclusions, add evidence or rethink your reasoning.

4. Proofread and Publish

Proofreading

Some transitional words and phrases need to be set off from the sentence with commas. Here are two examples:

- The Louisiana Territory was a huge region of land. *As a result,* the size of the United States almost doubled when the land was purchased.
- Jefferson wanted to know more about the land he had purchased. *Therefore,* he asked Congress to fund an expedition.

Check your paper to see if you need to add commas after or around any transitional words or phrases.

Publishing

Get together with a classmate and share causes and/or effects. Compare your lists to see whether you have identified different causes or effects. Share your findings with your class.

5. Practice and Apply

Use the steps and strategies outlined in this workshop to write your explanation of the causes or effects of the War of 1812.

TIP **Recognizing False Cause-and-Effect** In planning your essay, be careful to avoid false cause-and-effect relationships. The fact that one thing happened before or after another doesn't mean one caused the other. For example, the fact that James Madison was elected in 1808, just four years before the War of 1812, does not mean his election caused the War of 1812.

TIP **Using Transitions** Here are some transitional words and phrases that show cause or effect relationships: *because, as a result, therefore, for, since, so, consequently, for this reason.*

UNIT 4 1790–1860

The Nation Expands

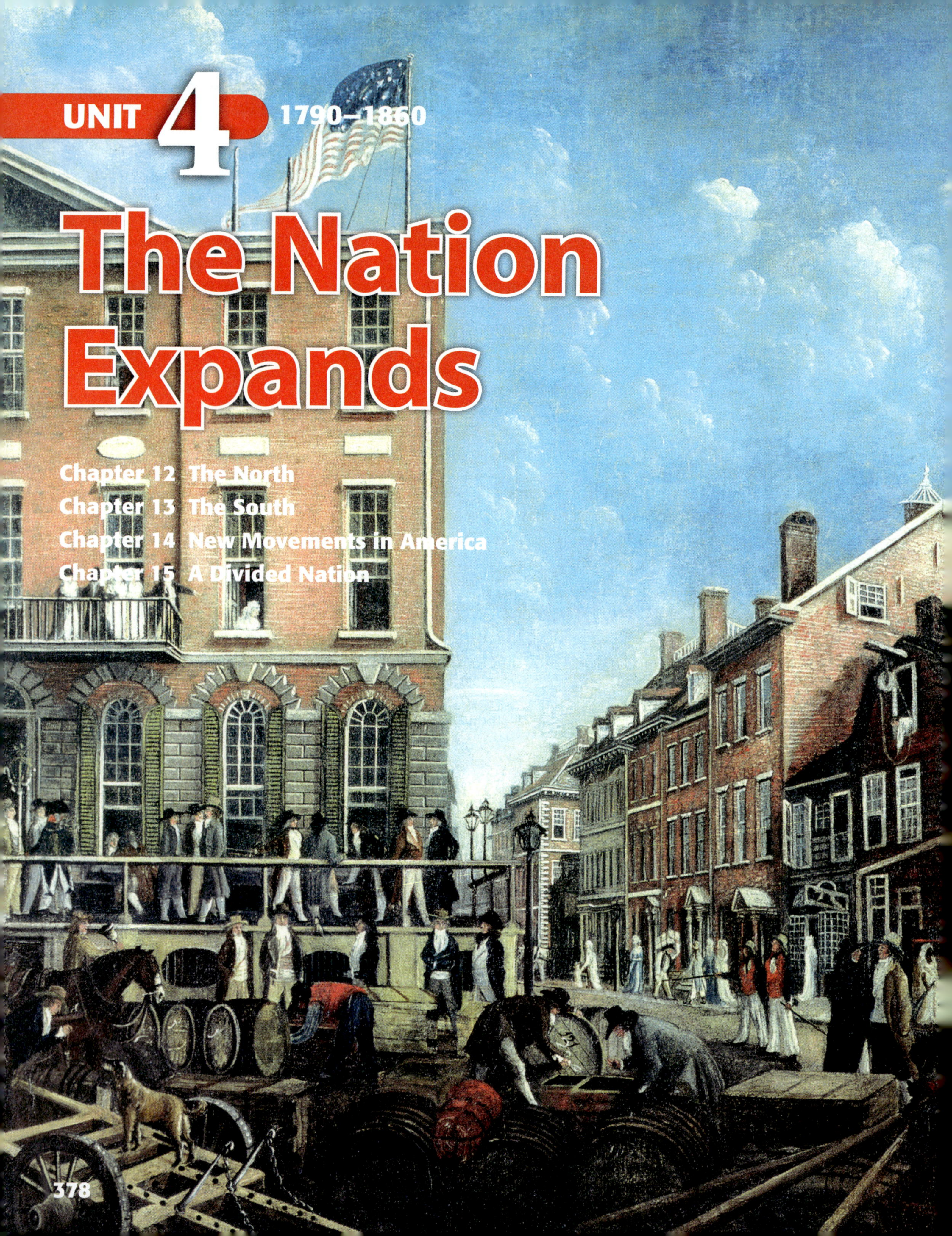

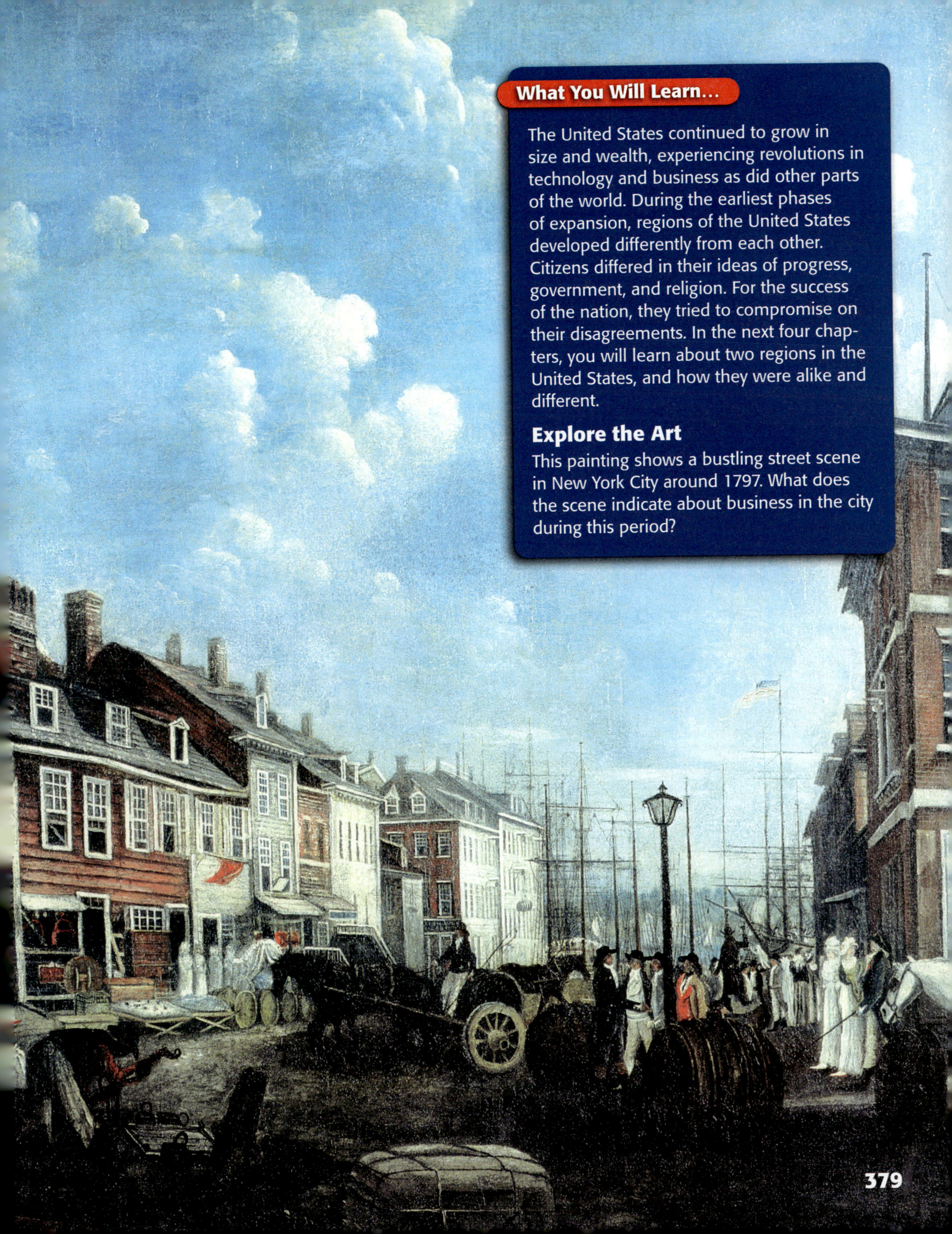

What You Will Learn...

The United States continued to grow in size and wealth, experiencing revolutions in technology and business as did other parts of the world. During the earliest phases of expansion, regions of the United States developed differently from each other. Citizens differed in their ideas of progress, government, and religion. For the success of the nation, they tried to compromise on their disagreements. In the next four chapters, you will learn about two regions in the United States, and how they were alike and different.

Explore the Art

This painting shows a bustling street scene in New York City around 1797. What does the scene indicate about business in the city during this period?

CHAPTER 12 1790–1860

The North

North Carolina Standards

Social Studies Objectives

3.08 Examine the impact of national events such as the Louisiana Purchase, the Lewis and Clark Expedition, the War with Mexico, and the California Gold Rush, and technological advances on North Carolina.

Language Arts Objectives

1.01 Narrate a personal account which:
- establishes a point of view and sharpens focus.
- uses remembered feelings.
- connects events to self/society.

1.02 Analyze expressive materials that are read, heard, and/or viewed by:
- monitoring comprehension for understanding of what is read, heard and/or viewed.

1.04 Reflect on learning experiences by:
- evaluating how personal perspectives are influenced by society, cultural differences, and historical issues.
- appraising changes in self throughout the learning process.
- evaluating personal circumstances and background that shape interaction with text.

3.01 Explore and evaluate argumentative works that are read, heard and/or viewed by:
- recognizing the effects of bias, emotional factors, and/or semantic slanting.

4.01 Analyze the purpose of the author or creator and the impact of that purpose by:
- evaluating any bias, apparent or hidden messages, emotional factors, and/or propaganda techniques.

go.hrw.com
North Carolina
KEYWORD: SC7 NC

FOCUS ON WRITING

Newspaper Advertisement The Industrial Revolution was a time when a great many new inventions were introduced. You work for an advertising agency, and your job is to design an advertisement for one of the inventions mentioned in this chapter. As you read, take notes on the inventions, their inventors, and how they changed life in the United States. Then choose one invention and design a newspaper advertisement to persuade readers to buy or use the invention.

UNITED STATES

1807 Robert Fulton's *Clermont* becomes the first commercially successful steamboat.

1790

WORLD

1790 The first steam-powered mill opens in Great Britain.

Textile mill workers were often women.

HOLT

History's Impact

video series

Watch the video to understand the impact of mass transportation.

What You Will Learn...

New machinery led to the construction of new mills, often along rivers. In this chapter you will learn about changes in the lives of Americans in the North as a result of rapid industrialization.

1830 The *Tom Thumb* becomes the first locomotive in the United States to carry passengers.

1838 The *Sirius* becomes the first ship to cross the Atlantic Ocean entirely under steam power.

1840 Federal government employees receive a 10-hour workday.

1845 Sarah Bagley is appointed secretary of the New England Working Men's Association.

1846 German astronomer Johann Galle observes that Neptune is a planet.

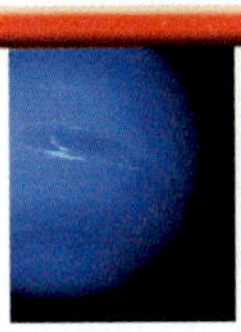

1851 London's Great Exhibition displays inventions from around the world in the Crystal Palace.

1856 Gail Borden patents a method of condensing milk so that it can be safely stored in cans.

1830 | 1840 | 1850 | 1860

Reading Social Studies

by Kylene Beers

Economics | Geography | Politics | Society and Culture | Science and Technology

Focus on Themes As you read this chapter, you will learn about how developments in **science and technology** brought about what is called the Industrial Revolution. As a result of the Industrial Revolution, you will see how American **economic** patterns changed. Next, you will read about how family life changed as more and more people went to work in factories. Finally, you will see how new methods of transportation changed where people lived and how new inventions affected daily life and work.

Causes and Effects in History

Focus on Reading Have you heard the saying, "We have to understand the past to avoid repeating it."? That is one reason we look for causes and effects in history.

Cause and Effect Chains You might say that all of history is one long chain of causes and effects. It may help you to understand the course of history better if you draw out such a chain as you read.

Since the 1790s, wars between European powers had interfered with U.S. trade. American customers were no longer able to get all the manufactured goods they were used to buying from British and European manufacturers . . . Americans began to buy the items they needed from American manufacturers instead of from foreign suppliers. As profits for American factories grew, manufacturers began to spend more money expanding their factories . . .

At the same time, many Americans began to realize that the United States had been relying too heavily on foreign goods. *(p. 389)*

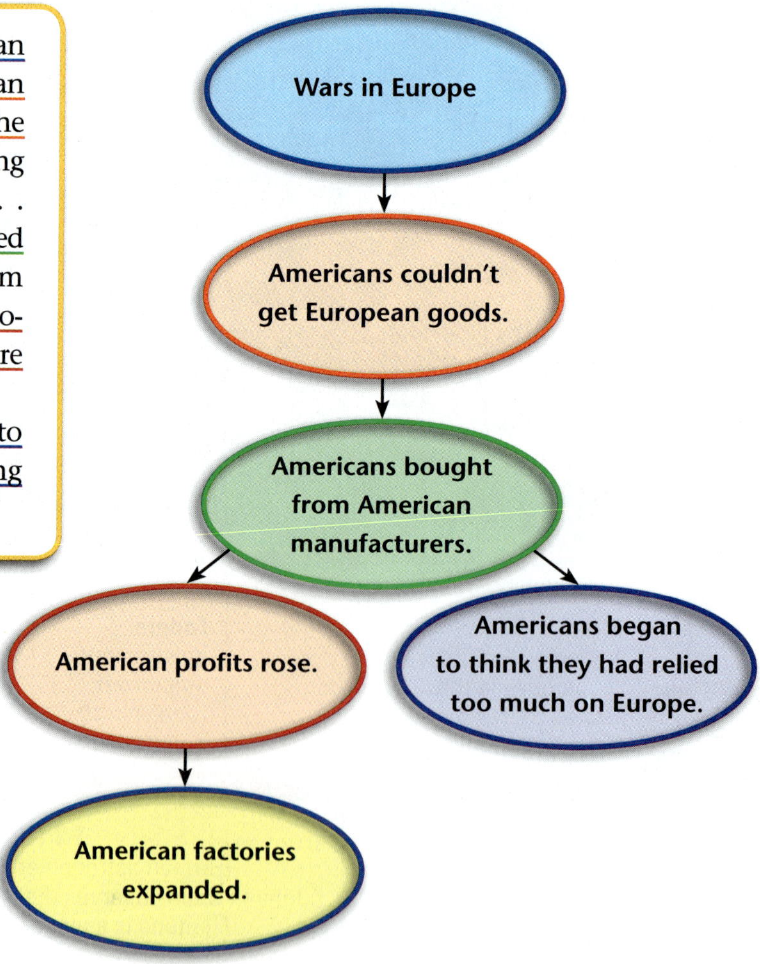

You Try It!

The following passage is from the chapter you are about to read. As you read each paragraph, ask yourself what is the cause and what is the effect of what is being discussed.

Workers Organize

From Chapter 12, p. 394

Factories continued to spread in the 1800s. Craftspeople, who made goods by hand, felt threatened. Factories quickly produced low-priced goods. To compete with factories, shop owners had to hire more workers and pay them less . . .

The wages of factory workers also went down as people competed for jobs. A wave of immigration in the 1840s brought people from other, poorer countries. They were willing to work for low pay. More immigrants came to the Northeast, where the mills were located, than to the South. Competition for jobs also came from people unemployed during the financial Panic of 1837.

After you have read the passage, answer the following questions.

1. What cause is being discussed in the first paragraph? What were its effects?
2. Draw a cause and effect chain that shows the events described in the first paragraph.
3. What main effect is discussed in the second paragraph? How many causes are given for it?
4. Draw a cause and effect chain that shows the events described in the second paragraph.

As you read Chapter 12, look for words that signal causes or effects. Picture these causes and effects as the links in a cause and effect chain.

Key Terms and People

Chapter 12

Section 1

Industrial Revolution *(p. 385)*
textiles *(p. 385)*
Richard Arkwright *(p. 385)*
Samuel Slater *(p. 386)*
technology *(p. 387)*
Eli Whitney *(p. 387)*
interchangeable parts *(p. 387)*
mass production *(p. 387)*

Section 2

Rhode Island system *(p. 391)*
Francis Cabot Lowell *(p. 392)*
Lowell system *(p. 392)*
trade unions *(p. 394)*
strikes *(p. 394)*
Sarah G. Bagley *(p. 395)*

Section 3

Transportation Revolution *(p. 396)*
Robert Fulton *(p. 397)*
Clermont *(p. 397)*
Gibbons v. *Ogden* *(p. 397)*
Peter Cooper *(p. 398)*

Section 4

Samuel F. B. Morse *(p. 402)*
telegraph *(p. 402)*
Morse code *(p. 403)*
John Deere *(p. 404)*
Cyrus McCormick *(p. 404)*
Isaac Singer *(p. 405)*

Academic Vocabulary

Success in school is related to knowing academic vocabulary—the words that are frequently used in school assignments and discussions. In this chapter, you will learn the following academic words:

efficient *(p. 385)*
concrete *(p. 395)*

SECTION 1

The Industrial Revolution in America

What You Will Learn…

Main Ideas

1. The invention of new machines in Great Britain led to the beginning of the Industrial Revolution.
2. The development of new machines and processes brought the Industrial Revolution to the United States.
3. Despite a slow start in manufacturing, the United States made rapid improvements during the War of 1812.

The Big Idea

The Industrial Revolution transformed the way goods were produced in the United States.

Key Terms and People

Industrial Revolution, *p. 385*
textiles, *p. 385*
Richard Arkwright, *p. 385*
Samuel Slater, *p. 386*
technology, *p. 387*
Eli Whitney, *p. 387*
interchangeable parts, *p. 387*
mass production, *p. 387*

TAKING NOTES As you read, make a list of the key contributions of the Industrial Revolution and who initiated them. Write your notes in a chart like the one below.

Contributor	Invention/improvement

If YOU were there...

You live in a small Pennsylvania town in the 1780s. Your father is a blacksmith, but you earn money for the family, too. You raise sheep and spin their wool into yarn. Your sisters knit the yarn into warm wool gloves and mittens. You sell your products to merchants in the city. But now you hear that someone has invented machines that can spin thread and make cloth.

Would you still be able to earn the same amount of money for your family? Why?

BUILDING BACKGROUND In the early 1700s making goods depended on the hard work of humans and animals. It had been that way for hundreds of years. Then new technology brought a change so radical that it is called a revolution. It began in Great Britain and soon spread to the United States.

The Industrial Revolution

At the beginning of the 1700s, the majority of people in Europe and the United States were farmers. They made most of what they needed by hand. For example, female family members usually made clothing. First, they used a spinning wheel to spin raw materials, such as cotton or wool, into thread. Then they used a hand loom to weave the thread into cloth.

Some families produced extra cloth to sell to merchants, who sold it for a profit. In towns, a few skilled workers made goods by hand in their own shops. These workers included blacksmiths, carpenters, and shoemakers. Their ways of life had stayed the same for generations.

A Need for Change

By the mid-1700s, however, changes in Great Britain led to a greater demand for manufactured goods. As agriculture and roads

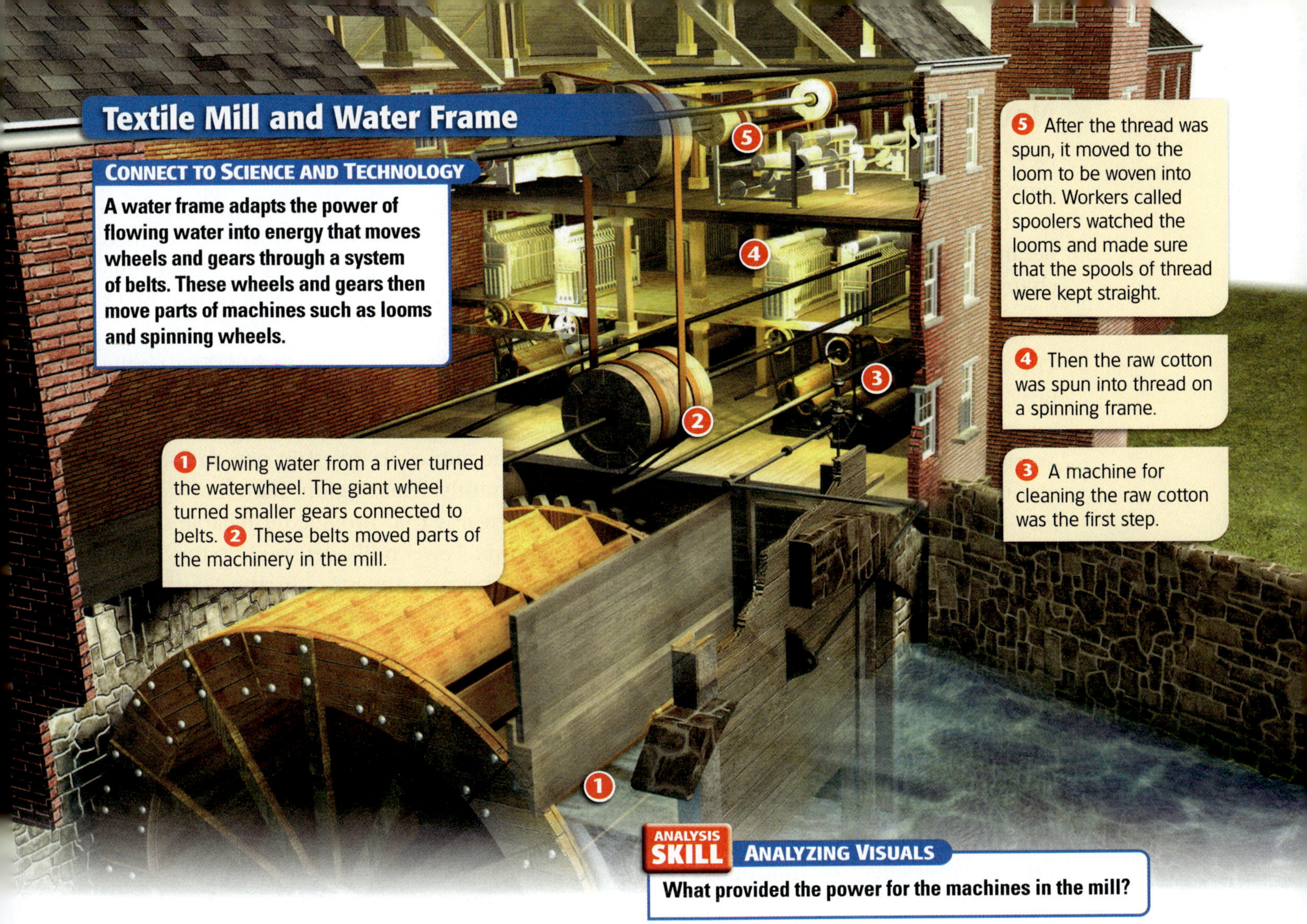

improved, cities and populations grew. Overseas trade also expanded. Traditional manufacturing methods did not produce enough goods to meet everyone's needs.

People began creating ways to use machines to make things more efficient. These developments led to the **Industrial Revolution**, a period of rapid growth in using machines for manufacturing and production that began in the mid-1700s.

Textile Industry

The first important breakthrough of the Industrial Revolution took place in how **textiles**, or cloth items, were made. Before the Industrial Revolution, spinning thread took much more time than making cloth. Several workers were needed to spin enough thread to supply a single weaver.

In 1769 Englishman **Richard Arkwright** invented a large spinning machine called a water frame. The water frame could produce dozens of cotton threads at the same time. It lowered the cost of cotton cloth and increased the speed of textile production.

The water frame used flowing water as its source of power. Merchants began to build large textile mills, or factories, near rivers and streams. The mills were filled with spinning machines. Merchants began hiring people to work in the mills.

Additional improvements also speeded up the spinning process. Britain soon had the world's most productive textile manufacturing industry.

ACADEMIC VOCABULARY
efficient productive and not wasteful

READING CHECK **Drawing Conclusions** How did machines speed up textile manufacturing?

New Machines and Processes

New machines encouraged the rise of new processes in business and manufacturing. As the machines used to make products became more efficient, the processes involved changed dramatically.

Slater and His Secrets

The new textile machines allowed Great Britain to produce cloth more quickly and inexpensively than other countries could. To protect British industry, the British Parliament had made it illegal for skilled mechanics or machine plans to leave the country. Disguised as a farmer, **Samuel Slater**, a skilled British mechanic, immigrated to the United States after carefully memorizing the designs of textile mill machines. Soon after arriving, he sent a letter to Moses Brown, who owned a textile business in New England. Slater claimed he could improve the way textiles were manufactured in the United States.

Brown had one of his workers test Slater's knowledge of machinery. Slater passed. Brown's son, Smith Brown, and son-in-law, William Almy, formed a partnership with Slater. In 1793 they opened their first mill in Pawtucket, Rhode Island. The production of cotton thread by American machines had begun. The Pawtucket mill became a success. Slater's wife also invented a new cotton thread for sewing. In 1798 Slater formed his own company to build a mill. By the time he died in 1835, he owned all or part of 13 textile mills.

Other Americans began building textile mills. Most were located in the Northeast. In New England in particular, merchants had the money to invest in new mills. More importantly, this region had many rivers and streams that provided a reliable supply of power. Fewer mills were built in the South, partly because investors in the South concentrated on expanding agriculture. There, agriculture was seen as an easier way to make money.

North Carolina took advantage of the new technology in a limited way. Entrepreneurs built 25 new cotton mills by 1840. Other industries grew in North Carolina as well. Businesspeople opened ironworks in the Piedmont area, especially in Lincoln County. These forges and furnaces helped supply the state's economy with the iron products it needed to grow.

Elements of Mass Production

CONNECT TO ECONOMICS

Mass-production techniques allow manufacturers to efficiently create more goods for the marketplace. Mass production requires the use of interchangeable parts, machine tools, and the division of labor.

Why are interchangeable parts important?

Interchangeable Parts

Eli Whitney developed the idea of using interchangeable parts. Interchangeable, or identical, parts are needed so each part does not have to be custom-made by hand.

Machine Tools

Machine tools like this one make parts that are identical and therefore interchangeable.

A Manufacturing Breakthrough

Despite these great changes, most manufacturing was still done by hand. In the late 1790s the U.S. government worried about a possible war with France, so it wanted more muskets for the army. Skilled workers made the parts for each weapon by hand. No two parts were exactly alike, and carefully fitting all the pieces together took much time and skill.

As a result, American gun makers could not produce the muskets quickly enough to satisfy the government's demand. Factories needed better **technology**, the tools used to produce items or to do work.

In 1798 inventor **Eli Whitney** tried to address some of these problems. Whitney gave officials a proposal for mass-producing guns for the U.S. government using water-powered machinery. Whitney explained the benefits of his ideas.

> "I am persuaded that machinery moved by water [and] adapted to this business would greatly reduce the labor and facilitate [ease] the manufacture of this article."
>
> —Eli Whitney, quoted in *Technology in America*, edited by Carroll W. Pursell

Whitney also came up with the idea of using **interchangeable parts**—parts of a machine that are identical. Using interchangeable parts made machines easier to assemble and broken parts easier to replace. Whitney promised to build 10,000 muskets in two years. The federal government gave him money to build his factory, and in 1801 Whitney was called to Washington, D.C., to give a demonstration.

Whitney stood before President John Adams and his secretary of war. He had an assortment of parts for 10 guns. He then randomly chose parts and quickly assembled them into muskets. To the audience's amazement, he repeated the process several times.

Whitney's Influence

Whitney had proven that American inventors could improve upon the new British technology. Machines that produced matching parts soon became standard in industry. Interchangeable parts sped up **mass production**, the efficient production of large numbers of identical goods.

READING CHECK **Summarizing** How did Eli Whitney influence American manufacturing?

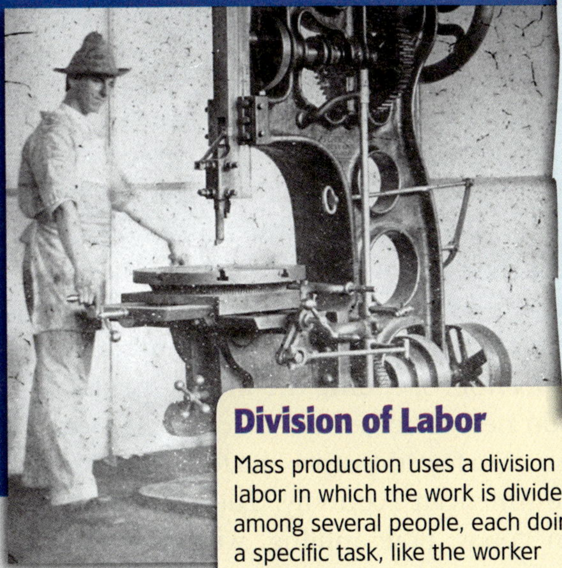

Division of Labor

Mass production uses a division of labor in which the work is divided among several people, each doing a specific task, like the worker shown here.

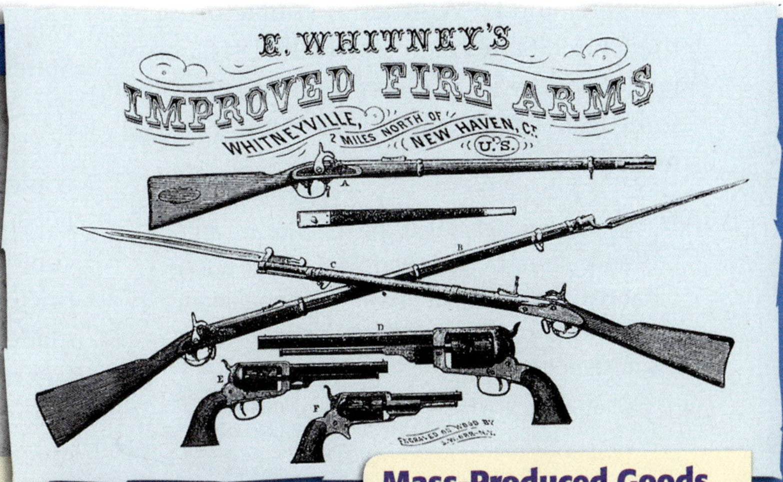

Mass-Produced Goods

The end result is goods that have been mass-produced. Eli Whitney used mass-production techniques to manufacture firearms.

LINKING TO TODAY

Modern Manufacturing

The word *manufacture* comes from Latin words that mean "to make by hand." Yet in modern manufacturing, machines—not human hands—do most of the work.

A key feature of modern manufacturing is the assembly line. An assembly line is a long conveyer belt. As the product moves along the belt, or "down the line," workers assemble it. Often, the workers use machines to help them. On a growing number of assembly lines, there are no workers at all: the product is assembled by computer-controlled robots.

Although a far cry from Eli Whitney's factory, modern factories use the same elements of mass production that Whitney did more than 200 years ago.

ANALYSIS SKILL **ANALYZING INFORMATION**

How do interchangeable parts help the modern assembly line work?

Manufacturing Grows Slowly

Despite the hard work of people such as Samuel Slater and Eli Whitney, manufacturing in the United States grew slowly. In 1810 Secretary of the Treasury Albert Gallatin suggested some reasons why there were so few factories in the United States.

> "[The reasons include] . . . the superior attractions of agricultural pursuits [farming], . . . the abundance of land compared with the population, the high price of labor, and the want [lack] of sufficient capital [investment]."
>
> —Albert Gallatin, quoted in *Who Built America?* by Bruce Levine et al.

Gallatin and others believed that few people would choose to work in a factory if they could own their own farm instead. In Great Britain, on the other hand, land was more scarce and more expensive than in the United States. As a result, fewer people were able to own farms. British factory workers generally were willing to work for lower wages than factory workers in the United States were.

Because British manufacturers had plenty of factory workers with technical skills, they could produce large amounts of goods less expensively than most American businesses could. As a result, they could charge lower prices for the goods. Lower British prices made it difficult for many American manufacturers to compete with British companies. This situation in turn discouraged American investors from spending the money needed to build new factories and machinery. As a result, only a few industries had found a place in the American economy. These included cotton goods, flour milling, weapons, and iron production.

These circumstances began to change around the time of the War of 1812. Since the 1790s, wars between European powers had interfered with U.S. trade. American customers were no longer able to get all the manufactured goods they were used to buying from British and European manufacturers. Then, during the War of 1812, British ships blockaded eastern seaports, preventing foreign ships from delivering goods. Americans began to buy the items they needed from American manufacturers instead of from foreign suppliers. As profits for American factories grew, manufacturers began to spend more money expanding their factories. State banks and private investors began to lend money to manufacturers for their businesses.

At the same time, many Americans began to realize that the United States had been relying too heavily on foreign goods. If the United States could not meet its own needs, it might be weak and open to attack. Former president Thomas Jefferson, who had once opposed manufacturing, changed his mind. He, too, realized that the United States was too dependent on imports.

> "To be independent for the comforts of life we must fabricate [make] them ourselves. We must now place the manufacturer by the side of the agriculturalist [farmer]."
>
> —Thomas Jefferson, from *The Writings of Thomas Jefferson*, edited by P. L. Ford

In February 1815, New Yorkers celebrated the end of the War of 1812 and the return of free trade. The streets were decorated and filled with merchants whose ships were loaded with goods. "With Peace and Commerce, America Prospers," declared one display. Eager businesspeople prepared to lead the United States into a period of industrial growth. They urged northern politicians to pass higher tariffs on foreign goods to protect American companies.

READING CHECK **Analyzing** How did the War of 1812 aid the growth of American manufacturing?

THE IMPACT TODAY

American dependence on some foreign goods, such as oil, is still being debated today.

SUMMARY AND PREVIEW The Industrial Revolution started with the textile industry in England but soon spread to the United States. In the next section you will learn about how the spread of factories changed the working lives of many Americans.

Section 1 Assessment

go.hrw.com
Online Quiz
KEYWORD: SC7 HP12

Reviewing Ideas, Terms, and People

1. a. Identify What was the first industry to begin to use machines to manufacture goods?
b. Predict In what ways might life for workers change as a result of the **Industrial Revolution**?

2. a. Recall In what part of the United States were most mills located? Why?
b. Draw Conclusions How did the ideas of **Samuel Slater** and **Eli Whitney** affect manufacturing in the United States?
c. Evaluate Whose contributions do you think were more important—Slater's textile machines or Whitney's **interchangeable parts**? Why?

3. a. Identify What event encouraged the growth of American manufacturing? Why?
b. Contrast Why was manufacturing in Great Britain in the early years more successful than that in the United States?

Critical Thinking

4. Drawing Conclusions Review your notes on key inventions and improvements during the Industrial Revolution. Then copy the chart below and use it to show how each contribution affected manufacturing.

Invention/improvement	Effect on Manufacturing

FOCUS ON WRITING

5. Noting Inventions In your notebook, create a three-column chart. In the first column, list any inventions mentioned in this section. In the second column, identify the inventor. In the third column, describe the invention and its benefits.

SECTION 2

Changes in Working Life

What You Will Learn...

Main Ideas

1. The spread of mills in the Northeast changed workers' lives.
2. The Lowell System revolutionized the textile industry in the Northeast.
3. Workers organized to reform working conditions.

The Big Idea

The introduction of factories changed working life for many Americans.

Key Terms and People

Rhode Island system, *p. 391*
Francis Cabot Lowell, *p. 392*
Lowell system, *p. 392*
trade unions, *p. 394*
strikes, *p. 394*
Sarah G. Bagley, *p. 395*

TAKING NOTES As you read, take notes on how mills changed workers' lives, and how workers organized to fight many of these changes.

Changes to workers' lives	→	Workers' reaction

If YOU were there...

You live on a dairy farm in Massachusetts in about 1820. On the farm, you get up at dawn to milk the cows, and your work goes on until night. But now you have a chance at a different life. A nearby textile mill is hiring young people. You would leave the farm and live with other workers. You could go to classes. Most important, you could earn money of your own.

Would you go to work in the textile mill? Why?

BUILDING BACKGROUND As factories and mills were established, the way people worked changed drastically. One dramatic change was the opportunity that factory work gave to young women. For young women in farm families, it was almost the only chance they had to earn their own money and a measure of independence.

Mills Change Workers' Lives

Workers no longer needed the specific skills of craftspeople to run the machines of the new mills. The lives of workers changed along with their jobs. Resistance to these changes sometimes sparked protests.

Many mill owners in the United States could not find enough people to work in factories because other jobs were available. At first, Samuel Slater and his two partners used apprentices—young men who worked for several years to learn the trade. However, they often were given only simple work. For example, their jobs might include feeding cotton into the machines and cleaning the mill equipment. They grew tired of this work and frequently left. Apprentice James Horton, for example, ran away from Slater's mill. "Mr. Slater . . . keep me always at one thing . . . ," Horton complained. "I might have stayed there until this time and never knew nothing."

Eventually, Slater began to hire entire families who moved to Pawtucket to work in the mills. This practice allowed Slater to fill his labor needs at a low cost. Children as well as adults worked in the mills.

Primary Source

NEWSPAPER ADVERTISEMENT

Family Wanted

This advertisement appeared in a Massachusetts newspaper in 1823. In it, a company requests that families come to work at a factory. The practice of hiring entire families was common at the time, especially in Britain. In America, it became known as the Rhode Island system.

FAMILIES WANTED.

THREE or four Families of large size, and good characters, may find employment at Blackstone Manufactory.

STEPHEN TRIPP,

Agent Blackstone Manufacturing Co.

Mendon, Nov. 27. tf.

ANALYSIS SKILL **ANALYZING PRIMARY SOURCES**

Drawing Conclusions Do you think advertisements like this one had the effect the companies wanted?

On most farms children worked to help their families. Therefore, few people complained about the hiring of children to work in factories. H. Humphrey, an author of books on raising children, told parents that children needed to be useful. Humphrey wrote, "If he [a child] will not study, put him on to a farm, or send him into the shop, or in some other way provide regular employment for him." The machines made many tasks in the mill simple enough for children to do. Mill owners profited because they paid children low wages. Adults usually earned as much in a day as most children did in a week.

To attract families to his mill, Slater built housing for the workers. He also provided them with a company store where they could buy necessities. In addition, he started the practice of paying workers with credit at the company store. Instead of paying the full price for an item all at once, small payments could be made over a period of time. This practice allowed Slater to reinvest his money in his business.

Slater's strategy of hiring families and dividing factory work into simple tasks became known as the **Rhode Island system**. Mill owners throughout the Northeast copied Slater's methods. Owners advertised with "Men with growing families wanted." They also sent recruiters to poor communities to find new workers. For many people, the chance to work in a factory was a welcome opportunity to earn money and to learn a new skill.

One of the earliest of the mill towns, Slatersville, was named after Samuel Slater. The town was built by Slater and his brother John. It included two houses for workers and their families, the owner's house, the company store, and the Slatersville Mill. The mill was the largest and most modern industrial building of its time.

The mills employed not only the textile workers who operated the machinery but also machine part makers and dam builders. Although the company store sold food and necessary items to workers, mill towns supported the same variety of businesses any other town needed to thrive. These included tailors and dressmakers, butchers, and other small workshops.

READING CHECK **Summarizing** What problem did Slater have in his mills, and how did he solve it?

The Lowell System

Not all mill owners followed this system. **Francis Cabot Lowell**, a businessman from New England, developed a very different approach. His ideas completely changed the textile industry in the Northeast.

The **Lowell system** was based on water-powered textile mills that employed young, unmarried women from local farms. The system included a loom that could both spin thread and weave cloth in the same mill. Lowell constructed boardinghouses for the women. Boardinghouse residents were given a room and meals along with their jobs.

With financial support from investors of the Boston Manufacturing Company, Lowell's first textile mill opened in Waltham, Massachusetts, in 1814. "From the first starting of the first power loom there was not . . . doubt about the success," wrote one investor. In 1822, the company built a larger mill in a Massachusetts town later named Lowell. Visitors to Lowell were amazed by the clean factories and neatly kept boardinghouses as well as the new machinery.

The young millworkers soon became known as Lowell girls. The mills paid them between $2 and $4 each week. The workers paid $1.25 for room and board. These wages were much better than those women could earn per week in other available jobs, such as domestic work.

Many young women came to Lowell from across New England. They wanted the chance to earn money instead of working on the family farm. "I must of course have something of my own before many more years have passed over my head," wrote one young woman. The typical Lowell girl worked at the mills for about four years.

Unlike other factory workers, the Lowell girls were encouraged to use their free time to take classes and form women's clubs. They even wrote their own magazine, the *Lowell Offering*. Lucy Larcom, who started working at Lowell at age 11, later praised her fellow workers.

No record exists today of the name of this girl, who worked in a mill around 1850. Judging from the photograph, if she were in school today, she would probably be in the seventh or eighth grade. Although hard to see in this photograph, her hands and arms are scratched and swollen—telltale signs of the hard labor required of young girls who worked up to 14 hours per day.

Time Table of the Lowell Mills

Morning Bells

First bell	4:30 AM
Second bell	5:30 AM
Third bell	6:20 AM

Dinner (Lunch) Bells

Ring out	12:00 PM
Ring in	12:35 PM

Evening Bells

Ring out	6:30 PM

Except on Saturday Evenings

—*The Table of the Lowell Mills, October 21, 1851*

History Close-up

Life of a Mill Girl

ANALYSIS SKILL **ANALYZING VISUALS**

Judging from the photograph on page 392, what might be the condition of the girl's hands in this illustration? Why?

Primary Source

MAGAZINE ARTICLE

Sarah G. Bagley and Workers' Rights

Lowell girl Sarah G. Bagley wrote magazine articles and made speeches about working in the mills. She organized workers to help change conditions.

Bagley believes that most mill girls would leave their jobs if they could.

"Is anyone such a fool as to suppose that out of six thousand factory girls in Lowell, sixty would be there if they could help it? Whenever I raise the point that it is immoral to shut us up in a close room twelve hours a day in the most monotonous and tedious of employment I am told that we have come to the mills voluntarily and we can leave when we will. Voluntarily! . . . the whip which brings us to Lowell is necessity. We must have money; a father's debts are to be paid, an aged mother to be supported, a brother's ambition to be aided and so the factories are supplied. Is this to act from free will?. . . Is this freedom? To my mind it is slavery."

—Sarah G. Bagley, quoted in *The Belles of New England: The Women of the Textile Mills and the Families Whose Wealth They Wove, by* William Moran

Bagley says that mill girls work to help their family members.

ANALYSIS SKILL **ANALYZING PRIMARY SOURCES**

How did Bagley view the idea that workers must endure poor conditions?

"I regard it as one of the privileges [advantages] of my youth that I . . . [grew] up among those active, interesting girls, whose lives . . . had principle [ideals] and purpose distinctly their own."

—Lucy Larcom, from *A New England Girlhood*

Mill life was hard, however. The workday was between 12 and 14 hours long, and daily life was carefully controlled. Ringing bells ordered workers to breakfast or lunch. Employees had to work harder and faster to keep up with new equipment. Cotton dust also began to cause health problems, such as chronic cough, for workers.

READING CHECK **Contrasting** How was the Lowell system different from the Rhode Island system?

THE IMPACT TODAY

In the 1950s, labor union membership reached its peak; about 40 percent of the workforce belonged to unions. Today only about 14 percent of the working population belongs to a labor union.

Workers Organize

Factories continued to spread in the 1800s. Craftspeople, who made goods by hand, felt threatened. Factories quickly produced low-priced goods. To compete with factories, shop owners had to hire more workers and pay them less. Shoemaker William Frazier complained about the situation in the mid-1840s. "We have to sit on our seats from twelve to sixteen hours per day, to earn one dollar."

The wages of factory workers also went down as people competed for jobs. A wave of immigration in the 1840s brought people from other, poorer countries. They were willing to work for low pay. More immigrants came to the Northeast, where the mills were located, than to the South. Competition for jobs also came from people unemployed during the financial Panic of 1837. For example, about 50,000 workers in New York City alone lost their jobs.

The Beginning of Trade Unions

Facing low wages and the fear of losing their jobs, skilled workers formed **trade unions**, groups that tried to improve pay and working conditions. Eventually, unskilled factory workers also formed trade unions. Most employers did not want to hire union workers. Employers believed that the higher cost of union employees prevented competition with other manufacturers.

Sometimes labor unions staged protests called **strikes**. Workers on strike refuse to work until employers meet their demands. Most early strikes were not successful, however. Courts and police usually supported companies, not striking union members.

Labor Reform Efforts

A strong voice in the union movement was that of millworker **Sarah G. Bagley**. She founded the Lowell Female Labor Reform Association in 1844 and publicized the struggles of factory laborers. The association's two main goals were to influence an investigation of working conditions by the Massachusetts state legislature and to obtain a 10-hour workday. Members of the association passed out pamphlets and circulated petitions.

President Martin Van Buren had granted a 10-hour workday in 1840 for many federal employees. Bagley wanted this rule to apply to employees of private businesses. These men and women often worked 12 to 14 hours per day, six days per week.

Many working men and women supported the 10-hour-workday campaign, despite the opposition of business owners. In 1845 Sarah Bagley was elected vice president of the New England Working Men's Association. She was the first woman to hold such a high-ranking position in the American labor movement.

Over time, the unions achieved some **concrete** legal victories. Connecticut, Maine, New Hampshire, Ohio, Pennsylvania, and a few other states passed 10-hour-workday laws.

ACADEMIC VOCABULARY
concrete specific, real

For factory workers in other states, long hours remained common. One witness described how children were "summoned by the factory bell before daylight" and worked until eight o'clock at night "with nothing but [a] recess of forty-five minutes to get their dinner." Union supporters continued to fight for work reforms such as an end to child labor in factories during the 1800s.

READING CHECK **Finding Main Ideas** Why did workers form unions, and what were the main goals of union reformers?

SUMMARY AND PREVIEW With the growth of factories, workers faced new opportunities and challenges. In the next section you will learn about how the Transportation Revolution brought changes to commerce and the daily lives of Americans.

Section 2 Assessment

go.hrw.com
Online Quiz
KEYWORD: SC7 HP12

Reviewing Ideas, Terms, and People

1. a. **Identify** What problems did many mill owners have in finding workers?
   b. **Analyze** How did Samuel Slater's **Rhode Island system** change employment practices in mills?
2. a. **Describe** What was life like for mill workers in the **Lowell system**?
   b. **Make Inferences** Why would young women have wanted to go to work in the Lowell mills?
3. a. **Recall** Why did workers form **trade unions**?
   b. **Predict** What are some possible problems that might arise between factory owners and trade unions?

Critical Thinking

4. **Drawing Conclusions** Review your notes on mills and workers' reactions to them. Then copy the graphic organizer to the right and use it to show how Slater, Lowell, and Sarah G. Bagley affected workers' lives.

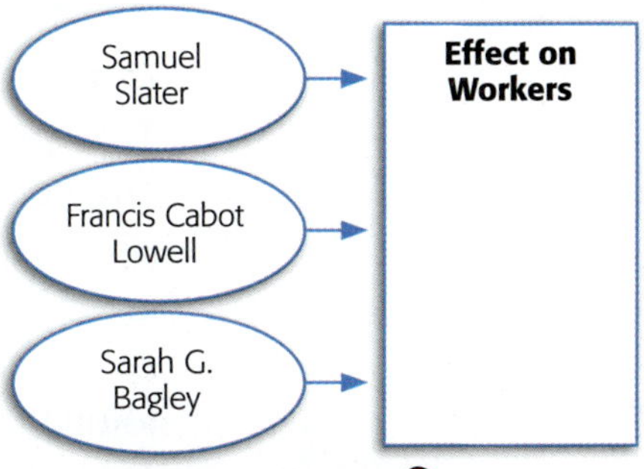

FOCUS ON WRITING

5. **Examining Working Conditions** This section tells about mill life and conditions for workers. In the chart you started for the first section, list the two labor systems used by mills, the person who developed each, and the benefits of each system.

SECTION 3

The Transportation Revolution

What You Will Learn...

Main Ideas

1. The Transportation Revolution affected trade and daily life.
2. The steamboat was one of the first developments of the Transportation Revolution.
3. Railroads were a vital part of the Transportation Revolution.
4. The Transportation Revolution brought many changes to American life and industry.

The Big Idea

New forms of transportation improved business, travel, and communication in the United States.

Key Terms and People

Transportation Revolution, *p. 396*
Robert Fulton, *p. 397*
Clermont, *p. 397*
Gibbons v. *Ogden*, *p. 397*
Peter Cooper, *p. 398*

TAKING NOTES Create a time line like the one below. As you read, fill in the time line with the key events in the development of the steamboat and the locomotive as vital forms of transportation.

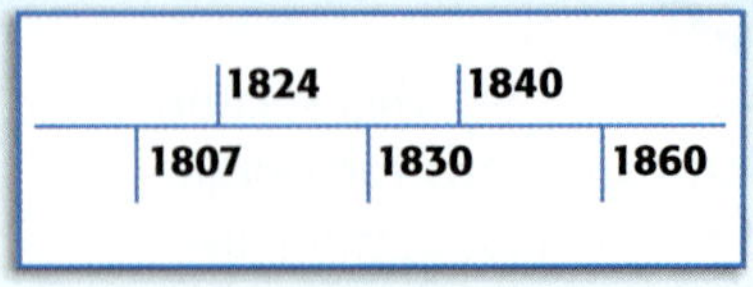

If YOU were there...

You live in a small town in Iowa in the 1860s. You've never been more than 30 miles from home and have always traveled by wagon or on horseback. Now there are plans to build a railroad westward from Chicago, 200 miles to the east. The tracks will come through your town! Twice a week, trains will bring goods from the city and take people farther west.

How would the coming of the railroad change your life?

BUILDING BACKGROUND The Industrial Revolution changed how goods were made. It brought great changes in the ways that many Americans lived. But developments in technology led to major changes in other areas of life, too. New forms of transportation would bring remote parts of America closer together.

Trade and Daily Life

During the 1800s the United States was transformed by a **Transportation Revolution**—a period of rapid growth in the speed and convenience of travel because of new methods of transportation. The Transportation Revolution created a boom in business across the country, particularly by reducing shipping time and costs. As one foreign observer declared in 1835, "The Americans . . . have joined the Hudson to the Mississippi, and made the Atlantic Ocean communicate with the Gulf of Mexico."

These improvements were made possible largely by the invention of two new forms of transportation: the steamboat and steam-powered trains. They enabled goods, people, and information to travel rapidly and efficiently across the United States.

READING CHECK **Finding Main Ideas** What benefits did the Transportation Revolution bring to trade and daily life?

Mississippi River Steamboats

Deckhands load a Mississippi River steamboat in Memphis, Tennessee. By the mid-1800s, hundreds of steamboats traveled up and down American rivers. Steamboats enabled Americans to ship more goods farther, faster, and for less money than ever before.

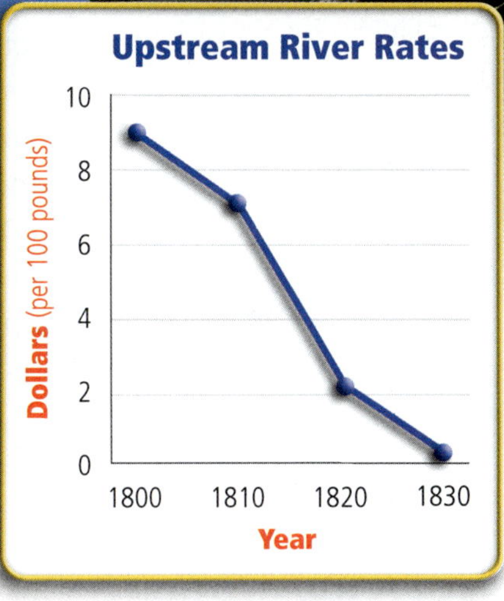

Steamboats

American and European inventors had developed steam-powered boats in the late 1700s. However, they were not in wide use until the early 1800s.

Steamboat Era

In 1803 American **Robert Fulton** tested his first steamboat design in France. Several years later, he tested the first full-sized commercial steamboat, called the ***Clermont***, in the United States. On August 9, 1807, the *Clermont* traveled against the current up the Hudson River without trouble. Demand for steamboat ferry service soon arose.

The steamboat was well suited for river travel. It could move upriver and did not rely on wind power. Steamboats increased trade and profits because goods could be moved quickly and thus more cheaply. More than 500 steamboats were in use in the United States by 1840. By the 1850s, steamboats were also being used to carry people and goods across the Atlantic Ocean.

Gibbons v. Ogden

Increased steamboat shipping led to conflict over waterway rights. In 1819 Aaron Ogden sued Thomas Gibbons for operating steamboats in New York waters that Ogden said he owned. Gibbons did not have a license to operate in New York, but argued that his federal license gave him the right to use New York waterways.

In the case of ***Gibbons* v. *Ogden***, which reached the Supreme Court in 1824, the Court reinforced the federal government's authority to regulate trade between the states by ending monopolistic control over waterways in several states. The ruling freed up waters to even greater trade and shipping.

READING CHECK **Summarizing** Explain the effects of the *Gibbons* v. *Ogden* ruling.

American Railroads

What the steamboat did for water travel, the train did for overland travel. Steam-powered trains had first been developed in Great Britain in the early 1800s. However, they did not become popular in the United States until the 1830s. In 1830 **Peter Cooper** built a small but powerful locomotive called the *Tom Thumb*. He raced the locomotive against a horse-drawn railcar. Eyewitness John Latrobe later described the race, in which *Tom Thumb* had a slow start and fell behind. Latrobe wrote, "The pace increased, the passengers shouted, the engine gained on the horse . . . then the engine passes the horse, and a great hurrah hailed the victory." Unfortunately for Cooper, victory was spoiled when *Tom Thumb* broke down and lost the race near the end.

Despite the defeat, the contest showed the power and speed of even a small locomotive. Railroad fever soon spread. By 1840 railroad companies had laid about 2,800 miles of track—more than existed in all of Europe. French economist Michel Chevalier described Americans as having "a perfect passion for railroads."

As more railroads were built, engineers and mechanics overcame many tough challenges. Most British railroads, for example, ran on straight tracks across flat ground. In the United States, however, many railroads had to run up and down steep mountains, around tight curves, and over swift rivers. Railroad companies also built the tracks quickly and often with the least expensive materials available. As time went on, engineers and mechanics built heavier, faster, and more powerful steam locomotives.

By 1860 about 30,000 miles of railroad linked almost every major city in the eastern United States. As a result, the economy surged forward. For example, American locomotives hauled more freight than those in any other country. The railroad companies quickly became some of the most powerful businesses in the nation. As the railroad

The Steam Train

CONNECT TO SCIENCE AND TECHNOLOGY

Boiling water produces steam, which pushes pistons back and forth in a steam engine. These pistons are connected to rods that rotate the wheels of the locomotive.

Why does the train have a firebox?

1 As steam follows the path of the white arrows into the cylinder, the pressure pushes the piston in the direction of the large blue arrow. Connecting rods turn the wheel half a turn.

2 When the small valve rod moves, the other valve is blocked, pushing steam into the other side of the cylinder. The pressure moves the piston in the direction of the large blue arrow and the wheel completes a turn.

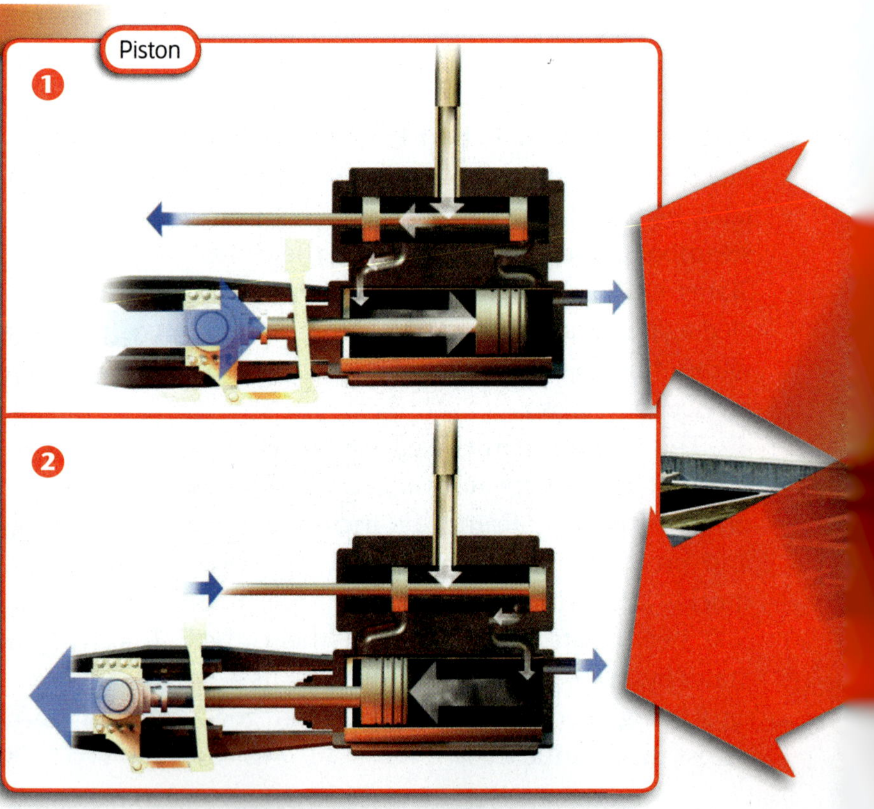

system grew, manufacturers and farmers could send their goods to distant markets.

In addition to their tremendous economic impact, the railroads made a powerful impression on the senses of passengers and observers. Trains were the fastest form of transportation most people had ever experienced. While wagons often traveled less than 2 miles per hour, locomotives averaged about 20 miles per hour. Writer George Templeton Strong of New York City described the thrill of a steam train passing by in the night:

> "Whizzing and rattling and panting, with its fiery furnace gleaming in front, its chimney vomiting fiery smoke above, and its long train of cars rushing along behind like the body and tail of a gigantic dragon— . . . and all darting forward at the rate of twenty miles an hour. Whew!"
>
> —George Templeton Strong, quoted in *The Market Revolution* by Charles Sellers

Riding on the early trains was often an adventure, but it could also be quite dangerous. Engineers trying to stay on time sometimes traveled too fast. English citizen Charles Richard Weld was on a railroad car that flew off the tracks. To his amazement, the other passengers did not complain about the accident. Instead, they praised the engineer for trying to keep on schedule!

Passengers accepted such risks because the railroads reduced travel time dramatically. Railroads also helped tie communities together. In 1847 Senator Daniel Webster spoke for many people in the United States when he declared that the railroad "towers above all other inventions of this or the preceding age."

READING CHECK **Drawing Inferences** In what ways did railroads affect the economy of the United States?

THE IMPACT TODAY

In 1883 four standard time zones were introduced in the United States to help railroads offer uniform train schedules. Today travelers might cross one or more time zones in a single airplane flight.

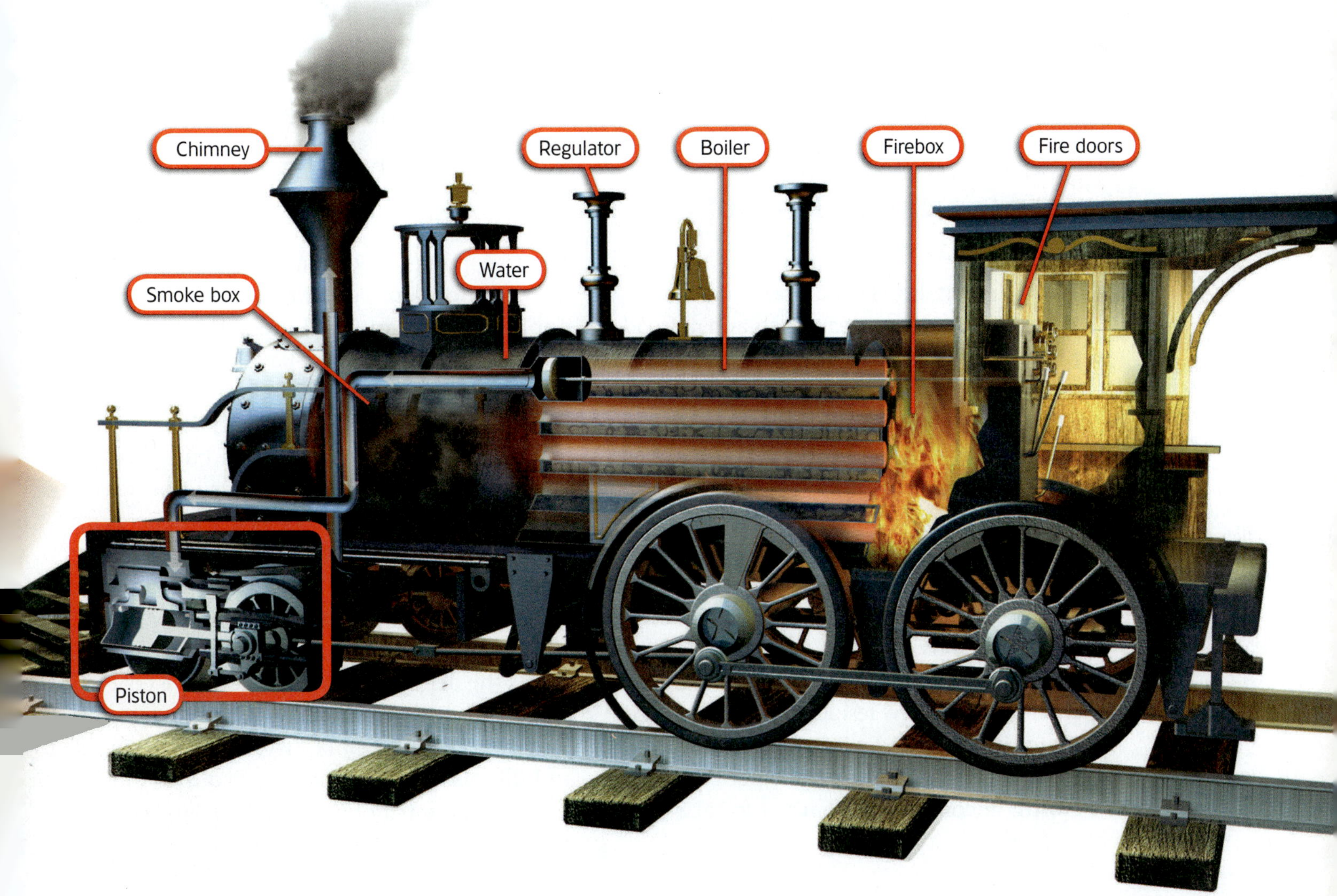

Interactive Map

Transportation Routes, 1850

By 1850 the United States already had about 9,000 miles of railroad track. Timber was needed for railroad ties, cars, and bridges and as fuel for steam locomotives.

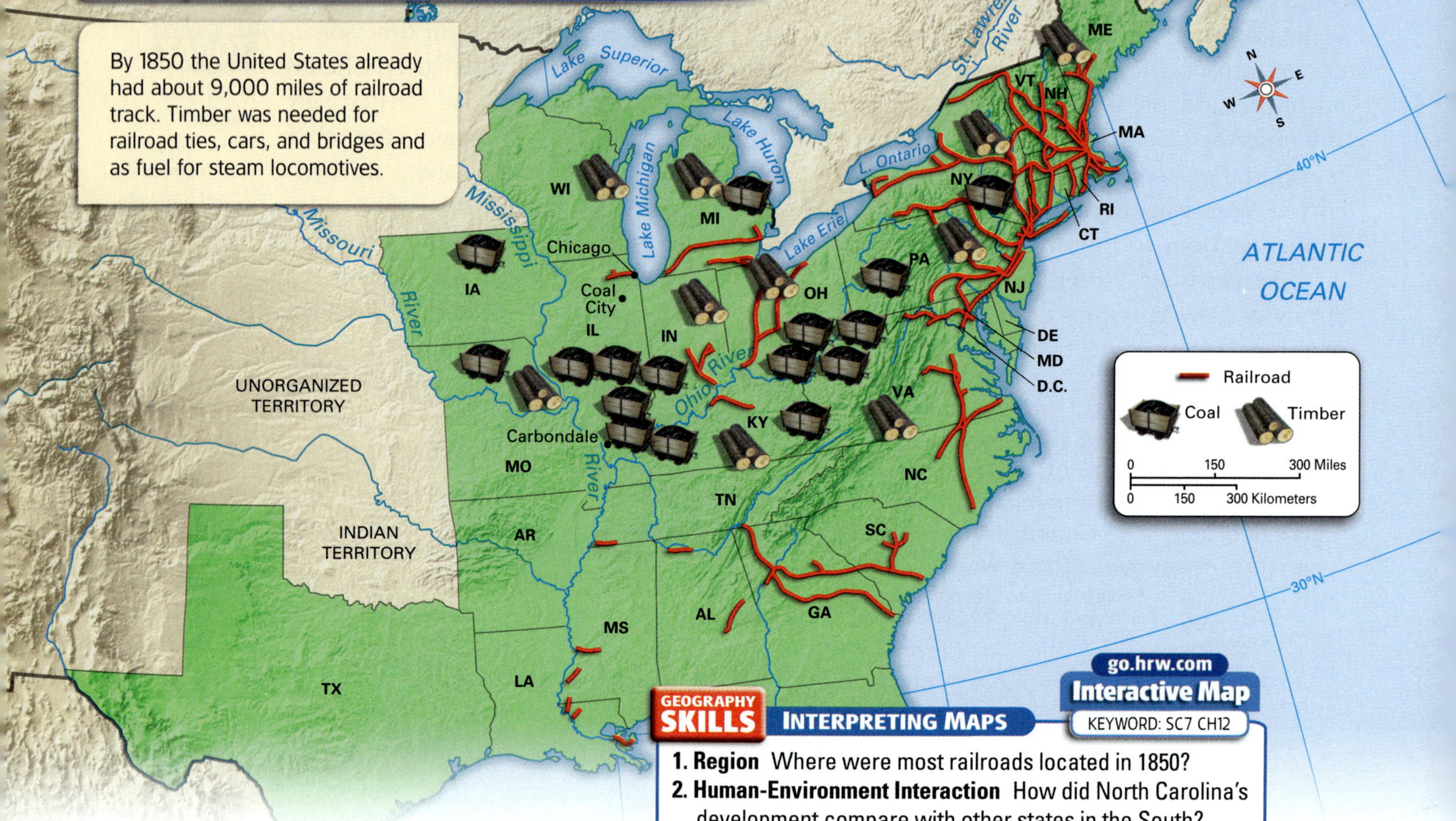

go.hrw.com
Interactive Map
KEYWORD: SC7 CH12

GEOGRAPHY SKILLS INTERPRETING MAPS

1. **Region** Where were most railroads located in 1850?
2. **Human-Environment Interaction** How did North Carolina's development compare with other states in the South?

Transportation Revolution Brings Changes

The Transportation Revolution brought many changes to America. Steamboats and railroads made getting goods to distant markets much easier and less costly. People in all areas of the nation now had access to products made and grown far away. More than ever before, there was a national economy. The wealth, however, was centered in the North.

Railroads contributed to the expansion of the borders of the nation and guided population growth. Towns sprang up at railroad junctions. Those towns that did not have railroads nearby suffered. Cities grew as trains brought new residents and raw materials for industry and construction. The growing prosperity of the nation, especially in the North, encouraged Americans to take pride in their country.

A New Fuel

The Transportation Revolution also increased the use of certain natural resources that had not been important until then. Throughout the early Transportation Revolution, wood was the primary source of fuel for trains and steamboats, as well as for cooking, light, and heat. As faster locomotives were built, coal replaced wood as the main source of power. A half ton of coal produces as much energy as two tons of wood but at half the cost. Coal also became popular for heating homes. Railroads transported the coal from mines to towns and cities.

As the demand for coal increased, a coal-mining industry developed in many states, including Pennsylvania, western Virginia, and Illinois. Coal mining changed the landscape in a number of ways. New towns, such as Coal City and Carbondale in Illinois,

FOCUS ON NORTH CAROLINA

Steamboats helped North Carolinians navigate the difficult rivers in the northeast part of the state, and the state helped fund railroad construction. Not every advance in transportation relied on new technology, however. The longest plank road in the United States was built between Fayetteville and Bethania, North Carolina.

sprang up in places where coal deposits could be mined. Miners made deep gashes in the earth removing the coal.

Later, in the 1870s, the demand for coal increased as the demand for steel grew. Steel is made through a smelting process—heating iron ore to very high temperatures. Coal was used to fire the furnaces. Steel, which is much stronger than iron, was increasingly used to build factories and the machines they produced. Steel was also used to make the rails that trains ride on.

The growing market for steel helped fuel the need for more railroads. Railroads transported steel to places where new factories were being built. Railroads also brought new steel farming tools and machines to farmers in the Midwest. Using the new equipment, farmers produced more crops. Railroads then transported their harvests to markets.

Effects of Railroads

The railroads also played a role in the growth of other businesses. The logging industry expanded as people in the growing towns and cities needed wood for houses and furniture. As newspaper publishing increased, demand for paper grew. Lumber items became the primary product of New England. Settlers spreading out across the Midwest cut down trees and plowed up prairies to make farmland. Deforestation, or cutting down and removing trees, took place on a large scale.

Railroads also caused cities to grow. Some cities became transportation hubs. Chicago was one such city. Its location on Lake Michigan made it an ideal transportation hub, linking the Midwest to the East and South.

READING CHECK **Analyzing Information** What role did railroads play in the growth of the coal industry?

SUMMARY AND PREVIEW The Transportation Revolution changed the way business was done. In the next section you will learn about more technological advances.

FOCUS ON READING

What causes and effects do you see in this section?

go.hrw.com
Online Quiz
KEYWORD: SC7 HP12

Section 3 Assessment

Reviewing Ideas, Terms, and People

1. a. **Identify** What forms of transportation were improved or invented at this time?
   b. **Explain** What effect did the **Transportation Revolution** have on the United States?
2. a. **Describe** What were the benefits of steamboat travel?
   b. **Analyze** What effect did the ruling in the ***Gibbons* v. *Ogden*** case have on federal government?
3. a. **Describe** What event showed the power and speed of locomotives?
   b. **Draw Conclusions** How did railroads affect trade and business in the United States?
   c. **Elaborate** Why do you think Americans were fascinated by railroads?
4. a. **Describe** What physical obstacles did railroad construction in the United States face?
   b. **Analyze** What effects did the Transportation Revolution have on the U.S. economy?
   c. **Elaborate** Do you think the Transportation Revolution played a role in deforestation? Explain.

Critical Thinking

5. **Identifying Effects** Review your time line on the steamboat and the locomotive. Then copy the chart below and use it to show how they affected business, travel, and communication in the United States.

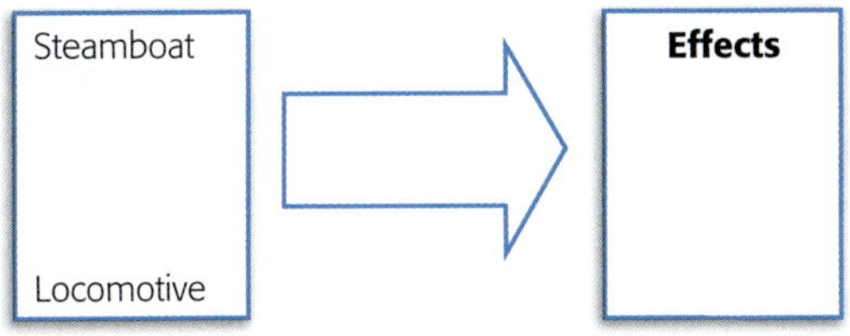

FOCUS ON WRITING

6. **Describing Travel Inventions** Add the steamboat and locomotive to your list. Note the individuals involved in their development as well as how these new methods of travel changed life for people in the United States.

SECTION 4

More Technological Advances

What You Will Learn...

Main Ideas

1. The telegraph made swift communication possible from coast to coast.
2. With the shift to steam power, businesses built new factories closer to cities and transportation centers.
3. Improved farm equipment and other labor-saving devices made life easier for many Americans.
4. New inventions changed lives in American homes.

The Big Idea

Advances in technology led to new inventions that continued to change daily life and work.

Key Terms and People

Samuel F. B. Morse, *p. 402*
telegraph, *p. 402*
Morse code, *p. 403*
John Deere, *p. 404*
Cyrus McCormick, *p. 404*
Isaac Singer, *p. 405*

TAKING NOTES As you read, take notes on the new advances in technology listed in the section. Create a graphic organizer like the one shown below that identifies the effects of each.

Inventions	Effects
Telegraph	
Steam Power	
Mass Production	
Home Inventions	

If YOU were there...

You own a small shop in Chicago, Illinois, in the 1850s. You sell ladies' hats and gowns. When you need more hats, you send a letter to the manufacturer in New York. Sometimes it takes weeks for the letter to get there. One day, the owner of the shop next door tells you about a wonderful new machine. It can send orders from Chicago to New York in just minutes!

How would a machine like this change your business?

BUILDING BACKGROUND The Industrial and Transportation Revolutions had far-reaching effects on Americans' lives. They led to still more innovations in technology. Some of the new machines and devices speeded up processes for business owners. Others made life easier for people at home.

Telegraph Speeds Communication

In 1832 **Samuel F. B. Morse** perfected the **telegraph**—a device that could send information over wires across great distances. To develop the telegraph, Morse studied electricity and magnetism. In

Time Line

American Inventions

1798 Eli Whitney proposed the idea of mass producing guns. Machines like this one made it possible for workers to make interchangeable parts efficiently.

1831 Cyrus McCormick invents the mechanical reaper. Harvesting grain becomes eight times more efficient.

time, Morse put the work of other scientists together in a practical machine.

The telegraph sent pulses, or surges, of electric current through a wire. The telegraph operator tapped a bar, called a telegraph key, that controlled the length of each pulse. At the other end of the wire, these pulses were changed into clicking sounds. A short click was called a dot. A long click was called a dash. Morse's partner, Alfred Lewis Vail, developed a system known as **Morse code**—different combinations of dots and dashes that represent each letter of the alphabet. For example, *dot dot dot, dash dash dash, dot dot dot* is the distress signal called SOS. Skilled telegraph operators could send and receive many words per minute.

Several years passed before Morse was able to connect two locations with telegraph wires. Despite that achievement, people doubted his machine. Some people did not think that he was reading messages sent from miles away. They claimed that he was making lucky guesses.

Morse's break came during the 1844 Democratic National Convention in Baltimore, Maryland. A telegraph wired news of the presidential candidate's nomination to politicians in Washington. The waiting politicians responded, "Three cheers for the telegraph!" Telegraphs were soon sending and receiving information for businesses, the government, newspapers, and private citizens.

BIOGRAPHY

Samuel F. B. Morse

(1791–1872)

Like steamboat creator Robert Fulton, Samuel F. B. Morse began his career as a painter rather than as an inventor. In 1832 Morse was a widower struggling to raise his three children alone. He became interested in the idea of sending messages electrically. Morse hoped he could invent a device that would earn him enough money to support his family. Eventually, earnings from the telegraph made Morse extremely wealthy.

Drawing Conclusions What motivated Morse to invent the telegraph?

The telegraph grew with the railroad. Telegraph companies strung their wires on poles along railroads across the country. They established telegraph offices in many train stations. Thousands of miles of telegraph line were added every year in the 1850s. The first transcontinental line was finished in 1861. By the time he died in 1872, Morse was famous across the United States.

READING CHECK **Identifying Cause and Effect** What event led to the widespread use of the telegraph, and what effect did the telegraph have on cross-country communications?

1832 Samuel F. B. Morse invents the telegraph. Long-distance communication becomes almost instantaneous.

1837 John Deere invents the steel plow. The tough prairie sod can be cut and the thick soil ploughed without having to constantly clean the plow.

Steam Power and New Factories

At the start of the Industrial Revolution, most factories ran on waterpower. In time, however, factory owners began using steam power. This shift brought major changes to the nation's industries. Water-powered factories had to be built near streams or waterfalls. In contrast, steam power allowed business owners to build factories almost anywhere. Yet the Northeast was still home to most of the nation's industry. By 1860 New England alone had as many factories as the entire South did.

Some companies decided to build their factories closer to cities and transportation centers. This provided easier access to workers, allowing businesses to lower wages. Being closer to cities also reduced shipping costs. Cities soon became the center of industrial growth. People from rural areas as well as foreign countries flocked to the cities for factory jobs.

Factory workers improved the designs of many kinds of machines. Mechanics invented tools that could cut and shape metal, stone, and wood with great precision. By the 1840s this new machinery was able to produce interchangeable parts. Within a short period of time, the growing machine-tool industry was even making customized equipment.

READING CHECK **Finding Main Ideas** What changes resulted from the shift to steam power?

Improved Farm Equipment

During the 1830s, technology began transforming the farm as well as the factory. In 1837 blacksmith **John Deere** saw that friends in Illinois had difficulty plowing thick soil with iron plows. He thought a steel blade might work better. His design for a steel plow was a success. By 1846 Deere was selling 1,000 plows per year.

In 1831 **Cyrus McCormick** developed a new harvesting machine, the mechanical reaper, which quickly and efficiently cut down wheat. He began mass producing his reapers in a Chicago factory. McCormick used new methods to encourage sales. His company advertised, gave demonstrations, and provided a repair and spare parts department. He also let customers buy on credit.

The combination of Deere's plow and McCormick's reaper allowed Midwestern farmers to plant and harvest huge crop fields. By 1860, U.S. farmers were producing more than 170 million bushels of wheat and more than 800 million bushels of corn per year.

READING CHECK **Summarizing** What marketing methods did McCormick use to help sell his farm equipment?

American Inventions (continued)

1849 Walter Hunt invents the safety pin.

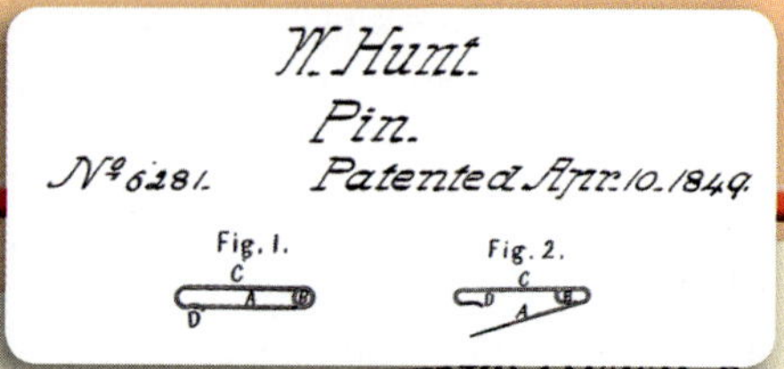

UNITED STATES PATENT OFFICE.

WALTER HUNT, OF NEW YORK, N. Y., ASSIGNOR TO WM. RICHARDSON AND JNO. RICHARDSON.

DRESS-PIN.

Specification of Letters Patent No. 6,281, dated April 10, 1849.

To all whom it may concern:

Be it known that I, WALTER HUNT, of the city, county, and State of New York, have invented a new and useful Improvement in the Make or Form of Dress-Pins, of which the following is a faithful and accurate

to the bar C, (see Figs. 6, 7 and 8,) which combined with the advantages of the spring and catch, renders it equally ornamental, and at the same time more secure and durable than any other plan of a clasp pin, heretofore in use, there being no joint to break or pivot to wear or get loose as in other plans. ... unknown in other

1851 Isaac Singer improves the sewing machine. The production and repair of clothing becomes much easier.

Changing Life at Home

Many inventions of the Industrial Revolution simply made life easier. When Alexis de Tocqueville of France visited the United States in the early 1830s, he identified what he called a very American quality.

> "[Americans want] to be always making life more comfortable and convenient, to avoid trouble, and to satisfy the smallest wants [desires] without effort and almost without cost."
>
> —Alexis de Tocqueville, from *Democracy in America*

The sewing machine, first invented by Elias Howe, a factory apprentice in Lowell, Massachusetts, was one of these conveniences. **Isaac Singer** then made improvements to Howe's design. Like McCormick, Singer allowed customers to buy his machines on credit and provided service. By 1860 Singer's company was the world's largest maker of sewing machines.

Other advances improved on everyday items. In the 1830s, iceboxes cooled by large blocks of ice became available. Iceboxes stored fresh food safely for longer periods. Iron cookstoves began replacing cooking fires and stone hearths.

Companies also began to mass produce earlier inventions. This allowed many families to buy household items, such as clocks, that they could not afford in the past. For example, a clock that cost $50 in 1800 was selling for only $1.50 by the 1850s. Additional useful items created during this period include matches, introduced in the 1830s, and the safety pin, invented in 1849. All of these inventions helped make life at home more convenient for an increasing number of Americans.

THE IMPACT TODAY

New inventions, such as cell phones, laptop computers, and microwave ovens, continue to make life easier and more convenient for people today.

READING CHECK **Analyzing** How did labor-saving inventions affect daily life?

SUMMARY AND PREVIEW New machines and inventions changed the way Americans lived and did business in the early 1800s. In the next section you will learn how agricultural changes affected the South.

1859 Manufactured goods become more valuable than agricultural goods in the country's economy for the first time. The United States is becoming a modern industrial nation.

ANALYSIS SKILL **READING TIME LINES**

Which two inventions improved American agriculture?

Section 4 Assessment

go.hrw.com
Online Quiz
KEYWORD: SC7 HP12

Reviewing Ideas, Terms, and People

1. a. **Describe** How did the **telegraph** work?
   b. **Predict** What impact might the telegraph have on the future of the United States?
2. a. **Describe** How did waterpowered factories differ from steam-powered factories?
   b. **Explain** How did the shift to steam power lead to the growth of cities?
3. a. **Identify** What contributions did **Cyrus McCormick** and **John Deere** make to farming?
   b. **Analyze** What effect did new inventions have on agriculture in the United States?
4. a. **Identify** What inventions improved life at home?
   b. **Evaluate** Which invention do you think had the greatest effect on the daily lives of Americans? Why?

Critical Thinking

5. **Supporting a Point of View** Review your notes on technological advances and their effects. Then create a graphic organizer like the one below that shows the top three advances you think are most important and why.

Most Important	Why

FOCUS ON WRITING

6. **Describing Technological Advances** Add notes about the inventions mentioned in this section to your chart. Think about which invention you will use for your newspaper advertisement.

Social Studies Skills

Analysis | Critical Thinking | **Civic Participation** | Study

North Carolina Skills
3.03 Detect bias.

Personal Conviction and Bias

Define the Skill

Everyone has *convictions,* or firmly held beliefs. However, when we let our beliefs automatically slant or shape our point of view on topics, we may be showing bias. *Bias* is a fixed idea or opinion about someone or something. Some bias is based on a set of ideas about a group to which the person or thing belongs. This type of bias is called a *stereotype*. If the group is defined by race, religion, age, gender, or similar characteristics, the bias is known as *prejudice*.

Bias, stereotypes, and prejudice are not always negative in nature. They include favorable opinions too. For example, the belief that a student is good at math because that person is male is a bias that shows both stereotyping and prejudice.

We should always be on guard for the presence of personal bias. Eliminating stereotyping and prejudice is particularly important. However, even "good" biases can slant how we view, judge, and communicate information. Honest and accurate communication requires that the information and ideas we express be as free of bias as possible.

Learn the Skill

Not all beliefs are biases, even if those beliefs are strongly held. Biases are beliefs that have little or no evidence to support them. The more unreasonable a person's view is in light of facts and evidence, the more likely it is that the belief is a bias.

Another characteristic of bias is the person's reluctance to question his or her belief if it is challenged by evidence. Sometimes people stubbornly cling to views that overwhelming evidence proves wrong. This is why bias is defined as a "fixed" idea or opinion. One of the most damaging effects of bias, and a good reason for trying to avoid it, is that it can prevent us from learning new things.

The following precautions can help you to reduce the amount of bias you hold and express.

1. When discussing a topic, keep in mind beliefs and experiences in your own background that might affect how you feel about the topic.
2. Try to not mix statements of fact with statements of opinion. Clearly separate and indicate what you *know* to be true from what you *believe* to be true.
3. Avoid using emotional, positive, or negative words when communicating factual information.

Practice the Skill

In 1834 Tennessee congressman Davy Crockett visited the textile mills at Lowell, Massachusetts. Read his account of the "Lowell girls" who worked in the factory and complete the activity below.

> "Here are thousands [of young women], useful to others, ...with the prospect before them of future comfort and respectability...There are more than five thousand females employed in Lowell; and when you come to see the amount of labour performed by them, in superintending [operating] the different machinery, you will be astonished."

Suppose that you were a "Lowell girl" who has just read this account of Crockett's visit. Write a letter to the editor of the *Lowell Offering* reacting to the biases and stereotypes about women that Crockett shows in his account.

CHAPTER 12

Chapter Review

HOLT

History's Impact

▶ **video series**

Review the video to answer the closing question:

How do you think ease of travel has affected U.S. population centers?

Visual Summary

QUICK FACTS

Use the visual summary below to help you review the main ideas of the chapter.

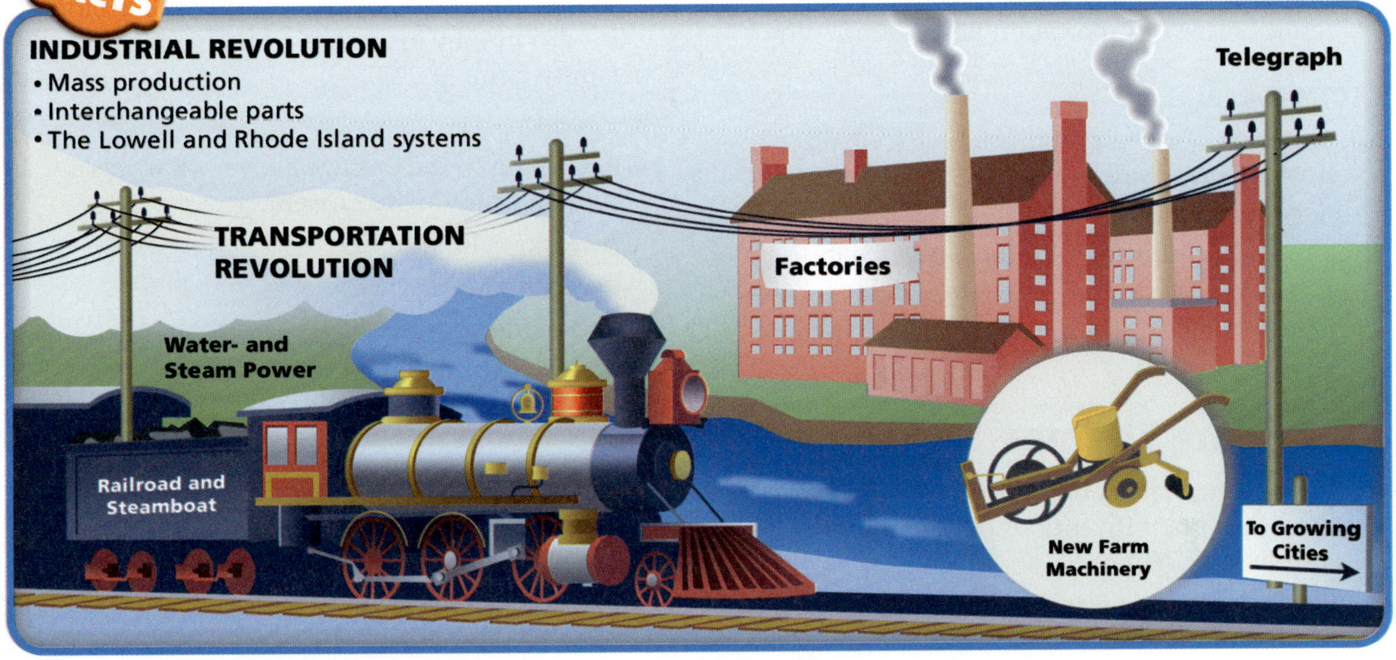

Reviewing Vocabulary, Terms, and People

Complete each sentence below by filling in the blank with the correct term or person from the chapter.

1. The system of ____________ was developed to represent letters of the alphabet when sending telegraph messages.
2. The first American woman to hold a high-ranking position in the labor movement was ______________________________.
3. The ____________ was a period of rapid growth in the use of machines and manufacturing.
4. The first locomotive in the United States was built by ______________________________.
5. Workers would sometimes go on __________ to force factory owners to meet their demands for better pay and working conditions.
6. The ____________ industry, which produced cloth items, was the first to use machines for manufacturing.

Comprehension and Critical Thinking

SECTION 1 *(Pages 384–389)*

7. a. Identify What ideas did Eli Whitney want to apply to the manufacture of guns?

b. Analyze How did the War of 1812 lead to a boom in manufacturing in the United States?

c. Elaborate Why do you think the Industrial Revolution began in Great Britain rather than in the United States?

SECTION 2 *(Pages 390–395)*

8. a. Describe What was mill life like?

b. Draw Conclusions How did the Rhode Island system and the Lowell system change the lives of American workers?

c. Evaluate Were reformers such as Sarah G. Bagley effective in improving labor conditions? Why?

SECTION 3 *(Pages 396–401)*

9. a. Describe How were Americans affected by the introduction of steamboats?

b. Make Inferences How did railroad companies become some of the most powerful businesses in the country?

c. Elaborate What was the most important result of the Transportation Revolution? Why?

SECTION 4 *(Pages 402–405)*

10. a. Recall What important change took place in how factories were powered?

b. Draw Conclusions How did the telegraph affect communication in the United States?

c. Evaluate Do you think moving factories close to cities helped or hurt working life? Explain.

Reviewing Themes

11. Science and Technology What are the three most important inventions of the Industrial Revolution? Why?

12. Economics What was the overall effect of the Industrial Revolution on the U.S. economy?

Using the Internet

go.hrw.com
KEYWORD: SC7 CH12

13. Activity: Marketing Plan The Industrial Revolution changed the way goods were produced. New inventions created easier, faster, or completely new ways of doing things. Enter the activity keyword and research inventions made between 1790 and 1860. Then create a plan for how to sell one of the inventions. In your plan, identify the problems the invention will fix, your target audience, and how the invention should be advertised and sold.

Reading Skills

Causes and Effects in History *Use the Reading Skills taught in this chapter to answer the question about the reading selection below.*

> Many young women came to Lowell from across New England. They wanted the chance to earn money instead of working on the family farm. *(p. 392)*

14. According to the passage above, what was a cause for moving to Lowell?

a. working long hours

b. earning money

c. meeting people

d. working on a farm

Social Studies Skills

Personal Conviction and Bias *Use the Social Studies Skills taught in this chapter to answer the question about the reading selection below.*

> "Is anyone such a fool as to suppose that out of six thousand factory girls in Lowell, sixty would be there if they could help it?"
>
> —Sarah G. Bagley, quoted in *The Belles of New England* by William Moran

15. Do you think that Bagley's opposition to the Lowell system was unfairly biased? Why or why not?

FOCUS ON WRITING

16. Writing Your Newspaper Advertisement Look over your chart, and choose one invention for your advertisement. Then answer these questions to help you plan your advertisement: Who is your audience? Who will buy this invention? How will the invention benefit this audience? What words or phrases will best persuade this audience? Once you have answered these questions, design your advertisement. To draw readers' attention to your ad, include an illustration, a catchy heading, and a few lines of text.

CHAPTER 12

Standardized Test Practice

DIRECTIONS: Read each question and write the letter of the best response.

1 The first machines of the Industrial Revolution were powered by

A electricity.

B water.

C animals.

D coal.

2 The earliest important evidence of the Industrial Revolution in the United States was found in the

A way cotton was processed for market.

B production of tobacco products.

C manufacture of cloth and thread.

D construction of the first steam railroads.

3 How did new industrial technology affect North Carolina?

A It led to a decrease in the number of farmers in North Carolina.

B It sparked a boom in cotton production.

C It encouraged state officials to open the first public schools.

D It led to the opening of cotton mills and ironworks in the state.

4 What change in technology allowed business owners to sell their goods in markets across the country?

A the Lowell system

B the growth of railroads

C the invention of the telegraph

D the Arkwright system

5 Eli Whitney's idea of interchangeable parts resulted in

A the dominance of American manufacturing.

B the beginning of the Industrial Revolution.

C a rapid expansion of railroads.

D the mass production of goods.

6 The inventions of John Deere and Cyrus McCormick

A improved communication.

B introduced two new factory labor systems.

C helped increase agricultural production in the United States.

D led to manufacturing breakthroughs in the textile industry.

7 Read the following passage written by a textile worker and use it to answer the question below.

> "The little money I could earn—one dollar a week, besides the price of my board—was needed in the family, and I must return [from home] to the mill . . . I began to reflect on life rather seriously for a girl of twelve or thirteen. What was I here for? What would I make of myself? . . . We did not forget that we were working girls . . . clearing away a few weeds from the overgrown track of independent labor for other women . . . [so that] no real odium [disrespect] could be attached to any honest toil that any self-respecting woman might undertake."
>
> —from *A New England Girlhood* by Lucy Larcom (1824–1893)

Document-Based Question How did Larcom see the role of women changing in the workforce?

CHAPTER 13 1790–1860

The South

North Carolina Standards

Social Studies Objectives

3.04 Describe the development of the institution of slavery in the State and nation, and assess its impact on the economic, social, and political conditions.

3.08 Examine the impact of national events such as the Louisiana Purchase, the Lewis and Clark Expedition, the War with Mexico, and the California Gold Rush, and technological advances on North Carolina.

9.02 Identify past and present state and local leaders from diverse cultural backgrounds and assess their influence in effecting change.

Language Arts Objectives

2.01 Analyze and evaluate informational materials that are read, heard, and/or viewed by:

- recognizing the characteristics of informational materials.
- summarizing information.

go.hrw.com
North Carolina
KEYWORD: SC7 NC

FOCUS ON WRITING

Biographical Sketch In this chapter you will learn about life in the South during the first half of the nineteenth century. Read the chapter, and then write a two-paragraph biographical sketch about a day in the life of a person living on a large cotton farm in the South. You might choose to write about a wealthy male landowner, his wife, or an enslaved man or woman working on the farm. As you read, think about what life would have been like for the different people who lived and worked on the farm. Take notes about farm life in your notebook.

UNITED STATES

1793 Eli Whitney invents the cotton gin.

1800

WORLD

1794 France ends slavery in its colonies.

HOLT

History's Impact

▶ **video series**
Watch the video to understand the impact of regional economies on the nation.

What You Will Learn...

These enslaved people were photographed on a South Carolina plantation in the year 1861. The issue of slavery would have a serious and dramatic impact on the history of the entire United States. In this chapter you will learn how the South developed an agricultural economy, and how that economy was dependent on the labor of enslaved people.

1807 Parliament bans the slave trade in the British Empire.

1808 A congressional ban on importing slaves into the United States takes effect.

1820

1831 Nat Turner's Rebellion leads to fears of further slave revolts in the South.

1835 Alexis de Tocqueville publishes *Democracy in America*.

1837 Victoria is crowned queen of Great Britain.

1840

1848 Joseph R. Anderson becomes the owner of the Tredegar Iron Works, the South's only large iron factory.

1858 A treaty at Tianjin, China, gives Hong Kong to the United Kingdom.

1860

Reading Social Studies

by Kylene Beers

Economics | Geography | Politics | Society and Culture | Science and Technology

Focus on Themes This chapter takes you into the heart of the South from 1800 through the mid-1800s. As you read, you will discover that the South depended on cotton as its **economic** backbone, especially after the invention of the cotton gin. You will also read about the slave system in the South during this time and about the harsh living conditions slaves endured. As you will see, the South was home to a variety of **societies and cultures**.

Online Research

Focus on Reading Researching history topics on the Web can give you access to valuable information. However, just because the information is on the Web doesn't mean it is automatically valuable.

Evaluating Web Sites Before you use information you find online, you need to evaluate the site it comes from. The checklist below can help you determine if the site is worth your time.

Evaluating Web Sites

Site: ____________ **URL:** ____________ **Date of access:** ____________

Rate each item on this 1–3 scale. Then add up the total score.

	No	Some	Yes
I. Authority			
a. Authors are clearly identified by name.	1	2	3
b. Contact information is provided for authors.	1	2	3
c. Authors' qualifications are clearly stated.	1	2	3
d. Site has been updated recently.	1	2	3
II. Content			
a. Site's information is useful to your project.	1	2	3
b. Information is clear and well-organized.	1	2	3
c. Information appears to be at the right level.	1	2	3
d. Links to additional important information are provided.	1	2	3
e. Information can be verified in other sources.	1	2	3
f. Graphics are helpful, not just decorative.	1	2	3
III. Design and Technical Elements			
a. Pages are readable and easy to navigate.	1	2	3
b. Links to other sites work.	1	2	3

Total Score ____________

36–28 = very good site **27–20 = average site** **below 20 = poor site**

You Try It!

The passage below is from the chapter you are about to read.

Cotton Becomes Profitable

From Chapter 13, pp. 414–415

Cotton had been grown in the New World for centuries, but it had not been a very profitable crop. Before cotton could be spun into thread for weaving into cloth, the seeds had to be removed from the cotton fibers.

Long-staple cotton, also called black-seed cotton, was fairly easy to process. Workers could pick the seeds from the cotton with relative ease. But long-staple cotton grew well in only a few places in the South. More common was short-staple cotton, which was also known as green-seed cotton. Removing the seeds from this cotton was difficult and time consuming. A worker could spend an entire day picking the seeds from a single pound of short-staple cotton.

After you read the passage, complete the following activity.

Suppose that after reading this passage you decide to do some research on cotton growing. You use a search engine that directs you to a site. At that site, you find the information described below. Using the evaluation criteria listed on the previous page, decide if this is a site you would recommend to others.

a. The authors of the site are listed as "Bob and Mack, good friends who enjoy working together."

b. The site was last updated on "the last time we got together."

c. The title of the site is "Cotton Pickin'." There are few headings.

d. This ten-page site includes nine pages about the authors' childhood on a cotton farm. No illustrations are included.

e. Pages are very long, but they load quickly, as there are no graphics. There is one link to a site selling cotton clothing.

Key Terms and People

Chapter 13

Section 1

cotton gin *(p. 415)*
planters *(p. 416)*
cotton belt *(p. 416)*
factors *(p. 417)*
Tredegar Iron Works *(p. 419)*

Section 2

yeomen *(p. 422)*

Section 3

folktales *(p. 427)*
spirituals *(p. 427)*
Nat Turner's Rebellion *(p. 428)*
Nat Turner *(p. 428)*

Academic Vocabulary

Success in school is related to knowing academic vocabulary—the words that are frequently used in school assignments and discussions. In this chapter, you will learn the following academic words:

primary *(p. 418)*
aspect *(p. 426)*

As you read Chapter 13, think about what topics would be interesting to research on the Web. If you do some research on the Web, remember to use the evaluation list to analyze the Web site.

SECTION 1

Growth of the Cotton Industry

What You Will Learn...

Main Ideas

1. The invention of the cotton gin revived the economy of the South.
2. The cotton gin created a cotton boom in which farmers grew little else.
3. Some people encouraged southerners to focus on other crops and industries.

The Big Idea

The invention of the cotton gin made the South a one-crop economy and increased the need for slave labor.

Key Terms and People

cotton gin, *p. 415*
planters, *p. 416*
cotton belt, *p. 416*
factors, *p. 417*
Tredegar Iron Works, *p. 419*

TAKING NOTES As you read, take notes on the causes of the cotton boom in the South. Record your notes in a graphic organizer like the one shown below.

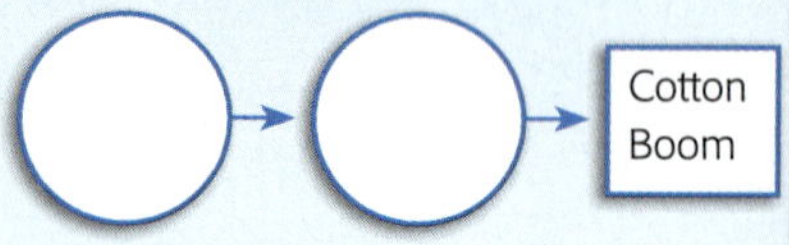

If YOU were there...

You are a field-worker on a cotton farm in the South in about 1800. Your job is to separate the seeds from the cotton fibers. It is dull, tiring work because the tiny seeds are tangled in the fibers. Sometimes it takes you a whole day just to clean one pound of cotton! Now you hear that someone has invented a machine that can clean cotton 50 times faster than by hand.

How might this machine change your life?

BUILDING BACKGROUND Sectional differences had always existed between different regions of the United States. The revolutionary changes in industry and transportation deepened the differences between North and South. The South remained mainly agricultural. New technology helped the region become the Cotton Kingdom.

Reviving the South's Economy

Before the American Revolution, three crops dominated southern agriculture—tobacco, rice, and indigo. These crops, produced mostly by enslaved African Americans, played a central role in the southern economy and culture.

After the American Revolution, however, prices for tobacco, rice, and indigo dropped. When crop prices fell, the demand for and the price of slaves also went down. In an effort to protect their incomes, many farmers tried, with little success, to grow other crops that needed less labor. Soon, however, cotton would transform the southern economy and greatly increase the demand for slave labor.

Cotton Becomes Profitable

Cotton had been grown in the New World for centuries, but it had not been a very profitable crop. Before cotton could be spun into thread for weaving into cloth, the seeds had to be removed from the cotton fibers.

Cotton Gin

Connect to Science and Technology

Eli Whitney's cotton gin enabled workers to easily remove seeds from cotton fibers. The result was a dramatic increase in cotton production in the South.

How did the cotton gin remove seeds from cotton fibers?

1. The operator turned the crank.
2. The crank turned a roller with teeth that stripped the seeds away from the cotton fiber.
3. Brushes on a second roller lifted the seedless cotton off the teeth of the first cylinder and dropped it out of the machine.
4. A belt connected the rollers so that they would both turn when the crank was turned.

Long-staple cotton, also called black-seed cotton, was fairly easy to process. Workers could pick the seeds from the cotton with relative ease. But long-staple cotton grew well in only a few places in the South. More common was short-staple cotton, which was also known as green-seed cotton. Removing the seeds from this cotton was difficult and time consuming. A worker could spend an entire day picking the seeds from a single pound of short-staple cotton.

By the early 1790s the demand for American cotton began increasing rapidly. For instance, in Great Britain, new textile factories needed raw cotton that could be used for making cloth, and American cotton producers could not keep up with the high demand for their cotton. These producers of cotton needed a machine that could remove the seeds from the cotton more rapidly.

Eli Whitney's Cotton Gin

Northerner Eli Whitney finally patented such a machine in 1793. The year before, Whitney had visited a Georgia plantation owned by Catherine Greene where workers were using a machine that removed seeds from long-staple cotton. This machine did not work well on short-staple cotton, and Greene asked Whitney if he could improve it. By the next spring, Whitney had perfected his design for the **cotton gin**, a machine that removes seeds from short-staple cotton. ("Gin" is short for engine.) The cotton gin used a hand-cranked cylinder with wire teeth to pull cotton fibers from the seeds.

Whitney hoped to keep the design of the gin a secret, but the machine was so useful that his patent was often ignored by other manufacturers. Whitney described how his invention would improve the cotton business.

The Impact Today

The same patent law that protected Whitney's invention of the cotton gin protects the rights of inventors today.

> “One man will clean ten times as much cotton as he can in any other way before known and also clean it much better than in the usual mode [method]. This machine may be turned by water or with a horse, with the greatest ease, and one man and a horse will do more than fifty men with the old machines.”
>
> —Eli Whitney, quoted in *Eli Whitney and the Birth of American Technology* by Constance McLaughlin Green

FOCUS ON NORTH CAROLINA

Most cotton was grown in the lower South. States of the upper South, like North Carolina, grew less cotton but had cotton mills that produced cloth. By 1860 North Carolina had 39 such mills.

Whitney's gin revolutionized the cotton industry. **Planters**—large-scale farmers who held more than 20 slaves—built cotton gins that could process tons of cotton much faster than hand processing. A healthy crop almost guaranteed financial success because of high demand from the textile industry.

READING CHECK **Drawing Conclusions** What effects did the cotton gin have on the southern economy?

The Cotton Boom

Whitney's invention of the cotton gin made cotton so profitable that southern farmers abandoned other crops in favor of growing cotton. The removal of Native Americans opened up more land, while the development of new types of cotton plants helped spread cotton production throughout the South as far west as Texas. This area of high cotton production became known as the **cotton belt**.

Production increased rapidly—from about 2 million pounds in 1791 to roughly a billion pounds by 1860. As early as 1840, the United States was producing more than half of the cotton grown in the entire world. The economic boom attracted new settlers, built up wealth among wealthy white southerners, and firmly put in place the institution of slavery in the South.

The Cotton Kingdom

After the invention of the cotton gin, the amount of cotton produced each year in the United States soared, as the chart below shows. The area of land devoted to growing cotton also increased dramatically between 1820 and 1860, as shown on the map.

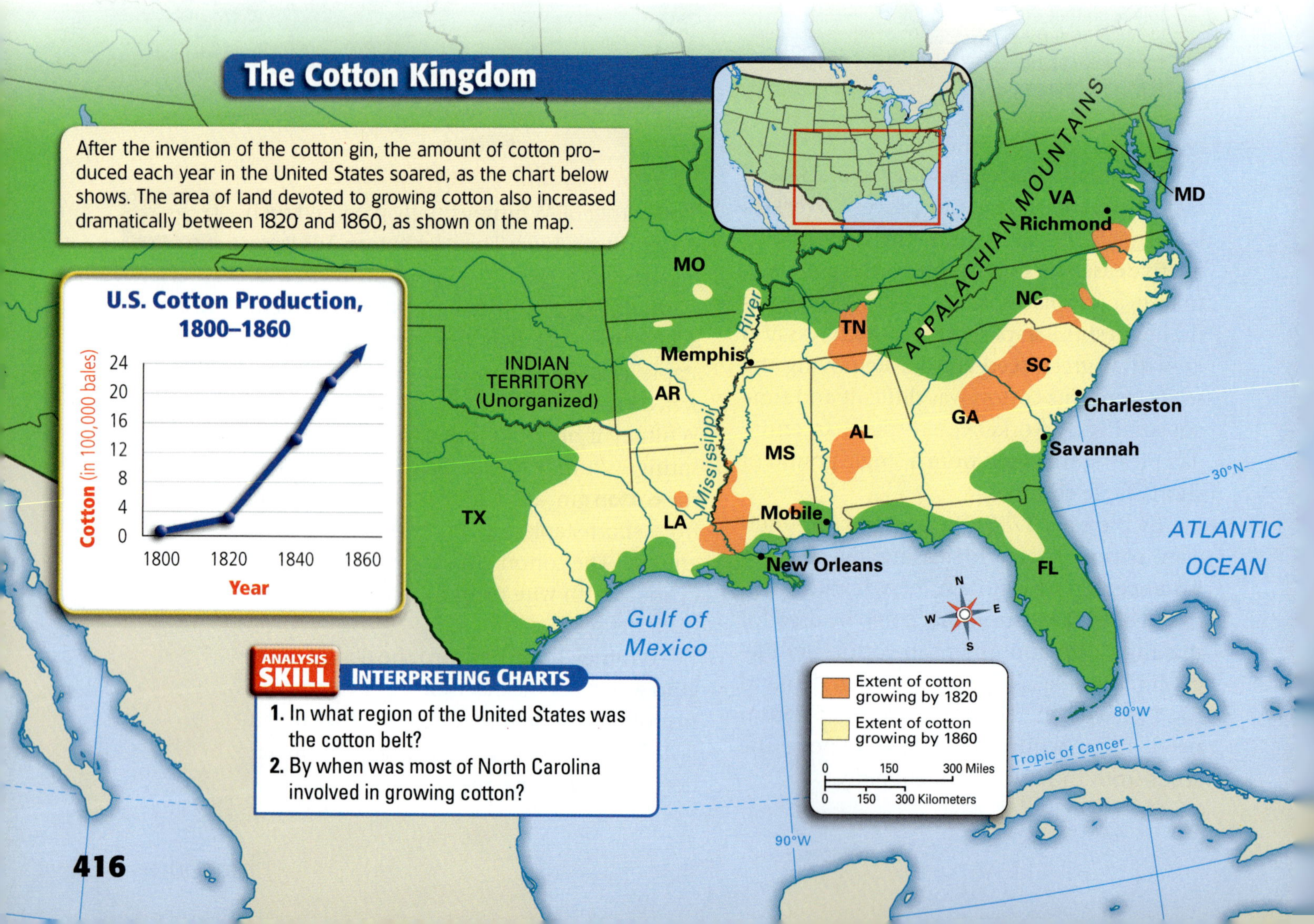

ANALYSIS SKILL **INTERPRETING CHARTS**

1. In what region of the United States was the cotton belt?
2. By when was most of North Carolina involved in growing cotton?

Cotton Belt

Cotton had many advantages as a cash crop. It cost little to market. Unlike food staples, harvested cotton could be stored for a long time. Because cotton was lighter than other staple crops, it also cost less to transport long distances.

Farmers eager to profit from growing cotton headed west to find land. Farmers also began to apply scientific methods to improve crop production. Cotton had one disadvantage as a crop—it rapidly used up the nutrients in the soil. After a few years, cotton could make the land useless for growing anything. Some agricultural scientists recommended crop rotation—changing the crop grown on a particular plot of land every few years. Different crops needed different nutrients, so crop rotation would keep the land fertile longer. Other agricultural scientists began to study soil chemistry, in an effort to keep the land rich and productive.

As the cotton belt grew, farmers continued trying to improve the crop. Agricultural scientists worked at crossbreeding short-staple cotton with other varieties. As a result, new, stronger types of cotton were soon growing throughout the cotton belt. This led to expansion of the cotton industry through the 1860s.

The cotton boom involved much more than growing and harvesting cotton. Harvested cotton had to be ginned, pressed into bales, and then shipped to market or to warehouses. Special agents helped do everything from marketing cotton to customers to insuring crops against loss or damage. Factories were built to produce items needed by cotton farmers, such as ropes to bale cotton.

Growing and harvesting cotton required many field hands. Rather than pay wages to free workers, planters began to use more slave labor. Congress had made bringing slaves into the United States illegal in 1808. However, the growing demand for slaves led to an increase in the slave trade within the United States.

Cotton Trade

In an 1858 speech before the U.S. Senate, South Carolina politician James Henry Hammond declared, "Cotton is King!" Without cotton, Hammond claimed, the global economy would fail. He believed that southern cotton was one of the most valuable resources in the world. Southern cotton was used to make cloth in England and the North. Many southerners shared Hammond's viewpoints about cotton. Southerner David Christy declared, "King cotton is a profound [learned] statesman, and knows what measures will best sustain [protect] his throne."

The cotton boom made the South a major player in world trade. Great Britain became the South's most valued foreign trading partner. Southerners also sold tons of cotton to the growing textile industry in the northeastern United States. This increased trade led to the growth of major port cities in the South, including Charleston, South Carolina; Savannah, Georgia; and New Orleans, Louisiana.

THE IMPACT TODAY

The Port of New Orleans remains a major seaport. It handles about 85 million tons of cargo annually.

In these cities, crop brokers called **factors** managed the cotton trade. Farmers sold their cotton to merchants, who then made deals with the factors. Merchants and factors also arranged loans for farmers who needed to buy supplies. They often advised farmers on how to invest profits. Once farmers got their cotton to the port cities, factors arranged for transportation aboard trading ships.

However, shipping cotton by land to port cities was very difficult in the South. The few major road projects at the time were limited to the Southeast. Most southern farmers had to ship their goods on the region's rivers. On the Ohio and Mississippi rivers, flatboats and steamboats carried cotton and other products to port. Eventually, hundreds of steamboats traveled up and down the mighty Mississippi River each day.

READING CHECK **Identifying Cause and Effect** What effect did the cotton boom have on the slave trade within the United States?

The South's Cotton Economy

Eli Whitney's cotton gin began the cotton boom. Soon, the Cotton Kingdom stretched across the South. For the cotton planters to succeed, they had to get their cotton to market.

Enslaved African Americans did most of the planting, harvesting, and processing of cotton.

Cotton was shipped on river steamboats to major ports such as Charleston.

From southern ports, sailing ships carried the cotton to distant textile mills.

Other Crops and Industries

Some leaders worried that the South was depending too much on cotton. They wanted southerners to try a variety of cash crops and investments.

ACADEMIC VOCABULARY

primary main, most important

Food and Cash Crops

One such crop was corn, the **primary** southern food crop. By the late 1830s the top three corn-growing states in the nation were all in the South. The South's other successful food crops included rice, sweet potatoes, wheat, and sugarcane.

Production of tobacco, the South's first major cash crop, was very time consuming because tobacco leaves had to be cured, or dried, before they could be shipped to market. In 1839 a slave discovered a way to improve the drying process by using heat from burning charcoal. This new, faster curing process increased tobacco production.

Partly as a result of the cotton boom, hemp and flax also became major cash crops. Their fibers were used to make rope and sackcloth. Farmers used the rope and sackcloth to bundle cotton into bales.

NC History Makers

Hinton Rowan Helper
Hinton Rowan Helper published the antislavery book *The Impending Crisis of the South* in 1857, which helped fuel secessionist feelings.

Industry

Many of the first factories in the South were built to serve farmers' needs by processing crops such as sugarcane. In 1803 the nation's first steam-powered sawmill was built in Donaldsonville, Louisiana. This new technology enabled lumber companies to cut, sort, and clean wood quickly.

By the 1840s, entrepreneurs in Georgia began investing in cotton mills. In 1840, there were 14 cotton mills; by the mid-1850s, there were more than 50. A few mill owners followed the model established by Francis Cabot Lowell. However, most built small-scale factories on the falls of a river for waterpower. A few steam-powered mills were built in towns without enough waterpower.

Southerners such as Hinton Rowan Helper encouraged industrial growth in the South.

> "We should . . . keep pace with the progress of the age. We must expand our energies, and acquire habits of enterprise and industry; we should rouse ourselves from the couch of lassitude [laziness] and inure [set] our minds to thought and our bodies to action."
>
> —Hinton Rowan Helper, *The Impending Crisis of the South: How to Meet It*

A large amount of cotton was sold to textile mills in the northeastern United States.

Textile mills in Great Britain were the largest foreign buyers of southern cotton.

ANALYSIS SKILL **DRAWING CONCLUSIONS**

Why do you think cotton was so important to the South's economy?

Joseph R. Anderson followed Helper's advice. In 1848 Anderson became the owner of the **Tredegar Iron Works** in Richmond, Virginia—one of the most productive iron works in the nation. It was the only factory to produce bridge materials, cannons, steam engines, and other products.

FOCUS ON READING

What kind of Web site would you look for to learn more about the Tredegar Iron Works?

Industry, however, remained a small part of the southern economy. Southern industry faced stiff competition from the North and from England, both of which could produce many goods more cheaply. And as long as agricultural profits remained high, southern investors preferred to invest in land.

READING CHECK **Making Inferences** Why were there fewer industries in the South?

SUMMARY AND PREVIEW You have read about how southern farmers worked to improve farming methods. In the next section you will read about the structure of southern society.

go.hrw.com
Online Quiz
KEYWORD: SC7 HP13

Section 1 Assessment

Reviewing Ideas, Terms, and People

1. a. **Describe** How did the **cotton gin** make processing cotton easier?
   b. **Draw Conclusions** Why had slavery been on the decline before the invention of the cotton gin? How did slavery change as a result of the cotton gin?
   c. **Predict** How might the rise of cotton production and slavery affect Southern society?
2. a. **Identify** What areas of the United States made up the **cotton belt**?
   b. **Evaluate** Do you think the South should have paid more attention to its industrial growth? Why?
3. a. **Describe** What other crops and industries were encouraged in the South?
   b. **Make Inferences** Why were some southern leaders worried about the South's reliance on cotton?

Critical Thinking

4. **Identifying Cause and Effect** Review your notes on the causes of the cotton boom. Then add to your graphic organizer by identifying the effects of the cotton boom on the South.

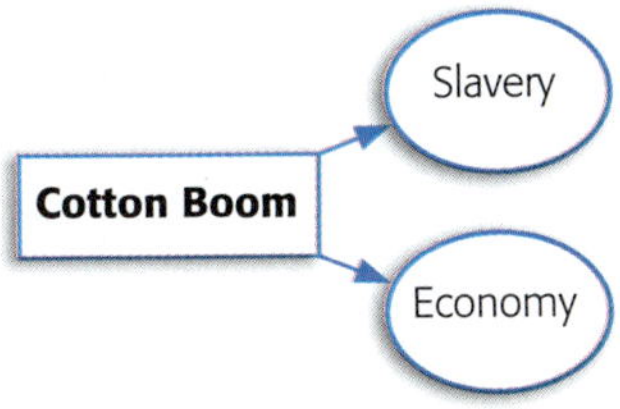

FOCUS ON WRITING

5. **Noting Life on the Cotton Farm** In your notebook, note how Whitney's gin changed life on the farm. Also note other details about cotton farming you could include in your sketch.

SECTION 2

Southern Society

What You Will Learn...

Main Ideas

1. Southern society and culture consisted of four main groups.
2. Free African Americans in the South faced a great deal of discrimination.

The Big Idea

Southern society centered around agriculture.

Key Term

yeomen, *p. 422*

TAKING NOTES As you read, take notes on the different segments of southern society. Record the information you find in a graphic organizer like the one below.

Group	Life
Planters	
Yeomen	
Poor Whites	
Free African Americans	

If YOU were there...

Your family owns a small farm in Georgia in the 1840s. Sometimes you work in the fields, but more often you tend the vegetable garden and peach orchard. Since you have no close neighbors, you look forward to Sundays. Going to church gives you a chance to socialize with other young people. Sometimes you wonder what it would be like to live in a city like Savannah.

How would life be different if you left the farm for the city?

BUILDING BACKGROUND Although the South had some industry, agriculture was the heart of the southern economy. Cotton was king. As a result, wealthy plantation families were the most prominent social class in southern society. Small farmers, however, made up the largest part of the population.

Southern Society and Culture

Popular fiction often made it seem that all white southerners had many slaves and lived on large plantations. Many fiction writers wrote about wealthy southern families who had frequent, grand parties. The ideal image of the Antebellum (before the war) South included hospitality and well-treated slaves on beautiful plantations that almost ran themselves.

This romantic view was far from the reality. During the first half of the 1800s, only about one-third of white southern families had slaves. Fewer families had plantations. Despite their small numbers, these planters had a powerful influence over the South. Many served as political leaders. They led a society made up of many different kinds of people, including yeomen farmers, poor whites, slaves, and free African Americans. Each of these segments of society contributed to the economic success of the South.

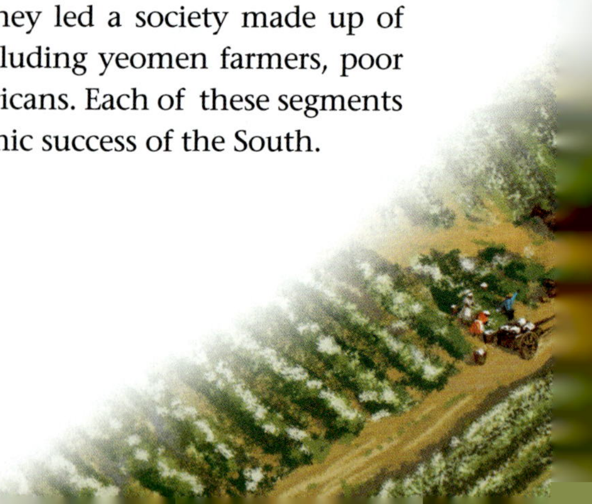

Planters

As the wealthiest members of southern society, planters also greatly influenced the economy. Some showed off their wealth by living in beautiful mansions. Many others chose to live more simply. A visitor described wealthy planter Alexander Stephens's estate as "an old wooden house" surrounded by weeds. Some planters saved all of their money to buy more land and slaves.

Male planters were primarily concerned with raising crops and supervising slave laborers. They left the running of the plantation household to their wives. The planter's wife oversaw the raising of the children and supervised the work of all slaves within the household. Slave women typically cooked, cleaned, and helped care for the planter's children. Wives also took on the important social duties of the family. For example, many southern leaders discussed political issues at the dances and dinners hosted by their wives.

Planters often arranged their children's marriages based on business interests. Lucy Breckinridge, the daughter of a wealthy Virginia planter, was married by arrangement in 1865. Three years earlier, she had described in her journal how she dreaded the very thought of marriage. "A woman's life after she is married, unless there is an immense amount of love, is nothing but suffering and hard work." How Breckinridge's life in her own arranged marriage would have turned out cannot be known. She died of typhoid fever just months after her wedding.

History Close-up

A Southern Plantation

A typical plantation had fields as well as many buildings where different work was done. This picture shows some of the more important buildings that were a part of the plantation system.

ANALYSIS SKILL ANALYZING VISUALS

How can you tell that the owner of this plantation was wealthy?

Free African Americans in the South

Collection of The American Numismatic Society, New York

In 1860 about 1 out of 50 African Americans in the South was free. Many worked in skilled trades, like this barber in Richmond, Virginia. In Charleston, South Carolina, a system of badges was set up to distinguish between free African Americans and slaves.

How would the work of the free African American in this picture be different from that of slaves in the South?

Yeomen and Poor Whites

Most white southerners were **yeomen**, owners of small farms. Yeomen owned few slaves or none at all. The typical farm averaged 100 acres. Yeomen took great pride in their work. In 1849 a young Georgia man wrote, "I desire above all things to be a 'Farmer.' It is the most honest, upright, and sure way of securing all the comforts of life."

Yeoman families, including women and children, typically worked long days at a variety of tasks. Some yeomen held a few slaves but worked alongside them.

The poorest of white southerners lived on land that could not grow cash crops. They survived by hunting, fishing, raising small gardens, and doing odd jobs for money.

Religion and Society

Most white southerners shared similar religious beliefs. Because of the long distances between farms, families often saw their neighbors only at church events, such as revivals or socials. Rural women often played volunteer roles in their churches. Wealthy white southerners thought that their religion justified their position in society and the institution of slavery. They argued that God created some people, like themselves, to rule others. This belief opposed many northern Christians' belief that God was against slavery.

Urban Life

Many of the largest and most important cities in the South were strung along the Atlantic coast and had begun as shipping centers. Although fewer in number, the southern cities were similar to northern cities. City governments built public water systems and provided well-maintained streets. Public education was available in a few places. Wealthy residents occasionally gave large sums of money to charities, such as orphanages and public libraries. Southern urban leaders wanted their cities to appear as modern as possible.

As on plantations, slaves did much of the work in southern cities. Slaves worked as domestic servants, in mills, in shipyards, and at skilled jobs. Many business leaders held slaves or hired them from nearby plantations.

READING CHECK **Summarizing** What different groups made up southern society?

Free African Americans and Discrimination

Although the vast majority of African Americans in the South were enslaved, more than 250,000 free African Americans lived in the region by 1860. Some were descendants of slaves who were freed after the American Revolution. Others were descendants of refugees from Toussaint L'Ouverture's Haitian Revolution in the late 1790s. Still others were former slaves who had run away, been freed by their slaveholder, or earned enough money to buy their freedom.

Free African Americans lived in both rural and urban areas. Most lived in the countryside and worked as paid laborers on plantations or farms. Free African Americans in cities often worked a variety of jobs, mostly as skilled artisans. Some, like barber William Johnson of Natchez, Mississippi, became quite successful in their businesses. Frequently, free African Americans, especially those in the cities, formed social and economic ties with one another. Churches often served as the center of their social lives.

Free African Americans faced constant discrimination from white southerners. Many governments passed laws limiting the rights of free African Americans. Most free African Americans could not vote, travel freely, or hold certain jobs. In some places, free African Americans had to have a white person represent them in any business transaction. In others, laws restricted where they were allowed to live or conduct business.

Many white southerners argued that free African Americans did not have the ability to take care of themselves, and they used this belief to justify the institution of slavery. "The status of slavery is the only one for which the African is adapted," wrote one white Mississippian. To many white southerners, the very existence of free African Americans threatened the institution of slavery.

READING CHECK **Finding Main Ideas** What challenges did free African Americans face in the South?

SUMMARY AND PREVIEW Southern society was led by rich planters but included groups of small farmers, slaves, and free African Americans as well. These groups each had their own culture. In the next section you will read about life under slavery.

Section 2 Assessment

go.hrw.com
Online Quiz
KEYWORD: SC7 HP13

Reviewing Ideas, Terms, and People

1. a. **Identify** What was the largest social group in the South? How did its members make a living?
   b. **Compare** In what ways were southern cities similar to northern cities?
   c. **Elaborate** Which southern social class do you think had the most difficult life? Why?
2. a. **Describe** What jobs were available to free African Americans in the South? Why were these jobs the only ones available?
   b. **Analyze** Why did many white southerners fear free African Americans?
   c. **Elaborate** Why do you think that discrimination against free African Americans was harsher in the South than in the North?

Critical Thinking

3. **Comparing and Contrasting** Review your notes on the different kinds of people who lived in the South. Then use a graphic organizer like the one below to identify the similarities and differences of the lives of planters, yeomen, and free African Americans.

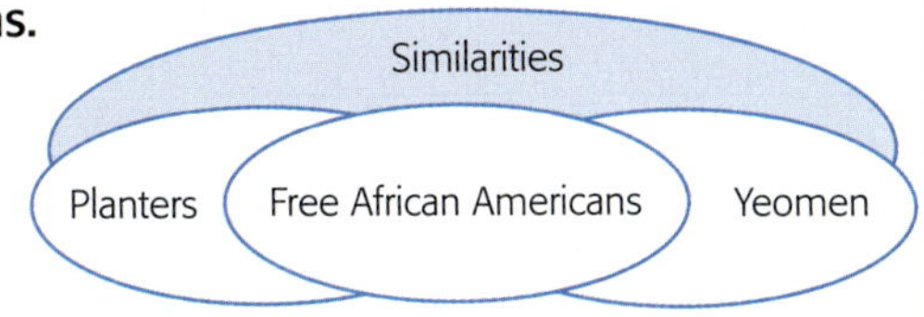

FOCUS ON WRITING

4. **Describing the Life of Cotton Farmers** In your notebook, describe the different roles played by male planters and their wives. What challenges would female planters have faced? When would the planters have had a chance to socialize?

SECTION 3

The Slave System

What You Will Learn...

Main Ideas

1. Slaves worked at a variety of jobs on plantations.
2. Life under slavery was difficult and dehumanizing.
3. Slave culture centered around family, community, and religion.
4. Slave uprisings led to stricter slave codes in many states.

The Big Idea

The slave system in the South produced harsh living conditions and occasional rebellions.

Key Terms and People

folktales, *p. 427*
spirituals, *p. 427*
Nat Turner's Rebellion, *p. 428*
Nat Turner, *p. 428*

TAKING NOTES As you read, take notes on the slavery system in a graphic organizer like the one shown below.

	Life as an Enslaved Person
Work	
Life	
Culture	

If YOU were there...

You are a reporter for a newspaper in Philadelphia in the 1850s. You are writing a series of articles about the slave system in the South. To get background for your stories, you are planning to interview some former slaves who now live in Philadelphia. Some have bought their freedom, while others have successfully escaped from slavery.

What questions will you ask in your interviews?

BUILDING BACKGROUND While most white southern families were not slaveholders, the southern economy depended on the work of slaves. This was true not only on large plantations but also on smaller farms and in the cities. Few chances existed for enslaved African Americans to escape their hard lives.

Slaves and Work

Most enslaved African Americans lived in rural areas where they worked on farms and plantations. Enslaved people on small farms usually did a variety of jobs. On large plantations, most slaves were assigned to specific jobs, and most worked in the fields. Most slaveholders demanded that slaves work as much as possible. Supervisors known as drivers, who were sometimes slaves themselves, made sure that slaves followed orders and carried out punishments.

Working in the Field

Most plantation owners used the gang-labor system. In this system, all field hands worked on the same task at the same time. They usually worked from sunup to sundown. Former slave Harry McMillan had worked on a plantation in South Carolina. He recalled that the field hands usually did not even get a break to eat lunch. "You had to get your victuals [food] standing at your hoe," he remembered.

Men, women, and even children older than about 10 usually did the same tasks. Sickness and poor weather rarely stopped the work. "The times I hated most was picking cotton when the frost was on the bolls [seed pods]," recalled former Louisiana slave Mary Reynolds. "My hands git sore and crack open and bleed."

Working in the Planter's Home

Some slaves worked as butlers, cooks, or nurses in the planter's home. These slaves often had better food, clothing, and shelter than field hands did, but they often worked longer hours. They had to serve the planter's family 24 hours a day.

Working at Skilled Jobs

On larger plantations, some enslaved African Americans worked at skilled jobs, such as blacksmithing or carpentry. Sometimes planters let these slaves sell their services to other people. Often planters collected a portion of what was earned but allowed slaves to keep the rest. In this way, some skilled slaves earned enough money to buy their freedom from their slaveholders. For example, William Ellison earned his freedom in South Carolina by working for wages as a cotton gin maker. For years, he worked late at night and on Sundays. He bought his freedom with the money he earned. Eventually, he was also able to buy the freedom of his wife and daughter.

READING CHECK **Summarizing** What were some types of work done by enslaved people on plantations?

Life Under Slavery

Generally, slaveholders viewed slaves as property, not as people. Slaveholders bought and sold slaves to make a profit. The most common method of sale was at an auction. The auction itself determined whether families would be kept together or separated. Sometimes a buyer wanted a slave to fill a specific job, such as heavy laborer, carpenter, or blacksmith. The buyer might be willing to pay for the slave who could do the work, but not for that slave's family. Families would then be separated with little hope of ever getting back together.

Slave traders sometimes even kidnapped free African Americans and then sold them into slavery. For example, Solomon Northup, a free African American, was kidnapped in Washington, D.C. He spent 12 years as a slave until he finally proved his identity and gained his release.

Living Conditions

Enslaved people often endured poor living conditions. Planters housed them in dirt-floor cabins with few furnishings and often leaky roofs. The clothing given to them was usually simple and made of cheap, coarse fabric. Some slaves tried to brighten up their

A Nurse's Work

Slaveholders' children were often cared for by enslaved women. At the time, women who looked after children were called nurses. This nurse is posing with her slaveholder's child in about 1850.

As a slave, what might have happened to this woman's family?

clothing by sewing on designs from discarded scraps of material. In this way, they expressed their individuality and personalized the clothing assigned to them by the planters.

Likewise, many slaves did what they could to improve their small food rations. Some planters allowed slaves to keep their own gardens for vegetables, and chickens for eggs. Other slaves were able to add a little variety to their diet by fishing or picking wild berries.

Punishment and Slave Codes

Some planters offered more food or better living conditions to encourage slaves' obedience. However, most slaveholders used punishment instead. Some would punish one slave in front of others as a warning to them all. Harry McMillan recalled some of the punishments he had witnessed.

> "The punishments were whipping, putting you in the stocks [wooden frames to lock people in] and making you wear irons and a chain at work. Then they had a collar to put round your neck with two horns, like cows' horns, so that you could not lie down . . . Sometimes they dug a hole like a well with a door on top. This they called a dungeon keeping you in it two or three weeks or a month, or sometimes till you died in there."
>
> —Harry McMillan, quoted in *Major Problems in the History of the American South, Volume I*, edited by Paul D. Escott and David R. Goldfield

Academic Vocabulary
aspect part

To further control slaves' actions, many states passed strict laws called slave codes. Some laws prohibited slaves from traveling far from their homes. Literacy laws in most southern states prohibited the education of slaves. Alabama, Virginia, and Georgia had laws that allowed the fining and whipping of anyone caught teaching enslaved people to read and write.

Reading Check **Summarizing** How did slaveholders control slaves?

A Slave's Daily Life

Typical Daily Schedule:

3:00 a.m.	*Out of bed, tend animals*
6:00 a.m.	*Prayers*
7:00 a.m.	*Start work*
12:00 p.m.	*Lunch*
1:00 p.m.	*Return to work*
7:00 p.m.	*Dinner*
8:00 p.m.	*Return to work*
11:00 p.m.	*Lights out*

Slave Culture

Many enslaved Africans found comfort in their community and culture. They made time for social activity, even after exhausting workdays, in order to relieve the hardship of their lives.

Family and Community

Family was the most important **aspect** of slave communities, and many slaves feared separation more than they feared punishment. Josiah Henson never forgot the day that he and his family were auctioned. His mother begged the slaveholder who bought her to buy Josiah, too. The slaveholder refused, and Henson's entire family was separated. "I must have been then between five or six years old," he recalled years later. "I seem to see and hear my poor weeping mother now."

The lives of slaves revolved around the work that was required of them. For many, this meant doing the backbreaking work of harvesting and loading tons of cotton. Most slaves found hope and a short escape from their daily misery in Sunday church services. Others sought to escape permanently and ran away, hoping to reach the freedom of the North. A failed escape attempt, however, could result in a cruel whipping–or worse.

What different aspects of slavery are shown in these pictures?

Hauling the Whole Week's Pickings by William Henry Brown, The Historic New Orleans Collection

Enslaved parents kept their heritage alive by passing down family histories as well as African customs and traditions. They also told **folktales**, or stories with a moral, to teach lessons about how to survive under slavery. Folktales often included a clever animal character called a trickster. The trickster—which often represented slaves—defeated a stronger animal by outwitting it. Folktales reassured slaves that they could survive by outsmarting more powerful slaveholders.

Religion

Religion also played an important part in slave culture. By the early 1800s many slaves were Christians. They came to see themselves, like the slaves in the Old Testament, as God's chosen people, much like the Hebrew slaves in ancient Egypt who had faith that they would someday live in freedom.

Some slaves sang **spirituals**, emotional Christian songs that blended African and European music, to express their religious beliefs. For example, "The Heavenly Road" reflected slaves' belief in their equality in the eyes of God.

> "Come, my brother, if you never did pray,
> I hope you pray tonight;
> For I really believe I am a child of God
> As I walk on the heavenly road."
>
> —Anonymous, quoted in *Afro-American Religious History*, edited by Milton C. Sernett

Slaves blended some aspects of their traditional African religions with those of the Christianity that the slaveholders followed. They worshipped in secret, out of sight of slaveholders. Some historians have called slave religion the invisible institution.

THE IMPACT TODAY

The musical influence of these inspirational slave songs can be heard today in gospel music.

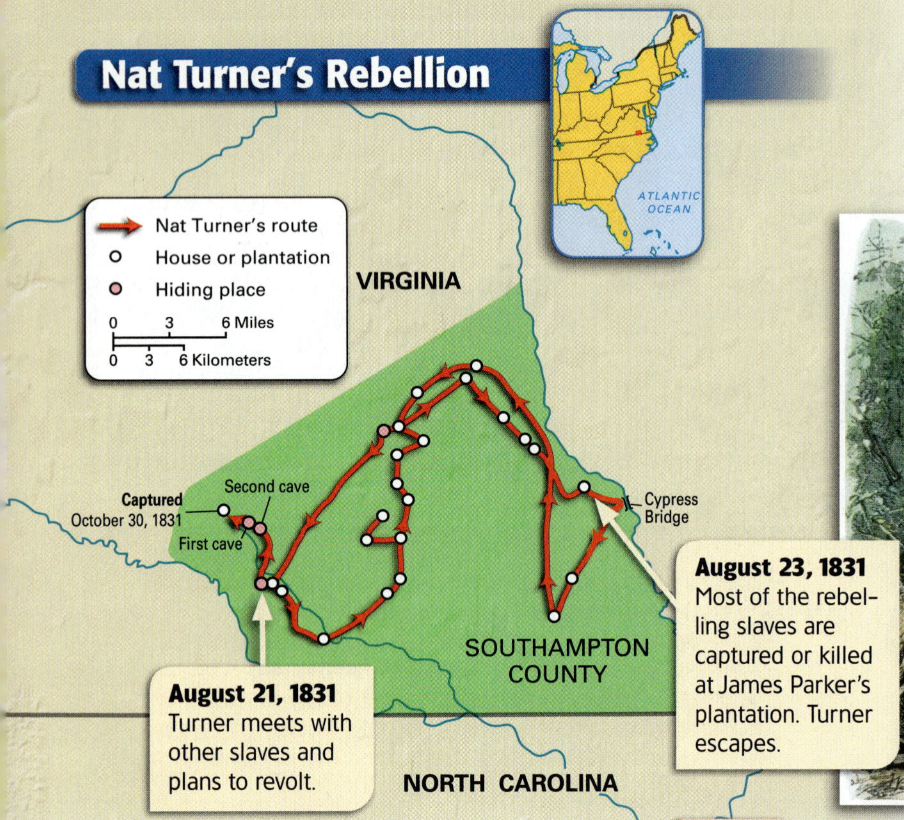

Slave Nat Turner led a revolt against white slaveholders in 1831. This is a map of his route and a depiction of his capture.

ANALYSIS SKILL **ANALYZING VISUALS**

1. **Location** Where did Nat Turner's Rebellion take place?
2. **Movement** How many days did it take to capture Nat Turner?

Seeds of Rebellion

Maintaining their own religious beliefs and practices was only one way in which enslaved people resisted slaveholders' attempts to control them completely. In small ways, slaves rebelled against the system daily. Sometimes they worked slower to protest long hours in the fields. Other times they ran away for a few days to avoid an angry slaveholder. Some slaves tried to escape permanently, but most left only for short periods, often to go and visit relatives.

Gaining freedom by escaping to the North was hard. If discovered, slaves were captured and sent back to their slaveholders, where they faced certain punishment or death. However, thousands of enslaved people succeeded in escaping.

READING CHECK **Summarizing** How did slaves' religious beliefs affect their attitudes toward slavery?

NC History Makers

Lunsford Lane
Born a slave in North Carolina, Lunsford Lane bought his freedom and became an abolitionist.

Slave Uprisings

Although violent slave revolts were relatively rare, white southerners lived in fear of them. Two planned rebellions were stopped before they began. Gabriel Prosser planned a rebellion near Richmond, Virginia, in 1800. Denmark Vesey planned one in Charleston, South Carolina, in 1822. Local authorities executed most of those involved in planning these rebellions. Though Vesey was executed as the leader of the Charleston conspiracy, several accounts written after his death by anti-slavery writers claimed he was a hero.

The most violent slave revolt in the country occurred in 1831 and is known as **Nat Turner's Rebellion**. **Nat Turner**, a slave from Southampton County, Virginia, believed that God had told him to end slavery. On an August night in 1831, Turner led a group of slaves in a plan to kill all of the slaveholders and their families in the county. First, they attacked the family that held Turner as a slave. Soon they had killed about 60 white people in the community.

More than 100 innocent slaves who were not part of Turner's group were killed in an attempt to stop the rebellion. Turner himself led authorities on a chase around the countryside for six weeks. He hid in caves and in the woods before he was caught and brought to trial. Before his trial, Turner made a confession. He expressed his belief that the revolt was justified and worth his death: "I am willing to suffer the fate that awaits me." Turner was executed on November 11, 1831. After the rebellion, many states strengthened their slave codes. The new codes placed stricter control on enslaved people. Despite resistance, slavery continued to spread.

READING CHECK **Finding Main Ideas** What was Nat Turner's Rebellion, and what happened as a result?

SUMMARY AND PREVIEW Several groups of African Americans attempted to end slavery by rebellion. All of the attempts failed. In the next chapter you will read about efforts to reform American society.

Primary Source

LETTER

Nat Turner's Rebellion

In 1831 a white southerner who had escaped the rebellion wrote a letter describing the mood of the area where Nat Turner had killed slaveholders.

"The oldest inhabitants of our county have never experienced such a distressing [terrible] time, as we have had since Sunday night last. The [slaves], about fifteen miles from this place, have massacred from 50 to 75 women and children, and some 8 or 10 men. Every house, room and corner in this place is full of women and children, driven from home, who had to take to the woods, until they could get to this place. We are worn out with fatigue [tiredness]."

—*Richmond Enquirer*, quoted in *The Southampton Slave Revolt of 1831* by Henry I. Tragle

The author believes no one in the county has been through a worse event.

The author says that many people went into hiding when the rebellion began.

ANALYSIS SKILL **ANALYZING PRIMARY SOURCES**

What emotions do you think the author of this letter was feeling?

Section 3 Assessment

go.hrw.com
Online Quiz
KEYWORD: SC7 HP13

Reviewing Ideas, Terms, and People

1. a. **Identify** What different types of work were done by slaves on plantations?
   b. **Elaborate** Do you think that skilled slaves had advantages over other slaves? Why or why not?
2. a. **Describe** What were living conditions like for most slaves?
   b. **Summarize** In what different ways did slaveholders encourage obedience from their slaves?
3. a. **Recall** What was the purpose of African American **folktales**?
   b. **Explain** How did slaves try to maintain a sense of community?
4. a. **Describe** What was the outcome of **Nat Turner's Rebellion**?
   b. **Elaborate** What do you think were some reasons why slaves rebelled?

Critical Thinking

5. **Evaluating** Review your notes on the slavery system. Then use a graphic organizer like the one shown below to identify the two most important reasons enslaved people challenged the system as well as how they did so.

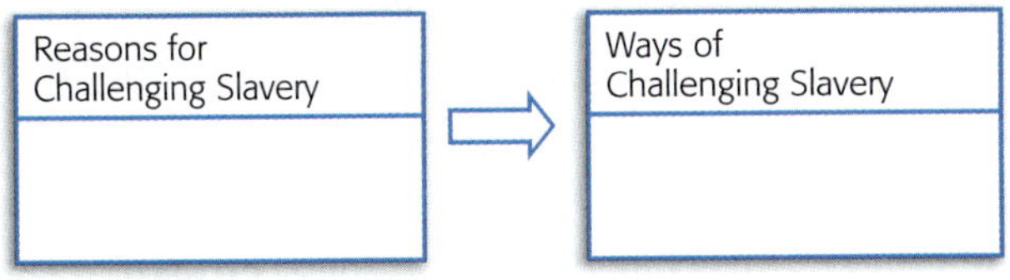

FOCUS ON WRITING

6. **Describing the Life of Slaves** Add notes about the life of slaves to your notebook. What would it have been like to be a slave? How would it have felt to have been separated from your family?

North Carolina Skills
3.02 Interpret graphs and charts.

Interpreting Graphs

Define the Skill

Graphs are drawings that classify and display data in a clear, visual format. There are three basic types of graphs. *Line graphs* and *bar graphs* plot changes in quantities over time. Bar graphs are also used to compare quantities within a category at a particular time. *Circle graphs,* also called *pie graphs,* have a similar use. The circle represents the whole of something, and the slices show what proportion of the whole is made by each part.

Being able to interpret graphs accurately lets you see and understand relationships more easily than in tables or in written explanations. This is especially true if the information is detailed or the relationships are complicated.

Learn the Skill

The following guidelines will help you interpret data that is presented as a graph.

1. Read the title to identify the subject and purpose of the graph. Note the kind of graph, remembering what each type is designed to indicate. Also note how the graph's subject relates to any printed material that accompanies it.

2. Study the graph's parts. Place close attention to the labels that define each axis. Note the units of measure. Identify the categories used. If there are different colors on bars or lines in the graph, determine what those differences mean.

3. Analyze the data in the graph. Note any increases or decreases in quantities. Look for trends, changes, and other relationships in the data.

4. Apply the information in the graph. Use the results of your analysis to draw conclusions. Ask yourself what generalizations can be made about the trends, changes, or relationships shown in the graph.

Practice the Skill

The graph below is a double-line graph. It shows both changes and relationships over time. This type of graph allows you to see how changes in one thing compare with changes in something else. Apply the guidelines to interpret the graph and answer the questions that follow.

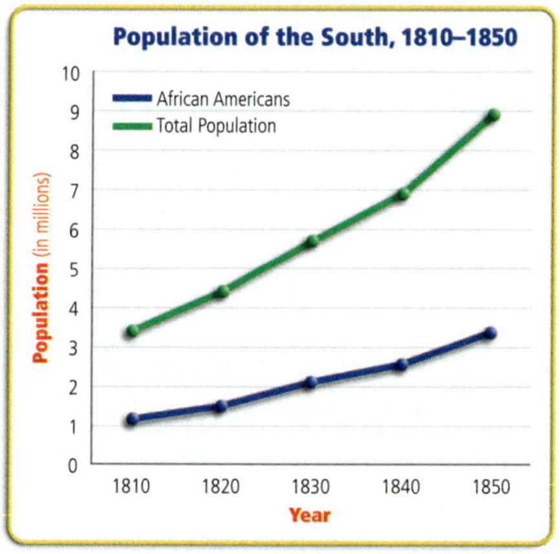

1. What is shown on each axis of this graph? What are the units of measure on each axis?
2. What do each of the lines represent?
3. What was the total population of the South in 1810? in 1850? By how much did the African American population grow during that period?
4. Was the white population or the African American population growing faster? Explain how you know.

CHAPTER 13

Chapter Review

HOLT
History's Impact
▶ **video series**
Review the video to answer the closing question:
What could Silicon Valley learn from the economic and industrial past (and present) of the South?

Visual Summary

QUICK FACTS

Use the visual summary below to help you review the main ideas of the chapter.

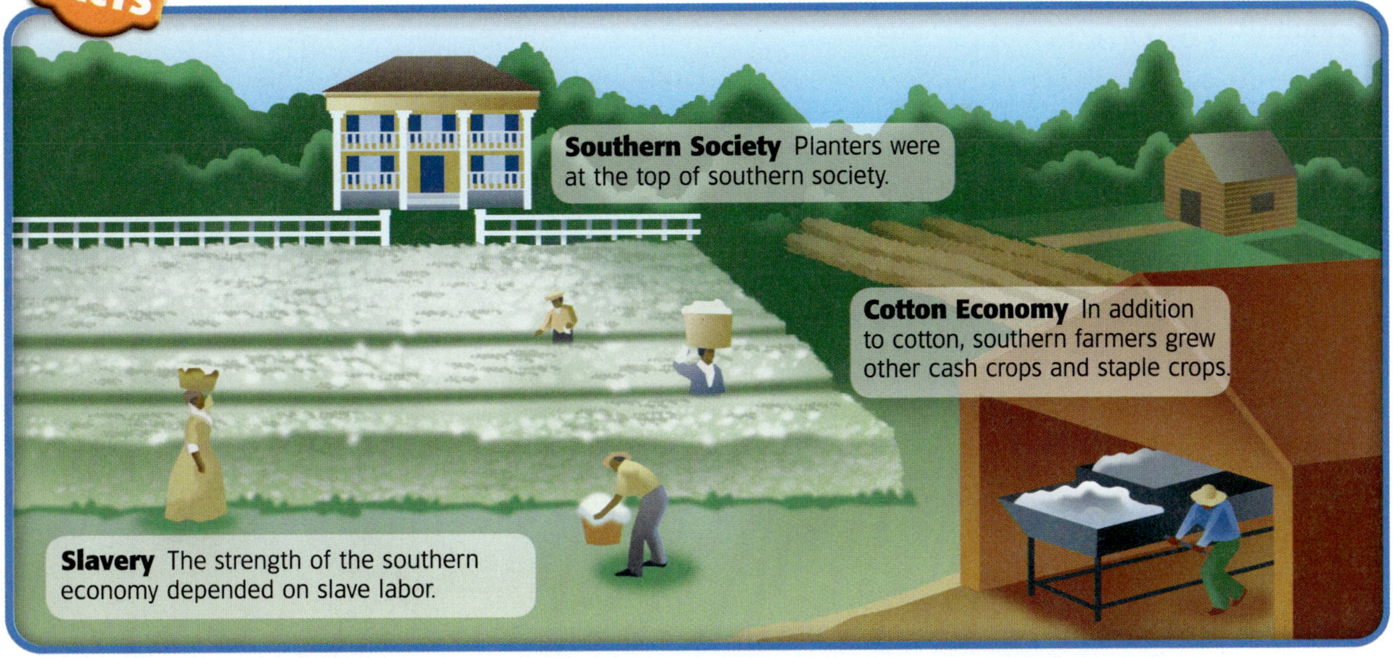

Reviewing Vocabulary, Terms, and People

Match the definition on the left with the correct term on the right.

1. A region of cotton-producing areas that stretched from South Carolina to Texas

2. Emotional songs that mixed African and European music and expressed religious beliefs

3. Owners of small farms who made up the largest social class in the South

4. Crop brokers who often managed the cotton trade in the South

5. Wealthy farmers and plantation owners

a. cotton belt

b. factors

c. planters

d. spirituals

e. yeomen

Comprehension and Critical Thinking

SECTION 1 *(Pages 414–419)*

6. a. Describe How did the cotton gin lead to a cotton boom in the South?

b. Analyze What were the positive and negative results of the cotton boom?

c. Evaluate Do you think that the South suffered as a result of its reliance on cotton? Why or why not?

SECTION 2 *(Pages 420–423)*

7. a. Describe What three groups made up white southern society?

b. Compare and Contrast In what ways were the lives of free African Americans and white southerners similar and different?

c. Predict What might have been the attitude of yeomen and poor white southerners toward slavery? Why?

SECTION 3 *(Pages 424–429)*

8. **a. Identify** What are some small ways in which slaves tried to challenge the slave system?

   b. Make Inferences How did religion and family help slaves cope with their lives?

   c. Predict What could be some possible results of stronger strengthening of slave codes in the South?

Reading Skills

Online Research *Use the Reading Skills taught in this chapter to answer the question below.*

9. Which of the following would be the best Web site to find information about life in the South before the Civil War?

   a. a Civil War historian's homepage

   b. a collection of autobiographies written by slaves

   c. a site with information about how to grow cotton

   d. a collection of biographies of inventors

Using the Internet

go.hrw.com
KEYWORD: SC7 CH13

10. **Activity: Writing Diary Entries** Enslaved African Americans faced harsh working and living conditions. Many tried to escape the slave system. Enter the activity keyword and research the attempts by enslaved African Americans to reach the North and the people who assisted them. Imagine you were trying to help slaves travel to freedom. Write four entries into a diary. In each entry, describe your experiences. Include thumbnail maps to trace their trip.

Reviewing Themes

11. **Society and Culture** How were the different social classes in the South affected by the cotton boom?

12. **Economics** How did the cotton boom affect the economy of the South?

Social Studies Skills

Interpreting Graphs *Use the Social Studies Skills taught in this chapter to answer the questions about the graph below.*

13. What span of time saw the largest increase in cotton production?

    a. 1800 to 1820 **c.** 1840 to 1860

    b. 1820 to 1840 **d.** after 1860

14. About what year did cotton production reach 1.2 million bales per year?

    a. 1800 **c.** 1840

    b. 1820 **d.** 1860

FOCUS ON WRITING

15. **Writing Your Biographical Sketch** Look over your notes about life on a cotton farm. Then choose an imaginary person to write about. Think about what life would have been like for this person. What might he or she have looked like? How might he or she have spoken? What might a typical day have been like? Once you have answered these questions, write two paragraphs about a day in the life of this person.

CHAPTER 13 Standardized Test Practice

DIRECTIONS: Read each question and write the letter of the best response.

1

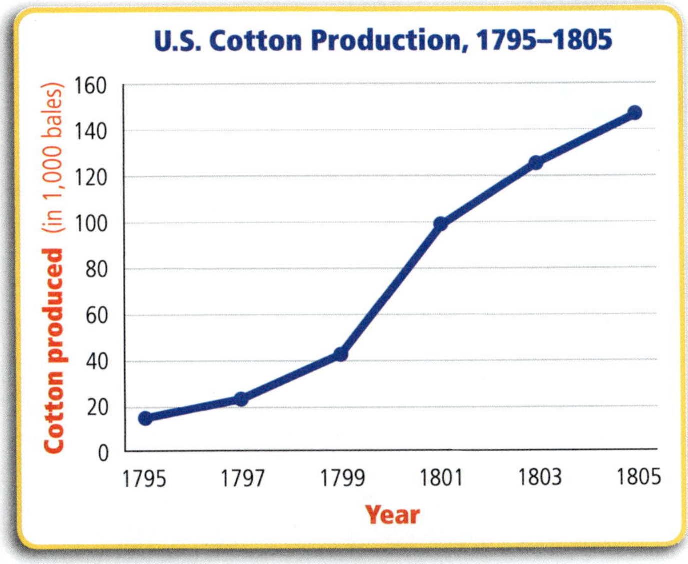

The *main* reason for the changes shown in the graph was

- **A** the invention and use of the cotton gin.
- **B** a decline in the number of slaves.
- **C** the end of the international slave trade.
- **D** a switch from food crops to cash crops.

2 Which of the following helped enslaved African Americans to endure and survive slavery?

- **A** their work
- **B** spirituals
- **C** slave codes
- **D** rebellions

3 States of the upper South, like North Carolina and Virginia, that grew less cotton still benefited from the cotton boom by

- **A** producing cloth in their many cotton mills.
- **B** increasing tariffs on cotton products.
- **C** concentrating on shipping cotton.
- **D** increasing the prices on the cotton they did produce.

4 Which statement accurately describes southern society in the mid-1800s?

- **A** Most white southerners owned slaves.
- **B** Yeomen were the wealthiest members of southern society.
- **C** Slaves made up the largest social group in the South.
- **D** Most white southerners were small farmers.

5 Free African Americans in the South in the early and mid-1800s

- **A** had the same rights and freedoms as white southerners.
- **B** had few rights and freedoms.
- **C** usually had escaped from slavery.
- **D** could travel freely in their home states.

6 Examine the following passage from a northern woman's journal of her stay in Georgia and then use it to answer the question below.

> "On my return from the river I had a long and painful talk with Mr. Butler on the subject of the whipping of Teresa [a slave worn out from childbearing and field work, who asked the author to try to get her workload reduced]. Those discussions are terrible. They throw me into great distress [worry] for the slaves, whose position is completely hopeless; for myself, whose efforts on their behalf sometimes seem to me worse than useless; and for Mr. Butler, whose part in this horrible system fills me by turns with anger and pity."
>
> –Frances Anne Kemble, adapted from *Journal of a Residence on a Georgian Plantation in 1838–1839*

Document-Based Question What might be the differences between Kemble and Butler on the question of slavery?

CHAPTER 14 1815–1850

New Movements in America

North Carolina Standards

Social Studies Objectives

3.03 Identify and evaluate the impact of individual reformers and groups and assess the effectiveness of their programs.

9.02 Identify past and present state and local leaders from diverse cultural backgrounds and assess their influence in effecting change.

Language Arts Objectives

1.04 Reflect on learning experiences by:

- evaluating how personal perspectives are influenced by society, cultural differences, and historical issues.
- appraising changes in self throughout the learning process.
- evaluating personal circumstances and background that shape interaction with text.

go.hrw.com
North Carolina
KEYWORD: SC7 NC

FOCUS ON WRITING

Persuasive Letter Your local newspaper is running a competition for students to answer the question, "What event or movement in history had the greatest impact on life in the United States?" This chapter tells about many important events and movements in the United States. As you read, take notes on each. Then decide which you believe has most affected life for people in the United States. Write a letter to the newspaper arguing your position.

UNITED STATES

1817 Thomas Gallaudet founds a school for people who have hearing impairments.

1820

WORLD

1824 British laws making trade unions illegal are repealed.

HOLT

History's Impact

▶ **video series**

Watch the video to understand the impact of individual rights and beliefs on society.

What You Will Learn...

In this chapter you will learn about dramatic changes in the United States in the early to mid-1800s. Ships filled with goods sailed back and forth across the Atlantic Ocean between Europe and the United States, as this painting of a busy port city shows. Many of these ships also brought people. The United States experienced a dramatic increase in immigration during this time period, particularly from Europe. Irish immigrants, forced from their homes by the potato famine, moved to the United States and built thriving communities. The photograph above shows a modern parade on Saint Patrick's Day, an Irish celebration day.

1831 William Lloyd Garrison begins publishing the abolitionist newspaper the *Liberator.*

1848 A major meeting for women's rights—the Seneca Falls Convention—is held in New York.

1850 Nathaniel Hawthorne publishes *The Scarlet Letter.*

1830 **1840** **1850**

1829 French educator Louis Braille creates a writing system of raised dots for people who are blind.

1845 A potato famine in Ireland increases Irish immigration to the United States.

1848 Revolutionaries attempt to unify German-speaking peoples in central Europe.

Focus on Themes The mid-1800s was a time of change in America. **Society and culture** changed for several reasons: thousands of immigrants arrived in America; women began to work hard for equal rights; and the North and South debated more and more over the slavery issue. Religious beliefs helped shape people's views toward abolition—the move to end slavery—and women's suffrage—the move to give women the right to vote. This chapter discusses these issues.

Information and Propaganda

Focus on Reading Where do you get information about historical events and people? One source is this textbook and others like it. You can expect the authors of your textbook to do their best to present the facts objectively and fairly. But some sources of historical information may have a totally different purpose in mind. For example, advertisements in political campaigns may contain information, but their main purpose is to persuade people to act or think in a certain way.

Recognizing Propaganda Techniques Propaganda is created to change people's opinions or get them to act in a certain way. Learn to recognize propaganda techniques, and you will be able to separate propaganda from the facts.

"People who don't support public education are greedy monsters who don't care about children!" → **Name Calling** Using loaded words, words that create strong positive or negative emotions, to make someone else's ideas seem inappropriate or wrong

"People all around the country are opening free public schools. It's obviously the right thing to do." → **Bandwagon** Encouraging people to do something because "everyone else is doing it"

"If we provide free education for all children, everyone will be able to get jobs. Poverty and unemployment will disappear." → **Oversimplification** Making a complex situation seem simple, a complex problem seem easy to solve

You Try It!

The flyer below was published in 1837. Read it and then answer the questions that follow.

Flyer from 1837

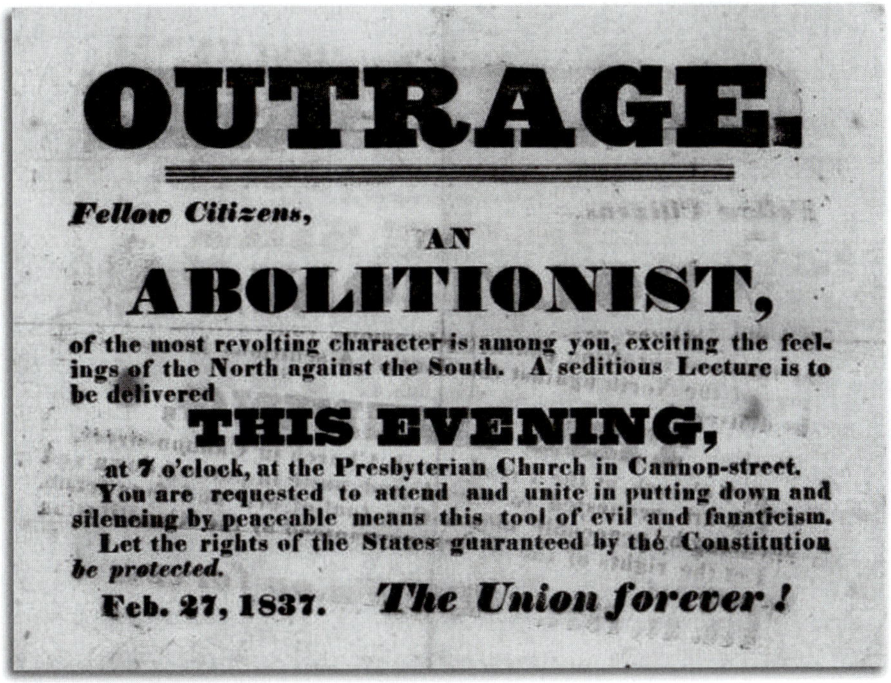

OUTRAGE.

Fellow Citizens,

AN

ABOLITIONIST,

of the most revolting character is among you, exciting the feelings of the North against the South. A seditious Lecture is to be delivered

THIS EVENING,

at 7 o'clock, at the Presbyterian Church in Cannon-street.

You are requested to attend and unite in putting down and silencing by peaceable means this tool of evil and fanaticism.

Let the rights of the States guaranteed by the Constitution *be protected.*

Feb. 27, 1837. *The Union forever!*

After studying the flyer, answer the following questions.

1. What is the purpose of this flyer?
2. Who do you think distributed this flyer?
3. Do you think this flyer is an example of propaganda? Why or why not? If you think it is propaganda, what kind is it?
4. If you were the subject of this flyer, how would you feel? How might you respond to it?

As you read Chapter 14, look carefully at all the primary sources. Do any of them include examples of propaganda?

Key Terms and People

Chapter 14

Section 1

nativists *(p. 440)*
Know-Nothing Party *(p. 440)*
middle class *(p. 440)*
tenements *(p. 442)*

Section 2

transcendentalism *(p. 443)*
Ralph Waldo Emerson *(p. 443)*
Margaret Fuller *(p. 443)*
Henry David Thoreau *(p. 443)*
utopian communities *(p. 444)*
Nathaniel Hawthorne *(p. 444)*
Edgar Allan Poe *(p. 445)*
Emily Dickinson *(p. 445)*
Henry Wadsworth Longfellow *(p. 445)*
Walt Whitman *(p. 445)*

Section 3

Second Great Awakening *(p. 448)*
Charles Grandison Finney *(p. 448)*
Lyman Beecher *(p. 448)*
temperance movement *(p. 449)*
Dorothea Dix *(p. 450)*
common-school movement *(p. 450)*
Horace Mann *(p. 450)*
Catharine Beecher *(p. 451)*
Thomas Gallaudet *(p. 451)*

Section 4

abolition *(p. 454)*
William Lloyd Garrison *(p. 455)*
American Anti-Slavery Society *(p. 455)*
Angelina and Sarah Grimké *(p. 455)*
Frederick Douglass *(p. 456)*
Sojourner Truth *(p. 456)*
Underground Railroad *(p. 456)*
Harriet Tubman *(p. 458)*

Section 5

Elizabeth Cady Stanton *(p. 464)*
Lucretia Mott *(p. 464)*
Seneca Falls Convention *(p. 464)*
Declaration of Sentiments *(p. 464)*
Lucy Stone *(p. 465)*
Susan B. Anthony *(p. 465)*

Academic Vocabulary

implicit *(p. 440)*
abstract *(p. 444)*

SECTION 1

Immigrants and Urban Challenges

What You Will Learn...

Main Ideas

1. Millions of immigrants, mostly German and Irish, arrived in the United States despite anti-immigrant movements.
2. Industrialization led to the growth of cities.
3. American cities experienced urban problems due to rapid growth.

The Big Idea

The population of the United States grew rapidly in the early 1800s with the arrival of millions of immigrants.

Key Terms

nativists, *p. 440*
Know-Nothing Party, *p. 440*
middle class, *p. 440*
tenements, *p. 442*

TAKING NOTES As you read, take notes on the causes of immigration and urban growth. Record your notes in a graphic organizer like the one shown below.

( ) →	**Immigration**
( ) →	**Urban Growth**

If YOU were there...

It is 1850, and you are a German immigrant standing on the deck of a steamboat, crossing Lake Erie. Other immigrants are on board, but they are strangers to you. Soon, you will arrive at your new home in Cleveland, Ohio. You've been told that other Germans have settled there. You hope to find friends and work as a baker. Right now, America seems very big and very strange.

What would you expect from your new life in America?

BUILDING BACKGROUND The revolutions in industry, transportation, and technology were not the only major changes in the United States in the mid-1800s. Millions of immigrants, mostly from Europe, swelled the population. Some settled in the rich farmland of the Midwest, while others moved to cities.

Millions of Immigrants Arrive

In the mid-1800s, large numbers of immigrants crossed the Atlantic Ocean to begin new lives in the United States. More than 4 million of them settled in the United States between 1840 and 1860, most from Europe. More than 3 million of these immigrants arrived from Ireland and Germany. Many of them were fleeing economic or political troubles in their native countries.

Fleeing the Irish Potato Famine

Most immigrants from the British Isles during that period were Irish. In the mid-1840s, potato blight, a disease that causes rot in potatoes, left many families in Ireland with little food. More than a million Irish people died of starvation and disease. Even more fled to the United States.

Most Irish immigrants were very poor. Many settled in cities in Massachusetts, New Jersey, New York, and Pennsylvania. They worked at unskilled jobs in the cities or on building canals and

Push-Pull Factors of Immigration

QUICK FACTS

Starvation and poverty pushed many Irish families such as this one from their homes, while economic opportunities pulled them toward the United States.

ANALYSIS SKILL ANALYZING VISUALS

How was freedom a push factor and a pull factor?

railroads. Irish women often worked as domestic servants for wealthy families, laboring 16 or more hours per day. In 1849 a Boston health committee reported that low wages forced most Irish immigrants to live in poor housing.

Still, many immigrants enjoyed a new feeling of equality. Patrick Dunny wrote home to his family about this situation.

> "People that cuts a great dash [style] at home ... think it strange [in the United States] for the humble class of people to get as much respect as themselves."
>
> —Patrick Dunny, quoted in *Who Built America?* by Bruce Levine et al.

A Failed German Revolution

Many Germans also came to the United States during this time. In 1848 some Germans had staged a revolution against harsh rule. Some educated Germans fled to the United States to escape persecution caused by their political activities. Most German immigrants, however, were working class, and they came for economic reasons. The United States seemed to offer both greater economic opportunity and more freedom from government control. While most Irish immigrants were Catholics, German immigrant groups included Catholics, Jews, and Protestants.

German immigrants were more likely than the Irish to become farmers and live in rural areas. They moved to midwestern states where more land was available. Unlike the Irish, a high percentage of German immigrants arrived in the United States with money. Despite their funds and skills, German immigrants often were forced to take low-paying jobs. Many German immigrants worked as tailors, seamstresses, bricklayers,

THE IMPACT TODAY

Many immigrants still come to the United States today. More than 16.4 million entered the United States between 1980 and 2000.

servants, clerks, cabinetmakers, bakers, and food merchants.

Anti-Immigration Movements

Industrialization and the waves of people from Europe greatly changed the American labor force. While many immigrants went to the Midwest to get farmland, other immigrants filled the need for cheap labor in towns and cities. Industrial jobs in the Northeast attracted many people.

Yet a great deal of native-born Americans feared losing their jobs to immigrants who might work for lower wages. Some felt **implicitly** threatened by the new immigrants' cultures and religions. For example, before Catholic immigrants arrived, most Americans were Protestants. Conflicts between Catholics and Protestants in Europe caused American Protestants to mistrust Catholic immigrants. Those Americans and others who opposed immigration were called **nativists**.

ACADEMIC VOCABULARY

implicit understood though not clearly put into words

In the 1840s and 1850s some nativists became politically active. An 1844 election flyer gave Americans this warning.

FOCUS ON READING

Look carefully at the quotation to the right from an election flyer. Does it include any examples of propaganda?

> "Look at the . . . thieves and vagabonds [tramps] roaming our streets . . . monopolizing [taking] the business which properly belongs to our own native and true-born citizens."
>
> —Election flyer, quoted in *Who Built America?* by Bruce Levine et al.

In 1849 nativists founded a political organization, the **Know-Nothing Party**, that supported measures making it difficult for foreigners to become citizens or hold office. Its members wanted to keep Catholics and immigrants out of public office. They also wanted to require immigrants to live in the United States for 21 years before becoming citizens. Know-Nothing politicians had some success getting elected during the 1850s. Later, disagreements over the issue of slavery caused the party to fall apart.

READING CHECK **Understanding Cause and Effect** Why did the Know-Nothing Party try to limit the rights of immigrants?

Rapid Growth of Cities

The Industrial Revolution led to the creation of many new jobs in American cities. These city jobs drew immigrants from many nations as well as migrants from rural parts of the United States. The Transportation Revolution helped connect cities and made it easier for people to move to them. As a result of these two trends, American cities grew rapidly during the mid-1800s. Cities in the northeastern and Middle Atlantic states grew the most. By the mid-1800s, three-quarters of the country's manufacturing jobs were in these areas.

The rise of industry and the growth of cities changed American life. Those who owned their own businesses or worked in skilled jobs benefited most from those changes. The families of these merchants, manufacturers, professionals, and master craftspeople made up a growing social class. This new **middle class** was a social and economic level between the wealthy and the poor. Those in the new middle class built large, dignified homes that demonstrated their place in society.

In the growing cities, people found entertainment and an enriched cultural life. Many enjoyed visiting places such as libraries and clubs, or attending concerts or lectures. In the mid-1800s people also attended urban theaters. Favorite pastimes included bowling, boxing, and playing cards. The rules of baseball were formalized in 1845, and the game became increasingly popular.

Cities during this time were compact and crowded. Many people lived close enough to their jobs that they could walk to work. Wagons carried goods down streets paved with stones, making a noisy, busy scene. One observer noted that the professionals in New York City always had a "hurried walk."

READING CHECK **Summarizing** How did the Industrial Revolution affect life in American cities?

History Close-up

New York City, Mid-1800s

In the mid-1800s, cities such as New York City lured thousands of people in search of jobs and a better life. Many city dwellers found life difficult in the crowded urban conditions.

Many city residents, particularly immigrants, lived in crowded, unsafe conditions.

Many immigrants and other poor city dwellers worked long hours in factories at dangerous jobs.

Women—and frequently children—labored all day in small rooms making clothing to be sold to the wealthy.

City streets were crowded with people buying, selling, and transporting goods.

The first floor of the building served many purposes—living quarters, kitchen, and work space. Here, garments were finished for sale.

ANALYSIS SKILL **ANALYZING VISUALS**

How is this scene similar to one you might see in a large American city today? How is it different?

Urban Problems

American cities in the mid-1800s faced many challenges due to rapid growth. Because public and private transportation was limited, city residents had to live near their workplaces. In addition, there was a lack of safe housing. Many city dwellers, particularly immigrants, could afford to live only in **tenements**—poorly designed apartment buildings that housed large numbers of people. These structures were often dirty, overcrowded, and unsafe.

Public services were also poor. The majority of cities did not have clean water, public health regulations, or healthful ways to get rid of garbage and human and animal waste. Under these conditions, diseases spread easily, and epidemics were common. In 1832 and 1849, for example, New York City suffered cholera epidemics that killed thousands.

City life held other dangers. As urban areas grew, they became centers of criminal activity. Most cities—including New York, Boston, and Philadelphia—had no permanent or organized force to fight crime. Instead, they relied on volunteer night watches, which offered little protection.

Fire was another constant and serious danger in crowded cities. There was little organized fire protection. Most cities were served by volunteer fire companies. Firefighters used hand pumps and buckets to put out fires. In addition, there were not enough sanitation workers and road maintenance crews. These shortages and flaws caused health and safety problems for many city residents.

READING CHECK **Analyzing** Why did so many American cities have problems in the mid-1800s?

SUMMARY AND PREVIEW Immigrants expected a better life in America, but not all Americans welcomed newcomers. The rapid growth of cities caused many problems. In the next section you will read about how America developed its own style of art and literature.

Section 1 Assessment

go.hrw.com
Online Quiz
KEYWORD: SC7 HP14

Reviewing Ideas, Terms, and People

1. a. **Identify** Who were the **nativists**?
   b. **Compare and Contrast** In what ways were Irish and German immigrants to the United States similar and different?
   c. **Predict** How might the rise of anti-immigrant groups lead to problems in the United States?
2. a. **Describe** What led to the growth of cities?
   b. **Analyze** How did the rise of industrialization and the growth of cities change American society?
3. a. **Describe** What were **tenements**?
   b. **Summarize** What problems affected American cities in the mid-1800s?
   c. **Evaluate** What do you think was the biggest problem facing cities in the United States? Why?

Critical Thinking

4. **Identifying Cause and Effect** Review your notes on the causes of immigration and urban growth. Then add the effects of each to your graphic organizer.

Immigration → Effects

Urban Growth → Effects

FOCUS ON WRITING

5. **Identifying Important Events** In your notebook, create a two-column chart. In the first column, list events described in this section. In the second column, write a description of each event and a note about how it changed life in the United States.

American Arts

SECTION 2

If YOU were there...

You are a teacher living in Massachusetts in the 1840s. Some of your neighbors have started an experimental community. They want to live more simply than present-day society allows. They hope to have time to write and think, while still sharing the work. Some people will teach, others will raise food. You think this might be an interesting place to live.

What would you ask the leaders of the community?

BUILDING BACKGROUND Great changes were taking place in American culture. The early 1800s brought a revolution in American thought. Artists, writers, and philosophers pursued their ideals and developed truly American styles.

What You Will Learn...

Main Ideas

1. Transcendentalists and utopian communities withdrew from American society.
2. American Romantic painters and writers made important contributions to art and literature.

The Big Idea

New movements in art and literature influenced many Americans in the early 1800s.

Key Terms and People

transcendentalism, *p. 443*
Ralph Waldo Emerson, *p. 443*
Margaret Fuller, *p. 443*
Henry David Thoreau, *p. 443*
utopian communities, *p. 444*
Nathaniel Hawthorne, *p. 444*
Edgar Allan Poe, *p. 445*
Emily Dickinson, *p. 445*
Henry Wadsworth Longfellow, *p. 445*
Walt Whitman, *p. 445*

TAKING NOTES Create a graphic organizer like the one shown below. Use it to take notes on the new movements in art and literature.

	Transcendentalism	Romanticism
What		
Who		

Transcendentalists

Some New England writers and philosophers found spiritual wisdom in **transcendentalism**, the belief that people could transcend, or rise above, material things in life. Transcendentalists also believed that people should depend on themselves and their own insights, rather than on outside authorities. Important transcendentalists included **Ralph Waldo Emerson**, **Margaret Fuller**, and **Henry David Thoreau**.

Walden Pond, where Thoreau lived for two years

Emerson was a popular writer and thinker who argued that Americans should disregard institutions and follow their own beliefs. "What I must do is all that concerns me, not what the people think," he wrote in an essay called "Self-Reliance." Fuller edited the famous transcendentalist publication *The Dial*. Thoreau advised even stronger self-reliance and simple living away from society in natural settings. He wrote his book *Walden* after living for two years at Walden Pond.

Some transcendentalists formed a community at Brook Farm, Massachusetts, in the 1840s. It was one of many experiments with **utopian communities**, groups of people who tried to form a perfect society. People in utopian communities pursued abstract spirituality and cooperative lifestyles. Communities sprang up in New Harmony, Oneida, and many other places. However, few communities lasted for long.

ACADEMIC VOCABULARY
abstract expressing a quality or idea without reference to an actual thing

READING CHECK **Drawing Inferences** Why did utopian communities last a short time?

American Romanticism

Ideas about the simple life and nature also inspired painters and writers in the early and mid-1800s. Some joined the Romantic movement that had begun in Europe. Romanticism involved a great interest in nature, an emphasis on individual expression, and a rejection of many established rules. These painters and writers felt that each person brings a unique view to the world. They believed in using emotion to guide their creative output. Some Romantic artists, like Thomas Cole, painted the American landscape. Their works showed the beauty and wonder of nature in the United States. Their images contrasted with the huge cities and corruption of nature that many Americans saw as typical of Europe.

Many female writers, like Ann Sophia Stephens, wrote historical fiction that was popular in the mid-1800s. New England writer **Nathaniel Hawthorne** wrote *The Scarlet Letter* during that period. One of the greatest classics of Romantic literature, it explored Puritan

Asher Durand's *The First Harvest in the Wilderness*

CONNECT TO THE ARTS

Artists of the Romantic movement celebrated nature in their dramatic paintings. Their work was made popular by their leader, Thomas Cole. Other important painters of the era were Frederick Church and Asher Durand.

What words would you use to describe this painting?

1 The light in the painting has a delicate, glowing quality. Artists of the Romantic movement pioneered this technique.

2 The human presence in this scene is dwarfed by nature but is in harmony with it.

life in the 1600s. Hawthorne's friend Herman Melville, a writer and former sailor, wrote novels about the sea, such as *Moby-Dick* and *Billy Budd*. Many people believe that *Moby-Dick* is one of the finest American novels ever written.

American Romantic authors also wrote a great deal of poetry. The poet **Edgar Allan Poe**, also a short story writer, became famous for a haunting poem called "The Raven." Other gifted American poets included **Emily Dickinson**, **Henry Wadsworth Longfellow**, and **Walt Whitman**. Most of Dickinson's short, thoughtful poems were not published until after her death. Longfellow, the best-known poet of the mid-1800s, wrote popular story-poems, like *The Song of Hiawatha*. Whitman praised American individualism and democracy in his simple, unrhymed poetry. In his poetry collection *Leaves of Grass*, he wrote, "The United States themselves are essentially the greatest poem."

READING CHECK **Summarizing** Who were some American Romantic authors, and why were they important?

SUMMARY AND PREVIEW American Romantic artists and authors were inspired by ideas about the simple life, nature, and spirituality. In the next section you will learn about ideas that changed American society.

Section 2 Assessment

go.hrw.com
Online Quiz
KEYWORD: SC7 HP14

Reviewing Ideas, Terms, and People

1. a. **Identify** What were the main teachings of **transcendentalism**?
   b. **Summarize** What was one **utopian community** established in the United States, and what was its goal?
   c. **Elaborate** Do you agree with transcendentalists that Americans put too much emphasis on institutions and traditions? Explain your answer.
2. a. **Recall** Who were some important American authors and poets at this time?
   b. **Explain** What ideas did artists in the Romantic movement express?
   c. **Evaluate** Do you think the Romantic movement was important to American culture? Explain.

Critical Thinking

3. **Comparing and Contrasting** Review your notes on art and literature. Then copy the graphic organizer below and use it to show the similarities and differences between the two movements.

Transcendentalism	Similarities	Romanticism

FOCUS ON WRITING

4. **Describing Artistic Movements** Two artistic movements are described in this section, transcendentalism and romanticism. Write these two movements in the first column of your chart. Then in the second column, write a brief description of each and explain how writings from each either described or influenced life in the United States.

Literature of the Young Nation: Romanticism and Realism

from "The Midnight Ride of Paul Revere"

by Henry Wadsworth Longfellow (1807–1882)

About the Reading *"The Midnight Ride of Paul Revere" was published in a book called* Tales of a Wayside Inn. *The book is a collection of poems that tell well-known stories from history and mythology. By including the story of Paul Revere with other famous stories, Longfellow helped increase the importance of Paul Revere's ride.*

AS YOU READ **Notice how Longfellow describes Revere as a hero.**

Listen my children and you shall hear
Of the midnight ride of Paul Revere,
On the eighteenth of April, in Seventy-five;
Hardly a man is now alive
Who remembers that famous day and year. ❶

He said to his friend, "If the British march
By land or sea from the town to-night,
Hang a lantern aloft in the belfry arch
Of the North Church tower as a signal light,—
One if by land, and two if by sea;
And I on the opposite shore will be,
Ready to ride and spread the alarm
Through every . . . village and farm,
For the country folk to be up and to arm." ❷

. . . .

Meanwhile, his friend, through alley and street
Wanders and watches with eager ears,
Till in the silence around him he hears
The muster of men at the barrack door,
The sound of arms, and the tramp of feet,
And the measured tread of the grenadiers,
Marching down to their boats on the shore. ❸

GUIDED READING

WORD HELP

belfry bell tower
muster gathering
barrack building where soldiers meet
grenadiers a soldier that throws grenades

❶ When the poem was written, there were still a few people alive who had lived during the Revolution.

❷ Longfellow uses poetic language to make Revere's story more dramatic.

❸ The sounds of the night are described to help the reader feel the excitement.

from *Little Women*

by Louisa May Alcott (1832–1888)

About the Reading Little Women *is a novel about four sisters living in a small New England town before the Civil War. Still popular with young people today,* Little Women *describes a family much like the one Louisa May Alcott grew up in. Alcott based the main character, Jo March, on herself. Like Alcott, Jo was different from most women of her time. She was outspoken, eager for adventure, and in conflict with the role her society expected her to play.*

AS YOU READ **Try to understand how Jo is different from Aunt March.**

Jo happened to suit Aunt March, who was lame and needed an active person to wait upon her. The childless old lady had offered to adopt one of the girls when the troubles came, and was much offended because her offer was declined . . .

The old lady wouldn't speak to them for a time, but happening to meet Jo at a friend's, . . . she proposed to take her for a companion.❶ This did not suit Jo at all, but she accepted the place since nothing better appeared, and to everyone's surprise, got on remarkably well with her irascible relative . . .

I suspect that the real attraction was a large library of fine books, which was left to dust and spiders since Uncle March died . . . The dim, dusty room, with the busts staring down from the tall bookcases, the cozy chairs, the globes, and, best of all, the wilderness of books, in which she could wander where she liked, made the library a region of bliss to her . . . ❷

Jo's ambition was to do something very splendid. What it was she had no idea, as yet, but left it for time to tell her, and, meanwhile, found her greatest affliction in the fact that she couldn't read, run, and ride as much as she liked.❸ A quick temper, sharp tongue, and restless spirit were always getting her into scrapes, and her life was a series of ups and downs, which were both comic and pathetic. But the training she received at Aunt March's was just what she needed, and the thought that she was doing something to support herself made her happy in spite of the perpetual "Josy-phine!"

GUIDED READING

WORD HELP

lame disabled
irascible difficult
bliss happiness
ambition hope for the future
affliction problem
pathetic very sad
perpetual constant

❶ ***Some women kept companions to help entertain them and perform small chores. Why might Jo not want to be a companion?***

❷ ***How does Jo differ from ideas about women in the 1880s?***

❸ ***What might Jo be able to do for work in the 1800s?***

CONNECTING LITERATURE TO HISTORY

1. **Drawing Conclusions** Henry Wadsworth Longfellow was the most popular American poet of his time. How does his version of Paul Revere's ride increase the importance of the story?

2. **Comparing and Contrasting** The lives of women in the 1800s were very different from the lives of women today. How does this excerpt of *Little Women* show some similarities and differences between now and then?

SECTION 3

Reforming Society

What You Will Learn...

Main Ideas

1. The Second Great Awakening sparked interest in religion.
2. Social reformers began to speak out about temperance and prison reform.
3. Improvements in education reform affected many segments of the population.
4. Northern African American communities became involved in reform efforts.

The Big Idea

Reform movements in the early 1800s affected religion, education, and society.

Key Terms and People

Second Great Awakening, *p. 448*
Charles Grandison Finney, *p. 448*
Lyman Beecher, *p. 448*
temperance movement, *p. 449*
Dorothea Dix, *p. 450*
common-school movement, *p. 450*
Horace Mann, *p. 450*
Catharine Beecher, *p. 451*
Thomas Gallaudet, *p. 451*

TAKING NOTES Create a time line like the one shown below. As you read, list the important events of the reform movements next to the appropriate date on the time line. Some dates might have more than one event.

1817	1821	1835	1837	1841

If YOU were there...

You live in New York State in the 1850s. You are the oldest daughter in your family. Since childhood you have loved mathematics, which puzzles your family. Your sisters are happy learning to sew and cook and run a household. You want more. You know that there is a female seminary nearby, where you could study and learn much more. But your parents are undecided.

How might you persuade your parents to send you to the school?

BUILDING BACKGROUND Along with changes in American culture, changes were also taking place in American society. A religious revival swept the country. Reform-minded men and women tried to improve all aspects of society, from schools to taverns. Reforms in education opened up new opportunities for young women.

Second Great Awakening

During the 1790s and early 1800s, some Americans took part in a Christian renewal movement called the **Second Great Awakening**. It swept through towns across upstate New York and through the frontier regions of Kentucky, Ohio, Tennessee, and South Carolina. By the 1820s and 1830s, this new interest in religion had spread to New England and the South.

Charles Grandison Finney was one of the most important leaders of the Second Great Awakening. After experiencing a dramatic religious conversion in 1821, Finney left his career as a lawyer and began preaching. He challenged some traditional Protestant beliefs, telling congregations that each individual was responsible for his or her own salvation. He also believed that sin was avoidable. Finney held revivals, emotional prayer meetings that lasted for days. Many people converted to Christianity during these revivals. Finney told new converts to prove their faith by doing good deeds.

Finney's style of preaching and his ideas angered some traditional ministers, like Boston's **Lyman Beecher**. Beecher wanted to prevent Finney from holding revivals in his city. "You mean to carry a streak of fire to Boston. If you attempt it, as the Lord liveth, I'll meet you . . . and fight every inch of the way." Despite the opposition of Beecher and other traditional ministers, Finney's appeal remained powerful. Also, the First Amendment guarantee of freedom of religion prevented the government from passing laws banning the new religious practices. Ministers were therefore free to spread their message of faith and salvation to whomever wished to listen.

Due to the efforts of Finney and his followers, church membership across the country grew a great deal during the Second Great Awakening. Many new church members were women and African Americans. The African Methodist Episcopal Church spread across the Middle Atlantic states. Although the movement had begun in the Northeast and on the frontier, the Second Great Awakening renewed some people's religious faith throughout America.

READING CHECK **Drawing Conclusions** What impact did the Second Great Awakening have on religion in America?

Social Reformers Speak Out

Renewed religious faith often led to involvement in movements to fix the problems created by urban growth. One solution was political action. For example, in 1844 New York City created the first city police force.

Members of the growing middle class, especially women, often led the efforts. Many of the women did not work outside the home and hired servants to care for their households. This gave them time to work in reform groups.

NC History Makers

Archibald D. Murphey
Archibald Murphey was an early leader in the calls for reform of North Carolina government, especially its education system.

Temperance Movement

Many social reformers worked to prevent alcohol abuse. They believed that Americans drank too much. In the 1830s, on average, an American consumed seven gallons of alcohol per year. Countless Americans thought that alcohol abuse caused social problems, such as family violence, poverty, and criminal behavior.

Americans' worries about the effects of alcohol led to the growth of a **temperance movement**. This reform effort urged people to use self-discipline to stop drinking hard liquor.

Reform Movements

Reform movements in America included religious meetings called revivals, where preachers urged huge crowds of people to seek salvation. The temperance movement, an effort to convince people to avoid drinking alcohol, promoted posters like the one shown here.

How might the scenes in this poster encourage people to stop drinking?

Reformers asked people to limit themselves to beer and wine in small amounts. Groups like the American Temperance Society and the American Temperance Union helped to spread the message. Minister Lyman Beecher spoke widely about the evils of alcohol. He claimed that people who drank alcohol were "neglecting the education of their families—and corrupting their morals."

FOCUS ON NORTH CAROLINA

Dorothea Dix traveled to North Carolina in 1848 and recommended a bill to the legislature that would provide hospitals for the mentally ill.

Prison Reform

Another target of reform was the prison system. **Dorothea Dix** was a middle-class reformer who visited prisons throughout Massachusetts beginning in 1841. Dix reported that mentally ill people frequently were jailed with criminals. They were sometimes left in dark cells without clothes or heat and were chained to the walls and beaten. Dix spoke of what she saw to the state legislature.

THE IMPACT TODAY

McGuffey's Readers were among the first "graded" textbooks. Organizing classes by grades was a new idea that is standard practice today.

In response, the Massachusetts government built facilities for the mentally ill. Dix's work had a nationwide effect. Eventually, more than 100 state hospitals were built to give mentally ill people professional care.

Prisons also held runaway children and orphans. Some had survived only by begging or stealing, and they got the same punishment as adult criminals. Boston mayor Josiah Quincy asked that young offenders receive different punishments than adults. In the 1820s, several state and local governments founded reform schools for children who had been housed in prisons. There, children lived under strict rules and learned useful skills.

FOCUS ON NORTH CAROLINA

In 1839 North Carolina passed its first public school law. It divided the state into districts and provided funds to build a school in each district. Many parents, however, kept their children out of school so that the children could work.

Some reformers also tried to end the overcrowding and cruel conditions in prisons. Their efforts led to the creation of houses of correction. These institutions did not use punishment alone to change behavior. They also offered prisoners education.

READING CHECK **Summarizing** How did reformers change the punishment of criminals?

Improvements in Education

Another challenge facing America in the early 1800s was poor public education. During this era, childhood was beginning to be viewed as a separate stage of life in which education was of the utmost importance in creating responsible citizens. However, many children worked in factories or on farms to help support their families. If children could read the Bible, write, and do simple math, that was often considered to be enough.

Education in the Early 1800s

The availability of education varied widely. New England had the most schools, while the South and West had the fewest. Few teachers were trained. Schoolhouses were small, and students of all ages and levels worked in one room.

McGuffey's Readers were the most popular textbooks. William Holmes McGuffey, an educator and minister, put selections from British and American literature in them as well as instruction in moral and social values.

Social background and wealth affected the quality of education. Rich families sent children to private schools or hired tutors. However, poor children had only public schools. Girls could go to school, but parents usually thought that girls needed little education and kept them home. Therefore, few girls learned to read.

Common-School Movement

People in the **common-school movement** wanted all children taught in a common place, regardless of background. **Horace Mann** was a leader of this movement.

In 1837 Mann became Massachusetts's first secretary of education. He convinced the state to double its school budget and raise teachers' salaries. He lengthened the school year and began the first school for teacher training. Mann's success set a standard for education reform throughout the country.

Women's Education

Education reform created greater opportunities for women. **Catharine Beecher** started an all-female academy in Hartford, Connecticut. The first college-level educational institution available to women was the Troy Female Seminary, opened by Emma Willard in 1821. Several other women's colleges opened during the 1830s, including Mount Holyoke College. The first medical college for women, who were barred from men's medical schools, opened in Boston in 1848.

Teaching People with Special Needs

Efforts to improve education also helped people with special needs. In 1831 Samuel Gridley Howe opened the Perkins School for the Blind in Massachusetts. Howe traveled widely, talking about teaching people with visual impairment. **Thomas Gallaudet** improved the education and lives of people with hearing impairments. He founded the first free American school for hearing-impaired people in 1817.

READING CHECK **Summarizing** What were Horace Mann's achievements?

BIOGRAPHY

Horace Mann

1796–1859

Born in Franklin, Massachusetts, Mann had little schooling, but he educated himself well enough at the local library to get into Brown University and attend law school. Despite a busy law practice, he served in the Massachusetts legislature for 10 years. He was also an outspoken advocate for public education. In 1837 the state created the post of secretary of education for him. His achievements in that office made him famous. He later served in the U.S. House of Representatives and as president of Antioch College in Ohio. His influence on education is reflected by the fact that many American schools are named for him.

Analyzing Information How do you think Mann's own education influenced his desire for public schools?

Primary Source

SPEECH

Horace Mann to the Board of Education

In a speech to the newly created Massachusetts Board of Education, Horace Mann, the board's first secretary, described the purpose of the public school system.

"[T]here should be a free district school, sufficiently safe, and sufficiently good, for all of the children... where they may be well instructed in the rudiments [basics] of knowledge, formed to propriety of demeanor [good behavior], and imbued [filled] with the principles of duty... It is on this common platform, that a general acquaintanceship [friendship] should be formed between the children of the same neighborhood. It is here, that the affinities [qualities] of a common nature should unite them together."

—Horace Mann, quoted in *The Republic and the School*, edited by Lawrence A. Cremin

Mann believed all students should receive free education.

Neighborhood children should attend school together to form a common bond.

ANALYSIS SKILL **ANALYZING PRIMARY SOURCES**

Besides knowledge, what purpose did Mann believe the public schools had?

African American Communities

Free African Americans usually lived in segregated, or separate, communities in the North. Most of them lived in cities such as New York, Boston, and Philadelphia. Community leaders were often influenced by the Second Great Awakening and its spirit of reform.

Founded by former slave Richard Allen, the Free African Religious Society became a model for other groups that pressed for racial equality and the education of blacks. In 1816 Allen became the first bishop of the African Methodist Episcopal Church, or AME Church. This church broke away from white Methodist churches after African Americans were treated poorly in some white congregations.

Other influential African Americans of the time, such as Alexander Crummel, pushed for the creation of schools for black Americans. The New York African Free School in New York City educated hundreds of children, many of whom became brilliant scholars and important African American leaders. Philadelphia also had a long history of educating African Americans. This was largely because Philadelphia was a center of Quaker influence, and the Quakers believed strongly in equality. The city ran seven schools for African American students by the year 1800. In 1820 Boston followed Philadelphia's lead and opened a separate elementary school for African American children. The city began allowing them to attend school with whites in 1855.

African Americans rarely attended college because few colleges would accept them. In 1835 Oberlin College became the first to do so. Harvard University soon admitted African Americans, too. Several African American colleges were founded beginning in the 1840s. In 1842 the Institute for Colored Youth opened in Philadelphia. Avery College, also in Pennsylvania, was founded in 1849.

This photograph (left) of the 1855 class at Oberlin College shows the slow integration of African Americans into previously white colleges. Some churches also became more integrated, and preachers like the one pictured above began calling for equality between races.

Why might preachers have been particularly influential in calls for greater integration?

While free African Americans had some opportunities to attend school in the North and Midwest, few had this chance in the South. Laws in the South barred most enslaved people from getting any education, even at the primary school level. While some slaves learned to read on their own, they almost always did so in secret. Slaveholders were fearful that education and knowledge in general might encourage a spirit of revolt among enslaved African Americans.

READING CHECK **Drawing Conclusions** Why was it difficult for African Americans to get an education in the South in the early 1800s?

SUMMARY AND PREVIEW The efforts of reformers led to improvements in many aspects of American life in the early to mid-1800s. In the next section you will learn about reform-minded people who opposed the practice of slavery.

Section 3 Assessment

go.hrw.com
Online Quiz
KEYWORD: SC7 HP14

Reviewing Ideas, Terms, and People

1. a. **Identify** What was the **Second Great Awakening**, and who was one of its leaders?
   b. **Summarize** What effects did the Second Great Awakening have on religion in the United States?
2. a. **Identify** What role did **Dorothea Dix** play in social reforms of the early 1800s?
   b. **Summarize** What different reforms helped improve the U.S. prison system?
   c. **Elaborate** How might the Second Great Awakening have led to the growth of social reform movements?
3. a. **Identify** What was the **common-school movement**, and who was one of its leaders?
   b. **Analyze** Why did reformers set out to improve education in the United States?
   c. **Evaluate** Do you think **Horace Mann**'s ideas for educational reform were good ones? Explain.
4. a. **Recall** In what cities were the first public schools for African Americans located?
   b. **Draw Conclusions** How did free African Americans benefit from educational reforms?

Critical Thinking

5. **Categorizing** Review the reform-movement events on the time line in your notes. Then use a chart like the one below to identify the leaders and accomplishments of each reform movement.

Movement	Leaders	Accomplishments
Prison and Mental Health Reform		
Temperance		
Education		

FOCUS ON WRITING

6. **Choosing Important Events** This section covers the reform of social issues such as religion, prisons, and education. Write the reforms described in your chart. Then write a note about each reform and about the important people involved in it. Think about how each one influenced life in the United States.

SECTION 4

The Movement to End Slavery

What You Will Learn...

Main Ideas

1. Americans from a variety of backgrounds actively opposed slavery.
2. Abolitionists organized the Underground Railroad to help enslaved Africans escape.
3. Despite efforts of abolitionists, many Americans remained opposed to ending slavery.

The Big Idea

In the mid-1800s, debate over slavery increased as abolitionists organized to challenge slavery in the United States.

Key Terms and People

abolition, *p. 454*
William Lloyd Garrison, *p. 455*
American Anti-Slavery Society, *p. 455*
Angelina and Sarah Grimké, *p. 455*
Frederick Douglass, *p. 456*
Sojourner Truth, *p. 456*
Underground Railroad, *p. 456*
Harriet Tubman, *p. 458*

TAKING NOTES As you read, take notes on the different abolitionist movements that existed, the leaders of each movement, and the methods used by each group to oppose slavery. Write your notes in a chart like the one below.

Movement	Members	Methods

If YOU were there...

You live in southern Ohio in the 1850s. A friend who lives across the river in Kentucky has asked you to join a network that helps escaping slaves. She reminds you that your house has a secret cellar where you could easily hide fugitives for a few days. You are opposed to slavery. But you know this might get you in trouble with your neighbors—and with the law.

Would you become an agent for the Underground Railroad? Why?

BUILDING BACKGROUND The early 1800s brought many movements for social reform in the United States. Perhaps the most important and far-reaching was the movement for the abolition of slavery. While reformers worked to end slavery, many also took risks to help slaves to escape.

Americans Oppose Slavery

Some Americans had opposed slavery since before the country was founded. Benjamin Franklin was the president of the first anti-slavery society in America, the Pennsylvania Society for Promoting the Abolition of Slavery. In the 1830s, Americans took more organized action supporting **abolition**, or a complete end to slavery.

Differences among Abolitionists

Abolitionists came from many different backgrounds and opposed slavery for various reasons. The Quakers were among the first groups to challenge slavery on religious grounds. Other religious leaders gave speeches and published pamphlets that moved many Americans to support abolition. In one of these, abolitionist Theodore Weld wrote that "everyman knows that slavery is a curse." Other abolitionists referred to the Declaration of Independence. They reminded people that the American Revolution had been fought in the name of liberty.

Antislavery reformers did not always agree on the details, however. They differed over how much equality they thought African Americans should have. Some believed that African Americans should receive the same treatment as white Americans. In contrast, other abolitionists were against full political and social equality.

Some abolitionists wanted to send freed African Americans to Africa to start new colonies. They thought that this would prevent conflicts between the races in the United States. In 1817 a minister named Robert Finley started the American Colonization Society, an organization dedicated to establishing colonies of freed slaves in Africa. Five years later, the society founded the colony of Liberia on the west coast of Africa. About 12,000 African Americans eventually settled in Liberia. However, many abolitionists who once favored colonization later opposed it. Some African Americans also opposed it. David Walker was one such person. In his 1829 essay, *Appeal to the Colored Citizens of the World*, Walker explained his opposition to colonization.

"The greatest riches in all America have arisen from our blood and tears: and they [whites] will drive us from our property and homes, which we have earned with our blood."

—David Walker, quoted in *From Slavery to Freedom* by John Hope Franklin and Alfred A. Moss Jr.

Spreading the Abolitionist Message

Abolitionists found many ways to further their cause. Some went on speaking tours or wrote pamphlets and newspaper articles. John Greenleaf Whittier wrote abolitionist poetry and literature. **William Lloyd Garrison** published an abolitionist newspaper, the *Liberator*, beginning in 1831. In 1833 he also helped found the **American Anti-Slavery Society**. Its members wanted immediate emancipation and racial equality for African Americans. Garrison later became its president.

Both the *Liberator* and the Anti-Slavery Society relied on support from free African Americans. Society members spread

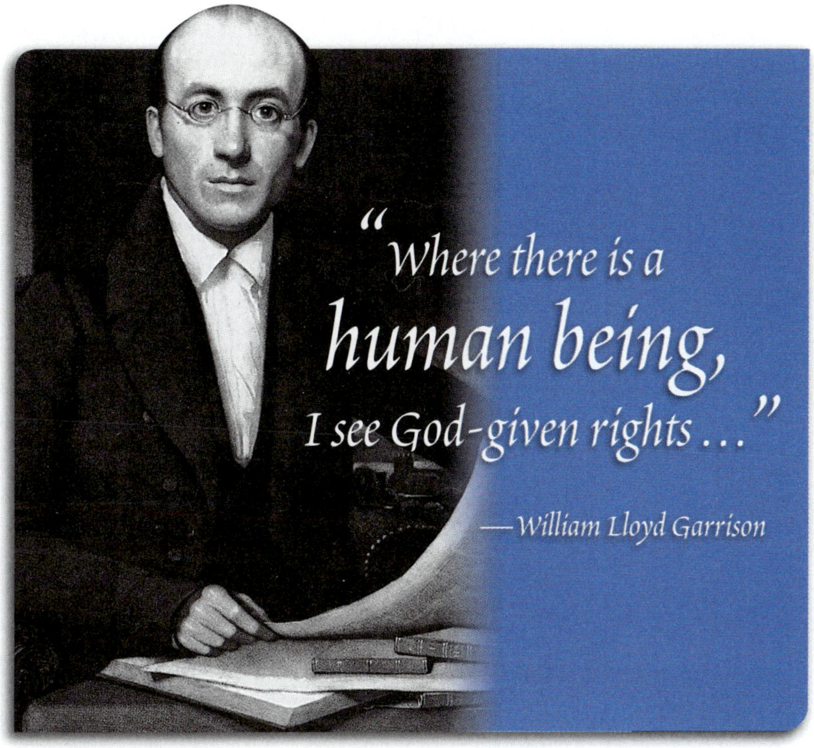

antislavery literature and petitioned Congress to end federal support of slavery. In 1840 the American Anti-Slavery Society split. One group wanted immediate freedom for enslaved African Americans and a bigger role for women. The others wanted gradual emancipation and for women to play only minor roles in the movement.

Angelina and Sarah Grimké, two white southern women, were antislavery activists of the 1830s. They came from a South Carolina slaveholding family but disagreed with their parents' support of slavery. Angelina Grimké tried to recruit other white southern women in a pamphlet called *Appeal to the Christian Women of the South* in 1836.

"I know you do not make the laws, but . . . if you really suppose you can do nothing to overthrow slavery you are greatly mistaken . . . Try to persuade your husband, father, brothers, and sons that slavery is a crime against God and man."

—Angelina Grimké, quoted in *The Grimké Sisters from South Carolina*, edited by Gerda Lerner

This essay was very popular in the North. In 1839 the Grimké sisters wrote *American Slavery As It Is*. The book was one of the most important antislavery works of its time.

African American Abolitionists

Many former slaves were active in the antislavery cause. **Frederick Douglass** escaped from slavery when he was 20 and went on to become one of the most important African American leaders of the 1800s. Douglass secretly learned to read and write as a boy, despite a law against it. His public-speaking skills impressed members of the Anti-Slavery Society. In 1841 they asked him to give regular lectures.

At a Fourth of July celebration in 1852, he captured the audience's attention with his powerful voice.

> "The blessings in which you, this day, rejoice, are not enjoyed in common ... This Fourth of July is *yours*, not *mine*. You may rejoice, I must mourn."
>
> —Frederick Douglass, quoted in *From Slavery to Freedom* by John Hope Franklin and Alfred A. Moss Jr.

In addition to his many speaking tours in the United States and Europe, Douglass published a newspaper called the *North Star* and wrote several autobiographies. His autobiographies were intended to show the injustices of slavery.

Another former slave, **Sojourner Truth**, also contributed to the abolitionist cause. She claimed God had called her to travel through the United States and preach the truth about slavery and women's rights. With her deep voice and quick wit, Truth became legendary in the antislavery movement for her fiery and dramatic speeches.

Other African Americans wrote narratives about their experiences as slaves to expose the cruelties that many slaves faced. In 1861 Harriet Jacobs, who had been a slave in North Carolina, published *Incidents in the Life of a Slave Girl*, one of the few slave narratives by a woman. William Wells Brown wrote an antislavery play as well as a personal narrative in the form of a novel called *Clotel*.

READING CHECK **Finding Main Ideas** In what ways did African Americans participate in the abolition movement?

FOCUS ON NORTH CAROLINA

In 1821 North Carolinian Levi Coffin tried to start a school for enslaved African Americans, but slaveholders would not let their slaves attend. Coffin eventually moved to Indiana, where he was active in the Underground Railroad and abolitionist activities.

The Underground Railroad

By the 1830s, a loosely organized group had begun helping slaves escape from the South. Free African Americans, former slaves, and a few white abolitionists worked together. They created what became known as the **Underground Railroad**. The organization was not an actual railroad but was a network of people who arranged transportation and hiding places for fugitives, or escaped slaves.

Fugitives would travel along "freedom trails" that led them to northern states or sometimes into Canada. At no time did the Railroad have a central leadership. No one person, or group of people, was ever officially in charge. Despite the lack of any real structure, the Underground Railroad managed to achieve dramatic results.

Often wearing disguises, fugitives moved along the "railroad" at night, led by people known as conductors. Many times, the fugitives had no other guideposts but the stars. They stopped to rest during the day at "stations," often barns, attics, or other places on property owned by abolitionists known as station masters. The station masters hid and fed the fugitives.

Harriet Tubman was a courageous conductor on the Underground Railroad.

The Underground Railroad

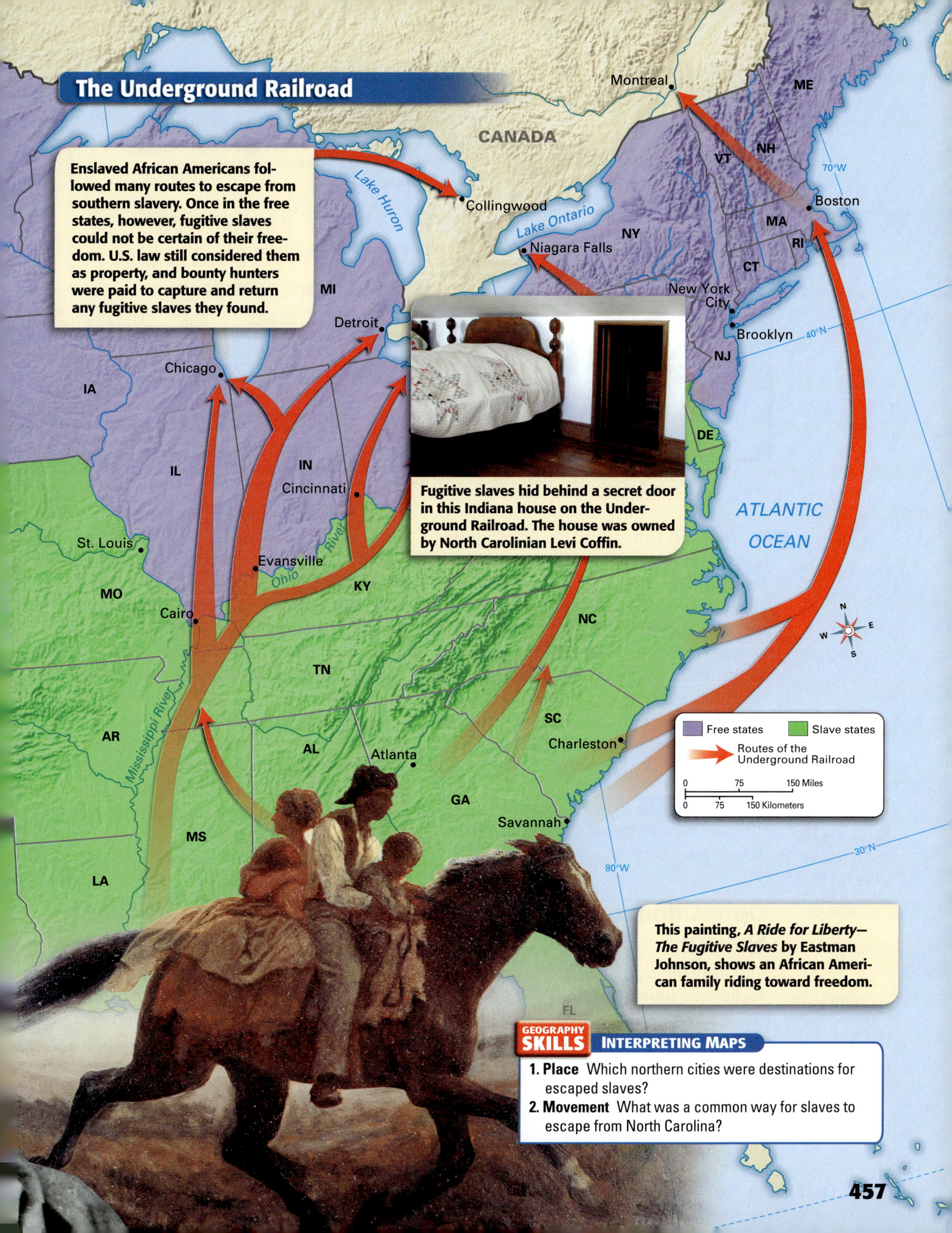

Enslaved African Americans followed many routes to escape from southern slavery. Once in the free states, however, fugitive slaves could not be certain of their freedom. U.S. law still considered them as property, and bounty hunters were paid to capture and return any fugitive slaves they found.

Fugitive slaves hid behind a secret door in this Indiana house on the Underground Railroad. The house was owned by North Carolinian Levi Coffin.

This painting, ***A Ride for Liberty—The Fugitive Slaves*** by Eastman Johnson, shows an African American family riding toward freedom.

GEOGRAPHY SKILLS **INTERPRETING MAPS**

1. **Place** Which northern cities were destinations for escaped slaves?
2. **Movement** What was a common way for slaves to escape from North Carolina?

Primary Source

HANDBILL

Anti-Abolitionist Rally

Members of an anti-abolitionist group used this flyer to call people together in order to disrupt a meeting of abolitionists in 1837.

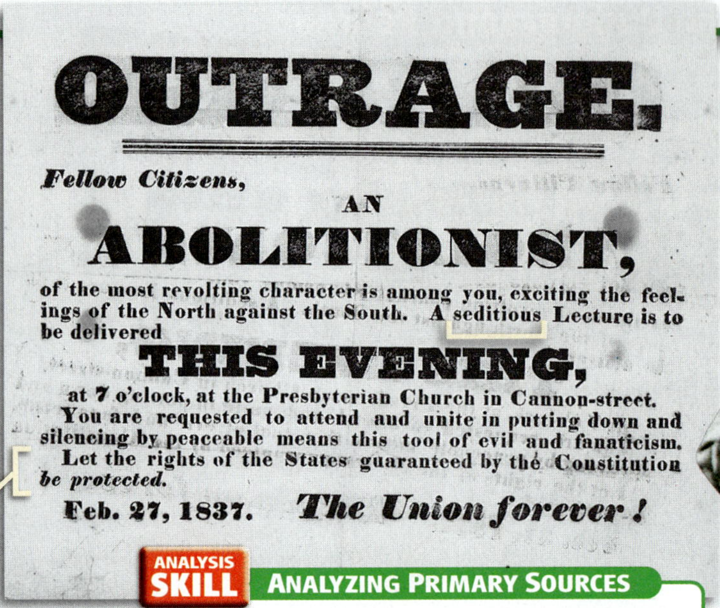

OUTRAGE.

Fellow Citizens,

AN

ABOLITIONIST,

of the most revolting character is among you, exciting the feelings of the North against the South. A seditious Lecture is to be delivered

THIS EVENING,

at 7 o'clock, at the Presbyterian Church in Cannon-street.

You are requested to attend and unite in putting down and silencing by peaceable means this tool of evil and fanaticism.

Let the rights of the States guaranteed by the Constitution *be protected.*

Feb. 27, 1837. ***The Union forever!***

Seditious means "guilty of rebelling against lawful authority."

The group believes abolition violates the Constitution.

ANALYSIS SKILL **ANALYZING PRIMARY SOURCES**

What emotional language does this handbill use to get its message across?

The most famous and daring conductor on the Underground Railroad was **Harriet Tubman**. When Tubman escaped slavery in 1849, she left behind her family. She swore that she would return and lead her whole family to freedom in the North. Tubman returned to the South 19 times, successfully leading her family and more than 300 other slaves to freedom. At one time the reward for Tubman's capture reportedly climbed to $40,000, a huge amount of money at that time.

READING CHECK **Drawing Inferences**

Why were the operations of the Underground Railroad kept secret?

NC History Makers

David Walker
Born as a free black in Wilmington, North Carolina, David Walker was an abolitionist who published a pamphlet called "Walker's Appeal to the Coloured Citizens of the World," which called for black pride.

Opposition to Ending Slavery

Although the North was the center of the abolitionist movement, many white northerners agreed with the South and supported slavery. Others disliked slavery but opposed equality for African Americans.

Newspaper editors and politicians warned that freed slaves would move north and take jobs from white workers. Some workers feared losing jobs to newly freed African Americans, whom they believed would accept lower wages. Abolitionist leaders were threatened with violence as some northerners joined mobs. Such a mob killed abolitionist Elijah Lovejoy in 1837 in Alton, Illinois.

The federal government also obstructed abolitionists. Between 1836 and 1844, the U.S. House of Representatives used what was called a gag rule. Congress had received thousands of antislavery petitions. Yet the gag rule forbade members of Congress from discussing them. This rule violated the First Amendment right of citizens to petition the government. But southern members of Congress did not want to debate slavery. Many northern members of Congress preferred to avoid the issue.

Eventually, representative and former president John Quincy Adams was able to get the gag rule overturned. His resolution to enact a constitutional amendment halting the expansion of slavery never passed, however.

Many white southerners saw slavery as vital to the South's economy and culture. They also felt that outsiders should not

Sojourner Truth was a former slave who became a leading abolitionist.

interfere with their way of life. After Nat Turner's Rebellion in 1831, when Turner led some slaves to kill slaveholders, open talk about slavery disappeared in the South. It became dangerous to voice antislavery sentiments in southern states. Abolitionists like the Grimké sisters left rather than air unpopular views to hostile neighbors. Racism, fear, and economic dependence on slavery made emancipation all but impossible in the South.

READING CHECK **Drawing Conclusions** Why did many northern workers oppose the abolition movement?

SUMMARY AND PREVIEW The issue of slavery grew more controversial in the United States during the first half of the nineteenth century. In the next section you will learn about women's rights.

Section 4 Assessment

go.hrw.com
Online Quiz
KEYWORD: SC7 HP14

Reviewing Ideas, Terms, and People

1. a. **Identify** What contributions did **William Lloyd Garrison** make to the **abolition** movement?
   b. **Draw Conclusions** In what ways did contributions from African Americans aid the struggle for abolition?
   c. **Elaborate** What do you think about the American Colonization Society's plan to return free African Americans to Liberia?
2. a. **Describe** How did the **Underground Railroad** work?
   b. **Explain** Why did **Harriet Tubman** first become involved with the Underground Railroad?
   c. **Evaluate** Do you think the Underground Railroad was a success? Why or why not?
3. a. **Describe** What action did Congress take to block abolitionists?
   b. **Analyze** Why did some Americans oppose equality for African Americans?
   c. **Predict** How might the debate over slavery lead to conflict in the future?

Critical Thinking

4. **Identifying Cause and Effect** Review your notes on the abolitionist movement. Then use a graphic organizer like the one below to show the reasons for opposition to the movement and the effects of that opposition.

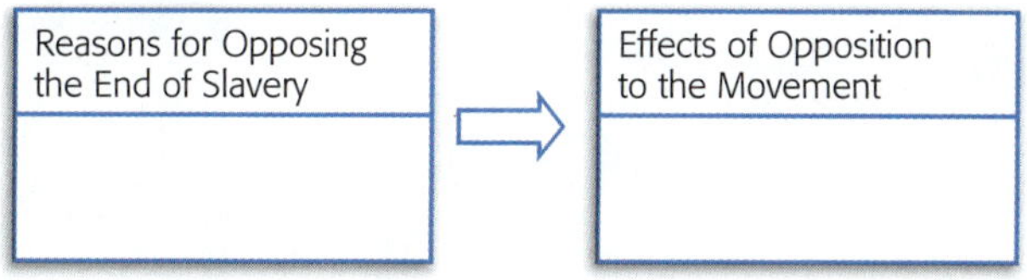

FOCUS ON WRITING

5. **Describing Abolition** Add notes about the abolitionist movement and its leaders to your chart. Be sure to note how abolitionists influenced life in the United States. What were they fighting for? Who opposed them, and why?

BIOGRAPHY

Frederick Douglass

As a freed slave, how would you help people still enslaved?

When did he live? 1817–1895

Where did he live? Frederick Douglass was born in rural Maryland. At age six he was sent to live in Baltimore, and at age 20 he escaped to New York City. For most of his life, Douglass lived in Rochester, New York, making his home into a stop along the Underground Railroad. He traveled often, giving powerful antislavery speeches to audiences throughout the North and in Europe.

What did he do? After hearing the abolitionist William Lloyd Garrison speak in 1841, Douglass began his own speaking tours about his experiences as a slave. In midlife he wrote an autobiography and started an abolitionist newspaper called the *North Star.* During the Civil War, Douglass persuaded black soldiers to fight for the North.

Why is he important? Douglass was the most famous African American in the 1800s. His personal stories and elegant speaking style helped the abolitionist movement to grow. His words remain an inspiration to this day.

Drawing Conclusions What made Frederick Douglass's speeches and writings so powerful?

KEY EVENTS

- **1817** Born a slave in Maryland
- **1837** Escapes slavery disguised as a sailor
- **1841** Begins his career as a speaker on abolition
- **1845** Writes *Narrative of the Life of Frederick Douglass*, his first autobiography
- **1847** Publishes first issue of the *North Star*
- **1863** Meets President Lincoln and becomes an adviser
- **1889** Named American consul general to Haiti
- **1895** Dies in Washington, D.C.

THE NORTH STAR.

VOL. I. NO. 22.

ROCHESTER, N. Y., FRIDAY, JUNE 2, 1848.

WHOLE NO.—22.

Frederick Douglass began publishing the *North Star,* an abolitionist newspaper, in 1847.

Women's Rights

SECTION 5

If YOU were there...

You are a schoolteacher in New York State in 1848. Although you earn a small salary, you still live at home. Your father does not believe that unmarried women should live alone or look after their own money. One day in a shop, you see a poster about a public meeting to discuss women's rights. You know your father will be angry if you go to the meeting. But you are very curious.

Would you attend the meeting? Why?

BUILDING BACKGROUND Women were active in the movements to reform prisons and schools. They fought for temperance and worked for abolition. But with all their work for social change, women still lacked many rights and opportunities of their own. Throughout the 1800s, the women's rights movement gradually became stronger and more organized.

What You Will Learn...

Main Ideas

1. Influenced by the abolition movement, many women struggled to gain equal rights for themselves.
2. Calls for women's rights met opposition from men and women.
3. The Seneca Falls Convention launched the first organized women's rights movement in the United States.

The Big Idea

Reformers sought to improve women's rights in American society.

Key Terms and People

Elizabeth Cady Stanton, *p. 464*
Lucretia Mott, *p. 464*
Seneca Falls Convention, *p. 464*
Declaration of Sentiments, *p. 464*
Lucy Stone, *p. 465*
Susan B. Anthony, *p. 465*

TAKING NOTES Create a graphic organizer like the one shown below. Use it to show some of the significant events in the struggle for women's rights.

Date	Events
1838 →	
1848 →	
1851 →	
1860 →	

Women's Struggle for Equal Rights

Fighting for the rights of African Americans led many female abolitionists to fight for women's rights. In the mid-1800s, these women found that they had to defend their right to speak in public, particularly when a woman addressed both men and women. For example, members of the press, the clergy, and even some male abolitionists criticized the Grimké sisters. These critics thought that the sisters should not give public speeches. They did not want women to leave their traditional female roles. The Grimkés protested that women had a moral duty to lead the antislavery movement.

Early Writings for Women's Rights

In 1838 Sarah Grimké published a pamphlet arguing for equal rights for women. She titled it *Letters on the Equality of the Sexes and the Condition of Women.*

> "I ask no favors for my sex ... All I ask our brethren [brothers] is that they will take their feet from off our necks, and permit us to stand upright on that ground which God designed us to occupy."
>
> —Sarah Grimké, quoted in *The Grimké Sisters from South Carolina,* edited by Gerda Lerner

Sarah Grimké also argued for equal educational opportunities. She pointed out laws that negatively affected women. In addition, she demanded equal pay for equal work.

Sarah Grimké never married. She explained that the laws of the day gave a husband complete control of his wife's property. Therefore, she feared that by marrying, she would become more like a slave than a wife. Her sister, Angelina, did marry, but she refused to promise to obey her husband during their marriage ceremony. She married Theodore Weld, an abolitionist. Weld agreed to give up his legal right to control her property after they married. For the Grimkés, the abolitionist principles and women's rights principles were identical.

In 1845 the famous transcendentalist Margaret Fuller published *Woman in the Nineteenth Century.* This book used well-known sayings to explain the role of women in American society. Fuller used democratic and transcendentalist principles to stress the importance of individualism to all people, especially women. The book influenced many leaders of the women's rights movement.

Sojourner Truth

Sojourner Truth was another powerful supporter of both abolition and women's rights. She had been born into slavery in about 1797. Her birth name was Isabella Baumfree. She took the name Sojourner Truth because she felt that her mission was to be a sojourner, or traveler, and spread the truth. Though she never learned to read or write, she impressed many well-educated people. One person who thought highly of her was the author Harriet Beecher Stowe. Stowe said that she had never spoken "with anyone who had more . . . personal presence than this woman." Truth stood six feet tall and was a confident speaker.

In 1851 Truth gave a speech that is often quoted to this day.

> "That man over here says that women need to be helped into carriages and lifted over ditches, and to have the best place everywhere. Nobody ever helps me into carriages or over mud puddles, or gives me any best place ... Look at me! I have ploughed and planted and ... no man could head [outwork] me. And ain't I a woman?"
>
> —Sojourner Truth, quoted in *A History of Women in America* by Carol Hymowitz and Michaele Weissman

Truth, the Grimké sisters, and other supporters of the women's movement were determined to be heard.

READING CHECK **Drawing Inferences** Why would reformers link the issues of abolition and women's rights?

Time Line

Women's Rights

1776 Abigail Adams asks her husband, John Adams, to "remember the ladies" and their rights in the Declaration of Independence.

1848 The Seneca Falls Convention is held, and the Declaration of Sentiments is written.

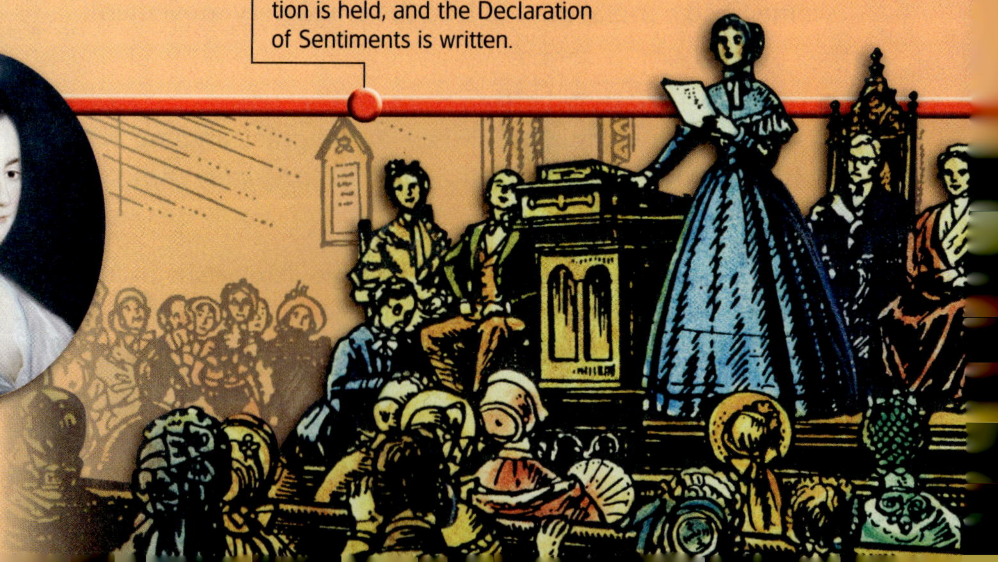

Opposing the Call for Women's Rights

Publications about women's rights first appeared in the United States shortly after the American Revolution. However, women's concerns did not become a national issue with strong opposition for many more years.

The Movement Grows

The change took place when women took a more active and leading role in reform and abolition. Other social changes also led to the rise of the women's movement. Women took advantage of better educational opportunities in the early 1800s. Their efforts on behalf of reform groups helped them learn how to organize more effectively and to work together.

Another benefit of reform-group work was that some men began to fight for women's rights. Many activists, both men and women, found it unacceptable that women were not allowed to vote or sit on juries. They were also upset that married women in many states had little or no control over their own property.

Opposition to Women's Rights

Like the abolitionist movement, the struggle for women's rights faced opposition. Many people did not agree with some of the goals of the women's rights movement. Some women believed that they did not need new rights. They said that women were not unequal to men, only different. Some critics believed that women should not try to work in public for social changes. Women were welcome to work for social change, but only from within their homes. "Let her not look away from her own little family circle for the means of producing moral and social reforms," wrote T. S. Arthur. His advice appeared in a popular women's magazine called *The Lady at Home*.

Some people also thought that women lacked the physical or mental strength to survive without men's protection. They believed that a woman should go from the protection of her father's home to that of her husband's. They also thought that women could not cope with the outside world; therefore, a husband should control his wife's property. Despite opposition, women continued to pursue their goal of greater rights.

READING CHECK **Drawing Conclusions** Why did some men and women think that the women's rights movement was misguided?

1872 Susan B. Anthony is arrested while trying to vote in New York.

1890 Wyoming's new state constitution includes women's suffrage.

1911 The National Association Opposed to Woman Suffrage is formed.

1920 On August 26, the Nineteenth Amendment is declared ratified by Congress, giving women the right to vote.

"There never will be complete equality until women themselves help to make laws and elect lawmakers."

Susan B. Anthony

ANALYSIS SKILL **READING TIME LINES**

Women in Wyoming could vote how many years before women in the rest of the country could?

Primary Source

HISTORIC DOCUMENT

Declaration of Sentiments

At the 1848 Seneca Falls Convention, 100 people signed the Declaration of Sentiments, a document declaring the rights of women. The wording of the document purposely echoed the Declaration of Independence.

We hold these truths to be self-evident: that all men and women are created equal; that they are endowed by their Creator with certain inalienable[1] rights; that among these are life, liberty, and the pursuit of happiness; that to secure these rights governments are instituted, deriving their just powers from the consent of the governed. Whenever any form of government becomes destructive of these ends, it is the right of those who suffer from it to refuse allegiance[2] to it, and to insist upon the institution of a new government, laying its foundation on such principles, and organizing its powers in such form, as to them shall seem most likely to effect their safety and happiness.

1. **inalienable** not able to be taken away 2. **allegiance** loyalty

The authors use the same words that are in the Declaration of Independence, but include women.

Here the women demand that they become a part of government.

ANALYSIS SKILL **ANALYZING PRIMARY SOURCES**

Why would women want to use the Declaration of Independence as a source for their own declaration?

Seneca Falls Convention

In 1840 **Elizabeth Cady Stanton** attended the World's Anti-Slavery Convention in London, England, while on her honeymoon. She discovered that, unlike her husband, she was not allowed to participate. All women in attendance had to sit behind a curtain in a separate gallery of the convention hall. William Lloyd Garrison, who had helped found the American Anti-Slavery Society, sat with them in protest.

The treatment of women abolitionists at the convention angered Stanton and her new friend, **Lucretia Mott**. Apparently, even many abolitionists did not think that women were equal to men. Stanton and Mott wanted to change this, so they planned to "form a society to advance the rights of women." Eight years passed before Stanton and Mott finally announced the **Seneca Falls Convention**, the first public meeting about women's rights held in the United States. It opened on July 19, 1848, in Seneca Falls, New York.

Declaration of Sentiments

The convention organizers wrote a **Declaration of Sentiments**. This document detailed beliefs about social injustice toward women. They used the Declaration of Independence as the basis for the language for their Declaration of Sentiments. The authors included 18 charges against men—the same number that had been charged against King George III. The Declaration of Sentiments was signed by some 100 people.

About 240 people attended the Seneca Falls Convention, including men such as abolitionist Frederick Douglass. Many other reformers who also worked in the temperance and abolitionist movements were present. Several women who participated in the convention worked in nearby factories. One of them, 19-year-old Charlotte Woodward, signed the Declaration of Sentiments. She worked long hours in a factory, making gloves. Her wages were very low, and she could not even keep her earnings. She had to turn her wages over to her father.

Women's Rights Leaders

After the convention, the struggle continued. Women's rights activists battled many difficulties and much opposition. Still, they kept working to obtain greater equality for women. Among the many women working for women's rights, three became important leaders: Lucy Stone, Susan B. Anthony, and Elizabeth Cady Stanton. Each brought different strengths to the fight for women's rights.

Lucy Stone was a well-known spokesperson for the Anti-Slavery Society. In the early years of the women's rights movement, Stone became known as a gifted speaker. Elizabeth Cady Stanton called her "the first who really stirred the nation's heart on the subject of women's wrongs."

Susan B. Anthony brought strong organizational skills to the women's rights movement. She did much to turn the fight for women's rights into a political movement. Anthony argued that women and men should receive equal pay for equal work. She also believed that women should be allowed to enter traditionally male professions, such as religion and law. Anthony was especially concerned with laws that affected women's control of money and property.

Anthony led a campaign to change laws regarding the property rights of women. She wrote in her diary that no woman could ever be free without "a purse of her own." After forming a network to cover the entire state of New York, she collected more than 6,000 signatures to petition for a new property-rights law. In 1860, due largely to the efforts of Anthony, New York finally gave married women ownership of their wages and property. Other states in the Northeast and Midwest soon created similar laws.

THE IMPACT TODAY

In the United States, as of the year 2000, women earned about 75 percent as much as men did.

The Antisuffragists

As the suffrage movement picked up speed, opponents to women's suffrage also began to organize. The antisuffragists, or "antis," formed statewide groups opposing the suffrage movement during the late 1800s. In 1911, Josephine Dodge united many of these groups' efforts by creating the National Association Opposed to Woman Suffrage in New York City. Dodge and other antisuffragists argued that women's suffrage would distract women from building strong families and improving communities.

Elizabeth Cady Stanton wrote many of the documents and speeches of the movement, which were often delivered by Anthony. Stanton was a founder and important leader of the National Woman Suffrage Association. This organization was considered one of the more radical groups because of its position that abolition was not a more important cause than women's rights.

Not every battle was won. Other major reforms, such as women's right to vote, were not achieved at this time. Still, more women than ever before became actively involved in women's rights issues. This increased activity was one of the movement's greatest accomplishments.

READING CHECK **Identifying Points of View** What did Susan B. Anthony mean when she said that no woman could be free without "a purse of her own"?

Lucy Stone worked for equal rights for women and African Americans.

SUMMARY AND PREVIEW Women's rights became a major issue in the mid-1800s, as women began to demand a greater degree of equality. In the next chapter you will read about western expansion.

Section 5 Assessment

go.hrw.com
Online Quiz
KEYWORD: SC7 HP14

Reviewing Ideas, Terms, and People

1. a. **Identify** What role did Sojourner Truth play in both the abolition and women's rights movements?
   b. **Analyze** How did the abolition movement influence women to demand equal rights?
2. a. **Identify** What limitations on women's rights did many activists find unacceptable?
   b. **Summarize** Why did many Americans oppose equal rights for women?
   c. **Elaborate** What arguments might you use to counter the arguments of men and women who opposed equal rights for women?
3. a. **Recall** Who were the three main leaders of the women's rights movement, and how did they each contribute to the movement?
   b. **Draw Conclusions** Why might working-class women like Charlotte Woodward have supported the **Seneca Falls Convention** and the **Declaration of Sentiments**?
   c. **Evaluate** Do you agree with **Susan B. Anthony** that women should receive equal pay for equal work? Explain your answer.

Critical Thinking

4. **Analyzing** Review your notes on events in the women's rights movement. Then copy the graphic organizer shown below and use it to show the goals of the movement, as well as the arguments against it.

Goals	Opponents' Arguments

FOCUS ON WRITING

5. **Describing Women's Suffrage** Add notes about the women's suffrage movement to your chart. Note important leaders and describe what they were fighting for. Ask yourself, "How did the women's suffrage movement change life in the United States?"

Elizabeth Cady Stanton

What steps would you take to bring about nationwide change?

When did she live? 1815–1902

Where did she live? Elizabeth Cady Stanton was born in Johnstown, New York. She married a prominent abolitionist and settled in Seneca Falls, New York, where she had seven children. Later in life she traveled widely, giving lectures and speeches across the country.

What did she do? Stanton and fellow activist Lucretia Mott organized the nation's first women's rights convention, at Seneca Falls in 1848. She and Susan B. Anthony founded the National Woman Suffrage Association in 1869. For nearly six decades, she spoke and wrote passionately about women's rights.

Why is she important? Stanton helped author the Declaration of Sentiments, which demanded equal rights for women, including the right to vote. A brilliant speaker and debater, Stanton spoke out against laws that kept married women from owning property, earning wages, and keeping custody of their children.

Finding Main Ideas What problems did Stanton try to correct? What problems did she face in accomplishing her goals?

KEY EVENTS

- **1815** Born in Johnstown, New York
- **1840** Meets Lucretia Mott at the World's Anti-Slavery Convention, where they are barred from participating
- **1848** Helps organize the first national meeting of women's suffrage reformers at Seneca Falls, New York
- **1851** Meets Susan B. Anthony, with whom she will later lead the National Woman Suffrage Association
- **1895** Publishes the Woman's Bible
- **1902** Dies in New York City

Elizabeth Cady Stanton helped author the Declaration of Sentiments at the Seneca Falls Convention.

A WOMAN'S DECLARATION OF INDEPENDENCE 1848

ELIZABETH CADY STANTON (1815–1902): After seeing the cruel and unjust treatment of women before the law, in the office of her father, Judge Cady, she vowed, even as a child, to find a way to help change these laws. Her marriage to the abolitionist leader, Henry B. Stanton, swept her swiftly into the current of national politics. This laid a firm foundation for the political experience to wage the battle for woman's rights in which she was to become a most inspiring leader. Together with friends, she planned and executed the first Woman's Rights Convention in Seneca Falls, New York, July 19th and 20th 1848. Her life story is truly the history of the Woman's Rights Movement.

Resolutions

Social Studies Skills

Analysis | Critical Thinking | **Civic Participation** | Study

Accepting Social Responsibility

Define the Skill

A *society* is an organized group of people who share a common set of activities, traditions, and goals. You are part of many societies—your school, community, and nation are just three. Every society's strength depends on the support and contributions of its members. *Social responsibility* is the obligation that every person has to the societies in which he or she is a member.

Learn the Skill

As a part of your school, community, and nation, you have obligations to the people around you. The most obvious is to do nothing to harm your society. You also have a duty to be part of it. At the very least, this means exercising the rights and responsibilities of membership. These include being informed about issues in your society.

Another level of social responsibility is support of change to benefit society. This level of involvement goes beyond being informed about issues to trying to do something about them. If you take this important step, here are some points to consider.

1. Few efforts to change society have everyone's support. Some people will want things to stay the same. They may treat you badly if you work for change. You must be prepared for this possibility if you decide to take action.
2. Sometimes efforts to improve things involve opposing laws or rules that need to be changed. No matter how just your cause is, if you break law or rules, you must be willing to accept the consequences of your behavior.
3. Remember that violence is *never* an acceptable method for change. People who use force in seeking change are not behaving in a socially responsible manner, even if their cause is good.

This chapter was filled with the stories of socially responsible people. Many of them devoted their lives to changing society for the better. Some did so at great personal risk. Boston abolitionist William Lloyd Garrison barely escaped with his life from a local mob that tried to lynch him because of his views.

Garrison and the other reformers you read about demonstrated the highest level of social responsibility. They saw an issue they believed to be a problem in society, and they worked tirelessly to change it and make society better.

Practice the Skill

Review the "If you were there" scene on page 454. Imagine yourself as that Ohioan. You believe slavery to be wrong. However, you also respect the law, and it is illegal to help an escaped slave. In addition, you know that most of your neighbors do not feel as you do about slavery. They might harm you or your property if you take this stand against it.

1. Would agreeing to your friend's request help benefit society? Explain why or why not.
2. Are you willing to risk the anger of your neighbors? Why or why not?
3. Is the idea of breaking the law or possibly going to jail a factor in your decision? Explain.
4. Would agreeing to your friend's request be a socially responsible thing to do? Explain why or why not.

CHAPTER 14 Chapter Review

HOLT

History's Impact

▶ **video series**

Review the video to answer the closing question:

Why does it make sense that the women's suffrage movement originated from the abolitionist movement?

Visual Summary

QUICK FACTS

Use the visual summary below to help you review the main ideas of the chapter.

Reviewing Vocabulary, Terms, and People

1. Which of the following authors wrote about Puritan life in *The Scarlet Letter*?

a. Emily Dickinson
b. Herman Melville
c. Thomas Gallaudet
d. Nathaniel Hawthorne

2. Which document expressed the complaints of supporters of women's rights?

a. Declaration of the Rights of Women
b. Declaration of Sentiments
c. Letters on Women's Rights
d. Seneca Falls Convention

3. As leader of the common-school movement, who worked to improve free public education?

a. Walt Whitman
b. Horace Mann
c. Lyman Beecher
d. Sojourner Truth

Comprehension and Critical Thinking

SECTION 1 *(Pages 438–442)*

4. a. Identify What political party was founded by nativists, and what policies did it support?

b. Analyze What factors caused U.S. cities to grow so fast?

c. Evaluate Do you think that the benefits of city life outweighed its drawbacks? Explain.

SECTION 2 *(Pages 443–445)*

5. a. Describe Who were some important transcendentalists, and what ideas did they promote?

b. Compare and Contrast In what ways were transcendentalists and Romantics similar and different?

c. Elaborate Which movement appeals to you more—American transcendentalism or Romanticism? Why?

SECTION 3 *(Pages 448–453)*

6. a. **Identify** What important reform movements became popular in the early 1800s?

   b. **Analyze** Why did education become an important topic for reformers in the 1800s?

   c. **Evaluate** Which reform movement do you think had the greatest effect on the United States? Why?

SECTION 4 *(Pages 454–459)*

7. a. **Recall** What are the different reasons why people supported abolition?

   b. **Make Inferences** How did northerners and southerners differ in their opposition to abolition?

   c. **Evaluate** Which of the methods used by abolitionists to oppose slavery do you think was most successful? Why?

SECTION 5 *(Pages 461–466)*

8. a. **Recall** What led many women to question their place in American society?

   b. **Make Inferences** Why did female factory workers like Charlotte Woodward support the women's rights movement?

   c. **Evaluate** By 1860 do you think the women's movement had been successful? Explain your answer.

Using the Internet

go.hrw.com
KEYWORD: SC7 CH14

9. **Activity: Creating Visuals** The *Liberator* and *North Star* were two newspapers that encouraged the end of slavery. Enter the activity keyword and research the influence of abolitionist newspapers, such as those written by William Lloyd Garrison and Frederick Douglass. Then create a visual display that illustrates how each newspaper represented the abolitionist point of view.

Reading Skills

Information and Propaganda *Use the Reading Skills taught in this chapter to answer the question below.*

10. Which of the following is *not* an example of propaganda?

    a. a flyer protesting new tax laws

    b. an ad about a political candidate

    c. a radio announcement sponsored by an interest group

    d. a list of camping rules from a park

Reviewing Themes

11. **Society and Culture** What social and cultural changes took place from 1800 to the mid-1800s?

Social Studies Skills

Accepting Social Responsibility *Use the Social Studies Skills taught in this chapter to fill in the chart below.*

12.

Action	Is it socially responsible?	Why or why not?
Removing litter from a park		
Voting		
Reading a political magazine		
Running a red light		

FOCUS ON WRITING

13. **Writing Your Persuasive Letter** You've described a number of important events and political, religious, and artistic movements in your notebook. Now, it's time to choose the one you consider most important. Think about how it changed life for people in the United States. Then write a two-paragraph persuasive letter to the newspaper, arguing for the event or movement you chose. In the first paragraph, identify the event or movement you chose as well as a thesis explaining why it is important. In the second paragraph, include details about the event or movement that support your thesis. Close with one or two sentences that sum up your points.

CHAPTER 14 Standardized Test Practice

DIRECTIONS: Read each question and write the letter of the best response.

1 U.S. cities experienced rapid growth in the mid-1800s as a result of

A the rise of a new middle class.

B new factory jobs that attracted workers.

C the lack of available land in the West.

D changes in immigration laws.

2 Which of the following statements best represents the ideas of transcendentalist thinkers?

A American institutions are crucial to the advancement of society.

B People should learn to be self-reliant and follow their own beliefs.

C Utopian communities are destined for failure.

D Art and poetry should depict the beauty of the American landscape.

3 Reformers like Archibald D. Murphey of North Carolina and Horace Mann of Massachusetts worked to improve

A prison systems.

B public education.

C living conditions in cities.

D the rights of free African Americans.

4 African American students in the North

A had less opportunity for education than those in the South.

B did not benefit from educational reforms.

C had opportunities to attend black colleges formed in the 1840's.

D usually attended the same schools as white students.

5 The temperance movement, efforts at prison reform, and the abolition movement were all elements of

A social reforms of the mid-1800s.

B the Second Great Awakening.

C transcendentalism.

D the women's rights movement.

6 Which of the following people would *most likely* have supported a law prohibiting foreigners from holding public office?

A an antisuffragist

B a nativist

C an abolitionist

D a transcendentalist

7 Examine the following cartoon about women breaking kegs of liquor and then use it to answer the question below.

Document-Based Question **What does the shield of the woman on horseback represent? How can you tell?**

CHAPTER 15 1848–1860

A Divided Nation

North Carolina Standards

Social Studies Objectives

4.01 Identify and analyze the significance of the causes of secession from the Union, and compare reactions in North Carolina to reactions in other regions of the nation.

Language Arts Objectives

1.02 Analyze expressive materials that are read, heard, and/or viewed by:

- monitoring comprehension for understanding of what is read, heard and/or viewed.
- reviewing the characteristics of expressive works.
- determining the importance of literary effects on the reader/viewer/listener.

go.hrw.com
North Carolina
KEYWORD: SC7 NC

FOCUS ON WRITING

Writing an Autobiographical Sketch When you read about history, it can be difficult to imagine how the events you read about affected ordinary people. In this chapter you will read about slavery in the United States. Then you will write an autobiography of a fictional character, telling how these events affected him or her. Your fictional character can live in any part of the United States. He or she might be an enslaved African, a southern plantation owner, a northern abolitionist, or a settler in one of the new territories. Your classmates are your audience.

UNITED STATES

1848
The Free-Soil Party is formed on August 9.

1848

1848
Revolutionary movements sweep across Europe.

WORLD

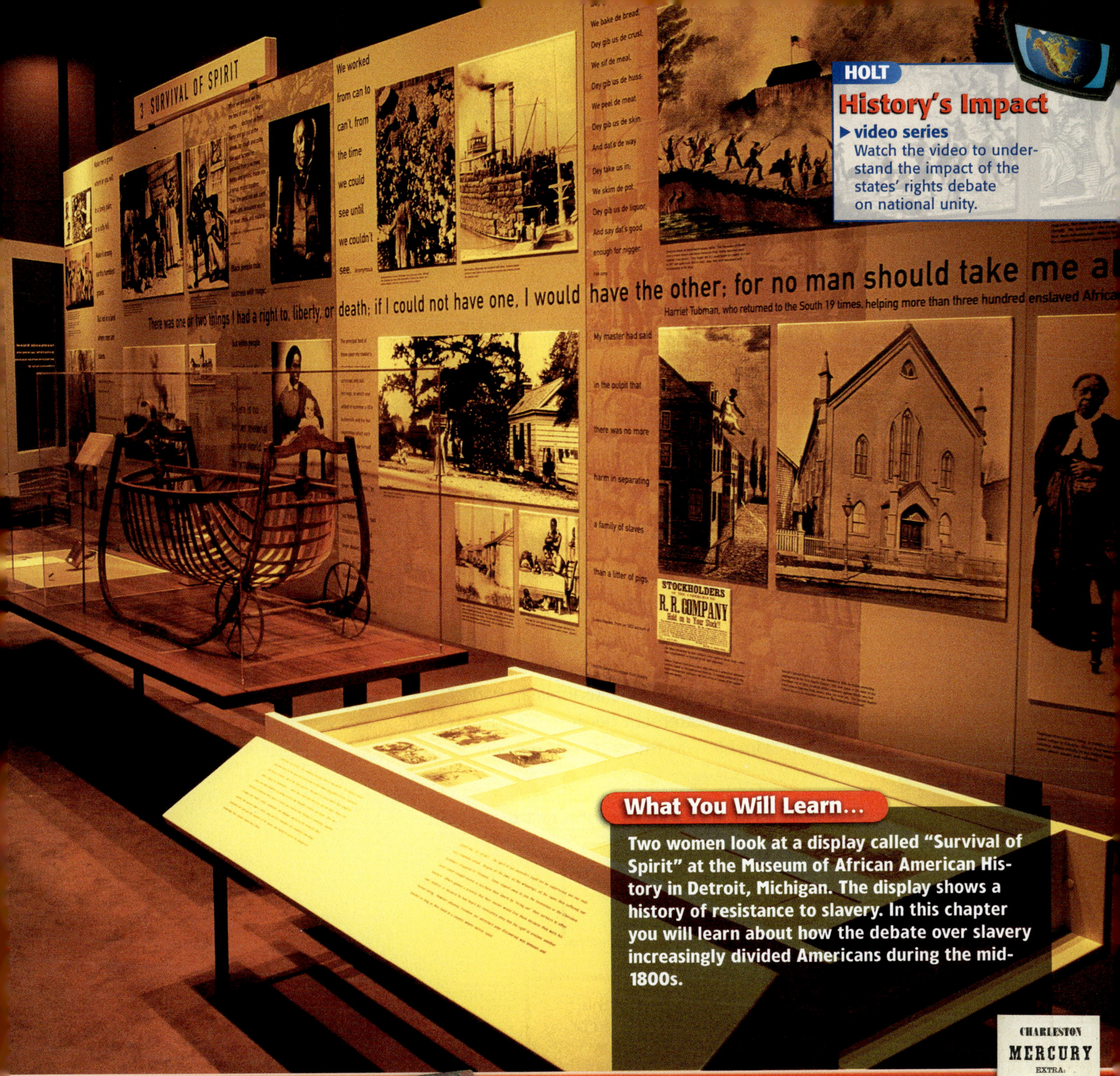

HOLT

History's Impact

▶ **video series**

Watch the video to understand the impact of the states' rights debate on national unity.

What You Will Learn...

Two women look at a display called "Survival of Spirit" at the Museum of African American History in Detroit, Michigan. The display shows a history of resistance to slavery. In this chapter you will learn about how the debate over slavery increasingly divided Americans during the mid-1800s.

1850 Congress passes the Fugitive Slave Act on September 18.

1852 *Uncle Tom's Cabin* is published by Harriet Beecher Stowe.

1856 In the Sack of Lawrence, pro-slavery forces attack the town of Lawrence, Kansas, on May 21.

1859 John Brown takes control of the federal arsenal at Harpers Ferry, Virginia.

1860 On December 20, South Carolina votes to secede from the United States.

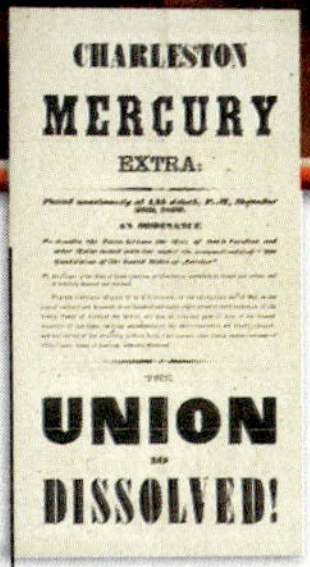

CHARLESTON
MERCURY
EXTRA:

UNION
DISSOLVED!

1850 — 1855 — 1860

1852 Louis-Napoléon declares himself Emperor Napoléon III of France.

1856 British and French forces defeat Russia in the Crimean War.

1857 Indian soldiers in the British army begin the Sepoy Mutiny against British control of India.

Reading Social Studies

by Kylene Beers

Economics | Geography | Politics | Society and Culture | Science and Technology

Focus on Themes This chapter describes the growing tension between the North and the South over the slavery issue. You will read what happened as more states were admitted to the Union and people argued if they should be slave states or not. You will read about events that widened the division between the North and South so that the South finally chose to secede from the Union. Throughout the chapter you will see that **cultural** differences influenced **political** decisions.

Facts, Opinions, and the Past

Focus on Reading When you are trying to learn about history, separating facts from opinions helps you know what really happened.

Identifying Facts and Opinions Something is a **fact** if there is a way to prove it. For example, research can prove or disprove the following statement: "Abraham Lincoln belonged to the Republican Party." But research can't prove the following statement because it is just an **opinion**, or someone's belief: "Lincoln was the greatest president in American history."

Use the process below to decide whether a statement is fact or opinion.

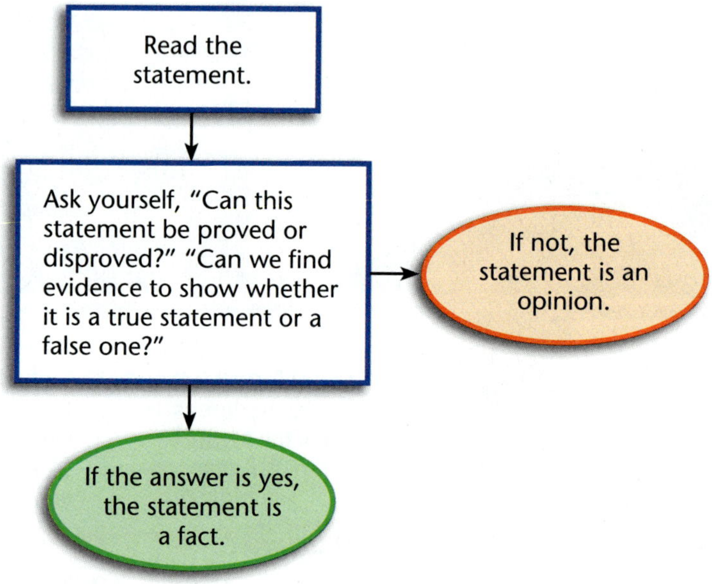

You Try It!

The following passage tells about the debates that Abraham Lincoln had with Stephen Douglas. All the statements in this passage are facts. What makes them facts and not opinions?

The Lincoln-Douglas Debates

From Chapter 15, p. 491

In 1858 Illinois Republicans nominated Abraham Lincoln for the U.S. Senate. His opponent was Democrat Stephen Douglas, who had represented Illinois in the Senate since 1847. Lincoln challenged Douglas in what became the historic Lincoln-Douglas debates.

In each debate, Lincoln stressed that the central issue of the campaign was the spread of slavery in the West. He said that the Democrats were trying to spread slavery across the nation.

Lincoln talked about the *Dred Scott* decision. He said that African Americans were "entitled to all the natural rights" listed in the Declaration of Independence, specifically mentioning "the right to life, liberty, and the pursuit of happiness."

Identify each of the following as a fact or an opinion and then explain your choice.

1. Lincoln accused the Democrats of trying to spread slavery across the nation.
2. The Lincoln-Douglas debates were the most important debates in the history of the nation.
3. Stephen Douglas was a U.S. senator from Illinois.
4. Abraham Lincoln ran against Douglas in the 1858 Senate election.
5. Most Americans believed that the *Dred Scott* decision was a good one.
6. Lincoln was the best debater people from Illinois had ever heard.

Key Terms and People

Chapter 15

Section 1

popular sovereignty *(p. 476)*
Wilmot Proviso *(p. 476)*
sectionalism *(p. 477)*
Free-Soil Party *(p. 477)*
secede *(p. 478)*
Compromise of 1850 *(p. 479)*
Fugitive Slave Act *(p. 479)*
Anthony Burns *(p. 480)*
Uncle Tom's Cabin *(p. 481)*
Harriet Beecher Stowe *(p. 481)*

Section 2

Franklin Pierce *(p. 483)*
Stephen Douglas *(p. 484)*
Kansas-Nebraska Act *(p. 485)*
Pottawatomie Massacre *(p. 487)*
Charles Sumner *(p. 487)*
Preston Brooks *(p. 487)*

Section 3

Republican Party *(p. 488)*
James Buchanan *(p. 488)*
John C. Frémont *(p. 489)*
Dred Scott *(p. 489)*
Roger B. Taney *(p. 490)*
Abraham Lincoln *(p. 490)*
Lincoln-Douglas debates *(p. 491)*
Freeport Doctrine *(p. 492)*

Section 4

John Brown's raid *(p. 493)*
John C. Breckinridge *(p. 495)*
Constitutional Union Party *(p. 495)*
John Bell *(p. 495)*
John J. Crittenden *(p. 496)*
Confederate States of America *(p. 497)*
Jefferson Davis *(p. 497)*

Academic Vocabulary

In this chapter, you will learn the following academic words:

implications *(p. 485)*
complex *(p. 489)*

As you read Chapter 15, look closely at quotes from historical figures. Are these quotes showing you facts or opinions?

SECTION 1

The Debate over Slavery

What You Will Learn...

Main Ideas

1. The addition of new land in the West renewed disputes over the expansion of slavery.
2. The Compromise of 1850 tried to solve the disputes over slavery.
3. The Fugitive Slave Act caused more controversy.
4. Abolitionists used antislavery literature to promote opposition.

The Big Idea

Antislavery literature and the annexation of new lands intensified the debate over slavery.

Key Terms and People

popular sovereignty, *p. 476*
Wilmot Proviso, *p. 476*
sectionalism, *p. 477*
Free-Soil Party, *p. 477*
secede, *p. 478*
Compromise of 1850, *p. 479*
Fugitive Slave Act, *p. 479*
Anthony Burns, *p. 480*
Uncle Tom's Cabin, *p. 481*
Harriet Beecher Stowe, *p. 481*

TAKING NOTES Copy the graphic organizer below. As you read, take notes on the sequence of events in the debate over slavery. Be sure to describe the effects of each event.

Significant Events in the Slavery Debate	
Event	Effect
1. 2. 3. 4. 5. 6.	

If YOU were there...

You live in a crowded neighborhood in New York City in 1854. Your apartment building is home to a variety of people—longtime residents, Irish immigrants, free African Americans. One day federal marshals knock on your door. They claim that one of your neighbors is a fugitive slave. The marshals say you must help them find her. If you don't, you will be fined or even sent to jail.

What would you tell the federal marshals?

BUILDING BACKGROUND Some reform movements of the 1800s drew stubborn and often violent opposition. This was especially true of the abolitionist movement. Pro-slavery supporters fought for laws to protect slavery and extend the slave system. These laws were a threat to African Americans in the North.

New Land Renews Slavery Disputes

The United States added more than 500,000 square miles of land as a result of winning the Mexican-American War in 1848. The additional land caused bitter debate about slavery. The Missouri Compromise of 1820 had divided the Louisiana Purchase into either free or slave regions. It prohibited slavery north of latitude 36°30′ but let Missouri become a slave state. In the 1840s President James K. Polk wanted to extend the 36°30′ line to the West coast, dividing the Mexican Cession into two parts—one free and one enslaved. Some leaders, including Senator Lewis Cass of Michigan, encouraged **popular sovereignty**, the idea that political power belongs to the people, who should decide on banning or allowing slavery.

Regional Differences about Slavery

Some northerners wanted to outlaw slavery in all parts of the Mexican Cession. During the war, Representative David Wilmot offered the **Wilmot Proviso**, a document stating that "neither slavery nor involuntary servitude shall ever exist in any part of [the] territory."

Upsetting the Balance

QUICK FACTS

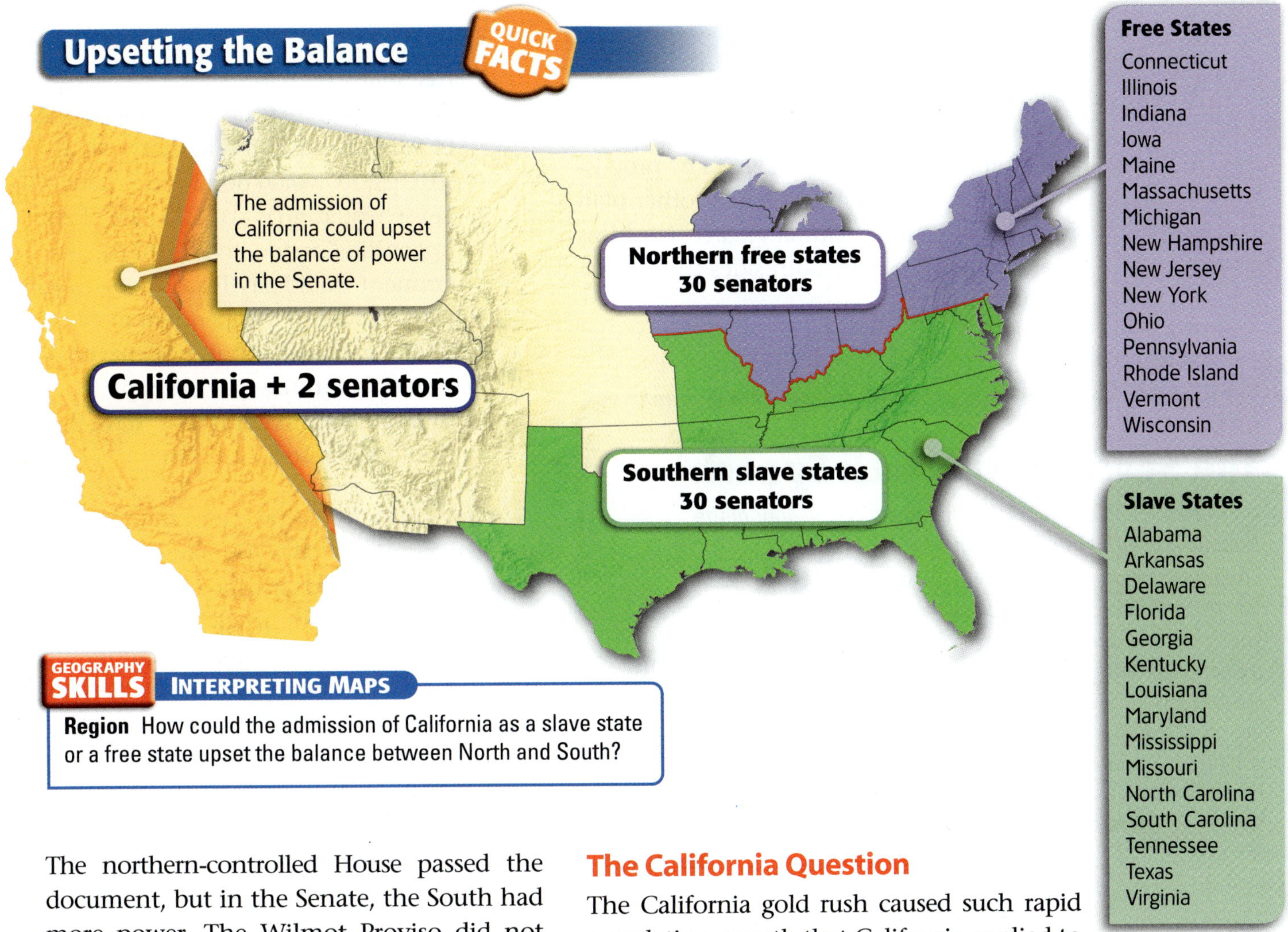

GEOGRAPHY SKILLS **INTERPRETING MAPS**

Region How could the admission of California as a slave state or a free state upset the balance between North and South?

The northern-controlled House passed the document, but in the Senate, the South had more power. The Wilmot Proviso did not pass. Before this time, politicians had usually supported the ideas of their political parties. However, the Wilmot Proviso spurred a debate that showed growing **sectionalism**, or favoring the interests of one section or region over the interests of the entire country.

To attract voters, the Democrats and the Whigs did not take a clear position on slavery in the presidential campaign of 1848. In response, antislavery northerners formed a new party, the **Free-Soil Party**, which supported the Wilmot Proviso. They worried that slave labor would mean fewer jobs for white workers. Party members chose former president Martin Van Buren as their candidate. The new party won 10 percent of the popular vote, drawing away votes from Democrat Lewis Cass. Whig candidate Zachary Taylor won a narrow victory.

The California Question

The California gold rush caused such rapid population growth that California applied to join the Union as a state instead of as a territory. But would California enter the Union as a free state or a slave state?

Most Californians opposed slavery, which had been illegal when the state was part of Mexico. Also, many forty-niners had come from free states. But if California became a free state, the balance between free and slave states would change, favoring the free states.

In the South, an imbalance was unacceptable. "We are about permanently to destroy the balance of power between the sections," said Senator Jefferson Davis of Mississippi. He and many other southerners did not want California to enter the Union as a free state.

READING CHECK **Drawing Inferences** Why did sectionalism in the United States increase in the late 1840s?

THE IMPACT TODAY

Small parties still affect presidential elections in a similar way today.

Compromise of 1850

Senator Henry Clay of Kentucky had helped to settle the Missouri crisis of 1819–20 and the nullification crisis of 1832–33 by proposing compromises. He now had another plan to help the nation maintain peace. His ideas were designed to give both sides things that they wanted:

1. California would enter the Union as a free state.
2. The rest of the Mexican Cession would be federal land. In this territory, popular sovereignty would decide on slavery.
3. Texas would give up land east of the upper Rio Grande. In return, the government would pay Texas's debts from when it was an independent republic.
4. The slave trade—but not slavery—would end in the nation's capital.
5. A more effective fugitive slave law would be passed.

Clay's plan drew attack, especially regarding California. Senator William Seward of New York defended antislavery views and wanted California admitted "directly, without conditions, without qualifications, and without compromise." However, Senator John C. Calhoun of South Carolina argued that letting California enter as a free state would destroy the nation's balance. He warned people of issues that would later start the Civil War. Calhoun asked that the slave states be allowed to **secede**—formally withdraw—from the Union.

Primary Source

SPEECH

The Seventh of March Speech

On March 7, 1850, Daniel Webster spoke on the floor of the Senate in favor of the Compromise of 1850.

I hear with distress and anguish the word "secession." Secession! Peaceable secession! Sir, your eyes and mine are never destined to see the miracle. The dismemberment [taking apart] of this vast country without convulsion! The breaking up of the fountains of the great deep without ruffing the surface! Who is so foolish, I beg every body's pardon, as to expect to see any such thing? . . . There can be no such thing as peaceable secession.

—quoted in *Daniel Webster: The Completest Man,* edited by Kenneth Shewmaker

Webster is upset by talk of secession.

Webster is saying that just as it is impossible to move water in the ocean without making waves, it is impossible for states to peacefully secede.

ANALYSIS SKILL **ANALYZING PRIMARY SOURCES**

Why did Webster support the Compromise of 1850?

In contrast, Senator Daniel Webster of Massachusetts favored Clay's plan:

> "I wish to speak today, not as a Massachusetts man, nor as a Northern man, but as an American ... I speak today for the preservation of the Union. Hear me for my cause."
>
> —Daniel Webster, quoted in *Battle Cry of Freedom* by James M. McPherson

Webster criticized northern abolitionists and southerners who talked of secession.

A compromise was enacted that year and seemed to settle most disputes between free and slave states. It achieved the majority of Clay's proposals. With the **Compromise of 1850**, California was able to enter the Union as a free state. The rest of the Mexican Cession was divided into two territories—Utah and New Mexico—where the question of whether to allow slavery would be decided by popular sovereignty.

Texas agreed to give up its land claims in New Mexico in exchange for financial aid from the federal government. The compromise outlawed the slave trade in the District of Columbia and established a new fugitive slave law.

READING CHECK **Analyzing** How was Texas affected by the Compromise of 1850?

Fugitive Slave Act

The newly passed **Fugitive Slave Act** made it a crime to help runaway slaves and allowed officials to arrest those slaves in free areas. Slaveholders were permitted to take suspected fugitives to U.S. commissioners, who decided their fate.

Details of the Fugitive Slave Act

Slaveholders could use testimony from white witnesses, but enslaved African Americans accused of being fugitives could not testify. Nor could people who hid or helped a runaway slave—they faced six months in jail and a $1,000 fine. Commissioners who rejected a slaveholder's claim earned $5 while those who returned suspected fugitives to slaveholders earned $10. Clearly, the commissioners benefited from helping slaveholders.

Reactions to the Fugitive Slave Act

Enforcement of the Fugitive Slave Act began immediately. In September 1850—the same month the law was passed—federal marshals arrested African American James Hamlet. They returned him to a slaveholder in

John C. Calhoun was weak and near death. He had his speech in support of slavery read to the Senate for him.

Primary Source

SPEECH

Southern View of the Compromise of 1850

John C. Calhoun from South Carolina wrote a speech saying that the proposed compromise did not go far enough to satisfy the South.

> "I have, senators, believed from the first that the agitation of the subject of slavery would, if not prevented by some timely and effective measure, end in disunion ... The South asks for justice, simple justice, and less she ought not to take. She has no compromise to offer but the Constitution, and no concession or surrender to make."

Agitation means "unrest."

Calhoun believes the South's position was supported by the Constitution.

ANALYSIS SKILL **ANALYZING PRIMARY SOURCES**

Why did Calhoun urge southern senators to vote against the compromise?

Primary Source

PHOTOGRAPH

A Fugitive Slave Convention

The Fugitive Slave Act enraged abolitionists. To protest the new law, they held many meetings to publicly denounce it. One such meeting was held in 1850 in the small town of Cazenovia in central New York, a center for abolitionist activity. About 2,000 people—including many former slaves—attended the convention. They listened to speeches, made plans, and raised their voices for freedom. This photo was a point of pride for the delegates, but it also was used by opponents of the movement as a symbol of the poor morals of abolitionists: Not only were whites allowed to mix with African Americans, women and men were allowed to mix as well. This angered many people.

ANALYSIS SKILL **ANALYZING PRIMARY SOURCES**

Why would the abolitionists want a photograph of their convention?

Maryland, although he had lived in New York City for three years.

Thousands of northern African Americans fled to Canada in fear. In the 10 years after Congress passed the Fugitive Slave Act, some 343 fugitive slave cases were reviewed. The accused fugitives were declared free in only 11 cases.

The Fugitive Slave Act upset northerners, who were uncomfortable with the commissioners' power. Northerners disliked the idea of a trial without a jury. They also disapproved of commissioners' higher fees for returning slaves. Most were horrified that some free African Americans had been captured and sent to the South.

Most northerners opposed to the Act peacefully resisted, but violence did erupt. In 1854 **Anthony Burns**, a fugitive slave from Virginia, was arrested in Boston. Abolitionists used force while trying to rescue him from jail, killing a deputy marshal. A federal ship was ordered to return Burns to Virginia after his trial. Many people in the North, particularly in Massachusetts, were outraged. The event persuaded many to join the abolitionist cause.

READING CHECK **Drawing Conclusions**

What concerns did northerners have about the Fugitive Slave Act?

Antislavery Literature

Abolitionists in the North used the stories of fugitive slaves like James Hamlet and Anthony Burns to gain sympathy for their cause. Slave narratives also educated people about their hardships.

Fiction also informed people about the evils of slavery. ***Uncle Tom's Cabin***, the antislavery novel written by **Harriet Beecher Stowe**, spoke out powerfully against slavery. Stowe, the daughter of Connecticut minister Lyman Beecher, moved to Ohio when she was 21. There she met fugitive slaves and learned about the cruelties of slavery. The Fugitive Slave Act greatly angered Stowe. She decided to write a book that would educate northerners about the realities of slavery.

Uncle Tom's Cabin was published in 1852. The main character, a kindly enslaved African American named Tom, is taken from his wife and sold "down the river" in Louisiana. Tom becomes the slave of cruel Simon Legree. In a rage, Legree has Tom beaten to death.

The novel electrified the nation and sparked outrage in the South. Louisa McCord, a famous southern writer, questioned the "foul imagination which could invent such scenes."

Within a decade, more than 2 million copies of *Uncle Tom's Cabin* had been sold in the United States. The book's popularity caused one northerner to remark that Stowe and her book had created "two millions of abolitionists." Stowe later wrote *A Key to Uncle Tom's Cabin* to answer those who had criticized her book.

The impact of Stowe's book is suggested by her reported meeting with Abraham Lincoln in 1862, a year after the start of the Civil War. Lincoln supposedly said to Stowe that she was "the little lady who made this big war." Her book is still widely read today as a source of information about the harsh realities of slavery.

READING CHECK **Identifying Cause and Effect** Why did abolitionists use antislavery literature to promote their cause, and what effect did it have on the slavery debate?

SUMMARY AND PREVIEW The United States experienced increasing disagreement over the issue of slavery. The Compromise of 1850 and the Fugitive Slave Act tried to address these disagreements with legislation. In the next section you will read about another disputed law concerning slavery, the Kansas-Nebraska Act, and the violence it sparked.

Section 1 Assessment

go.hrw.com
Online Quiz
KEYWORD: SC7 HP15

Reviewing Ideas, Terms, and People

1. a. **Describe** What ideas did the **Free-Soil Party** promote?
   b. **Predict** What are some possible results of the growing sectional debate over slavery?
2. a. **Describe** What were the major points of the **Compromise of 1850**?
   b. **Contrast** What differing opinions emerged toward Henry Clay's proposed compromise?
3. a. **Identify** What were the effects of the **Fugitive Slave Act**?
   b. **Draw Conclusions** Why did some Americans believe the Fugitive Slave Act was unfair?
4. a. **Identify** What are three examples of antislavery literature?
   b. **Elaborate** Do you think literature was an effective tool against slavery? Why or why not?

Critical Thinking

5. **Evaluating** Review your notes on the debate over slavery. Then evaluate how the Compromise of 1850, the Fugitive Slave Act, and antislavery literature affected the slavery debate. Use a graphic organizer like the one below.

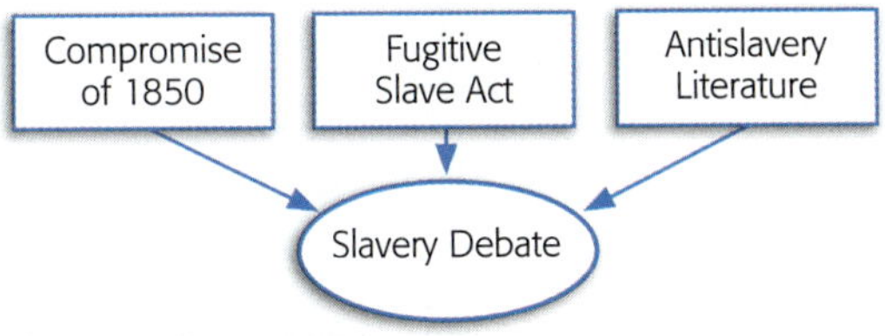

FOCUS ON WRITING

6. **Taking Notes on the Debate over Slavery** Make some notes on the Wilmot Proviso, the Free-Soil Party, the Compromise of 1850, and the Fugitive Slave Act. Decide how your character feels about each of these. How do the Compromise of 1850 and the Fugitive Slave Act affect your character?

Antislavery Literature
from Uncle Tom's Cabin

GUIDED READING

WORD HELP

conceive imagine
desolate alone
forlorn unhappy
slacking slowing down
thither there

❶ ***What detail tells you how long Eliza has walked up to this point?***

❷ ***Why do you think she chooses that escape route?***

by Harriet Beecher Stowe (1811–1896)

About the Reading *Published nine years before the outbreak of the Civil War,* Uncle Tom's Cabin *focused the nation's attention on the cruelties of slavery. In the following section, Stowe describes how a slave named Eliza is trying to escape to save her son from being sold.*

AS YOU READ **Look for details that appeal to your feelings.**

It is impossible to conceive of a human creature more wholly desolate and forlorn than Eliza when she turned her footsteps from Uncle Tom's cabin . . .

The boundaries of the farm, the grove, the wood lot passed by her dizzily as she walked on; and still she went, leaving one familiar object after another, slacking not, pausing not, till reddening daylight found her many a long mile from all traces of any familiar objects upon the open highway. ❶

She had often been, with her mistress, to visit some connections in the little town of T—, not far from the Ohio River, and knew the road well. ❷ To go thither, to escape across the Ohio River, were the first hurried outlines of her plan of escape; beyond that she could only hope in God . . .

CONNECTING LITERATURE TO HISTORY

1. **Slaves had no legal rights. They were considered to be property, not human beings.** How do the actions and description in this passage contradict these ideas about slaves?

2. **Frederick Douglass, Sojourner Truth, and other former slaves wrote narratives about their experiences. Yet these true stories did not have as much impact as Stowe's novel.** Why do you think this fictional story about slavery had more impact than true slave narratives?

Trouble in Kansas

SECTION 2

If YOU were there...

You live on a New England farm in 1855. You often think about moving West. But the last few harvests have been bad, and you can't afford it. Now the Emigrant Aid Society offers to help you get to Kansas. To bring in antislavery voters like you, they'll give you a wagon, livestock, and farm machines. Still, you know that Kansas might be dangerous.

Would you decide to risk settling in Kansas?

BUILDING BACKGROUND The argument over the extension of slavery grew stronger and more bitter. It dominated American politics in the mid-1800s. Laws that tried to find compromises ended by causing more violence. The bloodiest battleground of this period was in Kansas.

What You Will Learn...

Main Ideas

1. The debate over the expansion of slavery influenced the election of 1852.
2. The Kansas-Nebraska Act allowed voters to allow or prohibit slavery.
3. Pro-slavery and antislavery groups clashed violently in what became known as "Bleeding Kansas."

The Big Idea

The Kansas-Nebraska Act heightened tensions in the conflict over slavery.

Key Terms and People

Franklin Pierce, *p. 483*
Stephen Douglas, *p. 484*
Kansas-Nebraska Act, *p. 485*
Pottawatomie Massacre, *p. 487*
Charles Sumner, *p. 487*
Preston Brooks, *p. 487*

TAKING NOTES As you read, take notes on Stephen Douglas's plan for a railroad to the Pacific Ocean, southern congressmembers' views of his plan, and the resulting Kansas-Nebraska Act. Write details about each in a graphic organizer like the one shown below.

Douglas's plan	
Southern Congress members' reaction	

→

Kansas-Nebraska Act

Election of 1852

Four leading candidates for the Democratic presidential nomination emerged in 1852. It became clear that none of them would win a majority of votes. Frustrated delegates at the Democratic National Convention turned to **Franklin Pierce**, a little-known politician from New Hampshire. Pierce promised to honor the Compromise

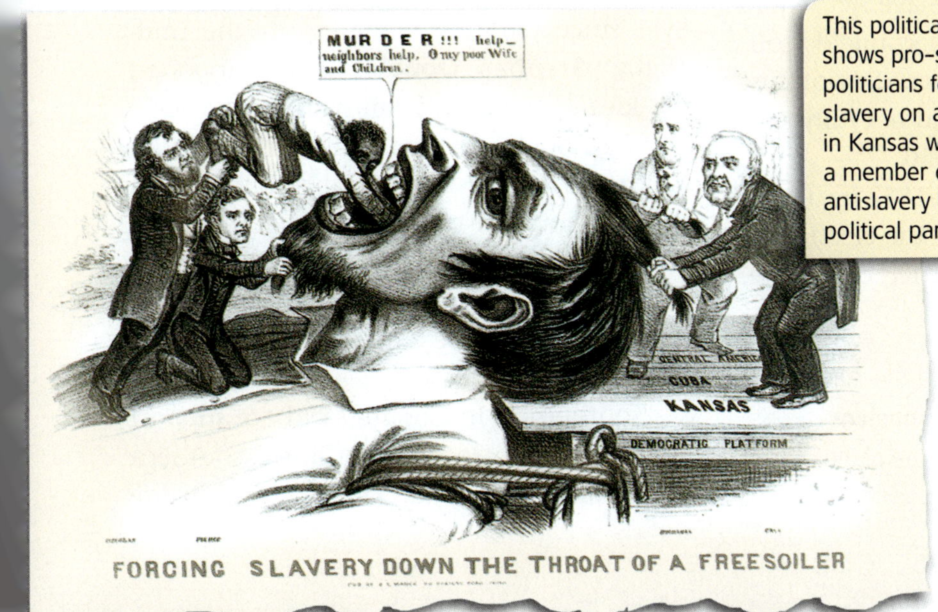

This political cartoon shows pro-slavery politicians forcing slavery on a settler in Kansas who is a member of the antislavery Free-Soil political party.

From Compromise to Conflict

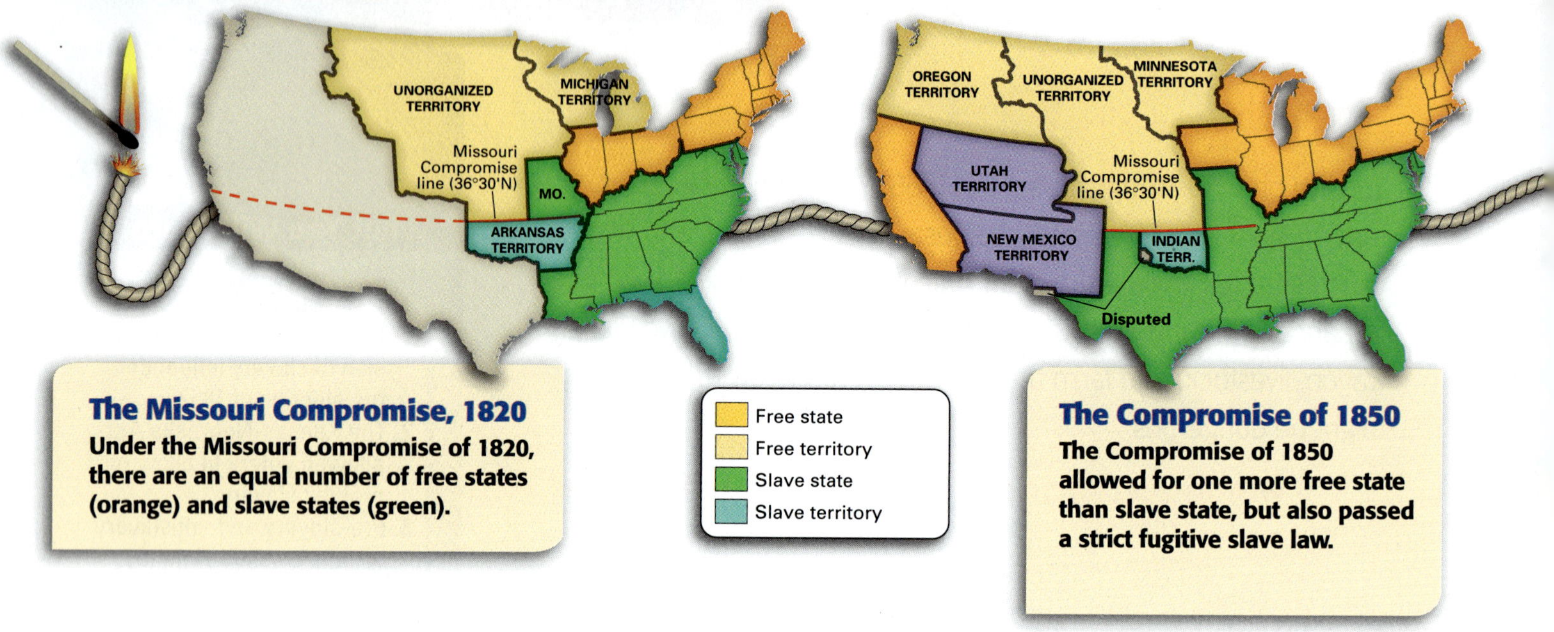

The Missouri Compromise, 1820
Under the Missouri Compromise of 1820, there are an equal number of free states (orange) and slave states (green).

The Compromise of 1850
The Compromise of 1850 allowed for one more free state than slave state, but also passed a strict fugitive slave law.

of 1850 and the Fugitive Slave Act. Therefore, southerners trusted Pierce on the issue of slavery.

FOCUS ON READING
What facts and what opinions are mentioned in this paragraph?

The opposing Whigs also held their convention in 1852. In other presidential elections, they had nominated well-known former generals such as William Henry Harrison and Zachary Taylor. This had been a good strategy, as both men had won. The Whigs decided to choose another war hero. They passed over the current president, Millard Fillmore, because they believed that his strict enforcement of the Fugitive Slave Act would cost votes. Instead, they chose Winfield Scott, a Mexican War hero. Southerners did not trust Scott, however, because he had not fully supported the Compromise of 1850.

Pierce won the election of 1852 by a large margin. Many Whigs viewed the election as a painful defeat, not just for their candidate, but for their party.

READING CHECK **Drawing Conclusions** What issues determined the outcome of the presidential election of 1852?

The Kansas-Nebraska Act

In his inaugural address, President Pierce expressed his hope that the slavery issue had been put to rest "and that no sectional . . . excitement may again threaten the durability [stability] of our institutions." Less than a year later, however, a proposal to build a railroad to the West coast helped revive the slavery controversy and opened a new period of sectional conflict.

Douglas and the Railroad

Ever since entering Congress in the mid-1840s, **Stephen Douglas** had supported the idea of building a railroad to the Pacific Ocean. Douglas favored a line running from Chicago. The first step toward building such a railroad would be organizing what remained of the Louisiana Purchase into a federal territory. The Missouri Compromise required that this land be free territory and eventually free states.

Southerners in Congress did not support Douglas's plan, recommending a southern route for the railroad. Their preferred line

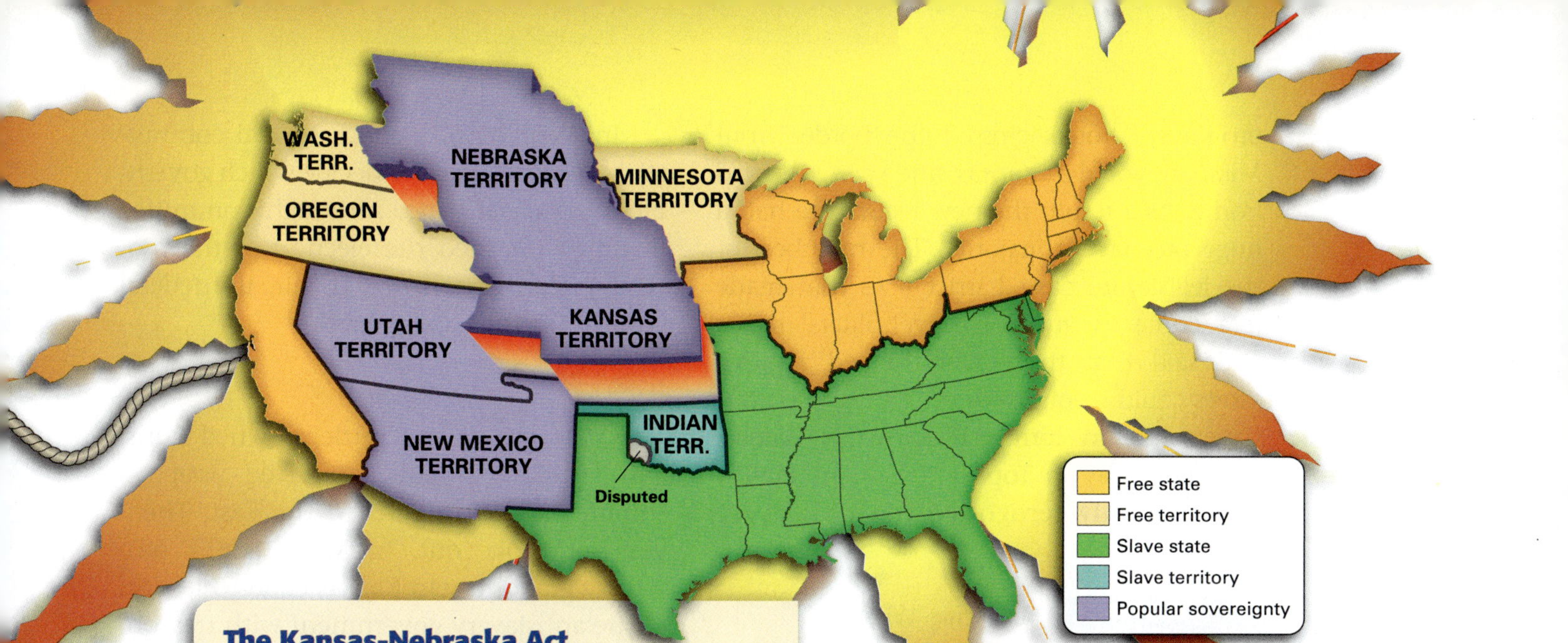

The Kansas-Nebraska Act

As a result of the Kansas-Nebraska Act, the question of slavery is to be decided by popular sovereignty—by the people who vote in the elections there—in the newly organized territories of Kansas and Nebraska. The act sparked violent conflict between pro-slavery and antislavery groups.

GEOGRAPHY SKILLS **INTERPRETING MAPS**

1. **Region** In what part of the United States were the slave states located?
2. **Place** What free state was added with the Compromise of 1850?

ran from New Orleans, across Texas and New Mexico Territory, to southern California. Determined to have the railroad start in Chicago, Douglas asked a few key southern senators to support his plan. They agreed to do so if the new territory west of Missouri was opened to slavery.

Two New Territories

In January 1854, Douglas introduced what became the **Kansas-Nebraska Act**, a plan that would divide the remainder of the Louisiana Purchase into two territories—Kansas and Nebraska—and allow the people in each territory to decide on the question of slavery. The act would eliminate the Missouri Compromise's restriction on slavery north of the 36° 30′ line.

Antislavery northerners were outraged by the **implications**. Some believed the proposal was part of a terrible plot to turn free territory into a "dreary region . . . inhabited by masters and slaves." All across the North, citizens attended protest meetings and sent anti-Nebraska petitions to Congress.

Even so, with strong southern support—and with Douglas and President Pierce pressuring their fellow Democrats to vote for it—the measure passed both houses of Congress and was signed into law on May 30, 1854. Lost amid all the controversy over the territorial bill was Douglas's proposed railroad to the Pacific Ocean. Congress would not approve the construction of such a railroad until 1862.

Kansas Divided

Antislavery and pro-slavery groups rushed their supporters to Kansas. One of the people who spoke out strongly against slavery in Kansas was Senator Seward.

> "Gentlemen of the Slave States . . . I accept [your challenge] in . . . the cause of freedom. We will engage in competition for . . . Kansas, and God give the victory to the side which is stronger in numbers as it is in right."
>
> —William Henry Seward, quoted in *The Impending Crisis, 1848–1861* by David M. Potter

Elections for the Kansas territorial legislature were held in March 1855. Almost 5,000

ACADEMIC VOCABULARY

implications things that are inferred or deduced

pro-slavery voters crossed the border from Missouri, voted in Kansas, and then returned home. As a result, the new legislature had a huge pro-slavery majority. The members of the legislature passed strict laws that made it a crime to question slaveholders' rights and said that those who helped fugitive slaves could be put to death. In protest, antislavery Kansans formed their own legislature 25 miles away in Topeka. President Pierce, however, only recognized the pro-slavery legislature.

READING CHECK **Analyzing** Why did northerners dislike the Kansas-Nebraska Act?

Bleeding Kansas

By early 1856 Kansas had two opposing governments, and the population was angry. Settlers had moved to Kansas to homestead in peace, but the controversy over slavery began to affect everyone.

In April 1856, a congressional committee arrived in Kansas to decide which government was legitimate. Although committee members declared the election of the pro-slavery legislature to be unfair, the federal government did not agree.

Attack on Lawrence

The new pro-slavery settlers owned guns, and antislavery settlers received weapons shipments from friends in the East. Then, violence broke out. In May 1856 a pro-slavery grand jury in Kansas charged leaders of the antislavery government with treason. About 800 men rode to the city of Lawrence to arrest the antislavery leaders, but they had fled. The posse took its anger out on Lawrence by setting fires, looting buildings, and destroying presses used to print antislavery newspapers. One man was killed in the pro-slavery attack that became known as the Sack of Lawrence.

John Brown's Response

Abolitionist John Brown was from New England, but he and some of his sons had moved to Kansas in 1855. The Sack of Lawrence made him determined to "fight fire with fire" and to "strike terror in the hearts of the pro-slavery people." On the night of May 24, 1856, along Pottawatomie Creek,

"Bleeding Kansas"

Abolitionists and pro-slavery forces clashed in Kansas, killing many people. Shown here is a group of abolitionists who took the law into their own hands to free one of their group from prison.

Why might these men have fought against slavery?

John Doy was imprisoned for his abolitionist activities but was freed by other abolitionists.

Brown and his men killed five pro-slavery men in Kansas in what became known as the **Pottawatomie Massacre**. Brown and his men dragged the pro-slavery men out of their cabins and killed them with swords. The abolitionist band managed to escape capture. Brown declared that his actions had been ordered by God.

Kansas collapsed into civil war, and about 200 people were killed. The events in "Bleeding Kansas" became national front-page stories. In September 1856, a new territorial governor arrived and began to restore order.

Brooks Attacks Sumner

Congress also reacted to the violence of the Sack of Lawrence. Senator **Charles Sumner** of Massachusetts criticized pro-slavery people in Kansas and personally insulted Andrew Pickens Butler, a pro-slavery senator from South Carolina. Representative **Preston Brooks**, a relative of Butler's, responded strongly.

On May 22, 1856, Brooks used a walking cane to beat Sumner unconscious in the Senate chambers. Dozens of southerners sent Brooks new canes, but northerners were outraged and called the attacker "Bully Brooks." Brooks only had to pay a $300 fine to the federal court. It took Sumner three years before he was well enough to return to the Senate.

The cartoon above shows Preston Brooks beating Charles Sumner with his cane. Sumner's only protection is a quill pen symbolically representing the law.

READING CHECK **Summarizing** What were some of the results of the intense division in Kansas?

SUMMARY AND PREVIEW The Kansas-Nebraska Act produced a national uproar. In the next section you will read about divisions in political parties.

Section 2 Assessment

go.hrw.com
Online Quiz
KEYWORD: SC7 HP15

Reviewing Ideas, Terms, and People

1. a. **Identify** What issues influenced the outcome of the election of 1852?
   b. **Draw Conclusions** Why did northern and southern Democrats support **Franklin Pierce**?
2. a. **Recall** What did the **Kansas-Nebraska Act** do?
   b. **Explain** Why did antislavery and pro-slavery groups encourage people to move to Kansas?
   c. **Evaluate** Would you have supported or opposed the Kansas-Nebraska Act? Why?
3. a. **Describe** What was the **Pottawatomie Massacre**?
   b. **Analyze** How did **Charles Sumner**'s views on "Bleeding Kansas" create conflict?
   c. **Elaborate** Do you think **Preston Brooks**'s punishment was reasonable? Why or why not?

Critical Thinking

4. **Sequencing** Review your notes on the Kansas-Nebraska Act. Then copy the graphic organizer shown below and use it to show how the act and later events led to violence in Kansas.

1.
2.
3.
4.
5. Violence in Kansas

Focus on Writing

5. **Taking Notes on the Trouble in Kansas** Make some notes on the election of 1852, the Kansas-Nebraska Act, and the events in Kansas. Decide how your character feels about each of these. How do these events affect your character?

SECTION 3

Political Divisions

What You Will Learn...

Main Ideas

1. Political parties in the United States underwent change due to the movement to expand slavery.
2. The *Dred Scott* decision created further division over the issue of slavery.
3. The Lincoln-Douglas debates brought much attention to the conflict over slavery.

The Big Idea

The split over the issue of slavery intensified due to political division and judicial decisions.

Key Terms and People

Republican Party, *p. 488*
James Buchanan, *p. 488*
John C. Frémont, *p. 489*
Dred Scott, *p. 489*
Roger B. Taney, *p. 490*
Abraham Lincoln, *p. 490*
Lincoln-Douglas debates, *p. 491*
Freeport Doctrine, *p. 492*

TAKING NOTES As you read, take notes on the effects of political divisions and the *Dred Scott* case on the debate over slavery. Write your notes in a graphic organizer like the one below.

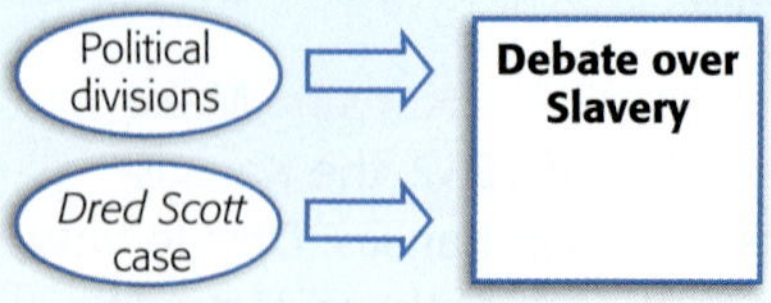

If YOU were there...

You are traveling through Michigan in July 1854. As you pass through the town of Jackson, you see a crowd of several hundred people gathered under the trees. You join them and find that it is a political rally. Antislavery supporters from different parties are meeting to form a new political party. Speakers promise to fight slavery "until the contest be terminated."

How do you think this new party will affect American politics?

BUILDING BACKGROUND The slavery question continued to divide the country and lead to violence. The issue not only dominated American politics in the mid-1800s but also brought changes in the makeup of American political parties.

Political Parties Undergo Change

Democrat Stephen Douglas had predicted that the Kansas-Nebraska Act would "raise a . . . storm." He was right. The Kansas-Nebraska Act brought the slavery issue back into the national spotlight. Some Whigs, Democrats, Free-Soilers, and abolitionists joined in 1854 to form the **Republican Party**, a political party united against the spread of slavery in the West.

Democrats were in trouble. Those who supported the Kansas-Nebraska Act were not re-elected. The Whig Party also fell apart when northern and southern Whigs refused to work together. A senator from Connecticut complained, "The Whig Party has been killed off . . . by that miserable Nebraska business." Some Whigs and Democrats joined the American Party, also known as the Know-Nothing Party. At the party's convention, delegates argued over slavery, then chose former president Millard Fillmore as their candidate for the election of 1856.

The Democrats knew they could not choose a strong supporter of the Kansas-Nebraska Act, such as President Pierce or Senator Douglas. They nominated **James Buchanan** of Pennsylvania. Buchanan had a great deal of political experience as Polk's secretary of state. Most importantly, he had been in Great Britain as ambassador during the Kansas-Nebraska Act dispute and had not been involved in the debate.

At their first nominating convention, the Republicans chose explorer **John C. Frémont** as their candidate. He had little political experience, but he stood against the spread of slavery. The public saw Republicans as a single-issue party. They had almost no supporters outside of the free states.

On election day, Buchanan won 14 of the 15 slave states and became the new president. Frémont won 11 of the 16 free states. Fillmore won only one state—Maryland. Buchanan had won the election.

READING CHECK **Summarizing** What were the major political parties in the election of 1856, and who was the candidate for each party?

Dred Scott Decision

Just two days after Buchanan became president, the Supreme Court issued a historic ruling about slavery. News of the decision threw the country back into crisis. The Court reviewed and decided the **complex** case involving an enslaved man named **Dred Scott**.

ACADEMIC VOCABULARY
complex difficult, not simple

Dred Scott Sues for Freedom

Dred Scott was the slave of Dr. John Emerson, an army surgeon who lived in St. Louis, Missouri. In the 1830s, Emerson had taken Scott on tours of duty in Illinois and the Wisconsin Territory. After they returned to Missouri, the doctor died, and Scott became the slave of Emerson's widow. In 1846 Scott sued for his freedom in the Missouri state courts, arguing that he had become free when he lived in free territory. Though a lower court ruled in

SUPREME COURT DECISIONS

Dred Scott v. *Sandford* (1857)

Background of the Case Born a slave in Virginia, Dred Scott moved with his slaveholder to the free state of Illinois and then to the Wisconsin Territory. After returning to the South, Scott sued for his freedom. He claimed that because he had lived in a state that banned slavery, he was no longer a slave.

The Court's Ruling
The Court ruled that African Americans, whether free or slave, were not considered citizens of the United States, and therefore had no right to sue in federal court. It also decided that the Missouri Compromise was unconstitutional.

The Court's Reasoning
Chief Justice Roger B. Taney wrote in the majority opinion that the Court did not believe that African Americans were included in the Constitution's definition of citizens and that they "had no rights which the white man was bound to respect." Addressing a side issue in the case, the opinion also stated that Congress could not outlaw slavery in the territories. This struck down the Missouri Compromise, which had made slavery illegal in territories north of the 36°30′ dividing line.

Why It Matters
The *Dred Scott* case was seen as a setback to abolitionist ideas against slavery. It reduced the status of free African Americans and upheld the view of slaves as property without rights or protection under the Constitution. It also took from Congress the power to ban slavery in its territories, which would aid the spread of slavery in new states. Because of its pro-slavery decision, the reputation of the Court suffered greatly in parts of the North.

ANALYSIS SKILL **ANALYZING INFORMATION**

1. **Why do you think the Court ruled that African Americans had no access to federal courts?**
2. **How did this case affect abolitionist efforts?**

A Growing Conflict

QUICK FACTS

Causes of Conflict

- Failure of Missouri Compromise
- Failure of Compromise of 1850
- Kansas-Nebraska Act
- *Dred Scott* decision

Short-Term Effects

- Political battles
- Sectional differences
- "Bleeding Kansas"
- Lincoln-Douglas debates

Long-Term Effect

- Civil War

his favor, the Missouri Supreme Court overturned this ruling.

Scott's case reached the U.S. Supreme Court 11 years later, in 1857. The justices—a majority of whom were from the South—had three key issues before them. First, the Court had to rule on whether Scott was a citizen. Only citizens could sue in federal court. Second, the Court had to decide if his time living on free soil made him free. Third, the Court had to determine the constitutionality of prohibiting slavery in parts of the Louisiana Purchase.

FOCUS ON NORTH CAROLINA

In 1857 North Carolinian Hinton Rowan Helper, an antislavery advocate, published a book called *The Impending Crisis of the South.* It attacked slavery on economic grounds and was praised by many northerners. Many southerners, on the other hand, accused Helper of betraying the South.

The Supreme Court's Ruling

Chief Justice **Roger B. Taney** (TAW-nee), himself from a slaveholding family in Maryland, wrote the majority opinion in the *Dred Scott* decision in March 1857. First, he addressed the issue of Dred Scott's citizenship. Taney said the nation's founders believed that African Americans "had no rights which a white man was bound to respect." He therefore concluded that all African Americans, whether slave or free, were not citizens under the U.S. Constitution. Thus, Dred Scott did not have the right to file suit in federal court.

Taney also ruled on the other issues before the Court. As to whether Scott's residence on free soil made him free, Taney flatly said it did not. Because Scott had returned to the slave state of Missouri, the chief justice said, "his *status,* as free or slave, depended on the laws of Missouri."

Finally, Taney declared the Missouri Compromise restriction on slavery north of 36°30′ to be unconstitutional. He pointed out that the Fifth Amendment said no one could "be deprived of life, liberty, or property without due process of law." Because slaves were considered property, Congress could not prohibit someone from taking slaves into a federal territory. Under this ruling, Congress had no right to ban slavery in any federal territory.

Most white southerners cheered this decision. It "covers every question regarding slavery and settles it in favor of the South," reported a Georgia newspaper. Another newspaper, the New Orleans *Picayune,* assured its readers that the ruling put "the whole basis of the . . . Republican organization under the ban of law."

The ruling stunned many northerners. The Republicans were particularly upset because their platform in 1856 had argued that Congress held the right to ban slavery in the federal territories. Now the nation's highest court had ruled that Congress did not have this right.

Indeed, some northerners feared that the spread of slavery would not stop with the federal territories. Illinois lawyer **Abraham Lincoln** warned that a future Court ruling, or what he called "the next *Dred Scott* decision," would prohibit states from banning slavery.

Primary Source

SPEECH

A House Divided

In 1858 Abraham Lincoln gave a passionate speech to Illinois Republicans about the dangers of the disagreement over slavery. Some considered it a call for war.

This line is a paraphrase of a line in the Bible.

"In my opinion, it [disagreement over slavery] will not cease [stop], until a crisis shall have been reached and passed. "A house divided against itself cannot stand." I believe this government cannot endure permanently half slave and half free. I do not expect the Union to be dissolved—I do not expect the house to fall—but I do expect it will cease to be divided."

—Abraham Lincoln,
quoted in *Abraham Lincoln: Speeches and Writings 1832–1858*
edited by Don E. Fehrenbacher

Lincoln expresses confidence that the Union will survive.

ANALYSIS SKILL **ANALYZING PRIMARY SOURCES**

What do you think Lincoln meant by "crisis"?

"We shall *lie down* pleasantly dreaming that the people of *Missouri* are on the verge of [close to] making their state *free*; and we shall *awake* to the *reality,* instead, that the 90 Supreme Court has made *Illinois* a *slave state.*"

—Abraham Lincoln, quoted in *The Collected Works of Abraham Lincoln*, edited by Roy P. Basler

READING CHECK **Summarizing** What were the major rulings of the *Dred Scott* decision?

Lincoln-Douglas Debates

In 1858 Illinois Republicans nominated Abraham Lincoln for the U.S. Senate. His opponent was Democrat Stephen Douglas, who had represented Illinois in the Senate since 1847. Lincoln challenged Douglas in what became the historic **Lincoln-Douglas debates**.

In each debate, Lincoln stressed that the central issue of the campaign was the spread of slavery in the West. He said that the Democrats were trying to spread slavery across the nation.

Lincoln talked about the *Dred Scott* decision. He said that African Americans were "entitled to all the natural rights" listed in the Declaration of Independence, specifically mentioning "the right to life, liberty, and the pursuit of happiness." However, Lincoln believed that African Americans were not necessarily the social or political equals of whites. Hoping to cost Lincoln votes, Douglas charged that Lincoln "thinks that the Negro is his brother . . ."

Douglas also criticized Lincoln for saying that the nation could not remain "half slave and half free." Douglas said that the statement revealed a Republican desire to make every state a free state. This, he warned, would only lead to "a dissolution [destruction] of the Union" and "warfare between the North and the South."

At the second debate, in the northern Illinois town of Freeport, Illinois, Lincoln pressed Douglas on the apparent contradiction between the Democrats' belief in popu-

THE IMPACT TODAY

Today political debates are televised and can be seen around the world.

Lincoln-Douglas Debates

Lincoln ran for the U.S. Senate in Illinois against Douglas in 1858. The two men debated seven times at various locations around the state. Lincoln lost the election but gained national recognition.

Abraham Lincoln

Stephen Douglas

lar sovereignty and the *Dred Scott* decision. Lincoln asked Douglas to explain how, if Congress could not ban slavery from a federal territory, Congress could allow the citizens of that territory to ban it.

Douglas responded that it did not matter what the Supreme Court decided about slavery. He argued that "the people have the lawful means to introduce it or exclude it as they please, for the reason that slavery cannot exist a day or an hour anywhere, unless it is supported by local police regulations."

This notion that the police would enforce the voters' decision if it contradicted the Supreme Court's decision in the Dred Scott case became known as the **Freeport Doctrine**.

The Freeport Doctrine put the slavery question back in the hands of American citizens. It helped Douglas win the Senate seat. Lincoln, while not victorious, made a strong, important leader of the Republican Party.

READING CHECK **Drawing Inferences** Why did Abraham Lincoln make slavery's expansion the central issue of the Lincoln-Douglas debates?

SUMMARY AND PREVIEW The *Dred Scott* decision and the Lincoln-Douglas debates dealt with the conflict over slavery in the western territories. In the next section you will read about how the conflict broke apart the Union.

Section 3 Assessment

go.hrw.com
Online Quiz
KEYWORD: SC7 HP15

Reviewing Ideas, Terms, and People

1. a. **Identify** What was the major issue of the newly formed **Republican Party**?
   b. **Draw Conclusions** How did the Kansas-Nebraska Act affect political parties?
   c. **Elaborate** Why do you think **James Buchanan** won the election of 1856?
2. a. **Identify** Who was **Roger B. Taney**, and why was he important?
   b. **Draw Conclusions** How did the *Dred Scott* decision affect the Missouri Compromise and the expansion of slavery?
   c. **Predict** What problems might result from the Supreme Court's ruling in the *Dred Scott* case?
3. a. **Recall** What was the major issue of the **Lincoln-Douglas debates**?
   b. **Make Inferences** Despite his loss in the election, how did Lincoln become the leader of the Republican Party?

Critical Thinking

4. **Identifying Points of View** Review your notes on political divisions and the Dred Scott decision. Then copy the graphic organizer below and use it to identify the views of Abraham Lincoln and Stephen Douglas on slavery.

Lincoln		Douglas
	vs.	

FOCUS ON WRITING

5. **Taking Notes on the Political Divisions** Make some notes on the Republican Party, the *Dred Scott* decision, and the Lincoln-Douglas debates. Decide how your character feels about each of these. How do these events affect your character?

The Nation Divides

SECTION 4

If YOU were there...

You work for the weekly newspaper in Harpers Ferry, Virginia. You strongly oppose slavery, but you think the question ought to be resolved by laws, not bloodshed. Now your paper has sent you to interview the famous abolitionist John Brown in prison. His raids in "Bleeding Kansas" killed several people. Now he is in jail for attacking a federal arsenal and taking weapons.

What questions would you ask John Brown?

BUILDING BACKGROUND Unpopular compromises and court decisions deepened the divisions between pro-slavery and antislavery advocates. The Lincoln-Douglas debates attracted more attention to the issue. As the disagreements grew, violence increased, though many Americans hoped to avoid it. But it was too late to keep the nation unified.

Raid on Harpers Ferry

In 1858 John Brown tried to start an uprising. He wanted to attack the federal arsenal in Virginia and seize weapons there. He planned to arm local slaves. Brown expected to kill or take hostage white southerners who stood in his way. He urged abolitionists to give him money so that he could support a small army. But after nearly two years, Brown's army had only about 20 men.

On the night of October 16, 1859, **John Brown's raid** began when he and his men took over the arsenal in Harpers Ferry, Virginia, in hopes of starting a slave rebellion. He sent several of his men into the countryside to get slaves to join him. However, enslaved African Americans did not come to Harpers Ferry, fearing punishment if they took part. Instead, local white southerners attacked Brown. Eight of his men and three local men were killed. Brown and some followers retreated to a firehouse.

Federal troops arrived in Harpers Ferry the following night. The next morning, Colonel Robert E. Lee ordered a squad of marines to storm the firehouse. In a matter of seconds, the marines killed two more of Brown's men and captured the rest—including Brown.

What You Will Learn...

Main Ideas

1. John Brown's raid on Harpers Ferry intensified the disagreement between free states and slave states.
2. The outcome of the election of 1860 divided the United States.
3. The dispute over slavery led the South to secede.

The Big Idea

The United States broke apart due to the growing conflict over slavery.

Key Terms and People

John Brown's raid, *p. 493*
John C. Breckinridge, *p. 495*
Constitutional Union Party, *p. 495*
John Bell, *p. 495*
John J. Crittenden, *p. 496*
Confederate States of America, *p. 497*
Jefferson Davis, *p. 497*

TAKING NOTES Create a chart like the one below. As you read, take notes on the significance of each of the people listed in the chart and his relationship to the events of the section.

Person	Significance
John Brown	
John C. Breckinridge	
John Bell	
Abraham Lincoln	
Jefferson Davis	
John J. Crittenden	

Primary Source

SPEECH

John Brown's Last Speech

At his trial, after being pronounced guilty, John Brown spoke in his own defense about his plan to free slaves.

"I intended certainly to have made a clean thing of that matter [freeing slaves] . . . I never did intend murder or treason, or the destruction of property, or to excite or incite the slaves to rebellion, or to make insurrection [revolt] . . . Had I interfered in the manner which I admit . . . in behalf of the rich, the powerful, the intelligent, the so-called great . . . it would have been all right, and every man in this Court would have deemed it an act worthy of reward rather than punishment . . . I believe that to have interfered as I have done . . . in behalf of His despised poor, is no wrong, but right."

–John Brown,

quoted in *The Life, Trial and Execution of Captain John Brown*

Brown says he never meant to start a rebellion.

By *His*, Brown means God's.

ANALYSIS SKILL **ANALYZING PRIMARY SOURCES**

How does Brown contrast his ideas with the Court's ideas?

Brown was quickly convicted of treason, murder, and conspiracy. Some of his men received death sentences. John A. Copeland, a fugitive slave, defended his actions. "If I am dying for freedom, I could not die for a better cause." Convinced that he also would be sentenced to death, Brown delivered a memorable speech.

> "Now, if it is deemed [thought] necessary that I should forfeit [give up] my life for the furtherance of the ends of justice, and mingle [mix] my blood . . . with the blood of millions in this slave country whose rights are disregarded by wicked, cruel, and unjust enactments, I say, let it be done."
>
> —John Brown, quoted in *John Brown, 1800–1859* by Oswald Garrison Villard

As expected, the judge ordered Brown to be hanged. The sentence was carried out one month later on December 2, 1859.

Many northerners mourned John Brown's death, but some abolitionists criticized his extreme actions. Abraham Lincoln said Brown "agreed with us in thinking slavery wrong." However, Lincoln continued, "That cannot excuse violence, bloodshed, and treason."

Most southern whites—both slaveholders and non-slaveholders—felt threatened by the actions of John Brown. They worried that a "John Brown the Second" might attack. One South Carolina newspaper voiced these fears: "We are convinced the safety of the South lies only outside the present Union." Another newspaper stated that "the sooner we get out of the Union, the better."

READING CHECK **Drawing Conclusions** Why did John Brown's raid lead some southerners to talk about leaving the Union?

Election of 1860

In this climate of distrust, Americans prepared for another presidential election in 1860. The northern and southern Democrats could not agree on a candidate. Northern Democrats chose Senator Stephen Douglas. Southern Democrats backed the current vice president, **John C. Breckinridge** of Kentucky, who supported slavery in the territories.

Meanwhile, a new political party emerged. The **Constitutional Union Party** recognized "no political principles other than the Constitution of the country, the Union of the states, and the enforcement of the laws." Members of this new party met in Baltimore, Maryland, and selected **John Bell** of Tennessee as their candidate. Bell was a slaveholder, but he had opposed the Kansas-Nebraska Act in 1854.

Senator William Seward of New York was the Republicans' leading candidate at the start of their convention. But it turned out that Lincoln appealed to more party members. A moderate who was against the spread of slavery, Lincoln promised not to abolish slavery where it already existed.

Douglas, Breckinridge, and Bell each knew he might not win the election. They hoped to win enough electoral votes to prevent Lincoln from winning in the electoral college. But with a unified Republican Party behind him, Lincoln won. Although he received the highest number of votes, he won only about 40 percent of the overall popular vote.

Lincoln won 180 of 183 electoral votes in free states. Douglas had the second-highest number of popular votes, but he won only one state. He earned just 12 electoral votes. Breckinridge and Bell split electoral votes in other slave states.

The election results angered southerners. Lincoln did not campaign in their region and did not carry any southern states, but he became the next president. The election signaled that the South was losing its national political power.

READING CHECK **Analyzing** Why was Lincoln viewed by many as a moderate candidate during his campaign for the presidency?

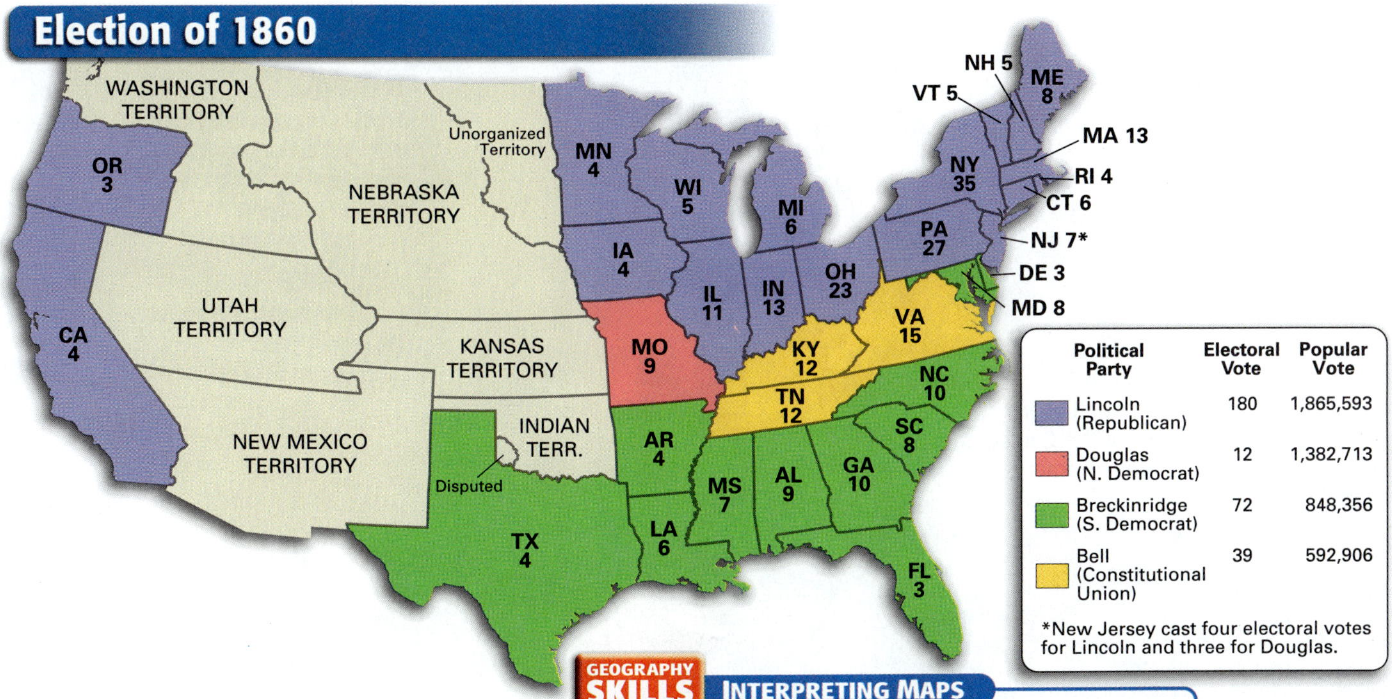

GEOGRAPHY SKILLS **INTERPRETING MAPS**

Region In which part of the country were most of the states that Lincoln won?

Source: Historical Statistics of the United States

The South Secedes

Lincoln insisted that he would not change slavery in the South. However, he said that slavery could not expand and thus would eventually die out completely. That idea angered many southerners.

FOCUS ON NORTH CAROLINA

North Carolina did not secede immediately. Debates arose between Unionists and secessionists. Unionists believed the state had a duty to try to maintain the Union with other states. Secessionists supported immediate withdrawal from the Union.

Southerners' Reactions

People in the South believed their economy and way of life would be destroyed without slave labor. They reacted immediately. Within a week of Lincoln's election, South Carolina's legislature called for a special convention. The delegates considered seccession. Southern secessionists believed that they had a right to leave the Union. They pointed out that each of the original states had voluntarily joined the Union by holding a special convention that had ratified the Constitution. Surely, they reasoned, states could leave the Union by the same process.

Critics of secession thought this argument was ridiculous. President Buchanan said the Union was not "a mere voluntary association of States, to be dissolved at pleasure by any one of the contracting parties." President-elect Abraham Lincoln agreed, saying, "No State, upon its own mere motion, can lawfully get out of the Union." Lincoln added, "They can only do so against [the] law, and by revolution."

While the South Carolina representatives were meeting in Charleston to discuss secession, Congress examined a plan to save the Union. Senator **John J. Crittenden** of Kentucky proposed a series of constitutional amendments that he believed would satisfy the South by protecting slavery. Crittenden hoped the country could avoid secession and a civil war.

Lincoln disagreed with Crittenden's plan. He believed there could be no compromise about the extension of slavery. Lincoln wrote, "The tug has to come and better now than later." A Senate committee voted on Crittenden's plan, and every Republican rejected it, as Lincoln had requested.

Jefferson Davis takes the oath of office for president of the Confederate States of America.

Rebel Government

This photograph is of the inauguration of Jefferson Davis as the president of the Confederate States of America. A former U.S. secretary of war, Davis was elected president of the confederacy in 1861.

How does this photo show the state of the southern government?

The Confederate States of America

South Carolina elected to dissolve "the union now subsisting [existing] between South Carolina and other States" on December 20, 1860. Mississippi, Florida, Alabama, Georgia, Louisiana, and Texas also seceded to form the **Confederate States of America**, also called the Confederacy. Its new constitution guaranteed citizens the right to own slaves.

Delegates from seceded states elected **Jefferson Davis** of Mississippi as president of the Confederacy. Davis had hoped to be the commanding general of Mississippi's troops. He responded to the news of his election with reluctance.

When the southern states seceded, the question of who owned federal property in the South arose. For instance, the forts in the harbor of Charleston, South Carolina, were federal property. However, Confederate president Davis and the Confederacy were ready to prevent the federal army from controlling the property.

Lincoln Takes Office

President Lincoln was inaugurated on March 4, 1861. In writing his inaugural address, Lincoln looked to many of the nation's founding documents. Referring to the idea that governments receive "their just powers from the consent of the governed," a line from the Declaration of Independence, Lincoln stated, "This country, with its institutions, belongs to the people who inhabit it. Whenever they grow weary of the existing Government, they can exercise their *constitutional* right of amending it or their *revolutionary* right to dismember [take apart] or overthrow it. I can not be ignorant of the fact that many worthy and patriotic citizens are desirous [wanting] of having the National Constitution amended . . ."

While he believed that U.S. citizens had the power to change their government through majority consent, he opposed the idea that southern states could leave the Union because they were unhappy with the government's position on slavery.

He announced in his inaugural address that he would keep all government property in the seceding states. However, he also tried to convince southerners that his government would not provoke a war. He hoped that, given time, southern states would return to the Union.

READING CHECK **Drawing Conclusions** Why did some southern states secede from the Union?

SUMMARY AND PREVIEW The secession of the southern states hinted at the violence to come. In the next chapter you will read about the Civil War.

Section 4 Assessment

go.hrw.com
Online Quiz
KEYWORD: SC7 HP15

Reviewing Ideas, Terms, and People

1. a. **Recall** Why did John Brown want to seize the federal arsenal at Harpers Ferry?
   b. **Explain** Why did some abolitionists disagree with Brown's actions?
2. a. **Identify** List the candidates in the presidential election of 1860, and what party each supported.
   b. **Predict** How might Abraham Lincoln's victory in the election of 1860 lead to future problems?
3. a. **Identify** What states made up the **Confederate States of America**?
   b. **Explain** Why did Lincoln disagree with **John J. Crittenden**'s plan to keep the Union together?
   c. **Elaborate** Do you believe that the southern states had the right to secede? Why or why not?

Critical Thinking

4. **Summarizing** Review your notes on the significant people in the section. Then copy the graphic organizer below and use it to summarize the causes of secession.

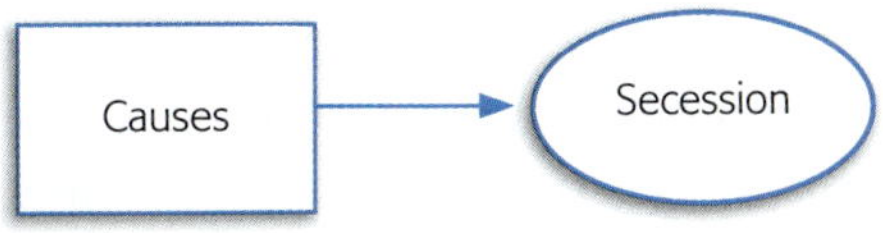

FOCUS ON WRITING

5. **Taking Notes on Secession** Make some notes on the raid on Harpers Ferry, the election of 1860, and the secession of the South. Decide how your character feels about each of these. How do these events affect your character?

Social Studies Skills

Analysis | Critical Thinking | Civic Participation | Study

North Carolina Skills
1.01 Read for literal meaning.

Assessing Primary and Secondary Sources

Define the Skill

All historical information comes from primary and secondary sources. *Primary sources* are documents written by someone who witnessed or took part in an event. They include diaries, letters, autobiographies, and newspaper reports. *Secondary sources* are accounts of events written after the events have occurred by someone who did not witness or take part in them. They retell, interpret, and summarize information from primary sources. History books and biographies are examples of secondary sources.

Historical sources often disagree. One writer's version of an event may be different from another writer's version. You must assess the reliability of a primary or secondary source in order to weigh its value to you as a source of accurate information.

Learn the Skill

Use these guidelines to analyze and evaluate primary and secondary sources.

1. Identify the nature of the material. Is it a first-hand, eyewitness account or is it based on information provided by others?
2. Evaluate the author. If the material is a secondary source, what qualifications does the author have to interpret the sources from which it came? If the material is a primary source, what was the author's connection to the event he or she is writing about?
3. Determine the audience. Was the source meant to be seen by the public? Was it meant for a friend, or for the writer alone? The intended audience can influence a source's content.
4. Determine the purpose. Even authors of primary sources can have reasons to distort the truth to suit their own purposes. Look for evidence of emotion, exaggeration, opinion, or bias that may have influenced the account.
5. Look for documentation. Look for other information or evidence that supports the source's account. Compare sources whenever possible.

Practice the Skill

The passage below concerns the attack on Lawrence, Kansas, that you read about in this chapter. The passage contains both a primary and a secondary source. The secondary account was written by John A. Garraty, a well-known historian. Review the information on page 486, analyze the passage, and answer the questions that follow.

"Sheriff Jones, at the head of an army of Missourians, marched into Lawrence. In broad daylight they threw the printing presses of two newspapers into a river. They burned down the Free State Hotel and other buildings. Antislavery Kansans seethed with rage. Here is how one eyewitness described the attack:

"Sheriff Jones, after looking at the flames rising from the hotel and saying that it was 'the happiest day of his life,' dismissed the troops and they began their lawless destruction.""

1. Did the author of the primary source likely support the attackers or the people of Lawrence? What clues in the passage suggest this?
2. For whom was the primary source likely written?
3. Which source is more reliable for information about this incident? Explain why.

CHAPTER 15 Chapter Review

HOLT
History's Impact
▶ **video series**
Review the video to answer the closing question:
What do the Tenth Amendment and the Civil Rights Act indicate about the powers of the federal and state governments?

Visual Summary

QUICK FACTS

Use the visual summary below to help you review the main ideas of the chapter.

Differing views on slavery in the North and South gradually tore the nation apart.

Reviewing Vocabulary, Terms, and People

Identify the correct term or person from the chapter that best fits each of the following descriptions.

1. belief that voters should be given the right to decide if slavery would be permitted or banned
2. chief justice of the Supreme Court who wrote the majority opinion for the *Dred Scott* decision
3. Democratic candidate for president in 1852 who promised to enforce the Compromise of 1850 and the Fugitive Slave Act
4. a fugitive slave whose arrest led to violence between government officials and abolitionists
5. Republican candidate for the presidency in 1856 who opposed the spread of slavery in the West
6. slave who sued for freedom, claiming that by living in free territory, he had earned his freedom
7. Stephen Douglas's claim that states and territories should determine the issue of slavery through popular sovereignty

Comprehension and Critical Thinking

SECTION 1 *(Pages 476–481)*

8. a. **Describe** How did literature aid the antislavery movement?
   b. **Draw Conclusions** How did the issue of slavery promote sectionalism?
   c. **Evaluate** Do you think the Compromise of 1850 was a good solution? Explain your answer.

SECTION 2 *(Pages 483–487)*

9. a. **Identify** Who were the candidates in the presidential election of 1852, and what issues did each support?
   b. **Analyze** How did the Kansas-Nebraska Act lead to growing hostility between pro-slavery and antislavery supporters?
   c. **Elaborate** Why do you think "Bleeding Kansas" produced intense controversy between many Americans?

SECTION 3 *(Pages 488–492)*

10. a. Identify Who was Dred Scott, and why was his case important?

b. Analyze How were political parties affected by the debate over slavery?

c. Elaborate Why do you think Republicans challenged Stephen Douglas's run for the Senate?

SECTION 4 *(Pages 493–497)*

11. a. Recall Why did the southern states secede, and what was the North's response?

b. Draw Conclusions Why did the results of the election of 1860 anger southerners?

c. Evaluate Do you think John Brown was right to use violence to protest slavery? Explain.

Reviewing Themes

12. Politics How did sectionalism affect American politics?

13. Society and Culture What effect did Harriet Beecher Stowe's book *Uncle Tom's Cabin* have on the debate over slavery?

Using the Internet

go.hrw.com
KEYWORD: SC7 CH15

14. Activity: Creating a Newspaper Harriet Beecher Stowe's novel and John Brown's raids were two important events that created more debate over slavery and heightened tension between sides. Enter the activity keyword and learn more about antislavery actions. Then create a newspaper with which to display your research. Remember to write from the point of view of someone from the mid-1800s.

Reading Skills

Facts, Opinions, and the Past *Use the Reading Skills taught in this chapter to answer the question about the reading selection below.*

> In 1858 John Brown tried to start an uprising. He wanted to attack the federal arsenal in Virginia and seize weapons there. He planned to arm local slaves. Brown expected to kill or take hostage white southerners who stood in his way. *(p. 493)*

15. Based on the reading selection above, which of the following statements is an opinion?

a. John Brown's raid was in 1858.

b. John Brown hated all slaveholders.

c. John Brown's raid took place in Virginia.

d. Local slaves helped John Brown.

Social Studies Skills

Assessing Primary and Secondary Sources *Use the Social Studies Skills taught in this chapter to answer the question below.*

16. Which of the following is *not* an example of a primary source used in this chapter?

a. *A People's History of the United States* by Howard Zinn

b. The Seventh of March speech by Daniel Webster

c. Abraham Lincoln's A House Divided speech

d. John Brown's last speech

FOCUS ON WRITING

17. Writing Your Autobiography Review your notes. Then write your autobiography, being sure to mention each of the events from your notes. Tell how your character heard about each event, what he or she was doing at the time, how he or she felt about the event, and how it affected him or her. What are your character's hopes and fears for the future?

CHAPTER 15 Standardized Test Practice

DIRECTIONS: Read each question and write the letter of the best response.

1 **Use the map below to answer the following question.**

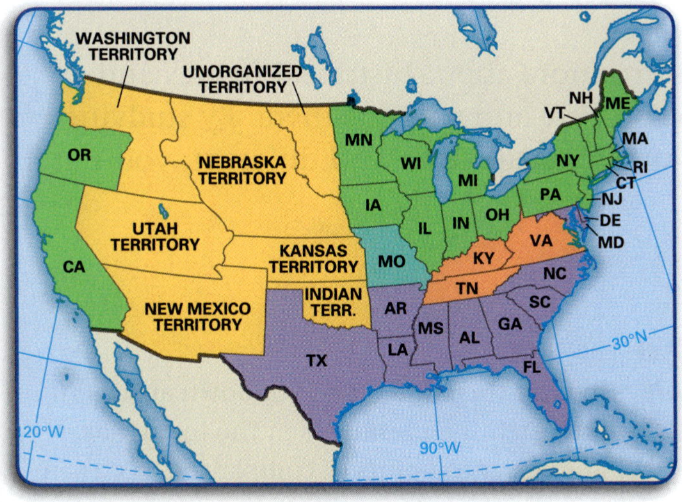

From the information in this map, you can conclude that it shows

A the provisions of the Compromise of 1850.

B the results of the election of 1860.

C the formation of the Confederacy.

D the results of the *Dred Scott* decision.

2 **Which leader was responsible for settling the dispute over the expansion of slavery that arose after the Mexican War?**

A David Wilmot

B Henry Clay

C Abraham Lincoln

D Jefferson Davis

3 **California's admission as a free state after the Mexican War aroused controversy because**

A many Californians already held slaves.

B it would upset the balance between free states and slave states.

C Mexico still claimed that California was part of Mexico's territory.

D most Californians wanted independence.

4 **Which of the following was an example of sectional differences in the United States?**

A the Lincoln-Douglas debates

B the Supreme Court's *Dred Scott* decision

C conflict in "Bleeding Kansas"

D the publication of *Uncle Tom's Cabin*

5 **Unlike most southern states, North Carolina**

A did not support slavery in the West.

B supported the election of Abraham Lincoln.

C opposed the Fugitive Slave Act.

D did not secede immediately.

6 **The Compromise of 1850 was *most* similar to what earlier compromise between free states and slave states?**

A the Great Compromise

B the Rush-Bagot Agreement

C the Northwest Ordinance

D the Missouri Compromise

7 **Examine the following passage written by a southerner before secession and then use it to answer the question below.**

> "As we sat around the long table today the talk turned to the [secession] convention, so soon to meet in Tallahassee [Florida]. Father said he considered this the most important year in the history of the South. He is for secession, and he does not think that war will necessarily [certainly] follow. Brother Junius is a strong Union man, and he thinks we will certainly have war. If the South secedes, the North will fight to keep us. If we do not secede, all property rights will be taken from us and we will be forced to fight to hold our own."
>
> –Susan Bradford, adapted from *Heroines of Dixie,* edited by Katharine Jones

Document-Based Question **What might be the outcome of this convention? Why?**

Writing Workshop

Comparing People and Events

Assignment

Write a paper comparing and contrasting one of the following: (1) America before and after the Industrial Revolution, (2) the lives of free blacks in the North with the lives of free blacks in the South.

One way to learn more about historical figures and events is to compare and contrast them. By studying how the figures or events are alike and different, you can begin to see each one more clearly.

TIP Using Graphic Organizers Venn diagrams help you focus on similarities and differences. Write details the subjects have in common in the overlapping area. Write details that make each subject different in the sections that do not overlap.

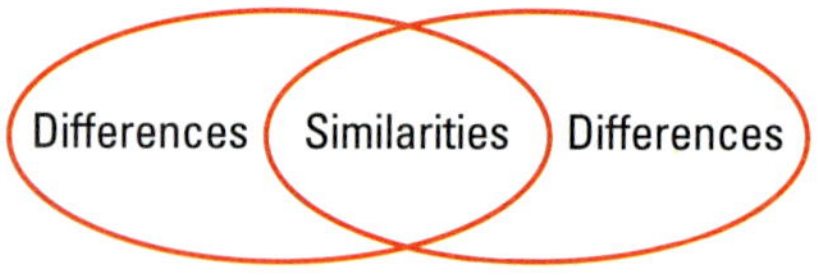

1. Prewrite

Getting Started

"How are they alike?" "How are they different?" Jot down answers to these questions as you research the presidents or the Industrial Revolution. Group your answers into points of comparison. For example, points of comparison for the lives of free blacks might be work, education, etc. Points of comparison for the Industrial Revolution might be factories or farming.

Organizing Your Information

There are two ways to organize a compare-and-contrast paper.

- **Block Style** Say everything you have to say about one subject. Then say everything you have to say about the second subject. Discuss the points of comparison in the same order for each subject.
- **Point-by-Point Style** Discuss the points of comparison one at a time. Explain how the subjects are alike and different on one point of comparison, then another, and so on. Discuss the subjects in the same order for each point of comparison.

2. Write

You can use this framework with your notes to help you write your first draft.

A Writer's Framework

Introduction
- Identify the two subjects and give background information to help readers understand your comparisons.
- State your big idea, or main purpose, in comparing and contrasting them.

Body
- Use block or point-by-point organization.
- Use three points of comparison.
- Support your points with specific historical facts, details, and examples.

Conclusion
- Restate your big idea.
- Summarize the points you made.
- Expand on your big idea, perhaps by relating it to later historical events or other historical figures.

3. Evaluate and Revise

Evaluating

Use these questions to discover ways to improve your paper.

Evaluation Questions for a Comparison/Contrast Paper

- Do you introduce both subjects in the first paragraph?
- Do you provide relevant background information in a clear and concise manner?
- Do you state your big idea in the introduction?
- Do you include three points of comparison between the subjects?
- Do you use either the block style or point-by-point style to organize your points of comparison?
- Do you support your points of comparison with appropriate historical facts, details, and examples?
- Do you restate your big idea and summarize your points?

TIP Making Meaning Clear

One way to make relationships between ideas clear is to repeat key or similar words and phrases in your writing. For example, you can use similar wording when comparing two historical figures on the same point of comparison.

EXAMPLE

Samuel Slater filled his labor needs by hiring entire families to work in the mills. Francis Lowell filled his labor needs by hiring young, unmarried women to work in the mills.

Revising

As you reread your paper, look for sentences that start with *There was* or *There were*. Sentences beginning with *There was/There were* tend to be weak: The verbs *was* and *were* do not convey any action.

Weak

There was a decline in southern agriculture after the American Revolution.

Stronger

Southern agriculture declined after the American Revolution.

4. Proofread and Publish

Proofreading

In a research report, you may be referring to the titles of your sources of information. Check to see whether you have punctuated any titles according to these guidelines.

- Underlining (if you are writing) or italics (if you are using a computer) for books, movies, TV programs, Internet sites, and magazines or newspapers
- Quotation marks for magazine articles, newspaper articles, chapters in a book

Publishing

Share your paper with one or more classmates. After reading each other's papers, you can compare and contrast them.

5. Practice and Apply

Use the steps and strategies outlined in this workshop to write your paper comparing and contrasting two people or events.

UNIT 5 1861–1877

The Nation Breaks Apart

Chapter 16 The Civil War
Chapter 17 Reconstruction

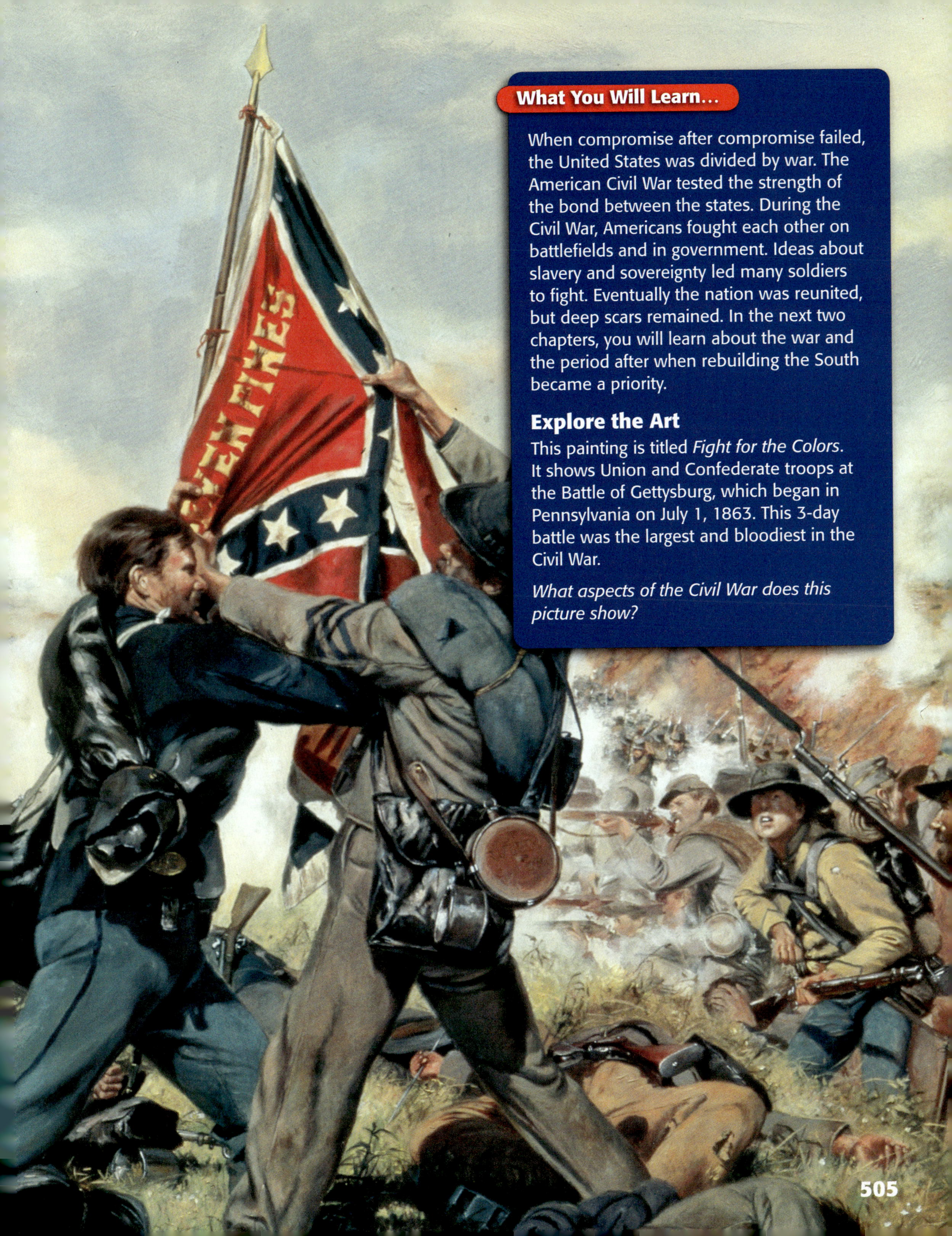

What You Will Learn...

When compromise after compromise failed, the United States was divided by war. The American Civil War tested the strength of the bond between the states. During the Civil War, Americans fought each other on battlefields and in government. Ideas about slavery and sovereignty led many soldiers to fight. Eventually the nation was reunited, but deep scars remained. In the next two chapters, you will learn about the war and the period after when rebuilding the South became a priority.

Explore the Art

This painting is titled *Fight for the Colors.* It shows Union and Confederate troops at the Battle of Gettysburg, which began in Pennsylvania on July 1, 1863. This 3-day battle was the largest and bloodiest in the Civil War.

What aspects of the Civil War does this picture show?

CHAPTER 16 1861–1865

The Civil War

North Carolina Standards

Social Studies Objectives

4.01 Identify and analyze the significance of the causes of secession from the Union, and compare reactions in North Carolina to reactions in other regions of the nation.

4.02 Describe the political and military developments of the Civil War and analyze their effect on the outcome of the war.

4.03 Assess North Carolina's role in the Civil War and analyze the social and economic impact of the war on the state.

4.04 Evaluate the importance of the roles played by individuals at the state and national levels during the Civil War and Reconstruction Period.

9.02 Identify past and present state and local leaders from diverse cultural backgrounds and assess their influence in affecting change.

Language Arts Objectives

2.01 Analyze and evaluate informational materials that are read, heard, and/or viewed by:

- monitoring comprehension for understanding of what is read, heard and/or viewed.
- recognizing the characteristics of informational materials.
- generating questions.
- extending ideas

go.hrw.com
North Carolina
KEYWORD: SC7 NC

FOCUS ON WRITING

Writing a Newspaper Article For most of this nation's history, newspapers have been an important way for citizens to learn about what is happening in the United States. In this chapter you will read about the main events of the Civil War. Then you will choose one of these events and write a newspaper article about it.

UNITED STATES

1861 Confederate guns open fire on Fort Sumter on April 12. Confederates win the first battle of the Civil War on July 21 at Bull Run in Virginia.

1861

WORLD

1861 Great Britain and France decide to buy cotton from Egypt instead of from the Confederacy.

HOLT

History's Impact

▶ **video series**
Watch the video to understand the impact of the Civil War.

What You Will Learn...

In this chapter you will learn how the resources of the North enabled it to defeat the South in the Civil War. Among those who marched off to war were these drummer boys of the Union army.

1862 The *Monitor* fights the *Virginia* on March 9.

1863 The Emancipation Proclamation is issued on January 1.

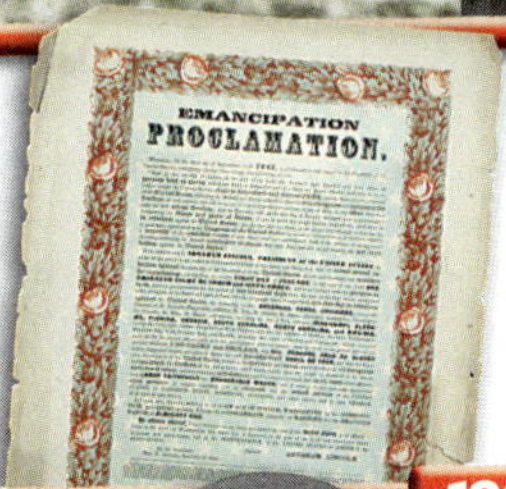

1865 General Robert E. Lee surrenders to General Ulysses S. Grant on April 9.

1862

1863

1864

1865

1862 An imperial decree expels foreigners from Japan.

1864 With the support of French troops, Archduke Maximilian of Austria becomes emperor of Mexico.

1864 The Taiping Rebellion in China ends after the capture of Nanjing in July.

Reading Social Studies

by Kylene Beers

Economics | Geography | **Politics** | **Society and Culture** | Science and Technology

Focus on Themes As you read this chapter about the Civil War, you will see that this was a time in our history dominated by two major concerns: **politics** and **society and culture**. You will not only read about the political decisions made during this war, but also you will see how the war affected all of American society. You will read about the causes and the key events during the war and the many consequences of this war. This chapter tells of one of the most important events in our history.

Supporting Facts and Details

Focus on Reading Main ideas and big ideas are just that, ideas. How do we know what those ideas really mean?

Understanding Ideas and Their Support A main idea or big idea may be a kind of summary statement, or it may be a statement of the author's opinion. Either way, a good reader looks to see what support—facts and various kinds of details—the writer provides. If the writer doesn't provide good support, the ideas may not be trustworthy.

Notice how the passage below uses facts and details to support the main idea.

Civil War armies fought in the ancient battlefield formation that produced massive casualties. Endless rows of troops fired directly at one another, with cannonballs landing amid them. When the order was given, soldiers would attach bayonets to their guns and rush toward their enemy. Men died to gain every inch of ground. . .

Despite the huge battlefield losses, the biggest killer in the Civil War was not the fighting. It was diseases such as typhoid, pneumonia, and tuberculosis. Nearly twice as many soldiers died of illnesses as died in combat.

From Chapter 16, p. 533

The main idea is stated first.

These sentences provide details about the challenges soldiers faced.

The writer concludes with some facts as support.

Writers support propositions with . . .

1. **Facts and statistics**—statements that can be proved; facts in number form
2. **Examples**—specific instances that illustrate the facts
3. **Anecdotes**—brief stories that help explain the facts
4. **Definitions**—explanation of unusual terms or words
5. **Comments from the experts or eyewitnesses**—statements from reliable sources

You Try It!

The following passage is from the chapter you are about to read. As you read it, look for the writer's main idea and support.

> In February 1862, Grant led an assault force into Tennessee. With help from navy gunboats, Grant's Army of the Tennessee took two outposts on key rivers in the west. On February 6, he captured Fort Henry on the Tennessee River. Several days later he took Fort Donelson on the Cumberland River.
>
> Fort Donelson's commander asked for the terms of surrender. Grant replied, "No terms except an unconditional and immediate surrender can be accepted." The fort surrendered. The North gave a new name to Grant's initials: "Unconditional Surrender" Grant.
>
> *From Chapter 16, pp. 522–523*

After you read the passage, answer the following questions.

1. Which sentence best states the writer's main idea?
   a. The fort surrendered.
   b. In February 1862, Grant led an assault force into Tennessee.
   c. Fort Donelson's commander asked for the terms of surrender.
2. Which method of support is not used to support the main idea?
   a. facts
   b. comments from experts or eyewitnesses
   c. anecdotes
3. Which sentence in this passage provides a comment from an expert or eyewitness?

As you read Chapter 16, pay attention to the details that the writers have chosen to support their main ideas.

Key Terms and People

Chapter 16

Section 1

Fort Sumter *(p. 511)*
border states *(p. 512)*
Winfield Scott *(p. 513)*
cotton diplomacy *(p. 513)*

Section 2

Thomas "Stonewall" Jackson *(p. 517)*
First Battle of Bull Run *(p. 517)*
George B. McClellan *(p. 517)*
Robert E. Lee *(p. 518)*
Seven Days' Battles *(p. 518)*
Second Battle of Bull Run *(p. 518)*
Battle of Antietam *(p. 519)*
ironclads *(p. 520)*

Section 3

Ulysses S. Grant *(p. 522)*
Battle of Shiloh *(p. 523)*
David Farragut *(p. 524)*
Siege of Vicksburg *(p. 524)*

Section 4

emancipation *(p. 529)*
Emancipation Proclamation *(p. 529)*
contrabands *(p. 531)*
54th Massachusetts Infantry *(p. 531)*
Copperheads *(p. 532)*
habeas corpus *(p. 532)*
Clara Barton *(p. 534)*

Section 5

Battle of Gettysburg *(p. 537)*
George Pickett *(p. 539)*
Pickett's Charge *(p. 539)*
Gettysburg Address *(p. 540)*
Wilderness Campaign *(p. 540)*
William Tecumseh Sherman *(p. 541)*
total war *(p. 542)*
Appomattox Courthouse *(p. 542)*

Academic Vocabulary

In this chapter, you will learn the following academic words:

innovation *(p. 520)*
execute *(p. 540)*

SECTION 1

The War Begins

What You Will Learn...

Main Ideas

1. Following the outbreak of war at Fort Sumter, Americans chose sides.
2. The Union and the Confederacy prepared for war.

The Big Idea

Civil war broke out between the North and the South in 1861.

Key Terms and People

Fort Sumter, *p. 511*
border states, *p. 512*
Winfield Scott, *p. 513*
cotton diplomacy, *p. 513*

TAKING NOTES As you read, take notes on the Civil War and how Americans chose sides and how each side prepared for the war.

	Choosing Sides	Preparing for War
North		
South		

If YOU were there...

You are a college student in Charleston in early 1861. Seven southern states have left the Union and formed their own government. All-out war seems unavoidable. Your friends have begun to volunteer for either the Union or the Confederate forces. You are torn between loyalty to your home state and to the United States.

Would you join the Union or the Confederate army?

BUILDING BACKGROUND The divisions within the United States reached a breaking point with the election of Abraham Lincoln in 1860. Several southern states angrily left the Union to form a new confederation. In border states such as Virginia and Kentucky, people were divided. The question now was whether the United States could survive as a disunified country.

Americans Choose Sides

Furious at Lincoln's election and fearing a federal invasion, seven southern states had seceded. The new commander in chief tried desperately to save the Union.

In his inaugural address, Lincoln promised not to end slavery where it existed. The federal government "will not assail [attack] you. You can have no conflict without being yourselves the aggressors," he said, trying to calm southerners' fears. However, Lincoln also stated his intention to preserve the Union. He believed that saving the Union would help to save democracy. If the Union and its government failed, then monarchs could say that people were unable to rule themselves. As a result, Lincoln refused to recognize secession, declaring the Union to be "unbroken."

In fact, after decades of painful compromises, the Union was badly broken. From the lower South, a battle cry was arising, born out of fear, rage—and excitement. Confederate officials began seizing branches of the federal mint, arsenals, and military outposts. In a last ditch effort to avoid war between the states, Secretary of State Seward suggested a united effort of threatening war against Spain and France for interfering in Mexico and the Caribbean. In the highly charged atmosphere, it would take only a spark to unleash the heat of war.

The first shots of the Civil War were fired at Fort Sumter, South Carolina. Although no one was killed there, the bloodiest war in the country's history had begun.

GEOGRAPHY SKILLS **INTERPRETING MAPS**

1. **Human-Environment Interaction** Why would the Union Army need to resupply Fort Sumter?
2. **Place** What advantages would a floating battery have?

In 1861, that spark occurred at **Fort Sumter**, a federal outpost in Charleston, South Carolina, that was attacked by Confederate troops, beginning the Civil War. Determined to seize the fortress—which controlled the entrance to Charleston harbor—the Confederates ringed the harbor with heavy guns. Instead of surrendering the fort, Lincoln decided to send in ships to provide badly needed supplies to defend the fort. Confederate officials demanded that the federal troops evacuate. The fort's commander, Major Robert Anderson, refused.

Before sunrise on April 12, 1861, Confederate guns opened fire on Fort Sumter. A witness wrote that the first shots brought "every soldier in the harbor to his feet, and every man, woman, and child in the city of Charleston from their beds." The Civil War had begun.

The fort, although massive, stood little chance. Its heavy guns faced the Atlantic Ocean, not the shore. After 34 hours of cannon blasts, Fort Sumter surrendered. "The last ray of hope for preserving the Union has expired at the assault upon Fort Sumter . . ." Lincoln wrote.

Reaction to Lincoln's Call

The fall of Fort Sumter stunned the North. Lincoln declared the South to be in a state of rebellion and asked state governors for 75,000 militiamen to put down the rebellion. States now had to choose: Would they secede, or would they stay in the Union? Democratic Senator Stephen Douglas, speaking in support of Lincoln's call for troops, declared, "There can be no neutrals in this war, *only patriots*—or *traitors*."

FOCUS ON NORTH CAROLINA

In reaction to Lincoln's call for troops, Democratic governor John Ellis replied, "You can get no troops from North Carolina." Even former Unionists were shocked by the call to arms, thinking the division should be resolved diplomatically. Once the state seceded, many Unionists accepted the government of the Confederacy.

North Versus South QUICK FACTS

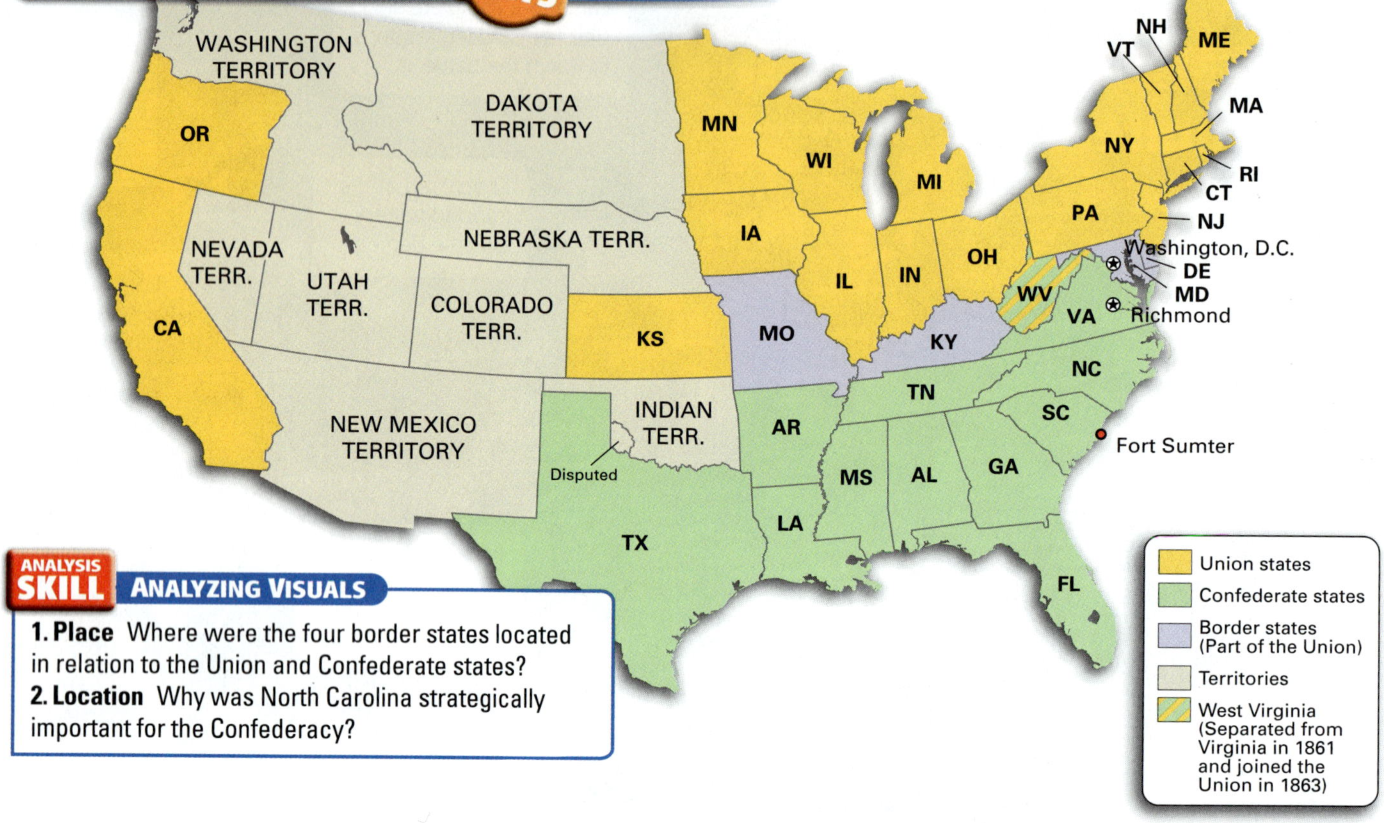

ANALYSIS SKILL **ANALYZING VISUALS**

1. Place Where were the four border states located in relation to the Union and Confederate states?
2. Location Why was North Carolina strategically important for the Confederacy?

Pennsylvania, New Jersey, and the states north of them rallied to the president's call. The crucial slave states of the Upper South—North Carolina, Tennessee, Virginia, and Arkansas—seceded. They provided soldiers and supplies to the South. North Carolina sent more soldiers than any other Confederate state, providing more than one-sixth of the entire Confederate force. North Carolina also lost the most men: 40,000. The state provided clothing, food, and other supplies to the war effort. Additionally, North Carolina citizens loyal to the Union organized several regiments to fight in the Union army.

Wedged between the North and the South were the key **border states** of Delaware, Kentucky, Maryland, and Missouri—slave states that did not join the Confederacy. Kentucky and Missouri controlled parts of important rivers. Maryland separated the Union capital, Washington, D.C., from the North.

People in the border states were deeply divided on the war. The president's own wife, Mary Todd Lincoln, had four brothers from Kentucky who fought for the Confederacy. Lincoln sent federal troops into the border states to help keep them in the Union. He also sent soldiers into western Virginia, where Union loyalties were strong. West Virginia set up its own state government in 1863.

Northern Resources

Numbers tell an important story about the Civil War. Consider the North's advantages. It could draw soldiers and workers from a population of 22 million. The South had only 5.5 million people to draw from. One of the greatest advantages in the North was the region's network of roads, canals, and railroads. Some 22,000 miles of railroad track could move soldiers and supplies throughout the North. The South had only about 9,000 miles of track.

In the North, the Civil War stimulated economic growth. To supply the military, the production of coal, iron, wheat, and wool increased. Also, the export of corn, wheat, beef, and pork to Europe doubled. In the South, the export of resources decreased because of the Union blockade.

Finally, the Union had money. It had a more developed economy, banking system, and a currency called greenbacks. The South had to start printing its own Confederate dollars. Some states printed their own money, too. This led to financial chaos.

Taking advantage of the Union's strengths, General **Winfield Scott** developed a two-part strategy: (1) destroy the South's economy with a naval blockade of southern ports; (2) gain control of the Mississippi River to divide the South. Other leaders urged an attack on Richmond, Virginia, the Confederate capital.

Southern Resources

The Confederacy had advantages as well. With its strong military tradition, the South put many brilliant officers into battle. Southern farms provided food for its armies. The South's best advantage, however, was strategic. It needed only to defend itself until the North grew tired of fighting.

The North had to invade and control the South. To accomplish this, the Union army had to travel huge distances. For example, the distance from northern Virginia to central Georgia is about the length of Scotland and England combined. Because of distances such as this, the North had to maintain long supply lines.

In addition, wilderness covered much of the South. Armies found this land difficult to cross. Also, in Virginia, many of the rivers ran from east to west. Because of this, they formed a natural defense against an army that attacked from the north to the south. As a result, Northern generals were often forced to attack Confederate troops from the side rather than from the front. Furthermore, because southerners fought mostly on their home soil, they were often familiar with the area.

The South hoped to wear down the North and to capture Washington, D.C. Confederate president Jefferson Davis also tried to win foreign allies through **cotton diplomacy**. This was the idea that Great Britain would support the Confederacy because it needed the South's raw cotton to supply its booming textile industry. Cotton diplomacy did not work as the South had hoped. Britain had large supplies of cotton, and it got more from India and Egypt.

READING CHECK **Comparing** What advantages did the North and South have leading up to the war?

Resources of the North and South

QUICK FACTS

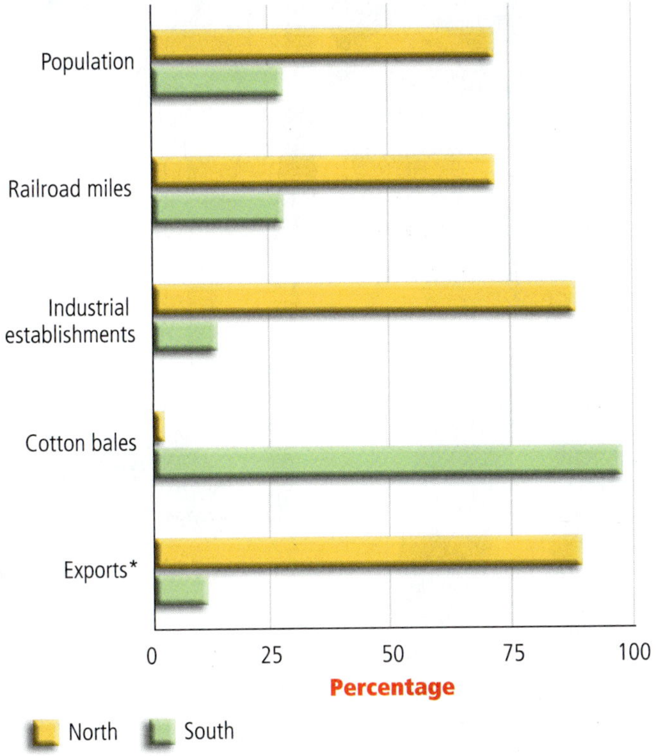

*Southern exports do not include Tennessee, Arkansas, and Mississippi.

ANALYSIS SKILL **ANALYZING VISUALS**

1. Do you think the North or the South could maintain better supply lines for their troops? Explain.
2. Do you think the North or the South could provide more weapons for their troops? Explain.

Union and Confederate Soldiers

Early in the war, uniforms differed greatly, especially in the Confederate army. Uniforms became simpler and more standard as the war dragged on.

ANALYSIS SKILL **ANALYZING VISUALS**

How are the Union and Confederate uniforms and equipment similar and different?

Preparing for War

The North and the South now rushed to war. Neither side was prepared for the tragedy to come.

Volunteer Armies

Volunteer militias had sparked the revolution that created the United States. Now they would battle for its future. At the start of the war, the Union army had only 16,000 soldiers. Within months that number had swelled to a half million. Southern men rose up to defend their land and their ways of life. Virginian Thomas Webber came to fight "against the invading foe [enemy] who now pollute the sacred soil of my beloved native state." When Union soldiers asked one captured rebel why he was fighting, he replied, "I'm fighting because you're down here."

Helping the Troops

Civilians on both sides helped those in uniform. They raised money, provided aid for soldiers and their families, and ran emergency hospitals. Dr. Elizabeth Blackwell, the first woman to receive a license to practice medicine, organized a group that pressured President Lincoln to form the U.S. Sanitary Commission in June 1861. The Sanitary, as it was called, was run by clergyman Henry Bellows. Tens of thousands of volunteers worked with the U.S. Sanitary Commission to send bandages, medicines, and food to Union army camps and hospitals. Some 3,000 women served as nurses in the Union army.

Training the Soldiers

Both the Union and Confederate armies faced shortages of clothing, food, and even rifles. Most troops lacked standard uniforms and simply wore their own clothes. Eventually, each side chose a color for their uniforms. The Union chose blue. The Confederates wore gray.

The problem with volunteers was that many of them had no idea how to fight. Schoolteachers, farmers, and laborers all had to learn the combat basics of marching, shooting, and using bayonets.

In a letter to a friend, a Union soldier described life in the training camp.

> "We have been wading through mud knee deep all winter ... For the last two weeks we have been drilled almost to death. Squad drill from 6 to 7 A.M. Company drill from 9 to 11 A.M. Batallion Drill from 2 to 4 1/2 P.M. Dress Parade from 5 to 5 1/2 P.M. and non-commissioned officers' school from 7 to 8 in the evening. If we don't soon become a well drilled Regiment, we ought to."
>
> —David R. P. Shoemaker, 1862

With visions of glory and action, many young soldiers were eager to fight. They would not have to wait long.

Discipline and drill were used to turn raw volunteers into an efficient fighting machine. During a battle, the success or failure of a regiment often depended on its discipline—how well it responded to orders.

Volunteers also learned how to use rifles. Eventually, soldiers were expected to be able to load, aim, and fire their rifles three times in one minute. The quality of the weapons provided varied greatly. Most soldiers favored the Springfield and Enfield rifles for their accuracy. On the other hand, soldiers often complained about their Austrian and Belgian rifles. A soldier remarked, "I don't believe one could hit the broadside of a barn with them."

The Union army provided the infantry with two-person tents. However, soldiers often discarded these tents in favor of more portable ones. The Confederate army did not usually issue tents. Instead, Confederates often used tents that were captured from the Union army.

READING CHECK **Summarizing** How did soldiers and civilians prepare for war?

SUMMARY AND PREVIEW As citizens chose sides in the Civil War, civilians and soldiers alike became involved in the war effort. In the next section you will learn about some early battles in the war, both on land and at sea.

NC History Makers

Daniel Harvey Hill
D. H. Hill was the superintendent of the North Carolina Military Institute and led North Carolina troops during the Civil War.

Section 1 Assessment

go.hrw.com
Online Quiz
KEYWORD: SC7 HP16

Reviewing Ideas, Terms, and People

1. **a. Identify** What event triggered the war between the Union and the Confederacy?
   b. Contrast How did the Union's strategy differ from that of the Confederacy?
   c. Evaluate Which side do you believe was best prepared for war? Explain your answer.
2. **a. Describe** How did women take part in the war?
   b. Summarize In what ways were the armies of the North and South unprepared for war?
   c. Elaborate Why did men volunteer to fight in the war?

Critical Thinking

3. **Comparing and Contrasting** Review your notes on the preparations for war by the North and the South. Then copy the graphic organizer shown below and use it to show the strengths and weaknesses of each side in the war.

	Union	Confederacy
Strengths		
Weaknesses		

FOCUS ON WRITING

4. **Taking Notes on the War's Beginning** As you read this section, take notes on the crisis at Fort Sumter and on the recruiting and training of the armies. Be sure to answer the following questions: Who? Where? When? Why? and How?

SECTION 2

The War in the East

What You Will Learn...

Main Ideas

1. Union and Confederate forces fought for control of the war in Virginia.
2. The Battle of Antietam gave the North a slight advantage.
3. The Confederacy attempted to break the Union naval blockade.

The Big Idea

Confederate and Union forces faced off in Virginia and at sea.

Key Terms and People

Thomas "Stonewall" Jackson, *p. 517*
First Battle of Bull Run, *p. 517*
George B. McClellan, *p. 517*
Robert E. Lee, *p. 518*
Seven Days' Battles, *p. 518*
Second Battle of Bull Run, *p. 518*
Battle of Antietam, *p. 519*
ironclads, *p. 520*

TAKING NOTES As you read, take notes on the battles in the east and at sea and the winners of each. Write your notes in a chart like the one below.

Battle	Winner

If YOU were there...

You live in Washington, D.C., in July 1861. You and your friends are on your way to Manassas, near Washington, to watch the battle there. Everyone expects a quick Union victory. Your wagon is loaded with food for a picnic, and people are in a holiday mood. You see some members of Congress riding toward Manassas, too. Maybe this battle will end the war!

Why would you want to watch this battle?

BUILDING BACKGROUND The shots fired at Fort Sumter made the war a reality. Neither the North nor the South was really prepared. Each side had some advantages—more industry and railroads in the North, a military tradition in the South. The war in the East centered in the region around the two capitals: Washington, D.C., and Richmond, Virginia.

War in Virginia

The troops that met in the first major battle of the Civil War found that it was no picnic. In July 1861, Lincoln ordered General Irvin McDowell to lead his 35,000-man army from the Union capital, Washington, to the Confederate capital, Richmond. The soldiers were barely trained. McDowell complained that they "stopped every moment to pick blackberries or get water; they would not keep in the ranks." The first day's march covered only five miles.

Bull Run/Manassas

McDowell's army was headed to Manassas, Virginia, an important railroad junction. If McDowell could seize Manassas, he would control the best route to the Confederate capital. Some 22,000 Confederate troops under the command of General Pierre G. T. Beauregard were waiting for McDowell and his troops along a creek called Bull Run. For two days, Union troops tried to find a way around the Confederates. During that time, Beauregard requested assistance, and

General Joseph E. Johnston headed toward Manassas with another 10,000 Confederate troops. By July 21, 1861, they had all arrived.

That morning, Union troops managed to cross the creek and drive back the left side of the Confederate line. Yet one unit held firmly in place.

"There is Jackson standing like a stone wall!" cried one southern officer. "Rally behind the Virginians!" At that moment, General **Thomas "Stonewall" Jackson** earned his famous nickname.

A steady stream of Virginia volunteers arrived to counter the attack. The Confederates surged forward, letting out their terrifying "rebel yell." One eyewitness described the awful scene.

> "There is smoke, dust, wild talking, shouting; hissings, howlings, explosions. It is a new, strange, unanticipated experience to the soldiers of both armies, far different from what they thought it would be."
>
> —Charles Coffin, quoted in *Voices of the Civil War* by Richard Wheeler

The battle raged through the day, with rebel soldiers still arriving. Finally, the weary Union troops gave out. They tried to make an orderly retreat back across the creek, but the roads were clogged with the fancy carriages of panicked spectators. The Union army scattered in the chaos.

The Confederates lacked the strength to push north and capture Washington, D.C. But clearly, the rebels had won the day. The **First Battle of Bull Run** was the first major battle of the Civil War, and the Confederates' victory. The battle is also known as the First Battle of Manassas. It shattered the North's hopes of winning the war quickly.

More Battles in Virginia

The shock at Bull Run persuaded Lincoln of the need for a better trained army. He put his hopes in General **George B. McClellan**. The general assembled a highly disciplined force of 100,000 soldiers called the Army of the Potomac. The careful McClellan spent months training. However, because he overestimated the size of the Confederate army, McClellan hesitated to attack. Lincoln grew impatient. Finally, in the spring of 1862, McClellan launched an effort to capture Richmond called the "Peninsular Campaign." Instead of marching south for a direct assault, McClellan slowly brought his force through the peninsula between the James and York rivers. More time slipped away.

The South feared that McClellan would receive reinforcements from Washington. To prevent this, Stonewall Jackson launched an attack toward Washington. Although the attack was pushed back, it prevented the Union from sending reinforcements to McClellan.

GEOGRAPHY SKILLS INTERPRETING MAPS

go.hrw.com
Interactive Map
KEYWORD: SC7 CH16

1. **Location** Which battle was fought in Maryland?
2. **Human-Environment Interaction** How did geography influence the movement of forces?

THE IMPACT TODAY

Many Americans continue to be fascinated by the Civil War. Some history buffs regularly stage re-enactments of famous battles, complete with uniforms, guns, and bayonets.

In June 1862, with McClellan's force poised outside Richmond, the Confederate army in Virginia came under the command of General **Robert E. Lee**. A graduate of the U.S. Military Academy at West Point, Lee had served in the Mexican War and had led federal troops at Harpers Ferry. Lee was willing to take risks and make unpredictable moves to throw Union forces off balance.

During the summer of 1862, Lee strengthened his positions. On June 26, he attacked, launching a series of clashes known as the **Seven Days' Battles** that forced the Union army to retreat from near Richmond. Confederate General D. H. Hill described one failed attack. "It was not war—it was murder," he said. Lee saved Richmond and forced McClellan to retreat.

A frustrated Lincoln ordered General John Pope to march directly on Richmond from Washington. Pope told his soldiers, "Let us look before us and not behind. Success and glory are in the advance."

Jackson wanted to defeat Pope's army before it could join up with McClellan's larger Army of the Potomac. Jackson's troops met Pope's Union forces on the battlefield in August in 1862. The three-day battle became known as the **Second Battle of Bull Run**, or the Second Battle of Manassas.

The first day's fighting was savage. Captain George Fairfield of the 7th Wisconsin regiment later recalled, "What a slaughter! No one appeared to know the object of the fight, and there we stood for one hour, the men falling all around." The fighting ended in a stalemate.

On the second day, Pope found Jackson's troops along an unfinished railroad grade. Pope hurled his men against the Confederates. But the attacks were pushed back with heavy casualties on both sides.

On the third day, the Confederates crushed the Union army's assault and forced it to retreat in defeat. The Confederates had won a major victory, and General Robert E. Lee decided it was time to take the war to the North.

READING CHECK **Sequencing** List in order the events that forced Union troops out of Virginia.

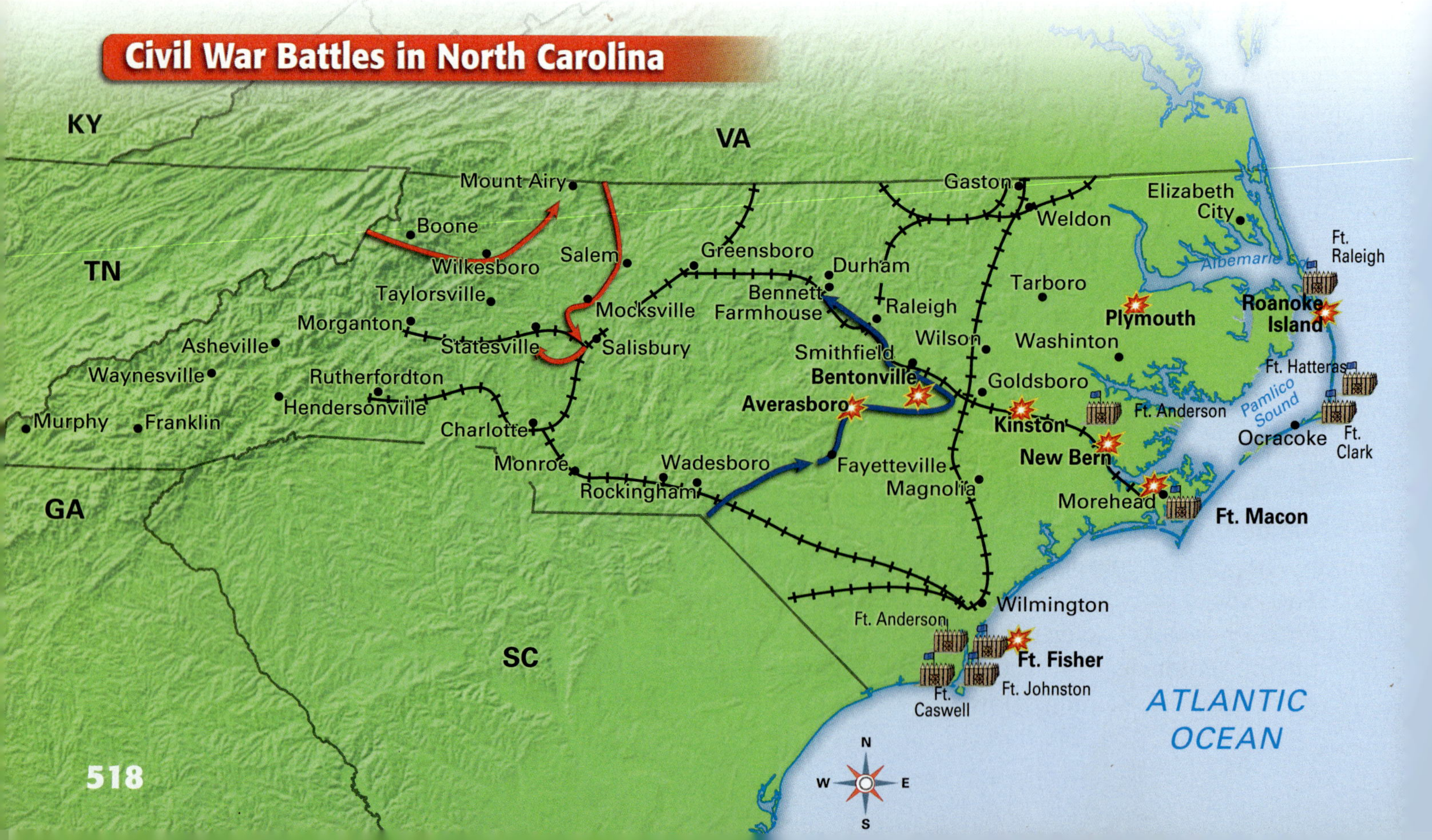

Battle of Antietam

Confederate leaders hoped to follow up Lee's successes in Virginia with a major victory on northern soil. On September 4, 1862, some 40,000 Confederate soldiers began crossing into Maryland. General Robert E. Lee decided to divide his army. He sent about half of his troops, under the command of Stonewall Jackson, to Harpers Ferry. There they defeated a Union force and captured the town. Meanwhile, Lee arrived in the town of Frederick and issued a Proclamation to the People of Maryland, urging them to join the Confederates. However, his words would not be enough to convince Marylanders to abandon the Union. Union soldiers, however, found a copy of Lee's battle plan, which had been left at an abandoned Confederate camp. General McClellan learned that Lee had divided his army in order to attack Harpers Ferry. However, McClellan hesitated to attack. As a result, the Confederates had time to reunite.

BIOGRAPHY

Robert E. Lee
(1807–1870)

Robert E. Lee was born into a wealthy Virginia family in 1807. Lee fought in the Mexican-American War, helping to capture Veracruz. When the Civil War began, President Lincoln asked Lee to lead the Union army. Lee declined and resigned from the U.S. Army to become a general in the Confederate army.

Drawing Conclusions How did Lee's choice reflect the division of the states?

The two armies met along Antietam Creek in Maryland on September 17, 1862. The battle lasted for hours. By the end of the day, the Union had suffered more than 12,000 casualties. The Confederates endured more than 13,000 casualties. Union officer A. H. Nickerson later recalled, "It seemed that everybody near me was killed." The **Battle of Antietam,** also known as the Battle of Sharpsburg, was the bloodiest single-day battle of the Civil War—and of U.S. history. More soldiers were killed and wounded at the Battle of Antietam than the deaths of all Americans in the American Revolution, War of 1812, and Mexican-American War combined.

During the battle, McClellan kept four divisions of soldiers in reserve and refused to use them to attack Lee's devastated army. McClellan was convinced that Lee was massing reserves for a counterattack. Those reserves did not exist. Despite this blunder, Antietam was an important victory. Lee's northward advance had been stopped.

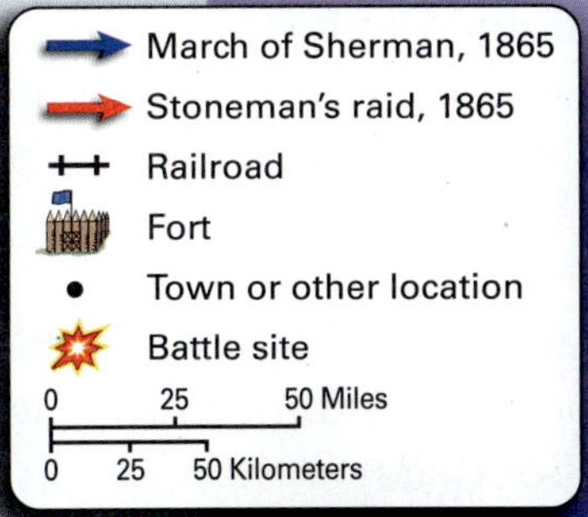

GEOGRAPHY SKILLS **Interpreting Maps**

Human-Environment Interaction Why was Wilmington such an important city to the Confederacy?

READING CHECK **Analyzing** Why was the Battle of Antietam significant?

Primary Source

POLITICAL CARTOON

Anaconda Plan

This cartoon shows visually the North's plan to cut off supplies to the South through naval blockades, a strategy called the Anaconda Plan.

Why is the snake's head red, white, and blue?

How does the cartoonist show what the snake represents?

ANALYSIS SKILL **ANALYZING PRIMARY SOURCES**

Why do you think the plan was called the Anaconda Plan?

Breaking the Union's Blockade

While the two armies fought for control of the land, the Union navy controlled the sea. The North had most of the U.S. Navy's small fleet, and many experienced naval officers had remained loyal to the Union. The North also had enough industry to build more ships. The Confederacy turned to British companies for new ships.

ACADEMIC VOCABULARY

innovation a new idea or way of doing something

The Union's Naval Strategy

The Union navy quickly mobilized to set up a blockade of southern ports. The blockade largely prevented the South from selling or receiving goods, and it seriously damaged the southern economy.

The blockade was hard to maintain because the Union navy had to patrol thousands of miles of coastline from Virginia to Texas. The South used small, fast ships to outrun the larger Union warships. Most of these blockade runners traveled to the Bahamas or Nassau to buy supplies for the Confederacy. These ships, however, could not make up for the South's loss of trade. The Union blockade reduced the number of ships entering southern ports from 6,000 to 800 per year.

The ports of North Carolina were home to many Confederate blockade runners like Captain John Newland Maffitt. He made several trips with supplies to the port of Wilmington. The rail line from Wilmington north to troops in Virginia was part of the supply line known as the lifeline of the Confederacy.

Clash of the Ironclads

Hoping to take away the Union's advantage at sea, the Confederacy turned to a new type of warship—**ironclads**, or ships heavily armored with iron. The Confederates had captured a Union steamship, the *Merrimack*, and turned it into an ironclad, renamed the *Virginia*. One Union sailor described the **innovation** as "a huge half-submerged crocodile." In early March 1862, the ironclad sailed into Hampton Roads, Virginia, an important waterway guarded by Union ships. Before nightfall, the *Virginia* easily sank two of the Union's wooden warships, while it received minor damage.

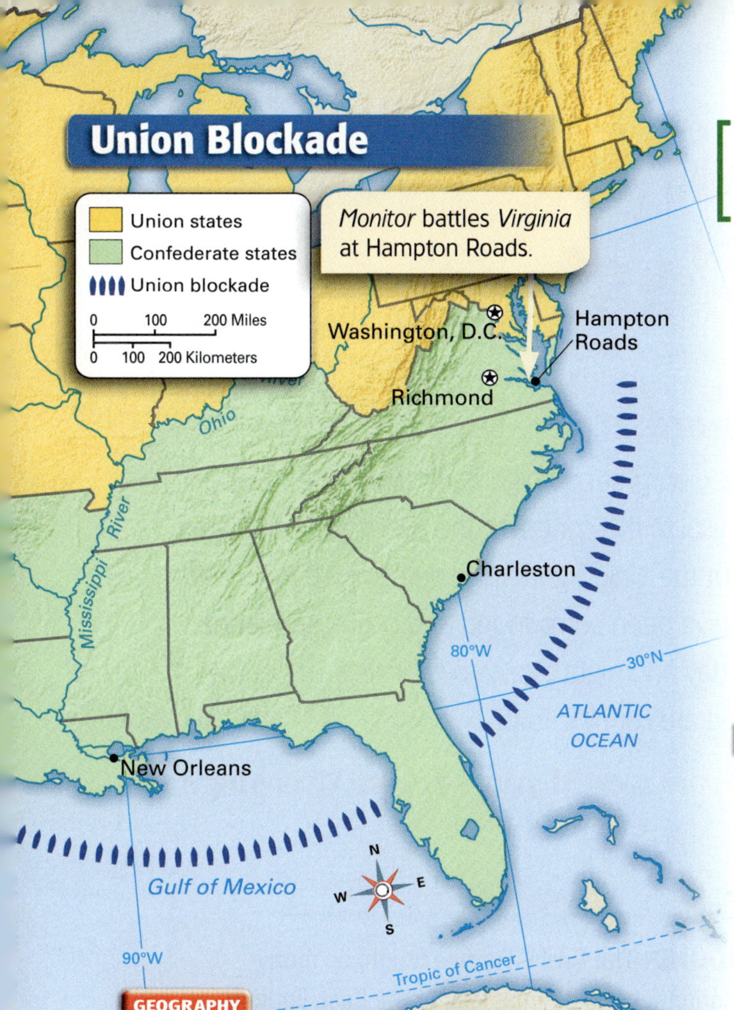

GEOGRAPHY SKILLS **INTERPRETING MAPS**

Location How was North Carolina affected by the blockade?

The Union navy had already built its own ironclad, the *Monitor*, designed by Swedish-born engineer John Ericsson. Ericsson's ship had unusual new features, such as a revolving gun tower. Although small, the *Monitor* carried powerful guns and had thick plating.

When the *Virginia* returned to Hampton Roads later that month, the *Monitor* was waiting. After several hours of fighting, the *Monitor* forced the *Virginia* to withdraw. This success saved the Union fleet and continued the blockade. The clash of the ironclads also signaled a revolution in naval warfare. The days of wooden warships powered by wind and sails were drawing to a close.

THE IMPACT TODAY

The *Monitor* sank in North Carolina in the winter of 1862. The shipwreck was located by scientists in 1973, and efforts to save it for further study continue today.

READING CHECK **Evaluating** How effective was the Union blockade?

SUMMARY AND PREVIEW The early battles of the Civil War were centered in the East. In the next section you will read about battles in the West.

Section 2 Assessment

go.hrw.com
Online Quiz
KEYWORD: SC7 HP16

Reviewing Ideas, Terms, and People

1. a. **Identify** List the early battles in the East and the outcome of each battle.
   b. **Elaborate** Why do you think the Union lost the **First Battle of Bull Run**?
2. a. **Describe** What costly mistake did the Confederacy make before the **Battle of Antietam**?
   b. **Analyze** What was the outcome of the Battle of Antietam, and what effect did it have on both the North and the South?
   c. **Elaborate** Why do you think General **George B. McClellan** did not finish off General **Robert E. Lee**'s troops when he had the chance?
3. a. **Describe** What was the Union's strategy in the war at sea?
   b. **Draw Conclusions** Why were **ironclads** more successful than older, wooden ships?

Critical Thinking

4. **Supporting a Point of View** Review your notes on the battles in the east and at sea. Then copy the graphic organizer below and use it to show which three conflicts you think were the most significant and why.

Most Significant	Why

Focus on Writing

5. **Taking Notes on the War in the East** As you read this section, take notes on the First Battle of Bull Run, the Seven Days' Battles, the Second Battle of Bull Run, and the Battle of Antietam. Be sure to answer the following questions: Who? Where? When? Why? and How?

SECTION 3

The War in the West

What You Will Learn...

Main Ideas

1. Union strategy in the West centered on control of the Mississippi River.
2. Confederate and Union troops struggled for dominance in the Far West.

The Big Idea

Fighting in the Civil War spread to the western United States.

Key Terms and People

Ulysses S. Grant, *p. 522*
Battle of Shiloh, *p. 523*
David Farragut, *p. 524*
Siege of Vicksburg, *p. 524*

TAKING NOTES As you read, take notes on Civil War battles in the West. Write your notes in a graphic organizer like the one below.

Battles in the West
1.
2.
3.
4.
5.
6.

If YOU were there...

You live in the city of Vicksburg, set on high bluffs above the Mississippi River. Vicksburg is vital to the control of the river, and Confederate defenses are strong. But the Union general is determined to take the town. For weeks, you have been surrounded and besieged. Cannon shells burst overhead, day and night. Some have fallen on nearby homes. Supplies of food are running low.

How would you survive this siege?

BUILDING BACKGROUND The Civil War was fought on many fronts, all across the continent and even at sea. In the East, fighting was at first concentrated in Virginia. In the West, cities and forts along the Mississippi River were the main target of Union forces. Northern control of the river would cut off the western states of the Confederacy.

Union Strategy in the West

While Lincoln fumed over the cautious, hesitant General McClellan, he had no such problems with **Ulysses S. Grant**. Bold and restless, Grant grew impatient when he was asked to lead defensive maneuvers. He wanted to be on the attack. As a commander of forces in the Union's western campaign, he would get his wish.

The western campaign focused on taking control of the Mississippi River. This strategy would cut off the eastern part of the Confederacy from sources of food production in Arkansas, Louisiana, and Texas. From bases on the Mississippi, the Union army could attack southern communication and transportation networks.

In February 1862, Grant led an assault force into Tennessee. With help from navy gunboats, Grant's Army of the Tennessee took two outposts on key rivers in the west. On February 6, he captured Fort Henry on the Tennessee River. Several days later he took Fort Donelson on the Cumberland River.

Fort Donelson's commander asked for the terms of surrender. Grant replied, "No terms except an unconditional and immediate

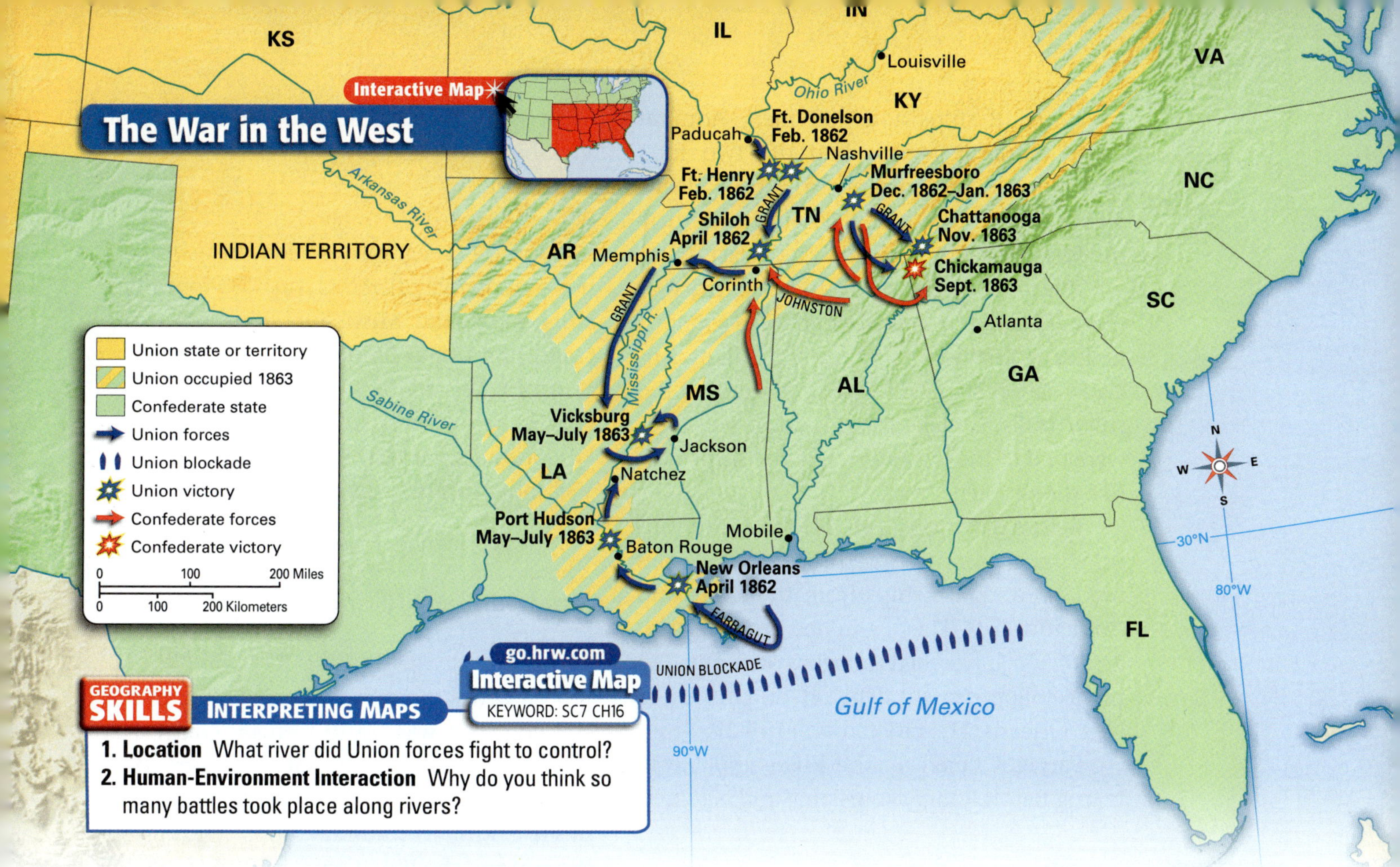

go.hrw.com
Interactive Map
KEYWORD: SC7 CH16

GEOGRAPHY SKILLS **INTERPRETING MAPS**

1. **Location** What river did Union forces fight to control?
2. **Human-Environment Interaction** Why do you think so many battles took place along rivers?

surrender can be accepted." The fort surrendered. The North gave a new name to Grant's initials: "Unconditional Surrender" Grant.

Advancing south in Tennessee, General Grant paused near Shiloh Church to await the arrival of the Army of Ohio. Grant knew that the large rebel army of General A. S. Johnston was nearby in Corinth, Mississippi, but he did not expect an attack. Instead of setting up defenses, he worked on drilling his new recruits.

In the early morning of April 6, 1862, the rebels sprang on Grant's sleepy camp. This began the **Battle of Shiloh**, in which the Union army gained greater control of the Mississippi River valley.

During the bloody two-day battle, each side gained and lost ground. Johnston was killed on the first day. The arrival of the Ohio force helped Grant regain territory and push the enemy back into Mississippi. The armies finally gave out, each with about 10,000 casualties. Both sides claimed victory, but, in fact, the victor was Grant.

The Fall of New Orleans

As Grant battled his way down the Mississippi, the Union navy prepared to blast its way upriver to meet him. The first obstacle was the port of New Orleans, the largest city in the Confederacy and the gateway to the Mississippi River.

BIOGRAPHY

David Farragut

(1801–1870)

David Farragut was born in Tennessee to a Spanish father and an American mother. At age seven Farragut was adopted by a family friend who agreed to train the young boy for the navy. Farragut received his first navy position—midshipman at large—at age nine and commanded his first vessel at 12. He spent the rest of his life in the U.S. Navy. Farragut led key attacks on the southern ports of Vicksburg and New Orleans.

Drawing Inferences How did Farragut help the war effort of the North?

With 18 ships and 700 men, Admiral **David Farragut** approached the two forts that guarded the entrance to New Orleans from the Gulf of Mexico. Unable to destroy the forts, Farragut decided to race past them.

The risky operation would take place at night. Farragut had his wooden ships wrapped in heavy chains to protect them like iron-clads. Sailors slapped Mississippi mud on the ships' hulls to make them hard to see. Trees were tied to the masts to make the ships look like the forested shore.

Before dawn on April 24, 1862, the warships made their daring dash. The Confederates fired at Farragut's ships from the shore and from gunboats. They launched burning rafts, one of which scorched Farragut's own ship. But his fleet slipped by the twin forts and made it to New Orleans. The city fell on April 29.

Farragut sailed up the Mississippi River, taking Baton Rouge, Louisiana, and Natchez, Mississippi. He then approached the city of Vicksburg, Mississippi.

The Siege of Vicksburg

Vicksburg's geography made invasion all but impossible. Perched on 200-foot-high cliffs above the Mississippi River, the city could rain down firepower on enemy ships or on soldiers trying to scale the cliffs. Deep gorges surrounded the city, turning back land assaults. Nevertheless, Farragut ordered Vicksburg to surrender.

> "Mississippians don't know, and refuse to learn, how to surrender . . . If Commodore Farragut . . . can teach them, let [him] come and try."
>
> —Colonel James L. Autry, military commander of Vicksburg

Farragut's guns had trouble reaching the city above. It was up to General Grant. His solution was to starve the city into surrender.

General Grant's troops began the **Siege of Vicksburg** in mid-May 1863, cutting off the city and shelling it repeatedly. As food ran out, residents and soldiers survived by eating horses, dogs, and rats. "We are utterly cut off from the world, surrounded by a circle of fire," wrote one woman. "People do nothing

Primary Source

SPEECH

Response to Farragut

The mayor of New Orleans considered the surrender of the city to the Union navy:

> "We yield to physical force alone and maintain allegiance to the Confederate States; beyond this, a due respect for our dignity, our rights and the flag of our country does not, I think, permit us to go."
>
> **–Mayor John T. Monroe,**
> quoted in *Confederate Military History, Vol. 10*

ANALYSIS SKILL — ANALYZING PRIMARY SOURCES

How does Monroe's statement reveal his attitude about surrender?

The Union navy played an important part in the Civil War. Besides blockading and raiding southern ports, the navy joined battles along the Mississippi River, as in this painting of Vicksburg.

but eat what they can get, sleep when they can, and dodge the shells."

The Confederate soldiers were also sick and hungry. In late June a group of soldiers sent their commander a warning.

> "The army is now ripe for mutiny [rebellion], unless it can be fed. If you can't feed us, you'd better surrender us, horrible as the idea is."
>
> —Confederate soldiers at Vicksburg to General John C. Pemberton, 1863

On July 4, Pemberton surrendered. Grant immediately sent food to the soldiers and civilians. He later claimed that "the fate of the Confederacy was sealed when Vicksburg fell."

READING CHECK **Summarizing** How did the Union gain control of the Mississippi River?

Struggle for the Far West

Early on in the war, the Union halted several attempts by Confederate armies to control lands west of the Mississippi. In August 1861, a Union detachment from Colorado turned back a Confederate force at Glorieta Pass. Union volunteers also defeated rebel forces at Arizona's Pichaco Pass.

Confederate attempts to take the border state of Missouri also collapsed. Failing to seize the federal arsenal at St. Louis in mid-1861, the rebels fell back to Pea Ridge in northwest Arkansas. There, in March 1862, they attacked again, aided by some 800 Cherokee. The Indians hoped the Confederates would give them greater freedom. In addition, slavery was legal in Indian Territory, and some Native Americans who were slaveholders supported the Confederacy. Despite being outnumbered, Union forces won the Battle of Pea Ridge. The Union defense of Missouri held.

Pro-Confederate forces remained active in the region throughout the war. They attacked Union forts and raided towns in Missouri and Kansas, forcing Union commanders to keep valuable troops stationed in the area.

READING CHECK **Analyzing** What was the importance of the fighting in the Far West?

SUMMARY AND PREVIEW The North and the South continued their struggle with battles in the West. A number of key battles took place in the Western theater, and several important Union leaders emerged from these battles. One, Ulysses S. Grant, would soon become even more important to the Union army. In the next section you will learn about the lives of civilians, enslaved Africans, and soldiers during the war.

Section 3 Assessment

go.hrw.com
Online Quiz
KEYWORD: SC7 HP16

Reviewing Ideas, Terms, and People

1. a. **Identify** What role did **Ulysses S. Grant** play in the war in the West?
   b. **Explain** Why was the **Battle of Shiloh** important?
   c. **Elaborate** Do you think President Lincoln would have approved of Grant's actions in the West? Why or why not?
2. a. **Describe** How did the Union take New Orleans, and why was it an important victory?
   b. **Draw Conclusions** How were civilians affected by the **Siege of Vicksburg**?
   c. **Predict** What might be some possible results of the Union victory at Vicksburg?

Critical Thinking

3. **Identifying Cause and Effect** Review your notes on Union strategy in the West. Then copy this graphic organizer and use it to show the causes and effects of each battle.

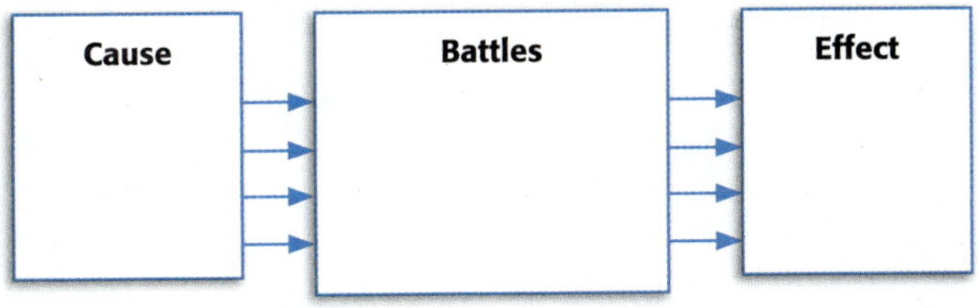

FOCUS ON WRITING

4. **Taking Notes on the War in the West** As you read this section, take notes on the fight for the Mississippi River and the Siege of Vicksburg. Be sure to answer the following questions: Who? Where? When? Why? and How?

History and Geography

The Vicksburg Strategy

"Vicksburg is the key!" President Abraham Lincoln declared. "The war can never be brought to a close until that key is in our pocket." Vicksburg was so important because of its location on the Mississippi River, a vital trade route and supply line. Union ships couldn't get past the Confederate guns mounted on the high bluffs of Vicksburg. Capturing Vicksburg would give the Union control of the Mississippi, stealing a vital supply line and splitting the Confederacy in two. The task fell to General Ulysses S. Grant.

1 Grant Crosses into Louisiana General Grant planned to attack Vicksburg from the North, but the swampy land made attack from that direction difficult. So, Grant crossed the Mississippi River into Louisiana and marched south.

2 Grant Moves East Grant's troops met up with their supply boats here and crossed back into Mississippi. In a daring gamble, Grant decided to move without a supply line, allowing his army to move quickly.

3 Port Gibson A skirmish at Port Gibson proved that the Confederates could not defend the Mississippi line.

5 The Siege of Vicksburg Grant now had 30,000 Confederate troops trapped in Vicksburg. After two assaults on the city failed, Grant was forced to lay siege. After six weeks of bombardment, the Confederates surrendered on July 4, 1863. Grant's bold campaign had given the Union control of the Mississippi River.

Ironclads

Union ironclads were vital to the Vicksburg campaign. These gunboats protected Grant's troops when they crossed the Mississippi. Later, they bombarded Vicksburg during the siege of the city.

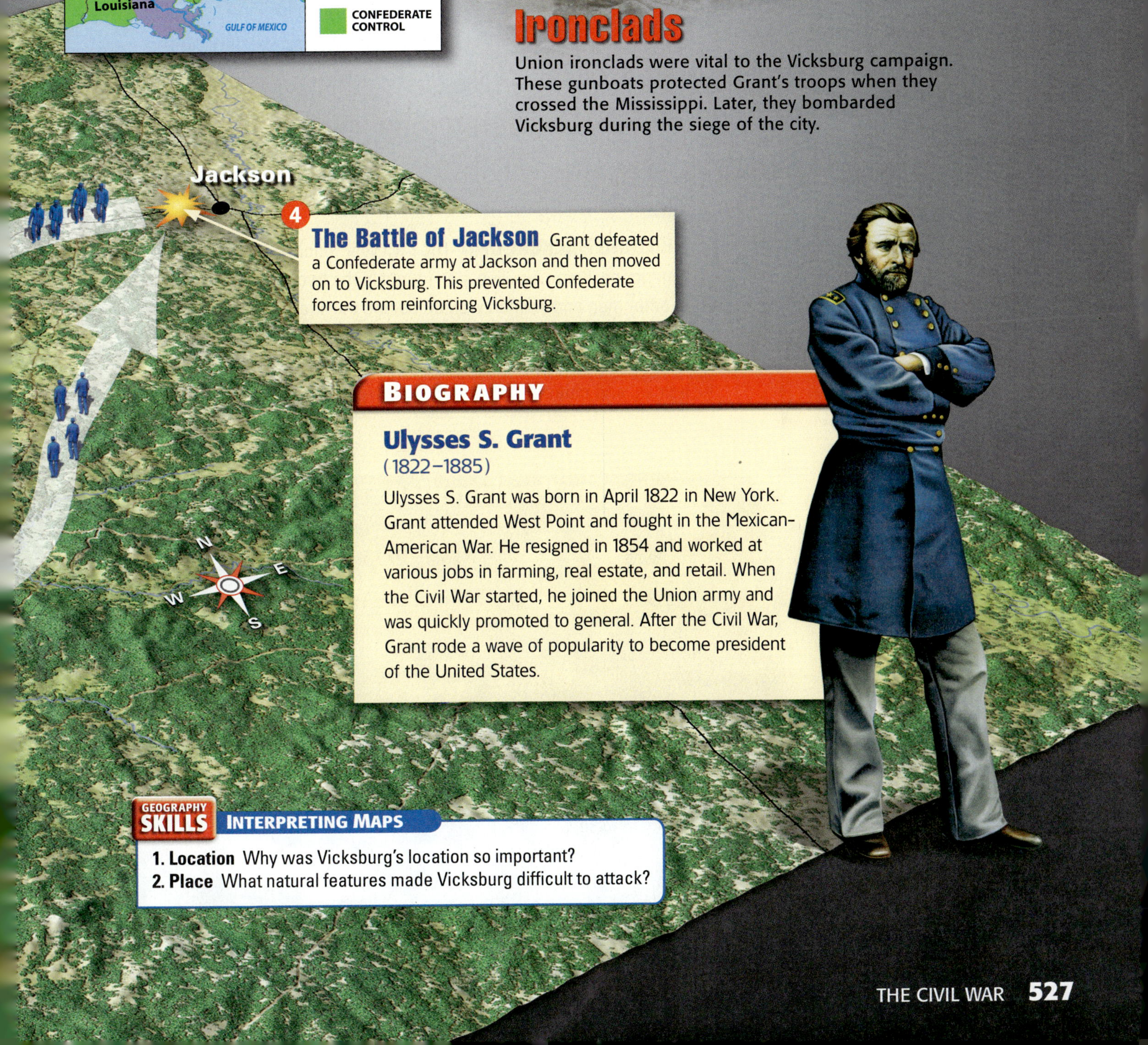

The Battle of Jackson Grant defeated a Confederate army at Jackson and then moved on to Vicksburg. This prevented Confederate forces from reinforcing Vicksburg.

BIOGRAPHY

Ulysses S. Grant
(1822–1885)

Ulysses S. Grant was born in April 1822 in New York. Grant attended West Point and fought in the Mexican-American War. He resigned in 1854 and worked at various jobs in farming, real estate, and retail. When the Civil War started, he joined the Union army and was quickly promoted to general. After the Civil War, Grant rode a wave of popularity to become president of the United States.

GEOGRAPHY SKILLS **INTERPRETING MAPS**

1. **Location** Why was Vicksburg's location so important?
2. **Place** What natural features made Vicksburg difficult to attack?

SECTION 4

Daily Life during the War

What You Will Learn...

Main Ideas

1. The Emancipation Proclamation freed slaves in Confederate states.
2. African Americans participated in the war in a variety of ways.
3. President Lincoln faced opposition to the war.
4. Life was difficult for soldiers and civilians alike.

The Big Idea

The lives of many Americans were affected by the Civil War.

Key Terms and People

emancipation, *p. 529*
Emancipation Proclamation, *p. 529*
contrabands, *p. 531*
54th Massachusetts Infantry, *p. 531*
Copperheads, *p. 532*
habeas corpus, *p. 532*
Clara Barton, *p. 534*

TAKING NOTES As you read, take notes on the effects of the Civil War on the lives of African Americans, soldiers, and women and children. Write your notes in a graphic organizer like the one below.

How the Civil War affected	
African Americans	
Soldiers	
Women and children	

If YOU were there...

You live in Maryland in 1864. Your father and brothers are in the Union army, and you want to do your part in the war. You hear that a woman in Washington, D.C., is supplying medicines and caring for wounded soldiers on the battlefield. She is looking for volunteers. You know the work will be dangerous, for you'll be in the line of fire. You might be shot or even killed.

Would you join the nurses on the battlefield?

BUILDING BACKGROUND The Civil War touched almost all Americans. Some 3 million men fought in the two armies. Thousands of other men and women worked behind the lines, providing food, supplies, medical care, and other necessary services. Civilians could not escape the effects of war, as the fighting destroyed farms, homes, and cities.

Emancipation Proclamation

Emancipation Proclamation

At the heart of the nation's bloody struggle were millions of enslaved African Americans. Abolitionists urged President Lincoln to free them.

In an 1858 speech, Lincoln declared, "There is no reason in the world why the negro is not entitled to all the natural rights numerated in the Declaration of Independence—the right to life, liberty, and the pursuit of happiness." Yet as president, Lincoln found **emancipation**, or the freeing of slaves, to be a difficult issue. He did not believe he had the constitutional power. He also worried about the effects of emancipation.

Lincoln Issues the Proclamation

Northerners had a range of opinions about abolishing slavery.

- The Democratic Party, which included many laborers, opposed emancipation. Laborers feared that freed slaves would come north and take their jobs at lower wages.
- Abolitionists argued that the war was pointless if it did not win freedom for African Americans. They warned that the Union would remain divided until the problem was resolved.

The painting at left shows Lincoln and his cabinet after the signing of the Emancipation Proclamation. Above is a photo of former slaves who were freed by the proclamation.

How do you think the Emancipation Proclamation would affect the Civil War?

Emancipation Proclamation

GEOGRAPHY SKILLS **INTERPRETING MAPS**

Place In which places was slavery still legal after the Emancipation Proclamation?

- Lincoln worried about losing support for the war. Previous wartime Confiscation Acts that had attempted to free the slaves had been unpopular in the border states.
- Others, including Secretary of War Edwin Stanton, agreed with Lincoln that the use of slave labor was helping the Confederacy make war. Therefore, as commander in chief, the president could free the slaves in all rebellious states. Freed African Americans could then be recruited into the Union army.

For several weeks in 1862, Lincoln worked intensely, thinking, writing, and rewriting. He finally wrote the **Emancipation Proclamation**, the order to free the Confederate slaves. The proclamation declared that:

> "...all persons held as slaves within any State or designated part of a State the people whereof shall then be in rebellion against the United States shall be then, thenceforward, and forever free."
>
> —Emancipation Proclamation, 1862

The Emancipation Proclamation was a military order that freed slaves only in areas

New Soldiers

African American soldiers, such as the 54th Massachusetts Infantry and Company E of the 4th U.S. Colored Infantry, shown here, fought proudly and bravely in the Civil War. At right is a flyer used to recruit African American soldiers.

controlled by the Confederacy. In fact, the proclamation had little immediate effect. It was impossible for the federal government to enforce the proclamation in the areas where it actually applied—the states in rebellion that were not under federal control. The proclamation did not stop slavery in the border states, where the federal government would have had the power to enforce it. The words written in the Emancipation Proclamation were powerful, but the impact of the document was more symbolic than real. It defined what the Union was fighting against, and discouraged Britain from aiding the Confederacy.

Lincoln wanted to be in a strong position in the war before announcing his plan. The Battle of Antietam gave him the victory he needed. He issued the Emancipation Proclamation on September 22, 1862. The proclamation went into effect on January 1, 1863.

Reaction to the Proclamation

New Year's Eve, December 31, 1862: In "night watch" meetings at many African American churches, worshippers prayed, sang, and gave thanks. When the clocks struck midnight, millions were free. Abolitionists rejoiced. Frederick Douglass called January 1, 1863, "the great day which is to determine the destiny not only of the American Republic, but that of the American Continent."

William Lloyd Garrison was quick to note, however, that "slavery, as a system" continued to exist in the loyal slave states. Yet where slavery remained, the proclamation encouraged many enslaved Africans to escape when the Union troops came near. They flocked to the Union camps and followed them for protection. The loss of slaves crippled the South's ability to wage war.

READING CHECK **Finding Main Ideas** How did northerners view the Emancipation Proclamation?

Primary Source

LETTER

June 23, 1863

Joseph E. Williams, an African American soldier and recruiter from Pennsylvania, wrote this letter describing why African Americans fought for the Union.

"We are now determined to hold every step which has been offered to us as citizens of the United States for our elevation [benefit], which represent justice, the purity, the truth, and aspiration [hope] of heaven. We must learn deeply to realize the duty, the moral and political necessity for the benefit of our race...Every consideration of honor, of interest, and of duty to God and man, requires that we should be true to our trust."

—quoted in *A Grand Army of Black Men*, edited by Edwin S. Redkey

ANALYSIS SKILL **ANALYZING PRIMARY SOURCES**

Why did Williams think being soldiers was so important for African Americans?

African Americans Participate in the War

As the war casualties climbed, the Union needed even more troops. African Americans were ready to volunteer. Not all white northerners were ready to accept them, but eventually they had to. Frederick Douglass believed that military service would help African Americans gain rights.

> "Once let the black man get upon his person the brass letters, U.S.; ... and a musket on his shoulder and bullets in his pocket, and there is no power on earth which can deny that he has earned the right to citizenship."
>
> —Frederick Douglass, quoted in *The Life and Writings of Frederick Douglass, Vol. 3*

Congress began allowing the army to sign up African American volunteers as laborers in July 1862. The War Department also gave **contrabands**, or escaped slaves, the right to join the Union army in South Carolina. Free African Americans in Louisiana and Kansas also formed their own units in the Union army. By the spring of 1863, African American army units were proving themselves in combat. They took part in a Union attack on Port Hudson, Louisiana, in May.

One unit stood out above the others. The **54th Massachusetts Infantry** consisted mostly of free African Americans. In July 1863 this regiment led a heroic charge on South Carolina's Fort Wagner. The 54th took heavy fire and suffered huge casualties in the failed operation. About half the regiment was killed, wounded, or captured. Edward L. Pierce, a correspondent for the *New York Tribune,* wrote, "The Fifty-fourth did well and nobly...They moved up as gallantly as any troops could, and with their enthusiasm they deserved a better fate." The bravery of the 54th regiment made it the most celebrated African American unit of the war.

About 180,000 African Americans served with the Union army. They received $10 a month, while white soldiers got $13. They were usually led by white officers, some from abolitionist families.

African Americans faced special horrors on the battlefield. Confederates often killed their black captives or sold them into slavery. In the 1864 election, Lincoln suggested rewarding African American soldiers by giving them the right to vote.

READING CHECK **Analyzing Information**
How did African Americans support the Union?

Growing Opposition

The deepening shadows in Lincoln's face reflected the huge responsibilities he carried. Besides running the war, he had to deal with growing tensions in the North.

Copperheads

As the months rolled on and the number of dead continued to increase, a group of northern Democrats began speaking out against the war. Led by U.S. Representative Clement L. Vallandigham of Ohio, they called themselves Peace Democrats. Their enemies called them Copperheads, comparing them to a poisonous snake. The name stuck.

FOCUS ON NORTH CAROLINA

Some southerners were also opposed to the war. William W. Holden ran for governor of North Carolina on a peace platform in 1864.

Many **Copperheads** were midwesterners that sympathized with the South and opposed abolition. They believed the war was not necessary and called for its end. Vallandigham asked what the war had gained, and then said, "Let the dead at Fredericksburg and Vicksburg answer."

Lincoln saw the Copperheads as a threat to support of the war effort. To silence them, he suspended the right of habeas corpus. **Habeas corpus** is a constitutional protection against unlawful imprisonment. Ignoring this protection, Union officials jailed their enemies, including some Copperheads, without evidence or trial. Lincoln's action greatly angered Democrats and some Republicans.

Northern Draft

In March 1863, war critics erupted again when Congress approved a draft, or forced military service. For $300, men were allowed to buy their way out of military service. For an unskilled laborer, however, that was nearly a year's wages. Critics of the draft called the Civil War a "rich man's war and a poor man's fight."

In July 1863, riots broke out when African Americans were brought into New York City to replace striking Irish dock workers. The city happened to be holding a war draft at the same time. The two events enraged rioters, who attacked African Americans and draft offices. More than 100 people died.

In this tense situation, the northern Democrats nominated former General George McClellan for president in 1864. They called

Infantry Family

While wealthy civilians could avoid military service, poorer men were drafted to serve in the Union army. This member of the 31st Pennsylvania Infantry brought his family along with him. His wife probably helped the soldier with many daily chores such as cooking and laundry.

Why would soldiers bring their families to live with them in camp?

for an immediate end to the war. Lincoln defeated McClellan in the popular vote, winning by about 400,000 votes out of 4 million cast. The electoral vote was not even close. Lincoln won 212 to 21.

READING CHECK **Identifying Cause and Effect** Who opposed the war, and how did Lincoln respond to the conflict?

Life for Soldiers and Civilians

Young, fresh recruits in both armies were generally eager to fight. Experienced troops, however, knew better.

On the Battlefield

Civil War armies fought in the ancient battlefield formation that produced massive casualties. Endless rows of troops fired directly at one another, with cannonballs landing amid them. When the order was given, soldiers would attach bayonets to their guns and rush toward their enemy. Men died to gain every inch of ground.

Doctors and nurses in the field saved many lives. Yet they had no medicines to stop infections that developed after soldiers were wounded. Many soldiers endured the horror of having infected legs and arms amputated without painkillers. Infections from minor injuries caused many deaths.

Despite the huge battlefield losses, the biggest killer in the Civil War was not the fighting. It was diseases such as typhoid, pneumonia, and tuberculosis. Nearly twice as many soldiers died of illnesses as died in combat.

Prisoners of War

Military prisoners on both sides lived in unimaginable misery. In prison camps, such as Andersonville, Georgia, and Elmira, New York, soldiers were packed into camps designed to hold only a fraction of their number. Soldiers had little shelter, food, or clothing. Starvation and disease killed thousands of prisoners.

LINKING TO TODAY

Battlefield Communications

The drummer was an essential member of every Civil War unit. Drummers served army commanders by drumming specific beats that directed troop movements during battle. Different beats were used to order troops to prepare to attack, to fire, to cease fire, and to signal a truce. Drummers had to stay near their commanders to hear orders. This meant that the drummers—some as young as nine years old—often saw deadly combat conditions.

The Civil War gave birth to the Signal Corps, the army unit devoted to communications. Today battlefield communications are primarily electronic. Radio, e-mail, facsimile, and telephone messages, often relayed by satellites, enable orders and other information to be transmitted nearly instantaneously all over the globe.

Union Signal Corps

Modern battlefield communications

ANALYSIS SKILL **ANALYZING INFORMATION**

Why is communication so important on the battlefield?

Life as a Civilian

The war effort involved all levels of society. Women as well as people too young or too old for military service worked in factories and on farms. Economy in the North boomed as production and prices soared. The lack of workers caused wages to rise by 43 percent between 1860 and 1865.

THE IMPACT TODAY

The American Red Cross today supplies victims of natural disasters with relief aid.

Women were the backbone of civilian life. On the farms, women and children performed the daily chores usually done by men. One visitor to Iowa in 1862 reported that he "met more women . . . at work in the fields than men." Southern women also managed farms and plantations.

One woman brought strength and comfort to countless wounded Union soldiers. Volunteer **Clara Barton** organized the collection of medicine and supplies for delivery to the battlefield. At the field hospitals, the "angel of the battlefield" soothed the wounded and dying and assisted doctors as bullets flew around her. Barton's work formed the basis for the future American Red Cross.

Clara Barton
founded the American Red Cross.

In the South, Sally Louisa Tompkins established a small hospital in Richmond, Virginia. By the end of the war, it had grown into a major army hospital. Jefferson Davis recognized her value to the war effort by making her a captain in the Confederate army.

READING CHECK **Analyzing** How did women help the war effort on both sides?

SUMMARY AND PREVIEW Many lives were changed by the war. In the next section you will learn about the end of the war.

Section 4 Assessment

go.hrw.com
Online Quiz
KEYWORD: SC7 HP16

Reviewing Ideas, Terms, and People

1. a. **Recall** Why did some Americans want to end slavery?
   b. **Contrast** How did reactions to the **Emancipation Proclamation** differ?
   c. **Elaborate** Do you think that the **emancipation** of slaves should have extended to the border states? Explain your answer.
2. a. **Recall** Why did some northerners want to recruit African Americans into the Union army?
   b. **Contrast** In what ways did African American soldiers face more difficulties than white soldiers did?
3. a. **Identify** Who were **Copperheads**, and why did they oppose the war?
   b. **Evaluate** Should President Lincoln have suspended the right to **habeas corpus**? Why?
4. a. **Describe** What were conditions like in military camps?
   b. **Draw Conclusions** How did the war change life on the home front?

Critical Thinking

5. **Identifying Effects** Review your notes. Then copy the graphic organizer below. Use it to summarize the reasons for the Emancipation Proclamation, its main points, and its effects on different people.

Reasons for the Emancipation Proclamation
↓
Main points of the Proclamation
↓
Effect on People's Lives
↓

FOCUS ON WRITING

6. **Taking Notes on Life During the War** As you read this section, take notes on the emancipation of the slaves, African American soldiers, and women who provided medical care for soldiers. Answer the following questions: Who? Where? When? Why? and How?

BIOGRAPHY

Abraham Lincoln

What would you do to save the struggling Union?

When did he live? 1809–1865

Where did he live? Abraham Lincoln was born in a log cabin to a poor family in Kentucky. Growing up in Kentucky and Illinois, Lincoln went to school for less than a year. He taught himself law and settled in Springfield, where he practiced law and politics. As president he lived in Washington, D.C. There, at age 56, his life was cut short by an assassin, John Wilkes Booth.

What did he do? The issue of slavery defined Lincoln's political career. He was not an abolitionist, but he strongly opposed extending slavery into the territories. In a series of famous debates against Senator Stephen Douglas of Illinois, Lincoln championed his views on slavery and made a brilliant defense of democracy and the Union. As president, Lincoln led the nation through the Civil War.

Why is he important? Lincoln is one of the great symbols of American democracy. "A house divided against itself cannot stand," he declared in a debate with Douglas. In 1863 Lincoln issued the Emancipation Proclamation. His address to commemorate the bloody battlefield at Gettysburg is widely considered to be one of the best political speeches in American history.

Summarizing Why is Lincoln such an important figure in American history?

KEY EVENTS

- **1834** Elected to the Illinois legislature
- **1842** Marries Mary Todd
- **1858** Holds series of famous debates with U.S. Senator Stephen Douglas
- **1860** Elected president on November 6
- **1863** Issues the Emancipation Proclamation on January 1
- **1863** Gives the Gettysburg Address on November 19
- **1865** Gives second inaugural address on March 4
- **1865** Shot on April 14; dies the next day

Lincoln's address at the dedication of the Gettysburg National Cemetery.

SECTION 5

The Tide of War Turns

What You Will Learn...

Main Ideas

1. The Union tried to divide the Confederate Army at Fredericksburg, but the attempt failed.
2. The Battle of Gettysburg in 1863 was a major turning point in the war.
3. During 1864, Union campaigns in the East and South dealt crippling blows to the Confederacy.
4. Union troops forced the South to surrender in 1865, ending the Civil War.

The Big Idea

Union victories in 1863, 1864, and 1865 ended the Civil War.

Key Terms and People

Battle of Gettysburg, *p. 537*
George Pickett, *p. 539*
Pickett's Charge, *p. 539*
Gettysburg Address, *p. 540*
Wilderness Campaign, *p. 540*
William Tecumseh Sherman, *p. 541*
total war, *p. 542*
Appomattox Courthouse, *p. 542*

TAKING NOTES Copy the graphic organizer. Use it to recall the events that led to the end of the Civil War.

July 1–3, 1863
May–June, 1864
September 2, 1864
December 10, 1864
April 2, 1865
April 9, 1865

If YOU were there...

You live in southern Pennsylvania in 1863, near a battlefield where thousands died. Now people have come from miles around to dedicate a cemetery here. You are near the front of the crowd. The first speaker impresses everyone with two hours of dramatic words and gestures. Then President Lincoln speaks—just a few minutes of simple words. Many people are disappointed.

Why do you think the president's speech was so short?

BUILDING BACKGROUND Many people, especially in the North, had expected a quick victory, but the war dragged on for years. The balance of victories seemed to seesaw between North and South, and both sides suffered terrible casualties. The last Confederate push into the North ended at Gettysburg in one of the bloodiest battles of the war.

Fredericksburg and Chancellorsville

Frustrated by McClellan's lack of aggression, Lincoln replaced him with General Ambrose E. Burnside as leader of the Army of the Potomac. Burnside favored a swift, decisive attack on Richmond by way of Fredericksburg. In November 1862, he set out with 120,000 troops.

Burnside's tactics surprised General Lee. The Confederate commander had divided his force of 78,000 men. Neither section of the Confederate army was in a good position to defend Fredericksburg. However, Burnside's army experienced delays in crossing the Rappahannock River. These delays allowed Lee's army to reunite and entrench themselves around Fredericksburg. Finally, the Union army crossed the Rappahannock and launched a series of charges. These attacks had heavy casualties and failed to break the Confederate line. Eventually, after suffering about 12,600 casualties, Burnside ordered a retreat. The Confederates had about 5,300 casualties.

Soon Burnside stepped down from his position. Lincoln made General Joseph Hooker the commander of the Army of the Potomac. At the end of April 1863, Hooker and his army of about 138,000 men launched a frontal attack on Fredericksburg. Then Hooker ordered about 115,000 of his troops to split off and approach the Confederate's flank, or side. Hooker's strategy seemed about to work. But for some reason he hesitated and had his flanking troops take a defensive position at Chancellorsville. This town was located a few miles west of Fredericksburg.

The following day, Lee used most of his army (about 60,000 men) to attack Hooker's troops at Chancellorsville. Stonewall Jackson led an attack on Hooker's flank while Lee commanded an assault on the Union front. The Union army was almost cut in two. They managed to form a defensive line, which they held for three days. Then Hooker ordered a retreat.

Lee's army won a major victory. But this victory had severe casualties. During the battle, Lee's trusted general, Stonewall Jackson, was accidentally shot by his own troops. He died a few days later.

READING CHECK **Comparing** What did generals McClellan, Burnside, and Hooker have in common?

Battle of Gettysburg

General Lee launched more attacks within Union territory. As before, his goal was to break the North's will to fight. He also hoped that a victory would convince other nations to recognize the Confederacy.

First Day

In early June 1863, Lee cut across northern Maryland into southern Pennsylvania. His forces gathered west of a small town called Gettysburg. Lee was unaware that Union soldiers were encamped closer to town. He had been suffering from lack of enemy information for three days because his cavalry chief "Jeb" Stuart was not performing his duties. Stuart and his cavalry had gone off on their own raiding party, disobeying Lee's orders.

Another Confederate raiding party went to Gettysburg for boots and other supplies. There, Lee's troops ran right into Union general George G. Meade's cavalry, triggering the **Battle of Gettysburg**, a key battle that finally turned the tide against the Confederates. The battle began on July 1, 1863, when the

Three Days at Gettysburg

Gettysburg was the largest and bloodiest battle of the Civil War. In three days, more than 51,000 soldiers were killed, wounded, captured, or went missing. It was an important victory for the Union, and it stopped Lee's plan of invading the North.

Artillery played a key role in the Battle of Gettysburg on July 1, 1863.

Day One: July 1, 1863

Confederate raiding party and the Union forces began exchanging fire. The larger Confederate forces began to push the Union troops back through Gettysburg.

The Union soldiers regrouped along the high ground of Cemetery Ridge and Culp's Hill. General Lee wanted to prevent the Union forces from entrenching themselves. He therefore ordered General Ewell to attack immediately. However, Ewell hesitated and thereby gave the Federals time to establish an excellent defensive position.

In fact, Confederate General James Longstreet thought that the Union position was almost impossible to overrun. Instead of attacking, he felt that the Confederate army should move east, take a strong defensive position themselves, and wait for the Union forces to attack them. However, General Lee was not convinced. He believed that his troops were invincible.

The Confederates camped at Seminary Ridge, which ran parallel to the Union forces. Both camps called for their main forces to reinforce them and prepare for combat the next day.

Second Day

On July 2, Lee ordered an attack on the left side of the Union line. Lee knew that he could win the battle if his troops captured Little Round Top from the Union forces. From this hill, Lee's troops could easily fire down on the line of Union forces. Union forces and Confederate troops fought viciously for control of Little Round Top. The fighting was particularly fierce on the south side of the hill. There the 20th Maine led by Colonel Joshua Chamberlain battled the 15th Alabama led by Colonel William Oates. Later, when describing the conflict, Oates said, "The blood stood in puddles in some places in the rocks." Eventually, the Union forced the Confederates to pull back from Little Round Top.

Then the Confederates attacked Cemetery Hill and Culp's Hill. The fighting lasted until nightfall. The assault on Cemetery Hill was unsuccessful. The Confederates did manage to take a few trenches on Culp's Hill. Even so, the Union forces still held a strong defensive position by the day's end.

Three Days at Gettysburg (continued)

Day Two: July 2, 1863, 10 a.m.

Union soldiers desperately defended Little Round Top from a fierce Confederate charge.

Pickett's Charge

On the third day of battle, Longstreet again tried to convince Lee not to attack. But Lee thought that the Union forces were severely battered and ready to break. Because of this, he planned to attack the center of the Union line on Cemetery Ridge. Such a tactic, he felt, would not be expected. Indeed, General Meade left only about 5,750 troops to defend the center.

For over an hour, the Confederates shelled Cemetery Ridge with cannon fire. For a while, the Union cannons fired back. Then they slacked off. The Confederates assumed that they had seriously damaged the Union artillery. In reality, the Confederate barrage did little damage.

The task of charging the Union center fell to three divisions of Confederate soldiers. General **George Pickett** commanded the largest unit. In late afternoon, nearly 15,000 men took part in **Pickett's Charge**. For one mile, the Confederates marched slowly up toward Cemetery Ridge. Showered with cannon and rifle fire, they suffered severe losses. But eventually, some of them almost reached their destination. Then Union reinforcements added to the barrage on the rebels. Soon the

Pickett's Charge, July 3, 1863

General George Pickett led his troops across Emmitsburg Road to attack the Union position. He lost more than half of his men in the 50-minute battle.

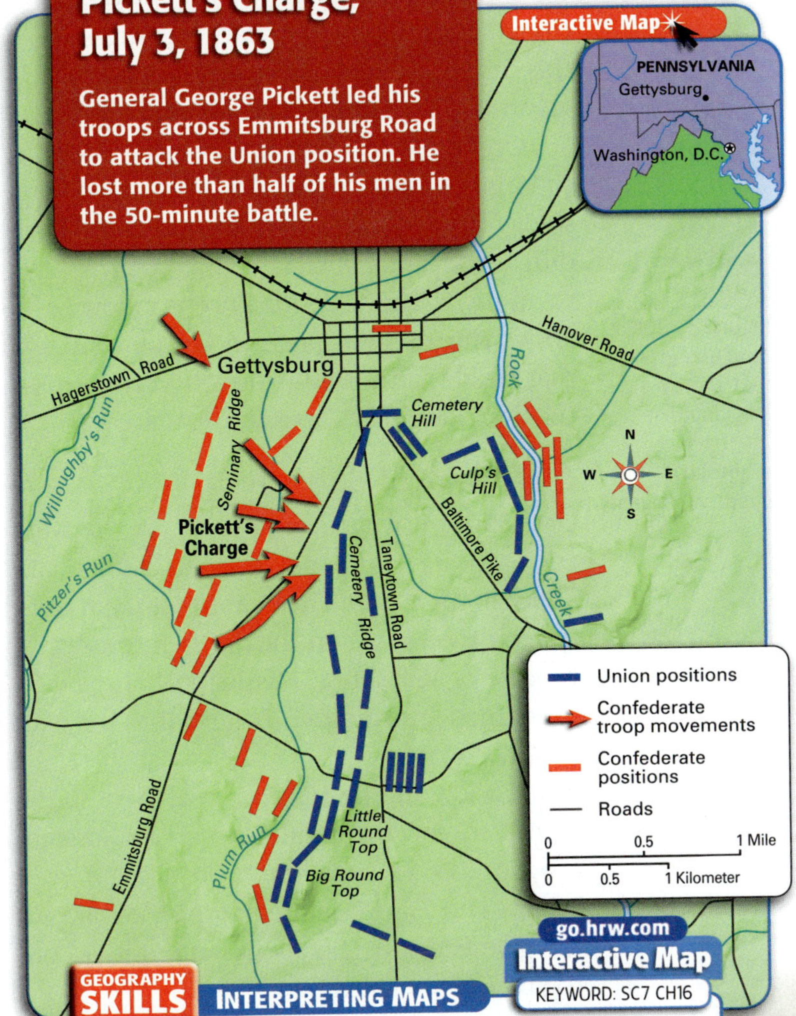

GEOGRAPHY SKILLS **INTERPRETING MAPS**

1. **Human-Environment Interaction** How do you think geography affected Pickett's Charge?
2. **Movement** In which direction did Pickett's soldiers charge?

Pickett's Charge

Pickett's Charge proved a disaster for the Confederate attackers. Fewer than half of them survived.

Day Three: July 3, 1863, 3 p.m.

Confederates retreated, leaving about 7,500 casualties on the field of battle. Distressed by this defeat, General Lee rode among the survivors and told them, "It is all my fault."

On the fourth day, Lee began to retreat to Virginia. In all, nearly 75,000 Confederate soldiers and 90,000 Union troops had fought during the Battle of Gettysburg.

Focus on Reading

The first sentence of the paragraph to the right is a main idea. The rest of this paragraph supports the idea.

General Meade decided not to follow Lee's army. This decision angered Lincoln. He felt that Meade had missed an opportunity to crush the Confederates and possibly end the war.

Aftermath of Gettysburg

Gettysburg was a turning point in the war. Lee's troops would never again launch an attack in the North. The Union victory at Gettysburg took place on the day before Grant's capture of Vicksburg, Mississippi. These victories made northerners believe that the war could be won.

In addition, the Union win at Gettysburg helped to end the South's search for foreign influence in the war. After Gettysburg, Great Britain and France refused to provide aid to the Confederacy. The South's attempt at cotton diplomacy failed.

The Gettysburg Address

On November 19, 1863, at the dedicating ceremony of the Gettysburg battlefield cemetery, President Lincoln gave a speech called the **Gettysburg Address**, in which he praised the bravery of Union soldiers and renewed his commitment to winning the Civil War. This short but moving speech is one of the most famous in American history. In one of its frequently quoted lines, Lincoln referenced the Declaration of Independence and its ideals of liberty, equality, and democracy. He reminded listeners that the war was being fought for those reasons.

Lincoln rededicated himself to winning the war and preserving the Union. A difficult road still lay ahead.

Academic Vocabulary

execute to perform, carry out

Reading Check **Analyzing** Why was Gettysburg a turning point?

Union Campaigns Cripple the Confederacy

Lincoln had been impressed with General Grant's successes in capturing Vicksburg. He transferred Grant to the East and gave him command of the Union army. In early 1864, Grant forced Lee to fight a series of battles in Virginia that stretched Confederate soldiers and supplies to their limits.

Wilderness Campaign in the East

From May through June, the armies fought in northern and central Virginia. Union troops launched the **Wilderness Campaign**—a series of battles designed to capture the Confederate capital at Richmond, Virginia. The first battle took place in early May, in woods about 50 miles outside of Richmond. Grant then ordered General Meade to Spotsylvania, where the fighting raged for five days.

Over the next month, Union soldiers moved the Confederate troops back toward Richmond. However, Grant experienced his worst defeat at the Battle of Cold Harbor in early June, just 10 miles northeast of Richmond. In only a few hours the Union army suffered 7,000 casualties. The battle delayed Grant's plans to take the Confederate capital.

Union forces had suffered twice as many casualties as the Confederates had, yet Grant continued his strategy. He knew he would be getting additional soldiers, and Lee could not. Grant slowly but surely advanced his troops through Virginia. He told another officer, "I propose to fight it out on this line if it takes all summer."

After Cold Harbor, General Grant moved south of Richmond. He had hoped to take control of the key railroad junction at Petersburg, Virginia. Lee's army, however, formed a solid defense, and Grant could not execute his attack. Grant was winning the war, but he still had not captured Richmond. Facing re-election, Lincoln was especially discouraged by this failure.

GEOGRAPHY SKILLS **INTERPRETING MAPS**

1. **Movement** About how long was Sherman's March to the Sea from Atlanta to Savannah?
2. **Movement** What challenges do you think Sherman faced on his southern attacks?

Sherman Strikes the South

Lincoln needed a victory for the Union army to help him win re-election in 1864. The bold campaign of General **William Tecumseh Sherman** provided this key victory. Sherman carried out the Union plan to destroy southern railroads and industries.

In the spring of 1864, Sherman marched south from Tennessee with 100,000 troops. His goal was to take Atlanta, Georgia, and knock out an important railroad link. From May through August, Sherman's army moved steadily through the Appalachian Mountains toward Atlanta. Several times, Sherman avoided defenses set up by Confederate general Joseph Johnston.

In July, Sherman was within sight of Atlanta. Confederate president Jefferson Davis gave General John Hood command of Confederate forces in the region. Hood repeatedly attacked Sherman in a final attempt to save Atlanta, but the Union troops proved stronger. The Confederate troops retreated as Sherman held Atlanta under siege.

Atlanta fell to Sherman's troops on September 2, 1864. Much of the city was destroyed by artillery and fire. Sherman ordered the residents who still remained to leave. Responding to his critics, Sherman later wrote, "War is war, and not popularity-seeking." The loss of Atlanta cost the South an important railroad link and its center of industry.

Many people in the North had been upset with the length of the war. However, the capture of Atlanta showed that progress was being made in defeating the South. This success helped to convince Union voters to re-elect Lincoln in a landslide.

Sherman did not wait long to begin his next campaign. His goal was the port city of Savannah, Georgia. In mid-November 1864,

FOCUS ON NORTH CAROLINA

After taking Savannah, Sherman began a march north through the Carolinas. When his troops arrived in North Carolina, they destroyed acres of forest by setting them on fire. The troops also took horses, food, and other supplies from the surrounding countryside. Troops under General Joseph Johnston tried to stop Sherman at Bentonville but were defeated in the largest battle on North Carolina soil.

Sherman left Atlanta with a force of about 60,000 men. He said he would "make Georgia howl!"

During his March to the Sea, Sherman practiced **total war**—destroying civilian and economic resources. Sherman believed that total war would ruin the South's economy and its ability to fight. He ordered his troops to destroy railways, bridges, crops, livestock, and other resources. They burned plantations and freed slaves.

Sherman's army reached Savannah on December 10, 1864. They left behind a path of destruction 60 miles wide. Sherman believed that this march would speed the end of the war. He wanted to break the South's will to fight by marching Union troops through the heart of the Confederacy. In the end, Sherman's destruction of the South led to anger and resentment toward the people of the North that would last for generations.

READING CHECK **Drawing Conclusions**

How did Sherman hope to help the Union with his total-war strategy?

Causes and Effects of the Civil War

QUICK FACTS

Causes

- Disagreement over the institution of slavery
- Economic differences
- Political differences

Effects

- Slavery ends
- 620,000 Americans killed
- Military districts created
- Southern economy in ruins

ANALYSIS SKILL **INTERPRETING CHARTS**

How important was slavery to the Civil War?

The South Surrenders

In early April, Sherman closed in on the last Confederate defenders in North Carolina. At the same time, Grant finally broke through the Confederate defenses at Petersburg. On April 2, Lee was forced to retreat from Richmond.

Fighting Ends

By the second week of April 1865, Grant had surrounded Lee's army and demanded the soldiers' surrender. Lee hoped to join other Confederates in fighting in North Carolina, but Grant cut off his escape just west of Richmond. Lee tried some last minute attacks but could not break the Union line. Lee's forces were running low on supplies. General James Longstreet told about the condition of Confederate troops. "Many weary soldiers were picked up . . . some with, many without, arms [weapons],—all asking for food."

Trapped by the Union army, Lee recognized that the situation was hopeless. "There is nothing left for me to do but go and see General Grant," Lee said, "and I would rather die a thousand deaths."

On April 9, 1865, the Union and Confederate leaders met at a home in the small town of **Appomattox Courthouse** where Lee surrendered to Grant, thus ending the Civil War.

During the meeting, Grant assured Lee that his troops would be fed and allowed to keep their horses, and they would not be tried for treason. Then Lee signed the surrender documents. The long, bloody war had finally ended. Grant later wrote that he found the scene at Appomattox Courthouse more tragic than joyful.

> "I felt . . . sad and depressed at the downfall of a foe [enemy] who had fought so long and valiantly [bravely], and had suffered so much for a cause, though that cause was, I believe, one of the worst for which a people ever fought."
>
> —Ulysses S. Grant, *Battle Cry of Freedom*

Surrender at Appomattox

Union general Grant rose to shake hands with Confederate general Lee after the surrender. Grant allowed Lee to keep his sword and Lee's men to keep their horses.

Was it important for Grant and Lee to shake hands? Why or why not?

As General Lee returned to his troops, General Grant stopped Union forces from cheering their victory. "The war is over," Grant said with relief. "The rebels are our countrymen again."

The Effects of the War

The Civil War had deep and long-lasting effects. Almost 620,000 Americans lost their lives during the four years of fighting.

The defeat of the South ended slavery there. The majority of former slaves, however, had no homes or jobs. The southern economy was in ruins.

A tremendous amount of hostility remained, even after the fighting had ceased. The war was over, but the question remained: How could the United States be united once more?

READING CHECK **Predicting** What problems might the Union face following the Civil War?

SUMMARY AND PREVIEW After four long years of battles, the Civil War ended with General Lee's surrender at Appomattox Courthouse. In the next chapter you will read about the consequences of the war in the South.

Section 5 Assessment

go.hrw.com
Online Quiz
KEYWORD: SC7 HP16

Reviewing Ideas, Terms, and People

1. a. **Identify** What Confederate general died from his wounds at Chancellorsville?
   b. **Draw Conclusions** Why was the Union army defeated at Chancellorsville?
2. a. **Identify** What was the **Gettysburg Address**?
   b. **Analyze** Why was geography important to the outcome of the Battle of Gettysburg?
3. a. **Recall** What was the purpose of the **Wilderness Campaign**?
   b. **Draw Conclusions** In what way was the capture of Atlanta an important victory for President Lincoln?
4. a. **Identify** What events led to Lee's surrender at **Appomattox Courthouse**?
   b. **Summarize** What problems did the South face at the end of the war?

Critical Thinking

5. **Supporting a Point of View** Review your notes on the end of the Civil War. Then copy the graphic organizer below. Use it to show the three events in this section that you think contributed most to the end of the Civil War and explain why.

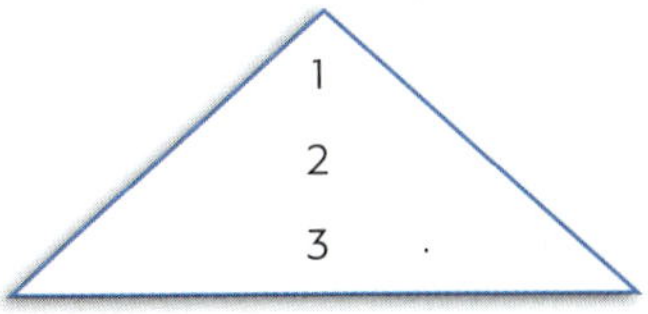

FOCUS ON WRITING

6. **Taking Notes on the End of the War** As you read this section, take notes on the Battle of Gettysburg, the Wilderness Campaign, the fall of Atlanta, and the South's surrender. Be sure to answer the following questions: Who? Where? When? Why? and How?

North Carolina Skills

3.04 Interpret social and political messages of cartoons.

Interpreting Political Cartoons

Define the Skill

Political cartoons are drawings that express views on important issues. They have been used throughout history to influence public opinion. The ability to interpret political cartoons will help you understand issues and people's attitudes about them.

Learn the Skill

Political cartoons use both words and images to convey their message. They often contain caricatures or symbolism. A caricature is a drawing that exaggerates the features of a person or object. Symbolism is the use of one thing to represent something else. Cartoonists use these techniques to help make their point clear. They also use titles, labels, and captions to get their message across.

Use these steps to interpret political cartoons.

1. Read any title, labels, and caption to identify the cartoon's general topic.
2. Identify the people and objects. Determine if they are exaggerated and, if so, why. Identify any symbols and analyze their meaning.
3. Draw conclusions about the message the cartoonist is trying to convey.

The following cartoon was published in the North in 1863. The cartoonist has used symbols to make his point. Lady Liberty, representing the Union, is being threatened by the Copperheads. The cartoonist has expressed his opinion of these people by drawing them as the poisonous snake for which they were named. This cartoon clearly supports the Union's continuing to fight the war.

Practice the Skill

Apply the guidelines to interpret the cartoon below and answer the questions that follow.

1. What do the tree and the man in it symbolize?
2. What policy or action of President Lincoln is this cartoon supporting?

LINCOLN'S LAST WARNING.
"Now, if you don't come down, I'll cut the Tree *from under you.*"
H.W. Oct. 11, 1862

CHAPTER 16 Chapter Review

HOLT
History's Impact
▶ **video series**
Review the video to answer the closing question:
How do you think the age of a country relates to its citizens' national pride?

Visual Summary

Use the visual summary below to help you review the main ideas of the chapter.

Reviewing Vocabulary, Terms, and People

Match the numbered definitions with the correct terms from the list below.

a. contrabands
b. cotton diplomacy
c. Second Battle of Bull Run
d. Siege of Vicksburg
e. Thomas "Stonewall" Jackson

1. Attack by Union general Ulysses S. Grant that gave the North control of the Mississippi River

2. Confederate general who held off Union attacks and helped the South win the First Battle of Bull Run

3. Important Confederate victory in which General Robert E. Lee defeated Union troops and pushed into Union territory for the first time

4. Southern strategy of using cotton exports to gain Britain's support in the Civil War

5. Term given to escaped slaves from the South

Comprehension and Critical Thinking

SECTION 1 *(Pages 510–515)*

6. a. Identify When and where did fighting in the U.S. Civil War begin?

b. Analyze How did civilians help the war effort in both the North and the South?

c. Elaborate Why do you think the border states chose to remain in the Union despite their support of slavery?

SECTION 2 *(Pages 516–521)*

7. a. Identify What was the first major battle of the war? What was the outcome of the battle?

b. Analyze What was the Union army hoping to accomplish when it marched into Virginia at the start of the war?

c. Evaluate Was the Union's naval blockade of the South successful? Why or why not?

SECTION 3 *(Pages 522–525)*

8. a. Identify Which side did the Cherokee support in the fighting at Pea Ridge? Why?

b. Draw Conclusions What progress did Union leaders make in the war in the West?

c. Evaluate Which victory in the West was most valuable to the Union? Why?

SECTION 4 *(Pages 528–534)*

9. a. Describe What responsibilities did women take on during the war?

b. Analyze What opposition to the war did President Lincoln face, and how did he deal with that opposition?

c. Predict What might be some possible problems that the newly freed slaves in the South might face?

SECTION 5 *(Pages 536–543)*

10. a. Recall When and where did the war finally end?

b. Compare and Contrast How were the efforts of Generals Grant and Sherman at the end of the war similar and different?

c. Elaborate What do you think led to the South's defeat in the Civil War? Explain.

Social Studies Skills

Interpreting Political Cartoons *Use the Social Studies Skills taught in this chapter to answer the question about the political cartoon below.*

11. What do you think the artist is saying about politicians with this cartoon?

Reading Skills

Supporting Facts and Details *Use the Reading Skills taught in this chapter to answer the question about the reading selection below.*

> Lee was unaware that Union soldiers were encamped closer to town. He had been suffering from lack of enemy information for three days because his cavalry chief "Jeb" Stuart was not performing his duties. Stuart and his cavalry had gone off on their own raiding party, disobeying Lee's orders. *(p. 537)*

12. What is the main idea of the above reading selection?

a. "Jeb" Stuart was not performing his duties.

b. Stuart and his cavalry had gone off on their own.

c. Stuart and his cavalry disobeyed Lee's orders.

d. Lee was suffering from a lack of enemy information.

Reviewing Themes

13. Society and Culture What effects did the Civil War have on American society?

14. Politics What political difficulties did the Emancipation Proclamation cause for President Lincoln?

Using the Internet

go.hrw.com
KEYWORD: SC7 CH16

15. Activity: Writing a Poem Soldiers in the Civil War came from all walks of life. Despite the hope for glory and adventure, many encountered dangerous and uncomfortable conditions. Enter the activity keyword to learn more about Civil War soldiers. After viewing photographs and reading letters, write a poem describing the life of a soldier. Your poem should reflect on the soldier's emotions and experiences.

FOCUS ON WRITING

16. Write Your Newspaper Article Review your notes. Then choose the subject you think would make the best newspaper article. Write an attention-grabbing headline. Then write your article, giving as many facts as possible.

CHAPTER 16 Standardized Test Practice

DIRECTIONS: Read each question and write the letter of the best response.

1 **Use the map below to answer the following question.**

The place where two major battles of the Civil War were fought is indicated on the map by which letter?

A W

B X

C Y

D Z

2 **What role did North Carolina play in the Civil War?**

A As a border state, North Carolina remained neutral in the war.

B Although part of the Confederacy, North Carolina did not play a big role in the war.

C North Carolina contributed the most troops of any Confederate state.

D North Carolina did not decide to enter the war until very late.

3 **Overall command of Confederate forces in Virginia during most of the Civil War was held by**

A Jefferson Davis.

B William Tecumseh Sherman.

C Thomas "Stonewall" Jackson.

D Robert E. Lee.

4 **Which of Lincoln's speeches and writings reflected the statement that "all men are created equal"?**

A the Emancipation Proclamation

B the first inaugural address (1861)

C the second inaugural address (1865)

D the Gettysburg Address

5 **The tactics that Sherman used against Confederate armies in the South were based on what strategy?**

A cutting off troops from their officers

B a naval blockade of southern ports

C destroying the South's resources and economy

D hit-and-run attacks on major southern cities

6 **In the War of 1812 the British navy blockaded American seaports in the hope that the U.S. economy would suffer and the United States would surrender. Which Civil War strategy was similar?**

A Scott's plan to destroy the southern economy

B Sherman's March to the Sea

C General Ulysses S. Grant's capture of Vicksburg

D Admiral David Farragut's defeat of New Orleans

7 **Read the following quote from a North Carolina Unionist and use it to answer the question below.**

> "[I] was pleading for the Union with hand upraised when news came of Fort Sumter and Lincoln's call for troops. When my hand came down from that impassioned gesticulation [gesture], it fell slowly and sadly by the side of a Secessionist."
>
> –Zebulon Vance, from *The Tar Heel State: A History of North Carolina*

Document-Based Question **What change of heart did the author have, and what brought about that change?**

CHAPTER 17 1865–1877

Reconstruction

North Carolina Standards

Social Studies Objectives

4.04 Evaluate the importance of the roles played by individuals at the state and national levels during the Civil War and Reconstruction Period.

4.05 Analyze the political, economic, and social impact of Reconstruction on the state and identify the reasons why Reconstruction came to an end.

5.01 Identify the role played by the agriculture, textile, tobacco, and furniture industries in North Carolina, and analyze their importance in the economic development of the state.

9.02 Identify past and present state and local leaders from diverse cultural backgrounds and assess their influence in affecting change.

go.hrw.com
North Carolina
KEYWORD: SC7 NC

FOCUS ON WRITING

Job History When the Civil War ended, it was time to rebuild. People were ready to get back to work. But life had changed for many people and would continue to change. As you read this chapter, think about jobs people may have had during Reconstruction.

UNITED STATES

1865
Abraham Lincoln is assassinated.

1865

WORLD

1865
Black Jamaicans rebel against the wealthy planter class.

HOLT

History's Impact

▶ **video series**
Watch the video to understand the impact of the preservation of the Union.

What You Will Learn...

The ruins of this Virginia plantation stand as a bleak reminder of the changes brought to the South by the Civil War. In this chapter you will learn about the challenges that faced the nation after the Civil War and attempts to meet those challenges.

1868
President Andrew Johnson is impeached and almost removed from office.

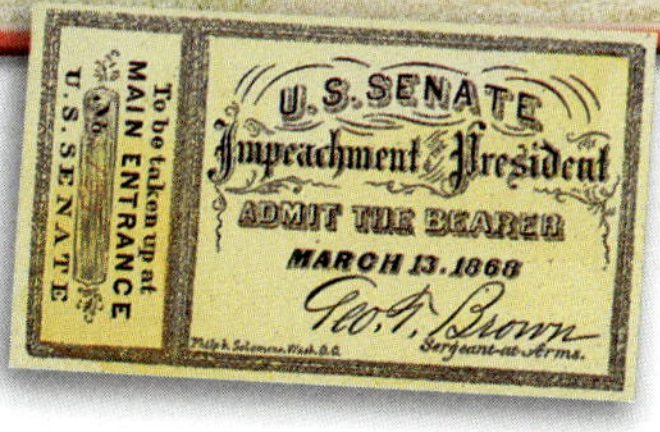

1870
Hiram Revels becomes the first African American to serve in the U.S. Senate.

1877
The Compromise of 1877 ends Reconstruction.

1870 — 1875 — 1880

1868
The Meiji dynasty returns to power in Japan.

1869
The Suez Canal opens, linking the Mediterranean and Red seas.

1871
Otto von Bismarck and Wilhelm I unite Germany.

Reading Social Studies

by Kylene Beers

Economics | Geography | Politics | Society and Culture | Science and Technology

Focus on Themes In this chapter you will read about the time immediately after the Civil War. You will see how the government tried to rebuild the South and will learn about how life changed for African Americans after slavery was declared illegal. You will read about the **political** conflicts that emerged as southern leadership worked to gain control of Reconstruction efforts. Throughout the chapter, you will read how the **culture** of the South changed after the War.

Analyzing Historical Information

Focus on Reading History books are full of information. As you read, you are confronted with names, dates, places, terms, and descriptions on every page. You don't want to have to deal with anything unimportant or untrue.

Identifying Relevant and Essential Information Information in a history book should be relevant to the topic you're studying. It should also be essential to understanding the topic and be verifiable. Anything else distracts from the material you are studying.

The first passage below includes several pieces of irrelevant and nonessential information. In the second, this information has been removed. Note how much easier the revised passage is to comprehend.

First Passage

President Abraham Lincoln, who was very tall, wanted to reunite the nation as quickly and painlessly as possible. He had proposed a plan for readmitting the southern states even before the war ended, which happened on a Sunday. Called the Ten Percent Plan, it offered southerners amnesty, or official pardon, for all illegal acts supporting the rebellion. Today a group called Amnesty International works to protect the rights of prisoners. Lincoln's plan certainly would have worked if it would have been implemented.

Lincoln's appearance and the day on which the war ended are not essential facts.

Amnesty International is not relevant to this topic.

There is no way to prove the accuracy of the last sentence.

Revised Passage

President Abraham Lincoln wanted to reunite the nation as quickly and painlessly as possible. He had proposed a plan for readmitting the southern states even before the war ended. Called the Ten Percent Plan, it offered southerners amnesty, or official pardon, for all illegal acts supporting the rebellion.

From Chapter 17, p. 553

You Try It!

The following passage is adapted from the chapter you are about to read. As you read, look for irrelevant, nonessential, or unverifiable information.

The Freedmen's Bureau

In 1865 Congress established the Freedmen's Bureau, an agency providing relief for freedpeople and certain poor people in the South. The Bureau had a difficult job. It may have been one of the most difficult jobs ever. At its high point, about 900 agents served the entire South. All 900 people could fit into one hotel ballroom today. Bureau commissioner Oliver O. Howard eventually decided to use the Bureau's limited budget to distribute food to the poor and to provide education and legal help for freedpeople. One common food in the South at that time was salted meat. The Bureau also helped African American war veterans. Today the Department of Veterans' Affairs assists American war veterans.

From Chapter 17, p. 556

After you read the passage, answer the following questions.

1. Which sentence in this passage is unverifiable and should be cut?

2. Find two sentences in this passage that are irrelevant to the discussion of the Freedmen's Bureau. What makes those sentences irrelevant?

3. Look at the last sentence of the passage. Do you think this sentence is essential to the discussion? Why or why not?

As you read Chapter 17, ask yourself what makes the information you are reading essential to a study of Reconstruction.

Key Terms and People

Chapter 17

Section 1

Reconstruction *(p. 552)*
Ten Percent Plan *(p. 553)*
Thirteenth Amendment *(p. 554)*
Freedmen's Bureau *(p. 556)*
Andrew Johnson *(p. 557)*

Section 2

Black Codes *(p. 558)*
Radical Republicans *(p. 559)*
Civil Rights Act of 1866 *(p. 560)*
Fourteenth Amendment *(p. 561)*
Reconstruction Acts *(p. 561)*
impeachment *(p. 562)*
Fifteenth Amendment *(p. 563)*

Section 3

Hiram Revels *(p. 565)*
Ku Klux Klan *(p. 566)*
Compromise of 1877 *(p. 567)*
poll tax *(p. 568)*
segregation *(p. 568)*
Jim Crow laws *(p. 568)*
Plessy v. *Ferguson* *(p. 569)*
sharecropping *(p. 569)*

Academic Vocabulary

Success in school is related to knowing academic vocabulary—the words that are frequently used in school assignments and discussions. In this chapter, you will learn the following academic words:

procedure *(p. 553)*
principle *(p. 560)*

SECTION 1

Rebuilding the South

What You Will Learn...

Main Ideas

1. President Lincoln and Congress differed in their views as Reconstruction began.
2. The end of the Civil War meant freedom for African Americans in the South.
3. President Johnson's plan began the process of Reconstruction.

The Big Idea

The nation faced many problems in rebuilding the Union.

Key Terms and People

Reconstruction, *p. 552*
Ten Percent Plan, *p. 553*
Thirteenth Amendment, *p. 554*
Freedmen's Bureau, *p. 556*
Andrew Johnson, *p. 557*

TAKING NOTES As you read, take notes on the different ways the U.S. government attempted to reconstruct the south after the Civil War. Write your notes in a graphic organizer like the one below.

Rebuilding and Reconstruction
1.
2.
3.
4.
5.
6.
7.

If YOU were there...

You are a young soldier who has been fighting in the Civil War for many months. Now that the war is over, you are on your way home. During your journey, you pass plantation manor homes, houses, and barns that have been burned down. No one is doing spring planting in the fields. As you near your family's farm, you see that fences and sheds have been destroyed. You wonder what is left of your home and family.

What would you think your future on the farm would be like?

BUILDING BACKGROUND When the Civil War ended, much of the South lay in ruins. Like the young soldier above, many people returned to destroyed homes and farms. Harvests of corn, cotton, rice, and other crops fell far below normal. Many farm animals had been killed or were roaming free. These were some of the challenges in restoring the nation.

Reconstruction Begins

After the Civil War ended in 1865, the U.S. government faced the problem of dealing with the defeated southern states. The challenges of **Reconstruction**, the process of readmitting the former Confederate states to the Union, lasted from 1865 to 1877.

Damaged South

Tired southern soldiers returned home to find that the world they had known before the war was gone. Cities, towns, and farms had been ruined. Because of high food prices and widespread crop failures, many southerners faced starvation. The Confederate money held by most southerners was now worthless. Banks failed, and merchants had gone bankrupt because people could not pay their debts.

Former Confederate general Braxton Bragg was one of many southerners who faced economic hardship. He found that "*all, all* was lost, except my debts." In South Carolina, Mary Boykin Chesnut wrote in her diary about the isolation she experienced after the war. "We are shut in here . . . All RR's [railroads] destroyed—bridges gone. We are cut off from the world."

Lincoln's Plan

President Abraham Lincoln wanted to reunite the nation as quickly and painlessly as possible. He had proposed a plan for readmitting the southern states even before the war ended. Called the **Ten Percent Plan**, it offered southerners amnesty, or official pardon, for all illegal acts supporting the rebellion. To receive amnesty, southerners had to do two things. They had to swear an oath of loyalty to the United States. They also had to agree that slavery was illegal. Once 10 percent of voters in a state made these pledges, they could form a new government. The state then could be readmitted to the Union.

Louisiana quickly elected a new state legislature under the Ten Percent Plan. Other southern states that had been occupied by Union troops soon followed Louisiana back into the United States.

Wade-Davis Bill

Some politicians argued that Congress, not the president, should control the southern states' return to the Union. They believed that Congress had the power to admit new states. Also, many Republican members of Congress thought the Ten Percent Plan did not go far enough. A senator from Michigan expressed their views.

> "The people of the North are not such fools as to . . . turn around and say to the traitors, 'all you have to do [to return] is . . . take an oath that henceforth you will be true to the Government.'"
>
> –Senator Jacob Howard, quoted in *Reconstruction: America's Unfinished Revolution, 1863–1877,* by Eric Foner

Two Republicans—Senator Benjamin Wade and Representative Henry Davis—had an alternative to Lincoln's plan. Following **procedures** of the Wade-Davis bill, a state had to meet two conditions before it could rejoin the Union. First, it had to ban slavery. Second, a majority of adult males in the state had to take the loyalty oath.

ACADEMIC VOCABULARY
procedure a series of steps taken to accomplish a task

War destroyed Richmond, Virginia, once the capital of the Confederacy.

Testing New Freedoms

aug5 Secretary.

SAML. DOVE wishes to know of the whereabouts of his mother, Areno, his sisters Maria, Neziah, and Peggy, and his brother Edmond, who were owned by Geo. Dove, of Rockingham county, Shenandoah Valley, Va. Sold in Richmond, after which Saml. and Edmond were taken to Nashville, Tenn., by Joe Mick; Areno was left at the Eagle Tavern, Richmond

Respectfully yours,
SAML. DOVE.
Utica, New York, Aug. 5, 1865–3m

U. S. Christian Commission,
Nashville, Tenn., July 19, 1865.

Under the Wade-Davis bill, only southerners who swore that they had never supported the Confederacy could vote or hold office. In general, the bill was much stricter than the Ten Percent Plan. Its provisions would make it harder for southern states to rejoin the Union quickly.

President Lincoln therefore refused to sign the bill into law. He thought that few southern states would agree to meet its requirements. He believed that his plan would help restore order more quickly.

READING CHECK **Contrasting** How was the Ten Percent Plan different from the Wade-Davis bill?

Freedom for African Americans

One thing Republicans agreed on was abolishing slavery. The Emancipation Proclamation had freed slaves only in areas that had not been occupied by Union forces, not in the border states. Many people feared that the federal courts might someday declare the proclamation unconstitutional.

Slavery Ends

On January 31, 1865, at President Lincoln's urging, Congress proposed the **Thirteenth Amendment**. This amendment made slavery illegal throughout the United States.

The freedpeople at left have packed their household belongings and are leaving Richmond. Many people traveled in search of relatives. Others placed newspaper advertisements looking for long-lost relatives. For other freedpeople, like the couple above, freedom brought the right to marry.

In what ways did former slaves react to freedom?

The amendment was ratified and took effect on December 18, 1865. When abolitionist William Lloyd Garrison heard the news, he declared that his work was now finished. He called for the American Anti-Slavery Society to break up. Not all abolitionists agreed that their work was done, however. Frederick Douglass insisted that "slavery is not abolished until the black man has the ballot [vote]."

Freedom brought important changes to newly freed slaves. Many couples held ceremonies to legalize marriages that had not been recognized under slavery. Many freedpeople searched for relatives who had been sold away from their families years earlier. Others placed newspaper ads seeking information about their children. Many women began to work at home instead of in the fields. Still others adopted children of dead relatives to keep families together. Church members established voluntary associations and mutual-aid societies to help those in need.

Now that they could travel without a pass, many freedpeople moved from mostly white counties to places with more African Americans. Other freedpeople traveled simply to test their new freedom of movement. A South Carolina woman explained this need. "I must go, if I stay here I'll never know I'm free."

For most former slaves, freedom to travel was just the first step on a long road toward equal rights and new ways of life. Adults took new last names and began to insist on being called Mr. or Mrs. as a sign of respect, rather than by their first names or by nicknames. Freedpeople began to demand the same economic and political rights as white citizens. Henry Adams, a former slave, argued that "if I cannot do like a white man I am not free."

Forty Acres to Farm?

Many former slaves wanted their own land to farm. Near the end of the Civil War, Union general William Tecumseh Sherman had issued an order to break up plantations in coastal South Carolina and Georgia. He wanted to divide the land into 40-acre plots and give them to former slaves as compensation for their forced labor before the war.

Many white planters refused to surrender their land. Some freedpeople pointed out that it was only fair that they receive some of this land because their labor had made the plantations prosper. In the end, the U.S. government returned the land to its original owners. At this time, many freedpeople were unsure about where they would live, what kind of work they would do, and what rights they had. Freedoms that were theirs by law were difficult to enforce.

Freedmen's Bureau

In 1865 Congress established the **Freedmen's Bureau**, an agency providing relief for freedpeople and certain poor people in the South. The Bureau had a difficult job. At its high point, about 900 agents served the entire South. Bureau commissioner Oliver O. Howard eventually decided to use the Bureau's limited budget to distribute food to the poor and to provide education and legal help for freedpeople. The Bureau also helped African American war veterans.

The Freedmen's Bureau played an important role in establishing more schools in the South. Laws against educating slaves meant that most freedpeople had never learned to read or write. Before the war ended, however, northern groups, such as the American Missionary Association, began providing books and teachers to African Americans. The teachers were mostly women who were committed to helping freedpeople. One teacher said of her students, "I never before saw children so eager to learn . . . It is wonderful how [they] . . . can have so great a desire for knowledge, and such a capacity for attaining [reaching] it."

After the war, some freedpeople organized their own education efforts. For example, Freedmen's Bureau agents found that some African Americans had opened schools in abandoned buildings. Many white southerners continued to believe that African Americans should not be educated. Despite opposition, by 1869 more than 150,000 African American students were attending more than 3,000 schools. The Freedmen's Bureau also helped establish a number of universities for African Americans, including Howard and Fisk universities.

Students quickly filled the new classrooms. Working adults attended classes in the evening. African Americans hoped that education would help them to understand and protect their rights and to enable them to find better jobs. Both black and white southerners benefited from the effort to provide greater access to education in the South.

READING CHECK **Analyzing** How did the Freedmen's Bureau help reform education in the South?

Helping the Freedpeople

Congress created the Freedmen's Bureau to help freedpeople and poor southerners recover from the Civil War. The Bureau assisted people by:

- **providing supplies and medical services**
- **establishing schools**
- **supervising contracts between freedpeople and employers**
- **taking care of lands abandoned or captured during the war**

What role did the Freedmen's Bureau play during Reconstruction?

President Johnson's Reconstruction Plan

While the Freedmen's Bureau was helping African Americans, the issue of how the South would politically rejoin the Union remained unresolved. Soon, however, a tragic event ended Lincoln's dream of peacefully reuniting the country.

A New President

On the evening of April 14, 1865, President Lincoln and his wife attended a play at Ford's Theater in Washington, D.C. During the play, John Wilkes Booth, a southerner who opposed Lincoln's policies, sneaked into the president's theater box and shot him. Lincoln was rushed to a boardinghouse across the street, where he died early the next morning. Vice President **Andrew Johnson** was sworn into office quickly. Reconstruction had now become his responsibility. He would have to win the trust of a nation shocked at its leader's death.

Johnson's plan for bringing southern states back into the Union was similar to Lincoln's plan. However, he decided that wealthy southerners and former Confederate officials would need a presidential pardon to receive amnesty. Johnson shocked Radical Republicans by eventually pardoning more than 7,000 people by 1866.

New State Governments

Johnson was a Democrat whom Republicans had put on the ticket in 1864 to appeal to the border states. A former slaveholder, he was a stubborn man who would soon face a hostile Congress.

Johnson offered a mild program for setting up new southern state governments. First, he appointed a temporary governor for each state. Then he required that the states revise their constitutions. Next, voters elected state and federal representatives. The new state government had to declare that secession was illegal. It also had to ratify the Thirteenth Amendment and refuse to pay Confederate debts.

By the end of 1865, all the southern states except Texas had created new governments. Johnson approved them all and declared that the United States was restored. Newly elected representatives came to Washington from each reconstructed southern state. However, Republicans complained that many new representatives had been leaders of the Confederacy. Congress therefore refused to readmit the southern states into the Union. Clearly, the nation was still divided.

READING CHECK **Summarizing** What was President Johnson's plan for Reconstruction?

FOCUS ON NORTH CAROLINA

President Johnson, a native of Raleigh, North Carolina, began his Reconstruction plan in his home state. He appointed William W. Holden as governor and soon pardoned Zebulon B. Vance, the state's wartime governor.

SUMMARY AND PREVIEW In this section you learned about early plans for Reconstruction. In the next section, you will learn that disagreements about Reconstruction became so serious that the president was almost removed from office.

Section 1 Assessment

go.hrw.com
Online Quiz
KEYWORD: SC7 HP17

Reviewing Ideas, Terms, and People

1. a. **Identify** What does **Reconstruction** mean?
   b. **Summarize** What was President Lincoln's plan for Reconstruction?
2. a. **Recall** What is the **Thirteenth Amendment**?
   b. **Elaborate** In your opinion, what was the most important accomplishment of the **Freedmen's Bureau**? Explain.
3. a. **Recall** Why was President Lincoln killed?
   b. **Analyze** Why did some Americans oppose President Johnson's Reconstruction plan?

Critical Thinking

4. **Summarizing** Review your notes on Reconstruction. Then copy the graphic organizer below and use it to show how African Americans were affected by the end of the war.

FOCUS ON WRITING

5. **Considering Historical Context** Many people planned to continue doing what they had done before the war. Others planned to start a new life. How do you think events and conditions you just read about might have affected their plans?

SECTION 2

The Fight over Reconstruction

What You Will Learn...

Main Ideas

1. Black Codes led to opposition to President Johnson's plan for Reconstruction.
2. The Fourteenth Amendment ensured citizenship for African Americans.
3. Radical Republicans in Congress took charge of Reconstruction.
4. The Fifteenth Amendment gave African Americans the right to vote.

The Big Idea

The return to power of the pre-war southern leadership led Republicans in Congress to take control of Reconstruction.

Key Terms and People

Black Codes, *p. 558*
Radical Republicans, *p. 559*
Civil Rights Act of 1866, *p. 560*
Fourteenth Amendment, *p. 561*
Reconstruction Acts, *p. 561*
impeachment, *p. 562*
Fifteenth Amendment, *p. 563*

TAKING NOTES As you read, take notes on how Republicans in Congress took over Reconstruction and how they changed Reconstruction policies. Write your notes in a graphic organizer like the one below.

Issues that Concerned Republicans	Changes by the Republican Congress

If YOU were there...

A member of Congress, you belong to the same political party as the president. But you strongly disagree with his ideas about Reconstruction and civil rights for African Americans. Now some of the president's opponents are trying to remove him from office. You do not think he is a good president. On the other hand, you think removing him would be bad for the unity of the country.

Will you vote to remove the president?

BUILDING BACKGROUND Americans were bitterly divided about what should happen in the South during Reconstruction. They disagreed about ending racial inequality and guaranteeing civil rights for African Americans. These conflicts split political parties. They led to showdowns between Congress and the president. Political fights even threatened the president's job.

Opposition to President Johnson

In 1866 Congress continued to debate the rules for restoring the Union. Meanwhile, new state legislatures approved by President Johnson had already begun passing laws to deny African Americans' civil rights. "This is a white man's government, and intended for white men only," declared Governor Benjamin F. Perry of South Carolina.

Black Codes

Soon, every southern state passed **Black Codes**, or laws that greatly limited the freedom of African Americans. They required African Americans to sign work contracts, creating working conditions similar to those under slavery. In most southern states, any African Americans who could not prove they were employed could be arrested. Their punishment might be one year of work without pay. African Americans were also prevented from owning guns. In addition, they were not allowed to rent property except in cities.

The Black Codes alarmed many Americans. As one Civil War veteran asked, "If you call this freedom, what do you call slavery?"

African Americans organized to oppose the codes. One group sent a petition to officials in South Carolina.

> “We simply ask . . . that the same laws which govern *white men* shall govern *black men* . . . that, in short, we be dealt with as others are—in equity [equality] and justice.”
>
> —Petition from an African American convention held in South Carolina, quoted in *There Is a River: The Black Struggle for Freedom in America* by Vincent Harding

Radical Republicans

The Black Codes angered many Republicans. They thought the South was returning to its old ways. Most Republicans were moderates who wanted the South to have loyal state governments. They also believed that African Americans should have rights as citizens. They hoped that the government would not have to force the South to follow federal laws.

Radical Republicans, on the other hand, took a harsher stance. They wanted the federal government to force change in the South. Like the moderates, they thought the Black Codes were cruel and unjust. The Radicals, however, wanted the federal government to be much more involved in Reconstruction. They feared that too many southern leaders remained loyal to the former Confederacy and would not enforce the new laws. Thaddeus Stevens

Primary Source

POLITICAL CARTOON

Supporting Radical Republican Ideas

Republicans were outraged to see former Confederates return to power as leaders of the Democratic Party. This 1868 political cartoon shows former Confederates Raphael Semmes and Nathan Bedford Forrest. Semmes was a Confederate admiral who had captured 62 Union merchant ships during the Civil War. Forrest was a cavalry officer known for brutality who later founded the Ku Klux Klan.

How do the actions of the people in these illustrations support the artist's point of view?

How do events in the background of these illustrations support the artist's point of view?

ANALYSIS SKILL **ANALYZING PRIMARY SOURCES**

Why do you think that the men are shown in their Confederate uniforms?

Primary Source

POINTS OF VIEW

Johnson vs. Stevens

President Andrew Johnson argued that the South should not be placed under military control.

"Military governments . . . established for an indefinite period, would have divided the people into the vanquishers and the vanquished, and would have envenomed [made poisonous] hatred rather than have restored affection."

—**Andrew Johnson**

Thaddeus Stevens believed that Congress had the power to treat the South as conquered territory.

"The future condition of the conquered power depends on the will of the conqueror. They must come in as new states or remain as conquered provinces. Congress . . . is the only power that can act in the matter."

—**Thaddeus Stevens**

ANALYSIS SKILL **IDENTIFYING POINTS OF VIEW**

How did Johnson's and Stevens's views on the South differ?

of Pennsylvania and Charles Sumner of Massachusetts were the leaders of the Radical Republicans.

A harsh critic of President Johnson, Stevens was known for his honesty and sharp tongue. He wanted economic and political justice for both African Americans and poor white southerners. Sumner had been a strong opponent of slavery before the Civil War. He continued to argue tirelessly for African Americans' civil rights, including the right to vote and the right to fair laws.

Both Stevens and Sumner believed that President Johnson's Reconstruction plan was a failure. Although the Radicals did not control Congress, they began to gain support among moderates when President Johnson ignored criticism of the Black Codes. Stevens believed the federal government could not allow racial inequality to survive.

READING CHECK **Comparing and Contrasting** How were Radical Republicans and moderate Republicans similar and different?

ACADEMIC VOCABULARY
principle basic belief, rule, or law

Fourteenth Amendment

Urged on by the Radicals in 1866, Congress proposed a new bill. It would give the Freedmen's Bureau more powers. The law would allow the Freedmen's Bureau to use military courts to try people accused of violating African Americans' rights. The bill's supporters hoped that these courts would be fairer than local courts in the South.

Johnson versus Congress

Surprising many members of Congress, Johnson vetoed the Freedmen's Bureau Bill. He insisted that Congress could not pass any new laws until the southern states were represented in Congress. Johnson also argued that the Freedmen's Bureau was unconstitutional.

Republicans responded with the **Civil Rights Act of 1866**. This act provided African Americans with the same legal rights as white Americans. President Johnson once again used his veto power. He argued that the act gave too much power to the federal government. He also rejected the **principle** of equal rights for African Americans. Congress, however, overrode Johnson's veto.

Many Republicans worried about what would happen when the southern states were readmitted. Fearing that the Civil Rights Act might be overturned, the Republicans proposed the **Fourteenth Amendment** in the summer of 1866. The Fourteenth Amendment included the following provisions.

1. It defined all people born or naturalized within the United States, except Native Americans, as citizens.
2. It guaranteed citizens the equal protection of the laws.
3. It said that states could not "deprive any person of life, liberty, or property, without due process of law."
4. It banned many former Confederate officials from holding state or federal offices.
5. It made state laws subject to federal court review.
6. It gave Congress the power to pass any laws needed to enforce it.

1866 Elections

President Johnson and most Democrats opposed the Fourteenth Amendment. As a result, civil rights for African Americans became a key issue in the 1866 congressional elections. To help the Democrats, Johnson traveled around the country defending his Reconstruction plan. Johnson's speaking tour was a disaster. It did little to win votes for the Democratic Party. Johnson even got into arguments with people in the audiences of some of his speaking engagements.

Two major riots in the South also hurt Johnson's campaign. On May 1, 1866, a dispute in Memphis, Tennessee, took place between local police and black Union soldiers. The dispute turned into a three-day wave of violence against African Americans. About three months later, another riot took place during a political demonstration in New Orleans. During that dispute, 34 African Americans and three white Republicans were killed.

READING CHECK **Summarizing** What issue did the Fourteenth Amendment address, and how did it affect the congressional elections of 1866?

Congress Takes Control of Reconstruction

The 1866 elections gave the Republican Party a commanding two-thirds majority in both the House and the Senate. This majority gave the Republicans the power to override any presidential veto. In addition, the Republicans became united as the moderates joined with the Radicals. Together, they called for a new form of Reconstruction.

Reconstruction Acts

In March 1867, Congress passed the first of several **Reconstruction Acts**. These laws divided the South into five districts. A U.S. military commander controlled each district.

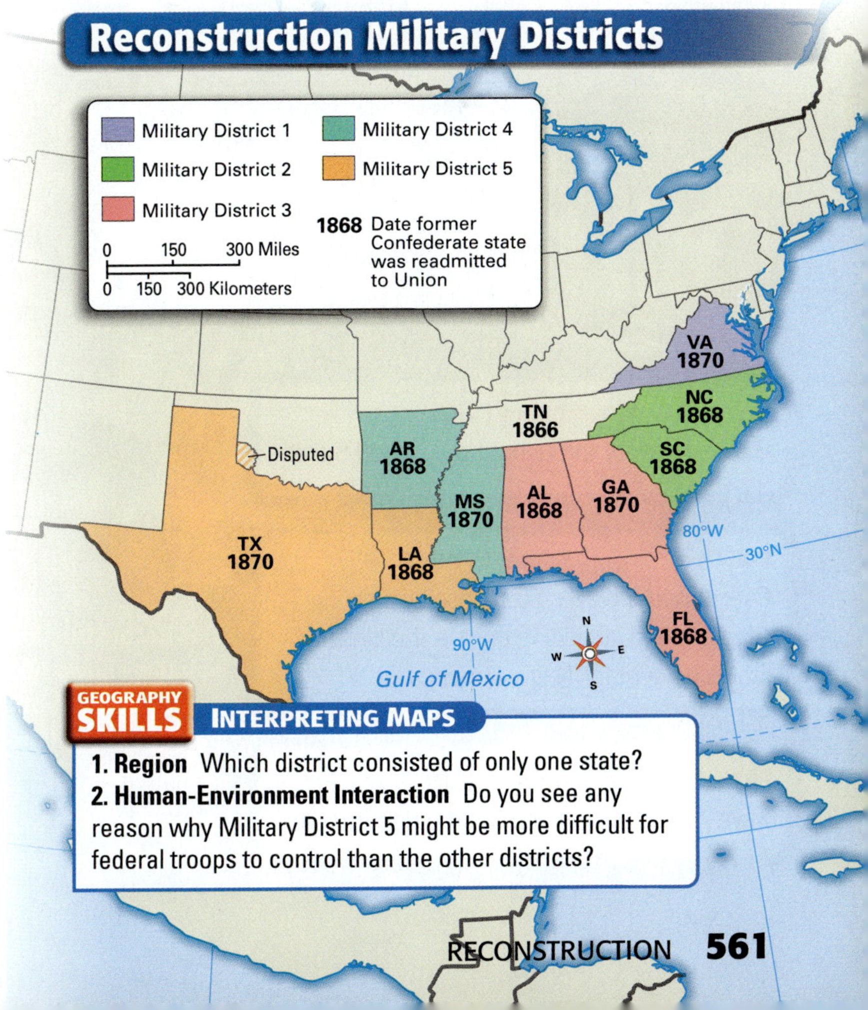

GEOGRAPHY SKILLS **INTERPRETING MAPS**

1. **Region** Which district consisted of only one state?
2. **Human-Environment Interaction** Do you see any reason why Military District 5 might be more difficult for federal troops to control than the other districts?

The military would remain in control of the South until the southern states rejoined the Union. To be readmitted, a state had to write a new state constitution supporting the Fourteenth Amendment. Finally, the state had to give African American men the right to vote.

Thaddeus Stevens was one of the new Reconstruction Acts' most enthusiastic supporters. He spoke in Congress to defend the acts.

> "Have not loyal blacks quite as good a right to choose rulers and make laws as rebel whites? Every man, no matter what his race or color . . . has an equal right to justice, honesty, and fair play with every other man; and the law should secure him those rights."
>
> –Thaddeus Stevens, quoted in *Sources of the American Republic*, edited by Marvin Meyers et al.

President on Trial

President Johnson strongly disagreed with Stevens. He argued that African Americans did not deserve the same treatment as white people. The Reconstruction Acts, he said, used "powers not granted to the federal government or any one of its branches." Knowing that Johnson did not support its Reconstruction policies, Congress passed a law limiting his power. This law prevented the president from removing cabinet officials without Senate approval. Johnson quickly broke the law by firing Edwin Stanton, the secretary of war.

For the first time in United States history, the House of Representatives responded by voting to impeach the president. **Impeachment** is the process used by a legislative body to bring charges of wrongdoing against a public official. The next step, under Article I of the Constitution, was a trial in the Senate. A two-thirds majority was required to find Johnson guilty and remove him from office.

Although Johnson was unpopular with Republicans, some of them believed he was being judged unfairly. Others did not trust the president pro tempore of the Senate, Benjamin Wade. He would become president if Johnson were removed from office. By a single vote, Senate Republicans failed to convict Johnson. Even so, the trial weakened his power as president.

Election of 1868

Johnson did not run for another term in 1868. The Democrats chose

The Reconstruction Amendments

QUICK FACTS

Thirteenth Amendment (1865)
Banned slavery throughout the United States

Fourteenth Amendment (1868)
Overturned the *Dred Scott* case by granting citizenship to all people born in the United States (except for Native Americans)

Fifteenth Amendment (1870)
Gave African American men the right to vote

This Reconstruction-era painting shows African American men voting after passage of the Fifteenth Amendment.

What right did the Fifteenth Amendment protect?

former New York governor Horatio Seymour as their presidential candidate. The Republicans chose Ulysses S. Grant. As a war hero, Grant appealed to many northern voters. He had no political experience but supported the congressional Reconstruction plan. He ran under the slogan "Let Us Have Peace."

Shortly after Grant was nominated, Congress readmitted seven southern states—Alabama, Arkansas, Florida, Georgia, Louisiana, North Carolina, and South Carolina. (Tennessee had already been readmitted in 1866.) Under the terms of readmission, these seven states approved the Fourteenth Amendment. They also agreed to let African American men vote. However, white southerners used violence to try to keep African Americans away from the polls.

Despite such tactics, hundreds of thousands of African Americans voted for Grant and the "party of Lincoln." The *New Orleans Tribune* reported that many former slaves "see clearly enough that the Republican party [is] their political life boat." African American votes helped Grant to win a narrow victory.

READING CHECK **Analyzing** To what voters did Grant appeal in the presidential election of 1868?

Fifteenth Amendment

After Grant's victory, Congressional Republicans wanted to protect their Reconstruction plan. They worried that the southern states might try to keep black voters from the polls in future elections. Also, some Radical Republicans argued that it was not fair that many northern states still had laws preventing African Americans from voting. After all, every southern state was required to grant suffrage to African American men.

In 1869 Congress proposed the **Fifteenth Amendment**, which gave African American men the right to vote. Abolitionist William Lloyd Garrison praised what he saw as "this wonderful, quiet, sudden transformation of four millions of human beings from . . . the auction block to the ballot-box." The amendment went into effect in 1870 as one of the last Reconstruction laws passed at the federal level.

The Fifteenth Amendment did not please every reformer, however. Many women were angry because the amendment did not also grant them the right to vote.

READING CHECK **Finding Main Ideas** How did Radical Republicans take control of Reconstruction?

THE IMPACT TODAY

The Voting Rights Act of 1965 enforces and expands the voting protections of the Fifteenth Amendment.

SUMMARY AND PREVIEW In this section you learned that Congress took control of Reconstruction and took steps to protect the rights of African Americans. In the next section you will learn about increasing opposition to Reconstruction.

Section 2 Assessment

go.hrw.com
Online Quiz
KEYWORD: SC7 HP17

Reviewing Ideas, Terms, and People

1. a. **Describe** What were **Black Codes**?
   b. **Make Inferences** Why did Republicans think Johnson's Reconstruction plan was a failure?
2. a. **Recall** What was the **Civil Rights Act of 1866**?
   b. **Summarize** Why was the **Fourteenth Amendment** important?
3. a. **Recall** Why was President Johnson impeached?
   b. **Evaluate** Which element of the **Reconstruction Acts** do you believe was most important? Why?
4. a. **Recall** What does the **Fifteenth Amendment** state?
   b. **Elaborate** Do you think that women should have been included in the Fifteenth Amendment? Explain.

Critical Thinking

5. **Identify** Review your notes on the issues that led Republicans to take over Reconstruction. Then copy the graphic organizer below and use it to identify the main provisions of the Fourteenth Amendment and their effects.

Provisions	Effects

FOCUS ON WRITING

6. **Recognizing Cause-and-Effect Relationships** As you have read in this section, social and political unrest continued long after the war ended. How could this unrest cause people to leave their jobs? What new jobs might they find?

SECTION 3

Reconstruction in the South

What You Will Learn...

Main Ideas

1. Reconstruction governments helped reform the South.
2. The Ku Klux Klan was organized as African Americans moved into positions of power.
3. As Reconstruction ended, the rights of African Americans were restricted.
4. Southern business leaders relied on industry to rebuild the South.

The Big Idea

As Reconstruction ended, African Americans faced new hurdles and the South attempted to rebuild.

Key Terms and People

Hiram Revels, *p. 565*
Ku Klux Klan, *p. 566*
Compromise of 1877, *p. 567*
poll tax, *p. 568*
segregation, *p. 568*
Jim Crow laws, *p. 568*
Plessy v. *Ferguson*, *p. 569*
sharecropping, *p. 569*

TAKING NOTES As you read, look for information related to the South's efforts to rebuild and the effects on African Americans.

Rebuilding the South	→	Effects on African Americans

If YOU were there...

You live on a farm in the South in the 1870s. Times are hard because you do not own your farm. Instead, you and your family work in a landowner's cotton fields. You never seem to earn enough to buy land of your own. Some of your neighbors have decided to give up farming and move to the city. Others are going to work in the textile mills. But you have always been a farmer.

Will you decide to change your way of life?

BUILDING BACKGROUND Reconstruction affected politics and economics in the South. Republican and Democratic politicians fought over policies and programs. New state governments began reforms, but later leaders ended many of them. Some parts of the southern economy improved. However, many farmers, like the family above, went through hard times.

Reconstruction Governments

After Grant became president in 1869, the Republicans seemed stronger than ever. They controlled most southern governments, partly because of the support of African American voters. However, most of the Republican officeholders were unpopular with white southerners.

Carpetbaggers and Scalawags

Some of these office-holders were northern-born Republicans who had moved South after the war. Many white southerners called them carpetbaggers. Supposedly, they had rushed South carrying all their possessions in bags made from carpeting. Many southerners resented these northerners, accusing them—often unfairly—of trying to profit from Reconstruction.

Southern Democrats cared even less for white southern Republicans. They referred to them as scalawags, or greedy rascals. Democrats believed that these southerners had betrayed the South by

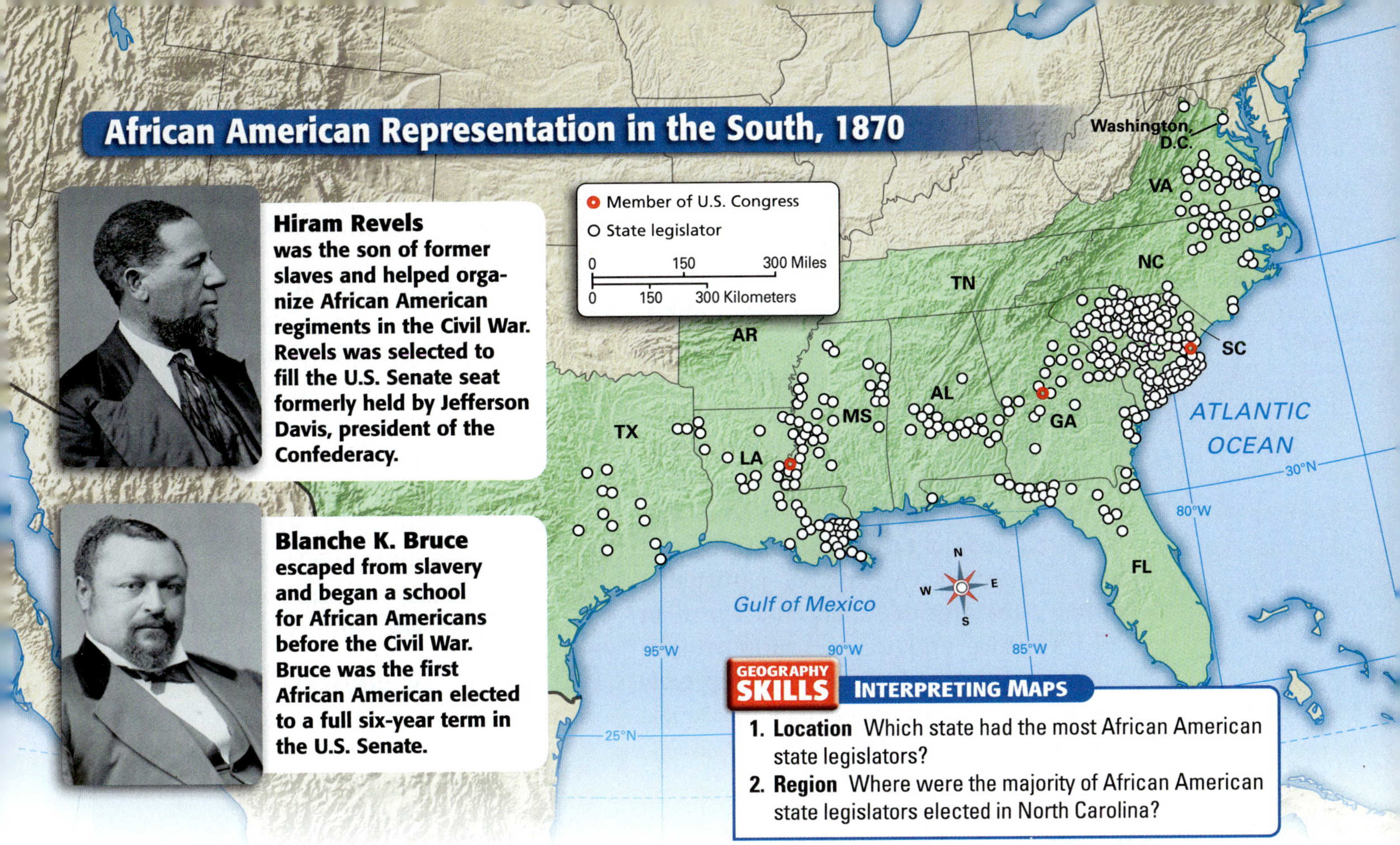

Hiram Revels was the son of former slaves and helped organize African American regiments in the Civil War. Revels was selected to fill the U.S. Senate seat formerly held by Jefferson Davis, president of the Confederacy.

Blanche K. Bruce escaped from slavery and began a school for African Americans before the Civil War. Bruce was the first African American elected to a full six-year term in the U.S. Senate.

GEOGRAPHY SKILLS **INTERPRETING MAPS**

1. **Location** Which state had the most African American state legislators?
2. **Region** Where were the majority of African American state legislators elected in North Carolina?

voting for the Republican Party. Many southern Republicans were small farmers who had supported the Union during the war. Others, like Mississippi governor James Alcorn, were former members of the Whig Party. They preferred to become Republicans rather than join the Democrats.

African American Leaders

African Americans were the largest group of southern Republican voters. During Reconstruction, more than 600 African Americans won election to state legislatures. Some 16 of these politicians were elected to Congress. Other African Americans held local offices in counties throughout the South.

African American politicians came from many backgrounds. **Hiram Revels** was born free in North Carolina and went to college in Illinois. He became a Methodist minister and served as a chaplain in the Union army. In 1870 Revels became the first African American in the U.S. Senate. He took over the seat previously held by Confederate president Jefferson Davis. Unlike Revels, Blanche K. Bruce grew up in slavery in Virginia. Bruce became an important Republican in Mississippi and served one term as a U.S. senator.

State Governments Change Direction

Reconstruction governments provided money for many new programs and organizations in the South. They helped to establish some of the first state-funded public school systems in the South. They also built new hospitals, prisons, and orphanages and passed laws prohibiting discrimination against African Americans.

Southern states under Republican control spent large amounts of money. They aided the construction of railroads, bridges, and public buildings. These improvements were intended to help the southern economy recover from the war. To get the money for these projects, the Reconstruction governments raised taxes and issued bonds.

READING CHECK **Summarizing** What reforms did Reconstruction state governments carry out?

FOCUS ON READING

How does the heading of this section tell you about what you will learn?

FOCUS ON NORTH CAROLINA

Republicans, northerners, and African Americans made up the convention that created the state constitution of 1868. Many conservatives in the state rallied against the constitution, but it served the state until 1971.

Ku Klux Klan

As more African Americans took office, resistance to Reconstruction increased among white southerners. Democrats claimed that the Reconstruction governments were corrupt, illegal, and unjust. They also disliked having federal soldiers stationed in their states. Many white southerners disapproved of African American officeholders. One Democrat noted, "'A white man's government' [is] the most popular rallying cry we have." In 1866 a group of white southerners in Tennessee created the **Ku Klux Klan**. This secret society opposed civil rights, particularly suffrage, for African Americans. The Klan used violence and terror against African Americans. The group's membership grew rapidly as it spread throughout the South. Klan members wore robes and disguises to hide their identities. They attacked—and even murdered—African Americans, white Republican voters, and public officials, usually at night.

Local governments did little to stop the violence. Many officials feared the Klan or were sympathetic to its activities. In 1870 and 1871 the federal government took action. Congress passed laws that made it a federal crime to interfere with elections or to deny citizens equal protection under the law.

Within a few years, the Klan was no longer an organized threat. But groups of whites continued to assault African Americans and Republicans throughout the 1870s.

READING CHECK **Drawing Conclusions** Why did southerners join the Ku Klux Klan?

The Ku Klux Klan

Members of the Ku Klux Klan often attacked under cover of darkness to hide their identities. This klansman from Tennessee, shown on the left, even disguised his horse.

Why do you think Klan members disguised themselves?

Reconstruction Ends

The violence of the Ku Klux Klan was not the only challenge to Reconstruction. Republicans slowly lost control of southern state governments to the Democratic Party. The General Amnesty Act of 1872 allowed former Confederates, except those who had held high ranks, to serve in public office. Many of these former Confederates, most of whom were Democrats, were soon elected to southern governments.

The Republican Party also began losing its power in the North. Although President Grant was re-elected in 1872, financial and political scandals in his administration upset voters. In his first term, a gold-buying scheme in which Grant's cousin took a leading role led to a brief crisis on the stock market called Black Friday. During his second term, his personal secretary was involved in the Whiskey Ring scandal, in which whiskey distillers and public officials worked together to steal liquor taxes from the federal government. Furthermore, people blamed Republican policies for the Panic of 1873.

Panic of 1873

This severe economic downturn began in September 1873 when Jay Cooke and Company, a major investor in railroads and the largest financier of the Union's Civil War effort, declared bankruptcy. The company had lied about the value of land along the side of the Northern Pacific Railroad that it owned and was trying to sell. When the truth leaked out, the company failed.

The failure of such an important business sent panic through the stock market, and investors began selling shares of stock more rapidly than people wanted to buy them. Companies had to buy their shares back from the investors. Soon, 89 of the nation's 364 railroads had failed as well. The failure of almost 18,000 other businesses followed within two years, leaving the nation in an economic crisis. By 1876 unemployment had risen to 14 percent, with an estimated 2 million people out of work. The high unemployment rate set off numerous strikes and protests around the nation, many involving railroad workers. In 1874 the Democrats gained control of the House of Representatives. Northerners were becoming less concerned about southern racism and more concerned about their financial well-being.

Election of 1876

Republicans could tell that northern support for Reconstruction was fading. Voters' attention was shifting to economic problems. In 1874 the Republican Party lost control of the House of Representatives to the Democrats. The Republicans in Congress managed to pass one last civil rights law. The Civil Rights Act of 1875 guaranteed African Americans equal rights in public places, such as theaters and public transportation. But as Americans became increasingly worried about economic problems and government corruption, the Republican Party began to abandon Reconstruction.

Republicans selected Ohio governor Rutherford B. Hayes as their 1876 presidential candidate. He believed in ending federal support of the Reconstruction governments. The Democrats nominated New York governor Samuel J. Tilden. During the election, Democrats in the South again used violence at the polls to keep Republican voters away.

The election between Hayes and Tilden was close. Tilden appeared to have won. Republicans challenged the electoral votes in Oregon and three southern states. A special commission of members of Congress and Supreme Court justices was appointed to settle the issue.

The commission narrowly decided to give all the disputed votes to Hayes. Hayes thus won the presidency by one electoral vote. In the **Compromise of 1877**, the Democrats agreed to accept Hayes's victory. In return, they wanted all remaining federal troops removed from the South. They also asked for funding for internal improvements in the South and

FOCUS ON NORTH CAROLINA

As in the rest of the South, the political and social reconstruction of North Carolina included violence against African Americans and white Republicans. Governor Holden tried to stop the violence with a militia during an incident called the "Kirk-Holden War." By the time of the incident, the Ku Klux Klan had accomplished its goal of getting conservatives into power in Alamance and Caswell Counties. Conservatives soon won control of the General Assembly, and conservative Democrat Zebulon Vance was elected governor in 1876. Reconstruction in North Carolina had ended.

Supreme Court Decisions

Plessy v. *Ferguson* (1896)

Background of the Case In 1892, Homer Plessy took a seat in the "whites only" car of a train in Louisiana. He was arrested, put on trial, and convicted of violating Louisiana's segregation law. Plessy argued that the Louisiana law violated the Thirteenth Amendment and denied him the equal protection of the law as guaranteed.

The Court's Ruling

The Court ruled that the Louisiana "separate-but-equal" law was constitutional.

The Court's Reasoning

The Court stated that the Thirteenth and Fourteenth Amendments did not apply. The Court decided that the case had nothing to do with the abolition of slavery mentioned in the Thirteenth Amendment. The justices also ruled that the Fourteenth Amendment was not designed to eliminate social barriers to equality between the races, only political barriers.

Justice John Marshall Harlan disagreed with the Court's ruling. In a dissenting opinion, he wrote that "in respect of civil rights, all citizens are equal before the law."

Why It Matters

Plessy was important because it approved the idea of separate-but-equal facilities for people based on race. The doctrine of separate-but-equal led to segregation in trains, buses, schools, restaurants, and many other social institutions.

The separate-but-equal doctrine led to unequal treatment of minority groups for decades. It was finally struck down by another Supreme Court ruling, *Brown* v. *Board of Education,* in 1954.

ANALYSIS SKILL **ANALYZING INFORMATION**

1. **Why did the Court reject Plessy's arguments?**
2. **Why was *Plessy* v. *Ferguson* an important Supreme Court case?**

the appointment of a southern Democrat to the president's cabinet. Shortly after he took office in 1877, President Hayes removed the last of the federal troops from the South.

Redeemers

Gradually, Democrats regained control of state governments in the South. In each state, they moved quickly to get rid of the Reconstruction reforms.

Democrats who brought their party back to power in the South were called Redeemers. They came from a variety of backgrounds. For instance, U.S. senator John T. Morgan of Alabama was a former general in the Confederate army. Newspaper editor Henry Grady of Georgia was interested in promoting southern industry.

Redeemers wanted to reduce the size of state government and limit the rights of African Americans. They lowered state budgets and got rid of a variety of social programs. The Redeemers cut property taxes and cut public funding for schools. They also succeeded in limiting African Americans' civil rights.

African Americans' Rights Restricted

Redeemers set up the poll tax in an effort to deny the vote to African Americans. The **poll tax** was a special tax people had to pay before they could vote.

Some states also targeted African American voters by requiring them to pass a literacy test. A so-called grandfather clause written into law affected men whose fathers or grandfathers could vote before 1867. In those cases, a voter did not have to pay a poll tax or pass a literacy test. As a result, almost every white man could escape the voting restrictions.

Redeemer governments also introduced legal **segregation**, the forced separation of whites and African Americans in public places. **Jim Crow laws**—laws that enforced segregation—became common in southern states in the 1880s.

African Americans challenged Jim Crow laws in court. In 1883, however, the U.S. Supreme Court ruled that the Civil Rights Act of 1875 was unconstitutional. The Court also ruled that the Fourteenth Amendment applied only to the actions of state governments. This ruling allowed private individuals and businesses to practice segregation.

Plessy v. *Ferguson*

In 1896 the U.S. Supreme Court returned to the issue of segregation. When Homer Plessy, an African American, refused to leave the whites-only Louisiana train car he was riding on, he was arrested and accused of breaking a state law requiring separate cars for blacks and whites. Plessy sued the railroad company and lost. His lawyers argued that the law violated his right to equal treatment under the Fourteenth Amendment. He then appealed to the U.S. Supreme Court. The Supreme Court ruled against Plessy in ***Plessy* v. *Ferguson***. Segregation was allowed, said the Court, if "separate-but-equal" facilities were provided. Among the justices, only John Marshall Harlan disagreed with the Court's decision. He explained his disagreement in a dissenting opinion:

> "In the eye of the law, there is in the country no superior, dominant [controlling], ruling class of citizens . . . Our constitution is color-blind, and neither knows nor tolerates classes among citizens. In respect of civil rights, all citizens are equal before the law."
>
> —John Marshall Harlan, quoted in *Plessy v. Ferguson: A Brief History with Documents,* edited by Brook Thomas

Despite Harlan's view, segregation became widespread across the country. African Americans were forced to use separate public schools, libraries, and parks. When they existed, these facilities were usually of poorer quality than those created for whites. In practice, these so-called separate-but-equal facilities were separate and unequal.

Farming in the South

Few African Americans in the South could afford to buy or even rent farms. Moving West also was costly. Many African Americans therefore remained on plantations. Others tried to make a living in the cities.

African Americans who stayed on plantations often became part of a system known as **sharecropping**, or sharing the crop. Landowners provided the land, tools, and supplies, and sharecroppers provided the labor. At harvest time, the sharecropper usually had to give most of the crop to the landowner. Whatever remained belonged to the sharecropper. Many sharecroppers hoped to save enough money from selling their share of the crops to one day be able to buy a farm. Unfortunately, only a few ever achieved this dream.

Instead, most sharecroppers lived in a cycle of debt. When they needed food, clothing, or supplies, most families had to buy goods on credit because they had little cash.

NC History Makers

Albion Tourgée
Albion Tourgée was a northerner who moved to North Carolina after the Civil War to fight segregation and help rebuild the South.

Hopes Raised and Denied

QUICK FACTS

Slavery

- No rights
- Forced labor
- No freedom of movement without permission
- Family members sold away from one another
- No representation in government

Freedom

- Slavery banned
- Free to work for wages
- Could move and live anywhere
- Many families reunited
- Could serve in political office

Rights Denied

- Sharecropping system put in place
- Ability to vote and hold office restricted
- White leadership regained control of southern state governments

The New South

When sharecroppers sold their crops, they hoped to be able to pay off these debts. However, bad weather, poor harvests, or low crop prices often made this dream impossible.

Sharecroppers usually grew cotton, one of the South's most important cash crops. When too many farmers planted cotton, however, the supply became excessive. As a result, the price per bale of cotton dropped. Many farmers understood the drawbacks of planting cotton. However, farmers felt pressure from banks and others to keep raising cotton. A southern farmer explained why so many sharecroppers depended on cotton:

> "Cotton is the thing to get credit on in this country ... You can always sell cotton ... [Y]ou load up your wagon with wheat or corn ... and I doubt some days whether you could sell it."
>
> –Anonymous farmer quoted in *The Promise of the New South,* by Edward L. Ayers

READING CHECK **Finding Main Ideas** How were African Americans' rights restricted?

FOCUS ON NORTH CAROLINA

The number of textile factories increased rapidly in North Carolina. Many were in the Piedmont area, where mill owners made use of the abundant water supply to drive the machines. By the early 1900s, about 200,000 people had moved from farms to work in textile mills.

Rebuilding Southern Industry

The southern economy suffered through cycles of good and bad years as cotton prices went up and down. Some business leaders hoped industry would strengthen the southern economy and create a New South.

Southern Industry

Henry Grady, an Atlanta newspaper editor, was a leader of the New South movement. "The new South presents . . . a diversified [varied] industry that meets the complex needs of this complex age," he wrote. Grady and his supporters felt that with its cheap and abundant labor, the South could build factories and provide a workforce for them.

The most successful industrial development in the South involved textile production. Businesspeople built textile mills in many small towns to produce cotton fabric. Many people from rural areas came to work in the mills, but African Americans were not allowed to work in most of them.

"The New South...is stirred with the breath of a new life."

—Henry Grady

Atlanta rebuilt quickly after the war, becoming a leading railroad and industrial center. Newspaper editor Henry Grady gave stirring speeches about the need for industry in the South. He became one of the best-known spokesmen of the "New South."

Why might Grady point to Atlanta as a model for economic change?

Southern Mill Life

Work in the cotton mills appealed to farm families who had trouble making ends meet. As one mill worker explained, "It was a necessity to move and get a job, rather than depend on the farm." Recruiters sent out by the mills promised good wages and steady work.

Entire families often worked in the same cotton mill. Mills employed large numbers of women and children. Many children started working at about the age of 12. Some children started working at an even earlier age. Women did most of the spinning and were valued workers. However, few women had the opportunity to advance within the company.

Many mill workers were proud of the skills they used, but they did not enjoy their work. One unhappy worker described it as "the same thing over and over again . . . The more you do, the more they want done." Workers often labored 12 hours a day, six days a week. Cotton dust and lint filled the air, causing asthma and an illness known as brown-lung disease. Fast-moving machinery caused injuries and even deaths. Despite the long hours and dangerous working conditions, wages remained low. However, mill work did offer an alternative to farming.

READING CHECK **Finding Main Ideas** What did southern business leaders hope industry would do?

SUMMARY AND PREVIEW In this section you learned about the end of Reconstruction. In the next chapter you will learn about America's continued westward expansion.

Section 3 Assessment

go.hrw.com
Online Quiz
KEYWORD: SC7 HP17

Reviewing Ideas, Terms, and People

1. a. **Identify** Who were some prominent African American leaders during Reconstruction?
   b. **Evaluate** What do you think was the most important change made by Reconstruction state governments? Explain your answer.
2. a. **Recall** For what reasons did some local governments not stop the **Ku Klux Klan**?
   b. **Draw Conclusions** How did the Ku Klux Klan's use of terror interfere with elections in the South?
3. a. **Recall** How did Reconstruction come to an end?
   b. **Explain** What was the relationship between **Jim Crow laws** and **segregation**?
4. a. **Identify** Who was Henry Grady, and why was he important?
   b. **Predict** What are some possible results of the rise of the "New South"?

Critical Thinking

5. **Identifying Causes and Effects** Review your notes on Reconstruction governments. Then copy the graphic organizer below and use it to show why Reconstruction ended, as well as the results of its end.

Causes	→	Effect/Cause	→	Effects
		End of Reconstruction		

WRITING JOURNAL

6. **Relating Historical Change to Individual Choice** Despite the difficulties of Reconstruction, the Freedmen's Bureau and plans to bring industry to the "New South" did create new jobs. What might have led people to leave their jobs for new ones?

Social Studies Skills

Analysis | Critical Thinking | Civic Participation | Study

North Carolina Skills
1.04 Detect cause and effect.

Chance, Oversight, and Error in History

Understand the Skill

Sometimes, history can seem very routine. One event leads to others which, in turn, lead to still others. You learn to look for cause-and-effect relationships among events. You learn how point of view and bias can influence decisions and actions. These approaches to the study of history imply that the events of the past are orderly and predictable.

In fact, many of the events of the past *are* orderly and predictable! They may seem even more so since they're over and done with, and we know how things turned out. Yet, predictable patterns of behavior *do* exist throughout history. Recognizing them is one of the great values and rewards of studying the past. As the philosopher George Santayana once famously said, "Those who cannot remember the past are condemned to repeat it."

At its most basic level, however, history is people, and people are "human." They make mistakes. Unexpected things happen to them, both good things and bad. This is the unpredictable element of history. The current phrase "stuff happens" is just as true of the past as it is today. Mistakes, oversights, and just plain "dumb luck" have shaped the course of history—and have helped to make the study of it so exciting.

Learn the Skill

California merchant John Sutter decided to build a sawmill along a nearby American river in 1848. He planned to sell the lumber it produced to settlers who were moving into the area. Sutter put James W. Marshall to work building the mill. To install the large water wheel that would power the saw, Marshall first had to deepen the river bed next to the mill. During his digging, he noticed some shiny bits of yellow metal in the water. The result of this accidental find was the California gold rush, which sent thousands of Americans to California, and speeded settlement of the West.

In 1863 the army of Confederate General Robert E. Lee invaded Maryland. The Civil War had been going well for the South. Lee hoped a southern victory on Union soil would convince the British to aid the South in the war. However, a Confederate officer forgot his cigars as his unit left its camp in the Maryland countryside. Wrapped around the cigars was a copy of Lee's battle plans. When a Union soldier came upon the abandoned camp, he spotted the cigars. This chance discovery enabled the Union army to defeat Lee at the Battle of Antietam. The Union victory helped keep the British out of the war. More importantly, it allowed President Lincoln to issue the Emancipation Proclamation and begin the process of ending slavery in the United States.

Practice the Skill

In April 1865 President Lincoln was assassinated while attending the theater in Washington, D.C. Bodyguard John Parker was stationed outside the door of the president's box. However, Parker left his post to find a seat from which he could watch the play. This allowed the killer to enter the box and shoot the unprotected president.

Write an essay about how this chance event altered the course of history. How might Reconstruction, North–South relations, and African Americans' struggle for equality have been different had Lincoln lived?

CHAPTER 17

Chapter Review

HOLT

History's Impact

▶ video series

Review the video to answer the closing question:

Name three ways the Thirteenth, Fourteenth, and Fifteenth Amendments are related.

Visual Summary

QUICK FACTS

Use the visual summary below to help you review the main ideas of the chapter.

Reform During Reconstruction, the Freedmen's Bureau opened schools for former slaves and performed other services to help the poorest southerners.

Dispute Differing ideas about how to govern the South led to conflicts between African Americans and white southerners, as well as between Republicans and Democrats.

Division After the Compromise of 1877 ended Reconstruction, segregation laws were enacted by southern governments and upheld by the U.S. Supreme Court.

Reviewing Vocabulary, Terms, and People

Complete each sentence by filling in the blank with the correct term or person from the chapter.

1. _______________ were laws that allowed racial segregation in public places.

2. The Radical Republicans were led by _______, a member of Congress from Pennsylvania.

3. The period from 1865 to 1877 that focused on reuniting the nation is known as _______.

4. Following the Civil War, many African Americans in the South made a living by participating in the _________ system.

5. After opposing Congress, Andrew Johnson became the first president to face _____ proceedings.

6. The _____ Amendment made slavery in the United States illegal.

7. In 1870 ________ became the first African American to serve in the U.S. Senate.

Comprehension and Critical Thinking

SECTION 1 *(Pages 552–557)*

8. a. Describe How did the lives of African Americans change after the Civil War?

b. Compare and Contrast How was President Johnson's Reconstruction plan similar and different from President Lincoln's Ten Percent Plan?

c. Evaluate Which of the three Reconstruction plans that were originally proposed do you think would have been the most successful? Why?

SECTION 2 *(Pages 558–563)*

9. a. Identify Who were the Radical Republicans, and how did they change Reconstruction?

b. Analyze How did the debate over the Fourteenth Amendment affect the election of 1866?

c. Elaborate Do you think Congress was right to impeach President Andrew Johnson? Explain.

SECTION 3 *(Pages 564–571)*

10. a. Describe What reforms did Reconstruction governments in the South support?

b. Draw Conclusions In what ways did southern governments attempt to reverse the accomplishments of Reconstruction?

c. Evaluate Do you think the South was successful or unsuccessful in its rebuilding efforts? Explain your answer.

Reviewing Themes

11. Politics Explain the political struggles that took place during Reconstruction.

12. Society and Culture How were the lives of ordinary southerners affected in the years after Reconstruction?

Using the Internet

go.hrw.com
KEYWORD: SC7 CH17

13. Activity: Drawing Conclusions A challenge for anyone trying to understand Reconstruction is drawing conclusions from primary and secondary sources from the time period. This activity will help you see how complex this can be. Enter the activity keyword, and then rate the credibility of the sources provided. Make sure you explain whether the source is a primary or secondary source, whether or not you think the source is credible, and the reasons for your thoughts.

Reading Skills

Analyzing Historical Information *Use the Reading Skills taught in this chapter to answer the question about the reading selection below.*

> Radical Republicans, on the other hand, took a harsher stance. They wanted the Federal government to force change in the South. Like the moderates, they thought the Black Codes were cruel and unjust. *(p. 559)*

14. Which of the following is relevant information for the passage above?

a. Thaddeus Stevens was a Radical Republican.

b. Andrew Johnson was a Democrat.

c. Radical Republicans wanted the federal government to make major changes in the South.

d. Radical Republicans were eventually removed from power.

Social Studies Skills

Chance, Oversight, and Error in History *Use the Social Studies Skills taught in this chapter to answer the question about the reading selection below.*

> Johnson's speaking tour was a disaster. It did little to win votes for the Democratic Party. Johnson even got into arguments with people in the audiences of some of his speaking engagements. *(p. 561)*

15. Which of the following is an example of chance, oversight, or error that affected history?

a. Johnson got into arguments with audiences.

b. The tour was a disaster.

c. The tour did not win votes.

d. Johnson spoke for the Democratic Party.

FOCUS ON WRITING

16. Writing a Job History Review your notes about the changing job scene during Reconstruction. Put yourself in the shoes of a person living then. It could be anyone—a returning soldier, a shopkeeper, a schoolteacher, or a politician. What jobs would that person seek? Why would he or she leave one job for another?

Write a brief job history for that person during Reconstruction. Include at least four jobs. Make each job description two to four sentences long. End each one with a sentence or two about why the person left that job. Add one sentence explaining why he or she took the next job. Be sure to include specific historical details.

CHAPTER 17

Standardized Test Practice

DIRECTIONS: Read each question and write the letter of the best response.

1 **Use the map below to answer the following question.**

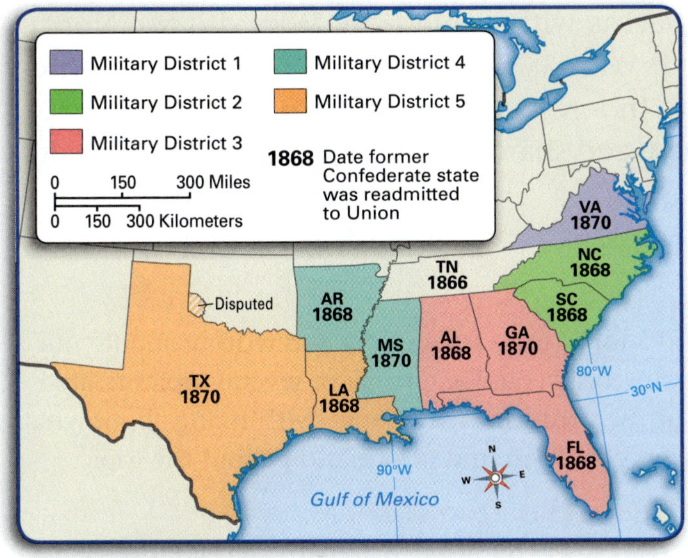

In what year was North Carolina readmitted to the Union?

A 1865

B 1866

C 1868

D 1870

2 **What can you infer from the map information?**

A South Carolina was difficult to reconstruct.

B The largest number of troops was in Military District 1.

C Military District 5 was the last district to end Reconstruction.

D Tennessee was readmitted to the Union before the other southern states.

3 **One result of Reconstruction in North Carolina was**

A the establishment of a public school system.

B the creation of a new constitution.

C a decrease in population.

D the introduction of new military technology.

4 **What development convinced Republicans in Congress to take control of Reconstruction from the president?**

A President Abraham Lincoln was assassinated by a southern sympathizer.

B President Andrew Johnson vetoed the Wade-Davis bill.

C Southern states began passing Black Codes to restrict African Americans' freedoms.

D White southern women refused to support the Fifteenth Amendment.

5 **Which of the following limited opportunities for African Americans in the South after Reconstruction ended?**

A Ten Percent plan

B Radical Republicans

C Jim Crow laws

D carpetbaggers

6 **Examine the following passage from a northern schoolteacher's letter home and then use it to answer the question.**

> "Wishing to work where there was the most need—there are so many places where nothing has been done for the freedmen, and where they are sorely persecuted—we came here. A schoolhouse built by the soldiers had just been destroyed by the citizens. The feeling is intensely bitter against anything northern. The affairs of the [Freedmen's] Bureau have been very much mismanaged in Columbus, and our government has been disgraced by the troops who were stationed here."
>
> –Sarah Chase, from *Dear Ones at Home*

Document-Based Question **What were some of the problems facing the Freedmen's Bureau in the South?**

Assignment
Collect information and write an informative report on a topic related to the Civil War.

A Social Studies Report

All research begins with a question. Why did the North win the Civil War? Why did Abraham Lincoln choose Ulysses S. Grant? In a research report, you find answers to questions like these and share what you learn with your reader.

TIP **Narrowing the Task** The key to a successful research report is picking a topic that is broad enough that you can find information, but narrow enough that you can cover it in detail. To narrow a subject, focus on one aspect of the larger subject. Then think about whether that one aspect can be broken down into smaller parts. Here's an example of how to narrow a topic:
Too Broad: Civil War Leaders
Less Broad: Civil War Generals
Narrower: Robert E. Lee's Role in the Civil War

1. Prewrite

Choosing a Subject

Since you will spend a lot of time researching and writing about your topic, pick one that interests you. First, think of several topics related to the Civil War. Narrow your list to one topic by thinking about what interests you and where you can find information about the topic.

Developing a Research Question

A guiding question related to your topic will help focus your research. For example, here is a research question for the topic "Robert E. Lee's Role in the Civil War": *How did Lee's decision to turn down the leadership of the Union army affect the Civil War?* The answer to this question becomes the thesis, or the big idea of your report.

Finding Historical Information

Use at least three sources of historical information besides your textbook. Good sources include

- books, maps, magazines, newspapers
- television programs, movies, Internet sites, CD-ROMs.

For each source, write down the kinds of information shown below. When taking notes, put a circled number next to each source.

Encyclopedia article
① "Title of Article." Name of Encyclopedia. Edition or year published.
Book
② Author. Title. City of Publication: Publisher, year published.
Magazine or newspaper article
③ Author. "Title of Article." Publication name. Date: page number(s).
Internet site
④ Author (if known). "Document title." Web site. Date of electronic publication. Date information was accessed <url>.

Taking Notes

As you read the source material, take thorough notes on facts, statistics, comparisons, and quotations. Take special care to spell names correctly and to record dates and facts accurately. If you use a direct quotation from a source, copy it word for word and enclose it in quotation marks. Along with each note, include the number of its source and its page number.

Organizing Your Ideas and Information

Informative research reports are usually organized in one of these ways:

- Chronological order (the order in which events occurred)
- Order of importance
- Causes (actions or situations that make something else happen) and effects (what happened as a result of something else).

Use one of these orders to organize your notes in an outline. Here is a partial outline for a paper on Robert E. Lee.

The Thesis/Big Idea: Robert E. Lee's decision to decline the leadership of the Union army had serious consequences for the path of the Civil War.

I. Lee's Military Expertise
   A. Achievements at the U.S. Military Academy
   B. Achievements during the Mexican War
II. Lee's Personality and Character
   A. Intelligence and strength
   B. Honesty and fairness
   C. Daring and courage
III. Lee's Military Victories
   A. Battle of Fredericksburg
   B. Battle of Chancellorsville

TIP Seeing Different Viewpoints Consult a variety of sources, including those with different points of view on the topic. Reading sources with different opinions will give you a more complete picture of your subject. For example, reading articles about Robert E. Lee written by a southern writer as well as a northern writer may give you a more balanced view of Lee.

TIP Recording Others' Ideas You will be taking three types of notes.
Paraphrases Restatements of all the ideas in your own words.
Summaries Brief restatements of only the most important parts.
Direct quotations The writer's exact words inside quotation marks.

2. Write

You can use this framework to help you write your first draft.

A Writer's Framework

Introduction

- Start with a quote or an interesting historical detail to grab your reader's attention.
- State the main idea of your report.
- Provide any historical background readers need to understand your main idea.

Body

- Present your information under at least three main ideas, using logical order.
- Write at least one paragraph for each of these main ideas.
- Add supporting details, facts, or examples to each paragraph.

Conclusion

- Restate your main idea, using slightly different words.
- Include a general comment about your topic.
- You might comment on how the historical information in your report relates to later historical events.

Studying a Model

Here is a model of a research report. Study it to see how one student developed a paper. The first and the concluding paragraphs are shown in full. The paragraphs in the body of the paper are summarized.

INTRODUCTORY PARAGRAPH

Attention grabber

Statement of thesis

"I cannot raise my hand against my birthplace, my home, my children." With these words, Robert E. Lee changed the course of the Civil War. Abraham Lincoln had turned to Lee as his first choice for commander of the Union army. However, Lee turned Lincoln down, choosing instead to side with his home state of Virginia and take command of the Confederate army. Lee's decision to turn Lincoln down weakened the North and strengthened the Confederates, turning what might have been an easy victory for the North into a long, costly war.

BODY PARAGRAPHS

In the first part of the body, the student points out that Lee graduated from the U.S. Military Academy at West Point, served in the Mexican War, and was a member of the Union army. She goes on to explain that he would have been a strong leader for the North, and his absence made the North weaker.

In the middle of the report, the writer discusses Lee's personality and character. She includes information about the strength of character he showed while in the military academy and while leading the Confederate army. She discusses and gives examples of his intelligence, his daring, his courage, and his honesty.

In the last part of the body of the report, the student provides examples of Lee leading the outnumbered Confederate army to a series of victories. The student provides details of the battles of Fredericksburg and Chancellorsville and explains how a lesser general than Lee may have lost both battles.

CONCLUDING PARAGRAPH

Summary of main points

Restatement of big idea

Lee's brilliant and resourceful leadership bedeviled a series of Union generals. He won battles that most generals would have lost. If Lee had used these skills to lead the larger and more powerful Union army, the Civil War might have ended in months instead of years.

3. Evaluate and Revise

Evaluating and Revising Your Draft

Evaluate your first draft by carefully reading it twice. Ask the questions below to decide which parts of your first draft should be revised.

Evaluation Questions for an Informative Report

- Does the introduction attract the readers' interest and state the big idea/thesis of your report?
- Does the body of your report have at least three paragraphs that develop your big idea? Is the main idea in each paragraph clearly stated?
- Have you included enough information to support each of your main ideas? Are all facts, details, and examples accurate? Are all of them clearly related to the main ideas they support?
- Is the report clearly organized? Does it use chronological order, order of importance, or cause and effect?
- Does the conclusion restate the big idea of your report? Does it end with a general comment about the importance or significance of your topic?
- Have you included at least three sources in your bibliography? Have you included all the sources you used and not any you did not use?

TIP **Organizing Your Time** By creating a schedule and following it, you can avoid that panicky moment when the due date is near and you haven't even started your research. To create your schedule and manage your time, include these six steps.

1 Develop a question and research your topic (10% of your total time).

2 Research and take notes (25%).

3 Write your main idea statement and create an outline (15%).

4 Write a first draft (25%).

5 Evaluate and revise your first draft (15%).

6 Proofread and publish your report (10%).

4. Proofread and Publish

Proofreading

To improve your report before sharing it, check the following:

- The spelling and capitalization of all proper names for people, places, things, and events.
- Punctuation marks around any direct quotation.
- Your list of sources (Works Cited or Bibliography) against a guide to writing research papers. Make sure you follow the examples in the guide when punctuating and capitalizing your source listings.

Publishing

Choose one or more of these ideas to publish your report.

- Share your report with your classmates by turning it into an informative speech.
- Submit your report to an online discussion group that focuses on the Civil War and ask for feedback.
- With your classmates, create a magazine that includes reports on several different topics or post the reports on your school Web site.

5. Practice and Apply

Use the steps and strategies outlined in this workshop to research and write an informative report on the Civil War.

UNIT 6 1850–1914

A Growing America

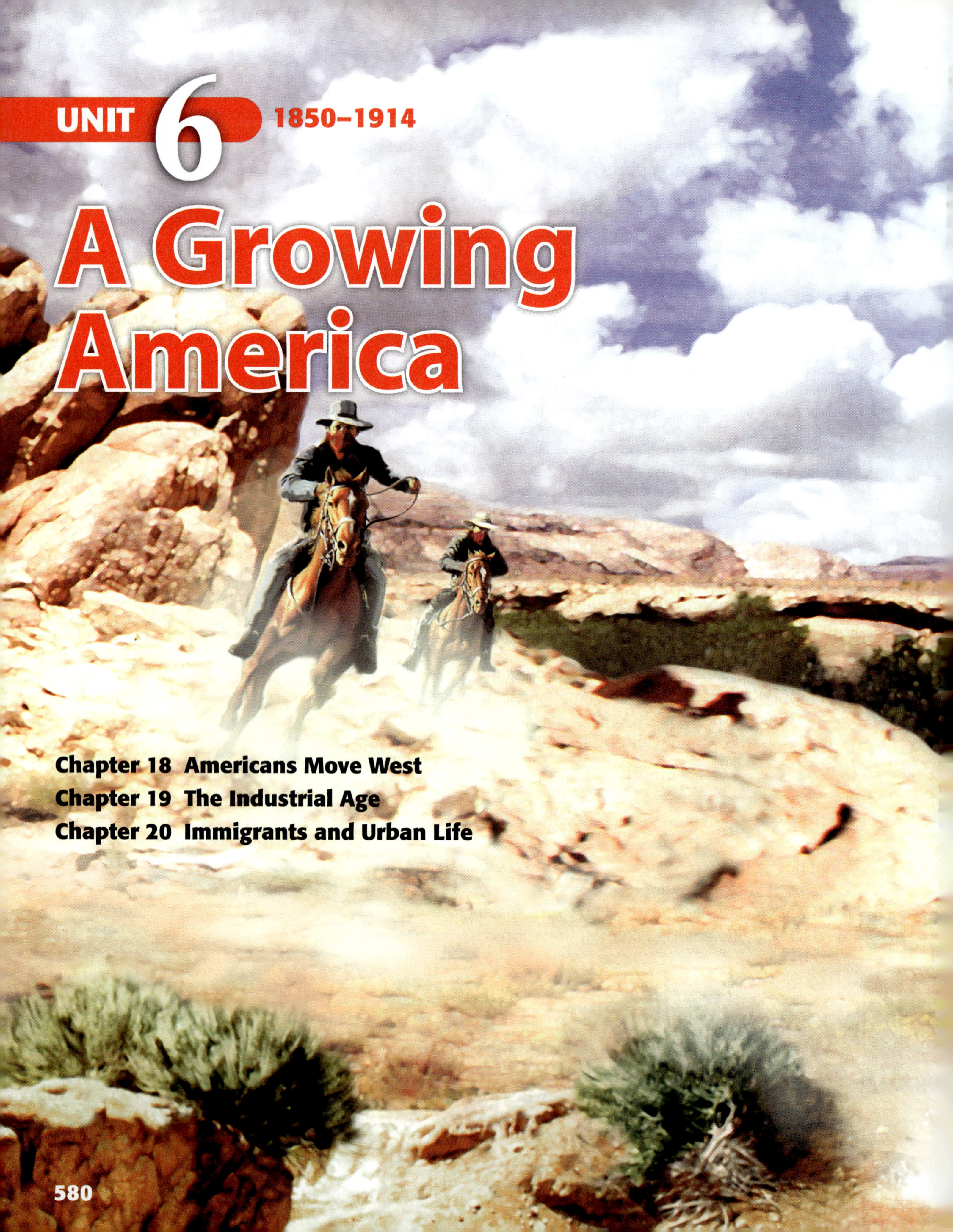

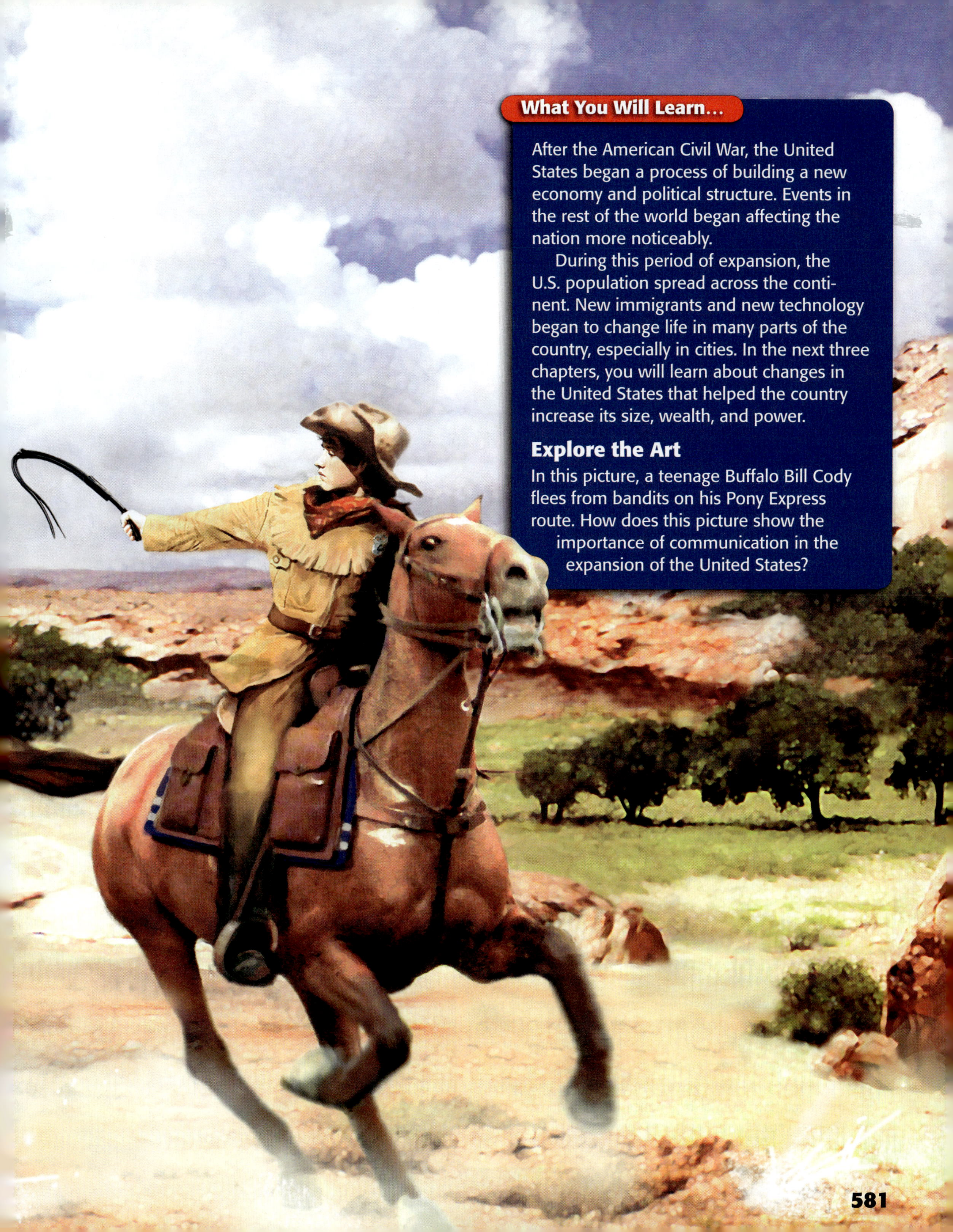

What You Will Learn...

After the American Civil War, the United States began a process of building a new economy and political structure. Events in the rest of the world began affecting the nation more noticeably.

During this period of expansion, the U.S. population spread across the continent. New immigrants and new technology began to change life in many parts of the country, especially in cities. In the next three chapters, you will learn about changes in the United States that helped the country increase its size, wealth, and power.

Explore the Art

In this picture, a teenage Buffalo Bill Cody flees from bandits on his Pony Express route. How does this picture show the importance of communication in the expansion of the United States?

CHAPTER 18 1850–1890

Americans Move West

North Carolina Standards

Social Studies Objectives

5.01 Identify the role played by the agriculture, textile, tobacco, and furniture industries in North Carolina, and analyze their importance in the economic development of the state.

5.02 Examine the changing role of educational, religious, and social institutions in the state and analyze their impact.

9.02 Identify past and present state and local leaders from diverse cultural backgrounds and assess their influence in affecting change.

Language Arts Objectives

2.01 Analyze and evaluate informational materials that are read, heard, and/or viewed by:

- monitoring comprehension for understanding of what is read, heard and/or viewed.
- recognizing the characteristics of informational materials.
- determining the importance and accuracy of information.
- making connections to related topics/information.
- drawing inferences and/or conclusions.

go.hrw.com
North Carolina
KEYWORD: SC7 NC

FOCUS ON WRITING

Writing a Letter Before telephones and e-mail, one way to communicate with people far away was by letter. In this chapter, you will read about the settlement of the West by European Americans. Suppose you were an Irish immigrant working on a railroad that crossed the Great Plains. What might you have seen or experienced? After you read the chapter, you will write a letter to your sister in Ireland telling her about your experiences.

UNITED STATES

1860 The Pony Express begins delivering mail between East and West.

1850 — 1860

1855 Paris holds a World's Fair.

WORLD

HOLT

History's Impact

▶ **video series**

Watch the video to understand the impact of the West on American culture.

What You Will Learn...

In this chapter you will learn about how the great American West changed in the late 1800s. Settlers poured into the region and built mines, ranches, farms, and railroads. In this photo, modern pioneers re-create a wagon journey from the 1800s.

1869 The first transcontinental railroad is completed.

1874 Gold is discovered in the Black Hills of the Dakotas.

1879 Thousands of African Americans migrate from the South to Kansas.

1890 The Massacre at Wounded Knee occurs.

1870 — 1880 — 1890

1864 French scientist Louis Pasteur invents the purification process of pasteurization.

1883 The Orient Express railway makes its first run from Paris to Istanbul.

1888 Brazil abolishes slavery.

Reading Social Studies

by Kylene Beers

Economics | **Geography** | Politics | Society and Culture | **Science and Technology**

Focus on Themes In this chapter you will follow the development of the United States from the mid-1800s through the 1890s. You will learn that California was admitted to the Union in 1850. You will find out about the struggles that people faced as the movement West continued and people settled the Great Plains. You will learn about the **technological** advancements made during this time as well as the difficult **geographical** obstacles miners and ranchers faced in the West.

Understanding through Questioning

Focus on Reading When newspaper reporters want to get to the heart of a story, they ask certain questions: who, what, when, where, why, and how. When you are reading a history book, you can use the same questions to get to the heart of what happened in the past.

Hypothetical Questions You can also use questions to dig deeper than what is in the text. You can ask hypothetical, or what if, questions. These questions ask what might have happened had events occurred differently. Sometimes asking such questions can help history come alive.

In 1862 Congress passed two important land acts that helped open the West to settlers. The Homestead Act gave government-owned land to small farmers. Any adult who was a U.S. citizen or planned to become one could receive 160 acres of land. In exchange, homesteaders promised to live on the land for five years. The Morrill Act granted more than 17 million acres of federal land to the states. *(p. 600)*

Who?
Congress

Where?
the West

How?
Congress gave land to anyone who agreed to settle on it for five years.

What?
encouraged new settlement

When?
1862

Why?
Perhaps Congress feared what would happen to western lands if they remained unsettled by U.S. citizens.

What if?
If Congress had not passed these laws, U.S. citizens might not have moved West. The United States might not have grown as quickly as it did.

You Try It!

Read the following passage and then answer the questions below.

Building Communities

Women were an important force in the settlement of the frontier. They joined in the hard work of farming and ranching and helped build communities out of the widely spaced farms and small towns. Their role in founding communities facilitated a strong voice in public affairs. Wyoming women, for example, were granted the vote in the new state's constitution, which was approved in 1869. Annie Bidwell, one of the founders of Chico, California, used her influence to support a variety of moral and social causes such as women's suffrage and temperance.

From Chapter 18, p. 602

Answer these questions based on the passage you just read.

1. Who is this passage about?
2. What did they do?
3. When did they do this?
4. How do you think they accomplished it?
5. Why do you think they were able to accomplish so much?
6. How can knowing this information help you understand the past?
7. What if women in the West had been given more rights? Fewer rights? How might the West have been different?

Key Terms and People

Chapter 18

Section 1

frontier *(p. 586)*
Comstock Lode *(p. 587)*
boomtowns *(p. 588)*
Cattle Kingdom *(p. 589)*
cattle drive *(p. 589)*
Chisholm Trail *(p. 589)*
Pony Express *(p. 590)*
transcontinental railroad *(p. 590)*

Section 2

Treaty of Fort Laramie *(p. 594)*
reservations *(p. 595)*
Crazy Horse *(p. 595)*
Treaty of Medicine Lodge *(p. 595)*
buffalo soldiers *(p. 596)*
George Armstrong Custer *(p. 596)*
Sitting Bull *(p. 596)*
Battle of the Little Bighorn *(p. 596)*
Massacre at Wounded Knee *(p. 597)*
Long Walk *(p. 597)*
Geronimo *(p. 597)*
Ghost Dance *(p. 598)*
Sarah Winnemucca *(p. 598)*
Dawes General Allotment Act *(p. 598)*

Section 3

Homestead Act *(p. 600)*
Morrill Act *(p. 600)*
Exodusters *(p. 601)*
sodbusters *(p. 601)*
dry farming *(p. 601)*
Annie Bidwell *(p. 602)*
National Grange *(p. 603)*
deflation *(p. 604)*
William Jennings Bryan *(p. 604)*
Populist Party *(p. 604)*

Academic Vocabulary

In this chapter, you will learn the following academic words:

establish *(p. 588)*
facilitate *(p. 602)*

As you read Chapter 18, ask questions like *who, what, when, where, why, how,* and *what if* to help you analyze what you are reading.

SECTION 1

Miners, Ranchers, and Railroads

What You Will Learn...

Main Ideas

1. A mining boom brought growth to the West.
2. The demand for cattle created a short-lived Cattle Kingdom on the Great Plains.
3. East and West were connected by the transcontinental railroad.

The Big Idea

As more settlers moved West, mining, ranching, and railroads soon transformed the western landscape.

Key Terms

frontier, *p. 586*
Comstock Lode, *p. 587*
boomtowns, *p. 588*
Cattle Kingdom, *p. 589*
cattle drive, *p. 589*
Chisholm Trail, *p. 589*
Pony Express, *p. 590*
transcontinental railroad, *p. 590*

TAKING NOTES As you read the following section, take notes on the kinds of economic oppportunities that people found in the West. Organize your notes in a table like the one below.

Opportunities in the West

If YOU were there...

You are a cowboy in Texas in 1875. You love life on the open range, the quiet nights, and the freedom. You even like the hard work of the long cattle drives to Kansas. But you know that times are changing. Homesteaders are moving in and fencing off their lands. Some of the older cowboys say it's time to settle down and buy a small ranch. You hope that they're not right.

What would make you give up a cowboy's life?

BUILDING BACKGROUND In the years following the Civil War, the U.S. population grew rapidly. Settlements in the West increased. More discoveries of gold and silver attracted adventurers, while the open range drew others. Thousands of former Civil War soldiers also joined the move West.

Mining Boom Brings Growth

During the years surrounding the War, most Americans had thought of the Great Plains and other western lands as the Great American Desert. In the years following the Civil War, Americans witnessed the rapid growth of the U.S. population and the spread of settlements throughout the West. With the admission of the state of California to the Union in 1850, the western boundary of the American **frontier**—an undeveloped area—had reached the Pacific Ocean.

The frontier changed dramatically as more and more people moved westward. Settlers built homes, fenced off land, and laid out ranches and farms. Miners, ranchers, and farmers remade the landscape of the West as they adapted to their new surroundings. The geography of the West was further changed by the development and expansion of a large and successful railroad industry that moved the West's natural resources to eastern markets. Gold and silver were the most valuable natural resources, and mining companies used the growing railroad network to bring these precious metals to the East.

Causes and Effects of Westward Expansion

QUICK FACTS

Causes
- New land for settlers and ranchers
- Mineral resources
- Businesses to support settlers, ranchers, and miners
- Immigration

Effects
- New towns
- Railroads across the continent
- Cattle Kingdom

ANALYSIS SKILL **INTERPRETING CHARTS**

What three economic activities attracted people to the West?

Posters like this one were designed to persuade people to move West.

Big Business

Most of the precious metals were located in western Nevada. In 1859 miner Henry Comstock discovered a huge deposit of gold and silver in Nevada that became called the **Comstock Lode**. The deposit was incredibly rich and deep. In just the first year after its discovery, the Comstock Lode lured thousands of California miners to Nevada. Over the next 20 years, the Comstock Lode produced more than $500 million worth of gold and silver.

Expensive equipment was needed to remove the silver and gold that were trapped within quartz rock. Larger mining companies bought up land claims from miners who could not afford this machinery. As a result, mining became a big business in the West.

As companies dug bigger and deeper mines, the work became more dangerous. Miners had to use unsafe equipment, such as elevator platforms without protective walls. They worked in dark tunnels and breathed hot, stuffy air. They suffered from lung disease caused by dusty air. Miners often were injured or killed by poorly planned explosions or by cave-ins. Fire was also a great danger. Mining was therefore one of the most dangerous jobs in the country. In the West, worries about safety and pay led miners to form several unions in the 1860s.

Settlers

People from all over the world came to work in the western mines. Some miners came from the eastern United States. Others emigrated from Europe, Central and South America, and Asia. Many Mexican immigrants and Mexican Americans were experienced miners. They were skilled in assaying, or testing, the contents of valuable ore. One newspaper reporter wrote, "Here were congregated the most varied elements of humanity . . . belonging to almost every nationality and every status of life."

New Towns

Mining booms also produced **boomtowns**, communities that grew suddenly when a mine opened. They disappeared just as quickly when the mine closed. Most boomtowns had general stores, saloons, and boardinghouses.

Few women or families lived in boomtowns. "I was never so lonely and homesick in all my life," wrote one young woman. Women washed, cooked, made clothes, and chopped wood. They also raised families, **established** schools, and wrote for newspapers. Their work helped turn some mining camps into successful, permanent towns.

ACADEMIC VOCABULARY

establish to set up or create

READING CHECK **Summarizing** What risks did miners face?

The Cattle Kingdom

The cattle industry was another area of rapid growth. Following the Civil War, a growing economy and population created a greater demand for beef in the East. Cattle worth $3 to $6 each in Texas could be sold for $38 each in Kansas. In New York, they could be sold for $80 each. The most popular breed of cattle was the longhorn. The longhorn spread quickly throughout western Texas. Because these animals needed very little water and could survive harsh weather, they were well-suited to the dry, desert-like environment of western Texas. But how could Texas ranchers move the longhorns to eastern markets?

In 1867 businessman Joseph McCoy discovered a solution. He built pens for cattle in the small town of Abilene, Kansas. The Kansas

Myth and Reality in the Wild West

No episode in American history has given rise to as many myths as the Wild West. Writers of dime novels, popular in the East, helped created the myths in the years after the Civil War. Even today, popular books, television shows, and movies continue to portray the West in ways that are more myth than reality.

Myth: The cowboy was a free-spirited individual.

Reality: Most cowboys were employees. Many joined labor unions and even went on strike.

Myth: Western cowtowns were wild places where cowboys had gunfights, and there was little law and order.

Reality: Most were orderly cities with active law enforcement. Showdowns rarely, if ever, occurred.

Myth: Almost all cowboys were Anglo Americans.

Reality: About 25 percent of cowboys were African Americans, and 12 percent were Hispanic.

Pacific Railroad line went through Abilene. As a result, cattle could be shipped by rail from there. Soon, countless Texas ranchers were making the trip north to Abilene to sell their herds of cattle.

Around the same time, cattle ranching began to expand in the Midwest. The Great Plains from Texas to Canada, where many ranchers raised cattle in the late 1800s, became known as the **Cattle Kingdom**. Ranchers grazed huge herds on public land called the open range. The land had once been occupied by Plains Indians and buffalo herds.

Importance of Cowboys

The workers who took care of the ranchers' cattle were known as cowhands or cowboys. They borrowed many techniques and tools from vaqueros (bah-KER-ohs), Mexican ranch hands who cared for cattle and horses. From vaqueros came the western saddle and the lariat—a rope used for lassoing cattle. The cowboys also borrowed the vaqueros' broad felt hat. However, they changed it into the familiar high-peaked cowboy hat.

One of the cowboy's most important and dangerous duties was the **cattle drive**. On these long journeys, cowboys herded cattle to the market or to the northern Plains for grazing. The trips usually lasted several months and covered hundreds of miles. The **Chisholm Trail**, which ran from San Antonio, Texas, to the cattle town of Abilene, Kansas, was one of the earliest and most popular routes for cattle drives. It was blazed, or marked, by Texas cowboy Jesse Chisholm in the late 1860s.

At times, rowdy cowboys made life in cattle towns rough and violent. There were rarely shoot-outs in the street, but there was often disorderly behavior. Law officials such as Wyatt Earp became famous for keeping the peace in cattle towns.

Marshal Wyatt Earp

Deadwood, South Dakota

End of the Open Range

As the cattle business boomed, ranchers faced more competition for use of the open range. Farmers began to buy range land on the Great Plains where cattle had once grazed. Small ranchers also began competing with large ranchers for land. Then in 1874, the invention of barbed wire allowed westerners to fence off large amounts of land cheaply. The competition between farmers, large ranchers, and small ranchers increased. This competition led to range wars, or fights for access to land.

FOCUS ON READING
Ask yourself questions about the information in this paragraph to help you understand the competition between farmers and ranchers.

Making matters worse, in 1885 and 1886, disaster struck the Cattle Kingdom. The huge cattle herds on the Plains had eaten most of the prairie grass. Unusually severe winters in both years made the ranching situation even worse. Thousands of cattle died, and many ranchers were ruined financially. The Cattle Kingdom had come to an end.

READING CHECK **Drawing Conclusions** Why did the Cattle Kingdom come to an end?

The Transcontinental Railroad

As more Americans began moving West, the need to send goods and information between the East and West increased. Americans searched for ways to improve communication and travel across the country.

In 1860 a system of messengers on horseback called the **Pony Express** began to carry messages west. The messengers carried mail between relay stations on a route about 2,000 miles long. However, telegraph lines, which sent messages faster, quickly put the Pony Express out of business.

Some Americans wanted to build a **transcontinental railroad**—a railroad that would cross the continent and connect the East to the West. The federal government, therefore, passed the Pacific Railway Acts in 1862 and in 1864. These acts gave railroad companies loans and large land grants that could be sold to pay for construction costs. Congress had granted more than 131 million acres of public land to railroad companies. In exchange, the government asked the railroads to carry U.S. mail and troops at a lower cost. Many railroad companies were inspired to begin laying miles of tracks.

Great Race

Two companies, the Central Pacific and the Union Pacific, led the race to complete the transcontinental railroad. In February 1863, the Central Pacific began building east from Sacramento, California. At the end of the year, the Union Pacific started building west from Omaha, Nebraska.

The Union Pacific hired thousands of railroad workers, particularly Irish immigrants. Chinese immigrants made up some 85 percent of the Central Pacific workforce. The railroad's part-owner Leland Stanford praised them, but he paid them less than other laborers. Chinese crews also were given the most dangerous tasks and had to work longer hours than other railroad laborers. They took the job, however, because the $30 a month

Routes West, 1870

When the two lines of the transcontinental railroad met in Promontory, Utah, Leland Stanford drove a celebratory golden spike into the rails.

GEOGRAPHY SKILLS **INTERPRETING MAPS**

Movement According to the map, what was the westernmost city on the transcontinental railroad?

that the Central Pacific paid was as much as 10 times what they could earn in China.

Railroad companies faced many geographic challenges. For example, workers for Central Pacific struggled to cross the Sierra Nevada mountain range in California. Breaking apart its rock formations required setting carefully controlled explosions using large amounts of blasting powder and the explosive nitroglycerin. And in the winter of 1866, snowdrifts more than 60 feet high trapped and killed dozens of workers. Faced with these obstacles, the Central Pacific took four years to lay the first 115 miles of track.

Meanwhile, Union Pacific workers faced harsh weather on the Great Plains. In addition, the company pressured them to work at a rapid pace—at times laying 250 miles of track in six months.

For both railroad companies, providing food and supplies for workers was vital. This job became more difficult in remote areas. The railroad companies consequently often relied on local resources. Professional hunters, such as William "Buffalo Bill" Cody, shot thousands of buffalo to feed Union Pacific workers.

Golden Spike

Congress required the two completed rail lines to connect at Promontory, Utah. On May 10, 1869, a golden spike was used to connect the railroad tie joining the two tracks. Alexander Toponce witnessed the event.

> "Governor Stanford, president of the Central Pacific, took the sledge [hammer], and the first time he struck he missed the spike and hit the rail. What a howl went up! Irish, Chinese, Mexicans, and everybody yelled with delight. 'He missed it'... Then Stanford tried it again and tapped the spike."
>
> —Alexander Toponce, quoted in *A Treasury of Railroad Folklore,* edited by B. A. Botkin and Alvin F. Harlo

The railroad companies were not finished, though. Following completion of the transcontinental railroad, companies continued building railroads until the West was crisscrossed with rail lines.

The Central Pacific and Union Pacific connected their tracks at Promontory, Utah, in 1869, completing the transcontinental railroad.

Effects of the Transcontinental Railroad

QUICK FACTS

- Increased settlement of the West
- Increased business activity and East-West trade
- Helped make the railroad industry one of the most powerful in the country

Results of the Railroad

The transcontinental railroad increased both economic growth and the population in the West. Railroad companies provided better transportation for people and goods. They also sold land to settlers, which encouraged people to move West.

THE IMPACT TODAY

Today's businesses ship goods across the country using railroads, the interstate highway system, and airplanes.

New railroads helped businesses. Western timber companies, miners, ranchers, and farmers shipped wood, metals, meat, and grain east by railroad. In exchange, eastern businesses shipped manufactured goods to the West. As trade between regions increased, the idea that the U.S. economy was interdependent became more widespread. Even perceptions of time became more formal as railroad schedules began to unite areas that had before existed under different times. Four continental time zones were established in 1883.

Railroad companies encouraged people to put their money into the railroad business, which they did—sometimes unwisely. Railroad speculation and the collapse of railroad owner Jay Cooke's banking firm helped start the Panic of 1873. By the 1880s, many small western railroads were deeply in debt. Despite such setbacks, Americans remained interested in railroad investments. By 1890 there were about 164,000 more miles of track in operation than in 1865. Railroads had become one of the biggest industries in the United States.

READING CHECK **Finding Main Ideas** How did the railroad affect the development of the West?

SUMMARY AND PREVIEW In this section you learned about the increased settlement of the West. In the next section you will learn about conflicts with Native Americans.

Section 1 Assessment

go.hrw.com
Online Quiz
KEYWORD: SC7 HP18

Reviewing Ideas, Terms, and People

1. a. **Recall** Why did Americans move West in the years following the Civil War?
   b. **Draw Conclusions** What effect did the discovery of the **Comstock Lode** have on the West?
   c. **Evaluate** Do you think women were important to the success of mining towns? Why or why not?
2. a. **Recall** What led to the cattle boom in the West?
   b. **Analyze** Why was there competition between ranchers and farmers to settle in the Great Plains?
   c. **Evaluate** What played the biggest role in ending the **Cattle Kingdom**? Why?
3. a. **Recall** When and where did the Union Pacific and Central Pacific lines meet?
   b. **Make Generalizations** How do you think the **transcontinental railroad** improved people's lives?

Critical Thinking

4. **Comparing** Review your notes about opportunities in the West. Then use a graphic organizer like the one below to list the effects of these opportunities.

Opportunity	Effect

FOCUS ON WRITING

5. **Taking Notes on Mining, Ranching, and the Railroads** As you read this section, take notes on how mining, ranching, and railroads changed the West. How might a railroad worker feel about these changes?

Wars for the West

SECTION 2

If YOU were there...

You are a member of the Sioux nation, living in Dakota Territory in 1875. These lands are sacred to your people, and the U.S. government has promised them to you. But now gold has been found here, and the government has ordered you to give up your land. Some Sioux leaders want to fight. Others say that it is of no use, that the soldiers will win.

Would you fight to keep your lands? Why?

BUILDING BACKGROUND Miners, ranchers, and farmers all moved West in the years after the Civil War. The arrival of settlers and the U.S. army to the Great Plains meant the end of the way of life of the Indians who lived there. The coming of the railroad began this destruction, with the killing of thousands of buffalo. Treaties were made but did not protect Indian lands from settlers.

Settlers Encounter the Plains Indians

As miners and settlers began crossing the Great Plains in the mid-1800s, they pressured the federal government for more access to western lands. To protect these travelers, U.S. officials sent agents to negotiate treaties with the Plains Indians.

The Plains Indians lived in the Great Plains, which stretch north into Canada and south into Texas. Indian groups such as the Apache and the Comanche lived in and around Texas and

The Plains Indians depended on two animals—the horse and the buffalo.

What You Will Learn...

Main Ideas

1. As settlers moved to the Great Plains, they encountered the Plains Indians.
2. The U.S. Army and Native Americans fought in the northern plains, the Southwest, and the Far West.
3. Despite efforts to reform U.S. policy toward Native Americans, conflict continued.

The Big Idea

Native Americans and the U.S. government came into conflict over land in the West.

Key Terms and People

Treaty of Fort Laramie, *p. 594*
reservations, *p. 595*
Crazy Horse, *p. 595*
Treaty of Medicine Lodge, *p. 595*
buffalo soldiers, *p. 596*
George Armstrong Custer, *p. 596*
Sitting Bull, *p. 596*
Battle of the Little Bighorn, *p. 596*
Massacre at Wounded Knee, *p. 597*
Long Walk, *p. 597*
Geronimo, *p. 597*
Ghost Dance, *p. 598*
Sarah Winnemucca, *p. 598*
Dawes General Allotment Act, *p. 598*

TAKING NOTES As you read this section, take notes on the major events in Native Americans' loss of land rights. Organize them in a chart like the one below.

Date	Event

what is now Oklahoma. The Cheyenne and the Arapaho lived in different regions across the central Plains. The Pawnee lived in parts of Nebraska. To the north were the Sioux. These groups spoke many different languages. However, they used a common sign language to communicate and they shared a similar lifestyle.

Hunting Buffalo

For survival, Plains Indians depended on two animals—the horse and the buffalo. The Spanish brought horses to America in the 1500s. Plains Indians learned to ride horses, and hunters used them to follow buffalo herds year-round. While on horseback, most Plains Indian hunters used a short bow and arrows to shoot buffalo from close range.

Plains Indians used buffalo for food, shelter, clothing, utensils, and tools. Women dried buffalo meat to make jerky. They made tepees and clothing from buffalo hides, and cups and tools from buffalo horns. As one Sioux explained, "When our people killed a buffalo, all of the animal was utilized [used] in some manner; nothing was wasted." The Plains Indians prospered. By 1850, some 75,000 Native Americans lived on the Plains.

Struggle to Keep Land

Miners and settlers were also increasing in numbers—and they wanted Indians' land. The U.S. government tried to avoid disputes by negotiating the **Treaty of Fort Laramie**, the first major treaty between the U.S. government and Plains Indians. Two years later, several southern Plains nations signed a treaty at Fort Atkinson in Nebraska. These treaties recognized Indian claims to most of the Great Plains. They also allowed the United States to build forts and roads and to travel across Indian homelands. The U.S. government promised to pay for any damages to Indian lands.

Interactive Map

Native American Land Loss in the West, 1850–1890

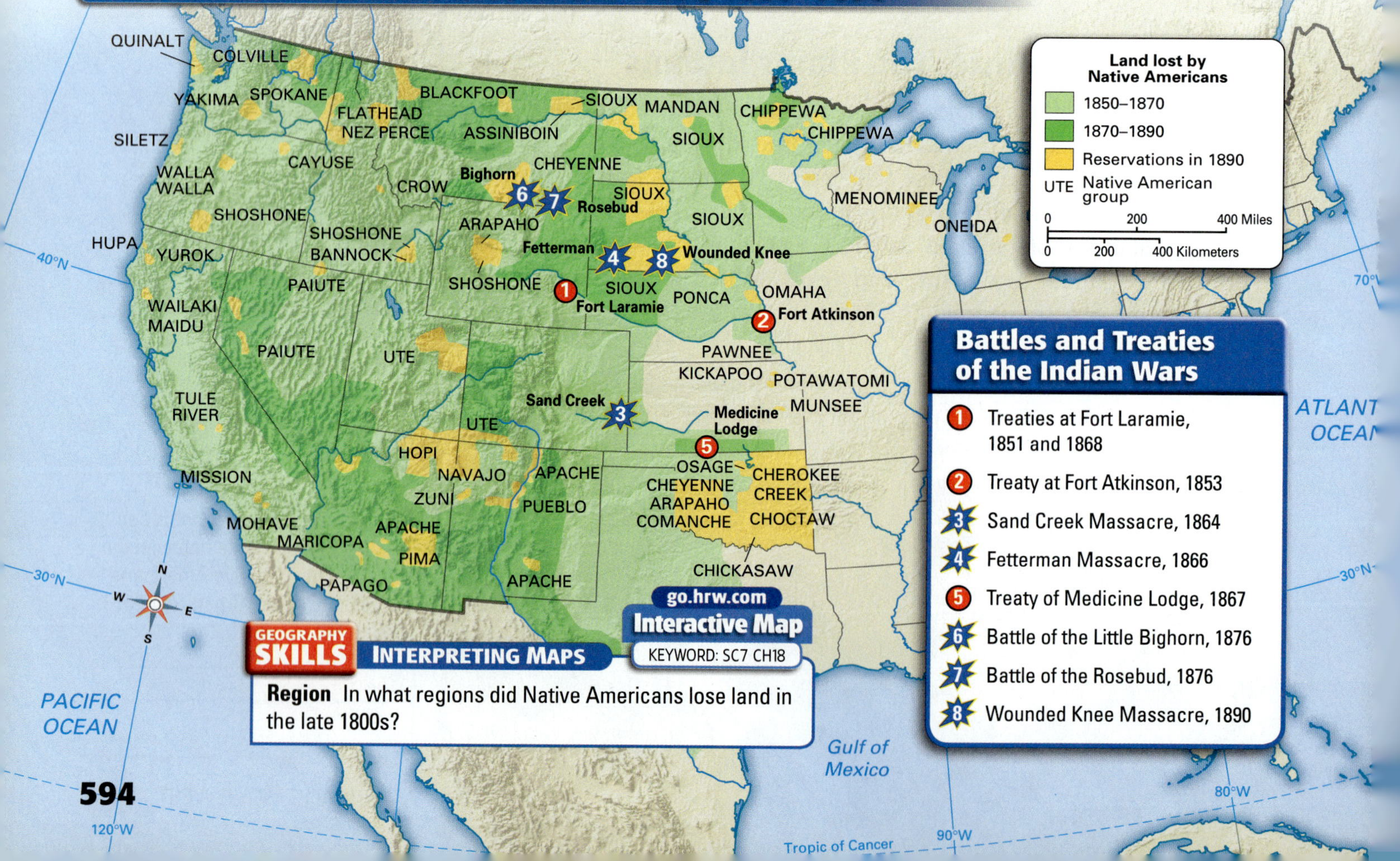

Battles and Treaties of the Indian Wars

1. Treaties at Fort Laramie, 1851 and 1868
2. Treaty at Fort Atkinson, 1853
3. Sand Creek Massacre, 1864
4. Fetterman Massacre, 1866
5. Treaty of Medicine Lodge, 1867
6. Battle of the Little Bighorn, 1876
7. Battle of the Rosebud, 1876
8. Wounded Knee Massacre, 1890

GEOGRAPHY SKILLS INTERPRETING MAPS

Region In what regions did Native Americans lose land in the late 1800s?

LINKING TO TODAY

Tribal Councils

Native Americans have long held tribal councils to make decisions on behalf of the group. Today this tradition of Native American government continues. There are more than 500 tribal governments in the United States. Tribal governments provide a wide range of services, including law enforcement, health care, and education. Here, a member of the Blackfoot Tribal Council addresses the Montana state legislature.

ANALYSIS SKILL **ANALYZING INFORMATION**

What types of services do tribal governments provide?

The treaties did not keep the peace for long. In 1858 the discovery of gold in what is now Colorado brought thousands of miners to the West. They soon clashed with the Cheyenne and the Arapaho. In 1861 the U.S. government negotiated new treaties with Plains Indians. These treaties created **reservations**, areas of federal land set aside for Native Americans. The government expected Indians to stay on the reservations, which made hunting buffalo almost impossible.

Pioneers and miners continued to cross the Great Plains. Many miners used the Bozeman Trail. To protect them, the U.S. Army built forts along the trail, which ran through favored Sioux hunting grounds. The Sioux responded with war. In late 1866, **Crazy Horse** and a group of Sioux ambushed and killed 81 cavalry troops.

In 1868, under the Second Treaty of Fort Laramie, the government agreed to close the Bozeman Trail, abandon the forts, and provide reservation land to the Sioux.

The U.S. government also negotiated for southern Plains Indians to move off their land. In the 1867 **Treaty of Medicine Lodge**, most southern Plains Indians agreed to live on reservations. However, many Indians did not want to give up their hunting grounds. Fighting soon broke out between the Comanche and Texans. The U.S. Army and the Texas Rangers were unable to defeat the Comanche, so they cut off the Comanche's access to food and water. In 1875 the last of the Comanche war leaders surrendered.

READING CHECK **Summarizing** What was the federal policy toward the Plains Indians in the 1860s and 1870s?

Two Views of a Historic Battle

CONNECT TO THE ARTS

Art historians have identified about 1,000 paintings of the Battle of the Little Bighorn. The painting on this page was painted in 1899. The painting on the next page is one of the many colored-pencil drawings of the battle done by Red Horse, who participated in the fight. He drew them five years after the battle.

How do these paintings show the influences of different cultures?

Fighting on the Plains

In the northern Plains, Southwest, and Far West, Native Americans continued to resist being moved to and confined on reservations. The U.S. government sent troops, including African American cavalry, who the Indians called **buffalo soldiers**, into the area to force the Indians to leave.

Battles on the Northern Plains

As fighting on the southern Plains came to an end, new trouble started in the north. In 1874 Lieutenant Colonel **George Armstrong Custer**'s soldiers discovered gold in the Black Hills of the Dakotas. **Sitting Bull**, a leader of the Lakota Sioux, protested U.S. demands for the land.

> "What treaty that the whites have kept has the red man broken? Not one. What treaty that the white man ever made with us have they kept? Not one."
>
> —Sitting Bull, quoted in *Touch the Earth* by T.C. McLuhan

Other Sioux leaders listened to Sitting Bull and refused to give up land. Fighting soon broke out between the army and the Sioux.

On June 25, 1876, Custer's scouts found a Sioux camp along the Little Bighorn River in Montana Territory. Leading 264 of his soldiers, Custer raced ahead without waiting for any supporting forces. In the **Battle of the Little Bighorn**, Sioux forces led by Crazy Horse and Sitting Bull surrounded and defeated Custer and his troops. Newspapers called the battle "Custer's Last Stand" because his entire command was killed. It was the worst defeat the U.S. Army suffered in the West. The Battle of the Little Bighorn was also the Sioux's last major victory.

In 1881 Sitting Bull and a few followers returned from Canada where they had moved. They had run out of food during the hard winter. They joined the Sioux on Standing Rock Reservation in Dakota Territory.

Almost a decade later, in 1890, while following orders to arrest Sitting Bull, reservation police killed him. Many Sioux left the reservations in protest. Later that year, the U.S. Army shot and killed about 150 Sioux near Wounded Knee Creek in South Dakota. This **Massacre at Wounded Knee** was the last major incident on the Great Plains.

Southwest

The Navajo lived in what became Arizona and New Mexico. In 1863 the Navajo refused to settle on a reservation. In response, U.S. troops made raids on the Navajo's fields, homes, and livestock.

When the Navajo ran out of food and shelter, they started surrendering to the U.S. Army. In 1864 the army led Navajo captives on the **Long Walk**. On this 300-mile march the Navajo were forced to walk across the desert to a reservation in Bosque Redondo, New Mexico. Along the way, countless Navajo died.

Far West

The United States had promised to let the peaceful Nez Percé keep their land in Oregon. Within a few years, however, the government ordered the Nez Percé to a reservation in what is now Idaho. Before leaving, a few angry Nez Percé killed some local settlers and tried to escape to Canada. Near the border, U.S. troops overtook them and sent them to a reservation in what is now Oklahoma.

Final Battles

By the 1880s, most Native Americans had stopped fighting. The Apache of the Southwest, however, continued to battle the U.S. Army. A Chiricahua Apache named **Geronimo** and his band of raiders avoided capture for many years. In September 1886 Geronimo surrendered, ending the Apache armed resistance.

READING CHECK **Contrasting** How did the Apache resistance differ from that of the Navajo?

Conflict Continues

Sarah Winnemucca spoke out for the fair treatment of her people.

By the 1870s, many Native Americans lived on reservations, where land was usually not useful for farming or buffalo hunting. Many Indians were starving.

A Paiute Indian named Wovoka began a religious movement, the **Ghost Dance**, that predicted the arrival of paradise for Native Americans. In this paradise, the buffalo herds would return and the settlers would disappear.

U.S. officials did not understand the meaning of the Ghost Dance. They feared it would lead to rebellion, so they tried to end the movement, which had spread to other groups, including the Sioux. After the massacre in 1890 at Wounded Knee, the Ghost Dance movement gradually died out.

In the late 1870s, a Paiute Indian named **Sarah Winnemucca** called for reform. She gave lectures on problems of the reservation system. Writer Helen Hunt Jackson published a book that pushed for reform of U.S. Indian policy in 1881.

Some reformers believed that Native Americans should adopt the ways of white people. The **Dawes General Allotment Act** of 1887 tried to lessen traditional influences on Indian society by making land ownership private rather than shared. The act also promised—but failed to deliver—U.S. citizenship to Native Americans. After breaking up reservation land, the government sold the acreage remaining. The Act took about two-thirds of Indian land.

READING CHECK **Evaluating** How did reformers try to influence Native Americans' lives?

SUMMARY AND PREVIEW In this section you read about conflict in the settlement of the West. In the next section you will learn more about Great Plains settlers.

Section 2 Assessment

go.hrw.com
Online Quiz
KEYWORD: SC7 HP18

Reviewing Ideas, Terms, and People

1. a. **Describe** What animals did Plains Indians depend on, and how did they use those animals?
   b. **Analyze** How did U.S. policy toward the Plains Indians change in the late 1850s?
   c. **Elaborate** Would you have agreed to move to a **reservation**? Why or why not?
2. a. **Describe** What events led to the **Battle of the Little Bighorn**?
   b. **Elaborate** Why do you think most Indian groups eventually stopped resisting the United States?
3. a. **Describe** How did the **Dawes General Allotment Act** affect American Indians?
   b. **Predict** What effect do you think the **Massacre at Wounded Knee** would have on relations between Plains Indians and the United States?

Critical Thinking

4. **Identifying Cause and Effect** Review your notes about Native American land losses. Organize the events in a time line like the one below.

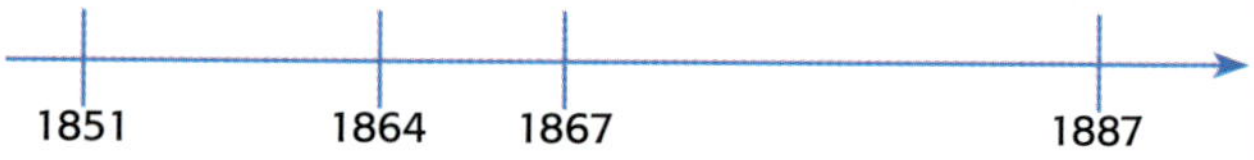

FOCUS ON WRITING

5. **Reading about the Wars for the West** As you read this section, take notes on the wars between the U.S. government and the Plains Indians. How might a railroad worker have experienced these conflicts?

BIOGRAPHY

Chief Joseph

What would you do to protect your home and your ways of life?

When did he live? 1840–1904

Where did he live? Chief Joseph lived in the Wallowa Valley, the Nez Percé homeland, in present-day Oregon.

What did he do? Chief Joseph led his people in an effort to hold on to the Nez Percé homeland and to avoid war with the United States. For years, Joseph and a band of Nez Percé refused to move as white settlers moved into the valley. Finally, after being threatened with attack, Joseph gave in. An army led by General Oliver Otis Howard eventually chased the Nez Percé across Idaho, Wyoming, and Montana. They were sent to a reservation in what is now Oklahoma, where many died.

Why is he so important? Chief Joseph's surrender speech earned him a place in American history. The band of 700 people, including only 200 warriors, made a courageous three-month, 1,400-mile trek, hoping to cross into Canada for protection. Exhausted, hungry, and freezing, Joseph's people collapsed just short of the Canadian border. In later years, the chief spoke about what had happened.

Cause and Effect What brought suffering to Chief Joseph and his people?

Chief Joseph of the Nez Percé nation tried to protect his people from the advancement of white settlers.

Speech

"I am tired of fighting. Our chiefs are killed . . . The old men are all dead . . . It is cold, and we have no blankets. The little children are freezing to death. My people, some of them, have run away to the hills, and have no blankets, no food. No one knows where they are—perhaps freezing to death. I want to have time to look for my children, and see how many of them I can find. Maybe I shall find them among the dead. Hear me, my chiefs! I am tired. My heart is sick and sad. From where the sun now stands I will fight no more forever."

—Chief Joseph of the Nez Percé, surrender speech, October 5, 1877

SECTION 3

Farming and Populism

What You Will Learn...

Main Ideas

1. Many Americans started new lives on the Great Plains.
2. Economic challenges led to the creation of farmers' political groups.
3. By the 1890s, the western frontier had come to an end.

The Big Idea

Settlers on the Great Plains created new communities and unique political groups.

Key Terms and People

Homestead Act, *p. 600*
Morrill Act, *p. 600*
Exodusters, *p. 601*
sodbusters, *p. 601*
dry farming, *p. 601*
Annie Bidwell, *p. 602*
National Grange, *p. 603*
deflation, *p. 604*
William Jennings Bryan, *p. 604*
Populist Party, *p. 604*

TAKING NOTES As you read this section, take notes on the reasons for the rise of populism. Organize your notes in a graphic organizer like the one below.

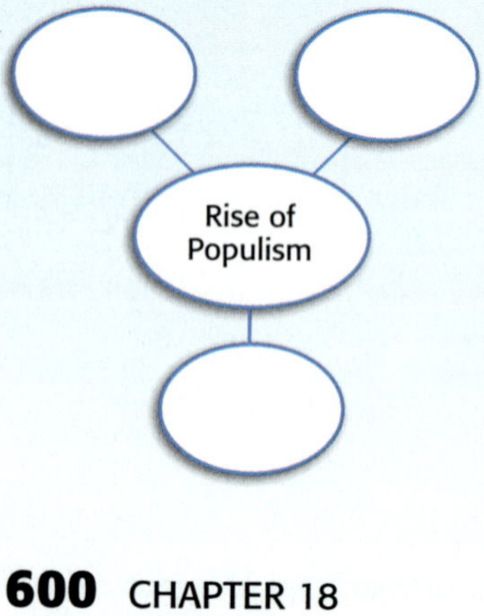

If YOU were there...

You are a female schoolteacher in Wisconsin in 1880. You live and teach in a small town, but you grew up on a farm and are used to hard work. Now you are thinking about moving West to claim free land from the government. You could teach in a school there, too. You think it would be an exciting adventure, but your family is horrified that a single woman would move West on her own.

Would you decide to become a homesteader?

BUILDING BACKGROUND By the 1870s and 1880s, the Great Plains had been "tamed" and made more welcoming to settlers. The end of the open cattle range was coming, and the Indian wars were nearly over. The government moved to encourage permanent settlements in the West by offering land to homesteaders.

New Lives on the Plains

In 1862 Congress passed two important land grant acts that helped open the West to settlers. The **Homestead Act** gave government-owned land to small farmers. Any adult who was a U.S. citizen or planned to become one could receive 160 acres of land. In exchange, homesteaders promised to live on the land for five years. The **Morrill Act** granted more than 17 million acres of federal land to the states. The act required each state to sell this land and to use the money to build colleges to teach agriculture and engineering.

Settling the Plains

People from all over the country moved West. Many farming families moved from areas where farmland was becoming scarce or expensive, such as New England. Many single women moved West. The Homestead Act granted land to unmarried women, which was unusual for the time.

The promise of land and a life free of discrimination also drew a large group of African Americans West. In 1879 some

20,000 to 40,000 southern African Americans moved to Kansas. Known as **Exodusters**, these southerners made a mass exodus, or departure, from the South. A number of black communities soon developed.

Western homesteads also were attractive to immigrants. Norwegian, Swedish, Danish, German, and Czech immigrants formed many small communities on the Great Plains.

Farming the Plains

Plains farmers had many unique challenges. The seasons were extreme. Weather could be extreme. Also, the root-filled sod, or dirt, beneath the Plains grass was very tough. The hard work of breaking up the sod earned Plains farmers the nickname **sodbusters**.

In the 1890s western Plains farmers began **dry farming**, a new method of farming that shifted the focus away from water-dependent crops such as corn. Instead, farmers grew more hardy crops like red wheat. In addition, by the 1880s mechanical farming was becoming common. By using machinery, farmers could work much more quickly on large fields with fewer workers. Farmers shipped their harvest east by train. From there, crops were shipped overseas. The Great Plains soon became known as the breadbasket of the world.

Primary Source

LETTER

Letter from the Plains, 1863

In a letter to her family in Norway, immigrant Gro Svendsen describes her new life as a farmer on the plains of Iowa.

"I remember I used to wonder when I heard that it would be impossible to keep the milk here as we did at home. Now I have learned that it is indeed impossible because of the heat here in the summertime . . . It's difficult, too, to preserve the butter. One must pour brine [salt water] over it or salt it.

The thunderstorms are so violent that one might think it was the end of the world . . . Quite often the lightning strikes down both cattle and people, damages property, and splinters sturdy oak trees into many pieces."

—quoted in *Sources in American History*

ANALYSIS SKILL **ANALYZING PRIMARY SOURCES**

What might be some of the differences between Norway and Svendsen's new home in Iowa?

Pioneers like this family often lived in houses made of sod because there were few trees for lumber on the Plains.

Building Communities

Women were an important force in the settlement of the frontier. They joined in the hard work of farming and ranching and helped build communities out of the widely spaced farms and small towns. Their role in founding communities **facilitated** a strong voice in public affairs. Wyoming women, for example, were granted the vote in the new state's constitution, which was approved in 1869. **Annie Bidwell**, one of the founders of Chico, California, used her influence to support a variety of moral and social causes such as women's suffrage and temperance.

ACADEMIC VOCABULARY

facilitate to make easier

FOCUS ON NORTH CAROLINA

The main political organization of farmers in North Carolina was the Farmers' Alliance, led by Leonidas L. Polk. He published a magazine to educate farmers and became the state's first commissioner of agriculture.

Many early settlers found life on their remote farms to be extremely difficult. Farmers formed communities so that they could assist one another in times of need. One of the first things that many pioneer communities did was establish a local church and school.

Children helped with many chores around the farm. Author Laura Ingalls Wilder was one of four children in a pioneer family. Wilder's books about settlers' lives on the prairie are still popular today.

READING CHECK **Comparing and Contrasting** How were settlers' lives alike and different from their lives in the East?

Farmers' Political Groups

From 1860 to 1900, the U.S. population more than doubled. To feed this growing population, the number of farms tripled. With modern machines, farmers in 1900 could harvest a bushel of wheat almost 20 times faster than they could in 1830.

Farm Incomes Fall

The combination of more farms and greater productivity, however, led to overproduction. Overproduction resulted in lower prices for crops. As their incomes decreased, many farmers found it difficult to pay bills. Farmers who could not make their mortgage payments lost their farms and homes. Many of these homeless farmers became tenant farmers who worked land owned by others. By 1880 one-fourth of all farms were rented by tenants, and the number continued to grow.

The National Grange

Many farmers blamed businesspeople—wholesalers, brokers, grain buyers, and especially railroad owners—for making money at their expense. As economic conditions worsened, farmers began to follow the example of other workers. They formed associations to protect and help their interests.

Time Line

Farming and the Rise of Populism

1862 President Lincoln signs the bill that authorizes the transcontinental railroad.

1867 The National Grange is founded.

1879 Exodusters move to Kansas.

One such organization was founded by Oliver Hudson Kelley, who toured the South in 1866 for the U.S. Department of Agriculture. Kelley saw firsthand how the country's farmers suffered. Afterward, Kelley and several government clerks formed the National Grange of the Patrons of Husbandry in 1867. The **National Grange** was a social and educational organization for farmers. (*Grange* is an old word for granary.) Local chapters were quickly founded, and membership grew rapidly.

The Grange campaigned for political candidates who supported farmers' goals. The organization also called for laws that regulated rates charged by railroads. The U.S. Supreme Court ruled in 1877 that the government could regulate railroads because they affected the public interest. In 1886 the Court said that the federal government could only regulate companies doing business across state lines. Rate regulation for railroad lines within states fell to the state governments.

In February 1887 Congress passed the Interstate Commerce Act, providing national regulations over trade between states and creating the Interstate Commerce Commission to ensure fair railroad rates. However, the commission lacked power to enforce its regulations.

Agriculture in North Carolina

Connect to Economics

Two of the crops that were most important to North Carolina's economy were tobacco and cotton. By 1880 both crops had recovered to pre–Civil War levels. *In which year shown on the graph was the most cotton and tobacco produced?*

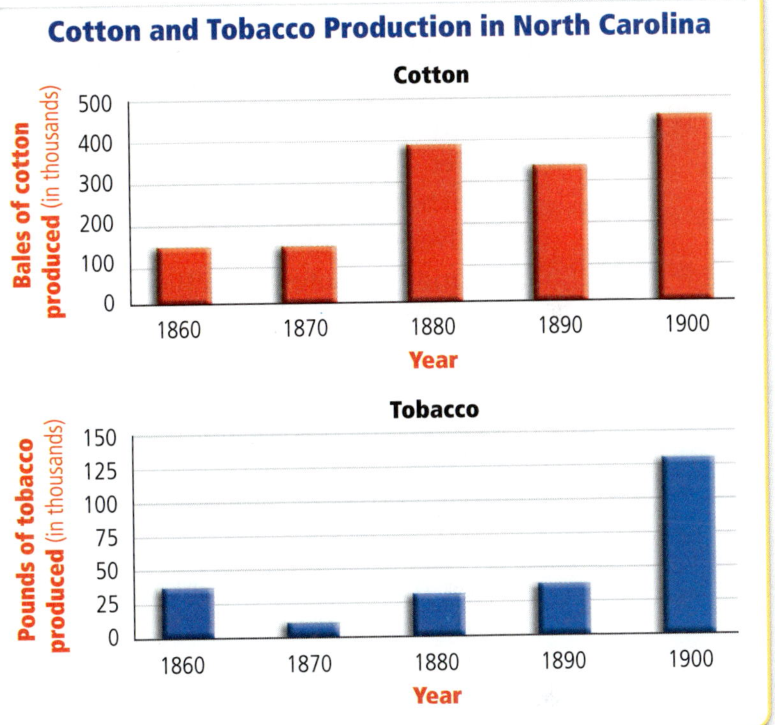

1887 The Interstate Commerce Commission is formed to regulate railroad prices.

1892 The national Populist Party is formed.

1896 The Populist Party backs William Jennings Bryan as the Democratic presidential candidate.

Analysis Skill: Reading Time Lines

How many years after the authorization of the transcontinental railroad was the Interstate Commerce Commission created?

Free Silver Debate

Money issues also caused problems for farmers. Many farmers hoped that help would come from new laws affecting the money supply.

Since 1873 the United States had been on the gold standard, meaning that all paper money had to be backed by gold in the treasury. As a result, the money supply grow more slowly than the nation's population and led to **deflation**—a decrease in the money supply and overall lower prices. One solution was to allow the unlimited coining of silver and to back paper currency with silver. This was the position of those in the Free Silver movement.

During the late 1870s, there was a great deal of support for the Free Silver movement. Many farmers began backing political candidates who favored free silver coinage. One such candidate was **William Jennings Bryan** of Nebraska.

The two major political parties, however, largely ignored the money issue. After the election of 1888, the Republican-controlled Congress passed the Sherman Silver Purchase Act. The act increased the amount of silver purchased for coinage. However, this did not help farmers as much as they had hoped.

BIOGRAPHY

William Jennings Bryan
1860–1925

William Jennings Bryan was born in Illinois but moved to Nebraska when he finished law school. He was elected Nebraska's first Democratic Congress member in 1890. Through his political campaigns and work as a newspaper editor, he became one of the best-known supporters of Populist ideas. After a dramatic speech at the 1896 Democratic National Convention, Bryan was nominated for the presidency. He was the youngest presidential candidate up to that time. Although he lost the election, he continued to be an influential speaker.

Making Inferences Why was Bryan's support of Populist ideas important?

Populist Party

To have greater power, many farmers organized to elect candidates that would help them. These political organizations became known as the Farmers' Alliances.

In the 1890 elections the Alliances were a strong political force. State and local wins raised farmers' political hopes. At a conference in Cincinnati, Ohio, in 1891, Alliance leaders met with labor and reform groups. Then, at a convention in St. Louis in February 1892, the Alliances formed a new national political party.

The new party was called the **Populist Party**, and it called for the government to own railroads and telephone and telegraph systems. It also favored the "free and unlimited coinage of silver." To gain the votes of workers, the Populists backed an eight-hour workday and limits on immigration.

The concerns of the Populists were soon put in the national spotlight. During the Panic of 1893, the U.S. economy experienced a crisis that some critics blamed on the shortage of gold. The failure of several major railroad companies also contributed to the economic problems.

The Panic of 1893 led more people to back the Populist call for economic reform. In 1896 the Republicans nominated William McKinley for president. McKinley was firmly against free coinage of silver. The Democrats nominated William Jennings Bryan, who favored free coinage.

The Populists had to decide between running their own candidate, and thus splitting the silver vote, or supporting Bryan. They decided to support Bryan. The Republicans had a well-financed campaign, and they won the election. McKinley's victory in 1896 marked the end of both the Populist Party and the Farmers' Alliances.

READING CHECK **Summarizing** Why did farmers, laborers, and reformers join to form the Populist Party?

Guthrie, Oklahoma

Oklahoma Land Rush

- The rush began at noon on April 22, 1889.
- Some witnesses said they could feel the ground shake as 50,000 people raced to claim land.
- Single women and widows could claim land on an equal basis with men.
- Many settlers were dismayed to find some people had claimed land before the rush legally began. These people were called sooners.

End of the Frontier

By 1870 only small portions of the Great Plains remained unsettled. For most of the next two decades, this land remained open range.

In March 1889, government officials announced that homesteaders could file claims on land in what is now the state of Oklahoma. This land had belonged to Creek and Seminole Indians. Within a month, about 50,000 people rushed to Oklahoma to stake their claims.

In all, settlers claimed more than 11 million acres of former Indian land in the famous Oklahoma land rush. This huge wave of pioneers was the last chapter of the westward movement. By the early 1890s, the frontier had ceased to exist in the United States.

READING CHECK **Finding Main Ideas** What event signaled the closing of the frontier?

SUMMARY AND PREVIEW In this section you read about the challenges settlers faced. In the next chapter you will read about the growth of America's industrial power and how that growth affected American lives.

Section 3 Assessment

go.hrw.com
Online Quiz
KEYWORD: SC7 HP18

Reviewing Ideas, Terms, and People

1. a. **Describe** What groups settled in the Great Plains?
   b. **Explain** How did the U.S. government make lands available to western settlers?
   c. **Elaborate** Would you have chosen to settle on the frontier? Why or why not?
2. a. **Recall** What was the goal of the **National Grange**?
   b. **Make Inferences** Why did the **Populist Party** want the government to own railroads and telegraph and telephone systems?
   c. **Evaluate** Do you think farmers were successful in bringing about economic and political change? Explain.
3. a. **Recall** What was the Oklahoma land rush?
   b. **Explain** Why did the frontier cease to exist in the United States?

Critical Thinking

4. **Comparing and Contrasting** Look back over your notes about the rise of populism. Use them to explain why Populists sought the changes they did in a chart like the one below.

Change sought	Reason why

FOCUS ON WRITING

5. **Farming the Great Plains** As you read this section, take notes on the growth of farming on the Great Plains. How did farmers interact with the railroads? What changes might have been apparent to a railroad worker?

Social Studies Skills

Analysis | Critical Thinking | Civic Participation | **Study**

North Carolina Skills
3.01 Use map and globe reading skills.

Comparing Migration Maps

Define the Skill

One of the best ways of using geography to learn history is by comparing maps. This skill allows you to see changes over time. It also helps you see relationships between one factor, such as population growth, and another factor, such as transportation routes or economic activities in an area.

Learn the Skill

Follow these steps to compare information on maps.

1. Apply basic map skills by reading the title and studying the legend and symbols for each map.
2. Note the date of each map and the area it covers. Maps compared for changes over time should include the same areas. Those used to look for relationships should have similar dates.
3. Note similarities or differences. Closely examine and compare each map's patterns and symbols.
4. Apply critical thinking skills. Make generalizations and draw conclusions about the relationships you find.

Practice the Skill

Use the maps below to answer the following questions.

1. What present-day state was unsettled by Americans in 1850 and almost completely settled in 1890?
2. Which other two present-day states show the most settlement by Americans from 1850 to 1890?
3. Why do you think the West coast was settled before the interior of the United States?
4. According to the maps, how might rivers have shaped the settlement of the West?

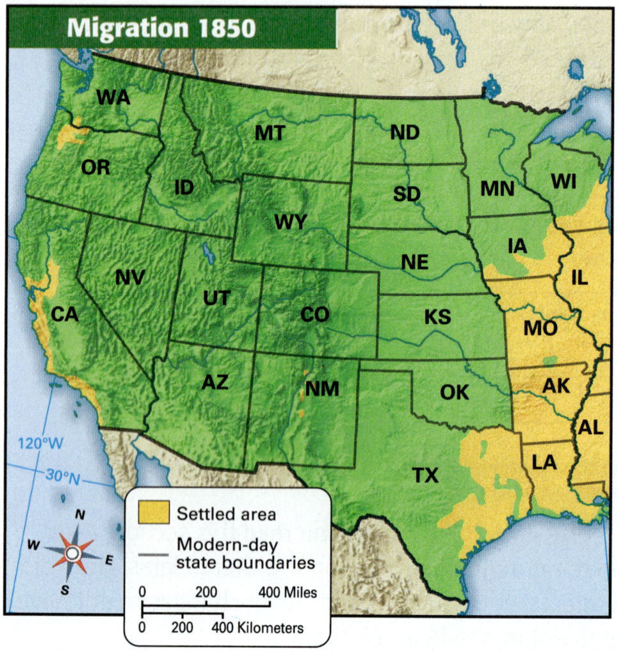

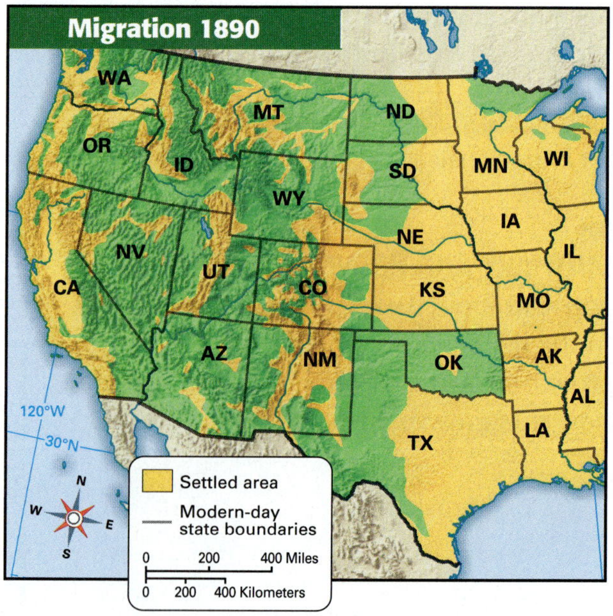

CHAPTER 18

Chapter Review

HOLT

History's Impact

▶ **video series**

Review the video to answer the closing question:

How was a cowboy's job essential to the American economy?

Visual Summary

QUICK FACTS

Use the visual summary below to help you review the main ideas of the chapter.

The American West

As settlers moved West, they came into conflict with American Indians. The U.S. government defeated Indian resistance and moved many tribes to reservations.

The completion of the transcontinental railroad in 1869 opened the West to more settlement. Gold and silver strikes also drew people hoping to get rich.

The railroads helped make the rise of the Cattle Kingdom possible. Cowboys drove huge herds of cattle from ranches to railway stations to be shipped to the East.

Farmers settled the Great Plains in large numbers. They overcame many hardships to make the Plains the breadbasket of America.

Reviewing Vocabulary, Terms, and People

1. Who was the leader of the 7th Cavalry in the Battle of the Little Bighorn?

a. Cyrus McCormick **c.** William Jennings Bryan

b. Leland Stanford **d.** George Armstrong Custer

2. What act gave millions of acres of federal lands to the states, which were to sell them and use those funds to build agricultural and engineering colleges?

a. Morrill Act **c.** Pacific Railway Act

b. Sherman Act **d.** Interstate Commerce Act

3. Which frontier woman was instrumental in supporting reform efforts in the West?

a. Sarah Winnemucca **c.** Annie Bidwell

b. Laura Ingalls Wilder **d.** Lucretia Mott

Comprehension and Critical Thinking

SECTION 1 *(Pages 586–592)*

4. a. Recall Why were many Americans eager to move to the western frontier?

b. Analyze How did railroads and ranching change the landscape of the West?

c. Elaborate In your opinion, which made the greatest changes to the West—mining, ranching, or railroads? Explain your answer.

SECTION 2 *(Pages 593–598)*

5. a. Describe What was life like for the Plains Indians before and after the arrival of large numbers of American settlers?

b. Draw Conclusions Why did the spread of the Ghost Dance movement cause concern for U.S. officials?

c. Elaborate What do you think about the reservation system established by the United States?

SECTION 3 *(Pages 600–605)*

6. **a. Identify** What political organizations did western farmers create? Why did farmers create these organizations?

   b. Analyze How did women participate in the settling of the American frontier?

   c. Predict How might the end of the frontier in the United States affect the nation?

Reviewing Themes

7. **Geography** What geographic obstacles did miners, ranchers, and railroad workers face in the West?

8. **Science and Technology** What types of technology did farmers on the Great Plains use, and how did it benefit them?

Using the Internet

go.hrw.com
KEYWORD: SC7 CH18

9. **Activity: Creating a Presentation** Our view of the settlement of the West is heavily influenced by popular culture. Writers, painters, and illustrators provided a steady flow of words and images that sensationalized life in the American West. Later, film makers and television producers also contributed to the myth of the Wild West. "When legend becomes fact," said one actor in the classic western movie *The Man Who Shot Liberty Valance,* "print the legend." How does legend affect our view of this part of our history? Enter the activity keyword. Analyze the myths and realities of the West and the ways in which they shaped our view of that time period. Then create a visual display or PowerPoint presentation to present your research.

Reading Skills

Understanding Through Questioning *Use the Reading Skills taught in this chapter to answer the question about the reading selection below.*

> For survival, Plains Indians depended on two animals—the horse and the buffalo. The Spanish brought horses to America in the 1500s. Plains Indians learned to ride horses, and hunters used them to follow buffalo herds year-round. *(p. 594)*

10. Write two or three questions you have about the information in the passage above. Remember to use the five W's—Who? What? When? Where? and Why?

Social Studies Skills

Comparing Migration Maps *Use the Social Studies Skills taught in this chapter to answer the questions about the map below.*

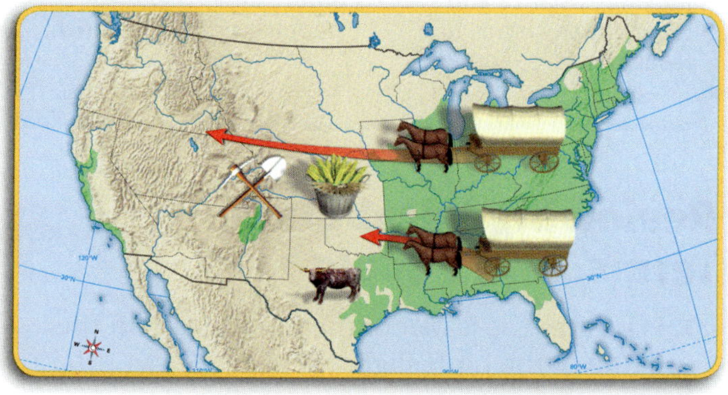

11. According to the map above, for what reasons did settlers migrate to the West?

    a. for mining, ranching, and farming

    b. for jobs in manufacturing

    c. for the homes in the major cities there

    d. for the fishing industry

Focus on Writing

12. **Writing Your Letter** Review your notes. Then write a letter to your sister back in Ireland about your experiences on the Great Plains. Describe all the changes you have seen. Use colorful language and precise details to make your sister feel as though she were there.

CHAPTER 18 Standardized Test Practice

DIRECTIONS: Read each question and write the letter of the best response.

1

- Government ownership of railroads
- Free and unlimited coinage of silver
- An eight-hour day for industrial workers
- Strict limits on foreign immigration
- Election of officials who will help farmers

Which of the following intended to accomplish the changes listed above in American society?

A the Morrill Act
B the Populist Party
C the National Grange
D the Homestead Act

2 The goal of many reformers who wanted to help Native Americans in the late 1800s was to

A get Indians to adopt the ways of white people.
B return to Indians all the land that had been taken from them.
C relocate all the nations to create an American Indian state in Oklahoma.
D negotiate treaties to bring peace to the frontier.

3 What played the *most important* part in the growth of the West's population and economy between 1865 and 1900?

A the mining industry
B the Cattle Kingdom
C the Populist Party
D the railroad

4 In general, the policy of the United States government toward Native Americans in the West was to

A send the army to track them down and engage them in battle.
B move them onto reservations and open their homelands to white settlers.
C kill all the buffalo so that they could not continue their traditional way of life.
D drive them into Canada or Mexico to settle.

5 The biggest problem facing western farmers in the late 1800s was

A a scarcity of good, cheap land to farm.
B their lack of organization to achieve change.
C overproduction and low crop prices.
D the threat of attacks by Native Americans.

6 Read the following excerpt from a speech by Leonidas L. Polk, president of the National Farmers' Alliance, and use it to answer the question below.

"These suffering millions must have relief. They ask for bread and will not be content with a stone. They are not asking for charity, but they are demanding justice . . . They demand that the heavy hand of oppressive discrimination be lifted from them, and that they be allowed an open field and an equal chance with the other great industries of the country."

—Leonidas L. Polk, speech before the Senate Committee on Agriculture and Forestry, 1890

Document-Based Question According to Polk, what hardships did farmers face?

CHAPTER 19 1876–1900

The Industrial Age

North Carolina Standards

Social Studies Objectives

5.04 Identify technological advances, and evaluate their influence on the quality of life in North Carolina.

go.hrw.com
North Carolina
KEYWORD: SC7 NC

FOCUS ON WRITING

A Business Plan You are an inventor in the late 1800s, and you want to start a business to sell your new inventions. Write a business plan for investors that will encourage them to lend you money to start your business. As you read this chapter, gather information about the new business practices that you can use to run your business. Then write your plan. Include information about what you will sell, how you will make it, and how you can avoid conflicts with the workers who make your product.

UNITED STATES

1879 Thomas Edison invents the first lightbulb.

1870

WORLD

1876 German engineer Nikolaus A. Otto perfects a gasoline-powered engine.

HOLT

History's Impact

▶ **video series**
Watch the video to understand the impact of the United States as the world's most powerful industrial nation.

What You Will Learn...

In this chapter you will learn about how the United States became an industrial power in the late 1800s. A new wave of immigrants provided the labor, and the combination of industry and immigration led to increased urbanization of the country. Cities like San Francisco, shown here, began to take the shape that they still have today. In fact, much of what we know as modern America developed during this important period.

1886 The American Federation of Labor is formed on December 8.

1890 Congress passes the Sherman Antitrust Act.

1892 On June 29 the Homestead strike begins. Carnegie Steel Company refuses to negotiate with the union.

1880 — 1890 — 1900

1883 The island volcano of Krakatau in the Pacific Ocean erupts in one of the world's greatest natural disasters.

1889 The Eiffel Tower is built in Paris.

1898 French scientists Pierre and Marie Curie discover radium.

Reading Social Studies

by Kylene Beers

Economics | **Geography** | **Politics** | **Society and Culture** | **Science and Technology**

Focus on Themes In this chapter, you will read about the advancements in transportation and communication made during what is called the Second Industrial Revolution. You will learn about the rise of powerful corporations. You will also read about the workers who organized in the late 1800s and will see what happened as unions began demanding better treatment for workers. Throughout the chapter, you will see how **society** was affected by the changing **economy**.

Organization of Facts and Information

Focus on Reading How are clothes organized in a department store? How are files arranged in a file cabinet? Clear organization helps us find the product we need, and it also helps us find facts and information.

Understanding Structural Patterns Writers use structural patterns to organize information in sentences or paragraphs. What's a structural pattern? It's simply a way of organizing information. Learning to recognize those patterns will make it easier for you to read and understand social studies texts.

Patterns of Organization

Pattern	Clue Words	Graphic Organizer
Cause-effect shows how one thing leads to another.	as a result, therefore, because, this led to	Cause → Effect; Cause → Effect; Cause → Effect
Chronological order shows the sequence of events or actions.	after, before, first, then, not long after, finally	First → Next → Last
Comparison-contrast points out similarities and/or differences.	although, but, however, on the other hand, similarly, also	Differences / Similarities
Listing presents information in categories such as size, location, or importance.	also, most important, for example, in fact	Category • Fact • Fact • Fact

To use text structure to improve your understanding, follow these steps:

1. Look for the main idea of the passage you are reading.
2. Then look for clues that signal a specific pattern.
3. Look for other important ideas and think about how the ideas connect. Is there any obvious pattern?
4. Use a graphic organizer to map the relationships among the facts and details.

You Try It!

The following passages are from the chapter you are about to read. As you read each set of sentences, ask yourself what structural pattern the writer used to organize the information.

Recognizing Structural Patterns

(A) Great advances in communication technologies took place in the late 1800s. By 1861, telegraph wires connected the East and West coasts. Five years later, a telegraph cable on the floor of the Atlantic Ocean connected the United States and Great Britain. *(p. 617)*

(B) Many business leaders justified their business methods through their belief in social Darwinism . . . Other business leaders, however, believed that the rich had a duty to aid the poor. *(p. 621)*

(C) During the late 1800s, several factors led to a decline in the quality of working conditions. Machines run by unskilled workers were eliminating the jobs of many skilled craftspeople. These low-paid workers could be replaced easily. *(p. 624)*

After you read the passages, answer the questions below:

1. Reread passage A. What structural pattern did the writer use to organize this information? How can you tell?

2. Reread passage B. What structural pattern did the writer use to organize this information? How can you tell? Why do you think the writer chose this pattern?

3. Reread passage C. What structural pattern did the writer use to organize this information? How can you tell? Why do you think the writer chose this pattern?

As you read Chapter 19, think about the organization of the ideas. Ask yourself why the writer chose to organize the information in this way.

Key Terms and People

Chapter 19

Section 1

Second Industrial Revolution *(p. 615)*
Bessemer process *(p. 615)*
Thomas Edison *(p. 616)*
patents *(p. 616)*
Alexander Graham Bell *(p. 617)*
Henry Ford *(p. 617)*
Wilbur and Orville Wright *(p. 618)*

Section 2

corporations *(p. 619)*
Andrew Carnegie *(p. 620)*
vertical integration *(p. 620)*
John D. Rockefeller *(p. 620)*
horizontal integration *(p. 621)*
trust *(p. 621)*
Leland Stanford *(p. 621)*
social Darwinism *(p. 621)*
monopoly *(p. 622)*
Sherman Antitrust Act *(p. 622)*

Section 3

Frederick W. Taylor *(p. 624)*
Knights of Labor *(p. 625)*
Terence V. Powderly *(p. 625)*
American Federation of Labor *(p. 625)*
Samuel Gompers *(p. 625)*
collective bargaining *(p. 626)*
Mary Harris Jones *(p. 626)*
Haymarket Riot *(p. 626)*
Homestead strike *(p. 627)*
Pullman strike *(p. 627)*

Academic Vocabulary

In this chapter, you will learn the following academic words:
implement *(p. 617)*
acquire *(p. 620)*

SECTION 1

The Second Industrial Revolution

What You Will Learn...

Main Ideas

1. Breakthroughs in steel processing led to a boom in railroad construction.
2. Advances in the use of oil and electricity improved communications and transportation.
3. A rush of inventions changed Americans' lives.

The Big Idea

The Second Industrial Revolution led to new sources of power and advances in transportation and communication.

Key Terms and People

Second Industrial Revolution, *p. 615*
Bessemer process, *p. 615*
Thomas Edison, *p. 616*
patents, *p. 616*
Alexander Graham Bell, *p. 617*
Henry Ford, *p. 617*
Wilbur and Orville Wright, *p. 618*

TAKING NOTES As you read this section, take notes on the inventors of the Second Industrial Revolution. Organize your notes in a table like the one below.

Inventor

If YOU were there...

You live in a small town but are visiting an aunt in the city in the 1890s. You are amazed when your aunt pushes a button on the wall to turn on electric lights. At home you still use kerosene lamps. You hear a clatter outside and see an electric streetcar traveling down the street. You are shocked when a telephone rings, and your aunt speaks to someone miles away!

Which of these inventions would you find most amazing?

BUILDING BACKGROUND The first Industrial Revolution in America began in the early 1800s. It changed the way products were made, from handwork to machines. It moved the workplace from cottages to factories. Later, it brought advances in transportation and communication. The Second Industrial Revolution built on these changes, introducing new technology and new sources of power.

Breakthroughs in Steel Processing

Technological advances were important to the **Second Industrial Revolution**, a period of rapid growth in U.S. manufacturing in the late 1800s. By the mid-1890s, the United States had become the world's industrial leader.

The Steel Industry

Some of the most important advances in technology happened in the steel industry. Steel is iron that has been made stronger by heat and the addition of other metals. In the mid-1850s Henry Bessemer invented the **Bessemer process**, a way to manufacture steel quickly and cheaply by blasting hot air through melted iron to quickly remove impurities. Before, turning several tons of iron ore into steel took a day or more. The Bessemer process took only 10 to 20 minutes.

The Bessemer process helped increase steel production. U.S. mills had produced 77,000 tons of steel in 1870. By 1879 production had risen to more than 1 million tons in one year.

Riding the Rails

As steel dropped in price, so did the cost of building railroads. Companies built thousands of miles of new steel track. The design of elegant passenger and sleeping cars improved passenger service. Manufacturers and farmers sent products to market faster than ever by rail in newly invented refrigerated shipping cars. Cities where major rail lines crossed, such as Chicago, grew rapidly. Railroads also increased western growth by offering free tickets to settlers. Finally, as rail travel and shipping increased, railroads and related industries began employing more people.

QUICK FACTS

Factors Affecting Industrial Growth

- Greater ability to use natural resources
- A growing population
- Transportation advances
- Rising immigration
- Inventions and innovations
- Increasing business investment
- Government policies assisting business, such as protective tariffs

READING CHECK **Identifying Cause and Effect** How did steel processing change in the 1850s, and how did this affect the United States?

Homestead Steel Mill

Steel mills like this one in Homestead, Pennsylvania, were the center of the new steel industry that led to advancements in rail travel. Workers used the Bessemer process to make steel more quickly.

How do you think mills like this one affected the surrounding area?

Time Line

The Spirit of Innovation

1850

1852 Elisha Otis invents the elevator safety brake, making elevators safe for people.

1854 Henry Bessemer patents a method for making cast steel.

1860

1869 John Roebling begins work on the Brooklyn Bridge.

FOCUS ON NORTH CAROLINA

Electric lights first lit the streets of Raleigh in 1885. The cities of Wilmington and Winston followed. Soon electricity was powering factories and homes in most North Carolina cities. However, some rural parts of the state did not receive electricity until the 1930s.

FOCUS ON READING

How does this paragraph show the cause and effect structure?

Use of Oil and Electricity

The Second Industrial Revolution was characterized by dramatic developments in the use and distribution of oil and electricity. These power sources fueled other changes.

Oil as a Power Source

An important technological breakthrough in the late 1800s was the use of petroleum, or oil, as a power source. People had known about oil for many years but had discovered few ways to use it. However, in the 1850s, chemists invented a way to convert crude, or unprocessed, oil into a fuel called kerosene. Kerosene could be used for cooking, heating, and lighting. Suddenly there was a demand for oil.

As demand grew, people began searching for a reliable source for oil. In 1859 Edwin L. Drake proved that it was possible to pump crude oil from the ground. Soon, wildcatters, or oil prospectors, drilled for oil in Ohio, Pennsylvania, and West Virginia. Oil became a big business as these states began producing millions of barrels per year. Oil companies built refineries to turn the crude oil into finished products like kerosene. One oil company supervisor referred to oil workers as "men who are supplying light for the world."

Electricity Spreads

In addition to kerosene, electricity became a critical source of light and power during the Second Industrial Revolution. The possible uses of electricity interested inventors like **Thomas Edison**. His research center in Menlo Park, New Jersey, was called an invention factory. Edison explained his practical approach to science.

> "I do not regard myself as a pure scientist, as so many persons have insisted that I am. I do not search for the laws of nature . . . for the purpose of learning truth. I am only a professional inventor . . . with the object [goal] of inventing that which will have commercial utility [use]."
>
> —Thomas Edison, quoted in *American Made,* by Harold C. Livesay

Edison eventually held more than 1,000 **patents**, exclusive rights to make or sell inventions. Patents allowed inventors to protect their inventions from being manufactured by others.

In 1878 Edison announced that he would soon invent a practical electric light. By the end of 1879 Edison and his team of inventors had created the electric lightbulb. The public was excited. However, Edison had a problem. At the time, few homes or businesses could get electricity. Edison therefore built a power plant that began supplying electricity to dozens of New York City buildings in

September 1882. The *New York Times* reported that with electric lighting in the newspaper offices, "it seemed almost like writing by daylight." However, Edison's equipment could not send electricity over long distances. As a result, his power company, Edison Electric, provided electricity mainly to central cities.

In the late 1880s, George Westinghouse built a power system that could send electricity across many miles. As Edison and Westinghouse competed, the use of electricity spread rapidly in the nation's cities. After a while, electricity soon lit homes and businesses and powered city factories. Electricity also was used to power streetcars in cities across the nation.

READING CHECK **Drawing Conclusions**
Why did people begin to pump oil from the ground?

Rush of Inventions

In the late 1800s, inventors focused on finding solutions to practical problems. Communication and transportation took the lead.

Advances in Communication

Great advances in communication technologies took place in the late 1800s. By 1861, telegraph wires connected the East and West coasts. Five years later, a telegraph cable on the floor of the Atlantic Ocean connected the United States and Great Britain.

However, the telegraph carried only written messages and was difficult for untrained people to use. These problems were solved in March 1876, when inventor **Alexander Graham Bell** patented the telephone. Bell was a Scottish-born speech teacher who studied the science of sound. He called the telephone a "talking telegraph."

Telephone companies raced to lay thousands of miles of phone lines. By 1880 there were about 55,000 telephones in the United States. Raleigh's first telephone exchange was constructed in 1879.

THE IMPACT TODAY
AT&T Corporation is a direct descendant of Bell's original company. AT&T pioneered the use of telephone cables across the oceans, satellite communications, and a radar system for the U.S. Defense Department.

Automobiles and Planes

In 1876 a German engineer invented an engine powered by gasoline, another fuel made from oil. In 1893 Charles and J. Frank Duryea used a gasoline engine to build the first practical motorcar in the United States. By the early 1900s, thousands of cars were being built in the United States.

At first, only the wealthy could buy these early cars. **Henry Ford** introduced the Model T in 1908. Ford was the first to **implement** the moving assembly line in manufacturing, a process that greatly reduced the cost of building a product, thus making cars more affordable.

ACADEMIC VOCABULARY
implement
to put in place

Time Line

The Spirit of Innovation

1893 George Ferris displays the first Ferris wheel at the World's Columbian Exposition in Chicago.

1900

1903 Orville Wright makes the first flight in a motorized airplane.

ANALYSIS SKILL **READING TIME LINES**

When was the telephone invented?

FOCUS ON NORTH CAROLINA

North Carolina takes its motto First in Flight from the Wright brothers' experiments at Kitty Hawk.

New engine technology helped make another breakthrough in transportation possible—air flight. Brothers **Wilbur and Orville Wright** built a lightweight airplane that used a small, gas-powered engine. In Kitty Hawk, North Carolina, Orville Wright made the first piloted flight in a gas-powered plane on December 17, 1903. This invention would change the way that many Americans traveled in the future and would increase the demand for oil production.

READING CHECK **Comparing** What new inventions excited the public in the 1800s, and how were they used?

SUMMARY AND PREVIEW The Second Industrial Revolution led to advances in energy sources, communication, and transportation. In the next section you will learn about the growth of big business.

Section 1 Assessment

go.hrw.com
Online Quiz
KEYWORD: SC7 HP19

Reviewing Ideas, Terms, and People

1. a. **Describe** What was the **Bessemer process**?
   b. **Summarize** How did improvements to railroads affect the economy and transportation in the United States?
   c. **Elaborate** What do you think was the most important effect of the Bessemer process? Why?
2. a. **Identify** What is kerosene, and for what could it be used?
   b. **Explain** What problem did **Thomas Edison** face regarding the use of electricity, and how did he solve it?
3. a. **Recall** What contribution did **Wilbur and Orville Wright** make to transportation?
   b. **Draw Conclusions** How did **Alexander Graham Bell**'s invention improve life in the United States?
   c. **Elaborate** Why do you think there was a rush of inventions in the late 1800s?

Critical Thinking

4. **Analyzing** Look over your notes on inventors. Use them to complete a table like the one below about inventors and their inventions.

Inventor	Invention

Focus on Writing

5. **Information on a Product** In your notes, list what kinds of new products became available at this time. What do you think would be a good thing to make and sell during the late 1800s?

Big Business

SECTION 2

If YOU were there...

It is 1895, and your town is home to a large corporation. The company's founder and owner, a wealthy man, lives in a mansion on a hill. He is a fair employer but not especially generous. Many townspeople work in his factory. You and other town leaders feel that he should contribute more to local charities and community organizations.

How could this business leader help the town more?

BUILDING BACKGROUND Advanced technology along with the use of oil and electric power helped American businesses grow. Soon the shape of the American economy changed. Some companies grew so large that they began to dominate entire industries.

What You Will Learn...

Main Ideas

1. The rise of corporations and powerful business leaders led to the dominance of big business in the United States.
2. People and the government began to question the methods of big business.

The Big Idea

The growth of big business in the late 1800s led to the creation of monopolies.

Key Terms and People

corporations, *p. 619*
Andrew Carnegie, *p. 620*
vertical integration, *p. 620*
John D. Rockefeller, *p. 620*
horizontal integration, *p. 621*
trust, *p. 621*
Leland Stanford, *p. 621*
social Darwinism, *p. 621*
monopoly, *p. 622*
Sherman Antitrust Act, *p. 622*

TAKING NOTES As you read this section, take notes on the new business practices you learn about. Keep them organized in a chart like the one below.

New Business Practice

Dominance of Big Business

In the late 1800s many entrepreneurs formed their businesses as **corporations**, or businesses that sell portions of ownership called stock shares. The leaders of these corporations were some of the most widely respected members of American society in the late 1800s. Political leaders praised prosperous businesspeople as examples of American hard work, talent, and success.

New sales techniques like those taught by John H. Patterson helped change business practices.

Corporations Generate Wealth

Successful corporations reward not only the people who found them but also investors who hold stock. Stockholders in a corporation typically get a percentage of profits based on the amount of stock they own. Although stockholders actually own the corporation, they do not run its day-to-day business. Instead, they elect a board of directors that chooses the corporation's main leaders, such as the president.

Corporations provided several important advantages over earlier business forms. Stockholders in a corporation are not responsible for business debts. If a corporation fails financially, the stockholders lose only the money that they invested. Stockholders are also usually free to sell their stock to whomever they want, whenever they want. As a result, corporations encouraged more investment in businesses. By 1900 more than 100 million shares per year were being traded on the New York Stock Exchange.

ACADEMIC VOCABULARY

acquire to get

Business Leaders

Countless business leaders became wealthy, powerful, and famous because of the business boom. **Andrew Carnegie** was one of the most admired businesspeople of the time. Born in Scotland, Carnegie came to the United States as a poor immigrant. As a teenager he took a job with a railroad company and quickly worked his way up to the position of railroad superintendent.

In 1873 he focused his efforts on steelmaking. Carnegie expanded his business by buying out competitors when steel prices were low. By 1901 Carnegie's mills were producing more steel than all of Great Britain's mills combined. Carnegie's businesses succeeded largely through **vertical integration**, or ownership of businesses involved in each step of a manufacturing process. For example, to lower production costs, Carnegie acquired the iron ore mines, coalfields, and railroads needed to supply and support his steel mills.

John D. Rockefeller was also successful in consolidating, or combining, businesses. By age 21, while a partner in a wholesale business, he decided to start an oil-refining company. In only 10 years Rockefeller's Standard Oil Company was the country's largest oil refiner. Like Carnegie, Rockefeller used ver-

The Rise of Investing

Investors purchased stock in corporations in record numbers in the late 1800s. They received stock certificates, like the one shown here, to document their part ownership in corporations. Corporations used the money raised by selling stocks to expand. Standard Oil Company financed the building of this refinery in Richmond, California, by selling stock.

Why did investors buy stock?

Primary Source

POLITICAL CARTOON

Trusts

The wealth and size of trusts such as Standard Oil made many Americans fear the influence of business leaders over government.

What do you think the smokestacks on the Capitol building represent?

What does the position of the White House suggest?

ANALYSIS SKILL **ANALYZING PRIMARY SOURCES**

How does the cartoonist show Rockefeller's power?

tical integration. For example, the company controlled most of the pipelines it used.

Rockefeller's company also developed **horizontal integration**, or owning all businesses in a certain field. By 1880 Rockefeller's companies controlled about 90 percent of the oil refining business in the United States. Rockefeller also formed a **trust**, a legal arrangement grouping together a number of companies under a single board of directors. To earn more money, trusts often tried to get rid of competition and to control production.

Leland Stanford was another important business leader of the late 1800s. He made a fortune selling equipment to miners. While governor of California, he became one of the founders of the state's Central Pacific railroad. Stanford also founded Stanford University.

Late in life, Stanford argued that industries should be owned and managed cooperatively by workers. He believed this would be the fulfillment of democracy.

READING CHECK **Comparing and Contrasting** Why did Andrew Carnegie use vertical integration?

Questioning the Methods of Big Business

By the late 1800s, people and the government were becoming uncomfortable with child labor, low wages, and poor working conditions. They began to view big business as a problem.

Social Darwinism

Many business leaders justified their business methods through their belief in **social Darwinism**, a view of society based on scientist Charles Darwin's theory of natural selection. Social Darwinists thought that Darwin's "survival of the fittest" theory decided which human beings would succeed in business and in life in general.

Other business leaders, however, believed that the rich had a duty to aid the poor. These leaders tried to help the less fortunate through philanthropy, or giving money to charities. Carnegie, Rockefeller, Stanford, and other business leaders gave away large sums. Carnegie gave away more than $350 million to charities, about $60 million of which went to fund public libraries to expand access to books. By the late 1800s, various charities had received millions of dollars from philanthropists.

The Antitrust Movement

Critics of big business said that many business leaders earned their fortunes through unfair business practices. These criticisms grew stronger in the 1880s as corporations became more powerful. Large corporations often used their size and strength to drive smaller competitors out of business. Carnegie and Rockefeller, for example, pressured railroads to charge their companies lower shipping rates. Powerful trusts also arranged to sell goods and services below market value. Smaller competitors went out of business trying to match those prices. Then the trusts raised prices again.

Some people became concerned when a trust gained a **monopoly**, or total ownership of a product or service. Critics argued that monopolies reduced necessary competition. They believed competition in a free market economy kept prices low and the quality of goods and services high.

Some Americans also worried about the political power of wealthy trusts. Many citizens and small businesses wanted the government to help control monopolies and trusts. People who favored trusts responded that trusts were more efficient and gave the consumer dependable products or services.

Many members of Congress favored big business. However, elected officials could not ignore the concerns of voters. In July 1890 Congress passed the **Sherman Antitrust Act**, a law that made it illegal to create monopolies or trusts that restrained trade. It stated that any "attempt to monopolize . . . any part of the trade or commerce among the several States" was a crime. However, the act did not clearly define a trust in legal terms. The antitrust laws were therefore difficult to enforce. Corporations and trusts kept growing in size and power.

READING CHECK **Analyzing** How did concerns about trusts lead to the Sherman Antitrust Act?

SUMMARY AND PREVIEW In the late 1800s some corporations became monopolies that dominated industries such as oil. In the next section you will learn about how industrial workers organized to improve working conditions.

Section 2 Assessment

go.hrw.com
Online Quiz
KEYWORD: SC7 HP19

Reviewing Ideas, Terms, and People

1. a. **Identify** What are **horizontal** and **vertical integration**?
   b. **Explain** What are the benefits of investing in **corporations**?
   c. **Evaluate** What do you think about the business methods of **Carnegie**, **Rockefeller**, and **Stanford**?
2. a. **Describe** What is **social Darwinism**?
   b. **Summarize** What concerns did critics of big business have regarding **trusts**?
   c. **Evaluate** Was the **Sherman Antitrust Act** successful? Why or why not?

Critical Thinking

3. **Contrasting** Look back over your notes about new business practices. Find examples of the new business practices. Use them to complete a graphic organizer like the one below.

New Practices	Example

FOCUS ON WRITING

4. **Gathering Information on Business** Look back over your notes and determine what new practices helped businesses expand during this time. Which practices could you use to start your business? Where would you try to sell your product?

BIOGRAPHY

Andrew Carnegie, John D. Rockefeller, and Leland Stanford

How would you go about building an industry?

Andrew Carnegie (1835–1919) Born in Scotland, Carnegie rose to become a multibillionaire in the steel industry. He brought new technologies to his steel mills and made them extremely efficient. In 1901 he sold Carnegie Steel Company for $250 billion, making him the richest man in the world.

John D. Rockefeller (1839–1937) Rockefeller got his start in the oil business in Cleveland, Ohio. Rockefeller's Standard Oil Company quickly bought out its competitors throughout the United States. To better control oil production and delivery, Rockefeller also bought railroad rights, terminals, and pipelines.

Leland Stanford (1825–1893) Leland Stanford was born to a New York farming family that sent him to excellent private schools. After practicing law in Wisconsin, he made his career in California. Stanford was instrumental in building the western section of the transcontinental railroad. He then plunged into politics, serving one term as governor. His political connections helped him obtain huge state land grants and other benefits for his railroad companies. As president of Central Pacific and Southern Pacific, he oversaw the laying of thousands of miles of track throughout the West.

Why are they so important? Carnegie, Rockefeller, and Stanford helped make America the world's greatest industrial power by the end of the 1800s. They built giant industries that made goods cheaply by keeping workers' wages low. They also engaged in ruthless business practices to defeat their competition and create monopolies. The Sherman Antitrust Act was passed in reaction to the Standard Oil monopoly. Later in life, all three men became philanthropists, people devoted to charity work. Rockefeller's philanthropies gave out $500 million in his lifetime. Carnegie spent $350 million, funding educational grants, concert halls, and nearly 3,000 public libraries. Stanford founded Stanford University in 1884.

Finding Main Ideas
Why are these three men important figures in U.S. history?

SECTION 3

Industrial Workers

What You Will Learn...

Main Ideas

1. The desire to maximize profits and become more efficient led to poor working conditions.
2. Workers began to organize and demand improvements in working conditions and pay.
3. Labor strikes often turned violent and failed to accomplish their goals.

The Big Idea

Changes in the workplace led to a rise in labor unions and workers' strikes.

Key Terms and People

Frederick W. Taylor, *p. 624*
Knights of Labor, *p. 625*
Terence V. Powderly, *p. 625*
American Federation of Labor, *p. 625*
Samuel Gompers, *p. 625*
collective bargaining, *p. 626*
Mary Harris Jones, *p. 626*
Haymarket Riot, *p. 626*
Homestead strike, *p. 627*
Pullman strike, *p. 627*

TAKING NOTES As you read this section, take notes about the problems workers faced in the new economy. Organize your notes in a chart like the one below.

Problems of Workers

If YOU were there...

You run a button machine in a clothing factory in the 1890s. You work from 7:00 in the morning until 6:00 at night, every day except Sunday. Your only break is 15 minutes for lunch. Now you hear about a movement to start a workers' union to bargain with your employer. Union members will ask for an eight-hour workday. But you think your employer might fire you if you join.

Would you join the union?

BUILDING BACKGROUND The rise of corporations and the establishment of monopolies gave big business a great deal of power. An antitrust movement arose to try to limit the power of trusts. Workers themselves began to organize and take action against bad working conditions and other problems.

Maximizing Profits and Efficiency

During the late 1800s, several factors led to a decline in the quality of working conditions. Machines run by unskilled workers were eliminating the jobs of many skilled craftspeople. These low-paid workers could be replaced easily. Factories began to focus on specialization, or workers repeating a single step again and again. Specialization brought costs down and caused production to rise. But it also made workers tired, bored, and more likely to be injured. Specialization allowed for Henry Ford's idea of a moving assembly line to speed production. Ford's use of the moving assembly line allowed automobiles to be made more quickly and cheaply. Automobiles soon became available to a wider segment of the population than ever before.

In 1909 **Frederick W. Taylor**, an efficiency engineer, published a popular book called *The Principles of Scientific Management*. He encouraged managers to view workers as interchangeable parts of the production process. In factories, managers influenced by Taylor paid less attention to working conditions. Injuries increased, and as conditions grew worse, workers looked for ways to bring about change.

READING CHECK **Identifying Cause and Effect** Why did companies begin to use scientific management, and how did it affect workers?

Poor Working Conditions

Small, crowded rooms. Stuffy air. Unsafe workplaces. Long hours. Low pay. No job security. These were the facts of working life for millions of Americans during the Second Industrial Revolution.

How did workers respond to these conditions?

Workers Organize

Workers formed labor unions to get better wages and working conditions for all workers in a factory or industry. The first national labor union, the **Knights of Labor**, was founded in the 1870s. It pushed for an eight-hour workday, equal pay for equal work, and an end to child labor. Union members also wanted the government to regulate trusts. Unlike most unions at the time, the Knights included both skilled and unskilled workers. The Knights of Labor was originally organized much like a secret society. In 1879 **Terence V. Powderly** became leader of the Knights. He ended all secrecy, creating the first truly national labor union in the United States.

Another early labor union was the **American Federation of Labor (AFL)**, led by **Samuel Gompers**. Unlike the Knights, the American Federation of Labor organized individual national unions, such as the mine-workers' and steelworkers' unions. The AFL

BIOGRAPHY

Samuel Gompers
1850–1924

Samuel Gompers was born in London. He came to the United States with his parents in 1863 at age 13. He worked as a cigar maker and joined a local union, eventually becoming its president. The Cigarmakers Union was reorganized and later joined the American Federation of Labor. Gompers became the AFL's first president and remained so, except for the year 1895, until his death. He campaigned for basic trade-union rights, such as the right to picket and to organize boycotts and strikes. His efforts on behalf of workers helped organized labor to gain respect.

Summarizing How did Samuel Gompers help the labor-union movement?

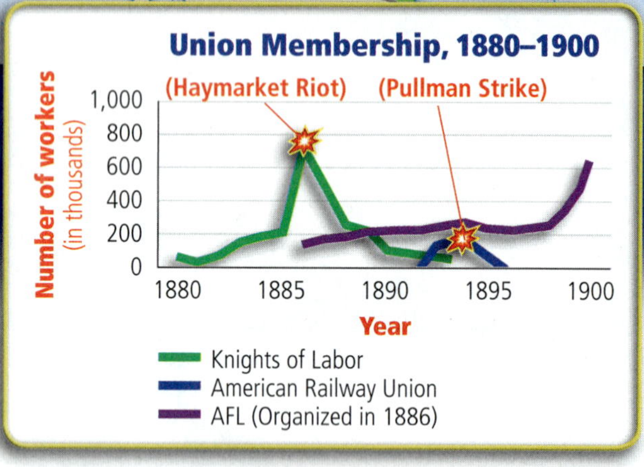

1 Haymarket Riot In May 1886 the Haymarket Riot erupted between protesters and police in Chicago. It resulted in the decline of the Knights of Labor.

2 Homestead Strike In 1892 a strike occurred at Carnegie Steel Company in Homestead, Pennsylvania. The resulting fight left workers and Pinkerton guards dead.

3 Colorado Miners' Strike In the summer of 1893, gold miners at Cripple Creek, Colorado, went on strike for higher wages and a shorter workday.

4 Pullman Strike The Pullman strike of 1894 began with workers who made Pullman train cars. It soon spread to workers who worked on trains pulling the sleeper cars.

5 California Railroad Strike In 1894 railroad workers in Oakland went on strike in the Bay Area's first major strike. Supporting Chicago Pullman workers, they halted passenger, freight, and mail trains for months.

go.hrw.com
Interactive Map
KEYWORD: SC7 CH19

ANALYSIS SKILL ANALYZING INFORMATION

How did conflicts between striking workers and authorities affect union membership?

also limited its membership to skilled workers. This gave the union great bargaining power but left out most workers. The AFL tried to get better wages, hours, and working conditions for laborers. By 1890 the AFL's membership was larger than that of the Knights. With **collective bargaining** —all workers acting collectively, or together—workers had a much greater chance of success in negotiating with management. Most employers opposed collective bargaining. One company president said, "I shall never give in. I would rather go out of business."

THE IMPACT TODAY

In 1955 the AFL merged with the Congress of Industrial Organizations to become the AFL-CIO. Today the organization has more than 13 million members.

Many women took active roles in unions. For example, **Mary Harris Jones**, an Irish immigrant, worked for better conditions for miners. A fiery speaker, she organized strikes and helped educate workers.

READING CHECK **Contrasting** How did the Knights of Labor and the AFL differ?

Labor Strikes

By the late 1800s, other unions were gaining strength. Major workers' strikes swept the country and included miners in Colorado, steel workers in Pennsylvania, and railroad workers in Illinois and California. The first major labor strike began in 1886 in Chicago.

In May 1886, thousands of union members in Chicago went on strike because they wanted an eight-hour workday. Two strikers were killed in a fight with police. The next night, workers met at Haymarket Square to protest the killings. In what became known as the **Haymarket Riot**, someone threw a bomb that wounded many police officers and killed eight. The police fired into the crowd, killing several people and wounding 100 others.

Eight people, some of whom were not at the riot, were arrested and convicted of conspiracy. One of them had a Knights of Labor membership card. Though Knights leadership had not supported the strike, several local chapters had. Membership in the Knights fell quickly.

Sometimes, business owners succeeded in breaking up unions. In 1892 a violent strike called the **Homestead strike** took place at Andrew Carnegie's Homestead steel factory in Pennsylvania. Union members there protested a plan to buy new machinery and cut jobs. The company refused to negotiate with the union and locked workers out of the plant, hiring strike breakers to perform their jobs. The workers responded by seizing control of the plant. Gunfire erupted on July 6, when Pinkerton detectives hired by the company tried to enter the plant. A fierce battle raged for 14 hours, leaving 16 people dead. The governor called out the state militia to restore order. Continuing for four more months, the union was eventually defeated.

Another major strike happened at George Pullman's Pullman Palace Car Company in the company town of Pullman, Illinois. Most of the company workers lived there, paying high rents. During a financial depression that began in 1893, Pullman laid off about half of the workers and cut pay for those that were left, without lowering their rents. On May 11, 1894, workers began the **Pullman strike**, which stopped traffic on many railroad lines until federal courts ordered the workers to return to their jobs. President Grover Cleveland sent federal troops to Chicago to stop the strike. Such defeats seriously damaged the labor movement for years.

READING CHECK **Analyzing** What were the effects of early major strikes on workers?

SUMMARY AND PREVIEW Workers formed unions to fight for better conditions and to keep their jobs. In the next section, you will learn about a new wave of immigrants in the late 1800s.

Section 3 Assessment

go.hrw.com
Online Quiz
KEYWORD: SC7 HP19

Reviewing Ideas, Terms, and People

1. a. **Recall** Why did conditions in factories begin to decline?
   b. **Draw Conclusions** How were workers affected by specialization and scientific management?
   c. **Evaluate** Do you think scientific management made businesses more successful? Explain.
2. a. **Identify** What role did **Mary Harris Jones** play in the labor movement?
   b. **Analyze** Why did workers demand **collective bargaining**, and why did business owners oppose it?
   c. **Elaborate** Do you think the demands made by labor unions were reasonable? Explain your answer.
3. a. **Describe** What major labor strikes took place in the late 1800s?
   b. **Evaluate** Do you think President Cleveland was right to use federal troops to end the **Pullman strike**? Explain.

Critical Thinking

4. **Analyzing** Review your notes about the problems workers faced. Use them to complete a table like the one below about how workers tried to solve the problems they faced.

Problem	Solution

FOCUS ON WRITING

5. **Taking Notes on Working Conditions** In your notebook, list some reasons why industrial workers were unhappy with working conditions. Can you think of ways to run your business so that you can avoid the problem of strikes?

Social Studies Skills

Analysis | Critical Thinking | Civic Participation | Study

North Carolina Skills
2.05 Transfer information from one medium to another such as written to visual and statistical to written.

Analyzing Costs and Benefits

Define the Skill

Everything you do has both costs and benefits connected to it. *Benefits* are things that you gain from something. *Costs* are what you give up to obtain benefits. For example, if you buy a video game, the benefits of your action include the game itself and the enjoyment of playing it. The most clear cost is what you pay for the game. However, there are other costs that do not involve money. One is the time you spend playing the game. This is a cost because you give up something else, such as doing your homework or watching a TV show, when you choose to play the game.

The ability to analyze costs and benefits is a valuable life skill as well as a useful tool in the study of history. Weighing an action's benefits against its costs can help you decide whether or not to take it.

Learn the Skill

Analyzing the costs and benefits of historical events will help you to better understand and evaluate them. Follow these guidelines to do a cost-benefit analysis of an action or decision in history.

1. First determine what the action or decision was trying to accomplish. This step is needed in order to determine which of its effects were benefits and which were costs.
2. Then look for the positive or successful results of the action or decision. These are its benefits.
3. Consider the negative or unsuccessful effects of the action or decision. Also think about what positive things would have happened if it had *not* occurred. All these things are its costs.
4. Making a chart of the costs and benefits can be useful. By comparing the list of benefits to the list of costs you can better understand the action or decision and evaluate it.

For example, you learned in Chapter 19 about the Second Industrial Revolution and its effects on the American economy. A cost-benefit analysis of the changes in American businesses might produce a chart like this one:

Benefits	Costs
New inventions made life easier. Communication became easier with new technologies. Efficient management reduced costs of products. Workers began to organize for better conditions.	New business methods ran smaller companies out of business. Workers received lower wages. Strikes resulted in violence and deaths.

Based on this chart, one might conclude that the Second Industrial Revolution was beneficial to the nation's economy.

Practice the Skill

Among the changes that occurred in the early 1900s was an increase in specialization and efficiency in the workplace. Use information from the chapter and the guidelines above to do a cost-benefit analysis of this development. Then write a paragraph explaining whether or not it was a wise one.

HOLT

History's Impact

▶ **video series**

Review the video to answer the closing question:

What advantages and disadvantages did the assembly line create? Do you think assembly lines still exist today?

CHAPTER 19 Chapter Review

Visual Summary

QUICK FACTS

Use the visual summary below to help you review the main ideas of the chapter.

Inventions
- Bessemer process
- Lightbulb
- Automobile

Big Business
- Growth of corporations
- Wealthy business owners
- Antitrust movements

Labor Movement
- Knights of Labor
- American Federation of Labor
- Haymarket Riot
- Homestead Strike

Reviewing Vocabulary, Terms, and People

Identify the descriptions below with the correct term or person from the chapter.

1. Labor organization that represented both skilled and unskilled laborers and was the first national labor union in the United States
2. Inventor who patented the telephone in 1876
3. A way of making steel quickly and cheaply by blasting hot air through melted iron to quickly remove waste
4. A system of business in which one company owns businesses in each step of the manufacturing process
5. Powerful business leader who helped to found the Central Pacific Railroad
6. Union speaker who worked to better the lives of mine workers
7. A method of negotiating for better wages or working conditions in which all workers act together to ensure a better chance for success

Comprehension and Critical Thinking

SECTION 1 *(Pages 614–618)*

8. a. Identify What was the Second Industrial Revolution?

b. Draw Conclusions Why were advances in transportation and communication important to the Second Industrial Revolution?

c. Elaborate Which invention do you think had the greatest effect on people's lives in the late 1800s? Explain your answer.

SECTION 2 *(Pages 619–622)*

9. a. Recall What criticisms were made of business leaders and trusts?

b. Analyze How did the rise of corporations and powerful business leaders lead to the growth of big business?

c. Evaluate Do you think the growth of big business helped or hurt ordinary Americans? Explain your answer.

SECTION 3 *(Pages 624–627)*

10. a. Recall What led to poor working conditions in factories during the Second Industrial Revolution?

b. Make Inferences Why did labor unions have a better chance of improving working conditions than laborers did on their own?

c. Evaluate Did the strikes of the 1880s and 1890s hurt or help the labor movement in the long run? Explain your answer.

Reviewing Themes

11. Economics How did the rise of big business affect consumers in the United States?

12. Society and Culture What changes in society were brought about by the organization of labor?

Using the Internet

go.hrw.com
KEYWORD: SC7 CH19

13. Activity: Creating a Time Line Technology in some sense has been part of human history since we began to write history. All tools are, in a sense, technology. In this chapter you read about new scientific discoveries that had positive and negative effects. Enter the activity keyword. Then choose one technological innovation mentioned in the chapter and trace its development to the present day. Create an illustrated time line to present your research.

Reading Skills

Organization of Facts and Information *Use the Reading Skills taught in this chapter to answer the question about the reading selection below.*

> Corporations provided several important advantages over earlier business forms. Stockholders in a corporation are not responsible for business debts. If a corporation fails financially, the stockholders lose only the money that they invested. Stockholders are also usually free to sell their stock to whomever they want, whenever they want. *(p. 620)*

14. By which structural pattern is the above passage organized?

a. Listing

b. Cause-effect

c. Chronological order

d. Comparison-contrast

Social Studies Skills

Analyzing Costs and Benefits *Use the Social Studies Skills taught in this chapter to answer the question below.*

15. Write two costs and two benefits of the Pullman strike from the point of view of the workers who participated.

FOCUS ON WRITING

16. Writing Your Business Plan Collect your notes and determine a good product to sell during the late 1800s. Decide which business practices you would use and which you would not. Write two to three paragraphs in which you explain why your product would sell, which business practices you can use to make your product, and how to avoid conflicts with workers. Remember to explain to the investors why your plan will work.

CHAPTER 19

Standardized Test Practice

DIRECTIONS: Read each question and write the letter of the best response. Use the map below to answer question 1.

1

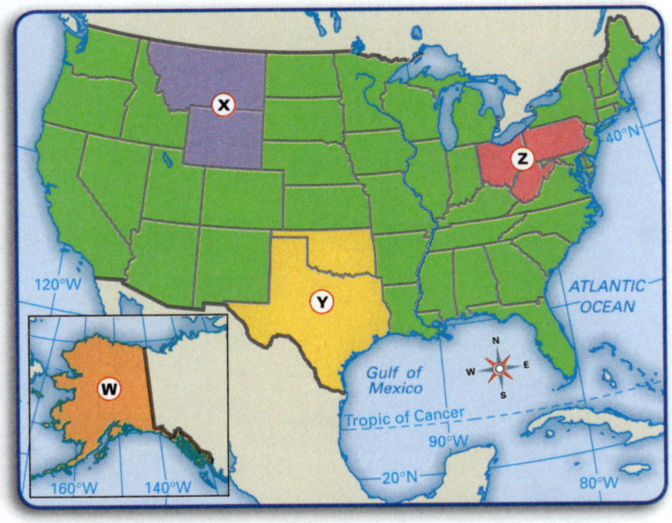

Which area on the map provided the petroleum for the oil-refining industry that arose in the United States in the mid- to late 1800s?

A the area labeled W
B the area labeled X
C the area labeled Y
D the area labeled Z

2 The person *most* responsible for making the steel industry a big business in the United States is

A John D. Rockefeller.
B Andrew Carnegie.
C Henry Bessemer.
D Leland Stanford.

3 Which of the following inventors built a small, gas-powered airplane that was first piloted in Kitty Hawk, North Carolina?

A Morse and Bell
B Orville and Wilbur Wright
C Edison and Westinghouse
D Charles and J. Frank Duryea

4 The development of corporations in America was helped by

A suburbs.
B vertical integration.
C the Sherman Antitrust Act.
D social Darwinism.

5 Which of the following was an inventor of the late 1800s?

A Andrew Carnegie
B Thomas Edison
C Leland Stanford
D John D. Rockefeller

6 One cause of labor strikes in the late 1800s was that workers sought

A shorter workdays.
B vertical integration.
C social Darwinism.
D lower wages.

7 Read the following excerpt from the 1889 book *Recent Economic Changes* and use it to answer the question below.

> "Machinery is now recognized as essential to cheap production. Nobody can produce effectively and economically without it, and what was formerly known as domestic manfacture is now almost obsolete. But machinery is one of the most expensive of all products, and its extensive purchase and use require an amount of capital far beyond the capacity [ability] of the ordinary individual to furnish."
>
> —David Wells, quoted in *Voices of the American Past*

Document-Based Question How might the large amounts of money needed for machinery affect the future of business?

CHAPTER 20 1872–1914

Immigrants and Urban Life

North Carolina Standards

Social Studies Objectives

5.03 Describe the social, economic, and political impact of migration on North Carolina.

Language Arts Objectives

4.03 Use the stance of a critic to:

- consider alternative points of view or reasons.
- remain fair-minded and open to other interpretations.
- constructing a critical response/review of a work/topic.

6.01 Model an understanding of conventional written and spoken expression by:

- using a variety of sentence types, punctuating properly, and avoiding fragments and run-ons.
- using subject-verb agreement and verb tense that are appropriate for the meaning of the sentence.
- determining the meaning of unfamiliar vocabulary words using context clues, a dictionary, a glossary, a thesaurus, and/or structural analysis (roots, prefixes, suffixes) of words.

go.hrw.com
North Carolina
KEYWORD: SC7 NC

Focus on Writing

A Memo You are a writer at a television network, and you have an idea for a TV drama series set in the late 1800s. Draft a memo telling your boss about your story idea. As you read this chapter, gather information about the people, places, and events of this time period. Tell about the cast of characters, the setting, and the basic plot of your series.

United States

1873 Olmsted designs the U.S. Capitol grounds.

1876 The Centennial Exposition opens in Philadelphia.

1870

World

1878 Electric streetlights are introduced in London.

HOLT

History's Impact

▶ **video series**

Watch the video to understand the impact of immigrants on the United States.

What You Will Learn...

Millions of immigrants from Europe came through Ellis Island, shown here. They came in search of jobs, freedom, and better lives for their families. Most settled in New York, Chicago, and other growing cities. American cities began to take the shape they still have today. In this chapter you will learn about the wave of immigration that changed the United States in the late 1800s and early 1900s.

1880 | **1890** | **1900** | **1910**

1886 Workers complete the Statue of Liberty.

1889 Jane Addams founds Hull House in Chicago.

1893 The Ferris Wheel is introduced at the 1893 Columbian Exposition in Chicago.

1886 Impressionists' exhibit opens in Paris.

1891 Construction begins on Russia's Trans-Siberian Railroad.

1901 The first Nobel Prizes are awarded in Stockholm, Sweden.

Reading Social Studies

by Kylene Beers

Economics | Geography | Politics | **Society and Culture** | Science and Technology

Focus on Themes In this chapter, you will read about the changes in **society and culture** in the late 1800s. Among these changes was an increase in immigration. New immigrants to America found a society full of **economic** opportunities and hardships. Immigration and technology combined to change the way of life in cities.

Understanding Historical Fact versus Historical Fiction

Focus on Reading When you read a book like *The Red Badge of Courage* or see a movie about World War II, do you ever wonder how much is fiction and how much is fact?

Distinguishing Fact from Fiction Historical fiction gives readers a chance to meet real historical people and real historical events in the framework of a made-up story. Some of what you read in historical fiction could be verified in an encyclopedia, but other parts existed only in the author's mind until he or she put it on paper. As a good reader of history, you should know the difference between facts, which can be proved or verified, and fiction.

Notice how one reader determined which details could be verified or proved.

That was a woman filling her pail by the hydrant you just bumped against. The sinks are in the hallway, that all the tenants may have access—and all be poisoned alike by their summer stenches. Hear the pump squeak! It is the lullaby of tenement house babes. In summer, when a thousand thirsty throats pant for a cooling drink in this block, it is worked in vain ...

— From *How the Other Half Lives*, by Jacob Riis

The woman filling her pail isn't a fact I can check. He's just using her as an example of what women did.

We could probably check city records to see whether the buildings really had sinks in the hallways.

The writer is generalizing here. We probably can't prove 1,000 thirsty throats. We could find out whether the city's water pumps actually went dry in the summer. That's verifiable.

You Try It!

The following passage is from *Bread Givers* by Anzia Yezierska, a young immigrant to New York. After you read it, answer the questions below.

> Mashah [Anzia's sister] came home with stories that in rich people's homes they had silver knives and forks, separate, for each person. And new-ironed tablecloths and napkins every time they ate on them. And rich people had marble bathtubs in their own houses, with running hot and cold water all day and night long so they could take a bath any time they felt like it, instead of having to stand on a line before the public bath-house, as we had to do when we wanted a bath for the holidays. But these millionaire things were so far over our heads that they were like fairy tales.
>
> That time when Mashah had work hemming towels in an uptown house, she came home with another new-rich idea, another money-spending thing, which she said she had to have. She told us that by those Americans, everybody in the family had a toothbrush and a separate towel for himself.
>
> —Anzia Yezierska, *Bread Givers*

1. Which facts from the paragraph above can be confirmed?

2. What sources might you check to confirm some of these facts?

3. List two things from the passage that could not be confirmed.

4. Why are these two things not able to be confirmed?

As you read Chapter 20, notice which facts you could easily confirm.

Key Terms and People

Chapter 20

Section 1

old immigrants *(p. 636)*
new immigrants *(p. 636)*
steerage *(p. 637)*
benevolent societies *(p. 639)*
tenements *(p. 639)*
sweatshops *(p. 640)*
Chinese Exclusion Act *(p. 641)*

Section 2

mass transit *(p. 644)*
suburbs *(p. 644)*
mass culture *(p. 644)*
Joseph Pulitzer *(p. 645)*
William Randolph Hearst *(p. 645)*
department stores *(p. 645)*
Frederick Law Olmsted *(p. 645)*

Section 3

Jacob Riis *(p. 646)*
settlement houses *(p. 648)*
Jane Addams *(p. 648)*
Hull House *(p. 648)*
Florence Kelley *(p. 648)*

Academic Vocabulary

advocate *(p. 641)*
factor *(p. 643)*

SECTION 1

A New Wave of Immigration

What You Will Learn...

Main Ideas

1. U.S. immigration patterns changed during the late 1800s as new immigrants arrived from Europe, Asia, and Mexico.
2. Immigrants worked hard to adjust to life in the United States.
3. Some Americans opposed immigration and worked to restrict it.

The Big Idea

A new wave of immigration in the late 1800s brought large numbers of immigrants to the United States.

Key Terms and People

old immigrants, *p. 636*
new immigrants, *p. 636*
steerage, *p. 637*
benevolent societies, *p. 639*
tenements, *p. 639*
sweatshops, *p. 640*
Chinese Exclusion Act, *p. 641*

TAKING NOTES As you read, look for information about new immigrants' lives in the United States. Take notes on the benefits and challenges immigrants found. Use a diagram like the one below.

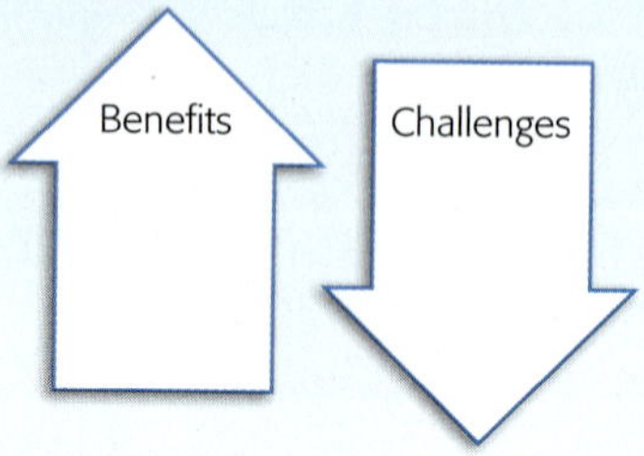

If YOU were there...

You live with your family on a small farm in Italy in the 1890s. You want to earn some money to help your parents, but there are not many jobs nearby. You have heard that jobs are easy to find in the booming factories of the United States. But you speak no English and know no one in America.

Would you travel to the United States in search of new opportunities?

BUILDING BACKGROUND From its beginnings, America has attracted people from many parts of the world. They came for many reasons, including land, religious freedom, and the chance to start new lives. In the late 1800s, jobs created by the rapid growth of the U.S. economy drew millions of new immigrants.

Changing Patterns of Immigration

Millions of immigrants came to the United States from northern Europe in the mid-1800s. They came mainly from Great Britain, Germany, Ireland, and the countries of Scandinavia. Except for the Irish, who were Roman Catholics, most were Protestants. Many were skilled workers. Others settled in rural areas and became farmers. By the late 1800s immigrants from northern Europe were known as **old immigrants**. A newer and larger wave of immigration—from different parts of the world—was arriving in the United States.

New Immigrants

During the 1880s more than 5 million immigrants arrived in the United States—about the same number of people as had arrived during the six decades from 1800 to 1860 combined. The majority of these **new immigrants** were from southern and eastern Europe. Thousands of Czechs, Greeks, Hungarians, Italians, Poles, Russians, and Slovaks came to the United States to find new opportunities and better lives. A young woman from Russia spoke for many of her fellow immigrants when she said she hoped "for all manner of miracles in a strange, wonderful land!"

New immigrants came from many different cultural and religious backgrounds. They included Orthodox Christians, Roman Catholics, and Jews. Some were escaping political or religious persecution. They were eager for the job opportunities created by the U.S. industrial boom of the late 1800s.

Arriving in a New Land

Immigrants usually faced a difficult journey by ship to America. Most traveled in **steerage**—an area below a ship's deck where steering mechanisms were located. Steerage tickets were inexpensive, but the cabins were hot, cramped, and foul-smelling. Unused to the rolling and crashing waves, many passengers were seasick for the entire journey. Some even died of diseases contracted along the way.

Once in the United States, new arrivals were processed through government-run immigration centers. The busiest center on the East Coast was Ellis Island, which opened in New York Harbor in 1892. Over the next 40 years, millions of European immigrants came through Ellis Island.

At immigration centers officials interviewed and examined immigrants to decide whether to let them enter the country. People with contagious diseases or legal problems could be turned away. "There was this terrible anxiety that one of us might be rejected," remembered one immigrant traveling with his family. "And if one of us was, what would the rest of the family do?" This rarely happened, however. Less than 2 percent of the people who arrived at Ellis Island were not allowed into the country.

On the West Coast, many Chinese immigrants entered the United States through Angel Island, which opened near San Francisco in 1910. Because laws limited immigration from China, only people whose fathers were U.S. citizens were allowed into the country.

Primary Source

AUTOBIOGRAPHY

An Immigrant's Story

Mary Antin and her family were Jewish. They moved from Russia to Boston in the 1890s to find religious freedom. Here, Antin writes about their journey.

For sixteen days the ship was our world ... [It] pitched and rolled so that people were thrown from their berths [beds] ... All this while the seasickness lasted. Then came happy hours on deck, with fugitive sunshine, birds atop the crested waves, band music and dancing and fun ... And so suffering, fearing, brooding [worrying], rejoicing, we crept nearer and nearer to the coveted [wished for] shore, until, on a glorious May morning, six weeks after our departure from Polotzk our eyes beheld the Promised Land [the United States].

—Mary Antin, *The Promised Land*

What do you think *fugitive* means here?

Antin describes a mix of emotions.

ANALYSIS SKILL **ANALYZING PRIMARY SOURCES**

Why do you think Antin was both "fearing" and "rejoicing" during her trip?

Chinese immigrants were often kept at Angel Island for weeks or months while officials investigated their families.

Mexican immigrants also came to the United States in large numbers in the late 1800s. The main processing center for immigrants from Mexico was in El Paso, Texas. Most settled in the Southwest. They found work in construction, steel mills, and mines, and on large commercial farms.

READING CHECK **Contrasting** How was the experience of immigrants at Ellis Island different from that of immigrants at Angel Island?

THE IMPACT TODAY

Almost half of all Americans today are related to someone who passed through Ellis Island. Visitors can now research their family origins at the Ellis Island Immigration Museum.

Coming to America

In this photo, Japanese men and Chinese women leave the detention center on Angel Island in San Francisco Bay. Angel Island was the processing center for many immigrants from Asia.

Augustin and Maria Lozano and their two children are shown after moving from Mexico to California. Many Mexican immigrants moved into the Southwest.

Adjusting to a New Life

Once they entered the United States, immigrants began the hard work of adjusting to life in a new country. They needed to find homes and jobs. They had to learn a new language and get used to new customs. This was all part of building a new life.

FOCUS ON READING
How could you verify the facts in this paragraph?

Immigrant Neighborhoods

Many immigrants moved into neighborhoods with others from the same country. In these neighborhoods, they could speak their native language and eat foods that reminded them of home. Immigrants could also practice the customs that their families had passed down from generation to generation. An Italian immigrant remembered that in his new neighborhood, "cheeses from Italy, sausage, salamis were all hanging in the window."

In their newly adopted neighborhoods, many immigrant groups published newspapers in their own languages. They founded schools, clubs, and places of worship to help preserve their customs. In New York City, for example, Jewish immigrants founded a theater that gave performances in Yiddish—the language spoken by Jews from central and eastern Europe.

Immigrants often opened local shops and small neighborhood banks. Business owners helped new arrivals by offering credit and giving small loans. Such aid was important for newcomers because there were few commercial banks in immigrant neighborhoods. In 1904 Italian immigrant Amadeo Peter Giannini started the Bank of Italy in San Francisco. This bank later grew and became the Bank of America.

Swedish immigrant Swan August Swanson followed his father to Wisconsin to help with the family farm. Like many new Americans, he married within the immigrant community.

The son of Italian immigrants, Amadeo Peter Giannini founded the Bank of Italy in San Francisco in 1904. Due to his guidance and perseverance, it became the largest privately owned bank in the world.

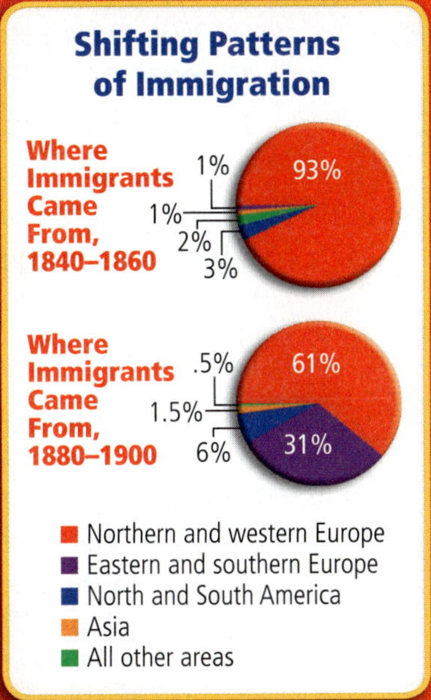

During the late 1800s the places people came from began to change. The charts above show the percentages of people who moved from different places. The total number of immigrants reached a peak in the 1880s, when about 5 million people came to the United States.

By how much did the percentage of immigrants from northern and western Europe change from 1840 to 1900?

Some immigrant communities formed **benevolent societies**. These aid organizations offered immigrants help in cases of sickness, unemployment, or death. At that time, few national government agencies provided such aid.

Even with neighborhood support, however, immigrants often found city life difficult. Many immigrants lived in **tenements**—poorly built, overcrowded apartment buildings. One young woman in New York City described the difference between her hopes and reality in the new land:

> "[I dreamed] of the golden stairs leading to the top of the American palace where father was supposed to live. [I] went 'home' to ... an ugly old tenement in the heart of the Lower East Side. There were stairs to climb but they were not golden."
>
> – Miriam Shomer Zusner, *Yesterday: A Memoir of a Russian Jewish Family*

Immigrants worked hard to adjust to their new country. Children often learned American customs more quickly than their parents. In public schools immigrant children learned English from McGuffey's Readers—illustrated textbooks that taught reading and writing.

Finding Work

Many new immigrants had worked on farms in their homelands. Few could afford to buy land in the United States, however. Instead, they found jobs in cities, where most of the country's manufacturing took place.

Having come from rural areas, few new immigrants were skilled in modern manufacturing or industrial work. They often had no choice but to take low-paying, unskilled jobs in garment factories, steel mills, or construction. Long hours were common.

FOCUS ON NORTH CAROLINA

Although the state set up the Board of Immigration in 1874 to encourage immigration, few immigrants came to North Carolina. After 1890, however, some groups established farm colonies like St. Helena (Italian immigrants), Castle Hayne and Van Eden (Dutch immigrants), and New Berlin (German immigrants).

Not all industrial labor took place in large factories. Some immigrants worked for little pay in small shops or mills located in their own neighborhoods. Often associated with the clothing industry, these workplaces were called **sweatshops** because of long hours and hot, unhealthy working conditions. One young immigrant worker remembered:

> "When the shirtwaists were finished at the machine . . . we were given scissors to cut the threads off. It wasn't heavy work, but it was monotonous [boring], because you did the same thing from seven-thirty in the morning till nine at night."
>
> – Pauline Newman, quoted in *American Mosaic: The Immigrant Experience in the Words of Those Who Lived It,* by Joan Morrison and Charlotte Fox Zabusky

Immigrants with skills that were in demand sometimes found work outside factories and sweatshops. For example, some immigrants worked as bakers, carpenters, masons, or skilled machinists. Others saved or borrowed money to open small businesses such as laundries, barbershops, or street vending carts. New immigrants often opened the same types of businesses in which other immigrants from the same country were already succeeding. They worked hard for long hours to become successful themselves.

READING CHECK **Summarizing** How did new immigrants help themselves and others to try to make successful lives in the United States?

LINKING TO TODAY

Asian Americans Today

Today, more than 12 million people in the United States are of Asian origin. They account for nearly 5 percent of the U.S. population—or about 1 in 20 Americans. Asian Americans trace their roots to various countries, including China, India, the Philippines, and, like this family, Vietnam. Most Asian Americans live in the West. California has by far the largest Asian American population of any state.

ANALYSIS SKILL **ANALYZING INFORMATION**

Why have so many people moved to the United States?

Opposition to Immigration

Some Americans welcomed new immigrants. Many business leaders, for example, wanted immigrant workers who were willing to work for low pay. In general, however, anti-immigrant feelings grew along with the rise in immigration in the late 1800s. Some labor unions opposed immigration because their members believed immigrants would take jobs away from native-born Americans.

Other Americans called nativists also feared that too many new immigrants were being allowed into the country. Many nativists held racial and ethnic prejudices. They thought that the new immigrants would not learn American customs, which might harm American society.

Some nativists were violent toward immigrants. Others **advocated** laws to stop or limit immigration. For example, in 1880 about 105,000 Chinese immigrants lived in the United States. Two years later, Congress passed the **Chinese Exclusion Act**, banning Chinese people from immigrating to the United States for 10 years. This law marked the first time a nationality was banned from entering the country. Although the law violated treaties with China, Congress continued to renew the law for decades to come. In 1892 another law was passed restricting convicts, immigrants with certain diseases, and those likely to need public assistance from entering the country.

Despite such opposition immigrants continued to arrive in large numbers. They worked for low pay in factories and built buildings, highways, and railroads. Their labor helped power the continuing indus trial growth of the late 1800s and early 1900s. Although they did not always achieve their dreams as quickly as they had hoped, most immigrants were still confident about the future for themselves and their families in the United States. An immigrant from Russia named Abraham Hyman expressed this idea, saying, "Your feeling is that a better time is coming, if not for yourself, for your families, for your children."

ACADEMIC VOCABULARY

advocate to plead in favor of

READING CHECK **Analyzing** Why did nativists oppose immigration?

SUMMARY AND PREVIEW Immigrants helped build the nation's economy and cities, but they met resistance from some native-born Americans. In the next section you will learn about what life was like in urban America.

Section 1 Assessment

go.hrw.com
Online Quiz
KEYWORD: SC7 HP20

Reviewing Ideas, Terms, and People

1. a. **Identify** What was Ellis Island?
   b. **Contrast** What differences existed between the **old immigrants** and the **new immigrants**?
2. a. **Identify** What job opportunities were available to new immigrants?
   b. **Summarize** How did immigrants attempt to adapt to their new lives in the United States?
   c. **Elaborate** Why do you think many immigrants tolerated difficult living and working conditions?
3. a. **Recall** What was the purpose of the **Chinese Exclusion Act**?
   b. **Explain** Why did some labor unions oppose immigration?
   c. **Predict** How might the growing opposition to immigration lead to problems in the United States?

Critical Thinking

4. **Categorizing** Review your notes on the benefits and challenges new U.S. immigrants faced. Then use the following graphic organizer to categorize the challenges into different areas of life.

FOCUS ON WRITING

5. **Writing about Immigrants and Their Lives** Make a list of potential characters for your TV series, and be sure to include new immigrants. Take notes about what life was like for them.

SECTION 2

The Growth of Cities

What You Will Learn...

Main Ideas

1. Both immigrants and native-born Americans moved to growing urban areas in record numbers in the late 1800s and early 1900s.
2. New technology and ideas helped cities change and adapt to rapid population growth.

The Big Idea

American cities experienced dramatic expansion and change in the late 1800s.

Key Terms and People

mass transit, *p. 644*
suburbs, *p. 644*
mass culture, *p. 644*
Joseph Pulitzer, *p. 645*
William Randolph Hearst, *p. 645*
department stores, *p. 645*
Frederick Law Olmsted, *p. 645*

TAKING NOTES As you read, take notes on the causes of the growth of cities.

Causes

→ Growth of Cities

If YOU were there...

The year is 1905 and you have just come to the city of Chicago from the small town where you grew up. People rush past as you stop to stare up at the skyscrapers. Elevated trains roar overhead, and electric streetcars clatter along streets already crowded with pushcarts and horse-drawn wagons.

Will you stay and look for work in this big city?

BUILDING BACKGROUND Industrial growth and a new wave of immigration swelled the populations of American cities in the late 1800s. Cities changed quickly to accommodate so many new people, offering urban residents excitement and new kinds of entertainment.

Growth of Urban Areas

In 1850 New York City was the only U.S. city with a population of more than 500,000. By 1900 New York City, Chicago, Philadelphia, St. Louis, Boston, and Baltimore all had more than half a million residents. More than 35 U.S. cities had populations greater than 100,000. About 40 percent of Americans now lived in urban areas.

As you have read, new immigrants were responsible for a lot of this urban growth. So were families from rural areas in the United States. As farm equipment replaced workers in the countryside, large numbers of rural residents moved to the cities in search of work. African Americans from the rural South also began moving to northern cities in the 1890s. They hoped to escape discrimination and find better educational and economic opportunities. Cities such as Chicago; Cleveland, Ohio; Detroit, Michigan; and New York saw large increases in their African American populations during the late 1800s and early 1900s.

Perhaps the most dramatic example of urban growth was the rise of Chicago. The city's population exploded from 30,000 in 1850 to 1.7 million in 1900. Chicago passed St. Louis as the

Primary Source

POSTCARD

Chicago, 1900

Postcards like this one were one way people shared the experience of visiting or living in a big city like Chicago. This scene shows a bustling street corner at which modern transportation like streetcars mingle with horse-drawn carts.

Streetcars move large numbers of people through the crowded cities.

ANALYSIS SKILL **ANALYZING PRIMARY SOURCES**

What changes does this picture show taking place in cities at the time?

Population Growth of Chicago, 1870–1900

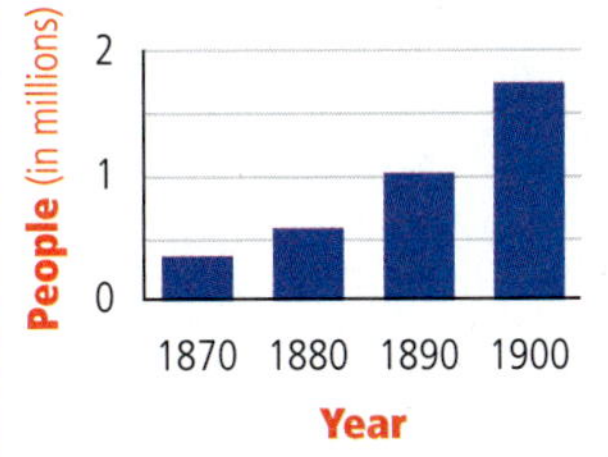

biggest city in the Midwest. Along with the large numbers of African Americans moving to the city, many of Chicago's new residents were immigrants from southern and eastern Europe. In 1900 immigrants and their children made up three quarters of Chicago's population.

Chicago's location was another **factor** in its rapid growth. Many of the new railroad lines connecting the East and West coasts ran through Chicago. This put Chicago at the heart of the nation's trade in lumber, grain, and meat. Thousands of new Chicago residents found work in the city's huge slaughterhouses and meatpacking plants. Here, meat from the West and Midwest was packed into refrigerated train cars and shipped to the growing cities of the East, where it could be sold in shops to customers.

READING CHECK **Identifying Cause and Effect** What factors led to massive population growth in urban areas during the late 1800s and early 1900s?

Changing Cities

American cities such as Chicago were ill-prepared for the rapid urban growth of the late 1800s and early 1900s. Where was everyone going to live? How were people going to get from home to work on crowded city streets? Several new technologies helped cities meet these challenges. These technologies forever changed the look and function of U.S. cities.

Building Skyscrapers

With so many people moving to urban areas, cities quickly ran out of building space in downtown areas. One solution would be to build taller buildings. Typical city buildings in the mid-1800s were only five stories tall, but taller structures were impossible to construct because the building materials available were either too weak or too heavy.

This changed with the rise of the American steel industry in the late 1800s.

ACADEMIC VOCABULARY

factor cause

FOCUS ON NORTH CAROLINA

Both the size of the middle class and the number of suburbs grew in North Carolina along with those in the rest of the nation. Although North Carolina cities grew during this period, many people left the state for the larger cities of the North.

THE IMPACT TODAY

Skyscrapers today use much of the same technology that was developed in the late 1800s—steel skeletons and elevators. Chicago's Sears Tower, with 110 stories, is one of the tallest buildings in the world.

Mills began producing tons of strong and inexpensive steel. Soon, architects such as Louis Sullivan of Chicago began designing multistory buildings called skyscrapers. Architects used steel beams to make sturdy frames that could support the weight of tall buildings. This allowed builders to use limited city space more efficiently.

The safety elevator, patented by Elisha Otis in the 1850s, helped make skyscrapers practical. Previous elevators had been unsafe because they would crash to the ground if the elevator cable snapped. Otis's safety elevator included a device to hold the elevator in place if the cable broke.

Getting Around

Taller buildings made it possible for more people to live and work in city centers. This increased the need for **mass transit**, or public transportation designed to move many people. By the late 1860s New York City had elevated trains running on tracks above the streets. Chicago followed in the 1890s.

Some cities built underground railroads, known as subways. In 1897 the first subway in the United States opened in Boston. In 1904 the first line of the New York City subway system began operation. Cable cars and electric trolleys also became common. These streetcars cheaply and quickly carried people in the cities to and from work.

Many Americans who could afford it moved to **suburbs**, residential neighborhoods outside of downtown areas that had begun springing up before the Civil War. Mass transit networks made such moves possible. People could live in the suburbs and take trolleys, subways, or trains into the cities.

New Ideas

In the late 1800s the United States also began to develop forms of **mass culture**, or leisure and cultural activities shared by many people. One factor contributing to mass culture was a boom in publishing. The invention of the Linotype, an automatic typesetting machine, greatly reduced the time and cost of printing. In 1850

Frederick Law Olmsted

CONNECT TO THE ARTS

Frederick Law Olmsted designed Central Park to serve as a place where New York City residents could relax, exercise, and enjoy nature. Olmsted included areas for horseback riding, ice-skating, boating, and baseball. The Children's District was designed as a place where parents could bring children to stay cool in the summer.

Why do you think a city dweller might be attracted to Central Park?

there were fewer than 300 daily newspapers in the country. Because of the use of Linotype machines, by 1900 there were more than 2,000 newspapers.

Big cities often had many newspapers, so publishers had to compete for readers. In 1896 **Joseph Pulitzer** added a color comic to his *New York World* newspaper. More people started buying Pulitzer's paper. **William Randolph Hearst**, publisher of the *New York Journal*, saw that comics helped sell newspapers. So he added a color comic strip to the *Journal*. Soon, newspapers across the country were adding comic strips.

Mass culture affected how people shopped as well. Giant retail shops, or **department stores**, appeared in some cities during the late 1800s. One of the earliest was Marshall Field in Chicago, which offered low prices and large quantities of products. It also was the first department store to offer its customers a restaurant where they could eat while shopping. Newspaper advertising was used to bring in customers. The public was also attracted by fancy window displays.

World fairs were another example of mass culture. Fairs brought merchants together, which sometimes resulted in new ideas and products. At the 1904 St. Louis World's Fair, for example, a Syrian food vendor began making cones for a nearby ice cream vendor who had run out of dishes. Ice cream cones became popular throughout the country.

The demand for public entertainment also led to the creation of amusement parks, such as New York's Coney Island. The inexpensive entry tickets made Coney Island a favorite destination for children and families. For a nickel, visitors could ride a new invention called the Switchback Railway—the country's first roller coaster.

As cities grew, people became aware of the need for open public space. Landscape architect **Frederick Law Olmsted** became nationally famous. He designed Central Park in New York City, as well as many state and national parks. Some of his other well-known projects include Prospect Park in Brooklyn, New York, and the U.S. Capitol grounds, which he worked on between 1874 and 1895.

READING CHECK **Summarizing** What forms of mass culture were available in urban areas?

SUMMARY AND PREVIEW Immigration and new technology helped cities grow in the late 1800s. In the next section you will learn about some of the problems caused by rapid urban growth.

Section 2 Assessment

go.hrw.com
Online Quiz
KEYWORD: SC7 HP20

Reviewing Ideas, Terms, and People

1. a. **Identify** What groups of people began moving to cities in the late 1800s?
   b. **Explain** Why did African Americans begin to move to northern cities in the 1890s?
   c. **Predict** Do you think cities such as Chicago continued to grow in the 1900s? Why or why not?
2. a. **Define** What is **mass transit**? What made mass transit necessary?
   b. **Explain** How did new inventions make it possible for people to build skyscrapers?
   c. **Evaluate** Which improvement to urban living do you think had the greatest impact on people's lives? Explain your answer.

Critical Thinking

3. **Identifying Cause and Effect** Review your notes on the causes for the growth of cities. Then copy the following graphic organizer and use it to identify the effects of city growth. You may need to add more circles.

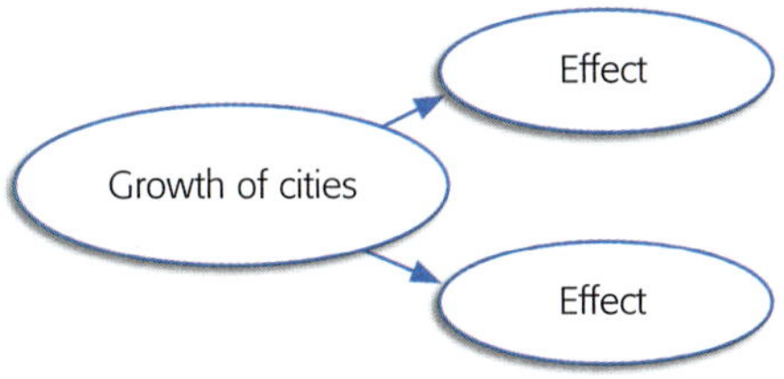

FOCUS ON WRITING

4. **Describing Setting** A city like those you have read about could serve as the setting of your TV series. How could you describe the city?

SECTION 3

City Life

What You Will Learn...

Main Ideas

1. Crowded urban areas faced a variety of social problems.
2. People worked to improve the quality of life in U.S. cities.

The Big Idea

The rapid growth of cities in the late 1800s created both challenges and opportunities.

Key Terms and People

Jacob Riis, *p. 646*
settlement houses, *p. 648*
Jane Addams, *p. 648*
Hull House, *p. 648*
Florence Kelley, *p. 648*

TAKING NOTES As you read, take notes on problems facing city residents. You can organize your notes in a table like this one.

Urban Problems

If YOU were there...

You live in a fast-growing city in 1895. When you walk the streets, you meet families that are packed into run-down apartments in crowded, filthy neighborhoods. You meet immigrants who want to study English but have no money for classes. You are determined to help these city residents improve their lives.

What would you do to help improve life in your city?

BUILDING BACKGROUND Despite the new public parks, skyscrapers, and mass transit systems, many cities were not ready for the rapid population growth that began taking place in the late 1800s. Overcrowding and poor living conditions forced people to search for solutions to these problems.

Urban Problems

In the late 1800s and early 1900s, shortages of affordable housing forced many poor families to squeeze into tiny tenement apartments, which were frequently unsafe and unsanitary. Journalist and photographer **Jacob Riis** became famous for exposing the horrible conditions in New York City tenements. Riis wrote about one typical tenement family:

> "There were nine in the family: husband, wife, an aged grandmother, and six children ... All nine lived in two rooms, one about ten feet square that served as parlor, bedroom, and eating-room, the other a small hall-room made into a kitchen."
>
> — Jacob Riis, *How the Other Half Lives*

This kind of overcrowding caused sanitation problems. Most cities did not have a good system for collecting trash, so garbage often piled up outside apartment buildings. An article in the *New York Tribune* described the garbage in front of one tenement as a "mass of air poisoning, death-breeding filth, reeking in the fierce sunshine."

Unsafe conditions were also common in tenements. Before 1900 most cities did not have laws requiring landlords to fix their tenements or to maintain safety standards. A fire on one floor could easily spread, and fire escapes were often blocked or broken.

Tenement Life

QUICK FACTS

Causes
- Overcrowding
- Unsafe buildings
- Unsanitary conditions
- Scarce running water
- Poor ventilation

Effects
- Diseases such as tuberculosis and cholera
- High child death rates
- Fire
- Crime

Tenement rooms had few or no windows to let in fresh air and sunshine. Comfort was also scarce, with so many people crowded into such small spaces. Running water and indoor plumbing were also scarce. So was clean water—cities often dumped garbage into local rivers that were used for drinking water.

Disease-causing bacteria grew easily in these conditions. Diseases such as cholera, typhoid, influenza, and tuberculosis spread quickly in crowded neighborhoods. Children were the most vulnerable to these diseases. For example, babies born in Chicago in 1870 had only a 50 percent chance of living to the age of five.

Air pollution was also a serious problem in many growing cities. This was a time when many business leaders were building huge oil refineries, steel mills, and other factories. The steel mills of Andrew Carnegie, for example, helped make Pittsburgh the nation's steel-making center in the late 1800s. Steel mills brought jobs and wealth to Pittsburgh, but they also caused some of the nation's worst air pollution. "Every street appears to end in a huge, black cloud," said one writer. "Pittsburgh is smoke, smoke, smoke—everywhere smoke." The air was so polluted at times that the city had to turn on outdoor lighting during the day.

The work of many city governments slowly helped to lessen some of these urban problems. By the late 1800s new sewage and water purification systems improved city sanitation. Many major cities also were hiring full-time firefighters and police officers. Police officers in cities were typically placed in one neighborhood. They knew the local residents and were frequently involved in local activities. They could spot local problems and, in many cases, provide help to immigrants.

THE IMPACT TODAY

Like many industrial cities, Pittsburgh has made great progress in cleaning its air and water. Today, Pittsburgh is ranked as one of the cleanest American cities.

READING CHECK **Summarizing** What challenges did many city residents face in the late 1800s?

Improving City Life

Jacob Riis hoped his book *How the Other Half Lives* would shock many Americans—and it did. A reformer named Lawrence Veiller helped lead the effort to improve conditions in tenements. Describing the effects of tenement living on children, he wrote:

> "A child living its early years in dark rooms, without sunlight or fresh air, does not grow up to be a normal, healthy person ... It is not of such material that strong nations are made."
>
> – Lawrence Veiller, quoted in *Readings in American History, Vol. 2*

Veiller worked with an organization called the Charity Organization Society (COS) to get changes made to New York laws. In 1900 he and the COS sponsored an exhibit of photographs and maps graphically showing the conditions of New York tenements. More than 10,000 people visited the exhibit, and they were shocked by what they saw. The work of Veiller and the COS helped to get the 1901 New York State Tenement House Act passed. This law required new buildings to have better ventilation and running water. The act became a model for housing reform in other states.

Because there was little government aid available in the 1800s, private organizations generally took on the task of helping the urban poor. Some individuals set up **settlement houses**, or neighborhood centers in poor areas that offered education, recreation, and social activities.

Settlement houses were staffed by professionals and volunteers. Many were educated women who came from wealthy families. In 1886 Charles B. Stover and Stanton Coit established the first settlement house in the United States. It was called Neighborhood Guild and was located on the Lower East Side in New York City. In 1889 **Jane Addams** and Ellen Gates Starr moved into a run-down building in a poor Chicago neighborhood and turned it into **Hull House**, the most famous settlement house of the period.

The Hull House staff focused on the needs of immigrant families, and by 1893 Hull House was serving 2,000 people a week. It provided services such as English classes, day care, and cooking and sewing classes. Children and adults came to take part in club meetings, art classes, plays, and sports.

Jane Addams and the staff at Hull House also worked for reforms. They studied the problems facing immigrants and poor city dwellers, then searched for ways to improve conditions. **Florence Kelley** was one important reformer at Hull House. She visited sweatshops and wrote about the problems there. Her work helped convince lawmakers to take action. Illinois passed a law in 1893 to limit working hours for women and to prevent child labor.

Kelley became the state's chief factory inspector and helped enforce the law. Although she believed more reforms were needed, she did report some improvements:

Hull House

Neighborhood children attended kindergarten at Hull House. Their parents typically had low-paying jobs, and many were children of immigrants. Children like these had few other options for education.

How did Hull House try to improve the lives of children?

"Previous to the passage of the factory law of 1893, it was the rule of [a candy] factory to work the children ... from 7 A.M. to 9 P.M., with twenty minutes for lunch, and no supper, a working week of eighty-two hours ... Since the enactment of the factory law, their working week has consisted of six days of eight hours each, a reduction of thirty-four hours a week."

– Florence Kelley and Alzina P. Stevens, from *Hull House Maps and Papers*

As Hull House gained recognition, the settlement house movement spread to other cities. Most settlement houses continued to provide programs and services for city dwellers through the early 1900s. Some, such as Germantown Settlement in Pennsylvania, remain active today.

READING CHECK **Drawing Conclusions** How did Hull House help improve city life?

SUMMARY AND PREVIEW Reformers in the late 1800s worked to solve urban problems. In the next chapter you will learn how Progressives pushed for further reforms.

BIOGRAPHY

Jane Addams

1860–1935

Jane Addams was born in Cedarville, Illinois. Like many upper-class women of the era, she received a college education but found few jobs open to her. In 1888, on a visit to England with classmate Ellen Gates Starr, she visited a London settlement house. On their return to the United States, Addams and Starr opened a settlement house in Chicago. They started a kindergarten and a public playground. Addams also became involved in housing safety and sanitation issues, factory inspection, and immigrants' rights. In 1931 she shared the Nobel Peace Prize for her work with the Women's International League for Peace and Freedom.

Summarizing How did Jane Addams try to improve the lives of workers?

Section 3 Assessment

go.hrw.com
Online Quiz
KEYWORD: SC7 HP20

Reviewing Ideas, Terms, and People

1. a. **Describe** What were conditions like in tenements?
   b. **Summarize** What problems resulted from the rapid growth of cities?
   c. **Draw Conclusions** Why do you think people lived in tenements?
2. a. **Define** What is a **settlement house**?
   b. **Explain** How did settlement houses help city dwellers?
   c. **Evaluate** Do you think settlement houses were successful? Why or why not?

Critical Thinking

3. **Categorizing** Review your notes on urban problems. Then copy the chart to the right onto your own sheet of paper and use it to identify the responses to those problems.

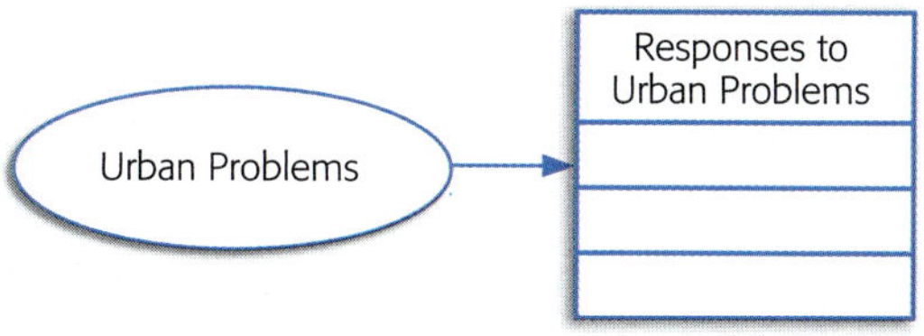

FOCUS ON WRITING

4. **Writing about Urban Problems** Finding solutions to problems is an important part of the plot of many stories. Take notes on scenes you could include in your TV series in which characters deal with the problems of urban life.

Analysis | Critical Thinking | Civic Participation | Study

North Carolina Skills
1.03 Draw inferences.

Making Comparisons

Define the Skill

Understanding similarities is important when studying history. Comparing two or more people, things, events, or ideas highlights the similarities between them. Making comparisons can help clarify larger historical issues. This is true when comparing different time periods or when comparing different things from the same time period. Making comparisons is important in identifying historical connections.

Learn the Skill

When you encounter similar people, things, events, or ideas in history, use the following guidelines to make comparisons.

1. Identify who or what you are going to compare.
2. Look for similarities between them. Find examples of what makes them alike. Note any differences as well.
3. Use comparison words such as "like," "both," and "similar" to point out similarities.

In this chapter, you have learned about several reformers, including Lawrence Veiller and Florence Kelley. Veiller helped lead the effort to improve conditions in tenements. Kelley was a reformer who worked at Hull House.

Lawrence Veiller and Florence Kelley were alike in many ways. Although Veiller focused on tenements and Kelley concentrated on factory work, both were concerned with problems that affected children. Both did research about their issues. Both then wrote about the poor conditions they found.

Both Veiller and Kelley worked successfully for laws that would improve those conditions. Kelley's work helped convince Illinois lawmakers to pass a law to limit child labor. Similarly, Veiller helped to get the 1901 New York State Tenement House Act passed.

Practice the Skill

Review the chapter to find two people, things, events, or ideas that are similar. Then apply the guidelines to answer the following questions.

1. Which people, events, or ideas will you compare? Why is each of them important?
2. How are they alike? How are they different?

CHAPTER 20

Chapter Review

HOLT
History's Impact
▶ **video series**
Review the video to answer the closing question:
Why do you think the United States had stricter immigration regulations for Asian immigrants?

Visual Summary

QUICK FACTS

Use the visual summary below to help you review the main ideas of the chapter.

People Arrived
- New immigrants, mostly from southern and eastern Europe
- Came for new opportunities and better lives
- Mostly found jobs in cities
- Faced opposition from some Americans

Cities Grew
- Massive urban growth
- New technologies emerged—skyscrapers and mass transit
- New urban culture

Problems Developed
- Overcrowded tenements
- Unsanitary conditions

Reviewing Vocabulary, Terms, and People

Identify the descriptions below with the correct term or person from the chapter.

1. Public transportation systems built to move many people and ease traffic in crowded cities
2. Founded Hull House with Ellen Gates Starr in 1889
3. Organizations created by immigrants to help each other in times of sickness, unemployment, or other troubles
4. Law banning Chinese people from moving to the United States
5. Neighborhood centers in poor urban areas that offered education, recreation, and social activities
6. Landscape architect who designed New York City's Central Park
7. Small shops or mills where immigrants worked for long hours in hot, unhealthy conditions

Comprehension and Critical Thinking

SECTION 1 *(Pages 636–641)*

8. a. Identify From what parts of the world did the wave of new immigrants come?

b. Analyze In what ways did immigration patterns in the United States change in the late 1800s?

c. Elaborate In your opinion, were the difficulties that immigrants faced worth the benefits of life in the United States? Explain.

SECTION 2 *(Pages 642–645)*

9. a. Recall Why did U.S. cities experience such rapid growth in the late 1800s?

b. Analyze How did new technologies help cities deal with population growth?

c. Elaborate Would you have preferred to live in a city or in a suburb? Why?

SECTION 3 *(Pages 646–649)*

10. a. Recall What were conditions like in tenements in the late 1800s?

b. Make Inferences Why did rapid population growth cause problems in cities?

c. Elaborate Why do you think the settlement house movement grew in the late 1800s and early 1900s?

Reviewing Themes

11. Economics What role did economics play in the growth of cities?

12. Society and Culture How did the lives of city dwellers change with the rise of mass culture?

Reading Skills

Understanding Historical Fact versus Historical Fiction *Use the Reading Skills taught in this chapter to answer the question about the reading selection below.*

> Mass culture affected how people shopped as well. Giant retail shops, or department stores, appeared in some cities during the late 1800s. One of the earliest was Marshall Field in Chicago, which offered low prices and large quantities of products. It also was the first department store to offer its customers a restaurant where they could eat while shopping. Newspaper advertising was used to bring in customers. The public was also attracted by fancy window displays. *(p. 645)*

13. Which facts above can be verified? Where would you look to verify them?

Social Studies Skills

Making Comparisons *Use the Social Studies Skills taught in this chapter to answer the question below.*

14. Choose two reforms that were discussed in this chapter. Make a comparison between the two.

Using the Internet

go.hrw.com
KEYWORD: SC7 CH20

15. Activity: Investigating Culture Mass culture developed in the late 1800s and early 1900s as a result of new and broader forms of communication taking root. Enter the activity keyword and explore some of the early influences on mass culture. Then research the ways in which modern culture is influenced by the media, the Internet, and other forms of mass communication. How does today's society experience mass culture? Create a visual display or computer-based presentation that compares mass culture then and now.

FOCUS ON WRITING

16. Writing Your Memo Look back over your notes about the people, places, and events of the late 1800s. Decide which of these you will include in your television drama series. Then draft a one- to two-paragraph memo to your boss describing the series. Remember to describe the basic plot, setting, and characters.

CHAPTER 20 Standardized Test Practice

DIRECTIONS: Read each question and write the letter of the best response.

1 Which of the following is associated with providing a better life for urban immigrants in the late 1800s and early 1900s?

A the department store
B the suburb
C the tenement
D the settlement house

2 Immigrants to the United States in the late 1800s and early 1900s came *mainly* from

A southern and eastern Europe.
B Japan, China, and the rest of Asia.
C Mexico and Central America.
D northern and western Europe.

3 Ellis Island and Angel Island were both

A locations of settlement houses.
B immigration processing centers.
C centers of shipping and industry.
D amusement parks.

4 Which of the following is an example of mass culture?

A newspaper comics
B immigrant neighborhoods
C Yiddish-language theaters
D subways

5 The *main* goal of Hull House was to

A provide jobs for wealthy women.
B pass the Tenement House Act of 1901.
C help poor immigrants.
D oppose the Chinese Exclusion Act.

6 Anti-immigrant feeling resulted in

A benevolent societies.
B the Chinese Exclusion Act.
C tenements.
D the Tenement House Act.

7 Which of the following groups moved from the southern United States to the North in large numbers during the 1890s?

A Chinese immigrants
B Mexican Americans
C African Americans
D Irish immigrants

8 Read this 1896 newspaper article describing poor conditions faced by many people and use it to answer the question below.

> "lack of family privacy … lack of light and air, and of sanitary accommodations, insuring a large death rate, and danger from fire … [These places are] infested with vermin [insects] and infected with disease germs, they are a disgrace to humanity and a menace, not only to the health of the unfortunate residents therein, but to the health of the whole community."
>
> —*The New York Times*, 1896

Document-Based Question **Based on this description, to what was this article most likely referring?**

Assignment

Write a persuasive essay either for or against one of these statements.

1. New laws should have limited immigration in the late 1800s.
2. The government should have done more to improve conditions in tenements.

TIP Using Order of Importance

How do you know whether to start or end with your most important or most convincing reason? If you are worried about getting your readers to read your entire paper, you might try to catch their attention by starting with the most convincing reason. If you are concerned that your readers remember one point after they finish reading, you may want to place that point, or reason, at the end of your paper.

Persuasion and History

You have probably heard people disagree about current political events—perhaps a new law or a government leader. People also disagree about events of the past. When we disagree about historical events, those of the past or those of the present, we can use persuasive arguments to convince others to agree with our opinion.

1. Prewrite

Stating Your Opinion

Persuasion starts with an opinion or a position on a topic. Choose one of the statements in the assignment and decide on your opinion, either for or against. Write your opinion in a statement: it will be the big idea of your persuasive paper. For example, here is an opinion statement about the first topic:

The government should not have limited immigration in the late 1800s.

Building and Organizing a Logical Argument

A strong persuasive essay includes a logical argument, sound reasoning, and proof in support of an opinion. Reasons tell *why* you have an opinion. Proof, or evidence, includes facts, examples, or expert opinions.

- **Opinion:** *Reformers' work improved Americans' lives.*
- **Reason:** *Reforms improved life in cities.*
- **Evidence:** *Lawrence Veiller influenced the passage of the 1901 New York State Tenement House Act.*

Persuasive writing is usually organized by order of importance.

2. Write

Here is a framework to help you write your first draft.

A Writer's Framework

Introduction
- Start with an interesting opener, such as a quotation or a surprising fact.
- Include your opinion statement, or big idea, for the paper.

Body
- Present one reason and its supporting evidence in each body paragraph.
- Address your reasons by order of importance.

Conclusion
- Restate your opinion in different words.
- Summarize your reasons.
- Make a connection to a current event.

3. Evaluate and Revise

Evaluating

Use these questions to discover ways to improve your draft.

Evaluation Questions for a Persuasive Essay

- Does your introduction include a clear statement of your opinion on the topic?
- Do you present your reasons by order of importance in the body paragraphs?
- Do you provide at least three reasons to support your opinion?
- Do you include facts, examples, or expert opinions to support each reason?
- Do you restate your opinion in different words in your conclusion?
- Does your conclusion include a summary of the reasons that support your opinion?

TIP **Fact vs. Opinion** Knowing the difference between a fact and an opinion is important for both writers and readers of persuasive essays.

- **Facts** are statements that can be proven true or false. *Jane Addams founded Hull House in 1889.*
- **Opinions** are statements of personal belief and cannot be proven. *Jane Addams was the greatest American woman of her time.*

Revising

Your essay will be more forceful if you write in the active voice.

Passive voice: *New parks were designed by Frederick Law Olmsted.*

Active voice: *Frederick Law Olmsted designed new parks.*

Active voice is more forceful, and often clearer, because it makes a stronger connection between the action and the actor. However, we may use passive voice because we do not know, or do not want to say, who the actor is or was.

Example: *New parks were designed in the late 1800s.*

4. Proofread and Publish

Proofreading

If you are writing your paper on a computer, you should use the spell-check feature to look for spelling errors. However, the spell-check feature will not help much if you have used the wrong word. Here are some examples to look for: *their/they're, its/it's, accept/except, affect/effect, advice/advise, altar/alter, capitol/capital.* When you spot one of these words in your paper, check your dictionary to make sure you have used the correct word.

Publishing

Share your essay with a classmate who took an opinion opposed to yours. Review each other's reasons. Can one of you persuade the other?

5. Practice and Apply

Use the steps and strategies in this workshop to write a persuasive essay.

UNIT 7 1867–1920

The Beginning of Modern America

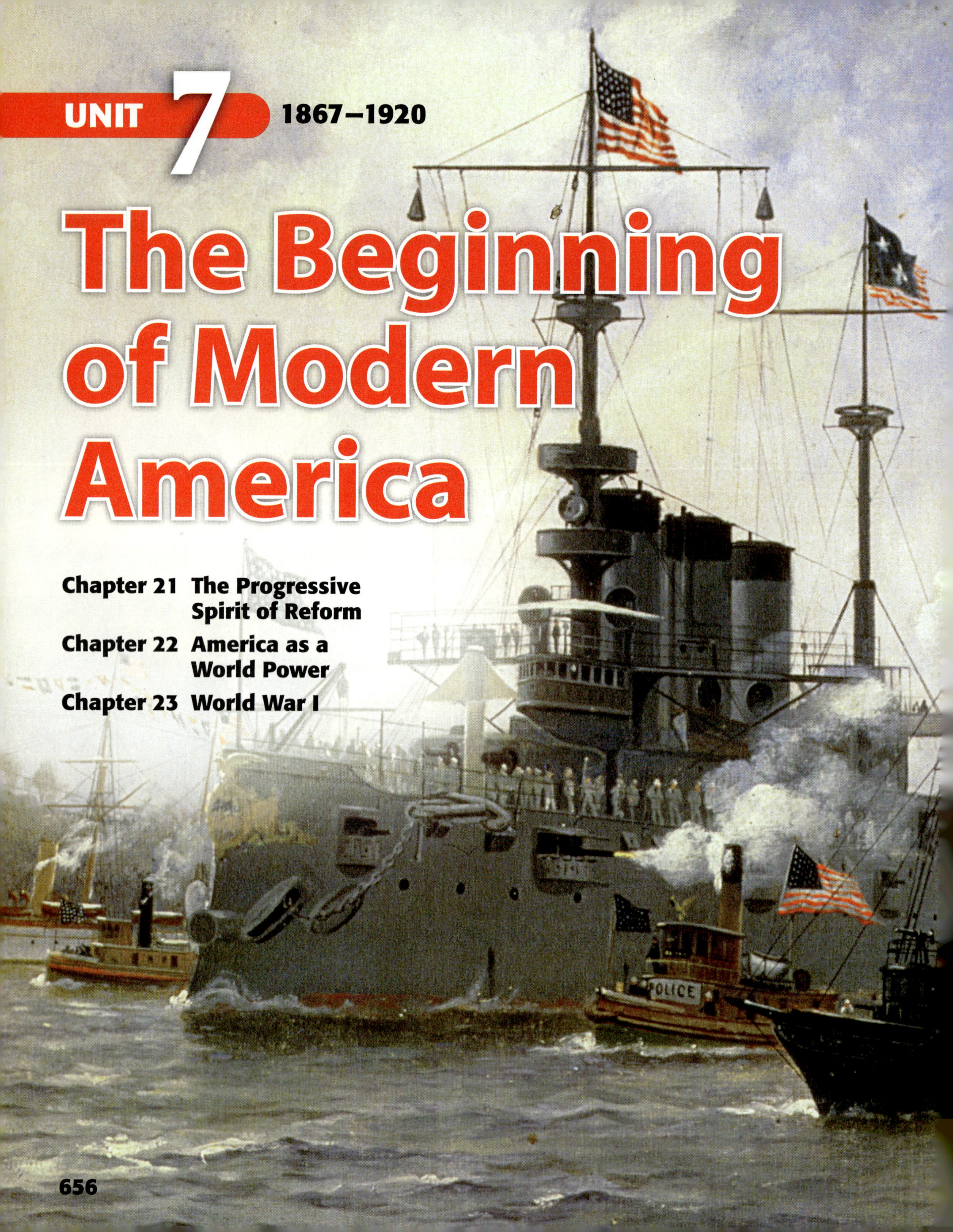

What You Will Learn...

As cities in the United States became more prosperous, people began to examine the inequalities in American society. A progressive spirit emerged that led to changes in American culture. The United States also began to expand its influence overseas.

Presidents were called upon to deal with many domestic and foreign challenges, including two wars that changed the landscape of international politics. During the Spanish-American War, the United States acquired overseas territories. During World War I, Americans fought in Europe for the first time.

Explore the Art

This painting shows the Great White Fleet, a group of U.S. ships that toured the world from 1907 to 1909. How might a tour of American ships affect foreign views of the United States?

CHAPTER 21 1868–1920

The Progressive Spirit of Reform

North Carolina Standards

Social Studies Objectives

5.05 Assess the influence of the political, legal, and social movements on the political system and life in North Carolina.

9.02 Identify past and present state and local leaders from diverse cultural backgrounds and assess their influence in effecting change.

go.hrw.com
North Carolina
KEYWORD: SC7 NC

Focus on Speaking

Campaign Promises In this chapter you will read about the political corruption of the Gilded Age and the reform movements that followed. Serious problems face the nation, and you must convince voters that you should be the one to tackle those problems. Create and present a list of campaign promises that you would make if you were a politician running for office in the United States in the late 1800s or early 1900s.

United States

1868 Ulysses S. Grant is elected president.

1865 — 1870

World

1871 The British Parliament legalizes labor unions.

HOLT

History's Impact

▶ **video series**
Watch the video to understand the impact of women's suffrage.

What You Will Learn...

In this chapter you will learn about how reform movements swept across the United States in the late 1800s and early 1900s. These movements had a variety of aims, from ending government corruption to abolishing child labor. Ordinary citizens, like these women calling for their right to vote, participated in the movements.

1881 Charles Guiteau, a frustrated federal job seeker, assassinates President James A. Garfield.

1888 Brazil officially ends slavery.

1901 President William McKinley is assassinated, and Vice President Theodore Roosevelt becomes president.

1912 The British luxury liner *Titanic* sinks after hitting an iceberg during its first voyage. About 1,500 passengers die.

1917 Mexico adopts a new constitution.

1920 Congress declares the Nineteenth Amendment ratified, giving women the right to vote.

1880 | 1890 | 1900 | 1910 | 1920

Reading Social Studies

by Kylene Beers

Economics | Geography | **Politics** | **Society and Culture** | Science and Technology

Focus on Themes In this chapter, you will read about the corrupt **politics** of the Gilded Age, a time marked by attempts at reform. You will learn how **society and culture** reacted and responded to the problems of corruption and inequality. Finally, you will read about several presidents of the early 1900s who supported ideas and initiatives that promoted social reform.

Evaluating Sources

Focus on Reading Historical texts and current history books are good sources of information about the past. However, some sources can be more reliable than others to learn the truth.

Evaluating Texts Sometimes people write texts with a specific purpose or viewpoint in mind. Determining what the author's goal was in writing a passage can help you evaluate whether to believe all of the text, or merely some of it. Knowing which parts you can believe and which you cannot will help you understand what really happened in history.

Notice how one reader evaluated the source below.

The man, therefore, who as the owner of newspapers, would corrupt public opinion is the most dangerous enemy of the State. We may talk about the perils incident [dangers attached] to the concentration of wealth, about the perils flowing from a disregard of fiduciary [financial] responsibility, about abuses of privilege, about exploiting the government for private advantage; but all of these menaces, great as they are, are nothing compared with a deliberate, persistent, artful, purchased endeavor to [change and direct] the public judgment.

–*Harper's Weekly*, October 20, 1906, quoted in *Yellow Journalism* by W. Joseph Campbell

The author is using strong words to describe his viewpoint. Maybe he isn't being as objective as he should be.

The article lists several ideas that the author seems to think are bad. Are these things really bad? Can that help me determine the author's viewpoint?

This magazine was widely read when the article appeared. I think that makes the article a good source for some viewpoints of the time.

You Try It!

Read the passage below and evaluate whether you would use it as a source for a paper.

> Space is no intervention now between communication. [N]ot only do the wires of copper bind the world together in closer communication, but with the telephone it is possible to converse [talk] with friends a thousand miles away, hearing distinctly every word and recognizing the individual voice. Closer acquaintance has thus wrought [created] vast changes in public opinions and policies. The entire civilized world has been drawn more closely together, old ideas and prejudices have been wiped out.
>
> –*Cincinnati Times-Star,* January 1, 1900, quoted in *Yellow Journalism* by W. Joseph Campbell

1. What viewpoint of new technology is the author taking in this article? How can you tell?
2. Do you believe that the telephone brought about "changes in public opinions and policies"? Why or why not? Why might the author say this?
3. Can you trust the author when he says that "old ideas and prejudices have been wiped out"? Why or why not? Why might the author say this?
4. Did this article appear in a well-known newspaper? Does this make it more trustworthy or less?
5. Would you use this article as a source for writing a paper about how new inventions affected life in the early 1900s? Explain your answer.

As you read Chapter 21, evaluate the primary sources for their usefulness in understanding history.

Key Terms and People

Chapter 21

Section 1
political machines *(p. 662)*
Progressives *(p. 664)*
muckrakers *(p. 664)*
Seventeenth Amendment *(p. 666)*
recall *(p. 666)*
initiative *(p. 666)*
referendum *(p. 666)*
Robert M. La Follette *(p. 667)*

Section 2
Triangle Shirtwaist Fire *(p. 673)*
workers' compensation laws *(p. 673)*
capitalism *(p. 674)*
socialism *(p. 674)*
William "Big Bill" Haywood *(p. 674)*
Industrial Workers of the World *(p. 674)*

Section 3
Eighteenth Amendment *(p. 676)*
National American Woman Suffrage Association *(p. 676)*
Alice Paul *(p. 677)*
Nineteenth Amendment *(p. 677)*
Booker T. Washington *(p. 677)*
Ida B. Wells *(p. 677)*
W. E. B. Du Bois *(p. 678)*
National Association for the Advancement of Colored People *(p. 678)*

Section 4
Theodore Roosevelt *(p. 680)*
Pure Food and Drug Act *(p. 681)*
conservation *(p. 681)*
William Howard Taft *(p. 682)*
Progressive Party *(p. 682)*
Woodrow Wilson *(p. 682)*
Sixteenth Amendment *(p. 683)*

Academic Vocabulary

In this chapter you will learn the following academic words:

motive *(p. 666)*
various *(p. 682)*

SECTION 1

The Gilded Age and the Progressive Movement

What You Will Learn...

Main Ideas

1. Political corruption was common during the Gilded Age.
2. Progressives pushed for reforms to improve living conditions.
3. Progressive reforms expanded the voting power of citizens.

The Big Idea

From the late 1800s through the early 1900s, the Progressive movement addressed problems in American society.

Key Terms and People

political machines, *p. 662*
Progressives, *p. 664*
muckrakers, *p. 664*
Seventeenth Amendment, *p. 666*
recall, *p. 666*
initiative, *p. 666*
referendum, *p. 666*
Robert M. La Follette, *p. 667*

TAKING NOTES As you read, take notes on progressive reforms and the problems they addressed. Organize your notes in a chart like the one below.

Progressive reform	Problem it addressed

If YOU were there...

You live in a big-city neighborhood in the 1890s. You and your brother are both looking for jobs. You know that the man down the street is the "ward boss." He can always get city jobs for his friends and neighbors. But in return you'll have to promise to vote the way he tells you to in the upcoming election.

Would you ask the ward boss for a job? Why or why not?

BUILDING BACKGROUND The late 1800s were a time of contrasts in American life. Great wealth created through business ventures existed alongside poverty and the difficulties of tenement life. In politics, money led to corruption and dishonesty. Reacting to these conditions, reformers worked to improve many areas of American life.

Political Corruption

The late 1800s in the United States are often called the Gilded Age. The term came from a novel by that name. *The Gilded Age* highlights the inequality between wealthy business owners, who profited from the Industrial Revolution, and workers, who often labored under terrible conditions for little pay. Many people began to believe that the government should help fix this inequality. The first step was to get rid of corruption in politics.

Political Machines

In the late 1800s city and county politics were dominated by **political machines**—powerful organizations that used both legal and illegal methods to get their candidates elected to public office. For example, members of political machines sometimes stuffed ballot boxes with extra votes for their candidates. They also paid people to vote a certain way and then bribed vote counters. Through such actions, political machines could control local governments.

Primary Source

POLITICAL CARTOON
The Tammany Ring

This political cartoon shows a ring of corrupt politicians known as Tammany Hall. The cartoonist shows how each person blames the one next to him for the corruption in government. As a result of political machines like Tammany Hall, many Americans began demanding political reforms.

The Granger Collection, New York

ANALYSIS SKILL **ANALYZING PRIMARY SOURCES**

Why are the men shown standing in a circle?

Political machines were run by leaders called bosses. The machine's boss frequently traded favors for votes. For example, the boss might hand out city jobs to unqualified people or allow an illegal business to operate. The bosses drew much of their support from immigrants. They became popular among poor families because of the services they provided, including jobs and social services such as a fire brigade. A Boston politician said that the role of the machine boss was "to be . . . somebody that any bloke [man] can come to . . . and get help."

New York City's political machine, Tammany Hall, was one of the most notorious. After winning city elections in 1888, members of Tammany Hall rewarded their supporters with about 12,000 jobs. As boss of Tammany Hall, William Marcy Tweed may have stolen up to $200 million from the city. One man remembered how Tammany Hall stayed in power by intimidating voters:

> "Father used to say, 'They know how you're voting. You can't fool them.' He was a Republican at heart, but he had to vote Democratic in order that they didn't find out and make it difficult for him."
>
> —Henry Fenner, quoted in *You Must Remember This,* edited by Jeff Kisseloff

Cleaning Up Political Corruption

Corruption was also a problem in the federal government. Many people thought that the corruption extended to the presidential administration of Ulysses S. Grant. During Grant's second term, federal officials were jailed for taking bribes from whiskey makers in exchange for allowing them to avoid paying taxes. Another scandal involved members of Congress who had taken bribes to allow the Union Pacific Railway to receive government funds. These scandals and others caused many Americans to question the honesty of national leaders.

In response, Americans began calling for changes in the civil service, the government job system. They disliked the spoils system, the practice of giving jobs to the winning candidates' supporters. Thomas Jefferson was the first to reward supporters with jobs. After his administration, each time a new party took power, it replaced many government officials. Many new employees were unqualified and untrained.

By the late 1800s government corruption was so widespread that reformers demanded that only qualified people be given government jobs. In response, President Rutherford B. Hayes

FOCUS ON NORTH CAROLINA

North Carolinian Republicans and Populists joined together to create the Fusionists. Their candidate was elected governor in 1896. His administration was marked by support of Populist goals and the appointment of African Americans to some posts. Democrats appealed to racial fears to deprive him of power. Violent bands of men called the "Red Shirts" attacked blacks, Republicans, and Fusionists during the 1898 election campaign. These attacks sparked a race riot in Wilmington that resulted in the expulsion from the city of white and black leaders opposed to Conservative Democratic governance.

Gilded Age Presidents

QUICK FACTS

Rutherford B. Hayes
Republican
In office: 1877–1881
Hayes promised to reform the government with "thorough, radical, and complete" changes.

James A. Garfield
Republican
In office: 1881
Garfield attempted reforms before he was assassinated.

Chester A. Arthur
Republican
In office: 1881–1885
Arthur supported a system for awarding federal jobs based on merit, not party loyalty.

Grover Cleveland
Democrat
In office: 1885–1889, 1893–1897
Cleveland was known for his honesty and for getting involved in the day-to-day details of government.

Benjamin Harrison
Republican
In office: 1889–1893
Harrison supported the Sherman Antitrust Act, which regulated business monopolies.

William McKinley
Republican
In office: 1897–1901
McKinley avoided scandals and helped win public trust in the government.

THE IMPACT TODAY

Tests are still required for many federal jobs, including secretarial positions, air traffic control, and law enforcement.

made minor reforms, such as firing a powerful member of the New York Republican political machine. President James A. Garfield also attempted reforms. But on July 2, 1881, Garfield was attacked and shot twice by a mentally unstable federal job seeker named Charles Guiteau. The president later died from his wounds, and Vice President Chester A. Arthur became president.

Arthur continued the push for reforms by backing the Pendleton Civil Service Act, which was passed in 1883. This law set up a merit system for awarding federal jobs. Under the Pendleton Act, more than 10 percent of government job applicants had to pass an exam before they could be hired. It was a start to reforming other government practices.

READING CHECK **Analyzing** What factors led to civil-service reform?

Progressives Push for Reforms

A group of reformers known as **Progressives** were also working to improve society in the late 1800s. Progressives tried to solve problems caused by rapid industrial and urban growth. Their goals were to eliminate the causes of problems such as crime, disease, and poverty. They fought for reforms ranging from better working conditions to education programs in poor neighborhoods.

Muckrakers at Work

Some journalists urged Progressives to action by writing stories that vividly described problems in U.S. society. These journalists were nicknamed **muckrakers** because they "raked up" and exposed the muck, or filth, of society. Muckrakers wrote about troubling issues such as child labor, racial discrimination, slum housing, and corruption in business and politics.

In 1902 and 1903 Lincoln Steffens wrote a series of articles in *McClure's Magazine* exposing corruption in city government. In one article, he described how government officials in St. Louis, Missouri, used their positions to earn extra money illegally:

> "Men empowered to issue peddlers' licenses and permits to citizens who wished to erect awnings or use a portion of the sidewalk for storage purposes charged an amount in excess of the prices stipulated [set] by law, and pocketed the difference."
>
> —Lincoln Steffens, *The Shame of the Cities*

Government Reforms

In addition to working for greater voter participation, Progressives attempted to change the way city government operated. Some reformers wanted city government to be run like a business. As a result of their efforts, several cities changed to council-manager governments. Under this system, voters elect a city council. The council then appoints a professional manager to run the city. Other business-minded reformers supported the commission form of government. Under this system, the city is headed by a group of elected officials. Each official manages a major city agency, such as housing or transportation.

One of the leaders of the effort to reform state government was Wisconsin's Republican governor **Robert M. La Follette**. La Follette decreased the power of political machines and used university professors and other experts to help write new laws and work in state agencies. He also made available to the public information on how politicians voted. That way, voters would know if leaders had kept their campaign promises. Called the Wisconsin Idea, La Follette's plan became a model for progressive reforms in other states.

Expanding Democracy — QUICK FACTS

Direct Primaries	Voters choose candidates.
Recall	Voters can remove an official from office.
Initiatives	Voters can propose laws by petition.
Referendum	Voters can overrule a law.
17th Amendment	Senators are elected directly by voters.

READING CHECK **Evaluating** How did Progressives work to change voting procedures?

SUMMARY AND PREVIEW Progressives worked to reform government and improve city life. In the next section you will learn about reforms in working conditions.

Section 1 Assessment

go.hrw.com
Online Quiz
KEYWORD: SC7 HP21

Reviewing Ideas, Terms, and People

1. a. **Recall** What was the main goal of **political machines** during the Gilded Age?
   b. **Draw Conclusions** Why do you think some immigrants supported political machines?
   c. **Predict** Do you think the system of testing created by the Pendleton Civil Service Act would work to reduce corruption in the spoils system? Why or why not?
2. a. **Identify** Who were **muckrakers**, and what effect did they have on reform?
   b. **Explain** How did **Progressives** try to improve education?
   c. **Evaluate** Which progressive reform do you think was most important? Why?
3. a. **Describe** What new ideas and practices were introduced to give voters more power?
   b. **Draw Conclusions** How did progressive reforms limit the power of political machines?

Critical Thinking

4. **Categorizing** Review your notes on the problems that progressive reforms addressed. Then copy the chart below and use it to categorize the various progressive reforms.

Progressive Reforms		
Social	Political	Urban

FOCUS ON SPEAKING

5. **Addressing Political and Social Problems** How would you address the problems of political corruption and urban growth during the late 1800s? Jot down notes about campaign promises you might make to assure voters that you would make the necessary reforms.

Reform Literature

from *How the Other Half Lives*

by Jacob Riis (1849–1914)

About the Reading How the Other Half Lives *describes the tenement houses where immigrants lived in New York City. Its author, Jacob Riis, was a newspaper reporter. His nonfiction book made Americans aware of the extremes of poverty suffered by working people. Riis believed that every human being deserved a decent, safe place to live.* How the Other Half Lives *led to reforms and new laws that improved housing conditions.*

AS YOU READ **Look for details that help you see, hear, and smell Cherry Street.**

Cherry Street. Be a little careful, please! ❶ The hall is dark and you might stumble over the children pitching pennies back there. Not that it would hurt them; kicks and cuffs are their daily diet. They have little else. Here where the hall turns and dives into utter darkness is a step, and another, another. A flight of stairs. You can feel your way, if you cannot see it. Close? Yes! What would you have? All the fresh air that ever enters these stairs comes from the hall door that is forever slamming, and from the windows of dark bedrooms that in turn receive from the stairs their sole supply of the elements God meant to be free . . . That was a woman filling her pail by the hydrant you just bumped against. The sinks are in the hallway, that all the tenants may have access—and all be poisoned alike by their summer stenches. Hear the pump squeak! It is the lullaby of tenement house babes. In summer, when a thousand thirsty throats pant for a cooling drink in this block, it is worked in vain . . . ❷

The sea of a mighty population, held in galling fetters, heaves uneasily in the tenements . . . If it rise once more, no human power may avail to check it. The gap between the classes in which it surges, unseen, unsuspected by the thoughtless, is widening day by day . . . I know of but one bridge that will carry us over safe, a bridge founded upon justice and built of human hearts.

GUIDED READING

WORD HELP

cuffs punches
utter complete
close stuffy
sole only
access right to use
stenches bad smells
in vain without success
galling causing pain; irritating
fetters chains
heaves rises and falls
avail help

❶ ***The writer wants you to imagine that he is taking you on a tour of the building. Why do you think he chooses this way to describe the place?***

❷ ***Find one detail that appeals to each sense: sight, sound, smell, taste, and touch. How would you sum up, in one sentence, the place that Riis describes?***

from *The Jungle*

by Upton Sinclair (1878–1968)

About the Reading The Jungle *focused the nation's attention on immigrant workers in the meatpacking industry. Upton Sinclair's novel showed bosses forcing human beings to live and work like animals. He also described, in shocking detail, how meat was handled. Sinclair published his book in 1906. Later that same year, the U.S. government passed the Pure Food and Drug Act and the Meat Inspection Act. Many Americans even gave up eating meat for a while.*

AS YOU READ **Look for details that create one overwhelming effect.**

There was never the least attention paid to what was cut up for sausage; there would come back from Europe old sausage that had been rejected, and that was mouldy and white—it would be dosed with borax and glycerine, and dumped into hoppers, and made over again for home consumption. There would be meat that had tumbled out on the floor, in the dirt and sawdust, where the workers had tramped and spit uncounted billions of consumption germs. ❶ There would be meat stored in great piles in rooms and the water from leaky roofs would drip over it, and thousands of rats would race about on it. It was too dark in these storage places to see well, but a man would run his hand over these piles of meat and sweep off handfuls of the dried dung of rats. ❷ These rats were nuisances, and the packers would put poisoned bread out for them; they would die, and then rats, bread, and meat would go into the hoppers together . . . ❸ There was no place for the men to wash their hands before they ate their dinner, and so they made a practice of washing them in the water that was to be ladled into the sausage. ❹

GUIDED READING

WORD HELP

borax white powder used in manufacturing and cleaning

glycerine sweet, sticky liquid

hoppers containers

consumption to eat or drink

consumption tuberculosis, a lung disease that was fatal at that time

ladled added with a large spoon

❶ ***What overall effect or mood does Sinclair create?***

❷ ***Based on the details in this passage, what were the packers most concerned about?***

❸ ***Why do you think rats were considered nuisances?***

❹ ***Find details that reveal how one improvement in working conditions might have resulted in healthier sausage.***

CONNECTING LITERATURE TO HISTORY

1. **Identify Cause and Effect** Jacob Riis and Upton Sinclair were both muckraking journalists. Why do you think so much muck existed in the tenements and in the meatpacking business? Why had people ignored those conditions for so long?
2. **Identify Cause and Effect** Both Riis and Sinclair believed that improving conditions for immigrants would benefit all of society. Explain how one specific change in the tenements might have a favorable effect on everyone. Then explain how one specific change in meat handling might affect everyone.
3. **Compare and Contrast** Both *How the Other Half Lives* and *The Jungle* inspired Progressives to work for reform. Which work do you think had the greater effect on its readers? Use details from each passage to explain your answer.

SECTION 2

Reforming the Workplace

What You Will Learn...

Main Ideas

1. Reformers attempted to improve conditions for child laborers.
2. Unions and reformers took steps to improve safety in the workplace and to limit working hours.

The Big Idea

In the early 1900s, Progressives and other reformers focused on improving conditions for American workers.

Key Terms and People

Triangle Shirtwaist Fire, *p. 673*
workers' compensation laws, *p. 673*
capitalism, *p. 674*
socialism, *p. 674*
William "Big Bill" Haywood, *p. 674*
Industrial Workers of the World, *p. 674*

TAKING NOTES As you read, take notes on important labor problems and the workers they affected. You can organize your notes in a table like this one.

Problems in the Workplace

If YOU were there...

You have been working in a hat factory since 1900, when you were eight years old. Now you are experienced enough to run one of the sewing machines. You don't earn as much as older workers, but your family needs every penny you bring home. Still, the long hours make you very tired. One day you hear that people are trying to stop children from doing factory work. They think that children should be at school or playing.

Would you be for or against this social reform? Why?

BUILDING BACKGROUND Since the Second Industrial Revolution, more and more people were working long hours in difficult conditions. With adult workers earning low wages, many children had to work full time to help support their families. Progressive reformers began to focus on these problems.

Improving Conditions for Children

In the early 1900s a reformer named Marie Van Vorst took a series of jobs in factories and clothing mills around the country. She wanted to investigate working conditions for children by living and working alongside them. In a South Carolina textile mill, Van Vorst met children as young as seven years old. She described working with one young child:

> "Through the looms I catch sight of ... my landlord's little child. She is seven; so small that they have a box for her to stand on ... I can see only her fingers as they clutch at the flying spools."
>
> – Marie Van Vorst, quoted in *A History of Women in America,* edited by Carol Hymowitz

This girl—and other children like her—provided cheap labor for manufacturers. Some children were paid as little as 40 cents per day. Marie Van Vorst helped focus attention on the problem of child labor. Eliminating the problems of child labor became a major issue for Progressives and other reformers.

Children at Work

Children did many jobs in the late 1800s. Boys sold newspapers and shined shoes on the streets. Girls often cooked or cleaned for boarders staying with their families. Girls also worked at home with their mothers, sewing clothes or making handicrafts.

Like the child Van Vorst encountered, many children worked in industry. In 1900 more than 1.75 million children age 15 and under worked in factories, mines, and mills, earning very low wages.

Calls for Reform

As reporters published shocking accounts of working conditions for children, more people became aware of the problem. Progressives began to call for new reforms. You have read about Florence Kelley's work against child labor in Illinois. Kelley also served as a board member of the National Consumers' League, the major lobbying group for women's and children's labor issues. A lobbying group works to influence legislators in favor of a cause.

During the early 1900s, reformers finally succeeded in getting some laws passed to ease the conditions of child laborers. In 1912 the state of Massachusetts passed the first minimum wage law, and a commission was created to establish rates for child workers.

In 1916 and 1919 Congress passed federal child labor laws. The laws banned products made with child labor from being shipped from one state to another. The Supreme Court, however, ruled that the laws were unconstitutional. The Court argued that the laws went beyond the federal government's legal power to regulate interstate commerce.

In any case, laws alone could not end child labor. Some parents ignored child labor laws so that their children could continue contributing to the family income. Children were often instructed to lie about their age to government inspectors and tell them they were older than they really were.

READING CHECK **Finding Main Ideas** How did reformers try to improve child labor conditions?

FOCUS ON NORTH CAROLINA

In 1901 more than 100 textile mills agreed to limit the workweek to 66 hours and not to hire children under the age of 12 during the school year. Many mills, however, failed to enforce the agreement. The state's first child labor laws were passed in 1903.

FOCUS ON READING

What do you think the author's goal is in this paragraph?

Child Labor

Young children did much of the work in the American factories of the late 1800s, like this girl in a North Carolina clothing factory. They were paid less than adult workers.

Why did some parents want their children to work?

History Close-up

Working Conditions for Children, Early 1900s

This illustration shows some of the jobs that children did in glass factories in the early 1900s. You can see that there were many ways for young workers to be injured on the job.

ANALYSIS SKILL **ANALYZING VISUALS**

Using the illustration, what can you tell about the life and work of these boys?

Safety and Working Conditions

Child labor reform was only part of the progressive effort to help American workers. Many Progressives also favored laws to ensure workers' safety, limit working hours, and protect workers' rights.

Workplace Safety

Workplace accidents were common in the 1800s and early 1900s. In 1900 some 35,000 people were killed in industrial accidents. About 500,000 suffered injuries. One child described how her sister was injured using a machine in a string factory. "You see you mustn't talk or look off a minute," she explained. "My sister was like me. She forgot and talked, and just that minute her finger was off, and she didn't even cry till she picked it up."

Accidents like this were not big news in the early 1900s, but in 1911 a much greater workplace tragedy shocked the nation. It took place at the Triangle Shirtwaist Company, a New York City clothing factory that employed mostly teenage immigrant women. On the afternoon of March 25, a fire started on the eighth floor of the factory. Workers tried to escape, but factory owners had locked the exit doors—to reduce theft of materials, they said.

By the time firefighters brought the fire under control, 146 workers had died. At a memorial service for the victims, union leader Rose Schneiderman called for action. "It is up to the working people to save themselves," she said. The **Triangle Shirtwaist Fire** and similar accidents led to the passage of laws improving factory safety standards.

Labor leaders and reformers also fought for **workers' compensation laws**, which guaranteed a portion of lost wages to workers injured on the job. In 1902 Maryland became the first state to pass such a law. However, new laws were not always strictly enforced. Working conditions remained poor in many places.

Primary Source

TRIAL TRANSCRIPT

Triangle Shirtwaist Fire

Ethel Monick was one of the teenage factory workers at the Triangle Shirtwaist Company. In the trial that followed the disaster, she described her experience in the fire. Rose Freedman, pictured, was the longest living survivor of the fire. She died in 2001.

I seen the fire and then I seen all the girls rushing down to the place to escape. So I tried to go through the Greene Street door, and there were quick girls there and I seen I can't get out there, so I went to the elevator, and then I heard the elevator fall down, so I ran through to the Washington Place side . . . I tried the door and I could not open it, so I thought I was not strong enough to open it, so I hollered girls here is a door, and they all rushed over and they tried to open it, but it was locked and they hollered "the door is locked and we can't open it!"

—Testimony of Ethel Monick, age 16

ANALYSIS SKILL ANALYZING PRIMARY SOURCES

According to Monick, what is the feeling in the factory?

The Courts and Labor

Not everyone supported the new workplace regulations. Some business leaders believed that the economy should operate without any government interference. They went to court to block new labor laws.

One important case began in New York in 1897, after the state passed a law limiting bakers to a 10-hour workday. Joseph Lochner, a bakery owner, challenged the law. The case eventually went to the U.S. Supreme Court in 1905. In *Lochner* v. *New York*, the Court ruled that states could not restrict the rights of employers and workers to enter into any type of labor agreement. The New York law was declared unconstitutional.

The Supreme Court did uphold some limits on working hours for women and children. In the 1908 *Muller* v. *Oregon* case, the Court upheld laws restricting women's work hours. The justices stated that such laws protected women's health, which was of public concern.

Labor Organizations

Labor unions were also a strong force for improving working conditions. Union membership rose from about 800,000 in 1900 to about 5 million in 1920. Led by Samuel Gompers, the American Federation of Labor (AFL) remained one of the strongest labor unions. The AFL focused on better working conditions and pay for skilled workers. Gompers supported the American system of **capitalism**, an economic system in which private businesses run most industries and competition determines the price of goods.

Some union members, however, believed in **socialism**—a system in which the government owns and operates a country's means of production. Socialists, led by Eugene V. Debs, hoped that the government would protect workers.

In 1905 a group of socialists and union leaders founded a union that welcomed immigrants, women, African Americans, and others not welcome in the AFL. Led by **William "Big Bill" Haywood**, this socialist union was called the **Industrial Workers of the World** (IWW). Its goal was to organize all workers into one large union that would overthrow capitalism. Staging strikes across the country, the IWW frightened many Americans with its aggressive tactics. Strong opposition led to its decline by 1920.

READING CHECK **Analyzing** How did reforms change the workplace?

SUMMARY AND PREVIEW Progressive reformers fought to improve working conditions. In the next section you will learn about how women and minorities struggled for their rights.

Section 2 Assessment

go.hrw.com
Online Quiz
KEYWORD: SC7 HP21

Reviewing Ideas, Terms, and People

1. a. **Recall** What jobs did child laborers often hold?
   b. **Explain** Why did businesses employ children in factories?
   c. **Elaborate** Why do you think reformers began to demand improvements to child labor conditions?
2. a. **Identify** What events led to the movement to improve workplace safety?
   b. **Make Inferences** Why did the **Industrial Workers of the World** frighten some people?
   c. **Predict** What conflicts might arise between supporters of **capitalism** and **socialism**?

Critical Thinking

3. **Analyzing** Review your notes on labor reforms and workers. Then copy the graphic organizer shown below. Use it to give specific examples of how Progressives tried to reform child labor, women's labor, and workplace conditions.

Labor Reform
- Child labor:
- Women's labor:
- Workplace conditions:

FOCUS ON SPEAKING

4. **Addressing Problems in the Workplace** How would you address problems in the workplace? Make notes on campaign promises you might make to assure voters that you would address issues of child labor and workplace safety.

The Rights of Women and Minorities

If YOU were there...

You are a member of the graduating class of 1912 from an excellent women's college. You have always been interested in science, especially biology. You would like to be a doctor, but you know that medical schools accept very few women. One career path for you is to go into social work. Yet that's not what you really want to do.

How would you want to use your education?

BUILDING BACKGROUND The Progressives had a wide variety of goals. Besides attacking social problems such as child labor, they worked to reform government and make it more democratic. Changes in women's education affected the movement, as college-educated women often became leaders in working for reforms.

Women Fight for Temperance and Voting Rights

New educational opportunities drew more women into the Progressive movement. In the late 1800s, women began attending women's colleges, such as Smith College in Massachusetts and Vassar College in New York, in record numbers. In 1870 only about 20 percent of college students were women. By 1910 that number had doubled. The goal of female students was "to develop as fully as may be the powers of womanhood," said Sophia Smith, founder of Smith College.

Many women graduates entered fields such as social work and teaching. They found it much harder to enter professions such as law and medicine, which were dominated by men. Denied access to such professions, women often put their education to use by becoming active in reform. Women's clubs campaigned for causes such as temperance, women's suffrage, child welfare, and political reform.

SECTION 3

What You Will Learn...

Main Ideas

1. Women fought for temperance and the right to vote.
2. African American reformers challenged discrimination and called for equality.
3. Progressive reforms failed to benefit all minorities.

The Big Idea

The Progressive movement made advances for the rights of women and some minorities.

Key Terms and People

Eighteenth Amendment, *p. 676*
National American Woman Suffrage Association, *p. 676*
Alice Paul, *p. 677*
Nineteenth Amendment, *p. 677*
Booker T. Washington, *p. 677*
Ida B. Wells, *p. 677*
W. E. B. Du Bois, *p. 678*
National Association for the Advancement of Colored People, *p. 678*

TAKING NOTES As you read, take notes on the causes supported by different groups of progressive reformers. In each circle of a diagram like the one below, fill in details about one cause or goal. You may need to add more circles.

The Temperance Movement

In the mid-1800s many of these reformers blamed social problems such as family violence and criminal behavior on a number of factors, including urbanization and immigration. They also blamed problems on alcohol consumption. As a result, many groups took up the cause of temperance, or avoidance of alcohol.

In 1874, reformers from many different backgrounds formed the Woman's Christian Temperance Union (WCTU), which fought for adoption of local and state laws restricting the sale of alcohol. Under the leadership of Frances Willard, the organization started 10,000 branches. More than 1,000 saloons were forced to shut down as a result of temperance supporters' efforts.

One especially radical temperance fighter chose more aggressive methods to fight for her cause. In the 1890s Carry Nation became famous for storming into saloons with a hatchet and smashing liquor bottles. Nation described destroying a Kansas saloon with bricks and rocks:

> "I threw as hard, and as fast as I could, smashing mirrors and bottles and glasses and it was astonishing how quickly this was done."
>
> —Carry Nation, quoted in *Witnessing America: The Library of Congress Book of Firsthand Accounts of Life in America, 1600–1900*

FOCUS ON NORTH CAROLINA

The North Carolina Woman's Christian Temperance Union split into two groups in 1889. The "WCTU No. 2" was the only African American women's temperance union in the United States.

In 1919 many years of temperance efforts led to the passage of the **Eighteenth Amendment**, banning the production, sale, and transportation of alcoholic beverages throughout the United States.

The Right to Vote

Women reformers also fought for suffrage, or the right to vote. Many people at this time opposed giving women the vote. Political bosses, for instance, worried about the anti-corruption efforts of women. Some business leaders worried that women voters would support minimum wage and child labor laws. Other people believed that women should only be homemakers and mothers and not politically active citizens.

In spite of such opposition, the women's suffrage movement began to gain national support in the 1890s. Elizabeth Cady Stanton and Susan B. Anthony founded the **National American Woman Suffrage Association** (NAWSA) in 1890 to promote the cause of women's suffrage. That same year, women

Time Line

The Nineteenth Amendment

Women had been seeking the right to vote since 1776. Finally, in 1920 they achieved success with the passage of the Nineteenth Amendment.

1919

May 21, 1919 The House of Representatives passes the Nineteenth Amendment by a vote of 304 to 89.

June 4, 1919 The Senate passes the Nineteenth Amendment by a vote of 56 to 25.

June 10, 1919 Illinois, Michigan, and Wisconsin become the first states to ratify the Nineteenth Amendment.

won the right to vote in Wyoming. Colorado, Idaho, and Utah followed.

Carrie Chapman Catt became president of the NAWSA in 1900. Catt mobilized more than 1 million volunteers for the movement. She argued that women should have a voice in creating laws that affected them. "We women demand an equal voice," she said. "We shall accept nothing less."

Some women believed that NAWSA did not go far enough. In 1913 **Alice Paul** founded what would become the National Woman's Party (NWP). The NWP used parades, public demonstrations, picketing, hunger strikes, and other means to draw attention to the suffrage cause. Paul even organized picketing in front of the White House. Paul and other NWP leaders were jailed for their actions.

Suffragists finally succeeded in gaining the vote. In 1919 the U.S. Congress passed the **Nineteenth Amendment**, granting American women the right to vote. The Nineteenth Amendment was ratified by the states the following year, making it law.

READING CHECK **Analyzing** How did reformers draw attention to the temperance and women's suffrage movements?

African Americans Challenge Discrimination

White reformers often overlooked issues such as racial discrimination and segregation. African American reformers took the lead in addressing these problems.

One of the most important African American leaders was **Booker T. Washington**. Born into slavery, he became a respected educator while in his twenties. Washington's strategy was not to fight discrimination directly. Instead, he encouraged African Americans to improve their educational and economic well-being. This, he believed, would eventually lead to the end of discrimination.

Other African Americans spoke out more directly against discrimination. Journalist **Ida B. Wells** wrote articles about the unequal education available to African American children. In her Memphis newspaper *Free Speech,* Wells also drew attention to the lynching of African Americans. During lynchings people were murdered by mobs instead of receiving a trial after being accused of a crime, or even for breaking social codes. More than 3,000 African Americans were lynched between 1885 and 1915.

Although death threats forced Wells to move to the North, she continued campaigning against lynching. In 1900 she wrote:

> "Our country's national crime is *lynching* . . . In fact, for all kinds of offenses—and, for no offenses—from murders to misdemeanors, men and women are put to death without judge or jury."
>
> —Ida B. Wells, from her article "Lynch Law in America"

1920

August 18, 1920 Tennessee becomes the thirty-sixth state to ratify the Nineteenth Amendment.

August 26, 1920 The secretary of state officially declares the Nineteenth Amendment ratified by three-fourths of the states, making it law.

November 2, 1920 The first national election in which all women can vote is held.

1921

Like Wells, **W. E. B. Du Bois** took a direct approach to fighting racial injustice. Born in Massachusetts, Du Bois was a college graduate who earned a doctorate from Harvard University. As part of his research, he studied and publicized cases of racial prejudice. Du Bois believed that African Americans should protest unjust treatment and demand equal rights.

In 1909 Du Bois and other reformers founded the **National Association for the Advancement of Colored People** (NAACP), an organization that called for economic and educational equality for African Americans. The NAACP attacked discrimination by using the courts. In 1915 it won the important case of *Guinn* v. *United States,* which made grandfather clauses illegal. These laws were used in the South to keep African Americans from voting. Grandfather clauses imposed strict qualifications on voters unless their grandfathers had been allowed to vote. Many white voters met this requirement and were therefore automatically permitted to vote in elections. However, most African Americans' grandfathers had been enslaved and could not vote.

THE IMPACT TODAY

Today the NAACP has around 2,200 adult branches and 1,700 branches for young people.

Another important organization, the National Urban League, was formed in 1911 by Dr. George Edmund Haynes. This organization aided many African Americans moving from the South by helping them find jobs and housing in northern cities. The League addressed many of the same problems faced by other Progressives, such as health, sanitation, and education.

READING CHECK **Finding Main Ideas** What was the purpose of the NAACP?

Primary Source

POINTS OF VIEW

Fighting Discrimination

Booker T. Washington and W. E. B. Du Bois had very different views on how African Americans should handle discrimination.

"Our greatest danger is that in the great leap from slavery to freedom we may overlook the fact that the masses of us are to live by the productions of our hands, and fail to keep in mind that we shall prosper in proportion as we learn to dignify and glorify common labour and put brains and skill into the common occupations of life . . . It is at the bottom of life we must begin, and not at the top."

–Booker T. Washington

"Is it possible, and probable, that nine millions of men can make effective progress in economic lines if they are deprived of political rights, made a servile caste,* and allowed only the most meager chance for developing their exceptional men? If history and reason give any distinct answer to these questions, it is an emphatic No."

*lower social rank

–W. E. B. Du Bois

ANALYSIS SKILL **ANALYZING POINTS OF VIEW**

Finding Main Ideas What is the primary difference between the views of Washington and Du Bois?

Failures of Reform

Other minority groups felt left behind by the Progressive movement. Although some reformers tried to aid such groups, the aim of many was to encourage other ethnicities to adopt the ways of European society. The Society of American Indians, formed in 1911, was one such attempt. Started by Native American doctors Carlos Montezuma and Charles Eastman, the society believed that integration into white society would end Native American poverty. Many Native Americans, however, wanted to preserve their traditional culture. They resisted the movement toward adopting white culture.

Immigrant groups from non-European countries also formed groups to help support their members. Chinese immigrants, for example, organized neighborhood associations in the communities in which they lived. District associations, cultural groups, churches, and temples provided public services that white reformers ignored. Such groups provided the money for building San Francisco's Chinese hospital in 1925. Chinese immigration dropped, however, due in part to anti-Chinese riots that occurred in some western towns and cities.

While fewer Chinese immigrants came to the United States, the number of Mexican immigrants increased. The northern and southern borders between the United States and its neighbors were fairly easy to cross in this period. Many Mexican immigrants moved to the South and Southwest, where they became an important part of the societies and economies of these regions. Many Mexican immigrants found jobs in the mining and railroad industries. Others began farms or became migrant workers. Progressive labor laws and factory reforms did nothing to improve the poor living and working conditions of migrant farm workers.

READING CHECK **Summarizing** What were the limitations of progressive reforms?

SUMMARY AND PREVIEW Many U.S. citizens worked for progressive reforms. In the next section you will read about presidents who also worked for progressive goals.

Section 3 Assessment

go.hrw.com
Online Quiz
KEYWORD: SC7 HP21

Reviewing Ideas, Terms, and People

1. a. **Identify** What did the **Eighteenth** and **Nineteenth Amendments** accomplish?
   b. **Summarize** How did **Alice Paul** and the National Woman's Party try to draw attention to the issue of women's suffrage?
2. a. **Identify** What role did **Ida B. Wells** play in reform efforts for African Americans?
   b. **Contrast** How did **Booker T. Washington** differ from other African American leaders?
   c. **Evaluate** Do you think the **National Association for the Advancement of Colored People** was successful in fighting discrimination? Explain.
3. a. **Describe** What discrimination did Chinese Americans face?
   b. **Summarize** How were some minority groups overlooked by the Progressive movement?

Critical Thinking

4. **Analyzing** Review your notes on Progressives' causes. Then copy the diagram shown and use it to identify the progressive reforms introduced by the temperance movement, the women's suffrage movement, and African Americans.

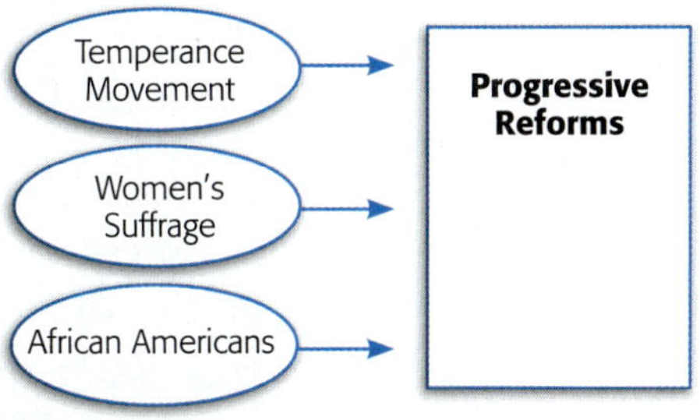

FOCUS ON SPEAKING

5. **Addressing the Rights of Women and Minorities** Review this section's material on education for women, women's suffrage, temperance, racial discrimination, and segregation. As a politician, what promises would you make regarding these issues? Think about how you would make your ideas acceptable to the American public. Would you be willing to compromise your ideals?

SECTION 4

The Progressive Presidents

What You Will Learn...

Main Ideas

1. Theodore Roosevelt's progressive reforms tried to balance the interests of business, consumers, and laborers.
2. William Howard Taft angered Progressives with his cautious reforms, while Woodrow Wilson enacted far-reaching banking and antitrust reforms.

The Big Idea

American presidents in the early 1900s did a great deal to promote progressive reforms.

Key Terms and People

Theodore Roosevelt, *p. 680*
Pure Food and Drug Act, *p. 681*
conservation, *p. 681*
William Howard Taft, *p. 682*
Progressive Party, *p. 682*
Woodrow Wilson, *p. 682*
Sixteenth Amendment, *p. 683*

TAKING NOTES As you read, take notes on the achievements of each of the progressive presidents. Use a table like the one below to organize your notes.

Roosevelt	Taft	Wilson

If YOU were there...

It is 1912 and you're voting in your first presidential election. This election is unusual—there are three major candidates. One is the popular former president Theodore Roosevelt, who is running as a third-party candidate. He thinks the Republican candidate will not make enough progressive reforms. But the Democratic candidate is a progressive reformer too.

How will you decide which candidate to support?

BUILDING BACKGROUND Political corruption was one early target of the progressive reformers. Some politicians who joined them believed that government—local, state, and national—should play an active role in improving society and people's lives.

Roosevelt's Progressive Reforms

During a summer tour after his second inauguration in 1901, President William McKinley met a friendly crowd in Buffalo, New York. Suddenly, anarchist Leon Czolgosz stepped forward and shot the president. A little more than a week later, McKinley died. Vice President **Theodore Roosevelt** took office.

Roosevelt's Square Deal

Roosevelt believed that the interests of businesspeople, laborers, and consumers should be balanced for the public good. He called this policy the Square Deal. He put the policy to the test in 1902 when faced by a coal miners' strike. Roosevelt knew the strike might leave the country without heating fuel for the coming winter. He threatened to take over the mines unless managers and strikers agreed to arbitration—a formal process to settle disputes. He felt this was the only fair way to protect Americans.

> "The labor unions shall have a square deal, and the corporations shall have a square deal, and in addition all private citizens shall have a square deal."
>
> —President Theodore Roosevelt, quoted in *The Presidency of Theodore Roosevelt*, by Lewis L. Gould

The National Park System

In 1872 Yellowstone National Park, located mostly in Wyoming, became the first national park in the United States—and the world. Today there are 55 national parks in the United States. They are managed by the National Park Service (NPS), an agency of the federal government established in 1916. The National Park Service administers almost 84 million acres (133,000 square miles) of land.

President Theodore Roosevelt and conservationist John Muir in Yosemite National Park in California

Cathedral Rocks, Yosemite National Park

Regulating Big Business

Roosevelt made regulating big business a top goal of his administration. Muckrakers helped build support for this regulation. The public was shocked, for instance, after reading Upton Sinclair's description of the meatpacking industry in *The Jungle*. Roosevelt opened an investigation and later convinced Congress to pass a meat inspection law.

In 1906 Congress passed the **Pure Food and Drug Act**. This law prohibited the manufacture, sale, and transport of mislabeled or contaminated food and drugs. Roosevelt also was the first president to successfully use the 1890 Sherman Antitrust Act to break up a monopoly. He persuaded Congress to regulate railroad shipping rates. The public largely supported this expansion of federal regulatory powers.

Conservation

Roosevelt's love of the outdoors inspired him to join other Progressives in supporting **conservation**, or the protection of nature and its resources. Roosevelt was the first president to consider conservation an important national priority.

People believed in conservation for various reasons. Preservationists such as John Muir thought that nature should be left untouched so that people could enjoy its beauty:

> "Thousands of tired, nerve-shaken, over-civilized people are beginning to find out that going to the mountains is going home; that wildness is a necessity; and that mountain parks and reservations are useful not only as fountains of timber and irrigating rivers, but as fountains of life."
>
> —John Muir, *Our National Parks*

Other conservationists wanted to make sure the nation used its natural resources efficiently. Gifford Pinchot, the first head of the newly created Forest Service, valued forests for the resources they provided to build "prosperous homes." The disagreement between the two ideals of conservation eventually widened.

While Roosevelt was in office, the Forest Service gained control of nearly 150 million acres of public land. Roosevelt doubled the number of national parks, created 18 national monuments, and started 51 bird sanctuaries.

READING CHECK **Summarizing** What reforms did Roosevelt support?

Reforms of Taft and Wilson

Theodore Roosevelt hoped that his secretary of war, **William Howard Taft**, would take his place as president in 1908. Like Roosevelt, Taft favored business regulation and opposed socialism. With Roosevelt's assistance, Taft defeated William Jennings Bryan in the election of 1908.

Taft Angers Progressives

Despite their friendship, Roosevelt and Taft held different ideas about how a president should act. Taft thought Roosevelt had claimed more power than a president was constitutionally allowed.

As president, therefore, Taft chose to move cautiously toward reform and regulation. This upset Roosevelt and various Progressives, who supported stricter regulation of big business. Although Taft's administration started twice as many antitrust lawsuits as Roosevelt's had, Progressives were not satisfied.

ACADEMIC VOCABULARY
various of many types

Taft angered Progressives further by signing the Payne-Aldrich Tariff of 1909. This tariff reduced some rates on imported goods, but it raised others. Progressives wanted all tariffs to be lowered, in order to lower prices for consumers.

Furious with Taft, Roosevelt decided to run for president again in 1912. After Taft won the Republican nomination, Roosevelt and his followers formed the **Progressive Party**. It was nicknamed the Bull Moose Party because Roosevelt said he was "as strong as a bull moose." The split between Taft and Roosevelt divided the Republican vote, and Democratic candidate **Woodrow Wilson** won the electoral vote by a wide margin.

Wilson's Reforms

In his inaugural address, Wilson spoke of the terrible social conditions under which many working-class Americans lived. "We have been proud of our industrial achievements," he said, "but we have not hitherto [yet] stopped thoughtfully enough to count the human cost." Passing reform legislation was Wilson's top goal. He pushed for two measures soon after taking office: tariff revision and banking reform.

Wilson backed the Underwood Tariff Act of 1913, which lowered tariffs. The act also introduced a version of the modern

The Election of 1912

	Electoral Vote	Popular Vote
Wilson (Democrat)	435	6,286,214
T. Roosevelt (Progressive)	88	4,126,020
Taft (Republican)	8	3,483,922

*California cast 11 electoral votes for Roosevelt and 2 for Wilson.

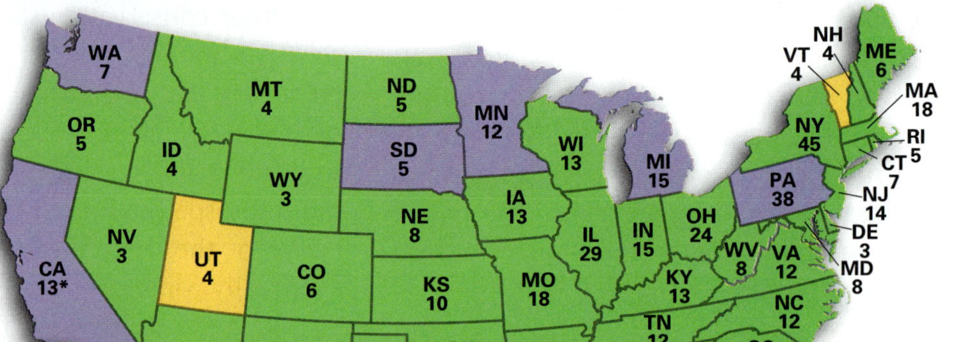

Wilson

Roosevelt

Taft

The Progressive Amendments, 1909–1920

QUICK FACTS

Number	Description	Proposed by Congress	Ratified by States
16th	Federal income tax	1909	1913
17th	Senators elected by people rather than state legislatures	1912	1913
18th	Manufacture, sale, and transport of alcohol prohibited	1917	1919
19th	Women's suffrage	1919	1920

income tax. The new tax was made possible in 1913 by the ratification of the **Sixteenth Amendment**. This amendment allows the federal government to impose direct taxes on citizens' incomes.

President Wilson next addressed banking reform with the 1913 Federal Reserve Act. This law created a national banking system called the Federal Reserve to regulate the economy.

Wilson also pushed for laws to regulate big business. The Clayton Antitrust Act of 1914 strengthened federal laws against monopolies. The Federal Trade Commission, created in 1914, had the power to investigate and punish unfair trade practices. Wilson's success in guiding reform programs through Congress helped him to win re-election in 1916.

READING CHECK **Analyzing** Why did Wilson win the election of 1912?

SUMMARY AND PREVIEW The progressive presidents tried to change American society for the better. In the next chapter you will learn how they also helped the United States become a world power.

Section 4 Assessment

go.hrw.com
Online Quiz
KEYWORD: SC7 HP21

Reviewing Ideas, Terms, and People

1. a. **Describe** How did **Theodore Roosevelt** support progressive reforms?
   b. **Analyze** Why did many Americans support **conservation**?
   c. **Evaluate** Do you think Roosevelt's reforms benefited the nation? Why or why not?
2. a. **Identify** What was the **Progressive Party**? Why was it created?
   b. **Compare and Contrast** How were the administrations of **William Howard Taft** and Roosevelt similar, and how were they different?
   c. **Evaluate** Which president do you think had the biggest influence on progressive reform—Roosevelt, Taft, or **Woodrow Wilson**? Explain your choice.

Critical Thinking

3. **Comparing and Contrasting** Review your notes on the progressive presidents. Then copy the diagram below and use it to compare and contrast the reforms of the progressive presidents.

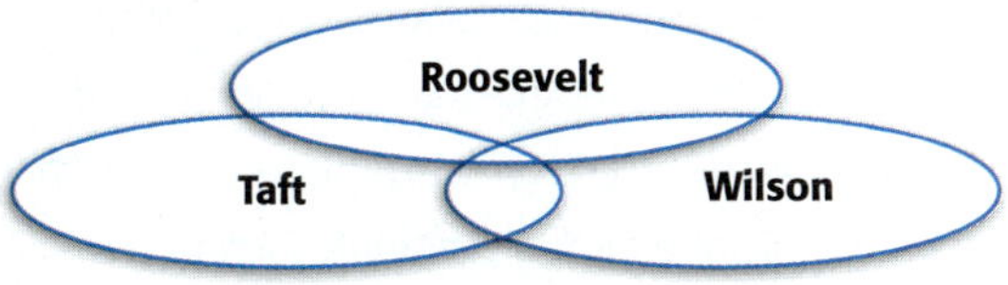

FOCUS ON SPEAKING

4. **The Ideas of Roosevelt, Taft, and Wilson** Do you agree or disagree with Presidents Roosevelt, Taft, and Wilson? Take notes on any of their ideas that you would include in your campaign promises.

Analysis | Critical Thinking | Civic Participation | Study

North Carolina Skills
1.06 Recognize and use social studies terms in written and oral reports.

Short- and Long-term Causal Relationships

Define the Skill

Most historical events are the result of other events. When something happens as a result of other things that occur, it is an effect of those things. Some events take place soon after the things that cause them. Such events are called *short-term effects*. In contrast, *long-term effects* can occur years, decades, or even hundreds of years after the events that caused them. Being able to recognize short-term and long-term cause-and-effect relationships will help you to better understand historical events.

Learn the Skill

Clue words can sometimes reveal a cause-and-effect relationship between events. Often, however, such language clues may not be present. Therefore, when you study history, you should always look for other clues that might explain why an action or event occurred.

Short-term effects are usually fairly easy to identify. In historical writing they are often closely linked to the event that caused them. For example, consider this passage from Chapter 21.

> "Some Progressives worked to change state and local governments in order to reduce the power of political machines. In many places, reformers replaced corrupt ballots that listed only one party's candidates with government-prepared ballots that listed all candidates. Under pressure from reformers, many states adopted secret ballots, giving every voter a private vote."

This passage contains no clue words. Yet it is clear that cause-and-effect relationships exist. The power of political machines created corrupt voting practices. Reformers wanted to change this. One effect of this situation was the government-prepared ballot, and another was the secret ballot.

Recognizing long-term causal relationships is often more difficult. Since long-term effects take place well after the event that caused them, they may not be discussed at the same time as their cause. This is why you should always question why an event occurred as you learn about it. For example, in 1971 Congress passed the first federal law to protect the health and safety of all workers. This law was a long-term result of efforts begun years earlier by the progressives you read about in this chapter.

Many long-term effects result from major forces running through history that make things happen. They include economics, science and technology, expansion, conflict and cooperation among people, cultural clashes and differences, and moral and religious issues. Ask yourself if one of these forces is involved in the event being studied. If so, the event may have long-term effects that you should be on the lookout for when studying later events.

Practice and Apply the Skill

Review the information in Chapter 21 and answer these questions to practice recognizing short- and long-term causal relationships.

1. All packaged food today must have its contents listed on the container. This requirement is a long-term effect of what progressive reform?
2. Write a paragraph explaining the effects of the muckrakers on the news media today.

CHAPTER 21 Chapter Review

HOLT

History's Impact

▶ **video series**

Review the video to answer the closing question:

How did the rights of women in individual states play a role in the women's suffrage movement?

Visual Summary

QUICK FACTS

Use the visual summary below to help you review the main ideas of the chapter.

Progressives hoped to improve society through reform. Their goals included

- Temperance
- Women's suffrage
- Big business regulation
- Conservation
- Tariff and banking reform

Reviewing Vocabulary, Terms, and People

Complete each sentence by filling in the blank with the correct term or person from the chapter.

1. Some Americans supported a _________ system, which proposed government ownership of the country's means of production.
2. Republican _________ began a program to reform state politics in Wisconsin.
3. The _________ granted women in the United States the right to vote.
4. The _________ prohibited the manufacture, sale, and transport of mislabeled or contaminated food and drugs.
5. During the Gilded Age, _________ often dominated local politics and used corruption to get their candidates elected.
6. _________ were journalists who wrote about troubling issues such as child labor, tenement housing, and political corruption.

Comprehension and Critical Thinking

SECTION 1 *(Pages 662–667)*

7. a. **Describe** What tactics did bosses and political machines use to gain control of local governments?

   b. **Analyze** What changes did Progressives make to city life?

   c. **Elaborate** Which progressive reform do you think had the greatest effect on Americans?

SECTION 2 *(Pages 670–674)*

8. a. **Identify** What reforms were made to improve working conditions, and who was affected by these reforms?

   b. **Contrast** What are the differences between capitalism and socialism?

   c. **Elaborate** If you were a business owner, would you have supported the progressive workplace reforms? Explain your answer.

SECTION 3 *(Pages 675–679)*

9. a. **Recall** What minority groups were overlooked by progressive reform efforts?

   b. **Analyze** How did women's involvement in the Progressive movement lead to constitutional change?

   c. **Elaborate** Do you agree with Booker T. Washington's approach to improving life for African Americans? Explain your answer.

SECTION 4 *(Pages 680–683)*

10. a. **Describe** How did William Howard Taft disappoint Progressives?

    b. **Compare** In what ways were the reforms of Presidents Roosevelt, Taft, and Wilson similar?

    c. **Elaborate** Would you have supported Wilson's progressive reforms? Explain your answer.

Reviewing Themes

11. **Politics** What role did political machines play in local politics during the Gilded Age?
12. **Society and Culture** How were children affected by the movement for workplace reforms?

Reading Skills

Evaluating Sources *Use the Reading Skills taught in this chapter to answer the question about the reading selection below.*

> The next day Rose went to town [Chicago] alone. The wind had veered [turned] to the south, the dust blew, and the whole terrifying panorama [view] of life in the street seemed some way blurred together, and forms of men and animals were like figures in tapestry. The grind and clang and clatter and hiss and howl of the traffic was all about her . . .
>
> —Hamlin Garland, from his novel *Rose of Dutcher's Coolly*, 1895

13. Is this a good source for understanding the experiences of Chicago in the late 1800s? Why or why not?

Social Studies Skills

Short- and Long-Term Causal Relationships *Use the Social Studies Skills taught in this chapter to answer the question about the reading selection below.*

> Despite their friendship, Roosevelt and Taft held different ideas about how a president should act. Taft thought Roosevelt had claimed more power than a president was constitutionally allowed.
>
> As president, therefore, Taft chose to move cautiously toward reform and regulation.
> *(p. 682)*

14. According to the passage above, what was a long-term cause of Taft's cautious reforms?

Using the Internet

go.hrw.com
KEYWORD: SC7 CH21

15. **Activity: Researching Progressives** Rapid industrial and urban growth in America in the late 1800s resulted in a number of problems. Progressives worked to address these issues in many ways, including efforts to clean up political corruption, improve working conditions, and enact social reforms. Enter the activity keyword and explore the lives of some of the leaders of the Progressive movement. Then write a profile of a Progressive leader that outlines his or her life and impact on American reform.

FOCUS ON SPEAKING

16. **Share Your Campaign Promises** Review your notes about possible campaign promises. Which promises will be most helpful in getting you elected? Look at your promises to see whether they focus on issues important to voters. Then write a speech including your campaign promises that you can deliver to your class.

CHAPTER 21 Standardized Test Practice

DIRECTIONS: Read each question and write the letter of the best response.

1

The people in this photograph would probably have been *most* interested in which of the following reforms?

A secret ballots

B the Pure Food and Drug Act

C child labor laws

D elimination of political machines

2 **One direct result of immigration and urban growth was the rise of**

A political machines.

B the civil-service system.

C the spoils system.

D primary elections.

3 **What was the *main* idea behind the creation of the civil-service system in the late 1800s?**

A Government jobs should be awarded to people who support the party in power.

B Government workers should be required to support the elected officials who hire them.

C Government employees should be qualified to do the jobs for which they were hired.

D Government jobs should not be filled with employees who serve in those jobs for life.

4 **Disagreements between North Carolina's Fusionists and Democrats resulted in the**

A election of a Republican governor.

B spread of violence.

C growth of political machines.

D creation of a new political party.

5 **Earlier in the book you learned how Frederick Douglass wrote and spoke against slavery and unfair treatment of African Americans. What later reformer also spoke out for equal rights for African Americans?**

A John Dewey

B W. E. B. Du Bois

C William Howard Taft

D Upton Sinclair

6 **Read the following excerpt from an interview with a boss at Tammany Hall and use it to answer the question below.**

> There's only one way to hold a district: you must study human nature and act accordin' . . . To learn real human nature you have to go among the people, see them and be seen. I know every man, woman, and child in the Fifteenth District, except them that's been born this summer—and I know some of them, too. I know what they like and what they don't like, what they are strong at and what they are weak in, and I reach them by approachin' at the right side.
>
> —George Washington Plunkitt, quoted in *Eyewitnesses and Others*

Document-Based Question How did Plunkitt say he kept his position in the political machine?

CHAPTER 22 1867–1920

America as a World Power

North Carolina Standards

Social Studies Objectives

5.06 Describe North Carolina's reaction to the increasing United States involvement in world affairs including participation in World War I, and evaluate the impact on the state's economy.

Language Arts Objectives

5.01 Increase fluency, comprehension, and insight through a meaningful and comprehensive literacy program by:

- using effective reading strategies to match type of text.

go.hrw.com
North Carolina
KEYWORD: SC7 NC

FOCUS ON WRITING

A List of Pros and Cons In the last half of the 1800s, the United States became more involved in international affairs. As you read this chapter, you will analyze the nation's new role and use the results of your analysis to guide U.S. policy in the future. In order to analyze the advantages and disadvantages of an aggressive foreign policy, you will need to create a list of the pros and cons of U.S. involvement with other nations in the late 1800s and early 1900s. As you create your list, note which items are facts and which are opinions—either yours or someone else's.

UNITED STATES

1867 The United States buys Alaska.

1867

WORLD

1868 Japan begins a time of modernization known as the Meiji Restoration.

HOLT

History's Impact

▶ **video series**

Watch the video to understand the impact of the United States as a world power.

What You Will Learn...

In this chapter you will learn about how the United States became a global power in the late 1800s and early 1900s. Through a combination of economic strength, military might, and aggressive foreign policy, America made its presence known in many parts of the world. One such place was Panama, where the United States built the Panama Canal, shown here. The United States has remained a powerful force on the international stage to this day.

1880

1885 The Indian National Congress is formed in British-controlled India.

1890

1890 Congress passes the McKinley Tariff, which gives a subsidy to U.S. sugar producers.

1895 Cubans rebel against Spanish rule.

1898 The United States wins the Spanish-American War, gaining the Philippine Islands and Puerto Rico.

1900

1900 The Boxer Rebellion erupts in China.

1903 Panama declares itself an independent nation.

1910

1910 The Mexican Revolution begins.

1914 The Panama Canal officially opens.

1920

Reading Social Studies

by Kylene Beers

Economics | Geography | Politics | Society and Culture | Science and Technology

Focus on Themes In this chapter, you will learn about how the physical **geography** of the United States changed as it acquired overseas territories. You will also read about how national and international **politics** affected foreign policy and brought new responsibilities to the government of the United States.

Comparing Historical Texts

Focus on Reading A good way to learn what people in the past thought is to read what they wrote. However, most documents will only tell you one side of the story. By comparing writings by different people, you can learn a great deal about various sides of a historical issue or debate.

Comparing Texts When you compare historical texts, you should consider two things: who wrote the documents and what the documents were meant to achieve. To do this, you need to find the writers' main point or points.

Document 1

"We have cherished the policy of non-interference with affairs of foreign governments wisely inaugurated [begun] by Washington, keeping ourselves free from entanglement, either as allies or foes, content to leave undisturbed with them the settlement of their own domestic concerns."

–President William McKinley, First Inaugural Address, 1897

Document 2

"Therefore, Mr. President, here is a war with terrible characteristics flagrant [obvious] at our very doors [in Cuba]. We have the power to bring it to an end. I believe that the whole American people would welcome steps in that direction."

–Senator Henry Cabot Lodge, Speech in Congress, 1896

Document 1	Document 2
Writer	
President William McKinley	Senator Henry Cabot Lodge
Main point	
The United States should not involve itself in the affairs of other countries.	The United States should go to war in Cuba.
Both Sides of the Issue	
Americans were torn over the war in Cuba. Some thought the United States should remain uninvolved as it always had. Others thought it was time for a change in foreign policy.	

You Try It!

Read the following passages, both taken from presidential addresses to Congress. As you read, look for the main point each president makes in his address.

Foreign Policy

In treating of our foreign policy and of the attitude that this great Nation should assume in the world at large, it is absolutely necessary to consider the Army and the Navy, and the Congress, through which the thought of the Nation finds its expression, should keep ever vividly in mind the fundamental fact that it is impossible to treat our foreign policy, whether this policy takes shape in the effort to secure justice for others or justice for ourselves, save as conditioned upon the attitude we are willing to take toward our Army, and especially toward our Navy.

—President Theodore Roosevelt, Message to Congress, 1904

The diplomacy of the present administration has sought to respond to modern ideas of commercial intercourse [involvement]. This policy has been characterized as substituting dollars for bullets. It is one that appeals alike to idealistic humanitarian sentiments [feelings], to the dictates [rules] of sound policy and strategy, and to legitimate [make real] commercial aims.

—President William Howard Taft, Message to Congress, 1912

After you read the passages, answer the following questions.

1. What was the main point Roosevelt made in his address?
2. What was the main point Taft made in his address?
3. How can a comparison of Roosevelt's and Taft's addresses to Congress help you understand the issues that shaped U.S. foreign policy in the early 1900s?

Key Terms and People

Chapter 22

Section 1

imperialism *(p. 692)*
isolationism *(p. 693)*
William H. Seward *(p. 693)*
Liliuokalani *(p. 694)*
spheres of influence *(p. 695)*
Open Door Policy *(p. 695)*
Boxer Rebellion *(p. 695)*

Section 2

yellow journalism *(p. 697)*
Teller Amendment *(p. 698)*
Emilio Aguinaldo *(p. 699)*
Anti-Imperialist League *(p. 700)*
Platt Amendment *(p. 701)*

Section 3

Panama Canal *(p. 705)*
Roosevelt Corollary *(p. 707)*
dollar diplomacy *(p. 708)*
Mexican Revolution *(p. 708)*
John J. Pershing *(p. 709)*
Francisco "Pancho" Villa *(p. 709)*

Academic Vocabulary

In this chapter, you will learn the following academic words:

process *(p. 695)*
role *(p. 707)*

As you read Chapter 22, organize your notes to help you point out the similarities and differences among events or policies.

SECTION 1

The United States Gains Overseas Territories

What You Will Learn...

Main Ideas

1. The United States ended its policy of isolationism.
2. Hawaii became a U.S. territory in 1898.
3. The United States sought trade with Japan and China.

The Big Idea

In the last half of the 1800s, the United States joined the race for control of overseas territories.

Key Terms and People

imperialism, *p. 692*
isolationism, *p. 693*
William H. Seward, *p. 693*
Liliuokalani, *p. 694*
spheres of influence, *p. 695*
Open Door Policy, *p. 695*
Boxer Rebellion, *p. 695*

TAKING NOTES As you read, make a list of examples of U.S. expansion in a chart like this one.

Areas or Trade Rights Gained

If YOU were there...

You are a Hawaiian living on Maui, one of the Hawaiian Islands, in 1890. Your parents work in a sugar mill owned by American planters. Although the mill supplies jobs, you don't trust the sugar planters. They have already made your king sign a treaty that gives them a lot of power in the islands. You are afraid they will take over the government.

What would you do if the planters took over your islands?

BUILDING BACKGROUND In the mid-1800s, most Americans had little interest in being involved with the rest of the world diplomatically. The Civil War and Reconstruction kept their focus on challenges at home. In the meantime, though, European nations were busily acquiring overseas territories. The United States would soon join them.

End of Isolation

In the 1800s powerful Western nations were busy building naval bases to protect their shipping routes around the world. This was an aspect of **imperialism**—building an empire by founding colonies or conquering other nations. Between 1870 and 1914, Europeans extended their colonial empires until they controlled most of Africa and Southeast Asia.

Roots of Imperialism

Several forces drove this wave of European imperialism. Countries wanted sources of raw materials—such as copper, rubber, and tin—to fuel industrial growth. Businesspeople wanted new markets for their manufactured goods. And many

Europeans saw colonies as a source of power and national pride.

In contrast, the United States followed a limited policy of **isolationism**—avoiding involvement in the affairs of other countries. In 1789 President George Washington had warned Americans "to steer clear of permanent alliances" with other countries. American leaders tried to follow this advice by staying out of overseas conflicts.

By the late 1800s, however, some Americans believed the United States needed to expand to keep its economy strong. In his 1890 book *The Influence of Sea Power upon History,* Alfred T. Mahan argued that the United States needed a strong navy to protect its economic interests. Mahan also explained that a strong navy needed overseas bases and coaling stations—places for ships to take on coal for fuel.

Seward's Folly

In 1867 the United States greatly expanded its North American territory when Secretary of State **William H. Seward** arranged the purchase of Alaska from Russia for $7.2 million. Some people thought Alaska was a frozen wasteland, calling the deal "Seward's Folly" [foolish act]. But Seward had purchased an area more than twice the size of Texas for two cents an acre. And as he had hoped, Alaska became a source of valuable natural resources such as fur, timber, and minerals. Gold was found in Alaska in the 1890s, bringing miners and settlers to the area.

Based on Seward's belief that the United States "must continue to move on westward," the nation also annexed the Midway Islands in 1867. The islands' location about halfway between the U.S. West Coast and Japan made Midway an excellent coaling station for the U.S. Navy.

The United States wanted the island group of Samoa for similar reasons. The United States and Germany agreed to divide Samoa in 1899.

THE IMPACT TODAY

The United States still has hundreds of military bases in foreign countries.

READING CHECK **Analyzing** Why did U.S. leaders end isolationist policies in the late 1800s?

U.S. Territories in the Pacific, 1856–1899

GEOGRAPHY SKILLS **INTERPRETING MAPS**

Between 1856 and 1898, Alaska and many Pacific islands, including Hawaii, became U.S. territories.

1. What U.S. territory was located below the equator?
2. In what year did the United States acquire the most territories?

Hawaii Becomes a Territory

Even more appealing than Samoa were the Hawaiian Islands. Hawaiians first saw Europeans in 1778. Trading and whaling ships in the Pacific soon began stopping in Hawaii. In the early 1800s American missionaries came and attempted to convert Hawaiians to Christianity. Missionaries opened businesses and raised crops, such as sugarcane. Some Americans became rich sugar planters.

By the 1840s most shops and shipyards in Hawaii were owned by Americans. Sugar became a leading export of the Hawaiian economy. An 1875 treaty allowed Hawaiian sugar to be shipped duty-free to the United States. (A duty is a tax on imported items.) This agreement helped the Hawaiian sugar industry prosper.

THE IMPACT TODAY

Today, sugarcane is Hawaii's most valuable crop.

The planters used their power to force the Hawaiian king to sign a new constitution in 1887. It became known as the Bayonet Constitution because the king was forced to sign it at gunpoint. The constitution granted more power to the planter-controlled legislature. Many Hawaiians feared the foreigners' increase in power.

BIOGRAPHY

Liliuokalani
(1838–1917)

Born in Honolulu, Queen Liliuokalani was proud of Hawaiian traditions. Even after being driven from power in 1883, she continued speaking out on behalf of native-born Hawaiians. In 1887 she traveled to Washington, D.C., meeting with President Grover Cleveland to argue against the annexation of Hawaii by the United States. Until her death, Liliuokalani served as a symbol of Hawaiian pride and a reminder of the islands' history as an independent nation.

Drawing Conclusions Why do you think Liliuokalani was a symbol of Hawaiian pride?

In 1891 the king died, and his sister, **Liliuokalani** (li-LEE-uh-woh-kuh-LAHN-ee), became queen. She proposed a new constitution that would return power to the monarchy. The planters revolted. John L. Stevens, U.S. minister to Hawaii, called 150 marines ashore to support the revolt, and it succeeded without a battle. The planters formed a new government. Congress voted to annex the Hawaiian Islands in 1898.

READING CHECK **Identifying Cause and Effect** What effect did the growing power of the planters have on the Hawaiian monarchy?

United States Seeks Trade with Japan and China

Economic interest also drew the United States to Japan and China. The United States wanted to open and secure trade markets in both Asian countries.

Opening Trade with Japan

By the mid-1800s European powers had formed strong trade ties with most East Asian countries. However, the island nation of Japan had isolated itself from the rest of the world for hundreds of years.

The United States wanted to open up trade with Japan before Europeans arrived. President Millard Fillmore sent Commodore Matthew Perry to Japan to secure "friendship, commerce, [and] a supply of coal and provisions." Perry attempted a peaceful alliance in 1853, but he was not successful.

Perry returned to Japan in 1854 with seven warships. He gave Japanese leaders gifts and tried to show some of the benefits that Japanese-American trade would have. For instance, Perry presented them with a telegraph transmitter and a model train. This effort—and the presence of U.S. naval power—persuaded Japanese officials to open trade with the United States. The two countries signed a trade agreement in 1858.

Perry Arrives in Japan

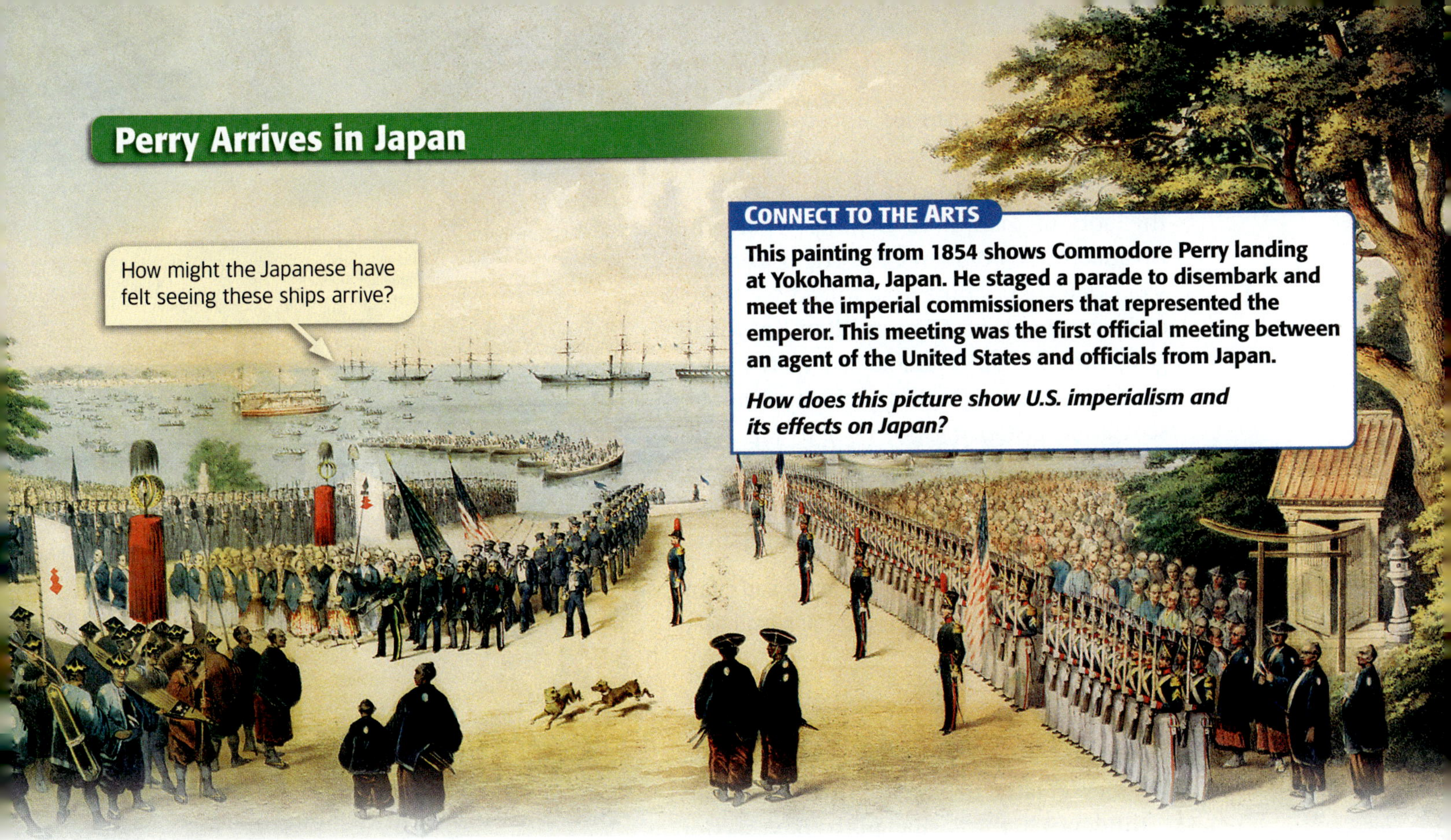

CONNECT TO THE ARTS

This painting from 1854 shows Commodore Perry landing at Yokohama, Japan. He staged a parade to disembark and meet the imperial commissioners that represented the emperor. This meeting was the first official meeting between an agent of the United States and officials from Japan.

How does this picture show U.S. imperialism and its effects on Japan?

Some Japanese leaders welcomed trade with the United States. In 1868 people who favored the industrialization process came to power in Japan, beginning a 40-year period of modernization. By the 1890s Japan was becoming a major imperial power. It defeated China in the Sino-Japanese War from 1894 to 1895. As a result, Japan gained new territory and enjoyed the same trading privileges in China as European countries. In 1904 Japan attacked Russian forces stationed in China. President Theodore Roosevelt helped to negotiate a peace treaty to end the Russo-Japanese War a year later. Japan gained control of Korea, a lease on Port Arthur in China, and other rights. Japan had become a world power.

Foreign Powers in China

After Japan defeated China, other countries took advantage of China's weakness by seizing **spheres of influence**—areas where foreign nations controlled resources. Germany, Great Britain, France, Japan, and Russia all took control of areas within China.

Some U.S. leaders feared that the United States would be closed out of Chinese markets. In 1899 Secretary of State John Hay sent notes to Japan and many European countries announcing the **Open Door Policy**. This policy stated that all nations should have equal access to trade in China. The policy was neither rejected nor accepted by European powers and Japan but made U.S. intentions clear.

Meanwhile, many Chinese resented the power and control held by foreign nations. This hostility sparked the **Boxer Rebellion**. The Boxers were Chinese nationalists who were angered by foreign involvement in China. In their language, the group was called the Fists of Righteous Harmony. Westerners called them Boxers because they used a clenched fist as their symbol. Although officially denounced, they were secretly supported by the Chinese government.

In June 1900 the Boxers took to the streets of Beijing, China's capital, and laid siege to the walled settlement where foreigners lived. They killed more than 200 people.

ACADEMIC VOCABULARY

process a series of steps by which a task is accomplished

The siege continued for two months. Foreign military forces, including United States Marines, fought their way from the port of Tianjin to Beijing, where they invaded the Forbidden City. The Boxers were soon defeated. China was forced to make a cash payment of $333 million to foreign governments, $25 million of which went to the United States. Secretary of State Hay then sent another Open Door note to Japan and the European nations. The Open Door Policy remained in effect until World War II again closed China's borders to foreign influence.

READING CHECK **Identifying Cause and Effect** What factors led to the Boxer Rebellion, and what was the result?

SUMMARY AND PREVIEW The United States greatly expanded its territory and influence in the Pacific. In the next section, you will learn about the causes and effects of the Spanish-American War.

Chinese nationalists attack the foreigners' compound in Beijing in this illustration of China's Boxer Rebellion.

Section 1 Assessment

go.hrw.com
Online Quiz
KEYWORD: SC7 HP22

Reviewing Ideas, Terms, and People

1. a. **Describe** What policy had the United States followed regarding other countries before the late 1800s?
   b. **Analyze** Why did the United States expand to Alaska and to islands in the Pacific?
   c. **Evaluate** Do you think **William H. Seward**'s purchase of Alaska was a good decision? Explain.
2. a. **Recall** What became Hawaii's leading export?
   b. **Sequence** What events led to Hawaii's annexation as a U.S. territory?
   c. **Elaborate** What do you think about the planters' revolt against Queen **Liliuokalani**?
3. a. **Describe** How did the United States persuade Japanese leaders to sign a trade treaty?
   b. **Contrast** How was the U.S. experience establishing trade with China different from U.S. attempts to open trade with Japan?
   c. **Evaluate** Do you think Japan made the right decision in agreeing to open trade with the United States? Explain your answer.

Critical Thinking

4. **Generalizing** Review your notes on the areas or trade rights gained by the United States. Then use the chart below to identify the benefits of these areas and trade rights.

American Expansion

Areas or Trade Rights Gained	Benefits for United States

FOCUS ON WRITING

5. **Identifying Pros and Cons of U.S. Involvement Overseas** What did the United States gain from its involvement in these areas of the world? What were the disadvantages? As you read this section, identify pros and cons to add to your list.

The Spanish-American War

SECTION 2

If YOU were there...

You live in New York City in 1898. Newspaper headlines are screaming about the start of war in Cuba. You hear that Theodore Roosevelt wants volunteers for a cavalry troop called the Rough Riders. You know how to ride a horse, and you've admired Roosevelt ever since he was New York's police commissioner. You know it will be dangerous, but it also sounds like a great adventure.

Would you join the Rough Riders? Why?

BUILDING BACKGROUND While the United States, Japan, and several European powers were gaining colonies, Spain's empire was declining. By the late 1800s Spain's once-extensive American empire was reduced to two island colonies—Cuba and Puerto Rico. Eager for independence, some Cubans revolted against Spanish rule. Many Americans sympathized with Cuba's fight for independence.

War with Spain

You read earlier that newspaper publishers Joseph Pulitzer and William Randolph Hearst were in a fierce competition for readers. In the late 1890s their newspapers published stories from Cuba, where Cuban rebels were fighting for independence from Spain. To attract readers, Pulitzer and Hearst printed sensational, often exaggerated news stories. This technique is called **yellow journalism**. Vivid stories about Spanish brutality in Cuba convinced many Americans that the U.S. military should support the Cuban rebels.

$50,000 REWARD.—WHO DESTROYED THE MAINE?—$50,000 REWARD.

EDITION FOR GREATER NEW YORK

NEW YORK JOURNAL AND ADVERTISER.

The Journal will give $50,000 for information, furnished to it exclusively, that will convict the person or persons who sank the Maine.

PRICE ONE CENT

NEW YORK, THURSDAY, FEBRUARY 17, 1898.—16 PAGES.

DESTRUCTION OF THE WAR SHIP MAINE WAS THE WORK OF AN ENEMY.

$50,000!

$50,000 REWARD!
For the Detection of the Perpetrator of the Maine Outrage!

Assistant Secretary Roosevelt Convinced the Explosion of the War Ship Was Not an Accident.

The Journal Offers $50,000 Reward for the Conviction of the Criminals Who Sent 258 American Sailors to Their Death.

$50,000!

$50,000 REWARD!
For the Detection of the Perpetrator of the Maine Outrage!

Newspapers such as this one encouraged Americans to seek war with Spain.

What You Will Learn...

Main Ideas

1. In 1898 the United States went to war with Spain in the Spanish-American War.
2. The United States gained territories in the Caribbean and Pacific.

The Big Idea

The United States expanded into new parts of the world as a result of the Spanish-American War.

Key Terms and People

yellow journalism, *p. 697*
Teller Amendment, *p. 698*
Emilio Aguinaldo, *p. 699*
Anti-Imperialist League, *p. 700*
Platt Amendment, *p. 701*

TAKING NOTES As you read, use a graphic organizer like this one to list the results of the Spanish-American War.

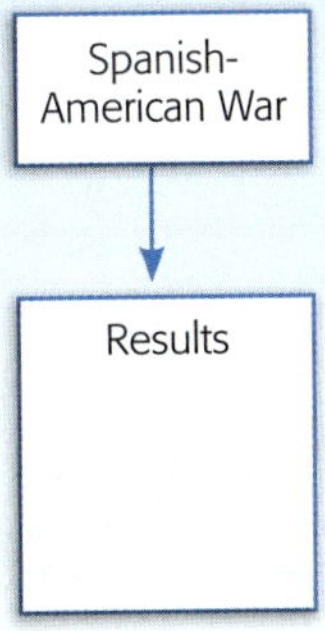

Despite growing support for military action in Cuba, President Grover Cleveland was opposed to U.S. involvement. In 1896 William McKinley, a supporter of Cuban independence, was elected president. Several events soon led to war.

In February 1898 Hearst's newspaper published a letter written by the Spanish minister to the United States, Enrique Dupuy de Lôme. In it, de Lôme called McKinley "weak and a bidder for the admiration of the crowd." Many Americans were outraged.

In January 1898, even before de Lôme's letter became public, the United States sent the battleship USS *Maine* to Havana Harbor. The *Maine*'s mission was to protect U.S. citizens and economic interests in Cuba. On February 15 the *Maine* exploded and sank, with a loss of 266 men. Although the cause of the explosion was unclear, the American press immediately blamed Spain. "Remember the *Maine*!" became a rallying cry for angry Americans.

President McKinley requested $50 million to prepare for war. Congress approved the money. Although Cuba was not a U.S. territory, Congress issued a resolution on April 20 declaring Cuba independent and demanding that Spain leave the island within three days. Attached to the resolution was the **Teller Amendment**, which stated that the United States had no interest in taking control of Cuba. In response to the resolution, Spain declared war on the United States. The next day, Congress passed, and McKinley signed, a declaration of war against Spain.

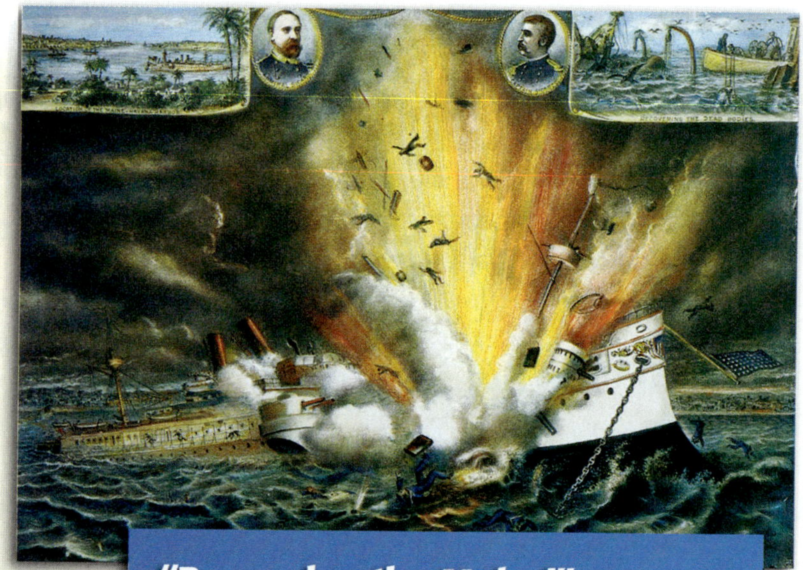

"Remember the *Maine*!"

Most of the men aboard the USS *Maine* were sleeping when a terrible explosion demolished the forward third of the ship at 9:40 P.M. on February 15, 1898. The rest of the ship sank quickly. Some 266 men were killed.

Whom did the United States blame for the explosion?

War in the Philippines

While attention was focused on Cuba, the U.S. Navy won a quick victory nearly halfway around the world in the Philippines, a Spanish colony in the Pacific. Filipinos, like Cubans, were rebelling against Spanish rule.

As soon as the Spanish-American War began, American commodore George Dewey raced to the Philippines with four large warships and two small gunboats. On May 1, ignoring reports that mines beneath the water barred his way, he sailed into Manila Bay and destroyed the Spanish Pacific fleet stationed there. Dewey's forces sank or captured 10 ships. The Spanish lost 381 lives, but none of Dewey's men were killed.

Dewey had defeated the Spanish, but he did not have enough troops to occupy and secure the Philippines. Troops eventually arrived, and on August 13, U.S. troops and Filipino rebels led by **Emilio Aguinaldo** (ahg-ee-NAHL-doh) took control of the Philippine capital, Manila.

GEOGRAPHY SKILLS **INTERPRETING MAPS**

1. **Region** Where did the United States achieve a victory?
2. **Movement** How far did Dewey travel to get to Manila?

War in the Caribbean

In contrast to the navy, the U.S. Army was unprepared for war. At the start of the conflict, the entire U.S. Army had only 28,000 soldiers. New volunteers quickly raised that figure to more than 280,000. The army did not have enough rifles or bullets for these soldiers. It did not even have appropriate clothing for the troops. Many soldiers received warm woolen uniforms to wear in Cuba's tropical heat.

The soldiers faced harsh living conditions in Cuba. They ate canned meat that one general called "embalmed beef," and many were stricken with yellow fever and other deadly diseases. More than 2,000 Americans died from diseases they contracted in Cuba. Fewer than 400 were killed in battle.

The most colorful group of soldiers was the Rough Riders. Second in command of this group was Lieutenant Colonel Theodore Roosevelt. Roosevelt had organized the Rough Riders to fight in Cuba. Volunteers included Native Americans, college athletes, cowboys, miners, and ranchers. Newspaper stories of their heroism earned the Rough Riders Americans' admiration. Four privates of the African American 10th Cavalry, who served with the Rough Riders, received the Congressional Medal of Honor.

Landing on June 22, 1898, the U.S. troops captured the hills around the main Spanish forces at Santiago. At the village of El Caney on July 1, some 7,000 U.S. soldiers, aided by Cuban rebels, overwhelmed about 600 Spanish defenders.

The main U.S. force then attacked and captured San Juan Hill. The Rough Riders and the African American 9th and 10th cavalries captured nearby Kettle Hill. The many accounts of the battle became popular with the American public back home. A journalist on the scene described the soldiers' charge:

FOCUS ON READING

How might accounts of the war written by these various soldiers have been different?

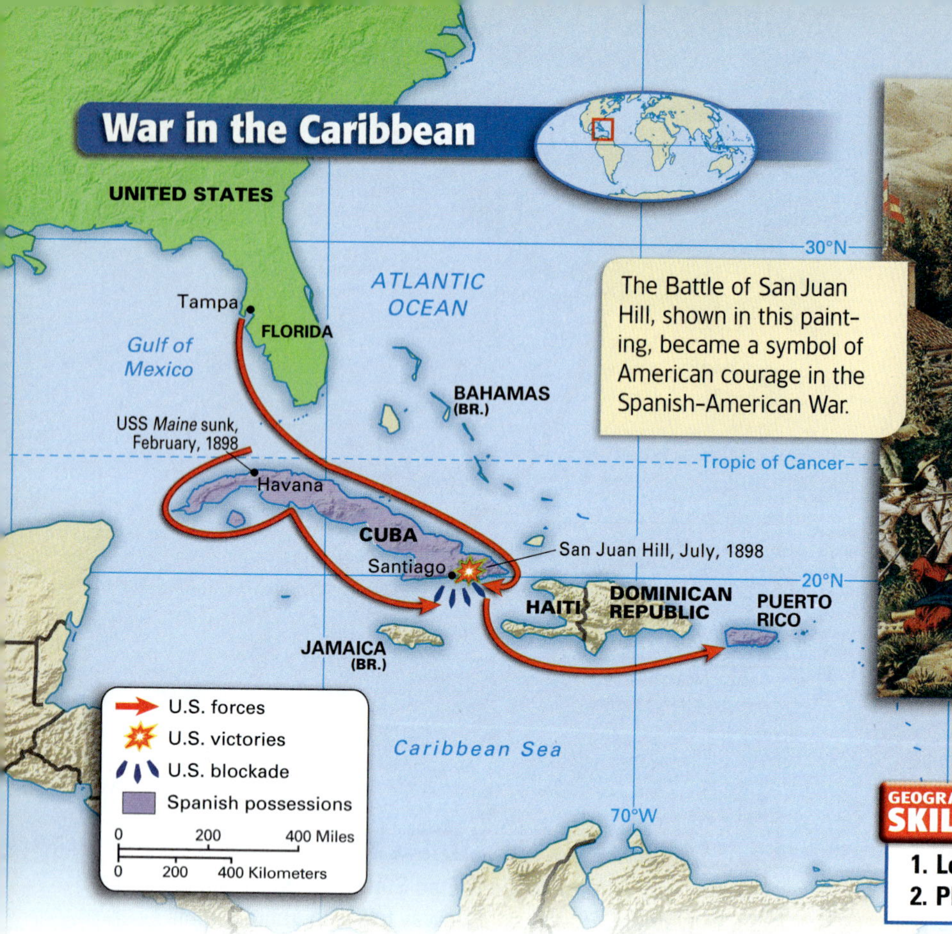

The Battle of San Juan Hill, shown in this painting, became a symbol of American courage in the Spanish-American War.

GEOGRAPHY SKILLS **INTERPRETING MAPS**

1. **Location** About how far is Havana from Tampa?
2. **Place** When was the victory at San Juan Hill?

FOCUS ON NORTH CAROLINA

President McKinley requested two infantry regiments from North Carolina, but three were raised. The First and Second were made up of white soldiers, while the Third was one of only three African American regiments created in the nation during the Spanish-American War.

"It was a miracle of self-sacrifice, a triumph of bulldog courage . . . The fire of the Spanish riflemen . . . doubled and trebled [tripled] in fierceness, the crests of the hills crackled and burst in amazed roars and rippled with waves of tiny flame. But the blue line [of United States soldiers] crept steadily up and on."

—Richard Harding Davis, quoted in *The American Reader*, edited by Paul M. Angle

On July 3 the commander of the Spanish fleet decided to try breaking through the U.S. blockade. Though every Spanish ship was destroyed in the battle, American forces suffered only two casualties. Santiago surrendered two weeks later. President McKinley began peace negotiations with Spain, which was assured of defeat. A few days later, U.S. troops invaded Spanish-held Puerto Rico, which surrendered with little resistance. Spain signed a cease-fire agreement on August 12, 1898.

READING CHECK **Comparing** How was fighting in the Pacific and the Caribbean similar?

United States Gains Territories

The peace treaty placed Cuba, Guam, Puerto Rico, and the Philippines under U.S. control. In reaction, some Americans formed the **Anti-Imperialist League**, a group that opposed the treaty and the creation of an American colonial empire. They argued that the treaty threatened democracy because it denied self-government to the people living in the newly acquired territories. The Senate approved the peace treaty by a vote of 57 to 27—just one vote more than the two-thirds majority needed to ratify treaties.

Cuba

The Teller Amendment had declared that the United States would not annex Cuba. However, McKinley wanted to create stability and increase U.S. economic activity there, so he set up a military government. He appointed Leonard Wood, who had commanded the Rough Riders during the war, as governor.

Wood quickly began building schools and a sanitation system.

Even with the new sanitation system, disease remained a major problem. Dr. Walter Reed, head of the army's Yellow Fever Commission, was sent to Cuba in 1900 to help fight the disease. He and his volunteers conducted experiments, including allowing themselves to be bitten by infected insects. They soon proved that yellow fever was transmitted by mosquitoes. Getting rid of the standing water where mosquitoes lived helped health officials to control the disease.

Governor Wood also oversaw the writing of a Cuban constitution. The document included the **Platt Amendment**, which limited Cuba's right to make treaties and allowed the United States to intervene in Cuban affairs. It also required Cuba to sell or lease land to the United States. Cuban leaders compared the Platt Amendment to "handing over the keys to our house so that they [the Americans] can enter it at any time, whenever the desire seizes them." The Cubans reluctantly accepted the amendment, and U.S. troops withdrew. The amendment remained in force until 1934, and the U.S. government stayed actively involved in Cuban affairs until the late 1950s.

Puerto Rico

Like Cubans, Puerto Ricans had hoped for independence after the war. Instead, the U.S. government made the island a territory. On April 12, 1900, the Foraker Act established a civil government in Puerto Rico. It was headed by a governor and included a two-house legislature.

A debate over the new territory soon arose. People who lived in Puerto Rico were

LINKING TO TODAY

Puerto Ricans Today

Today about 3.7 million Puerto Ricans live on the mainland United States. This is the second-largest Hispanic population in the country, behind people of Mexican descent. Puerto Ricans live throughout the United States, but about one-third live in New York State. Puerto Rican culture is very strong in New York—the National Puerto Rican Day Parade in New York City is one of the largest parades for any ethnic group in the city.

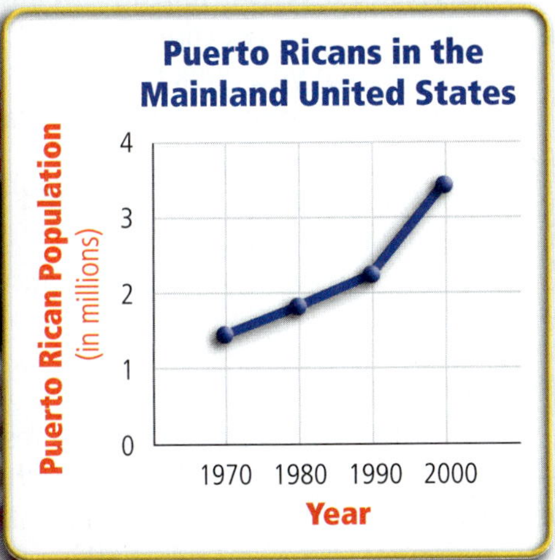

ANALYSIS SKILL — ANALYZING INFORMATION

How are the people in the picture celebrating Puerto Rican culture?

considered citizens of the island but not of the United States. In 1917 the Jones Act gave Puerto Ricans U.S. citizenship and made both houses of the legislature elective. However, another 30 years passed before Puerto Ricans could elect their own governor. Today the island has its own constitution and elected officials but remains associated with the United States as what is known as a commonwealth.

The Philippines

Spain had surrendered the Philippines in return for a $20 million payment from the United States. Many Americans agreed with President McKinley, who said that the United States would benefit from the islands' naval and commercial value and that annexing the islands would keep Europeans from seizing them.

Filipino rebels, however, had expected to gain independence after the war. They had helped U.S. forces to capture Manila. When the United States decided instead to keep the islands, rebels led by Emilio Aguinaldo started a guerrilla war against the American forces. More than 4,200 U.S. soldiers and hundreds of thousands of Filipinos died before the conflict ended in 1902.

That same year, Congress passed the Philippine Government Act. It provided that an appointed governor and a two-house legislature would rule the Philippines. In 1946 the United States granted full independence to the Philippines.

READING CHECK **Summarizing** What areas did the United States control as a result of the war?

SUMMARY AND PREVIEW The United States fought a war with Spain and gained new territories in the Pacific and Caribbean regions. In the next section you will learn about U.S. interests in Latin America.

Section 2 Assessment

go.hrw.com
Online Quiz
KEYWORD: SC7 HP22

Reviewing Ideas, Terms, and People

1. a. **Recall** What was the cause of the conflict between Cuba and Spain?
   b. **Analyze** How did **yellow journalism** affect public support for U.S. military action in Cuba?
   c. **Elaborate** Why do you think the United States was so successful in defeating Spain? Explain your answer.
2. a. **Identify** What territories did the United States gain as a result of the war?
   b. **Analyze** Why did some Americans oppose the annexation of the Philippines?

Critical Thinking

3. **Categorizing** Review your notes on the results of the Spanish-American War. Then copy the graphic organizer to the right. Use your notes to identify arguments for and against taking control of foreign territories.

Arguments for Imperialism		Arguments against Imperialism
	vs.	

FOCUS ON WRITING

4. **Identifying Pros and Cons of the Spanish-American War** As you read this section, add to your pros and cons list by identifying American losses and gains as a result of the Spanish-American War. What were the costs in human lives? What were the gains in territory? Can you identify any other losses and gains? For example, how did the United States handle the issues of self-rule involved in the war?

Theodore Roosevelt

What would you do to reform your country and make it stronger?

When did he live? 1858–1919

Where did he live? Theodore Roosevelt was born into a wealthy family in New York City. He spent two years on a ranch in the Dakota Territory, where he became an avid hunter and conservationist. His political career then took him to Albany, New York, where he served as state governor, and Washington, D.C., where he served as vice president and president.

What did he do? Roosevelt became a national hero while leading the Rough Riders in the Spanish-American War. After serving less than a year as vice president, the 42-year-old Roosevelt became the youngest president in U.S. history when President William McKinley was killed in 1901. As president, Roosevelt fought for progressive reforms and set aside millions of acres as national parks and forests. Roosevelt's aggressive foreign policy expanded American power in the world.

Why is he so important? "I believe in a strong executive," Roosevelt once declared. "While president, I have been president, emphatically [forcefully]; I have used every ounce of power there was in the office." As this quote suggests, Roosevelt was a strong leader who set a precedent for a more active and powerful presidency.

Drawing Conclusions What characteristics made Theodore Roosevelt a successful leader?

KEY EVENTS

1882
Elected to the New York State Assembly at age 23

1898
Becomes a hero in the Spanish-American War; elected governor of New York

1900
Elected vice president

1901
Becomes president when McKinley is assassinated

1903
Gains Panama Canal Zone for the United States

1906
Visits Panama, becoming the first president to travel outside the country while in office

1919
Dies at home in New York

President Theodore Roosevelt and the Rough Riders

SECTION 3

The United States and Latin America

What You Will Learn...

Main Ideas

1. The United States built the Panama Canal in the early 1900s.
2. Theodore Roosevelt changed U.S. policy toward Latin America.
3. Presidents Taft and Wilson promoted U.S. interests in Latin America.

The Big Idea

The United States expanded its role in Latin America in the early 1900s.

Key Terms and People

Panama Canal, *p. 705*
Roosevelt Corollary, *p. 707*
dollar diplomacy, *p. 708*
Mexican Revolution, *p. 708*
John J. Pershing, *p. 709*
Francisco "Pancho" Villa, *p. 709*

TAKING NOTES As you read, take notes on changing U.S. policies toward Latin America. List each policy in an outer circle of a web like this one.

If YOU were there...

You are an engineer, and you've been working on the Panama Canal for almost eight years. Your work crews used huge steam shovels to slice through a ridge of mountains and built a huge artificial lake. You planned a system to move ships through different water levels. Now your work is done. You can watch massive ships travel from the Atlantic to the Pacific.

Which part of the work on the canal was the most challenging?

BUILDING BACKGROUND When the Spanish-American War began in 1898, the U.S. battleship *Oregon* set out from Washington State to join the fighting in Cuba. The approximately 12,000-mile trip around the southern tip of South America took more than two months. This delay convinced many U.S. leaders that the United States needed to build a canal linking the Atlantic and Pacific oceans.

Building the Panama Canal

A canal across the narrow neck of Central America would link the Atlantic and Pacific oceans and cut some 8,000 miles off the voyage by ship from the West to the East coasts of the United States. It would also allow the U.S. Navy to link its Atlantic and Pacific naval fleets quickly.

Revolution in Panama

No one was a stronger supporter of a Central American canal than President Theodore Roosevelt. Roosevelt knew that the best spot for the canal was the Isthmus of Panama, which at the time was part of the nation of Colombia. But he was unable to convince the Colombian senate to lease a strip of land across Panama to the United States.

Roosevelt considered other ways to gain control of the land. He learned that Panamanian revolutionaries were planning a revolt against Colombia. On November 2, 1903, a U.S. warship arrived outside Colón, Panama. The next day the revolt began. Blocked by the U.S. warship, Colombian forces could not reach Panama to stop the rebellion. Panama declared itself an independent country. The United States then recognized the new nation.

The new government of Panama supported the idea of a canal across its land. The United States agreed to pay Panama $10 million plus $250,000 a year for a 99-year lease on a 10-mile-wide strip of land across the isthmus.

Building the Canal

Canal construction began in 1904. The first obstacle to overcome was tropical disease. The canal route ran through 51 miles of forests and swamps filled with mosquitoes, many of which carried the deadly diseases malaria and yellow fever.

Dr. William C. Gorgas, who had helped Dr. Walter Reed stamp out yellow fever in Cuba, organized a successful effort to rid the canal route of disease-carrying mosquitoes. If Gorgas had not been successful, the canal's construction would have taken much longer. It also would have cost much more in terms of both lives and money.

Even with the reduced risk of disease, the work was very dangerous. Most of the canal had to be blasted out of solid rock with explosives. Workers used dozens of steam shovels to cut a narrow, eight-mile-long channel through the mountains of central Panama. Sometimes workers died when their shovels struck explosive charges. "The flesh of men flew in the air like birds every day," recalled one worker from the West Indies.

Some 6,000 lives were lost during the American construction of the **Panama Canal**. It was finally opened to ships on August 15, 1914, linking the Atlantic and Pacific oceans. An opening ceremony was held the next year. It had taken 10 years to complete, and the cost was $375 million. In the end, however, the world had its "highway between the oceans."

THE IMPACT TODAY

Today the Panama Canal Zone is threatened by deforestation and erosion because of heavy use. Decreased rainfall is also hurting the canal.

READING CHECK **Drawing Conclusions** Why did building the canal cost so many lives?

The massive Gatun Locks, shown here under construction in 1914, raise ships 85 feet onto Gatun Lake, an inland waterway on the Panama Canal.

Interactive Map

The Panama Canal

CONNECT TO ECONOMICS

Increasing Exports The Panama Canal did not just increase trade between the East and West coasts of the United States. By shortening the trip from many U.S. ports to other parts of the world, the canal also led to increased exports of agricultural and manufactured goods.

By how many miles did the Panama Canal shorten the shipping distance between New York City and San Francisco?

go.hrw.com
Interactive Map
KEYWORD: SC7 CH22

GEOGRAPHY SKILLS — INTERPRETING MAPS

1. **Place** Why was Panama chosen as the site for a canal?
2. **Movement** How many locks did ships have to travel through from Balboa to Colón?

U.S. Policy Toward Latin America

As president, Theodore Roosevelt actively pursued progressive reforms at home. He also believed the United States should play a more active role in the Western Hemisphere. In 1900 Roosevelt said, "I have always been fond of the West African proverb: 'Speak softly and carry a big stick; you will go far.'" Roosevelt wanted everyone to know he would use a "big stick"—meaning U.S. military force—to protect U.S. interests in Latin America.

This was a change from the policies of previous presidents. In the 1823 Monroe Doctrine, President James Monroe had warned European nations not to interfere in the Western Hemisphere. And while the Monroe Doctrine became a major principle of U.S. foreign policy, the United States did not have the military strength to enforce it. By the time Roosevelt became president, however, this situation was changing. The United States was growing stronger and expanding its influence. The United States was becoming a world power.

How should the United States use its new power in Latin America? This question came up often in the early 1900s. European banks had made loans to a number of Latin American countries. Venezuela, for example, fell deeply in debt to British and German investors. Venezuela refused to repay these debts in 1902. A similar situation arose in the Caribbean nation of the Dominican Republic in 1904. European powers prepared to use military force to collect the debts.

Roosevelt insisted the countries must repay their debts. But he did not want to allow Europeans to intervene in Latin America. The presence of European forces there would violate the Monroe Doctrine and threaten U.S. power in the region.

Roosevelt knew that U.S. officials would have to force debtor nations to repay their loans in order to keep European nations from directly intervening in Latin America. In December 1904 he announced what became known as the **Roosevelt Corollary** to the Monroe Doctrine. This addition warned that in cases of "wrongdoing" by Latin American countries, the United States might exercise "international police power."

The Roosevelt Corollary asserted a new **role** for the United States as an "international police power" in the Western Hemisphere. Roosevelt actively enforced the corollary throughout the rest of his presidency.

ACADEMIC VOCABULARY
role assigned behavior

READING CHECK **Finding Main Ideas** Why did Roosevelt announce the Roosevelt Corollary?

Primary Source

POLITICAL CARTOON

Roosevelt's Imperialism

Theodore Roosevelt's foreign policy is shown visually in this cartoon. Roosevelt is the giant leading a group of ships that represent debt collection. The U.S. president is patrolling the Caribbean Sea and Latin American countries, trying to enforce the payment of debts to European countries.

ANALYSIS SKILL **ANALYZING PRIMARY SOURCES**

Analyzing How does the cartoonist portray the parts of the Roosevelt Corollary?

GEOGRAPHY SKILLS **INTERPRETING MAPS**

1. **Region** What parts of this region does the United States still control?
2. **Place** Which country was a U.S. protectorate for the longest period of time?

U.S. Interests in Latin America

William Howard Taft, who became president in 1909, also acted to protect U.S. interests in Latin America. Taft used a policy called **dollar diplomacy**—influencing governments through economic, not military, intervention.

President Taft described dollar diplomacy as "substituting dollars for bullets. It is . . . directed to the increase of American trade." He wanted to encourage stability and keep Europeans out of Latin America by expanding U.S. business interests there.

For example, in 1911 Nicaragua failed to repay a loan from British investors. American bankers lent Nicaragua $1.5 billion in return for control of the National Bank of Nicaragua and the government-owned railway. When local anger over this deal led to revolt in Nicaragua, Taft sent U.S. Marines to protect American interests.

When President Woodrow Wilson took office in 1913, he rejected Taft's dollar diplomacy. He believed the United States had a moral obligation to promote democracy in Latin America. Like Roosevelt, Wilson was willing to use military force to protect U.S. interests in the region.

In 1910 many Mexicans revolted against the harsh rule of Mexican dictator Porfirio Díaz. This was the start of the **Mexican Revolution**, a long, violent struggle for power in Mexico. The war affected U.S. interests

U.S. Foreign Policy

QUICK FACTS

Departing from the example set by the nation's first president, George Washington, future presidents increased U.S. involvement around the world, particularly in Latin America.

Washington's Farewell Address
The United States will not become involved in European affairs.

Monroe Doctrine
The United States will defend its interests in the Western Hemisphere and keep European powers out.

Roosevelt Corollary
The United States will police wrongdoing by nations in the Western Hemisphere.

Taft's Dollar Diplomacy
The United States will use economic means to aid its interests in Latin America.

Wilson and Democracy
The United States will promote and protect democracy in the Western Hemisphere.

because Americans had invested more than $1 billion in Mexican land, mining, oil, and railways. American business leaders feared they would lose their investments.

In 1914 President Wilson learned that a German ship carrying weapons was headed to the port of Veracruz, Mexico. To keep the weapons from reaching the rebels, Wilson ordered the navy to seize Veracruz. Wilson acted again in 1916, sending General **John J. Pershing** and 15,000 U.S. soldiers into Mexico. Pershing's mission was to catch the rebel leader **Francisco "Pancho" Villa**, who had killed 17 Americans in New Mexico. Pershing failed to capture Villa, and Wilson recalled the troops.

In 1917 a new constitution began to bring order to Mexico. The violence caused more than 120,000 Mexicans to flee to the United States between 1905 and 1915.

READING CHECK **Summarizing** How did Wilson respond to events in Mexico?

SUMMARY AND PREVIEW The United States and Latin America established relationships through both conflicts and agreements. In the next chapter, you will learn how the United States became involved in conflict in Europe.

Section 3 Assessment

go.hrw.com
Online Quiz
KEYWORD: SC7 HP22

Reviewing Ideas, Terms, and People

1. a. **Recall** Why did the United States want to build a canal?
   b. **Analyze** What challenges did the builders of the **Panama Canal** face, and how did they overcome them?
   c. **Elaborate** Defend or criticize the U.S. decision to support the revolution in Panama.
2. a. **Describe** What problem was causing conflict between European and Latin American nations?
   b. **Summarize** How and why did Theodore Roosevelt change U.S. policy toward Latin America?
3. a. **Recall** What did Woodrow Wilson believe was the United States's obligation to Latin America?
   b. **Compare and Contrast** How were the policies of Taft and Wilson toward Latin America similar, and how were they different?

Critical Thinking

4. **Categorizing** Review your notes on U.S. policies toward Latin America. Then copy the web diagram below. Use it to identify American policies toward Latin America.

FOCUS ON WRITING

5. **Identifying Pros and Cons of U.S. Intervention** What were the pros and cons of the construction of the Panama Canal and interventionist U.S. policies toward Latin America? Take notes for your list as you read this section.

History and Geography

America's Global Influence 1900

By 1900 most of the current boundaries of the United States had been established. But the world had become a much smaller place. American inventions were spreading, changing daily life in countries around the world. In addition, U.S. troops stationed in China were displaying the increasing importance of the United States in global affairs.

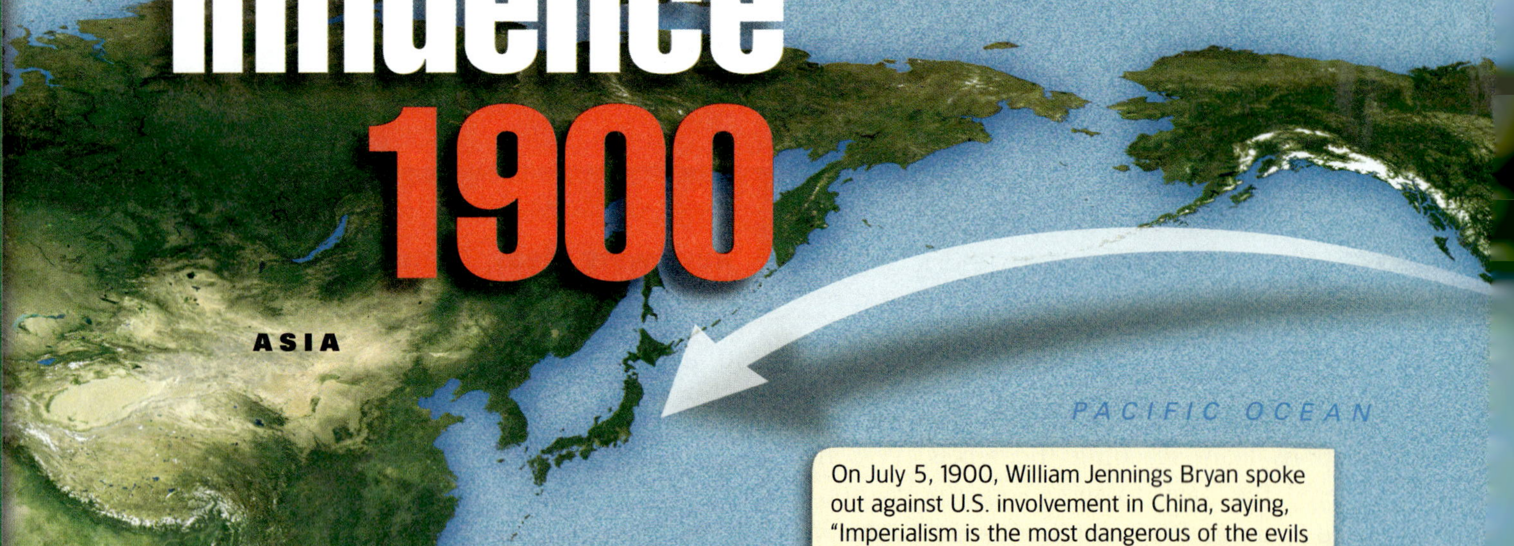

Asia Before 1898, U.S. troops had never been sent outside the Western Hemisphere. But in 1900, some 5,000 troops were in Asia, fighting alongside European troops.

On July 5, 1900, William Jennings Bryan spoke out against U.S. involvement in China, saying, "Imperialism is the most dangerous of the evils now menacing [threatening] our country."

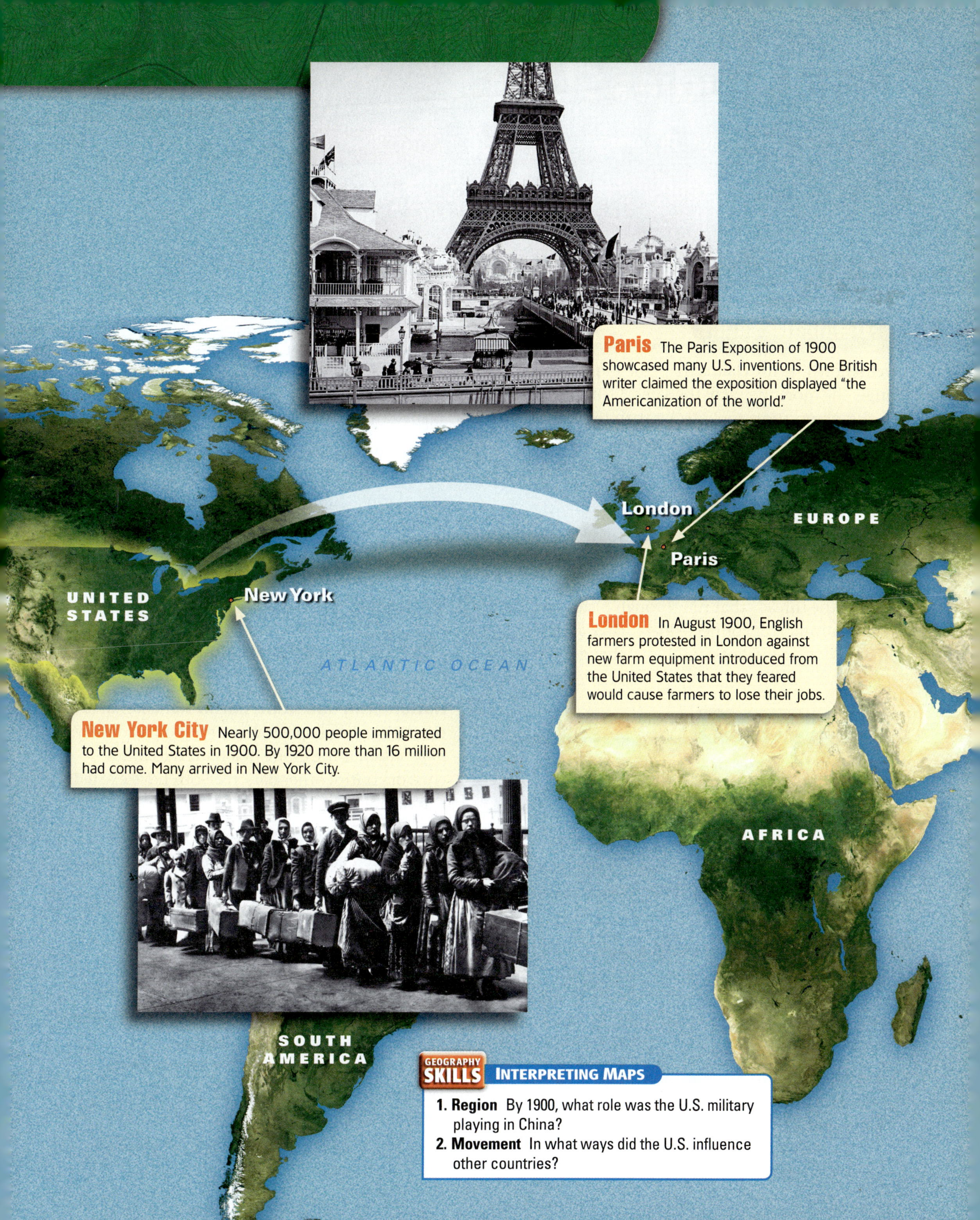

Paris The Paris Exposition of 1900 showcased many U.S. inventions. One British writer claimed the exposition displayed "the Americanization of the world."

London In August 1900, English farmers protested in London against new farm equipment introduced from the United States that they feared would cause farmers to lose their jobs.

New York City Nearly 500,000 people immigrated to the United States in 1900. By 1920 more than 16 million had come. Many arrived in New York City.

GEOGRAPHY SKILLS INTERPRETING MAPS

1. **Region** By 1900, what role was the U.S. military playing in China?
2. **Movement** In what ways did the U.S. influence other countries?

Social Studies Skills

Analysis | Critical Thinking | Civic Participation | Study

Continuity and Change in History

Define the Skill

A well-known saying claims that "the more things change, the more they stay the same." Nowhere does this observation apply better than to the study of history. Any examination of the past will show many changes—nations expanding or shrinking, empires rising and falling, changes in leadership, or people on the move, for example.

The reasons for change have not changed, however. The same general forces have driven the actions of people and nations across time. These forces are the threads that run through history and give it continuity, or connectedness. They are the "sameness" in a world of continuous change.

Learn the Skill

You can find the causes of all events of the past in one or more of these major forces or themes that connect all history.

1. **Cooperation and Conflict** Throughout time, people and groups have worked together to achieve goals. They have also opposed others who stood in the way of their goals.

2. **Cultural Invention and Interaction** The values and ideas expressed in peoples' art, literature, customs, and religion have enriched the world. But the spread of cultures and their contact with other cultures have produced conflict as well.

3. **Geography and Environment** Physical environment and natural resources have shaped how people live. Efforts to gain, protect, or make good use of land and resources have been major causes of cooperation and conflict in history.

4. **Science and Technology** *Technology,* or the development and use of tools, has helped humans across time make better use of their environment. Science has changed their knowledge of the world, and changed their lives, too.

5. **Economic Opportunity and Development** From hunting and gathering to herding, farming, manufacturing, and trade, people have tried to make the most of their resources. The desire for a better life has also been a major reason people have moved from one place to another.

6. **The Impact of Individuals** Political, religious, military, business, and other leaders have been a major influence in history. The actions of many ordinary people have also shaped history

7. **Nationalism and Imperialism** *Nationalism* is the desire of a people to have their own country. *Imperialism* is the desire of a nation to influence or control other nations. Both have existed across time.

8. **Political and Social Systems** People have always been part of groups—families, villages, nations, or religious groups, for example. The groups to which people belong shape how they relate to others around them.

Practice the Skill

Check your understanding of continuity and change in history by answering the following questions.

1. What forces of history are illustrated by the events in Chapter 22? Explain with examples.
2. How do the events in this chapter show continuity with earlier periods in U.S. history?

CHAPTER 22

Chapter Review

HOLT

History's Impact

▶ **video series**

Review the video to answer the closing question:

How would you characterize the current policy of the United States: isolationist or imperialist?

Visual Summary

QUICK FACTS

Use the visual summary below to help you review the main ideas of the chapter.

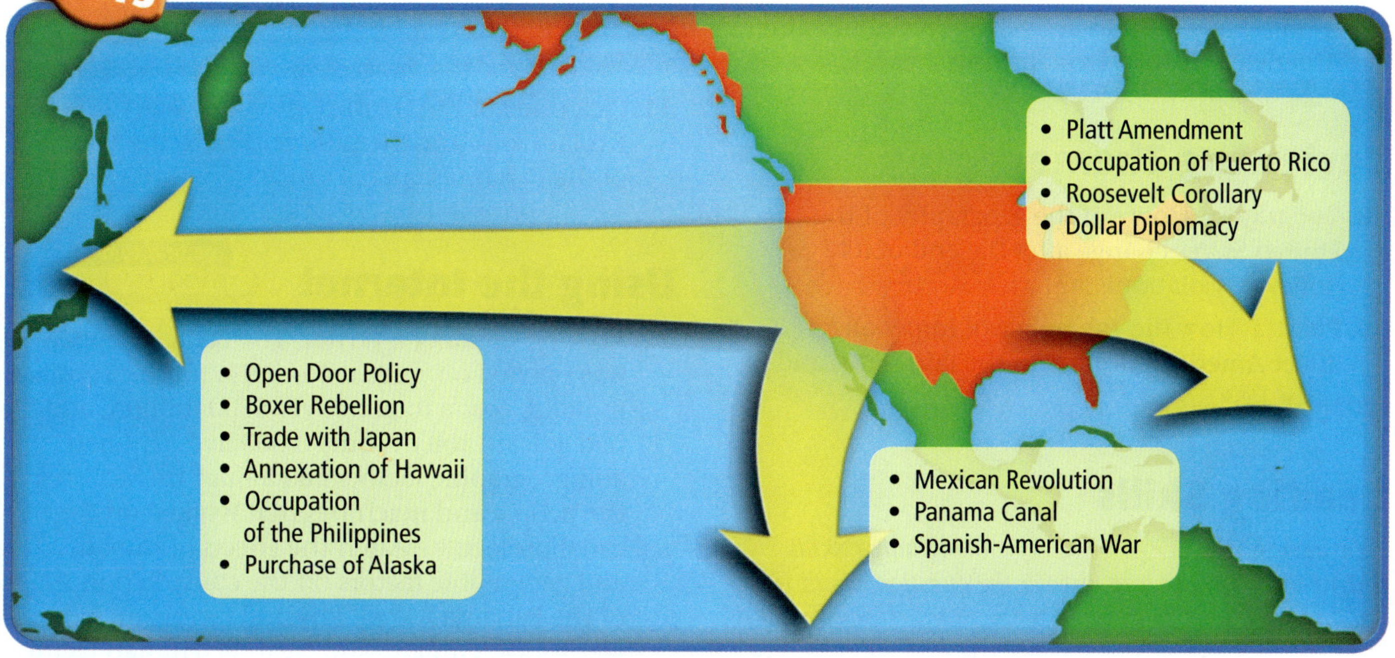

Reviewing Vocabulary, Terms, and People

1. In which of the following did the United States declare that it had no interest in taking control of Cuba?

a. Roosevelt Corollary **c.** Open Door Policy

b. Monroe Doctrine **d.** Teller Amendment

2. Which leader upset sugar planters in Hawaii by proposing a plan to return power to the monarchy?

a. Liliuokalani **c.** Millard Fillmore

b. John L. Stevens **d.** Woodrow Wilson

3. Which president supported Panama's revolt against Colombia in 1903?

a. Woodrow Wilson **c.** William Howard Taft

b. William McKinley **d.** Theodore Roosevelt

4. Who led U.S. forces into Mexico after attacks against U.S. citizens by Mexican rebels?

a. John Hay **c.** John J. Pershing

b. William H. Seward **d.** Theodore Roosevelt

Comprehension and Critical Thinking

SECTION 1 *(Pages 692–696)*

5. a. Identify Into what areas did the United States expand in the late 1800s?

b. Draw Conclusions How did the United States benefit from contact with foreign nations and territories?

c. Elaborate Which policy would you have supported—isolationism or imperialism? Explain your answer.

SECTION 2 *(Pages 697–702)*

6. a. Describe What events led the United States to declare war on Spain?

b. Analyze How did the United States benefit from the Spanish-American War?

c. Predict How might foreign countries view the actions of the United States in the Spanish-American War?

SECTION 3 *(Pages 704–709)*

7. **a. Identify** In what ways did the United States become involved in Latin American affairs?

   b. Draw Conclusions Why did the United States expand its role in Latin America in the early 1900s?

   c. Elaborate Do you think the United States should have been as actively involved in Latin America as it was? Explain your answer.

Reviewing Themes

8. **Geography** How did the geography of the United States change after the end of its policy of isolationism?
9. **Politics** How did the policy of imperialism affect American politics in the late 1800s and early 1900s?

Reading Skills

Comparing Historical Texts *Use the Reading Skills taught in this chapter to answer the question about the reading selections below.*

A. "Sad to say, this most precious and sublime feature of the Yosemite National Park (Hetch Hetchy Valley), one of the greatest of all our natural resources for the uplifting joy and peace and health of the people, is in danger of being dammed and made into a reservoir to help supply San Francisco with water and light . . ."

—John Muir, *The Yosemite*, 1912

B. "As we all know, there is no use of water that is higher than the domestic use. Then, if there is, as the engineers tell us, no other source of supply that is anything like so reasonably available as this one; if this is the best, and, within reasonable limits of cost, the only means of supplying San Francisco with water, we come straight to the question of whether the advantage of leaving this valley in a state of nature is greater than the advantage of using it for the benefit of the city of San Francisco."

—Gifford Pinchot, address to Congress, 1913

10. How do the two men quoted above differ on the issue of building a dam in the Hetch Hetchy Valley?

Social Studies Skills

Continuity and Change in History *Use the Social Studies Skills taught in this chapter to answer the question below.*

11. Pick three of the themes listed on page 712. Explain how the themes connect to the history of the Panama Canal.

Using the Internet

go.hrw.com
KEYWORD: SC7 CH22

12. **Activity: Creating a Poster** The Panama Canal was opened on August 15, 1914. It took 10 years to build, cost a total of over $600 million, and had a death toll of some 6,000 lives. Human and geographic factors had a huge impact on the people and machines that worked on the canal project. Research the effects of human and geographic factors on the construction of the Panama Canal. Physical factors include landforms, climate, and weather. Human factors should focus on the use of technology and the reasons humans modified the environment, along with the hazards they faced. Then create a poster about the canal, highlighting the most important details.

FOCUS ON WRITING

13. **Writing Your List of Pros and Cons** Review your notes and choose the pros and cons to include in your final list. Decide whether you want to include only facts, only opinions, or some of each. How can your analysis of history help guide U.S. foreign policy in the future? When you have finished your list, use it as the basis for a paragraph recommending either that the United States continue to involve itself in the affairs of other nations or that it pull back from such involvement.

CHAPTER 22

Standardized Test Practice

DIRECTIONS: Read each question and write the letter of the best response. Use the map below to answer question 1.

1

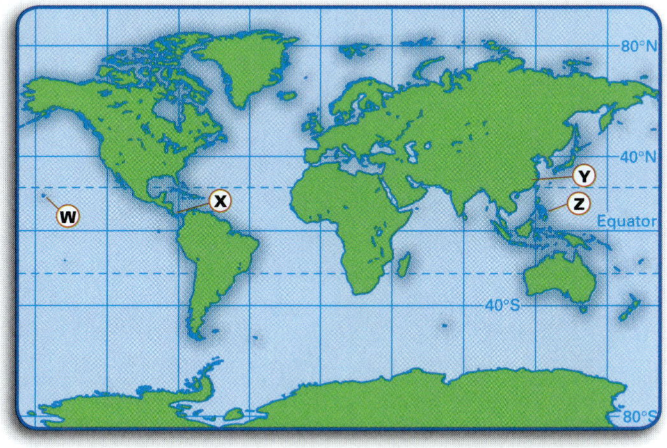

The only area in which the United States did not control territory in the late 1800s and early 1900s is shown on the map by which letter?

A W

B X

C Y

D Z

2 **The practice of using U.S. businesses and economic aid to influence foreign governments and achieve U.S. goals in Latin America is known as**

A imperialism.

B dollar diplomacy.

C isolationism.

D the big stick.

3 **During the Mexican Revolution, President Wilson sent U.S. forces to Veracruz, Mexico. Which U.S. policy did this act best express?**

A Roosevelt Corollary

B dollar diplomacy

C Teller Amendment

D isolationism

4 **Which two nations did the United States hope to trade with rather than annex in the late 1800s?**

A Hawaii and Japan

B Japan and China

C China and Cuba

D Cuba and Hawaii

5 **Exaggerated newspaper stories about events in Cuba resulted in**

A public support for war with Spain.

B the election of President Roosevelt.

C the opening of trade with Japan.

D financial support for the Panama Canal.

6 **The opening of the Panama Canal was important because it**

A triggered war between the United States and Spain.

B provided hundreds of jobs for Latin American workers.

C improved relations between the United States and Latin America.

D shortened the time for transporting many goods.

7 **Read the following passage from a letter from President Fillmore and use it to answer the question below.**

> "I am desirous that our two countries should trade with each other, for the benefit of both Japan and the United States. We know that the ancient laws of your imperial majesty's government do not allow of foreign trade, except with the Chinese and the Dutch; but as the state of the world changes . . . it seems to be wise, from time to time, to make new laws."
>
> —Letter from U.S. President Millard Fillmore to Japan, 1852

Document-Based Question **What is President Fillmore asking the Japanese to do?**

CHAPTER 23 1914–1920

World War I

North Carolina Standards

Social Studies Objectives

5.06 Describe North Carolina's reaction to the increasing United States involvement in world affairs including participation in World War I, and evaluate the impact on the state's economy.

Language Arts Objectives

2.01 Analyze and evaluate informational materials that are read, heard, and/or viewed by:

- monitoring comprehension for understanding of what is read, heard and/or viewed.
- recognizing the characteristics of informational materials.
- summarizing information.
- determining the importance and accuracy of information

go.hrw.com
North Carolina
KEYWORD: SC7 NC

FOCUS ON SPEAKING

Persuasive Speech Before the United States entered World War I in 1917, Americans heatedly debated joining the fight. Many were torn between either helping Britain and France or remaining isolated from world conflict. In this chapter, you will read about U.S. involvement in World War I. Then you will make a speech presenting your point of view on whether the United States should have entered the war.

UNITED STATES

1914 President Wilson issues a proclamation of neutrality in the European war.

1914

1914 Archduke Francis Ferdinand is assassinated.

WORLD

HOLT
History's Impact
▶ **video series**
Watch the video to understand the impact of modern warfare on the outcome of World War I.

What You Will Learn...

In this chapter you will learn how an assassination in Europe sparked the deadliest war the world had ever seen. You will find out how the United States was drawn into the fighting and will read about new battle strategies, such as trench warfare. The photograph on this page shows the terrible conditions soldiers faced as they fought the enemy from their trench positions.

1916 Jeannette Rankin becomes the first woman elected to Congress.

1917 The Selective Service Act is passed, introducing the draft.

1918 President Wilson announces the Fourteen Points.

1919 The U.S. Senate refuses to approve the Treaty of Versailles.

1916 — 1918 — 1920

1915 A German U-boat sinks the *Lusitania.*

1917 The United States declares war on Germany.

1918 Germany agrees to an armistice, ending World War I.

Reading Social Studies

by Kylene Beers

Economics | Geography | Politics | Society and Culture | Science and Technology

Focus on Themes In this chapter, you will read about World War I and the changes it brought to the United States and the world. Many of the **political** tensions that led to the war were caused by the rise of nationalism in European countries. You will read about how the war devastated European **economies**, and how peace affected European countries.

Recognizing Fallacies in Reasoning

Focus on Reading As part of evaluating a historical argument, you can judge whether the reasoning is sound. A *fallacy* is a false or mistaken idea.

Recognizing Fallacies As you identify a main idea, judge its soundness. Look for cause-and-effect relationships that support the idea. Decide whether you think the argument is logical.

Notice how a reader explained the logical reasoning behind the main idea in the following paragraph.

Three main factors led to a shortage of labor in the United States during the war. First, American factories were working nonstop to produce weapons and supplies for the Allied forces. Factories needed new workers to meet this huge demand. Second, the war almost completely cut off immigration. As you know, immigrants had provided a steady source of labor to American industry. And third, many of the young men who would normally take factory jobs were off fighting in Europe.

From Chapter 23, p. 728

If factories were working overtime, they would need more workers. This supports the main idea of a labor shortage.

If factories were used to having immigrants to hire, and there were fewer immigrants, it would make sense that there was a labor shortage.

Here's a third reason for a labor shortage: many men became soldiers. It makes sense that there was a labor shortage during the war.

You Try It!

The man who assassinated Archduke Francis Ferdinand was a Serb.

↓

All Serbians wanted war with Austria-Hungary.

Wilson wanted to establish the League of Nations

↓

because he thought it would help ensure peace.

Trench warfare was a new kind of warfare.

↓

Therefore, trench warfare was more horrible than any other kind of warfare.

1. Is the first conclusion reasonable? Why or why not? How can you tell?
2. Do you think the second conclusion is logical or illogical? What makes you think so?
3. Is the third conclusion a fallacy of reason? What reasonable conclusions can you draw from the statement?

Key Terms and People

Chapter 23

Section 1

militarism *(p. 721)*
Archduke Francis Ferdinand *(p. 721)*
mobilize *(p. 721)*
Central Powers *(p. 721)*
Allied Powers *(p. 721)*
trench warfare *(p. 722)*
stalemate *(p. 723)*
U-boats *(p. 724)*

Section 2

Lusitania (p. 726)
Zimmermann Note *(p. 726)*
Selective Service Act *(p. 727)*
Liberty bonds *(p. 727)*
National War Labor Board *(p. 729)*

Section 3

American Expeditionary Force *(p. 730)*
Communists *(p. 731)*
armistice *(p. 734)*

Section 4

League of Nations *(p. 737)*
reparations *(p. 737)*
Treaty of Versailles *(p. 738)*
Henry Cabot Lodge *(p. 738)*

Academic Vocabulary

In this chapter, you will learn the following academic words:

neutral *(p. 724)*
strategy *(p. 733)*

As you read Chapter 23, notice how the authors use logical reasoning to support their main ideas.

SECTION 1

The Road to War

If YOU were there...

You are walking past a newspaper stand when a headline catches your eye: "Austria-Hungary's Archduke Francis Ferdinand Assassinated in Sarajevo." Your first thought is, "Who's he?" You pick up the paper and read about the archduke and about the rising tensions in Europe related to his death. The article makes it sound like Europe is about to explode into war.

At this point, do you think the assassination will affect the United States? Why or why not?

What You Will Learn...

Main Ideas

1. Many factors contributed to the outbreak of World War I.
2. European nations suffered massive casualties in the war's early battles.

The Big Idea

In 1914 tensions in Europe exploded into the deadliest war the world had ever seen.

Key Terms and People

militarism, *p. 721*
Archduke Francis Ferdinand, *p. 721*
mobilize, *p. 721*
Central Powers, *p. 721*
Allied Powers, *p. 721*
trench warfare, *p. 722*
stalemate, *p. 723*
U-boats, *p. 724*

TAKING NOTES As you read, identify the major battles of the beginning of World War I. In a chart like the one below, list the battles and where they were fought.

Battle	Location

BUILDING BACKGROUND European nations had not been involved in a major war in the region since the 1870s. Rising political tensions during the early 1900s threatened this peace, however, and nations began to build up their military forces. Even a small incident might trigger a major war.

Outbreak of War

Though Europe was at peace in the early 1900s, relations between European nations were not necessarily friendly. In fact, feelings of fear and distrust were growing among European powers such as Germany, France, Great Britain, Russia, and Austria-Hungary. This dangerous tension had several important causes.

Tensions in Europe

One cause of tension was the rise of nationalism in the 1800s. Nationalism is a strong sense of pride and loyalty to one's nation or culture. Nationalism inspired people who shared a language or culture to want to unite politically. In 1871, for example, Chancellor Otto von Bismarck and Kaiser Wilhelm I brought together several German states to form the nation of Germany.

While nationalism helped bring stability to Germany, it caused instability in other places. The empire of Austria-Hungary included people from many different cultural groups. One of these groups was the Slavs. Slavic nationalists wanted to break away from Austria-Hungary and join the independent Slavic country of Serbia on the

Balkan Peninsula. Leaders of Austria-Hungary reacted angrily, seeing this movement as a threat to their empire.

Another source of tension in Europe was imperialism. Britain's huge empire, stretching from Africa to Asia, brought it wealth and power. Eager to share in such benefits, other European powers competed for control of overseas territories. Fierce competition for territory took place within Europe as well. For example, Germany had taken the Alsace-Lorraine region from France in the Franco-Prussian War in 1871. France wanted it back.

In this competitive atmosphere, nations focused their resources on **militarism**—the aggressive strengthening of armed forces. European nations raced to build armies and navies that were larger than ever before.

As nations became more powerful, they sought to protect themselves by forming new alliances. Germany formed an alliance with Austria-Hungary in 1879. Each promised to defend the other in case of enemy attack. Concerned with Germany's growing power, France and Russia created their own alliance in 1893. Britain joined France and Russia in 1907.

The Spark

With so much hostility dividing the nations of Europe, a German general felt that "a European war is bound to come sooner or later." All that was needed was a spark to set Europe on fire. That spark flew from the Balkan province of Bosnia and Herzegovina.

Bosnia and Herzegovina had gained independence from Turkish rule in 1878. In 1908, however, Austria-Hungary annexed the province. Slavic nationalists resisted violently—they wanted the region to be part of Serbia.

On June 28, 1914, **Archduke Francis Ferdinand**, heir to the throne of Austria-Hungary, visited the province's capital of Sarajevo with his wife, Sophie. While riding through the streets, they were shot and killed by a 19-year-old Serb nationalist named Gavrilo Princip.

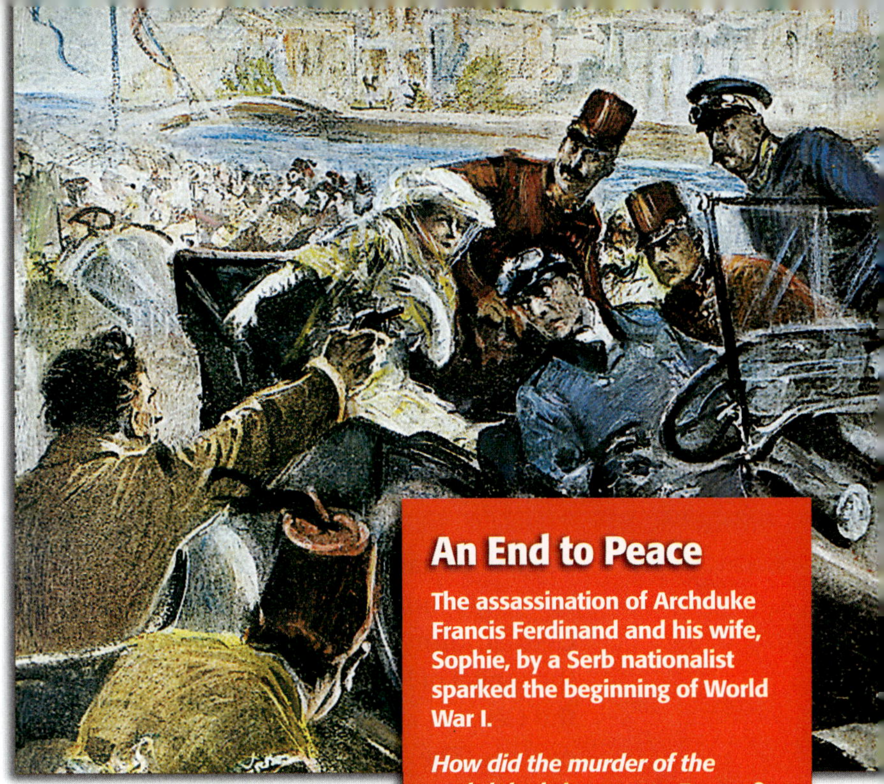

An End to Peace

The assassination of Archduke Francis Ferdinand and his wife, Sophie, by a Serb nationalist sparked the beginning of World War I.

How did the murder of the archduke bring war to Europe?

The assassination shattered Europe's fragile peace. Determined to crush Serbia and the Slavic nationalists, Austria-Hungary declared war on Serbia. Very quickly, other countries were pulled into the fighting. Russia had promised to support Serbia in case of war. It began to **mobilize**, or prepare its military for war. On August 1 Germany, Austria-Hungary's ally, declared war on Russia. Two days later, Germany also declared war on France, Russia's ally. To reach France quickly, the German army marched into Belgium on August 4. Britain, which had promised to support Belgium, then declared war on Germany.

As the fighting started, the alliance between Austria-Hungary and Germany came to be known as the **Central Powers**. Bulgaria and the Ottoman Empire later sided with the Central Powers. France, Russia, and Britain were known as the **Allied Powers**. Italy joined them in 1915. Over the next several years, soldiers from 30 nations and six continents would fight in what was then called the Great War. The conflict later became known as World War I.

READING CHECK **Identifying Cause and Effect** How did nationalism contribute to political tensions in Europe?

Early Battles of the War

Focus on Reading
What mistake did the German leaders make in their reasoning?

Both sides expected the war to be over in a few months. German leaders planned to defeat France quickly, before Russia could join the fighting. But as the Germans marched toward France, they met fierce resistance from Belgian soldiers. This gave Britain and France time to mobilize their own troops.

The First Battle of the Marne

Belgian resistance slowed the German advance but could not stop it. On September 3 the German army was just 25 miles from Paris, the capital of France. The French army blocked the German advance at the Marne River, east of Paris. The First Battle of the Marne raged for several days before the Germans were pushed back.

By mid-September French and German troops faced each other along a long battle line called the western front. The western front stretched from the North Sea all the way to Switzerland. Meanwhile, the Russian and German armies were struggling back and forth along the eastern front, which reached from the Black Sea to the Baltic Sea. It quickly became clear that this war would be longer and deadlier than anyone had expected.

A New Kind of War

Part of what made World War I so long and deadly was a new technique called **trench warfare**—defending a position by fighting from the protection of deep ditches. When the French defeated the Germans in the First Battle of the Marne, the Germans did not retreat far. Instead, they dug trenches nearby. Opposite them, the French dug their own trenches. A 400-mile-long network of trenches soon stretched across the western front.

Soldiers fought in these cold, wet, and muddy ditches, sometimes for months at a time. The filthy trenches were perfect breeding

History Close-up

Trench Warfare

grounds for germs, and soldiers on both sides died from disease. An American in the French army described life in the trenches:

> "The impossibility of the simplest kind of personal cleanliness makes vermin [bugs] a universal ill, against which there is no remedy. Cold, dirt, discomfort, are the ever present conditions, and the soldier's life comes to mean ... the most misery that the human organism [body] can support."
>
> —Alan Seeger, *Letters and Diary of Alan Seeger*

The empty patch of ground between enemy trenches came to be known as "no-man's-land." This area was quickly stripped of trees and blasted full of holes by artillery shells. Anyone who ventured into no-man's-land was likely to be killed by enemy fire.

Another factor that made World War I deadlier than previous wars was the use of modern technology. New machine guns, for example, could fire 400 to 600 bullets a minute. Enormous artillery guns fired shells over the trenches, where they exploded and sent speeding scraps of metal onto the soldiers below. Other shells spread poisonous gases. If soldiers were not wearing gas masks, the gas destroyed their lungs, causing slow, painful deaths. Poisonous gases were originally banned but came into use by both sides by the end of the war.

Other new weapons included tanks and airplanes. Tanks are armored combat vehicles that can cause heavy damage but cannot be destroyed easily. Airplanes were used to fire down on soldiers in trenches and to gather information about enemy locations. Airplanes also battled each other in fights called "dogfights."

THE IMPACT TODAY

Many of the weapons first used in World War I, such as tanks and airplanes, are still used in warfare today. The use of poison gas, however, has been outlawed by international treaties.

Land and Sea Battles

After a year of vicious fighting, the war had become a **stalemate**—a situation in which neither side can win a decisive victory. Determined to break the stalemate, both sides launched massive attacks in 1916. In February 1916 the Germans attacked the French city of Verdun, at the southern end of the western front. That summer, the Allies staged an attack along the Somme River, in northeastern

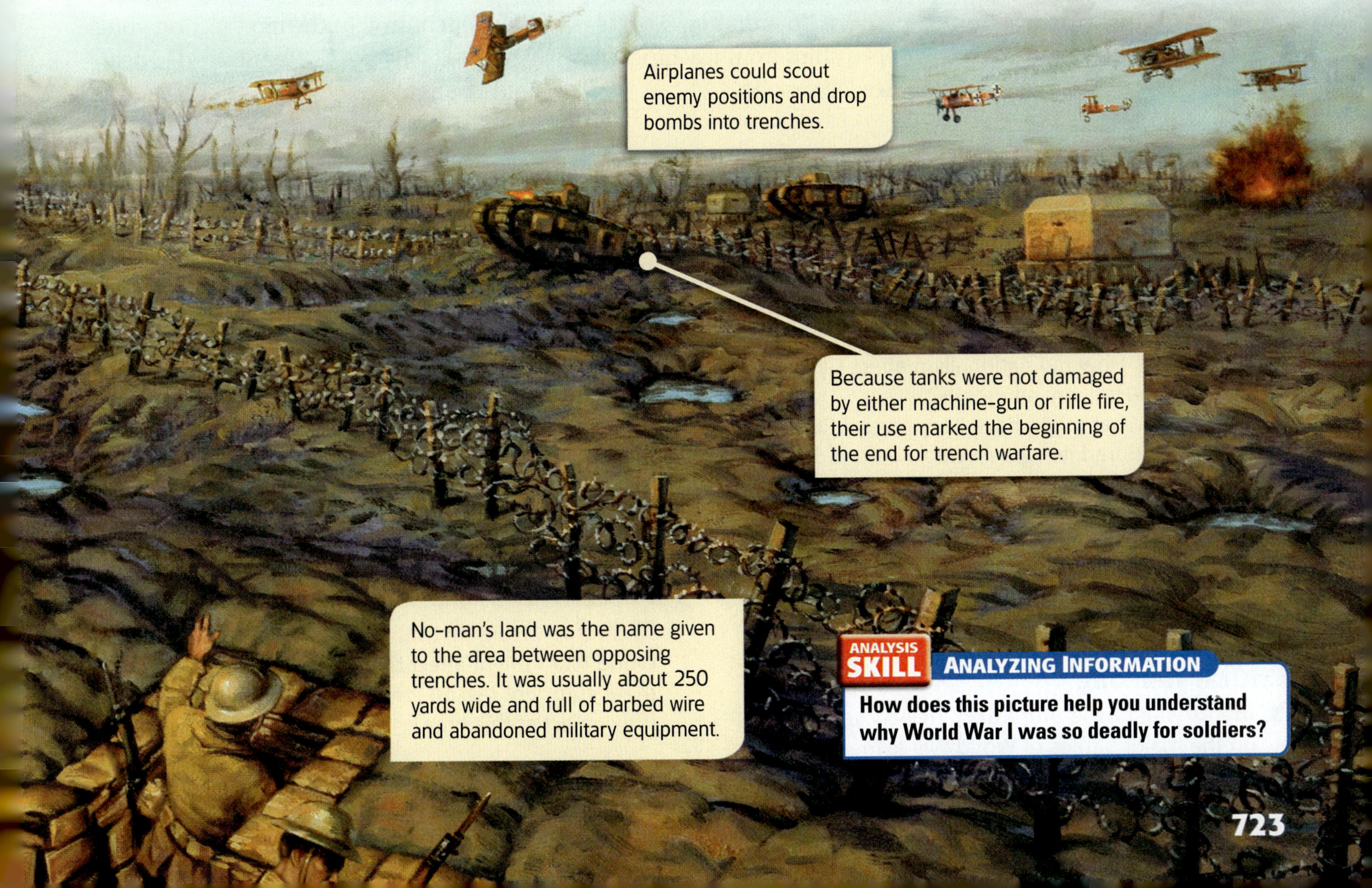

Airplanes could scout enemy positions and drop bombs into trenches.

Because tanks were not damaged by either machine-gun or rifle fire, their use marked the beginning of the end for trench warfare.

No-man's land was the name given to the area between opposing trenches. It was usually about 250 yards wide and full of barbed wire and abandoned military equipment.

ANALYSIS SKILL **ANALYZING INFORMATION**

How does this picture help you understand why World War I was so deadly for soldiers?

German U-boats

Germany developed small submarines called U-boats as part of its war strategy. U-boats could strike Allied ships without being seen. They destroyed around 10 million tons of Allied and neutral ships and cargo from 1914 to 1918.

Why might U-boats have been so effective against the Allies?

France. Both battles raged for months, as the armies attacked and counterattacked.

By the end of the year, the Germans had failed to take Verdun. At the Somme River, the Allies had advanced just seven miles. Almost nothing had changed on the western front. But nearly 1 million men had been killed at Verdun and the Somme River.

ACADEMIC VOCABULARY
neutral unbiased, not favoring either side in a conflict

As the stalemate on land dragged on, sea battles in the Atlantic Ocean and the North Sea became even more important. The powerful British navy blockaded the ports of the Central Powers and laid explosive mines in the North Sea. These could blow a huge hole in a ship, sinking it in minutes. The tactic effectively stopped ships from reaching German ports with needed supplies.

The Germans responded by using submarines called **U-boats**. U-boats launched torpedoes against Allied supply ships, causing heavy losses. The Germans also attacked ships belonging to **neutral** countries they believed were helping the Allies. This would soon pull the United States into World War I.

READING CHECK **Categorizing** What new technologies did armies in World War I use?

SUMMARY AND PREVIEW World War I became a stalemate by 1916 as countries battled for control. In the next section you will find out why the United States decided to join the fighting.

Section 1 Assessment

go.hrw.com
Online Quiz
KEYWORD: SC7 HP23

Reviewing Ideas, Terms, and People

1. a. **Describe** What factors contributed to the outbreak of World War I?
   b. **Contrast** How did nationalism affect Germany and Austria-Hungary differently?
   c. **Predict** What might have happened if Russia had not honored its agreement to defend Serbia?
2. a. **Identify** What were the outcomes of the early battles of the war?
   b. **Explain** How did Belgian resistance affect the German war plan?
   c. **Evaluate** How successful was **trench warfare** as a strategy?

Critical Thinking

3. **Identifying Cause and Effect** Review your notes on the major battles of World War I. Then copy the graphic organizer below and use it to show the outcomes of these early battles and how they affected the war.

Battle	Outcome	Results

FOCUS ON SPEAKING

4. **Analyzing Rising Tensions** Start a list of ways that World War I might affect the United States. Was there sufficient reason for the United States to join the conflict at this time?

Americans Prepare for War

SECTION 2

If YOU were there...

Everywhere you go people are talking about the war in Europe. The United States has just joined the fighting on the side of the Allied Powers. Many young men you know are volunteering to fight. Women are signing up to drive ambulances or work as nurses. You know that the situation in Europe is dangerous, but you want to serve your country.

Will you volunteer for service in World War I?

BUILDING BACKGROUND When World War I began, the United States had a long history of avoiding involvement in European conflicts. Most Americans wanted the United States to remain neutral in this war as well. But as tensions with Germany increased, it became clear that distance from Europe would not keep Americans out of battle.

The United States Enters World War I

Millions of Americans at this time were immigrants or children of immigrants. Many came from countries belonging to the Allied or Central Powers. They naturally sympathized with their former homelands. This did not change the fact that most Americans viewed World War I as a European conflict. They did not want American soldiers sent to the bloody battlefields of Europe. Shortly after World War I began, President Woodrow Wilson announced that the United States would remain neutral. Most Americans agreed that America should stay out of the war.

American Neutrality Threatened

Although the United States had a policy of neutrality, its merchants continued to trade with European nations. American ships carried supplies and war materials to the Allies. U.S. banks invested $2 billion in European war bonds, nearly all of it in Allied countries.

The Germans used U-boat attacks to try to stop supplies from reaching the Allies. Sometimes they attacked ships without

What You Will Learn...

Main Ideas

1. The United States entered the war after repeated crises with Germany.
2. The United States mobilized for war by training troops and stepping up production of supplies.
3. Labor shortages created new wartime opportunities for women and other Americans.

The Big Idea

After entering World War I in 1917, Americans began the massive effort of preparing for war.

Key Terms and People

Lusitania, *p. 726*
Zimmermann Note, *p. 726*
Selective Service Act, *p. 727*
Liberty bonds, *p. 727*
National War Labor Board, *p. 729*

TAKING NOTES As you read, take notes on the new laws and government programs created to prepare for World War I. In each outer circle of this web, name one new law or program. You may need to add more circles.

warning. In May 1915 a German U-boat sank the ***Lusitania***, a British passenger liner. Nearly 1,200 people, including 128 Americans, were killed. The incident fueled anti-German feeling in the United States. Throughout the coming war, German Americans faced nativist attacks, including anti-German speeches, discrimination, and physical attacks.

Secretary of State William Jennings Bryan resigned over President Wilson's handling of the affair. Bryan thought that Wilson's protest note to the Germans was designed to bring the United States into the war.

In March 1916 a U-boat attacked the *Sussex,* a French passenger ship. Several of the 80 casualties were Americans. Wilson demanded that the Germans stop attacking nonmilitary ships. German leaders responded with the *Sussex* pledge, agreeing not to attack merchant ships without warning.

Congress Declares War

When Wilson ran for reelection in 1916, the promise to remain neutral helped him win the election. Nearly a year after the *Sussex* pledge, however, the Germans again began launching attacks on ships, including American vessels. In response, Wilson broke off diplomatic relations with Germany.

The United States stepped closer to war when Americans found out about the **Zimmermann Note**. This secret telegram to Mexico sent by the German foreign minister, Arthur Zimmermann, was decoded and then published by American newspapers in March 1917. In the note, Zimmermann proposed an alliance against the United States. He promised that Germany would help Mexico recapture areas that Mexico had lost during the Mexican-American War.

The American public was outraged by the telegram. President Wilson asked Congress to declare war on Germany. "The world must be made safe for democracy," he proclaimed. Congress declared war on April 6, 1917.

READING CHECK **Finding Main Ideas** What events challenged U.S. neutrality?

Primary Source

NEWSPAPER ARTICLE

Sinking of the *Lusitania*

In 1915 German U-boats sank the Lusitania, *an event that pushed the United States toward entry into World War I. Newspapers quickly spread news of the disaster.*

The accounts which have so far been received are fragmentary, and give no clear idea of the disaster. There is, however, no doubt that two torpedoes were fired without warning into the starboard side of the ship soon after 2 o'clock yesterday afternoon. There were conflicting accounts of the period during which the *Lusitania* remained afloat, but the Cunard Company states that she sunk 40 minutes after being struck.

—*The Register*, quoted in the *Times of London*

The ship was treated as an enemy warship.

The ship sank before enough rescue ships could arrive.

ANALYSIS SKILL **ANALYZING PRIMARY SOURCES**

How might this disaster draw the United States into war with Germany?

Supreme Court Decisions

Schenck v. *United States* (1919)

Background of the Case Charles Schenck was arrested for violating the Espionage Act. He had printed and distributed pamphlets urging resistance to the draft. Schenck argued that the First Amendment, which guarantees freedom of speech and freedom of the press, gave him the right to criticize the government.

The Court's Ruling

The Supreme Court ruled that the pamphlet was not protected by the First Amendment and that the Espionage Act was constitutional.

The Court's Reasoning

The Supreme Court decided that under certain circumstances, such as a state of war, Congress could limit free speech. The Court created a test to distinguish between protected and unprotected speech. Unprotected speech would have to present "a clear and present danger" to national security. For example, the First Amendment would not protect a person who created a panic by yelling "Fire!" in a crowded theater.

Why It Matters

Schenck v. *United States* was important because it was the first case in which the Supreme Court interpreted the First Amendment. The Court concluded that certain constitutional rights, such as free speech, could be limited under extraordinary conditions, such as war. Later rulings by the Court narrowed the test of "clear and present danger" to speech advocating violence. The nonviolent expression of ideas and opinions—however unpopular—was thereby protected.

ANALYSIS SKILL **ANALYZING INFORMATION**

1. According to the Supreme Court, when could free speech be limited?
2. How do you think this case affected other people who opposed the war?

Mobilizing for War

In order to persuade the public to support the war effort, President Wilson formed the Committee on Public Information (CPI). The CPI organized rallies and parades and published posters and pamphlets. Speakers known as "four-minute men" gave short patriotic speeches in movie theaters and churches.

The U.S. government's war effort also involved limiting some freedoms in the United States. The Espionage Act of 1917 and the Sedition Act of 1918 restricted free speech and allowed the government to arrest opponents of the war. Antiwar mail was prohibited and seized. About 900 opponents of the war were jailed for violating these laws. The Sedition Act was later repealed, but the Espionage Act is still in effect today.

To prepare the U.S. military, Congress passed the **Selective Service Act** in 1917. The act required men between the ages of 21 and 30 to register to be drafted. Almost 3 million Americans were drafted into service in World War I. A number of the draftees were African Americans. Altogether, about 400,000 African Americans served in the war. Their units were segregated from white forces and were commanded by white officers. Eventually, African Americans were trained as officers. During World War I, however, they were never placed in command of white troops.

Preparations for war were very expensive. Troops had to be trained, supplied, transported, and fed. Ships and airplanes had to be built and fueled. The government raised taxes and issued war bonds. Money from the sale of these **Liberty bonds** provided billions of dollars in loans to the Allies.

The government took other actions to supply the troops. The War Industries Board (WIB) oversaw the production and distribution of steel, copper, cement, and rubber. The Food Administration worked to increase food supplies for the troops. It guaranteed farmers high prices for their crops. To conserve food at home, citizens were encouraged to practice "meatless Mondays" and "wheatless Wednesdays." Many people also grew their own vegetables in "victory gardens" at home.

READING CHECK **Analyzing** How did the U.S. government gain public support for the war?

FOCUS ON NORTH CAROLINA

In 1918 Camp Bragg was established as a U.S. military installation. Many soldiers who fought in World War I were trained at Camp Bragg and two other camps in North Carolina. After the war the two other camps closed, but in 1922 Camp Bragg was recommissioned as Fort Bragg. It has since become the largest artillery base in the world and the home of several airborne units.

THE IMPACT TODAY

To conserve fuel used for lighting for the war effort, daylight saving time was first introduced in March 1918. The plan is still in effect today.

Linking to Today

Women on the Battlefield

The role of women in World War I was much like their roles in previous wars—providing support for male troops. Women drove ambulances and entered the battlefield as nurses and medics. Red Cross volunteers were often responsible for the first stage of treatment of the wounded. Today, women may also serve in the military as soldiers. They are not allowed to fight in ground combat, but they do serve as guards and pilots, and in the navy.

Red Cross volunteers in World War I

Soldier on duty in Iraq

ANALYSIS SKILL: ANALYZING INFORMATION

How have wartime roles for women changed since World War I?

New Wartime Opportunities

Three main factors led to a shortage of labor in the United States during the war. First, American factories were working nonstop to produce weapons and supplies for the Allied forces. Factories needed new workers to meet this huge demand. Second, the war almost completely cut off immigration. As you know, immigrants had provided a steady source of labor to American industry. And third, many of the young men who would normally take factory jobs were off fighting in Europe.

Women's War Efforts

This labor shortage created new opportunities for many workers. American women took on new roles to help the war effort. Some 1 million women joined the U.S. workforce during the war years. For many, this was their first experience working outside the home.

Women also worked for the war effort in Europe. About 25,000 American women volunteered as nurses, telephone operators, signalers, typists, and interpreters in France. Women were not given jobs in combat, but they braved gunfire at the front lines as nurses and ambulance drivers. One female driver described her World War I experiences:

> "We had our first air-raid work last night. I was the night driver on duty . . . Some bombs fell very near just as I got to the [hospital] . . . when shrapnel [metal fragments] whizzed past my head and there was a tremendous crash close beside . . . Then an ambulance call came and I tore off."
>
> —Mrs. Guy Napier-Martin, quoted in *The Overseas War Record of the Winsor School, 1914–1919*

Other women, meanwhile, spoke out against U.S. participation in the war. Social reformer Jane Addams was against U.S. entry into the war. Jeannette Rankin of Montana, the first female member of Congress, was one of 50 House members to cast a vote against declaring war in 1917. "I want to stand by my country," she said, "but I cannot vote for war."

Labor and the War

Even with so many women joining the workforce, factories needed additional workers. New job opportunities encouraged Mexican Americans from the West and African Americans from the South to move to northern industrial cities.

Because labor was scarce, workers were in a good position to demand better wages and conditions. Union membership increased. More than 4 million unionized workers went on strike during the war. Because factory owners could not easily replace workers, they often agreed to demands.

President Wilson set up the **National War Labor Board** in April 1918. The board helped workers and management avoid strikes and reach agreements. The board settled more than 1,000 labor disputes. Its members were generally sympathetic to workers. They helped establish a minimum wage and limited work hours. They also required fair pay for women.

READING CHECK **Finding Main Ideas** How did war mobilization benefit American workers?

Patriotic Posters

Posters like this one encouraged American citizens to participate in the effort to provide weapons and food to soldiers fighting in World War I.

How does this poster inspire patriotism?

SUMMARY AND PREVIEW The war effort created new opportunities for women and other Americans. In the next section you will learn about what life was like for soldiers overseas.

Section 2 Assessment

go.hrw.com
Online Quiz
KEYWORD: SC7 HP23

Reviewing Ideas, Terms, and People

1. **a. Explain** Why did the United States enter World War I?
   b. Evaluate Do you think the United States was right to stay neutral for so long? Why or why not?
2. **a. Explain** How did the United States prepare for war?
   b. Recall What was the purpose of the Committee on Public Information?
   c. Summarize How did the government exercise control over the economy during the war?
3. **a. Describe** How did women help the war effort abroad?
   b. Predict How do you think the end of the war affected labor unions? Explain your answer.

Critical Thinking

4. **Problem Solving** Review your notes on new laws and government programs during World War I. Then copy the graphic organizer below and use it to identify the challenges the United States faced when mobilizing for World War I. List which new laws, government programs, and other changes responded to those challenges.

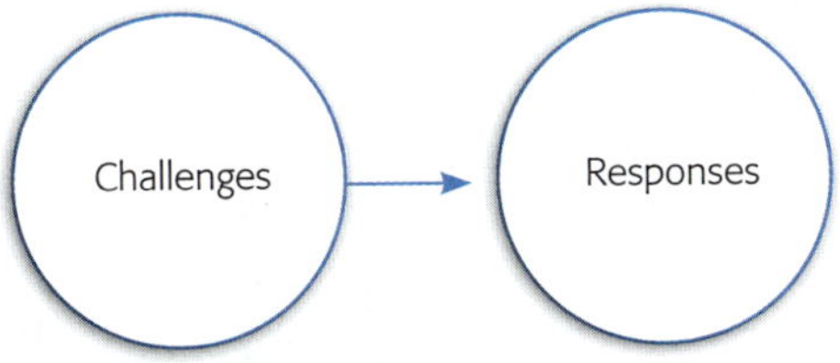

FOCUS ON SPEAKING

5. **Analyzing Wilson's Policies** Add to your list examples of causes of growing tension between Germany and the United States. What events led President Wilson to support war with Germany? Do you agree with his view? Why or why not?

SECTION 3

Americans in World War I

What You Will Learn...

Main Ideas

1. American soldiers started to arrive in Europe in 1917.
2. The Americans helped the Allies win the war.
3. Germany agreed to an armistice after suffering heavy losses.

The Big Idea

American troops helped the Allies achieve victory in World War I.

Key Terms and People

American Expeditionary Force, *p. 730*
Communists, *p. 731*
armistice, *p. 734*

TAKING NOTES As you read, take notes on the achievements and victories of the American Expeditionary Force (AEF). Organize your notes in a chart like this one.

Achievements of the AEF

If YOU were there...

It is April 1918. You are marching into Paris with your army unit on your way to the front lines. Women and children throw flowers from windows and balconies as you pass through the city. You want to do whatever it takes to defend this city and its residents. You know that defeating Germany will be difficult and very dangerous.

Do you think American forces can help the Allies win the war?

BUILDING BACKGROUND Preparations for war helped make the United States a strong military power. By 1918 nearly 5 million Americans were serving in the army, navy, and marine corps. While this huge armed force was being trained, however, the fighting in Europe was going badly for the Allies. French and British leaders were eager for help from America.

American Soldiers Arrive

By the time U.S. troops started to arrive in Europe in 1917, the Allies were dangerously near defeat. German forces were advancing in France, once again driving toward Paris. The German navy was destroying Allied ships at sea. And on the eastern front, the Russians were desperately struggling to hold back the Germans.

Joining the Fight

French and British generals called for immediate help on the front lines. They wanted the U.S. troops, known as the **American Expeditionary Force** (AEF), to join French and British units. But General John J. Pershing, leader of the American troops, insisted that the Americans join the fight as a separate force. He refused to have the AEF "scattered among the Allied forces where it will not be an American army at all."

Pershing also demanded that his troops be thoroughly trained for combat before rushing to the front lines. The AEF included many well-trained regular army and National Guard troops. But it also included a large number of inexperienced volunteers and draftees. Pershing gave the men three months of intense training in army discipline and trench warfare. He believed that taking the time to train his soldiers would help the Allies achieve victory.

Russia Leaves the War

While Pershing trained his troops, the Allies' position became even more dangerous. In November 1917 a group of Russians called the Bolsheviks overthrew the Russian government and seized power. The Bolsheviks were **Communists**—people who favor the equal distribution of wealth and the end of all forms of private property.

Led by Vladimir Lenin, the new Russian government faced a desperate situation. Around 8 million Russians had been killed or wounded during the war. Soldiers were deserting from the eastern front, and sailors were leaving naval bases. Food riots raged in the cities. The Russians could not keep fighting under these conditions. In March 1918 Russia signed the Treaty of Brest-Litovsk, a peace agreement with the Central Powers. A civil war then broke out in Russia between the Communists and forces loyal to the czar (ZAHR), Russia's emperor. The United States and other Allied countries sent aid to the czarist forces. Russia, however, one of the main Allied Powers, was out of World War I.

READING CHECK **Drawing Inferences** Why do you think General Pershing refused to put American troops in foreign units?

Winning the War

With Russia out of the fighting, German generals saw a chance to win the war. In the spring of 1918 Germany transferred many of its divisions of troops from the eastern front to the western front. Germany planned to smash the stalemate.

World War I U.S. Soldier

ANALYSIS SKILL **ANALYZING VISUALS**

How did clothing and supplies help a U.S. soldier in the battlefield?

The Final Battles

At the same time, American soldiers arrived. Even training had not prepared them for the realities of war. The troops lived on dried beef, hard biscuits, and canned emergency rations. The men shared the trenches with rats, lice, and sometimes the bodies of dead soldiers. A soldiers' song of the time described the situation:

> "Sing me to sleep where bullets fall,
> Let me forget the war and all;
> Damp is my dug-out [trench], cold my feet,
> Nothing but bully [canned meat] and biscuits
> to eat."
>
> —Quoted in *Great Push: An Episode of the Great War,* by Patrick MacGill

GEOGRAPHY SKILLS **INTERPRETING MAPS**

1. **Human-Environment Interaction** Why was the British naval blockade located where it was?
2. **Location** In which country were the most battles fought, according to this map?

On March 21, 1918, the Germans began blasting more than 6,000 heavy guns at Allied troops along the Somme River in northern France. German forces drove 40 miles into Allied lines before the advance stalled. Some 250,000 Germans had been killed or wounded. British and French casualties totaled 133,000.

The Germans then attacked farther south, advancing to the Marne River and pushing the French line back toward Paris. At this critical moment, General Pershing promised Allied commander Ferdinand Foch: "Infantry, artillery, aviation—all that we have . . . The American people would be proud to be engaged in the greatest battle of history." Two divisions of the AEF joined French forces.

The Germans were unprepared for the fresh energy and fighting skills of the Americans. The U.S. soldiers succeeded in stopping the German advance less than 50 miles from Paris. Then, at Belleau Wood, the Allies attacked and gradually drove the Germans back.

German generals became desperate. In July 1918 they launched their final offensive—one last attempt to cross the Marne River. Terrible losses on the German side stopped the German offensive and protected Paris from invasion. Although they suffered about 12,000 casualities, American troops had helped force a major turning point in the war.

Driving the Germans Back

Now the Allies drove toward victory. There were more than 1 million U.S. troops in France, and they played a key role in the later battles of the war. In September 1918 Allied forces attacked and defeated the Germans at the town of Saint-Mihiel on the border of France and Germany. Along the Meuse River and in the Argonne Forest, near the French-Belgian border, American and Allied troops again attacked German forces.

Among the many heroes of these battles was a young man from Tennessee named Alvin York. In October 1918 York killed 25 German gunners and captured 132 prisoners. His heroism earned him fame and many awards, including the Congressional Medal of Honor. His life story even became the basis for a popular movie in 1941.

Also among the brave American troops were the African American soldiers of the 369th Infantry. Known as the Harlem Hellfighters, the 369th spent more time in combat than any other American unit. Its members were the first to reach the Rhine River on the German border. France awarded them the prized Croix de Guerre (Cross of War) medal for their bravery.

The Allies were also winning the war at sea. Allied war planners used a new **strategy** called the convoy system to protect their ships. This meant that destroyers capable of sinking U-boats escorted and protected groups of Allied merchant ships.

ACADEMIC VOCABULARY

strategy a plan for fighting a battle or war

By November 1918, American soldiers were making rapid advances toward Germany. "For the first time the enemy lines were completely broken through," reported General Pershing.

READING CHECK **Sequencing** Identify significant events leading to the turning of the tide in the war.

Armistice

At home and on the battlefield, Germans were tired of war. Food was so scarce in Germany that more than 800 German civilians were dying of starvation every day. In Germany and other nations of the Central Powers, food riots and strikes occurred. Germany was also running out of soldiers. In addition to those killed or wounded in 1918, one quarter of Germany's fighting men had been captured by the Allies.

Germany's allies were also eager to end the war. Bulgaria and the Ottoman Empire quit the war in the fall of 1918. Austria-Hungary reached a peace agreement with the Allies on November 3. Seeing that his country was beaten, the German leader, Kaiser Wilhelm II, gave up his throne and fled to the Netherlands.

FOCUS ON NORTH CAROLINA

The war drove up prices for many consumer goods and agricultural products. After the war, North Carolina experienced a recession as the demand for agricultural products, textiles, and tobacco fell. Larger producers weathered the economic downturn easily, but smaller farms and factories were put out of business by the falling prices.

The 369th Infantry

The 369th Infantry spent 191 days in combat, longer than any other American force sent to Europe during World War I. Its members aided French forces at Château-Thierry and Belleau Wood, receiving the Croix de Guerre for their bravery. The "Harlem Hellfighters" became famous throughout Europe and America for their valor.

The Croix de Guerre was created by France in 1915 to reward bravery by members of the Allied armed forces—French citizens and foreigners alike.

The Germans then agreed to a cease-fire. The Allies demanded that Germany pull back from all its conquered territory. They insisted that Germany destroy its aircraft, tanks, and big guns, and surrender its U-boats. The Germans had no choice but to accept these demands to disarm. The **armistice**, or truce, went into effect on the 11th hour of the 11th day of the 11th month of 1918. "At eleven o'clock everything got so quiet that the silence was nearly unbearable," remembered an American soldier. Then the silence was broken with shouts like "I've lived through the war!"

READING CHECK **Analyzing** How did Allied troops break the stalemate with Germany?

SUMMARY AND PREVIEW America's entry into World War I helped the Allies achieve victory. In the next section, you will learn about the effort to work out a permanent peace agreement.

Section 3 Assessment

go.hrw.com
Online Quiz
KEYWORD: SC7 HP23

Reviewing Ideas, Terms, and People

1. a. **Define** What was the **American Expeditionary Force**?
   b. **Analyze** How did the Russian Revolution change the course of the war?
   c. **Evaluate** Why did Russia leave the war?
2. a. **Analyze** How did U.S. troops make a difference in the final battles of the war?
   b. **Recall** How was the Second Battle of the Marne a turning point in the war?
3. a. **Describe** What was Germany required to surrender in the **armistice**?
   b. **Interpret** Were the terms of the armistice fair? Explain your answer.

Critical Thinking

4. **Categorizing** Review your notes on the victories of the American Expeditionary Force. Then copy the graphic organizer below and use it to list challenges the Allies faced from 1917 to 1918. List the Allies' achievements during the same time period.

Allied Challenges	
Allied Achievements	

FOCUS ON SPEAKING

5. **Analyzing the War's Effects on Soldiers** What examples from this section could you add to your list of how World War I events affected the United States? How did American soldiers contribute to the Allied war effort? What were conditions like for American soldiers? Do you think U.S. involvement was justified?

Establishing Peace

SECTION 4

If YOU were there...

Your older brother was drafted in 1917 and sent to fight on the western front in Europe. He has written home about the terrible conditions in the trenches and the horror of seeing men killed in battle. Now the war is over. You read in the newspaper that a peace treaty is being negotiated in Paris, France.

What do you hope the peace treaty will say?

BUILDING BACKGROUND After World War I, many questions about the future remained. Who would pay for the huge costs of the war? How should defeated powers' territories be divided? How could countries work together to avoid another world war? Leaders began discussing and debating these questions.

The Costs of War

While soldiers and civilians around the world celebrated the end of World War I in November 1918, the tragedy of war was never far from people's minds. When asked what the armistice meant, one British soldier simply said, "Time to bury the dead."

War Dead

The number of soldiers killed in World War I was beyond anything the world had ever experienced. About 5 million Allied soldiers and 3.5 million soldiers from the Central Powers died in combat. More than 20 million soldiers on both sides were wounded. The war devastated an entire generation of young men in many European nations. In France, for example, 90 percent of the healthy young men had served in World War I. More than 7 out of 10 of these men were killed or wounded. While the United States escaped this extreme level of devastation, American forces did suffer heavy losses. Some 116,000 U.S. troops died, and about 200,000 were wounded.

Financial Losses

Along with the shocking human losses, the war brought financial disaster to many parts of Europe. Factories and farms were left in ruins. "For mile after mile nothing was left," said one British visitor

What You Will Learn...

Main Ideas

1. The costs of war included millions of human lives as well as financial burdens.
2. President Woodrow Wilson and European leaders met to work out a peace agreement.
3. The U.S. Senate rejected the Treaty of Versailles.

The Big Idea

The United States and the victorious Allied Powers clashed over postwar plans.

Key Terms and People

League of Nations, *p. 737*
reparations, *p. 737*
Treaty of Versailles, *p. 738*
Henry Cabot Lodge, *p. 738*

TAKING NOTES As you read, take notes on the provisions of the Treaty of Versailles. You can use a graphic organizer like the one below to keep track of your notes.

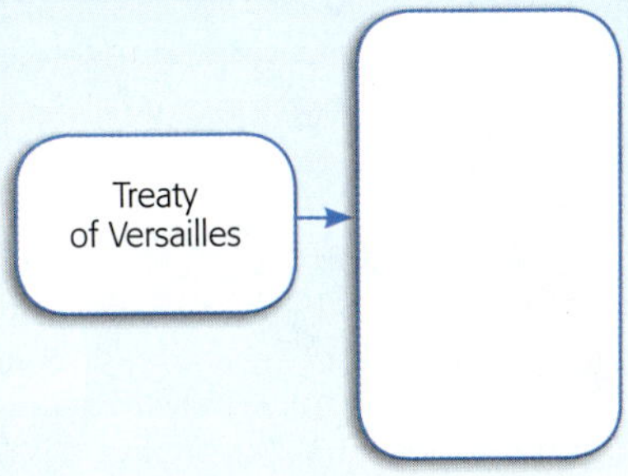

THE IMPACT TODAY

Today, vaccinations help prevent major outbreaks of the flu and other contagious diseases.

about the French countryside. "No building was habitable [livable] and no field fit for the plow." With farmers unable to raise crops, severe food shortages occurred.

The overall economic cost of the war was huge. Property worth $30 billion had been destroyed. The Allies had spent $145 billion on the war effort, and the Central Powers had spent $63 billion. France and Britain had borrowed large amounts of money to fight the war, and now they were deeply in debt to American banks. Germany was also in debt, and its people faced starvation.

The Influenza Epidemic

The world was in for another shock in 1918 when a worldwide epidemic of influenza, or flu, broke out. The virus was extremely contagious and deadly. Over the next two years, it spread around the world, killing approximately 30 million people—even more than the war itself.

The epidemic started in an army training camp in Kansas. Because the flu is transmitted through the air, it spread rapidly. American soldiers unknowingly spread the disease to other army camps, to American civilians, and eventually to soldiers and civilians in Europe. One American doctor said that seeing stacks of bodies at an army camp in Massachusetts "beats any sight they ever had in France after a battle." Half of the Americans who died during this period died from influenza.

The epidemic changed life everywhere in the United States. In Chicago, for example, the flu more than doubled the normal death rate in the fall of 1918. Many of those killed were young and strong. State and local governments took measures to prevent the spread of the disease. Kearney, Nebraska, imposed a quarantine, forbidding people who were ill from leaving their homes. Many cities banned public gatherings, including school classes. A man named Dan Tonkel remembered what life was like for children in his hometown of Goldsboro, North Carolina:

> "I felt like I was walking on eggshells. I was afraid to go out, to play with my playmates, my classmates, my neighbors . . . I remember I was actually afraid to breathe. People were afraid to talk to each other. It was like—don't breathe in my face, don't even look at me, because you might give me germs that will kill me."
>
> —Dan Tonkel, quoted in *Influenza 1918: The Worst Epidemic in American History,* by Lynette Lezzoni

Although there was no cure for the flu, people would try anything. One woman surrounded her daughter with raw onions. Another remembered, "We hung bags of . . . garlic about our necks. We smelled awful, but it was okay, because everyone smelled bad." By the time the influenza epidemic ended in 1919, it had killed 800,000 Americans at home and abroad.

READING CHECK **Finding Main Ideas** What made the influenza epidemic of 1918 so deadly?

Memorials to soldiers killed in World War I, like this one at Somme, France, are located throughout Europe.

ANALYSIS SKILL **ANALYZING VISUALS**

Did the Allied or Central Powers have more casualties?

The Peace Agreement

Even before the United States entered World War I, President Woodrow Wilson began making plans for a peace agreement. He was determined to do everything possible to prevent another world war. On January 8, 1918, Wilson outlined his vision for the postwar world in a plan known as the Fourteen Points.

Wilson's Fourteen Points

Wilson's Fourteen Points were a list of specific proposals for postwar peace. Several of the points would settle national border disputes. Others called for military cutbacks, proposed lower tariffs, and banned secret agreements between nations. Another proposed settlements for colonial peoples who wished to be independent. This reflected Wilson's strong belief in self-determination—the right of people to choose their own political status. The final point called for the creation of an international assembly of nations called the **League of Nations**. The League's mission would be to work to settle international disputes and encourage democracy.

European leaders disagreed with Wilson's vision for the peace settlement, wanting it to clearly punish Germany for its role in the war. They wanted to prevent Germany from ever again becoming a world power.

The Treaty of Versailles

President Wilson traveled to Europe to attend the Paris Peace Conference, which was held at the palace of Versailles (ver-SY), outside of Paris. Wilson felt it was his duty to "play my full part in making good what [our soldiers] offered their lives to obtain."

The leaders, called the Big Four—President Wilson, British prime minister David Lloyd George, French premier Georges Clemenceau, and Italian prime minister Vittorio Orlando—took control of the conference. No representatives from Russia or the Central Powers attended.

Many Allied leaders defended their own country's interests and insisted on severe punishment for Germany. They wanted Germany to accept complete blame for the war and pay for the damage it had caused. These **reparations**, or payments for war damages, were set at $33 billion. France and the other Allies also wanted to take control of large parts of German territory.

BIOGRAPHY

Woodrow Wilson

1856–1924

Woodrow Wilson was born in Virginia in 1856. The terrible destruction he saw as a child during the Civil War would later influence his response to World War I. As president, he backed reforms such as child-labor restrictions and an eight-hour workday for railroad workers. Although he eventually abandoned American neutrality during World War I, Wilson was committed to world peace after the war. For his role in helping found the League of Nations, Wilson won the Nobel Peace Prize in 1919.

Making Inferences How did Wilson's childhood experiences affect his reaction to World War I?

Key Goals of the Fourteen Points QUICK FACTS

- End secret alliances
- Encourage free shipping
- Remove barriers to trade
- Reduce armies and navies
- Resolve colonial claims
- Support the right of people to choose their own government
- Settle border disputes
- Establish the League of Nations

Europe after World War I

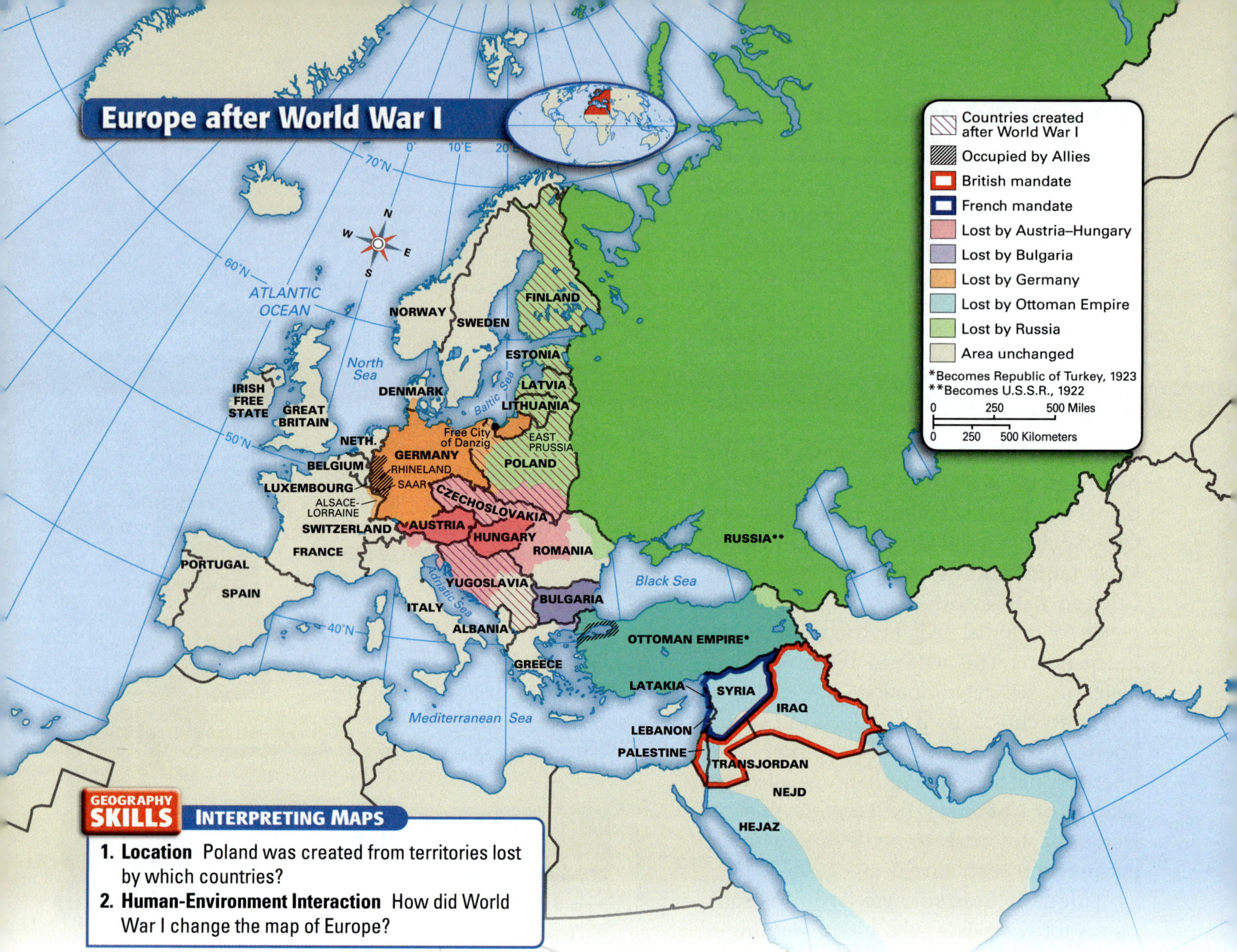

GEOGRAPHY SKILLS **INTERPRETING MAPS**

1. **Location** Poland was created from territories lost by which countries?
2. **Human-Environment Interaction** How did World War I change the map of Europe?

Wilson reluctantly agreed to the **Treaty of Versailles**, the peace settlement of World War I. In it, the League of Nations was established. Estonia, Finland, Latvia, Lithuania, Czechoslovakia, and Yugoslavia became independent countries. Poland was restored as a nation. The Central Powers turned over their colonies to the League of Nations, which assigned other European powers to rule. Though the Treaty of Versailles did not give Wilson everything he wanted, he hoped the League of Nations would solve remaining problems.

READING CHECK **Identifying Points of View** Why did Allied leaders object to Wilson's plan?

Versailles Treaty Rejected

The U.S. Constitution states that treaties must be ratified by at least two-thirds of the members of the Senate. Wilson knew he was going to have a hard time convincing some senators to vote to ratify the Versailles Treaty. Republican senator **Henry Cabot Lodge** declared: "No peace that satisfied Germany in any degree can ever satisfy us." Lodge wanted the winners to set the terms of the peace.

Republicans insisted on changes to the treaty before they would ratify it. Their main objection was the League of Nations' power to use military force. They were worried that as a member of the League, the United States could be forced to send troops to war based on decisions made by the League of Nations. This, they argued, conflicted with Congress's constitutional power to declare war.

Wilson refused to compromise. He insisted that the treaty be ratified exactly as it was written. He traveled around the country, trying to convince the public to pressure Republican senators to vote for the treaty. Before he completed his tour, however, Wilson was weakened by a stroke.

Lodge announced that he was prepared to accept most of the treaty, though he still wanted to limit U.S. military commitment to the League of Nations. Wilson demanded that Democrats in the Senate refuse to change the treaty. When the vote was taken on November 19, 1919, neither the Democrats nor the Republicans would compromise. The Treaty of Versailles was defeated in the Senate.

It was a bitter disappointment for President Wilson. The United States signed separate peace treaties with Austria, Hungary, and Germany and never joined the League of Nations.

Causes and Effects of World War I
QUICK FACTS

Causes
- Nationalism
- Militarism
- Competition for territory
- Alliance system in Europe

Effects
- U.S. entry into the war in 1917
- Millions of deaths and widespread destruction in Europe
- Treaty of Versailles
- Creation of several new nations
- League of Nations

READING CHECK **Supporting a Point of View** Do you think Wilson should have compromised with Republicans in the Senate on the Treaty of Versailles? Why or why not?

SUMMARY AND PREVIEW World War I changed the world map and affected the lives of millions. In the next chapter you will learn about American social, political, and economic conditions after the war.

Section 4 Assessment

go.hrw.com
Online Quiz
KEYWORD: SC7 HP23

Reviewing Ideas, Terms, and People

1. a. **Recall** Approximately how many soldiers were killed or wounded in World War I?
   b. **Draw Conclusions** How did the war affect the European economy?
   c. **Summarize** How did Americans try to fight the influenza epidemic of 1918?
2. a. **Define** What was the **League of Nations**?
   b. **Explain** How did the **Treaty of Versailles** change the map of Europe?
   c. **Elaborate** Which countries did not attend the Paris Peace Conference? How do you think this affected the outcome?
3. a. **Identify** Who was **Henry Cabot Lodge**?
   b. **Predict** How might Wilson have ensured that the U.S. Senate would ratify the Treaty of Versailles?

Critical Thinking

4. **Identifying Points of View** Review your notes on the Treaty of Versailles. Then copy the graphic organizer below and use it to compare the positions of Woodrow Wilson, Allied leaders, and Senate Republicans. Fill in the results of each person's or group's goals.

	Goals	Results
Woodrow Wilson		
Allied Leaders		
Senate Republicans		

FOCUS ON SPEAKING

5. **Analyzing the Peace** Add to your list ways the United States was affected by World War I. How many American lives were lost? What were the results of the war? Do you think U.S. involvement in the war could have been avoided? Should the United States have joined the League of Nations?

Social Studies Skills

Analysis | Critical Thinking | Civic Participation | **Study**

North Carolina Skills
2.02 Explore print and non-print materials.

Using Visual Resources

Define the Skill

A major part of history is understanding the events and ideas of the past. Visual resources are often good sources of information about the past. Visual resources include paintings, drawings, cartoons, posters, and photographs. The symbols and images in these resources tell us about the ideas and values of a time period. They often provide different information and points of view than do written documents.

Learn the Skill

Visual resources can have special purposes. For example, the poster above was produced by the U.S. government to inspire patriotism and encourage support for the war effort. It uses symbols and images to suggest that all Americans can contribute to the war effort.

You know from reading the chapter that conserving food to provide supplies for troops was an important part of the war effort. This poster encourages Americans to can fruits and vegetables. The pictures show canned tomatoes and peas in glass jars.

The poster also shows the German kaiser in a jar. He cannot reach his sword, which is outside the jar. He is helpless. This suggests that, by canning fruit and vegetables, Americans can help defeat the German leader.

Practice the Skill

Study the World War I poster below. Like the poster above, it was produced by the U.S. government to encourage support for the war effort. Write a paragraph describing the poster. Your paragraph should include the specific purpose of the poster, the symbols it uses, and whether it conveys its message effectively. You can use the text above as a model.

CHAPTER 23

Chapter Review

HOLT

History's Impact

▶ **video series**

Review the video to answer the closing question:

How did the U.S. entry into World War I affect the war's outcome and define the U.S. role in the global community?

Visual Summary

QUICK FACTS

Use the visual summary below to help you review the main ideas of the chapter.

The assassination of Archduke Francis Ferdinand threw Europe into a state of war.

Brutal fighting took place across Europe.

President Wilson thought a League of Nations would prevent future wars.

Reviewing Vocabulary, Terms, and People

Identify the descriptions below with the correct term or person from the chapter.

1. International assembly of nations designed to settle international disputes and encourage democracy

2. Strategy of defending a position by fighting from the protection of deep ditches

3. American fighting force trained and led by General John J. Pershing

4. Law that required men between the ages of 21 and 30 to register to be drafted into the armed forces

5. Senate leader who opposed the Treaty of Versailles

6. Truce between warring nations

7. Telegram from the German foreign minister proposing an alliance between Germany and Mexico against the United States

Comprehension and Critical Thinking

SECTION 1 *(Pages 720–724)*

8. a. Identify What event sparked World War I?

b. Explain How did tensions in Europe lead to war?

c. Draw Conclusions Why did the war in Europe become a stalemate?

SECTION 2 *(Pages 725–729)*

9. a. Recall What happened to the *Lusitania*? How did the American public react?

b. Analyze How did the country's mobilization for war affect American women?

c. Evaluate Do you think U.S. efforts to prepare for war were successful? Why or why not?

SECTION 3 *(Pages 730–734)*

10. a. Define How did the American Expeditionary Force prepare for war?

b. Contrast How was the Second Battle of the Marne different from the First Battle of the Marne?

c. Draw Conclusions Do you think the Allies would have won World War I without American help? Explain your answer.

SECTION 4 *(Pages 735–739)*

11. a. Recall Which nations' leaders dominated the Paris Peace Conference?

b. Summarize What were the main ideas of Wilson's Fourteen Points?

c. Predict How effective do you think the League of Nations was? Why?

Using the Internet

go.hrw.com
KEYWORD: SC7 CH23

12. Activity: Researching the Technology of War Many new technologies were introduced in World War I. The introduction of new weapons, like poison gas and machine guns, and combat vehicles, such as tanks and aircraft, made this war deadlier than any previous one. Enter the activity keyword. Research new battlefield technologies in World War I. Then write three journal entries from the point of view of a soldier in the trenches. Your entries should describe what the soldier who experienced these technologies and inventions for the first time saw, felt, and thought. Remember to use facts from your research in your journal entries.

Reviewing Themes

13. Economics How did World War I affect the economy of the United States?

14. Politics What lasting political changes were brought about by World War I?

Social Studies Skills

Using Visual Resources *Use the Social Studies Skills taught in this chapter to answer the question below.*

15. What parts of the U.S. war effort are shown in this poster?

Reading Skills

Recognizing Fallacies in Reasoning *Use the Reading Skills taught in this chapter to answer the question about the reading selection below.*

> The number of soldiers killed in World War I was beyond anything the world had ever experienced. About 5 million Allied soldiers and 3.5 million soldiers from the Central Powers died in combat. More than 20 million soldiers on both sides were wounded. *(p. 735)*

16. Which of the following is an example of a false conclusion drawn from the selection above?

a. More soldiers were killed in World War I than in any war up to that point.

b. World War I devastated the European population.

c. Europe would never recover from World War I.

d. The number of soldiers wounded was more than two times the number of soldiers killed.

FOCUS ON SPEAKING

17. Presenting Your Persuasive Speech Review your notes and form an opinion on whether the United States should have entered World War I. You will have about five minutes to present your point of view. Use note cards to organize your ideas. Begin by writing a one-sentence introduction clearly stating your opinion. Then write several sentences with details and examples from the chapter that support your point of view. Conclude your speech with a sentence that summarizes your ideas. Practice your speech and then present it to the class.

CHAPTER 23

Standardized Test Practice

DIRECTIONS: Read each question and write the letter of the best response.

1 Which of the following was made up of Germany, Austria-Hungary, the Ottoman Empire, and Bulgaria?

A Central Powers

B Allied Powers

C League of Nations

D Big Four

2 The Communist takeover of the Russian government caused

A the armistice to go into effect.

B a German victory at the Second Battle of the Marne.

C the United States to remain neutral.

D Russia to leave the war.

3 During the war, many African Americans

A gained equal rights because of their military service.

B served in segregated units in the military.

C were removed from jobs in war industries and the military.

D volunteered to serve in the military without pay.

4 One reason the United States entered World War I was Germany's violation of

A the Treaty of Versailles.

B the Zimmermann Note.

C the *Sussex* pledge.

D Wilson's Fourteen Points.

5 How was North Carolina's economy affected by the end of World War I?

A The high demand for agricultural products led to an economic boom.

B The return of soldiers from the war led to a dramatic rise in unemployment rates.

C The end of the war had little effect on North Carolina's economy.

D The demand for goods decreased and prices fell, forcing some farms and factories out of business.

6 Which of the following technologies was *most* important to warfare at sea during World War I?

A U-boats

B bayonets

C ironclads

D poison gas

7 Examine the fourth of Woodrow Wilson's Fourteen Points and use it to answer the question below:

> "Adequate guarantees given and taken that national armaments [weapons] will be reduced to the lowest point consistent with domestic safety."
>
> —Woodrow Wilson, Fourteen Points

Document-Based Question **Why do you think Wilson wanted to reduce the amount of weapons in nations around the world?**

Writing Workshop

Assignment

Find a primary source from World War I and write an analysis of it.

Analyzing a Primary Source

Primary sources are often the best sources of information available to historians. Primary sources provide answers to questions about the past. They also provide a unique point of view from the past. Analyzing a primary source allows you to share that information.

TIP **Using the Internet** If you find a primary source on the Internet, make sure it is accurate. You should be able to identify the person or institution that runs the Web site and make sure that person or institution is trustworthy. The Web site should include basic information about the source, such as its author, when it was written, and where it first appeared. University and library Web sites are excellent places to find primary sources.

1. Prewrite

Locating Primary Sources

Many primary sources are available in libraries and on the Internet. Letters, diaries, autobiographies, memoirs, newspaper articles, public speeches, and legal documents are good examples of primary sources.

Reading the Primary Source

Take notes on these questions to better understand the document.

- Who wrote the document?
- What kind of document is it?
- When was it written? Where did it originally appear?
- What was the author's point of view? What was his or her experience during the war?
- Why did the author write the document?

As you read the primary source, take notes on these questions.

- Why is the document important? The answer to this question will be the main idea of your essay.
- What questions about World War I does it answer? Answering this question will help you write your body paragraphs.

2. Write

You can use this framework to help you write your first draft.

A Writer's Framework

Introduction

- Introduce your primary source and its main purpose.
- Introduce the author of the source and include the date it was written.
- State your main idea, explaining why this source is important.

Body

- Explain how the source answers at least two questions about World War I.
- Include examples from the document.

Conclusion

- Summarize the information in the source.
- Restate why the document is important for historians.

3. Evaluate and Revise

Evaluating

Use these questions to discover ways to improve your paper.

Evaluation Questions for Analyzing a Primary Source

- Do you introduce your primary source with its main purpose?
- Do you introduce the author of the source and the document's date?
- Do you state a main idea explaining why this source is important?
- Do you explain how the source answers at least two questions about World War I?
- Do you include examples from the document?
- Do you summarize the information in the source?

Revising

Make sure each paragraph has a topic sentence at the beginning. Then check the information in the paragraph. It should all relate to the topic sentence. If it does not, there are several ways to fix the paragraph. First, you can remove unrelated information. If the information is related but not clearly explained, add a more detailed explanation. You can also change the topic sentence to include all the information in the paragraph.

4. Proofread and Publish

Proofreading

Reread your paper carefully to make sure all the verbs are in the same tense. The past tense is usually best for history writing. Summaries of primary sources should also be in the past tense. A direct quotation from a primary source, however, should remain in its original tense.

Publishing

Share your paper with a classmate. Read each other's papers. Then write a one-paragraph summary of the new information you each learned.

5. Practice and Apply

Use the steps and strategies in this workshop to analyze your primary source.

TIP Using Pronouns Effectively

Use pronouns such as *he, she,* and *it* to replace frequently used nouns and proper nouns. This will help you vary your sentences. Make sure that the person or thing to which each pronoun refers is clear. If it is not, repeat the original noun or name.

EXAMPLE

Woodrow Wilson proposed a peace plan called the Fourteen Points. He wanted to make sure the postwar peace would last.

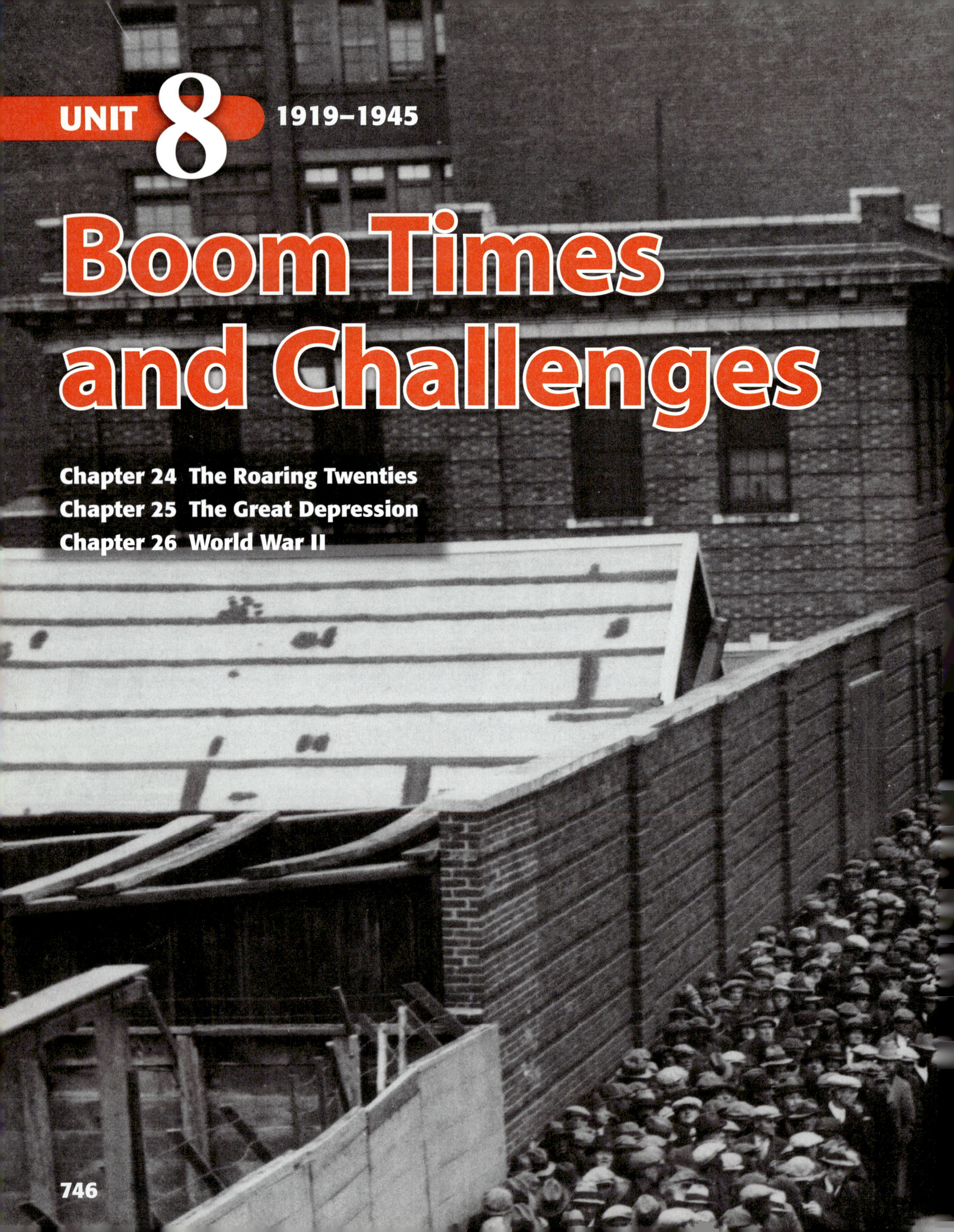

UNIT 8 1919–1945

Boom Times and Challenges

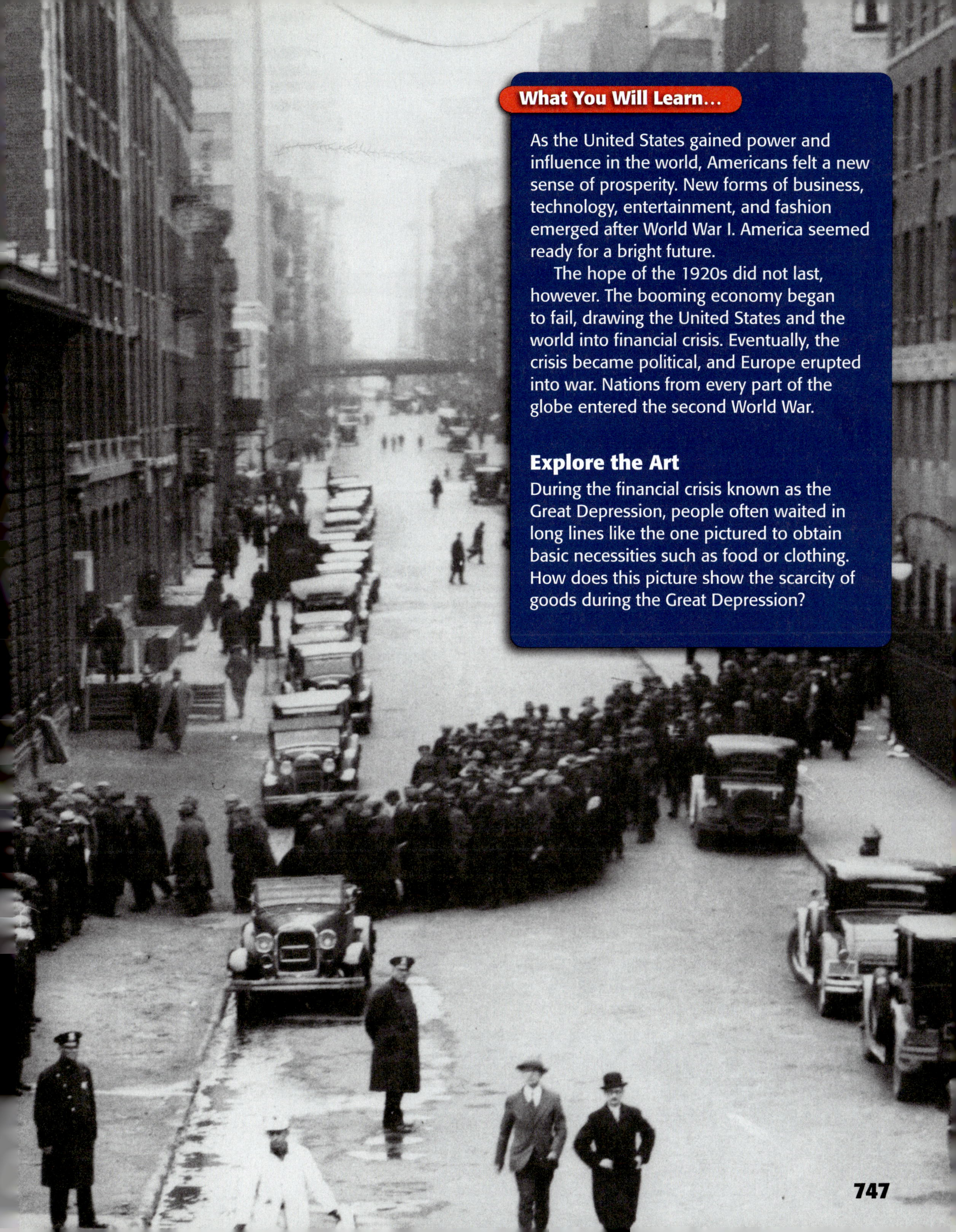

What You Will Learn...

As the United States gained power and influence in the world, Americans felt a new sense of prosperity. New forms of business, technology, entertainment, and fashion emerged after World War I. America seemed ready for a bright future.

The hope of the 1920s did not last, however. The booming economy began to fail, drawing the United States and the world into financial crisis. Eventually, the crisis became political, and Europe erupted into war. Nations from every part of the globe entered the second World War.

Explore the Art

During the financial crisis known as the Great Depression, people often waited in long lines like the one pictured to obtain basic necessities such as food or clothing. How does this picture show the scarcity of goods during the Great Depression?

CHAPTER 24 1919–1929

The Roaring Twenties

North Carolina Standards

Social Studies Objectives

9.02 Identify past and present state and local leaders from diverse cultural backgrounds and assess their influence in affecting change.

Language Arts Objectives

2.01 Analyze and evaluate informational materials that are read, heard, and/or viewed by:

- monitoring comprehension for understanding of what is read, heard and/or viewed by.
- drawing inferences and/or conclusions.
- generating questions.
- extending ideas.

go.hrw.com
North Carolina
KEYWORD: SC7 NC

Focus on Writing

Radio Advertisement Radio stations began to air regular broadcasts in the 1920s. Radios linked Americans from coast to coast, allowing them to hear the same programs—and the same advertisements. In the 1920s Americans with means had new choices in entertainment, travel, fashion, and convenience. In this chapter, you will read about these new choices. You will then write a radio advertisement for a new product or form of entertainment of the 1920s.

United States

1920 Warren Harding wins the presidency in a landslide victory.

1920

World

1920 The League of Nations is established.

HOLT

History's Impact

▶ **video series**

Watch the video to understand the impact of younger generations on national culture.

What You Will Learn...

In this chapter you will learn about the ways that American life changed in the decade following World War I. With a booming economy, many people had money to spend on exciting new forms of entertainment. People flocked to bustling city centers like New York City's Times Square, shown in this painting.

1922 The tomb of King Tutankhamen is discovered.

1924 Native Americans are granted the right of U.S. citizenship.

1924 Joseph Stalin becomes dictator of Communist Russia.

1926 Ernest Hemingway publishes *The Sun Also Rises.*

1926 Prince Hirohito becomes emperor of Japan.

1928 Alexander Fleming discovers penicillin.

1929 Construction begins on the Empire State Building.

1922 — 1924 — 1926 — 1928 — 1930

Reading Social Studies

by Kylene Beers

Economics | Geography | Politics | Society and Culture | Science and Technology

Focus on Themes In this chapter, you will learn about the decade of the 1920s, a period called the Roaring Twenties. During this time, many in **society** thought that the Great War would be the last major war and that the future was bright. Also during this time, **science and technology** made leaps forward that would make life easier for millions of Americans.

Synthesizing Information

Focus on Reading Learning about history means synthesizing, or combining, many different sources about the past. When you read this textbook, you are reading a synthesis of other sources, accounts, and ideas about history.

Synthesizing Once you have identified the subject you are studying, you should try to read as many different accounts of the story as you can. Be sure to investigate the author of a source to learn what his or her goals might be. Compare and contrast the different sources and evaluate which ones you believe. Finally, use all the various stories you have read to form your own interpretation of what happened in history.

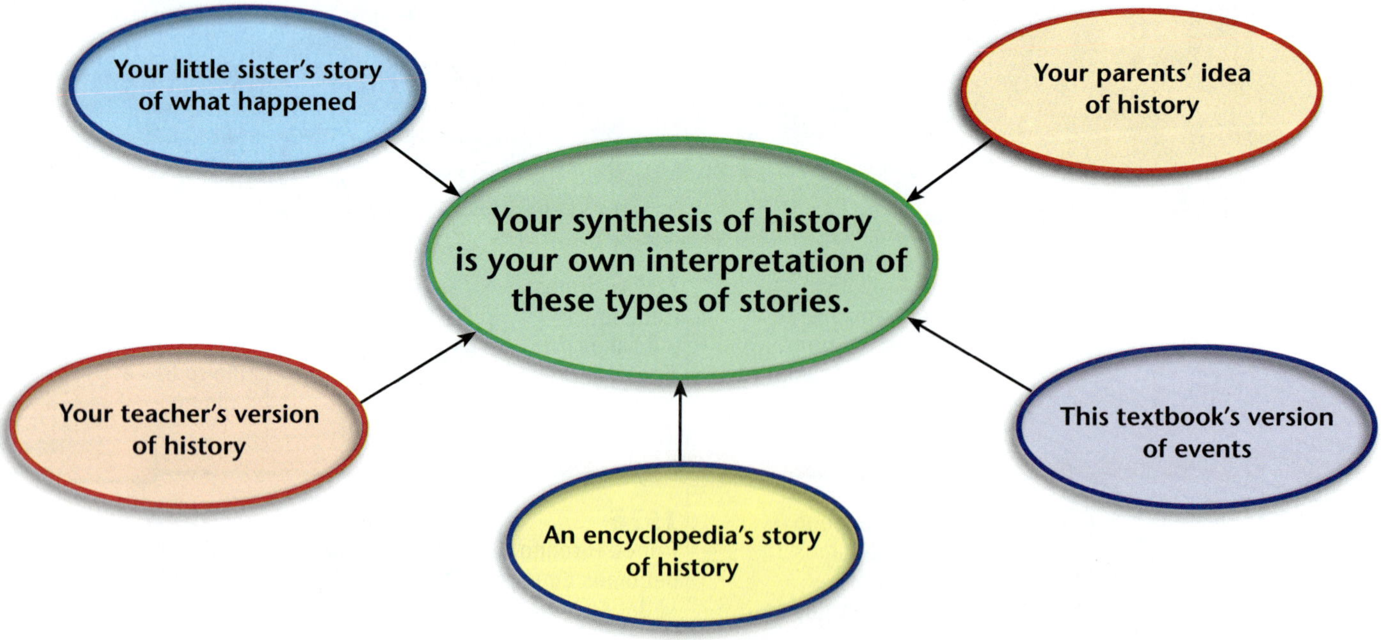

You Try It!

Read these varying accounts of the assassination of Archduke Francis Ferdinand and his wife, Sophie. Then write your own version of the story.

"Two bullets fired on a Sarajevo street on a sunny June morning in 1914 set in motion a series of events that shaped the world we live in today. World War One, World War Two, the Cold War and its conclusion all trace their origins to the gunshots that interrupted that summer day."

–Anonymous

"As the car came abreast he stepped forward from the curb, drew his automatic pistol from his coat and fired two shots. The first struck the wife of the Archduke, the Archduchess Sofia, in the abdomen . . . She died instantly. The second bullet struck the Archduke close to the heart. He uttered only one word, 'Sofia'—a call to his stricken wife. Then his head fell back and he collapsed. He died almost instantly."

–conspirator Borijove Jevtic

"As I was pulling out my handkerchief to wipe the blood away from his mouth, the duchess cried out to him, 'In Heaven's name, what has happened to you?' At that she slid off the seat and lay on the floor of the car ... I had no idea that she too was hit and thought she had simply fainted with fright. Then I heard His Imperial Highness say, "Sopherl, Sopherl, don't die. Stay alive for the children!"

–guard Count Franz von Harrach,
quoted in "Assassination of an Archduke," *Eyewitness to History*

1. What differences do you notice between accounts?
2. Why might these different authors have a different view of the assassination?
3. How can you tell what each author's viewpoint is?
4. Write your own version of what might have happened. Use details that you believe from the sources above.

As you read Chapter 24, notice any differing views from different sources.

Key Terms and People

Chapter 24

Section 1

Warren G. Harding *(p. 752)*
Calvin Coolidge *(p. 752)*
Teapot Dome scandal *(p. 753)*
Kellogg-Briand Pact *(p. 754)*
Model T *(p. 755)*
moving assembly line *(p. 755)*
Herbert Hoover *(p. 757)*

Section 2

flappers *(p. 759)*
Red Scare *(p. 760)*
Twenty-first Amendment *(p. 761)*
fundamentalism *(p. 762)*
Scopes trial *(p. 762)*
Great Migration *(p. 763)*
Marcus Garvey *(p. 763)*

Section 3

talkie *(p. 766)*
Jazz Age *(p. 767)*
Harlem Renaissance *(p. 768)*
Langston Hughes *(p. 768)*
Lost Generation *(p. 768)*
expatriates *(p. 768)*
Georgia O'Keeffe *(p. 769)*

Academic Vocabulary

In this chapter, you will learn the following academic words:

incentive *(p. 753)*
traditional *(p. 762)*
innovation *(p. 767)*

SECTION 1

Boom Times

What You Will Learn...

Main Ideas

1. President Harding promised a return to peace and prosperity.
2. Calvin Coolidge supported a probusiness agenda.
3. American business boomed in the 1920s.
4. In 1928, Americans elected Herbert Hoover, hoping he would help good financial times continue.

The Big Idea

American industries boomed in the 1920s, changing many Americans' way of life.

Key Terms and People

Warren G. Harding, *p. 752*
Calvin Coolidge, *p. 752*
Teapot Dome scandal, *p. 753*
Kellogg-Briand Pact, *p. 754*
Model T, *p. 755*
moving assembly line, *p. 755*
Herbert Hoover, *p. 757*

TAKING NOTES As you read, take notes on the presidents of the 1920s. Record your notes in a chart like this one.

President	Year Elected	Political Party

If YOU were there...

You have been working in a car factory for years, and now you have finally bought a car of your own—a shiny new 1920 Ford Model T. As you set out on your first drive, the car rattles and bounces over unpaved roads that were designed for horse-and-buggy travel. But you don't mind the rough ride. You now have the freedom to drive anywhere you want to go!

How will owning a car change your life?

BUILDING BACKGROUND The American economy boomed during World War I, as industries raced to produce weapons and supplies for the Allied armies. With more than 4 million men serving in the armed forces, there was a shortage of workers in American factories, and many people found jobs. When the war ended, however, conditions changed quickly, and the economy faced a difficult adjustment.

Return to Peace and Prosperity

The end of World War I had an immediate impact on the American economy. Because the government no longer needed war supplies, it canceled billions of dollars' worth of contracts with American factories. This meant that factories cut back on production at the very moment that millions of soldiers left the military and began looking for jobs. The result was a sharp rise in unemployment. Meanwhile, many people who did have jobs rushed to buy products they could not buy during the war. This caused prices to soar. Wages could not keep up with the rising prices, and thus workers could no longer afford to buy the goods they needed and wanted. Many went on strike for higher wages—more than 4 million in 1919 alone.

As the 1920 presidential election approached, the economic difficulties were bad news for the party in power, Woodrow Wilson's Democratic Party. Many voters blamed the Democrats for the hard times. Sensing the public's anger, the Republicans looked for a candidate who would offer new hope for American voters. They chose **Warren G. Harding**, a senator from Ohio. Harding picked Governor **Calvin Coolidge** of Massachusetts as his running mate.

Primary Source

POLITICAL CARTOON

Teapot Dome

During the Teapot Dome scandal, people began to question the judgment and honesty of government leaders. This cartoon, called "Juggernaut," was published in 1924 to show how harmful the scandal had been. A juggernaut is an indestructible force that crushes everything in its path.

How do the images in the cartoon illustrate the destructive force of the scandal?

ANALYSIS SKILL **ANALYZING PRIMARY SOURCES**

Why do you think the artist called this cartoon "Juggernaut"?

Harding based his campaign strategy on a promise to return the country to stability and prosperity, what he called "normalcy." His conservative policies contrasted with the reform-minded policies of the Progressive Era. Harding summed up his ideas in a campaign speech:

> "America's present need is not heroics, but healing; not nostrums [uncertain cures] but normalcy [normal times]; not revolution, but restoration."
>
> —Warren G. Harding, 1920

Democrats believed there was still support for Wilson's ideas for reform. They ran Ohio governor James M. Cox for president, and New York's Franklin D. Roosevelt for vice president. But Harding's promise of a return to normalcy captured the public's mood in 1920. Harding won a landslide victory with about 60 percent of the popular vote.

Harding worked quickly to help strengthen the economy. He put together a cabinet of experts who believed in reducing money owed by the government and limiting government involvement in the economy. Secretary of the Treasury Andrew Mellon pushed for tax cuts for wealthy Americans. Mellon believed that this policy would give the wealthy an **incentive** to invest in new businesses and create new jobs for other Americans. Mellon's opponents called this idea the trickle-down theory, arguing that money would only "trickle down" in small drops to less-well-off Americans.

While Harding was president, businesses did in fact bounce back from the postwar recession. The economy created new, better-paying jobs, leading to an economic boom that lasted for most of the decade.

Harding faced problems in other areas, however. He had appointed many of his trusted friends to high positions. Some of these men used their positions to gain wealth through illegal means. "I have no trouble with my enemies," Harding once said. "But my . . . friends . . . keep me walking the floor nights."

What came to be known as the **Teapot Dome scandal** involved Secretary of the Interior Albert Fall, who accepted large sums of money and valuable gifts from private oil companies. In exchange, Fall allowed the companies to control government oil reserves in Elk Hills, California, and Teapot Dome, Wyoming. The U.S. Senate soon began investigating Fall, who was convicted of accepting bribes. He was the first cabinet member ever to be convicted of a crime for his actions while in office.

READING CHECK **Summarizing** What did Harding mean when he promised a return to normalcy?

ACADEMIC VOCABULARY

incentive something that encourages people to behave a certain way

Coolidge's Probusiness Administration

Just before details of the Teapot Dome scandal became public, President Harding died of a heart attack. In August 1923 Vice President Calvin Coolidge took charge. Coolidge had a strong reputation as an honest and trustworthy leader. These qualities helped him restore confidence in the government.

Coolidge acted quickly to fire all officials who had been involved in the bribery scandals of Harding's administration. This helped him win the presidential election in 1924. He received nearly twice as many votes as the Democratic candidate, John W. Davis.

THE IMPACT TODAY

Countries still try to prevent wars with international agreements. More than 180 nations have signed the Treaty on the Non-Proliferation of Nuclear Weapons, an agreement to prevent the spread of nuclear weapons.

Coolidge proved to be even more probusiness than Harding had been. He once declared that "the business of America is business." He expanded the policies started under Harding, such as tax cuts for wealthier citizens. He also supported raising tariffs on foreign goods to decrease competition with domestic products. Despite higher tariffs, trade with other countries actually increased under Coolidge. This was mainly because many nations depended on trade with the United States to rebuild their economies after World War I. Not everyone profited from Coolidge's efforts, however. Coolidge vetoed congressional attempts to provide aid to farmers through the regulation of prices.

Like the United States, European nations wanted a return to prosperity. Europeans also wanted to avoid another devastating war. In 1928 the United States and 14 other nations signed the **Kellogg-Briand Pact**, an agreement that outlawed war. Eventually 62 nations accepted the pact. There was no way to enforce the pact, however. One U.S. senator complained that the treaty would be "as effective to keep down war as a carpet would be to smother an earthquake." Still, it was a sign that most countries wanted to prevent another global conflict.

READING CHECK **Comparing and Contrasting** How were Harding and Coolidge similar, and how were they different?

The Model T Assembly Line

CONNECT TO SCIENCE AND TECHNOLOGY

Early assembly lines involved workers moving down a line of parts. On a moving assembly line, workers along the line specialize in one or two simple assembly tasks that they perform as parts move past them. The moving assembly line greatly increases the efficiency of mass production.

These workers are attaching the leather seat covers to the carriage and are stuffing them with horsehair.

Business Booms

The 1920s were years of rapid economic growth in the United States. Between 1921 and 1929, U.S. manufacturing nearly doubled. As jobs and wages increased, so did people's ability to buy new products. Some of these products changed the way Americans lived.

Ford's Model T

Today we think of cars as a major part of American life. In the early 1900s, though, cars were seen as luxury items that only the wealthy could afford. Henry Ford, an inventor and business leader from Detroit, helped to change this. Ford dreamed of building a car that most Americans could afford:

> "I will build a motor car for the great multitude [most of the people]. It will be large enough for the family but small enough for the individual to run and care for. It ... will be so low in price that no man making a good salary will be unable to own one."
>
> —Henry Ford, quoted in *Daily Life in the United States, 1920–1940,* by David E. Kyvig

Ford achieved his goal by building a sturdy and reliable car called the **Model T**, nicknamed the Tin Lizzie. In 1908 the Model T sold for $850. By 1925 it cost just $290. Ford was able to make his car affordable by cutting costs of production. For example, every car looked the same. The Model T came only in black for many years.

To decrease the time it took to make the cars, Ford also began using a **moving assembly line**. This system used conveyer belts to move parts and partly assembled cars from one group of workers to another. The workers stood in one place and did a specialized job.

The chassis, or frame, and the engine are assembled on separate lines. Workers on a third line then attach them.

The assembled chassis is then connected to the body of the car.

From the Collections of Henry Ford Museum and Greenfield Village

ANALYSIS SKILL **ANALYZING VISUALS**

How does the moving assembly line reduce the time it takes to build a car?

The Model T

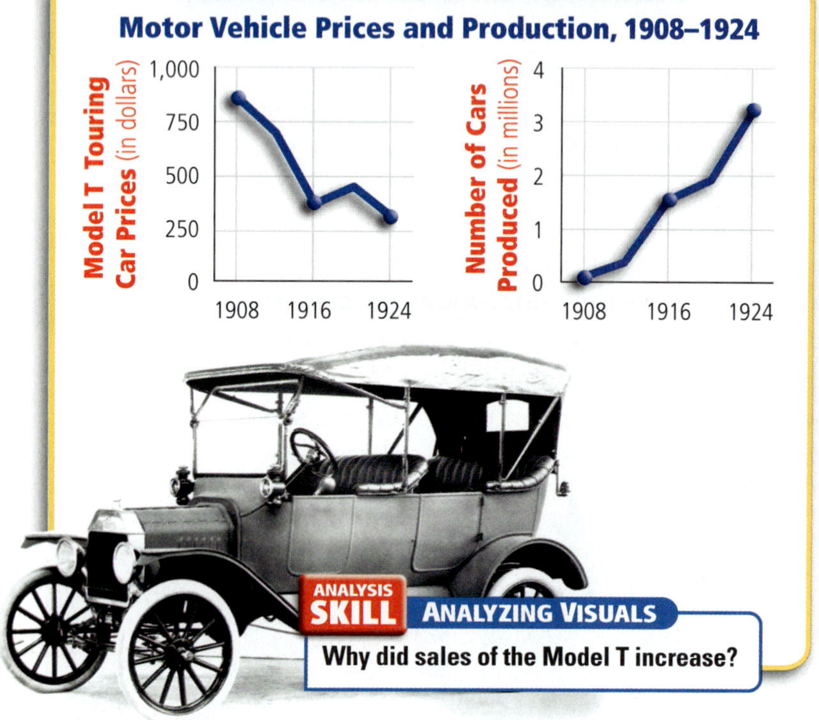

ANALYSIS SKILL **ANALYZING VISUALS**

Why did sales of the Model T increase?

In 1914 Ford raised the wages for his factory workers to $5 a day. This was good pay, compared with the $2 or $3 per day offered by many other factories. Ford believed the wage increase would keep his employees from quitting. He also lowered the workday to eight hours and employed people that other factories would not hire, such as African Americans and people with disabilities.

NC History Makers

Harriet M. Berry Known as the "Mother of Good Roads," Harriet Berry headed the Good Roads Association. Through her efforts, the State Highway Commission was founded in 1921. Today, North Carolina is known for its extensive highway system.

Even with the good wages, many workers had a hard time adjusting to the fast-paced and repetitive work on Ford's assembly line. One wife of an autoworker wrote to Ford saying, "My husband has come home and thrown himself down and won't eat his supper—so done out [tired]! . . . That $5 a day is a blessing—a bigger one than you know, but oh they earn it."

To help make his cars more affordable, Ford allowed customers to buy cars using an installment plan. Most people were used to saving up for years to buy items. Installment plans let people pay a small amount of the cost every month until the entire car was paid for. Ford's competitors also allowed customers to pay with installment plans. For a slightly higher price than the Model T, companies such as General Motors offered cars in a variety of colors and with more power.

FOCUS ON READING

How is this paragraph an example of synthesized information?

The automobile changed the way Americans lived. They could now go on long drives or take jobs farther away from where they lived. Cars gave people a sense of freedom and adventure. As *Motor Car* magazine told drivers, "You are your master, the road is ahead . . . your freedom is complete."

Growing Industries

The rise of the automobile affected the entire American economy. Millions of Americans found work making steel for car bodies, rubber for tires, or glass for windows. To improve road safety, the government spent millions of dollars paving highways and building new bridges. People opened roadside businesses to serve travelers, such as gas stations, restaurants, and motels. The rising number of cars also created a demand for car repair shops and car insurance.

Following Ford's example, other manufacturers began using assembly lines and allowing customers to pay on installment plans. Many companies also took advantage of the increasing number of homes with electricity. By 1929 about 85 percent of all Americans living in towns or cities had electricity. Companies responded by building new electrical appliances designed to make household chores easier, such as washing machines, vacuum cleaners, and refrigerators.

As companies competed to sell these new goods, the advertising industry boomed. Companies advertised in magazines and on the radio to convince people that their lives would be improved if they owned a certain product. Many advertisers targeted women, hoping to convince them that they needed the newest labor-saving products. For example, one advertisement for an electric dishwasher called its product "the greatest gift of electricity to the modern housewife."

READING CHECK **Identifying Cause and Effect**
How did the automobile change society?

Hoover Elected

With the economy booming, public support for the Republican Party remained strong. When President Coolidge decided not to run for reelection in 1928, the party chose his secretary of commerce, **Herbert Hoover**, as its nominee. The Democrats nominated New York governor Alfred E. Smith.

Hoover told voters that he was the right choice to maintain economic prosperity. Hoover boldly claimed that "we in America today are nearer to the final triumph over poverty than ever before in the history of any land."

Smith's campaign focused mainly on issues facing city dwellers. This concerned some rural voters. Smith's religious faith also became an issue. He was the first Catholic to run for president. His opponents stirred up fears that Smith would be controlled by the pope and other church officials. In the end, Hoover won easily, gaining 58 percent of the popular vote.

READING CHECK **Drawing Conclusions** What helped Herbert Hoover win the presidency in 1928?

Republican Herbert Hoover defeated Democrat Alfred E. Smith in the 1928 presidential election.

SUMMARY AND PREVIEW In this section you learned about politics and the economy in the 1920s. In the next section you will learn more about how society changed during the decade.

FOCUS ON NORTH CAROLINA

Hoover was the first Republican since 1872 to win North Carolina's electoral votes.

Section 1 Assessment

go.hrw.com
Online Quiz
KEYWORD: SC7 HP24

Reviewing Ideas, Terms, and People

1. a. **Describe** What was the result of the 1920 presidential election, and why?
   b. **Summarize** What did the **Teapot Dome scandal** reveal about **Warren G. Harding**'s administration?
2. a. **Identify** Who succeeded Harding as president, and what were his main policies?
   b. **Analyze** What was the main weakness of the **Kellogg-Briand Pact**?
3. a. **Recall** Why did American businesses grow during the 1920s?
   b. **Explain** Why were Model T prices low?
4. a. **Recall** Why was **Herbert Hoover** elected?
   b. **Elaborate** Who would you have voted for in the 1928 election? Explain your answer.

Critical Thinking

5. **Summarizing** Review your notes on the presidents from the 1920s. Then copy the graphic organizer below and expand on your notes by summarizing the main ideas or achievements of each president.

President	Ideas/ Achievements

FOCUS ON WRITING

6. **Taking Notes on Consumer Goods** Make a list of new products people had access to in this decade, including cheaper automobiles and appliances for the home. Be sure to note how these products improved the lives of Americans. Use the information about advertising in this section to help you with ideas for your radio advertisement.

SECTION 2

Life during the 1920s

What You Will Learn...

Main Ideas

1. In the 1920s many young people found new independence in a changing society.
2. Postwar tensions occasionally led to fear and violence.
3. Competing ideals caused conflict between Americans with traditional beliefs and those with modern views.
4. Following the war, minority groups organized to demand their civil rights.

The Big Idea

Americans faced new opportunities, challenges, and fears as major changes swept the country in the 1920s.

Key Terms and People

flappers, *p. 759*
Red Scare, *p. 760*
Twenty-first Amendment, *p. 761*
fundamentalism, *p. 762*
Scopes trial, *p. 762*
Great Migration, *p. 763*
Marcus Garvey, *p. 763*

TAKING NOTES As you read, look for changes that affected American life in the 1920s. Record your notes in a diagram like this one.

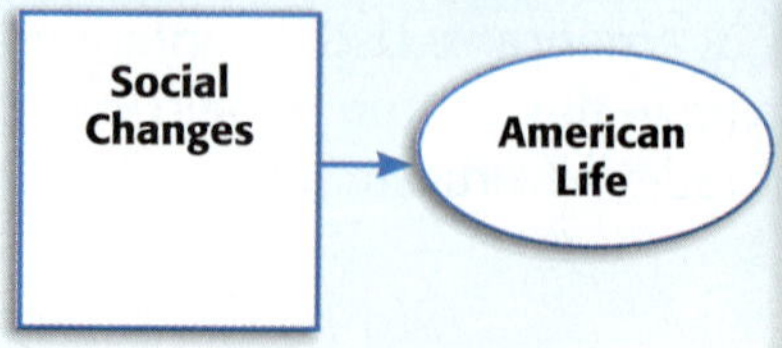

If YOU were there...

The year is 1925. You have just finished school and you are visiting a big city for the first time. You and your friends go to a club and watch young people dancing energetically to popular music. The women have short hair and wear makeup, trying to copy the glamorous style of movie stars. Some of your friends start talking about finding an apartment and looking for jobs in the city.

Would you want to move to a big city in 1925? Why?

BUILDING BACKGROUND The United States enjoyed nearly a decade of economic expansion during the 1920s. American society changed rapidly during this period. Although many people welcomed the new opportunities, others felt their traditional beliefs were being challenged. Conflicts between competing ideals and different groups of people ruffled the surface of America's peace and prosperity.

A Changing Society

The experience of living through World War I changed the way many young people saw the world around them. Young men returning from Europe had visited far-off countries and learned about other cultures. Many of them came home with a desire to continue expanding their horizons. The title of one popular song in 1919 asked, "How 'Ya Gonna Keep 'em Down on the Farm after They've Seen Paree [Paris]"?

Many young people moved away from farms and small towns to cities. By 1920, for the first time in American history, more than half of the country's population lived in urban areas. Young people took advantage of the economic opportunities of the 1920s to gain independence. In the past most young people had lived and worked at home until they got married. Now more young adults were experiencing a time of freedom before settling down. A new youth culture developed, which included going to parties and dance clubs, listening to popular music, and driving fast cars.

For many young Americans, access to education was an important part of this new independence. High school attendance doubled during the decade. The percentage of students going on to college was higher in the United States than in any other country. This included women, who were attending college in higher numbers than ever before.

The number of women in the workforce continued to grow as well. Women with college degrees worked as nurses, teachers, librarians, and social workers. Women were also finding new opportunities in politics. In 1925 Nellie Tayloe Ross (Wyoming) and Miriam "Ma" Ferguson (Texas) became the first women to serve as governors in the United States. Three years later, there were 145 women serving in state legislatures. Five women had won terms in the U.S. House of Representatives.

Women were still discouraged from pursuing fields such as medicine, law, and architecture, however. By the end of the 1920s, less than 5 percent of the country's doctors, lawyers, and architects were women. The percentage was small—but it was beginning to rise.

Some young women found other ways to express their freedom. Young women known as **flappers** cut their hair short and wore makeup and short dresses, openly challenging traditional ideas of how women were supposed to behave. Many older Americans considered this behavior scandalous. One 1920s writer expressed her admiration for flappers, saying:

> "I want my girl to do what she pleases, be what she pleases ... I want [my daughter] to be a flapper, because flappers are brave."
>
> —Zelda Fitzgerald, quoted in *Zelda*, by Nancy Milford

Fashion magazines, Hollywood movies, and advertising helped promote these new images and ideas of youthful freedom.

READING CHECK **Generalizing** How did women in the 1920s express their independence?

Focus on Women

In 1923 suffrage leader Alice Paul introduced the Equal Rights Amendment to Congress, calling for equality of rights regardless of a person's gender. The U.S. Senate passed the amendment 49 years later, but it was never ratified by the states.

Bryn Mawr and other colleges provided education to women in new fields.

Bessie Coleman became the first African American woman to obtain her international pilot's license. She traveled the United States, performing stunts under the name "Brave Bessie."

Flappers challenged many of society's ideas about womanhood. They established new rules of speech, dress, and behavior.

ANALYSIS SKILL **ANALYZING VISUALS**

How do these images reflect new roles for women during the 1920s?

Sacco and Vanzetti

Supporters of Sacco and Vanzetti held rallies and raised money for the immigrants' defense. The men were found guilty and were executed in 1927.

Why did the Sacco and Vanzetti case become so famous?

Fear and Violence

Not all social changes during the 1920s were peaceful. You have read about the hard times that hit the U.S. economy after World War I—unemployment, inflation, and labor disputes that resulted in large strikes. These troubles worried many Americans. In this atmosphere, suspicion of foreigners and radicals, or people who believe in an extreme change in government, sometimes led to violence.

The Red Scare

After the Communists took power in Russia in 1917, many Americans began to fear Communist ideas. They worried that Communists would soon try to gain power in the United States. This fear increased when millions of American workers went on strike in 1919. Many Americans blamed Communists and radicals for the upheaval.

These attitudes led to a **Red Scare**, a time of fear of Communists, or Reds. The Red Scare began in April 1919, when U.S. postal workers found bombs hidden in several packages addressed to famous Americans. Officials never found out who sent the bombs, but they suspected members of the Communist Party.

In June a bomb exploded outside the home of Attorney General A. Mitchell Palmer. Palmer responded by organizing police raids to break up Communist and other groups. In what became known as the Palmer raids, government agents arrested thousands of suspected radicals, often without evidence. Palmer frightened the public by warning that radicals were planning a revolution.

The Red Scare led to one of the best-known criminal cases in American history. In 1920 police arrested Italian-born anarchists Nicola Sacco and Bartolomeo Vanzetti for the robbery and murder of a factory paymaster and his guard. (Anarchists are people opposed to organized government.) Though both men declared themselves innocent of the crime, Sacco and Vanzetti were found guilty. The American Civil Liberties Union (ACLU), founded in 1920 to defend people's civil rights, tried unsuccessfully to get the verdict overturned. Sacco and Vanzetti were convicted. They were executed in 1927.

Restricting Immigration

Some people thought the Sacco and Vanzetti case was influenced by a general fear of foreigners. Many recent immigrants were poor and did not speak English. Some Americans saw them as a threat to their jobs and culture. Immigrants "fill places that belong to the loyal wage-earning citizens of America," said Alabama senator James Thomas Heflin.

The government responded to these concerns with new laws. The Emergency Quota Act of 1921 limited the total number of immigrants allowed into the country. It also favored immigrants from western Europe. The National Origins Act of 1924 banned immigration from East Asia entirely and further reduced the number of immigrants allowed to enter the country. These laws caused a dramatic drop in immigration to the United States.

READING CHECK **Drawing Conclusions** Why were new immigration laws passed in the 1920s?

Competing Ideals

Fear of radical ideas and foreigners was part of a larger clash over ideals and values in America. Differences were growing between older, rural traditions and the beliefs and practices of modern urban society. Americans had very different ideas about what was best for the country's future.

Prohibition

An issue that highlighted this conflict was prohibition. The Eighteenth Amendment—which outlawed the manufacture, sale, and transportation of alcoholic beverages—went into effect in 1920. Support for prohibition was strongest in rural areas, while opposition was strongest in cities.

Government officials found it nearly impossible to enforce prohibition. Congress passed the Volstead Act, which set fines and punishments for disobeying prohibition. Even respectable citizens, however, broke the law. Many people found ways to make alcohol at home using household products. Others bought alcohol at speakeasies, or illegal bars.

Organized criminals called bootleggers quickly seized control of the illegal alcohol business. They made their own alcohol or smuggled it in from Canada or Mexico. Gangsters were able to avoid arrest by bribing local police and politicians. Competition between gangs often led to violent fighting. In Chicago gangster Al "Scarface" Capone gained control of the alcohol trade by murdering his rivals. By 1927 Capone was earning more than $60 million a year from his illegal businesses.

By the end of the decade, the nation was weary of the effects of prohibition. The law had reduced alcohol consumption but had not stopped Americans from drinking. Prohibition had also created new ways for criminals to grow rich. Without government supervision of alcohol production, much of the alcohol consumed in speakeasies was more dangerous than what had been produced before prohibition. Many people came to believe that it would be better to have a legal alcohol trade that could be monitored by the government. In 1933 state and federal governments responded with the **Twenty-first Amendment**, which ended prohibition.

THE IMPACT TODAY

The Twenty-first Amendment made the manufacture and sale of alcohol legal again, but laws today still regulate drinking. The National Minimum Drinking Age Act of 1984 raised the minimum drinking age from 18 to 21 in every state.

Primary Source

PHOTOGRAPH

Prohibition

Agents of federal and state governments tried to enforce the Eighteenth Amendment against great odds. They usually destroyed any liquor that they found. This photograph shows an illegal barrel of beer being broken with an axe. More illegal beer and liquor would soon turn up, however. Faced with a lack of public support and an impossible task of enforcing the ban on alcohol, prohibition was repealed with the Twenty-first Amendment in 1933.

ANALYSIS SKILL **ANALYZING PRIMARY SOURCES**

Why was enforcing prohibition such a hard task?

Religious Ideals

ACADEMIC VOCABULARY
traditional customary, time-honored

Youth culture of the 1920s and prohibition's failure concerned many religious leaders. They saw these changes as movements away from **traditional** values. This led to a Protestant religious movement known as **fundamentalism**—characterized by the belief in a literal, or word-for-word, interpretation of the Bible. Popular preachers like Aimee Semple McPherson used the radio and modern marketing tools to draw followers. Fundamentalism was especially strong in rural areas and small towns, where people often blamed society's problems on the culture of urban areas.

Many fundamentalists believed that modern scientific theories, such as Charles Darwin's theory of evolution, conflicted with the teachings of the Bible. Darwin's theory states that species evolve over time by adapting to their environment. To fundamentalists, this contradicted the biblical account of how the world was made. They opposed the teaching of evolution in public schools. Many cities and states passed laws to prevent the teaching of evolution.

In May 1925 a Dayton, Tennessee, high school science teacher named John T. Scopes was put on trial for teaching evolution in what became known as the **Scopes trial**. National interest in the event was heightened by the fact that famous Americans represented each side. Criminal attorney Clarence Darrow led the ACLU defense team. Three-time presidential candidate William Jennings Bryan assisted the prosecution.

Over live radio, Darrow and Bryan attacked each other's ideas. After more than a week on trial, Scopes was convicted and fined $100 for breaking the law. The state supreme court later overturned his conviction, but the debate over evolution continued.

READING CHECK **Evaluating** What cultural conflict did the Scopes trial represent?

Primary Source

POINTS OF VIEW

The Scopes Trial

Although the focus of the Scopes trial was whether or not John Scopes had broken the law, prosecution witness William Jennings Bryan saw the conflict as one between science and faith.

"Science is a magnificent force, but it is not a teacher of morals. It can perfect machinery, but it adds no moral restraints to protect society from the misuse of the machine . . . The [Scopes] case has assumed the proportions of a battle-royal [a struggle involving many people] between unbelief that attempts to speak through so-called science and the defenders of the Christian faith."

Clarence Darrow saw the conflict as a battle over free speech.

"If today you can take a thing like evolution and make it a crime to teach it in the public school, tomorrow you can make it a crime to teach it in the private schools, and the next year you can make it a crime to teach it . . . in the church. At the next session you may ban books and the newspapers. Soon you may set Catholic against Protestant and Protestant against Protestant, and try to foist [force] your own religion upon the minds of men."

ANALYSIS SKILL **ANALYZING POINTS OF VIEW**

Why did Darrow believe the Scopes trial was about free speech?

The Great Migration

CONNECT TO THE ARTS

From 1940 to 1941 artist Jacob Lawrence created a series of paintings that told the story of African Americans moving from the South to northern cities in search of jobs and equality. This is one of 60 paintings in the Migration Series. It shows African Americans about to begin their journey.

Where are the people in the painting going?

Minority Rights

During World War I large numbers of African Americans began leaving the South to take jobs in northern factories. This movement, called the **Great Migration**, continued during the economic boom of the 1920s. While African Americans found jobs in the North, they did not escape racism.

Racial Tensions

The economic recession that followed the war led to increased racial tensions. Many white laborers feared the competition for jobs. Several race riots broke out in 1919, including one in Chicago that left 38 dead.

Racial tensions and fear of foreigners helped give rise to a new form of the Ku Klux Klan, the racist group that had terrorized African Americans during Reconstruction. The new Klan harassed Catholics, Jews, and immigrants, as well as African Americans. It also worked against urbanization, women's rights, and modern technology. By the mid-1920s the Klan had become an influential force in American politics, with more than 5 million members. Its influence then began to decline as news of financial corruption became public.

Protecting Rights

People who were the targets of the Klan's hatred found new ways to protect their rights. In 1922, for example, the NAACP began placing advertisements in newspapers that presented the harsh facts about the large number of lynchings taking place across the South.

Another way minorities attempted to protect their rights was to strengthen their culture. During the 1910s and 1920s, **Marcus Garvey** encouraged black people around the world to express pride in their culture. Garvey argued that black people should establish economic independence by building their own businesses and communities. These ideas were the basis of a movement known as black nationalism. The New York *Amsterdam News* praised Garvey's work, saying he "made black people proud of their race."

Hispanic Americans also organized to fight prejudice and promote civil rights. In 1929 Mexican American leaders met in Corpus Christi, Texas, to form the League of United Latin American Citizens (LULAC). This group worked to end unfair treatment such as segregation in schools and voting restrictions.

BIOGRAPHY

Marcus Garvey

1887–1940

Marcus Garvey grew up in Jamaica and moved to the United States in 1916. A talented speaker, he quickly became one of the country's most famous and controversial black leaders. His newspaper *Negro World* promoted the idea of building an independent black economy. To encourage world-wide trade among black people, he created the Black Star Steamship Line. Some black leaders, including W. E. B. Du Bois, considered Garvey's ideas dangerous and extremist. After a series of legal problems related to his steamship company, Garvey was arrested in 1922 and was later deported.

Drawing Inferences How did Marcus Garvey try to help African Americans?

Most Native Americans lacked the legal protections of citizenship and the right to vote because they were not citizens of the United States. The fact that thousands of Native Americans had performed military service in World War I helped bring about change. In 1924 Congress passed the Indian Citizenship Act, granting citizenship to all Native Americans. However, the federal government also attempted to buy or take back some of the reservation lands. Native Americans successfully organized to stop these attempts, which were part of a larger effort to encourage Indians to adopt the culture of white Americans.

READING CHECK **Finding Main Ideas** How did minorities react to discrimination in the 1920s?

SUMMARY AND PREVIEW Americans saw many conflicts as their culture changed. In the next section you will learn about entertainment and the arts in the 1920s.

Section 2 Assessment

go.hrw.com
Online Quiz
KEYWORD: SC7 HP24

Reviewing Ideas, Terms, and People

1. a. **Recall** How did **flappers** express their freedom?
   b. **Elaborate** How were young people of the 1920s more independent than their parents?
2. a. **Identify** What caused the **Red Scare,** and what was its result?
   b. **Explain** Describe the results of the immigration laws of the 1920s.
3. a. **Recall** What kinds of social conflicts developed during the 1920s?
   b. **Describe** What did the **Twenty-first Amendment** accomplish?
   c. **Analyze** How did **fundamentalism** influence the **Scopes trial**?
4. a. **Identify** How did minorities fight for their rights in the 1920s?
   b. **Define** What was the **Great Migration**?
   c. **Draw Conclusions** Why did **Marcus Garvey** call for black people to build their own businesses?

Critical Thinking

5. **Identifying Cause and Effect** Review your notes on social changes that took place in the 1920s. Then copy the graphic organizer below and use it to identify the causes and effects of several changes in American society.

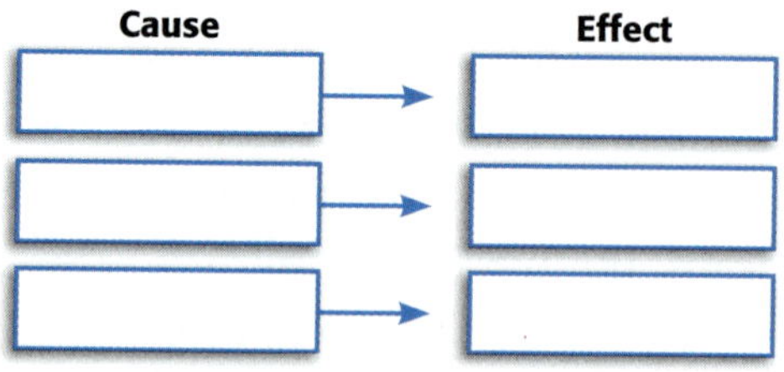

FOCUS ON WRITING

6. **Taking Notes on New Fashions** In the 1920s many women wore fashions that reflected their new independence. Look back at the example of flapper fashion on page 759. Think of how a radio advertisement could describe clothing like this to an audience that cannot see it.

The Jazz Age

SECTION 3

If YOU were there...

The year is 1924, and the New York Giants are playing the Washington Senators in the World Series. You just bought your first radio, and you are listening to an announcer describe the tense action as the seventh and deciding game goes into extra innings. You used to have to wait to read about the games in the newspaper. Now you can follow your favorite team pitch by pitch!

What other forms of entertainment could the radio bring to you?

BUILDING BACKGROUND You read earlier about the rise of mass culture in the United States in the late 1800s. Newspapers, department stores, and world's fairs allowed millions of Americans to share the same cultural activities. In the 1920s technologies such as radio broadcasts and movies helped the rise of mass culture continue.

A National Culture

On November 2, 1920, KDKA, the first commercial radio station, announced that Warren Harding had won the presidential election held that day. Just one year later, stations broadcast the action from the 1921 World Series. One newspaper writer predicted, "It might not be too long before farmers at the four corners of the Union may sit in their own houses and hear the president of the United States." Such an event seemed amazing to Americans in the early 1900s. But it quickly became a reality, as hundreds of radio stations began broadcasting all over the United States.

National radio networks, such as the National Broadcasting Company (NBC) and Columbia Broadcasting System (CBS), allowed people all over the country to listen to the same programs. People suddenly had access to music, news, weather reports, children's bedtime stories, sports broadcasts, and political speeches without leaving their homes. Business owners loved this technology because it allowed their advertisements to reach millions of listeners. Radio helped build a new national culture by allowing Americans everywhere to share common experiences.

What You Will Learn...

Main Ideas

1. Radio and movies linked the country in a national culture.
2. Jazz and blues music became popular nationwide.
3. Writers and artists introduced new styles and artistic ideas.

The Big Idea

Musicians, artists, actors, and writers contributed to American popular culture in the 1920s.

Key Terms and People

talkie, *p. 766*
Jazz Age, *p. 767*
Harlem Renaissance, *p. 768*
Langston Hughes, *p. 768*
Lost Generation, *p. 768*
expatriates, *p. 768*
Georgia O'Keeffe, *p. 769*

TAKING NOTES As you read, look for examples of popular culture in the 1920s. Record your notes in a diagram like this.

1920s Popular Culture
1.
2.
3.
4.

THE IMPACT TODAY

The Academy of Motion Picture Arts and Sciences has held the Oscar ceremony every year since 1929. It was first broadcast over the radio in 1930, and in 1953 the Academy Awards were first televised.

Movies also became a major national passion in the 1920s. Though early motion pictures had no sound, they opened a new world of exciting adventures for audiences. People packed theaters to see Westerns, romances, and stories about bootlegging gangsters. Movie fans were even more thrilled by the 1927 movie *The Jazz Singer*, in which actor Al Jolson shouted the line "You ain't heard nothin' yet!" This was the first **talkie**, or motion picture with sound.

The movies quickly became big business. By the end of the decade, Americans were buying 95 million movie tickets each week, an amazing figure considering that the U.S. population was only 123 million. Young movie fans copied hair and clothing styles of movie stars. Fans felt a personal connection to stars like Douglas Fairbanks, Charlie Chaplin, and Mary Pickford, who was known as "America's Sweetheart." Few fans at the time realized that Pickford was also a smart businesswoman. She was one of the highest paid actors in Hollywood and a founder of United Artists, one of the nation's most successful film companies.

Movie stars were not the only national heroes. Fans packed baseball stadiums to watch the great players of the 1920s, especially George Herman "Babe" Ruth. Ruth shattered home-run records, drawing thousands of new fans to the sport. Because baseball was segregated, African American players and business leaders started their own league. Negro League stars such as Satchel Paige and Josh Gibson are considered to be among the best baseball players in history.

Fans always loved to see athletes break records. In 1926 American swimmer Gertrude Ederle became the first woman to swim the English Channel between England and France, beating the men's world record by almost two hours.

Pilots also became national heroes in the 1920s. Charles Lindbergh dominated the national news in 1927 when he completed the first nonstop solo flight across the Atlantic Ocean, traveling from New York to Paris. A few years later, Amelia Earhart became the first woman to fly solo across the Atlantic.

New ideas like psychoanalysis became more popular. Developed by psychologist Sigmund Freud, psychoanalysis is a method for examining human behavior to find out why people behave the way they do.

READING CHECK **Summarizing** How did American culture change during the 1920s?

Time Line

Popular Culture of the 1920s

1920 Babe Ruth begins playing for the New York Yankees.

1920

1924 First Negro-League World Series is played.

Popular Music

With a booming economy and exciting forms of entertainment, the 1920s became known as the Roaring Twenties. An explosion in the popularity of jazz music gave the decade another nickname—the **Jazz Age**.

Jazz developed in New Orleans, where African American musicians blended spirituals with European harmonies and West African rhythms. When blacks moved north during the Great Migration, they brought their music with them.

As with many new forms of popular culture, jazz sparked arguments between older and younger generations. "When my grandmother found out that I was playing jazz music . . . she told me that I had disgraced the family," remembered "Jelly Roll" Morton, an early jazz composer. But young Americans loved the music and the wild, fast-paced dances that went along with it. Dance crazes sweeping the nation included the Charleston, the Toddle, and the Shimmy. New magazines arose that taught dance steps to subscribers.

Jazz musicians such as Louis Armstrong experimented with various sounds and rhythms to create a new kind of music. Armstrong, who played the trumpet, was known for his solo numbers. His method of stepping out from the band to perform a solo was an innovation that is still copied by musicians today. Another major figure of the Jazz Age was conductor and composer Edward "Duke" Ellington. His "big band" sound blended many instruments together in songs such as "Take the A Train." Ellington described the exciting life of Jazz Age musicians in New York City:

> "A lot of guys liked to play so much that in spite of being on a regular job, they'd still hire out to work matinees, or breakfast dances . . . Nobody went to bed at nights and round three or four in the mornings you'd find everyone making the rounds bringing their horns with them."
>
> — Duke Ellington, quoted in *Reminiscing in Tempo*, by Stuart Nicholson

Blues music, which came from the rural South of the Mississippi Delta, also gained national popularity in the 1920s. Blues began as an expression of the suffering of African Americans during slavery. One of the leading blues singers of the 1920s was Bessie Smith, nicknamed the Empress of the Blues. "She had music in her soul," said Louis Armstrong.

ACADEMIC VOCABULARY

innovation a new idea or way of doing something

READING CHECK **Finding Main Ideas** Where did jazz originate, and what musical styles influenced it?

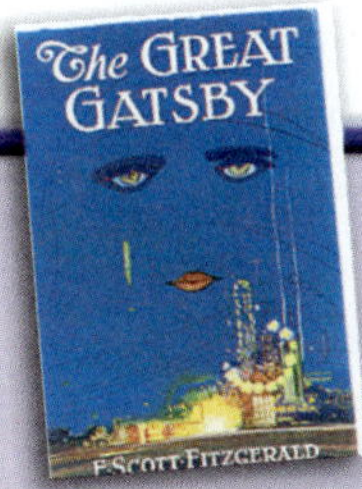

1925 F. Scott Fitzgerald's *The Great Gatsby* is published.

1925 Louis Armstrong begins recording with his band, the Hot Five.

1926 Gertrude Ederle becomes the first woman to swim across the English Channel.

1926 NBC, the first national radio network, begins broadcasting.

1927 Charles Lindbergh completes the first non-stop solo flight across the Atlantic Ocean.

1927 *The Jazz Singer*, the first full-length talkie, is released.

1928

ANALYSIS SKILL **READING TIME LINES**

Which events reflected people's interest in breaking records?

Writers and Artists

While musicians were creating new forms of music, writers and artists were also reshaping American culture. Many creative works of the 1920s are still admired today.

NC History Makers

Thomas Wolfe
Author Thomas Wolfe wrote about growing up in North Carolina and is today regarded as the state's most famous native author.

The Harlem Renaissance

Many of the African Americans who came north in the Great Migration built a thriving community in the Harlem neighborhood of New York City. This community became the center of the **Harlem Renaissance**, a period of African American artistic accomplishment.

Primary Source

POEM

"I, Too"

In one of his most celebrated poems, Langston Hughes expressed both pride in being African American and faith in the American dream.

"I, Too

I, too, sing America.
I am the darker brother.
They send me to eat in the kitchen
When company comes,
But I laugh,
And eat well,
And grow strong.

Tomorrow,
I'll be at the table
When company comes.
Nobody'll dare
Say to me,
'Eat in the kitchen,'
Then.

Besides,
They'll see how beautiful I am
And be ashamed—
I, too, am America."

ANALYSIS SKILL **ANALYZING PRIMARY SOURCES**

Analyzing Who do you think Hughes is referring to when he speaks of "they"?

Harlem Renaissance writers included **Langston Hughes** and Claude McKay. Hughes produced poems, plays, and novels about African American life. His works often incorporated African American slang and jazz rhythms. McKay was a poet and activist who spoke out against racial discrimination and called on African Americans to stand up against lynchings and other violence.

Another important writer of the Harlem Renaissance was Zora Neale Hurston. Her novels, such as *Their Eyes Were Watching God,* reflected the experiences of African American women.

The Lost Generation

Other Americans also wrote of their experiences living in the United States and in places around the world. Soon after he graduated from high school in Illinois, Ernest Hemingway volunteered as an ambulance driver in World War I. Hemingway called the war "the most colossal, murderous, mismanaged butchery that had ever taken place on earth." He began writing short stories and novels, and soon he gained fame for his powerful and direct writing style. Hemingway was among a group of young American writers who expressed feelings of disillusionment in the American society that they felt denied them a voice in their own futures. Author Gertrude Stein called these writers "a lost generation." Writers who criticized American society in the 1920s thus became known as the **Lost Generation**.

Many members of the Lost Generation moved to Paris in the 1920s and formed a community of **expatriates**—people who leave their home country to live elsewhere. Hemingway wrote about the expatriate community in his best-selling novel *The Sun Also Rises*. Another Lost Generation writer was F. Scott Fitzgerald. His novel *The Great Gatsby* focused on what he saw as the loss of morality behind the seemingly fun and free-spirited times of the Jazz Age. Criticizing a glamorous couple, Fitzgerald wrote:

"They were careless people . . . they smashed up things and creatures and then retreated back into their money or their vast carelessness or whatever it was that kept them together, and let other people clean up the mess they had made."

—F. Scott Fitzgerald, *The Great Gatsby*

Another writer of the time, Sinclair Lewis, became the first American to receive the Nobel Prize in literature.

New Directions in Art

Painters were also experimenting with new artistic styles in the 1920s. Edward Hopper painted images of the loneliness of modern urban life. **Georgia O'Keeffe** was well known for her detailed paintings of flowers and of the Southwest.

Architects of the 1920s embraced a style they called art deco. Buildings constructed in this style had clean, sharp lines that resembled machines. Today art-deco skyscrapers still stand out in American city skylines.

READING CHECK **Comparing and Contrasting** How were the artists of the Harlem Renaissance and the Lost Generation similar and different?

BIOGRAPHY

Georgia O'Keeffe

1887–1986

Georgia O'Keeffe grew up in Wisconsin and studied art in Chicago and New York. While teaching art at a college in Canyon, Texas, she would sometimes hike in Palo Duro Canyon, where she sketched scenes of amazing colors and rock formations. This was the start of a lifelong fascination with the beauty of the desert landscape. O'Keeffe lived much of her life in rural New Mexico, where many of her paintings were created. Animal bones, rocks, and desert flowers fill her works. She would often paint these objects in close-up view, showing tiny details. O'Keeffe said, "Most people in the city rush around so, they have no time to look at a flower. I want them to see it whether they want to or not."

Finding Main Ideas How did Georgia O'Keeffe's life influence her painting?

SUMMARY AND PREVIEW Americans became interested in new forms of entertainment and art in the 1920s. In the next chapter you will learn about how life changed in the 1930s.

Section 3 Assessment

go.hrw.com
Online Quiz
KEYWORD: SC7 HP24

Reviewing Ideas, Terms, and People

1. a. **Recall** What new forms of entertainment dominated American society during the 1920s?
   b. **Identify** What was the first **talkie**?
2. a. **Explain** Why were the 1920s called the **Jazz Age**?
   b. **Make Inferences** Why do you think jazz music became so popular?
3. a. **Recall** How did writers and artists express new ideas during the 1920s?
   b. **Describe** What did the **Lost Generation** writers express in their works?
   c. **Predict** How might the artists of the **Harlem Renaissance** influence African American artists of later generations?

Critical Thinking

4. **Categorizing** Review your notes on examples of popular culture in the 1920s. Then copy the graphic organizer below. Use it to categorize examples of popular culture in the 1920s.

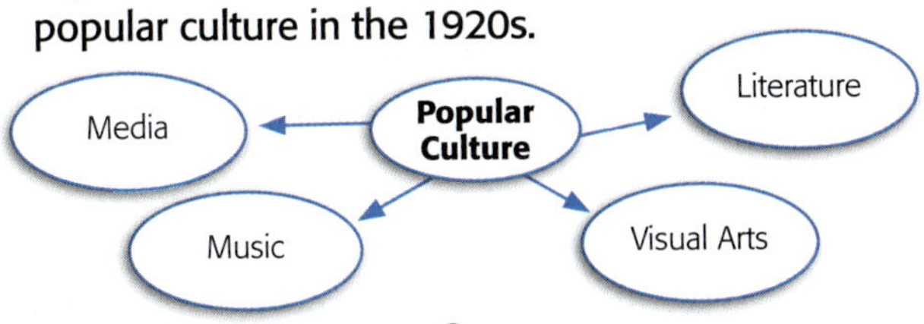

FOCUS ON WRITING

5. **Taking Notes on Entertainment** Make a list of popular forms of entertainment in the 1920s. How would you persuade people to attend a sports event, a talkie, or a jazz club? Begin to think about which product or form of entertainment you will choose for your radio advertisement.

North Carolina Skills
3.02 Interpret graphs and charts.

Comparing Graphs

Define the Skill

Graphs are often a very useful way to organize historical information. They can present a large amount of detailed information clearly. Graphs can be an especially good way of showing how something like population or average income changed over time.

When information is organized in a graph, it is often easy to see patterns. Looking at two related graphs, you can compare patterns and make conclusions. For example, you can ask yourself, "Do the numbers in the graphs go up or down for the same reasons? What are the causes behind the changes shown by these graphs?"

Learn the Skill

These guidelines will help you to compare information in two or more graphs.

1. Use your basic graph-interpreting skills. Identify each graph's subject, purpose, and type. Study its parts and categories.
2. Analyze the data in each graph. Then compare any increases, decreases, changes, or patterns you find.
3. Finally, draw conclusions about the relationship between the information in each graph. Think about what could cause such relationships. It will probably help you to review what you know about related events at the same time.

Practice the Skill

Compare the graphs below to answer the following questions.

1. What are the topics of these graphs?
2. What percentage of American households had electricity in 1922? What was the first year when more than half of American households had electricity?
3. Based on the information in the graphs, draw a conclusion about how electricity changed American households.

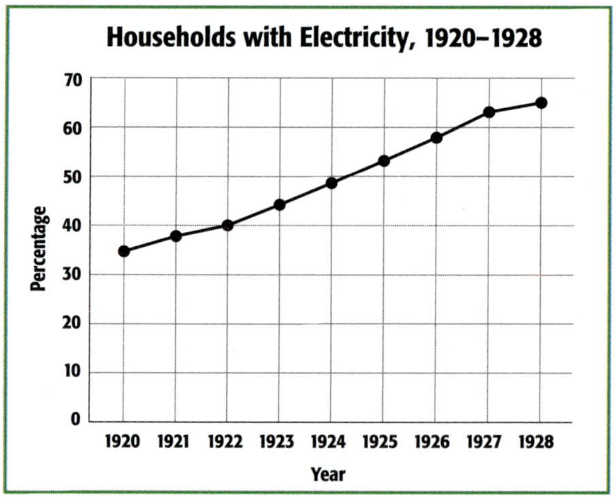

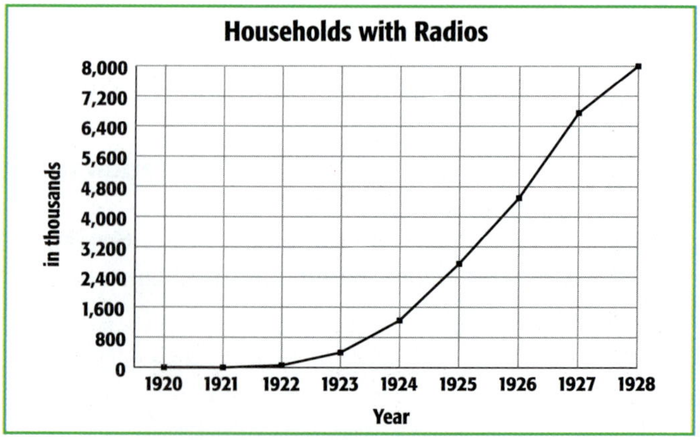

Source: *Historical Atlas of the United States*

CHAPTER 24 Chapter Review

HOLT

History's Impact

▶ **video series**

Review the video to answer the closing question:

How did the post–World War I economy have an impact on film, literature, and music?

Visual Summary

QUICK FACTS *Use the visual summary below to help you review the main ideas of the chapter.*

Political leaders tried to create economic prosperity during the 1920s.

Women found new freedom and opportunity in post–World War I America.

People enjoyed new forms of entertainment during the 1920s.

Reviewing Vocabulary, Terms, and People

Complete each sentence by filling in the blank with the correct term or person from the chapter.

1. Harlem Renaissance writer __________ wrote poems, plays, and novels about African American life.

2. The United States and other nations signed the __________, which outlawed war.

3. In the __________, Clarence Darrow defended a high school teacher tried for teaching evolution.

4. The __________ repealed prohibition.

5. Writers who criticized American culture during the 1920s were known as the __________.

6. African Americans moved north for jobs during the __________.

Comprehension and Critical Thinking

SECTION 1 *(Pages 752–757)*

7. a. Describe What was President Warren Harding's plan for strengthening the U.S. economy?

b. Explain What methods did Henry Ford's competitors use to attract customers?

c. Elaborate What do you think might have made the Kellogg-Briand Pact more effective?

SECTION 2 *(Pages 758–764)*

8. a. Recall What was the Red Scare?

b. Analyze What are some reasons women had more opportunities in the 1920s?

c. Evaluate Would you have become involved in the youth culture if you had lived during the 1920s? Why or why not?

SECTION 3 *(Pages 765–769)*

9. a. **Identify** What were talkies?

   b. **Explain** How did African Americans play an important role in Jazz Age culture?

   c. **Predict** How do you think new aspects of American culture affected life after the 1920s?

Reviewing Themes

10. **Society and Culture** How did the prosperity of the 1920s change American culture?

11. **Science and Technology** What new forms of technology emerged in the 1920s?

Social Studies Skills

Comparing Graphs *Use the Social Studies Skills taught in this chapter to answer the question below.*

12. Look back at the line graphs on page 770. Do you think a graph showing the number of radio stations in the United States during the 1920s would look similar to these graphs? Explain your answer.

Using the Internet

go.hrw.com
KEYWORD: SC7 CH24

13. **Activity: Experiencing the Jazz Age** The arts flourished in America during the 1920s. There were amazing developments in the literary and visual arts, and new forms of performing arts, like blues and jazz, became popular. Enter the activity keyword. Use the Internet links provided to research some of the most influential writers, artists, and musicians of the 1920s. Choose one and conduct an imaginary interview with that person about his or her work and impact on American culture. Document your conversation by creating an audio recording or by writing a transcript.

Reading Skills

Synthesizing Information *Use the Reading Skills taught in this chapter to answer the question below.*

> The number of women in the workforce continued to grow as well. Women with college degrees worked as nurses, teachers, librarians, and social workers . . . Women were still discouraged from pursuing fields such as medicine, law, and architecture, however. By the end of the 1920s, less than 5 percent of the country's doctors, lawyers, and architects were women. The percentage was small—but it was beginning to rise. *(p. 759)*

14. Which of the following sources might have been used to synthesize the information above?

   a. a history of architecture

   b. an instructional manual for nurses

   c. a history of working women in the 1920s

   d. the list of graduates from a women's college in 1910

Focus on Writing

15. **Writing Your Radio Advertisement** Look over your notes and choose one product that was popular in the 1920s. Think about these questions as you design your radio ad: Who is your audience? How will this product improve people's lives? What words or sounds will best describe your product? Write the dialogue for your ad, including directions for the actors. Also, include information about music or sound effects you want to use.

CHAPTER 24 Standardized Test Practice

DIRECTIONS: Read each question and write the letter of the best response.

1 President Warren Harding's secretary of the interior was convicted and jailed for his participation in the

A Scopes trial.

B Teapot Dome scandal.

C Red Scare.

D Kellogg-Briand Pact.

2 Marcus Garvey was a leader in which of the following movements?

A black nationalism

B fundamentalism

C socialism

D communism

3 Which of the following is a reason why consumers bought more manufactured products in the 1920s?

A More Americans had electricity in their homes, so they could use new electric appliances.

B Radio and print advertising made it easier to buy products.

C Immigrants came to the United States in record numbers and bought new goods.

D The Lost Generation felt separated from American culture.

4 Which of the following was a famous Jazz Age writer from North Carolina?

A Thomas Wolfe

B Mary Pickford

C Charles Lindbergh

D Edward "Duke" Ellington

5 One effect of the Red Scare was

A the election of Herbert Hoover in 1928.

B the trial and execution of Nicola Sacco and Bartolomeo Vanzetti.

C new opportunities for women, immigrants, and minorities.

D the Scopes trail.

6 President Calvin Coolidge once said, "The business of America is business." Which of the following statements *most likely* explains his views?

A The United States is very wealthy.

B Big businesses run the U.S. government.

C The U.S. economy is driven by private businesses.

D Private businesses will be eliminated.

7 Read the following excerpt from a 1928 campaign speech by Herbert Hoover and use it to answer the question below.

> "We in America today are nearer to the final triumph over poverty than ever before in the history of any land . . . We have not yet reached the goal, but given a chance to go forward with the policies of the last eight years, we shall soon with the help of God be in sight of the day when poverty will be banished from this nation."
>
> — Herbert Hoover, 1928 inaugural speech

Document-Based Question What did Hoover believe about poverty in the United States?

CHAPTER 25 1929–1939

The Great Depression

North Carolina Standards

Social Studies Objectives

6.01 Identify the causes and effects of the Great Depression and analyze the impact of New Deal policies on Depression Era life in North Carolina.

9.02 Identify past and present state and local leaders from diverse cultural backgrounds and assess their influence in affecting change.

Language Arts Objectives

1.03 Interact in group activities and/or seminars in which the student:
- shares personal reactions to questions raised.
- gives reasons and cites examples from text in support of expressed opinions.
- clarifies, illustrates, or expands on a response when asked to do so, and asks classmates for similar expansion.

2.02 Use multiple sources of print and non-print information to explore and create research products in both written and presentational forms by:
- determining purpose, audience, and context.

3.01 Explore and evaluate argumentative works that are read, heard and/or viewed by:
- comparing the argument and counter-argument presented.
- identifying/evaluating the effectiveness of tone, style, and use of language.
- evaluating the author's purpose and stance.

go.hrw.com
North Carolina
KEYWORD: SC7 NC

Focus on Writing

Journal Entry We know a lot about life during the Great Depression because many Americans described their experiences in journals and letters. In this chapter you will read about how people struggled through hard times in the 1930s. Read the chapter and then write a one-page journal entry as if you were a person living during the Depression. You may choose to write from the point of view of a student, artist, farmer, or other individual. As you read, think about how the events in the 1930s may have affected this person.

STAGE BROADWAY SCREEN
VARIETY 25¢
WALL ST. LAYS AN EGG

UNITED STATES

1929 The U.S. stock market crashes on Black Tuesday.

1930

WORLD

1930 Mahatma Gandhi and a group of followers begin the Salt March.

HOLT

History's Impact

▶ **video series**
Watch the video to understand the impact of the 1929 stock market crash.

What You Will Learn...

The prosperity of the Roaring Twenties came crashing to an end in October 1929. Americans who had been dreaming of growing rich were suddenly forced to focus on day-to-day survival. Many Americans, like the man in this photo, had to sell prized possessions just to eat. In this chapter you will learn how Americans coped with the economic difficulties of the 1930s.

1932 Franklin D. Roosevelt wins his first presidential election, beating Herbert Hoover.

1935 The CIO is organized.

1937 The first Social Security payments are made.

1939 The film *The Wizard of Oz* is released.

1932 | 1934 | 1936 | 1938 | 1940

1932 At least 30 million people worldwide are unemployed.

1933 Adolf Hitler becomes chancellor of Germany.

1936 Jesse Owens wins four gold medals at the Berlin Olympics.

1937 War officially begins between Japan and China.

1938 Violence against German Jews erupts into Kristallnacht ("night of broken glass").

Reading Social Studies

by Kylene Beers

Economics | Geography | Politics | Society and Culture | Science and Technology

Focus on Themes In this chapter, you will learn about the Great Depression, one of the most serious **economic** crises in America's history. You will also learn about the **politics** that arose to try to deal with this crisis. Finally, you will read about how the Depression affected the global economy and how world leaders responded to it.

Recognizing Implied Main Ideas

Focus on Reading When you read, you will notice that not every paragraph has a main idea sentence. Sometimes the main idea is implied.

Implied Main Ideas While main ideas give a basic structure to a paragraph, supporting details help convince the reader of the author's point. Main ideas can be presented in a sentence, or simply implied. Usually, a paragraph without a main idea sentence will still have an implied main idea that ties the sentences together.

Notice how one reader found the main idea of the following paragraph.

During the boom years of the 1920s, one General Motors executive boldly declared: "Anyone not only can be rich, but ought to be rich." For almost all of the Roaring Twenties, the stock market was a bull market, or one with rising stock values. It seemed easy to make money by investing in stocks. For example, you could have bought shares in the Radio Corporation of America for $85 each at the beginning of 1928. You could have sold them a year later for $549 each. *(p. 778)*

This quote is about making money and being rich. Maybe the main idea is about money or economics.

This sentence is about making money through the stock market. I guess the main idea has to do with investing.

Here is a great example of how easy it was to make money in the late 1920s. I think the main idea is something like "The stock market provided an easy way for many to become rich in the 1920s."

You Try It!

Read the following paragraph and then answer the questions below.

> The action began when Roosevelt called Congress into a special session. Known as the Hundred Days, the session started just after the inauguration and lasted until the middle of June. During the Hundred Days, Roosevelt and Congress worked together to create new programs to battle the Depression and aid economic recovery. These programs became known as the New Deal.
>
> *From Chapter 25, p. 784*

1. List two ideas that this paragraph discusses.
2. How are these two ideas related to each other?
3. Write an example of the main idea of this paragraph.
4. Which details support your main idea?

As you read Chapter 25, think of a main idea for any paragraph that does not have a main idea sentence.

Key Terms and People

Chapter 25

Section 1

buying on margin *(p. 778)*
Black Tuesday *(p. 779)*
business cycle *(p. 780)*
Great Depression *(p. 780)*
Bonus Army *(p. 781)*
Franklin D. Roosevelt *(p. 782)*

Section 2

New Deal *(p. 784)*
fireside chats *(p. 785)*
Tennessee Valley Authority *(p. 785)*
Frances Perkins *(p. 785)*
Eleanor Roosevelt *(p. 787)*
Social Security Act *(p. 787)*
Congress of Industrial Organizations *(p. 788)*
sit-down stike *(p. 788)*

Section 3

Dust Bowl *(p. 790)*
Mary McLeod Bethune *(p. 792)*
John Steinbeck *(p. 793)*
Woody Guthrie *(p. 793)*

Academic Vocabulary

In this chapter you will learn the following academic words:

implement *(p. 781)*
authority *(p. 786)*

SECTION 1

The End of Prosperity

What You Will Learn...

Main Ideas

1. The U.S. stock market crashed in 1929.
2. The economy collapsed after the stock market crash.
3. Many Americans were dissatisfied with Hoover's reaction to economic conditions.
4. Roosevelt defeated Hoover in the election of 1932.

The Big Idea

The collapse of the stock market in 1929 helped lead to the start of the Great Depression.

Key Terms and People

buying on margin, *p. 778*
Black Tuesday, *p. 779*
business cycle, *p. 780*
Great Depression, *p. 780*
Bonus Army, *p. 781*
Franklin D. Roosevelt, *p. 782*

TAKING NOTES As you read, look for information about the American economy in the 1920s and 1930s. Take notes about your findings in a diagram like the one shown.

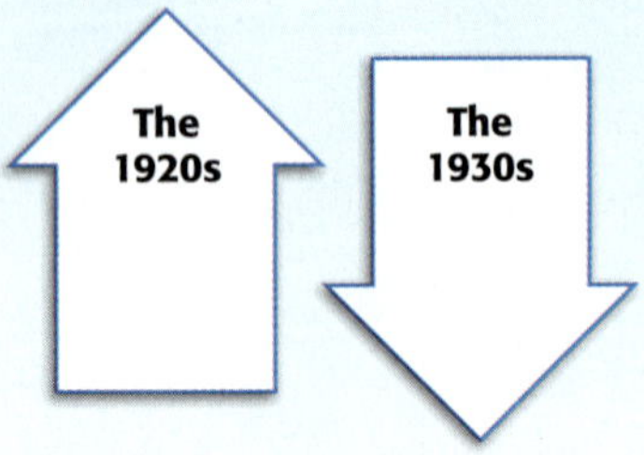

If YOU were there...

For almost a year you've been working part-time at a neighborhood store. You earn money for your family and still have time to go to school. But when you arrive at work today, your boss says business has been so bad that he can't afford to pay you anymore. With your father out of work, your family had been counting on your income from this job.

How can you continue earning money to help your family?

BUILDING BACKGROUND By the late 1920s many Americans were used to year after year of economic expansion. It was easy to believe that the prosperity of the 1920s would last forever. But the U.S. economy historically has experienced periods of prosperity followed by periods of economic downturn. This cycle would continue in a way that shocked Americans in the 1930s.

The Stock Market Crashes

During the boom years of the 1920s, one General Motors executive boldly declared: "Anyone not only can be rich, but ought to be rich." For almost all of the Roaring Twenties, the stock market was a bull market, or one with rising stock values. It seemed easy to make money by investing in stocks. For example, you could have bought shares in the Radio Corporation of America for $85 each at the beginning of 1928. You could have sold them a year later for $549 each.

The chance to make huge profits from small investments encouraged many people to buy stocks. Some who could not afford the stocks' full price began **buying on margin**—purchasing stocks on credit, or with borrowed money. These stockholders planned to sell the stocks at a higher price, pay back the loan, and keep what remained as profit. But this plan only worked if stock values went up. Few considered what would happen if the bull market turned into a bear market, or one with declining stock prices.

Black Tuesday

More than 16 million shares were traded on Wall Street on Black Tuesday, a record that stood for 39 years. Just weeks later, roughly one-third of the value of the stock market had disappeared.

How are the events of Black Tuesday shown on the chart?

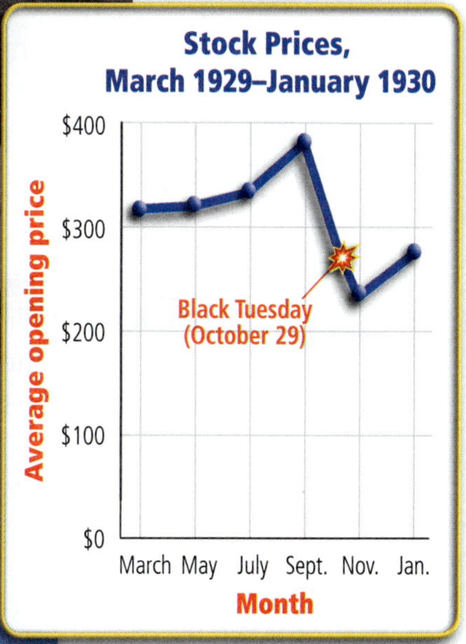

Stock prices peaked in the late summer of 1929. Then prices started to drop. Frightened investors who had bought stocks on margin rushed to sell their stocks in order to pay off their loans. On Thursday, October 24, panic hit the stock market. Within three hours the market had lost $11 billion in value. The following Monday, prices dropped again. On Tuesday, October 29—a day that became known as **Black Tuesday**—the stock market crashed. So many people wanted to sell their stocks, and so few wanted to buy, that stock prices collapsed. One journalist described the nightmare:

> "The wires to other cities were jammed with frantic orders to sell [stock]. So were the cables, radio, and telephones to Europe and the rest of the world. Buyers were few, sometimes wholly absent . . . This was real panic . . . When the closing bell rang, the great bull market was dead and buried."
>
> —Jonathan Norton Leonard, from *Three Years Down*

In September 1929 the total value of all stocks was $87 billion. Less than two months later, more than $30 billion in stock value had disappeared.

READING CHECK **Analyzing Information** Why was buying on margin risky?

The Economy Collapses

President Herbert Hoover tried to calm public fears by assuring Americans that the economy was still strong. "The fundamental business of the country . . . is on a sound and prosperous basis," he said. But this was just the beginning of more than 10 years of economic hard times.

The Banking Crisis

One immediate effect of the stock market crash was a banking crisis. Banks had invested heavily in the stock market, so they lost heavily when the market crashed. Banks had also lent their customers money to buy stocks on margin. Now those customers were unable to pay back their loans. Some banks went out of business. People who had deposited their life savings in those banks lost everything.

This created a panic all over the country, as customers rushed to their banks to withdraw their money. But since banks usually do not keep enough cash on hand to cover all deposits, the banks soon ran out of money. Many had to close their doors. In 1931 alone, more than 2,200 banks closed. The banking crisis contributed to a business crisis. Some businesses lost their savings in failed banks and had to close. Others were forced to cut back production, which meant they needed fewer workers. In the last three months of 1929, U.S. unemployment soared from under half a million workers to more than 4 million.

FOCUS ON NORTH CAROLINA

The furniture industry of North Carolina was especially hard hit by the Depression. Production fell by about half between 1929 and 1933.

The Causes

Throughout the history of the United States, the economy has followed a pattern of ups and downs. When businesses produce more than they can sell, unsold goods pile up. Businesses then cut back on their production and lay off workers. People who have lost their jobs, and others who are afraid they might soon lose their jobs, buy fewer goods. This causes more businesses to fail. This economic event is called a recession. Deep and long-lasting recessions are known as depressions.

As time passes, an economy will tend to bounce back. Consumers buy surplus goods, and companies increase production to meet the demand. Soon, more workers are hired and unemployment drops. This up-and-down pattern is known as the **business cycle**.

The United States had experienced recessions and depressions before 1929. Each time, the economy followed the business cycle and recovered. But the economy did not recover quickly from the downturn that began in 1929. Because of its severity and length, it was called the **Great Depression**.

Historians and economists still debate the exact causes of the Great Depression. Some believe that the government's monetary policy was a cause. Most agree that a major factor was the overproduction of goods at a time when the market for those goods was shrinking. Companies built millions of cars and appliances during the 1920s. By the late 1920s, however, most people who could afford these products already had them. That meant that American businesses were producing far more goods than people were consuming.

Uneven distribution of wealth made this problem worse. In 1929 the wealthiest 5 percent of Americans earned one-third of all income, while the bottom 40 percent earned only one-eighth of all income. Millions of Americans simply did not earn enough money to buy expensive new products.

Declining world trade also hurt American manufacturers. Europeans were still recovering from World War I and could not afford many American goods. At the same time, high tariffs made it difficult for European nations to sell products to the United States. As a result, Europeans had even less money to buy American goods.

READING CHECK **Making Predictions** Do you think the Great Depression could have been avoided? How?

Unemployment during the Depression

CONNECT TO ECONOMICS

People are considered unemployed if they are trying to find work but do not have a job. High rates of unemployment hurt the economy because unemployed people cannot buy many goods and services. This causes businesses to lose money.

During what year was unemployment the highest?

Primary Source

POLITICAL CARTOON

"Blame It on Hoover"

Presidents can affect the economy to some degree through their policies. During the Great Depression, President Hoover was blamed for the financial crisis. Political cartoons like this one gave voice to those Americans who thought Hoover could have prevented the crisis or could have brought it to an end quickly through government programs.

How does the cartoonist show Hoover reacting to the crisis?

What kind of people are blaming Hoover?

A Most Vicious Circle

—Costello in the Albany "News."

ANALYSIS SKILL **ANALYZING PRIMARY SOURCES**

Why is this cartoon useful for showing the feelings of the American public during the Great Depression?

Hoover's Reaction

As unemployment skyrocketed, more and more Americans struggled just to feed themselves and their families. Hungry people searched city dumps for scraps of food. One woman remembered taking off her glasses when she cooked so she could not see the maggots in the meat her family was about to eat. Private charities, as well as state and local governments, set up soup kitchens and breadlines. But the need far exceeded the available resources. Many people turned to President Herbert Hoover and the federal government to lead the relief effort.

Hoover knew that many Americans needed help. He did not believe, however, that it was the federal government's role to provide direct relief to Americans. Hoover felt it was up to private individuals and institutions, not the government, to offer relief. Despite this belief, Hoover did **implement** some new government programs. In 1932 he created the Reconstruction Finance Corporation (RFC). That year, the RFC loaned $1.2 billion to 5,000 different financial institutions, including banks and farm mortgage companies. Hoover continued to resist giving direct assistance to individuals.

This angered Americans who believed the president should do more to fix the economy. People bitterly referred to empty pockets turned inside out as Hoover flags. Groups of tin and cardboard shacks built by homeless families were nicknamed Hoovervilles.

In 1932 a new Hooverville was built in Washington, D.C. Its more than 17,000 residents were World War I veterans, some with their families. Called the **Bonus Army**, they had come to the capital to demand early payment of a military bonus. After the government denied the payment, most of the veterans returned home. About 2,000, however, stayed in their shantytown.

President Hoover authorized General Douglas MacArthur to use U.S. troops to evict the Bonus Army. MacArthur used force, including tear gas and tanks, to scatter the veterans. Several veterans were killed. The public reacted with outrage to the government's treatment of war veterans. Americans would have a chance to express this frustration in the upcoming election.

READING CHECK **Making Generalizations**
How would you describe President Hoover's response to the Depression?

FOCUS ON NORTH CAROLINA

Governor O. Max Gardner introduced the "Live-at-Home" program in 1929. This program urged farm families to grow their own food and taught them how to preserve food for later use through canning. The program was eventually copied in other states.

ACADEMIC VOCABULARY

implement put in place

Election of 1932

The Republican Party nominated Herbert Hoover again for president in 1932, but few people believed he could win. Regarding his chances of re-election, even Hoover realized that "the prospects are dark." Still, he began campaigning hard for a second term.

THE IMPACT TODAY

Before 1932, candidates did not attend their party's nominating convention. Roosevelt broke with this tradition, setting a new precedent. Today presidential candidates give televised speeches at party conventions.

He called the election "a contest between two philosophies of government." He warned that the government aid programs Democrats were promising would weaken Americans' spirit of self-reliance.

By 1932, however, much of the public had lost confidence in Hoover. Many even blamed him for the Depression. In contrast, as governor of New York during the first years of the Depression, **Franklin D. Roosevelt** had taken active steps to provide aid. He directed the state government to provide relief for the state's citizens, especially farmers. He also helped establish the Temporary Emergency Relief Administration, which gave unemployment assistance to many out-of-work New Yorkers.

Roosevelt's confident and optimistic personality appealed to many voters. At the Democratic Party convention, Roosevelt declared to Americans: "I pledge you, I pledge myself, to a new deal for the American people." Voters responded overwhelmingly to this message of hope. Roosevelt won the 1932 election in a landslide. In addition, the Democrats won strong majorities in both houses of Congress.

READING CHECK **Analyzing Information** How did Franklin D. Roosevelt win the 1932 presidential election?

SUMMARY AND PREVIEW After the stock market crash and the start of the Great Depression, Franklin Roosevelt offered hope for the future. In the next section you will learn about his programs for relief.

Section 1 Assessment

go.hrw.com
Online Quiz
KEYWORD: SC7 HP25

Reviewing Ideas, Terms, and People

1. a. **Recall** Why did the stock market crash in 1929?
   b. **Compare** How is **buying on margin** similar to buying on an installment plan?
2. a. **Recall** What happened to the economy as a result of the stock market crash?
   b. **Explain** Why did many banks close in the late 1920s and early 1930s?
   c. **Draw Conclusions** What do you think was the goal of U.S. tariffs?
3. a. **Make Inferences** Why did many Americans blame President Hoover for the Depression?
   b. **Describe** What did the **Bonus Army** want?
   c. **Elaborate** Do you think Americans were justified in blaming Hoover for the hard times?
4. a. **Identify** Which party was more successful in the 1932 elections?
   b. **Make Inferences** Why do you think voters did not listen to Hoover's ideas about government?
   c. **Elaborate** How do you think **Franklin D. Roosevelt**'s experiences as governor of New York helped him appeal to voters?

Critical Thinking

5. **Identifying Cause and Effect** Review your notes on the American economy in the 1920s and 1930s. Then copy the graphic organizer below and use it to identify the economic causes of the Depression and their effects.

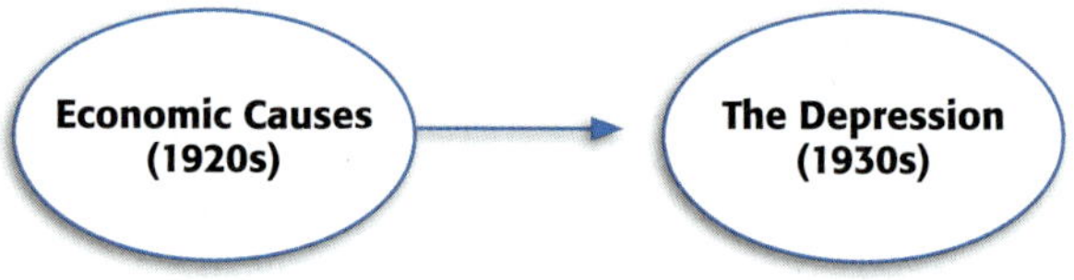

FOCUS ON WRITING

6. **Taking Notes on the End of Prosperity** To begin thinking about creating a character for your journal entry, answer the question at the end of the "If YOU Were There" on page 778. Then make some notes on the stock market crash, the banking crisis, and rising unemployment. Decide how your character would feel about these developments.

BIOGRAPHY

Franklin Delano Roosevelt

How would you try to lead your country through times of national crisis?

When did he live? 1882–1945

Where did he live? Roosevelt lived much of his life in New York State, where he served in the state senate and as governor. He also lived in Washington, D.C., while he was serving as assistant secretary of the navy and later as president. He had a second home in Warm Springs, Georgia.

What did he do? He began the New Deal, a set of government programs designed to help the country survive and recover from the Great Depression. He gave many Americans hope for the future when he spoke to them in his fireside chats. Roosevelt also led the country through World War II. His support for strong ties between the Allied countries helped the Allies achieve victory.

Why is he so important? Roosevelt led the United States during two of the most serious crises that our country has ever faced: the Great Depression and World War II. He served as president for 12 years, longer than any other. Many of the programs he began in the 1930s expanded the role of government in American life.

Making Predictions How do you think Franklin Roosevelt's experience as president during the Depression might have helped him lead the country during World War II?

KEY EVENTS

1905
Marries Eleanor Roosevelt

1921
Stricken with polio; unable to walk without leg braces and canes for the rest of his life

1928
Elected governor of New York

1932
Elected president; reelected in 1936, 1940, and 1944

1941
U.S. entry into World War II

1945
Dies at his home in Warm Springs, Georgia

"The only thing we have to fear is fear itself, nameless, unreasoning, unjustified terror."

Franklin Roosevelt, 1933 inaugural address

SECTION 2

Roosevelt's New Deal

What You Will Learn...

Main Ideas

1. Congress approved many new programs during the Hundred Days.
2. Critics expressed concerns about the New Deal.
3. New Deal programs continued through Roosevelt's first term in what became known as the Second New Deal.
4. Roosevelt clashed with the Supreme Court over the New Deal.

The Big Idea

Franklin Roosevelt's New Deal included government programs designed to relieve unemployment and help the economy recover.

Key Terms and People

New Deal, *p. 784*
fireside chats, *p. 785*
Tennessee Valley Authority, *p. 785*
Frances Perkins, *p. 785*
Eleanor Roosevelt, *p. 787*
Social Security Act, *p. 787*
Congress of Industrial Organizations, *p. 788*
sit-down strike, *p. 788*

TAKING NOTES As you read, take notes on the challenges the nation and President Roosevelt faced during the Great Depression in a chart like the one below.

The Nation	President Roosevelt

If YOU were there...

It has been five months since you lost your job. One of your friends has found work in a new government program that is hiring young people to work in national parks and forests. The pay is low, and you would have to leave home, but you would have enough food, a place to live, and a little money to send back to your family every month.

Would you take a job with the Civilian Conservation Corps? Why or why not?

BUILDING BACKGROUND When he ran for president in 1932, Franklin D. Roosevelt promised to provide relief to people suffering from the Depression. Even before he took office, Roosevelt began making plans with his Brain Trust, a group of expert advisers. People endured the harsh winter of 1932–1933, looking forward to Roosevelt's inauguration.

The Hundred Days

Immediately after taking the oath of office in March 1933, President Franklin Roosevelt spoke to the nation. In his first inaugural address, Roosevelt told nervous Americans that economic recovery was possible. "The only thing we have to fear is fear itself," he said, "nameless, unreasoning, unjustified terror." It was only fear of the future, he argued, that could keep America from moving forward. Roosevelt spoke openly of the severe problems facing the American people—unemployment, failing banks, and products with no markets. He promised that the government would help. "This nation asks for action," he said, "and action now."

The action began when Roosevelt called Congress into a special session. Known as the Hundred Days, the session started just after the inauguration and lasted until the middle of June. During the Hundred Days, Roosevelt and Congress worked together to create new programs to battle the Depression and aid economic recovery. These programs became known as the **New Deal**.

Tennessee Valley Authority, 1933–1945

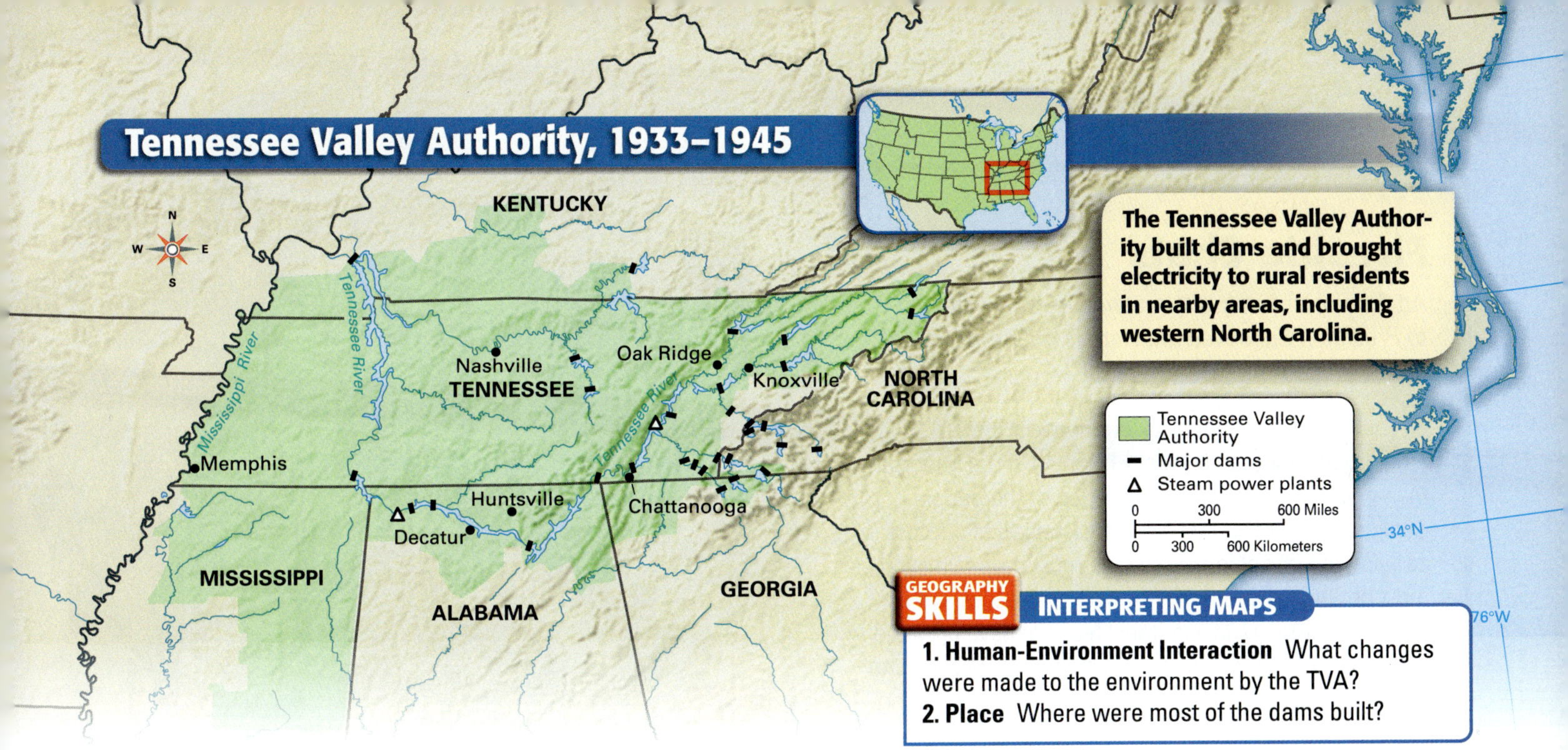

The Tennessee Valley Authority built dams and brought electricity to rural residents in nearby areas, including western North Carolina.

GEOGRAPHY SKILLS **INTERPRETING MAPS**

1. **Human-Environment Interaction** What changes were made to the environment by the TVA?
2. **Place** Where were most of the dams built?

Restoring Confidence

One of Roosevelt's first goals was to restore confidence in American banks. The day after his inauguration, Roosevelt announced a "bank holiday," ordering all banks to close temporarily. Three days later, Congress's special session began. Congress quickly passed the Emergency Banking Relief Act, and President Roosevelt signed it into law.

That Sunday, President Roosevelt gave the first of his **fireside chats**—radio addresses in which he spoke directly to the American people. In this first fireside chat, he explained the new bank relief law. The government would inspect the finances of every bank and allow only healthy banks to reopen. The new bank law and Roosevelt's fireside chat helped Americans trust banks with their money again. As banks reopened, there were no rushes to withdraw money. Over the next month, Americans deposited almost $1 billion in banks.

Relief and Recovery

Roosevelt next turned his attention to other serious problems. In 1933 some 13 million Americans—about 25 percent of the nation's workforce—were unemployed. New Deal programs helped to get Americans back to work. The Civil Works Administration (CWA) employed more than 4 million Americans, building roads and airports. One grateful CWA worker expressed the feelings of many when he said, "I was working, and I could again hold my head up when I met people." The Civilian Conservation Corps (CCC) provided jobs for hundreds of thousands of people through projects such as planting trees and improving national parks.

Another federal project, the **Tennessee Valley Authority** (TVA), hired people to build dams and generators, bringing electricity and jobs to communities in the Tennessee River valley. The New Deal also included programs to help farmers. The Farm Credit Administration (FCA) helped farmers refinance their mortgages so they could keep their farms. The Agricultural Adjustment Act (AAA) helped stabilize agricultural prices.

The National Industrial Recovery Act (NIRA) addressed business concerns by eliminating unfair competition among companies. This law was passed with support from Secretary of Labor **Frances Perkins**, the nation's first woman cabinet member.

READING CHECK **Categorizing** Which New Deal programs employed people to build public projects?

FOCUS ON READING

What is the main idea of this paragraph?

FOCUS ON NORTH CAROLINA

The Agricultural Adjustment Act of 1933 helped North Carolina farmers more than double their income by 1936. In general, tobacco farmers were helped more than cotton farmers.

Primary Source

RADIO BROADCAST

Fireside Chats

An American family sits around the radio listening to President Roosevelt answer his critics in his first fireside chat.

"There is an element in . . . our financial system more important than currency [money], more important than gold, and that is the confidence of the people. Confidence and courage are the essentials of success in carrying out our plan. You people must have faith; you must not be stampeded by rumors or guesses. Let us unite in banishing [driving away] fear. We have provided the machinery to restore our financial system; it is up to you to support and make it work. It is your problem no less than it is mine. Together we cannot fail."

ANALYSIS SKILL **ANALYZING PRIMARY SOURCES**

According to Roosevelt, how should the American people help the government deal with the banking crisis?

New Deal Critics

While many Americans approved of the New Deal, others criticized President Roosevelt's programs. New Deal critics fell into two main groups—those who believed the New Deal went too far, and those who believed it did not go far enough.

Those who felt the New Deal went too far criticized the enormous expansion of the federal government. For example, members of the American Liberty League said that New Deal laws gave the president too much **authority**. Many business leaders were concerned that the high cost of new government programs would lead to new taxes. As one writer explained:

ACADEMIC VOCABULARY

authority power, right to rule

"It's simple arithmetic to figure that taxpayers must pay the bills for current billions of emergency expenditures. The question is, Which taxpayers? Under this administration the answering finger points pretty much in the direction of business interests. Thus higher taxes of the future will eat into profits."

—W. H. Kiplinger, quoted in *The New Deal and the American People,* edited by Frank Freidel

One critic who thought the New Deal did not go far enough was a U.S. senator from Louisiana, Huey Long. Long proposed a program called "Share Our Wealth," which would tax rich Americans and use the money to help the poor. Every family would be guaranteed an annual income of $5,000. As Long prepared to challenge Roosevelt in the 1936 election, he announced his goal "to break up the swollen fortunes of America and to spread the wealth among all our people." Long's White House dreams ended when an assassin shot him in 1935.

Another fierce critic of Roosevelt's New Deal was Father Charles Edward Coughlin. Coughlin was a Roman Catholic priest in Detroit who developed a large following by broadcasting sermons over the radio. Although he initially supported Roosevelt and his programs, Coughlin eventually decided that the New Deal helped only business interests. Coughlin wanted the government to nationalize, or take over, all of the country's wealth and natural resources.

READING CHECK **Supporting a Point of View**

Do you agree with any of the New Deal critics? Why or why not?

The New Deal Continues

Despite criticism of the New Deal, Democrats increased their majorities in both houses of Congress in the 1934 election. With this show of support from the American people, Roosevelt continued to introduce additional New Deal legislation. These later laws were known as the Second New Deal.

The Second New Deal

After the Civil Works Administration ended in 1934, Congress formed a new agency to provide jobs for unemployed Americans. Between 1935 and 1943, the Works Progress Administration (WPA) employed some 8.5 million people on tens of thousands of projects all over the country. WPA employees built more than 650,000 miles of roads; 75,000 bridges; 8,000 parks; and 800 airports. WPA workers also built the Grand Coulee Dam in Washington and New York City's Lincoln Tunnel, as well as prisons, swimming pools, hospitals, and courthouses nationwide.

First Lady **Eleanor Roosevelt** was an active supporter of New Deal programs. She was concerned, however, that the WPA was not solving the problem of unemployment among young Americans in their teens and early twenties. "I live in real terror when I think we may be losing this generation," she said. "We have got to bring these young people into the active life of the community and make them feel that they are necessary." The first lady helped convince the president to create the National Youth Administration (NYA). The NYA gave part-time jobs to many students. These jobs allowed young workers to stay in school and help their families. One NYA worker said, "I tell you, the first time I walked through the front door with my paycheck, I was somebody!"

President Roosevelt also wanted to help those who were "unable . . . to maintain themselves independently . . . through no fault of their own." The **Social Security Act**, passed in 1935, provided some financial security for the elderly, the disabled, children, and the unemployed. To help pay for these programs, the law placed a new tax on workers and employers. The passage of the Social Security Act marked the first time the federal government took direct responsibility

THE IMPACT TODAY

Social Security today is a matter of great debate. Some Americans support the continuation of the program, while others believe that the government spends too much on the program and it should be privatized.

Selected New Deal Programs — QUICK FACTS

Program	Purpose
Emergency Banking Relief Act	Gave the executive branch the right to regulate banks
Farm Credit Act (FCA)	Refinanced loans to keep farmers from losing their land
Civilian Conservation Corps (CCC)	Created jobs for single, unemployed young men
Agricultural Adjustment Act (AAA)	Paid farmers to grow less (declared unconstitutional)
Tennessee Valley Authority (TVA)	Built dams and power plants in the Tennessee Valley
Federal Deposit Insurance Corporation (FDIC)	Guaranteed deposits in individual bank accounts
National Industrial Recovery Act (NIRA)	Established fair competition laws (declared unconstitutional)
Civil Works Administration (CWA)	Provided jobs for the unemployed
Works Progress Administration (WPA)	Created jobs in construction, research, and the arts
National Youth Administration (NYA)	Provided part-time jobs to students
National Labor Relations Act (Wagner Act)	Recognized unions' right to bargain collectively
Social Security Act	Provided government aid to the retired and unemployed

for many citizens' economic well-being. In a national radio address, Secretary of Labor Perkins told Americans she believed Social Security was "a most significant step in our national development, a milestone in our progress toward the better-ordered society."

FOCUS ON NORTH CAROLINA

In 1934 textile workers in North Carolina participated in a general strike that involved 400,000 American workers. The strike was the largest labor action in American history up to that time. The strike lasted about three weeks and resulted in many workers losing their jobs and homes. The defeat of the union left the South largely anti-union for the next 50 years.

New Deal Labor Programs

The National Industrial Recovery Act of 1933 helped regulate business by requiring minimum wage and allowing collective bargaining. In 1935, however, the Supreme Court declared the NIRA unconstitutional.

In response to this setback, Congress passed the National Labor Relations Act (NLRA). This law is sometimes called the Wagner Act after its sponsor, Senator Robert F. Wagner of New York. This law allowed workers to join labor unions and take part in collective bargaining. It also established the National Labor Relations Board to oversee union activities. Union membership grew after the passage of the Wagner Act. Organized labor became a powerful political force.

At the start of the Depression, many skilled workers belonged to craft unions. Such unions were often associated with the American Federation of Labor, which had existed since the 1880s. Unskilled workers, however, such as those who worked on assembly lines, did not qualify to belong to AFL unions. In 1935 a new union called the **Congress of Industrial Organizations** (CIO) organized workers into unions based on industry, not skill level. For example, all workers in the automobile industry would belong to the same union. The CIO also welcomed African American and Hispanic members, as well as women and immigrants.

Unions led a number of major strikes during the Depression. On New Year's Eve 1936, the CIO went on strike against General Motors for 44 days. Instead of leaving the buildings as strikers usually did, workers stayed in the factories so they could not be replaced by new workers. This strategy became known as the **sit-down strike**. The success of the General Motors strike attracted more workers to CIO unions.

READING CHECK **Comparing and Contrasting** How were the WPA and the Social Security Act similar, and how were they different?

National Youth Administration

A New Deal program called the National Youth Administration (NYA) helped thousands of young people continue their education while working to support their families. Eleanor Roosevelt was a strong supporter of the program, which aimed to teach young people the skills they would need to remain part of the workforce.

How did the NYA demonstrate the ideals of the New Deal?

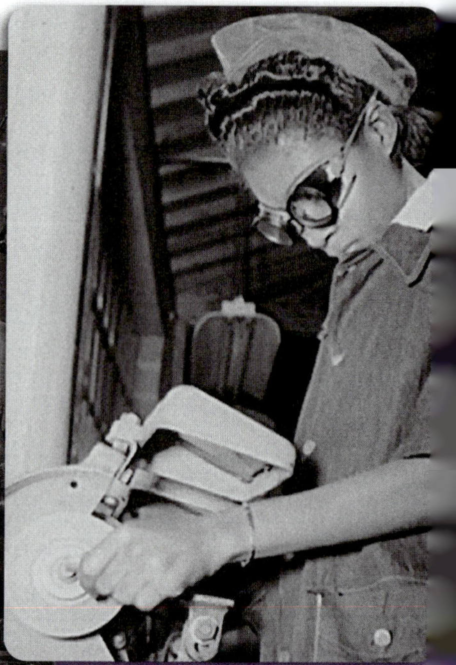

Clashes with the Court

Roosevelt won re-election by a huge margin in 1936, carrying every state but Maine and Vermont. Democrats expanded their dominant control of Congress. But Roosevelt and the Democrats in Congress could not control the Supreme Court.

In 1935 the Supreme Court issued a series of rulings declaring several New Deal programs, including the AAA, unconstitutional. Roosevelt and his advisers felt that the entire New Deal was in danger. "Mr. President, they mean to destroy us," said Attorney General Homer Cummings.

Roosevelt decided to propose a plan for reorganizing the federal judiciary that was soon to be labeled the "court-packing" bill. This bill would allow the president to appoint a new Supreme Court justice for every justice who was 70 years old or older. Roosevelt would be able to appoint six new justices immediately.

Roosevelt's judiciary plan drew harsh criticism from Congress and the public. Critics charged that Roosevelt was trying to change the balance of power so carefully defined in the U.S. Constitution. After a heated debate, Congress rejected the bill. The Supreme Court, however, did not overturn any more New Deal legislation. Roosevelt eventually had the opportunity to nominate nine new Supreme Court justices to replace those who had retired or died.

READING CHECK **Analyzing Information** Why did Roosevelt try to alter the Supreme Court?

SUMMARY AND PREVIEW Roosevelt's New Deal programs brought economic relief to many Americans. In the next section you will read about how the country continued to suffer the effects of the Depression.

Section 2 Assessment

go.hrw.com
Online Quiz
KEYWORD: SC7 HP25

Reviewing Ideas, Terms, and People

1. a. **Recall** What were the Hundred Days?
   b. **Make Inferences** What was the purpose of the bank holiday Roosevelt declared?
   c. **Evaluate** Which of the **New Deal** programs that passed during the Hundred Days was most effective? Why?
2. a. **Describe** Who were some of the critics of the New Deal?
   b. **Contrast** How were the ideas of Huey Long and the American Liberty League different?
   c. **Elaborate** Why do you think people supported New Deal critics such as Huey Long and Father Coughlin?
3. a. **Identify** What programs were part of the Second New Deal?
   b. **Make Inferences** Why did the Wagner Act encourage people to join unions?
4. a. **Recall** What happened to some of the New Deal programs when they were challenged in court?
   b. **Make Inferences** What was the purpose of Roosevelt's judiciary reorganization bill?

Critical Thinking

5. **Problem Solving** Review your notes on the challenges faced by the nation and the president during the Depression. Then copy the graphic organizer below and use it to identify Depression problems and New Deal solutions.

Problems	New Deal solutions

FOCUS ON WRITING

6. **Thinking about New Deal Programs** Take notes on the New Deal programs. Think about how your character might be affected by one or more of the programs. For instance, how do you think he or she would feel about getting a construction job with the Works Progress Administration?

SECTION 3

Americans Face Hard Times

What You Will Learn...

Main Ideas

1. Parts of the Great Plains came to be known as the Dust Bowl as severe drought destroyed farms there.
2. Families all over the United States faced hard times.
3. Depression-era culture helped lift people's spirits.
4. The New Deal had lasting effects on American society.

The Big Idea

All over the country, Americans struggled to survive the Great Depression.

Key Terms and People

Dust Bowl, *p. 790*
Mary McLeod Bethune, *p. 792*
John Steinbeck, *p. 793*
Woody Guthrie, *p. 793*

TAKING NOTES As you read, take notes on people's lives during the Depression. In each circle of a diagram like the one below, fill in details about their challenges, struggles, and culture.

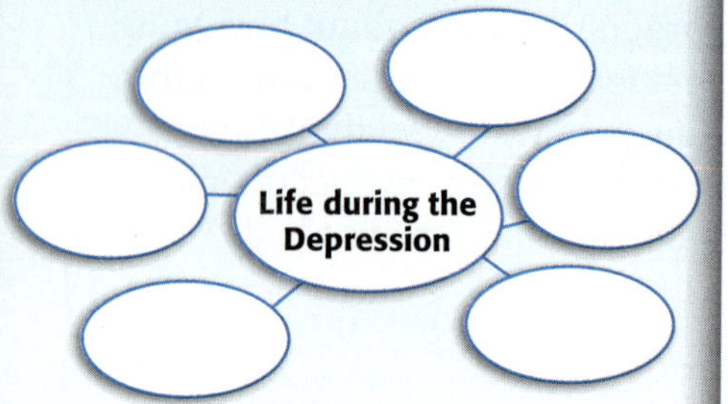

If YOU were there...

You own a wheat farm on the Great Plains, where you and your family live and work. Wheat prices have been low for years, and you have managed to get by only by borrowing thousands of dollars. Now the region is suffering through a terrible drought. Without water, you have been unable to grow any wheat at all. But if you do not start paying your debts, you will lose your farm.

Would you stay on your farm or leave and start a new life somewhere else?

BUILDING BACKGROUND The New Deal provided jobs and relieved suffering for many Americans, but it did not end the Great Depression. Unemployment fell to about 14 percent in 1937 but then rose again to about 17 percent in 1939. All over the country, people still struggled to survive.

The Dust Bowl

For American farmers, hard times began well before the start of the Great Depression. Despite the widespread prosperity of the 1920s, prices for farm products remained low. The Depression worsened this already bad situation. Conditions worsened again when a severe drought hit the Great Plains in the early 1930s and lasted most of the decade. From North Dakota to Texas, crops withered away. With no roots to hold it in place, topsoil began to blow away.

Massive dust storms swept the region, turning parts of the Great Plains into the **Dust Bowl**. "These storms were like rolling black smoke," recalled one Texas schoolboy. "We had to keep the lights on all day. We went to school with the headlights on, and with dust masks on." A woman from Kansas remembered dust storms "covering everything—including ourselves—in a thick, brownish gray blanket . . . Our faces were as dirty as if we had rolled in the dirt; our hair was gray and stiff and we ground dirt between our teeth."

Unable to raise crops, farmers in the Dust Bowl region could not pay their mortgages. Many lost their farms. Several New Deal programs tried to assist farmers by offering loans and by working to stabilize prices for farm products. Scientists also began thinking of ways to prevent dust storms during future droughts. Soil conservation experts encouraged farmers to adopt new farming methods to protect the soil. Grass was planted to hold soil in place, and rows of trees were planted to help break the wind. These changes have helped prevent another Dust Bowl in the years since the Great Depression.

For many farmers in the 1930s, however, the new programs came too late. After losing their crops and livestock to dust storms, about 2.5 million people left the area. Many packed up whatever they could fit in the family car or truck and drove to California to look for any kind of work they could find. Once there, they often found that there were already more workers than available jobs.

READING CHECK **Identifying Cause and Effect** How did the Dust Bowl affect farmers?

Hard Times

The Great Depression took a heavy toll on families all over the United States. Many families were forced to split up, as individual members roamed the country in search of work. To help their families buy food, children often had to drop out of school and take very low-paying jobs. Others left home

Primary Source

PERSONAL ACCOUNT

The Dust Bowl

Lawrence Svobida was a Kansas wheat farmer who saw his life's work destroyed in the 1930s.

"When I knew that my crop was irrevocably [forever] gone I experienced a deathly feeling which, I hope, can affect a man only once in a lifetime. My dreams and ambitions . . . and my shattered ideals seemed gone forever. The very desire to make a success of my life was gone, the spirit and urge to strive were dead within me. Fate had dealt me a cruel blow above which I felt utterly unable to rise."

ANALYSIS SKILL **ANALYZING PRIMARY SOURCES**

How did Svobida feel after his crop was destroyed?

Interactive Map

The Dust Bowl

go.hrw.com
Interactive Map
KEYWORD: SC7 CH25

Dust Bowl
Other areas with severe wind erosion
Migration routes
0 300 600 Miles
0 300 600 Kilometers

ANALYSIS SKILL **ANALYZING VISUALS**

Which part of the United States was affected by wind erosion?

Severe drought during the 1930s destroyed the livelihood of many Great Plains farmers. Here, a black cloud of dust rages toward the outbuildings of a farm.

to fend for themselves. One boy wrote this diary entry in 1932:

> "Slept in paper box. Bummed swell breakfast three eggs and four pieces meat . . . Rode freight [train] to Roessville. Small burg [town], but got dinner. Walked Bronson . . . Couple a houses. Rode to Sidell . . . Hit homes for meals and turned down. Had to buy supper 20 cents. Raining."
>
> —Anonymous, quoted in *The Great Depression*, by Thomas Minehan

The Great Depression was especially hard on minority groups. As white families moved west in search of jobs, Mexican Americans found it harder to get work. In California local leaders and unions convinced the government to deport many Mexican-born workers. Some of the workers' children were American-born, which made them U.S. citizens, but they were deported anyway.

African Americans also faced discrimination. Many lost jobs to unemployed white workers. One man recalled traveling around Michigan in search of work. He went into a factory that was hiring workers:

> "They didn't hire me because I didn't belong to the right kind of race. Another time I went into Saginaw, it was two white fellas and myself made three. The fella there hired the two men and didn't hire me. I was back out on the streets. That hurt me pretty bad, the race part."
>
> —Louis Banks, quoted in *Hard Times: An Oral History of the Great Depression*, by Studs Terkel

In spite of this type of discrimination, hundreds of thousands of African Americans were able to find work though relief programs such as the CCC and WPA. President Roosevelt also consulted with African American leaders, including educator **Mary McLeod Bethune**. Bethune was one of several African Americans who Roosevelt appointed to his administration. Other members included Walter White and William Henry Hastie. These advisers became known as the Black Cabinet. Their role was to advance the concerns of African Americans in the Roosevelt White House.

First Lady Eleanor Roosevelt was a strong supporter of equal rights. She encouraged the president to include African Americans in his recovery programs. In 1939 the Daughters of the American Revolution (DAR) refused to rent their auditorium to the African American singer Marian Anderson. In protest, Eleanor Roosevelt resigned her membership in the DAR. She then helped Anderson arrange a concert at the base of the Lincoln Memorial. Some 75,000 people attended.

READING CHECK **Drawing Inferences** What weakened families during the Depression?

Primary Source

PHOTOGRAPH

"Migrant Mother"

Photographer Dorothea Lange gained fame in the 1930s for documenting the conditions of the poor during the Depression. Lange took this famous photograph of a widowed migrant worker and two of her seven children. The woman worked in the pea fields of Nipomo, California. Her family survived by eating frozen peas and birds the children caught. The woman had just sold her car's tires for money to buy food.

ANALYSIS SKILL **ANALYZING PRIMARY SOURCES**

How would you describe the expression on the face of the woman in the photograph?

Depression-Era Culture

Starting in 1935, new Works Progress Administration projects began to put the country's painters, sculptors, writers, and actors to work. When he was criticized for hiring artists, WPA director Henry Hopkins said, "They've got to eat just like other people."

Some of the work done by WPA artists has become an important part of American culture. For example, WPA musicians went into the nation's rural areas to record cowboy ballads, folk songs, and African American spirituals. This music might have been lost without these recordings. Artists employed by the WPA made more than 2,500 murals and 17,000 pieces of sculpture for public spaces. WPA writers created a permanent record of American life by interviewing Americans of many different backgrounds about their lives and memories.

Like many people at the time, author **John Steinbeck** was deeply affected by the Great Depression. Depression life became a main theme of Steinbeck's most famous novel, *The Grapes of Wrath*. The novel tells the story of the Joads, a family of farmers who are forced to move to California for work.

Some of the music of the day expressed themes similar to Steinbeck's. Oklahoma-born folk singer **Woody Guthrie** crisscrossed the country singing his songs of loss and struggle. One contained the line, "All along your green valley I'll work till I die"—a grim reality for some Americans.

Swing music, meanwhile, became popular for a different reason. Instead of focusing on the sadness of the Depression, swing helped people forget their troubles. Big band leaders such as Duke Ellington, Benny Goodman, and Count Basie helped make swing wildly popular in the 1930s. People tuned into swing music shows on inexpensive radios and danced to the fast-paced rhythms. Radios provided people with other forms of entertainment as well. Every week millions of Americans put aside their worries to listen to radio shows such as *Little Orphan Annie* and *The Lone Ranger.*

Movies offered Americans another welcome escape from reality. One boy remembered how he and his friends would save their pennies for movie tickets. "[It] was two for a nickel," he said. "You'd come to the movie in the summer like 8:30 in the mornin' and you'd see about 200 kids." For 25 cents or less, adults, too, could forget their troubles as they watched historical dramas, gangster films, comedies, and musicals.

READING CHECK **Evaluating** How was the work of writers and musicians affected by the Great Depression?

Escape to the Movies

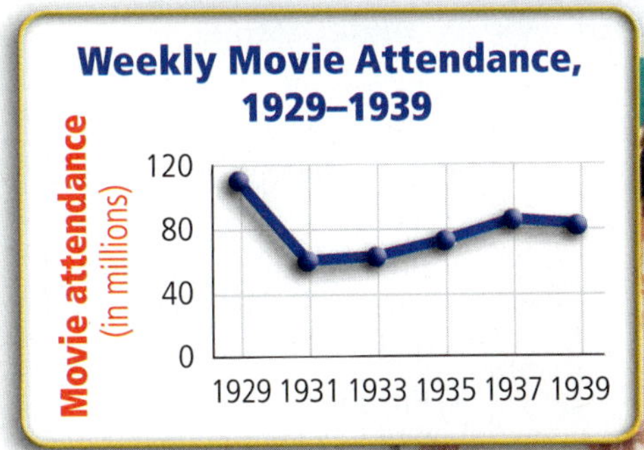

ANALYSIS SKILL **ANALYZING INFORMATION**

How many Americans attended movies in 1930?

THE IMPACT TODAY

Today many of the thousands of interviews conducted by WPA writers are available on the Internet. You can read the stories of former slaves, pioneers, Native American leaders, and others in their own words.

Causes and Effects of the New Deal

QUICK FACTS

Causes
- Stock market crash
- Banking crisis
- Soaring unemployment
- Farmers' troubles
- Widespread poverty

Effects
- Expanded role of federal government
- Created major programs such as Social Security and the FDIC
- Provided hope and relief to many Americans but did not end the Great Depression

Effects of the New Deal

People are still debating the effects of the New Deal today. New Deal critics point out that Roosevelt's programs did not end the Great Depression. Full recovery occurred in the early 1940s, after the United States entered World War II. Roosevelt's supporters, however, believe that the New Deal gave Americans help and hope in a time of severe economic crisis.

People today do agree that the New Deal greatly expanded the role of the federal government. Some of the programs and agencies created as part of the New Deal, such as Social Security and the Federal Deposit Insurance Corporation (FDIC), remain part of our lives. Social Security still provides economic relief to the elderly, children, and those with disabilities. The FDIC protects the savings of bank customers.

READING CHECK **Finding the Main Idea** What are some current government programs that began during the New Deal?

SUMMARY AND PREVIEW The New Deal helped Americans but did not end the Great Depression. The Depression finally ended after the United States entered World War II, which you will learn about in the next chapter.

Section 3 Assessment

go.hrw.com
Online Quiz
KEYWORD: SC7 HP25

Reviewing Ideas, Terms, and People

1. a. **Identify** What was the **Dust Bowl**?
   b. **Explain** What factors contributed to farmers' difficulties in the 1920s and 1930s?
2. a. **Recall** What were some of the problems people faced during the Depression?
   b. **Compare** How was the experience of African Americans and Mexican Americans in the Depression similar?
   c. **Evaluate** Do you think President Roosevelt did enough to help African Americans? Explain your answer.
3. a. **Draw Conclusions** Why do you think swing music, radio shows, and movies were popular during the Great Depression?
   b. **Identify** How did the WPA help the arts?
4. a. **Recall** What are the different viewpoints on the success of the New Deal?
   b. **Elaborate** How are Social Security and the FDIC still important today?

Critical Thinking

5. **Categorizing** Review your notes on life during the Great Depression. Then copy the graphic organizer below and use it to identify challenges people faced during the Depression and the ways they coped.

Challenges people faced	Ways people coped with challenges

FOCUS ON WRITING

6. **Taking Notes on the Hard Times** As you read this section, add notes about the Dust Bowl, family life, and Depression-era culture. What would it have been like to be a farmer at this time? How would you describe your experiences?

Depression-Era Literature

GUIDED READING

WORD HELP

migrant a person who moves regularly

Divide The Continental Divide separates rivers that flow east from those that flow west.

tributary stream that feeds into a larger river or lake (Steinbeck applies the word to the road system.)

1. ***From what are people on Highway 66 fleeing?***

2. ***How does Steinbeck describe what people are running from?***

from *The Grapes of Wrath*

by John Steinbeck (1902–1968)

About the Reading *Published in 1939,* The Grapes of Wrath *described the impact of the Great Depression on the nation. In this passage, Steinbeck describes a journey of Dust Bowl families to California.*

AS YOU READ **Look for details that appeal to the five senses.**

Highway 66 is the main migrant road. 66—the long, concrete path across the country, waving gently up and down the map, from the Mississippi [River] to Bakersfield [California]—over the red lands and the gray lands, twisting up into the mountains, crossing the Divide and down into the bright and terrible desert to the mountains again, and into the rich California valleys.

66 is the path of people in flight,[1] refugees from dust and shrinking land, from the thunder of tractors and shrinking ownership, from the desert's slow northward invasion, from the twisting winds that howl up out of Texas, from the floods that bring no richness to the land and steal what little richness is there.[2] From all of these the people are in flight, and they come into 66 from the tributary side roads, from the wagon tracks and the rutted country roads. 66 is the mother road, the road of flight.

CONNECTING LITERATURE TO HISTORY

1. **Steinbeck describes in vivid detail the fear that people on the road felt.** According to this passage, why might driving between towns be a terror? What does this tell you about the migrants?

2. ***The Grapes of Wrath* became a favorite among readers for its honest portrayal of the realities of the Depression.** Based on Steinbeck's description and on what you already know, how might people traveling on Route 66 have felt? Why?

Social Studies Skills

Analysis | Critical Thinking | **Civic Participation** | Study

North Carolina Skills
4.02 Examine, understand, and evaluate conflicting viewpoints.

Having a Debate

Define the Skill

The First Amendment to the U.S. Constitution guarantees freedom of speech, assembly, and the press. These freedoms have become a key part of American democracy. They guarantee that both government officials and citizens can express their opinions. People also have the right to express disagreement with leaders or the government.

The ability to discuss opposing points of views is key to a democratic society. In the United States, citizens vote for their leaders. Having access to different points of view helps people decide which candidates to support in elections.

One way to express opposing points of view is to have a debate. Debates are organized to present two sides of an issue. Debate rules make sure that both sides are treated fairly. By learning about the strengths and weaknesses of two positions on an issue, people can decide which position is more convincing.

Learn the Skill

Think about the opposition President Franklin D. Roosevelt faced when he tried to begin new programs during the Great Depression. He had to convince people to support his ideas. Roosevelt and members of his administration used radio programs and newspaper articles to promote their point of view and answer questions from their critics.

In a debate, it is important to make your point of view clear. Explain why you support a certain position or give specific reasons why you oppose it. The more detailed the argument, the more persuasive it will be. When you are in a debate, make sure to prepare plenty of evidence and examples to support your case.

Debaters have the chance not only to present a case but also to argue against the opposite point of view. One way to get ready for this is to think of possible arguments against your position. Prepare responses to each of these arguments in advance. Having good answers to criticism makes your position stronger.

In a debate, it is important to follow any rules that have been set up. Not all debates have the same rules. They do share some basic guidelines, however. Only one person is allowed to speak at once, and speaking time is limited. The two sides take turns presenting their arguments. Debates may have additional rules as well.

Practice the Skill

Suppose that your class is the Senate in 1933. President Roosevelt has already begun several new government programs. Now he is asking you to pass more new laws, which he believes will help the economy. Follow the guidelines above to have a debate about the New Deal. One group should support expanding the New Deal, and one group should oppose it. When the debate is over, answer the following questions.

1. Did your group make its point of view clear? Did it explain the reasons for taking that position? What do you think was your group's most persuasive supporting detail or example?
2. Did your group prepare arguments against the other side in advance? Were any of these arguments particularly effective?

CHAPTER 25 Chapter Review

HOLT

History's Impact

▸ **video series**

Review the video to answer the closing question:

How did some of Roosevelt's programs lessen the damage caused by the recessions of 1987 and the early 2000s?

Visual Summary

QUICK FACTS

Use the visual summary below to help you review the main ideas of the chapter.

The economy began to decline when the stock market crashed in 1929.

Many farmers from the Great Plains moved elsewhere to escape the devastation of the Dust Bowl.

President Roosevelt and Congress tried to end the financial crisis.

Reviewing Vocabulary, Terms, and People

Read each question and write the letter of the best response.

1. Which of the following refers to a severe economic downturn that lasted for more than 10 years?

a. the Bonus Army **c.** the bull market
b. the Great Depression **d.** the business cycle

2. Who was Franklin Roosevelt's secretary of labor and the first woman Cabinet member?

a. Frances Perkins **c.** Eleanor Roosevelt
b. Mary McLeod Bethune **d.** Dorothea Lange

3. Parts of the Great Plains where a severe drought struck were known as the

a. Tennessee Valley. **c.** Dust Bowl.
b. New Deal. **d.** Hoovervilles.

4. Which of the following means purchasing stocks on credit with a loan?

a. the installment plan **c.** the banking crisis
b. buying on margin **d.** bear market

Comprehension and Critical Thinking

SECTION 1 *(Pages 778–782)*

5. a. Describe What happened on Black Tuesday—October 29, 1929?

b. Summarize How did President Hoover respond to the Depression?

c. Elaborate Why do you think Americans were so unprepared for difficult times?

SECTION 2 *(Pages 784–789)*

6. a. Recall What New Deal programs did lawmakers create during the Hundred Days?

b. Explain How did the Works Progress Administration help Americans?

c. Evaluate Do you think the New Deal was successful? Explain your answer.

SECTION 3 *(Pages 790–794)*

7. a. **Recall** How did the Great Depression affect Mexican Americans?

   b. **Contrast** How did Depression-era culture show both hope and the difficulties of everyday life?

   c. **Draw Conclusions** Why do you think many African Americans supported President Roosevelt, even though they continued to face discrimination and segregation?

Reviewing Themes

8. **Economics** How did the economy of the country change during the Great Depression?
9. **Politics** What role did politics play in easing the Great Depression?

Reading Skills

Recognizing Implied Main Ideas *Use the Reading Skills taught in this chapter to answer the question about the reading selection below.*

> Banks had invested heavily in the stock market, so they lost heavily when the market crashed. Banks had also lent their customers money to buy stocks on margin. Now those customers were unable to pay back their loans. Some banks went out of business. People who had deposited their life savings in those banks lost everything. *(p. 779)*

10. Write a main idea for the paragraph above.

Using the Internet

go.hrw.com
KEYWORD: SC7 CH25

11. **Activity: Writing an Article** During the 1930s, part of the Great Plains region of the United States became known as the Dust Bowl. The troubled region earned its nickname from the dust storms that swept through the dry, drought-stricken area. Enter the activity keyword. Research accounts of the Dust Bowl and write a magazine feature article about it. Your article should include references to your research and quotations from accounts of the Depression, and it should have correct spelling, punctuation, and grammar.

Social Studies Skills

Having a Debate *Use the Social Studies Skills taught in this chapter to answer the question below.*

12. Suppose you have been invited to participate in a debate on Franklin Roosevelt's plan to "pack" the Supreme Court by adding extra justices. First decide on your position. Then prepare several supporting arguments. Summarize the main points of your argument in a paragraph.

FOCUS ON WRITING

13. **Writing Your Journal Entry** Review your notes. Then decide on a fictional character and a set of circumstances for your character. Choose one or more events from the Great Depression for your character to talk about. Write a one-page journal entry about the life of this person. Begin by placing a date from the 1930s at the top of the page. Think about what life would have been like for this person. Remember to describe how the character feels about his or her experiences. What are your character's hopes and fears for the future?

CHAPTER 25

Standardized Test Practice

DIRECTIONS: Read each question and write the letter of the best response.

1 President Roosevelt successfully used his fireside chats to

A promote the American movie industry.

B hold negotiations between labor unions and business owners.

C persuade many Americans to vote for him in the election of 1932.

D convince people that it was safe to keep their money in reopened banks.

2 Which of the following was *not* a cause of the Great Depression?

A World War I

B banks closing

C overproduction of goods

D high unemployment

3 How did the National Labor Relations Act affect organized labor?

A It increased the power of labor unions and helped them grow.

B It banned all strikes and increased the power of big business.

C It created new government jobs but did not affect labor unions.

D It gave relief money directly to labor unions to help unemployed workers.

4 Which of the following was a part of the New Deal?

A nationalizing businesses

B relieving unemployment

C guaranteeing every family an income of at least $5,000

D discouraging negotiations between labor unions and business owners

5 North Carolina's "Live at Home" program was *most likely* intended to

A put unemployed North Carolinians to work.

B create more factory jobs.

C show support for President Roosevelt's New Deal.

D help farm families become self-sufficient.

6 Which of the following was a way many families coped with the Depression?

A They bought stocks on margin.

B They sent their children to boarding schools in California.

C They moved to the Dust Bowl looking for farm jobs.

D They separated to look for work.

7 Read the excerpt from John Steinbeck's *The Grapes of Wrath* and use it to answer the question below.

"66 is the path of people in flight, refugees from dust and shrinking land, from the thunder of tractors and shrinking ownership, from the desert's slow northward invasion, from the twisting winds that howl up out of Texas, from the floods that bring no richness to the land and steal what little richness is there."

—John Steinbeck, *The Grapes of Wrath*

Document-Based Question Why did people travel on Highway 66, according to Steinbeck?

CHAPTER 26 1938–1945

World War II

North Carolina Standards

Social Studies Objectives

6.02 Describe the significance of major events and military engagements associated with World War II and evaluate the impact of the war on North Carolina.

6.03 Examine the significance of key ideas and individuals associated with World War II.

6.04 Assess the impact of World War II on the economic, political, social, and military roles of different groups in North Carolina including women and minorities.

Language Arts Objectives

2.02 Use multiple sources of print and non-print information to explore and create research products in both written and presentational forms by:

- understanding the focus.
- recognizing and/or choosing a relevant topic.
- researching and organizing information to achieve purpose.
- using notes and/or memory aids to structure information.

go.hrw.com
North Carolina
KEYWORD: SC7 NC

Focus on Writing

A Radio News Broadcast During World War II, millions of Americans had relatives fighting overseas. They relied on radio broadcasts for up-to-date news from the battlefronts around the world. In this chapter, you will read about American involvement in World War II. Then you will write a radio news broadcast about an event from the war.

United States

1938 Orson Welles broadcasts "War of the Worlds."

1938

World

HOLT

History's Impact

▶ **video series**
Watch the video to understand the impact of the GI Bill.

What You Will Learn...

In this chapter, you will learn how the United States prepared for and fought in World War II. Life changed at home, as U.S. industries worked around the clock to supply the Allied armies. Life also changed for the 16 million Americans who served in the military around the world, like these soldiers who took part in the D-Day invasion of Normandy, France.

1940 — 1942 — 1944 — 1946

1940 Alan Turing devises a way to break the code of the German Enigma machine.

1941 On December 7, the Japanese attack the U.S. fleet at Pearl Harbor, Hawaii.

1942 German submarines begin attacking the United States.

1943 Mussolini is overthrown and executed in Italy.

1944 U.S. forces participate in the D-Day invasion.

1944 The Allies enter Paris.

1945 The United States drops atomic bombs on Hiroshima and Nagasaki, Japan.

1945 Hideki Tojo, prime minister of Japan, attempts suicide after atomic bombs are dropped on Japan.

Reading Social Studies

by Kylene Beers

Economics | Geography | Politics | Society and Culture | Science and Technology

Focus on Themes In this chapter, you will read about the causes and consequences of World War II. You will learn about how **geography** played an important role in the fighting of the war. You will also read about how **society and culture** reacted to the Second World War.

Categorizing

Focus on Reading Have you ever read a schoolbook and been overwhelmed by the amount of information it contained? Categorizing events, people, and ideas can help you make sense of the facts you learn in this book.

Understanding Categorizing Ideas, people, events, and things can all be categorized in many different ways. For the study of history, some of the most useful ways are by time period and by similarity between events. Categorizing events by the people involved can also be helpful. Within a category, you can make subcategories to further organize the information.

People involved in WWII	Events of WWII
• Winston Churchill • Franklin D. Roosevelt • Adolf Hitler • Benito Mussolini • Hideki Tojo • Soldiers • Civilians	• Key battles • Treaties • Invasions ↓ **Invasions** • China • Rhineland • Czechoslovakia • Poland • Dunkirk • French Indochina • D-Day

You Try It!

The following passage is from the chapter you are getting ready to read. As you read the passage, look for ways to organize the information.

Japan Advances

American and Filipino forces under the command of American general Douglas MacArthur could not stop Japan's advance in the Philippines. MacArthur left the islands in March 1942, vowing to return. More than 70,000 American and Filipino soldiers surrendered to the Japanese. The exhausted soldiers were forced to march 63 miles up the Bataan Peninsula to prison camps. Many prisoners were starved and beaten by Japanese soldiers. More than 600 Americans and about 10,000 Filipinos died in the Bataan Death March.

From Chapter 26, p. 820

After you read the passage, answer the following questions.

1. What are two categories you could use to organize the information in this passage?

2. How many different kinds of people are mentioned in this passage?

3. What different places are mentioned in this passage?

4. Complete the chart below using the information from the passage above.

People involved	Countries involved	Places mentioned

As you read Chapter 26, remember to look for categories that can help you organize the information you read.

Key Terms and People

Chapter 26

Section 1
totalitarianism *(p. 804)*
Benito Mussolini *(p. 804)*
fascism *(p. 804)*
Adolf Hitler *(p. 805)*
Nazis *(p. 805)*
Joseph Stalin *(p. 805)*
Axis Powers *(p. 806)*
appeasement *(p. 806)*
Winston Churchill *(p. 806)*
Allied Powers *(p. 806)*
Lend-Lease Act *(p. 808)*
Pearl Harbor *(p. 808)*

Section 2
War Production Board *(p. 810)*
A. Philip Randolph *(p. 812)*
Tuskegee Airmen *(p. 812)*
Benjamin O. Davis *(p. 812)*
zoot-suit riots *(p. 813)*
internment *(p. 813)*

Section 3
Battle of El Alamein *(p. 816)*
Dwight D. Eisenhower *(p. 816)*
Battle of Stalingrad *(p. 817)*
D-Day *(p. 819)*

Section 4
Douglas MacArthur *(p. 820)*
Bataan Death March *(p. 820)*
Chester Nimitz *(p. 821)*
Battle of the Coral Sea *(p. 821)*
Battle of Midway *(p. 821)*
island hopping *(p. 822)*
Battle of Leyte Gulf *(p. 822)*
kamikaze *(p. 822)*

Section 5
Battle of the Bulge *(p. 826)*
Harry S. Truman *(p. 826)*
Holocaust *(p. 827)*
genocide *(p. 827)*
Manhattan Project *(p. 828)*
atomic bomb *(p. 828)*

Academic Vocabulary

In this chapter, you will learn the following academic word:
execute *(p. 822)*

SECTION 1

The War Begins

What You Will Learn...

Main Ideas

1. During the 1930s, totalitarian governments rose to power in Europe and Japan.
2. German expansion led to the start of World War II in Europe in 1939.
3. The United States joined the war after Japan attacked Pearl Harbor in 1941.

The Big Idea

The rise of aggressive totalitarian governments led to the start of World War II.

Key Terms and People

totalitarianism, *p. 804*
Benito Mussolini, *p. 804*
fascism, *p. 804*
Adolf Hitler, *p. 805*
Nazis, *p. 805*
Joseph Stalin, *p. 805*
Axis Powers, *p. 806*
appeasement, *p. 806*
Winston Churchill, *p. 806*
Allied Powers, *p. 806*
Lend-Lease Act, *p. 808*
Pearl Harbor, *p. 808*

TAKING NOTES As you read, take notes on the countries in which totalitarian governments gained power before World War II. Use a graphic organizer like the one below.

Totalitarianism before WW II	
Country	Leader

If YOU were there...

The year is 1933 and your family is struggling through the Great Depression along with millions of others. Sometimes your parents wonder if they should have left Italy to come to the United States. But conditions in Italy are far from ideal. A dictator rules the country, and the people have little personal freedom.

What would you say to your parents?

BUILDING BACKGROUND The devastating effects of the Great Depression reached well beyond the United States. In Europe, war debt and the huge costs of rebuilding after World War I made economic recovery even more difficult.

The Rise of Totalitarianism

Desperate to end the hard times, many people were willing to give up their individual rights to leaders who promised to deliver prosperity and national glory. As a result, in the 1920s and 1930s, several European countries moved toward **totalitarianism**, a political system in which the government controls every aspect of citizens' lives.

Italy

In the years after World War I, the people of Italy suffered through economic depression, unemployment, strikes, and riots. Many Italians looked for a strong leader who could bring stability to the country. They found such a leader in **Benito Mussolini**, who gained complete control of Italy in 1922. Mussolini's rule was based on **fascism**, a political system in which the "state"—or government—is seen as more important than individuals. Fascist systems are typically militaristic and headed by a strong leader.

Mussolini restored order to Italy and improved the economy through public works projects. But the fascist government violently crushed all opposition, destroying basic individual rights such as freedom of speech. In 1935 Mussolini tried to expand Italy's territory by attacking the nation of Ethiopia, making it a colony. Haile Selassie, Ethiopia's overthrown emperor, warned the world, "It is us today. It will be you tomorrow."

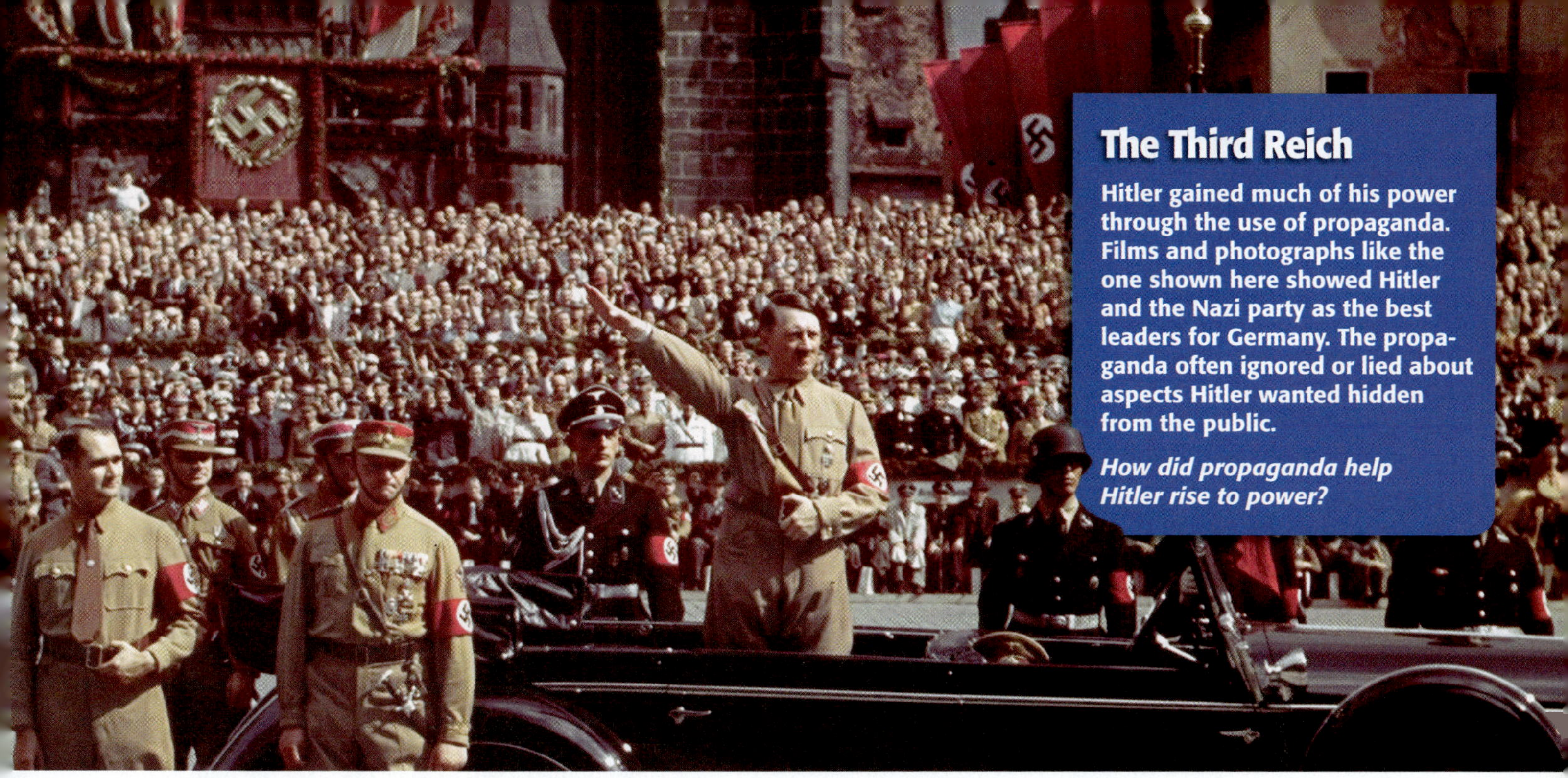

The Third Reich

Hitler gained much of his power through the use of propaganda. Films and photographs like the one shown here showed Hitler and the Nazi party as the best leaders for Germany. The propaganda often ignored or lied about aspects Hitler wanted hidden from the public.

How did propaganda help Hitler rise to power?

Germany

Germany was also suffering the effects of the global depression. In addition, many Germans were furious about the Treaty of Versailles, which forced Germany to make crippling reparation payments for its role in World War I. Politician and World War I veteran **Adolf Hitler** took advantage of public anger to gain power. A fiery speaker, he inspired huge audiences by vowing to restore Germany to prosperity and a position of international power.

Hitler also offered Germans a scapegoat, or someone to blame for their problems. He accused intellectuals, Communists, and especially Jews of causing Germany's defeat in World War I and its economic problems after the war. Only by ridding itself of Jews, Hitler declared, would Germany again rise to greatness. Hitler's National Socialist Party, or **Nazis**, gained a large following. Hitler became chancellor in 1933 and quickly seized all government power.

The Soviet Union

Hitler spoke with fury of his hatred of communism. But he had something in common with the Communist ruler of the Soviet Union—both ruled as ruthless dictators. By 1928 **Joseph Stalin** had become dictator of the Soviet Union. In the 1930s Stalin terrorized those he saw as political enemies, killing or imprisoning millions of Soviet citizens. As one Soviet artist put it, "There isn't a single thinking adult in this country who hasn't thought that he might get shot."

Japan

Though Japan never had one single dictator, a group of military leaders slowly gained complete control over the government during the early 1900s. By the early 1930s this group had more influence than the Japanese emperor. The military leaders wanted to build a large Japanese empire in East Asia. In 1931 Japan invaded and conquered a region in northern China and called it Manchukuo. From 1937 to 1938, at least 360,000 Chinese were killed by the invading Japanese in the fall of Nanjing. The United States protested the invasion. Fearful of another world war, however, most Americans opposed using force to help China.

READING CHECK **Comparing and Contrasting** What did the leaders of totalitarian governments have in common?

Germany Expands

Hitler dreamed of avenging Germany's defeat in World War I. "The lost land will never be won back by solemn appeals to God," he told Germans, "nor by hopes in any League of Nations, but only by force of arms." Hitler wanted to build an empire, uniting all German-speaking people in Europe. He also wanted "living space" for the growing German population.

In violation of the Treaty of Versailles, Hitler began to rebuild the German military. In 1936 Nazi troops invaded the Rhineland, a former German territory lost during World War I. That year he also signed an alliance with Mussolini, forming the **Axis Powers**. Japan later joined this pact. In 1938 Hitler forced Austria to unite with Germany. Then he demanded control of the Sudetenland, a region in Czechoslovakia where many Germans lived. When the Czechs refused, Hitler threatened war.

Nazi planes bombed London from September 1940 to May 1941. During that time, residents of London sought shelter wherever they could, including subway stations. Here, a relief effort passes out food to Londoners who have lost their homes.

Appeasement Fails

Czech leaders looked to their allies in France and Great Britain for help. But neither country wanted to be pulled into an armed conflict. British prime minister Neville Chamberlain organized a meeting with Hitler to work out a peaceful solution. At the 1938 Munich Conference, Germany was given control over the Sudetenland in return for a promise not to demand more land. This approach was known as **appeasement**—a policy of avoiding war with an aggressive nation by giving in to its demands. British admiral **Winston Churchill** was convinced that this strategy would not stop Hitler. "The government had to choose between shame and war," Churchill warned. "They have chosen shame. They will get war."

Churchill was right. In March 1939, German troops seized the rest of Czechoslovakia and began demanding territory from Poland. Great Britain and France pledged to defend Poland if Hitler attacked. To keep the Soviets out of the conflict, Hitler signed a nonaggression pact with Joseph Stalin in August 1939. In addition to promising not to attack each other, the two countries secretly agreed to divide Poland between them.

On September 1, 1939, Hitler's troops and tanks rushed into Poland. This was the start of World War II. Two days later, Britain and France, known as the **Allied Powers**, declared war on Germany. Neville Chamberlain spoke bitterly of the failure of appeasement, saying, "Everything that I believed in during my public life has crashed into ruins."

Hitler Moves West

The Allied Powers had little time to organize their forces to protect Poland. Using a strategy called *blitzkrieg,* or "lightning war," German tanks and airplanes broke through Polish defenses. As German forces drove into Poland from the west, the Soviets attacked from the east. Within a month, the two powers had taken control of Poland.

With Poland secure, Hitler turned toward western Europe. In the spring of 1940, Germany quickly conquered Denmark, Norway,

World War II in Europe, 1939–1941

GEOGRAPHY SKILLS INTERPRETING MAPS

go.hrw.com Interactive Map KEYWORD: SC7 CH26

1. **Place** Which countries shown on the map remained neutral during World War II?
2. **Human-Environment Interaction** What major British city was affected by the Battle of Britain?

Belgium, Luxembourg, and the Netherlands. German troops then invaded France, trapping hundreds of thousands of Belgian, British, and French soldiers in the French port city of Dunkirk. British ships raced to Dunkirk and carried the soldiers across the English Channel to safety in Britain.

German forces, meanwhile, continued their march through France. As the Germans approached the French capital of Paris, Italy declared war on the Allied powers. France surrendered to Germany on June 22, 1940. Many of the French soldiers who had escaped at Dunkirk, however, continued to resist Germany's occupation of France. In London, French general Charles de Gaulle organized a "Free French" army to fight alongside the Allies. "France has lost a battle," de Gaulle declared. "But France has not lost the war!"

The Battle of Britain

Great Britain now stood alone against Hitler's war machine. "The final German victory over England is now only a question of time," said German general Alfred Jodl. Hitler prepared to invade Britain. To safely move troops and equipment across the English Channel, Germany first had to defeat the British Royal Air Force (RAF). In July 1940 the Luftwaffe, or German air force, began attacking British planes and airfields in what became known as the Battle of Britain.

In August Hitler ordered the Luftwaffe to begin bombing British cities in the hope of crushing British morale. But Winston Churchill, the new prime minister, refused to give in. "We shall fight on the beaches," he vowed. "We shall fight in the fields and in the streets, we shall never surrender." Using the new technology of radar, the RAF was able to detect and destroy some 2,300 of the Luftwaffe's aircraft. Hitler canceled the invasion of Britain.

READING CHECK **Sequencing** What event sparked World War II?

FOCUS ON NORTH CAROLINA

Americans tuned in to their radios to listen to reports of the bombing of London. North Carolinian Edward R. Murrow broadcast from London, giving Americans vivid descriptions of the bombing and devastation. Murrow became one of the most respected journalists of the twentieth century, in part because of these reports.

The United States Joins the War

Most Americans opposed Hitler's actions, but they did not want to join the war. When President Franklin Roosevelt ran for re-election in 1940, he told voters that "your boys are not going to be sent into any foreign wars." Privately, however, Roosevelt was convinced that the United States would soon be at war.

THE IMPACT TODAY

Pearl Harbor is still the headquarters of the U.S. Pacific Fleet today. The sunken USS *Arizona*, still visible beneath the harbor waters, is a national memorial to the victims of the Pearl Harbor attack.

Helping the Allies

In 1941 Roosevelt proposed new programs to assist the Allies. "We must be the great arsenal [arms supply] of democracy," he told Congress. In March 1941 Congress passed the **Lend-Lease Act**, allowing the president to aid any nation believed vital to U.S. defense. Under Lend-Lease, the United States sent billions of dollars' worth of aid in the form of weapons, tanks, airplanes, and food to Great Britain, the Nationalists in China, and other Allied countries. In June 1941 Hitler violated his nonaggression pact with Stalin and invaded the Soviet Union. The Soviets then joined the Allies in the fight against Germany. In November the United States extended the Lend-Lease program to the Soviet Union, though many Americans worried about giving aid to a Communist country.

Japan Attacks Pearl Harbor

Like Germany and Italy, Japan was quickly building an empire. After conquering much of China in the 1930s, Japanese forces moved into Southeast Asia. Japan's leaders wanted control of oil and other resources there.

When Japanese forces captured French Indochina in July 1941, Roosevelt protested. He demanded that Japan withdraw. Then the United States froze Japanese funds in its banks and cut off exports to Japan.

Japanese military leaders had already begun planning a large-scale attack to destroy the U.S. naval fleet stationed at **Pearl Harbor**, in Hawaii. This would give Japan time to secure control of East Asia before the U.S. military could respond.

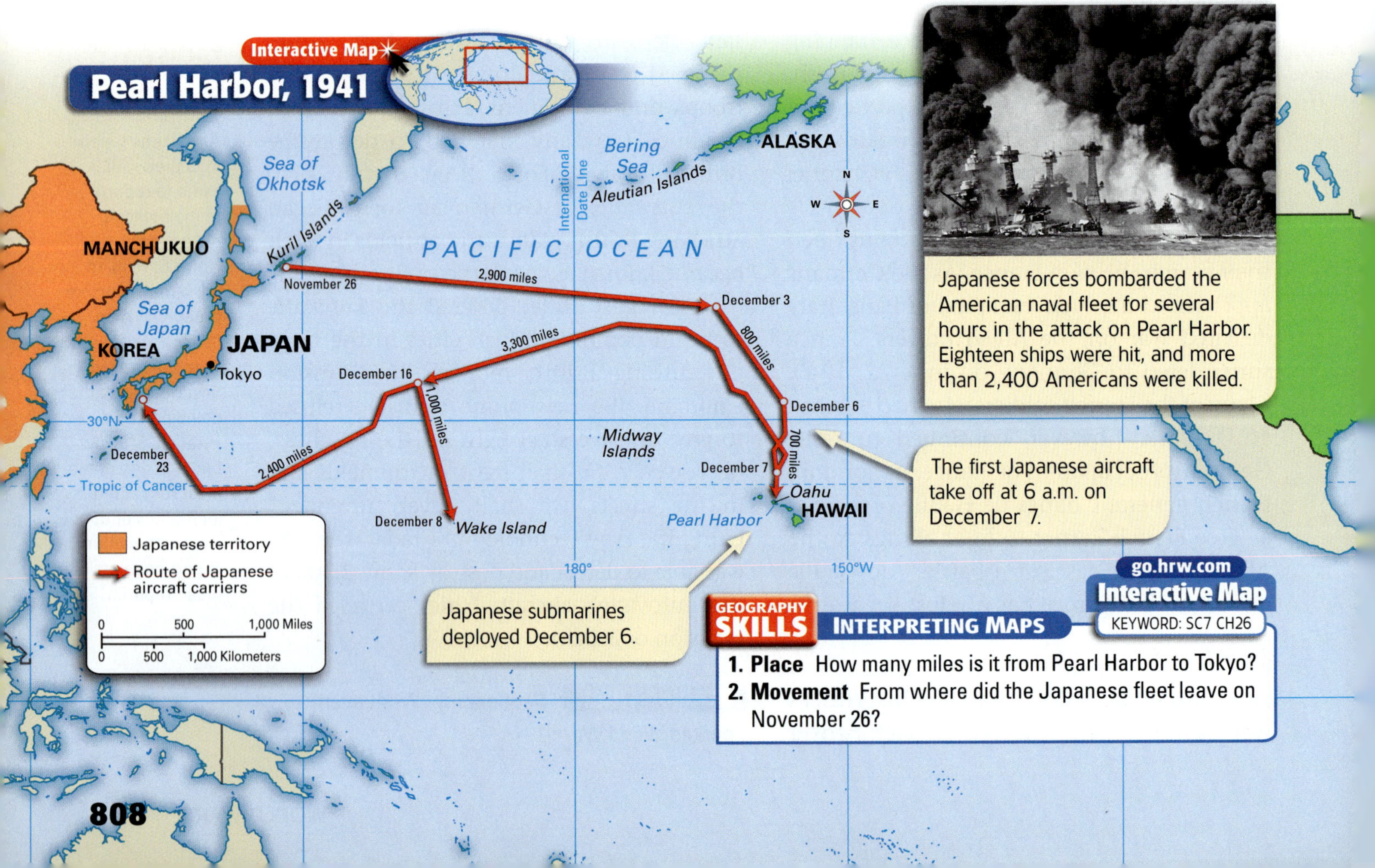

Japanese forces bombarded the American naval fleet for several hours in the attack on Pearl Harbor. Eighteen ships were hit, and more than 2,400 Americans were killed.

GEOGRAPHY SKILLS INTERPRETING MAPS

1. **Place** How many miles is it from Pearl Harbor to Tokyo?
2. **Movement** From where did the Japanese fleet leave on November 26?

At 7:55 A.M. on Sunday, December 7, 1941, Japanese airplanes dove from the sky and attacked Pearl Harbor. An American sailor aboard the USS *Arizona* remembered how quickly his battleship was hit and destroyed:

> "I began to realize there were dead men all around me . . . it was obvious the ship was doomed. I made my way to the side of the ship, which by this time was sinking fast, and jumped off."
>
> —George D. Phraner, quoted in *World War II*, by H. P. Willmott

In just a few hours, the Japanese sank or damaged all of the battleships anchored at Pearl Harbor. More than 2,400 Americans were killed. Almost 200 airplanes were destroyed.

Speaking to Congress the next day, President Roosevelt called December 7, 1941, "a date which will live in infamy [disgrace]." Congress voted to declare war on Japan. Germany then declared war on the United States. Less than 25 years after entering World War I, the United States joined the Allies in another global war. This one would be even more devastating.

BIOGRAPHY

Daniel Inouye

1924–

Daniel Inouye was born in Honolulu, Hawaii, to Japanese parents. When the Japanese attacked Pearl Harbor, the 17-year-old Inouye used his medical aid training to help treat victims. He joined the army the next year, winning several medals for bravery in combat. In an attack in Italy, Inouye was shot three times, and his right arm had to be amputated. After the war, Inouye studied law and entered politics. In 1959 he became Hawaii's first representative in Congress, as well as the first Japanese American to serve in Congress. He was elected to the U.S. Senate in 1962 and became an important figure in U.S. politics.

Drawing Conclusions Why do you think Inouye went into politics?

READING CHECK **Identifying Cause and Effect** What did Japan hope to gain by attacking Pearl Harbor?

SUMMARY AND PREVIEW Military aggression in Europe and Asia drew the United States into war. In the next section you will learn how the war affected the home front.

Section 1 Assessment

go.hrw.com
Online Quiz
KEYWORD: SC7 HP26

Reviewing Ideas, Terms, and People

1. a. **Identify** What types of leaders came to power in Italy, Germany, and the Soviet Union before World War II?
   b. **Explain** Why did some Europeans have faith in these leaders?
2. a. **Summarize** What did **Adolf Hitler** promise the German people, and how did he act on this promise?
   b. **Recall** Which countries formed the **Axis Powers** and the **Allied Powers**?
   c. **Elaborate** Do you think **Winston Churchill** was a good choice for Britain's prime minister? Explain your answer.
3. a. **Explain** What event brought the United States into World War II?
   b. **Describe** How did the **Lend-Lease Act** help the Allies?

Critical Thinking

4. **Identifying Cause and Effect** Review your notes on totalitarian countries and their leaders prior to World War II. Then copy the graphic organizer below and use it to give details on the causes of World War II.

FOCUS ON WRITING

5. **Taking Notes on Pearl Harbor** Look back at what you have read about the attack on Pearl Harbor. Take notes on who attacked Pearl Harbor, where the attack took place, and when. What were the results of the attack?

SECTION 2

The Home Front

What You Will Learn...

Main Ideas

1. Businesses, soldiers, and citizens worked to prepare the United States for war.
2. The war brought new opportunities for many women and minorities.
3. Japanese Americans faced internment during the war.

The Big Idea

American involvement in World War II helped the U.S. economy and changed the lives of many Americans.

Key Terms and People

War Production Board, *p. 810*
A. Philip Randolph, *p. 812*
Tuskegee Airmen, *p. 812*
Benjamin O. Davis, *p. 812*
zoot-suit riots, *p. 813*
internment, *p. 813*

TAKING NOTES As you read, look for information about how the war brought both opportunities and challenges to minorities. Record your notes in a graphic organizer like the one below.

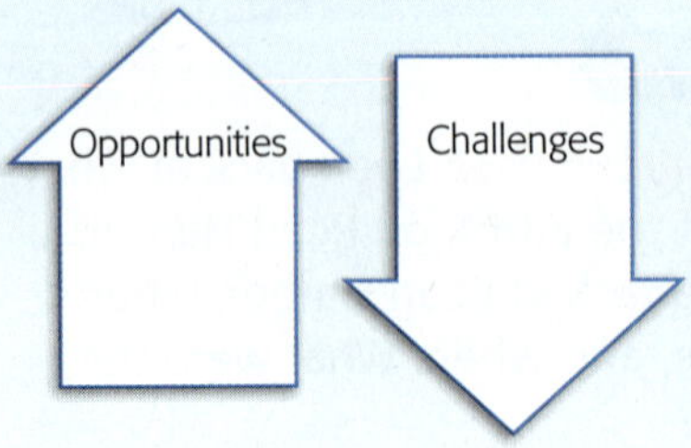

If YOU were there...

Shopping for food has become a whole new experience since the United States entered World War II. When your mother sends you to the grocery store these days, she gives you government-issued ration stamps. These stamps limit the amount of sugar, butter, and meat each family can buy. The sacrifice is difficult, but you know it will help the soldiers fighting overseas.

In what other ways can you help the war effort?

BUILDING BACKGROUND As World War II raged in 1940 and 1941, the Allies relied on war supplies and food from the United States. President Roosevelt and Congress also increased defense spending at home, believing that the United States would soon join the fighting. The increased spending boosted the U.S. economy.

Preparing for War

The United States was still experiencing the effects of the Great Depression when the Japanese attacked Pearl Harbor in December 1941. The enormous effort of mobilizing for war finally brought the Depression to an end. Factories ran 24 hours a day, producing ships, tanks, jeeps, guns, and ammunition. Americans turned their knowledge of mass production toward the production of war supplies. One remarkable example was the building of Liberty ships—transport vessels for troops and supplies. Workers could build an entire 441-foot-long Liberty ship in as little as four days.

American workers were soon doubling the war production of Germany, Japan, and all other Axis Power countries combined. Unemployment fell to 1 percent in 1944. Agricultural production increased as well, as farmers sent food overseas to feed Allied soldiers. To organize the war effort, the government created the **War Production Board** (WPB) to oversee the conversion of factories to war production. In 1942, for example, the WPB banned the production of cars so that auto plants could produce military equipment.

The United States also needed millions of soldiers. Congress had begun to prepare for war by passing the Selective Training and Service Act in 1940. This was the first peacetime draft in the country's history.

Men from the ages of 21 to 35 (later 18 to 38) were required to register for the draft. More than 16 million Americans served during the war.

To finance the war effort, the government increased taxes and sold war bonds. War bonds were essentially loans that people made to the government. People who bought war bonds in 1942, for example, would get their money back 10 years later, with interest.

Americans also contributed to the war effort by collecting scrap metal that could be used in weapons factories. People learned to adjust to government rations limiting the supply of gasoline, rubber, shoes, and some foods. Posters urged Americans to "Use it up, wear it out, make it do, or do without."

READING CHECK **Identifying Cause and Effect** How did the war affect the U.S. economy?

Wartime Opportunities

You read that wartime production during World War I created new opportunities for many women and minorities. The same thing happened on an even larger scale during World War II.

New Roles for Women

With so many men leaving home to fight in World War II, factories badly needed new workers. The government urged women to fill these positions. Women found themselves doing work that had traditionally been considered "unladylike."

Women in North Carolina helped build submarine chasers, minesweepers, and merchant ships in the shipyards in Wilmington, Elizabeth City, and New Bern. They worked at factories that made ammunition, rockets, bomb clusters, and radar components. In all, women helped fulfill about $2 billion worth of government contracts in the state. A federal official said at the time, "So wide is the variety of production . . . that every soldier and sailor in the service of the Nation either wears or carries some article manufactured in North Carolina."

Women also filled new roles in military service. About 300,000 women served in the armed forces through special divisions such as the Women's Auxiliary Army Corps (WAAC) and Women's Airforce Service Pilots (WASP). WASP pilots flew test flights and ferried planes between factories and air bases. Army and navy nurses served in combat areas.

Civilians and the War Effort

Soon after Germany declared war on the United States, German U-boats headed for the U.S. Atlantic coast. Their mission was to attack Allied merchant ships. During the first months of 1942, so many ships were sunk off the coast of Cape Hatteras, North Carolina, that the area became known as Torpedo Junction. Threats such as these prompted cities to organize blackouts, or nights when all artificial light was extinguished to prevent targets from being seen by the enemy. Communities across the nation practiced Civil Defense drills designed to protect themselves in case of attack. Civilians made important contributions to the nation's war strategy by executing blackouts, growing extra food, and following rules of rationing.

Ships attacked at Torpedo Junction

FOCUS ON NORTH CAROLINA

The first African American paratroopers completed their training in North Carolina and were stationed at Camp Mackall. The 555th Parachute Infantry Battalion, or "Triple Nickels," was moved to the West Coast to fight possible forest fires from potential Japanese attacks. Its members pioneered the techniques of smoke-jumping.

African Americans

The Great Migration that began during World War I continued as African Americans moved to northern cities to find factory jobs. In most cases, however, black workers received lower pay than did white workers. They also were restricted in what kinds of jobs they were hired to perform.

To protest this unfair treatment, African American labor leader **A. Philip Randolph** began to organize a march to Washington, D.C., in 1941. "If freedom and equality are not [granted for] the peoples of color, the war for democracy will not be won," he argued. Randolph canceled the march, however, after President Roosevelt issued an order prohibiting racial discrimination in the government and in companies producing war goods.

Struggles at Home

Although members of every race participated in the war as American soldiers, life for minorities at home changed very little. African Americans were still subject to segregation, and Mexican Americans continued to have very little economic opportunity. After the attack on Pearl Harbor, Japanese Americans were removed from their communities and ordered into internment camps far away from the West Coast.

Primary Source

AUTOBIOGRAPHY

Tuskegee Airmen

Benjamin O. Davis was a graduate of West Point who became the first African American Air Force officer to achieve the rank of general. During World War II he led the first African American flying unit, the 99th Fighter Squadron. These men had been trained at the Tuskegee Institute in Alabama.

"While no AAF [American Air Force] unit had gone into combat better trained or better equipped than the 99th Fighter Squadron, we lacked actual combat experience. So as we approached our first missions, my own inexperience and that of my flight commanders was a major source of concern. On the other hand, we had averaged about 250 hours per man in a P-40 (quite a lot for pilots who had not yet flown their first missions), and we possessed an unusually strong sense of purpose and solidarity."

—Benjamin O. Davis, *Benjamin O. Davis, American: An Autobiography*

ANALYSIS SKILL ANALYZING PRIMARY SOURCES

What advantages did the Tuskegee Airmen bring to battle?

About 1 million African Americans served in the armed forces during the war, mostly in segregated units. In the Navy, African Americans were assigned only to support positions and denied the right to participate in combat. Despite this, many black soldiers became national heroes during the war, including Dorie Miller. Leaving his post as ship's cook, Miller manned a machine gun on the deck of the USS *West Virginia* until he was ordered to abandon the ship because it was sinking.

The **Tuskegee Airmen** were African American pilots who trained at the Tuskegee Army Air Field in Alabama. **Benjamin O. Davis**, who later became the first African American general in the U.S. Air Force, led the group. Davis and his pilots had to overcome prejudice in the military as well as the hazards of war. He later described the pilots as "outstanding Americans who served their country unselfishly. Despite treatment that would have demoralized men of lesser strength and character, they persisted through humiliations and dangers to earn the respect of their fellows." The Tuskegee Airmen flew thousands of successful combat missions in North Africa and Italy.

Mexican Americans

About 300,000 Mexican Americans served in the military during the war. Many Mexican Americans also found wartime jobs on the West Coast and in the Midwest. Because of a shortage of farm workers, the federal government asked Mexico to provide agricultural workers. The workers, called *braceros*, were guaranteed a minimum wage, food, shelter, and clean living conditions. About 200,000 Mexicans worked in the *bracero* program.

Young Mexican Americans of the time created their own culture by blending different music styles and clothing styles. Some men wore zoot suits—fancy, loose-fitting outfits with oversized hats. Despite their aiding of the war effort, many faced discrimination. In Los Angeles in June 1943, groups of sailors attacked Mexican Americans wearing zoot suits, beginning the **zoot-suit riots**. During the 10-day period, white mobs attacked many Mexican Americans.

READING CHECK **Evaluating** How did the war create both opportunities and challenges for minorities?

Japanese American Internment

Japanese Americans faced a different form of prejudice during World War II. After the Japanese attack on Pearl Harbor, some Americans began to look at Americans of Japanese descent with fear and suspicion. Most Japanese Americans lived on the West Coast at this time. It was feared that they would serve as secret agents for Japan and help Japan prepare an invasion of the West Coast or try to sabotage U.S. war efforts.

The U.S. government had no evidence to support these fears. In spite of this fact, President Roosevelt issued Executive Order 9066. This order allowed the government to begin the process of **internment**, or forced relocation and imprisonment, of Japanese Americans. About 115,000 Japanese Americans were evacuated from their homes and held in isolated internment camps. Half of those held in the camps were children. A smaller number of Americans of German and Italian ancestry were also held in internment camps during the war.

THE IMPACT TODAY

Congress passed the Civil Liberties Act of 1988 to compensate victims of internment. Each living Japanese American who had been interned—60,000 in all—received $20,000 and a formal apology signed by President Ronald Reagan.

At this time, some Japanese Americans were *Issei*, or immigrants born in Japan. But most were *Nisei*, American citizens born in the United States to Japanese immigrant parents. Whether they were U.S. citizens or not, Japanese Americans lost their jobs, homes, and belongings when they were forced to move to internment camps. A farm owner named Yuri Tateishi spoke of feeling betrayed by his government. "You hurt," he said. "You give up everything that you worked for that far, and I think everybody was at the point of just having gotten out of the Depression and was just getting on his feet. And then all that happens! You have to throw everything away."

After the Pearl Harbor attack, the government banned young Japanese American men from serving in the military. But Roosevelt reversed this policy in 1943. Daniel Inouye remembered the excitement he and his fellow Japanese Americans in Hawaii felt when they heard that the government was going to form an all-*Nisei* combat team. An army recruiter had prepared a pep talk for the young Japanese Americans, but this proved to be unnecessary:

> "As soon as he said that we were now eligible to volunteer, that room exploded into a fury of yells and motion. We went bursting out of there and ran—ran!—the three miles to the draft board . . . jostling for position, like a bunch of marathoners gone berserk."
>
> —Daniel Inouye, quoted in *Only What We Could Carry*, edited by Lawson Fusao Inada

Inouye was one of about 33,000 *Nisei* who served in World War II. The Japanese American 100th/442nd Regimental Combat Team received more than 18,000 decorations for bravery—more than any other unit of its size in U.S. military history. Many of the soldiers of the 100th/442nd served while their families were held in internment camps back home.

READING CHECK **Evaluating** Why were Japanese Americans interned?

SUMMARY AND PREVIEW The war effort changed life on the home front. In the next section you will learn about the fighting in Europe and North Africa.

Section 2 Assessment

go.hrw.com
Online Quiz
KEYWORD: SC7 HP26

Reviewing Ideas, Terms, and People

1. a. **Describe** How did people on the home front support the war effort?
   b. **Identify** What government agency oversaw factory production during the war?
2. a. **Recall** What were the WAAC and the WASP?
   b. **Explain** Why did **A. Philip Randolph** organize a march on Washington and then cancel it?
   c. **Elaborate** How did the *bracero* program benefit both Mexicans and Americans?
3. a. **Define** What was the **internment** program?
   b. **Contrast** How did the U.S. government change its policy toward Japanese Americans serving in the military? How did many respond?

Critical Thinking

4. **Categorizing** Review your notes on challenges and opportunities for different groups of people in America during World War II. Then copy the graphic organizer below and use it to list opportunities that women, African Americans, and Mexican Americans found during the war.

Wartime Opportunities

Women	African Americans	Mexican Americans

FOCUS ON WRITING

5. **Taking Notes on the Home Front** Radio broadcasts often reminded Americans to "Do your part" in winning World War II. Take notes on the ways ordinary citizens helped the troops by supporting the war effort on the home front. How might you convince someone to support the effort?

War in Europe and North Africa

SECTION 3

If YOU were there...

The year is 1943 and you are a senior in high school. You know that you will be drafted into the armed forces as soon as you graduate. Every day after school you listen to radio reports about the battles being fought around the world. Your future, and the future of the whole world, seems so uncertain.

How do you feel about fighting in this war?

BUILDING BACKGROUND By the time the United States entered the war, the Allies were in trouble. The Axis Powers controlled much of western Europe and were advancing in North Africa and the Soviet Union. German submarine attacks on Allied ships were making it difficult to get American supplies to the British.

What You Will Learn...

Main Ideas

1. The Allies fought back against the Axis Powers in North Africa and Europe.
2. Key Allied victories halted the German advance.
3. In the D-Day invasion, Allied forces attacked German-controlled France.

The Big Idea

After fierce fighting in North Africa and Europe, the Allies stopped the German advance and slowly began driving back German forces.

Key Terms and People

Battle of El Alamein, *p. 816*
Dwight D. Eisenhower, *p. 816*
Battle of Stalingrad, *p. 817*
D-Day, *p. 819*

TAKING NOTES As you read, make a list of the major battles and campaigns in different areas of the world. You may want to organize your list in a table like this one.

North Africa	Italy	Eastern Europe	Western Europe

The Allies Fight Back

In December 1941, soon after the United States entered the war, President Roosevelt met with British prime minister Winston Churchill to work out a plan to defeat the Axis Powers. Roosevelt agreed that the United States would place "Europe first" in its plans to defeat the Axis, while still aiding China in the fight against Japan in the Pacific. In addition, Roosevelt and Churchill agreed on two initial strategies: a buildup of troops in Great Britain to be used to invade France, and an assault on German forces in North Africa.

Meanwhile, the Soviets had been demanding Allied help on the eastern front, where they had borne the brunt of the European war for months after Hitler's invasion. Stalin wanted the Allies to attack

The Allies began using sonar to destroy German U-boats, shown here in a German harbor.

in Europe immediately, to take some of the pressure off of the Soviet forces in the east. In July 1942, however, the Allies decided to put a European invasion on hold and launch an initial offensive in North Africa. Stalin was angry. The Soviets would have to continue to fight the war on the eastern front without a western European assault to distract the Germans.

As they prepared their battle plans, the Allies faced many obstacles. One major threat the Allies had to combat was U-boat attacks. In 1942 alone German U-boats sank more than 6,000,000 tons of Allied materials. To prevent further damage, the Allies used the convoy system of multiple ships traveling at once, along with new sonar technology. Sonar, which uses sound waves to detect objects underwater, helped Allied ships find and destroy German U-boats. In addition, new long-range Allied planes protected the convoys from the air. Long-range planes could also fly into German territory to drop bombs on factories, railroads, and cities, inflicting tremendous damage on German targets.

FOCUS ON READING
What categories could you use to organize the information in this paragraph?

READING CHECK **Explaining** What battle plan did the Allies agree to pursue after American entry into the war?

BIOGRAPHY

Dwight D. Eisenhower
1890–1969

Dwight D. Eisenhower was born in Denison, Texas. "Ike," as his friends called him, attended the U.S. Military Academy at West Point and trained soldiers for tank warfare during World War I. With a strong ability to organize and plan strategies, as well as a persuasive and optimistic personality, Eisenhower rose to the rank of general during World War II. He was named supreme commander of Allied forces in western Europe in 1943. His standing as a war hero helped him win the presidential elections of 1952 and 1956.

Drawing Inferences What were some of Eisenhower's strengths?

Halting the German Advance

Churchill predicted that the road to victory would be long and difficult. By winning several key battles, however, Allied forces finally stopped the German advance.

North Africa and Italy

As you have read, a main focus for the Allies when the United States entered the war was North Africa. The Germans and British were battling for control there because Axis leaders wanted to grab control of the Suez Canal, a crucial supply route in Egypt. Germany's Afrika Korps was led by General Erwin Rommel, nicknamed the Desert Fox for his bold, surprise attacks.

In the summer of 1942, Rommel began an offensive to take Egypt. General Bernard Montgomery led the British forces to stop the Germans. The British stopped the Afrika Korps in July at the **Battle of El Alamein**. At the same time, U.S. and British troops, led by American general **Dwight D. Eisenhower**, came ashore in Morocco and Algeria, west of Egypt. Caught between two Allied forces, the Afrika Korps surrendered in May 1943.

With North Africa under their control, the Allies prepared to attack the Axis Powers in Europe. Churchill identified Italy as the "soft underbelly" of the Axis. Allied forces invaded the island of Sicily in July 1943 and moved from there to the Italian mainland. Italian leaders overthrew Mussolini and surrendered to the Allies. But Hitler refused to recognize the Axis defeat. He sent German troops to Italy to block the Allied advance.

In January 1944, Allied forces tried to get behind the Germans with a surprise attack at Anzio, on the western coast of Italy. American and British troops landed at Anzio but were pinned down on the beach for several months. The "soft underbelly" proved to be much tougher than expected. Finally, the Allied forces in southern Italy battled north to Anzio. The combined forces captured Rome, the capital of Italy, in June

Major Leaders of the War in Europe

QUICK FACTS

Winston Churchill
Prime Minister of Great Britain

Franklin Roosevelt
President of the United States

Joseph Stalin
Premier of the Soviet Union

Adolf Hitler
Chancellor of Germany

Benito Mussolini
Prime Minister of Italy

1944. Early in 1945, German forces were driven out of Italy. Italian freedom fighters executed Mussolini.

The Battle of Stalingrad

Meanwhile, massive German and Soviet armies were battling on the eastern front. By the middle of 1942, Axis armies had driven deep into Soviet territory. Millions of Soviet soldiers had been killed or captured.

German forces then advanced to the key industrial city of Stalingrad. German firebombs set much of the city on fire. But Soviet leader Joseph Stalin was determined to hold on to Stalingrad at all costs. Savage street fighting dragged on for months. Soviet snipers used the ruined buildings to their advantage, firing at German soldiers from behind piles of stone and brick.

German supplies began to run desperately low as the harsh Russian winter began. Hitler remained obsessed with capturing Stalingrad, however. He ordered his troops to keep fighting, though he did not send enough new supplies or soldiers. Thousands of Germans froze or starved to death. In late January 1943 the German commander at Stalingrad defied Hitler and surrendered to save his remaining troops. The **Battle of Stalingrad** thus became a key turning point of the war.

The Soviet victory came at an enormous cost—more than 1 million Soviet soldiers died at Stalingrad. About 800,000 Axis soldiers were killed. After Stalingrad, the Soviets won another victory in the city of Kursk, in the biggest tank battle ever fought. The Axis Powers now began to retreat from the Soviet Union. The tide of the war in the east had turned.

READING CHECK **Sequencing** What events led to the Allied victories in Italy and Russia?

The D-Day Invasion

After hard-fought victories in North Africa and Italy, the Allies were ready for an even tougher task—the invasion of German-occupied France. This was the first step toward the goal of liberating Europe and forcing Hitler to surrender.

World War II in Europe, 1942–1945

Interactive Map

Tanks thundered across Europe, destroying much of what lay in their paths.

Airplanes dropped millions of bombs on opposing forces. They were also used for moving troops and for spying on the enemy.

go.hrw.com
Interactive Map
KEYWORD: SC7 CH26

1942

November 1942
Allies win the Battle of El Alamein.

February 1943
Final German troops surrender at Stalingrad.

May 1943
Axis forces in North Africa surrender.

July 1943
Allies begin an invasion of Sicily.

Dwight Eisenhower was in charge of planning what would be the largest sea-to-land invasion ever attempted. Eisenhower knew that German forces were expecting an invasion of France. The Germans had planted mines and stretched barbed wire along the French coastline. Heavily armed German soldiers waited on the beaches in bombproof bunkers. Eisenhower warned his troops of the danger but expressed confidence in their ability to succeed. "The hopes and prayers of liberty-loving people everywhere march with you," he told them.

American, British, and Canadian troops invaded France on June 6, 1944—known as **D-Day**, or "designated day." They crossed the choppy waters of the English Channel and landed on five beaches in Normandy. More than 6,000 ships, 11,000 planes, and 156,000 men were part of the invasion. Soldiers jumped from boats and waded ashore, often under heavy fire.

The Americans landed on two beaches, codenamed Utah and Omaha. Fighting was especially fierce on Omaha Beach, where almost 3,000 men were killed or wounded. "The entire beach was strewn with mines," wrote one U.S. soldier to his wife. "With a stream of lead coming towards us, we were at the mercy of the Germans."

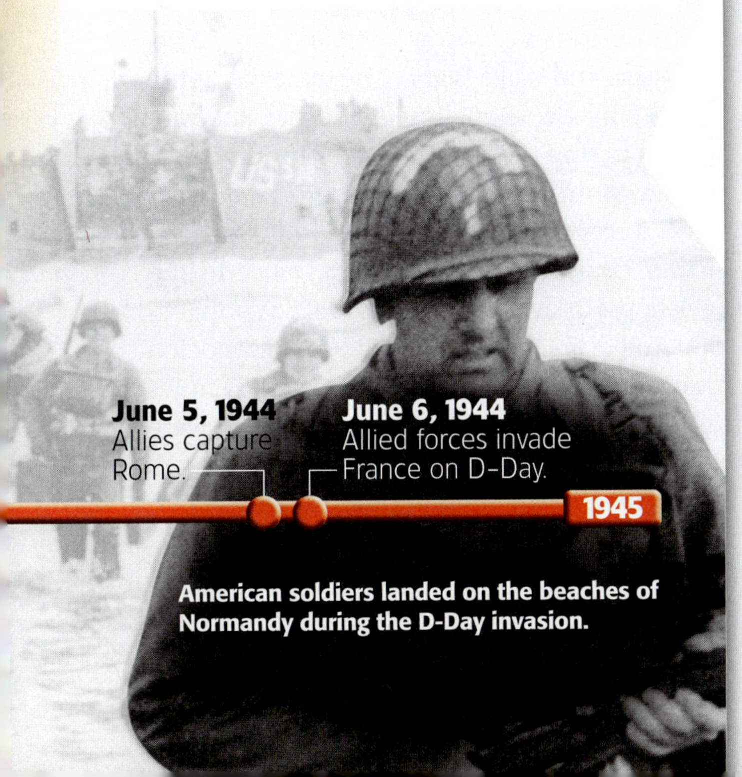

American soldiers landed on the beaches of Normandy during the D-Day invasion.

By the end of D-Day, all five beaches were secured. The Allies then began driving east through French villages and countryside toward Germany.

READING CHECK **Summarizing** What was the goal of the D-Day invasion?

SUMMARY AND PREVIEW Allied victories led to the D-Day invasion. In the next section you will read about the Pacific war.

Section 3 Assessment

go.hrw.com
Online Quiz
KEYWORD: SC7 HP26

Reviewing Ideas, Terms, and People

1. a. **Describe** What new strategies did the Allies use in the fight in Europe and North Africa?
   b. **Draw Conclusions** Why was it important for no individual Allied Power to make peace with the Axis countries?
2. a. **Recall** What role did **Dwight D. Eisenhower** play in the North Africa campaign?
   b. **Analyze** Why did the Allies decide to invade North Africa and Italy?
   c. **Evaluate** Why do you think people call the **Battle of Stalingrad** a turning point in the war?
3. a. **Define** What was **D-Day**?
   b. **Elaborate** What did Eisenhower mean when he said, "The hopes and prayers of liberty-loving people everywhere march with you"?

Critical Thinking

4. **Categorizing** Review your list of the major battles and campaigns in different areas of the world. Then copy the graphic organizer below and use it to explain the significance of each event shown.

Event	Significance
Battle of El Alamein	
Capture of Rome	
Battle of Stalingrad	
D-Day invasion	

FOCUS ON WRITING

5. **Taking Notes on the Progress of the War** Take notes on the major battles involving American soldiers. How did American leaders, strategies, and individual soldiers contribute to victories in Europe and North Africa?

SECTION 4

War in the Pacific

What You Will Learn...

Main Ideas

1. The Japanese continued advancing across the Pacific in 1942.
2. The Allies stopped Japan's advance with key victories over the Japanese navy.
3. The Allies began battling toward Japan.

The Big Idea

Allied forces reversed Japan's expansion in the Pacific and battled toward the main Japanese islands.

Key Terms and People

Douglas MacArthur, *p. 820*
Bataan Death March, *p. 820*
Chester Nimitz, *p. 821*
Battle of the Coral Sea, *p. 821*
Battle of Midway, *p. 821*
island hopping, *p. 822*
Battle of Leyte Gulf, *p. 822*
kamikaze, *p. 822*

TAKING NOTES As you read, take notes on the main events of the war in the Pacific. You may want to organize your list in a chart like this one.

Pacific War
1.
2.
3.
4.

If YOU were there...

It is spring 1945, and your older brother is fighting the Japanese in the Pacific. You've been following the news reports closely and you know that fighting in the Pacific is terribly fierce. You hear that the Japanese soldiers often refuse to surrender, fighting to the death instead. Your brother reveals in his letters that he is lonely and suffering many hardships. Now you are writing to him.

What would you say to encourage him?

BUILDING BACKGROUND Japan attacked China in the early 1930s, leading to all-out war between Japan and China in 1937. Japanese forces captured key Chinese cities, including Nanjing, where they killed up to 300,000 civilians. Under the command of General Hideki Tojo, Japanese forces continued to expand the Japanese empire in Asia.

Japan Advances

Japan's attack on Pearl Harbor left the U.S. Pacific Fleet so weakened that it could not immediately respond to the Japanese advance. While the United States recovered from Pearl Harbor, Japan conquered Thailand, Burma, the British colonies of Hong Kong and Singapore, and the U.S. territories of Guam and Wake Island. The same day as the attack on Pearl Harbor, Japan invaded Hong Kong. British, Canadian, and Indian forces attempting to stop the invasion were outnumbered. Japan attacked the American-controlled Philippines the same day.

American and Filipino forces under the command of American general **Douglas MacArthur** could not stop Japan's advance in the Philippines. MacArthur left the islands in March 1942, vowing to return. More than 70,000 American and Filipino soldiers surrendered to the Japanese. The exhausted soldiers were forced to march 63 miles up the Bataan Peninsula to prison camps. Many prisoners were starved and beaten by Japanese soldiers. More than 600 Americans and about 10,000 Filipinos died in the **Bataan Death March**.

READING CHECK **Identifying Cause and Effect** Why could the U.S. Pacific Fleet not immediately stop the Japanese advance?

Code Talkers

More than 40,000 Native Americans served in the U.S. armed forces during the war. About 400 Navajo Native Americans served as "Code Talkers," relaying coded messages based on the complex Navajo language. Japan's expert code breakers were never able to crack the Navajo code.

Why might the Japanese have been unable to break the Navajo code?

Key Allied Victories

The Allies feared the Japanese might next attack India, Australia, or even the United States mainland. Admiral **Chester Nimitz** led the U.S. Pacific Fleet. Nimitz was determined to stop the Japanese advance, and he had an important advantage—the ability to crack secret Japanese codes.

American code breakers helped the Allies in two key naval battles in the Pacific. Nimitz learned that the Japanese were planning an attack on Port Moresby, New Guinea, an island just north of Australia. If the Japanese took New Guinea, they would have a base from which to invade Australia. In May 1942 Nimitz sent Allied forces to stop the Japanese fleet. American and Japanese aircraft carriers and fighter planes clashed in the **Battle of the Coral Sea**. Neither side won a clear victory, but the Japanese assault on Port Moresby was stopped.

Allied leaders then learned that the Japanese planned a surprise attack on the Midway Islands. Nimitz was prepared. The **Battle of Midway** began on June 4, 1942, when Japan started bombing the islands. American aircraft carriers launched their planes, catching the Japanese aircraft carriers while many of their planes were refueling on deck. American dive bombers destroyed four of Japan's aircraft carriers, severely weakening Japanese naval power. "Pearl Harbor has now been partially avenged," said Nimitz.

The Allies then began the enormous and difficult task of recapturing territory from Japan. In August 1942 American marines invaded Guadalcanal, one of the Solomon Islands northeast of Australia. Intense fighting raged for nearly six months. Marine Louis Ortega remembered that enemy bombs and bullets were only part of the danger in the hot, rainy jungles of Guadalcanal. Soldiers also suffered from diseases, such as malaria, and from hunger due to lack of supplies. "I had gone to Guadalcanal weighing about 150," Ortega said. "I left weighing about 110." American forces finally took control of the island in February 1943.

READING CHECK **Drawing Conclusions** How did the Allied victory at Midway change the course of the war in the Pacific?

Battling toward Japan

Allied victories at Midway and Guadalcanal helped change the course of the war in the Pacific. The Allies now saw their chance to go on the offensive, with the goal of reaching Japan itself.

Island Hopping

To fight their way toward Japan, Allied war planners developed a strategy called **island hopping**, where Allied forces took only the most strategically important islands, instead of each Japanese-held island. They could use each captured island as a base for the next attack, while isolating the Japanese forces on the bypassed islands.

ACADEMIC VOCABULARY

execute perform, carry out

Island hopping proved to be a successful strategy, though very costly to execute. Japanese forces fortified key islands and fought fiercely to hold on to them. In November 1943, U.S. Marines leapt off their boats and waded toward Tarawa, one of the Gilbert Islands. They advanced into ferocious fire from Japanese machine guns. "The water seemed never clear of . . . men," one Marine said. "They kept falling, falling, falling." Both sides sustained heavy casualties at Tarawa, but the Marines captured the island. The Allies won similar victories in the Marshall, Mariana, Volcano, and Bonin islands.

In October 1944 General MacArthur led a mission to retake the Philippines. The Japanese navy confronted the Allies at the **Battle of Leyte Gulf**, the largest naval battle in history. The Allies crushed the Japanese fleet, crippling Japan's naval power for the remainder of the war. It also gave the Allies a base from which to attack the main shipping routes that supplied Japan. After splashing ashore on Leyte, MacArthur proudly declared: "People of the Philippines: I have returned." Securing the Philippines took many more months of fighting. Allied forces and Filipino guerrillas finally drove out or captured all of the Japanese defenders by the summer of 1945.

Final Battles

With key islands close to Japan secured, Allied planes began bombing targets in Japan in November 1944. American B-29 bombers, able to carry 20,000 pounds of explosives each, led bombing raids on more than 60 major Japanese cities. A March 1945 raid set Japan's capital city of Tokyo on fire, leaving 1 million people homeless. Japanese factories were destroyed, and food became so scarce that many people neared starvation. Still, Japan refused to surrender.

Two of the war's fiercest battles occurred on Japan's outer islands early in 1945. In February U.S. Marines stormed the beaches of Iwo Jima. Japanese defenders were dug into caves, with orders to fight to the death. "On Iwo, we hardly ever saw the enemy," recalled one marine. After the Marines raised the American flag on Iwo Jima, a month of bloody fighting followed. Of more than 20,000 Japanese defenders on Iwo Jima, about a thousand were taken prisoner—the rest were killed or wounded in battle. Around 6,800 Americans had died.

Beginning in April an even deadlier battle was fought for the island of Okinawa. There were an estimated 100,000 Japanese soldiers on the island when U.S. forces began their attack. One U.S. Marine officer described the hard fighting at the Battle of Okinawa:

> "We poured a tremendous amount of metal in on those positions . . . It seemed nothing could possibly be living in that churning mass where the shells were falling and roaring but when we next advanced, [Japanese troops] would still be there and madder than ever."
>
> —Colonel Wilburt S. Brown, quoted in *The Final Campaign: Marines in the Victory on Okinawa* by Colonel Joseph H. Alexander

In the waters near the island, Japanese planes struck U.S. ships with the tactic of **kamikaze**—purposely crashing piloted planes into enemy ships. In wave after wave, kamikaze pilots flew planes loaded with explosives straight down onto the decks of Allied ships. An American sailor who was on the deck of an aircraft carrier when a kamikaze attacked the ship described the scene.

War in the Pacific, 1941–1945

Kamikaze pilots as young as 17 flew their airplanes directly into enemy targets, committing suicide to fulfill their duty.

GEOGRAPHY SKILLS INTERPRETING MAPS

1. **Location** Did the area controlled by Japan by July 1942 include the Hawaiian Islands? How can you tell?
2. **Human-Environment Interaction** Which major battles occurred south of the equator?

Six Marines are shown raising the American flag atop Mt. Suribachi on the island of Iwo Jima after an important battle there. They were instructed to raise the flag on the highest point of the island so that all the men still fighting could see it.

The plane "cartwheeled the length of the carrier and plowed into the planes we had on the [flight deck]. We were burning bow to stern . . . All the guys manning the guns were dead. Standing up. Pointing their guns. They never left their posts."

More than 2,500 kamikaze missions were flown, killing more than 4,000 Allied sailors. The fighting on Okinawa lasted nearly three months and led to terrible casualties. By the time the island was secure, some 12,000 Allied troops were dead and 36,000 wounded. The Japanese losses were staggering—some 110,000 troops and 80,000 civilians had been killed.

After their victories at Iwo Jima and Okinawa, the Allies were one step closer to final victory. Allied leaders began to plan for an all-out assault on the main Japanese islands.

READING CHECK **Analyzing** How did the Allied strategy in the Pacific change starting in 1943?

SUMMARY AND PREVIEW The Allies made major gains in the Pacific war, moving closer to Japan. In the next section, you will learn how the Allies achieved full victory.

Section 4 Assessment

go.hrw.com
Online Quiz
KEYWORD: SC7 HP26

Reviewing Ideas, Terms, and People

1. a. **Identify** Why were the Japanese able to advance in the Pacific in 1942?
   b. **Explain** Why did so many prisoners die on the **Bataan Death March**?
2. a. **Recall** What Allied victories halted Japan's advance?
   b. **Analyze** Why was the **Battle of the Coral Sea** important?
   c. **Elaborate** How do you think the war might have been different if the Allies had lost at Midway?
3. a. **Define** What was **island hopping**?
   b. **Sequence** What event led to the retaking of the Philippines?
   c. **Evaluate** Why do you think someone would serve as a **kamikaze** pilot?

Critical Thinking

4. **Sequencing** Review your notes on the main events of the Pacific war. Then copy the graphic organizer below and use it to put the events in the correct sequence.

1942	→	1943	→	1944	→	1945

FOCUS ON WRITING

5. **Taking Notes on Military Achievements** Take notes on the challenges U.S. soldiers faced in the Pacific. How was fighting in the Pacific different from and similar to fighting in Africa and Europe? How might you describe a Pacific battle to someone?

Victory and Consequences

If YOU were there...

It is August 1944. You are an American soldier in France. You have seen the horrors of battle up close, but today is a day to rejoice. You and other Allied soldiers are marching through the streets of Paris, celebrating its liberation from Nazi control. It seems as if the whole city has come out to greet the Americans. People rush up to shake your hand. Children cheer and hand you flowers.

How does it feel to be part of this moment in history?

BUILDING BACKGROUND By late 1944 Allied forces were advancing in Europe and Asia. But Germany and Japan were both resisting, showing no signs of being willing to surrender. Allied leaders knew there was much more fighting still to be done.

Germany Surrenders

In the weeks after the successful D-Day invasion, hundreds of thousands of Allied troops landed in France. Led by American general Omar Bradley, Allied forces began fighting their way across France toward Germany. At the same time, the Soviets were closing in on Germany from the east. Although Germany's defeat seemed certain to the Allies, Hitler refused to surrender.

In July 1944 Allied tank forces led by American general George Patton broke through German lines on the western front. While Patton drove forward, more Allied forces invaded southern France. Both groups of Allied forces fought their way toward Paris. Encouraged by the Allies' success, the citizens of Paris rebelled against the German occupying force. By the end of August, General Bradley was leading Allied troops through the streets of the freed city. "All Paris surged out to meet the Allied columns and welcome their liberators," remembered one witness. After securing Paris, the Allies continued driving through Belgium and Luxembourg, making their way toward Germany. Hitler drafted every able-bodied German man from the age of 16 to 60 and planned one last desperate attack.

SECTION 5

What You Will Learn...

Main Ideas

1. The Allies gained victory in Europe with Germany's surrender.
2. Nazis murdered millions of Jews and other people in the Holocaust.
3. Victory in the Pacific came after the United States dropped atomic bombs on Japan.

The Big Idea

The Allies won World War II, the most devastating war in world history.

Key Terms and People

Battle of the Bulge, *p. 826*
Harry S. Truman, *p. 826*
Holocaust, *p. 827*
genocide, *p. 827*
Manhattan Project, *p. 828*
atomic bomb, *p. 828*

TAKING NOTES As you read, take notes on the final days of the war in both Europe and the Pacific. You may want to use a graphic organizer like the one below.

Europe	Pacific

Hitler's goal was for German forces to drive through a weak spot in the Allied lines and capture the city of Antwerp, Belgium. On December 16 the Germans seized a moment when Allied planes were grounded due to bad weather. In heavy snow some 25 German divisions attacked the Ardennes (ahr-DEN), a densely forested region defended by just a few American divisions. The Germans quickly pushed the Allied forces back about 65 miles, creating a huge bulge in the Allied lines. This gave the battle its name—the **Battle of the Bulge**.

Allied forces recovered rapidly and stopped the German advance. When the skies cleared in late December, Allied planes began pounding German troops. In early January 1945 the Germans began to retreat. American losses were heavy—between 70,000 and 81,000 casualties. Germany's losses were even greater, and Hitler's ability to wage offensive war was now completely crushed.

FOCUS ON NORTH CAROLINA

The Allies took prisoners of war after winning battles. More than 400,000 were brought to camps across the United States. North Carolina had several POW camps, and prisoners sometimes worked on nearby farms.

In the final months of the war, Allied bombing raids devastated major German cities such as Berlin and Hamburg. Both sides in World War II had used these kinds of bombing raids against the enemy's cities. German raids, for example, killed about 30,000 civilians in the British capital of London. In February 1945 Allied bombers attacked the German city of Dresden, igniting a firestorm that destroyed the city and killed more than 35,000 civilians. "Dresden was an inferno," recalled one U.S. soldier. "I have nightmares, even today."

As Allied forces surrounded Berlin, Hitler retreated to an underground bunker in the heart of the ruined city. On April 30, as Soviet troops entered Berlin, Hitler committed suicide. A week later, the Germans surrendered. The war in Europe had finally come to an end. The Allies celebrated May 8, 1945, as V-E (Victory in Europe) Day.

President Franklin Roosevelt, who had led the United States throughout World War II, did not live to see V-E Day. He died of a stroke on April 12. **Harry S. Truman** became president and immediately faced the challenge of winning the war in the Pacific.

READING CHECK **Sequencing** What events led to Germany's surrender?

Primary Source

INTERVIEW TRANSCRIPT

Battle of the Bulge

In the Battle of the Bulge, American soldiers faced a strong German attack in snowy forests during the coldest winter northern Europe had seen in 40 years. Private Dave Nutt described the long, tense nights on the front lines:

> "The cold, the snow, and the darkness were enough to set young nerves on edge. The thud of something as innocuous [harmless] as snow plopping to the ground from a tree branch could be terrifying. Was it snow? Was it maybe a German patrol? Should you fire at the sound and risk giving away your position, or worse, hitting one of your own men? But did the Germans have us surrounded?"
>
> —Dave Nutt, quoted in *Citizen Soldiers*, by Stephen Ambrose

ANALYSIS SKILL **ANALYZING PRIMARY SOURCES**

What factors made the Battle of the Bulge especially hard on soldiers?

Buchenwald

Jews, Gypsies, and other victims of Hitler and the Nazis were sent to concentration camps. Many were killed immediately upon arrival at the camps, while others were executed later. Families were forced apart, and prisoners were poorly fed and clothed. Some were used as subjects for medical experiments. This photo shows survivors of the Buchenwald concentration camp after their liberation.

How did Hitler use the concentration camps to fulfill part of his goals for Germany?

Horrors of the Holocaust

When Allied forces liberated Europe, they uncovered evidence of horrifying Nazi crimes against humanity. In a program of mass murder that became known as the **Holocaust**, Hitler and the Nazis had attempted to exterminate the entire Jewish population of Europe in the name of Aryan supremacy.

The Final Solution

Soon after gaining power in Germany, Hitler began his campaign of terror against the Jews. The Nazis stripped German Jews of their citizenship and seized their property. On the "night of broken glass," or *Kristallnacht*, many Jewish homes and businesses were destroyed. Many Jews who did not escape the country were imprisoned in concentration camps such as Dachau (DAH-kow), near Munich.

When Germany conquered huge sections of Europe and the Soviet Union early in World War II, nearly 10 million Jews came under Hitler's control. The Nazis forced many Jews into urban centers called ghettos. Others were sent to concentration camps and used as slave labor. Many died from hunger or disease. The Nazis also formed special killing squads that rounded up groups of Jews, shot them, and buried them in mass graves. When the Germans invaded the Soviet Union, these squads murdered more than 33,000 Soviet Jews near Kiev in three days. By the end of 1941, the death squads had executed nearly 1 million people.

The Death Camps

In January 1942 senior Nazi officials met to plan what they called "a final solution to the Jewish question." Hitler's "final solution" was **genocide**, or the extermination of an entire group of people. The Nazi plan was to kill the Jews in specially built death camps, mainly in German-occupied Poland. The camps were equipped with gas chambers designed to kill large numbers of people, and furnaces were used to cremate the bodies of victims.

By mid-1942 the Nazis had begun to ship Jews from throughout German-occupied Europe to the camps. Several hundred thousand Jews, for example, were transported by train from the ghetto in the Polish capital of Warsaw to a death camp called Treblinka. In April 1943 Jews in the Warsaw ghetto staged a violent uprising, attacking the Germans with guns and homemade bombs. It took German troops nearly a month to crush the revolt. Survivors were sent to Treblinka.

THE IMPACT TODAY

There are more than 50 museums in the world that honor victims of the Holocaust. The United States Holocaust Memorial Museum in Washington, D.C., displays historical film footage and artifacts from the Holocaust.

At the death camps most children, the elderly, and the sick were immediately executed. Those strong enough to work were used as laborers. When they became too weak to work, they too were sent to the gas chambers. Moritz Vegh was 13 when his family was sent from Czechoslovakia to Auschwitz, one of the most notorious of the death camps. He later described what happened to his mother and sister:

> "When we got off the cattle truck, they ordered, 'Men, right; women, left.' . . . I went with my father. My little sister, Esther, she went with my mother. Esther was only eleven. She was holding my mother's hand. When they made a selection of the women, Esther clung to my mother. My mother wouldn't give her up . . . They went straight to the gas chamber."
>
> —Moritz Vegh, quoted in *The Boys: Triumph over Adversity*

Moritz survived the war, working as a laborer at Auschwitz.

The Allied soldiers who liberated the death camps were horrified by what they found. About 6 million Jews—some two-thirds of Europe's prewar Jewish population—had been killed in the Holocaust. The Nazis had also murdered millions of others, including Gypsies, Slavs, political opponents, and people with physical or mental disabilities.

READING CHECK **Summarizing** What was the purpose of the Nazis' "final solution"?

Victory in the Pacific

In the Pacific Allied war planners prepared for an invasion of Japan. They estimated that the invasion could result in more than 1 million Allied casualties.

The Allies had another option. Since 1942 Allied scientists had been working on a secret program known as the **Manhattan Project**. The goal was to develop an **atomic bomb**, a weapon that produces tremendous power by splitting atoms. On July 16, 1945, the Allies successfully tested the first atomic bomb in the New Mexico desert. The massive explosion melted the desert sand into glass for 800 yards in all directions.

When Japanese leaders refused the Allies' demand for an unconditional surrender, President Truman gave the order to use the atomic bomb. On August 6, 1945, the B-29 bomber *Enola Gay* dropped an atomic bomb above the city of Hiroshima. "When I saw a very strong light, a flash, I put my arms over my face unconsciously," said one Japanese survivor. "Almost instantly I felt my face was inflating . . . I saw people looking for water and they died soon after they drank it . . . The whole city was destroyed and burning. There was no place to go." The explosion killed almost 80,000 people instantly. Thousands more died later from burns and radiation poisoning.

The atomic blast over Hiroshima destroyed the city. Over 80,000 people were killed instantly, and thousands more died later from the effects of radiation.

Japanese leaders still refused to surrender. On August 9 U.S. forces dropped a second atomic bomb on the city of Nagasaki. About one-third of the city was destroyed, and approximately 22,000 people died immediately. The Japanese announced their surrender on August 15, 1945.

After six years, World War II was finally over. More than 50 million people had been killed—more than half of them civilians. National economies in Europe and Asia were devastated, and millions of people were left without food, water, or shelter. Since the war had been fought far from American soil, the United States escaped this level of destruction. As the strongest power left in the world, much of the responsibility for postwar rebuilding fell to the United States.

READING CHECK **Drawing Conclusions** Why did Japan surrender?

SUMMARY AND PREVIEW In this section you learned how World War II ended. In the next chapter you will learn how the world recovered from the war and worked to prevent such wars in the future.

Causes and Effects of World War II

QUICK FACTS

Causes

- Global and local economic problems
- Totalitarian governments
- Germany's aggression in Europe
- Japanese aggression in Asia and the Pacific

Effects

- Millions of deaths worldwide
- Widespread destruction of cities and industries
- The Holocaust
- Rise of the United States as the leading world power

Section 5 Assessment

go.hrw.com
Online Quiz
KEYWORD: SC7 HP26

Reviewing Ideas, Terms, and People

1. a. **Identify** What was the last major battle of the war in Europe?
   b. **Evaluate** What was the biggest task facing **Harry S. Truman** when he became president?
2. a. **Define** What was the **Holocaust**?
   b. **Elaborate** How did the oppression of Jews increase during the war?
3. a. **Recall** What was the purpose of the **Manhattan Project**, and how did it result in the end of the war against Japan?
   b. **Explain** What was the status of the United States after the war?
   c. **Predict** How do you think the invention of the **atomic bomb** changed people's views of war?

Critical Thinking

4. **Identifying Causes** Review your notes on the final days of the war in both Europe and the Pacific. Then copy the graphic organizer below and use it to show the short-term causes of Germany's and Japan's surrenders.

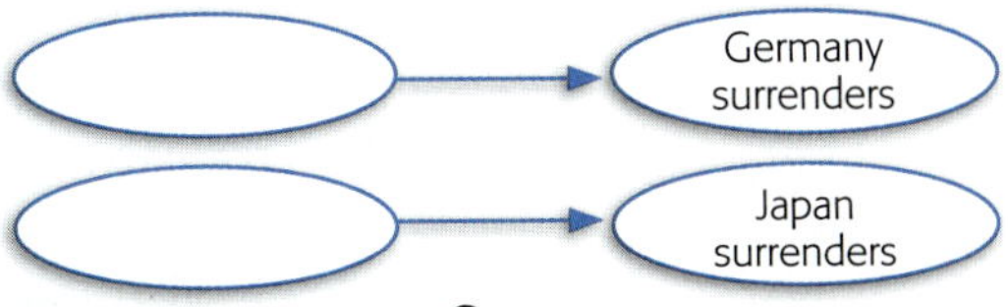

FOCUS ON WRITING

5. **Taking Notes on the Impact of the War** Take notes on the last days of World War II. How did the Allies finally win the war? What impact did the war have on people and countries around the world?

Literature of the Holocaust

from *Diary of Anne Frank*

by Anne Frank (1929–1945)

About the Reading *Anne Frank was a Jewish teenager in Amsterdam who experienced the Nazi occupation of the Netherlands firsthand. Frank and her family hid for more than two years in the sealed-off back room of an office. The family was betrayed to the Gestapo in 1944. Frank and her family members were sent to concentration camps in Germany. Frank died in 1945 at the Bergen-Belsen concentration camp.*

AS YOU READ **Notice how Frank describes the oppression of Jews.**

19th November, 1942

Mr. Dussel has told us much about the outside world we've missed for so long. He had sad news. Countless friends and acquaintances have been taken off to a dreadful fate. ❶ Night after night, green and grey military vehicles cruise the streets. They knock on every door, asking whether any Jews live there. If so, the whole family is immediately taken away. If not, they proceed to the next house. It's impossible to escape their clutches unless you go into hiding. They often go around with lists, knocking only on those doors where they know there's a big haul to be made... In the evenings when it's dark, I often see long lines of good, innocent people, accompanied by crying children, walking on and on, ordered about by a handful of men who bully and beat them until they nearly drop. No one is spared. The sick, the elderly, children, babies and pregnant women—all are marched to their death. ❷

9th October, 1942

Our many Jewish friends and acquaintances are being taken away in droves. The Gestapo is treating them very roughly and transporting them in cattle-trucks to Westerbork, the big camp in Drenthe to which they're sending all the Jews. ❸

GUIDED READING

WORD HELP

Mr. Dussel a friend of Anne's father

droves large numbers

Gestapo German military police

Westerbork a concentration camp on the Dutch-German border

Drenthe a province of the Netherlands

❶ Jews in hiding knew that they would be sent to concentration camps if discovered.

❷ Anne cannot hide her feelings at seeing innocent victims of the Germans being treated poorly.

❸ Jews suffered harsh treatment before and after arrest.

from *Night*

by Elie Wiesel (1928–), translated by Stella Rodway

About the Reading *Elie Wiesel was taken to Auschwitz when he was age 15. Though he survived the camp, not all of his family did. Years after the war, Wiesel wrote about his time spent imprisoned at Auschwitz.*

AS YOU READ **Look for ways that Wiesel describes the trauma of being taken away.**

By eight o'clock in the morning, a weariness like molten lead began to settle in the veins, the limbs, the brain. I was in the midst of my prayers when suddenly there were shouts in the street. I tore myself from my phylacteries and ran to the window. Hungarian police had entered the ghetto and were shouting in the neighboring street:

"All Jews outside! Hurry!"

Some Jewish police went into the houses, saying in broken voices:

"The time's come now . . . you've got to leave all this . . . "

The Hungarian police struck out with truncheons and rifle butts, to right and left, without reason, indiscriminately, their blows falling upon old men and women, children and invalids alike. ❶

One by one the houses emptied, and the street filled with people and bundles. By ten o'clock, all the condemned were outside. The police took a roll call, once, twice, twenty times. The heat was intense. Sweat streamed from faces and bodies.

Children cried for water.

Water? There was plenty, close at hand, in the houses, in the yards, but they were forbidden to break the ranks. "Water! Mummy! Water!"

The Jewish police from the ghetto were able to go and fill a few jugs secretly. Since my sisters and I were destined for the last convoy and we were still allowed to move about, we helped them as well as we could.

GUIDED READING

WORD HELP

molten melted

phylacteries wooden prayer devices

ghetto neighborhood set aside for Jews

truncheons sticks

indiscriminately without care

invalids people who are ill

convoy military escort

❶ ***The Hungarian police used physical force to gather people together.***

CONNECTING LITERATURE TO HISTORY

1. **The Nazi oppression of Jews eventually led to the Gestapo taking Jews from their homes.** How does Frank describe the job that the Gestapo did?
2. **The oppression soon changed to removal.** How does Wiesel describe the removal of the Jews from his hometown?
3. **Jews were treated with physical violence by Nazi supporters.** Give two examples of violence against Jews found in these passages.

Social Studies Skills

Analysis | Critical Thinking | Civic Participation | Study

North Carolina Skills
2.01 Use appropriate sources of information.

Constructing Time Lines

Define the Skill

Time lines are a good way to organize historical information. Time lines clearly show a sequence of historical events over a certain period of time. Many time lines focus on a specific theme within a time period.

When you construct a time line, it often makes the sequence of events easier to follow. Time lines show events in the order they happened and the amount of time between events. Constructing a time line can therefore help you better understand events' context. For example, organizing events on a time line can help you determine their causes and effects.

Learn the Skill

When you construct a time line, you need to make some basic decisions. First, the time line needs a topic. This topic can be general or specific. One example of a general topic is the 1940s. A more specific topic might be major battles of World War II. The time line should cover a time period that includes the main events related to the topic. For example, it would make sense for a time line on American battles in World War II to cover the period 1941 to 1945.

The next step in constructing a time line is gathering information. This includes taking notes on events from the chosen time period related to the topic. It is important to write down the date when each event happened. Putting the events in order before making the time line is often helpful. If there are too many events, it is a good idea to include only the most important ones.

The first step in actually constructing the time line is to draw a straight line using a ruler. The next step is to mark even intervals on the line. Intervals are dates that divide the time line into smaller, equal time periods. For example, a time line of the 1940s might include two-year intervals: 1940, 1942, 1944, and so on. Then add events in the correct places on the time line. The beginning and end of the time line, each interval, and each event should be labeled with dates. The finished time line should include at least six events. As a final touch, the time line needs a title. The title tells what the entries in the time line are about and may include the dates the time line covers.

Practice the Skill

Follow these instructions to construct a time line.

1. Using your textbook, choose a topic related to World War II for your time line. Decide on the dates your time line will need to cover.
2. Use your textbook to take notes on events to include in your time line and their dates. Put the events in order.
3. Following the steps described above, construct your time line. The finished time line should include clearly labeled dates, at least six events, and a title.

CHAPTER 26

Chapter Review

HOLT

History's Impact

▶ **video series**

Review the video to answer the closing question:

Why do you think the United States made the GI Bill of Rights a permanent policy?

Visual Summary

QUICK FACTS

Use the visual summary below to help you review the main ideas of the chapter.

The bombing of Pearl Harbor drew the United States into World War II.

To help supply the troops, women worked in jobs usually held by men.

American soldiers helped defeat the Axis Powers in Europe and the Pacific.

Reviewing Vocabulary, Terms, and People

Identify the term or person from the chapter that best fits each of the following descriptions.

1. The first African American flying unit in the U.S. military
2. American general who retreated from and then retook the Philippines
3. The dictator of the Soviet Union
4. A weapon that produces a massive explosion by splitting atoms
5. Battle at which British troops stopped the German *Afrika Korps*
6. Policy of avoiding war with an aggressive nation by giving in to its demands
7. Extermination of an entire group of people

Comprehension and Critical Thinking

SECTION 1 *(Pages 804–809)*

8. a. **Define** What is fascism?

   b. **Make Inferences** Before Pearl Harbor, what U.S. policies suggested that the United States would join the Allies?

   c. **Evaluate** How well did the policy of appeasement work? Explain your answer.

SECTION 2 *(Pages 810–814)*

9. a. **Recall** What happened during the zoot-suit riots?

   b. **Analyze** Why was the War Production Board important to the war effort?

   c. **Elaborate** How do you think Japanese Americans felt about internment?

SECTION 3 *(Pages 815–819)*

10. a. Identify What led the Axis powers to retreat from the Soviet Union?

b. Summarize In which regions and countries did the Allies win major victories against Germany?

c. Draw Conclusions Why do you think D-Day succeeded?

SECTION 4 *(Pages 820–824)*

11. a. Describe What did kamikaze pilots do?

b. Explain How did cracking Japanese codes help the Allies in the Pacific?

c. Draw Conclusions Why do you think Japan was determined to continue fighting?

SECTION 5 *(Pages 825–829)*

12. a. Recall What were the effects of the atomic bombs on Hiroshima and Nagasaki?

b. Contrast How was the Holocaust different from other wartime tragedies?

c. Evaluate Do you think the strategy of bombing civilian centers was fair? Why or why not?

Reviewing Themes

13. Geography How did geography affect the course of World War II?

14. Society and Culture What changes in society did World War II bring about?

Using the Internet

go.hrw.com
KEYWORD: SC7 CH26

15. Activity: Understanding Code Talkers Guns and bombs were not the only weapons of World War II. Cryptography, or the use of secret codes, was also an important tool for the Allied forces. Some Native Americans in the U.S. military used their own language as a form of cryptography. They spoke Navajo, a complex language, and adapted it for battlefield communications and to transmit secret information by radio and telephone. Soldiers who could speak it became known as "code talkers." Enter the activity keyword. Research the Navajo code talkers of World War II and then create a poster to present your findings.

Reading Skills

Categorizing *Use the Reading Skills taught in this chapter to answer the question from the reading selection below.*

> American, British, and Canadian troops invaded France on June 6, 1944—known as D-Day or "designated day." They crossed the choppy waters of the English Channel and landed on five beaches in Normandy. More than 6,000 ships, 11,000 planes, and 156,000 men were part of the invasion. Soldiers jumped from boats and waded ashore, often under heavy fire. *(p. 819)*

16. Which of the following general categories could help you organize this information?

a. generals of the American forces

b. types of ammunition used

c. resources of invading forces

d. leaders of Allied nations

Social Studies Skills

Constructing Time Lines *Use the Social Studies Skills taught in this chapter to answer the question below.*

17. Make a time line about the end of World War II, covering the events of 1945.

FOCUS ON WRITING

18. Writing Your Radio News Broadcast Review your notes. Choose one event or story from World War II as the focus of your radio broadcast. You can include quotes from soldiers or national leaders. Remember that people cannot see your broadcast, so use descriptive language. Be sure to answer the following questions: *Who? What? Where? When? Why?* and *How?*

CHAPTER 26

Standardized Test Practice

DIRECTIONS: ***Read each question and write the letter of the best response. Use the map below to answer question 1.***

1

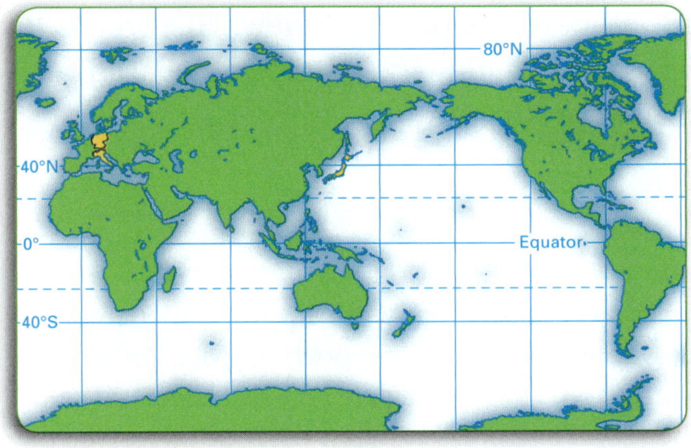

The yellow countries above represent the

A Central Powers.

B Allied Powers.

C Axis Powers.

D Big Three.

2 What led the United States to enter the war?

A Great Britain requested help from the United States.

B Germany attacked a U.S. ship in the Pacific Ocean.

C Germany sent U-boats to attack the U.S. Atlantic coast.

D The Japanese bombed the U.S. base at Pearl Harbor, Hawaii.

3 During the war, many women in North Carolina

A went to work in the state's many shipyards.

B spoke out in opposition to the war.

C joined the armed forces.

D refused to work outside the home.

4 The Allies' successful 1944 invasion of France is known as

A D-Day.

B the Desert Fox.

C sonar.

D the Battle of Britain.

5 Who became president when Franklin D. Roosevelt died in 1945?

A Eleanor Roosevelt

B Harry S. Truman

C Winston Churchill

D Douglas MacArthur

6 The majority of Holocaust victims were

A Slavs.

B Japanese.

C disabled people.

D Jews.

7 Read the following excerpt from the diary of Anne Frank, a Dutch Jew who died in the Holocaust, and use it to answer the question below.

> July 15, 1944
>
> "It's a wonder I haven't abandoned all my ideals, they seem so absurd and impractical. Yet I cling to them because I still believe, in spite of everything, that people are truly good at heart."
>
> —Anne Frank, *The Diary of Anne Frank*

Document-Based Question **Why does Frank call her ideals "absurd and impractical"?**

Assignment

Write an essay describing either Hoovervilles or the Dust Bowl during the Great Depression.

A Descriptive Essay

Vivid descriptions of a place and time can help us understand history. Primary sources often provide such descriptions from one person's point of view. Historians provide a different point of view in descriptions based on many primary and secondary sources.

1. Prewrite

Getting Started

Descriptive essays depend on details that will help the reader create a mental picture. The quotes about the Dust Bowl on page 790 are examples of vivid descriptions. The passage from *The Grapes of Wrath* on page 795 is another good example. For your description, review Chapter 25 and look in the encyclopedia and other sources. Collect as many details as you can about Hoovervilles or the Dust Bowl. Try to find details that involve all of the five senses (sight, sound, smell, touch, and taste). Good description depends on strong details.

TIP **Using Visual Images** Look at visual images such as photographs from the 1930s. What do they show about Hoovervilles or the Dust Bowl and the people who lived there? Use this information in your description.

Organizing Information

Make one generalization that sums up all your details. This will be your main idea. Then organize the details and examples you have found into two, three, or four categories. These will become the body paragraphs of the essay. All of these categories should support the main idea.

For example, the main idea of an essay could be that the name *Dust Bowl* was an accurate description of the area. One detail might be that the gritty dirt often became caught in people's skin, hair, and clothing. This detail could fit into the category of people in the Dust Bowl.

2. Write

You can use this framework to help you write your first draft.

A Writer's Framework

Introduction
- Make a generalization about your topic.
- List the categories that will be included in the body paragraphs.

Body
- Separate details into paragraphs by category.
- Use vivid details that involve the five senses.
- Use details from different sources.

Conclusion
- Summarize your information.
- Explain how your topic is related to larger issues.

3. Evaluate and Revise

Evaluating

Use these questions to discover ways to improve your essay.

Evaluation Questions for a Descriptive Essay

- Do you begin with a generalization about your topic?
- Do you separate details into separate paragraphs by category?
- Do you use vivid details that involve the five senses?
- Do you use details from different sources?
- Do you explain how your topic is related to larger issues?

TIP **Show, Don't Tell** Writers are often advised, "Show, don't tell." This phrase means that writers should use strong words, details, and examples to make a point. Choose vivid, clear examples for your description. They should not need much explanation.

Revising

When you revise your essay, make examples and details as specific as possible. This will make your description more vivid.

General: *People built flimsy houses in Hoovervilles.*

Specific: *In Hoovervilles, people built shelters out of scraps of lumber, tin, and cardboard.*

4. Proofread and Publish

Proofreading

Check your sentences for fragments and run-ons. A fragment is an incomplete sentence. Adding a subject or a verb can often make a fragment into a complete sentence. A run-on has too many subjects and verbs for one sentence. It usually needs to be broken into two or more separate sentences.

Publishing

Share your essay with one or more classmates. Make illustrations based on the descriptions in each other's essays.

5. Practice and Apply

Use the steps and strategies in this workshop to write your descriptive essay.

UNIT 9 1945–1975

Postwar America

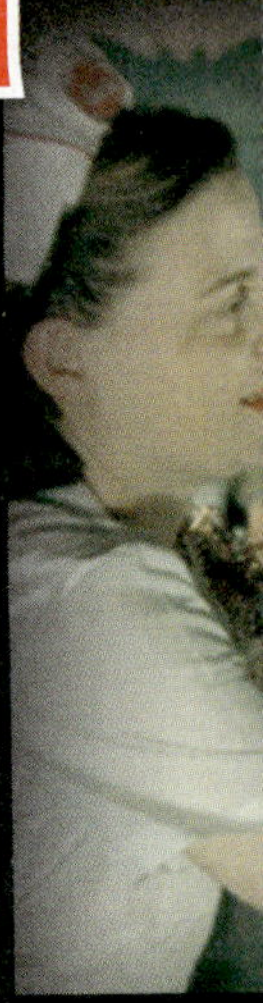

What You Will Learn...

After the end of World War II, Americans became concerned with the global spread of communism. The government began taking steps to defend the nation against possible aggression from Communist nations. At home, many Americans enjoyed the economic prosperity of 1950s society. Not everyone benefited, however. Some Americans spoke out against American society and a government that did not guarantee equality to all citizens.

During the civil rights movement many Americans demanded equal rights for minority groups. Despite sometimes violent opposition, many successes were achieved. Differing viewpoints within society were further exposed, however, by reactions to the Vietnam War, a war fought in Southeast Asia over Communist expansion.

Explore the Art

The movies of the 1950s often portrayed American life as prosperous and content, although this was not true for everyone. What does this image suggest about the prosperity of postwar America?

CHAPTER 27 1945–1959

Early Years of the Cold War

North Carolina Standards

Social Studies Objectives

7.01 Analyze the extent and significance of economic changes in North Carolina.

7.03 Assess the influence of technological advances on economic development and daily life.

7.04 Compare and contrast the various political viewpoints surrounding issues of the post World War II era.

9.02 Identify past and present state and local leaders from diverse cultural backgrounds and assess their influence in effecting change.

Language Arts Objectives

2.01 Analyze and evaluate informational materials that are read, heard, and/or viewed by:

- monitoring comprehension for understanding of what is read, heard and/or viewed.
- determining the importance and accuracy of information.
- making connections to related topics/information.

go.hrw.com
North Carolina
KEYWORD: SC7 NC

Focus on Writing

Song Lyrics The end of World War II brought economic prosperity to the United States, along with new fears and challenges. Americans adjusted to changes in their everyday lives and the new threat of nuclear war. In this chapter you will read about life at the beginning of the Cold War. Then you will write the words to a song that reflects some aspect of American life in the 1950s.

United States

1945 After Roosevelt's death, Harry S. Truman becomes president.

1945

World

1946 Winston Churchill declares an "iron curtain" between Western powers and the Soviet Union.

HOLT

History's Impact

▶ **video series**
Watch the video to understand the impact of television on the United States.

What You Will Learn...

After World War II, the United States and the Soviet Union became involved in a nuclear arms race between the two nations. Here, American students practice a "duck-and-cover" drill, designed to protect them from a nuclear bomb blast, shown in the government poster above. In this chapter, you will learn how American life changed as a result of the Cold War.

1952 Grace Hopper creates the first compiler, which translates English into computer language.

1953 Julius and Ethel Rosenberg are executed for Communist activities.

1956 Fats Domino's "Blueberry Hill" tops the charts.

1958 The National Aeronautics and Space Administration (NASA) is formed.

1950 · 1955 · 1960

1948 The nation of Israel is established.

1955 The Warsaw Pact is formed between Eastern European powers.

1957 The Soviet Union launches the first satellite, *Sputnik*, into orbit.

1959 Fidel Castro takes over Cuba.

Reading Social Studies

by Kylene Beers

Economics | Geography | **Politics** | Society and Culture | **Science and Technology**

Focus on Themes In this chapter, you will learn about the Cold War between the United States and the Soviet Union. This war was unlike other wars in that it was often fought between **politicians** instead of soldiers. Each country used developments in **science and technology** to declare itself superior. You will also read about U.S. society and its reaction to the Cold War.

Visualizing

Focus on Reading Visualizing how your life might have been different if you had been alive during a period in history can help you understand life at that time.

Understanding Visualizing Using clues about everyday life that you find in a history book like this one can help you imagine what life was like in the past. You can imagine yourself and your life, and how life would have been different if you had lived in the past. Or, you can try to imagine what life was like for the people alive then.

Notice the clues in this passage that give you an idea of how people felt living during the Cold War.

> All the time, in the homely [plain], cluttered rooms of our private lives the television displayed the continuing spectacle of public life—all of it still going on in the windless places on the other side of the screen. Presidents and First Secretaries trod [climbed] down the metal staircases from the bellies of great aircraft to shake hands on the tarmac [runway] and climb into big black cars. Tanks wheeled down blind streets and across muddy fields. Rolls of heavy wire netting were unwound and veered [turned] upwards against a dawn sky.
>
> —From *The Cruel Peace*, by Fred Inglis

The author is using description to inform the reader about the feeling of watching the Cold War unfold on television.

Here the author uses frightening images to help the reader understand the fear of the Cold War.

You Try It!

The following passage is from the chapter you are getting ready to read. As you read the passage, look for details that help you visualize the past.

> In 1946 Winston Churchill described how Soviet control cut these countries off from the Western world. "An iron curtain has descended [fallen] across the [European] Continent," he said. The term *iron curtain* thus came to be used to describe this division. Presidential adviser Bernard Baruch warned of the seriousness of the Soviet threat, saying, "Let us not be deceived—we are today in the midst of a cold war." The phrase *Cold War* came to be used often to describe the long struggle for global power between the United States and the Soviet Union.
>
> *From Chapter 27, p. 846*

After you read the passage, answer the following questions.

1. Which details help you understand the attitude existing between the United States and the Soviet Union?
2. How does the quote by Winston Churchill help you visualize the political atmosphere of the time?
3. How does the phrase *Cold War* help you visualize the political atmosphere of the time?

As you read Chapter 27, look for details that help you visualize the past.

Key Terms and People

Chapter 27

Section 1

Yalta Conference *(p. 844)*
Nuremberg trials *(p. 845)*
United Nations *(p. 846)*
Cold War *(p. 846)*
containment *(p. 847)*
Truman Doctrine *(p. 847)*
Marshall Plan *(p. 847)*
North Atlantic Treaty Organization *(p. 848)*
GI Bill of Rights *(p. 848)*
Fair Deal *(p. 850)*

Section 2

Mao Zedong *(p. 852)*
38th parallel *(p. 852)*
Joseph McCarthy *(p. 855)*
hydrogen bomb *(p. 856)*
arms race *(p. 856)*
Sputnik (p. 856)
brinkmanship *(p. 856)*

Section 3

baby boom *(p. 858)*
Sun Belt *(p. 858)*
urban renewal *(p. 859)*
beats *(p. 861)*

Academic Vocabulary

In this chapter, you will learn the following academic words:
concrete *(p. 855)*

SECTION 1

Adjusting to Peace

What You Will Learn...

Main Ideas

1. As World War II ended, leaders began planning the future of the postwar world.
2. The United States and the Soviet Union went from being allies to enemies after World War II.
3. Americans adjusted to postwar life.

The Big Idea

After World War II, Americans adjusted to new challenges both at home and around the world.

Key Terms and People

Yalta Conference, *p. 844*
Nuremberg trials, *p. 845*
United Nations, *p. 846*
Cold War, *p. 846*
containment, *p. 847*
Truman Doctrine, *p. 847*
Marshall Plan, *p. 847*
North Atlantic Treaty Organization, *p. 848*
GI Bill of Rights, *p. 848*
Fair Deal, *p. 850*

TAKING NOTES As you read, take notes on the results of the end of World War II. Organize your notes in a diagram like this one.

End of World War II → Results

If YOU were there...

You are an adviser to President Harry S. Truman in July 1945. You have traveled with him to Potsdam, outside the ruined city of Berlin, where Allied leaders are discussing postwar plans. Everyone agrees that steps must be taken to prevent another world war. But you are worried that Soviet leader Joseph Stalin cannot be trusted.

What advice would you give to President Truman?

BUILDING BACKGROUND U.S. leaders had mistrusted the Soviet government before World War II. The goals of the totalitarian, Communist Soviet state conflicted with American democratic, capitalistic ideals. In addition, Soviet dictator Joseph Stalin used brutal tactics, including murder, to maintain power and control political opposition. During the war, the rivals put aside their differences to defeat Germany. After the war, however, old tensions resurfaced.

The Future of the Postwar World

As 1945 began, it was becoming clear that the Allies were going to win World War II. In February Allied leaders known as the Big Three—Franklin D. Roosevelt of the United States, Winston Churchill of Great Britain, and Joseph Stalin of the Soviet Union—met in the Soviet city of Yalta to discuss plans for peace.

At the **Yalta Conference**, the three leaders made important decisions about the future of European governments. They expressed support for the creation of an international peacekeeping organization. They also agreed that nations freed from Germany should have the right "to create democratic institutions of their own choice." Stalin promised to allow free elections in the Soviet-occupied countries in Eastern Europe. However, after driving German troops out of Poland, Soviet forces set up a pro–Soviet Communist government.

In July 1945 President Truman met with British and Soviet leaders near Berlin, Germany, at the Potsdam Conference. The Allied leaders divided conquered Germany into four zones. Britain, France, the United States, and the Soviet Union would each occupy one zone. The capital city of Berlin—located deep inside the Soviet zone—was also divided into four zones.

War Crimes Trials

After World War II, Allied leaders formed a special court, called the International Military Tribunal, to try Axis leaders accused of war crimes. In November 1945 the tribunal put high-ranking Nazis on trial in the German city of Nuremberg in what became known as the **Nuremberg trials**. U.S. Supreme Court justice Robert H. Jackson served as the chief American attorney. In his opening statement, Jackson explained the importance of the trials:

> "The wrongs which we seek to condemn and punish have been so calculated [well planned], so malignant [evil] and devastating, that civilization cannot tolerate their being ignored because it cannot survive their being repeated."
>
> —Robert H. Jackson, quoted in *The Nuremberg Trial*, edited by Mitchell Bard

The court charged Nazi officials with "crimes against humanity." One defendant was Hermann Goering, a key planner of Hitler's "final solution." Another was Hans Frank, Poland's wartime governor, who had organized the killing of hundreds of thousands of Poles and Polish Jews. The tribunal found 19 Nazi leaders guilty. Of these, 12, including Goering and Frank, were sentenced to death.

The International Military Tribunal for the Far East held trials in Japan. Japan's wartime leader Hideki Tojo was convicted and executed. Seven other Japanese leaders were also sentenced to death. The trials in Germany and Japan helped establish the principle that individuals must be held responsible for committing war crimes, even when acting on behalf of a government.

FOCUS ON READING

How does the quote from Robert H. Jackson help you visualize the atmosphere of the Nuremberg trials?

The United Nations

During the war, President Roosevelt had spoken of the need for a new international organization to promote world peace. Roosevelt did not believe the United States alone could bring peace to the whole world. "The structure of world peace," he said, "must be a peace which rests on the cooperative effort of the whole world."

QUICK FACTS

Yalta Conference, February 1945

Who attended?

- Franklin Roosevelt, United States
- Winston Churchill, Great Britain
- Joseph Stalin, Soviet Union

What was the outcome?

- Free elections for countries liberated from German control
- Strong support for creation of an international peacekeeping organization

Winston Churchill, Franklin Roosevelt, and Joseph Stalin (seated left to right) met at Yalta in 1945.

QUICK FACTS

Potsdam Conference, July 1945

Who attended?

- Harry S. Truman, United States
- Winston Churchill and Clement Attlee, Great Britain
- Joseph Stalin, Soviet Union

What was the outcome?

- Germany and the city of Berlin would be divided into four zones. Britain, France, the United States, and the Soviet Union would each control one zone.

Clement Attlee, Harry Truman, and Joseph Stalin (seated left to right) met at Potsdam in 1945.

Linking to Today

The United Nations

Written in 1945, the United Nations Charter declared the organization's commitment "to unite our strength to maintain international peace and security." Since 1945 the UN has grown from 51 member nations to more than 190. In addition to working to prevent war, the United Nations today works to provide disaster relief, prevent hunger and disease, and combat international terrorism.

Analysis Skill: Analyzing Information

How have the goals of the United Nations expanded since 1945?

In 1944 American, British, Soviet, and Chinese representatives met to draft a plan for the **United Nations** (UN)—an organization dedicated to resolving international conflicts. In 1945, representatives from 50 countries met to write the UN Charter. President Truman appointed Eleanor Roosevelt as one of the first U.S. delegates to the UN.

One of the UN's first actions concerned Palestine, occupied by the British after World War I. The UN General Assembly voted to divide the area into separate Arab and Jewish states. Jews had begun moving to Palestine, an area important to the Jewish, Christian, and Islamic religions, after World War I. Many more moved there before and during World War II. On May 14, 1948, Jewish leaders announced the creation of the nation of Israel.

The United States quickly recognized the new Jewish state. Arab leaders refused to do so and claimed the land as their own. Armies from five Arab states attacked Israel. Israeli forces drove them back, and the two sides reached a truce in 1949. Israel then joined the UN. But tensions remained high.

Reading Check **Finding Main Ideas** What steps did world leaders take to establish peace?

From Allies to Enemies

During World War II, the United States and the Soviet Union cooperated to win the war. Afterward, the differences between the two nations led to new hostility. The Soviet Union hoped to spread communism around the world. Americans remained committed to capitalism and democracy.

The Iron Curtain

After Stalin created a Communist government in Poland, the Soviet Union expanded its control over Eastern Europe by creating "satellite states"—countries under complete Soviet control. In 1946 Winston Churchill described how Soviet control cut these countries off from the Western world. "An iron curtain has descended [fallen] across the [European] Continent," he said. The term *iron curtain* thus came to be used to describe this division. Presidential adviser Bernard Baruch warned of the seriousness of the Soviet threat, saying, "Let us not be deceived—we are today in the midst of a cold war." The phrase **Cold War** came to be used to describe the struggle for global power between the United States and the Soviet Union.

Cold War Policies

The United States quickly developed a new foreign policy to deal with the Cold War. It was based on the goal of **containment**, or preventing the Soviet Union from expanding its influence around the world.

In 1945 the Soviet Union began demanding control over areas in the Mediterranean Sea that were under Turkish authority. In 1946 Communist rebels in Greece threatened to topple the Greek monarchy. At Truman's request, Congress passed an aid package worth millions of dollars for Greece and Turkey. The money, the president said, would "support free peoples who are resisting attempted subjugation [conquest] by armed minorities or outside pressures." U.S. aid helped the Greek army defeat the Communist rebels and protected Turkey from Soviet expansion. This policy of providing aid to help foreign countries fight communism became known as the **Truman Doctrine**.

The nations of Europe, meanwhile, were still devastated from World War II. American secretary of state George C. Marshall saw this as a threat both to stability in Europe and to the U.S. economy, which depended on trade with Europe. Marshall called on European leaders to develop plans for economic recovery, which the United States would help fund. Under the **Marshall Plan**, Western Europe received more than $13 billion in U.S. loans and grants for European economic recovery between 1948 and 1952. Soviet leaders rejected Marshall Plan aid. They also kept Eastern European nations from participating.

Cold War tensions rose further in 1948 when France, Britain, and the United States

This cartoon shows Czechoslovakia's freedom being crushed by the Soviet Union.

Cold War Europe, 1955

GEOGRAPHY SKILLS **INTERPRETING MAPS**

1. **Place** Which countries remained nonaligned during the Cold War?
2. **Location** What is the northernmost NATO member country shown on the map?

decided to join their occupation zones of Germany into one unit. The Soviet Union had good reason to fear the creation of a strong West German state. On June 24, the Soviet Union suddenly blocked all rail, highway, and water traffic between western Germany and the city of Berlin. West Berlin's 2 million residents were trapped behind the iron curtain.

To respond to this crisis without using military force, U.S. and British planes began airlifting supplies into West Berlin. For more than a year, planes delivered lifesaving food, fuel, and machinery to West Berliners. The Soviet Union made no determined effort to stop the airlift, fearing a war. It then lifted the blockade in May 1949.

That same year, the United States joined nine Western European countries, along with Iceland and Canada, to form the **North Atlantic Treaty Organization** (NATO). NATO members promised to defend each other if attacked. In 1955 the Soviet Union created the Warsaw Pact, which provided a unified system of military command between the Soviet Union and its Eastern European satellite countries for their mutual defense.

THE IMPACT TODAY

When the Cold War ended, many former Warsaw Pact nations joined NATO. Today NATO has 26 member nations.

FOCUS ON NORTH CAROLINA

The idea of bringing research and industry together would eventually lead to the construction of Research Triangle Park between Durham, Chapel Hill, and Raleigh. By 1969 there were 21 companies with locations in the park, and by 1979 there were 17 more.

READING CHECK **Comparing** How were NATO and the Warsaw Pact similar?

BIOGRAPHY

Harry S. Truman

1884–1972

Harry S. Truman grew up in Independence, Missouri. He was an artillery officer in France during World War I, then he returned to Missouri and later became active in politics. He was elected to the U.S. Senate in 1934, where he served until becoming vice president in 1945. When President Roosevelt died, Truman was sworn in as president of the United States. "I felt like the moon, the stars, and all the planets had fallen on me," he said. Truman later called his first year in office a "year of decisions," as he led the country through the end of World War II and the start of the Cold War.

Analyzing Information What made Truman's first year as president especially challenging?

Postwar America

You have read about the economic depression that followed the end of World War I. As World War II ended, President Truman was worried about a similar downturn. More than 16 million Americans had served in the armed forces during the war. Now they were coming home, and most would be looking for work.

The Postwar Economy

To provide jobs for returning veterans, the government urged the millions of women who had gone to work during the war to give up their jobs. New laws also eased the transition for returning soldiers. The Servicemen's Readjustment Act, or **GI Bill of Rights**, offered veterans money for school as well as loans for houses, farms, and businesses. The GI Bill's home loans enabled veterans to buy about 20 percent of the new houses built right after the war. Some 8 million veterans used the GI Bill's educational benefits to attend colleges and technical schools.

Another major postwar change was Truman's decision to end the rationing of scarce products. Prices skyrocketed as people rushed to buy gasoline and other products that had been limited during the war. The inflation rate in 1946 rose above 18 percent. The U.S. economy remained strong, however.

North Carolina continued to be the nation's leading manufacturer of textiles, tobacco products, and wood furniture between 1945 and 1970. However, leaders worried that the state was too dependent on these industries. They made efforts to attract new and different industries to the state.

In 1949 the legislature approved Governor W. Kerr Scott's "Go Forward" program. It provided funding to build and improve roads, schools, and port facilities. Leaders also began discussing the creation of a place where research and industry could come together.

Jackie Robinson

On April 15, 1947, Jackie Robinson played his first game for the Brooklyn Dodgers. Robinson became a hero to millions by ending segregation in major league baseball. He went on to be a Hall of Fame player—and an outspoken supporter of equal rights. "The right of every American to first-class citizenship is the most important issue of our time," Robinson said.

How did Robinson show his support for equal rights for all Americans?

Labor Unrest

More than 35 percent of all nonfarm workers were members of unions in 1946, more than ever before. With prices rising quickly, workers went on strike to demand higher wages. In 1946 alone, 4.5 million workers participated in nearly 5,000 strikes.

The strikes became a problem for Truman. Many people began to wonder if he could handle the presidency. In April 1946 the 400,000-member United Mine Workers Union went on strike. When Truman was unable to negotiate a settlement, he placed the mines under government control. In May Truman threatened to draft striking railroad workers into the army.

To reduce the power of labor unions, Congress passed the Taft-Hartley Act in 1947. This act outlawed closed shops—businesses that could hire only union members. It also allowed the president to order an 80-day "cooling-off" period before a strike began. In addition, union leaders had to swear they were not Communists. Truman thought this bill went too far to weaken unions. He vetoed the bill, but Congress overrode his veto.

Civil Rights

After serving their country in World War II, many African Americans faced prejudice and segregation at home. "Black servicemen were overseas dying for this country," said civil rights lawyer Constance Baker Motley. "And . . . they would be coming home to a situation that said, in effect, You're a second-class citizen." African American veterans helped lead a major effort to gain equal rights.

Truman responded in 1946 by appointing the Committee on Civil Rights to investigate discrimination and suggest solutions. As a result of the committee's report, Truman recommended that Congress pass anti-lynching laws, outlaw segregation, and protect civil rights. Congress failed to act on Truman's ideas. But in 1948, under pressure from African American groups, Truman issued an executive order ending segregation in the armed forces. He also banned discrimination in the hiring of federal employees.

The Election of 1948

As the election of 1948 drew near, President Truman's chances of re-election looked bleak. The Republicans had gained control of Congress in 1946. They felt confident that their presidential candidate, New York governor Thomas Dewey, could beat Truman.

Truman faced challenges from within the Democratic Party as well. Some southern Democrats protested Truman's support for civil rights laws by walking out of the 1948

Democratic National Convention. Many joined the States' Rights Party, or Dixiecrats, which favored racial segregation. The Dixiecrats nominated their own presidential candidate—South Carolina governor Strom Thurmond.

Truman took his case for re-election directly to the American people. He traveled more than 30,000 miles by train and delivered hundreds of speeches. He attacked what he called the "do-nothing, good-for-nothing" Congress for refusing to pass his legislation. "I spoke I believe altogether to between fifteen and twenty million people," he later said. "I met them face to face, and I convinced them, and they voted for me." Truman won a surprise victory. The Democratic Party also regained control of both houses of Congress.

In his 1949 State of the Union Address, Truman urged Congress to support his plans for the nation. Truman's domestic program, called the **Fair Deal**, included a higher minimum wage, the creation of a national health insurance plan for all Americans, and expanded Social Security benefits for the elderly. It also asked for federal protection of civil rights and an end to racial discrimination in hiring.

Congress approved some parts of the Fair Deal, such as a higher minimum wage and expanded Social Security benefits. Congress rejected other Fair Deal proposals. These included civil rights legislation that would have created a permanent Fair Employment Practices Committee.

QUICK FACTS

The Fair Deal

The Fair Deal included
- National health insurance
- Expanded social security
- Higher minimum wage
- Public housing
- Civil rights legislation
- Federal aid to education

READING CHECK **Analyzing** How did the GI Bill help returning soldiers?

SUMMARY AND PREVIEW The United States faced a series of new challenges after World War II. In the next section you will learn how the fear of communism grew in the 1950s.

Section 1 Assessment

go.hrw.com
Online Quiz
KEYWORD: SC7 HP27

Reviewing Ideas, Terms, and People

1. a. **Describe** How did the Allies divide Germany at the Potsdam Conference?
   b. **Explain** Why were the **Nuremberg trials** important?
   c. **Predict** Based on its founding and early years, do you think the **United Nations** would be an effective organization?
2. a. **Define** What was the **Truman Doctrine**?
   b. **Analyze** How did the **Marshall Plan** help stabilize Western Europe?
   c. **Elaborate** Why do you think the United States and Western European countries were concerned about Soviet expansion?
3. a. **Recall** What kinds of programs were included in President Truman's **Fair Deal**?
   b. **Explain** What was the purpose of the Taft-Hartley Act?
   c. **Evaluate** Do you think President Truman did enough to promote civil rights? Why or why not?

Critical Thinking

4. **Categorizing** Review your notes on the results of World War II. Then copy the graphic organizer below and use it to identify the effects of the war's end on the United States and the world.

Results of World War II	
In the United States	In the World

FOCUS ON WRITING

5. **The Postwar World** Take notes on postwar developments in the United States and the world. Which events might have given Americans hope? Which might have made them concerned? If you had lived during the 1950s, which issue would have been of the most interest to you?

BIOGRAPHY

Eleanor Roosevelt

How would you work for human rights for all?

When did she live? 1884–1962

Where did she live? She lived much of her life in New York, where she married Franklin D. Roosevelt in 1905. She also lived in Washington, D.C., when her husband was assistant secretary of the navy and, later, president.

What did she do? During the Great Depression, Eleanor Roosevelt acted as President Roosevelt's "eyes and ears" by traveling around the United States to study conditions among the people. She investigated New Deal programs and reported on their effectiveness. She also worked for equal rights for African Americans. Serving on the UN Commission on Human Rights from 1946 to 1951, she helped write the Universal Declaration of Human Rights, which the UN adopted in 1948. In 1961 President John F. Kennedy chose her to chair his Commission on the Status of Women.

Why is she so important? She changed the role of first lady by acting as a public figure. She held her own press conferences, made speeches, and wrote newspaper columns. She was a leading figure in the movements to promote human rights, children's welfare, and equal rights for women and minorities.

Making Inferences How did Eleanor Roosevelt's different jobs and activities reflect her values and beliefs?

KEY EVENTS

1905
Marries Franklin D. Roosevelt

1921
Becomes active in politics

1936
Begins writing daily newspaper columns; holds press conferences for women correspondents

1945
Appointed delegate to the UN

1946
Becomes chair of the UN Commission on Human Rights

1961
Appointed chair of the Commission on the Status of Women

1962
Dies in New York City

SECTION 2

War in Korea and a New Red Scare

What You Will Learn...

Main Ideas

1. The United States fought Communist North Korea in the Korean War.
2. Fear of Communists led to a new Red Scare at home.
3. President Eisenhower faced Cold War crises around the world.

The Big Idea

During the Cold War, the U.S. government confronted communism globally and within the United States.

Key Terms and People

Mao Zedong, *p. 852*
38th parallel, *p. 852*
Joseph McCarthy, *p. 855*
hydrogen bomb, *p. 856*
arms race, *p. 856*
Sputnik, *p. 856*
brinkmanship, *p. 856*

TAKING NOTES As you read, take notes on Cold War conflicts and crises. In each circle of a diagram like the one below, describe one conflict or crisis. You may need to add more circles.

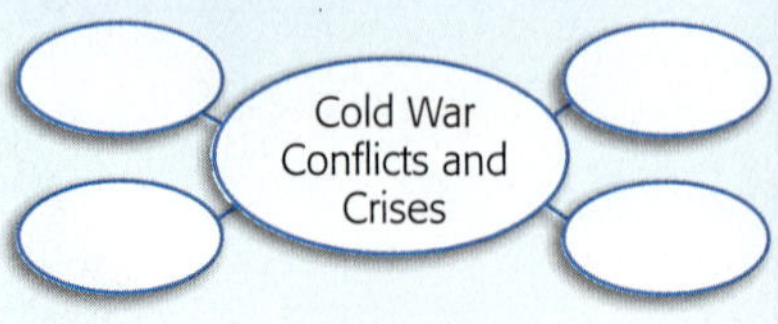

If YOU were there...

A radio broadcast on June 26, 1950, delivers a shocking announcement. Communist forces from North Korea have just invaded South Korea. President Truman has demanded that the North Koreans halt their invasion, but they seem to be ignoring this demand. Now Truman has to decide whether to use American military force to stop the North Koreans.

Do you think the United States should send troops to Korea? Why or why not?

BUILDING BACKGROUND The earliest Cold War conflicts were in Central and Eastern Europe, where countries were divided by the Iron Curtain. But the Truman Doctrine committed the United States to containing communism on a wider scale. The Communist takeover of China in 1949 soon focused Cold War fears on Asia.

The Korean War

The Cold War began in Europe but quickly spread to the Asian nations of China and Korea. In China, the Communist Party and the Nationalist Party had been struggling for control of the country since the early 1900s. The two rivals joined forces against Japan during World War II but then resumed their civil war after Japan's defeat. The United States, as part of its commitment to stop the spread of communism, backed the Nationalists. The Nationalists were defeated, however, and were forced to flee to the island of Taiwan. Led by **Mao Zedong**, the Communists officially established the People's Republic of China on October 1, 1949. Many Americans saw this as a disastrous failure of U.S. foreign policy. They feared that all of Asia might soon fall to communism.

These fears were heightened by a crisis in Korea. Japan had controlled Korea from 1910 to the end of World War II. After the war, the Allies divided Korea at the **38th parallel**. The Soviet Union

GEOGRAPHY SKILLS **INTERPRETING MAPS**

1. **Location** Why do you think the Demilitarized Zone is located where it is?
2. **Movement** Which two forces advanced into South Korea?

BIOGRAPHY

Douglas MacArthur

1880–1964

Douglas MacArthur grew up on a series of military bases, where his father served in the U.S. Army. "It was here I learned to ride and shoot even before I could read or write," he later said. After graduating first in his class at West Point, MacArthur began an army career that would last more than 50 years. He reached the rank of general in 1918 and commanded troops in World War I, World War II, and the Korean War. "When I joined the Army," he told Congress in 1951, "it was the fulfillment of all my boyhood hopes and dreams."

Drawing Inferences How can you tell how MacArthur felt about the U.S. Army?

controlled the northern part of Korea, and the United States occupied the south. Both sides set up governments, neither of which recognized the other as legitimate.

Fighting in Korea

On June 25, 1950, North Korea's Soviet-trained and equipped army stormed across the 38th parallel and invaded South Korea. The United Nations called for a cease-fire. But the North Koreans continued their attack.

President Truman had to make an immediate decision: Should the United States use force to try to stop the North Korean invasion? On June 27 Truman announced: "I have ordered United States air and sea forces to give the [South] Korean government troops cover and support." That same day, the UN decided to help South Korea "to repel the armed attack." American general Douglas MacArthur was put in command of the UN forces, which included troops from the United States and 15 other countries. The majority of the troops were from the United States and South Korea.

In the early battles, MacArthur's forces were driven back to the southeastern tip of the Korean Peninsula, near the city of Pusan. Fierce fighting raged for six weeks before the UN troops turned the tide of the war with a surprise attack. Landing at the port city of Inchon on September 15, UN forces attacked the North Koreans from behind. About a month later, MacArthur's troops captured Pyongyang, North Korea's capital. They then advanced north to the Yalu River, the border between North Korea and China. MacArthur told Truman he would "have the boys home by Christmas."

Then China suddenly sent hundreds of thousands of soldiers across the border to join the North Koreans. They drove UN forces south again, back below the 38th parallel. MacArthur suggested air strikes on Chinese cities and an attack on mainland China. Truman refused permission. He was determined to contain the war in Korea.

When MacArthur publicly criticized the president's strategy, Truman relieved the general of command. "I fired General MacArthur because he wouldn't respect the authority of the president," Truman said. This was a very unpopular decision with the American public. MacArthur came home to a hero's welcome.

FOCUS ON NORTH CAROLINA

A graduate of the University of North Carolina, Junius I. Scales, was arrested in 1954 for being a member of the Communist Party. He appealed his conviction, and the case was eventually decided against Scales by the U.S. Supreme Court. However, President Kennedy commuted his sentence after he had spent 15 months in prison.

The War Ends

By the spring of 1951 the fighting in Korea settled into a violent stalemate. The UN forces had driven the North Koreans and Chinese back across the 38th parallel. But neither side seemed able to win the war.

Americans' frustration with the war dominated the 1952 presidential election. The Republicans nominated war hero Dwight D. Eisenhower. He promised to end the increasingly unpopular conflict, saying, "The first task of a new administration will be to . . . bring the Korean War to an early and honorable end."

This promise helped Eisenhower win the election. Eisenhower visited Korea, but the conflict dragged on. A cease-fire finally ended the fighting on July 27, 1953. After three years of fighting, North and South Korea were again divided near the 38th parallel. More than 130,000 Americans had been killed or wounded. Korean and Chinese casualties topped 2 million.

READING CHECK **Summarizing** What were the effects of the Korean War?

Primary Source

POLITICAL CARTOON

Fear of Communism

In the 1950s the fear of communism caused some government leaders to ignore the civil liberties of suspected Communists. Some critics, like this cartoonist, believed these tactics threatened the freedom of all Americans. Here, a frightened man climbs the arm of the Statue of Liberty to put out her torch.

"FIRE!" from *Herblock: A Cartoonist's Life* (Times Books 1998)

ANALYSIS SKILL **ANALYZING PRIMARY SOURCES**

Why is the man shown to be putting out Liberty's torch?

A New Red Scare

The first Red Scare swept America after the Russian Revolution in 1917. Cold War fears led to another Red Scare in the late 1940s and 1950s. Attorney General J. Howard McGrath summed up these fears when he said, "There are today many Communists in America. They are everywhere—in factories, offices, butcher shops, on street corners."

Fear of Communists

A congressional committee called the House Un-American Activities Committee (HUAC) investigated Communist influence in America. In 1947 HUAC launched a series of hearings to expose what it believed was Communist influence in the Hollywood movie industry. The committee branded as "red," or Communist, actors and writers who would not answer questions or who refused to reveal the names of suspected Communists. People suspected of Communist sympathies were often blacklisted, or denied work. Some of these people never worked in movies again.

Explosive spy cases also fed the fears that Communists were at work in the United States. In 1950 a German-born physicist was convicted of providing the Soviets information about the atomic bomb project at Los Alamos, New Mexico, that allowed them

Primary Source

POINTS OF VIEW

McCarthyism

Journalist Edward R. Murrow frequently criticized Senator McCarthy's tactics. This drew a furious response from McCarthy.

"If none of us ever read a book that was 'dangerous,' nor had a friend who was 'different,' or never joined an organization that advocated 'change,' we would all be just the kind of people Joe McCarthy wants. Whose fault is that? Not really [McCarthy's]. He didn't create this situation of fear. He merely exploited [took advantage of] it, and rather successfully."

—Edward R. Murrow

"Murrow is a symbol—the leader and the cleverest of the jackal [wild dog] pack which is always found at the throat of anyone who dares to expose individual Communists and traitors. I am compelled by the facts to say to you that Mr. Edward R. Murrow, as far back as twenty years ago, was engaged in propaganda for Communist causes."

—Joseph McCarthy

ANALYSIS SKILL **ANALYZING POINTS OF VIEW**

How would you describe Murrow's criticism of McCarthy's ideas?

to develop an atomic bomb at least one year earlier than they would have. In 1951 Julius and Ethel Rosenberg also were tried for providing Soviet spies with secret details about atomic bomb design. The Rosenbergs denied the charges but were found guilty and executed in 1953.

The Rise of McCarthy

Wisconsin senator **Joseph McCarthy** contributed to fears in the early 1950s by charging that Communists were working inside the State Department. He claimed to have the names of 57 people who were "either card-carrying members or certainly loyal to the Communist Party."

McCarthy produced no concrete proof of crimes. When challenged, he made up new charges, labeling those who questioned him as "soft on communism." This method of making aggressive accusations without proof became known as McCarthyism.

McCarthy finally went too far in 1954. In televised Senate hearings, he charged that there were Communists in the U.S. Army. For five weeks, Americans watched McCarthy's bullying tactics. At one point, McCarthy tried to discredit Joseph Welch, the army's attorney, by attacking a young assistant in Welch's law firm. This shocked Welch—and the nation. "Let us not assassinate this lad further, Senator," Welsh said. "Have you left no sense of decency?" A later Senate vote condemned McCarthy's actions, but it came too late for those whose careers had been ruined by his attacks.

READING CHECK **Comparing** How were HUAC's and McCarthy's actions similar?

ACADEMIC VOCABULARY

concrete specific, real

NC History Makers

Edward R. Murrow
Edward R. Murrow became a trusted journalist during World War II and successfully confronted Senator McCarthy.

Eisenhower and the Cold War

Cold War tensions increased around the world during the presidency of Dwight Eisenhower. In this hostile atmosphere, Americans adjusted to the reality of living with the constant threat of nuclear war.

The Arms Race

In 1950 President Truman approved work on the **hydrogen bomb**, a weapon far more powerful than the atomic bombs used in World War II. American scientists tested the first hydrogen bomb in the South Pacific in 1952. "The fireball expanded to three miles in diameter," said a test observer. He soon saw that the entire island on which the bomb exploded "had vanished, vaporized."

The Soviet Union tested its first atomic bomb in 1949 and its first hydrogen bomb in 1953. In what became a nuclear **arms race**, both the United States and the Soviet Union rushed to build more and more weapons. American school children practiced "duck and cover" drills, in which they were taught to crouch under their desks in case of nuclear attack. Some families built underground bomb shelters in their backyards.

THE IMPACT TODAY

Today Americans, Russians, and astronauts from other countries work side by side on the International Space Station, which has been in orbit since 1998.

In October 1957 the Soviets launched ***Sputnik,*** the world's first artificial satellite. Americans feared that if the Soviet Union could launch a satellite, it could launch missiles to attack the United States. In January 1958 the United States responded by launching its own satellite. Later that year, the U.S. government established the National Aeronautics and Space Administration (NASA) to conduct space research.

Cold War Crises

President Eisenhower modified Truman's policy of containment. He and Secretary of State John Foster Dulles supported **brinkmanship**—a willingness to go to the brink of war to oppose communism. "The ability to get to the verge [edge] without getting into war is the necessary art," Dulles explained. The president and Dulles also

History Close-up

Inside a Bomb Shelter

Many families built personal bomb shelters for use in a nuclear emergency. The shelters were stocked with essentials like food and water and were often located in the family's backyard.

threatened the Soviet Union with "massive retaliation" against Soviet advances.

As part of his effort, Eisenhower used covert, or secret, operations around the world. In 1953, for example, the Central Intelligence Agency (CIA) helped overthrow the premier of Iran. American officials had feared he was a Communist. In 1954 the CIA helped organize the removal of the Guatemalan president for similar reasons.

In 1956 a crisis in Egypt seemed to push the world to the brink of a third world war. Egyptian leader Gamal Abdel Nasser nationalized the Suez Canal, a vital waterway connecting the Mediterranean and Red seas, in an attempt to collect tolls from the canal to finance a major dam project. Britain and France, which relied on the canal for trade, allied with Israel, a longtime enemy of Egypt, and invaded the area around the canal. The Soviet Union, an ally of Egypt, threatened to crush the invaders. This would force the United States to defend its allies. Finally, the Americans and the Soviet Union agreed to condemn the invasion, and the Suez crisis ended. After the brief moment of cooperation, the Cold War continued.

READING CHECK **Analyzing** How was the arms race a display of brinkmanship?

Families practiced getting into their shelters as quickly as possible. Some families spent free time in the shelters to adjust to spending weeks or months there.

ANALYSIS SKILL **ANALYZING INFORMATION**

Which essentials did families keep in their bomb shelters?

SUMMARY AND PREVIEW After World War II, Americans responded to Communist threats at home and abroad. In the next section you will read about how America prospered during these challenging times.

Section 2 Assessment

go.hrw.com
Online Quiz
KEYWORD: SC7 HP27

Reviewing Ideas, Terms, and People

1. a. **Identify** What is the **38th parallel**, and why was it important in the Korean War?
   b. **Analyze** How did the outcome of China's civil war affect the U.S. response to North Korea's attack?
   c. **Evaluate** Do you think President Truman should have fired MacArthur? Explain your answer.
2. a. **Describe** Why did a second Red Scare occur in the late 1940s and 1950s?
   b. **Explain** How did television affect **Joseph McCarthy**'s power?
   c. **Elaborate** Why do you think the Red Scare lasted so long?
3. a. **Recall** How did Eisenhower deal with Cold War crises during his administration?
   b. **Make Inferences** How can you tell that the U.S. government took the launch of ***Sputnik*** seriously?
   c. **Elaborate** Why do you think the United States and the Soviet Union were able to cooperate during the Suez crisis?

Critical Thinking

4. **Categorizing** Review your notes on Cold War conflicts and crises. Then copy the graphic organizer below and use it to list each event under its appropriate location.

Asia	Soviet Union	United States	Other

FOCUS ON WRITING

5. **Taking Notes on Challenges at Home and Abroad** Take notes on the challenges and fears Americans faced during the Korean War, McCarthy era, and Eisenhower presidency. How did the government and individuals respond to these challenges and fears?

SECTION 3

The Nation Prospers

What You Will Learn...

Main Ideas

1. America's economy boomed in the 1950s.
2. Americans enjoyed new forms of popular culture.
3. Social critics found fault with 1950s society.

The Big Idea

An expanding economy led to new ways of life for many Americans in the 1950s.

Key Terms and People

baby boom, *p. 858*
Sun Belt, *p. 858*
urban renewal, *p. 859*
beats, *p. 861*

TAKING NOTES As you read, take notes on the suburban lifestyle and culture of the 1950s. You can organize your notes in a table like this one.

Suburban Life and Culture

If YOU were there...

You live with your parents in an apartment building in 1954. You have grown up in the city, and you are used to walking or taking the subway everywhere you need to go. But your parents are talking about moving out to the suburbs. They like the idea of having a house of their own, with a driveway and a backyard. They ask what you think about moving to the suburbs.

How would you respond?

BUILDING BACKGROUND A long economic boom after World War II led to a rapid rise in the income of many Americans. By the mid-1950s nearly 60 percent of the U.S. population qualified as middle class, with annual incomes between $3,000 and $10,000. The prosperity of the 1950s brought many changes to American life.

America's Economy in the 1950s

The American economy boomed during the 1950s. Millions of Americans earned more money than ever before and, therefore, had more money to spend on homes, cars, vacations, and large appliances. Feeling better off than they had during the Depression and World War II, many young Americans were getting married and starting families. This led to a **baby boom**, or a significant increase in the number of babies born.

A Nation on the Move

Americans were also on the move in the 1950s, as people relocated to new parts of the country to take jobs and improve the quality of their lives. Many businesses and workers moved to the **Sun Belt**—southern and western states that offered a warm climate year-round and low tax rates. As a result, the region's population doubled in the 30 years after World War II.

The 1956 Highway Act also encouraged travel. This new law provided billions of dollars for the construction of a 41,000-mile

Postwar Boom, 1945–1960 — QUICK FACTS

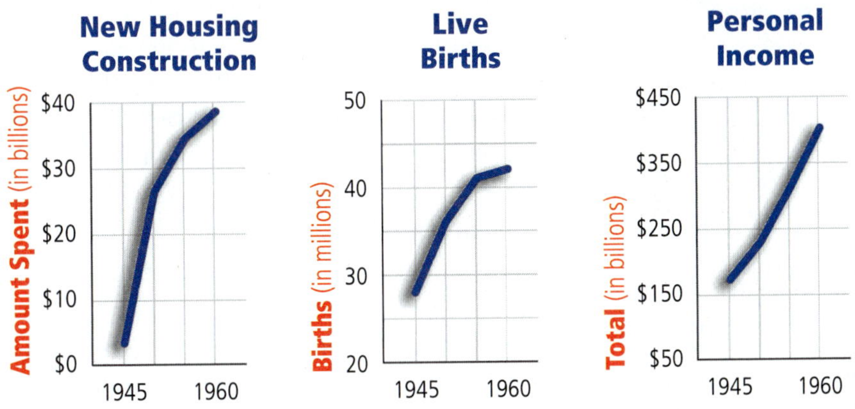

ANALYSIS SKILL — ANALYZING VISUALS

How did rising wealth affect families in the 1950s?

Many American families used their newfound wealth to buy consumer products like houses, automobiles, and appliances. Advertisements like this one used an idealized version of an American family to sell products.

interstate highway system. New highways helped to greatly increase both business and personal travel between cities throughout the country. The roads also made it easier for people to move to suburbs and commute to jobs in cities.

Suburbs and Cities

The rising demand for homes in the suburbs encouraged developers to build new suburban neighborhoods. On Long Island, New York, William Levitt created Levittown, one of the nation's first preplanned suburbs. Between 1946 and 1951, Levitt built more than 17,000 low-priced, mass-produced houses. Like Henry Ford's Model T, Levitt's homes were designed to be simple and affordable. By the mid-1950s, builders were constructing similar suburban homes all over the country. By 1970 more Americans lived in suburbs than in cities.

Many families welcomed the comfort and convenience of suburban living. Suburban homes usually had driveways, large lawns, and labor-saving appliances. Suburban children could participate in a wide variety of sports and other activities. Many mothers spent so much time driving their children from one activity to another that one commentator referred to the task as "motherhood on wheels."

Some critics of suburbs complained that suburban life was too heavily based on consumer culture. They also criticized the suburbs for encouraging conformity, or sameness. Most of the people living in the suburbs were white and middle class. In fact, some communities—including Levittown—refused to sell homes to black families.

As middle-class families moved to the suburbs, cities collected fewer tax dollars. This led to a decline in city services. Those who were unable to afford a move to the suburbs lived in increasingly decaying urban areas. As conditions worsened, the federal government began an **urban renewal** program—a plan to improve life in cities. Urban renewal projects focused on improving city services and urban housing. In reality, however, the programs sometimes led to more problems for urban residents.

READING CHECK **Contrasting** How was life different in suburbs and cities?

FOCUS ON NORTH CAROLINA

North Carolina's economy changed focus in the 1950s and 1960s, with more laborers becoming involved in manufacturing and fewer involved in agricultural production. New industries required workers to have new skills, and the state began one of the nation's first state-sponsored job training programs in 1957.

Life in the 1950s

Life for the average citizen in the United States changed dramatically in the prosperous years after World War II. More money was available to buy a wider variety of products, and technological advances made life safer and easier for many.

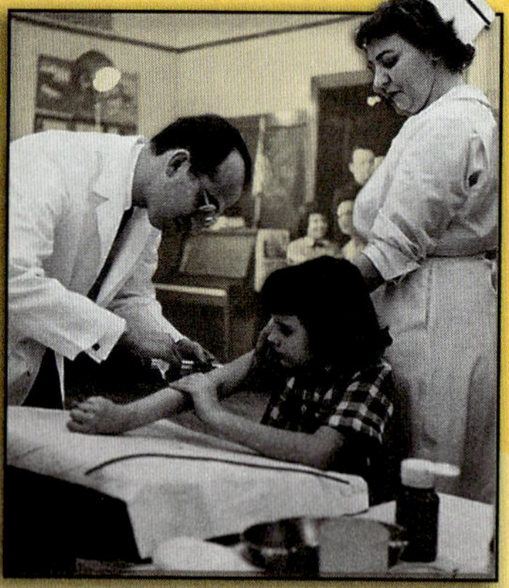

In 1952 Dr. Jonas Salk developed a vaccine for the paralyzing disease of polio.

Teenagers enjoyed the music of Elvis Presley and other rock 'n' roll stars.

North Carolinian Thelonious Monk was one of many African American jazz musicians who became famous during the 1950s. Today he is considered one of the best jazz pianists of all time.

Drive-in movie theaters became increasingly popular during the 1950s. Movies were shown on large outdoor screens as patrons watched from their cars. The largest drive-ins could accommodate 3,000 cars.

American Pop Culture

American life was changing quickly in the 1950s as new technology developed. Many people began shopping in malls and eating at new fast-food restaurants. By the end of the decade, nearly 90 percent of all American families owned at least one television set. On average, American families watched about six hours of television a day.

Americans all over the country shared the experience of watching the same news, comedies, and sports programs. Many shows, such as *The Lone Ranger*, were versions of shows that began on the radio. Early hits included Milton Berle's variety show *Texaco Star Theater* and the Western drama *Gunsmoke*. But the most popular show was *I Love Lucy*, a situation comedy (or sitcom) starring Lucille Ball and her real-life husband, Cuban American bandleader Desi Arnaz. About 44 million Americans tuned in to one episode of *I Love Lucy* in 1953 to see the birth of their son—twice the number that watched President Eisenhower's inauguration the next day.

New styles of music also helped reshape American culture in the 1950s. African American jazz greats Charlie Parker and Dizzy Gillespie became known as the Fathers of Bebop, a complex jazz style often played at a rapid pace. Meanwhile, musicians like Elvis Presley, Buddy Holly, Chuck Berry, and Little Richard helped rock 'n' roll sweep the nation. Teenage music fans powered the rock 'n' roll revolution, buying more than 70 percent of all records sold in the late 1950s. Just like jazz in the 1920s, rock music drew criticism from some adults. One journalist even labeled rock 'n' roll "a menace to morals." An Arizona teenager responded to this type of criticism by saying, "Man, I believe the older generation just doesn't want the younger generation to have any fun."

READING CHECK **Finding Main Ideas** What changes took place in American pop culture during the 1950s?

Social Critics

Though the postwar years were happy and productive for many Americans, not everyone was happy with American society in the 1950s. Some women, for instance, were frustrated that they could only find work in a limited number of fields such as teaching, nursing, or office work. Others were discouraged by the expectation that they would give up their jobs when they got married. One woman recalled,

> "There was always the assumption, even when I was getting my graduate degree in education, that any work I did was temporary, something to do until I assumed [began] my principal role in life which was to be the perfect wife and mother, supported by my husband."
>
> —Sally Ann Carter, quoted in *The Fifties: A Women's Oral History*, by Brett Harvey

Many writers commented on 1950s society in their work. In 1951 J. D. Salinger published *The Catcher in the Rye*. The novel's teenage narrator, Holden Caulfield, criticizes the "phoniness" of the adults around him, who he believed loved only money and wanted everyone to be the same. In his 1952 novel *Invisible Man*, Ralph Ellison wrote about how African Americans felt left out by American society. "I am an invisible man," Ellison wrote. "I am invisible, understand, simply because people refuse to see me."

Young people known as beatniks, or **beats**, criticized society with unusual writing styles and rebellious behavior. The works of beat poet Allen Ginsberg and novelist Jack Kerouac inspired many young people to question the rules of mainstream American society. Many young people also identified with rebellious characters in popular movies of the 1950s. In the 1953 film *The Wild One,* actor Marlon Brando plays Johnny, a wild biker who challenges the rules of society. When asked, "Hey Johnny, what are you rebelling against?" Johnny replies, "Whadda ya got?"

READING CHECK **Finding Main Ideas** Why did people criticize 1950s society?

SUMMARY AND PREVIEW In the 1950s, suburban life, television, and pop culture changed American society. In the next chapter you will learn how the civil rights movement affected the United States.

Section 3 Assessment

go.hrw.com
Online Quiz
KEYWORD: SC7 HP27

Reviewing Ideas, Terms, and People

1. a. **Recall** How did a booming economy affect life in the United States in the 1950s?
   b. **Explain** How did the growth of suburbs affect cities?
   c. **Elaborate** How do you think the **baby boom** affected 1950s society?
2. a. **Identify** How did American pop culture change in the 1950s?
   b. **Make Inferences** Based on what you have read, how was teenage culture in the 1950s different from adult culture?
3. a. **Describe** What was *Invisible Man* about?
   b. **Compare** What did J. D. Salinger and Jack Kerouac have in common?
   c. **Predict** How do you think some women in the 1950s might have wanted to change their lives?

Critical Thinking

4. **Analyzing Information** Review your notes on 1950s suburban life and culture. Then copy the graphic organizer below and use it to list the benefits and challenges of suburban life and culture.

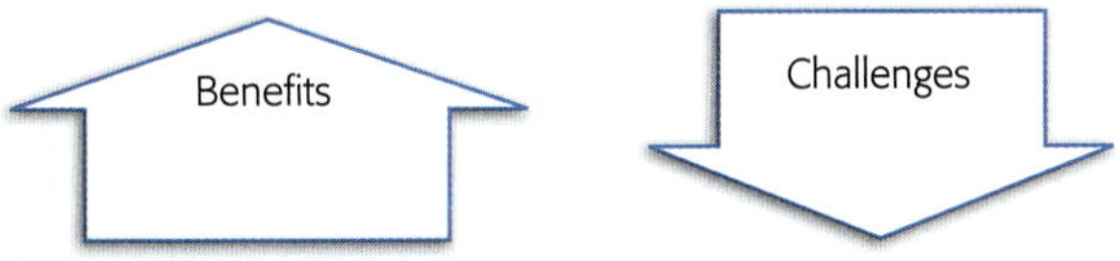

FOCUS ON WRITING

5. **Taking Notes on Daily Life and Culture** Take notes on daily life and pop culture during the 1950s. What did Americans want, and what was important to them? What kind of music would be appropriate for a song about the 1950s?

Social Studies Skills

Analysis | Critical Thinking | Civic Participation | **Study**

North Carolina Skills
3.01 Use map and globe reading skills.

Interpreting Battle Maps

Define the Skill

Battle maps show events during a battle or war. They may show army movements or locations of battles. A single battle map often shows events that occurred at different times. Reading the map key is very important when you interpret battle maps. Battle maps usually include many different symbols. The map key explains the symbols used on the map.

Learn the Skill

Follow these steps to interpret battle maps.

1. Read the title to determine what the map is about.
2. Study the map key to understand what the symbols on the map mean. Locate the symbols from the key on the map.
3. Look for labels and other information on the map. Use what you already know about the time period to determine the importance of these features.
4. Use the map to make a generalization about a battle or war, such as which side won.

Practice the Skill

1. What is this map about?
2. What does the solid blue line on this map represent? What does the solid red line represent?
3. What does the green line on the 38th parallel show? Why is this important?

Based on this map, make a generalization about the Korean War.

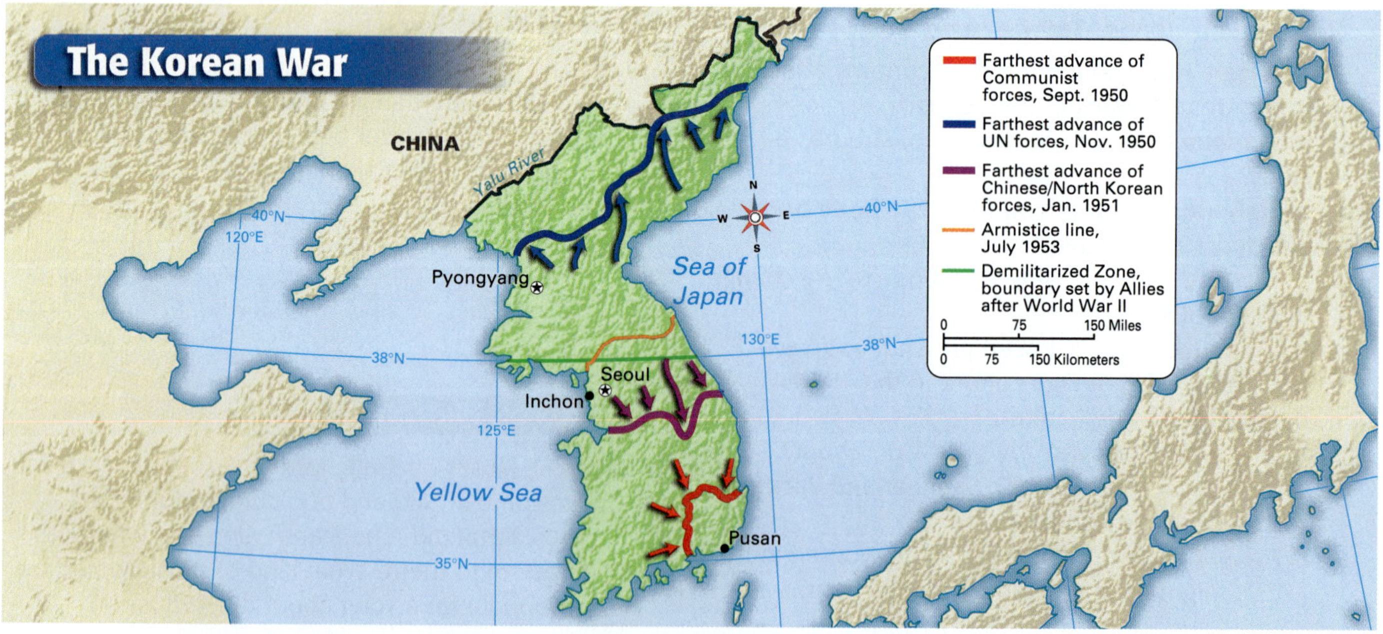

CHAPTER 27

Chapter Review

HOLT

History's Impact

▶ **video series**

Review the video to answer the closing question:

How might Americans' awareness of world events have changed once television became popular?

Visual Summary

QUICK FACTS

Use the visual summary below to help you review the main ideas of the chapter.

American prosperity during the 1950s was sometimes overshadowed by a fear of communism.

Reviewing Vocabulary, Terms, and People

Match the numbered person or term with the correct lettered definition.

1. GI Bill of Rights
2. Yalta Conference
3. Truman Doctrine
4. Joseph McCarthy
5. Fair Deal

a. U.S. senator who unfairly accused many citizens of being Communists
b. meeting at which Franklin Roosevelt, Winston Churchill, and Joseph Stalin discussed strategy for postwar peace
c. package of domestic reforms proposed by President Truman
d. U.S. policy of containing communism through economic aid
e. program that offered veterans money for school after World War II

Comprehension and Critical Thinking

SECTION 1 *(Pages 844–850)*

6. a. Recall What is the United Nations?

b. Explain Why did Franklin Roosevelt support the formation of the UN?

c. Elaborate Would you have supported the policy of containment? Why or why not?

SECTION 2 *(Pages 852–857)*

7. a. Identify How did the United States battle communism in Asia in the 1950s?

b. Explain What effect did the launch of *Sputnik* have on the United States?

c. Evaluate What were some risks and advantages of the strategy of brinkmanship?

SECTION 3 *(Pages 858–861)*

8. a. **Describe** How did life in the United States change in the 1950s?

   b. **Summarize** Why were some women frustrated with 1950s society?

   c. **Elaborate** How has American popular culture changed since the 1950s? How has it stayed the same?

Reviewing Themes

9. **Politics** How did the Cold War affect political relations between the United States and the Soviet Union?

10. **Science and Technology** How did science and technology advance during the 1950s?

Reading Skills

Visualizing *Use the Reading Skills taught in this chapter to answer the question below.*

> Wisconsin senator Joseph McCarthy contributed to fears in the early 1950s by charging that Communists were working inside the State Department. He claimed to have the names of fifty-seven people who were "either card-carrying members or certainly loyal to the Communist Party." *(p. 855)*

11. What elements of the selection above help you visualize the feelings created by the Red Scare?

Social Studies Skills

Interpreting Battle Maps *Use the Social Studies Skills taught in this chapter to answer the question below.*

12. Look back at the battle map on page 853. In what year did North Korean forces make their farthest advance?

Using the Internet

go.hrw.com
KEYWORD: SC7 CH27

13. **Activity: Researching the Second Red Scare** Fear of communism and spies grew during the late 1940s and 1950s. What were Americans' fears? How did Senator Joseph McCarthy and congressional hearings affect the lives of those accused of Communist activities? What did the hearings accomplish? Enter the activity keyword to learn about the second Red Scare. Then write a journal entry from the point of view of Senator McCarthy, a blacklisted writer, or Joseph Welch, attorney for the U.S. Army. Your journal entry should include direct references to your research.

FOCUS ON WRITING

14. **Writing Your Song Lyrics** Review your notes. Decide on a theme for your song about the 1950s. It can focus either on one event or idea, or on several. Remember that the lyrics should address something specific about what it was like to live in the United States in the 1950s. You may even want to write from the point of view of a young person living in the 1950s. What would that person think about? What would be his or her hopes and fears?

CHAPTER 27

Standardized Test Practice

DIRECTIONS: Read each question and write the letter of the best response.

1 At the Yalta Conference, Joseph Stalin promised

A to allow free elections in the Soviet Union.

B to allow free elections in Eastern Europe.

C to prosecute Soviet war criminals.

D that the Soviet Union would join the United Nations.

2 Research Triangle Park began with an idea to

A bring together research and industry.

B prepare North Carolina for the "Go Forward" program.

C revive North Carolina's textile and furniture industries.

D improve North Carolina's road system.

3 Why was McCarthyism criticized by opponents?

A It denied people work.

B It was a type of communism.

C It brought the United States to the brink of nuclear war.

D It brought accusations of Communist activity without proof.

4 Which president decided to use U.S. troops to help defend South Korea in 1950?

A Franklin Roosevelt

B Dwight Eisenhower

C Harry Truman

D Herbert Hoover

5 What new kind of music was popular with teenagers in the 1950s?

A suburban swing

B big band jazz

C rock 'n' roll

D beatnik

6 Which country aided North Korean forces in the Korean War?

A Japan

B China

C the United States

D the Soviet Union

7 Which of the following was a noted critic of Joseph McCarthy?

A Thelonious Monk

B the United Nations

C Douglas MacArthur

D Edward R. Murrow

8 Read the following excerpt from a 1953 speech by President Eisenhower and use it to answer the question below.

> "Every gun that is made, every warship launched, every rocket fired signifies, in the final sense, a theft from those who hunger and are not fed, those who are cold and not clothed. This world in arms is not spending money alone. It is spending the sweat of its laborers, the genius of its scientists, the hopes of its children."
>
> —Dwight D. Eisenhower, April 16, 1953

Document-Based Question What desire do you think Eisenhower was expressing in this passage?

CHAPTER 28 1945–1975

The Civil Rights Movement

North Carolina Standards

Social Studies Objectives

7.02 Evaluate the importance of social changes to different groups in North Carolina.

7.04 Compare and contrast the various political viewpoints surrounding issues of the post World War II era.

Language Arts Objectives

1.01 Narrate a personal account which:
- selects details that best illuminate the topic.
- connects events to self/society.

2.02 Use multiple sources of print and non-print information to explore and create research products in both written and presentational forms by:
- researching and organizing information to achieve purpose.
- using notes and/or memory aids to structure information.

3.03 Evaluate and create arguments that persuade by:
- anticipating and addressing reader/listener concerns and counterarguments.
- recognizing and/or creating an organizing structure appropriate to purpose, audience, and context.

6.02 Continue to identify and edit errors in spoken and written English by:
- producing final drafts/presentations that demonstrate accurate spelling and the correct use of punctuation, capitalization, and format.

go.hrw.com
North Carolina
KEYWORD: SC7 NC

WRITING JOURNAL

A Civil Rights Bill In the 1950s and 1960s, African Americans began successfully to challenge the discrimination they had faced for so many years. In this chapter, you will read about the civil rights movement and about the passage of new civil rights laws. Imagine that you are a member of Congress at this time. You will write a new civil rights bill to help people gain fair treatment under the law.

UNITED STATES

1954 Thurgood Marshall argues against segregation in the Supreme Court case *Brown* v. *Board of Education.*

1945

WORLD

1953 Soviet leader Joseph Stalin dies.

HOLT

History's Impact

▶ **video series**

Watch the video to understand the impact of equal rights and justice for all Americans.

What You Will Learn...

African Americans launched a major civil rights movement in the years following World War II. Members of the movement organized demonstrations to protest unfair treatment, like the March on Washington shown here. In this chapter, you will learn about the efforts of African Americans and others to gain civil rights protections in the 1950s, 1960s, and 1970s.

1963 Lee Harvey Oswald assassinates President John F. Kennedy.

1966 The National Organization for Women is formed.

1969 La Raza Unida is organized to support the rights of Mexican Americans.

1973 The American Indian Movement protests at Wounded Knee.

1960

1970

1957 The Soviets launch *Sputnik*, the first human-made satellite.

1961 The Berlin Wall divides East and West Berlin.

1966 Indira Gandhi becomes prime minister of India.

Reading Social Studies

by Kylene Beers

Economics | Geography | Politics | Society and Culture | Science and Technology

Focus on Themes In this chapter, you will read about the important changes in American **society** during the period called the civil rights era. You will learn about how many people came to see **politics** as a way to correct social inequalities that existed for minority groups in the United States such as African Americans, women, Mexican Americans, Native Americans, and people with disabilities. You will also read about life in the 1960s.

Using Context Clues: Synonyms

Focus on Reading Some words mean almost the same thing. Understanding the similarities can help you understand words whose meaning you may not know.

Understanding Synonyms Words that have similar meanings are called synonyms. Often, a synonym is given as a definition. The synonym will probably be a word you already understand. This will help you learn the new word through context clues.

Notice how one reader uses synonyms to understand words she does not understand.

An AIM leader described the group's goals, saying, "We don't want civil rights in the white man's society—we want our own *sovereign [self-governing]* rights."

This is a word I don't know the meaning of.

These brackets mean that the word inside is a synonym of the word or phrase that comes before. The word inside is a synonym of *sovereign.*

The word *sovereign* must mean to govern on one's own.

You Try It!

The following passage is from the chapter you are getting ready to read. As you read the passage, look for synonyms in the definitions of unfamiliar words.

> On February 1, 1960, the students went into Woolworth and staged a sit-in—a demonstration in which protesters sit down and refuse to leave. They sat in the "whites-only" section of the lunch counter and ordered coffee. They were not served, but they stayed until the store closed. The next day, they returned with dozens more students to continue the sit-in. Soon, another sit-in began at the lunch counter of a nearby store.
>
> *From Chapter 28, p. 874*

After you read the passage, answer the following questions.

1. What word is a synonym of "sit-in" that is given in that word's definition?
2. What clue is given that helps you find the synonym in the above passage?
3. Can you think of another synonym for sit-in that might have been used?

As you read Chapter 28, look for synonyms that can help you define words you don't know.

Key Terms and People

Chapter 28

Section 1

Thurgood Marshall *(p. 871)*
Brown v. *Board of Education (p. 871)*
Little Rock Nine *(p. 871)*
Rosa Parks *(p. 872)*
Montgomery bus boycott *(p. 873)*
Martin Luther King Jr. *(p. 873)*
sit-in *(p. 874)*
Student Nonviolent Coordinating Committee *(p. 874)*

Section 2

John F. Kennedy *(p. 876)*
Freedom Rides *(p. 877)*
March on Washington *(p. 878)*
Lyndon B. Johnson *(p. 879)*
Civil Rights Act of 1964 *(p. 879)*
Voting Rights Act of 1965 *(p. 879)*
Great Society *(p. 880)*
Black Power *(p. 880)*
Malcolm X *(p. 880)*

Section 3

Cesar Chavez *(p. 882)*
United Farm Workers *(p. 882)*
Betty Friedan *(p. 883)*
National Organization for Women *(p. 883)*
Shirley Chisholm *(p. 883)*
Equal Rights Amendment *(p. 883)*
Phyllis Schlafly *(p. 883)*
American Indian Movement *(p. 885)*
Disabled in Action *(p. 885)*

Academic Vocabulary

In this chapter, you will learn the following academic words:

implement *(p. 871)*
consequences *(p. 883)*

SECTION 1

The Civil Rights Movement Takes Shape

What You Will Learn...

Main Ideas

1. Civil rights leaders battled school segregation in court.
2. The Montgomery bus boycott helped end segregation on buses.
3. Students organized sit-ins to protest segregation.

The Big Idea

Civil rights activists used legal challenges and public protests to confront segregation.

Key Terms and People

Thurgood Marshall, *p. 871*
Brown v. *Board of Education, p. 871*
Little Rock Nine, *p. 871*
Rosa Parks, *p. 872*
Montgomery bus boycott, *p. 873*
Martin Luther King Jr., *p. 873*
sit-in, *p. 874*
Student Nonviolent Coordinating Committee, *p. 874*

TAKING NOTES As you read, take notes on key events in the fight against segregation in a web diagram like the one below. In each outer circle of the web, describe one event. You may need to add more circles.

If YOU were there...

You are an African American student in the 1950s. You get up early every day and take a long bus ride across the city to an African American public school. There is another school just three blocks from your home, but only white students are welcome there. You have heard, however, that this school will soon be opening its doors to black students as well.

Would you want to be one of the first African Americans to attend this school? Why or why not?

BUILDING BACKGROUND African Americans continued to face segregation and discrimination after World War II. Early victories in the civil rights movement included the end of segregation in baseball in 1947 and President Truman's ban on segregation in the military in 1948. These successes were the beginning of a national movement for civil rights.

Battling School Segregation

The 1896 Supreme Court case *Plessy* v. *Ferguson* established the "separate-but-equal" doctrine. This doctrine stated that federal, state, and local governments could allow segregation as long as separate facilities were equal. One result of this ruling was that states in both the North and South maintained separate schools for white and black students. Government officials often insisted that though these schools were separate, they were equal in quality.

In fact, however, schools for black children typically received far less funding. Early civil rights leaders, led by members of the National Association for the Advancement of Colored People (NAACP), focused on ending segregation in America's public schools.

Brown v. *Board of Education*

The NAACP's strategy was to show that separate schools were unequal. The NAACP attorneys **Thurgood Marshall**, who went on to become Supreme Court justice, and Jack Greenberg led the courtroom battles against segregation. In the early 1950s, five school segregation cases from Delaware, Kansas, South Carolina, Virginia, and Washington, D.C., came together under the title of ***Brown* v. *Board of Education*.** The "Brown" in the case title was a seven-year-old African American girl from Topeka, Kansas, named Linda Brown. Though she lived near a school for white children, Linda Brown had to travel across town to a school for black children. Linda's father and the NAACP sued to allow Linda to attend the school closer to her home.

On May 17, 1954, the Supreme Court issued a unanimous ruling on *Brown* v. *Board of Education*. Segregation in schools and other public facilities was illegal.

The next year, the Court ordered public schools to desegregate, or integrate, "with all deliberate speed." These rulings would prove difficult to enforce.

Little Rock Nine

In the entire South, only three school districts began desegregating in 1954. Most others implemented gradual integration plans. In Little Rock, Arkansas, the school board started by integrating one high school. It allowed nine outstanding black students to attend Central High School. These students became known as the **Little Rock Nine**. Arkansas governor Orval Faubus worked to prevent desegregation at Central High School, however. He used National Guard troops to block the Little Rock Nine from entering the school.

On the morning of September 4, 1957, eight of the nine students arrived at the school together and were turned away by the National Guard. Then the ninth student, 15-year-old Elizabeth Eckford, arrived at the school by herself. She found the entrance blocked by the National Guard. Turning around, she faced a screaming mob. Someone began yelling, "*Lynch her! Lynch her!*" Finally, a white man and woman guided Eckford to safety.

Elizabeth Eckford and the rest of the Little Rock Nine went home. For weeks, Governor

Academic Vocabulary

implement put in place

Focus on Reading

What is a synonym for *desegregrate*?

Focus on North Carolina

North Carolina desegregated its schools slowly but without violence, for the most part. In 1969 a federal district judge ordered a Mecklenburg County school to use busing to aid in desegregation, if needed. Busing became a national political issue when the U.S. Supreme Court upheld the ruling in *Swann* v. *Charlotte-Mecklenburg County Board of Education*.

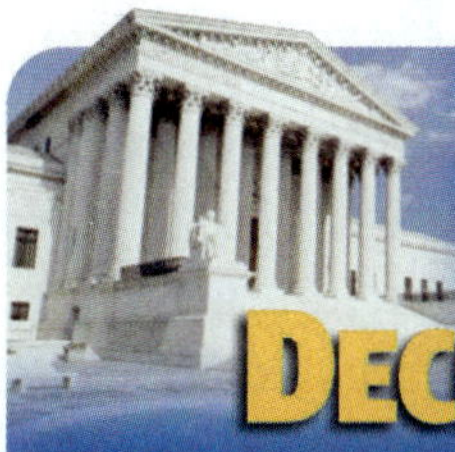

Supreme Court Decisions

Brown v. *Board of Education* (1954)

Background of the Case In 1896 the Supreme Court had ruled in *Plessy* v. *Ferguson* that "separate-but-equal" facilities were constitutional. In 1951 the NAACP sued the Board of Education of Topeka, Kansas. It argued that segregated schools did not give equal opportunities to black and white children. After hearing many arguments, the Court made its ruling in 1954.

The Court's Ruling

The Supreme Court overturned the *Plessy* doctrine of "separate-but-equal." It ruled that racially segregated schools were not equal and were therefore unconstitutional. All of the justices agreed to the ruling, making it unanimous.

The Court's Reasoning

The Supreme Court decided that segregation violated the Fourteenth Amendment's guarantee of "equal protection of the laws." Its opinion stated, "We conclude that, in the field of public education, the doctrine of 'separate-but-equal' has no place. Separate educational facilities are inherently [naturally] unequal."

Why It Matters

The ruling in *Brown* v. *Board of Education* led to integrated public schools. It also opened the door to other successful challenges to segregation in public places.

Linda Brown, age 9

Analysis Skill — Analyzing Information

1. How did the ruling in *Brown* v. *Board of Education* overturn the 1896 Supreme Court ruling in *Plessy* v. *Ferguson*?
2. How might parents of both black and white children at the time have reacted to the ruling in *Brown* v. *Board of Education*?

LINKING TO TODAY

An Apology

The famous photograph to the right shows Elizabeth Eckford walking to Little Rock's Central High School on September 4, 1957. The young woman shouting at Eckford is Hazel Massery. Massery was later sorry for what she had done. She decided that she did not want to be, she said, the "poster child of the hate generation, trapped in the image captured in the photograph." In 1963 Massery apologized to Eckford. The two women, shown below, have since become friends and have spoken publicly together about their experiences.

Faubus refused to allow them to attend the school. The tense situation lasted until President Eisenhower sent federal troops to escort the students into the school.

The Little Rock Nine began attending classes, but resistance to integration continued. Some white students insulted, harassed, and attacked the black students. In spite of these obstacles, eight of the nine remained at the school. In May 1958 Ernest Green became the first African American student to graduate from Central High. When Green's name was called at the graduation ceremony, no one clapped. "But I figured they didn't have to," he later said. "After I got that diploma, that was it. I had accomplished what I had come there for."

READING CHECK **Summarizing** What obstacles faced supporters of desegregation?

Montgomery Bus Boycott

The victory in *Brown* v. *Board of Education* was part of a larger struggle against segregation. Most facilities in the South, including public transportation, remained segregated.

The NAACP decided to continue the battle against segregation in Montgomery, Alabama. Black passengers there were required to sit in the back of city buses. If the whites-only front section filled up, black passengers had to give up their seats.

On December 1, 1955, a seamstress and NAACP worker named **Rosa Parks** boarded a bus and sat in the front row of the section reserved for black passengers. When the bus became full, the driver told Parks and three others to give their seats to white passengers. Parks refused. The bus driver called the police, and Parks was taken to jail.

ANALYSIS SKILL **FINDING THE MAIN IDEA**

Why did Hazel Massery apologize to Elizabeth Eckford?

To protest Parks's arrest, African American professor Jo Ann Robinson organized a boycott of Montgomery buses. Local leaders formed the Montgomery Improvement Association (MIA) to help strengthen the boycott. In the **Montgomery bus boycott**, thousands of African Americans stopped riding the buses. Some white residents supported the boycott as well. Bus ridership fell by 70 percent.

To lead the MIA, African American leaders turned to **Martin Luther King Jr.**, a young Baptist minister. The 26-year-old King already had a reputation as a powerful speaker whose words could motivate and inspire listeners.

As the boycott continued, bus drivers guided nearly empty buses down the city streets. Leaders planned a carpool system that helped people find rides at more than 40 locations throughout Montgomery. For 381 days, boycotters carpooled, took taxis, rode bicycles, and walked. Still, Montgomery's leaders refused to integrate the bus system.

As in Little Rock during the school segregation fight, many white residents were angry about the attempt to end segregation. Some people resorted to violence. King's home was bombed, and he received hate mail and phone calls threatening him and his family. The police also harassed and arrested carpool drivers. In spite of this intimidation, the boycott gained national attention, sparking similar protests in other cities.

Finally, in November 1956 the Supreme Court ruled that segregation on public transportation was illegal. The next month, King joined other black and white ministers to ride the first integrated bus in Montgomery. "It . . . makes you feel that America is a great country and we're going to do more to make it greater," remembered Jo Ann Robinson.

The Montgomery bus boycott helped make Martin Luther King Jr. a nationally known civil rights leader. He formed the Southern Christian Leadership Conference (SCLC), which led campaigns for civil rights throughout the South.

READING CHECK **Identifying Cause and Effect** What event sparked the Montgomery bus boycott?

BIOGRAPHY

Rosa Parks

1913–2005

Rosa Parks was born in Tuskegee, Alabama, and spent most of her childhood in Montgomery. While working as a seamstress, Parks became an active member of the NAACP.

She was fired from her seamstress job for her leading role in the Montgomery bus boycott. After the boycott succeeded, she and her husband moved to Detroit, Michigan. She continued working for fair treatment for all Americans and started a program to teach children about the Underground Railroad and the civil rights movement.

Finding the Main Idea How did Rosa Parks work for equal rights?

Sit-ins and the SNCC

Like public schools and buses, many private businesses in the South were segregated. In Greensboro, North Carolina, four students decided to challenge this form of segregation. They targeted a lunch counter at Woolworth, a popular department store. Black customers were supposed to eat standing up at one end of the counter. White customers sat down to eat at the other end.

On February 1, 1960, the students went into Woolworth and staged a **sit-in**—a demonstration in which protesters sit down and refuse to leave. They sat in the whites-only section of the lunch counter and ordered coffee. They were not served, but they stayed until the store closed. The next day, they returned with dozens more students to continue the sit-in. Soon, another sit-in began at the lunch counter of a nearby store.

People across the country read newspaper stories about the Greensboro sit-ins. Other black students in the South began to hold similar protests. The student protesters practiced the strategy of nonviolent resistance. No matter how much they were insulted or threatened, they refused to respond with violence. They were inspired by Martin Luther King Jr., who was a strong supporter of nonviolent action.

Over time, some restaurants and businesses, including Woolworth, began the process of integration. To continue the struggle for civil rights, the leaders of the student protests formed the **Student Nonviolent Coordinating Committee** (SNCC) in the spring of 1960. The SNCC activists trained protesters and organized civil rights demonstrations. Bob Moses, a leader of the SNCC, helped organize sit-ins and voter registration drives.

READING CHECK **Comparing** How were sit-ins similar to other civil rights protests?

SUMMARY AND PREVIEW In the 1950s court rulings and protests challenged segregation. In the next section you will learn how the civil rights movement continued the fight against inequality.

FOCUS ON NORTH CAROLINA

The Greensboro Four, as they became known, were students at North Carolina A&T State University, a historically black college in Greensboro.

THE IMPACT TODAY

Today Bob Moses runs the Algebra Project. Its goals include helping students in poor communities become skilled in math, get into college, and compete for jobs.

Section 1 Assessment

go.hrw.com
Online Quiz
KEYWORD: SC7 HP28

Reviewing Ideas, Terms, and People

1. a. **Summarize** How did the Supreme Court impact the desegregation of public schools?
   b. **Identify** Who were the **Little Rock Nine**?
2. a. **Recall** What was the purpose of the **Montgomery bus boycott**?
   b. **Analyze** Why was the arrest of **Rosa Parks** a turning point in the civil rights movement?
   c. **Elaborate** Why do you think the bus boycott lasted so long?
3. a. **Identify** What means did the **Student Nonviolent Coordinating Committee** use to protest segregation?
   b. **Make Inferences** What might have inspired the Greensboro students to stage a **sit-in**?
   c. **Evaluate** Do you think nonviolent resistance is an effective form of protest? Why or why not?

Critical Thinking

4. **Sequencing** Review your notes on events that challenged segregation. Then copy the graphic organizer below and use it to show the sequence of major events in the civil rights movement described in this section.

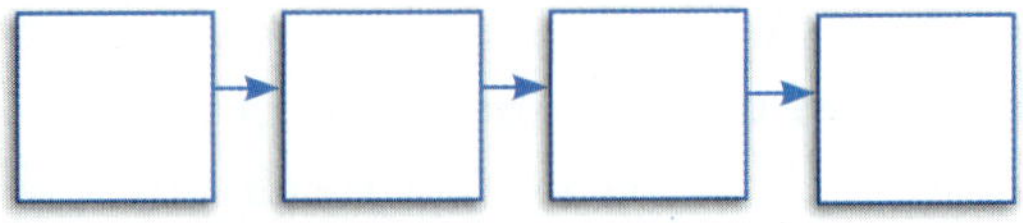

FOCUS ON WRITING

5. **Explaining Major Issues** Take notes on the major issues behind the civil rights movement. What were these issues? Why were they important to African Americans? What changes did the movement try to make?

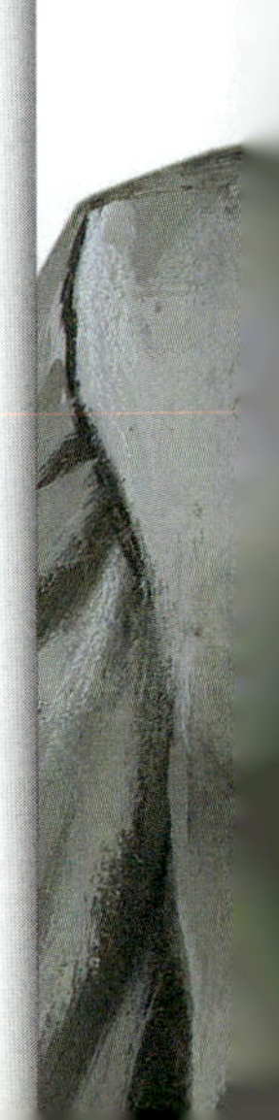

BIOGRAPHY

Martin Luther King Jr.

How would you help lead a national movement?

When did he live? 1929–1968

Where did he live? King grew up in Atlanta, Georgia, where his father was a pastor. He studied to become a minister in Pennsylvania. He received his doctorate in Massachusetts, then became pastor of a church in Alabama. He traveled throughout the country as a civil rights leader.

What did he do? As a powerful and moving speaker, King became one of the leading voices of the civil rights movement. He was committed to achieving equality through nonviolent protest. He led a series of successful marches and protests, including the 1955 Montgomery bus boycott and the 1963 March on Washington.

Why is he so important? His leadership helped make the civil rights movement a success. His belief in and passion for nonviolence led to the boycotts, sit-ins, and marches that helped African Americans gain equal treatment. King's work helped bring an end to legal segregation and led to new laws guaranteeing equal rights for all Americans.

Evaluating Which of Martin Luther King Jr.'s contributions to the civil rights movement was most important? Why?

KEY EVENTS

- **1953** Marries Coretta Scott
- **1955** Becomes leader of the Montgomery Improvement Association
- **1957** Founds Southern Christian Leadership Conference
- **1963** Writes "Letter from Birmingham Jail"; gives the "I Have a Dream" speech at the March on Washington
- **1964** Wins the Nobel Peace Prize; Civil Rights Act of 1964 is passed
- **1968** Shot and killed in Memphis, Tennessee
- **1986** Martin Luther King Jr. Day becomes a national holiday.

"I have a dream that my four children will one day live in a nation where they will not be judged by the color of their skin but by the content of their character."

—Martin Luther King Jr., speech at March on Washington

SECTION 2

Kennedy, Johnson, and Civil Rights

What You Will Learn...

Main Ideas

1. John F. Kennedy was elected president in 1960.
2. Civil rights leaders continued to fight for equality.
3. Lyndon B. Johnson became president when Kennedy was assassinated.
4. Changes occurred in the civil rights movement in the late 1960s.

The Big Idea

The civil rights movement made major advances during the presidencies of John F. Kennedy and Lyndon B. Johnson.

Key Terms and People

John F. Kennedy, *p. 876*
Freedom Rides, *p. 877*
March on Washington, *p. 878*
Lyndon B. Johnson, *p. 879*
Civil Rights Act of 1964, *p. 879*
Voting Rights Act of 1965, *p. 879*
Great Society, *p. 880*
Black Power, *p. 880*
Malcolm X, *p. 880*

TAKING NOTES As you read, take notes on the names of leaders who supported civil rights. Use a chart like this one for your notes on these leaders and their goals.

Leaders	Goals

If YOU were there...

You are a civil rights activist living and working in the South. It is 1960, a presidential election year. The battle for fair treatment has been difficult, and you hope that the next president will support civil rights. Both major presidential candidates will be visiting your area soon, and you might have a chance to meet them and ask some questions.

What questions would you ask the candidates?

BUILDING BACKGROUND In the 1960 presidential election Republican Richard M. Nixon, who had served as Eisenhower's vice president, ran against Democrat John F. Kennedy, a senator from Massachusetts. For the first time, presidential candidates debated each other on television. Kennedy's performance in the televised debates helped him win a very close election.

Kennedy Elected

When **John F. Kennedy** won the election of 1960, he became the youngest person ever elected president of the United States. For many Americans, Kennedy and his wife, Jacqueline, brought a sense of style and excitement to the White House. Kennedy was also the first Roman Catholic to become president.

In his inaugural address, Kennedy spoke of the opportunities and dangers facing Americans. "Man holds in his mortal hands the power to abolish all forms of human poverty and all forms of human life," he said. He encouraged all Americans to support freedom throughout the world, saying, "And so, my fellow Americans, ask not what your country can do for you—ask what you can do for your country."

As president, Kennedy pursued a set of proposals he called the New Frontier. His plan included a higher minimum wage and tax cuts to help stimulate economic growth. It called for new spending on the military and on the space program, and new programs to help

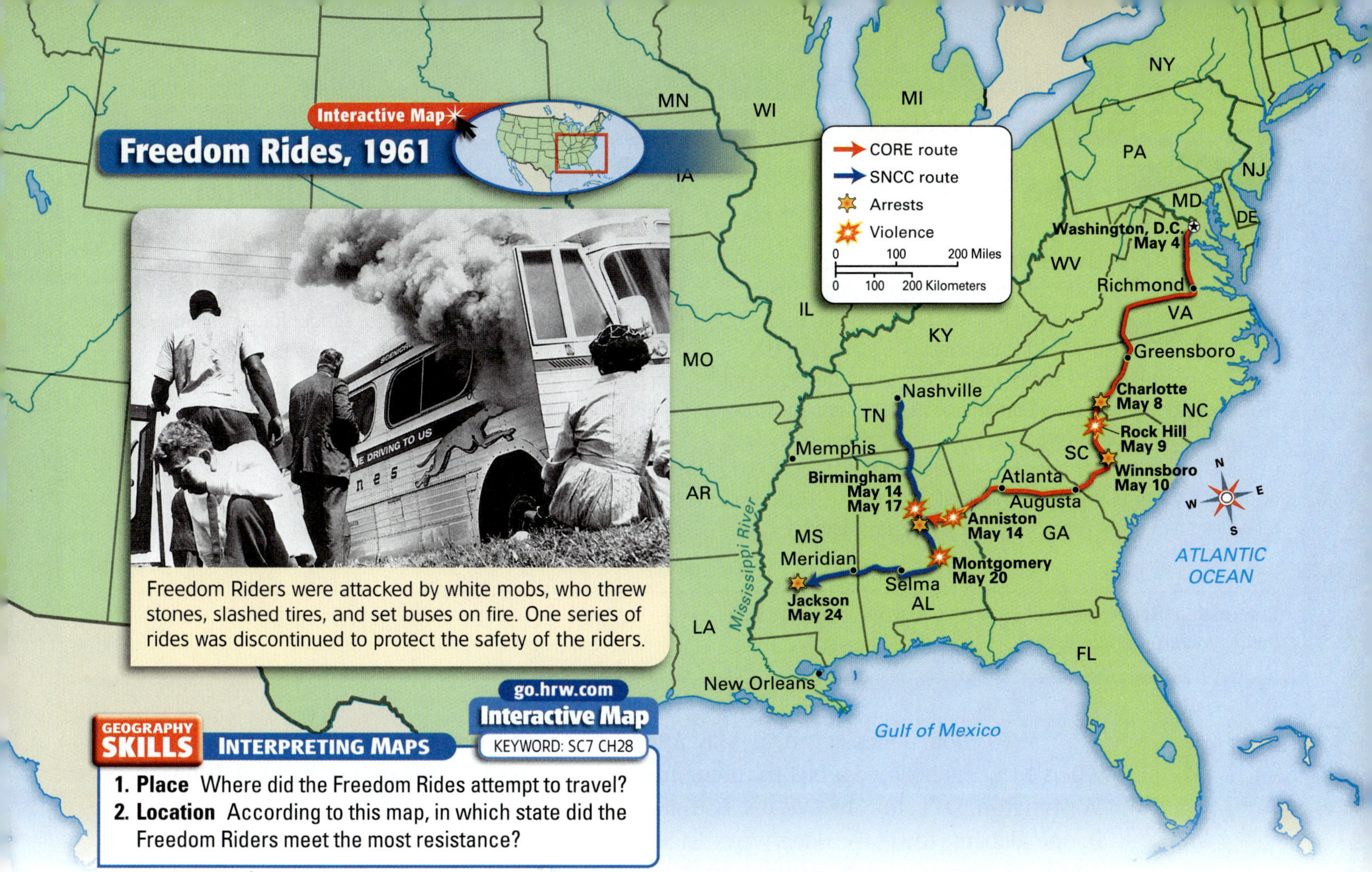

Freedom Riders were attacked by white mobs, who threw stones, slashed tires, and set buses on fire. One series of rides was discontinued to protect the safety of the riders.

go.hrw.com
Interactive Map
KEYWORD: SC7 CH28

GEOGRAPHY SKILLS **INTERPRETING MAPS**

1. **Place** Where did the Freedom Rides attempt to travel?
2. **Location** According to this map, in which state did the Freedom Riders meet the most resistance?

poor and unemployed Americans. Kennedy also proposed providing greater financial help to public schools. Fearing a budget imbalance, Republicans and conservative southern Democrats blocked much of the legislation Kennedy introduced.

Kennedy also spoke of his support for the goals of the civil rights movement. This had helped convince many African Americans to vote for him in the election of 1960. As president, however, Kennedy moved slowly on civil rights legislation. He was reluctant to anger Republicans and conservative southern Democrats in Congress, whose support he needed to pass other items on his agenda. Kennedy was also busy dealing with foreign policy crises, as you will read in the next chapter.

READING CHECK **Drawing Inferences** What do you think African American voters hoped for from the new president?

The Fight for Rights Continues

Public schools and some businesses had begun to desegregate. But other facilities remained strictly segregated.

Freedom Rides

In 1947 a civil rights group called the Congress of Racial Equality (CORE) began protests in which African Americans rode in the whites-only section of interstate buses. In 1960 the Court ruled that segregation of bus stations was illegal. CORE decided to put pressure on President Kennedy to enforce this ruling.

To accomplish this, CORE organized a series of protests called the **Freedom Rides**, in which black and white bus riders traveled together to segregated bus stations in the South. White riders planned to use facilities set aside for African Americans in bus stations. Black riders would use whites-only facilities.

BIOGRAPHIES

John F. Kennedy
1917–1963

John F. Kennedy was born to a politically powerful and wealthy family in Massachusetts. He graduated from Harvard University, then joined the U.S. Navy. He commanded a patrol boat in the South Pacific during World War II and was wounded in a sea battle. Kennedy was elected to the House of Representatives at the age of 29 and to the Senate six years later. He was elected president in 1960, bringing a youthful energy to the White House. He had served for fewer than three years when he was assassinated.

Lyndon B. Johnson
1908–1973

Lyndon B. Johnson grew up in rural Texas. After working his way through college, Johnson taught school for a year. In 1937, at the age of 29, he was elected to the House of Representatives. He was elected to the Senate in 1948. Johnson was known for his ability to guide bills through Congress by convincing members from both political parties to support them. As one fellow member of Congress said, "Lyndon got me by the lapels [jacket collar] and put his face on top of mine and he talked and talked." Johnson was elected vice president in 1960 and became president in 1963.

Contrasting How were Kennedy's and Johnson's careers similar, and how were they different?

The Freedom Rides began in May 1961, when 13 riders boarded a bus travel-ing from Washington, D.C., to New Orleans, Louisiana. In one Alabama town, the riders were viciously attacked by a white mob. After more attacks, CORE leaders decided to stop the protest to protect the riders' lives.

The leaders of the SNCC decided to continue the Freedom Rides. The SNCC activists faced the same violence as the CORE riders. Arriving in Montgomery, Alabama, in late May, they were attacked by a furious mob. Many freedom riders were jailed in Jackson, Mississippi. That same month, President Kennedy ordered the Interstate Commerce Commission to enforce strict bans on segregation in interstate bus terminals.

King in Birmingham

In 1963 Martin Luther King Jr. organized marches in Birmingham, Alabama. King was arrested and jailed for marching without a permit. While jailed, he wrote a "Letter from Birmingham Jail," explaining his commitment to nonviolence. "We will reach the goal of freedom in Birmingham and all over the nation, because the goal of America is freedom."

King was released from prison and led a new round of marches. In May 1963, some 2,500 demonstrators marched through downtown Birmingham. Police commissioner Eugene "Bull" Connor ordered his officers to unleash their attack dogs and blast the marchers with high-pressure water hoses. Televised images of their tactics shocked Americans.

The March on Washington

Pressure for civil rights legislation continued to grow. President Kennedy called racial discrimination "a moral crisis." In June 1963 he announced support for a sweeping civil rights bill to end racial discrimination completely.

To demonstrate support for the civil rights bill, African American leaders held the **March on Washington**—a massive demonstration for civil rights. On August 28, 1963, Martin Luther King Jr. stood at the Lincoln Memorial before a diverse crowd of more than 200,000 people. In his famous "I Have a Dream" speech, King expressed his hope for a future in which all Americans would enjoy equal rights and opportunities.

READING CHECK **Summarizing** How did the Birmingham marches affect public opinion?

Johnson and Civil Rights

After he became president, Lyndon Johnson promised to continue Kennedy's plans for civil rights legislation. Johnson worked with Congress and African American leaders to create and pass laws that would help ensure equality for all Americans. Here, Johnson is shown signing the Civil Rights Act of 1964 as Martin Luther King, Jr. and other leaders look on.

How did Johnson work to continue Kennedy's campaign promises?

Johnson Becomes President

In the months following the March on Washington, Congress debated Kennedy's civil rights legislation. In November 1963 Kennedy began a quick tour of Texas cities.

Kennedy Assassinated

On November 22, 1963, Kennedy rode through Dallas in a convertible, waving to supporters in the streets. Suddenly, gunshots rang out. Kennedy had been shot twice, and he died soon afterward in a Dallas hospital. Vice President **Lyndon B. Johnson** was quickly sworn in as president. Dallas police arrested an alleged assassin, Lee Harvey Oswald.

The assassination stunned Americans, who grieved the young president's death. Many of Kennedy's goals were left unfinished. Vowing to continue Kennedy's work, President Johnson urged Congress to pass a civil rights bill.

Civil Rights Laws

On July 2, 1964, President Johnson signed the **Civil Rights Act of 1964**. The act banned segregation in public places. It also outlawed discrimination in the workplace on the basis of color, gender, religion, or national origin.

That summer, activists began to push for equal voting rights for African Americans in the South. Legally, of course, African Americans had the right to vote. But in much of the South, threats and unfair election rules often kept them from the polls. During the "Freedom Summer" of 1964, hundreds of volunteers, including many white college students, came to Mississippi. Their goal was to help African Americans register to vote.

Volunteers were threatened and attacked. On June 21 three civil rights workers—James Chaney, a young black Mississippian plasterer's apprentice; Andrew Goodman, a Jewish Queens College student; and Michael Schwerner, a Jewish social worker from New York City—were murdered by members of the Ku Klux Klan. Martin Luther King, Jr. organized a voting rights march from Selma, Alabama, to Montgomery, during which many marchers were beaten and jailed. Violence against civil rights workers convinced many people to support voter registration efforts.

Congress approved the **Voting Rights Act of 1965**, which Johnson signed into law in August. This law gave the federal government new powers to protect African Americans' voting rights. Within three years, more than half of all qualified African Americans in the South registered to vote.

THE IMPACT TODAY

In June 2005 a judge in Mississippi sentenced Edgar Ray Killen to 60 years in prison for his role in the murder of the three civil rights workers. The 1967 case had ended in a deadlocked jury.

QUICK FACTS

The Great Society

Great Society Legislation:

- Civil Rights Act of 1964
- Voting Rights Act of 1965
- Elementary and Secondary Education Act of 1965
- Medicare and Medicaid Bill, 1965
- Department of Housing and Urban Development Act of 1965

The Great Society

President Johnson won the election of 1964 by a huge margin. He saw this as a vote of approval for his program of domestic reforms that he called the **Great Society**. "The Great Society rests on abundance and liberty for all," Johnson said.

Congress quickly passed most of Johnson's Great Society legislation. Great Society programs included Medicare and Medicaid, which help senior citizens and low-income citizens afford health care. Another act gave local schools more than $1 billion to help students with special needs. The Department of Housing and Urban Development (HUD) was created to help low-income families get better housing. Robert Weaver served as HUD's secretary, becoming the first African American appointed to a presidential cabinet.

READING CHECK **Summarizing** How did President Johnson support civil rights?

Changes in the Rights Movement

Many young civil rights reformers found the pace of change too slow. Others entirely rejected the goal of racial integration.

New Directions

One such activist was Stokely Carmichael, who had participated in the Freedom Rides and many marches. But in the mid-1960s, he broke with the goal of nonviolence. Carmichael was a founder of the **Black Power** movement, which called for African American independence. Black Power activists believed that blacks should reject integration, focusing instead on controlling their own communities.

Malcolm X helped inspire the Black Power movement. He was a leader of the Nation of Islam, an organization that combined ideas about African American independence with the teachings of Islam. Malcolm X argued that African Americans should work for social and political independence. He believed that African Americans had the right to defend themselves, using violence if necessary.

Time Line

Civil Rights Movement, Key Events

1955 An African American tailor's assistant named Rosa Parks refused to give up her seat on a Montgomery, Alabama, bus, sparking a citywide bus boycott that would last more than a year.

1950

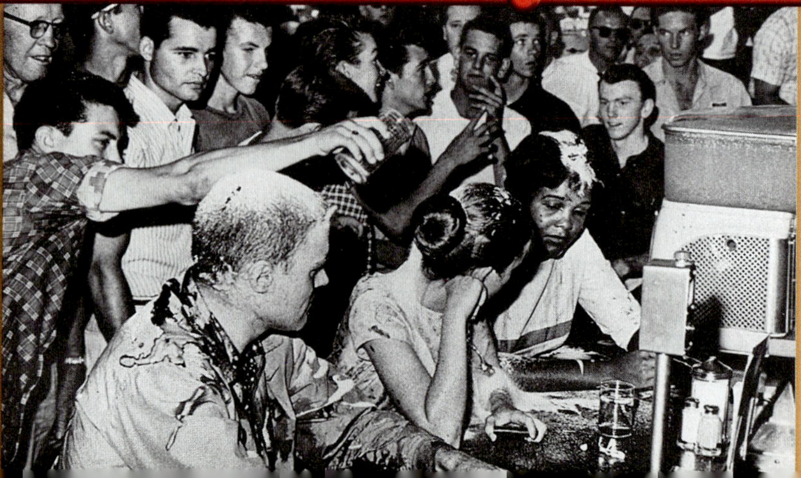

1960 The first sit-in at a lunch counter occurs in Greensboro, North Carolina. During these sit-ins, young African Americans sat at segregated lunch counters along with their white counterparts and asked to be served.

In 1964 Malcolm X traveled to the Muslim holy city of Mecca, where he met Muslims of many races. He began to hope that different races could coexist in peace, although he still supported freedom "by any means necessary." But in 1965 Malcolm X broke with the Nation of Islam and was killed by three of its members.

Violence in the Streets

Slow progress in the civil rights movement frustrated many members of the black community. In some U.S. cities, tensions exploded into violent, sometimes deadly, riots. One such riot occurred in August 1965 in the Watts section of Los Angeles. Twenty-four people were killed, and much of Watts was destroyed.

In April 1968 Martin Luther King Jr. was shot and killed in Memphis, Tennessee. As televised reports spread the news of King's assassination, furious rioters took to the streets in more than 100 American cities. The movement had lost its most visible leader.

1963 Four young girls die in the racially motivated bombing of a Birmingham, Alabama, church. The deaths lead to riots and civil unrest during which police attack African Americans. Televised images of the events shocked many people.

1965

1964 Civil rights leader Martin Luther King Jr. receives the Nobel Peace Prize for his work in nonviolent demonstrations against segregation.

READING CHECK **Contrasting** How did Malcolm X's goals differ from Martin Luther King Jr.'s?

SUMMARY AND PREVIEW Under Kennedy and Johnson, major civil rights legislation was passed. In the next section, you will learn how more groups began to push for equal rights.

Section 2 Assessment

go.hrw.com
Online Quiz
KEYWORD: SC7 HP28

Reviewing Ideas, Terms, and People

1. a. **Describe** How was **John F. Kennedy** different from previous presidents?
   b. **Analyze** Why did many African Americans vote for Kennedy?
2. a. **Identify** What were the **Freedom Rides**?
   b. **Explain** How did television influence public opinion about the civil rights movement?
3. a. **Recall** What happened in Dallas, Texas, on November 22, 1963?
   b. **Draw Conclusions** Based on Johnson's plans for the **Great Society**, what do you think he believed was the purpose of government?
4. a. **Recall** What challenges did the civil rights movement face in the late 1960s?
   b. **Elaborate** Why did **Malcolm X** reject the goal of racial integration?

Critical Thinking

5. **Evaluating** Review your notes on the goals and achievements of leaders who supported civil rights. Then copy the graphic organizer below and use it to evaluate the leaders discussed in the section. Tell whether or not you think the leaders' actions were effective.

Leader	Evaluation

FOCUS ON WRITING

6. **Listing Laws** List new civil rights laws passed in the 1960s. What were the goals of these laws? What problems or events did they respond to? As a member of Congress, would you have approved of these laws? Why or why not?

SECTION 3

Rights for Other Americans

What You Will Learn...

Main Ideas

1. Hispanic Americans organized for civil rights and economic opportunities.
2. The women's movement worked for equal rights.
3. Other Americans also fought for change.

The Big Idea

Encouraged by the success of the civil rights movement, many groups worked for equal rights in the 1960s.

Key Terms and People

Cesar Chavez, *p. 882*
United Farm Workers, *p. 882*
Betty Friedan, *p. 883*
National Organization for Women, *p. 883*
Shirley Chisholm, *p. 883*
Equal Rights Amendment, *p. 883*
Phyllis Schlafly, *p. 883*
American Indian Movement, *p. 885*
Disabled in Action, *p. 885*

TAKING NOTES As you read, make a list of major events that occurred as various groups worked for equal rights. You may want to organize your list in a table like this one.

Social Movements in the 1960s

If YOU were there...

Your parents came to the United States from Mexico, and you were born in California in the 1950s. You and your family work year-round picking crops—the work is hard, and the pay is low. You're trying to put aside some money for school, but your family barely makes enough to get by. Some farmworkers are talking about going on strike for better wages.

Would you join the strike? Why or why not?

BUILDING BACKGROUND Many Americans faced unfair treatment in the 1960s. Women were paid lower wages and had fewer job opportunities than men. Hispanic Americans had long faced discrimination as well. The victories of the civil rights movement inspired many groups to struggle for equal rights as well.

Hispanic Americans Organize for Change

The Hispanic population of the United States grew to 4 million by 1960, and to more than 10 million by 1970. Though people of Mexican descent made up the majority of this population, Hispanic Americans were a diverse group. Many people from Puerto Rico, Cuba, and other Latin American countries also lived in the United States.

The success of African Americans encouraged Hispanic Americans to fight for their own rights. **Cesar Chavez** was one of many Hispanic Americans who worked to improve conditions. In 1962 Chavez formed a union that would later become the **United Farm Workers** (UFW). This union was committed to the goal of better pay and working conditions for migrant farm workers—those who move seasonally from farm to farm for work. Chavez led the UFW in a five-year strike and boycott against California grape growers. The workers finally won better wages and benefits in 1970. The UFW became a national organization in 1976.

Chavez shared the commitment to nonviolent protest. To those who complained about the slow pace of change, he replied:

“Nonviolence takes time … I despise exploitation [unfair gain] and I want change, but I'm willing to pay the price in terms of time. There's a Mexican saying, 'Hay más tiempo que vida'—there's more time than life. We've got all the time in the world.”

—Cesar Chavez, quoted in *Chávez, César: Autobiography of La Causa*

Chavez helped inspire young leaders in what became known as the Chicano movement. To fight discrimination and gain greater political influence, Chicano activists formed a political party called *La Raza Unida*, or the United Race. The Hispanic civil rights movement had important **consequences**. A 1968 amendment to the Elementary and Secondary Education Act required schools to teach students whose first language was not English in both languages until they learned English. The Voting Rights Act of 1975 required communities with large immigrant populations to print ballots in the voters' preferred language.

READING CHECK **Sequencing** What group helped inspire the Chicano movement?

The Women's Movement

Activists also brought public attention to women's position in society. In 1963 a government commission reported that women had fewer job opportunities than men and were often paid less for the same work. President Kennedy responded by ordering an end to discrimination based on gender in civil service jobs. That same year Congress passed the Equal Pay Act, which required many employers to pay men and women equal salaries for the same work. The Civil Rights Act of 1964 banned discrimination based on both gender and race.

Some women also began to question their traditional roles in society. In her 1963 book *The Feminine Mystique*, **Betty Friedan** described the dissatisfaction some women felt with their traditional roles of wife, mother, and homemaker.

BIOGRAPHY

Cesar Chavez

1927–1993

Cesar Chavez was born on a small family ranch in Arizona. After losing their land during the Great Depression, Chavez and his family began working as migrant farm workers. Moving from town to town in search of work, Chavez went to more than 30 different schools. He served in the U.S. Navy during World War II, then returned to the fields to help migrant workers fight for better pay and working conditions. The soft-spoken Chavez seemed to many an unlikely leader of a protest movement. But Chavez quickly became an influential leader, continuing to lead the struggle for farm workers' rights into the 1990s. Before his death, Chavez insisted, "It's not me who counts, it's the Movement."

Making Inferences Why do you think Chavez began the farm workers' movement?

Friedan became a leader of the modern women's rights movement. In 1966 she helped found the **National Organization for Women** (NOW) to fight for equal educational and career opportunities for women. Other women worked for change by running for public office. In 1968 **Shirley Chisholm** was elected to represent a New York City district in the House of Representatives. She was the first African American woman elected to the U.S. Congress.

In the early 1970s, NOW and other women's rights activists supported an amendment to the Constitution. The **Equal Rights Amendment** (ERA) would outlaw all discrimination based on sex. The ERA was approved by Congress in 1972.

For an amendment to go into effect, it must be ratified by three-fourths of the states—or 38 out of 50 states. The ERA was ratified by 30 state legislatures by the end of 1973. But many opponents came forward to block the ERA. **Phyllis Schlafly**, a conservative activist, founded the group STOP ERA to prevent its ratification. Schlafly and her supporters argued that the ERA would hurt

ACADEMIC VOCABULARY

consequences the effects of a particular event or events

THE IMPACT TODAY

Eighty-two women were elected to Congress in 2004, the highest total in U.S. history.

Debate over Women's Rights

In the 1960s, women began to organize to demand equal rights. The movement became known as women's liberation. Many activists supported a woman's right to equal pay and equal protection under the law. Some opposing activists worked to maintain what they saw as women's protected status under the law.

Shirley Chisholm became the first African American woman elected to Congress in 1968.

Betty Friedan authored *The Feminine Mystique*, a book declaring that many women wanted achievements beyond those of becoming a wife and mother.

Phyllis Schlafly argued against the Equal Rights Amendment, saying it would reduce the legal rights of wives and mothers.

families by encouraging women to focus on careers rather than on motherhood. Such opposition weakened support for the ERA. In June 1982 the amendment fell three states short of ratification.

Despite this failure, the women's movement achieved many of its goals. Women found new opportunities in education and the workplace. For example, women began attending many formerly all-male universities. Increasing numbers of women pursued careers in traditionally all-male fields such as law and medicine. Many women also won political office at all levels of government.

READING CHECK **Finding Main Ideas**
What were some achievements of the women's movement of the 1960s?

Other Voices for Change

Other Americans also began to demand change in laws and other discriminating practices during the 1960s and 1970s. In 1974 the Asian American Legal Defense and Education Fund was founded with the purpose of building an "informed and active Asian America." The National Italian American Foundation (1975) advocates for Italian Americans. League of United Latin American Citizens, which was founded much earlier, played an important activist role for Hispanic Americans during this period as well and continues to do so today. Native Americans and people with disabilities were also inspired by the civil rights movement.

Native Americans

One major issue for Native Americans was their lack of control over tribal lands. Many worked through the National Congress of American Indians (NCAI) to gain more control over reservation lands from the federal government. They helped win passage of the Indian Civil Rights Act of 1968.

Other activists thought that groups like the NCAI worked too slowly. In November 1969 a group of young Native Americans occupied Alcatraz Island in San Francisco Bay to protest the government's takeover of Native American lands.

One of the groups that participated in the Alcatraz protest was the **American Indian Movement** (AIM), founded in 1968 to fight for Native Americans' rights. In February 1973 AIM activists seized a trading post and church at Wounded Knee, South Dakota—the site of the U.S. Army's massacre of Sioux Indians in 1890. Federal marshals surrounded Wounded Knee, and the standoff ended with a gun battle killing two protesters and wounding one federal agent.

Such protests brought attention to issues facing Native Americans. In the early 1970s Congress began passing laws granting Native Americans greater self-government on tribal lands.

The Disability Rights Movement

In 1970 Judy Heumann and other activists created **Disabled in Action** (DIA) to make people aware of challenges facing people with disabilities. People with disabilities often lacked access to both job opportunities and to public places. The DIA's work led to the passage of new laws. The Rehabilitation Act of 1973 banned federal agencies from discriminating against people with disabilities. The Education of Handicapped Children Act of 1975 required public schools to provide a quality education to children with disabilities. In 1990 the Americans with Disabilities Act (ADA) outlawed all discrimination against people with disabilities.

Disabled in Action

Judy Heumann and other activists formed Disabled in Action in 1970. The group promotes legislation and access to independent living for people with disabilities.

What kind of rights might people with disabilities seek?

READING CHECK **Contrasting** How were the tactics of AIM and DIA different?

SUMMARY AND PREVIEW The fight for equal rights had far-reaching effects on American society. In the next chapter you will learn about world conflicts that also affected Americans.

Section 3 Assessment

go.hrw.com
Online Quiz
KEYWORD: SC7 HP28

Reviewing Ideas, Terms, and People

1. a. **Evaluate** How did Hispanic Americans fight for civil rights?
   b. **Describe** Who benefited from laws like the Elementary and Secondary Education Act of 1968 and the Voting Rights Act of 1975?
2. a. **Recall** What were the goals of the women's movement?
   b. **Explain** What happened during the ratification process of the **Equal Rights Amendment**?
   c. **Elaborate** Do you think we need the ERA today? Explain your answer.
3. a. **Compare** In what way was the **American Indian Movement** similar to the Black Power movement?
   b. **Identify** What laws banned discrimination against people with disabilities?

Critical Thinking

4. **Categorizing** Review your notes on the achievements of groups that worked for equal rights. Then copy the graphic organizer below and use it to identify the achievements of each group.

Hispanic Americans	Women	Native Americans	People with Disabilities

FOCUS ON WRITING

5. **Describing New Movements** Describe new rights movements inspired by the success of the African American civil rights movement. What groups did these movements represent? What were their goals? What did they accomplish?

Social Studies Skills

Analysis | Critical Thinking | Civic Participation | Study

North Carolina Skills
2.06 Create written, oral, musical, visual, and theatrical presentations of social studies information.

Making Speeches

Define the Skill

In a democracy, activists, government leaders, and candidates for public office often need to address people directly. Speeches allow public figures to deliver a message to many people at once. People can use speeches to make their views known. They can use speeches to try to persuade people to support their ideas or programs.

Learn the Skill

Think about the role of speeches in the civil rights movement. Speakers increased awareness of and support for the movement's goals. Civil rights leader Martin Luther King Jr. is remembered as a powerful and effective speaker. His words moved and inspired many listeners—and continue to do so today. Here is a brief excerpt from King's famous "I Have a Dream" speech, delivered during the March on Washington on August 28, 1963:

"I have a dream that one day on the red hills of Georgia the sons of former slaves and the sons of former slaveowners will be able to sit down together at the table of brotherhood."

"I have a dream that my four little children will one day live in a nation where they will not be judged by the color of their skin but by the content of their character."

"I have a dream today."

In his speech, King followed one basic idea. He used the same words over and over to emphasize his hopes for racial equality. Every time he said "I have a dream," however, King gave a different example of equality. With these different examples on the same topic, King laid out a powerful vision for the future.

The words of the "I Have a Dream" speech are powerful, but King's delivery made the speech even stronger. King spoke with confidence in a loud, clear voice. He also looked at his audience and connected with them.

Following these steps can help you make a persuasive speech.

1. **Write the speech.** Make sure it includes a clear main idea, good examples, and convincing language.
2. **Practice.** Practice reading your speech out loud to a friend. You can also practice at home in front of a mirror.
3. **Give the speech.** Remember to speak loudly and clearly and to look at your audience.

Practice the Skill

Suppose that you are a civil rights leader in the 1960s. Following the steps above, write a short speech in favor of equal rights for African Americans, Hispanic Americans, women, Native Americans, or Americans with disabilities. After you have written and practiced your speech, give the speech to the class.

CHAPTER 28 Chapter Review

HOLT

History's Impact

▶ **video series**

Review the video to answer the closing question:

How did the Civil Rights Act of 1964 inspire a push for equality among other minority groups?

Visual Summary

QUICK FACTS

Use the visual summary below to help you review the main ideas of the chapter.

Many groups of Americans organized to demand their civil rights during the 1960s and 1970s.

Reviewing Vocabulary, Terms, and People

Complete each sentence by filling in the blank with the correct term or person from the chapter.

1. __________ was an African American civil rights leader and minister who believed in nonviolent, direct action.

2. In 1960, black students staged a __________ at a Woolworth lunch counter in Greensboro, North Carolina.

3. The Congress of Racial Equality organized the __________ to protest segregation in bus stations throughout the South.

4. The __________ protected the voting rights of African Americans.

5. The __________ worked to get better pay and working conditions for migrant farm workers.

6. __________ was the first African American woman elected to the United States Congress.

Comprehension and Critical Thinking

SECTION 1 *(Pages 870–874)*

7. a. Describe What was the Court's ruling in the *Brown* v. *Board of Education* case?

b. Explain What did the Student Nonviolent Coordinating Committee do to fight segregation?

c. Draw Conclusions Why do you think Martin Luther King Jr. was chosen to lead the MIA?

SECTION 2 *(Pages 876–881)*

8. a. Recall What was the New Frontier?

b. Contrast What roles did leaders from CORE and SNCC play in the Freedom Rides?

c. Contrast How did Malcolm X's ideas about integration differ from those of Martin Luther King Jr.?

SECTION 3 *(Pages 882–885)*

9. a. **Identify** What is the National Organization for Women?

   b. **Summarize** How did Cesar Chavez help migrant farm workers?

   c. **Elaborate** How did the Americans with Disabilities Act help disabled Americans?

Reviewing Themes

10. **Politics** How did political changes help minorities achieve their goals?

11. **Society and Culture** How did society change during the civil rights era?

Reading Skills

Using Context Clues: Synonyms *Use the Reading Skills taught in this chapter to answer the question below.*

> The Little Rock Nine began attending classes, but resistance to integration continued. Some white students insulted, harassed, and attacked the black students. In spite of these obstacles, eight of the nine remained at the school. *(p. 872)*

12. Which of the following would be a good synonym for the word *harassed*?
    - **a.** comforted
    - **b.** assisted
    - **c.** helped
    - **d.** insulted

Social Studies Skills

Making Speeches *Use the Social Studies Skills taught in this chapter to answer the question below.*

13. What steps should you follow to make a persuasive speech?

Using the Internet

go.hrw.com
KEYWORD: SC7 CH28

14. **Activity: Creating a Newspaper** Even after the ruling in *Brown* v. *Board of Education*, integration was slow to take effect. Many districts began gradual integration plans, as in Little Rock, Arkansas, where local leaders chose the Little Rock Nine to start the process. Enter the activity keyword. Research the Little Rock Nine and then create a two pages of a newspaper. Make sure your newspaper articles include direct references to your research. Include quotations from the historical figures that were involved in the integration of Central High School.

FOCUS ON WRITING

15. **Writing Your Bill** Review your notes. Then start writing your civil rights bill. What is its goal? Explain how it will expand civil rights. Is it designed to help a certain group of people? Discuss the reasons you believe it is important to expand civil rights in this way. You may refer to problems or events the bill responds to, as well as to earlier civil rights laws and legal decisions.

CHAPTER 28

Standardized Test Practice

DIRECTIONS: Read each question and write the letter of the best response.

1 **Use the following graph to answer the question below.**

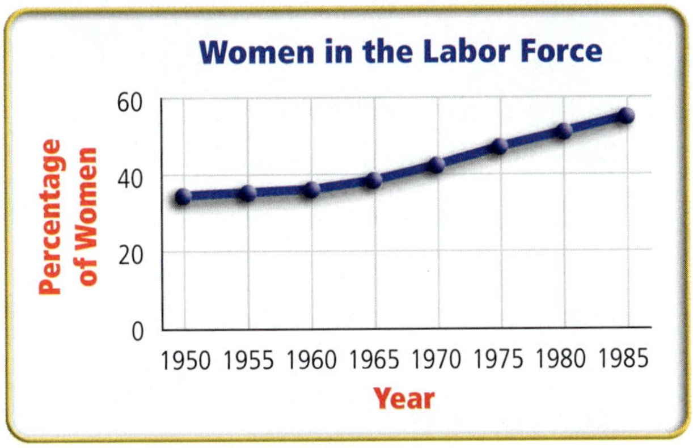

By about how much did the percentage of women in the workforce increase between 1960 and 1980?

A 5 percent
B 25 percent
C 15 percent
D 50 percent

2 **Why was the Mecklenburg busing case so important?**

A It led to segregated schools in the South.
B It forced schools to integrate.
C It created funds for school buses.
D It led to equal rights for women.

3 **Leaders of the MIA organized the Montgomery Bus Boycott after**

A black students staged a sit-in at a Woolworth lunch counter.
B Martin Luther King Jr. founded the Southern Christian Leadership Conference.
C Rosa Parks was arrested for sitting in the whites-only section of a public bus.
D the Little Rock Nine began attending Central High School.

4 **In the 1960s Cesar Chavez became**

A the first Hispanic American to serve in the U.S. Congress.
B a nationally recognized Hispanic rights leader.
C a member of President Johnson's cabinet.
D a leader of the Native American rights movement.

5 **Where did the first civil rights sit-in in the South occur?**

A Montgomery, Alabama
B Greensboro, North Carolina
C Selma, Alabama
D New Orleans, Louisiana

6 **Read the following excerpt from Martin Luther King Jr.'s "I Have a Dream" speech and use it to answer the question below.**

> "When we allow freedom to ring, when we let it ring from every village and every hamlet [community], from every state and every city, we will be able to speed up that day when all of God's children, black men and white men, Jews and Gentiles [non-Jews], Protestants and Catholics, will be able to join hands and sing in the words of the old Negro spiritual, 'Free at last! Free at last! Thank God Almighty, we are free at last!'"
>
> —Martin Luther King Jr., speech at the March on Washington

Document-Based Question **What is the main idea King is expressing in this passage?**

CHAPTER 29 1960–1975

The Vietnam War Years

North Carolina Standards

Social Studies Objectives

7.02 Evaluate the importance of social changes to different groups in North Carolina.

7.04 Compare and contrast the various political viewpoints surrounding issues of the post World War II era.

Language Arts Objectives

2.01 Analyze and evaluate informational materials that are read, heard, and/or viewed by:
- drawing inferences and/or conclusions.
- generating questions.
- extending ideas.

3.01 Explore and evaluate argumentative works that are read, heard and/or viewed by:
- comparing the argument and counter-argument presented.
- identifying/evaluating the effectiveness of tone, style, and use of language.
- evaluating the author's purpose and stance.

4.01 Analyze the purpose of the author or creator and the impact of that purpose by:
- drawing conclusions based on evidence, reasons, or relevant information.
- considering the implications, consequences, or impact of those conclusions.

go.hrw.com
North Carolina
KEYWORD: SC7 NC

WRITING JOURNAL

Newscast Writing in the 1960s, Michael Arlen called the Vietnam War the first American "living room war." For the first time, Americans could sit in their homes and watch scenes from the war on TV newscasts. In this chapter, you will read about American involvement in Cold War conflicts, such as the Cuban missile crisis and the Vietnam War. Then you will present a newscast on major events of the Cold War.

UNITED STATES

1961 Kennedy sends military advisers to Vietnam.

1960

WORLD

1960 Cuba and the Soviet Union sign a trade agreement and establish diplomatic relations.

HOLT
History's Impact
▶ **video series**
Watch the video to understand the impact of public opinion on foreign policy.

What You Will Learn...

Tensions between the United States and the Soviet Union continued to cause conflicts in the 1960s. In this chapter you will read about the major Cold War crises of the 1960s. You will also learn how the commitment to stop the spread of communism worldwide led the United States into a long and costly war in Vietnam. Here, soldiers in the U.S. 173 Airborne are shown taking part in the Iron Triangle assault.

1968 Martin Luther King Jr. and Robert Kennedy are assassinated.

1969 Joan Baez, The Who, and Jimi Hendrix headline the Woodstock Music Festival.

1973 Last U.S. ground troops leave Vietnam.

1965 — 1970 — 1975

1965 North Vietnamese leader Ho Chi Minh refuses peace talks with President Lyndon Johnson.

1969 Ho Chi Minh dies in Hanoi.

1975 North Vietnamese troops capture Saigon.

Reading Social Studies

by Kylene Beers

Economics | **Geography** | Politics | Society and Culture | Science and Technology

Focus on Themes In this chapter, you will learn about the Vietnam War years. American soldiers faced many obstacles in Vietnam, including the country's **geography**. Jungles and mountains prevented Americans from gaining an easy victory. You will read about how the long, drawn-out conflict caused divisions between the nation's leaders and many Americans.

Setting a Purpose

Focus on Reading Setting a purpose for your reading can help you to understand the things that you read. Understanding the author's goal is often an important part of this task.

Setting a Purpose When you open this book to a page you have been assigned to read, there will be clues about what you will be learning. The information in this book is organized under headings that help explain the text. When you read a section like the one below, try to determine how the text explains the heading.

Notice how one reader used the headings to determine his purpose for reading the passage below.

Society in the 1960s

As the Vietnam War continued, growing numbers of Americans began to criticize the war . . .

From Chapter 29, p. 908

This large heading lets me know that the text below will be about everyday life during the 1960s.

Antiwar Protests

College students often took the lead in organizing antiwar protests . . .

The text below this heading might answer questions about what antiwar protests are and who took part in them.

I guess protests were frequent during the 1960s. I should read to find out what they were and why they took place.

You Try It!

The following passage is from the chapter you are getting ready to read. As you read the passage, look for information in the headings that tell you what to look for.

The Vietnam War Ends

While Nixon was running for reelection in 1972, Henry Kissinger started peace negotiations with the North Vietnamese . . .

From Chapter 29, pp. 911–912

The Impact in Southeast Asia

The war ended when North Vietnamese forces captured Saigon in April 1975 . . .

The Impact at Home

The Vietnam War carried heavy costs for the United States as well . . .

After you read the passage, answer the following questions.

1. After reading the headings, what do you think this section is going to be about?
2. What are some questions you might ask before reading this section?
3. What information do you think you will learn from the section?

Key Terms and People

Chapter 29

Section 1

Peace Corps *(p. 894)*
Fidel Castro *(p. 895)*
Berlin Wall *(p. 896)*
Cuban missile crisis *(p. 896)*
Neil Armstrong *(p. 898)*
Edwin "Buzz" Aldrin *(p. 898)*
Ho Chi Minh *(p. 898)*
domino theory *(p. 898)*
Vietcong *(p. 899)*

Section 2

Tonkin Gulf Resolution *(p. 902)*
Ho Chi Minh Trail *(p. 902)*
escalation *(p. 902)*
William Westmoreland *(p. 903)*
search-and-destroy missions *(p. 903)*
Tet Offensive *(p. 904)*
doves *(p. 904)*
hawks *(p. 904)*

Section 3

Students for a Democratic Society *(p. 908)*
hippies *(p. 909)*
Richard M. Nixon *(p. 910)*
Henry Kissinger *(p. 910)*
Vietnamization *(p. 910)*
Twenty-sixth Amendment *(p. 911)*
War Powers Act *(p. 913)*
Vietnam Veterans Memorial *(p. 913)*

Academic Vocabulary

In this chapter, you will learn the following academic words:

aspect *(p. 896)*
values *(p. 909)*

As you read Chapter 29, set a purpose before you read each section.

SECTION 1

Kennedy and Foreign Policy

What You Will Learn...

Main Ideas

1. President Kennedy confronted Communist threats around the world.
2. The United States and the Soviet Union raced to send a person to the moon.
3. The Cold War conflict in Vietnam led the United States into war.

The Big Idea

The United States confronted Communist nations in Cold War conflicts around the world.

Key Terms and People

Peace Corps, *p. 894*
Fidel Castro, *p. 895*
Berlin Wall, *p. 896*
Cuban missile crisis, *p. 896*
Neil Armstrong, *p. 898*
Edwin "Buzz" Aldrin, *p. 898*
Ho Chi Minh, *p. 898*
domino theory, *p. 898*
Vietcong, *p. 899*

TAKING NOTES As you read, take notes on Cold War crises that took place during the Kennedy administration. You may want to use a graphic organizer like this one.

Bay of Pigs	Berlin Wall	Cuban Missile Crisis

If YOU were there...

You are a student in 1960. Whenever you discuss current events in class, students talk nervously about the ongoing nuclear arms race between the United States and the Soviet Union. If Cold War tensions ever spark an all-out nuclear war, entire cities and populations could be destroyed in just a matter of minutes.

Do you think Cold War tensions will lead to a nuclear war?

BUILDING BACKGROUND In the 1950s some Americans feared that the United States was falling behind the Soviet Union in missile production. The United States began using U-2 spy planes to gather information about Soviet military technology. On May 1, 1960, a U-2 plane was shot down over Soviet territory. Soviet leaders reacted angrily. Cold War tensions were running high as the Kennedy presidency began in 1961.

Kennedy Confronts Communism

As president, John F. Kennedy was committed to the Cold War policy of stopping the spread of communism worldwide. He maintained strong military forces and expanded the nation's supply of nuclear weapons. He also sought nonmilitary ways to defeat communism. For example, in a program called the Alliance for Progress, the United States pledged $20 billion in aid to countries in Latin America. This assistance did little to improve conditions in Latin America or U.S.–Latin American relations, however. Another nonmilitary program was more successful. Beginning in 1961, the **Peace Corps** sent volunteers to developing countries to help with projects such as digging wells and building schools.

Bay of Pigs

Much of Kennedy's attention, in his early days as president, involved confronting communism with U.S. military forces. The first Cold

This map of Cuba was marked by President Kennedy during a cabinet briefing on the Cuban missile crisis.

GEOGRAPHY SKILLS **INTERPRETING MAPS**

1. **Location** How far is Havana from Miami?
2. **Human-Environment Interaction** Why was the Cuban military presence so dangerous for the United States?

War crisis during his administration took place in Cuba. In the late 1950s Cuban rebel **Fidel Castro** had led a revolution against an unpopular dictator. In 1959 he overthrew the dictator and soon established a Communist government allied to the Soviet Union. Many Cubans who had opposed Castro fled to the United States.

Castro's close ties with the Soviet Union worried Kennedy, especially since Cuba is only about 90 miles from Florida. Soviet leaders could use Cuba as a base from which to attack the United States.

While president, Dwight Eisenhower had developed a plan to remove Castro from power. The Central Intelligence Agency began training Cuban exiles to invade the island and overthrow Castro. Kennedy learned of the plan when he became president. He approved the operation.

On April 17, 1961, about 1,500 Cuban exiles landed by boat at Cuba's Bay of Pigs. Castro's forces quickly responded, killing about 300 of the invaders and capturing the rest. Many Americans criticized Kennedy for the disastrous invasion attempt. His administration was off to a shaky start.

The Berlin Wall

Located behind the Iron Curtain in East Germany, the city of Berlin was the site of Kennedy's second crisis. East Berlin was part of Communist East Germany. West Berlin remained a part of democratic West Germany and stood as a model of prosperity and freedom. Desperate for freedom and better economic opportunities, about 2.5 million East Germans fled to West Berlin between 1949 and 1961. The steady loss of skilled workers alarmed Communist officials. Calling the open border between East and West Berlin a "handy escape route," Soviet premier Nikita Khrushchev demanded that the border be closed.

Khrushchev threatened to take over West Berlin. President Kennedy responded by vowing to defend the free city. "We cannot and will not permit the Communists to drive us out of Berlin," he warned. Then, on the night of August 12–13, 1961, the East German government began building the **Berlin Wall**, a barrier of concrete and barbed wire between East and West Berlin. Kennedy rushed American troops to West Berlin. But he was unwilling to go to war with the Soviet Union over the Berlin Wall. The wall stood as a symbol of the Cold War for nearly three decades.

The Cuban Missile Crisis

In October 1962 Kennedy faced yet another problem in Cuba when American U-2 spy planes discovered that the Soviets were installing nuclear missiles in Cuba. If launched, the missiles could reach, and possibly destroy, American cities within minutes.

At a press conference on October 22, Kennedy demanded that the Soviet Union remove the missiles. During the **Cuban missile crisis**, the U.S. Navy formed a blockade around Cuba to prevent Soviet ships from bringing in more weapons. As Soviet ships approached the blockade, terrified Americans waited tensely for news updates. Then came some welcome news—the Soviet ships had turned back.

ACADEMIC VOCABULARY
aspect
part

After the crisis ended, Khrushchev agreed to remove the nuclear missiles from Cuba. In return, Kennedy promised not to invade Cuba. He also agreed to remove some missiles in Italy and Turkey. To improve future communication, Kennedy and Khrushchev set up a telephone "hotline" so the leaders could talk directly to each other at a moment's notice. They also signed the Limited Nuclear Test Ban Treaty, which banned the testing of new nuclear weapons aboveground.

READING CHECK **Sequencing** When did Kennedy's three Cold War crises occur?

Race to the Moon

Although Kennedy and Khrushchev had taken some steps to prevent conflicts, the Cold War continued. One **aspect** of the Cold War that heated up in the 1960s was the space race—the competition between the United

Primary Source

BOOK

Thirteen Days

During the Cuban missile crisis, President Kennedy considered several options: blockade Cuba, invade the island, or bomb missile sites by air. After choosing the blockade, Kennedy and his advisers could only wait to see how Khrushchev would respond. The president's brother, Attorney General Robert F. Kennedy, later described these tense moments in the White House.

I think these few minutes were the time of gravest concern for the President. Was the world on the brink of a holocaust? Was it our error? A mistake? Was there something further that should have been done? Or not done?. . . The minutes in the Cabinet Room ticked slowly by. What could we say now—what could we do?

Then it was 10:25—a messenger brought in a note . . . 'Mr. President . . . some of the Russian ships have stopped dead in the water . . . Six ships . . . have stopped or have turned back toward the Soviet Union' . . .

Then we were back to the details. The meeting droned on. But everyone looked like a different person. For a moment the world had stood still, and now it was going around again.

—Robert F. Kennedy, from *Thirteen Days: A Memoir of the Cuban Missile Crisis*

Robert Kennedy describes the doubts he and others in the room felt.

ANALYSIS SKILL **ANALYZING PRIMARY SOURCES**

What details from the passage show that the moment was tense?

States and the Soviet Union to explore space. The Soviet Union pulled ahead in April 1961 when Soviet cosmonaut Yuri Gagarin became the first person to travel into space, orbiting Earth once.

The United States was determined to catch up to and surpass the Soviet Union in the space race. Kennedy outlined a bold plan in a 1961 speech to Congress:

> "I believe that this nation should commit itself to achieving the goal, before this decade is out, of landing a man on the moon and returning him safely to the earth."
>
> —John F. Kennedy, speech to Congress, May 25, 1961

It is difficult for us to imagine what it was like for Kennedy's audience to hear these words. Space travel seems normal to us today. But to people in the early 1960s, the idea of humans landing on the moon seemed like something out of a science fiction novel. Still, Americans supported the project. Congress provided NASA with billions of dollars to fund the development of new technology.

In May 1961 astronaut Alan Shepard Jr. became the first U.S. astronaut in space. The next year, John Glenn became the first American to orbit Earth. Then NASA pushed ahead with Project Apollo, with the goal of landing an astronaut on the moon. Even with careful planning, Apollo astronauts faced great danger. Three astronauts died in a fire during a prelaunch test in 1967.

Mission to the Moon

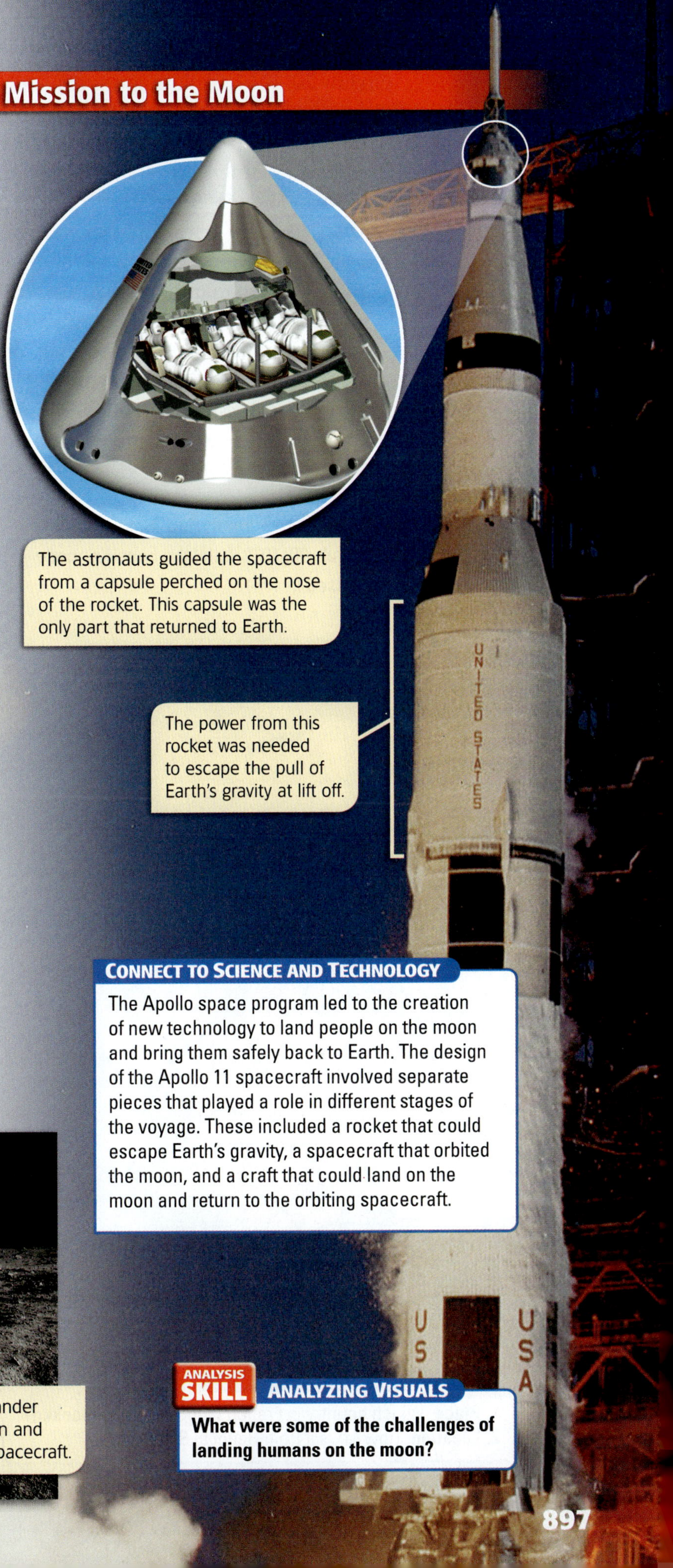

The astronauts guided the spacecraft from a capsule perched on the nose of the rocket. This capsule was the only part that returned to Earth.

The power from this rocket was needed to escape the pull of Earth's gravity at lift off.

CONNECT TO SCIENCE AND TECHNOLOGY

The Apollo space program led to the creation of new technology to land people on the moon and bring them safely back to Earth. The design of the Apollo 11 spacecraft involved separate pieces that played a role in different stages of the voyage. These included a rocket that could escape Earth's gravity, a spacecraft that orbited the moon, and a craft that could land on the moon and return to the orbiting spacecraft.

A vehicle known as the moon lander took two astronauts to the moon and returned them to the orbiting spacecraft.

ANALYSIS SKILL **ANALYZING VISUALS**

What were some of the challenges of landing humans on the moon?

On July 20, 1969, while millions of people around the world watched on television, the lunar module *Eagle* landed on the surface of the moon. American astronauts **Neil Armstrong** and **Edwin "Buzz" Aldrin** climbed out and became the first people to walk on the moon. "That's one small step for [a] man, one giant leap for mankind," said Armstrong as he touched the lunar surface. Armstrong and Aldrin planted the American flag on the moon's surface and collected samples of moon rocks. The Apollo program continued, achieving five more successful moon landings by 1972.

READING CHECK **Analyzing** How did the events of July 20, 1969, fulfill the hope Kennedy had expressed in 1961?

French Indochina

France combined its protectorates of Laos, Cambodia, and Vietnam in 1891 to create French Indochina.

GEOGRAPHY SKILLS **INTERPRETING MAPS**

1. **Place** Which country in French Indochina is landlocked?
2. **Location** How far is it from Hanoi to Saigon?

Conflict in Vietnam

The most serious and deadly event of the Cold War took place in Vietnam, a country in Southeast Asia. The Vietnamese struggled against the domination of China for centuries. By the early 1880s all of Vietnam was conquered by France. The French combined Vietnam with neighboring Laos and Cambodia to create a colony called French Indochina. French leaders imposed harsh taxes and put limits on political freedoms. Vietnamese nationalists began a struggle for independence in the early 1900s.

France and Vietnam

One of the leading Vietnamese nationalists was **Ho Chi Minh**. Ho believed that only a Communist revolution could free the Vietnamese people.

During World War II, Japan drove the French out of Indochina. Ho Chi Minh did not want Vietnam to be controlled by yet another foreign power. He organized a group called the Vietminh to resist Japanese occupation. When Japan was defeated by the Allies in 1945, Ho declared Vietnamese independence. Using words echoing those of the American Declaration of Independence, he said, "All men are born equal: the Creator has given us inviolable rights, life, liberty, and happiness." In reality, Ho did not believe in the democratic principles outlined in the American document.

Vietnam was still not free of foreign rule. France insisted that Vietnam was a French colony. French forces moved to regain control of Vietnam, leading to new fighting between the two sides.

Presidents Truman and Eisenhower both supported France with military aid. They were concerned that a Vietminh victory would lead to the spread of communism in Asia. American leaders feared that if one country became Communist, nearby countries would also fall to communism. This was called the **domino theory**. Americans had already watched Communist victories in China and North Korea. They did not want Vietnam to be next.

The Vietminh had fewer weapons and supplies than the French, but they used hit-and-run guerrilla tactics to gradually weaken French forces. In May 1954 the Vietminh trapped a French army at Dien Bien Phu, where the French surrendered. In July French and Vietnamese leaders worked out an agreement called the Geneva Accords. This compromise temporarily divided Vietnam into North and South. It also called for democratic elections in July 1956 that would unite the two countries under one government.

North and South Vietnam

North Vietnam became a Communist dictatorship led by Ho Chi Minh. South Vietnam had a Western-style government led by Ngo Dinh Diem (en-GOH DIN de-EM) and supported by the United States. U.S. officials hoped Diem would win control of the country in the 1956 elections.

Diem, however, quickly proved to be a disappointing leader. He put his own family members in top government positions and used his security forces to imprison and torture his political enemies. President Eisenhower was concerned, but he and his advisers saw Diem as the only realistic alternative to a Communist Vietnam.

In North Vietnam, meanwhile, Ho Chi Minh introduced land redistribution plans. Like Diem, Ho and the Vietminh violently persecuted their opponents. During the land redistribution process, they imprisoned and killed thousands of landowners.

As the 1956 reunification elections approached, however, a growing number of South Vietnamese supported Ho and the Vietminh. Diem refused to allow South Vietnam to participate in the elections. The United States backed this decision. Diem also arrested thousands of people who supported Ho.

In 1960 members of the North Vietnamese government formed the National Liberation Front (NLF). The NLF recruited South Vietnamese who were opposed to Diem to fight against the South Vietnamese government. The NLF relied on Communist guerrilla forces called the **Vietcong** as its army, which was supplied and funded by the North Vietnamese.

South Vietnamese soldiers plot a firing pattern under the guidance of American military personnel.

American Involvement

President Eisenhower sent aid, weapons, and military advisers to South Vietnam to aid Diem. Soon after taking office in 1961, President Kennedy sent more advisers and special forces. Although they were not official combat troops, the U.S. military advisers often accompanied the South Vietnamese army on combat missions. Some were killed in action. By late 1963 about 16,000 U.S. military personnel were serving in Vietnam.

The increased U.S. support did not help Diem, who was becoming less and less popular in South Vietnam. Several attempts were made to overthrow his government, all of which failed. Diem would not hold elections, and his opponents began to consider violence as their only option. He lost more support when he ordered his troops to fire on Buddhist demonstrators.

Some Buddhist monks protested by setting themselves on fire. Horrifying images of these protests helped turn U.S. public opinion against Diem.

In November 1963 a group of South Vietnamese army officers seized power and killed Diem and his brother. Only weeks later, Kennedy was assassinated, and Vice President Lyndon Johnson became president. Johnson immediately faced tough decisions about how to handle an increasingly unstable South Vietnam.

READING CHECK **Evaluating** Why did the United States see the Vietnam conflict as a Cold War struggle?

SUMMARY AND PREVIEW In the 1950s and early 1960s, Cold War tensions caused conflicts around the world. In the next section you will read about increased U.S. involvement in Vietnam.

The Beginning of the Vietnam War

QUICK FACTS

Causes

- French lose control of Vietnam
- Cold War tensions
- Civil war in Vietnam
- Assassination of President Diem

Effects

- Eisenhower and Kennedy send military advisers
- Gulf of Tonkin Resolution

Section 1 Assessment

go.hrw.com
Online Quiz
KEYWORD: SC7 HP29

Reviewing Ideas, Terms, and People

1. a. **Describe** What nonmilitary tactics did President Kennedy use to confront communism?
   b. **Explain** How was the **Cuban missile crisis** resolved?
   c. **Evaluate** In which Cold War crisis do you think President Kennedy showed the strongest leadership? Explain your answer.
2. a. **Recall** How did the Soviet Union take the lead in the space race in 1961?
   b. **Predict** How do you think the Soviet Union responded to the successful U.S. landing of a man on the moon?
3. a. **Identify** Who was **Ho Chi Minh**?
   b. **Describe** According to the **domino theory**, what did U.S. leaders think might happen if Vietnam became a Communist country?
   c. **Analyze** Do you think the United States was justified in supporting Ngo Dinh Diem? Why or why not?

Critical Thinking

4. **Identifying Cause and Effect** Review your notes on Cold War crises during the Kennedy administration. Then copy the graphic organizer below and use it to list the causes and effects of each crisis.

Cause →	Bay of Pigs	→ Effect
Cause →	Berlin Wall	→ Effect
Cause →	Cuban Missile Crisis	→ Effect

FOCUS ON WRITING

5. **Listing Cold War Conflicts** List Cold War conflicts the United States faced during the 1960s. Who was involved in each conflict? How could you explain each conflict to a television audience? What could you show in your newscast to illustrate the conflicts?

Escalation in Vietnam

If YOU were there...

It is 1965, and you have just been elected to Congress. You know voters are concerned about events in Vietnam, and you are carefully following the progress of the war. No one knows what will happen if the United States gets more deeply involved in the conflict. It might turn back the tide of communism. On the other hand, thousands of young soldiers might die.

Would you support sending U.S. troops to Vietnam? Why or why not?

BUILDING BACKGROUND Lyndon Johnson had spent most of his political career focused on domestic issues. After becoming president, he dedicated himself to civil rights legislation and his Great Society programs. But Johnson also had the same goal as presidents before him—to stop the spread of communism around the world.

Johnson Commits to Victory

Lyndon Johnson was determined to prevent Communists from taking over in South Vietnam. "We have the resources and the will to follow this course as long as it may take," Johnson said. He waited for a spark that might allow him to take action.

The Tonkin Gulf Resolution

In the summer of 1964, a naval skirmish led to a rapid expansion of U.S. involvement in Vietnam. On August 2, 1964, the USS *Maddox* reportedly exchanged gunfire with North Vietnamese torpedo boats in the Gulf of Tonkin, off the North Vietnamese coast. Two days later, during a night of thunderstorms, U.S. ships reported a second attack. The captain of the *Maddox* was not sure his ship had actually been attacked, but the USS *Turner Joy* claimed to have picked up high-speed vessels on its radar. Despite the conflicting stories, President Johnson declared the incident an act of war.

SECTION 2

What You Will Learn...

Main Ideas

1. President Johnson committed the United States to victory in Vietnam by expanding U.S. involvement.
2. American soldiers faced new challenges fighting the Vietnam War.
3. The Tet Offensive was an important turning point in the war.

The Big Idea

Johnson quickly expanded U.S. involvement in Vietnam, but American soldiers faced a determined enemy.

Key Terms and People

Tonkin Gulf Resolution, *p. 902*
Ho Chi Minh Trail, *p. 902*
escalation, *p. 902*
William Westmoreland, *p. 903*
search-and-destroy missions, *p. 903*
Tet Offensive, *p. 904*
doves, *p. 904*
hawks, *p. 904*

TAKING NOTES As you read, list the events that led to the escalation of U.S. involvement in the Vietnam War. Write your notes in a table like this one.

Events that led to escalation:
1.
2.
3.
4.

Johnson asked Congress to give him the authority to take military action. Congress passed the **Tonkin Gulf Resolution**, giving the president the authority "to take all necessary measures to repel any armed attack against the forces of the United States." Johnson used the Tonkin Gulf Resolution to greatly expand the U.S. role in Vietnam.

FOCUS ON NORTH CAROLINA

More than 200,000 soldiers were trained at Fort Bragg near Fayetteville between 1966 and 1970. Many of these troops served in Vietnam.

Air Strikes Begin

Johnson sent the first U.S. combat troops to South Vietnam in March 1965. At the same time, he ordered Operation Rolling Thunder, a series of air strikes on war industries in North Vietnam. The air strikes were also designed to disrupt the **Ho Chi Minh Trail**, a supply route used by the North Vietnamese. The trail was a network of paths and tunnels that led from North Vietnam, through Laos and Cambodia, and into South Vietnam.

Because some of the Ho Chi Minh Trail was located in neutral countries, U.S. soldiers could not surround it on the ground. Instead, U.S. airplanes bombed the route, sometimes with napalm, or jellied gasoline, to kill troops and destroy supplies. Planes also released chemicals such as Agent Orange to kill the dense forests on the trail and to increase visibility from the air. American veterans and Vietnamese civilians later suffered serious health problems from exposure to these chemicals.

By late 1968 more than a million tons of explosives had been dropped on North and South Vietnam. Many Vietnamese soldiers and civilians were killed. The Communists' ability to wage war, however, was not destroyed.

READING CHECK **Summarizing** What authority did the Tonkin Gulf Resolution give to President Johnson?

U.S. Soldiers in Vietnam

From 1965 to 1968, President Johnson pursued a policy of **escalation**, or increased involvement, in the war. By 1968 more than 500,000 U.S. troops were serving in Vietnam. Backed by superior military technology, U.S. generals expected to win a quick victory. But the Vietnam War proved to be different from previous wars.

Strategies and Tactics

In Vietnam, there was rarely a front line where armies met face to face. Much of the war was

BIOGRAPHY

John McCain

1936–

John McCain's father and grandfather were both U.S. Navy admirals. The younger McCain also attended the Naval Academy and later served in Vietnam as a combat pilot. While on a bombing mission over Hanoi in 1967, his plane was shot down and he was captured. McCain was held as a prisoner of war (POW) for more than five years and was often tortured and kept in solitary confinement. McCain entered politics after the war. In 2004 he was elected to his fourth term as U.S. senator from Arizona. One of his priorities as a senator was to help repair and strengthen U.S. relations with Vietnam.

Drawing Inferences If you were John McCain, would you want to establish good relations with Vietnam? Why or why not?

As a lieutenant, John McCain served as a flight instructor.

fought in the jungles and villages of South Vietnam. General **William Westmoreland** commanded the U.S. ground forces involved in Vietnam. He developed a strategy based on **search-and-destroy missions**, where U.S. patrols searched for hidden enemy camps, then destroyed them with massive firepower and air raids.

To make up for their disadvantage in firepower, Vietcong and North Vietnamese Army (NVA) troops used guerrilla warfare tactics. Moving quickly, they set deadly traps and land mines. They also knew the local geography, which allowed them to make quick surprise assaults on small groups of U.S. soldiers. Though the Vietcong and NVA suffered high casualty rates, they were able to match U.S. escalation by continuing to send new troops into combat. They also received supplies and weapons from Communist China and the Soviet Union.

The civilians of South Vietnam were often caught in the middle of the fighting. Vietcong forces entered villages at night and killed people they believed were cooperating with the South Vietnamese government. South Vietnamese and American troops attacked villages they suspected of assisting the Vietcong. About 4 million South Vietnamese were driven from their homes. This undermined the crucial U.S. goal of winning the support and loyalty of South Vietnamese civilians.

Soldiers' Stories

More than 2 million American soldiers served in the Vietnam War. Their average age was 18–21, several years younger than in previous American wars. About one-quarter of the soldiers were drafted, many from minority groups and poor families. College students—most of whom were white and from wealthier families—were able to get draft releases called deferments.

American troops patrolled jungles and rice paddies, carrying 75–90 pounds of equipment through 100-degree heat and rainstorms that could last for days. They never knew when they might run into enemy fire. Soldiers also faced the constant danger of land mines and booby traps. "We required this kind of instant hair-trigger alertness," said marine Philip Caputo. "You simply trusted absolutely no one. I mean, from a 5-year-old kid to a 75-year-old woman."

While American troops were often able to win individual battles, they were rarely able to control the territory they had won for long. "You were just constantly walking out over the same ground," Caputo explained. "The enemy you were supposed to be defeating statistically kept coming back for more."

READING CHECK **Comparing and Contrasting**

How was Vietnam different from previous wars for U.S. soldiers?

Primary Source

ORAL HISTORY

Vietnam War

Charley Trujillo was a soldier in the Vietnam War. He later became a writer and filmmaker, focusing on the experiences of Latinos and Chicanos in the Vietnam War. Below he describes a day in Vietnam.

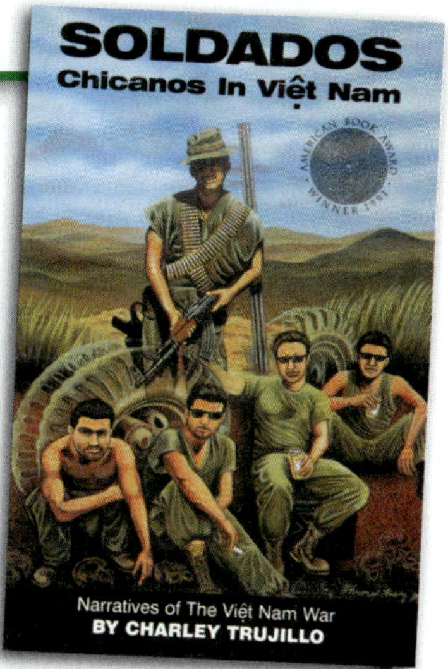

"Throughout the day we received mortar and sniper fire. By that evening we had suffered more casualties. The one I remember most was a guy we called the yippie. He was totally against the war and usually tried to avoid any violence. He was even thinking, for a while, of not carrying a rifle. It didn't help him much because the dude lost his leg that afternoon."

—Charley Trujillo, quoted in *Soldados: Chicanos In Việt Nam*

ANALYSIS SKILL **ANALYZING PRIMARY SOURCES**

Why might Trujillo have remembered this casualty the most?

Turning Points in Vietnam

By the end of 1967, U.S. military leaders argued that they were nearing victory in Vietnam. General Westmoreland said that he saw "a light at the end of the tunnel." But events in 1968 weakened the American public's confidence in this claim.

The Tet Offensive

On January 30, 1968, the Vietnamese celebrated their New Year, called Tet. In previous years, a cease-fire had halted fighting on this holiday. In 1968, however, Vietcong and North Vietnamese forces launched the **Tet Offensive**—surprise attacks all over South Vietnam, including an attack on the U.S. Embassy in Saigon, South Vietnam's capital.

GEOGRAPHY SKILLS INTERPRETING MAPS

1. **Place** In which countries did major U.S. air strikes occur?
2. **Human-Environment Interaction** Which country experienced most of the fighting in the Vietnam War?

South Vietnamese and U.S. forces successfully fought off the enemy strikes. Still, the massive size of the Tet Offensive shocked Americans. They had been told that the war would soon be over. Now they saw that the enemy was still strong and determined. Many began to wonder if government officials were being honest about the war. One poll taken after the Tet Offensive showed that only 33 percent of Americans believed that the United States was winning the war in Vietnam. About 49 percent said that the United States should never have become involved in the war.

In February 1968 Westmoreland asked for some 200,000 more troops. Many Americans questioned the wisdom of further escalation in Vietnam. President Johnson denied the general's request.

Hawks and Doves

Television reports had an important impact on public opinion about the war. Americans could watch action from the battlefield and see real images of the war's brutality on nightly news broadcasts. Many were dismayed by what they saw.

Gradually, some Americans who had been supporters of the Vietnam War began to call for an end to U.S. involvement. Opponents of the war were called **doves**—named after the birds that symbolize peace. Many doves believed that the war was draining money that should be spent on social programs at home. Supporters of the war were called **hawks**. Hawks called for increased military spending, based on the belief that winning the Cold War took priority over domestic programs.

The bitter divisions between hawks and doves deepened as the Vietnam War continued. On March 16, 1968, a company of U.S. soldiers under the command of

Lieutenant William Calley entered the South Vietnamese village of My Lai. Calley and his men expected to find Vietcong forces in My Lai. Their search-and-destroy mission turned into a massacre when American soldiers opened fire, killing about 500 unarmed villagers, including women and children.

At first, U.S. military officials tried to cover up news of the massacre. But former soldiers eventually made details of the events public. Lieutenant Calley was tried by the military and convicted of murder. As with the Tet Offensive, the My Lai massacre caused many Americans to question U.S. involvement in Vietnam.

READING CHECK **Summarizing** What events made some Americans oppose the war?

SUMMARY AND PREVIEW The Vietnam War escalated steadily under President Johnson. In the next section, you will learn about the final years of the war.

A Reporter in the Field

Millions of Americans watched correspondent Walter Cronkite report the Vietnam War from the field. When Cronkite called the war a stalemate, or tie, President Johnson said "I've lost middle America."

How did Cronkite affect American's view of the war?

Section 2 Assessment

go.hrw.com
Online Quiz
KEYWORD: SC7 HP29

Reviewing Ideas, Terms, and People

1. a. **Recall** What events led Johnson to ask Congress for authority to take military action in Vietnam?
   b. **Explain** Why was the **Ho Chi Minh Trail** the target of U.S. air strikes?
   c. **Predict** What problems might arise from giving a president powers such as those defined in the **Tonkin Gulf Resolution**?
2. a. **Define** What was **escalation**?
   b. **Contrast** How did strategies and tactics of U.S. troops differ from those of the NVA and Vietcong?
3. a. **Describe** What were the goals of the **doves** and the **hawks** during the Vietnam War?
   b. **Analyze** How did television influence public opinion during the Vietnam War?
   c. **Elaborate** Why was the Tet Offensive such a surprise to U.S. forces?

Critical Thinking

4. **Sequencing** Review your notes on events that led to increased U.S. involvement in the Vietnam War. Then copy the graphic organizer below and use it to put these events in the correct order.

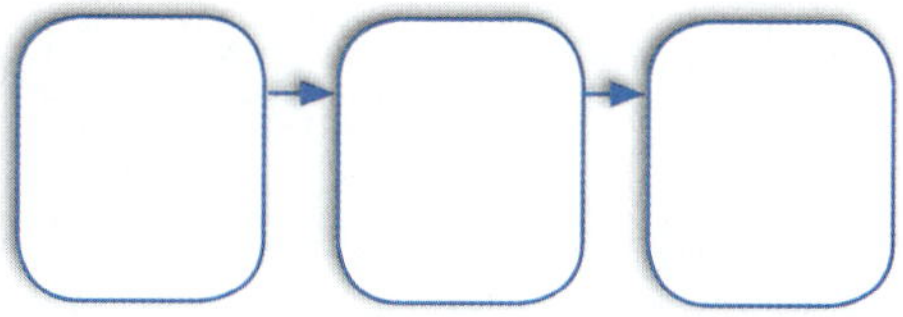

FOCUS ON WRITING

5. **Comparing Points of View** Take notes on different people's points of view on the war. What different points of view should you present in your newscast to give a complete picture of the war in Vietnam? What kinds of people might you want to interview?

History and Geography

The Vietcong Tunnels

Besides knowing the geography and terrain much better than U.S. forces, the Vietcong had the advantage of an underground system of tunnels. One large system of tunnels was installed some 47 miles north of Saigon in the Cu Chi district of South Vietnam. The picture on these pages is a re-created representation of these tunnels. The tunnels provided a place from which to fight that the Americans could not attack. A tunnel complex included special rooms in which to sleep, eat, plan, store weapons and supplies, and tend wounded soldiers.

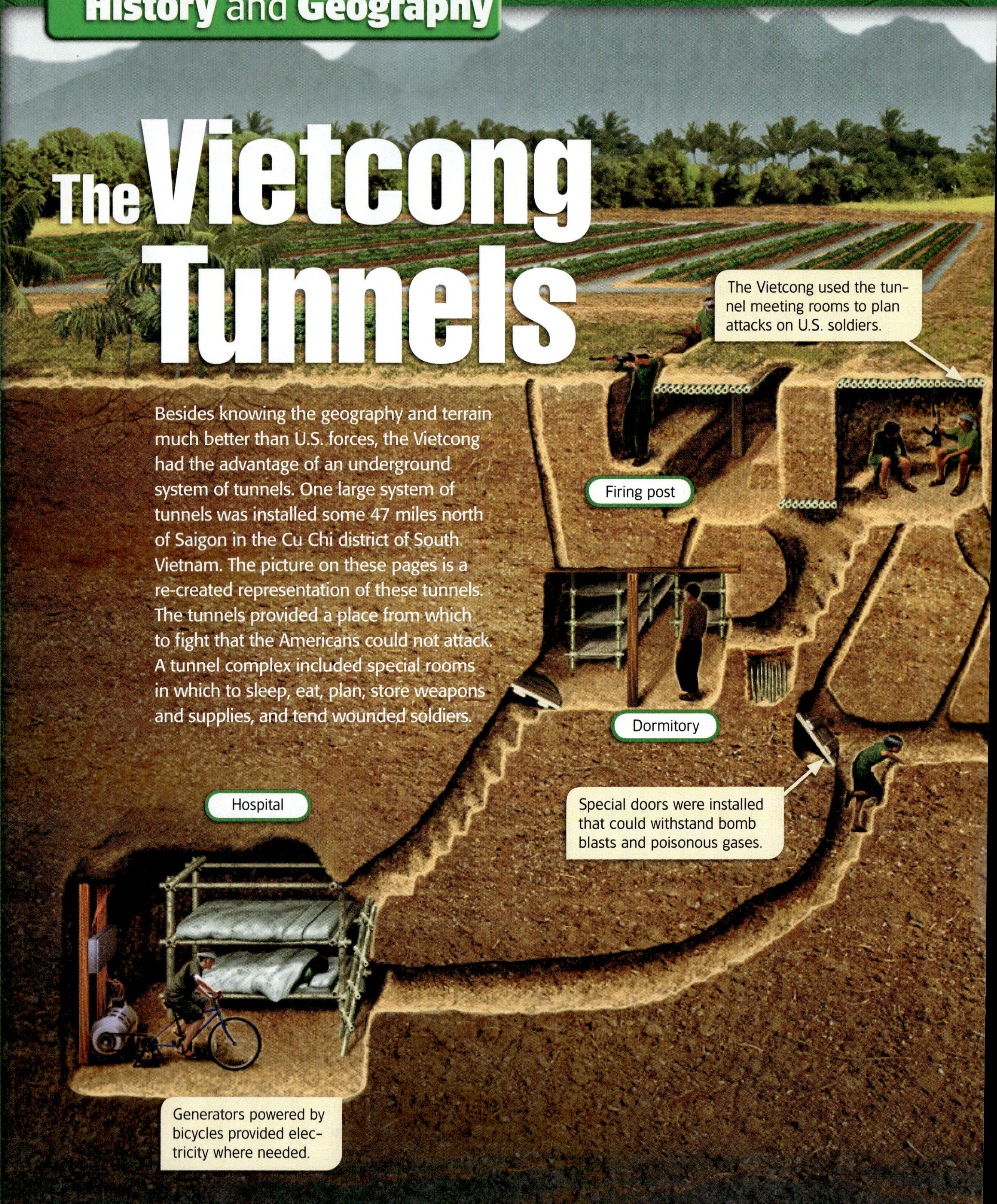

American soldiers had trouble finding the hidden tunnel entrances, like the one in this photograph.

ANALYSIS SKILL **ANALYZING VISUALS**

How did the Vietcong's tunnel system help their soldiers fight U.S. forces?

SECTION 3

The End of the War

What You Will Learn...

Main Ideas

1. Opinions about the Vietnam War divided American society in the 1960s.
2. The war under Nixon expanded from Vietnam to Laos and Cambodia.
3. The Vietnam War ended in 1973, but it had lasting effects on Vietnam and the United States.

The Big Idea

Growing antiwar feelings in the United States helped convince the government to end U.S. involvement in the Vietnam War.

Key Terms and People

Students for a Democratic Society, *p. 908*
hippies, *p. 909*
Richard M. Nixon, *p. 910*
Henry Kissinger, *p. 910*
Vietnamization, *p. 910*
Twenty-sixth Amendment, *p. 911*
War Powers Act, *p. 913*
Vietnam Veterans Memorial, *p. 913*

TAKING NOTES As you read, take notes on the causes of the end of the Vietnam War. Organize your notes in a graphic organizer like the one below.

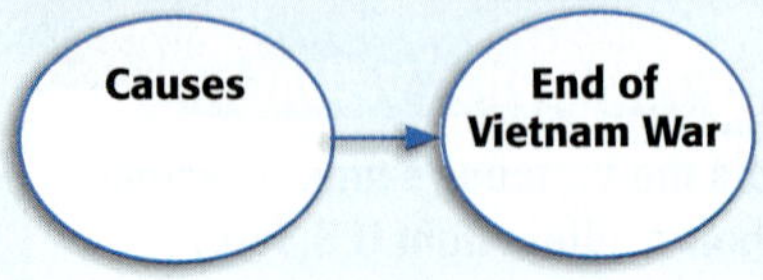

If YOU were there...

You are a high school student in 1969. You follow events in Vietnam very closely and often talk about the war with your friends. Some of your friends are active in the antiwar movement, but you also have friends who support the war. You think each group makes good points, but you are having a hard time deciding which position you support.

Would you join the antiwar protests? Why or why not?

BUILDING BACKGROUND Should the United States continue fighting in Vietnam? The debate over this question caused deep divisions in American society in the late 1960s. Antiwar demonstrators marched in cities and on college campuses. Others demonstrated in support of the war.

Society in the 1960s

As the Vietnam War continued, growing numbers of Americans began to criticize the war. "The peaceniks [war protesters] these days are legion [many]," said Charlotte Keyes, who helped organize a group called Women Strike for Peace. "They are ninety-years-old and fifteen, heads of families and housewives with babies, students, [and] young people."

Antiwar Protests

College students often took the lead in organizing antiwar protests. One of the most active protest groups was **Students for a Democratic Society** (SDS). Members of SDS protested the draft, as well as companies that made weapons used in Vietnam.

By the end of 1968, students had held antiwar demonstrations on nearly 75 percent of college campuses. Some young men protested by publicly burning their draft cards. Others avoided military service by moving to Canada. Many Americans, however, criticized the antiwar movement as anti-American. In 1970, for example, thousands of construction workers marched in New York City, shouting, "All the way with the U.S.A."

A Society Divided

Some young Americans supported the war in Vietnam. Many saw it as the only way to stop the spread of communism.

Other young Americans protested the war. They believed the United States should not be involved in a violent conflict far from home.

ANALYSIS SKILL **ANALYZING INFORMATION**

What differing views did young Americans have about the Vietnam War?

For some Americans, the antiwar movement was part of a rejection of traditional **values** and government authority. Some young people chose to "drop out" of mainstream society and built a counterculture—a culture with its own values and ways of behaving. Members of this counterculture, called **hippies**, emphasized individual freedom, nonviolence, and communal sharing. Hippies expressed their rejection of traditional society by growing their hair long and wearing unusual clothes. The views of hippies and war protesters upset many Americans. Commentators described a "generation gap," or division between older and younger Americans. "I know of no time in our history when the gap between the generations has been wider," said one university professor.

The Election of 1968

News of the Tet Offensive led to a sharp drop in the popularity of President Johnson. In early 1968 the percentage of Americans who approved of Johnson's performance as president fell from 48 to 36. The number of Americans who approved of the way Johnson was handling the war was even lower. As the 1968 presidential election approached, Johnson was even losing support within his own Democratic Party. On March 31 he went on live television and told Americans: "I shall not seek, and I will not accept, the nomination of my party for another term as president."

Several other candidates campaigned for the Democratic nomination. Johnson backed his vice president, Hubert Humphrey. Eugene McCarthy, a senator from Minnesota, ran as an outspoken antiwar candidate. Senator Robert F. Kennedy of New York argued that the United States should do everything possible to negotiate a quick and peaceful end to the war.

Kennedy won the California primary on June 5, 1968—an important step before the upcoming Democratic National Convention in Chicago. After giving his victory speech that night, he was assassinated by a man named Sirhan Sirhan.

The Democrats were badly divided going into their party's convention in Chicago.

ACADEMIC VOCABULARY

values ideas that people hold dear and try to live by

FOCUS ON NORTH CAROLINA

Like many other colleges in the nation, North Carolina universities witnessed student protests during the Vietnam War. In 1969 the University of North Carolina at Chapel Hill enacted regulations that would suspend or expel any student for participation in activities that interfered with education. Protests continued, however.

Vice President Humphrey seemed certain to win the nomination. But many delegates disliked his close ties with President Johnson and the Vietnam War. Angry debates inside the convention hall were matched by antiwar protests on the streets. When police officers moved in to stop the demonstrations, a riot broke out. Television cameras broadcast live images of the violent chaos in Chicago. More than 100 police and 100 demonstrators were injured.

Humphrey won the Democratic nomination for president, but the events in Chicago damaged his chances of victory. Republican nominee **Richard M. Nixon** promised to restore order to American society and bring "peace with honor" to Vietnam. Nixon won the election, receiving 301 electoral votes to Humphrey's 191. Southern voters gave 46 electoral votes to George Wallace, a segregationist candidate of the American Independent Party.

READING CHECK **Summarizing** Who were the candidates in the 1968 election? What was the outcome of the election?

The War under Nixon

President Nixon wanted to get U.S. troops out of Vietnam without creating the appearance of an American defeat. "I will not be the first president of the United States to lose a war," he told his fellow Republicans. With his national security adviser, **Henry Kissinger**, Nixon created a plan to pull U.S. troops from Vietnam and have the South Vietnamese Army take over all the fighting. This strategy was called **Vietnamization**.

Nixon began slowly withdrawing American troops from Vietnam. Without the knowledge of Congress or the American public, however, he approved bombing raids on Cambodia and Laos. The goal of these raids was to disrupt Vietcong supply lines. On April 30, 1970, Nixon announced that he had sent U.S. troops into Cambodia to attack Communist bases. "If, when the chips are down," he said, "the United States of America acts like a pitiful helpless giant, the forces of totalitarian anarchy will threaten free nations." Many Americans were furious. Rather than seeking peace, Nixon seemed to be expanding the war.

LINKING TO TODAY

The United States and Vietnam Today

Since the end of the Vietnam War, relations between the United States and Vietnam have slowly improved. In 1994 the United States lifted its long-standing trade embargo against Vietnam. In 1995 the former enemies officially established diplomatic relations. It became more common for American veterans and tourists to visit Vietnam.

According to the 2000 census, more than a million Vietnamese immigrants now live in the United States. Vietnamese, Laotian, and Cambodian immigrants to the United States have made significant contributions to the communities they join, many of which are along the West and Gulf coasts.

GEOGRAPHY SKILLS **ANALYZING INFORMATION**

How did the relationship between Vietnam and the United States change from the end of the war to today?

The Election of 1972

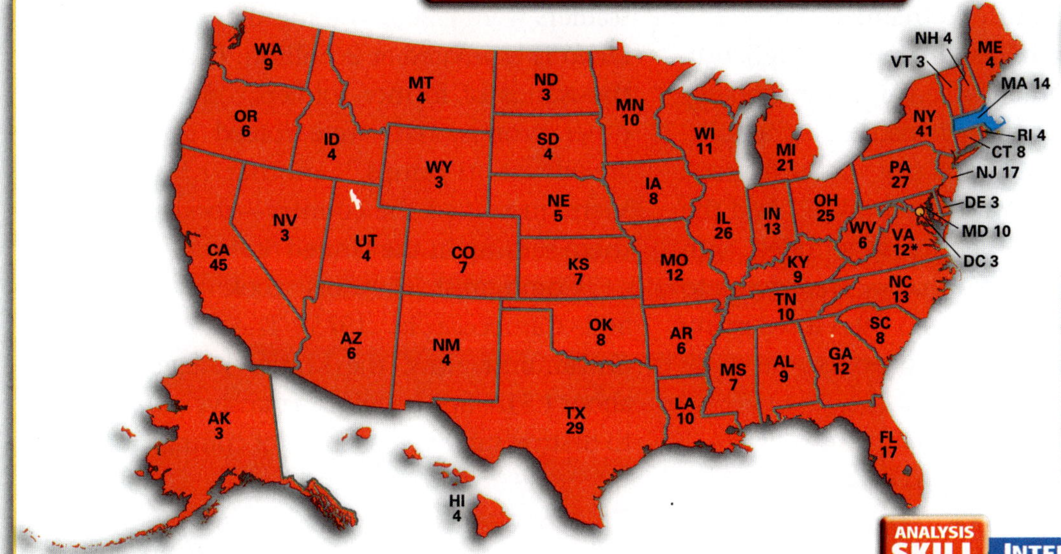

Richard M. Nixon

George McGovern

Candidate (Political Party)	Electoral Vote	Popular Vote
Nixon (Republican)	520	47,165,234
McGovern (Democrat)	17	29,170,774

*One elector from Virginia cast his vote for John Hospers of California.

ANALYSIS SKILL **INTERPRETING CHARTS**

Location Why was the 1972 election considered a landslide victory for Nixon?

Student protests erupted on hundreds of college campuses. On May 4, at Kent State University in Ohio, the National Guard was called in to break up a demonstration. When the students refused to leave, guard troops used tear gas. Some students began throwing rocks at the National Guard. Several guard troops then opened fire into the crowd. Four students were killed. Horrified by the killings, antiwar activists expanded their protests all over the nation.

Antiwar feelings grew in June 1971 when the *New York Times* published secret government documents known as the Pentagon Papers. These documents revealed that U.S. officials had been lying to the American public about the progress of the war for years.

Public opinion was hardening against the war as the 1972 presidential race began. Democratic candidate George McGovern was an outspoken opponent of the war who promised voters an immediate U.S. troop withdrawal from Vietnam. "The doors of government will be opened, and that brutal war will be closed," he said.

McGovern hoped to appeal to young voters, many of whom would be voting for the first time. The **Twenty-sixth Amendment**, which was ratified in 1971, lowered the federal voting age from 21 to 18. McGovern did win a majority of these younger voters in 1972, but a majority of voters over 21 from both parties supported Nixon. Many of these voters feared that a McGovern victory would lead to greater disorder and protests. Nixon won by a landslide, receiving 520 electoral votes to McGovern's 17.

READING CHECK **Drawing Conclusions** Why did McGovern lose in a landslide?

The Vietnam War Ends

While Nixon was running for re-election in 1972, Henry Kissinger continued peace negotiations with the North Vietnamese. On January 27, 1973, the United States signed a cease-fire called the Paris Peace Accords with representatives of North Vietnam, South Vietnam, and the Vietcong. The United States agreed to withdraw all its troops from Vietnam. North Vietnam agreed to return all American prisoners of war. Despite the peace agreement, fighting broke out between North and South Vietnam

FOCUS ON READING
What is a purpose you can set for reading this section?

in 1974. The United States refused to send troops back to South Vietnam.

In 1975 North Vietnam invaded the South. Thousands of panic-stricken American Embassy workers and South Vietnamese scrambled to evacuate Saigon. "The city was in flames," remembered one American worker. "And the Communists had the city surrounded with missiles . . . We realized that we were down to hours if not minutes." Helicopters lifted many people to ships waiting off the coast.

THE IMPACT TODAY

Today the U.S. government is more prepared to meet the needs of veterans with post-traumatic stress disorder. It offers counseling and information to vets and their families on how to deal with symptoms of trauma.

The Impact in Southeast Asia

The war ended when North Vietnamese forces captured Saigon in April 1975. Communist leaders created the Socialist Republic of Vietnam, uniting the former countries of North and South Vietnam. Hanoi became the capital, and Saigon was renamed Ho Chi Minh City.

Life remained extremely difficult in Vietnam. Cities, villages, forests, and farms had been destroyed. Some 250,000 South Vietnamese soldiers died in the war. About 1 million North Vietnamese and Vietcong soldiers were killed. The number of civilians killed is estimated at 2 million. Hundreds of thousands of former soldiers, officials, and other professionals were forced to live in "re-education camps." Another 1.5 million Vietnamese fled the country—about half of them settling in the United States.

Communist dictators took over Laos and Cambodia in 1975. The Cambodian Communist army, the Khmer Rouge, killed about 1.5 million people in a massive campaign to destroy supposed enemies of communism.

The Impact at Home

The Vietnam War carried heavy costs for the United States as well. Some 58,000 Americans were killed, and more than 300,000 were wounded.

Returning American soldiers were not always welcomed home as heroes as other war veterans had been. Some were insulted by antiwar protesters. As veterans struggled

BIOGRAPHY

Maya Ying Lin

1959–

Ohio-born Maya Lin was a 21-year-old architecture student when she designed the Vietnam Veterans Memorial. Her design was chosen from more than 1,400 proposed memorial designs. The memorial is a V-shaped black granite wall that lists the names of more than 58,000 dead and missing Americans. Explaining the design, Lin said, "It was important to me to be extremely honest; not be concerned with the politics of war, but the results. I wanted to bring the visitor a concrete realization of the great loss." The memorial is now one of the most-visited spots in Washington, D.C. Many visitors leave letters, flowers, or other objects at the memorial to honor loved ones.

Drawing Conclusions How does Lin's design achieve the goal she describes?

to readjust to civilian life, many suffered from post-traumatic stress disorder. This condition includes symptoms such as nightmares and flashbacks to traumatic experiences.

Another effect of the war was that Americans had less trust in government officials, including the president. This led to passage in 1973 of the **War Powers Act**, which requires the president to get congressional approval before committing U.S. troops to an armed struggle.

Americans took a step toward healing the wounds of the war with the 1982 dedication of the **Vietnam Veterans Memorial**. Designed by Maya Ying Lin, the black granite memorial lists the names of dead or missing American soldiers.

READING CHECK **Summarizing** What were the long-term effects of the Vietnam War?

SUMMARY AND PREVIEW American society was deeply divided by the Vietnam War. In the next chapter, you will read about how American life changed in the 1970s and 1980s.

Causes and Effects of the Vietnam War

QUICK FACTS

Long-Term Causes

- Fear of Communist expansion
- U.S. support of South Vietnam's government

Immediate Causes

- Gulf of Tonkin incident
- Communist attacks against South Vietnam

Vietnam War

Effects

- Many thousands of Americans and millions of Vietnamese killed and injured
- Vietnam united as a Communist nation
- Political divisions created in the United States
- Increased Vietnamese immigration to the United States

Section 3 Assessment

go.hrw.com
Online Quiz
KEYWORD: SC7 HP29

Reviewing Ideas, Terms, and People

1. a. **Identify** What was **Students for a Democratic Society**?
   b. **Elaborate** How did **hippies** express their disapproval of traditional culture?
   c. **Evaluate** How did the Republicans win the presidential election of 1968?
2. a. **Explain** What was **Vietnamization**?
   b. **Summarize** Why did the Pentagon Papers fuel antiwar feelings?
   c. **Elaborate** How did the **Twenty-sixth Amendment** affect the 1972 presidential election?
3. a. **Recall** How did the Vietnam War end?
   b. **Describe** What was the experience of veterans returning home from Vietnam?
   c. **Analyze** Do you think U.S. leaders made the right decision in signing the Paris Peace Accords? Why or why not?

Critical Thinking

4. **Identifying Effects** Review your notes on the causes of the end of the Vietnam War. Then copy the graphic organizer below and use it to list the effects of the end of the war.

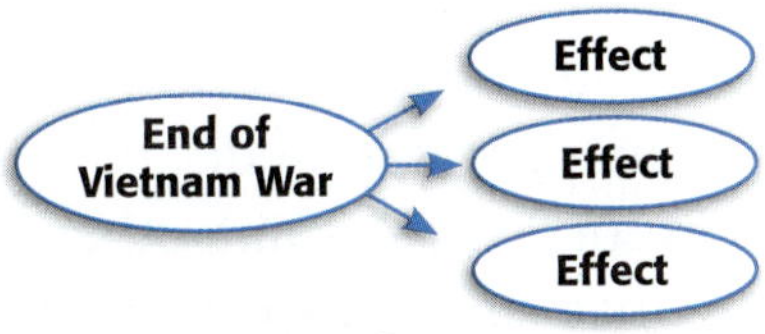

FOCUS ON WRITING

5. **Taking Notes on the Effects of the War** Take notes on the effects of the Vietnam War. How did it affect American politics? How did it affect American culture? How did it affect the American and Vietnamese people? How will you explain these effects to television viewers?

Social Studies Skills

Analysis | Critical Thinking | Civic Participation | Study

North Carolina Skills
2.04 Utilize community-related resources such as field trips, guest speakers, and interviews.

Using Primary Sources: Oral Histories

Define the Skill

An important part of history is understanding the lives and experiences of people in the past. Oral histories and personal memoirs are primary sources that help historians understand how people in the past acted and felt.

Oral histories are interviews in which people talk about events they participated in or witnessed. In personal memoirs, people write about their memories of such events. Both oral histories and personal memoirs are different from other kinds of primary sources because they can be written long after an event takes place. However, they both include descriptions of firsthand experiences.

Learn the Skill

Follow these guidelines to analyze oral histories and personal memoirs.

1. Identify the situation that the oral history or memoir describes.
2. Find the emotions or events that stand out in the description.
3. Make a generalization about how the individual's experience helps us understand the time period or event. Do you think other people might have had similar experiences?

In the following quotation, Diana Dwan Poole describes her experience serving in the Army Nurse Corps in Vietnam.

> "One of my rules was that nurses were not allowed to cry. The wounded and dying men in our care need our strength, I told them. We couldn't indulge in the luxury of our own feelings ... I was always straight with the soldiers. I would never say, 'Oh, you're going to be just fine,' if they were on their way out. I didn't lie."

Poole was a nurse in Vietnam. In this quotation, she describes working with other nurses and with wounded and dying patients. Her strength in the face of sadness and her honesty stand out.

Other nurses might have had experiences similar to Poole's. The nurses' situation—treating the wounded and the dying—also suggests the dangers soldiers faced.

Practice the Skill

Harold Bryant was a combat engineer in Vietnam. Read the primary source quotation from Bryant below.

> "Today I'm constantly thinking about the war. I walk down streets different. I look at places where individuals could hide. Maybe assault me or rob me or just harass me. I hear things that other people can't hear. My wife, she had a habit at one time of buying cheap watches and leaving them on top of the dresser. I could hear it ticking, so she would put it in a drawer. I could still hear it ticking."

1. What situation does Bryant describe?
2. Based on this description, how do you think Bryant felt at the time?
3. How can Bryant's experience help us better understand soldiers serving in Vietnam?

CHAPTER 29 Chapter Review

HOLT
History's Impact
▶ **video series**
Review the video to answer the closing question:
How was the passing of the War Powers Act a reaction to the Vietnam War?

Visual Summary

QUICK FACTS

Use the visual summary below to help you review the main ideas of the chapter.

The spread of communism encouraged the United States to escalate the Vietnam War.

The Vietcong's superior knowledge of the geography helped them win the war.

Richard Nixon won the 1968 presidential election and pulled troops out of Vietnam.

Reviewing Vocabulary, Terms, and People

Identify the descriptions below with the correct term or person from the chapter.

1. The Cuban rebel who overthrew an unpopular dictator and established a Communist government
2. A barrier made of concrete and barbed wire that separated East Berlin and West Berlin
3. The commander of U.S. ground forces in Vietnam who developed the strategy of search-and-destroy missions
4. Supporters of the Vietnam War who believed winning the Cold War took priority over domestic reform
5. The Republican nominee who won the 1968 election for president of the United States
6. The amendment that lowered the voting age from 21 to 18

Comprehension and Critical Thinking

SECTION 1 *(Pages 894–900)*

7. a. Recall What is the Peace Corps?

b. Sequence Describe the sequence of events that led to American astronauts landing on the moon in 1969.

c. Evaluate How do you think the Cuban missile crisis would have ended had the United States pursued air strikes or an invasion of Cuba?

SECTION 2 *(Pages 901–905)*

8. a. Define What is guerrilla warfare?

b. Describe How did the American military try to disrupt the Ho Chi Minh Trail?

c. Predict Do you think Americans' opinions about the war would have been different had there been no television reporting? Explain your answer.

SECTION 3 *(Pages 908–913)*

9. a. **Identify** What was the War Powers Act?

   b. **Explain** What was Henry Kissinger's role in the Vietnam War?

   c. **Summarize** What long-term effects did the Vietnam War have on the United States?

Reviewing Themes

10. **Geography** How did the geography of Vietnam help the Vietcong?

11. **Geography** How did the geography of Vietnam affect American forces?

Reading Skills

Setting a Purpose *Use the Reading Skills taught in this chapter to answer the question about the reading selection below.*

Johnson Commits to Victory

Lyndon B. Johnson was determined to prevent Communists from taking over in South Vietnam. "We have the resources and the will to follow this course as long as it may take," Johnson said . . .

The Tonkin Gulf Resolution

In the summer of 1964, a naval skirmish led to a rapid expansion of U.S. involvement in Vietnam. On August 2, 1964, the USS *Maddox* reportedly exchanged gunfire with North Vietnamese torpedo boats in the Gulf of Tonkin, off the North Vietnamese coast . . . *(p. 901)*

12. Which of the following is an example of a purpose you could set for the passage above?

    a. Find out why the Vietnam War was fought.

    b. Find out Johnson's view of the Vietnam War.

    c. Find out when the Vietnam War ended.

    d. Find out what the Vietnam Veterans Memorial is.

Social Studies Skills

Using Primary Sources: Oral Histories *Read this passage from marine officer Philip Caputo. Then use the Social Studies Skills taught in this chapter to answer the question below.*

"You simply trusted absolutely no one. I mean, from a 5-year-old kid to a 75-year-old woman." *(p. 903)*

13. How do you think Caputo felt about not being able to trust anyone? Do you think he felt safe? Why or why not?

Using the Internet

go.hrw.com
KEYWORD: SC7 CH29

14. **Activity: Mapping the Terrain** Geography played a very important role in the Vietnam War. American soldiers struggled to fight against enemy soldiers who knew the land and were able to use that knowledge to their advantage. Enter the activity keyword and find information about the geography of Southeast Asia. Then create a map showing the area's various geographic features. Include notes on the map that describe some of the geographical challenges American soldiers faced.

FOCUS ON WRITING

15. **Presenting Your Newscast** Review your notes and prepare your newscast. You will have about five minutes for your newscast. Include several segments on different topics from the chapter. One could be an interview with a friend in the role of a soldier back from Vietnam, a government official, or an antiwar protester. You can also use pictures to illustrate the events you are reporting. Write your script and practice reading it before your presentation.

CHAPTER 29 Standardized Test Practice

DIRECTIONS: Read each question and write the letter of the best response.

1 How did the University of North Carolina react to students protesting the Vietnam War?

A It encouraged protests.

B It enacted rules against protesting.

C It sent armed security officers to stop protesters.

D It called for a debate between opponents and supporters of the war.

2 Ho Chi Minh was the leader of

A Laos.

B Cambodia.

C North Vietnam.

D South Vietnam.

3 President Johnson's policy of escalation called for

A a gradual withdrawal of U.S. troops from Vietnam.

B an immediate withdrawal of U.S. troops from Vietnam.

C a rapid buildup of U.S. forces in Vietnam.

D expanding the war into Laos and Cambodia.

4 During the war, the Vietcong and NVA fought using what tactics?

A quick, surprise assaults

B air strikes

C search-and-destroy missions

D blockades

5 How were young people affected by the constitutional amendment in the Vietnam era?

A Their rights were restricted.

B They were forced to work at a younger age.

C The Vietnam War was brought to an end by their protests.

D The voting age was reduced to 18.

6 The Pentagon Papers revealed that

A the Bay of Pigs invasion was a disaster.

B U.S. officials had been lying about the progress of the war.

C the USS *Maddox* was attacked by North Vietnamese torpedo boats.

D the 1968 election was won by Richard Nixon.

7 What was the main purpose of the War Powers Act?

A It allowed President Kennedy to blockade Cuba.

B It allowed President Johnson to expand the U.S. role in Vietnam.

C It repealed the Tonkin Gulf Resolution.

D It limited the right of any president to commit troops to an armed struggle.

8 Read the following quote from Attorney General Robert F. Kennedy and use it to answer the question below.

> "On Tuesday morning, October 16, 1962, shortly after 9:00, President Kennedy called and asked me to come to the White House. He said only that we were facing great trouble. Shortly afterward, in his office, he told me that a U-2 had just finished a photographic mission and that the Intelligence Community had become convinced that Russia was placing missiles and atomic weapons in Cuba."
>
> —Robert F. Kennedy, *Thirteen Days: A Memoir of the Cuban Missile Crisis*

Document-Based Question What clues can you read that tell you how frightening the Cuban missile crisis was for Americans?

Writing Workshop

Assignment

Write a news article about the anniversary of either (1) the Nuremberg trials, (2) the Supreme Court's *Brown* v. *Board of Education* decision, or (3) the opening of the Vietnam Veterans Memorial.

A News Article

You have probably read many news articles in newspapers and magazines. News articles keep people informed about events in their communities, the nation, and the world. Sometimes they also remind people about important events from the past.

1. Prewrite

Considering Purpose and Audience

Remember that you are writing for people who have a choice about what to read. Your story must keep readers interested. How will you relate the topic of your story to their lives or emotions? At the same time, your story should give people information they need. In order to share information effectively, you must choose the most important details to include in your article.

TIP **Brainstorming** Brainstorm ways to interest people in the topic of your article. Take a few minutes to review what you know about the topic. Then write down as many questions, interesting points, and examples as you can.

Writing a Compelling Article

Make your article vivid and compelling by including

- **A short headline** showing what the article is about.
- **A "hook"**—an interesting fact or detail—to get the reader's attention at the beginning of the article.
- **Clear descriptions** of people and events.
- **Specific examples and quotations.**
- **Reasons** why the event is important.

2. Write

You can use this framework to help you write the first draft of your article.

A Writer's Framework

Introduction
- Grab your reader's attention with a strong headline.
- Begin with a striking detail or quotation for a hook.
- Introduce the event and its importance to people today.

Body
- Describe what happened, who was involved, and where, when, and why the event took place.
- Explain the significance of the event.
- Use details to connect the event to readers' lives or emotions.

Conclusion
- Finish any incomplete thoughts.
- End with a quotation or example that sums up the main point of the article.

3. Evaluate and Revise

Evaluating

Use these questions to discover ways to improve your news article.

Evaluation Questions for a News Article

- Do you begin with a strong headline and hook?
- Do you introduce the event and its importance to people today?
- Do you describe what happened, who was involved, and where, when, and why the event took place?
- Do you explain the significance of the event?
- Do you use details to connect the event to readers' lives or emotions?
- Do you end with a quotation or example that sums up the main point of the article?

Revising

Newspapers and magazines often have limited space. News articles must express a sharply focused idea briefly. To make sure that your article does this, read each sentence carefully. Each sentence should

- Be clear and to-the-point.
- Contain no unnecessary words or phrases.
- Use only precise words. Eliminate words such as *very* unless they add meaning to the sentence.

TIP **Vivid Writing** Make sentences more interesting by using vivid words and images. Use strong words that help readers create a mental picture.

4. Proofread and Publish

Proofreading

Read your essay aloud to catch any mistakes in your spelling or grammar. If something looks or sounds wrong, mark it. Come back to it later to correct the mistake. This is also a good strategy for identifying and fixing awkward sentences.

Publishing

Exchange articles with a classmate who wrote about a different topic. Did you learn from your classmate's article? Did you find it interesting? Put together a class newspaper that includes all the articles and headlines. Add pictures, and display the newspaper on a bulletin board.

5. Practice and Apply

Use the steps and strategies in this workshop to write your news article.

UNIT 10 1968–PRESENT

Modern America

What You Will Learn...

By the end of the Vietnam War, Americans were living in a society very different from previous eras. Economic and political changes continue today. People are choosing new kinds of jobs in new industries, and the role of the United States in international affairs is increasing. Rapid advances in technology will also affect the future of American society. As the population becomes larger and more diverse, new solutions are needed to provide all Americans with equality and opportunity.

Explore the Art

The city skyline of Charlotte displays the importance of banking and other service industries to the modern economy of North Carolina and the rest of the United States. How does the skyline of Charlotte show the prosperity of the city and state?

CHAPTER 30 1968–1988

Searching for Order

North Carolina Standards

Social Studies Objectives

7.05 Evaluate the major changes and events that have affected the roles of local, state, and national governments.

9.02 Identify past and present state and local leaders from diverse cultural backgrounds and assess their influence in effecting change.

Language Arts Objectives

1.02 Analyze expressive materials that are read, heard, and/or viewed by:

- making connections between works, self and related topics.
- drawing inferences.

4.01 Analyze the purpose of the author or creator and the impact of that purpose by:

- evaluating the underlying assumptions of the author/creator.
- evaluating the effects of author's craft on the reader/viewer/listener.

4.02 Analyze and develop (with limited assistance) and apply appropriate criteria to evaluate the quality of the communication by:

- considering the implications, consequences, or impact of those conclusions.

5.01 Increase fluency, comprehension, and insight through a meaningful and comprehensive literacy program by:

- extending understanding by creating products for different purposes, different audiences, and within various contexts.

go.hrw.com
North Carolina
KEYWORD: SC7 NC

FOCUS ON WRITING

Historical Novel Suppose you have decided to write a historical novel set during the 1970s or 1980s. You want your story to bring one or more of the major events of this time period to life for readers. As you read this chapter, you will take notes on the important people and conflicts of this time. You will choose which historical figures and events to include in your story. Then you will write the first page of your novel.

UNITED STATES

1968 Richard Nixon is elected president.

1969

WORLD

1969 Golda Meir becomes prime minister of Israel.

HOLT

History's Impact

▶ **video series**

Watch the video to understand the impact of checks and balances.

What You Will Learn...

Americans celebrated their nation's 200th birthday on July 4, 1976, with celebrations across the country. As you will read in the chapter, this celebration was a welcome distraction from difficult times. A major political scandal had weakened Americans' trust in government. Economic troubles, soaring oil prices, and international crises shook many Americans' confidence in the future.

1970 America celebrates its first Earth Day.

1973 Egypt and Syria attack Israel.

1974 Nixon resigns the presidency. Gerald Ford is sworn in.

1975 South Vietnam surrenders to North Vietnam.

1976 Jimmy Carter is elected president.

1979 The Three Mile Island accident creates doubts about nuclear energy.

1979 The Soviet Union invades Afghanistan.

1985 Ronald Reagan is sworn in to his second term as president.

1970 | 1975 | 1980 | 1985

Reading Social Studies

by Kylene Beers

Economics | Geography | Politics | Society and Culture | Science and Technology

Focus on Themes In this chapter, you will learn about issues faced by several modern presidents. You will also read about crises in the **economy** and in **politics** that changed the way Americans viewed their role as a nation. Finally, you will learn about American society in the 1970s.

Summarizing

Focus on Reading After reading a large amount of information, you can summarize it into a shorter amount that is easier for you to understand.

Understanding Summarizing Using the ideas and information presented in a book can be easier if you summarize what the author is saying. When you summarize, you can use some of the key ideas and words to write your own sentences that explain the information. When you write a summary, some details can be left out.

Read the following passage and its summary. Notice which details the author chose to include and which to leave out.

The American population was changing in the 1970s. Throughout American history, most immigrants to the United States had come from Europe. Beginning in the 1970s, however, a majority of new immigrants came from the Americas and Asia. This pattern continues today.

From Chapter 30, p. 932

Summary:

The population immigrating to the United States began changing during the 1970s. Now the majority of immigrants come from Latin America and Asia.

This passage contains most of the same information but is shorter. Not all of the information is included.

You Try It!

The following passage is from the chapter you are getting ready to read. As you read the passage, look for information that is important enough to go in a summary.

> "Are you better off than you were four years ago?" That was the question Republican candidate Ronald Reagan asked voters during the 1980 presidential campaign. Millions of voters answered "No," giving Reagan an easy victory over President Carter. Reagan won 489 electoral votes to Carter's 49. On January 20, 1981—the day of Reagan's inauguration—Iran finally released the American hostages after 444 days in captivity.
>
> *From Chapter 30, p. 937*

After you read the passage, answer the following questions.

1. Do you think the campaign slogan from the passage above is essential information for a summary of the election?
2. Do you think the number of electoral votes should be included in your summary?
3. Write a two-sentence summary of the passage above.

As you read Chapter 30, practice summarizing the information from several paragraphs.

Key Terms and People

Chapter 30

Section 1

stagflation *(p. 927)*
Organization of Petroleum Exporting Countries *(p. 927)*
realpolitik *(p. 928)*
Strategic Arms Limitation Talks *(p. 928)*
détente *(p. 928)*
Watergate *(p. 929)*
Gerald Ford *(p. 930)*
pardon *(p. 931)*

Section 2

affirmative action *(p. 933)*
Rachel Carson *(p. 933)*
Jimmy Carter *(p. 934)*
human rights *(p. 935)*
apartheid *(p. 935)*
sanctions *(p. 935)*
Camp David Accords *(p. 935)*
Iran hostage crisis *(p. 936)*

Section 3

Ronald Reagan *(p. 937)*
supply-side economics *(p. 938)*
deficit *(p. 938)*
Iran-Contra affair *(p. 939)*
Mikhail Gorbachev *(p. 940)*

Academic Vocabulary

In this chapter, you will learn the following academic words:

consequences *(p. 930)*
implications *(p. 938)*

SECTION 1

Nixon's Presidency and Watergate

What You Will Learn...

Main Ideas

1. Americans faced domestic challenges, including an energy and economic crisis.
2. Nixon's foreign policy led to improved relations with Communist powers.
3. The Watergate scandal forced Nixon to resign.
4. Gerald Ford became president upon Nixon's resignation and faced many challenges.

The Big Idea

Richard Nixon's policies helped ease Cold War tensions before the Watergate scandal brought down his presidency.

Key Terms and People

stagflation, *p. 927*
Organization of Petroleum Exporting Countries, *p. 927*
realpolitik, *p. 928*
Strategic Arms Limitation Talks, *p. 928*
détente, *p. 928*
Watergate, *p. 929*
Gerald Ford, *p. 930*
pardon, *p. 931*

TAKING NOTES Create a concept web like the one below. Fill in the outer ovals with facts about Nixon's domestic policy, foreign policy, and the Watergate scandal.

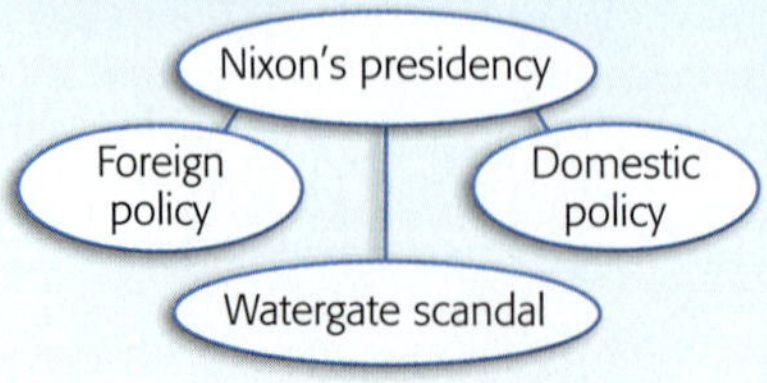

If YOU were there...

You experienced a decade of conflict and change in the 1960s. You were a witness to major events in the civil rights movement, and you lived through frightening Cold War crises. You saw leaders assassinated and astronauts walk on the moon. You have some friends who fought in Vietnam and others who led antiwar protests.

Do you think the United States is now headed in the right direction? Why or why not?

BUILDING BACKGROUND Protests over the Vietnam War led to bitter divisions among Americans in the 1960s. When Republican Richard Nixon ran for president in 1968, he said he would work to restore law and order to American society. Nixon won a close election over Democratic candidate Hubert Humphrey.

Domestic Challenges

As president, Richard Nixon promised to work on behalf of Americans who opposed protests and supported his plan for ending the war. Nixon called these Americans the "Silent Majority." He criticized student protesters and called on them to stop their activities. He did not believe Americans should leave Vietnam quickly.

New Federalism

Nixon also had a new plan for government. Nixon knew that his supporters blamed the federal government for setting high taxes and interfering in citizens' lives. He proposed a plan called the New Federalism, which would limit the power of the federal government. His policies represented a major shift in direction from Lyndon Johnson's Great Society ideas. Under Nixon's plan, grants of money from the federal government went directly to state and local governments, who decided how to spend the money. This plan reflected Nixon's conservatism, or a belief in limiting the involvement of government in citizens' lives.

The Energy Crisis

CONNECT TO ECONOMICS

Rising oil prices in the early 1970s had a major impact on the U.S. economy. Because oil was more expensive, the cost of everything made from oil—gasoline, heating oil, electricity, and other key products—also shot up. These higher prices led to rising inflation.

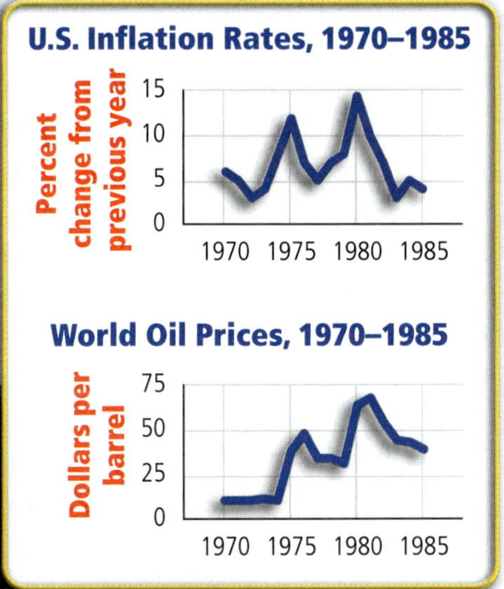

ANALYSIS SKILL ANALYZING GRAPHS

Comparing How were trends in oil prices and inflation similar during the 1970s?

President Nixon promised to reduce welfare spending and to restore law and order. He supported policies that gave more power to police and to the courts.

His political philosophy affected the Supreme Court as well. As president, he appointed four new justices. Many Court decisions soon began to reflect a more conservative point of view.

Nixon did not push for new civil rights legislation. He believed that the government had done enough in the 1960s, saying, "The laws have caught up with our consciences."

Economic Troubles

Nixon faced the difficult economic challenge of so-called **stagflation**—the economic condition of combined stagnant economic growth and high inflation. From 1967 to 1974, rising prices reduced the purchasing power of the U.S. dollar by more than 30 percent.

One cause of inflation was the rising cost of oil. By the early 1970s, the United States was importing about one-third of its oil. Much of this oil was purchased from Middle Eastern nations that were members of the **Organization of Petroleum Exporting Countries**, or OPEC. This group worked to control the production and sale of oil to keep prices high.

Most OPEC countries were Arab countries that had been opposed to the creation of the Jewish state of Israel. On October 6, 1973, the Jewish holy day of Yom Kippur, Egypt and Syria attacked Israel in what would become known as the Yom Kippur War. The United States sent military supplies to help Israel.

OPEC members responded angrily to support for Israel by declaring an embargo, or ban, on oil sales to the United States. The oil embargo and soaring oil prices caused an energy crisis. This worsened an already weak U.S. economy.

READING CHECK **Identifying Cause and Effect** What was one cause of inflation?

THE IMPACT TODAY

Today about half of U.S. oil imports comes from OPEC countries.

FOCUS ON NORTH CAROLINA

Dramatic changes took place in North Carolina's government during the 1960s and 1970s. In 1971 a new constitution was approved. The document made possible a more streamlined government by allowing the governor to combine more than 350 state agencies into fewer than 20 governmental departments. The new constitution also eliminated outdated references to race.

Nixon's Foreign Policy

As the energy crisis demonstrated, international events could have a serious impact on life in the United States. Henry Kissinger, a German American professor who became Nixon's senior foreign policy adviser, helped Nixon develop a new approach to foreign policy. Nixon's foreign policy decisions would be based on practical American interests, not on moral or political ideals. This approach was known as **realpolitik**, the German term meaning "actual politics." Nixon credited his realpolitik strategies with bringing an end to the Vietnam War by using political pressure from the Soviet Union and China to convince the North Vietnamese to negotiate.

Realpolitik was controversial. In several Latin American countries, for example, the United States backed harsh military governments because they were friendly to U.S. interests.

In the ongoing Cold War rivalries with China and the Soviet Union, the realpolitik approach led to important changes. American officials had long feared China and the Soviet Union would work together to spread communism. But by 1970, it was clear that these two Communist powers had become bitter rivals. Nixon believed it was in America's interest to widen this split and to improve U.S. relations with both Communist powers.

Nixon first turned his attention to China. He lifted restrictions on trade and travel, and opened negotiations with its leaders. In 1972 Nixon became the first U.S. president to make an official visit to China. Newscasts showed Nixon and Chinese leader Mao Zedong shaking hands and trading jokes.

Nixon's trip led to improved U.S.–China relations. It also caught the attention of Soviet leaders, who became more open to talks with the United States. In May 1972 Nixon flew to Moscow, where he and Soviet leader Leonid Brezhnev participated in the **Strategic Arms Limitation Talks** (SALT). These talks led to a treaty limiting each country's nuclear weapons. The SALT agreement opened a period of **détente** (day-TAHNT), or less hostile relations, between the United States and the Soviet Union. Détente brought economic benefits, as the Soviets began buying millions of tons of grain from American farmers.

READING CHECK **Supporting a Point of View** Do you think realpolitik was a good strategy? Why or why not?

The Watergate Scandal

On June 17, 1972, five men were arrested while breaking in to the Democratic National Committee's offices at the Watergate Hotel in Washington, D.C. The burglars were carrying camera equipment and secret recording devices. Police soon discovered that some of them had ties to the Nixon administration. One had worked for the Committee to Re-elect the President (CRP).

Nixon denied that anyone in his administration was involved in the Watergate break-in. He went on to win the 1972 election in a landslide. But early in Nixon's second term,

Watergate Scandal

Microphones hidden in tubes of lip balm were used in the burglary.

On May 28, 1972, five men burglarized the Democratic National Committee headquarters in the Watergate Hotel, shown here. They took pictures of files and bugged telephones. The burglars returned for more information on June 17 and were arrested.

the seemingly minor break-in exploded into a massive political scandal that became known as **Watergate**.

Americans watched the Watergate drama unfold through the intense media coverage of the scandal.

Investigating the Break-in

Did Nixon administration officials have anything to do with the Watergate break-in? Reporters Bob Woodward and Carl Bernstein investigated that question in a series of articles in the *Washington Post.* Key figures in the Nixon administration refused to talk to the reporters. Then Woodward was contacted by a government official who had inside information on the Watergate investigation. To protect the identity of their source, Woodward called him by a secret codename. With the informant's information, Woodward and Bernstein began publishing stories about illegal activities by Nixon administration officials. The stories revealed that the CRP had hidden illegal campaign contributions and spread false rumors about Democratic candidates. They also presented evidence that officials in the Nixon White House were trying to cover-up the facts of the Watergate break-in.

A Senate committee led by North Carolina Senator Sam Ervin launched its own investigation of Watergate. When the committee began televised hearings in May 1973, millions of Americans tuned in. The most damaging witness was former White House attorney John Dean, who testified that Nixon was personally involved in the Watergate cover-up. Dean could not prove this, however. Then another witness revealed that Nixon had tape-recorded almost all of his Oval Office conversations.

THE IMPACT TODAY

The identity of the *Post's* informant remained confidential for more than 30 years. In 2005 W. Mark Felt, second-in-command at the FBI during Watergate, revealed that he was the inside source for information.

Washington Post reporters soon linked the break-in to the presidential re-election campaign. A White House cover-up began.

The Senate formed a committee to investigate the break-in and possible cover-up. Its hearings (shown above) were televised.

Faced with impeachment for an illegal cover-up of the break-in, Nixon resigned. He was later pardoned by President Gerald Ford.

ANALYSIS SKILL **ANALYZING INFORMATION**

Why was Nixon threatened with impeachment by the House?

Supreme Court Decisions

United States v. Nixon (1974)

Background of the Case During the Watergate investigation, a special prosecutor asked for the tapes of President Nixon's Oval Office conversations. Nixon claimed that he did not have to obey court orders to turn over the tapes because of executive privilege. On July 8, 1974, the case went before the Supreme Court.

The Court's Ruling

The Supreme Court announced its unanimous decision on July 24. It stated, "the legitimate [lawful] needs of the judicial process may outweigh presidential privilege." Nixon could not use executive privilege to avoid the subpoenas.

The Court's Reasoning

The Court decided to hear the case more quickly than most cases because of its importance to the functioning of government and the interest of the American public. The Supreme Court ruled that to claim executive privilege a president would have to show a compelling national security reason. Nixon had no such reason for refusing to hand over the tapes.

Why It Matters

The Supreme Court ruling showed that, despite their unique and important position, presidents do have to obey the law. It also showed that the government could use the powers defined in the Constitution to prevent one branch from becoming too powerful. Less than a week later, the House Judiciary Committee voted to impeach Nixon.

ANALYSIS SKILL — ANALYZING INFORMATION

1. How is this case an example of the checks and balances system?
2. What do you think was the most important impact of this Supreme Court decision?

Committee members asked Nixon to allow them to listen to the tapes. Nixon refused to hand the tapes over to a special prosecutor, claiming executive privilege—a president's right to keep information secret for reasons of national security. In July 1974 the Supreme Court ordered Nixon to turn over the tapes. The recordings proved that Nixon had directed the Watergate cover-up and lied about it to Congress and the public.

While this investigation was unfolding, Vice President Spiro Agnew resigned amid charges that he had taken bribes and failed to pay taxes. Nixon appointed Michigan congressman **Gerald Ford** as vice president.

ACADEMIC VOCABULARY
consequences the effects of a particular event or events

Nixon Resigns

After studying the case, the House Judiciary Committee recommended impeachment. Judiciary Committee member Barbara Jordan of Texas explained why she thought Nixon should be impeached:

> "My faith in the Constitution is whole, it is complete, it is total. And I am not going to sit here and be an idle spectator to the . . . destruction of the Constitution."
>
> —Barbara Jordan, in a speech before Congress, 1974

On July 27, 1974, the committee approved its first article of impeachment, charging Nixon with obstruction of justice. Within the next week, two more articles were approved by the committee, one for the abuse of power and one for contempt of Congress.

On August 8, 1974, Nixon appeared on national television and announced, "I shall resign the presidency effective at noon tomorrow." He became the first president in American history to resign from office. Gerald Ford was sworn in as president on August 9.

One of the consequences of Watergate was that many Americans lost faith in government officials. In a poll taken in 1974, just 36 percent of Americans said they trusted the government. Others, however, saw a more positive side of Watergate. Senator Sam Ervin viewed the hearings and Nixon's resignation as evidence that the government was able to rid itself of corruption. "Watergate . . . proved our Constitution works," he said.

READING CHECK **Sequencing** What events led to Nixon's resignation?

Ford as President

Vice President Gerald Ford became the first modern president to hold the office without being elected to it. Ford lost some public support when he granted Richard Nixon a **pardon**, or freedom from punishment. He declared it was best for the nation that Nixon not be tried for his crime because he would be "cruelly and excessively penalized" and "ugly passions would again be aroused [stirred]."

Adding to Ford's difficulties, oil prices and unemployment remained high, and stagflation continued. The United States also had an increasing trade deficit, an imbalance in which a country imports more than it exports.

Arguing that inflation was the main cause of the economic troubles, Ford began a campaign called Whip Inflation Now (WIN). WIN encouraged people to save money and businesses to hold down wages and prices. Ford's plan met with resistance from many members of Congress, who wanted to increase spending to help the poor and unemployed. In 1975 Ford and Congress began to compromise. Still, inflation and unemployment remained high.

A U.S. Marine changes the official presidential photograph from one of Nixon to one of Ford.

READING CHECK **Evaluating** Do you think President Ford was right to pardon Nixon?

SUMMARY AND PREVIEW Gerald Ford became president after the Watergate scandal ended Nixon's presidency. In the next section you will learn about life in the 1970s.

Section 1 Assessment

go.hrw.com
Online Quiz
KEYWORD: SC7 HP30

Reviewing Ideas, Terms, and People

1. a. **Describe** What challenges did the United States face during President Nixon's terms of office?
   b. **Make Inferences** Why do you think the **Organization of Petroleum Exporting Countries** objected to U.S. support for Israel?
2. a. **Identify** Who was Henry Kissinger?
   b. **Contrast** How was **realpolitik** different from other foreign policy approaches?
   c. **Draw Conclusions** Why do you think improved U.S.–China relations made the Soviets more open to talks with the United States?
3. a. **Recall** What was the **Watergate** scandal?
   b. **Explain** Why were President Nixon's tapes important?
   c. **Elaborate** Why do you think President Nixon decided to resign?
4. a. **Describe** How did **Gerald Ford** become president of the United States?
   b. **Predict** Do you think WIN was effective in helping the economy?

Critical Thinking

5. **Sequencing** Review your notes on Richard Nixon's presidency. Then copy the graphic organizer below and use it to list, in order, events in his presidency.

Event	Date

FOCUS ON WRITING

6. **Describing Major Events** Take notes on Nixon's domestic policy, Cold War strategy, and the Watergate scandal. What were the major events of this time period? Who were the major public figures involved, and what roles did they play? Which of these events and people do you find the most interesting?

SECTION 2

America in the 1970s

What You Will Learn...

Main Ideas

1. American society debated key social issues during the 1970s.
2. Jimmy Carter was elected president in 1976.
3. Carter had successes as well as failures in foreign policy during his administration.

The Big Idea

Americans faced major challenges both at home and around the world in the 1970s.

Key Terms and People

affirmative action, *p. 933*
Rachel Carson, *p. 933*
Jimmy Carter, *p. 934*
human rights, *p. 935*
apartheid, *p. 935*
sanctions, *p. 935*
Camp David Accords, *p. 935*
Iran hostage crisis, *p. 936*

TAKING NOTES As you read, take notes on new government policies in the 1970s. Write your notes in a chart like this one.

New Policies

If YOU were there...

It is July 4, 1976. Today the entire nation is celebrating the 200th anniversary of the signing of the Declaration of Independence. As you sit with your family watching a spectacular fireworks show, you think about the challenges this country has faced throughout its history. You think about the economic and foreign policy challenges facing Americans right now.

What are your hopes for the nation's future?

BUILDING BACKGROUND The celebration of the country's bicentennial, or 200th birthday, was a much-needed break from worries about political scandals, economic troubles, and Cold War dangers. This was a moment of renewal and hope—though many Americans still disagreed about how the country should move forward.

Social Issues of the 1970s

The American population was changing in the 1970s. Throughout American history, most immigrants to the United States had come from Europe. Beginning in the 1970s, however, a majority of new immigrants came from the Americas and Asia. This pattern continues today. Another change was that the birthrate, or number of births per 1,000 people, was declining. By 1970 Americans 65 and older became one of the fastest-growing population groups.

As the population grew and changed, American society faced the challenges of how to balance the views of all Americans. You read earlier that the Equal Rights Amendment caused nationwide debate in the 1970s. Although the ERA was not ratified, the women's movement did make important gains. A 1972 federal law known as Title IX banned discrimination on the basis of sex in educational programs that receive federal funds. The number of women admitted to medical and law schools climbed quickly. Title IX also opened the door for many more women to participate in college sports and earn athletic scholarships. In 1973 the Supreme Court legalized abortion in the case *Roe* v. *Wade*.

In the 1970s Americans also debated **affirmative action**, the practice of giving special consideration to nonwhites or women to make up for past discrimination. Supporters of affirmative action argued that it was needed to improve educational and job opportunities for minorities and women. Opponents insisted that any race- or gender-based preferences were unfair.

Many African Americans benefited from new opportunities in the 1970s. For example, the number of African Americans attending college in 1976 was four times higher than it had been a decade earlier. Many people credited affirmative action programs with this increase.

The environment also became a major issue in the 1970s. In her book *Silent Spring*, biologist **Rachel Carson** brought attention to the dangers of pollution. She explained how chemicals used to kills insects travelled through the food chain and affect people's health.

> "Man, however much he may like to pretend the contrary, is part of nature. Can he escape a pollution that is now so thoroughly distributed throughout our world?"
>
> —Rachel Carson, *Silent Spring*

First published in 1962, *Silent Spring* helped inspire a nationwide movement to improve the environment. Environmentalists in the United States celebrated the first Earth Day on April 22, 1970. "Earth Day is to remind each person of his [or her] . . . equal responsibility . . . to preserve and improve the Earth," explained activists.

Congress passed new laws to limit the release of pollutants. The Environmental Protection Agency (EPA) was established in 1970 to enforce these laws. As protections increased, debates sprung up about how to balance business interests with environmental concerns.

READING CHECK **Comparing and Contrasting** How are Title IX and affirmative action similar and different?

Issues of the 1970s

Environmental protection, women's rights, and affirmative action were among the major issues of the 1970s.

Activists brought the environment to the forefront of national debate, urging legislation and individual action to help protect the Earth.

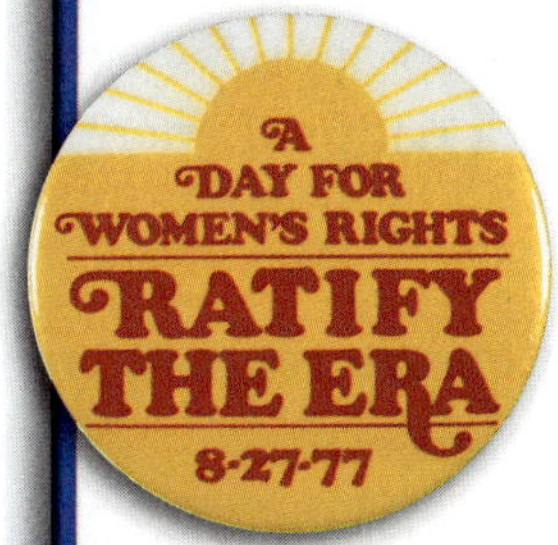

Supporters of the Equal Rights Amendment urged states to ratify the amendment they believed would ensure equal protection to women under the Constitution.

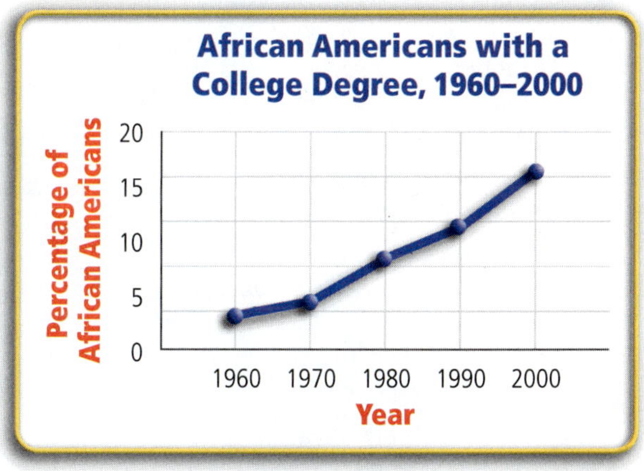

Affirmative action helped African Americans and other minorities gain access to universities and certain jobs but also created much debate.

Carter Elected

To oppose Republican Gerald Ford in the 1976 presidential election Democrats nominated **Jimmy Carter**, a little-known former governor of Georgia. The Democrats purposely chose a candidate who was untouched by the recent scandals. Carter knew that the Vietnam War and Watergate had badly shaken American voters' trust in government. "I will never lie to you," he told voters.

Carter defeated Ford in a close election. As president, Carter wanted to show a new spirit of informality and openness at the White House. On inauguration day, he and his family broke with tradition by walking to the inauguration rather than riding in a limousine.

While Americans seemed to respond positively to his straightforward style, Carter faced serious challenges. High unemployment and inflation continued. The ongoing energy crisis also kept oil prices high. Many Americans became frustrated with the president's inability to solve these problems.

Although Democrats controlled Congress, Carter had a hard time convincing members to support his proposals. For example, Carter proposed a national energy plan that called for conservation and the use of alternative fuels such as solar energy. Congress demanded changes to the complex plan. The plan was never fully enacted.

One way Carter hoped to decrease the country's dependence on imported oil was by expanding the use of nuclear power. But an accident at the Three Mile Island nuclear power plant in Pennsylvania caused new worries about the safety of nuclear energy. On March 28, 1979, a reactor core at Three Mile Island overheated, and the plant released a small amount of radioactive gas into the air. This frightening incident damaged the nuclear power industry, and the federal government put in place a ban on building new reactors.

Reading Check **Drawing Conclusions** How did the Three Mile Island incident affect Carter's energy plan?

Carter and Foreign Policy

President Carter rejected Nixon's realpolitik approach to foreign policy. He argued that "fairness, not force, should lie at the heart of our dealings with the nations of the world."

The Election of 1976

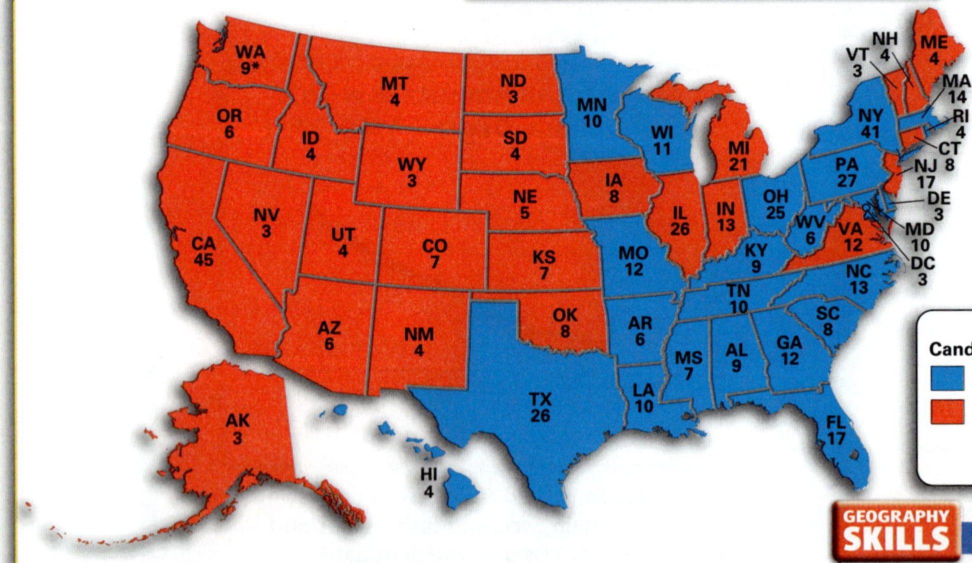

Jimmy Carter

Gerald Ford

Candidate	Party	Electoral Vote	Popular Vote	% Popular Vote
Carter	Democrat	297	40,828,929	50.1
Ford	Republican	240	39,148,940	48.0

*One electoral vote was cast for Ronald Reagan.

Source: *World Almanac and Book of Facts, 2004*

Geography Skills **Interpreting Maps**

Place Which areas of the country did Carter win in 1976?

Primary Source

HISTORIC DOCUMENT

The Camp David Accords

During the long and often bitter Camp David negotiations, Carter worked hard to keep Israel's Menachem Begin and Egypt's Anwar el-Sadat from walking out. He later wrote about one moment when the talks nearly broke down.

"Within a few minutes Sadat announced angrily that a stalemate [standstill] had been reached. He saw no reason for the discussions to continue. As far as he was concerned, they were over . . . They [Sadat and Begin] were moving toward the door, but I got in front of them to partially block the way. I urged them not to break off their talks, to give me another chance to use my influence and analysis, to have confidence in me. Begin agreed readily. I looked straight at Sadat; finally, he nodded his head. They left without speaking to each other."

Leaders Anwar el-Sadat (left), Jimmy Carter, and Menachem Begin reached a peace agreement for the Middle East in the Camp David Accords.

ANALYSIS SKILL **ANALYZING PRIMARY SOURCES**

Why do you think Begin and el-Sadat agreed to continue their negotiations?

Changing Policies

Carter favored policies that promoted **human rights**—the basic rights and freedoms of all people. He reduced U.S. aid to several former allies that committed human rights violations. In South Africa, Carter hoped to pressure the government into ending **apartheid**, a system of laws requiring racial segregation. He called for **sanctions**, or economic penalties, to encourage reform.

Carter's approach to foreign policy had effects in Latin America as well. Many Latin Americans resented previous U.S. interference in their countries. American control of the Panama Canal stood as a symbol of power in the region. In 1977 Carter signed treaties that would transfer control of the canal to Panama by the year 2000.

Carter had less success improving relations with the Soviet Union. Détente broke down when he criticized the Soviet Union for committing human rights abuses. Then in 1979 the Soviet Union invaded Afghanistan. Carter responded by breaking off arms-control talks and refusing to allow U.S. athletes to participate in the 1980 Summer Olympics in Moscow.

The Middle East

While Cold War tensions increased, Carter worked to ease tensions in the Middle East. Egypt and Israel had been at war for 30 years. In 1978 Carter invited Egyptian president Anwar el-Sadat and Israeli prime minister Menachem Begin (men-AHK-uhm BAY-guhn) to the presidential retreat at Camp David, Maryland. After 13 days of meetings, the two leaders reached a peace agreement called the **Camp David Accords**, considered by many to be Carter's greatest achievement.

Carter also experienced disaster in the Middle East. Since the 1950s, the United States had supported the pro–American shah, or king, of Iran. Many Iranians resented the shah's reform efforts and the country's shift from a traditional and agricultural society to a more urban and industrial one. The government severely punished its opponents and controlled all political participation. Many members of the opposition supported the views of Islamic spiritual leader Ruhollah Khomeini, who had been forced to leave the country because of his criticisms of the shah's policies. In 1979 Khomeini's supporters drove

Hostages Released

Approximately 52 Americans were held hostage by Iranian militants during the Iran hostage crisis. The men and women were kept blindfolded by their captors. After 444 days in captivity, the Americans were released.

How do these photographs show the experiences of the hostages?

the shah out of Iran, and a month later, Khomeini took control of the government. On November 4, a group of Iranian students attacked the U.S. embassy in Tehran, the capital of Iran, seizing about 90 American hostages. The **Iran hostage crisis** lasted for more than a year.

In the early days of the crisis, some hostages were released. These remaining hostages were often blindfolded and beaten by their Iranian captors. Carter ended Iranian oil imports and froze Iranian assets in American banks. After a failed rescue attempt in April 1980, many Americans lost confidence in Carter's leadership.

READING CHECK **Making Generalizations** Overall, do you think President Carter's foreign policy was effective? Why or why not?

SUMMARY AND PREVIEW President Carter's policies included both successes and failures. In the next section, you will learn about the policies of Ronald Reagan.

Section 2 Assessment

go.hrw.com
Online Quiz
KEYWORD: SC7 HP30

Reviewing Ideas, Terms, and People

1. a. **Define** What social issues did Americans debate during the 1970s?
   b. **Contrast** How had immigration patterns changed by the 1970s?
   c. **Draw Conclusions** Why do you think *Silent Spring* remained important in the 1970s?
2. a. **Describe** How did **Jimmy Carter** break with tradition at his inauguration?
   b. **Analyze** Why did Carter's promise of honesty appeal to voters?
   c. **Elaborate** How did the Three Mile Island accident affect the energy crisis?
3. a. **Recall** Describe the successes and failures of President Carter's foreign policy.
   b. **Explain** What did the treaties Carter signed about the Panama Canal promise?
   c. **Draw Conclusions** Why do you think many people consider the **Camp David Accords** Carter's greatest achievement?

Critical Thinking

4. **Evaluating** Review your notes on new policies in the 1970s. Then copy the graphic organizer below and use it to show President Carter's successes and failures.

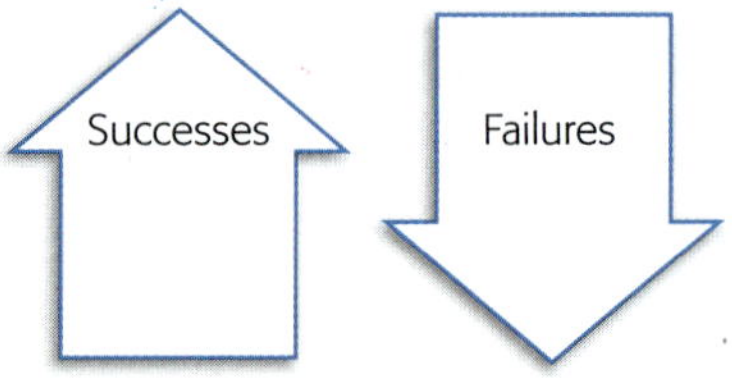

FOCUS ON WRITING

5. **Identifying Important Issues** Identify important issues and challenges facing Americans during the 1970s. Which of these issues or challenges do you think you will write about? What do you know about this subject? What more would you have to learn before writing about it?

The Reagan Presidency

If YOU were there...

It is 1980 and you are a top adviser to the newly elected president, Ronald Reagan. You think about the challenges Reagan will face. High inflation and unemployment are plaguing the economy. Relations with the Soviet Union are falling apart. And 52 Americans are still being held hostage in Iran.

What would be your first recommendation to the president?

BUILDING BACKGROUND Many Americans blamed President Carter for the nation's economic problems and the continuing hostage crisis in Iran. These became major issues in the presidential election of 1980. Republican candidate Ronald Reagan promised to take the country in a new direction.

Reagan and Conservative Ideas

"Are you better off than you were four years ago?" That was the question Republican candidate **Ronald Reagan** asked voters during the 1980 presidential campaign. Millions of voters answered "No," giving Reagan an easy victory over President Carter. Reagan won 489 electoral votes to Carter's 49. On January 20, 1981—the day of Reagan's inauguration—Iran finally released the American hostages after 444 days in captivity.

Reagan's approach to government was based on conservative ideas. He wanted to cut taxes and reduce regulations on businesses. He promised to scale back the size of government, arguing that government involvement in business and society harmed individual ambition. "Government is not the solution to our problem; government is the problem," Reagan declared in his inaugural address.

Just two months into his presidency, Reagan was shot and severely wounded in an assassination attempt by John Hinckley Jr. Reagan was released from the hospital within two weeks, and returned to work.

SECTION 3

What You Will Learn...

Main Ideas

1. President Reagan based his policies on conservative ideas.
2. Reagan took a tough stand against communism in his foreign policy.

The Big Idea

President Reagan enacted conservative policies at home and took a strong anti-Communist stance in the Cold War.

Key Terms and People

Ronald Reagan, *p. 937*
supply-side economics, *p. 938*
deficit, *p. 938*
Iran-Contra affair, *p. 939*
Mikhail Gorbachev, *p. 940*

TAKING NOTES As you read, take notes on President Reagan's domestic and foreign policies. Organize your notes in a diagram like this one.

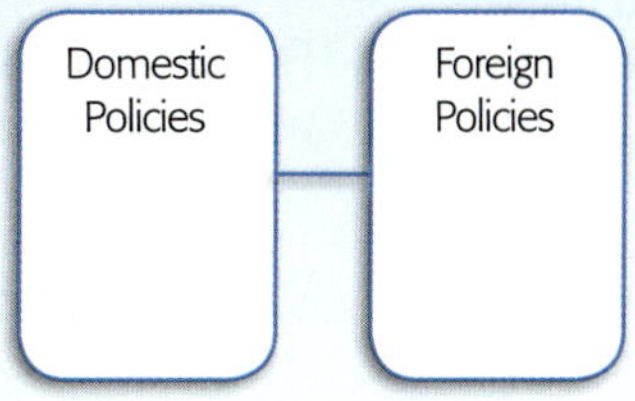

BIOGRAPHY

Sandra Day O'Connor
1930–

Sandra Day O'Connor grew up on a ranch in Arizona and entered Stanford University at age 16. She graduated third in her class from Stanford Law School in 1952. When she applied for jobs as a lawyer, however, she found that law firms were not willing to hire women. She turned instead to public service in Arizona, holding jobs including assistant attorney general, state senator, and judge. She was serving on the Arizona Court of Appeals when she was nominated to the Supreme Court by Ronald Reagan. The Senate confirmed O'Connor's appointment by a vote of 99–0. O'Connor retired from the bench in 2005.

Analyzing Information Why did Sandra Day O'Connor begin working in public service?

Reaganomics

Reagan's economic policies, which some called Reaganomics, were based on a theory called **supply-side economics**. This theory calls for sharp tax cuts with the goal of increasing the amount of money people and businesses have to invest. This investment would lead to economic growth and the creation of new jobs. Over time, the expanding economic activity would produce increased tax revenues for the government.

ACADEMIC VOCABULARY
implications effects of a decision

Though many Democrats opposed this theory, Congress approved most of Reagan's plan for large cuts in business and personal taxes. To help balance the budget, Reagan called for spending cuts as well. Congress agreed to cut the rate of the growth of spending on social programs such as school lunches, low-income housing, and food stamps.

NC History Makers
Jesse Helms Senator Jesse Helms from North Carolina was a leader in the influential conservative movement.

The economy experienced a brief recession early in Reagan's presidency. Then in 1983 the economy rebounded and began a long period of expansion. Business profits and tax revenues increased.

At the same time, spending on defense was increased dramatically, from $180 billion in 1981 to nearly $280 billion in 1985. The new spending outpaced the new tax revenues. The result was a rapidly rising **deficit**—the amount by which a government's spending exceeds its revenues.

Conservative Goals

One of Reagan's conservative goals was to reduce government regulation of key industries. Reagan hoped fewer rules would encourage expansion in those industries, thereby improving the U.S. economy. Congress responded by reducing regulations on industries such as television, airlines, and banking.

Reagan was also able to move the Supreme Court in a more conservative direction by appointing politically conservative judges. In 1981 he appointed Sandra Day O'Connor to the Court. She became the first woman to serve as a Supreme Court justice. Reagan later appointed two more conservative justices: Antonin Scalia and Anthony M. Kennedy.

Election of 1984

President Reagan ran for re-election in 1984 against Democratic candidate Walter Mondale, who had served as Jimmy Carter's vice president. Mondale chose Geraldine Ferraro as his running mate. Ferraro was the first woman to run for vice president on a major-party ticket. She spoke of the implications of her nomination:

> "By choosing an American woman to run for our nation's second-highest office, you send a powerful signal to all Americans ... We will place no limits on achievement. If we can do this, we can do anything."
>
> —Geraldine Ferraro, *Ferraro: My Story*

The economy was booming as the election approached. Mondale argued that Reagan's economic policies unfairly favored the wealthy. Voters, however, gave Reagan a landslide victory. Reagan received 59 percent of the popular vote and captured 525 of the 538 electoral votes.

READING CHECK **Summarizing** What theories did Reaganomics include?

Reagan and Foreign Policy

President Reagan was an outspoken critic of communism and the Soviet Union, which he called an "evil empire." He saw the Cold War as a fight of "good versus evil, right versus wrong."

Conflicts in Central America

Civil wars raged in several Central American countries in the 1980s as communism spread in the area. Reagan supported anti-Communist governments in El Salvador and Guatemala with financial aid. Critics of this policy charged that the aid went to military governments that committed major human rights violations.

In Nicaragua, a revolutionary group called the Sandinistas overthrew the country's pro-American dictator in 1979. U.S. leaders became concerned when the Sandinistas formed closer ties with Communist Cuba. Reagan cut all U.S. aid to Nicaragua and began supporting anti-Sandinista rebels known as the Contras. This led to fears that the United States could be drawn into war. In 1984 Congress passed a ban on further U.S. military aid to the Contras.

A group of Reagan administration officials secretly found a way to continue funding the Contras. One member of the group was Oliver North, a marine officer serving as a national security aide. North helped arrange the sale of U.S. missiles to Iran. In exchange, Iran released U.S. hostages that had been taken by Iranian terrorists. Profits from this secret deal were sent to the Contras, in violation of the congressional ban. The so-called **Iran-Contra affair** became a national controversy when it was exposed in 1986. Congressional hearings concluded that President Reagan was not guilty of illegal activity. Several White House officials, however, were convicted of crimes related to the affair.

The United States provided military aid to the Contras in Nicaragua.

GEOGRAPHY SKILLS **INTERPRETING MAPS**

1. **Location** In which two countries did the United States intervene in 1983?
2. **Human-Environment Interaction** Why might the United States have intervened in the countries it did?

An Easing of Tensions

President Reagan and his wife Nancy developed a friendship with Mikhail Gorbachev and his wife Raisa that symbolized the easing of Cold War tensions between their countries. Gorbachev's policies helped greatly to bring about this change in foreign affairs.

How did the friendship between the Reagans and the Gorbachevs help unite the two countries?

Reagan and Gorbachev

During his first term, President Reagan took a tough stand against the Soviet Union. He halted arms negotiations and quickly expanded the U.S. military.

The Soviet Union tried to keep up with American spending in the arms race. This contributed to desperate economic times in the Soviet Union during the 1980s. In 1985 **Mikhail Gorbachev** became the new Soviet leader. To deal with his country's economic problems, he began a process of political and economic reforms called *perestroika*. He also adopted a new policy of political openness called *glasnost*. The newfound freedoms introduced by Gorbachev's policies threatened other leaders of the Soviet Union but were mostly supported by its citizens and by leaders in the West.

Reagan became convinced of Gorbachev's desire for change. In 1987 the two leaders signed the Intermediate-Range Nuclear Forces Treaty, eliminating all medium-range nuclear weapons in Europe. Cold War tensions were decreasing for the first time since the early 1970s.

READING CHECK **Identifying Cause and Effect** Why did President Reagan change his tough stand toward the Soviet Union?

SUMMARY AND PREVIEW Conservative ideas influenced many of Ronald Reagan's policies. In the next chapter, you will learn about the policies of presidents in the 1990s.

Section 3 Assessment

go.hrw.com
Online Quiz
KEYWORD: SC7 HP30

Reviewing Ideas, Terms, and People

1. a. **Recall** What was **Ronald Reagan**'s view of government?
   b. **Analyze** Why did the federal budget deficit rise during Reagan's presidency?
   c. **Draw Conclusions** Why do you think so many Americans voted for Reagan in the 1984 election?
2. a. **Recall** What changes did **Mikhail Gorbachev** make in the Soviet Union?
   b. **Explain** How did Reagan administration officials violate the law in the **Iran-Contra affair**?
   c. **Predict** Do you think Reagan's policies were effective in fighting communism?

Critical Thinking

3. **Categorizing** Review your notes on Ronald Reagan's domestic and foreign policies. Then copy the graphic organizer below and use it to list each policy with its correct geographic focus.

United States	Central America	Soviet Union

FOCUS ON WRITING

4. **Describing Characters** How would you describe President Reagan's approach to government? What major decisions did he make during his presidency? How did these decisions influence government, politics, and foreign relations? Make notes on what you will use in your historical novel.

BIOGRAPHY

Ronald Reagan

How would you lead your country during the Cold War?

When did he live? 1911–2004

Where did he live? Ronald Reagan grew up in Illinois. In 1937 he moved to California, where he became a well-known movie actor. He later entered politics and was elected governor of California. After serving eight years as president, he retired to his California ranch.

What did he do? Reagan worked to reshape the American government and economy based on conservative principles. In foreign policy, he took an aggressive stand toward communism and the Soviet Union. In a famous speech at the Berlin Wall, he challenged the Soviet leader to allow freedom in Eastern Europe, saying, “Mr. Gorbachev, open this gate! Mr. Gorbachev, tear down this wall!” Reagan and Gorbachev later signed the Intermediate-Range Nuclear Forces (INF) Treaty, the first treaty reducing the number of nuclear weapons held by both countries.

Why is he so important? Nicknamed “the Great Communicator,” Reagan inspired many Americans with his sense of humor and his optimistic view of America’s future. Many voters credited him with restoring their confidence after the difficulties of the 1970s. Reagan’s buildup of the U.S. military is believed by many to have contributed to major changes in the Cold War and the eventual fall of Communist governments in the Soviet Union and Eastern Europe.

Finding Main Ideas What was Reagan’s biggest foreign policy achievement? Use evidence from the reading to support your answer.

KEY EVENTS

1937
Becomes a movie actor

1952
Marries his second wife, Nancy Davis

1966
Elected governor of California

1980
Elected president

1981
Shot by John Hinckley Jr.

1984
Elected to second term

1987
Signs INF Treaty

2004
Dies in California

Ronald Reagan used his California ranch as a retreat during his years in the White House.

Social Studies Skills

Analysis | **Critical Thinking** | Civic Participation | Study

North Carolina Skills
4.03 Recognize and analyze values upon which judgements are made.

Determining the Strength of an Argument

Define the Skill

Studying history often involves learning about different opinions. In order to understand these opinions, it is important to recognize strong arguments. Strong arguments are based on convincing supporting evidence. Examples and points should be true and should make sense in the context of the argument. For example, supporting points should relate to the main idea of the argument. It is also important to consider any evidence against the argument.

Many people in the past have made decisions based on the strength of an argument. Determining the strength of an argument is important for the present as well. Your judgments can help you decide whether or not to support a policy, idea, or candidate.

During the 1970s, Americans had to determine the strength of arguments during the Watergate scandal. If Nixon had not resigned, for example, members of the House of Representatives would have had to decide whether or not to vote to impeach the president. They would have had to weigh the evidence and determine the strength of arguments for and against him.

Learn the Skill

In *Silent Spring,* Rachel Carson argued that environmental pollution was harmful and had to be stopped. Here is part of her argument:

> "Man, however much he may like to pretend the contrary, is part of nature. Can he escape a pollution that is now so thoroughly distributed throughout our world?"

How strong is Carson's argument? In *Silent Spring,* she gives many examples of the harmful effects of pollutants and insect poisons. This makes her argument stronger. In the quotation above, Carson points out that humans rely upon nature. As nature becomes polluted, she argues, humans will not be able to avoid the harmful health effects of that pollution.

Carson's argument was strong enough to convince the American people and Congress to take action. The environmental movement grew, and new laws were passed to protect the nation's air and water.

Practice the Skill

Suppose that you are a member of Congress during the Watergate scandal. You have to decide whether or not to impeach President Nixon. Your decision will depend on the strength of the arguments in favor of impeachment. Review the chapter and answer the following questions to help determine the strength of those arguments.

1. What is the evidence against President Nixon? How does this evidence strengthen or weaken the case against him?
2. Is there any evidence that President Nixon is innocent? How strong is this evidence?
3. Would you vote to impeach the president? Explain your answer.

CHAPTER 30 Chapter Review

HOLT

History's Impact

▶ **video series**

Review the video to answer the closing question:

How did the Supreme Court contribute to the series of checks and balances that eventually led to President Nixon's resignation?

Visual Summary

QUICK FACTS

Use the visual summary below to help you review the main ideas of the chapter.

Positives and Negatives of the Presidencies

Richard Nixon

Positive: Nixon brought China and the United States together diplomatically.

Negative: His administration ended because of the Watergate scandal.

Jimmy Carter

Positive: Carter helped create the Camp David Accords.

Negative: He also faced the Iran hostage crisis.

Ronald Reagan

Positive: Reagan signed a major arms treaty with several countries.

Negative: His administration was linked to the Iran-Contra affair.

Reviewing Vocabulary, Terms, and People

Read each question and write the letter of the best response.

1. Which of the following refers to a period of less hostile U.S.–Soviet relations in the 1970s?

a. détente **c.** realpolitik

b. stagflation **d.** *perestroika*

2. The South African government's system of official racial segregation was known as

a. Title IX. **c.** sanctions.

b. the ERA. **d.** apartheid.

3. Which of the following was a theory that influenced President Reagan's policies?

a. Whip Inflation Now **c.** SALT

b. supply-side economics **d.** *glasnost*

Comprehension and Critical Thinking

SECTION 1 *(Pages 926–931)*

4. a. Identify Who were the reporters who uncovered the Watergate scandal?

b. Analyze What were some results of Nixon's visit to China?

c. Elaborate Why do you think Nixon called his supporters the Silent Majority?

SECTION 2 *(Pages 932–936)*

5. a. Recall What happened at Three Mile Island?

b. Contrast How were the foreign policies of Nixon and Carter different?

c. Draw Conclusions Why do you think many Americans responded to *Silent Spring*?

SECTION 3 *(Pages 937–940)*

6. a. **Describe** What happened in the election of 1980?

   b. **Summarize** What were some results of Reagan's conservative policies?

   c. **Evaluate** Do you think Congress was right to ban aid to the Contras in Nicaragua?

Reviewing Themes

7. **Economics** How did the energy crisis affect the economy of the United States?
8. **Politics** How did the politics of the presidents discussed in this chapter affect the foreign policy of the United States?

Reading Skills

Summarizing *Use the Reading Skills taught in this chapter to answer the question below.*

Carter also experienced disaster in the Middle East. Since the 1950s, the United States had supported the pro–American shah, or king, of Iran. Many Iranians resented the shah's reform efforts and the country's shift from a traditional and agricultural society to a more urban and industrial one. The government severely punished its opponents and controlled all political participation. Many members of the opposition supported the views of Islamic spiritual leader Ruhollah Khomeini, who had been forced to leave the country because of his criticisms of the shah's policies. In 1979 Khomeini's supporters drove the shah out of Iran, and a month later, Khomeini took control of the government. On November 4, a group of Iranian students attacked the U.S. embassy in Tehran, the capital of Iran, seizing about 90 American hostages. The Iran hostage crisis lasted for more than a year. *(p. 935–936)*

9. Summarize the beginning of the Iran hostage crisis in three sentences.

Using the Internet

go.hrw.com
KEYWORD: SC7 CH30

10. **Activity: Making Connections** The cost of oil rose steadily in the early 1970s, and it reached a new high after OPEC nations placed an embargo on oil exports to the United States. Americans felt the impact as costs increased for all products that were made from oil, and the already weakened U.S. economy struggled to survive. Enter the activity keyword. Research the causes, effects, results, and connections between the Yom Kippur War and the OPEC oil embargo. Create a model or diagram to illustrate your research. You should label your model or diagram and be prepared to explain it to the class.

Social Studies Skills

Determining the Strength of an Argument *Use the Social Studies Skills taught in this chapter to answer the question about the selection below.*

In this chapter, you have read about the Supreme Court case *United States v. Nixon.* Nixon argued that executive privilege, a president's right to keep information secret for reasons of national security, protected him from having to give up tapes of his official conversations.

11. In your opinion, how strong was Nixon's argument?

FOCUS ON WRITING

12. **Writing Your Historical Novel** Review your notes about important events and people from the 1970s and 1980s. Choose a subject that you would like to focus on in your novel. Think about the main events you will describe and main characters your story will include. Then write the first page of your novel. Be sure to describe where and when your story is taking place. Since this is a novel, you should feel free to write dialogue for historical figures who appear in your story.

CHAPTER 30

Standardized Test Practice

DIRECTIONS: Read each question and write the letter of the best response.

1 The Camp David Accords were

A secret deals supplying Iran with weapons and the Nicaraguan Contras with money.

B the negotiations that ended the Iran hostage crisis.

C U.S.–Soviet nuclear arms reduction treaties.

D a set of peace agreements between Israel and Egypt.

2 Which of the following was a result of Reagan's economic plan?

A The deficit decreased.

B Tax rates were lowered.

C Military spending was cut.

D Unemployment and inflation rose.

3 Which president participated in the 1972 Strategic Arms Limitation Talks?

A Gerald Ford

B Richard Nixon

C Ronald Reagan

D Jimmy Carter

4 The *main* job of the Environmental Protection Agency is to

A enforce the laws that help protect air and water quality.

B raise environmental awareness through Earth Day celebrations.

C negotiate arms-control agreements.

D prevent inflation and unemployment.

5 What was one aspect of Reagan's tough stance against communism?

A He dramatically increased military spending.

B He made peace agreements in the Middle East.

C He visited and established diplomatic relations with China.

D He focused on human rights.

6 How did the state constitution of 1971 change government in North Carolina?

A It allowed the direct election of the governor.

B It streamlined government by combining many state agencies.

C It eliminated restrictions on property ownership.

D It instituted a state income tax.

7 How were Nixon's and Reagan's influences on the Supreme Court similar?

A Both tried to give the Supreme Court more power.

B Both denied the authority of the Supreme Court to issue subpoenas.

C Both appointed women as Supreme Court justices.

D Both appointed conservative Supreme Court justices.

8 *Stagflation* refers to the unusual economic condition of

A high oil prices but low inflation.

B stagnant economic growth and high inflation.

C low unemployment and low inflation.

D stagnant deficits and falling exports.

9 Read the following quote from a U.S. senator urging Nixon's impeachment and use it to answer the question below.

> "What the president has done threatens to destroy our system of law. It smacks of dictatorship. Unless Congress responds in the only way provided in the Constitution for resisting such a usurpation [stealing] of authority, we endanger our country's future."
>
> —Senator Edmund S. Muskie, quoted in the *Washington Post*, October 21, 1973

Document-Based Question **Why did Muskie feel Nixon should be impeached?**

CHAPTER 31 1988–PRESENT

America Looks to the Future

North Carolina Standards

Social Studies Objectives

8.01 Describe the changing demographics in North Carolina and analyze their significance for North Carolina's society and economy.

8.02 List economic and technological advances occurring in North Carolina since 1970, and assess their influence on North Carolina's role in the nation and the world.

8.03 Describe the impact of state and national issues on the political climate of North Carolina.

8.04 Assess the importance of regional diversity on the development of economic, social, and political institutions in North Carolina.

9.01 Describe contemporary political, economic, and social issues at the state and local levels and evaluate their impact on the community.

9.02 Identify past and present state and local leaders from diverse cultural backgrounds and assess their influence in effecting change.

Language Arts Objectives

4.03 Use the stance of a critic to:
- consider alternative points of view or reasons.
- remain fair-minded and open to other interpretations.
- constructing a critical response/review of a work/topic.

go.hrw.com
North Carolina
KEYWORD: SC7 NC

FOCUS ON WRITING

Web Site The popularity of the Internet dramatically increased in the 1990s, changing the way we communicate and share information. The attacks of September 11, 2001, made terrorism a major concern for Americans. In this chapter you will learn about these and other important events that have taken place in your lifetime. Then you will write the text for a Web site about late twentieth century and early twenty-first century America.

UNITED STATES

1988 George H. W. Bush is elected president.

1980

WORLD

1989 Most of the Berlin Wall is dismantled.

HOLT

History's Impact

▶ **video series**

Watch the video to understand the impact of government in our daily lives.

What You Will Learn...

Young people like those pictured here are helping to shape the future of the United States. In this chapter, you will read about the amazing events that have changed our world in recent years. From the end of the Cold War to the rising terrorist threat and the development of new technology, life in the United States has been changing quickly. Today Americans are working together to face new challenges and take advantage of new opportunities.

1990 U.S. and UN forces liberate Kuwait from Iraqi control in the Persian Gulf War.

1995 Extremists bomb a federal building in Oklahoma.

2001 Terrorists attack the World Trade Center and the Pentagon on September 11.

2005 The Cassini-Huygens Mission photographs Saturn's moon Titan.

1990 — **2000** — **PRESENT**

1991 Nelson Mandela is elected president of South Africa.

1997 Hong Kong returns to Chinese control.

2005 Pope John Paul II dies.

Reading Social Studies

by Kylene Beers

Economics | Geography | Politics | Society and Culture | Science and Technology

Focus on Themes In this chapter, you will read about the most recent presidents and their administrations. You will learn about the changing role the United States has gained in global **politics** and the global **economy.** You will also read about September 11, 2001, and learn how that tragedy helped shape the world you live in today.

Predicting

Focus on Reading Often when you are reading, predicting what might come next can help you understand what is happening in the story of history.

Understanding Summarizing Predicting what may come next in the logical progression of a story relies on understanding what has happened in the past. You have learned many different responses to crises that have occurred throughout U.S. history. You can use this knowledge to predict what may come in the future.

Notice how one reader uses information from the past to predict what may happen

In October 2001 the United States began air strikes on Taliban targets and al Qaeda bases in Afghanistan. By December U.S. forces had driven the Taliban from power. Many of al Qaeda's members were captured, though Osama bin Laden remained at large. The United States began helping Afghanistan in the long and difficult process of establishing a democratic government and rebuilding the nation.

Most Americans supported the use of force in Afghanistan. Disagreement soon arose, however, about how best to move forward in the war against terrorism.

From Chapter 31, p. 957

After reading this section, one reader thought:

I have read about other wars in which the American public was divided over the action the country should take. In the War of 1812, there was a convention of delegates opposed to the war. During the Civil War, President Lincoln silenced antiwar Democrats by imprisoning them. In the 1960s and 1970s, many citizens publicly protested the Vietnam War, while others supported the war. What happened in these past wars that might happen in the war against terrorism?

You Try It!

The following passage is from the chapter you are getting ready to read. As you read the passage, look for the facts that can help you predict what might happen in the future.

> The Internet was first developed in 1969 by scientists at the U.S. Department of Defense. Early computer networks were used mainly by government and university researchers. Then, in the 1990s, computer programmers developed the World Wide Web, enabling people to access information from computers around the world. Internet use exploded in the 1990s. Computers and the Internet made it easier and faster for people at home, work, and school to access and share information. This important development was known as the Information Revolution.

From Chapter 31, p. 961

After you read the passage, answer the following questions.

1. What other revolutions have you read about in the study of American history, and how have they affected American society?

2. Is the Information Revolution similar to any other revolution you have read about?

3. How might the Information Revolution affect American society in the future?

As you read Chapter 31, use the information given to predict what may happen in American society in the next 10 years.

Key Terms and People

Chapter 31

Section 1

George H. W. Bush *(p. 950)*
Saddam Hussein *(p. 951)*
Operation Desert Storm *(p. 951)*
Colin Powell *(p. 951)*
Bill Clinton *(p. 952)*
North American Free Trade Agreement *(p. 952)*
Madeleine Albright *(p. 953)*
terrorism *(p. 953)*

Section 2

Al Gore *(p. 954)*
George W. Bush *(p. 954)*
World Trade Center *(p. 956)*
Pentagon *(p. 956)*
al Qaeda *(p. 956)*
Osama bin Laden *(p. 956)*
weapons of mass destruction *(p. 957)*

Section 3

service economy *(p. 960)*
globalization *(p. 960)*
Internet *(p. 961)*
Information Revolution *(p. 961)*
AIDS *(p. 961)*
ozone layer *(p. 962)*
global warming *(p. 962)*

Academic Vocabulary

In this chapter, you will learn the following academic words:

facilitate *(p. 961)*
ideals *(p. 963)*

SECTION 1

The End of the Twentieth Century

What You Will Learn...

Main Ideas

1. Major global changes took place during the presidency of George H. W. Bush.
2. During Bill Clinton's presidency, the nation experienced scandal, economic growth, and the rise of terrorist threats.

The Big Idea

The United States and the world faced many new challenges at the end of the 20th century.

Key Terms and People

George H. W. Bush, *p. 950*
Saddam Hussein, *p. 951*
Operation Desert Storm, *p. 951*
Colin Powell, *p. 951*
Bill Clinton, *p. 952*
North American Free Trade Agreement, *p. 952*
Madeleine Albright, *p. 953*
terrorism, *p. 953*

TAKING NOTES As you read, look for information about key events that happened during the presidencies of George H. W. Bush and Bill Clinton. Use a diagram like the one below to help you organize your notes.

Bush	Clinton

If YOU were there...

You are visiting the city of West Berlin in 1989. Just after midnight on November 9, you see huge crowds of people pouring into the streets to celebrate. You rush outside to find out what's going on. "The wall is falling!" people shout. You run toward the Berlin Wall, and there you see East and West Germans working together to rip down the hated wall.

What might the fall of the Berlin Wall mean for the future?

BUILDING BACKGROUND Mikhail Gorbachev began a process of political and economic reforms in the Soviet Union in the late 1980s. Encouraged by these changes, people from many Eastern European countries continued to demand change as well. They were eager to break free from Soviet domination and establish their own democratic governments.

George H. W. Bush

Ronald Reagan was popular with a majority of voters as his second term as president came to an end. Republicans hoped this would help Reagan's vice president, **George H. W. Bush**, win the election of 1988. Bush's Democratic opponent was Massachusetts governor Michael Dukakis. After a hard-fought campaign, Bush won the election with 426 electoral votes to Dukakis's 111.

The Cold War Ends

As Bush began his presidency, Mikhail Gorbachev continued his reform programs in the Soviet Union. In the Soviet-controlled states of Eastern Europe, people demanded even faster change and more freedom. Prodemocracy movements in Hungary, Poland, and other nations put increasing pressure on Communist governments. This pressure produced world-changing results in 1989, as pro-Soviet governments across Eastern Europe began to fall.

In October 1989 massive protests in East Germany lead to the resignation of Communist leader Erich Honecker. The new government agreed to open the borders of East Germany—including the border guarded by the Berlin Wall. At midnight on November 9, a wild celebration broke out as East and West Berliners jumped onto the Berlin Wall, shouting and dancing. Some smashed through parts of the wall with hammers and chisels. The wall, which had stood as a symbol of the Cold War since 1961, began crumbling to the ground. Within a year, the two Germanys reunited as one democratic country.

Several Soviet republics soon declared independence from the Soviet regime. In a desperate attempt to hold on to power, hard-line Communists took Gorbachev hostage and tried to seize the government. Thousands of Soviets took to the streets in protest. Ignoring orders to stop the protesters, many soldiers joined the crowds. Prodemocracy leader Boris Yeltsin encouraged the protesters to stand strong. The Soviet Union soon broke apart, confirming the end of the Cold War.

GEOGRAPHY SKILLS **INTERPRETING MAPS**

1. **Place** Where did Iraqi forces invade?
2. **Location** From which country did UN ground forces attack Iraq?

The Persian Gulf War

President Bush called for all countries to work together, especially during times of crisis. A major crisis soon developed in the Middle East. In August 1990 Iraq's dictator, **Saddam Hussein**, invaded neighboring oil-rich Kuwait.

Members of the United Nations called for the immediate withdrawal of Iraqi troops. President Bush, with strong public support, began assembling a coalition of nations to drive Iraq from Kuwait by force.

When Saddam refused to withdraw from Kuwait, a U.S.-led multinational coalition launched **Operation Desert Storm**. This air offensive was led by U.S. generals Norman Schwarzkopf and **Colin Powell**—chair of the joint chiefs of staff and the highest-ranking African American ever to serve in the U.S. military. After a six-week bombing campaign, ground forces entered Kuwait. Within days, Iraq agreed to a cease-fire.

About 22,300 Iraqi soldiers and civilians were killed in the Persian Gulf War. The coalition forces lost around 223 soldiers, 148 of whom were American. More than 35,000 American women served in the war, though federal laws prevented them from serving in combat.

President Bush explained the importance of the war, telling Congress:

> "Now, we can see a new world coming into view. A world in which there is the very real prospect of a new world order . . . A world in which freedom and respect for human rights find a home among all nations."
>
> —George H. W. Bush, March 6, 1991

READING CHECK **Summarizing** How did the world change between 1989 and 1991?

Clinton's Presidency

An overwhelming majority of Americans supported President Bush's handling of the Gulf War. By the time of the 1992 election, however, the struggling U.S. economy had become a more important issue for most voters. The Democratic nominee, Arkansas governor **Bill Clinton**, told voters he would focus on improving the economy. Clinton won a three-way race against Bush and H. Ross Perot, who ran as an independent candidate.

THE IMPACT TODAY

In 2005 Congress approved a similar accord with the Central American countries of Costa Rica, El Salvador, Guatemala, Honduras, and Nicaragua. The treaty is known as CAFTA.

Clinton and Congress

Under President Clinton's leadership, Congress passed a budget designed to reduce the deficit by cutting spending and raising taxes. He also convinced Congress to support the **North American Free Trade Agreement** (NAFTA), which eliminated trade barriers between the United States, Canada, and Mexico.

In the 1994 congressional elections, House minority leader Newt Gingrich of Georgia helped lead Republicans to an important victory. Gingrich and other Republicans promoted a set of policies called the Contract with America, promising lower taxes and smaller government. Republicans gained control of both houses of Congress for the first time since 1952.

A growing economy helped Clinton win a second term in 1996 over Senator Bob Dole of Kansas. By 1998 the U.S. government was taking in more money than it was spending. Clinton's second term, however, was dominated by questions about his personal and official conduct. Government investigators charged that the president had conducted an improper relationship with a White House intern and then lied about it under oath. In 1998 the House of Representatives voted to impeach Clinton for obstruction of justice. The Senate acquitted him of the charges in 1999. The scandal damaged Clinton's public image, though his approval ratings remained high, due in part to the booming economy.

Primary Source

POINTS OF VIEW

NAFTA

Just before Congress voted on NAFTA in 1993, Vice President Al Gore and former presidential candidate H. Ross Perot debated the controversial issue on national television.

"If we keep shifting our manufacturing jobs across the border [to Mexico] and around the world and deindustrializing our country, we will not be able to defend this great country, and that is a risk we will never take."

—H. Ross Perot

"Everything that he [Perot] is worried about will get worse if NAFTA is defeated. We want jobs for America's working men and women. We want to get rid of the barriers that have prevented us from selling what we make in other countries. This is an historic opportunity to do that."

—Al Gore

ANALYSIS SKILL **ANALYZING POINTS OF VIEW**

According to Perot, how would NAFTA affect the United States? Why does Gore disagree?

A Dangerous World

The collapse of the Soviet Union left the United States as the world's only superpower. In 1997 President Clinton appointed **Madeleine Albright** as the first woman to be secretary of state. Albright had been born in Prague before her family moved to the United States, fleeing the Holocaust. She helped adapt U.S. foreign policy to this complex new world.

The United States worked to protect global peace and democracy. In the Balkan region of Europe, for example, the former nation of Yugoslavia broke apart. Different ethnic and religious groups fought for control of territory. U.S. diplomats helped negotiate an end to the bloody war. President Clinton then sent 20,000 U.S. troops to the region to help maintain peace.

In the 1990s **terrorism**—the use of violence by individuals or small groups to advance political goals—became a major issue. In April 1995 American terrorists bombed the Alfred P. Murrah Federal Building in Oklahoma City, killing 168 people. The United States also faced increasingly deadly attacks by extremist Islamic groups. Hundreds were killed in bomb attacks on U.S. embassies in Africa in 1998.

BIOGRAPHY

Bill Clinton

1946–

Bill Clinton was born in Hope, Arkansas. As a teenager he met and shook hands with President John Kennedy—an experience that heightened his interest in becoming a politician. He became a Rhodes scholar at Oxford after graduating from college. After graduating from Yale Law School, Clinton returned to Arkansas and was elected governor in 1978. He lost his bid for reelection in 1980 but ran again in 1982 and won, serving 10 more years as governor. Clinton was elected president in 1992 and reelected in 1996. The country experienced the longest period of continued economic growth during his presidency. In 1998, however, Clinton became only the second president in U.S. history to be impeached.

Drawing Conclusions Why might meeting President Kennedy have influenced Clinton?

READING CHECK **Identifying Cause and Effect** How did the end of the Cold War change the U.S. role in the world?

SUMMARY AND PREVIEW The Cold War ended in 1990. In the next section you will learn about new world challenges.

Section 1 Assessment

go.hrw.com
Online Quiz
KEYWORD: SC7 HP31

Reviewing Ideas, Terms, and People

1. a. **Summarize** What were some of the major world events during **George H. W. Bush**'s presidency?
   b. **Identify** What was the purpose of **Operation Desert Storm**?
   c. **Evaluate** How did the Persian Gulf War test President Bush's vision of a new world order?
2. a. **Recall** What were some of the high points and low points of **Bill Clinton**'s presidency?
   b. **Contrast** How is **terrorism** different from standard warfare?
   c. **Elaborate** Do you think Congress was right to pass the **North American Free Trade Agreement**? Explain your answer.

Critical Thinking

3. **Sequencing** Review your notes on the presidencies of George H. W. Bush and Bill Clinton. Then copy the graphic organizer below and use it to identify major events and the year they occurred.

Year	Event

FOCUS ON WRITING

4. **Identifying Important Figures** Take notes on the main people in the chapter. Identify why each of these people was important. In what major events was each person involved? How did he or she affect the United States?

SECTION 2

George W. Bush in Office

What You Will Learn...

Main Ideas

1. George W. Bush won the disputed 2000 presidential election.
2. Americans debated the future of the War on Terror that began after terrorists attacked the United States.
3. The nation faced difficult challenges during President Bush's second term.

The Big Idea

George W. Bush led the country in response to terrorist attacks and through domestic challenges.

Key Terms and People

Al Gore, *p. 954*
George W. Bush, *p. 954*
World Trade Center, *p. 956*
Pentagon, *p. 956*
al Qaeda, *p. 956*
Osama bin Laden, *p. 956*
weapons of mass destruction, *p. 957*

TAKING NOTES As you read, take notes on the major policies of George W. Bush. Use a diagram like the one below. You may need to add more circles.

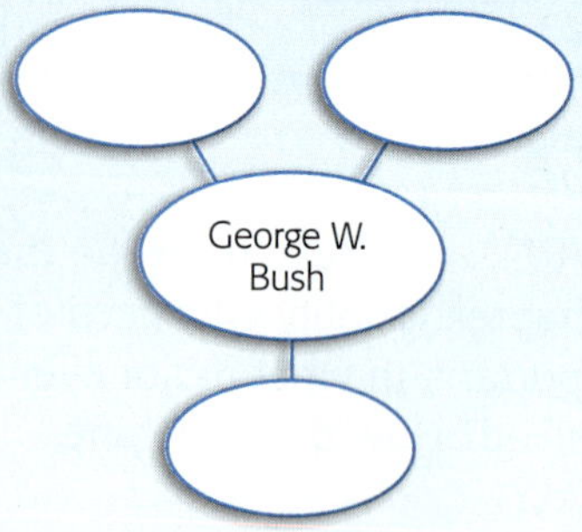

If YOU were there...

It is the December after the presidential election between George W. Bush and Al Gore. For weeks, people have been talking about whether the votes can be recounted by hand. The race was too close to call on election night, and now the candidates are involved in a court case that will decide who the next president will be.

How would you solve the problem of recounting votes?

BUILDING BACKGROUND In the 1990s extremist Islamic groups in the Middle East vowed to attack the United States. They carried out deadly attacks on U.S. embassies in Africa and against the ship the USS *Cole*. Terrorism was not a major issue in the 2000 presidential election, but it would soon begin to dominate American politics.

The 2000 Presidential Election

The United States was at peace and enjoying economic prosperity as the 2000 presidential election neared. The Democrats chose **Al Gore**, who had served as Bill Clinton's vice president, as their nominee. The Republican candidate was Texas governor **George W. Bush**, the son of former president George H. W. Bush.

Campaign Issues

One major campaign issue was how to use the federal budget surplus, which totaled nearly $100 billion in 1999. Gore said he would use the money for education and health care and to pay off a part of the national debt. Bush promised to return the money to taxpayers in the form of tax cuts. Bush and Gore also debated the role that the United States—now the world's only superpower—should play in global affairs. Campaign polls showed that the race was very close.

On election night, the voting in some states was so close that no winner could be declared. It soon became clear that Florida's 25 electoral votes would determine the outcome of the election. The popular vote

The Election of 2000

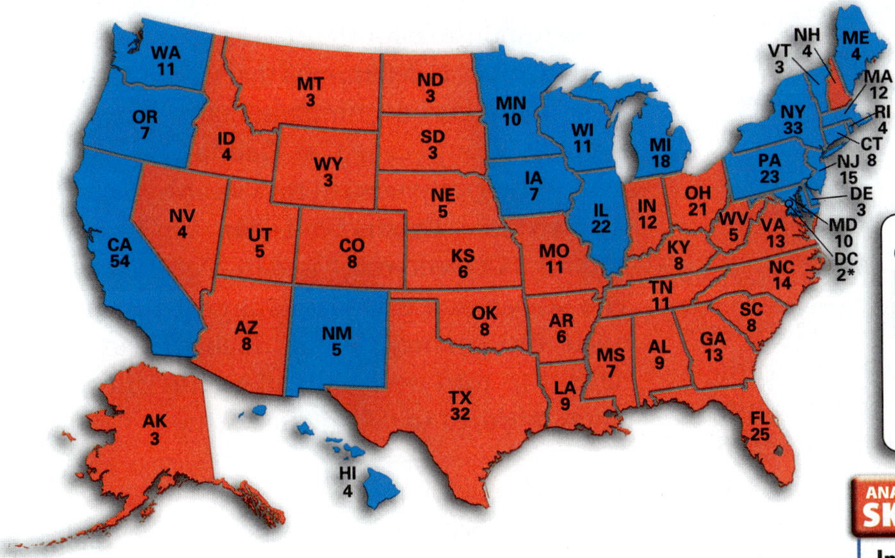

George W. Bush

Al Gore

Candidate	Party	Electoral Vote	Popular Vote	% Popular Vote
Bush	Republican	271	50,459,211	47.89
Gore	Democrat	266	51,003,894	48.41
Nader	Green		2,834,410	2.69
Other			1,062,745	1.01

*One elector from the District of Columbia abstained.

Source: *The World Almanac and Book of Facts*, 2002

ANALYSIS SKILL **INTERPRETING CHARTS**

Interpreting Charts By how many electoral votes did Bush win? How many more popular votes did Gore have than Bush?

in Florida was so close that state law required the votes to be recounted. A machine recount found that Bush had received a few hundred more votes than Gore. But Gore supporters wanted the votes in four counties to be counted by hand, arguing that this would ensure all votes were counted. The Bush campaign challenged this manual recount in court.

After several weeks of suspense, the Supreme Court ruled that the manual recounts could not ensure that all votes would be counted the same way. They ordered the recount to stop. Florida's electoral votes went to Bush, making him the winner of the election. He was the first president in more than 100 years to win the electoral vote while receiving fewer popular votes than his opponent.

At his inauguration, President Bush urged Americans to come together.

> "This is my solemn pledge: I will work to build a single nation of justice and opportunity … Today, we affirm a new commitment to live out our nation's promise through civility, courage, compassion, and character."
>
> —George W. Bush, January 20, 2001

Bush's Early Days in Office

The disputed election, however, caused lingering bitterness between Democrats and Republicans. Republicans held a small majority in the House of Representatives, while the Senate was split 50–50. When votes in the Senate are tied, the vice president casts the tie-breaking vote. This gave Vice President Dick Cheney an important role in helping to pass Republican legislation.

Bush put together his cabinet, appointing Colin Powell to the key position of secretary of state. Powell became the first African American to hold this office. Bush carried through with his campaign promise to cut taxes. Six months after taking office, he signed into law a $1.35 trillion tax-cut plan. He also signed into law an education reform plan called No Child Left Behind. This act created a national set of standards for every student and every school to meet. It also raised funding for schools.

READING CHECK **Analyzing** What was unusual about the outcome of the 2000 presidential election?

NC History Makers

Elizabeth Dole
Elizabeth Dole has served the citizens of the United States in numerous positions, including as a U.S. senator from North Carolina.

Fighting Terrorism

Despite many plans for educational and economic reform, President Bush was soon faced with the challenge of confronting terrorism. His administration became focused on developing a foreign policy to protect Americans from the growing threat of terrorist attacks after the events of September 11, 2001.

September 11, 2001

On September 11, 2001, terrorists took control of four commercial airliners, using them as weapons to attack sites in Washington, D.C., and New York City. The hijackers flew an airplane into each of two towers that made up the **World Trade Center**, an important business center in New York City. The resulting fires caused the buildings, which had been the tallest in the United States, to crumble to the ground. About 2,500 people were killed in the collapsing buildings.

Another hijacked airplane was flown into the **Pentagon**—the headquarters of the Department of Defense located outside of Washington, D.C. A fourth hijacked airplane crashed in a Pennsylvania field.

The tragedy brought Americans together, and the nation received support from foreign leaders and citizens. One French newspaper's headline read, "WE ARE ALL AMERICANS." President Bush promised to find and punish those responsible for the attacks.

U.S. officials determined that the hijackers were members of a fundamentalist Islamic terrorist group called **al Qaeda**, or "the Base." The group was led by a wealthy Saudi Arabian exile, **Osama bin Laden**. Bin Laden and his followers were based in Afghanistan. The Taliban, an extreme Islamic government, ruled the country. When Taliban leaders refused to turn over bin Laden, the United States prepared to take military action.

War in Afghanistan

In October 2001 the United States began air strikes in Afghanistan. By December U.S. forces had driven the Taliban from power and captured many of al Qaeda's members. Osama bin Laden remained at large. The United States began helping Afghanistan to rebuild and establish a democratic government.

War in Iraq

Although most Americans supported the use of force in Afghanistan, disagreement arose about how best to move forward in the war against terrorism. President Bush argued that

Time Line

9/11 and Beyond

2001

September 11, 2001 About 3,000 Americans are killed in terrorist attacks on the United States.

October 7, 2001 The war in Afghanistan begins.

November/December 2001 The Taliban regime is driven from power in Afghanistan.

January 2003 The Department of Homeland Security is created to oversee domestic security.

March 20, 2003 The air war in Iraq begins.

Saddam Hussein, the dictator of Iraq, posed the most immediate threat to U.S. security.

When the Persian Gulf War ended in 1991, Saddam had agreed to give up Iraq's **weapons of mass destruction**—chemical, biological, or nuclear weapons that can kill thousands. Saddam agreed to allow United Nations inspectors to enter the country to ensure that these weapons were not being produced. He then refused to cooperate with the inspectors.

Members of the UN Security Council debated how to handle the renewed crisis. Leaders from France, Germany, Russia, and other countries argued that the UN inspectors should be given more time to search for weapons. President Bush and British prime minister Tony Blair insisted that UN inspections alone were not working. They said force should be used to ensure Iraq was complying with the weapons ban.

On March 20, 2003, the United States and a coalition of allies launched a ground attack on Iraq. After just a few weeks of fighting, U.S. forces occupied the Iraqi capital of Baghdad. Saddam's government collapsed, and Saddam was captured in December.

As in Afghanistan, U.S. officials began working with Iraqis to establish a democratic government. Violence continued in Iraq, however. Supporters of Saddam carried out deadly attacks on U.S. soldiers and Iraqis who were working to rebuild the country. Iraqi voters elected new government leaders and approved a new constitution in 2005. Deep divisions among Iraqis remained an issue and threatened the stability of the new government. The violence continued after Saddam was executed by the Iraqi government in 2006.

Debates at Home

The war in Iraq caused fierce debate at home. Supporters of the war argued that removing Saddam from power was a key part of the war on terror. Critics, however, doubted that Saddam had posed a serious threat to the United States. Months of searching uncovered no weapons of mass destruction, and no concrete ties to al Qaeda could be proved.

These were major issues in the presidential election of 2004. The Democratic nominee, Senator John Kerry of Massachusetts, argued that Bush had rushed to war. Bush insisted that the war had made Americans safer and brought freedom to Iraqis. Bush defeated Kerry, with 286 electoral votes to Kerry's 251.

READING CHECK **Summarizing**
What led to the war in Iraq?

NC History Makers

John Edwards
North Carolina Senator John Edwards was the vice-presidential candidate on the 2004 Democratic ticket with John Kerry.

FOCUS ON NORTH CAROLINA

Eastern counties in North Carolina tend to vote Democratic, while western counties favor Republicans. National issues such as the war in Iraq and issues surrounding illegal immigration have created debate between the political parties. State and local issues such as the Education Lottery have divided the parties as well.

December 13, 2003 Saddam Hussein is captured.

October 9, 2004 Afghanistan holds elections for a new government.

2005

October 29, 2004 Osama bin Laden, still at large, releases a videotaped message criticizing and threatening the United States.

January 30, 2005 Iraqis choose new leaders in a democratic election. Violence continues.

July 2005 Suicide bombers attack the mass transit system in London.

ANALYSIS SKILL **READING TIME LINES**

How long did it take American forces to capture Saddam Hussein after the war in Iraq began?

BIOGRAPHY

George W. Bush

1946–

George W. Bush was born in Connecticut and grew up mainly in Texas. His family has a long history of political success—his grandfather was a U.S. senator and his father served as president from 1989 to 1993. Bush was a member of the National Guard during the Vietnam War, then attended Harvard Business School. After running unsuccessfully for Congress in 1978, he started several oil businesses in Texas and became part owner of the Texas Rangers baseball team. He was elected governor of Texas in 1994 and re-elected in 1998. In 2000 he defeated Al Gore in one of the closest presidential races in American history.

Sequencing What did George W. Bush do before he was elected president?

Domestic Issues

After the 2004 election Secretary of State Colin Powell resigned. Bush appointed Condoleezza Rice as his replacement. She became the first African American woman to hold the office. Bush's other new cabinet appointees included Alberto Gonzales, the first Hispanic attorney general. After the resignation of Supreme Court Justice Sandra Day O'Connor and the death of Chief Justice William Rehnquist in 2005, Bush nominated two new justices to the Supreme Court. John Roberts replaced Rehnquist as chief justice. In January 2006 Samuel Alito was approved by the Senate to replace O'Connor.

Bush's administration faced major domestic challenges when Hurricane Katrina hit the Gulf Coast in August 2005. Hardest hit was New Orleans, where thousands of residents who weathered the storm in the city were left with few or no resources and no way to evacuate. Many people criticized the local, state, and federal governments for what they believed was an inadequate response to the crisis. As the disaster unfolded, the Bush administration worked to step up the response to the states hardest hit by the disaster.

READING CHECK **Analyzing** What issues did Bush face in his second term?

SUMMARY AND PREVIEW Terrorism became a major concern after September 11, 2001. In the next section you will learn about other debates in America today.

Section 2 Assessment

go.hrw.com
Online Quiz
KEYWORD: SC7 HP31

Reviewing Ideas, Terms, and People

1. a. **Describe** What was the outcome of the 2000 presidential election?
   b. **Explain** How did **George W. Bush** promise to use the government surplus?
   c. **Elaborate** How do you think the election of 2000 shows the importance of voting?
2. a. **Identify** What is al Qaeda?
   b. **Explain** Why did the United States enter into the war with Iraq?
   c. **Predict** What do you think the future holds for the war on terror?
3. a. **Recall** Who is Condoleezza Rice?
   b. **Interpret** How might Hurricane Katrina have affected people's view of government?

Critical Thinking

4. **Categorizing** Review your notes on the major policies of George W. Bush. Then copy the graphic organizer below and use it to describe George W. Bush's approach to dealing with terrorism.

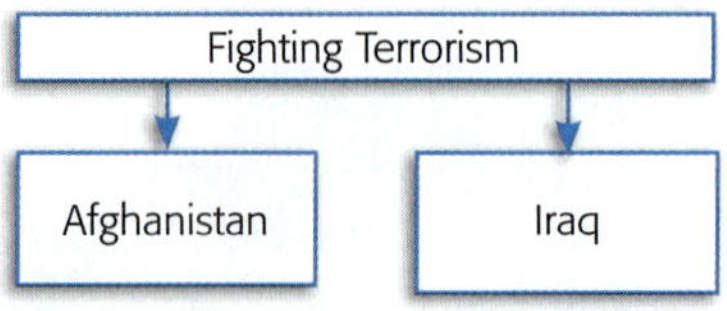

FOCUS ON WRITING

5. **Describing the Effects of September 11** Take notes on the effects of the September 11, 2001, terrorist attacks. What are your own memories of that day? How did Americans respond to the attacks? How did the attacks change the focus of the American people? How did they affect the presidency of George W. Bush?

The Road Ahead

SECTION 3

If YOU were there...

You are a student studying American history. You have read about the dramatic impact that inventions, new industries, political changes, and wars have had on daily life over the years. In your own life, you have seen how much things can change in just a few years. Now picture yourself living in the United States 50 years from now.

What will be different about life in America?

BUILDING BACKGROUND Think of the challenges Americans have faced throughout our history. Consider how much the country has changed since it was founded and how much progress has been made. Today the United States continues to face challenges and to search for solutions.

What You Will Learn...

Main Ideas

1. The American economy and job market are changing.
2. Technological advances continue to solve everyday problems.
3. Americans are a diverse people united by shared ideals.

The Big Idea

The United States continues to grow and change as we move ahead in the twenty-first century.

Key Terms and People

service economy, *p. 960*
globalization, *p. 960*
Internet, *p. 961*
Information Revolution, *p. 961*
AIDS, *p. 961*
ozone layer, *p. 962*
global warming, *p. 962*

TAKING NOTES As you read, look for information about changes taking place in the United States. Use a diagram like the one below to help you organize your notes.

Changes		
Economy	Technology	Population

America's Changing Economy

In public opinion polls taken in 2005, Americans listed terrorism and the continuing violence in Iraq among the most important challenges facing the United States. Other major concerns included the economy and the availability of jobs, health care costs, education, immigration, and the environment. The growing national debt was another key concern. After several years of surpluses, the government began running a deficit again in 2002. Slow economic growth, the cost of the war in Iraq, and tax cuts all contributed to the rising budget imbalance.

The American economy and job market have also experienced important ups and downs in recent years. During the 1990s the United States enjoyed the longest period of economic growth in its history. The stock market boomed, and unemployment fell to its lowest level in 30 years. Much of this economic growth was powered by Internet companies and other high-tech firms. When some high-tech firms failed to earn profits, however, their stocks lost value, and many went out of business. Unemployment began rising again. North Carolina was hit by the decline of the high-tech industry, and leaders looked at ways to diversify the economy. Charlotte has meanwhile become the second-largest banking center in the nation.

Although high-tech industries have remained a key part of the U.S. economy, other industries have declined in importance. In recent years, for example, many textile companies have closed mills and shifted their operations to countries where labor is less expensive. This is part of a larger trend in which the percentage of Americans working in manufacturing has steadily fallen. The U.S. economy has moved toward becoming a **service economy**. This means that most people have jobs providing services, such as medical care or entertainment, rather than producing goods.

By the end of the 1900s, about 75 percent of American workers were employed in service jobs. Economists predict that service industries will continue to grow in the 2000s. Health care, computer engineering, and education are expected to be among the fastest-growing fields. Such predictions are based partly on population trends. As the number of older Americans increases, for example, so will the need for nurses and other health-care professionals.

Another ongoing change in our economy is the process of **globalization**—growing connections among economies and cultures all over the world. Multinational corporations—companies that do business in more than one country—play a large part in globalization. For example, you can find American fast-food restaurants in Russia and Japanese car factories in the United States. Increasing international trade has also contributed to globalization. In 1995 more than 120 nations joined to form the World Trade Organization (WTO). The WTO's goal is to promote international trade by removing political and economic trade barriers between nations.

Americans have different opinions about how globalization will affect the United States. Supporters believe globalization will lead to increased U.S. exports and new jobs at home. Opponents worry that Americans will lose jobs as U.S. companies move their operations to countries where wages are lower. North Carolina has experienced growth in manufacturing jobs since the 1970s, but recently many of these jobs have been moved to other countries. New jobs have been created in service industries, however.

READING CHECK **Identifying Cause and Effect** What economic trend led to the creation of the World Trade Organization?

The North Carolina Economy

Agriculture continues to be an important part of the North Carolina economy.

The textile industry has experienced many changes in technology but still thrives in North Carolina.

Technology Moves Forward

As you have seen throughout this book, technological changes and new inventions have dramatic effects on life in the United States and around the world. This continues to be true of our lives today. Just think about all the ways you use technology every day.

One of the new technologies that has changed everyday life is the **Internet**—a global system of computer networks through which people anywhere in the world can communicate and share information. The Internet was first developed in 1969 by scientists at the U.S. Department of Defense. Early computer networks were used mainly by government and university researchers. Then in the 1990s, computer programmers developed the World Wide Web, enabling people to access information from computers around the world.

Internet use exploded in the 1990s. Computers and the Internet made it easier and faster for people at home, work, and school to access and share information. This important development was known as the **Information Revolution**. Bill Gates, a leader in the computer industry, described the exciting changes this revolution promised:

> "We are watching something historic happening, and it will affect the world . . . the same way the scientific method, the invention of printing, and the arrival of the Industrial Age did."
>
> —Bill Gates, quoted in *Newsweek*

Excitement about the Internet and the Information Revolution helped fuel the economic boom of the 1990s. Although not all Internet companies succeeded, the Internet has changed the way we find information and communicate with each other. Internet use continues to grow rapidly around the world today.

Technology is also helping to **facilitate** new medical research. For example, researchers have made important breakthroughs in understanding connections between genetics and illness. In 2003 scientists completed the Human Genome Project, a project to identify more than 30,000 genes in human DNA. Medical researchers hope to use this information to find treatments for a wide range of diseases.

Another ongoing challenge for medical reasearchers is fighting **AIDS**—acquired immune deficiency syndrome. Caused by the human immunodeficiency virus (HIV), AIDS shuts down the body's immune system.

FOCUS ON READING

Predict how the use of the Internet might change American society.

ACADEMIC VOCABULARY

facilitate bring about

Banking and financial services contribute to a strong economy that continues to adapt to the changing world.

North Carolina is known worldwide for its fine furniture industry.

New industries such as pharmaceutical research have strengthened North Carolina's economy.

The Freedom Tower

CONNECT TO THE ARTS

The Freedom Tower in New York City was designed to reflect the events of 9/11. The design combines symbols of American freedom with a construction designed for safety. The antenna will reach 1,776 feet into the air, a number that recalls the date 1776, the year America declared its independence. The spire will cast a ray of light that mirrors the Statue of Liberty's torch.

How does the design of the tower reflect the ideals of freedom?

FOCUS ON NORTH CAROLINA

Residents of North Carolina have been worried about the environmental impact of acid rain created by factories at home and in neighboring states.

This makes it more likely that people with AIDS will contract other illnesses and die. As of 2004, more than 20 million people worldwide had died from AIDS. Scientists have developed drugs that help control the HIV virus but have not yet found a cure. In 2002 leaders from around the world founded the Global Fund to Fight AIDS, Tuberculosis, and Malaria. The Global Fund provides money to treat these deadly diseases and search for cures.

Scientists are also searching for ways to help protect the environment. In our increasingly global society, environmental problems often require international solutions. In the 1980s, for example, many people became concerned about the condition of the **ozone layer**—a thin layer of gas in the upper atmosphere that blocks harmful solar rays. The United States joined with more than 100 other nations to ban the use of chemicals that were harming the ozone layer. By 2004 some scientists reported that damage to the ozone layer was slowly being repaired.

Another environmental issue facing the world is climate change, or **global warming**. The burning of fossil fuels such as gasoline and coal releases carbon dioxide into Earth's atmosphere. Many scientists warn that rising levels of carbon dioxide are causing a greenhouse effect that traps heat from the sun in Earth's atmosphere. This could cause temperatures to rise, which could cause rising sea levels and more severe weather patterns. A 2001 United Nations scientific report predicted that Earth's average temperature could rise between 2 and 10 degrees by 2100.

Concerns about global warming and high oil prices have encouraged development of new transportation technologies. In 2005 Americans bought record numbers of hybrid cars, which run partially on electricity. Scientists are also developing vehicles that will run entirely on hydrogen and release almost no pollution.

Even as some scientists take on issues facing our planet, others look to the challenge of exploring space. In 2004 NASA landed two robotic vehicles on Mars. The rovers began exploring the Martian surface, sending back images that people could see on NASA's Web site. Human exploration of space continues on the International Space Station and with successful shuttle flights. NASA has faced challenges in the complicated task of sending people into space, however. In 1986 the space shuttle *Challenger* exploded, and in 2003 the *Columbia* shuttle broke apart. Fourteen astronauts were killed in these accidents.

READING CHECK **Summarizing** In what key areas is technology changing modern life?

The American People

The American population will continue to grow and change in the twenty-first century. The U.S. Census Bureau reports that our population is more ethnically diverse than ever before. In 2005 the bureau reported that Hispanics made up 14 percent of the country's total population, making them the country's largest minority group. African Americans made up just over 13 percent of the American population, and Asian Americans about 5 percent.

These changes are greatly influenced by immigration patterns. Of the more than 32.5 million foreign-born residents, 52 percent were born in Latin America and 25 percent were born in Asia. Based on these trends, the Census Bureau predicts that the country's white and nonwhite populations will be about equal by the year 2050.

Increased diversity is reflected not only in American society but also in individual Americans. In the year 2000 the Census Bureau began allowing people to indicate in official surveys that they were of more than one race. In the 2000 census, more than 6.8 million Americans listed themselves as belonging to more than one race.

While the diversity of our population grows, Americans of all backgrounds share a belief in many basic **ideals**. Our shared commitment to the ideals of freedom, equality, and justice helps keep our nation strong. So does our shared dedication to the responsibilities of citizenship. Americans also share many of the same hopes and dreams for the future.

READING CHECK **Predicting** How do you think the U.S. population will change over the next 100 years?

SUMMARY The United States continues to create opportunities and face challenges. How would you like to contribute to your country's future?

ACADEMIC VOCABULARY
ideals ideas or goals that people try to live up to

FOCUS ON NORTH CAROLINA
North Carolina has one of the fastest-growing Hispanic populations in the nation.

Section 3 Assessment

go.hrw.com
Online Quiz
KEYWORD: SC7 HP31

Reviewing Ideas, Terms, and People

1. a. **Recall** How has the American economy changed in the past several decades?
   b. **Explain** What caused government deficits to rise in the early 2000s?
   c. **Draw Conclusions** How do you think **globalization** has changed the U.S. economy?
2. a. **Identify** What are some of the world's most recent technological advances?
   b. **Explain** How did the **Internet** spark an **Information Revolution**?
   c. **Predict** Do you think **global warming** will affect your life in the future? Why or why not?
3. a. **Describe** Describe the U.S. population today.
   b. **Make Inferences** Why do you think the Census Bureau started allowing people to mark more than one race?
   c. **Elaborate** How do you think diversity and shared ideals affect America?

Critical Thinking

4. **Categorizing** Review your notes on changes taking place in the United States. Then copy the graphic organizer below and use it to describe major technological challenges for the future.

FOCUS ON WRITING

5. **Elaborating on Key Themes** Identify key elements of American life today. In your opinion, what are some great things about life in America? What do you think are the major challenges facing Americans today? What are some possible solutions? Which subjects would you like to read more about? Think about links you could include on your Web site that would provide readers with more information about these topics.

History and Geography

North Carolina TODAY

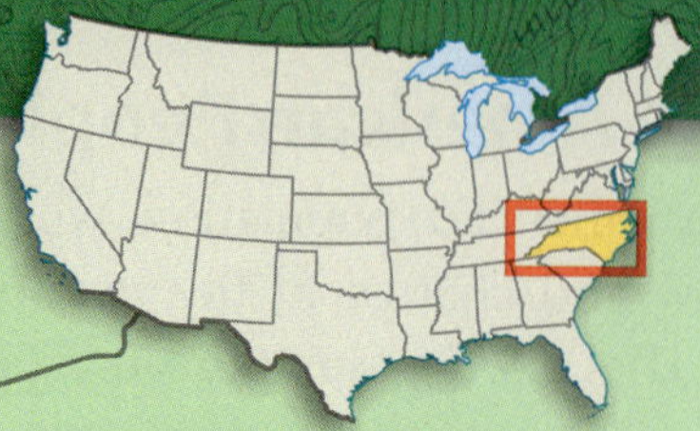

North Carolina today is experiencing tremendous growth. Since 1980 the state population has grown by about 40 percent. Newcomers to the state include Hispanic and Asian immigrants and retirees from other states.

North Carolina's economy has experienced similar growth. The banking, technology, and tourism industries have all helped spark this economic boom. The state's three geographic regions each face their own issues as a result of rapid growth.

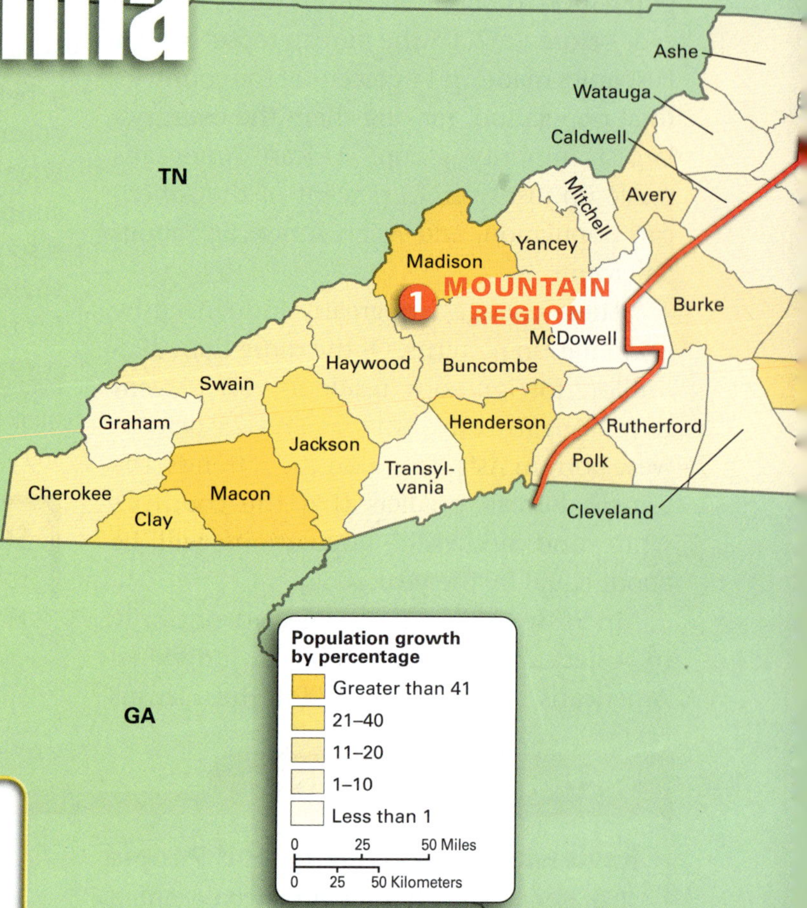

Ethnic Diversity in North Carolina

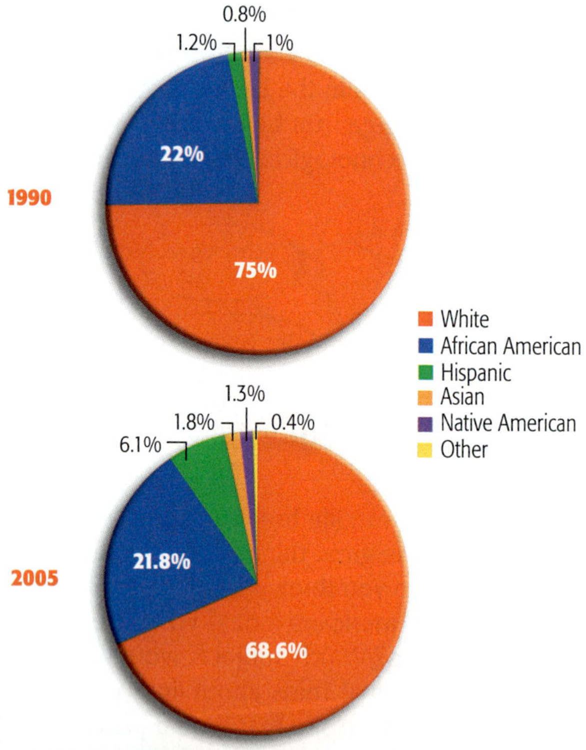

1 Mountain Region The mountain region in western North Carolina relies heavily on the tourism industry. This canoeing company on the banks of the Nantahala River attracts hundreds of tourists each year.

Population Change by County, 1995–2005

ANALYSIS SKILL **ANALYZING VISUALS**

1. **Human-Environment Interaction** Which group has experienced the highest growth rate since 1990?
2. **Location** Which region of North Carolina has experienced the greatest population growth since 1995?

2 Piedmont Region The Piedmont region is home to North Carolina's high-tech industry. Areas like Research Triangle Park lure big businesses and workers to the region.

3 Coastal Region
Residents of North Carolina's coastal region face environmental issues, such as the erosion, or wearing away, of coastlines along the Outer Banks. In 1999, officials had the Cape Hatteras Lighthouse moved some 2,900 feet, or more than a half mile, to avoid its being damaged by coastal erosion.

Social Studies Skills

Analysis | Critical Thinking | **Civic Participation** | Study

North Carolina Skills
4.02 Examine, understand, and evaluate conflicting viewpoints.

Confronting Controversial Issues

Define the Skill

The United States and the world face many challenges in the twenty-first century. People often have different opinions on how to deal with these challenges, which can lead to controversy. Some of the issues discussed in this book remain controversial.

As citizens of a democracy, Americans have a responsibility to confront controversial issues. This includes learning about different issues and why they are controversial. It also involves discussing the issues and forming opinions about them. Part of the democratic system is listening to other people's ideas about how to solve controversial issues and presenting your own ideas in a helpful way. In this way, everyone's ideas can be heard and discussed, so that the best course of action can be followed.

Learn the Skill

To confront controversial issues, it is important to understand them. You can start by identifying them. For example, one controversial issue in the 21st century is globalization—the process of economies and cultures becoming more closely connected. Some people think that globalization is a good way to improve the lives of all the world's citizens. Others think that globalization destroys what is unique about individual cultures.

Once the issue has been identified, you can learn more about it. Books, news reports, and articles are good sources of information on controversial issues. They can provide different points of view on an issue. Gathering different opinions about globalization, for example, can help you see why it is controversial. It can also help you determine your own point of view on the issue.

Follow these guidelines to confront other controversial issues.

1. Identify the issue.
2. Learn about the issue. Gather information on the subject from different sources. Determine why the issue is controversial.
3. Figure out your own point of view on the issue.
4. Discuss the issue with others. Because the issue is controversial and may lead to disagreements, it is important to be respectful of differences of opinion.

Practice the Skill

Follow these instructions to confront the controversial issue of how to deal with terrorism.

1. Find at least three articles showing different points of view about dealing with terrorism.
2. Read and take notes on the articles you have found. Based on what you have learned, determine your own point of view.
3. Have a class discussion about dealing with terrorism. Listen to opposing points of view. Share your own ideas and explain how you arrived at your point of view.

CHAPTER 31 Chapter Review

HOLT

History's Impact

▶ **video series**

Review the video to answer the closing question:

The National Park Service is constantly challenged to find a balance between wildlife and visitors. Why is this?

Visual Summary

QUICK FACTS

Use the visual summary below to help you review the main ideas of the chapter.

The United States today acts as a member of the global community as it faces the future.

Challenges

- Environmental issues
- Diseases
- Terrorism

Benefits

- Technology
- Political alliances

Reviewing Vocabulary, Terms, and People

Match the numbered person or term with the correct lettered definition.

1. World Trade Center
2. Colin Powell
3. Al Gore
4. global warming
5. Saddam Hussein
6. Madeleine Albright
7. AIDS
8. terrorism

a. 2000 Democratic presidential candidate
b. the rise in average temperatures around the world
c. dictator of Iraq overthrown in 2003
d. buildings attacked on September 11, 2001
e. deadly disease that shuts down the body's immune system
f. the use of violence by individuals or small groups to achieve political goals
g. the first woman secretary of state
h. the first African American secretary of state

Comprehension and Critical Thinking

SECTION 1 *(Pages 950–953)*

9. a. Recall What important Cold War symbol was destroyed in Germany in 1989?

b. Explain How did U.S. foreign policy change in the Clinton administration?

c. Evaluate Do you think NAFTA helped the U.S. economy? Why?

SECTION 2 *(Pages 954–958)*

10. a. Identify Who was responsible for the September 11, 2001, terrorist attacks on the United States?

b. Explain Why was the 2000 U.S. presidential election controversial?

c. Evaluate Do you think the United States was right to go to war with Iraq in 2003? Why?

SECTION 3 *(Pages 959–963)*

11. a. Identify What trend is responsible for increasing diversity in the United States?

b. Analyze Why are some people concerned about globalization?

c. Predict What aspects of life do you think will be most affected by new technology in the future?

Reviewing Themes

12. Economics How have changes in the economy affected American society since the 1990s?

13. Politics How have international politics changed over the course of George W. Bush's presidency?

Reading Skills

Predicting *Use the Reading Skills taught in this chapter to answer the question below.*

14. What might you predict for the future of society in the United States? What about the U.S. economy? How might American politics stay the same or change? What ideas in the chapter lead you to these conclusions?

Using the Internet

go.hrw.com
KEYWORD: SC7 CH31

15. Activity: Ending the Cold War By the 1980s, the Cold War had been going on for decades. But times were changing—communism was falling apart, and the Soviet Union would never be the same again. Enter the activity keyword. Research the factors that led to the decline of the Soviet Union's political and economic power. Then create a brochure on the fall of communism in the Soviet Union, the factors that led to this decline, and the impact on Russian society.

Social Studies Skills

Confronting Controversial Issues *Use the Social Studies Skills taught in this chapter to answer the question below.*

16. Name one controversial issue today. What are two different points of view on the issue?

FOCUS ON WRITING

17. Designing Your Web Site Review your notes and plan your Web site. Decide whether it will be just one page or multiple linked pages. Remember to include information on significant people, events, and ideas. Include ideas for photos, audio, or video you would like to place on your site. You might also want to provide links to other Web sites where viewers can find more information. Make sure your links connect to reliable Web sites, such as government sites or those for newspapers or museums. Finally, choose the Web site address you would like to use.

CHAPTER 31 Standardized Test Practice

DIRECTIONS: Read each question and write the letter of the best response.

1 Madeleine Albright and Colin Powell both

A conducted breakthrough medical research.

B lost close presidential elections.

C served as secretary of state.

D commanded troops in Iraq.

2 One way the U.S. economy is changing is that

A more people are working in service industries.

B more people are working in manufacturing.

C the health care and computer industries are shrinking.

D textile mills are hiring thousands of new workers.

3 What was one cause of the debate over the war in Iraq that began in 2003?

A Many Americans believed that Saddam Hussein should remain in power.

B Opponents of the war believed the Taliban should fight the war in Iraq, not U.S. troops.

C Many Americans did not want the United Nations to help pay for a costly foreign war.

D Critics of the war doubted that Saddam Hussein posed a serious threat to the United States.

4 What is one way in which globalization has affected the economy of North Carolina?

A Local jobs have been moved to foreign countries.

B Local businesses have been taken over by companies from other states.

C Troops from North Carolina have taken part in fighting in Afghanistan and Iraq.

D Most people in the state now work in service industries.

5 What trend did the Internet help bring about?

A terrorism

B the Information Revolution

C a service economy

D global warming

6 Which of the following was one of Bill Clinton's achievements as president?

A gaining the passage of the North American Free Trade Agreement

B creating the Department of Homeland Security

C allowing women in the military to serve in combat

D setting new education standards in the No Child Left Behind act

7 Read the following speech by New York City mayor Rudolph Giuliani following the 9/11 attacks and use it to answer the question below.

> "We're a city of immigrants unlike any other city, within a nation of immigrants. Like the victims of the World Trade Center attack, we're of every race, we're of every religion, we're of every ethnicity . . . It's the thing that renews us and revives us in every generation, our openness to new people from all over the world."
>
> —Rudolph Giuliani, quoted in *The Washington Post*

Document-Based Question What did Mayor Giuliani say was a unique strength of New York City? Why was this an important message to deliver after the attacks of September 11?

Assignment

Write an oral history, based on an interview with an adult you know, about one of the events in this chapter.

An Oral History

Oral histories can provide excellent sources of information about events in the recent past. An oral history is a report based on an interview with a person who experienced or remembers a historical event. Oral histories preserve personal experiences and memories for future generations.

1. Prewrite

Getting Started

Think about all the events you read about in this unit. Which ones interested you the most? Which ones do you think made the strongest impression on people at the time? Choose one as your subject.

TIP Use question words like *Who? What? When? Where? Why?* and *How?* in your interview questions.

Writing Questions

- Focus on finding out how the person you are interviewing experienced the event you chose.
- Write at least 10 questions.

Conducting an Interview

- Find an adult family member or friend to interview who remembers participating in or reacting to the event.
- Come prepared with your questions, paper, and something to write with.
- Take notes on the answers. Indicate direct quotations with quotation marks.
- Ask follow-up questions, even if you did not prepare them in advance.

2. Write

You can use this framework, along with your interview notes, to help you write your first draft.

A Writer's Framework

Introduction

- Grab your reader's attention with an interesting quote from your interview.
- Introduce the event you chose and why it was important.
- Explain how the event affected the person you interviewed.

Body

- Describe the memories and experiences of the person you interviewed about the event.
- Summarize what you learned from the interview.
- Use quotes from the interview.

Conclusion

- Make a generalization about how people reacted to the event.
- Draw conclusions about how people's reactions to the event affected history.

3. Evaluate and Revise

Evaluating

Use these questions to discover ways to improve your oral history.

Evaluation Questions for an Oral History

- Do you introduce the event and the person you interviewed in the first paragraph?
- Do you focus on the event from a personal point of view?
- Do you describe the memories and experiences of the person you interviewed about the event?
- Do you summarize what you learned and use quotes from the interview?
- Do you make generalizations and draw conclusions about people's reactions to the event?

Revising

When you revise your oral history, you may need to add background information. Check the material you have included from your interview. If anything is unclear, add more details about the event or time period. Make sure to explain clearly the connections between the personal experience and the event.

4. Proofread and Publish

Proofreading

In your oral history, you have been using quotations from the person you interviewed. Check the punctuation marks around these direct quotations. Also check the spelling and capitalization of all proper names, such as the name of the person you interviewed.

Publishing

Share your oral history with classmates who wrote about the same event. How were the experiences of the people you interviewed similar and different? Share your oral history with the class. The person you interviewed would probably also like to see the finished project.

5. Practice and Apply

Use the steps and strategies in this workshop to write your oral history.

TIP **Using Quotations Effectively** Quotations from your interview will make your oral history more interesting. Introduce quotations with a phrase or a sentence that makes it clear what they are about. Always identify the person who is quoted.

EXAMPLE

Simon remembered taking part in a demonstration in Washington, D.C., the night before President Nixon resigned. "There were thousands of people in Lafayette Park across from the White House," Simon recalled.

TIP **Using Ellipses** To make a quotation shorter, you can delete some words and replace them with an ellipsis—the symbol "...". Make sure the quotation still makes sense after you do this.

EXAMPLE

Original quotation: "On the morning of September 11, I woke up, brushed my teeth, ate breakfast, and did everything like any other day."

Quotation with an ellipsis: "On the morning of September 11, I ... did everything like any other day."

Credits and Acknowledgments

For permission to reproduce copyrighted material, grateful acknowledgment is made to the following sources:

Saint Martin's Press: Quote by Sarah G. Bagley from *The Belles of New England: The Women of the Textile Mills and the Families Whose Wealth They Wove* by William Moran. Copyright © 2002 by William Moran.

Doubleday, a division of Random House, Inc., www.randomhouse.com: From *The Diary of a Young Girl: The Definitive Edition* by Anne Frank, edited by Otto H. Frank and Mirjam Pressler, translated by Susan Massotty. Copyright © 1995 by Doubleday, a division of Random House, Inc.

Hill and Wang, a division of Farrar, Straus & Giroux, LLC and electronic format by permission of ***Georges Borchardt, Inc., for Les Editions de Minuit:*** From *Night* by Elie Wiesel, translated by Stella Rodway. Copyright © 1958 by Les Editions de Minuit; English translation copyright © 1960 by MacGibbon & Kee, renewed © 1988 by The Collins Publishing Group. Originally published as *La Nuit.* All rights reserved.

Alfred A. Knopf, a division of Random House, Inc., www.randomhouse.com: "I, Too, Sing America" from *The Collected Poems of Langston Hughes.* Copyright © 1994 by the Estate of Langston Hughes.

W. W. Norton & Company, Inc., www.wwnorton.com: *Thirteen Days: A Memoir of the Cuban Missile Crisis* by Robert F. Kennedy. Copyright © 1969, 1971 by W. W. Norton & Company, Inc. Copyright © 1968 by McCall Corporation.

Persea Books, Inc.: *Bread Givers* by Anzia Yezierska. Copyright © 1925 by Doubleday & Co., Inc.; copyright renewed 1952 by Anzia Yezierska, transferred to Louise Levitas Henriksen in 1970. Revised edition copyright © 1999 by Persea Books, Inc. Foreward and Introduction copyright © 1999 by Alice Kessler-Harris.

Scribner, an imprint of Simon & Schuster Adult Publishing Group: From *The Great Gatsby* by F. Scott Fitzgerald. Copyright 1925 by Charles Scribner's Sons; renewed copyright 1953 by Frances Scott Fitzgerald Lanahan.

Viking Penguin, a division of Penguin Group (USA) Inc.: From *The Grapes of Wrath* by John Steinbeck. Copyright 1939 and renewed © 1967 by John Steinbeck.

Sources Cited:

Quote by an Aztec messenger from *The Broken Spears: The Aztec Account of the Conquest of Mexico,* Expanded and Updated Edition, edited by Miguel León-Portilla. Published by Beacon Press, Boston, 1992

Quote by Harold Bryant from *Bloods: An Oral History of the Vietnam War by Black Veterans* by Wallace Terry. Published by Ballantine Books, New York, 1985.

From *Keeping The Faith* by Jimmy Carter. Published by Bantam Books, New York, 1982.

Quote by Maya Lin from "Architect Maya Lin Describes the thoughts Behind the Vietnam Veterans Memorial" by Fernando Quintero from *The Berkeleyan,* 1995.

Quote by Philip Caputo from *CNN Cold War: Interviews,* accessed at http://www.cnn.com/SPECIALS/cold.war/episodes/11/interviews/caputo/

From "The Fall of Saigon" by Ken Moorefield from *To Bear Any Burden: The Vietnam War and Its Aftermath in the Words of Americans and Southeast Asians* by Al Santoli. Published by E.P. Dutton, Inc., 1985.

From quote by Henry Fenner from *You Must Remember This: An Oral History of Manhattan from the 1890s to World War II* by Jeff Kisseloff. Published by Harcourt, Inc., Orlando, 1989.

From *Yesterday: A Memoir of a Russian Jewish Family* by Miriam Shomer Zunser, edited by Emily Wortis Leider. Published by HarperCollins Publishers, New York, 1978.

From "Now I Lay Me Down to Sleep" by Diana Dwan Poole from *Chicken Soup for the Veteran's Soul* by Jack Canfield, Mark Victor Hansen, and Sidney R. Slagter. Published by Health Communications, Inc., Deerfield Beach, FL, 2001.

From *A Life is More than a Moment: The Desegregation of Little Rock's Central High* by Will Counts, Will Campbell, Ernest Dumas and Robert S. McCord. Published by Indiana University Press, Bloomington, 1999.

Quote by Dave Reinemen from "60 Years Later, Okinawa Memories Still Burn" by Tom Berg from *Orange County Register,* 2005.

Quote by Frank Hall from "Hundreds tread site of bloody battle" by Steve Limtiaco. Published in *Pacific Daily News,* accessed at http://www.guampdn.com/apps/pbcs.dll/article?AID=/20050314/NEWS01/503140301/1002.

Quote from *Hard Times: An Oral History of the Great Depression* by Studs Terkel. Published by Pantheon Books, New York, 1970.

Quote by Lawrence Svobida from "Farming the Dust Bowl" from *The American Experience, Surviving the Dust Bowl,* accessed at http://www.pbs.org/wgbh/amex/dustbowl/sfeature/eyewitness.html.

Quote by Louis Ortega from *WWII: The People's Story* edited by Nigel Fountain. Published by Reader's Digest, Pleasantville, NY, 2003.

Quote by Boris Pilnyak from *Our Times,* edited by Loraine Glennon. Published by Turner Publishing, Inc., Atlanta, GA, 1995.

Quote by Michiko Yamaoka, interviewed by Mitsuru Ohba from *Voices of A-Bomb Survivors* web site, accessed at http://www.csi.ad.jp/ABOMB/Hibakusha/h03.html.

Illustration and Photo Credits

Frontmatter: vii (t) Mireille Vautier/Cherokee Indian Museum North Carolina/The Art Archive; xix The Granger Collection, New York; xxi From the Collections of Henry Ford Museum and Greenfield Village; xxiii (t) Flip Schulke/Corbis (c) Bizuayehu Tesfaye/AP/Wide World Photos; xxix Kelly Culpepper/Transparencies, Inc.; xxxv Adam Jones/Photodisc/Getty Images; xxxvi TIME Inc./Courtesy of the general libraries, The University of Texas at Austin/HRW photo by Victoria Smith; xxxvii Arthur Schatz/Time Life Pictures/Getty Images; xxxviii Richard A. Cooke/Corbis.

Prologue: NC0 Andre Jenny/Alamy; NC1 (l) Private Collection/Boltin Picture Library/Bridgeman Art Library, (r) The Granger Collection, New York; NC2 Hulton Archive/Getty Images; NC3 (tl) John Pineda/Getty Images, (tr) Lee Snider/Photo Images/Corbis, (b) The Granger Collection, New York; NC4 (tl) Courtesy of the North Carolina Division of Archives and History, (tr) Library of Congress, (b) Kelly Culpepper/Transparencies, Inc.; NC5 (t) Hulton Archive/Getty Images, (b) Digital Vision/Getty Images; NC6 (t,b) Courtesy of the North Carolina Division of Archives and History; NC7 (t) Jane Faircloth/Transparencies, Inc., (b) Courtesy of the North Carolina Division of Archives and History; NC8 Culver Pictures/The Art Archive; NC9 (l) Oberlin College Archives, Oberlin, Ohio, (r) North Carolina Collection, University of North Carolina, Library at Chapel Hill; NC10 (t) The Granger Collection, New York, (b) David Muench/Corbis; NC11 Science Museum/SSPL/The Image Works; NC12 (l) Courtesy of the North Carolina Division of Archives and History, (r) Getty Images; NC13 (tl) Marie Hansen/Time Life Pictures/Getty Images, (tr) Bettmann/Corbis, (b) Gabriel Benzur/Getty Images; NC14 (l) PRNewsFoto/NewsCom, (r) News & Observer Publishing Company Collection/Courtesy North Carolina Division of Archives and History; NC15 (l) Shepard Sherbell/Corbis Saba, (r) Brooks Kraft/Corbis.

Unit 1: 00-01 © Burstein Collection/Corbis. **Chapter 1:** Pages 2-3 (t)© Annie Griffiths/CORBIS; 2 (br) The Art Archive/National Anthropological Museum Mexico/Dagli Orti; 3 (bc) ©Yoshio Tomii/SuperStock, (br) ©Rabatti - Domingie/akg-images; 7 (t) Smithsonian Institution, Washington, DC. Photograph by Chip Clark # 90-14563, (c) PRC Archive, (b) Getty Images; 11 © David Muench/CORBIS; 13 (tr) From the Collection of Gilcrease Museum, Tulsa, 13 (bl) © 2000 The Art Institute of Chicago (detail), (tl) Ohio Historical Society; 14 (tl) Marilyn Wynn/Nativestock Pictures, 14 (tr) The Granger Collection, New York; 17 (tl) Carol Beckwith & Angela Fisher/HAGA/The Image Works, Inc., 17 (tl) © John Elk III Photography; 19 (bc) Reuters/Corbis, (br) AFP/Getty Images; 21 (br) The Granger Collection, New York; 23 (b) Ben Mangor/SuperStock; 24 (bc) © Archivo Iconografico, S.A./CORBIS, (bl) ©Christopher Groenhout/Lonely Planet Images; 25 (bl) © Bettmann/CORBIS, (br) ©G K & Vikki Hart/PhotoDisc, (bc) The Granger Collection, New York. **Chapter 2:** Pages 34-35 (all) © Rebecca Marvil/Index Stock Imagery, Inc.; 34 (b) National Maritime Museum; 35 (cl) SuperStock, (c) Tate Gallery, London/Art Resource, NY, (bl) Fundacion Miguel Mujica Gallo, Museo do Oro del Peru, (bc) G. Tortoli/Ancient Art & Architecture Collection, Ltd., (br) Victoria & Albert Museum, London/Art Resource, NY, (cr) David Muench/Corbis; 40 (bkgd) © Royalty Free/CORBIS; 44 SuperStock; 47 (br) © Scott Nelson/Getty Images; 49 The Granger Collection, New York; 51 (cr) PRC Archive; 52 (bl) Saint Bride Printing Library; 53 (bl) AKG-Images, (br) Mary Evans Picture Library; 54 (t) Tate Gallery, London/Art

Resource, NY; 59 (br) Copyright The New York Public Library / Art Resource, NY; 60 (tr) **Chapter 3:** Pages 68-69 (t) Ted Curtin for Plimoth Plantation, (c) Courtesy of the Pilgrim Society, Plymouth, Massachusetts; 68 (bl) © David Ball/CORBIS; 69 (br) © Culver Pictures, Inc., (bl) © SuperStock, (cr) Courtesy of the Burton Historical Collection, Detroit Public Library; 75 North Wind Picture Archives/Alamy; 82 (t) Art Reference: PRC Archive; 85 (b) © SuperStock; 86 (bl) Art Reference: Historical Society of Pennsylvania; 88 (l) SuperStock, (t) NASA, (b) © SuperStock, Inc./SuperStock; 93 (r) Art Reference: Royal Albert Memorial Museum, Exeter, Devon, UK/ Bridgeman Art Library, (l) Private Collection/ www.bridgeman.co.uk; 94 (t) National Portrait Library, London/Bridgeman Art Library; 97 (tr) Art Reference: Courtesy of the Burton Historical Collection, Detroit Public Library; 99 (t) Virginia Historical Society; 101 (t) Peter Newark's American Pictures; 102 (tr) Courtesy of the Massachusetts Historical Society, (tl) © Hulton-Deutsch Collection/CORBIS; 103 (tl) © Bettmann/CORBIS, (tr) American Antiquarian Society. **Chapter 4:** Pages 108-109 (t) © James Lemass/Index Stock Imagery; 108 (cl) The Granger Collection, New York; 109 (br) © Christie's Images, (cr) North Wind Picture Archives; 113 (b) © Concord Museum/Photograph by Chip Fanelli, (t) The Granger Collection, New York; 117 (br) © Robert Llewellyn/SuperStock; 119 Courtesy of The North Carolina State Archives; 120 (t) © Bettmann/CORBIS; 123 (br) The Granger Collection, New York; 127 (l) #1921.101, ©Collection of The New-York Historical Society, (r) ©Collection of The New-York Historical Society, neg. 31665; 128-129 (t) © SuperStock; 130 (r) Chateau de Versailles, France/Giraudon/ Bridgeman Art Library, (l) Saratoga National Historic Park; 131 (r) Hotel Galvez, Galveston, Texas, (l) Falmouth Art Gallery, Cornwall, UK/The Bridgeman Art Library; 132 © SuperStock, Inc. / SuperStock; 136 (t) The Granger Collection, New York; 138 The Granger Collection, New York.

Unit 2. Chapter 5: Pages 148-149 (t) Joe Marquette/AP/Wide World Photos; 148 (b) Library of Congress/PRC Archive; 149 (br) © Andrea Jemolo/CORBIS, (bl) © Nik Wheeler/CORBIS, (c) Collection of the American Numismatic Society, New York; 153 The Granger Collection, New York; 156 (t) © Bettmann/CORBIS, (b) © Bettmann/ CORBIS; 157 (t) © Bettmann/CORBIS, (c) © Michael Nicholson/CORBIS , (br) © Archivo Iconografico, S.A./CORBIS; 160-161 (b) The Granger Collection, New York; 163 © Dennis Degnan/CORBIS; 164 (t) Hall of Representatives, Washington, DC/ Bridgeman Art Library, (bl) Independence National Historical Park , (bc) Stock MontageStrock, (br) Portrait by Robert S. Susan, Collection of the Supreme Court of the United States; 166 (l) South Carolina Legal History Collection, (r) City of Bristol Museum and Art Gallery/ Bridgeman Art Library; 167 © Alex Wong/ Getty Images; 169 (br) American Antiquarian Society; 171 (r) © Bettmann/CORBIS, (l) Stock Montage, Inc., (bkgd) © Alan Schein Photography/CORBIS. **Chapter 6:** Pages 178-179 (t) Sam Dudgeon/HRW Photo; 179 (b) © Bettmannn/CORBIS, (cl) PRC Archive, (cr) © Tony Freeman/PhotoEdit; 185 Getty Images; 187 (bc) National Archives (NARA), (br) National Archives/PRC Archive; 192 (br) Dennis Cook/AP/Wide World Photos; 192-193 (bc) © Mark Wilson/Getty Images, (t) © Miles Ertman/Masterfile; 193 (br) © Brooks Kraft/ CORBIS; 194 © Royalty-Free/CORBIS; 204 (bl) © Yang Liu/CORBIS, (bc) Norm Detlaff, Las Cruces Sun-News/AP/Wide World Photos; 205 (bl) ©Alex Webb/Magnum Photos, (bc) © David Young-Wolff/PhotoEdit, (br) © Bettmann/CORBIS; © Royalty-Free/CORBIS; 209 (t) Library of Congress/PRC Archive; 211 (tr) Library of Congress; 213 (l) © Bettmann/ CORBIS, (r) © Oscar White/CORBIS; 214 (tr) ©1978 Matt Herron/TakeStock, (tc) Texas State Library & Archives Commission, (tl) Dr. Hector P. Garcia Papers, Special Collections & Archives, Texas A&M University-Corpus Christi, Bell Library; 217 (b) © Daily News Pix; 219 © Spencer Grant/PhotoEdit; 220-221 (b) © Ariel Skelley/CORBIS; 223 (t) © David Butow/CORBIS; 224 (tl) ©James Pickerell/The Image Works, (tr) © Brownie Harris/CORBIS; 225 (l) © Ariel Skelly/CORBIS, (c) Janet Knott/ The Boston Globe. Republished with permission of The Globe Newspaper Company, Inc., (r) © Jeff Greenberg/PhotoEdit. **Chapter 7:** Pages 230 (b) © Christie's Images; 231 (bl) Giraudon/Art Resource, NY ,(r) Art Resource, NY; 235 (r) Library of Congress/PRC Archive; 237 (inset) © Collection of The New-York Historical Society, 31907.32; 240 (b) © Joseph Sohm; Chromosohm, Inc./CORBIS, (c) Photo ©2004 Roger Foley; 241 (r) Stock Montage/ Getty Images, (l) Stock Montage, Inc.; 243 (b) Réunion des Musées Nationaux/Art Resource, NY; 244 (l) Chicago Historical Society, (r) Library of Congress/PRC Archive, (c) Chicago Historical Society, #i35980aa; 245 (l) HRW Photo Research Library; 246 Courtesy Ohio Historical Society; 248 © Museum of the City of New York/CORBIS; 251 (tl) ©The New York Historical Society, New York, NY/ Bridgeman Art Library, (tc) The Art Archive/Chateau de Biernacourt/Dagli Orti, (bl) Independence National Historical Park Collection, (bc) The Henry Luce III Center for the Study of American Culture/SuperStock, (tr) ©The New-York Historical Society, New York, NY/ Bridgeman Art Library, (br) National Portrait Gallery, Smithsonian Institution, Washington, DC/Art Resource, NY; 252 Library of Congress/PRC Archive.

Unit 3. Chapter 8: Pages 262 (b) The Granger Collection, New York; 262-263 (t) Superstock; 263 (cl) Benninghoff Collection of the American Revolution, (cr) Portrait of the Founder, Munetada Kurozumi. Image courtesy of Kurozumikyo Shinto, (cr) Library of Congress, LC-USZC4-6466; 267 (l) The Art Archive/Chateau de Blernacourt/Dagli Orti, (r) © Bettmann/CORBIS, (bkgd) © Alan Schein Photography/CORBIS; 269 (b) Getty Images; 270 Washington and Lee University; 275 (r) © Jeff Vanuga/CORBIS, (l) © Joseph Sohm/Chromosohm, Inc./CORBIS; 280 (l) The Mariners Museum, (r) North Wind Picture Archives; 281 (t) North Wind Picture Archives, (br) © 1993 Mickey Osterreischer/ Black Star, (bl) The Granger Collection, New York; 282 (r) National Portrait Gallery, Smithsonian Institution; gift of Mrs. Herbert Lee Pratt, Jr, (l) ©The Field Museum, Neg #A93851.1c, Chicago; 286 (inset) © New-York Historical Society/ Bridgeman Art Library, (b) © Bettmann/CORBIS; 288 Louis Orr/Library of Congress; 289 (l) Corbis, (r) Bettmann/ Corbis; **Chapter 9:** Pages 294 (tl) National Portrait Gallery, Smithsonian Institution, Washington, DC/Art Resource, NY; 294-295 (t) © Lee Snider/Photo Images/CORBIS; 295 (bl) Courtesy PRC Archive, (c) Library of Congress #LC-USZC4-5801, (br) The Granger Collection, New York; 302 (t) © Bettmann/ CORBIS, (b) Maryland Historical Society, Baltimore, Maryland; 306 (r) Jane Faircloth/ Transparencies, Inc., (inset) Digital Vision/ Getty Images; 307 (t) SuperStock, (inset) Collection of the American Numismatic Society, New York; 308 © Andre Jenny/Alamy Photos; 309 Library of Congress/PRC Archive; 310 (c) Smithsonian American Art Museum, Washington DC/Art Resource, NYSmithsonian American Art Museum, Washington DC/Art Resource, NY, (l) American Antiquarian Society; 311 (r) © Francis G. Mayer/CORBIS. **Chapter 10:** Pages 318 (b) The Granger Collection, New York; 318-319 (t) Detroit Publishing Company Collection, from Birth of A Century, KEA Publishing Services Ltd.; 319 (cl) Janice L. and David J. Frent Collection of Political Americana, (bl) The Stapleton Collection, UK/ Bridgeman Art Library, (cr) National Portrait Gallery, Smithsonian Institution/Art Resource, NY, (br) The Art Archive; 323 (r) R.W. Norton Art Gallery, Shreveport, LA. Used by permission., (l) David Young-Wolff/PhotoEdit; 325 (br) The Hermitage, Home of Andrew Jackson; 327 (l) American Museum of Textile History, (c) Christie's Images/ Bridgeman Art Library, (r) The Fine Arts Museum of San Francisco, Gift of Eleanor Martin, 37566; 330 The Granger Collection, New York; 333 © SuperStock, Inc. / SuperStock; 336 (l) Mireille Vautier/ Cherokee Indian Museum North Carolina/ The Art Archive, (r) Danita Delimont/Alamy; 337 (t) Richard A. Cooke/Corbis, (b) Global Book Publishing/The Art Archive. **Chapter 11:** Pages 342-343 (t) Seaver Center for Western History Research, Natural History Museum of Los Angeles County; 343 (cr) © The Oakland Museum, The City of Oakland, (br) Library of Congress, LC-USZC4-1307/PRC Archive, (cl) Panhandle-Plains Historical Museum, Research Center, Canyon, Texas; 347 (c) © Bettmann/CORBIS; 348 (t) Used by permission, Utah State Historical Society, all rights reserved.; 351 (tl) Institute of Texan Cultures, University of Texas at San Antonio (colorized), (tr) Courtesy Texas General Land Office, HRW Photo by Peter Van Steen; 352 (b) Jack Lewis/TxDOT, (bl) The Center For American History, University of Texas at Austin; 355 (t) Library of Congress/PRC Archive; 356 (b) James Walker, Vaqueros in a Horse Corral, 1877, #0126.1480, From the Collection of Gilcrease Museum, Tulsa, Oklahoma.; 357 (t) Society of California Pioneers; 360-361 (t) Texas State Library and Archives Commission; 362 (t) J. Griffiths Smith/TxDOT; 365 (br) Collection of Matthew Isenburg, (bl) Collection of Matthew Isenburg; 366 (t) Courtesy of the California History Room, California State Library, Sacramento, California; 367 (tl) Seaver Center for Western History Research; 369 (t) Library of Congress. #LC-USZC4-7421; 370 (c) © George F. Mobley/Getty Images; 371 (t) © Bettmann/ CORBIS, (b) © Lester Lefkowitz/CORBIS , (c) © SuperStock, Inc./SuperStock; 375 (br) The Granger Collection, New York.

Unit 4: 378-379 Tontine Coffee House, c. 1797 (oil on linen), Guy Francis (1760–1820)/© New York Historical Society, New York, USA/Bridgeman Art Library. **Chapter 12:** Pages 380-381 (c) © Marilyn Root/Index Stock Imagery, Inc.; 380 (b) New York State Historical Association, Cooperstown; 381 (bl) NASA, (cr) © Southeast Museum, (cl) PRC Archive, (br) © CORBIS; 386 (l) Samuel Finley Breese Morse, Eli Whitney (1765-1825), Yale University Art Gallery. Gift of George Hoadley, B.A. 1801., (r) Museum of Connecticut History; 387 (l) Museum of Connecticut History, (r) New Haven Colony Historical Society; 388 © Bob Krist/CORBIS;

391 Rhode Island Historical Society; 392 Jack Naylor Collection; 397 Library of Congress, Detroit Publishing Company Collection, #LC-D401-19395; 402 Museum of Connecticut History; 403 (bl) Smithsonian Institution, Washington, DC (Photograph by Charles Phillips), (br) Courtesy John Deere & Company Archives; 404 (r) National Museum of American History, Smithsonian Institution, Washington, DC (#89-6626), (c) U.S. Patent Office, (l) U.S. Patent Office; Pate. **Chapter 13:** Pages 410 (b) National Museum of American History, Smithsonian Institution, Washington, DC. Photo by Kim Neilson, #83-2953; 410-411 (t) Penn School Papers, Southern Historical Collection, University of North Carolina at Chapel Hill, Wilson Library, #P.3615/0824(A); 411 (c) Library of Congress, (b) © Hulton-Deutsch Collection/CORBIS; 422 (tl) The Valentine Museum, (tr) Collection of the American Numismatic Society, New York; 425 The J. Paul Getty Museum, Los Angeles; 426-427 (t) Hauling the Whole Week's Picking by WIlliam Henry Brown, The Historic New Orleans Collection; 427 (tr) South Carolina Historical Society; 428 (tr) North Wind Picture Archives; 432 Sam Dudgeon/HRW. **Chapter 14:** Pages 434-435 (t) The Metropolitan Museum of Art, Gift of I.N. Phelps Stokes, Edward S. Hawes, Alice Mary Hawes, Marion Augusta Hawes, 1937.[37.14.22]. All rights reserved, The Metropolitan Museum of Art.; 435 (cl) Courtesy of the Massachusetts Historical Society, (cr) PRC Archive, (bl) Photo © David Modica, courtesy American Printing House for the Blind Museum, (br) Peter Newark's American Pictures; 437 Library of Congress; 439 (c) Wiliam B. Becker Collection/American Museum of Photography; 443 © Royalty-Free/CORBIS; 444 Brooklyn Museum of Art, Gift of the Brooklyn Institute of Arts and Sciences/ Bridgeman Art Library; 449 (inset) Hulton Archive/Getty Images, (b) The Granger Collection, New York; 452 Courtesy of Oberlin Archives; 453 Oberlin College Archives, Oberlin, Ohio; 455 (t) Trustees of the Boston Public Library; 456 Library of Congress; 457 (t) Courtesy of the Levi Coffin House Association and Waynet, (b) Courtesy of The Brooklyn Museum of Art [40.59]; 458 Library of Congress; 459 Courtesy of the Massachusetts Historical Society; 460 (r) Library of Congress, Manuscript Division; 462 (l) Courtesy of the Massachusetts Historical Society, (r) The Granger Collection, New York; 463 (l) Courtesy of the Susan B. Anthony House, Rochester, NY, (r) Library of Congress/ PRC Archive; 465 Stock Montage, Inc.; 466 © Bettmann/CORBIS; 467 (r) © 1973 Historical Documents Co. Harcourt Photo by Maria Paraskevas.; 470 Sam Dudgeon/HRW; 471 © CORBIS. **Chapter 15:** Pages 472-473 (t) © Dave G. Houser; 473 (bl) The Art Archive/Private Collection/Dagli Orti, (br) India Office Library & Records, The British Library, (cr) Chicago Historical Society, (cl) PRC Archive; 478 (b) PRC Archive; 480 (t) The J. Paul Getty Museum, Los Angeles.; 483 (b) Library of Congress, LC-USZ62-92043; 486 (b) Kansas State Historical Society, Topeka, Kansas; 487 (t) The Granger Collection, New York; 489 (b) Missouri Historical Society, (cl) Getty Images; 491 (tr) Library of Congress/PRC Archive; 492 (t) The Museum of American Political Life, University of Hartford, West Hartford, CT.; 494 (t) Ohio Historical Society; 496 (b) Boston Athenaeum.

Unit 5 Chapter 16: Pages 506 (b) Confederate Museum, United Daughters of the Confederacy; 506-507 (t) Library of Congress, Brady Civil War Photo Collection, #LC-B8171-7514; 507 (b) Chicago Historical Society, # i26736aa, (cl) © SuperStock, (cr) © SuperStock; 518-519 (b) National Park Service; 519 (br) Library of Congress/PRC Archive; 520 (t) Library of Congress/ PRC Archive; 524 (b) © 1989, The Greenwich Workshop, Inc., Reproduced with the permission of the Greenwich Workshop, Inc., Shelton, CT; 528 (b) SuperStock; 529 (b) South Carolina Historical Society; 530 (inset) Courtesy of the Massachusetts Historical Society, (t) Library of Congress; 532 (b) © Bettmann/CORBIS; 533 (t) National Museum of American History, Smithsonian Institution, Washington, DC (ID#84-9312), (b) © REUTERS/Kai Pfaffenbach/CORBIS; 534 (t) American Antiquarian Society; 543 (t) © SuperStock; 544 The Granger Collection, New York, (b). **Chapter 17:** Pages 548 (b) © Kean Collection/Getty Images; 548-549 (t) © Paul Rocheleau; 549 (bl) © Michael Maslan Historic Photographs/CORBIS, (cr) Herbert F. Johnson Museum of Art, Cornell University, (cl) The Granger Collection, New York; 552-553 (b) National Archives (NARA); 554 (inset) Chicago Historical Society; 554-555 (t) Library of Congress; 555 (t) University of Texas at El Paso Library, Special Collections Department, Ada Tharp Photograph Collection.; 556 (b) © William Gladstone Collection; 559 (b) Library of Congress, #LC-USZ62-43958; 560 (l) Library of Congress, (r) © CORBIS; 562 (b) North Wind Picture Archives; 565 (t) Library of Congress, (b) Library of Congress; 566 (r) The Granger Collection, New York, (l) Tennessee State Museum Collection. Photography by June Dorman; 568 (t) Getty Images; 570 (t) Courtesy of The Charleston Renaissance Gallery, Robert M. Hicklin, Jr. Inc., Charleston, South Carolina; 571 © Bettmann/CORBIS.

Unit 6. Chapter 18: Pages 582-583 © James L. Amos/CORBIS; 582 (b) Courtesy Wells Fargo Bank; 583 (bl) The Art Archive / Musée d'Orsay Paris/ Dagli Orti, (cl) Southern Pacific Lines/PRC Archive, (cr) © CORBIS, (br) The Granger Collection, New York; 587 (tr) © Collection of the New-York Historical Society, [neg. 41800]; 588 (l) Denver Public Library, Western History Collection; 588-589 (r) Nebraska State Historical Society, Photograph Collections; 589 (inset) Bob Boze Bell, True West Magazine; 590 (inset) © James L. Amos/CORBIS; 591 Union Pacific Historical Collection; 592 (t) The Granger Collection, New York; 592-593 (b) SuperStock; 595 (t) George Lane/AP/Wide World Photos; 596 (t) © Bettmann/CORBIS; 597 (t) Western History Division, National Museum of American History/Smithsonian Institution, Washington, DC; 598 The Granger Collection, New York; 599 (l) (art Reference) all LOC -no credit needed, (r); 601 (b) Western History Collections, University of Oklahoma; 602 (bl) Library of Congress, (tr) Elias Carr Papers, East Carolina Manuscript Collection, J.Y. Joyner Library, East Carolina University, Greenville, NC. Photo by Dewane Frutiger., (br) Nebraska State Historical Society; 603 (l) Culver Pictures; 604 (art reference) LOC/ PRC No credit needed; 605 (t) © CORBIS; 608 (bl) Sam Dudgeon/HRW. **Chapter 19:** Pages 610-611 (t) PRC Archive; 611 (bl) © Bettmann/CORBIS, (br) Archives Larousse, Paris, France/ Bridgeman Art Library, (c) George Meany Memorial Archives; 614-615 (b) Library of Congress; 616 (r) [neg. #40578] ©Collection of The New-York Historical Society, (l) Whittier Museum; 617 (l) Property of AT&T Archives. Printed with permission of AT&T., (r) © Hulton Archive/Getty Images; 618 (l) © CORBIS, (r) Library of Congress/PRC Archive; 619 (b) Montgomery County Historical Society; 620 (b) © CORBIS, (inset) Courtesy of the Rockefeller Archive Center; 621 (t) [#71880T] © Collection of The New-York Historical Society; 623 (l) (Art Reference) AP/Wide World Photos & © Bettmann/CORBIS, (c) (Art Reference) AP/ Wide World Photos, (r) (Art Reference) Photo courtesy Union Pacific Historical Collection; 625 (b) (Art Reference) © Bettmann/CORBIS, (t) Brown Brothers. **Chapter 20:** Pages 632-633 © Bettmann/CORBIS; 633 (cl) © Joseph Sohm, Chromosohm, Inc./CORBIS, (cr) © CORBIS, (br) © Ted Spiegel/CORBIS; 637 (t) PictureHistory/NewsCom; 638 (cr) Shades of L.A. Archives/Los Angeles Public Library, (cl) National Archives, #90-G-152-2038; 639 (tc) Col. Ernest Swanson Papers, Swenson Swedish Immigration Research Center, Augustana College, Rock Island, IL, (cl) © CORBIS; 640 (bl) Library of Congress, Arnold Genthe Collections, #LC-G403-T01-0363, (br) Library of Congress, Arnold Genthe Collections, #LC-G403-T01-0363; 643 (t) Lake County (IL) Museum /Curt Teich Postcard Archives; 644 (bc) New York State Historical Association, (br) © David Bell/CORBIS; 647 The Granger Collection, New York; 648 Jane Addams Memorial Collection (JAMC neg 227), Special Collections, University Library, University of Illinois at Chicago.

Unit 7: 656-657 Courtesy of the U.S. Naval Academy Museum. **Chapter 21:** 658-659 (t) Elizabeth Cady Stanton Trust; 659 (cl, cr) Janice L. and David J. Frent Collection of Political Americana, (b) The Granger Collection, New York; 663 (t) The Granger Collection, New York; 664 (tl) PRC Archive, (tr) PRC Archive, (cl) PRC Archive, (cr) PRC Archive, (bl) PRC Archive, (br) PRC Archive; 665 (t) © Bettmann/CORBIS; 668 (t) Barnes & Noble, Inc.; 669 (t) Library of Congress/PRC Archive; 671 Lewis Wickes Hine/Library of Congress; 673 (t) Courtesy of Steve Latham; 676 (b) © Bettmann/CORBIS; 677 (b) Library of Congress; 681 (tc) Leroy Radanovich/ Yosemite Museum, (tl) © W. Perry Conway/ CORBIS; 682 (br) White House Collection, copyright White House Historical Association, (bl) White House Collection, copyright White House Historical Association, (bc) White House Collection, copyright White House Historical Association; 687 (t) Library of Congress. **Chapter 22:** Pages 688 (b) © Charles Sleicher; 688-689 (t) © Bettmann/CORBIS; 689 (bl) Press Information Bureau of India, (c) Denver Public Library, Western History Collection; 694 (c) © Douglas Peebles/ CORBIS; 695 National Portrait Gallery, Smithsonian Institution/Art Resource, NY; 696 Trustees of the British Museum; 698 (b) © Bettmann/CORBIS, (c) PRC Archive; 700 (tr) Library of Congress; 701 (bl) © Richard Cohen/CORBIS; 703 (br) © CORBIS; 704-705 (b) Library of Congress; 707 The Granger Collection, New York; 708 (inset) © Bettmann/CORBIS; 710 (b) © Bettmann/ CORBIS, (c) © Bettmann/CORBIS; 711 (tr, b) © Bettmann/CORBIS. **Chapter 23:** Pages 716-717 (t) © Bettmann/CORBIS; 717 (cl) Culver Pictures, Inc., (br) Collection of Colonel Stuart S. Corning/Courtesy of PRC Archive, (bl) Stock Montage, Inc.; 721 The Granger Collection, New York; 724 (t) © CORBIS; 726 ©SuperStock; 728 (t) © Underwood & Underwood/CORBIS, (b) © Patrick BazGetty Images; 729 (t) © K.J. Historical/CORBIS; 731

Sam Dudgeon/HRW; 734 (c) © Hulton/Getty Images, (t) ©Dorling Kindersley Ltd./Courtesy of Spink & Son Ltd., London; 736 (bl) © Michael St. Maur Sheil/CORBIS.

Unit 8: 746-747 Everett Collection. **Chapter 24:** Pages 748 (b) HRW Photo by Lance Schriner; 748-749 (t) The Great White Way, Times Square, 1925 (oil on canvas), Thain, Howard A. (1891-1959)/© New-York Historical Society, New York, USA,;/Bridgeman ARt Library; 749 (bl) Egyptian National Museum, Cairo, Egypt/SuperStock, (cr) Brown Brothers, (bc) © Bettmann/CORBIS, (c) The Granger Collection, New York; 753 The Granger Collection, New York; 754-755 (b) From the Collections of Henry Ford Museum and Greenfield Village; 756 (c) From the Collections of Henry Ford Museum and Greenfield Village; 757 (tr) Janice L. and David J. Frent Collection of Political Americana, (tl) Janice L. and David J. Frent Collection of Political Americana; 759 (t) Library of Congress, (b) TIME Inc./Courtesy of the general libraries, The University of Texas at Austin/HRW photo by Victoria Smith, (c) © Underwood & Underwood/CORBIS; 760 Library of Congress; 761 © Bettmann/ CORBIS; 763 The Phillips Collection, Washington, D.C.; 766 (bl) © Bettmann/ CORBIS, (br) The Negro Leagues Baseball Museum; 767 (cl) The Granger Collection, New York, (bl) © Hulton/Getty Images, (cr) The Granger Collection, New York; 768 © Getty Images; 769 © Georgia O'Keeffe Museum, Santa Fe / Art Resource. **Chapter 25:** Pages 774 (b) The Granger Collection, New York; 774-775 (t) © Bettmann/CORBIS; 775 (cl) Janice L. and David J. Frent Collection of Political Americana, (cr) Courtesy Everett Collection, (bl) © Bettmann/CORBIS; 779 (t) © Bettmann/CORBIS; 780 (br) Milton (Pete) Brooks/The Detroit News; 781 (t) Brown Brothers; 786 (t) © Bettmann/CORBIS; 788 (br) Library of Congress, (bl) Library of Congress; 791 (b) NOAA George E. Marsh Album; 792 Library of Congress; 793 (t) Twentieth Century Fox; 795 The Granger Collection, New York. **Chapter 26:** Pages 800 (b) (c) Bridgeman Art Library; 800-801 (t) © CORBIS; 801 (cr) Reuters/HO/Hulton Archive/ Getty Images, (bl) AKG-Images, London, (bc) © MPI/Getty Images; 805 © Hugo Jaeger/ Timepix/Time Life Pictures/Getty Images; 806 © CORBIS; 808 (cr) © CORBIS; 809 (t) © Brooks Kraft/Corbis; 811 (bl) National Archives; (bc) Picture Research Consultants & Archives, (br) Library of Congress; 812 (bl) © U.S. Air Force/Collection of David Ethell, (t) CORBIS/Bettman; 813 (tr) © Seattle Post-Intelligencer Collection; Museum of History and Industry/CORBIS; 815 (b) Everett Collection; 816 © Bettmann/CORBIS; 817 (tl) Bettmann/CORBIS, (tcl) Bettmann/CORBIS, (tc) Bettmann/CORBIS, (tcr) Bettmann/ CORBIS, (tr) Bettmann/CORBIS, (bkgd) Bettmann/CORBIS; 818 (tl) © CORBIS, (cr) Library of Congress; 818-819 (b) © Keystone/ Getty Images; 821 National Archives (NARA); 823 (bl) © Hulton-Deutsch Collection/ CORBIS, (tl) © Hulton-Deutsch Collection/ CORBIS; 824 ©PHOTOGRAPHER/SuperStock; 826 © CORBIS; 827 © H. Miller/Hulton Archive/Getty Images; 828 © Bettmann/ CORBIS; 831 Bantam Books.

Unit 9: 838-839 (bkgd) © New York Times Co./Hulton Archive/Getty Images, 839 (inset) © Lazlo Willinger/SuperStock. **Chapter 27:** Pages 840-841 (tc) © Bettmann/ CORBIS; 841 (bl) © Bettman/CORBIS, (cr) AP/Wide World Photos, (bl) © Carl & Ann Purcell/CORBIS, (cl) © Hulton Archive/ Getty Images, (cl) © Bettmann/CORBIS; 841 (c) Civil Defense Museum; 845 (bl) © Hulton-Deutsch Collection/CORBIS, (br) UPI/Corbis-Bettmann; 846 (tc) © CORBIS, (tr) AP Photo/United Nations; 847 (cr) Editorial cartoon by Tom Little, 1948; courtesy of the Nashville Tennessean.; 848 The White House, Courtesy Harry S. Truman Library; 849 The Granger Collection, New York; 851 (bl) The Granger Collection, New York; 853 (tc) © ohn Florea/Time & Life Pictures/Getty Images; 854 "FIRE!" From *Herblock: A Cartoonist's Life* (Times Books, 1998)/ Library of Congress; 856 (cl) © Bettmann/CORBIS; 859 (tr) Image courtesy of The Advertising Archives; 860 (tl) © Bettmann/CORBIS, (cl) Time Life Pictures/ Getty Images; (bl) © Bettmann/CORBIS. **Chapter 28:** Pages 866 (br) Photo by Hank Walker//Time Life Pictures/Getty Images; 866-867 (t) Jack Moebes/Corbis; 867 (bc) © Bettmann/CORBIS, (cr) AIMovement, (bl) Sovfoto/Eastfoto; 871 (br) AP/Wide World Photos; 872 (cl) Photos by Will Counts from A LIFE IS MORE THAN A MOMENT; 872-873 (c) Photos by Will Counts from A LIFE IS MORE THAN A MOMENT; 877 (tl) © Bettmann/CORBIS; 878 (all) © Bettmann/ CORBIS; 879 (t) LBJ Library Collection; 880 (cl) Gene Herrick/AP/Wide World Photos, (bl) Wisconsin Historical Society; 881 (cl) Bill Hudson/AP/Wide World Photos, (bl) AP/Wide World Photos; 883 © Arthur Schatz/Time Life Pictures/Getty Images; 884 (all) © Bettmann/CORBIS; 885 William Philpott/REUTERS/NewsCom. **Chapter 29:** Pages 890-891 (t) AP/Wide World Photos; 891 (bl) © Hulton Archive/Getty Images, (br) © Dirck Halstead/Getty Images, (c) © Blank Archives/Getty Images; 897 (r) NASA, (bl) © 1996 CORBIS; Original image courtesy of NASA/CORBIS; 900 AP/Wide World Photos; 902 (br) © Sygma/CORBIS, (bl) © LARRY DOWNING/Reuters/Corbis; 903 Courtesy of Charley Trujillo/Chusma House Publications; 905 © CBS Photo Archive/Getty Images; 907 (tr) National Archives (NARA); 909 (tcl) © Leif Skoogfors/CORBIS, (tcr) © Dick Swanson/ Time Life Pictures/Getty Images, (tl, tr) © David J. & Janice L. Frent Collection/CORBIS, (bkgd) © The Image Bank/Getty Images; 910 © Paula Bronstein/Getty Images; 911 (tr) © CORBIS, (tc) © Bettmann/CORBIS; 912 (b) © James P. Blair/CORBIS, (cl) © Richard Howard/ Time Life Pictures/Getty Images.

Unit 10: 920-921 Jack Harris/Transparency, Inc. **Chapter 30:** Pages 922 (cl) © Bill Pierce/ Getty Images, (b) © Bettmann/CORBIS; 922-923 (t) Wally McNamee/Woodfin Camp & Associates;923 (cr) Tim Shaffer/ AP/Wide World Photos, (br) Lehtikuva Oy/ Woodfin Camp & Associates; 927 (t) Jason Laure/Woodfin Camp & Associates; 929 (t) Republished with permission of Globe Newspaper Company, Inc.; 931 AP/Wide World Photos; 933 (t) Bernard Gotfryd/ Woodfin Camp & Associates, (c) Janice L. and David J. Frent Collection of Political Americana; 934 (bl) White House Collection, copyright White House Historical Association, (bc) White House Collection, copyright White House Historical Association; 935 Courtesy, Jimmy Carter Library; 936 (t) AP/Wide World Photos, (inset) © Bettmann/CORBIS; 938 Leste Sloan/Woodfin Camp & Associates; 939 (inset) © Bill Gentile/CORBIS; 940 Joh Ficara/Woodfin Camp & Associates; 941 (br) Courtesy Ronald Reagan Library, (br) © Robert Nickelsberg/Getty Images, (bc) NASA, (bl) Chuck Nacke/Woodfin Camp & Associates. **Chapter 31:** Pages 946 (b) Smithsonian Institution, Washington, DC Harold Dorwin 2004-55788; 946-947 (t) © Jeff Greenberg/PhotoEdit; 947 (cl) © Peter Turnley/CORBIS, (bl) David Modell-Katz/ Woodfin Camp & Associates, (br) © Derrick Ceyrac/Getty Images; 952 (c) © AFP/Getty Images, (b) © Shelly Katz/Time Life/Getty Images; 953 The White House; 955 (all) © Brooks Kraft/CORBIS; 956 (bl) © Ricky Flores/CORBIS, (bc) © Oleg Nikishin/Getty Images; 957 (bl) © Mirrorpix/Getty Images, (cr) Hasan Sarbakhshian/AP/WideWorld, (bc) Al-Jazeera via APTN/AP/Wide World Photos; 958 Courtesy the White House/Photo by Eric Draper; 960 (l) Eriko Sugita/Corbis, (r) Martin Heitner/Stock Connection Distribution/ Alamy; 961 (l) Steven McBride/Picturesque, (c) Jane Faircloth/Transparencies, Inc., (r) Kelly Culpepper/Transparencies, Inc.; 962 Skidmore, Owings and Merrill Ltd.; 964 Lynne Siler Photography/Alamy; 965 (l) Index Stock Imagery/NewsCom, (r) Bob Jordan/AP/ Wide World Photos.

State Facts: R33 (t) Getty Images, (b) Stockbyte, (bkgd) PhotoDisc/Getty Images.

Staff Credits. The people who contributed to ***The Creation and Development of North Carolina in United States History*** are listed below. They represent editorial, design, intellectual property resources, production, emedia, and permissions.

Melanie Baccus, Charles Becker, Jessica Bega, Kristina Bigelow, Ed Blake, Gillian Brody, Shirley Cantrell, Erin Cornett, Rose Degollado, Mescal Evler, Rhonda Fariss, Marsh Flournoy, Leanna Ford, Bob Fullilove, Matthew Gierhart, Janet Harrington, Betsy Harris, Kristin Hay, Rhonda Haynes, Wilonda Ieans, Cathy Jenevein, Kadonna Knape, Cathy Kuhles, Debbie Lofland, Bob McClellan, Joe Melomo, Richard Metzger, Cynthia Munoz, Holly Norman, Nathan O'Neal, Karl Pallmeyer, Shelly Ramos, Peter Reid, Curtis Riker, Marleis Roberts, Diana Rodriguez, Nancy Rogier, Gene Rumann, Annette Saunders, Kay Selke, Ken Shepardson, Michele Shukers, Chris Smith, Elaine Tate, Jeannie Taylor, Joni Wackwitz, Ken Whiteside, Nadyne Wood

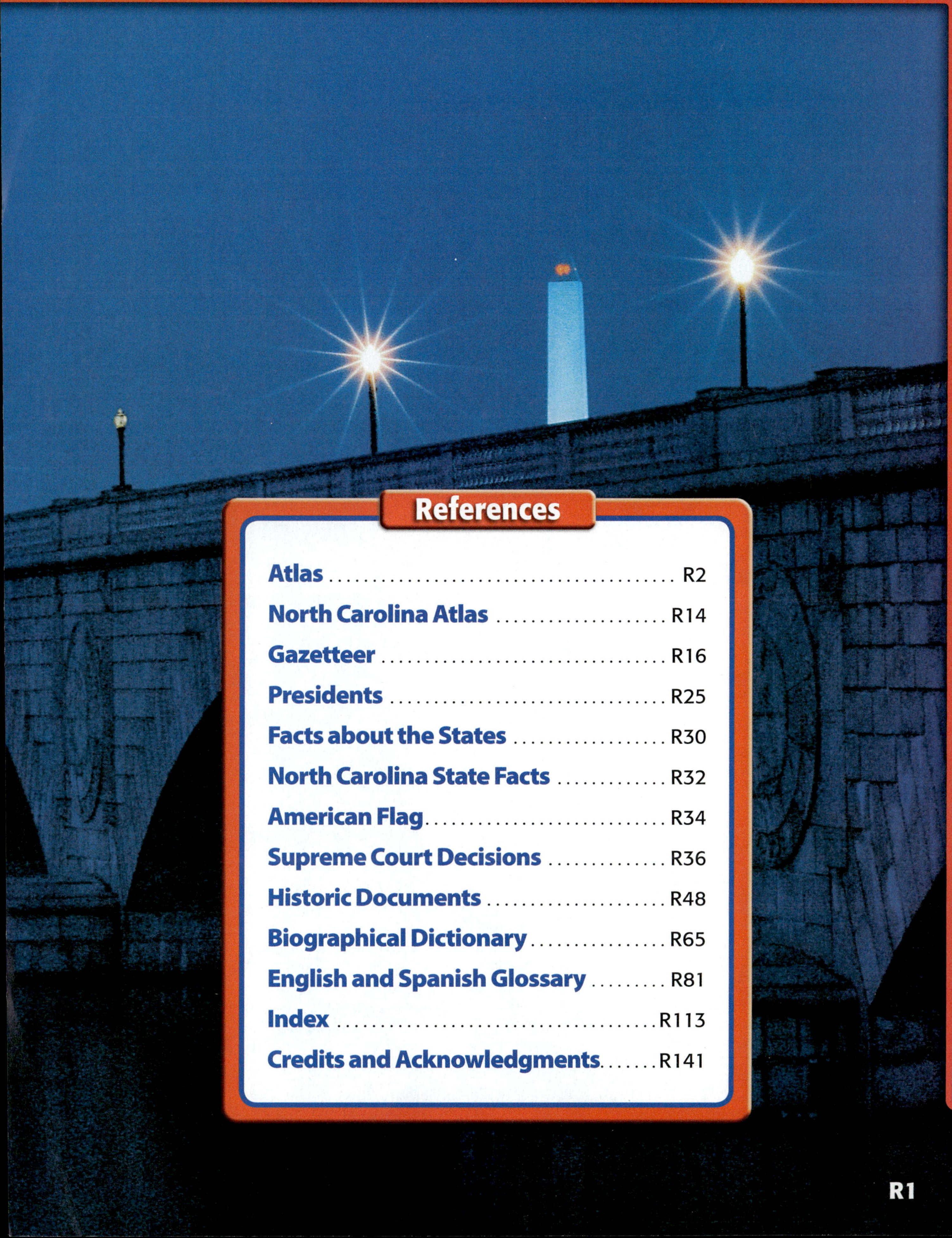

References

The United States of America: Political

To understand the relative locations of Alaska and Hawaii, as well as the vast distances separating them from the rest of the United States, see the world map.

CANADA
MINNESOTA
WISCONSIN
MICHIGAN
IOWA
ILLINOIS
INDIANA
OHIO
MISSOURI
KENTUCKY
TENNESSEE
ARKANSAS
MISSISSIPPI
ALABAMA
GEORGIA
FLORIDA
LOUISIANA
SOUTH CAROLINA
NORTH CAROLINA
VIRGINIA
WEST VIRGINIA
PENNSYLVANIA
NEW YORK
MAINE
VT
NH
MA
CT
RI
NJ
DE
MD
THE BAHAMAS
ATLANTIC OCEAN
Gulf of Mexico
Lake Superior
Lake Michigan
Lake Huron
Lake Erie
Lake Ontario
Lake Champlain
Lake Okeechobee
Lake of the Ozarks
Lake Barkley
Kentucky Lake
Keystone Lake
Eufaula Lake
Lake Texoma
Toledo Bend Reservoir
Red River
Minnesota River
Mississippi River
Missouri River
Illinois River
Ohio River
Hudson R.
Connecticut R.
St. Lawrence River
Susquehanna River
Savannah River
Chattahoochee R.
Delaware Bay
Chesapeake Bay
Long Island Sound
Long Island
Cape Cod
Cape Hatteras
Cape Canaveral
Cape Sable
Florida Keys
Straits of Florida
Sea Islands
Chandeleur Islands
Grand Forks
Fargo
Duluth
Superior
Minneapolis
St. Paul
Sioux Falls
Sioux City
Omaha
Lincoln
Topeka
Kansas City
Wichita
Tulsa
Dallas
Waco
Houston
Beaumont
Galveston
Marquette
Sault Ste. Marie
Green Bay
Madison
Milwaukee
Grand Rapids
Lansing
Saginaw
Detroit
Ann Arbor
Toledo
Cedar Rapids
Davenport
Des Moines
Rockford
Chicago
Gary
South Bend
Fort Wayne
Peoria
Springfield
Indianapolis
Dayton
Columbus
Cincinnati
Cleveland
Youngstown
Akron
Erie
Pittsburgh
St. Louis
East St. Louis
Jefferson City
Springfield
Louisville
Evansville
Frankfort
Lexington
Charleston
Nashville
Knoxville
Memphis
Chattanooga
Fayetteville
Little Rock
Pine Bluff
Huntsville
Birmingham
Atlanta
Macon
Columbus
Savannah
Vicksburg
Jackson
Meridian
Montgomery
Shreveport
Baton Rouge
New Orleans
Biloxi
Mobile
Pensacola
Tallahassee
Jacksonville
Gainesville
Orlando
Tampa
St. Petersburg
Fort Myers
Fort Lauderdale
Miami
Greenville
Columbia
Charleston
Asheville
Charlotte
Winston-Salem
Greensboro
Durham
Raleigh
Richmond
Newport News
Norfolk
Virginia Beach
Washington, D.C.
Baltimore
Annapolis
Dover
Atlantic City
Camden
Trenton
Philadelphia
Harrisburg
Allentown
Newark
Jersey City
New York City
Yonkers
Bridgeport
New Haven
Hartford
Springfield
Providence
Worcester
Boston
Manchester
Concord
Portland
Augusta
Burlington
Montpelier
Albany
Syracuse
Rochester
Buffalo
National capital
State capitals
Other cities
0 100 200 Miles
0 100 200 Kilometers
Projection: Albers Equal Area
N
S
E
W
40°N
35°N
30°N
25°N
95°W
90°W
85°W
80°W
75°W
70°W

The United States of America: Physical

To understand the relative locations of Alaska and Hawaii, as well as the vast distances separating them from the rest of the United States, see the world map.

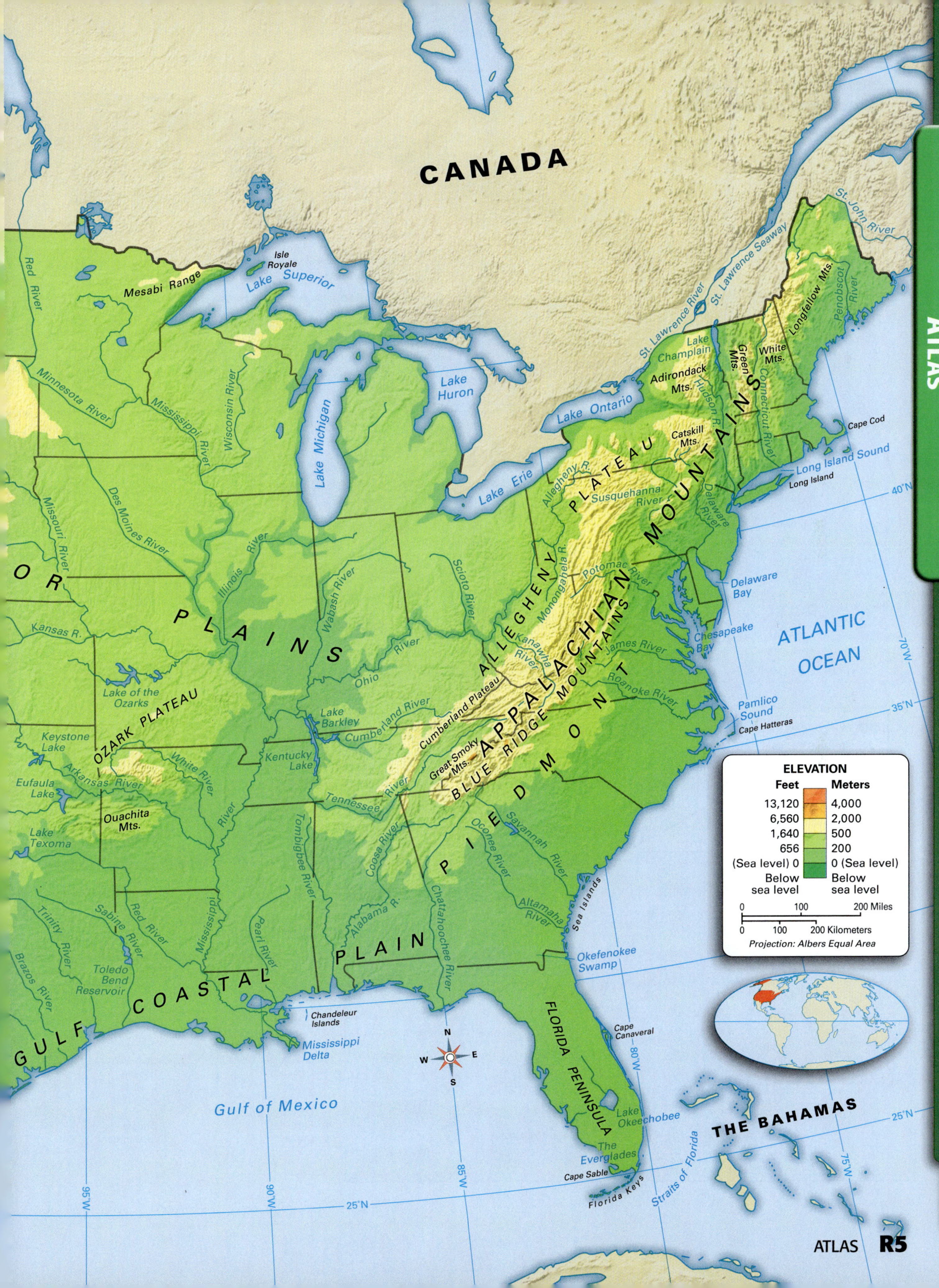
CANADA
Isle Royale
Lake Superior
Mesabi Range
Red River
Minnesota River
Mississippi River
Wisconsin River
Lake Michigan
Lake Huron
Lake Ontario
Lake Erie
St. Lawrence River
St. Lawrence Seaway
St. John River
Penobscot River
Longfellow Mts.
White Mts.
Green Mts.
Lake Champlain
Adirondack Mts.
Hudson R.
Connecticut River
Catskill Mts.
Cape Cod
Long Island Sound
Long Island
40°N
Allegheny R.
PLATEAU
Susquehanna River
Delaware River
MOUNTAINS
Des Moines River
Missouri River
Illinois River
Wabash River
Scioto River
Monongahela R.
Potomac River
Delaware Bay
ALLEGHENY
APPALACHIAN
Chesapeake Bay
ATLANTIC OCEAN
70°W
Kansas R.
PLAINS
Ohio River
Kanawha River
James River
BLUE RIDGE MOUNTAINS
Roanoke River
Pamlico Sound
Cape Hatteras
35°N
Lake of the Ozarks
OZARK PLATEAU
Lake Barkley
Cumberland River
Cumberland Plateau
Great Smoky Mts.
Keystone Lake
Kentucky Lake
PIEDMONT
Eufaula Lake
Arkansas River
White River
Tennessee River
Ouachita Mts.
Lake Texoma
Tombigbee River
Coosa River
Oconee River
Savannah River
Altamaha River
Sea Islands
Trinity River
Sabine River
Red River
Mississippi River
Pearl River
Alabama R.
Chattahoochee River
Brazos River
Toledo Bend Reservoir
COASTAL PLAIN
GULF
Okefenokee Swamp
Chandeleur Islands
Mississippi Delta
FLORIDA PENINSULA
Cape Canaveral
N
W
E
S
80°W
Gulf of Mexico
Lake Okeechobee
THE BAHAMAS
25°N
The Everglades
Cape Sable
Florida Keys
Straits of Florida
95°W
90°W
85°W
75°W
ELEVATION
Feet
Meters
13,120
6,560
1,640
656
(Sea level) 0
Below sea level
4,000
2,000
500
200
0 (Sea level)
Below sea level
0
100
200 Miles
0
100
200 Kilometers
Projection: Albers Equal Area

World: Political

	COUNTRY	CAPITAL
1	Antigua and Barbuda	St. Johns
2	St. Kitts and Nevis	Basseterre
3	Dominica	Roseau
4	St. Lucia	Castries
5	St. Vincent and the Grenadines	Kingstown
6	Barbados	Bridgetown
7	Grenada	St. George's

COUNTRY	CAPITAL
1 Czech Republic	Prague
2 Slovakia	Bratislava
3 Slovenia	Ljubljana
4 Croatia	Zagreb
5 Bosnia and Herzegovina	Sarajevo
6 Macedonia	Skopje
7 Serbia	Belgrade
8 Montenegro	Podgorica
9 Lithuania	Vilnius
10 Latvia	Riga
11 Estonia	Tallinn

North America: Political

South America: Political

ATLAS

Europe: Political

Asia: Political

Africa: Political

Australia and New Zealand: Political

North Carolina: Physical

ATLAS

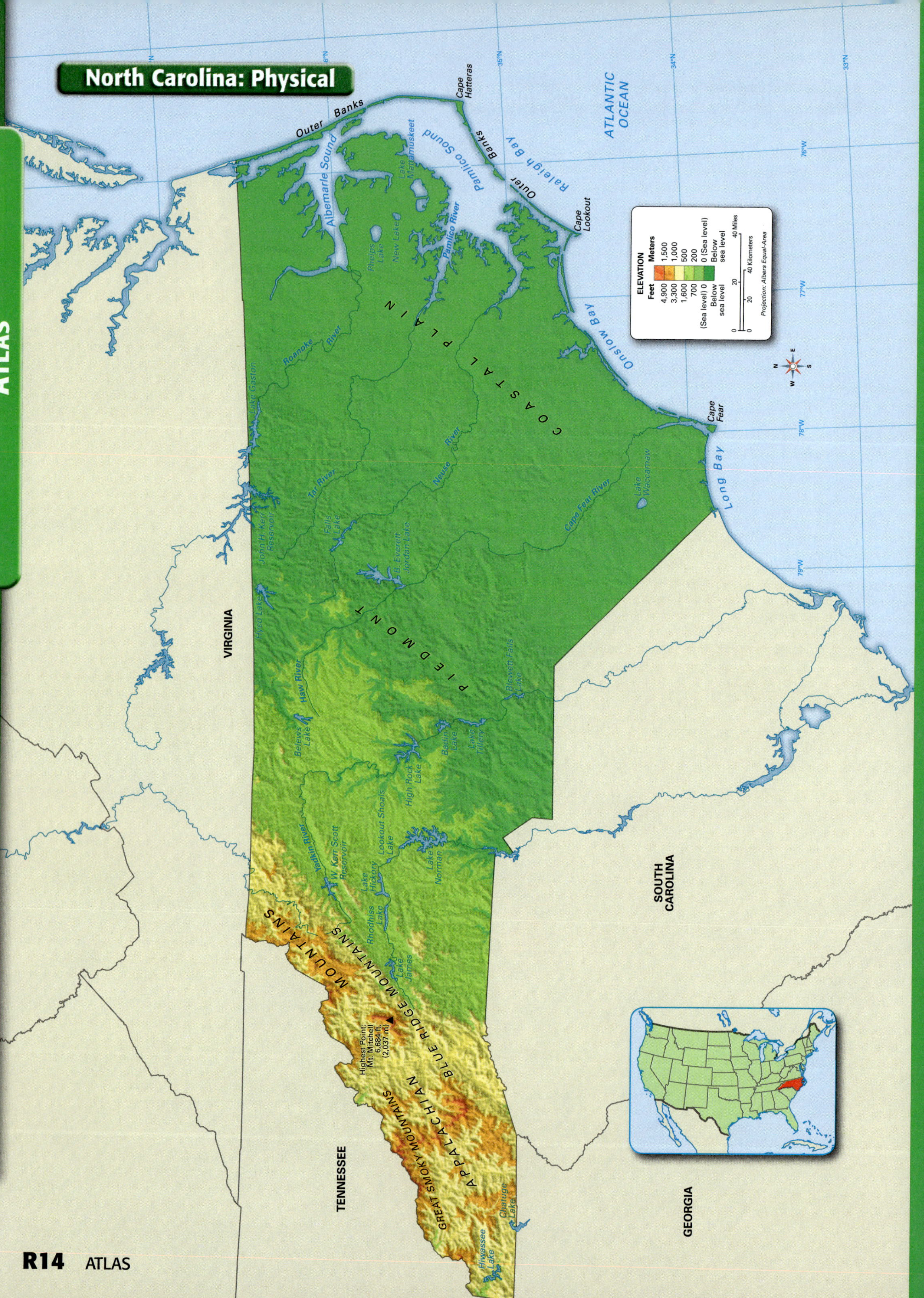

North Carolina: Political

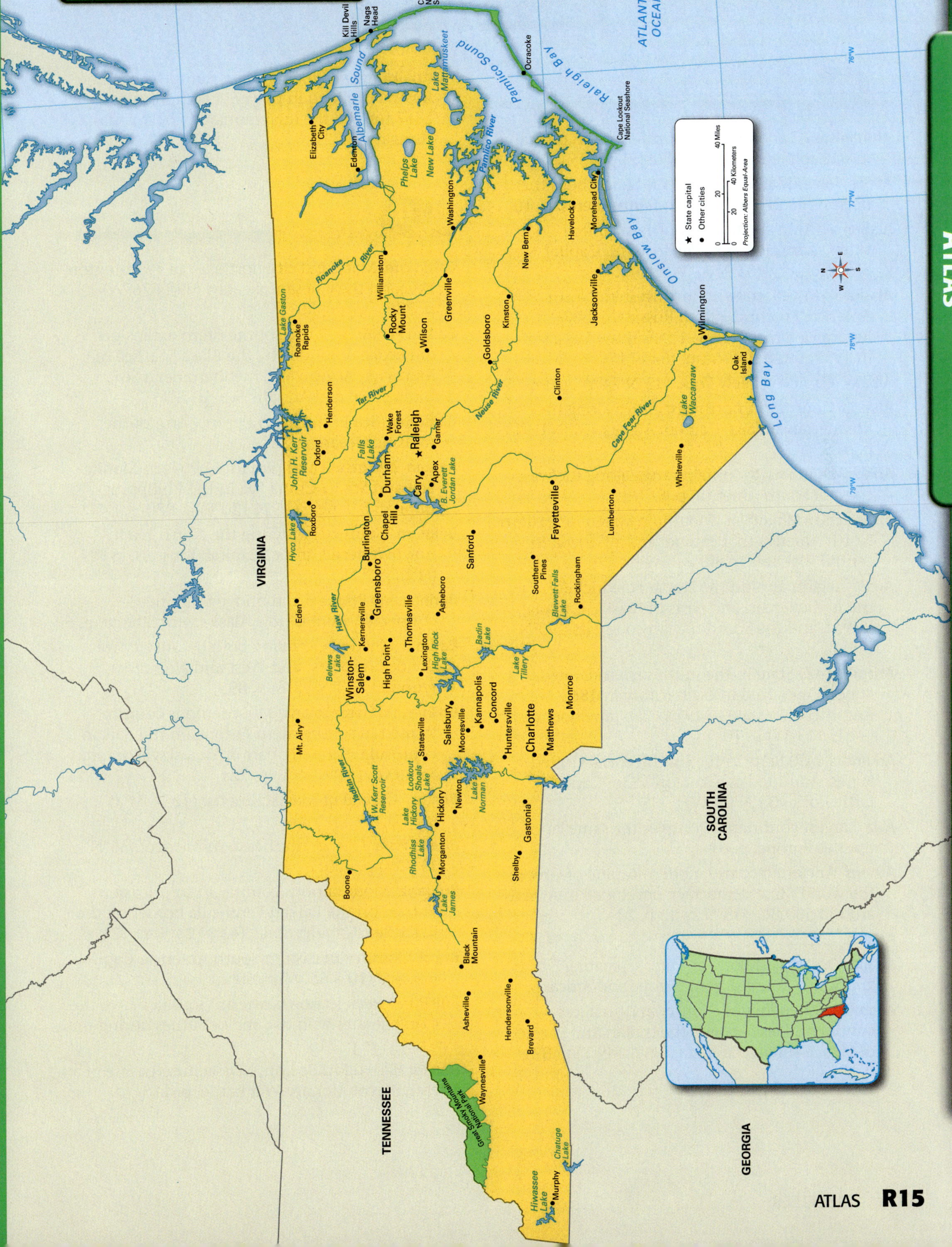

Gazetteer

A

Afghanistan Landlocked country in south central Asia. Capital: Kabul. (35°N 69°E) p. 935

Africa Second-largest continent. Lies in both the northern and the southern hemispheres. p. 16

Alabama (AL) State in the southern United States. Admitted as a state in 1819. Capital: Montgomery. (33°N 87°W) p. 426

Alaska (AK) U.S. state in northwestern North America. Purchased from Russia in 1867. Became a territory in 1912. Admitted as a state in 1959. Capital: Juneau. (64°N 150°W) p. 6

Albany Capital of New York. (42°N 74°W) p. 96

Algeria Country in northwest Africa along the Mediterranean Sea. Capital: Algiers. (37°N 03°E) p. 816

Andes Mountains Mountain range along the west coast of South America. p. 8

Appalachian Mountains Mountain system in eastern North America that extends from Canada to central Alabama. p. 48

Arctic Region around the North Pole including the Arctic Ocean and parts of Alaska, Canada, Russia, and the Scandinavian countries. (90°N 0°E) p. 12

Arizona (AZ) State in the southwestern United States. Organized into a territory in 1863. Admitted as a state in 1912. Capital: Phoenix. (34°N 113°W) p. 10

Arkansas (AR) State in the south-central United States. Admitted as a state in 1836. Capital: Little Rock. (35°N 93°W) p. 55

Asia Largest continent. Occupies the same land mass as Europe. p. 6

Athens Ancient city and modern capital of Greece; the world's first democracy developed in Athens around 500 BC. (38°N 24°E) p. 23

Atlanta Capital of Georgia. (33°N 84°W) p. 541

Atlantic Ocean Vast body of water separating North and South America from Europe and Africa. p. 44

Australia Independent country and smallest continent. Lies between the Indian and Pacific oceans. Capital: Canberra. (35°S 149°E) p. 821

Austria-Hungary Once a major European empire, Austria declined in power. A compromise in 1867 formed the dual monarchy of Austria-Hungary. p.720

B

Baltimore Maryland city northeast of Washington, D.C., on the Chesapeake Bay. (39°N 76°W) p. 286

Balkan Peninsula Most southeastern extension of Europe, bounded by the Black Sea, Sea of Marmara, Aegean Sea, Mediterranean Sea, Ionian Sea, and Adriatic Sea. p. 721

Baltic Sea Sea in northern Europe. Arm of the Atlantic Ocean. p. 722

Bataan Peninsula and province between Manila Bay and South China Sea in the Philippines. Capital: Balanga. (15°N 120°E) p. 820

Belgium Country bordering the North Sea in northwestern Europe. Capital: Brussels. (51°N 04°E) p. 721

Bering Land Bridge Land bridge that once connected what is now Alaska with Siberia. p. 6

Berlin Capital of Germany both before city was divided into East and West and after it was reunited. (53°N 13°E) p. 895

Bosnia and Herzegovina Mountainous country located in southeastern Europe on the Balkan Peninsula. Formerly part of Yugoslavia. Capital: Sarajevo. (44°N 18°E) p. 721

Boston Capital of Massachusetts. (42°N 71°W) p. 100

Buena Vista City in northeastern Mexico. (33°N 117°W) p. 360

Bulgaria Mountainous country in southeastern Europe on the Balkan Peninsula bordering the Black Sea. Capital: Sofia. (43°N 23°E) p. 721

Brazil Country in eastern South America. Capital: Brasília. (10°S 55°W) p. 60

Bull Run Creek in northeastern Virginia where the Confederates won two major battles during the Civil War. p. 516

Bunker Hill Hill in Boston, Massachusetts. Site of an early Revolutionary War battle. p. 115

Burma Renamed Myanmar, the largest nation in southeastern Asia. Capital: Yangon. (17°N 96°E) p. 820

C

Cahokia Site in modern-day Missouri where the Mississippian culture built large settlements. (38°N 90°W) p. 11

California (CA) State in the western United States. Admitted as a state in 1850. Capital: Sacramento. (38°N 121°W) p. 12

Cambodia Country in southeastern Asia on the Indochina Peninsula and the Gulf of Thailand. Capital: Phnom Penh. (12°N 105°E) p. 898

Camp David Presidential retreat in the middle of Catoctin Mountain National Park in Maryland. p. 935

Canada Country in northern North America. Capital: Ottawa. (50°N 100°W) p. 6

Cape of Good Hope Southern tip of Africa. p. 40

Caribbean Sea Arm of the Atlantic Ocean between North and South America. p. 48

Central America Region of land connecting North and South America. p. 8

Charleston Port city in southeastern South Carolina. Originally called Charles Town. (33°N 80°W) p. 136

Chesapeake Bay Inlet of the Atlantic Ocean in Virginia and Maryland. p. 75

Chicago Large U.S. city in northeastern Illinois on Lake Michigan. Major port. (41°N 87°W) p. 401

Chile Country in western South America; the Inca Empire stretched into central Chile. Capital: Santiago. p. 9

China Country in East Asia with the world's largest population. Capital: Beijing. (Official name: People's Republic of China) p. 25

Colombia Country in northwest South America. Capital: Bogotá. (4°N 72°W) p. 705

Columbia River River in the northwestern United States and southwestern Canada. Forms part of boundary between Oregon and Washington. p. 276

Colorado (CO) State in the southwestern United States. Admitted as a state in 1876. Capital: Denver. (39°N 107°W) p. 10

Concord One of two northeastern Massachusetts towns (along with Lexington) where the first fighting of the American Revolution took place in 1775. (42°N 71°W) p. 113

Connecticut (CT) State in the northeastern United States. One of the original thirteen colonies. Admitted as a state in 1788. Capital: Hartford. (41°N 73°W) p. 57

Coral Sea Home to the Great Coral Reef. Arm of southwest Pacific Ocean. p. 821

Cuba Westernmost country of the West Indies, an island republic in the northern Caribbean Sea. Capital: Havana. (23°N 82°W) p. 697

Cuzco City in Peru; it was the capital of the Inca Empire. (14°S 72°W) p. 8

Czechoslovakia Former name of the country in central Europe that included the current Czech and Slovak republics. Capital: Prague. (15°N 14°E) p. 806

D

Delaware (DE) State in the eastern United States. One of the original thirteen colonies. Capital: Dover. (38°N 75°W) p. 57

Denmark Southernmost Scandinavian country in northern Europe. Peninsula and island kingdom between the North and Baltic Seas. Capital: Copenhagen. (56°N 12°E) p. 806

Detroit Largest city in Michigan. (42°N 83°W) p. 642

District of Columbia Federal district between Maryland and Virginia where the capital of the United States is located. (39°N 77°W) p. 240

Dominican Republic West Indies country that occupies approximately the eastern two-thirds of Hispaniola. Capital: Santo Domingo. (19°N 71°W) p. 707

E

Ecuador Country in northwest South America. Capital: Quito. (2°S 78°W) p. 9

Egypt Middle East country in northeast Africa along the Mediterranean and Red Sea coasts. Capital: Cairo. (30°N 31°E) p. 816

El Alamein Village in northwest Egypt where Germany's Africa Korps was defeated by the Allies during World War II. (31°N 29°E) p. 816

Ellis Island New York Bay island. Part of Statue of Liberty National Monument. U.S. immigration center. Entry point for millions of people from 1892–1954. (41°N 74°W) p. 637

England Region of the United Kingdom that makes up most of the southern part of the island of Great Britain. Capital: London. (51°N 1°W) p. 53

Erie Canal Early 1800s building project created a waterway between New York cities of Albany, the capital, and Buffalo, on Lake Erie. p. 303

Ethiopia Country, once known as Abyssinia, in northeastern Africa. Capital: Addis Ababa. (9°N 39°E) p. 804

Europe Continent occupying the same land mass as Asia. p. 22

F

Florence City in Italy; ruled by the Medici family in the 1400s, it was a major center for culture and trade. (44°N 11°E) p. 27

Florida (FL) State in the southeastern United States. Organized as a territory in 1822. Admitted as a state in 1845. Capital: Tallahassee. (30°N 84°W) p. 299

Fort McHenry U.S. fort that guarded Baltimore, Maryland. The British attacked the fort in the War of 1812. p. 286

Fort Necessity Site where the French defeated British colonists in 1754, in what was the first battle of the French and Indian War. p. 96

Fort Sumter Fort on Charleston Harbor, South Carolina. Attack by Confederate forces here began the American Civil War. p. 511

France Country in Western Europe. Capital: Paris. (46°N 0°W) p. 24

G

Georgia (GA) State in the southeastern United States. Admitted as a state in 1788. One of the original thirteen colonies. Capital: Atlanta. (32°N 84°W) p. 76

Germany Country in Western Europe. Capital: Berlin. (51°N 8°E) p. 53

Gettysburg Town in southern Pennsylvania. (40°N 77°W) p. 537

Ghana West African country located between the Niger and Senegal Rivers; it was the site of a powerful empire established around AD 300. Capital: Accra. p. 16

Great Basin Elevated region made up of parts of California, Idaho, Nevada, Oregon, Utah, and Wyoming that was home to many Native American nations. p. 12

Great Britain Country in western Europe that includes England, Scotland, and Wales. Capital: London. p. 93

Great Lakes Chain of lakes located in central North America that extends across the U.S.-Canada border. Includes Lake Superior, Lake Michigan, Lake Huron, Lake Erie, and Lake Ontario. p. 55

Great Plains Region of central North America that lies between the Mississippi River and the Rocky Mountains. p. 14

Greece Country in southern Europe with mountains, rugged coastlines, and scenic islands; the country is called the birthplace of democracy. Capital: Athens. p. 22

Greenland Island in the North Atlantic that was settled by the Vikings. Capital: Godthåb. p. 38

Guam Unincorporated U.S. territory that is the southernmost and largest of the Mariana Islands in the west Pacific Ocean. Capital: Agana. (13°N 145°E) p. 700

Gulf of Mexico Gulf on the southeastern coast of North America, bordered by the United States, Mexico, and Cuba. p. 48

H

Hartford Capital of Connecticut. (41°N 72°W) p. 287

Harlem A neighborhood in upper Manhattan in New York City that became a political and cultural hub for many African Americans in the early 1900s. (41°N 74°W) p. 768

Hawaii Largest of group of eight large and many smaller Hawaiian Islands in the Pacific Ocean admitted to the Union in 1959 as the 50th state. Capital: Honolulu. (21°N 158°W) p. 694

Herzegovina See Bosnia-Herzegovina

Hiroshima A city in Japan where the first atomic bomb was dropped. (34°N 132°E) p. 828

Hispaniola Island that includes the countries of Haiti and the Dominican Republic. p. 43

Ho Chi Minh Trail Network of trails of more than 12,000 miles through eastern Laos and Cambodia into South Vietnam used by the North Vietnamese during the Vietnam War. p. 902

Hong Kong City located on this south coast of China and a special administrative zone of China. Former British colony. Capital: Victoria. (22°N 114°E) p. 820

Hudson Bay Inland sea in east-central Canada. Explored by Henry Hudson in 1610. p. 96

Hudson River River flowing from northeastern to southern New York. p. 57

Hungary Central European nation. Capital: Budapest. (48°N 19°E) p. 950

I

Idaho (ID) State in the northwestern United States. Admitted as a state in 1890. Capital: Boise. (44°N 115°W) p. 364

Illinois (IL) State in the north-central United States. Admitted as a state in 1819. Capital: Springfield. (40°N 90°W) p. 11

India Large country in southern Asia. Capital: New Delhi. (28°N 77°E) p. 40

Indiana (IN) State in the north-central United States. Admitted as a state in 1816. Capital: Indianapolis. (40°N 86°W) p. 155

Indian Ocean Vast body of water east of Africa, south of Asia, west of Australia, and north of Antarctica. p. 44

Iowa (IA) State in the north-central United States. Admitted as a state in 1846. Capital: Des Moines. (42°N 94°W) p. 348

Iran Islamic country in the Persian Gulf region. Formerly Persia. Capital: Tehran. (27°N 55°E) p. 936

Iraq Persian Gulf nation known in ancient times as Mesopotamia. Capital: Baghdad. (33°N 44°E) p. 951

Ireland Island in the British Isles. Divided into Northern Ireland (Capital: Belfast), and the Republic of Ireland (Capital: Dublin). (54°N 8°W) p. 438

Israel Modern Middle Eastern country on the Mediterranean Sea formed in 1948. Capital: Jerusalem. (32°N 35°E) p. 846

Italy Country in southern Europe. Capital: Rome. (44°N 11°E) p. 26

J

Jamestown First successful English colony in America. Established in eastern Virginia in 1607. p. 72

Japan Island chain nation of East Asia. Japan in Chinese means "Land of the rising sun." Capital: Tokyo. (36°N 140°E) p. 694

K

Kansas (KS) State in the central United States. Organized as a territory in 1854. Admitted as a state in 1861. Capital: Topeka. (38°N 99°W) p. 483

Kentucky (KY) State in the east-central United States. Admitted as a state in 1792. Capital: Frankfort. (37°N 87°W) p. 253

Korea See North Korea and South Korea

Kuwait Persian Gulf country on the Arabian Peninsula. Capital: Al-Kuwait, also known as Kuwait City. (29°N 48°E) p. 951

L

Lake Erie One of the Great Lakes. Located in the United States and Canada. p. 285

Latin America Spanish-speaking countries of North and South America that were once claimed by Spain and Portugal. p. 60

Laos Landlocked country in southeast Asia. Capital (Administrative): Vientiane (18°N 103°E) Capital (Historic royal): Luang Phabang. (18°N 108°E) p. 898

Leyte Gulf Large inlet of the Philippine Sea in the Pacific Ocean. (11°N 125°E) p. 822

Lexington One of two northeastern Massachusetts towns (along with Concord) where the first fighting of the American Revolution took place in 1775. (42°N 71°W) p. 114

Liberia Country on the west coast of Africa. Capital: Monrovia. (6°N 10°W) p. 455

Little Rock Capital city in central Arkansas on the Arkansas River. (35°N 92°W) p. 871

London Capital of the United Kingdom, in England. (52°N 0°W) p. 72

Los Angeles Large city in southern California. (34°N 118°W) p. 367

Louisiana (LA) State in the southeastern United States carved out of the Louisiana Territory. Admitted as a state in 1812. Capital: Baton Rouge. (31°N 92°W) p. 273

Luxembourg Also, Grand Duchy of Luxembourg. Small European country between France, Germany, and Belgium. Capital: Luxembourg City. (50°N 6°E) p. 807

M

Maine (ME) State in the northeastern United States. Admitted as a state in 1820. Capital: Augusta. (45°N 70°W) p. 305

Mali West African country located on the Niger River; it was the location of an empire that reached its height around 1300. Capital: Bamako. p. 18

Manhattan Island Island at the north end of New York Bay. One of the five boroughs that make up New York City. p. 57

Maryland (MD) State in the east-central United States. One of the original thirteen colonies. Admitted as a state in 1788. Capital: Annapolis. (39°N 76°W) p. 75

Massachusetts (MA) State in the northeastern United States. One of the original thirteen colonies. Admitted as a state in 1788. Capital: Boston. (42°N 72°W) p. 79

Mecca Ancient city in Arabia and the birthplace of Muhammad. (21°N 40°E) p. 18

Mediterranean Sea Large sea bordered by southern Europe, Southwest Asia, and northern Africa. p. 25

Mesoamerica Area from Mexico to North Central American during pre-Spanish culture. p. 8

Mexico Country in southern North America. Capital: Mexico City. (23°N 104°W) p. 6

Michigan (MI) State in the north-central United States. Admitted as a state in 1837. Capital: Lansing. (46°N 87°W) p. 155

Midway Coral atoll consisting of two islands in central Pacific Ocean west of the Hawaiian chain. Site of Battle of Midway, an Allied victory during World War II. p. 821

Minnesota (MN) State in the north-central United States. Admitted as a state in 1858. Capital: St. Paul. (46°N 90°W) p. 155

Mississippi (MS) State in the southeastern United States. Admitted as a state in 1817. Capital: Jackson. (32°N 89°W) p. 332

Mississippi River River that flows from Minnesota south to the Gulf of Mexico. p. 11

Missouri (MO) State in the central United States. Admitted as a state in 1821. Capital: Jefferson City. (38°N 93°W) p. 11

Missouri River River that flows from southern Montana and joins the Mississippi River. p. 11

Montana (MT) State in the northwestern United States. Admitted as a state in 1889. Capital: Helena. (47°N 112°W) p. 599

Montgomery Capital of Alabama. (32°N 86°W) p. 873

Montreal City in southeastern Canada founded by the French in 1642. (46°N 74°W) p. 128

Morocco Country in northwest Africa bounded by the western Sahara, the Mediterranean Sea, and the Atlantic Ocean. Capital: Rabat. (34°N 07°W). p. 18

N

Nebraska (NE) State in the central United States. Admitted as a state in 1867. Capital: Lincoln. (41°N 101°W) p. 484

Netherlands Country in northwestern Europe. Capital: Amsterdam. (52°N 5°E) p. 53

Nevada (NV) State in the western United States. Organized as a territory in 1861. Admitted as a state in 1864. Capital: Carson City. (39°N 117°W) p. 356

New Amsterdam Dutch settlement on the island of Manhattan. Founded in 1626. p. 57

New England Northeastern section of the United States. Made up of Connecticut, Maine, Massachusetts, New Hampshire, Rhode Island, and Vermont. p. 81

New Hampshire (NH) State in the northeastern United States. One of the original thirteen colonies. Admitted as a state in 1788. Capital: Concord. (44°N 71°W) p. 83

New Jersey (NJ) State in the northeastern United States. One of the original thirteen colonies. Admitted as a state in 1787. Capital: Trenton. (40°N 75°W) p. 57

New Mexico (NM) State in the southwestern United States. Admitted as a state in 1912. Capital: Santa Fe. (34°N 107°W) p. 10

New Orleans Port city in southeastern Louisiana. (30°N 90°W) p. 57

New Spain Vast area of North America controlled by Spain. p. 47

New Sweden Swedish colony in North America that was located along the Delaware River. p. 57

New York (NY) State in the northeastern United States. One of the original thirteen colonies. Admitted as a state in 1788. Capital: Albany. (42°N 78°W) p. 57

New York City Largest city in the United States. (41°N 74°W) p. 57

Nicaragua Country between Caribbean Sea and Pacific Ocean in Central America. Capital: Managua. (12°N 86°W) p. 708

Niger River Major river in West Africa. p. 18

North America Continent in the northern Western Hemisphere. p. 6

North Carolina (NC) State in the southeastern United States. One of the original thirteen colonies. Admitted as a state in 1789. Capital: Raleigh. p. 76

North Dakota (ND) State in north-central United States. Admitted as a state in 1889. Capital: Bismarck. (47°N 102°W) p. 790

North Korea Country in East Asia consisting of the northern half of Korean peninsula. Capital: P'yōngyang. (39°N 126°E) p. 853

North Sea Arm of the Atlantic Ocean, between the east coast of Britain and the area northwest of the central European mainland. (Between 51°N and 62°N) p. 722

Norway Country on the northwestern part of Scandinavia in northern Europe. Capital: Oslo. (60°N 11°E) p. 806

Nuremberg Also, Nūrnberg. City in southern Germany. Site of trials of German World War II war criminals. (49°N 11°E) p. 845

O

Ohio (OH) State in the north-central United States. Originally part of the Northwest Territory. Admitted as a state in 1803. Capital: Columbus. (40°N 83°W) p. 155

Ohio River River that flows through Pennsylvania, Ohio, Indiana, and Illinois. p. 11

Oklahoma (OK) State in the south-central United States. Organized as a territory in 1890. Admitted as a state in 1907. Capital: Oklahoma City. (36°N 98°W) p. 48

Ottoman Empire Vast former Turkish empire that expanded to include much of southeastern Europe, the Middle East, and North Africa between the 1300s and 1900s. p. 721

Oregon (OR) State in the northwestern United States. Admitted as a state in 1859. Capital: Salem. (43°N 122°W) p. 348

P

Pacific Ocean Body of water extending from the Arctic Circle to Antarctica and from western North and South America to Australia, the Malay Archipelago, and East Asia. p. 44

Palestine Region between the Jordan River and the Mediterranean Sea containing modern-day Israel, the West Bank, and the Gaza Strip. Often called "The Holy Land." p. 846

Panama Country in southern Central America. Location of the Panama Canal. Capital: Panama City. (8°N 81°W) p. 49

Pearl Harbor An inlet on the Pacific island of Oahu, Hawaii. p. 808

Pennsylvania (PA) State in the eastern United States. One of the original thirteen colonies. Admitted as a state in 1787. Capital: Harrisburg. (41°N 78°W) p. 86

Persian Gulf Arm of the Arabian Sea in the Indian Ocean between the Arabian Peninsula and the Asian mainland. Called the Arabian Gulf by Arabs. p. 951

Peru Country in western South America. Capital: Lima. (10°S 75°W) p. 47

Philadelphia City in southeastern Pennsylvania. Capital of the United States from 1790 to 1800. (40°N 75°W) p. 86

Philippines Country in the western Pacific Ocean. Made up of about 7,100 islands. Capital: Manila. (14°N 125°E) p. 44

Pittsburgh Second largest city and major port in Pennsylvania. (40°N 80°W) p. 647

Plymouth Site in Massachusetts where the Pilgrims first landed in North America in 1620. (42°N 70°W) p. 79

Poland Country in central Europe on the Baltic Sea. Capital: Warsaw. (52°N 21°E) p. 806

Portugal Country in southwestern Europe on the western Iberian Peninsula. Capital: Lisbon. (38°N 8°W) p. 39

Providence Capital of Rhode Island. (42°N 71°W) p. 82

Puerto Rico Island east of Cuba and southeast of Florida. A U.S. territory acquired in the Spanish-American War. Capital: San Juan. (18°N 67°W) p. 48

R

Rhode Island (RI) State in the northeastern United States. One of the original thirteen colonies. Admitted as a state in 1790. Capital: Providence. (41°N 71°W) p. 82

Richmond Capital of Virginia. Capital of the Confederate States of America during the Civil War. (37°N 7°W) p. 428

Rio Grande Spanish for *Great River*. Forms the border between Texas and Mexico. p. 357

Roanoke Island Island off the coast of North Carolina. Site of Britain's first settlement in North America. p. 56

Rocky Mountains Mountain range in western North America that extends from Alaska south to New Mexico. p. 14

Rome A city in Italy near the Mediterranean Sea; it was the capital of the Roman Empire. (42°N 13°E) p. 22

Russia Vast country that extends from Eastern Europe through northwestern Asia. Capital: Moscow. (61°N 60°E) p. 347

S

Sacramento River River in northwest California. Sacramento, capital of California, sits at its head. (38°N 121°W) p. 365

Sahara The world's largest desert, located in northern Africa. p. 16

St. Louis City in Missouri on the Mississippi River. (39°N 90°W) p. 642

San Antonio City in southern Texas. Site of the Mexican victory over Texas forces at the Alamo during the Texas Revolution. (29°N 99°W) p. 362

San Diego City in southern California. Located on San Diego Bay. (33°N 117°W) p. 358

San Francisco City in western California on a peninsula between the Pacific Ocean and San Francisco Bay. (37°N 122°W) p. 358

San Juan Hill Hill close to the city of Santiago, Cuba. Site of a battle in the Spanish-American War. p. 699

Santa Fe Capital of New Mexico. (35°N 106°W) p. 349

Saratoga Site in eastern New York of the Revolutionary War's Battle of Saratoga, the turning point of the war. p. 129

Savannah Port city in southeastern Georgia. Founded by James Oglethorpe in 1733. (32°N 81°W) p. 136

Scandinavia Large peninsula in northern Europe. p. 38

Serbia (Serbia and Montenegro). Balkan republic. About 80 percent of former Yugoslavia. Capital: Belgrade. (45°N 21°E) p. 721

Seneca Falls Village in west-central New York State. Site of the first women's rights convention in the United States in 1848. (43°N 77°W) p. 464

Sierra Nevada Large mountain range in eastern California. p. 12

Singapore Island republic in southeast Asia. Capital: Singapore City. (1°N 104°E) p. 820

Songhai Large and powerful empire in West Africa during the 1400s and 1500s. p. 19

South America Continent in the southern Western Hemisphere. p. 6

South Carolina (SC) State in the southeastern United States. One of the original thirteen colonies. Admitted as a state in 1788. Capital: Columbia. (34°N 81°W) p. 76

South Dakota (SD) State in the north-central United States. Organized as part of the Dakota Territory in 1861. Admitted as a state in 1889. Capital: Pierre. (44°N 102°W) p. 597

South Korea Country in East Asia consisting of the southern half of Korean peninsula. Capital: Seoul. (38°N 127°E) p. 853

Soviet Union Former federation of republics succeeding the Russian empire. First Communist state. Full name: Union of Soviet Socialist Republics (USSR). p. 805

Spain Country in southwestern Europe that occupies the greater part of the Iberian Peninsula. Capital: Madrid. (40°N 4°W) p. 43

Stalingrad Russian city. Renamed Volgograd in 1961. (49°N 42°E) p. 817

Sun Belt Term given to the warmer climate region of southern U.S. states stretching between east and west coasts. p. 858

Switzerland Also known as Swiss Confederation. Alpine country in central Europe. Capital: Bern. (47°N 7°E) p. 722

Syria Ancient country and formerly larger region. Modern Middle East Arab country on the Mediterranean Sea. Capital: Damascus. (35°N 38°E) p. 927

T

Teapot Dome Rock formation rising above an oil field in Wyoming named for teapot-like shape. Known for a scandal during President Harding's administration. (43°N 116°W) p. 753

Tennessee (TN) State in the south-central United States. Admitted as a state in 1796. Capital: Nashville. (36°N 88°W) p. 282

Tenochtitlán Aztec island-city that was located on the site of what is now Mexico City. p. 8

Texas (TX) State in the south-central United States. Independent republic from 1836 to 1845. Admitted as a state in 1845. Capital: Austin. (31°N 101°W) p. 350

Thailand Country in central southeast Asia. Capital: Bangkok. (14°N 101°E) p. 820

Timbuktu City in West Africa that began as a camp for traders around AD 1100 and became a major center of culture and learning. (17°N 3°W) p. 18

Tonkin, Gulf of Arm of South China Sea between Vietnam and China. p. 901

Tuskegee City in Alabama. Home of Tuskegee Institute historic site. (32°N 86°W) p. 812

U

United States of America Country in central North America. Capital: Washington, D.C. (38°N 110°W) p. 6

Utah (UT) State in the western United States. Admitted as a state in 1896. Capital: Salt Lake City. (39°N 112°W) p. 10

V

Valley Forge Site in southeastern Pennsylvania where General George Washington and his troops spent the harsh winter of 1777–1778. p. 132

Venezuela Country in South America. Capital: Caracas. (11°N 67°W) p. 707

Vermont (VT) State in the northeastern United States. Admitted as a state in 1791. Capital: Montpelier. (44°N 73°W) p. 89

Vicksburg City in western Mississippi on the bluffs above the Mississippi River. (42°N 85°W) p. 522

Vietnam Country along east coast of Southeast Asian peninsula. North and South united in 1976 after Vietnam War ended. Capital: Hanoi. (21°N 106°E) p. 898

Virginia (VA) State in the eastern United States. One of the original thirteen colonies. Admitted as a state in 1788. Capital: Richmond. (37°N 80°W) p. 72

W

Washington (WA) State in the northwestern United States. Admitted as a state in 1889. Capital: Olympia. (47°N 121°W) p. 362

Washington, D.C. Capital of the United States. Located on the Potomac River between Virginia and Maryland. (39°N 77°W) p. 240

West Virginia (WV) State in the east-central United States. Part of Virginia until the area refused to join the Confederacy in 1861. Admitted as a state in 1863. Capital: Charleston. (39°N 81°W) p. 303

Western Hemisphere Term given to that half of the earth's sphere that contains the Americas. p. 707

Wisconsin (WI) State in the north-central United States. Became part of the Northwest Territory in 1787. Admitted as a state in 1848. Capital: Madison. (44°N 91°W) p. 155

Wyoming (WY) State in the northwestern United States. Admitted as a state in 1890. Capital: Cheyenne. (43°N 108°W) p. 361

Y

Yalta Ukrainian city on south shore of the Crimean peninsula by the Black Sea. Meeting place of Churchill, Roosevelt, and Stalin near end of World War II. (45°N 34°E) p. 844

Yugoslavia Former country of the Balkan peninsula in southeast Europe created in 1918 that crumbled during the late 1900s. Capital: Belgrade. (45°N 21°E) p. 953

Presidents

1 GEORGE WASHINGTON
Born: 1732 **Died:** 1799
Years in Office: 1789–97
Political Party: None
Home State: Virginia
Vice President: John Adams

2 JOHN ADAMS
Born: 1735 **Died:** 1826
Years in Office: 1797–1801
Political Party: Federalist
Home State: Massachusetts
Vice President: Thomas Jefferson

3 THOMAS JEFFERSON
Born: 1743 **Died:** 1826
Years in Office: 1801–09
Political Party: Republican*
Home State: Virginia
Vice Presidents: Aaron Burr, George Clinton

4 JAMES MADISON
Born: 1751 **Died:** 1836
Years in Office: 1809–17
Political Party: Republican
Home State: Virginia
Vice Presidents: George Clinton, Elbridge Gerry

5 JAMES MONROE
Born: 1758 **Died:** 1831
Years in Office: 1817–25
Political Party: Republican
Home State: Virginia
Vice President: Daniel D. Tompkins

6 JOHN QUINCY ADAMS
Born: 1767 **Died:** 1848
Years in Office: 1825–29
Political Party: Republican
Home State: Massachusetts
Vice President: John C. Calhoun

7 ANDREW JACKSON
Born: 1767 **Died:** 1845
Years in Office: 1829–37
Political Party: Democratic
Home State: Tennessee
Vice Presidents: John C. Calhoun, Martin Van Buren

8 MARTIN VAN BUREN
Born: 1782 **Died:** 1862
Years in Office: 1837–41
Political Party: Democratic
Home State: New York
Vice President: Richard M. Johnson

* The Republican Party of the third through sixth presidents is not the party of Abraham Lincoln, which was founded in 1854.

9 William Henry Harrison
Born: 1773 **Died:** 1841
Years in Office: 1841
Political Party: Whig
Home State: Ohio
Vice President: John Tyler

10 John Tyler
Born: 1790 **Died:** 1862
Years in Office: 1841–45
Political Party: Whig
Home State: Virginia
Vice President: None

11 James K. Polk
Born: 1795 **Died:** 1849
Years in Office: 1845–49
Political Party: Democratic
Home State: Tennessee
Vice President: George M. Dallas

12 Zachary Taylor
Born: 1784 **Died:** 1850
Years in Office: 1849–50
Political Party: Whig
Home State: Louisiana
Vice President: Millard Fillmore

13 Millard Fillmore
Born: 1800 **Died:** 1874
Years in Office: 1850–53
Political Party: Whig
Home State: New York
Vice President: None

14 Franklin Pierce
Born: 1804 **Died:** 1869
Years in Office: 1853–57
Political Party: Democratic
Home State: New Hampshire
Vice President: William R. King

15 James Buchanan
Born: 1791 **Died:** 1868
Years in Office: 1857–61
Political Party: Democratic
Home State: Pennsylvania
Vice President: John C. Breckinridge

16 Abraham Lincoln
Born: 1809 **Died:** 1865
Years in Office: 1861–65
Political Party: Republican
Home State: Illinois
Vice Presidents: Hannibal Hamlin, Andrew Johnson

17 Andrew Johnson
Born: 1808 **Died:** 1875
Years in Office: 1865–69
Political Party: Republican
Home State: Tennessee
Vice President: None

18 Ulysses S. Grant
Born: 1822 **Died:** 1885
Years in Office: 1869–77
Political Party: Republican
Home State: Illinois
Vice Presidents: Schuyler Colfax, Henry Wilson

19 Rutherford B. Hayes
Born: 1822 **Died:** 1893
Years in Office: 1877–81
Political Party: Republican
Home State: Ohio
Vice President: William A. Wheeler

20 James A. Garfield
Born: 1831 **Died:** 1881
Years in Office: 1881
Political Party: Republican
Home State: Ohio
Vice President: Chester A. Arthur

21 Chester A. Arthur
Born: 1829 **Died:** 1886
Years in Office: 1881–85
Political Party: Republican
Home State: New York
Vice President: None

22 Grover Cleveland
Born: 1837 **Died:** 1908
Years in Office: 1885–89
Political Party: Democratic
Home State: New York
Vice President: Thomas A. Hendricks

23 Benjamin Harrison
Born: 1833 **Died:** 1901
Years in Office: 1889–93
Political Party: Republican
Home State: Indiana
Vice President: Levi P. Morton

24 Grover Cleveland
Born: 1837 **Died:** 1908
Years in Office: 1893–97
Political Party: Democratic
Home State: New York
Vice President: Adlai E. Stevenson

25 William McKinley
Born: 1843 **Died:** 1901
Years in Office: 1897–1901
Political Party: Republican
Home State: Ohio
Vice Presidents: Garret A. Hobart, Theodore Roosevelt

26 Theodore Roosevelt
Born: 1858 **Died:** 1919
Years in Office: 1901–09
Political Party: Republican
Home State: New York
Vice President: Charles W. Fairbanks

27 William Howard Taft
Born: 1857 **Died:** 1930
Years in Office: 1909–13
Political Party: Republican
Home State: Ohio
Vice President: James S. Sherman

28 Woodrow Wilson
Born: 1856 **Died:** 1924
Years in Office: 1913–21
Political Party: Democratic
Home State: New Jersey
Vice President: Thomas R. Marshall

29 Warren G. Harding
Born: 1865 **Died:** 1923
Years in Office: 1921–23
Political Party: Republican
Home State: Ohio
Vice President: Calvin Coolidge

30 Calvin Coolidge
Born: 1872 **Died:** 1933
Years in Office: 1923–29
Political Party: Republican
Home State: Massachusetts
Vice President: Charles G. Dawes

31 Herbert Hoover
Born: 1874 **Died:** 1964
Years in Office: 1929–33
Political Party: Republican
Home State: California
Vice President: Charles Curtis

32 Franklin D. Roosevelt
Born: 1882 **Died:** 1945
Years in Office: 1933–45
Political Party: Democratic
Home State: New York
Vice Presidents: John Nance Garner, Henry Wallace, Harry S Truman

33 Harry S Truman
Born: 1884 **Died:** 1972
Years in Office: 1945–53
Political Party: Democratic
Home State: Missouri
Vice President: Alben W. Barkley

34 Dwight D. Eisenhower
Born: 1890 **Died:** 1969
Years in Office: 1953–61
Political Party: Republican
Home State: Kansas
Vice President: Richard M. Nixon

35 John F. Kennedy
Born: 1917 **Died:** 1963
Years in Office: 1961–63
Political Party: Democratic
Home State: Massachusetts
Vice President: Lyndon B. Johnson

36 LYNDON B. JOHNSON
Born: 1908 **Died:** 1973
Years in Office: 1963–69
Political Party: Democratic
Home State: Texas
Vice President: Hubert H. Humphrey

37 RICHARD M. NIXON
Born: 1913 **Died:** 1994
Years in Office: 1969–74
Political Party: Republican
Home State: California
Vice Presidents: Spiro T. Agnew, Gerald R. Ford

38 GERALD R. FORD
Born: 1913 **Died:** 2006
Years in Office: 1974–77
Political Party: Republican
Home State: Michigan
Vice President: Nelson A. Rockefeller

39 JIMMY CARTER
Born: 1924
Years in Office: 1977–81
Political Party: Democratic
Home State: Georgia
Vice President: Walter F. Mondale

40 RONALD REAGAN
Born: 1911 **Died:** 2004
Years in Office: 1981–89
Political Party: Republican
Home State: California
Vice President: George Bush

41 GEORGE BUSH
Born: 1924
Years in Office: 1989–93
Political Party: Republican
Home State: Texas
Vice President: J. Danforth Quayle

42 BILL CLINTON
Born: 1946
Years in Office: 1993–2001
Political Party: Democratic
Home State: Arkansas
Vice President: Albert Gore Jr.

43 GEORGE W. BUSH
Born: 1946
Years in Office: 2001–
Political Party: Republican
Home State: Texas
Vice President: Richard B. Cheney

Facts about the States

State	Year of Statehood	2003 Population	Area (Sq. Mi.)	Population Density (Sq. Mi.)	Capital
 Alabama	1819	4,500,752	50,744	88.7	Montgomery
 Alaska	1959	648,818	571,951	1.1	Juneau
 Arizona	1912	5,580,811	113,635	49.1	Phoenix
 Arkansas	1836	2,725,714	52,068	52.3	Little Rock
 California	1850	35,484,453	155,959	227.5	Sacramento
 Colorado	1876	4,550,688	103,718	43.9	Denver
 Connecticut	1788	3,483,372	4,845	719.0	Hartford
 Delaware	1787	817,491	1,954	418.4	Dover
 District of Columbia	—	563,384	61	9,235.8	—
 Florida	1845	17,019,068	53,927	315.6	Tallahassee
 Georgia	1788	8,684,715	57,906	150.0	Atlanta
 Hawaii	1959	1,257,608	6,423	195.8	Honolulu
 Idaho	1890	1,366,332	82,747	16.5	Boise
 Illinois	1818	12,653,544	55,584	227.6	Springfield
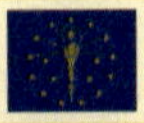 Indiana	1816	6,195,643	35,867	172.7	Indianapolis
 Iowa	1846	2,944,062	55,869	52.7	Des Moines
 Kansas	1861	2,723,507	81,815	33.3	Topeka
 Kentucky	1792	4,117,827	39,728	103.7	Frankfort
 Louisiana	1812	4,496,334	43,562	103.2	Baton Rouge
 Maine	1820	1,305,728	30,862	42.3	Augusta
 Maryland	1788	5,508,909	9,774	563.6	Annapolis
 Massachusetts	1788	6,433,422	7,840	820.6	Boston
 Michigan	1837	10,079,985	56,804	177.5	Lansing
 Minnesota	1858	5,059,375	79,610	63.6	St. Paul

State	Year of Statehood	2003 Population	Area (Sq. Mi.)	Population Density (Sq. Mi.)	Capital
Mississippi	1817	2,881,281	46,907	61.4	Jackson
Missouri	1821	5,704,484	68,886	82.8	Jefferson City
Montana	1889	917,621	145,552	6.3	Helena
Nebraska	1867	1,739,291	76,872	22.6	Lincoln
Nevada	1864	2,241,154	109,826	20.4	Carson City
New Hampshire	1788	1,287,687	8,968	143.6	Concord
New Jersey	1787	8,638,396	7,417	1,164.7	Trenton
New Mexico	1912	1,874,614	121,356	15.4	Santa Fe
New York	1788	19,190,115	47,214	406.4	Albany
North Carolina	1789	8,407,248	48,711	172.6	Raleigh
North Dakota	1889	633,837	68,976	9.2	Bismarck
Ohio	1803	11,435,798	40,948	279.3	Columbus
Oklahoma	1907	3,511,532	68,667	51.1	Oklahoma City
Oregon	1859	3,559,596	95,997	37.1	Salem
Pennsylvania	1787	12,365,455	44,817	275.9	Harrisburg
Rhode Island	1790	1,076,164	1,045	1,029.8	Providence
South Carolina	1788	4,147,152	30,109	137.7	Columbia
South Dakota	1889	764,309	75,885	10.1	Pierre
Tennessee	1796	5,841,748	41,217	141.7	Nashville
Texas	1845	22,118,509	261,797	84.5	Austin
Utah	1896	2,351,467	82,144	28.6	Salt Lake City
Vermont	1791	619,107	9,250	66.9	Montpelier
Virginia	1788	7,386,330	39,594	186.6	Richmond
Washington	1889	6,131,445	66,544	92.1	Olympia
West Virginia	1863	1,810,354	24,078	75.2	Charleston
Wisconsin	1848	5,472,299	54,310	100.8	Madison
Wyoming	1890	501,242	97,100	5.2	Cheyenne

Governors of the State of North Carolina

Richard Caswell (1776–1780)
Abner Nash (1780–1781)
Thomas Burke (1781–1782)
Alexander Martin (1782–1785)
Richard Caswell (1784–1787)
Samuel Johnston (1787–1789)
Alexander Martin (1789–1792)
Richard Dobbs Spaight, Sr. (1792–1795)
Samuel Ashe (1795–1798)
William Richardson Davie (1798–1799)
Benjamin Williams (1799–1802)
James Turner (1802–1805)
Nathaniel Alexander (1805–1807)
Benjamin Williams (1807–1808)
David Stone (1808–1810)
Benjamin Smith (1810–1811)
William Hawkins (1811–1814)
William Miller (1814–1817)
John Branch (1817–1820)
Jesse Franklin (1820–1821)
Gabriel Holmes (1821–1824)
Hutchins Gordon Burton (1824–1827)
James Iredell, Jr. (1827–1828)
John Owen (1828–1830)
Montford Stokes (1830–1832)
David Lowry Swain (1832–1835)
Richard Dobbs Spaight, Jr. (1835–1836)
Edward Bishop Dudley (1836–1841)
John Motley Morehead (1841–1845)
William Alexander Graham (1845–1849)
Charles Manly (1849–1850)
David Settle Reid (1851–1854)
Warren Winslow (1854–1855)
Thomas Bragg (1855–1859)
John Willis Ellis (1859–1861)
Henry Toole Clark (1861–1862)
Zebulon Baird Vance (1862–1865)
William Woods Holden (1865)
Jonathan Worth (1865–1868)
William Woods Holden (1868–1870)
Tod Robinson Caldwell (1870–1874)
Curtis Hooks Brogden (1874–1877)
Zebulon Baird Vance (1877–1879)
Thomas Jordan Jarvis (1879–1885)
Alfred Moore Scales (1885–1889)
Daniel Gould Fowle (1889–1891)
Thomas Michael Holt (1891–1893)
Elias Carr (1893–1897)
Daniel Lindsay Russell (1897–1901)
Charles Brantley Aycock (1901–1905)
Robert Broadnax Glenn (1905–1909)
William Walton Kitchin (1909–1913)
Locke Craig (1913–1917)
Thomas Walter Bickett (1917–1921)
Cameron Morrison (1921–1925)
Angus Wilton McLean (1925–1929)
Oliver Max Gardner (1929–1933)
John Christoph Blucher Ehringhaus (1933–1937)
Clyde Roark Hoey (1937–1941)
Joseph Melville Broughton (1941–1945)
Robert Gregg Cherry (1945–1949)
William Kerr Scott (1949–1953)
William Bradley Umstead (1953–1954)
Luther Hartwell Hodges (1954–1961)
Terry Sanford (1961–1965)
Dan Killian Moore (1965–1969)
Robert Walter Scott (1969–1973)
James Eubert Holshouser, Jr. (1973–1977)
James Baxter Hunt, Jr. (1977–1985)
James Grubbs Martin (1985–1993)
James Baxter Hunt, Jr. (1993–2001)
Michael F. Easley (2001–Present)

North Carolina Government

Executive Branch

Carries out the laws and policies of state government

Governor

- Elected by voters to a four-year term
- Limited to two terms
- Appoints cabinet and some judges
- Chairs the Council of State

Lieutenant Governor

- Elected by voters to a four-year term
- Holds various responsibilities, including replacing the governor should he or she leave office

Cabinet

- Consists of officials appointed by governor
- Offers advice to governor on specific areas of knowledge

Legislative Branch

Makes state laws

Bicameral System

- General Assembly has two houses—Senate and House of Representatives
- Both houses take part in presenting and passing laws
- General Assembly can override the governor's veto with a three-fifths vote in both houses

State Senate

- 50 members
- Elected to two-year terms
- No term limits

State House of Representatives

- 120 members
- Elected to two-year terms
- No term limits

Judicial Branch

Decides conflicts and questions about the law

Trial Courts

- Hear civil and criminal cases

Appellate Courts

- North Carolina Court of Appeals is only intermediate appellate court in the state
- Consists of fifteen judges who rule in rotating panels of three

Supreme Court of North Carolina

- Highest appellate court in the state
- Determines statewide principles of law in deciding specific lawsuits
- Consists of seven justices
- Justices elected by voters to eight-year terms
- No term limits

North Carolina Facts

THE WORLD ALMANAC

State tree	Pine
State bird	Cardinal
State reptile	Eastern box turtle
State mammal	Gray squirrel
State fish	Channel bass
State shell	Scotch bonnet
State flower	Dogwood
State vegetable	Sweet potato
Capital	Raleigh
Year of Statehood	1789 (12th state)
Nickname	The Old North State, Tar Heel State
Motto	Esse Quam Videri (To be rather than to seem)
Song	"The Old North State"
Highest Elevation	Mt. Mitchell, 6,684 feet above sea level
Lowest Elevation	Sea level
Total area	53,819 square miles
National rank in total area	28
Total Coastline	301 miles
Largest city	Charlotte
Largest lake	Mattamuskeet
Number of counties	100
Population	8,683,242 (as of 2005)
National rank in population	11
Length (North to South)	190 miles
Width (East to West)	505 miles

The cardinal is the North Carolina state bird.

The coast of North Carolina

American Flag

The American flag is a symbol of the nation. It is recognized instantly, whether as a big banner waving in the wind or a tiny emblem worn on a lapel. The flag is so important that it is a major theme of the national anthem, "The Star-Spangled Banner." One of the most popular names for the flag is the Stars and Stripes. It is also known as Old Glory.

THE MEANING OF THE FLAG

The American flag has 13 stripes—7 red and 6 white. In the upper-left corner of the flag is the union—50 white five-pointed stars against a blue background.

The 13 stripes stand for the original 13 American states, and the 50 stars represent the states of the nation today. According to the U.S. Department of State, the colors of the flag also are symbolic:

Red stands for courage.

White symbolizes purity.

Blue is the color of vigilance, perseverance, and justice.

DISPLAYING THE FLAG

It is customary not to display the American flag in bad weather. It is also customary for the flag to be displayed outdoors only from sunrise to sunset, except on certain occasions. In a few special places, however, the flag is always flown day and night. When flown at night, the flag should be illuminated.

Near a speaker's platform, the flag should occupy the place of honor at the speaker's right. When carried in a parade with other flags, the American flag should be on the marching right or in front at the center. When flying with the flags of the 50 states, the national flag must be at the center and the highest point. In a group of national flags, all should be of equal size and all should be flown from staffs, or flagpoles, of equal height.

The flag should never touch the ground or the floor. It should not be marked with any insignia, pictures, or words. Nor should it be used in any disrespectful way—as an advertising decoration, for instance. The flag should never be dipped to honor any person or thing.

SALUTING THE FLAG

The United States, like other countries, has a flag code, or rules for displaying and honoring the flag. For example, all those present should stand at attention facing the flag and salute it when it is being raised or lowered or when it is carried past them in a parade or procession. A man wearing a hat should take it off and hold it with his right hand over his heart. All women and hatless men should stand with their right hands over their hearts to show their respect for the flag. The flag should also receive these honors during the playing of the national anthem and the reciting of the Pledge of Allegiance.

THE PLEDGE OF ALLEGIANCE

The Pledge of Allegiance was written in 1892 by Massachusetts magazine (*Youth's Companion*) editor Francis Bellamy. (Congress added the words "under God" in 1954.)

I pledge allegiance to the flag of the United States of America and to the republic for which it stands, one nation under God, indivisible, with liberty and justice for all.

Civilians should say the Pledge of Allegiance with their right hands placed over their hearts. People in the armed forces give the military salute. By saying the Pledge of Allegiance, we promise loyalty ("pledge allegiance") to the United States and its ideals.

"THE STAR-SPANGLED BANNER"

"The Star-Spangled Banner" is the national anthem of the United States. It was written by Francis Scott Key during the War of 1812. While being detained by the British aboard a ship on September 13–14, 1814, Key watched the British bombardment of Fort McHenry at Baltimore. The attack lasted 25 hours. The smoke was so thick that Key could not tell who had won. When the air cleared, Key saw the American flag that was still flying over the fort. "The Star-Spangled Banner" is sung to music written by British composer John Stafford Smith. In 1931 Congress designated "The Star-Spangled Banner" as the national anthem.

I

Oh, say, can you see, by the dawn's early light,
What so proudly we hailed at the twilight's last gleaming,
Whose broad stripes and bright stars through the perilous fight,
O'er the ramparts we watched were so gallantly streaming?
And the rockets' red glare, the bombs bursting in air,
Gave proof through the night that our flag was still there.
Oh, say, does that star-spangled banner yet wave
O'er the land of the free, and the home of the brave?

II

On the shore, dimly seen through the mists of the deep,
Where the foe's haughty host in dread silence reposes,
What is that which the breeze, o'er the towering steep,
As it fitfully blows, half conceals, half discloses?
Now it catches the gleam of the morning's first beam,
In full glory reflected, now shines on the stream.
'Tis the star-spangled banner; oh, long may it wave
O'er the land of the free, and the home of the brave!

III

And where is that band who so vauntingly swore
That the havoc of war and the battle's confusion
A home and a country should leave us no more?
Their blood has washed out their foul footsteps' pollution.
No refuge could save the hireling and slave
From the terror of flight, or the gloom of the grave:
And the star-spangled banner in triumph doth wave
O'er the land of the free, and the home of the brave!

IV

Oh! thus be it ever when freemen shall stand
Between their loved homes and the war's desolation!
Blest with victory and peace, may the heaven-rescued land
Praise the Power that hath made and preserved us a nation!
Then conquer we must, for our cause it is just,
And this be our motto: "In God is our trust!"
And the star-spangled banner in triumph shall wave,
O'er the land of the free, and the home of the brave!

Sheet music to the national anthem

"AMERICA, THE BEAUTIFUL"

One of the most beloved songs celebrating our nation is "America, the Beautiful." Katharine Lee Bates first wrote the lyrics to the song in 1893 after visiting Colorado. The version of the song we know today is set to music by Samuel A. Ward. The first and last stanzas of "America, the Beautiful" are shown below.

O beautiful for spacious skies,
For amber waves of grain,
For purple mountain majesties
Above the fruited plain!
America! America!
God shed his grace on thee
And crown thy good with brotherhood
From sea to shining sea!

O beautiful for patriot dream
That sees beyond the years
Thine alabaster cities gleam
Undimmed by human tears!
America! America!
God shed his grace on thee
And crown thy good with brotherhood
From sea to shining sea!

Supreme Court Decisions

SUPREME COURT DECISIONS

Marbury v. *Madison* (1803)

Significance This ruling established the Supreme Court's power of judicial review, by which the Court decides whether laws passed by Congress are constitutional. This decision greatly increased the prestige of the Court and gave the judiciary branch a powerful check against the legislative and executive branches.

Background William Marbury and several others were commissioned as judges by Federalist president John Adams during his last days in office. This act angered the new Democratic-Republican president, Thomas Jefferson. Jefferson ordered his secretary of state, James Madison, not to deliver the commissions. Marbury took advantage of a section in the Judiciary Act of 1789 that allowed him to take his case directly to the Supreme Court. He sued Madison, demanding the commission and the judgeship.

Decision This case was decided on February 24, 1803, by a vote of 5 to 0. Chief Justice John Marshall spoke for the Court, which decided against Marbury. The court ruled that although Marbury's commission had been unfairly withheld, he could not lawfully take his case to the Supreme Court without first trying it in a lower court. Marshall said that the section of the Judiciary Act that Marbury had used was actually unconstitutional and that the Constitution must take priority over laws passed by Congress.

McCulloch v. *Maryland* (1819)

Significance This ruling established that Congress had the constitutional power to charter a national bank. The case also established the principle of national supremacy, which states that the Constitution and other laws of the federal government take priority over state laws. In addition, the ruling reinforced the loose-construction interpretation of the Constitution favored by many Federalists.

Background In 1816 the federal government set up the Second Bank of the United States to stabilize the economy following the War of 1812. Many states were opposed to the competition provided by the new national bank. Some of these states passed heavy taxes on the Bank. The national bank refused to pay the taxes. This led the state of Maryland to sue James McCulloch, the cashier of the Baltimore, Maryland, branch of the national bank.

Decision This case was decided on March 6, 1819, by a vote of 7 to 0. Chief Justice John Marshall spoke for the unanimous Court, which ruled that the national bank was constitutional because it helped the federal government carry out other powers granted to it by the Constitution. The Court declared that any attempt by the states to interfere with the duties of the federal government could not be permitted.

Gibbons v. *Ogden* (1824)

Significance This ruling was the first case to deal with the clause of the Constitution that allows Congress to regulate interstate and foreign commerce. This case was important because it reinforced both the authority of the federal government over the states and the division of powers between the federal government and the state governments.

Background Steamboat operators who wanted to travel on New York waters had to obtain a state license. Thomas Gibbons had a federal license to travel along the coast, but not a state license for New York. He wanted the freedom to compete with state-licensed Aaron Ogden for steam travel between New Jersey and the New York island of Manhattan.

Decision This case was decided on March 2, 1824, by a vote of 6 to 0. Chief Justice John Marshall spoke for the Court, which ruled in favor of Gibbons. The Court stated that the congressional statute (Gibbons's federal license) took priority over the state statute (Ogden's state-monopoly license). The ruling also defined commerce as more than simply the exchange of goods, broadening it to include the transportation of people and the use of new inventions (such as the steamboat).

Supreme Court Building, Washington, D.C.

Worcester v. *Georgia* (1832)

Significance This ruling made Georgia's removal of the Cherokee illegal. However, Georgia, with President Andrew Jackson's support, defied the Court's decision. By not enforcing the Court's ruling, Jackson violated his constitutional oath as president. As a result, the Cherokee and other American Indian tribes continued to be forced off of lands protected by treaties.

Background The state of Georgia wanted to remove Cherokee Indians from lands they held by treaty. Samuel Worcester, a missionary who worked with the Cherokee Nation, was arrested for failing to take an oath of allegiance to the state and to obey a Georgia militia order to leave the Cherokee's lands. Worcester sued, charging that Georgia had no legal authority on Cherokee lands.

Decision This case was decided on March 3, 1832, by a vote of 5 to 1 in favor of Worcester. Chief Justice John Marshall spoke for the Supreme Court, which ruled that the Cherokee were an independent political community. The Court decided that only the federal government, not the state of Georgia, had authority over legal matters involving the Cherokee people.

Scott v. *Sandford* (1857)

Significance This ruling denied enslaved African Americans U.S. citizenship and the right to sue in federal court. The decision also invalidated the Missouri Compromise, which had prevented slavery in territories north of the 36° 30′ line of latitude. The ruling increased the controversy over the expansion of slavery in new states and territories.

Background John Emerson, an army doctor, took his slave Dred Scott with him to live in Illinois and then Wisconsin Territory, both of which had banned slavery. In 1842 the two moved to Missouri, a slave state. Four years later, Scott sued for his freedom according to a Missouri legal principle of "once free, always free." The principle meant that a slave was entitled to freedom if he or she had once lived in a free state or territory.

Decision This case was decided March 6-7, 1857, by a vote of 7 to 2. Chief Justice Roger B. Taney spoke for the Court, which ruled that slaves did not have the right to sue in federal courts because they were considered property, not citizens. In addition, the Court ruled that Congress did not have the power to abolish slavery in territories because that power was not strictly defined in the Constitution. Furthermore, the Court overturned the once-free, always-free principle.

SUPREME COURT DECISIONS

Civil Rights Cases (1883)

Significance This ruling struck down the Civil Rights Act of 1875. It allowed private businesses to discriminate based on race or color. The Court ruled that Congress could only make laws preventing states, not private individuals or companies, from discriminating.

Background Five separate cases were combined under this one decision. After the Civil Rights Act of 1875 was passed, individuals and private businesses continued to discriminate against former slaves and other African Americans. In the five separate cases, African Americans were denied the same accommodations that whites were provided.

Decision The case was decided on October 15, 1883, by a vote of 8 to 1. Justice Joseph P. Bradley wrote the opinion, which said of the 14th Amendment, "Individual invasion of individual rights is not the subject-matter of the amendment." Justice John Marshall Harlan was the lone dissenter, claiming that the 13th Amendment gave Congress the right to make the law. "The letter of the law is the body," he said. "[T]he sense and reason of the law is the soul."

Wabash, St. Louis & Pacific Railroad v. *Illinois* (1886)

Significance This ruling reversed an earlier decision in *Munn* v. *Illinois* and removed the power from the states to regulate railroad rates. It reasserted the authority of Congress over interstate commerce and led to the creation of the Interstate Commerce Commission.

Background The state of Illinois passed a law attempting to regulate the shipping rates of railroads that passed through the state, including the Wabash, St. Louis & Pacific line. In an attempt to operate without regulation, the railroad company sued the state.

Decision The Court struck down the Illinois law, saying that the state was able to regulate businesses that operated only within its boundaries. Businesses that operated between states were subject to regulation by the national government.

United States v. *E.C. Knight Co.* (1895)

Significance This ruling effectively put most monopolies out of the reach of the Sherman Antitrust Act of 1890. It declared that local manufacturing was out of the scope of the interstate-commerce regulatory power of Congress.

Background The E. C. Knight Company enjoyed a virtual monopoly of sugar refining within the United States. The federal government sued the company under the Sherman Antitrust Act in an attempt to break this monopoly and allow other companies to refine sugar.

Decision The court ruled that although the act was legal, it did not apply to manufacturing. Justice Melville Fuller said that manufacturing was not interstate commerce and could therefore not be regulated by Congress.

In Re Debs (1895)

Significance In this ruling the Court upheld the right of the federal government to halt strikes organized by union workers. After losing his case, Debs ran for president from his jail cell.

Background Railway union official Eugene V. Debs had organized a strike of union workers. The government petitioned him to halt the strike, and a court held him in contempt when he refused. Debs fought his conviction.

Decision In a unanimous decision, the Court declared that the federal government did have the power to order Debs to halt the strike. Justice David J. Brewer wrote the opinion of the Court, which stated the U.S. government "acts directly upon each citizen."

Plessy v. *Ferguson* (1896)

Significance This case upheld the constitutionality of racial segregation by ruling that separate facilities for different races were legal as long as those facilities were equal to one another. This case provided a legal justification for racial segregation for nearly 60 years until it was overturned by *Brown* v. *Board of Education* in 1954.

Background An 1890 Louisiana law required that all railway companies in the state use "separate-but-equal" railcars for white and African American passengers. A group of citizens in New Orleans banded together to challenge the law and chose Homer Plessy to test the law in 1892. Plessy took a seat in a whites-only coach, and when he refused to move, he was arrested. Plessy eventually sought review by the U.S. Supreme Court, claiming that the Louisiana law violated his Fourteenth Amendment right to equal protection.

Decision This case was decided on May 18, 1896, by a vote of 7 to 1. Justice Henry Billings Brown spoke for the Court, which upheld the constitutionality of the Louisiana law that segregated railcars. Justice John M. Harlan dissented, arguing that the Constitution should not be interpreted in ways that recognize class or racial distinctions.

Northern Securities Co. v. *United States* (1904)

Significance In this ruling the Court declared that the federal government had the right to break up companies if their formation was illegal, whether or not dissolving the company would have a harmful impact on the business community.

Background The Northern Securities Company held stock in several major railroads. Although President Theodore Roosevelt claimed the company was a trust and therefore illegal under the Sherman Antitrust Act, some disagreed that the idea of trusts extended into the realm of owning stocks.

Decision In a 5-to-4 decision, the Court ruled that the formation of the company was illegal, and that the federal government had the power to disband it. Writing for the majority, Justice John Marshall Harlan said, "every corporation created by a state is necessarily subject to the supreme law of the land," meaning the federal government.

Lochner v. *New York* (1905)

Significance This decision established the Supreme Court's role in overseeing state regulations. For more than 30 years, Lochner was often used as a precedent in striking down state laws such as minimum-wage laws, child labor laws, and regulations placed on the banking and transportation industries.

Background In 1895 the state of New York passed a labor law limiting bakers to working no more than 10 hours per day or 60 hours per week. The purpose of the law was to protect the health of bakers, who worked in hot and damp conditions and breathed in large quantities of flour dust. In 1902 Joseph Lochner, the owner of a small bakery in New York, claimed that the state law violated his Fourteenth Amendment rights by unfairly depriving him of the liberty to make contracts with employees. This case went to the U.S. Supreme Court.

Decision This case was decided on April 17, 1905, by a vote of 5 to 4 in favor of Lochner. The Supreme Court judged that the Fourteenth Amendment protected the right to sell and buy labor, and that any state law restricting that right was unconstitutional. The Court rejected the argument that the limited workday and workweek were necessary to protect the health of bakery workers.

Muller v. *Oregon* (1908)

Significance A landmark for cases involving social reform, this decision established the Court's recognition of social and economic conditions (in this case, women's health) as a factor in making laws.

Background In 1903 Oregon passed a law limiting workdays to 10 hours for female workers in laundries and factories. In 1905 Curt Muller's Grand Laundry was found guilty of breaking this law. Muller appealed, claiming that the state law violated his freedom of contract (the Supreme Court had upheld a similar claim that year in *Lochner* v. *New York*). When this case came to the Court, the National Consumers' League hired lawyer Louis D. Brandeis to present Oregon's argument. Brandeis argued that the Court had already defended the state's police power to protect its citizens' health, safety, and welfare.

Decision This case was decided on February 24, 1908, by a vote of 9 to 0 upholding the Oregon law. The Court agreed that women's well-being was in the state's public interest and that the 10-hour law was a valid way to protect their well-being.

Schechter Poultry Corporation v. United States (1935)

Significance This ruling declared that the United States could not regulate businesses that operated only within one state. It dealt a severe blow to President Franklin Roosevelt's New Deal.

Background In an attempt to lessen the effects of the Great Depression, Roosevelt encouraged Congress to pass a Recovery Act that set a minimum wage and restricted working hours. The Schechter Poultry Corporation, which operated only within New York City, maintained that the federal government did not have a constitutional right to regulate its businesses practices.

Decision In a unanimous decision, the Court upheld the Schechter Corporation's claim. Chief Justice Charles Evans Hughes wrote the opinion, which stated that the transactions in the case—wages, salaries, and working hours—were a local concern outside of the scope of federal regulation.

Korematsu v. U.S. (1944)

Significance This case addressed the question of whether government action that treats a racial group differently from other people violates the Equal Protection Clause of the Fourteenth Amendment. The ruling in the case held that distinctions based on race are "inherently suspect," and that laws and rules based on race must withstand "strict scrutiny" by the courts. The Court still applies the "strict scrutiny" standard today to cases involving race and other groups.

Background When the United States declared war on Japan in 1941, about 112,000 Japanese Americans lived on the West Coast. About 70,000 of these Japanese Americans were citizens. In 1942 the U.S. military was afraid that these people could not be trusted in wartime. They ordered most of the Japanese Americans to move to special camps far from their homes. Fred Korematsu, a Japanese American and an American citizen, did not go to the camps as ordered. He stayed in California and was arrested. He was sent to a camp in Utah. Korematsu then sued, claiming that the government acted illegally when it sent people of Japanese descent to camps.

Decision By a 6-to-3 margin, the Supreme Court said the orders moving the Japanese-Americans into the camps were constitutional. Justice Hugo Black wrote the opinion for the Court. He said that the unusual demands of wartime security justified the orders. However, he made it clear that distinctions based on race are "inherently suspect," and that laws based on race must withstand "strict scrutiny" by the courts. Justice Robert H. Jackson dissented; he wrote that Korematsu was "convicted of an act not commonly a crime ... being present in the state [where] he is a citizen, near where he was born, and where all his life he has lived." Justice Frank Murphy, another dissenter, said the military order was based on racial prejudice.

Brown v. Board of Education (1954)

Significance This ruling reversed the Supreme Court's earlier position on segregation set by *Plessy* v. *Ferguson* (1896). The decision also inspired Congress and the federal courts to help carry out further civil rights reforms for African Americans.

Background Beginning in the 1930s, the National Association for the Advancement of Colored People (NAACP) began using the courts to challenge racial segregation in public education. In 1952 the NAACP took a number of school segregation cases to the Supreme Court. These included the Brown family's suit against the school board of Topeka, Kansas, over its "separate-but-equal" policy.

Decision This case was decided on May 17, 1954, by a vote of 9 to 0. Chief Justice Earl Warren spoke for the unanimous Court, which ruled that segregation in public education created inequality. The Court held that racial segregation in public schools was by nature unequal, even if the school facilities were equal. The Court noted that such segregation created feelings of inferiority that could not be undone. Therefore, enforced separation of the races in public education is unconstitutional.

Watkins v. *United States* (1957)

Significance The decision limited the inquiry powers of Congress. It was expected not to engage in law enforcement (an executive function), nor to act as a trial agency (a judicial function), but to inquire only as far as was necessary for the functioning of Congress.

Background Watkins was a labor union officer who appeared before the House Un-American Activities Committee during the 1950s Red Scare. Although he was willing to answer personal questions about himself and others whom he knew to be members of the Communist Party, he would not answer questions about past members of the Communist Party. He was therefore held in contempt of Congress.

Decision In a vote of 6 to 1 handed down on June 17, 1957, the Court threw out the charge of contempt against Watkins. Congress, it said, did not have the right to invade the private lives of individuals.

Mapp v. *Ohio* (1961)

Significance In this ruling the Court declared that evidence discovered in the process of an illegal search could not be used in state courts.

Background While searching for a bombing suspect, police found evidence of a separate crime in the house of Dollree Mapp. The police did not have permission to enter the home, nor did they have a search warrant. Upon conviction for the separate crime, Mapp appealed her case to the Supreme Court.

Decision In a 5-to-3 decision, the Court stated that convictions based on illegally obtained evidence must be overturned. Justice Tom Clark wrote for the majority, "all evidence obtained by searches and seizures in violation of the Constitution is … inadmissible in a state court."

Baker v. *Carr* (1962)

Significance Through this decision, the Court ruled that the judiciary branch may involve itself in hearing cases about political matters.

Background Voters from Tennessee sued their state in federal court, arguing that the way the state drew the boundary lines between representative districts created unequal representation within the legislature, and therefore unequal protection under the laws of the state. Tennessee argued that the federal court did not have the jurisdiction to hear the case.

Decision By a 6-to-2 margin, the Court decided that the federal court did have the right to hear the case and that the voters had the right to sue over the issue. Writing for the majority, Justice William Brennan said that the voters "are entitled to a trial and a decision" on whether they were denied equal protection.

Engel v. *Vitale* (1962)

Significance This case deals with the specific issue of organized prayer in schools and the broader issue of the proper relationship between government and religion under the First Amendment. The question in the case was whether a state violates the First Amendment when it composes a prayer that students must say at the beginning of each school day.

Background The state of New York recommended that public schools in the state begin the day by having students recite a prayer written by the state government. A group of parents sued to stop the official prayer, saying that it was contrary to their beliefs and their children's beliefs. They believed the law was unconstitutional because it "established" (officially supported) religion. Though students were permitted to remain silent, the parents claimed that there would always be pressure on students to pray.

Decision By a 6-to-1 margin (two justices did not take part in the case), the Court agreed with the parents. It struck down the state law. Justice Hugo Black wrote for the decision for the majority. He pointed out that the prayer was clearly religious. He said that under the First Amendment, "it is no part of the business of government to compose official prayers for any group of American people to recite as part of a religious program carried on by government." Black, referring to Jefferson and Madison, said "These men knew that the First Amendment, which tried to put an end to governmental control of religion and prayer, was not written to destroy either."

Gideon v. Wainwright (1963)

Significance This ruling was one of several key Supreme Court decisions establishing free legal help for those who cannot otherwise afford representation in court.

Background Clarence Earl Gideon was accused of robbery in Florida. Gideon could not afford a lawyer for his trial, and the judge refused to supply him with one for free. Gideon tried to defend himself and was found guilty. He eventually appealed to the U.S. Supreme Court, claiming that the lower court's denial of a court-appointed lawyer violated his Sixth and Fourteenth Amendment rights.

Decision This case was decided on March 18, 1963, by a vote of 9 to 0 in favor of Gideon. The Court agreed that the Sixth Amendment (which protects a citizen's right to have a lawyer for his or her defense) applied to the states because it fell under the due process clause of the Fourteenth Amendment. Thus, the states are required to provide legal aid to those defendants in criminal cases who cannot afford to pay for legal representation.

Heart of Atlanta Motel v. United States (1964)

Significance This ruling upheld the public accommodations clause of the Civil Rights Act of 1964. It enforced the right of African Americans to receive access to the same accommodations as whites and gave Congress judicial backing for passing more civil rights legislation.

Background The owner of the Heart of Atlanta Motel routinely discriminated against African Americans. He claimed that his business was not an interstate business and therefore not subject to regulation by congressional acts.

Decision In a unanimous decision, the Court declared that as a business that served people from across state boundaries, the Heart of Atlanta Motel was in fact an interstate business and that, therefore, congressional acts did apply.

Miranda v. Arizona (1966)

Significance This decision ruled that an accused person's Fifth Amendment rights begin at the time of arrest. The ruling caused controversy because it made the questioning of suspects and collecting evidence more difficult for law enforcement officers.

Background In 1963 Ernesto Miranda was arrested in Arizona for a kidnapping. Miranda signed a confession and was later found guilty of the crime. The arresting police officers, however, admitted that they had not told Miranda of his right to talk with an attorney before his confession. Miranda appealed his conviction on the grounds that by not informing him of his legal rights the police had violated his Fifth Amendment right against self-incrimination.

Decision This case was decided on June 13, 1966, by a vote of 5 to 4. Chief Justice Earl Warren spoke for the Court, which ruled in Miranda's favor. The Court decided that an accused person must be given four warnings after being taken into police custody: (1) the suspect has the right to remain silent, (2) anything the suspect says can and will be used against him or her, (3) the suspect has the right to consult with an attorney and to have an attorney present during questioning, and (4) if the suspect cannot afford a lawyer, one will be provided before questioning begins.

Tinker v. Des Moines Independent Community School District (1969)

Significance This ruling established the extent to which American public school students can take part in political protests in their schools. The question the case raised is whether, under the First Amendment, school officials can prohibit students from wearing armbands to symbolize political protest.

Background Students in Des Moines, Iowa, decided to wear black armbands to protest the Vietnam War. Two days before the protest, the school board created a new policy. The policy stated that any student who wore an armband to school and refused to remove it would be suspended. Three students wore armbands and were suspended. They said that their First Amendment right to freedom of speech had been violated. In 1969 the United States Supreme Court decided their case.

The Decision By a 7-to-2 margin, the Court agreed with the students. Justice Abe Fortas wrote the decision for the majority. He said that students do not "shed their constitutional rights to freedom of speech ... at the schoolhouse gate." Fortas admitted that school officials had the right to set rules. However, their rules must be consistent with the First Amendment. In this case, Des Moines school officials thought their rule was justified. They feared that the protest would disrupt learning. Fortas's opinion held that wearing an armband symbolizing political protest was a form of speech called symbolic speech. Symbolic speech is conduct that expresses an idea. Symbolic speech is protected in the same manner as the spoken word. Fortas wrote that student symbolic speech could be punished only if it disrupts the learning process. Fortas also noted that school officials allowed other political symbols, such as campaign buttons, to be worn in school.

Reed v. Reed (1971)

Significance This ruling was the first in a century of Fourteenth Amendment decisions to say that gender discrimination violated the equal protection clause. This case was later used to strike down other statutes that discriminated against women.

Background Cecil and Sally Reed were separated. When their son died without a will, the law gave preference to Cecil to be appointed the administrator of the son's estate. Sally sued Cecil for the right to administer the estate, challenging the gender preference in the law.

Decision This case was decided on November 22, 1971, by a vote of 7 to 0. Chief Justice Warren Burger spoke for the unanimous Supreme Court. Although the Court had upheld laws based on gender preference in the past, in this case it reversed its position. The Court declared that gender discrimination violated the equal protection clause of the Fourteenth Amendment and therefore could not be the basis for a law.

New York Times v. United States (1971)

Significance In this ruling the Court dismissed the idea of "prior restraint," or attempting to stop an action before it happens, by the government as unconstitutional. The ruling allowed the *New York Times* to continue publishing documents that were critical of the government's handling of the Vietnam War.

Background The *New York Times* began publishing a series of papers called the Pentagon Papers that were critical of the government. The government attempted to stop publication of the papers with a court order, citing national security. Because of the national importance of the case, the Supreme Court agreed to hear the case quickly.

Decision In a 6-to-3 decision, the Court declared that the government could not stop publication of the Pentagon Papers. Although the government did have the right to stop publication if it could prove the danger to national security, the Court said that in this case the government had not met the burden of proof.

Roe v. *Wade* (1973)

Significance This ruling made abortions available to women during their first trimester of pregnancy, even when their health was not in danger.

Background The case was brought in the name of Jane Roe against the restrictive abortion laws of Texas. Until this case, states had widely varying laws about the availability of abortions, some restricting them altogether.

Decision With a 7 to 2 decision, the Court said that elective abortions must be available to any woman in her first three months of pregnancy. Because of the variety of moral opinions about when life begins, the court ruled that a fetus does not have the same rights as an infant.

United States v. *Nixon* (1974)

Significance This ruling forced President Nixon to turn over tapes of White House conversations to the congressional committee investigating his wrongdoing in the Watergate breakin. Nixon resigned shortly after.

Background Nixon had been secretly taping every conversation that took place in the Oval Office. After the president was implicated in the cover-up of the Watergate Hotel break in, Congress wanted to hear these tapes. Nixon refused to hand them over, claiming "executive privilege" to keep some information secret.

Decision In a unanimous decision, the Court ruled that Nixon must turn the tapes over to the prosecution as requested. Writing for the court, Chief Justice Warren Burger stated that finding the truth requires that courts have all the evidence they need, even if it includes presidential communication.

New Jersey v. *TLO* (1985)

Significance In this ruling, the Court declared that searches of juveniles on school grounds are not subject to the same standards of "reasonableness" and "probable cause" that protect other citizens.

Background T. L. O. was a fourteen year old who was caught smoking in the girls' bathroom of her school. A principal at the school questioned the girl and searched her purse, finding marijuana and other drug paraphernalia.

Decision In a 7 to 2 decision, the Court ruled that the suspension of the rules of "reasonable" search and seizure as defined by the Fourth Amendment and later court rulings applied only to school officials and not to law enforcement officers.

Texas v. *Johnson* (1989)

Significance This ruling answered the question of whether the First Amendment protects burning the U.S. flag as a form of symbolic speech. It deals with the limits of symbolic speech. This case is particularly important because it involves burning the flag, one of our national symbols.

Background At the 1984 Republican National Convention in Texas, Gregory Lee Johnson doused a U.S. flag with kerosene. He did this during a demonstration, as a form of protest. Johnson was convicted of violating a Texas law that made it a crime to desecrate [treat disrespectfully] the national flag. He was sentenced to one year in prison and fined $2,000. The Texas Court of Criminal Appeals reversed the conviction because, it said, Johnson's burning of the flag was a form of symbolic speech protected by the First Amendment. Texas then appealed to the U.S. Supreme Court.

Decision The Court ruled for Johnson, five to four. Justice William Brennan wrote for the majority. He said that Johnson was within his constitutional rights when he burned the U.S. flag in protest. As in Tinker v. Des Moines Independent Community School District (1969), the Court looked at the First Amendment and "symbolic speech." Brennan concluded that Johnson's burning the flag was a form of symbolic speech—like the students wearing armbands in Des Moines—is protected by the First Amendment. According to Brennan, "Government may not prohibit the expression of an idea [because it is] offensive." Chief Justice Rehnquist dissented. He said the flag is "the visible symbol embodying our Nation. It does not represent the views of any particular political party, and it does not represent any particular political philosophy. The flag is not simply another 'idea' or 'point of view' competing for recognition in the marketplace of ideas." Since this decision, several amendments banning flag burning have been proposed in Congress, but so far all have failed.

Cruzan v. Director, Missouri Department of Health (1990)

Significance This ruling helped define who may refuse medical treatment. Although the issue is still undecided, this case began a series of efforts to provide legislative and judicial guidelines for the "right to die."

Background The parents of comatose patient Nancy Cruzan wanted to remove her life support system. The Department of Health ruled that Cruzan had not previously made clear her desire to refuse medical treatment in the event of brain damage.

Decision By a 5-to-4 margin, the Court ruled that Cruzan's parents could not remove her from life support because she had not clearly expressed her desires previously. Writing for the majority, Chief Justice William Rehnquist stated that it was Nancy's demand to be removed from life support, not her parents' wishes, that the state must respect in such cases.

Planned Parenthood of Southeastern Pennsylvania, et al. v. Casey (1992)

Significance In this ruling the Court upheld its decision in *Roe* v. *Wade* of the right to elective abortion, but allowed the state of Pennsylvania to impose restrictions of notification and consent upon minors.

Background In 1988 and 1989, Pennsylvania revised its laws to require that, to receive an abortion, minors must receive consent from a parent, and married women must notify their husbands. The laws were challenged by several abortion clinics and physicians.

Decision In a 5-to-4 decision, the Court upheld its previous ruling of *Roe* v. *Wade* that women have the right to an abortion in the first trimester of pregnancy, but provided that a state may require that minors have the consent of one parent 24 hours before the procedure. The Court struck down the part of the Pennsylvania laws that required married women to notify their husbands, saying that it could be an "undue burden" upon women.

Vernonia School District v. Acton (1995)

Significance This ruling allowed random drug testing of minors on school property as a safety measure.

Background James Acton, a student athlete in the Vernonia School District, refused to participate in drug testing, stating that the policy invaded his right to privacy and was an illegal search and seizure.

Decision In a 6-to-3 decision, the Court ruled that while on school property, students are subject to greater control of personal rights than are free adults. Furthermore, concern over the safety of minors under governmental supervision outweighs the minimal intrusion into a student's privacy.

Bush v. *Gore* (2000)

Significance In this ruling, the question before the court was whether ballots that could not be read by voting machines should be recounted by hand. The broader issues were whether the Supreme Court can overrule state court decisions on state laws, and whether an appointed judiciary can affect the result of democratic elections.

Background The 2000 presidential election between Democrat Al Gore and Republican George Bush was very close. Ultimately, the outcome would be determined by votes in the state of Florida. People in Florida voted by punching a hole in a ballot card. The votes were counted by a machine that detected these holes. According to that count, Bush won the state of Florida by a few hundred votes. Florida's Election Commission declared that Bush had won Florida. However, about 60,000 ballots were not counted because the machines could not detect a hole in the ballot. Gore argued in the Florida Supreme Court that these votes should be recounted by hand. The Florida Supreme Court ordered counties to recount all those votes. Bush appealed to the United States Supreme Court, which issued an order to stop the recounts while it made a decision.

The Decision On December 12, 2000, the Supreme Court voted 5 to 4 to end the hand recount of votes ordered by the Florida Supreme Court. The majority said that the Florida Supreme Court had ordered a recount without setting standards for what was a valid vote. Different vote-counters might use different standards. The Court said that this inconsistency meant that votes were treated arbitrarily—based on a person's choice rather than on standards. This arbitrariness, said the Court, violated the due process clause and the equal protection clause of the Constitution. Also, the justices said that Florida law required the vote count to be finalized by December 12. The justices said that rules for recounts could not be made by that date, so they ordered election officials to stop recounting votes.

Gratz v. *Bollinger* and *Grutter* v. *Bollinger* (2003)

Significance These cases considered whether a university violates the Constitution by using race as a factor for admitting students to its undergraduate school and its law school. The ruling affects use of affirmative action programs in higher education. The decisions gave colleges guidelines as to what is permitted and what is not. The decisions were limited to higher education and may not apply to other affirmative action programs such as those for applying for a job or for a government contract.

Background Jennifer Gratz and Barbara Grutter are both white. They challenged the University of Michigan's affirmative action admissions policies. Gratz said that the university violated the Constitution by considering race as a factor in its undergraduate admissions programs. Grutter claimed that the University of Michigan Law School did so.

Decisions In Gratz, the Court ruled 6 to 3 that the undergraduate program—which gave each minority applicant an automatic 20 points toward admission—was unconstitutional. Chief Justice William Rehnquist's opinion held that the policy violated the equal protection clause because it did not consider each applicant individually. "The ... automatic distribution of 20 points has the effect of making 'the factor of race ... decisive' for virtually every minimally qualified underrepresented minority applicant." The result was different when the Court turned to the affirmative action policy of Michigan's Law School, however, which used race as one factor for admission. In Grutter, by a 5-to-4 margin, the Court held that this policy did not violate the equal protection clause. Justice Sandra Day O'Connor wrote for the majority. "Truly individualized consideration demands that race be used in a flexible, nonmechanical way ... Universities can ... consider race or ethnicity ... as a 'plus' factor [when individually considering] each and every applicant." Thus, the law school's policy was constitutional.

United States v. *American Library Association* (2003)

Significance This case deals with the constitutionality of a federal law called the Children's Internet Protection Act (CIPA). The law was designed to protect children from being exposed to pornographic Web sites while using computers in public libraries. The question before the court was this: Does a public library violate the First Amendment by installing Internet filtering software on its public computers?

Background CIPA applies to public libraries that accept federal money to help pay for Internet access. These libraries must install filtering software to block pornographic images. Some library associations sued to block these filtering requirements. They argued that by linking money and filters, the law required public libraries to violate the First Amendment's guarantees of free speech. The libraries argued that filters block some nonpornographic sites along with pornographic ones. That, they said, violates library patrons' First Amendment rights. CIPA does allow anyone to ask a librarian to unblock a specific Web site. It also allows adults to ask that the filter be turned off altogether. But, the libraries argued, people using the library would find these remedies embarrassing and impractical.

Decision In this case, Chief Justice William Rehnquist authored a plurality opinion. He explained that the law does not require any library to accept federal money. A library can choose to do without federal money. If the library makes that choice, it does not have to install Internet filters. And Rehnquist did not think that filtering software's tendency to overblock nonpornographic sites was a constitutional problem. Adult patrons could simply ask a librarian to unblock a blocked site or could have the filter disabled entirely.

The Dissents Justice John Paul Stevens viewed CIPA "as a blunt nationwide restraint on adult access to an enormous amount of valuable" and often constitutionally protected speech. Justice David Souter noted that he would have joined the plurality if the First Amendment interests raised in this case were those of children rather than those of adults.

Hamdi v. *Rumsfeld* and *Rasul* v. *Bush* (2004)

Significance These cases addressed the balance between the government's powers to fight terrorism and the Constitution's promise of due process. Each case raised a slightly different question:

1. Can the government hold American citizens for an indefinite period as "enemy combatants" and not permit them access to American courts, and

2. Do foreigners captured overseas and jailed at Guantánamo Bay, Cuba, have the right to take their cases to American courts to decide if they are being held legally?

Background In *Hamdi* v. *Rumsfeld*, Yaser Hamdi, an American citizen, was captured in Afghanistan in 2001. The U.S. military said Hamdi was an enemy combatant and claimed that "it has the authority to hold ... enemy combatants captured on the battlefield ... to prevent them from returning to the battle." Hamdi's attorney said that Hamdi deserved the due process rights that other Americans have, including a hearing in court to argue that he was not an enemy combatant.

The prisoners in *Rasul* v. *Bush* also claimed they were wrongly imprisoned. They wanted a court hearing, but Guantánamo Bay Naval Base is on Cuban soil. Cuba leases the base to the United States. In an earlier case, the Court had ruled that "if an alien is outside the country's sovereign territory, then ... the alien is not permitted access to the courts of the United States to enforce the Constitution."

Decision In *Hamdi*, the Court ruled 6 to 3 that Hamdi had a right to a hearing. Justice Sandra Day O'Connor wrote that the Court has "made clear that a state of war is not a blank check for the president when it comes to the rights of the nation's citizens." The government decided not to prosecute Hamdi. In *Rasul*, also decided 6 to 3, Justice John Paul Stevens wrote that the prisoners had been held for more than two years in territory under U.S. control. Thus, even though the prisoners are not on U.S. soil, they can ask U.S. courts if their detention is legal. The *Rasul* cases were still pending when this book was printed.

Historic Documents

Magna Carta

England's King John angered many people with high taxes. In 1215 a group of English nobles joined the archbishop of Canterbury to force the king to agree to sign Magna Carta. This document stated that the king was subject to the rule of law, just as other citizens of England were. It also presented the ideas of a fair and speedy trial and due process of law. These principles are still a part of the U.S. Bill of Rights.

1. In the first place have granted to God, and by this our present charter confirmed for us and our heirs for ever that the English church shall be free, and shall have its rights undiminished and its liberties unimpaired . . . We have also granted to all free men of our kingdom, for ourselves and our heirs for ever, all the liberties written below, to be had and held by them and their heirs of us and our heirs.
2. If any of our earls or barons or others holding of us in chief by knight service dies, and at his death his heir be of full age and owe relief he shall have his inheritance on payment of the old relief, namely the heir or heirs of an earl 100 for a whole earl's barony, the heir or heirs of a baron 100 for a whole barony, the heir or heirs of a knight 100s, at most, for a whole knight's fee; and he who owes less shall give less according to the ancient usage of fiefs.
3. If, however, the heir of any such be under age and a ward, he shall have his inheritance when he comes of age without paying relief and without making fine.

40. To no one will we sell, to no one will we refuse or delay right or justice.
41. All merchants shall be able to go out of and come into England safely and securely and stay and travel throughout England, as well by land as by water, for buying and selling by the ancient and right customs free from all evil tolls, except in time of war and if they are of the land that is at war with us . . .
42. It shall be lawful in future for anyone, without prejudicing the allegiance due to us, to leave our kingdom and return safely and securely by land and water, save, in the public interest, for a short period in time of war—except for those imprisoned or outlawed in accordance with the law of the kingdom and natives of a land that is at war with us and merchants (who shall be treated as aforesaid).

62. And we have fully remitted and pardoned to everyone all the ill–will, indignation and rancour that have arisen between us and our men, clergy and laity, from the time of the quarrel. Furthermore, we have fully remitted to all, clergy and laity, and as far as pertains to us have completely forgiven, all trespasses occasioned by the same quarrel between Easter in the sixteenth year of our reign and the restoration of peace. And, besides, we have caused to be made for them letters testimonial patent of the lord Stephen archbishop of Canterbury, of the lord Henry archbishop of Dublin and of the aforementioned bishops and of master Pandulf about this security and the aforementioned concessions.
63. An oath, moreover, has been taken, as well on our part as on the part of the barons, that all these things aforesaid shall be observed in good faith and without evil disposition. Witness the above–mentioned and many others. Given by our hand in the meadow which is called Runnymede between Windsor and Staines on the fifteenth day of June, in the seventeenth year of our reign.

From "English Bill of Rights." Britannica Online. Vers. 99.1. 1994–1999.

The Mayflower Compact

In November 1620, the Pilgrim leaders aboard the Mayflower *drafted the Mayflower Compact. This was the first document in the English colonies to establish guidelines for self-government. This excerpt from the Mayflower Compact describes the principles of the Pilgrim colony's government.*

The Mayflower Compact

We whose names are underwritten, the loyal subjects of our dread Sovereign Lord King James, by the Grace of God of Great Britain, France and Ireland, King, Defender of the Faith, etc.

Having undertaken, for the Glory of God and advancement of the Christian Faith and Honour of our King and Country, a Voyage to plant the First Colony in the Northern Parts of Virginia, do by these presents solemnly and mutually in the presence of God and one of another, Covenant and Combine ourselves together into a Civil Body Politic, for our better ordering and preservation and furtherance of the ends aforesaid; and by virtue hereof to enact, constitute and frame such just and equal Laws, Ordinances, Acts, Constitutions and Offices, from time to time, as shall be thought most meet and convenient for the general good of the Colony, unto which we promise all due submission and obedience. In witness whereof we have hereunder subscribed our names at Cape Cod, the 11th of November, in the year of the reign of our Sovereign Lord King James, of England, France and Ireland the eighteenth, and of Scotland the fifty-fourth. Anno Domini 1620.

From William Bradford, *Of Plymouth Plantation,* 1620–1647 (Samuel Eliot Morison, ed., 1952), 75–76.

Fundamental Orders of Connecticut

In January 1639, settlers in Connecticut led by Thomas Hooker drew up the Fundamental Orders of Connecticut—America's first written constitution. It is essentially a compact among the settlers and a body of laws.

Forasmuch as it hath pleased the All-mighty God by the wise disposition of his divyne pruvidence so to Order and dispose of things that we the Inhabitants and Residents of Windsor, Harteford and Wethersfield are now cohabiting and dwelling in and uppon the River of Conectecotte and the Lands thereunto adioyneing; As also in our Civell Affaires to be guided and governed according to such Lawes, Rules, Orders and decrees as shall be made, ordered & decreed, as followeth:—

1. It is Ordered . . . that there shall be yerely two generall Assemblies or Courts, the one the second thursday in Aprill, the other the second thursday in September, following; the first shall be called the Courte of Election, wherein shall be yerely Chosen . . . soe many Magestrats and other publike Officers as shall be found requisitte: which choise shall be made by all that are admitted freemen and have taken the Oath of Fidelity, and doe cohabitte within this Jurisdiction, (having beene admitted Inhabitants by the major part of the Towne wherein they live,) or the major parte of such as shall be then present . . .

From F. N. Thorpe, ed., *Federal and State Constitutions,* vol. 1 (1909), 519.

HISTORIC DOCUMENTS

The English Bill of Rights

In 1689, after the Glorious Revolution, Parliament passed the English Bill of Rights, which ensured that Parliament would have supreme power over the monarchy. The bill also protected the rights of English citizens.

Whereas the late King James the Second, by the assistance of divers evil counsellors, judges and ministers employed by him, did endeavour to subvert and extirpate the Protestant religion and the laws and liberties of this kingdom;

By assuming and exercising a power of dispensing with and suspending of laws and the execution of laws without consent of Parliament;

By committing and prosecuting divers worthy prelates for humbly petitioning to be excused from concurring to the said assumed power;

By issuing and causing to be executed a commission under the great seal for erecting a court called the Court of Commissioners for Ecclesiastical Causes;

By levying money for and to the use of the Crown by pretence of prerogative for other time and in other manner than the same was granted by Parliament;

By raising and keeping a standing army within this kingdom in time of peace without consent of Parliament, and quartering soldiers contrary to law; . . .

By violating the freedom of election of members to serve in Parliament;

By prosecutions in the Court of King's Bench for matters and causes cognizable only in Parliament, and by divers other arbitrary and illegal courses;

And whereas of late years partial corrupt and unqualified persons have been returned and served on juries in trials, and particularly divers jurors in trials for high treason which were not freeholders;

And excessive bail hath been required of persons committed in criminal cases to elude the benefit of the laws made for the liberty of the subjects;

And excessive fines have been imposed;

And illegal and cruel punishments inflicted;

And several grants and promises made of fines and forfeitures before any conviction or judgment against the persons upon whom the same were to be levied;

All which are utterly and directly contrary to the known laws and statutes and freedom of this realm; ...

That the pretended power of suspending of laws or the execution of laws by regal authority without consent of Parliament is illegal;

That the pretended power of dispensing with laws or the execution of laws by regal authority, as it hath been assumed and exercised of late, is illegal;

That the commission for erecting the late Court of Commissioners for Ecclesiastical Causes, and all other commissions and courts of like nature, are illegal and pernicious;

That levying money for or to the use of the Crown by pretence of prerogative, without grant of Parliament, for longer time, or in other manner than the same is or shall be granted, is illegal;

That it is the right of the subjects to petition the king, and all commitments and prosecutions for such petitioning are illegal;

That the raising or keeping a standing army within the kingdom in time of peace, unless it be with consent of Parliament, is against law;

That the subjects which are Protestants may have arms for their defence suitable to their conditions and as allowed by law;

That election of members of Parliament ought to be free;

That the freedom of speech and debates or proceedings in Parliament ought not to be impeached or questioned in any court or place out of Parliament;

(continued next page)

That excessive bail ought not to be required, nor excessive fines imposed, nor cruel and unusual punishments inflicted;

That jurors ought to be duly impanelled and returned, and jurors which pass upon men in trials for high treason ought to be freeholders;

That all grants and promises of fines and forfeitures of particular persons before conviction are illegal and void;

And that for redress of all grievances, and for the amending, strengthening and preserving of the laws, Parliaments ought to be held frequently.

From "English Bill of Rights." Britannica Online. Vers. 99.1. 1994–1999.

Mecklenburg Resolves

A committee of concerned North Carolina citizens met at Charlotte in May 1775. They agreed upon an official statement that declared the laws of England void in the colony, one of the first steps toward independence taken in the English colonies.

Mecklenburg County May 31, 1775
This day the Committee of this county met, and passed the following Resolves:
WHEREAS, By an Address presented to His Majesty by both Houses of Parliament, in February last, the American colonies are declared to be in a state of actual rebellion, we conceive, that all laws and commissions confirmed by, or derived from the authority of the King or Parliament, are annulled and vacated, and the former civil constitution of these colonies, for the present, wholly suspended. To provide, in some degree, for the exigencies of these colonies, in the present alarming period, we deem it proper and necessary to pass the following Resolves, viz.:

That all commissions, civil and military, heretofore granted by the Crown, to be exercised in these colonies, are null and void, and the constitution of each particular colony wholly suspended.

That the Provincial Congress of each province, under the direction of the great Continental Congress, is invested with all legislative and executive powers within their respective provinces, and that no other legislative or executive power, does, or can exist, at this time, in any of these colonies.

As all former laws are now suspended in this province, and the Congress have not yet provided others, we judge it necessary, for the better preservation of good order, to form certain rules and regulations for the internal government of this county, until laws shall be provided for us by the Congress.

That the inhabitants of this county do meet on a certain day appointed by this Committee, and having formed themselves into nine companies (to-wit), eight in the county, and one in the town of Charlotte, do choose a Colonel and other military officers, who shall hold and exercise their several powers by virtue of this choice, and independent of the Crown of Great Britain, and former constitution of this province.

That for the better preservation of the peace and administration of justice, each of those companies do choose from their own body, two discreet freeholders, who shall be empowered, each by himself and singly, to decide and determine all matters of controversy, arising within said company, under the sum of twenty shillings; and jointly and together, all controversies under the sum of forty shillings; yet so as that their decisions may admit of appeal to the Convention of the Select-Men of the county, and also that any one of these men shall have power to examine and commit to confinement persons accused of petit larceny.

(continued next page)

That those two Select-Men, thus chosen, do jointly and together choose from the body of their particular company, two persons properly qualified to act as Constables, who may assist them in the execution of their office.

That upon the complaint of any persons to either of these Select-Men, he do issue his warrant, directed to the Constable, commanding him to bring the aggressor before him or them, to answer said complaint.

That these eighteen Select-Men, thus appointed, do meet every third Thursday in January, April, July, and October, at the Court-House, in Charlotte, to hear and determine all matters of controversy, for sums exceeding forty shillings, also appeals; and in cases of felony, to commit the person or persons convicted thereof to close confinement, until the Provincial Congress shall provide and establish laws and modes of proceeding in all such cases.

That these eighteen Select-Men, thus convened, do choose a Clerk to record the transactions of said Convention, and that said Clerk, upon the application of any persons aggrieved, do issue his warrant to one of the Constables of the company to which the offender belongs, directing said Constable to summons and warn said offender to appear before the Convention, at their next meeting, to answer the aforesaid complaint.

That any person making complaint upon oath, to the Clerk, or any member of the Convention, that he has reason to suspect, that any person or persons indebted to him, in a sum above forty shillings, intend clandestinely to withdraw from the county, without paying such debt, the Clerk or such member shall issue his warrant to the Constable, commanding him to take said person or persons into safe custody, until the next sitting of the Convention.

That when a debtor for a sum below forty shillings shall abscond and leave the county, the warrant granted as aforesaid, shall extend to any goods or chattels of said debtor, as may be found, and such goods or chattels be seized and held in custody by the Constable, for the space of thirty days; in which time, if the debtor fail to return and discharge the debt, the Constable shall return the warrant to one of the Select-Men of the company, where the goods are found, who shall issue orders to the Constable to sell such a part of said goods as shall amount to the sum due; That when the debt exceeds forty shillings, the return shall be made to the Convention, who shall issue orders for sale.

That all receivers and collectors of quit-rents, public and county taxes, do pay the same into the hands of the chairman of this Committee, to be by them disbursed as the public exigencies may require; and that such receivers and collectors proceed no further in their office, until they be approved of by, and have given to, this Committee, good and sufficient security, for a faithful return of such monies when collected.

That the Committee be accountable to the county for the application of all monies received from such public officers.

That all these officers hold their commissions during the pleasure of their several constituents.

That this committee will sustain all damages that ever hereafter may accrue to all or any of these officers thus appointed, and thus acting, on account of their obedience and conformity to these Resolves.

That whatever person shall hereafter receive a commission from the Crown, or attempt to exercise any such commission heretofore received, shall be deemed an enemy to his country, and upon information being made to the Captain of the company in which he resides, the said company shall cause him to be apprehended, and conveyed before the two Select-Men of the said company, who, upon proof of the fact, shall commit him, the said offender, to safe custody, until the next sitting of the Committee, who shall deal with him as prudence may direct.

That any person refusing to yield obedience to the above Resolves, shall be considered equally criminal, and liable to the same punishment, as the offenders above last mentioned.

(continued next page)

That these Resolves be in full force and virtue, until instructions from the Provincial Congress, regulating the jurisprudence, of the Province shall provide otherwise, or the legislative body of Great Britain, resigns its unjust and arbitrary pretensions with respect to America.

That the eight militia companies in the county, provide themselves with proper arms and accoutrements. and hold themselves in readiness to execute the commands and directions of the General Congress of this province and this Committee.

That the Committee appoint Colonel Thomas Polk, and Doctor Joseph Kennedy, to purchase 300 lb. of powder, 600 lb. of lead, 1,000 flints, for the use of the militia of this county, and deposit the same in such place as the Committee may hereafter direct.

Signed by order at the Committee. EPH. BREVARD, Clerk of the Committee

From http://www.americanrevolution.com/MecklenburgResolve.htm

Halifax Resolves

In April 1776 the Fourth Provincial Congress, made of delegates from around North Carolina, authorized the colony's delegates to the Continental Congress in Philadelphia to vote for independence from Britain. This was the first official action by a colony calling for independence. The congress at Halifax unanimously adopted the resolution.

The Select Committee taking into Consideration the usurpations and violences attempted and committed by the King and Parliament of Britain against America, and the further Measures to be taken for frustrating the same, and for the better defence of this province reported as follows, to wit,

It appears to your Committee that pursuant to the Plan concerted by the British Ministry for subjugating America, the King and Parliament of Great Britain have usurped a Power over the Persons and Properties of the People unlimited and uncontrouled and disregarding their humble Petitions for Peace, Liberty and safety, have made divers Legislative Acts, denouncing War Famine and every Species of Calamity daily employed in destroying the People and committing the most horrid devastations on the Country. That Governors in different Colonies have declared Protection to Slaves who should imbrue their Hands in the Blood of their Masters. That the Ships belonging to America are declared prizes of War and many of them have been violently seized and confiscated in consequence of which multitudes of the people have been destroyed or from easy Circumstances reduced to the most Lamentable distress.

And whereas the moderation hitherto manifested by the United Colonies and their sincere desire to be reconciled to the mother Country on Constitutional Principles, have procured no mitigation of the aforesaid Wrongs and usurpations and no hopes remain of obtaining redress by those Means alone which have been hitherto tried, Your Committee are of Opinion that the house should enter into the following Resolve, to wit

Resolved that the delegates for this Colony in the Continental Congress be impowered to concur with the other delegates of the other Colonies in declaring Independency, and forming foreign Alliances, resolving to this Colony the Sole, and Exclusive right of forming a Constitution and Laws for this Colony, and of appointing delegates from time to time (under the direction of a general Representation thereof to meet the delegates of the other Colonies for such purposes as shall be hereafter pointed out.

From http://statelibrary.dcr.state.nc.us/NC/HISTORY/HISTORY.HTM#Halifax

Articles of Confederation

After winning the Revolutionary War in 1777, the newly formed United States of America created a government under the Articles of Confederation. This government allowed the states to have more power than the central government, a situation that would lead to problems later.

Articles of Confederation and perpetual Union between the states of New Hampshire, Massachusetts-bay Rhode Island and Providence Plantations, Connecticut, New York, New Jersey, Pennsylvania, Delaware, Maryland, Virginia, North Carolina, South Carolina and Georgia.

I.
The Stile of this Confederacy shall be
"The United States of America".

II.
Each state retains its sovereignty, freedom, and independence, and every power, jurisdiction, and right, which is not by this Confederation expressly delegated to the United States, in Congress assembled.

III.
The said States hereby severally enter into a firm league of friendship with each other, for their common defense, the security of their liberties, and their mutual and general welfare, binding themselves to assist each other, against all force offered to, or attacks made upon them, or any of them, on account of religion, sovereignty, trade, or any other pretense whatever.

VI.
No State, without the consent of the United States in Congress assembled, shall send any embassy to, or receive any embassy from, or enter into any conference, agreement, alliance or treaty with any King, Prince or State; nor shall any person holding any office of profit or trust under the United States, or any of them, accept any present, emolument, office or title of any kind whatever from any King, Prince or foreign State; nor shall the United States in Congress assembled, or any of them, grant any title of nobility.

VIII.
All charges of war, and all other expenses that shall be incurred for the common defense or general welfare, and allowed by the United States in Congress assembled, shall be defrayed out of a common treasury, which shall be supplied by the several States in proportion to the value of all land within each State, granted or surveyed for any person, as such land and the buildings and improvements thereon shall be estimated according to such mode as the United States in Congress assembled, shall from time to time direct and appoint.

The taxes for paying that proportion shall be laid and levied by the authority and direction of the legislatures of the several States within the time agreed upon by the United States in Congress assembled.

Federalist Paper No. 51

In 1788 the newly written Constitution faced opponents who believed it gave too much power to the federal government. James Madison, Alexander Hamilton, and John Jay wrote, anonymously, a collection of essays that became known as the Federalist Papers. *The following essay, written by James Madison, outlines reasons why the division of power written into the Constitution would keep the government from harming citizens.*

In order to lay a due foundation for that separate and distinct exercise of the different powers of government, which to a certain extent is admitted on all hands to be essential to the preservation of liberty, it is evident that each department should have a will of its own; and consequently should be so constituted that the members of each should have as little agency as possible in the appointment of the members of the others. Were this principle rigorously adhered to, it would require that all the appointments for the supreme executive, legislative, and judiciary magistracies should be drawn from the same fountain of authority, the people, through channels having no communication whatever with one another. Perhaps such a plan of constructing the several departments would be less difficult in practice than it may in contemplation appear. Some difficulties, however, and some additional expense would attend the execution of it. Some deviations, therefore, from the principle must be admitted. In the constitution of the judiciary department in particular, it might be inexpedient to insist rigorously on the principle: first, because peculiar qualifications being essential in the members, the primary consideration ought to be to select that mode of choice which best secures these qualifications; secondly, because the permanent tenure by which the appointments are held in that department, must soon destroy all sense of dependence on the authority conferring them.

Washington's Farewell Address

In 1796 at the end of his second term as president, George Washington wrote his farewell address with the help of Alexander Hamilton and James Madison. In it he spoke of the dangers facing the young nation. He warned against the dangers of political parties and sectionalism, and he advised the nation against permanent alliances with other nations.

In contemplating the causes, which may disturb our Union, it occurs as matter of serious concern, that any ground should have been furnished for characterizing parties by geographical discriminations-Northern and Southern-Atlantic and Western . . .

No alliances, however strict, between the parts can be an adequate substitute; they must inevitably experience the infractions and interruptions which all alliances in all times have experienced . . .

The great rule of conduct for us, in regard to foreign nations, is, in extending our commercial relations, to have with them as little political connexion as possible. So far as we have already formed engagements, let them be fulfilled with perfect good faith. Here let us stop.

From *Annals of Congress*, 4th Congress, pp. 2869–2880. American Memory. Library of Congress. 1999.

Monroe Doctrine

In 1823 President James Monroe proclaimed the Monroe Doctrine. Designed to end European influence in the Western Hemisphere, it became a cornerstone of U.S. foreign policy.

With the existing colonies or dependencies of any European power we have not interfered and shall not interfere. But with the governments who have declared their independence and maintained it, and whose independence we have, on great consideration and on just principles, acknowledged, we could not view any interposition for the purpose of oppressing them, or controlling in any other manner their destiny, by any European power in any other light than as the manifestation of an unfriendly disposition toward the United States. . . .

Our policy in regard to Europe, which was adopted at an early stage of the wars which have so long agitated that quarter of the globe, nevertheless remains the same, which is not to interfere in the internal concerns of any of its powers; to consider the government de facto as the legitimate government for us; to cultivate friendly relations with it, and to preserve those relations by a frank, firm, and manly policy, meeting in all instances the just claims of every power, submitting to injuries from none.

From "The Monroe Doctrine" by James Monroe. Reprinted in *The Annals of America: Volume 5, 1821–1832*.

Seneca Falls Declaration of Sentiments

One of the first documents to express the desire for equal rights for women is the Declaration of Sentiments, issued in 1848 at the Seneca Falls Convention in Seneca Falls, New York. Led by Elizabeth Cady Stanton and Lucretia Mott, the delegates adopted a set of resolutions modeled on the Declaration of Independence.

When, in the course of human events, it becomes necessary for one portion of the family of man to assume among the people of the earth a position different from that which they have hitherto occupied, but one to which the laws of nature and of nature's God entitle them, a decent respect to the opinions of mankind requires that they should declare the causes that impel them to such a course.

We hold these truths to be self–evident: that all men and women are created equal; that they are endowed by their Creator with certain inalienable rights; that among these are life, liberty, and the pursuit of happiness; that to secure these rights governments are instituted, deriving their just powers from the consent of the governed. Whenever any form of government becomes destructive of these ends, it is the right of those who suffer from it to refuse allegiance to it, and to insist upon the institution of a new government, laying its foundation on such principles, and organizing its powers in such form, as to them shall seem most likely to effect their safety and happiness.

From "Seneca Falls Declaration on Women's Rights." Reprinted in *The Annals of America: Volume 7, 1841–1849*.

The Emancipation Proclamation

When the Union army won the Battle of Antietam, President Abraham Lincoln decided to issue the Emancipation Proclamation, which freed all enslaved people in states under Confederate control. The proclamation, which went into effect on January 1, 1863, was a step toward the Thirteenth Amendment (1865), which ended slavery in all of the United States.

That on the 1st day of January, in the year of our Lord 1863, all persons held as slaves within any state or designated part of a state, the people whereof shall then be in rebellion against the United States, shall be then, thenceforward, and forever free; and the executive government of the United States, including the military and naval authority thereof, will recognize and maintain the freedom of such persons and will do no act or acts to repress such persons, or any of them, in any efforts they may make for their actual freedom. . . .

And I further declare and make known that such persons of suitable condition will be received into the armed service of the United States to garrison forts, positions, stations, and other places, and to man vessels of all sorts in said service.

And upon this act, sincerely believed to be an act of justice, warranted by the Constitution upon military necessity, I invoke the considerate judgment of mankind and the gracious favor of Almighty God.

Lincoln's Gettysburg Address

On November 19, 1863, Abraham Lincoln addressed a crowd gathered to dedicate a cemetery at the Gettysburg battlefield. His short speech, which is excerpted below, reminded Americans of the ideals on which the Republic was founded.

FOUR SCORE AND SEVEN YEARS ago our fathers brought forth on this continent a new nation, conceived in liberty and dedicated to the proposition that all men are created equal.

Now we are engaged in a great civil war, testing whether that nation or any nation so conceived and so dedicated can long endure. We are met on a great battlefield of that war. We have come to dedicate a portion of that field as a final resting–place for those who here gave their lives that that nation might live. It is altogether fitting and proper that we should do this.

But in a larger sense, we cannot dedicate—we cannot consecrate—we cannot hallow—this ground. The brave men, living and dead, who struggled here have consecrated it far above our poor power to add or detract. The world will little note nor long remember what we say here, but it can never forget what they did here. It is for us, the living, rather, to be dedicated here to the unfinished work which they who fought here have thus far so nobly advanced.

It is rather for us to be here dedicated to the great task remaining before us—that from these honored dead we take increased devotion to that cause for which they gave the last full measure of devotion; that we here highly resolve that these dead shall not have died in vain; that this nation, under God, shall have a new birth of freedom; and that government of the people, by the people, for the people shall not perish from the earth.

"I Will Fight No More Forever"

In 1877 Chief Joseph and his group of Nez Percé surrendered to General Oliver Otis Howard. With this surrender, the Nez Percé were removed from their native lands in Idaho to a reservation in Oklahoma.

Tell General Howard I know his heart. What he told me before I have in my heart. I am tired of fighting. Our chiefs are killed. Looking Glass is dead. Toohoolhoolzote is dead. The old men are all killed. It is the young men who say yes or no. He who led the young men is dead. It is cold and we have no blankets. The little children are freezing to death. My people, some of them, have run away to the hills, and have no blankets, no food; no one knows where they are -- perhaps freezing to death. I want time to look for my children and see how many of them I can find. Maybe I shall find them among the dead. Hear me, my chiefs. I am tired; my heart is sick and sad. From where the sun now stands, I will fight no more forever.

Wilson's Fourteen Points

Even before the end of World War I, President Woodrow Wilson announced a 14-point plan to help maintain peace throughout Europe and the world. The goal of his plan was to provide "peace without victory."

Gentlemen of the Congress:

It will be our wish and purpose that the processes of peace, when they are begun, shall be absolutely open and that they shall involve and permit henceforth no secret understandings of any kind. The day of conquest and aggrandizement is gone by; so is also the day of secret covenants entered into in the interest of particular governments and likely at some unlooked-for moment to upset the peace of the world. It is this happy fact, now clear to the view of every public man whose thoughts do not still linger in an age that is dead and gone, which makes it possible for every nation whose purposes are consistent with justice and the peace of the world to avow now or at any other time the objects it has in view.

We entered this war because violations of right had occurred which touched us to the quick and made the life of our own people impossible unless they were corrected and the world secured once for all against their recurrence. What we demand in this war, therefore, is nothing peculiar to ourselves. It is that the world be made fit and safe to live in; and particularly that it be made safe for every peace-loving nation which, like our own, wishes to live its own life, determine its own institutions, be assured of justice and fair dealing by the other peoples of the world as against force and selfish aggression. All the peoples of the world are in effect partners in this interest, and for our own part we see very clearly that unless justice be done to others it will not be done to us. The program of the world's peace, therefore, is our program; and that program, the only possible program, as we see it, is this:

I. Open covenants of peace, openly arrived at, after which there shall be no private international understandings of any kind but diplomacy shall proceed always frankly and in the public view.

II. Absolute freedom of navigation upon the seas, outside territorial waters, alike in peace and in war, except as the seas may be closed in whole or in part by international action for the enforcement of international covenants.

III. The removal, so far as possible, of all economic barriers and the establishment of an equality of trade conditions among all the nations consenting to the peace and associating themselves for its maintenance.

(continued next page)

IV. Adequate guarantees given and taken that national armaments will be reduced to the lowest point consistent with domestic safety.

V. A free, open-minded, and absolutely impartial adjustment of all colonial claims, based upon a strict observance of the principle that in determining all such questions of sovereignty the interests of the populations concerned must have equal weight with the equitable claims of the government whose title is to be determined.

VI. The evacuation of all Russian territory and such a settlement of all questions affecting Russia as will secure the best and freest cooperation of the other nations of the world in obtaining for her an unhampered and unembarrassed opportunity for the independent determination of her own political development and national policy and assure her of a sincere welcome into the society of free nations under institutions of her won choosing; and, more than a welcome, assistance also of every kind that she may need and may herself desire. The treatment accorded Russia by her sister nations in the months to come will be the acid test of their good will, of their comprehension of her needs as distinguished from their own interests, and of their intelligent and unselfish sympathy.

VII. Belgium, the whole world will agree, must be evacuated and restored, without any attempt to limit the sovereignty which she enjoys in common with all other free nations. No other single act will serve as this will serve to restore confidence among the nations in the laws which they have themselves set and determined for the government of their relations with one another. Without this healing act the whole structure and validity of international law is forever impaired.

VIII. All French territory should be freed and the invaded portions restored, and the wrong done to France by Prussia in 1871 in the matter of Alsace-Lorraine, which has unsettled the peace of the world for nearly fifty years, should be righted, in order that peace may once more be made secure in the interest of all.

IX. A readjustment of the frontiers of Italy should be effected along clearly recognizable lines of nationality.

X. The peoples of Austria-Hungary, whose place among the nations we wish to see safeguarded and assured, should be accorded the freest opportunity of autonomous development.

XI. Rumania, Serbia and Montenegro should be evacuated; occupied territories restored; Serbia accorded free and secure access to the sea; and the relations of the several Balkan states to one another determined by friendly counsel along historically established lines of allegiance and nationality; and international guarantees of the political and economic independence and territorial integrity of the several Balkan states should be entered into.

XII. The Turkish portions of the present Ottoman Empire should be assured a secure sovereignty, but the other nationalities which are now under Turkish rule should be assured an undoubted security of life and an absolutely unmolested opportunity of autonomous development, and the Dardanelles should be permanently opened as a free passage to the ships and commerce of all nations under international guarantees.

XIII. An independent Polish state should be erected which should include the territories inhabited by indisputably Polish populations, which should be assured a free and secure access to the sea, and whose political and economic independence and territorial integrity should be guaranteed by international covenant.

XIV. A general association of nations must be formed under specific covenants for the purpose of affording mutual guarantees of political independence and territorial integrity to great and small states alike.

In regard to these essential rectifications of wrong and assertions of right we feel ourselves to be intimate partners of all the governments and peoples associated together against the Imperialists. We cannot be separated in interest or divided in purpose. We stand together until the end.

Brown v. Board of Education

In 1954 a collection of cases came before the Supreme Court under the name Brown v. Board of Education. *These cases challenged segregation in public schools based on the equal protection clause of the Fourteenth Amendment. Chief Justice Earl Warren wrote the majority opinion, which reversed the earlier decision in* Plessy v. Ferguson *that instituted the "separate but equal" doctrine."*

In the instant cases, that question is directly presented. Here, unlike Sweatt v. Painter, there are findings below that the Negro and white schools involved have been equalized, or are being equalized, with respect to buildings, curricula, qualifications and salaries of teachers, and other "tangible" factors. Our decision, therefore, cannot turn on merely a comparison of these tangible factors in the Negro and white schools involved in each of the cases. We must look instead to the effect of segregation itself on public education.

In approaching this problem, we cannot turn the clock back to 1868 when the Amendment was adopted, or even to 1896 when Plessy v. Ferguson was written. We must consider public education in the light of its full development and its present place in American life throughout the Nation. Only in this way can it be determined if segregation in public schools deprives these plaintiffs of the equal protection of the laws.

Today, education is perhaps the most important function of state and local governments. Compulsory school attendance laws and the great expenditures for education both demonstrate our recognition of the importance of education to our democratic society. It is required in the performance of our most basic public responsibilities, even service in the armed forces. It is the very foundation of good citizenship. Today it is a principal instrument in awakening the child to cultural values, in preparing him for later professional training, and in helping him to adjust normally to his environment. In these days, it is doubtful that any child may reasonably be expected to succeed in life if he is denied the opportunity of an education. Such an opportunity, where the state has undertaken to provide it, is a right which must be made available to all on equal terms.

We come then to the question presented: Does segregation of children in public schools solely on the basis of race, even though the physical facilities and other "tangible" factors may be equal, deprive the children of the minority group of equal educational opportunities? We believe that it does.

We conclude that in the field of public education the doctrine of "separate but equal" has no place. Separate educational facilities are inherently unequal. Therefore, we hold that the plaintiffs and others similarly situated for whom the actions have been brought are, by reason of the segregation complained of, deprived of the equal protection of the laws guaranteed by the Fourteenth Amendment.

John F. Kennedy's Inaugural Address

John F. Kennedy became president in 1961, during the middle of the Cold War. In his inaugural address, he spoke to citizens of the United States and the world, asking for peace to be restored for the good of humanity.

[W]e observe today not a victory of party, but a celebration of freedom—symbolizing an end, as well as a beginning—signifying renewal, as well as change. For I have sworn before you and Almighty God the same solemn oath our forebears prescribed nearly a century and three quarters ago.

The world is very different now. For man holds in his mortal hands the power to abolish all forms of human poverty and all forms of human life. And yet the same revolutionary beliefs for which our forebears fought are still at issue around the globe—the belief that the rights of man come not from the generosity of the state, but from the hand of God.

We dare not forget today that we are the heirs of that first revolution. Let the word go forth from this time and place, to friend and foe alike, that the torch has been passed to a new generation of Americans—born in this century, tempered by war, disciplined by a hard and bitter peace, proud of our ancient heritage—and unwilling to witness or permit the slow undoing of those human rights to which this Nation has always been committed, and to which we are committed today at home and around the world.

Let every nation know, whether it wishes us well or ill, that we shall pay any price, bear any burden, meet any hardship, support any friend, oppose any foe, in order to assure the survival and the success of liberty.

This much we pledge—and more.

So let us begin anew—remembering on both sides that civility is not a sign of weakness, and sincerity is always subject to proof. Let us never negotiate out of fear. But let us never fear to negotiate.

Let both sides explore what problems unite us instead of belaboring those problems which divide us.

Let both sides, for the first time, formulate serious and precise proposals for the inspection and control of arms—and bring the absolute power to destroy other nations under the absolute control of all nations.

Let both sides seek to invoke the wonders of science instead of its terrors. Together let us explore the stars, conquer the deserts, eradicate disease, tap the ocean depths, and encourage the arts and commerce.

Let both sides unite to heed in all corners of the earth the command of Isaiah—to "undo the heavy burdens ... and to let the oppressed go free."

And so, my fellow Americans: ask not what your country can do for you—ask what you can do for your country.

My fellow citizens of the world: ask not what America will do for you, but what together we can do for the freedom of man.

I Have a Dream

In 1963 civil rights leaders organized a march on Washington, D.C., that brought attention to the difference between the ideals of the United States and the reality faced by millions of African American citizens. Martin Luther King, Jr. gave the following speech in front of the more than 200,000 demonstrators at the Lincoln Memorial.

I say to you today, my friends, that in spite of the difficulties and frustrations of the moment, I still have a dream. It is a dream deeply rooted in the American dream.

I have a dream that one day this nation will rise up and live out the true meaning of its creed: "We hold these truths to be self-evident; that all men are created equal."

I have a dream that one day on the red hills of Georgia the sons of former slaves and the sons of former slaveowners will be able to sit down together at a table of brotherhood.

I have a dream that one day even the state of Mississippi, a desert state sweltering with the heat of injustice and oppression, will be transformed into an oasis of freedom and justice.

I have a dream that my four children will one day live in a nation where they will not be judged by the color of their skin but by the content of their character.

I have a dream today.

I have a dream that one day the state of Alabama, whose governor's lips are presently dripping with the words of interposition and nullification, will be transformed into a situation where little black boys and black girls will be able to join hands with little white boys and white girls and walk together as sisters and brothers.

I have a dream today.

I have a dream that one day every valley shall be exalted, every hill and mountain shall be made low, the rough places will be made plain, and the crooked places will be made straight, and the glory of the Lord shall be revealed, and all flesh shall see it together.

This is our hope. This is the faith with which I return to the South. With this faith we will be able to hew out of the mountain of despair a stone of hope. With this faith we will be able to transform the jangling discords of our nation into a beautiful symphony of brotherhood.

With this faith we will be able to work together, to pray together, to struggle together, to go to jail together, to stand up for freedom together, knowing that we will be free one day.

This will be the day when all of God's children will be able to sing with a new meaning, "My country, 'tis of thee, sweet land of liberty, of thee I sing. Land where my fathers died, land of the Pilgrim's pride, from every mountainside, let freedom ring."

Let freedom ring from every hill and every molehill of Mississippi. From every mountainside, let freedom ring.

When we let freedom ring, when we let it ring from every village and every hamlet, from every state and every city, we will be able to speed up that day when all of God's children, black men and white men, Jews and Gentiles, Protestants and Catholics, will be able to join hands and sing in the words of the old Negro spiritual, "Free at last! Free at last! Thank God Almighty, we are free at last!"

HISTORIC DOCUMENTS

President Bush's Address to the Nation

On September 11, 2001, terrorists hijacked four passenger planes and used them to attack sites in the United States, including the World Trade Center in New York City. President George W. Bush addressed the country's citizens that evening.

Good evening. Today, our fellow citizens, our way of life, our very freedom came under attack in a series of deliberate and deadly terrorist acts. The victims were in airplanes, or in their offices; secretaries, businessmen and women, military and federal workers; moms and dads, friends and neighbors. Thousands of lives were suddenly ended by evil, despicable acts of terror.

The pictures of airplanes flying into buildings, fires burning, huge structures collapsing, have filled us with disbelief, terrible sadness, and a quiet, unyielding anger. These acts of mass murder were intended to frighten our nation into chaos and retreat. But they have failed; our country is strong.

A great people has been moved to defend a great nation. Terrorist attacks can shake the foundations of our biggest buildings, but they cannot touch the foundation of America. These acts shattered steel, but they cannot dent the steel of American resolve.

America was targeted for attack because we're the brightest beacon for freedom and opportunity in the world. And no one will keep that light from shining.

Today, our nation saw evil, the very worst of human nature. And we responded with the best of America—with the daring of our rescue workers, with the caring for strangers and neighbors who came to give blood and help in any way they could.

Immediately following the first attack, I implemented our government's emergency response plans. Our military is powerful, and it's prepared. Our emergency teams are working in New York City and Washington, D.C. to help with local rescue efforts.

Our first priority is to get help to those who have been injured, and to take every precaution to protect our citizens at home and around the world from further attacks.

The functions of our government continue without interruption. Federal agencies in Washington which had to be evacuated today are reopening for essential personnel tonight, and will be open for business tomorrow. Our financial institutions remain strong, and the American economy will be open for business, as well.

The search is underway for those who are behind these evil acts. I've directed the full resources of our intelligence and law enforcement communities to find those responsible and to bring them to justice. We will make no distinction between the terrorists who committed these acts and those who harbor them.

I appreciate so very much the members of Congress who have joined me in strongly condemning these attacks. And on behalf of the American people, I thank the many world leaders who have called to offer their condolences and assistance.

America and our friends and allies join with all those who want peace and security in the world, and we stand together to win the war against terrorism. Tonight, I ask for your prayers for all those who grieve, for the children whose worlds have been shattered, for all whose sense of safety and security has been threatened. And I pray they will be comforted by a power greater than any of us, spoken through the ages in Psalm 23: "Even though I walk through the valley of the shadow of death, I fear no evil, for You are with me."

This is a day when all Americans from every walk of life unite in our resolve for justice and peace. America has stood down enemies before, and we will do so this time. None of us will ever forget this day. Yet, we go forward to defend freedom and all that is good and just in our world.

Thank you. Good night, and God bless America.

Biographical Dictionary

A

Adams, John (1735–1826) American statesman, he was a delegate to the Continental Congress, a member of the committee that drafted the Declaration of Independence, vice president to George Washington, and the second president of the United States. (p. 266)

Adams, John Quincy (1767–1848) Son of President John Adams and the secretary of state to James Monroe, he largely formulated the Monroe Doctrine. He was the sixth president of the United States and later became a representative in Congress. (p. 305)

Adams, Samuel (1722–1803) American revolutionary who led the agitation that led to the Boston Tea Party; he signed the Declaration of Independence. (p. 99)

Addams, Jane (1860–1935) American social worker and activist, she was the co-founder of Hull House, an organization that focused on the needs of immigrants. She helped found the American Civil Liberties Union and won the Nobel Peace Prize in 1931. (p. 648)

Aguinaldo (ahg-ee-NAHL-doh), Emilio (1869–1964) Filipino leader and commander of forces in rebellion against Spain, he led an insurrection against the authority of the United States. (p. 699)

Albright, Madeleine (1937–) First woman to serve as secretary of state, she was appointed by Bill Clinton and sworn into office in 1997. (p. 953)

Aldrin, Edwin "Buzz" (1930–) Copiloted the first lunar landing mission, he was the second man to walk on the moon. (p. 898)

Anthony, Susan B. (1820–1906) American social reformer, she was active in the temperance, abolitionist, and women's suffrage movements and was co-organizer and president of the National Woman Suffrage Association. (p. 465)

Aristotle (384 BC–322 BC) Greek philosopher, he thought that people should live in moderation and use reason. (p. 22)

Arkwright, Richard (1732–1792) English inventor, he patented the water-powered spinning frame, improving the production of cotton thread. (p. 385)

Armstrong, Neil (1930–) Commander of the first lunar landing mission, he was also the first person to step on the surface of the moon. (p. 898)

Askia the Great (c. 1443–1538) Songhai ruler, he overthrew Sunni Baru. Originally named Muhammad Ture, he took the military title askia and became known as Askia the Great. (p. 19)

Astor, John Jacob (1763–1848) American fur trader and financier, he founded the fur-trading post of Astoria and the American Fur Company. (p. 346)

Austin, Stephen F. (1793–1836) American colonizer in Texas, he was imprisoned for urging Texas statehood after Santa Anna suspended Mexico's constitution. After helping Texas win independence from Mexico, he became secretary of state for the Texas Republic. (p. 351)

B

Banneker, Benjamin (1731–1806) African American architect and city planner, he helped design the city of Washington, D.C. after the site was chosen by George Washington. (p. 240)

Barker, Penelope (1728–1796) Led the women of Edenton, North Carolina, during a 1774 protest of the British tax on tea. The women said they would not drink British tea until the tax was lifted.

Barton, Clara (1821–1912) Founder of the American Red Cross, she obtained and administered supplies and care to the Union soldiers during the American Civil War. (p. 534)

Batts, Nathaniel (1620?–1679?) The first recorded permanent European settler in the area that became North Carolina. He was a fur-trapper from Virginia who settled near the Great Dismal Swamp in 1665.

Beckwourth, Jim (1798–1866?) African American explorer and mountain man who spent time in the unsettled western United States and later recounted his exciting life in a book. (p. 347)

Beecher, Catharine (1800–1878) American educator and the daughter of Lyman Beecher, she promoted education for women in such writings as An Essay on the Education of Female Teachers. She founded the first all-female academy. (p. 451)

Beecher, Lyman (1775–1863) American clergyman, he disapproved of the style of preaching of the Great Awakening ministers. He served as president of the Lane Theological Seminary and supported female higher education. (p. 448)

Bell, Alexander Graham (1847–1922) American inventor and educator, his interest in electrical and mechanical devices to aid the hearing-impaired led to the development and patent of the telephone. (p. 617)

Bell, John (1797–1869) Senator from Tennessee, he supported the Union over slavery and helped found the Constitutional Union Party. (p. 495)

Berry, Harriet M. (1877–1940) Born near Chapel Hill, North Carolina. She ran the Good Roads Association and supported building a better road system in the state.

Bethune, Mary McLeod (1875–1955) An African American educator and leader who rose to national prominence during the presidency of Franklin Roosevelt, who appointed her director of the National Youth Administration's Division of Negro Affairs. (p. 792)

Bidwell, Annie (1839–1918) American pioneer activist, she worked for social and moral causes and for women's suffrage. (p. 602)

Bingham, George Caleb (1811–1879) American painter who specialized in painting scenes of everyday life in the West. (p. 310)

bin Laden, Osama (1957–) A Saudi millionaire and leader of al-Qaeda, the terrorist organization that claimed responsibility for the September 11 attacks on the United States. (p. 956)

Black Hawk (1767–1838) Native American leader of Fox and Sauk Indians, he resisted the U.S.-ordered removal of Indian nations from Illinois and raided settlements and fought the U.S. Army. (p. 335)

Blalock, Sarah Pritchard (1840?–1901) A Unionist from North Carolina who joined the Confederate Army with her husband to obtain military training. They planned to join the Union Army later, but her husband's illness ended the plan.

Bolívar, Simon (1783–1830) South American revolutionary leader who was nicknamed the Liberator, he fought many battles for independence, winning the support of many U.S. leaders. (p. 300)

Bonny, Anne (1697?–?) A pirate who was born in Ireland but raided ships along the coast of the Carolinas during the first half of the eighteenth century.

Bradham, Caleb (1867–1934) Pharmacist who invented Pepsi-Cola ® at his New Bern, North Carolina, drugstore in 1867. He originally sold the soft drink only in syrup form.

Breckinridge, John C. (1821–1875) Vice president under James Buchanan, he was also a senator from Kentucky. He later served as a general in the Confederate army. (p. 495)

Brooks, Preston (1819–1857) American congressman, he assaulted and beat Senator Charles Sumner for his antislavery speeches and for insulting a pro-slavery relative. He was nicknamed Bully Brooks by northerners. (p. 487)

Brown, John (1800–1859) American abolitionist who helped fuel the violence in Bleeding Kansas and was executed for his role in organizing a slave revolt at Harpers Ferry, Virginia. (p. 486)

Bryan, William Jennings (1860–1925) American lawyer and Populist politician, he favored free silver coinage, an economic policy expected to help farmers. He was a Democratic nominee for president in 1896 and was defeated by William McKinley. (p. 604)

Buchanan, James (1791–1868) American politician and fifteenth president of the United States, he was chosen as the Democratic nominee for president in 1854 for being politically experienced and not offensive to slave states. (p. 488)

Burns, Anthony (1834–1862) American enslaved African, he ran away and was arrested in Boston. His arrest became the center of violent protests by northern opponents of the Fugitive Slave Act. (p. 480)

Burns, Otway (1775–1850) American privateer during the War of 1812 and owner of the first steamship in North Carolina.

Bush, George H. W. (1924–) The 41st president of the United States, also served as vice president to Ronald Reagan. He led the nation through the Persian Gulf War. (p. 950)

Bush, George W. (1946–) The 43rd president of the United States and son of George H. W. Bush, he was president during the September 11, 2001 terrorist attacks. (p. 954)

C

Calhoun, John C. (1782–1850) American politician and supporter of slavery and states' rights, he served as vice president to Andrew Jackson and was instrumental in the South Carolina nullification crisis. (p. 323)

Carnegie, Andrew (1835–1919) American industrialist and humanitarian, he focused his attention on steelmaking and made a fortune through his vertical integration method. (p. 620)

Carson, Rachel (1907–1964) Author of *Silent Spring* and one of the founders of the modern environmental conservation movement. (p. 933)

Carter, Jimmy (1924–) The 39th president of the United States, his presidency saw a dramatic energy crisis. (p. 934)

Carteret, John, Earl Granville (1690–1763) One of the original eight Lords Proprietors of the Carolina colony. He did not sell his share to the Crown along with the other seven Proprietors, and his eighth became known as the Granville District.

Cartier, Jacques (1491–1557) French navigator who made three voyages to Canada for France. He explored the St. Lawrence River. (p. 54)

Castro, Fidel (1926–) Communist leader of Cuba, came to power through a revolution in 1959. (p. 895)

Caswell, Richard (1729–1789) Represented North Carolina in both the First and Second Continental Congresses and became the first governor of the state in 1776.

Chavez, Cesar (1927–1993) Social activist and founder of the United Farm Workers, a leader in the movement for Hispanic Americans' civil rights. (p. 882)

Chesnutt, Charles W. (1858–1932) Writer and social activist who grew up in Fayetteville, North Carolina. He wrote novels and short stories examining racism and other social themes.

Chisholm, Shirley (1924–2005) First African American woman to be elected to Congress, as a Representative from New York. (p. 883)

Churchill, Winston (1874–1965) The prime minister of Britain during much of World War II, he is well-remembered for many speeches made in support of the Allies. (p. 806)

Clark, George Rogers (1752–1818) American Revolutionary soldier and frontier leader, he captured the British trading village of Kaskaskia during the Revolution and encouraged Indian leaders to remain neutral. (p. 133)

Clark, William (1770–1838) American soldier and friend of Meriwether Lewis, he was invited to explore the Louisiana Purchase and joined what became known as the Lewis and Clark expedition. (p. 275)

Clay, Henry (1777–1852) American politician from Kentucky, he was known as the Great Pacificator because of his support of the Missouri Compromise. He developed the Compromise of 1850 to try to avoid civil war. (p. 302)

Clinton, Bill (1946–) The 42nd president of the United States, he became the second president impeached by the House of Representatives but found not guilty of the charges. (p. 952)

Cole, Thomas (1801–1848) American painter, he was the founder of the Hudson River school, a group of artists who emphasized the beauty of the American landscape, especially the Hudson River valley. (p. 310)

Columbus, Christopher (1451–1506) Italian explorer, he was convinced that he could reach Asia by sailing westward across the Atlantic Ocean. He gained the support of Spain's monarchs and commanded a small fleet that reached the so-called New World, setting off a tide of European exploration of the area. (p. 42)

Coolidge, Calvin (1872–1933) The 30th president of the United States, his presidency helped restore faith in government leaders after the scandals of the Harding administration. (p. 752)

Cooper, James Fenimore (1789–1851) Well-known Early American novelist, he wrote the *Last of the Mohicans* and many stories about the West. (p. 309)

Cooper, Peter (1791–1883) American ironworks manufacturer who designed and built Tom Thumb, the first American locomotive. (p. 398)

Cortés, Hernán (1485–1547) Spanish conquistador, he conquered Mexico and brought about the fall of the Aztec Empire. (p. 46)

Crazy Horse (1842?–1877) Native American chief of Oglala Sioux, he took part in the Battle of the Little Bighorn, in which General Custer was surrounded and killed. He was killed after surrendering and resisting imprisonment. (p. 595)

Crittenden, John J. (1787–1863) Kentucky senator, he attempted to save the Union by reconciling differences between northern and southern states in the Senate proposal known as Crittenden's Compromise. (p. 496)

Custer, George Armstrong (1839–1876) American army officer in the Civil War, he became a Native American fighter in the West and was killed with his troops in the Battle of the Little Bighorn. (p. 596)

D

Dare, Virginia (1587–?) First child to be born in America of English parents. She was born on Roanoke Island and disappeared with the Lost Colony.

da Vinci, Leonardo (1452–1519) Italian painter, sculptor, architect, engineer, scientist, and inventor. (p. 26)

Davis, Benjamin O. (1912–2002) The first African American general in the United States military, he led the Tuskegee Airmen through World War II. (p. 812)

Davis, Jefferson (1808–1889) First and only president of the Confederate States of America after the election of President Abraham Lincoln in 1860 led to the secession of many southern states. (p. 497)

Deere, John (1804–1886) American industrialist; he developed a steel plow to ease difficulty of turning thick soil on the Great Plains. (p. 404)

Dickinson, Emily (1830–1886) American poet, she lived a reclusive life, and her poems were not widely acclaimed until after her death. (p. 445)

Dix, Dorothea (1802–1887) American philanthropist and social reformer, she helped change the prison system nationwide by advocating the development of state hospitals for treatment for the mentally ill instead of imprisonment. (p. 450)

Dole, Elizabeth (1936–) Republican Senator from North Carolina. She held numerous important government posts, including Secretary of Transportation under Ronald Reagan. She was the first woman to hold the position of Secretary of Transportation.

Douglas, Stephen (1813–1861) American politician and pro-slavery nominee for president, he debated Abraham Lincoln about slavery during the Illinois senatorial race. He proposed the unpopular Kansas-Nebraska Act, and he established the Freeport Doctrine, upholding the idea of popular sovereignty. (p. 484)

Douglass, Frederick (1817–1895) American abolitionist and writer, he escaped slavery and became a leading African American spokesman and writer. He published his biography, *The Narrative of the Life of Frederick Douglass,* and founded the abolitionist newspaper, the *North Star.* (p. 456)

Du Bois, W. E. B. (1868–1963) African American educator, editor, and writer, he led the Niagara Movement, calling for economic and educational equality for African Americans. He helped found the National Association for the Advancement of Colored People (NAACP). (p. 678)

Duke, Washington (1820–1905) A tobacco manufacturer from Durham, North Carolina. He gave Trinity College a gift of $100,000 in 1896 under the condition that it would accept women. The college was renamed Duke University.

E

Earnhardt, Dale, Sr. (1951–2001) A NASCAR driver from North Carolina who won seven Winston Cup titles during his career. He was killed in the last lap of the Daytona 500 race in 2001.

Edison, Thomas Alva (1847–1931) American inventor of over 1,000 patents, he invented the lightbulb and established a power plant that supplied electricity to parts of New York City. (p. 616)

Edwards, Jonathan (1703–1758) Important and influential revivalist leader in the Great Awakening religious movement, he delivered dramatic sermons on the choice between salvation and damnation. (p. 94)

Eisenhower, Dwight D. (1890–1969) The 34th president of the United States, he used his popularity as a war hero of World War II to become president, in which position he led the nation through the Korean War. (p. 816)

Emerson, Ralph Waldo (1803–1882) American essayist and poet, he was a supporter of the transcendentalist philosophy of self-reliance. (p. 443)

Equiano, Olaudah (c.1750–1797) African American abolitionist, he was an enslaved African who was eventually freed and became a leader of the abolitionist movement and writer of *The Interesting Narrative of the Life of Olaudah Equiano.* (p. 77)

Eriksson, Lief (c. 1000) Norwegian explorer, son of Erik the Red, was first European to explore the Americas. (p. 38)

Ervin, Sam (1896–1985) A Democratic United States Senator from North Carolina. He headed the committee that voted to impeach President Nixon in 1974.

F

Farragut, David (1801–1870) American soldier, he was the first commissioned American admiral, and in the Civil War he captured New Orleans and maintained a blockade along the Gulf Coast against Confederate forces. (p. 524)

Finney, Charles Grandison (1792–1875) American clergyman and educator, he became influential in the Second Great Awakening after a dramatic religious experience and conversion. He led long revivals that annoyed conventional ministers. (p. 448)

Ford, Gerald (1913–2006) The 38th president of the United States, he became president upon Richard Nixon's resignation. Ford later pardoned Nixon for his involvement in the Watergate scandal. (p. 930)

Ford, Henry (1863–1947) Founder of Ford Motor Company, he created the moving assembly line and is often credited with helping to create a middle class in American culture. (p. 617)

Francis Ferdinand (Archduke) (1863–1914) Heir apparent to the Austrian emperor, the assassination of him and his wife led to the beginning of World War I. (p. 721)

Franklin, Benjamin (1706–1790) Early American politician and inventor, he took a central role in helping form the government of the new United States, and acted as a foreign diplomat on behalf of the new nation. (p. 169)

Franklin, John Hope (1915–) An African American historian who published the influential book *From Slavery to Freedom.* He is Professor Emeritus of History at Duke University and was awarded the Presidential Medal of Freedom in 1995.

Frémont, John C. (1813–1890) American explorer, army officer, and politician, he was chosen as the first Republican candidate for president. He was against the spread of slavery, and he was rejected by all but the free states as a "single issue" candidate in the election of 1856. (p. 489)

Friedan, Betty (1921–2006) Author of *The Feminine Mystique,* she pointed out women's dissatisfaction with traditional roles and became a leader of the women's rights movement of the 1960s and 1970s. (p. 883)

Fuller, Margaret (1810–1850) A journalist, critic, and women's rights activist, she was a member of the Transcendentalist group of authors. (p. 443)

Fulton, Robert (1765–1815) American engineer and inventor, he built the first commercially successful full-sized steamboat, the Clermont, which led to the development of commercial steamboat ferry services for goods and people. (p. 397)

G

Gallaudet, Thomas (1787–1851) American educator, he studied techniques for instructing hearing impaired people and established the first American school for the hearing impaired. (p. 451)

Gálvez, Bernardo de (1746–1786) Governor of Spanish Louisiana, he captured key cities from the British, greatly aiding the American Patriot movement and enabling the Spanish acquisition of Florida. (p. 131)

Garrison, William Lloyd (1805–1879) American journalist and reformer; he published the famous antislavery newspaper, the Liberator, and helped found the American Anti-Slavery Society, promoting immediate emancipation and racial equality. (p. 455)

Garvey, Marcus (1887–1940) African American leader of the black nationalism movement. (p. 763)

Marcus Garvey

Gatling, Richard Jordan (1818–1903) North Carolinian who invented the first successful rapid-repeating firearm. The weapon became known as the Gatling gun.

George III (1738–1820) King of England, 1760–1820, during the American Revolution. King against which American colonists claimed to be rebelling. (p. 97)

Geronimo (1829–1909) Chiricahua Apache leader, he evaded capture for years and led an extraordinary opposition struggle against white settlements in the American Southwest until his eventual surrender. (p. 597)

Gompers, Samuel (1850–1924) American labor leader, he helped found the American Federation of Labor to campaign for workers' rights, such as the right to organize boycotts. (p. 625)

Gorbachev, Mikhail (1931–) Leader of the Soviet Union who introduced perestroika and oversaw the dismantling of the Communist government there. (p. 940)

Gore, Al (1948–) Vice president of the United States and Democratic presidential nominee in 2000. (p. 954)

Grant, Ulysses S. (1822–1885) Eighteenth president of the United States, he received a field promotion to lieutenant general in charge of all Union forces after leading a successful battle. He accepted General Lee's surrender of Confederate forces at Appomattox Courthouse, ending the Civil War. (p. 522)

Grimké, Angelina (1805–1879) and **Sarah** (1792–1873) American sisters and reformers, they were the daughters of a slaveholding family from South Carolina who became antislavery supporters and lecturers for the American Anti-Slavery Society. They also took up the women's rights campaign. (p. 455)

Gutenberg, Johannes (c. 1400–1468) Credited with the invention of the movable type printing press. (p. 27)

Guthrie, Woody (1912–1967) Folksinger who expressed the desperation felt by millions of Americans during the Great Depression, especially those rural residents hit by the Dust Bowl. (p. 793)

H

Hamilton, Alexander (1755–1804) American statesman and member of the Continental Congress and the Constitutional Convention, he was an author of the Federalist Papers, which supported ratification of the Constitution. He was the first secretary of treasury under George Washington and developed the Bank of the United States. (p. 238)

Harding, Warren G. (1865–1923) The 29th president of the United States, his administration was full of scandals. He died during his presidency while in California. (p. 752)

Harrison, William Henry (1773–1841) American politician, he served as the governor of Indian Territory and fought Tecumseh in the Battle of Tippecanoe. He was the ninth president of the United States. (p. 331)

Hawthorne, Nathaniel (1804–1864) American writer, he is famous for his many stories and books, including *The Scarlet Letter,* and he is recognized as one of the first authors to write in a uniquely American style. (p. 444)

Haywood, William "Big Bill" (1869–1928) One of the leaders of the International Workers of the World, a Socialist labor union active in the early 1900s. (p. 674)

Hearst, William Randolph (1863–1951) American journalist, he was famed for sensational news stories, known as yellow journalism, that stirred feelings of nationalism and formed public opinion for the Spanish-American War. (p. 645)

Helms, Jesse (1921–) A five-term Republican Senator from North Carolina. He helped the Christian conservative movement to become an important political force.

Helper, Hinton Rowan (1829–1909) A North Carolina native who was critical of slavery. He published the abolitionist book *The Impending Crisis of the South and How to Meet It* in 1857.

Henry the Navigator (1394–1460) King of Portugal who established a school of navigation and financed trips of exploration. (p. 39)

Hidalgo y Costilla, Father Miguel (1753–1811) Mexican priest and revolutionist, he led a rebellion of about 80,000 impoverished Indians and mestizos against Spain in the hope of improving living conditions; though defeated, the rebellion eventually grew and helped lead to Mexican independence. (p. 350)

Hill, Daniel Harvey (1821–1889) A Confederate general who led North Carolina troops during the Civil War. He was also the superintendent of the North Carolina Military Academy.

Hitler, Adolf (1889–1845) Leader of Nazi Germany during World War II, he rose to power on a platform of intolerance and nationalism. (p. 805)

Ho Chi Minh (1890–1969) Communist leader of North Vietnam during the Vietnam War, his government aided the Vietcong. (p. 898)

Holden, William W. (1818–1892) Publisher of the North Carolina Standards newspaper. He was appointed governor by Andrew Johnson during Reconstruction, and won election to the office in 1868.

Hoover, Herbert (1874–1964) The 31st president of the United States, he was president during the stock market crashes that helped lead to the Great Depression. (p. 757)

Horton, George Moses (1797?–1883?) Born a slave in North Carolina. He was illiterate but composed poems in his head. In 1829 a collection of his poems that had been copied by University of North Carolina students was published.

Howe, Robert (1732–1786) A major general in the Continental Army and the highest ranking officer from North Carolina during the Revolutionary War. He briefly commanded the southern Patriot troops.

Hughes, Langston (1902–1967) African American writer who achieved fame during the Harlem Renaissance for his poetry, which discussed the alienation of African Americans from white American society. (p. 768)

Hussein, Saddam (1937–2006) Socialist president of the Iraqi Republic until captured as a prisoner of war by U.S. forces in 2003. (p. 951)

Hutchinson, Anne (1591–1643) Puritan leader who angered other Puritans by claiming that people's relationship to God did not need guidance from ministers; she was tried and convicted of undermining church authorities and was banished from Massachusetts Bay Colony; she later established the colony of Portsmouth in present-day Rhode Island. (p. 82)

BIOGRAPHICAL DICTIONARY

I

Ibn Said, Omar (1773?–1864) Born in Senegal, Africa, and spent 25 years studying with Muslim scholars. He was enslaved in 1807 and taken to North Carolina. He wrote an autobiography in Arabic.

Inouye, Daniel (1924–) Japanese American who served as Hawaii's first United States senator. He also served in the U.S. Army during World War II. (p. 809)

Iredell, James (1751–1799) Even though he worked as a British official, Iredell was a strong supporter of independence. He was the most famous Revolutionary era pamphleteer in North Carolina. President Washington appointed him to the first Supreme Court.

Irving, Washington (1783–1859) Early American satirical writer, he was the first American writer to gain international acclaim. His works include Rip Van Winkle and The Legend of Sleepy Hollow. He often used American history and authentic American settings and characters. (p. 308)

J

Jackson, Andrew (1767–1845) Nicknamed Old Hickory, he was an American hero in the Battle of New Orleans. As commander of the Tennessee militia, he defeated the Creek Indians, securing 23 million acres of land. His election as the seventh president of the United States marked an era of democracy called Jacksonian Democracy. (p. 286, 325)

Jackson, Thomas "Stonewall" (1824–1863) American Confederate general, he led the Shenandoah Valley campaign and fought with Lee in the Seven Days' Battles and the First and Second Battles of Bull Run. (p. 517)

Jacobs, Harriet (1813–1897) Born a slave in Edenton, North Carolina. She escaped to freedom in the North and published her autobiography in 1860.

Jefferson, Thomas (1743–1826) American statesman, and member of two Continental Congresses, chairman of the committee to draft the Declaration of Independence, the Declaration's main author and one of its signers, and the third president of the United States. (pp. 119, 239, 266, 271)

Johnson, Andrew (1808–1875) American politician and the seventeenth president of the United States upon the assassination of Lincoln, he was impeached for his unpopular ideas about Reconstruction. He held onto the office by a one-vote margin. (p. 557)

Johnson, Lyndon (1908–1973) The 36th president of the United States, became president after the assassination of John Kennedy. Johnson led the nation through the civil rights movement, signing many antidiscrimination bills into law. (p. 879)

Jones, John Paul (1747–1792) American naval officer famed for bravery, his most famous victory was the defeat of the British warship *Serapis,* during which he declared, "I have not yet begun to fight!" (p. 133)

Jordan, Michael (1963–) An African American basketball player who attended University of North Carolina. He achieved fame as a player for the Chicago Bulls and holds numerous records. Many consider him the best basketball player of all time.

Joseph (1840–1904) Native American chief of the Nez Percé group, he became involved in a war with the U.S. Army when his people were removed to a reservation in Idaho. (p. 599)

K

Kelley, Florence (1859–1932) American reformer, she was active in the settlement house movement and led progressive reforms in labor conditions for women and children. (p. 648)

Kennedy, John F. (1917–1963) The 35th president of the United States, led the country through several cold war crises, but was assassinated in 1963. (p. 876)

Key, Francis Scott (1749–1843) American lawyer who was imprisoned on a British ship during the War of 1812. His poem written about the battle he witnessed has become the national anthem of the United States. (p. R31)

King, Martin Luther, Jr. (1929–1968) Civil rights leader who was committed to a nonviolent approach in bringing about the dramatic change of racial integration. He was assassinated in 1968. (p. 873)

Kissinger, Henry (1923–) Served as secretary of state under President Nixon and helped form the policy of realpolitik. (p. 910)

L

Lafayette, Marquis de (1757–1834) French statesman and officer who viewed the American Revolution as important to the world, he helped finance the Revolution and served as major general. p. 131)

La Follette, Robert M. (1855–1925) Progressive American politician, he was active in local Wisconsin issues and challenged party bosses. As governor, he began the reform program called the Wisconsin Idea to make state government more professional. (p. 667)

Lane, Lunsford (1803–1863?) Born a slave in Raleigh, Lane began a tobacco trading company that allowed him arrange for his freedom. He eventually moved to the North and became an abolitionist.

Las Casas, Bartolomé de (1474–1566) Spanish missionary and historian, he became the first ordained Catholic priest in the New World and advocated for the welfare and protection of Native Americans as well as preached against the slavery system. (p. 51)

Lee, Robert E. (1807–1870) American soldier, he refused Lincoln's offer to head the Union Army and agreed to lead Confederate forces. He successfully led several major battles until his defeat at Gettysburg, and he surrendered to the Union's commander General Grant at Appomattox Courthouse. (p. 518)

Lewis, Meriwether (1774–1809) Former army captain selected by President Jefferson to explore the Louisiana Purchase, he led the expedition that became known as the Lewis and Clark expedition. (p. 275)

Liliuokalani (li-lee-uh-who-kuh-LAHN-ee) (1838–1917) Queen of the Hawaiian Islands, she opposed annexation by the United States but lost power in a U.S.-supported revolt by planters that led to a new government. (p. 694)

Lin, Maya Ying (1959–) Chinese American sculptor and architect, designed the Vietnam Veterans' Memorial in Washington, D.C. (p. 912)

Lincoln, Abraham (1809–1865) Sixteenth presi dent of the United States, he promoted equal rights for African Americans in the famed Lincoln-Douglas debates. He issued the Emancipation Proc lamation and set in motion the Civil War, but he was determined to preserve the Union. He was assassinated in 1865. (p. 490)

Little Turtle (c. 1752–1812) Miami chief who led a Native American alliance that raided settlements in the Northwest Territory, he was defeated and forced to sign the Treaty of Greenville, and he later became an advocate for peace. (p. 246)

Lodge, Henry Cabot (1850–1924) A U.S. senator from Massachusetts, he was opposed to President Wilson's plan for the League of Nations, fearing it would draw the United States into wars not in the nation's interest. (p. 738)

Longfellow, Henry Wadsworth (1807–1882) American poet in the mid-nineteenth century, he is best known for his story-poems, such as "Paul Revere's Ride" in Tales of a Wayside Inn and The Song of Hiawatha. (p. 445)

Lowell, Francis Cabot (1775–1817) American industrialist who developed the Lowell system, a mill system that included looms that could both weave thread and spin cloth. He hired young women to live and work in his mill. (p. 392)

BIOGRAPHICAL DICTIONARY

M

MacArthur, Douglas (1880–1964) A U.S. general who achieved fame for his actions in the Pacific during World War II and the Korean War. (p. 820)

Macon, Nathaniel (1757–1837) Born to a wealthy North Carolina family of planters. He fought in the Revolutionary War and served in Congress for more than 30 years. He helped write the state constitution of 1835.

Madison, Dolley (1768–1849) Born in North Carolina, Madison grew up in Virginia and Philadelphia. She was first lady during the war of 1812 and helped save important papers when the British burned the White House.

Madison, James (1751–1836) American statesman, he was a delegate to the Constitutional Convention, the fourth president of the United States, the author of some of the Federalist Papers, and is called the father of the Constitution for his proposals at the Constitutional Convention. He led the United States through the War of 1812. (p. 164, 187, 216, 283)

Magellan (muh-JEL-uhn), Ferdinand (1480–1521) Portuguese captain of a Spanish fleet that sought a western route to Asia via the "Southern Ocean", he found a passage through South America, now known as the Strait of Magellan, but died during the expedition. His crew of 18 people with one remaining ship successfully circumnavigated the world. (p. 44)

Malcolm X (1925–1965) African American civil rights leader who advocated using violence if necessary to secure equal rights. Originally a leader of the Nation of Islam, when he broke with the organization, three of its members assassinated him. (p. 880)

Mann, Horace (1796–1859) American educator, he is considered the father of American public education. He was a leader of the common-school movement, advocating education for all children. (p. 450)

Mansa Musa (d. 1332?) Emperor of Mali, grandson or grandnephew of Sundiata, made pilgrimage to Mecca in 1324. (p. 18)

Marion, Francis (1732?–1795) Revolutionary War commander of Marion's Brigade, a group of guerrilla soldiers in South Carolina that used surprise raids against British communications and supply lines. (p. 136)

Marshall, John (1755–1835) Federalist leader who served in the House of Representatives and as U.S. Secretary of State, he later became the Chief Justice of the U.S. Supreme Court, establishing in Marbury v. Madison the Supreme Court's power of judicial review. (p. 270)

Marshall, Thurgood (1908–1993) First African American U.S. Supreme Court Justice, he represented as a lawyer the National Association for the Advancement of Colored People and fought racial segregation. (p. 186, 871)

Mason, George (1725–1792) American Patriot who became an Antifederalist and refused to sign the Constitution (p. 170)

McCain, John (1936–) American who served as Arizona's United States senator beginning in 1987. He also served in the U.S. Army during the Vietnam War. (p. 902)

McCarthy, Joseph (1908–1957) A U.S. senator from Wisconsin, he led investigations into the spread of communism in American society and within the government itself. He was eventually discredited when he could produce no evidence. (p. 855)

McClellan, George B. (1826–1885) American army general put in charge of Union troops and later removed by Lincoln for failure to press Lee's Confederate troops in Richmond. (p. 517)

McCormick, Cyrus (1809–1884) American inventor and industrialist, he invented the mechanical reaper and harvesting machine that quickly cut down wheat. (p. 404)

McKimmon, Jane Simpson (1867–1957) A pioneer of the home demonstration program in the United States. Her emphasis on gardening and canning helped women improve their families' lives.

Michelangelo (1475–1564) Italian sculptor, painter, architect, and poet. (p. 26)

Moctezuma II (1466–1520) Emperor of Mexico's Aztec Empire, he welcomed explorer Cortés as a god but was taken prisoner by him. He was later killed, and the Aztec capital was destroyed during the following Aztec uprising. (p. 46)

Monroe, James (1758–1831) Leading Revolutionary figure and negotiator of the Louisiana Purchase, he was the fifth president of the United States. He put forth the Monroe Doctrine establishing the U.S. sphere of influence in the Western Hemisphere that became the foundation of U.S. foreign policy. (p. 299)

Morse, Samuel F. B. (1791–1872) American artist and inventor, he applied scientists' discoveries of electricity and magnetism to develop the telegraph, which soon sent messages all across the country. (p. 402)

Mott, Lucretia (1793–1880) American reformer, she planned the Seneca Falls Convention with Elizabeth Cady Stanton, the first organized meeting for women's rights in the United States. (p. 464)

Murphey, Archibald (1777?–1832) A lawyer and professor from North Carolina. He made early calls for reforms of the state education system and is known as the father of North Carolina public schools.

Murrow, Edward R. (1908–1965) A journalist from North Carolina who gained national prominence during World War II after his reports from London. He was among the most respected people in the nation, and later helped to end McCarthyism.

Mussolini, Benito (1883–1945) Fascist leader of Italy during World War II. (p. 804)

N

Nimitz, Chester (1885–1966) Commander of the U.S. fleet in the Pacific during World War II, his strategy helped defeat Japan. (p. 821)

Nixon, Richard M. (1913–1994) The 37th president of the United States, he withdrew troops from Vietnam, ending the hugely unpopular war. He became the first president to resign, after the Watergate scandal affected his credibility. (p. 910)

O

O'Connor, Sandra Day (1930–) Associate justice of the U.S. Supreme Court, she was the first woman appointed to the Court. (p. 186)

O'Keeffe, Georgia (1887–1986) American artist whose works of flowers and cow skulls became famous. (p. 769)

Olmsted, Frederick Law (1822–1903) American landscape architect who promoted the idea of recreational parks across the nation and helped design Central Park in New York City. (p. 645)

Osceola (c.1804–1838) Florida Seminole leader, he resisted removal by the U.S. government despite an earlier treaty that Seminole leaders had been forced to sign. He was eventually captured and died in prison. (p. 335)

P

Paine, Thomas (1737–1809) American political philosopher and author, he urged an immediate declaration of independence from England in his anonymously and simply written pamphlet, Common Sense. (p. 118)

Parks, Rosa (1913– 2005) African American seamstress and civil rights activist who began the Montgomery bus boycott by refusing to give up her seat on a segregated city bus. (p. 872)

Patterson, Mary Jane (1840–1894) First African American woman to earn a B.A. degree. She graduated from Oberlin in 1862 and became a teacher and principal.

Paul, Alice (1885–1977) American social reformer, suffragist, and activist, she was the founder of the organization that became the National Woman's Party (NWP) that worked to obtain women's suffrage. (p. 677)

Penn, William (1644–1718) Quaker leader who founded a colony for Quakers in Pennsylvania; the colony provided an important example of representative self-government and became a model of freedom and tolerance. (p. 86)

BIOGRAPHICAL DICTIONARY

Perkins, Frances (1882–1962) Secretary of Labor under Franklin Roosevelt, she helped draft New Deal legislation and was the first female Cabinet member. (p. 785)

Perry, Oliver Hazard (1785–1819) American naval captain who put together the fleet that defeated the British at the Battle of Lake Erie in the War of 1812. (p. 285)

Pershing, John J. (1860–1948) American army commander, he commanded the expeditionary force sent into Mexico to find Pancho Villa. He was the major general and commander in chief of the American Expeditionary Forces in World War I. (p. 709)

Pickett, George (1825–1875) American general in the Confederate army, he was famed for Pickett's Charge, a failed but heroic effort at Cemetery Ridge in the Battle of Gettysburg, often considered a turning point of the Civil War. (p. 539)

Pierce, Franklin (1804–1869) Democratic candidate for president in 1852 and the fourteenth president of the United States, he made the Gadsden Purchase, which opened the Northwest for settlement, and passed the unpopular Kansas-Nebraska Act. (p. 483)

Pike, Zebulon (1779–1813) Army officer sent on a mission to explore the West, he was ordered to find the headwaters of the Red River. He attempted to climb what is now known as Pikes Peak in Colorado. (p. 276)

Pizarro (puh-ZAHR-oh), Francisco (c. 1475–1541) Spanish conquistador who sailed with Balboa on the discovery of the Pacific Ocean, he later pursued rumors of golden cities in the Andes Mountains of South America and conquered the Inca Empire. (p. 47)

Plato (c. 428–348 BC) Greek philosopher, student of Plato and teacher of Aristotle, wrote The Republic. (p. 22)

Pocahontas (c.1595–1617) American Indian princess, she saved the life of John Smith when he was captured and sentenced to death by the Powhatan. She was later taken prisoner by the English, converted to Christianity, and married colonist John Rolfe. (p. 73)

Poe, Edgar Allan (1809–1849) American writer, he is famed for his haunting poem "The Raven," as well as many other chilling or romantic stories and poems. He is credited with creating the first detective story, "The Gold Bug." (p. 445)

Polk, James K. (1795–1849) Eleventh president of the United States, he settled the Oregon boundary with Great Britain and successfully conducted the Mexican-American War. (p. 355)

Pontiac (c.1720–1769) Ottawa chief who united the Great Lakes' Indians to try to halt the advance of European settlements, he attacked British forts in a rebellion known as Pontiac's Rebellion; he eventually surrendered in 1766. (p. 97)

Powderly, Terence V. (1849–1924) American labor leader for the Knights of Labor, he removed the secrecy originally surrounding the organization, leading to its becoming the first truly national American labor union. (p. 625)

Powell, Colin (1937–) Appointed the first African American secretary of state by George W. Bush in 2000, he resigned his position over the handling of the Iraq war. (p. 951)

Pulitzer, Joseph (1847–1911) American journalist and newspaper publisher, he established the Pulitzer Prize for public service and advancement of education. (p. 645)

R

Randolph, A. Philip (1889–1979) African American labor leader who proposed a March on Washington during Franklin Roosevelt's presidency. It was called off when Roosevelt barred discrimination in defense industries. (p. 812)

Reagan, Ronald (1911–2004) The 40th president of the United States, his presidency was the result of a rise in conservatism after the dramatic changes of the 1960s and 1970s. (p. 937)

Revels, Hiram (1822–1901) American clergyman, educator, and politician, he became the first African American in the U.S. Senate. (p. 565)

Reynolds, R. J. (1850–1918) Born to a North Carolina tobacco farmer, Reynolds founded a tobacco manufacturing business in Winston-Salem in 1874. He was soon one of the wealthiest people in Winston-Salem.

Riis, Jacob (1849–1914) Photographer and journalist who took shocking pictures of the lives of poverty-stricken immigrants, sweatshop workers, and tenement dwellers. These photos were published in *How the Other Half Lives.* (p. 646)

Rochambeau, Comte de (1725–1807) French soldier who commanded the French troops in the American Revolutionary War. He was with General George Washington at the Battle of Yorktown. (p. 137)

Rockefeller, John D. (1839–1937) American industrialist and philanthropist, he made a fortune in the oil business and used vertical and horizontal integration to establish a monopoly on the steel business. (p. 620)

Roosevelt, Eleanor (1884–1962) Author, diplomat, humanitarian, and First Lady of Franklin D. Roosevelt, she supported much New Deal legislation aimed at young people and minorities. (p. 787)

Roosevelt, Franklin D. (1882–1945) The 32nd president of the United States, he led the country through the Great Depression and World War II. He served four terms, more than any other president. (p. 782)

Roosevelt, Theodore (1858–1919) Twenty-sixth president of the United States after William McKinley was assassinated, he organized the first volunteer cavalry regiment known as the Rough Riders who fought in Cuba during the Spanish-American War. As President, he acquired the Panama Canal Zone, and announced the Roosevelt Corollary, making the United States the defender of the Western Hemisphere. (p. 680)

S

Sacagawea (sak-uh-juh-WEE-uh) (1786?–1812) Shoshone woman who, along with her French fur-trapper husband, accompanied and aided Lewis and Clark on their expedition. (p. 276)

Santa Anna, Antonio López de (1794–1876) Mexican general and politician, he was president of Mexico and became a dictator. He fought in the Texas Revolution and seized the Alamo but was defeated and captured by Sam Houston at San Jacinto. (p. 351)

Schafly, Phyllis (1924–) A leader of the conservative movement against the Equal Rights Amendment, she spoke out against the forces of feminism that emerged in the 1970s. (p. 883)

Scott, Dred (1795?–1858) Enslaved African who filed suit for his freedom stating that his time living in a free state made him a free man; the Supreme Court ruling known as the Dred Scott decision upheld slavery and found the Missouri Compromise unconstitutional. (p. 489)

Scott, Winfield (1786–1866) American general, he served as commander in the Mexican War and used a two-part strategy against the South in the Civil War; he wanted to destroy the South's economy with a naval blockade and gain control of the Mississippi River. (p. 513)

Sequoya (between 1760 and 1770–1843) American Indian scholar and craftsman, he created a writing system for the Cherokee language and taught literacy to many Cherokee. (p. 333)

Seward, William H. (1801–1872) Secretary of state under Abraham Lincoln, he also was responsible for the purchase of Alaska from Russia. (p. 693)

Shays, Daniel (1747?–1825) Revolutionary War officer who led Shays's Rebellion, an uprising of farmers in western Massachusetts that shut down the courts so that farmers would not lose their farms for tax debts. He was defeated and condemned to death, but pardoned. (p. 161)

Sherman, William Tecumseh (1820–1891) American Union army officer, his famous March to the Sea captured Atlanta, Georgia, marking an important turning point in the war. (p. 541)

Singer, Isaac (1811–1875) American inventor; he patented an improved sewing machine and by 1860, was the largest manufacturer of sewing machines in the country. (p. 405)

Sitting Bull (c.1831–1890) American Indian leader who became the head chief of the entire Sioux nation, he encouraged other Sioux leaders to resist government demands to buy lands on the Black Hills reservations. (p. 596)

Slade, Stephen (1823–1906) An enslaved African American. He discovered a way to cure bright-leaf tobacco in 1839 that revolutionized the tobacco industry.

Slater, Samuel (1768–1835) English industrialist who brought a design for a textile mill to America, he is considered the founder of the American cotton industry. (p. 386)

Smith, John (c.1580–1631) English colonist to the Americas who helped found the Jamestown Colony and encouraged settlers to work harder and build better housing. (p. 73)

Socrates (c. 470–399 BC) Greek philosopher and teacher who wanted to make people question their own beliefs and think for themselves. (p. 22)

Spaight, Richard Dobbs (1758–1802) Born in New Bern, North Carolina. He served as a delegate to the Continental Congress, the Senate, the House of Representatives, in the North Carolina General Assembly, and as governor of the state.

Squanto (?–1622) Patuxet Indian who was captured and enslaved in Spain but later escaped to England and then America; he taught the Pilgrims native farming methods and helped them establish relations with the Wampanoag, the Indians at the feast later known as Thanksgiving. (p. 79)

Stalin, Joseph (1879–1953) Communist dictator of the Soviet Union, led that nation through World War II and greatly affected the postwar decisions made about Europe at the Yalta and Potsdam conferences. (p. 805)

Stanford, Leland (1824–1893) American railroad builder and politician, he established the California Central Pacific Railroad and founded Stanford University. (p. 621)

Stanton, Elizabeth Cady (1815–1902) American woman suffrage leader, she organized the Seneca Falls Convention with Lucretia Mott. The convention was the first organized meeting for women's rights in the United States, which launched the suffrage movement. (p. 464)

Steinbeck, John (1902–1968) Writer who captured the desperation of Americans struggling through the Great Depression, especially those affected by the Dust Bowl. (p. 793)

Steuben, Baron Friedrich von (1730–1794) Prussian soldier who helped train American forces at Valley Forge during the American Revolutionary War. (p. 131)

Stone, Lucy (1818–1893) American woman suffragist, she was a well-known and accomplished antislavery speaker who supported the women's rights movement. (p. 465)

Stowe, Harriet Beecher (1811–1896) American author and daughter of Lyman Beecher, she was an abolitionist and author of the famous antislavery novel, *Uncle Tom's Cabin*. (p. 481)

Stuyvesant (STY-vi-suhnt), Peter (c.1610–1672) Director general of the Dutch New Netherland colony, he was forced to surrender New Netherland to the English. (p. 85)

Sumner, Charles (1811–1874) A Senator from Massachusetts, he was attacked by Preston Brooks with a cane over the issue of slavery. (p. 487)

Sutter, John (1803–1880) American pioneer who built Sutter's Fort, a trading post on the California frontier; gold was discovered, leading to the California gold rush. (p. 365)

T

Taft, William Howard (1857–1930) Twenty-seventh president of the United States, he angered progressives by moving cautiously toward reforms and by supporting the Payne–Aldrich Tariff, which did not lower tariffs very much. He lost Roosevelt's support and was defeated for a second term. (p. 682)

Taney (TAW-nee), Roger B. (1777–1864) U.S. Supreme Court Chief Justice, he wrote the majority opinion in the *Dred Scott* decision, stating that African Americans were not citizens and that the Missouri Compromise was unconstitutional. (p. 490)

Taylor, Frederick W. (1856–1915) American efficiency engineer, he introduced the manufacturing system known as scientific management that viewed workers as mechanical parts of the production process, not as human beings. (p. 624)

Teach, Edward (1680?–1718) Also known as Blackbeard. A pirate that raided ships in the Caribbean and along the coast of North Carolina in the early 1700s.

Tecumseh (1768–1813) Shawnee chief who attempted to form an Indian confederation to resist white settlement in the Northwest Territory. (p. 280)

Thoreau, Henry David (1817–1862) American writer and transcendentalist philosopher, he studied nature and published a magazine article, "Civil Disobedience," as well as his famous book, Walden Pond. (p. 443)

Tourgée, Albion (1838–1905) A northerner and Radical Republican who moved to North Carolina to aid freedpeople during Reconstruction. He published a book entitled *A Fool's Errand by One of the Fools* about his experiences there.

Truman, Harry S. (1884–1972) The 33rd president of the United States, he became president after the death of Franklin Roosevelt. Truman ended World War II after dropping atomic bombs on Japan. (p. 826)

Truth, Sojourner (c.1797–1883) American evangelist and reformer, she was born an enslaved African but was later freed and became a speaker for abolition and women's suffrage. (p. 456)

Tubman, Harriet (c.1820–1913) American abolitionist who escaped slavery and assisted other enslaved Africans to escape; she is the most famous Underground Railroad conductor and is known as the Moses of her people. (p. 458)

Turner, Nat (1800–1831) American slave leader, he claimed that divine inspiration had led him to end the slavery system. Called Nat Turner's Rebellion, the slave revolt was the most violent one in U.S. history; he was tried, convicted, and executed. (p. 428)

Tweed, William Marcy (1823–1878) New York city politician known for his control of the corrupt political machine called the Tammany Ring. (p. 663)

V

Vallejo, Mariano Guadalupe (1808–1890) Californio leader who urged equal rights for Mexicans living in California after the state was captured in the Mexican-American War. (p. 357)

Van Buren, Martin (1782–1862) American politician and secretary of state under Andrew Jackson, he later became the eighth president of the United States. (p. 324)

Vance, Zebulon B. (1830–1894) Born in Buncombe County, North Carolina. He was elected to Congress but resigned his seat when it became apparent that North Carolina would secede. During the Civil War he commanded troops, and then won the office of governor. His dedication to his state caused conflict with the Confederate government.

Vanderbilt, George W., II (1862–1914) Member of the wealthy Vanderbilt family. He built the largest home in the United States, the Biltmore estate near Asheville, North Carolina.

Villa, Francisco "Pancho" (1878–1923) Mexican bandit and revolutionary leader, he led revolts against Carranza and Huerta. He was pursued by the U.S. but evaded General Pershing. (p. 709)

W

Walker, David (1785–1830) An African American abolitionist from North Carolina. He published a pamphlet called *Walker's Appeal* which called for black pride and defended violent rebellion.

Washington, Booker T. (1856–1915) African American educator and civil rights leader, he was born into slavery and later became head of the Tuskegee Institute for career training for African Americans. He was an advocate for conservative social change. (p. 677)

Washington, George (1732–1799) Revolutionary War hero and Patriot leader, he served as a representative to the Continental Congresses, commanded the Continental Army, and was unanimously elected to two terms as president of the United States. (pp. 114, 234)

Washington, Martha (1731–1802) Wife of George Washington, she was the first First Lady. (p. 234)

Webster, Daniel (1782–1852) American lawyer and statesman, he spoke out against nullification and states' rights, believing that the country should stay unified. (p. 328)

BIOGRAPHICAL DICTIONARY

Wells, Ida B. (1862–1931) African American journalist and anti-lynching activist, she was part owner and editor of the Memphis Free Speech. (p. 677)

Westmoreland, William (1914–2005) Commander of all U.S. forces in Vietnam during the Vietnam War, he began the strategy of search-and-destroy missions. (p. 903)

Whitman, Walt (1819–1892) American poet, he gained recognition abroad and later at home for unrhymed works of poetry praising the United States, Americans, democracy, and individualism. (p. 445)

Whitney, Eli (1765–1825) American inventor whose cotton gin changed cotton harvesting procedures and enabled large increases in cotton production; he introduced the technology of mass production through the development of interchangeable parts in gun-making. (p. 387)

Willard, Frances (1839–1898) American reformer who helped found the Women's Christian Temperance Union and was also active in the Women's suffrage movement. (p. 676)

Wilson, Woodrow (1856–1924) Twenty-eighth president of the United States, his reform legislation was given the name New Freedom, and it included three constitutional amendments: direct election of senators, prohibition, and women's suffrage. He created the Federal Reserve System, the Federal Trade Commission, and he enacted child labor laws. (p. 682)

Winnemucca, Sarah (1844–1891) Paiute Indian reformer, she was an activist for Indian rights and lectured specifically about the problems of the reservation system. (p. 598)

Winthrop, John (1588–1649) Leader of the Massachusetts Bay Colony who led Puritan colonists to Massachusetts to establish an ideal Christian community; he later became the colony's first governor. (p. 80)

Wolfe, Thomas (1900–1938) A novelist from North Carolina. He wrote about growing up in the state. His novels were written during the Great Depression, but two of them were not published until after his death.

Wright, Orville (1871–1948) and **Wilbur** (1867–1912) American pioneers of aviation, they went from experiments with kites and gliders to piloting the first successful gas-powered airplane flight and later founded the American Wright Company to manufacture airplanes. (p. 618)

Y

Young, Brigham (1801–1877) American religious leader who headed the Mormon Church after the murder of Joseph Smith, he moved the community to Utah, leading thousands along what came to be known as the Mormon Trail to the main settlement at Salt Lake City. (p. 349)

Z

Zedong, Mao (1893–1976) Communist leader of China, he defeated a nationalist army for control of China. (p. 852)

English and Spanish Glossary

MARK	AS IN	RESPELLING	EXAMPLE
a	alphabet	a	*AL-fuh-bet
ā	Asia	ay	AY-zhuh
ä	cart, top	ah	KAHRT, TAHP
e	let, ten	e	LET, TEN
ē	even, leaf	ee	EE-vuhn, LEEF
i	it, tip, British	i	IT, TIP, BRIT-ish
ī	site, buy, Ohio	y	SYT, BY, oh-HY-oh
	iris	eye	EYE-ris
k	card	k	KAHRD
ō	over, rainbow	oh	OH-vuhr, RAYN-boh
u̇	book, wood	ooh	BOOHK, WOOHD
ȯ	all, orchid	aw	AWL, AWR-kid
ȯi	foil, coin	oy	FOYL, KOYN
au̇	out	ow	OWT
ə	cup, butter	uh	KUHP, BUHT-uhr
ü	rule, food	oo	ROOL, FOOD
yü	few	yoo	FYOO
zh	vision	zh	VIZH-uhn

*A syllable printed in small capital letters receives heavier emphasis than the other syllable(s) in a word.

Phonetic Respelling and Pronunciation Guide

Many of the key terms in this textbook have been respelled to help you pronounce them. The letter combinations used in the respelling throughout the narrative are explained in the following phonetic respelling and pronunciation guide. The guide is adapted from *Merriam-Webster's Collegiate Dictionary, 11th Edition; Merriam-Webster's Geographical Dictionary;* and *Merriam-Webster's Biographical Dictionary.*

A

abolition an end to slavery (p. 454)
abolición fin de la esclavitud (pág. 454)

Adams-Onís Treaty (1819) an agreement in which Spain gave East Florida to the United States (p. 299)
Tratado de Adams y Onís (1819) acuerdo en el que España le dio el territorio del este de Florida a Estados Unidos (pág. 299)

affirmative action an active effort to improve the employment or educational opportunities of members of minority groups and women (p. 933)
acción afirmativa iniciativas para mejorar las oportunidades laborales o educativas de las minorías y de las mujeres (pág. 933)

AIDS Acquired Immunodeficincy Syndrome, a disease that affects the immune system, making patients vulnerable to infections (p. 961)
SIDA síndrome de inmunodeficiencia adquirida; enfermedad que afecta al sistema inmunológico y hace que los pacientes sean vulnerables a infecciones (pág. 961)

African Diaspora the population of displaced Africans and their descendants around the world (p. 60)
diáspora africana población de africanos desplazados y sus descendientes en todo el mundo (pág. 60)

Alamo Spanish mission in San Antonio, Texas, that was the site of a famous battle of the Texas Revolution in 1836 (p. 352)
El Álamo misión española en San Antonio, Texas; escenario de una famosa batalla durante la Revolución Texana de 1836 (pág. 352)

Alien and Sedition Acts (1798) laws passed by a Federalist-dominated Congress aimed at protecting the government from treasonous ideas, actions, and people (p. 253)
Leyes de Extranjeros y Sedición (1798) leyes aprobadas por un Congreso mayormente federalista para proteger al gobierno de la influencia de ideas, acciones y personas desleales (pág. 253)

Allied Powers a group of nations that allied to fight the Central Powers in World War I, and those countries in opposition to the Axis Powers in World War II (pp. 721, 806)
potencias aliadas grupo de naciones que se aliaron para luchar contra las potencias centrales en la Primera Guerra Mundial, y los países que se oponían a las potencias del Eje en la Segunda Guerra Mundial (págs. 721, 806)

al Qaeda the name of the terrorist organization headed by Osama bin Laden and responsible for the September 11, 2001, attacks (p. 956)
al-Qaeda nombre de la organización terrorista encabezada por Osama bin Laden, responsable de los ataques del 11 de septiembre de 2001 (pág. 956)

amendment official change, correction, or addition to a law or constitution (p. 173)
enmienda cambio, corrección o adición oficial a una ley o constitución (pág. 173)

American Anti-Slavery Society an organization started by William Lloyd Garrison whose members wanted immediate emancipation and racial equality for African Americans (p. 455)
Sociedad Americana contra la Esclavitud organización fundada por William Lloyd Garrison cuyos miembros pedían la emancipación inmediata y la igualdad racial de los afroamericanos (pág. 455)

American Expeditionary Force the U.S. military forces sent to Europe during World War I and led by General John J. Pershing (p. 730)
Fuerza Expedicionaria Estadounidense fuerzas armadas de Estados Unidos bajo el mando del general John J. Pershing que fueron enviadas a Europa en la Primera Guerra Mundial (pág. 730)

American Federation of Labor (AFL) an organization that united skilled workers into national unions for specific industries (p. 625)
Federación Americana del Trabajo (AFL, por sus siglas en inglés) organización que unió a obreros especializados en sindicatos nacionales para industrias específicas (pág. 625)

American Indian Movement (AIM) a civil rights group organized to promote the interests of Native Americans (p. 885)
Movimiento de los Indígenas Americanos (AIM, por sus siglas en inglés) agrupación a favor de los derechos civiles que promueve los intereses de los indígenas norteamericanos (pág. 885)

American System Henry Clay's plan for raising tariffs to pay for internal improvements such as better roads and canals (p. 302)
Sistema Estadounidense plan de alza de aranceles creado por Henry Clay para hacer mejoras internas como la reparación de caminos y canales (pág. 302)

Antifederalists people who opposed ratification of the Constitution (p. 170)
antifederalistas personas que se oponían a la aprobación de la Constitución (pág. 170)

Anti-Imperialist League a group of citizens opposed to imperialism, and, specifically, to the peace treaty that gave the United States control of Cuba, Guam, Puerto Rico, and the Philippines (p. 700)
Liga Antiimperialista grupo de ciudadanos que se oponían al imperialismo y, más específicamente, al tratado de paz que daba a Estados Unidos el control de Cuba, Guam, Puerto Rico y Filipinas (pág. 700)

apartheid a system of segregation practiced in South Africa (p. 935)
apartheid sistema de segregación practicado en Sudáfrica (pág. 935)

appeasement the policy of giving into the demands of a nation in order to avoid war (p. 806)
apacigua miento contemporizacióno política de ceder ante las exigencias de una nación para evitar la guerra (pág. 806)

Appomattox Courthouse the location where General Robert E. Lee was forced to surrender, thus ending the Civil War (p. 542)
Appomattox Courthouse poblado de Virginia donde el general Robert E. Lee fue obligado a rendirse, dando fin a la Guerra Civil (pág. 542)

armistice a truce or cease-fire agreement between warring nations (p. 734)
armisticio tregua o acuerdo de cese del fuego entre dos naciones en guerra (pág. 734)

arms race a growth in weapons based on the number of weapons an enemy country has (p. 856)
carrera armamentística aumento de armamentos según la cantidad de armas que tiene un país enemigo (pág. 856)

Articles of Confederation (1777) the document that created the first central government for the United States; was replaced by the Constitution in 1789 (p. 154)
Artículos de Confederación (1777) documento que creó el primer gobierno central en Estados Unidos; fue reemplazado por la Constitución en 1789 (pág. 154)

astrolabe a device that enabled navigators to learn their ship's location by charting the position of the stars (p. 40)
astrolabio aparato que permitía a los navegantes saber la ubicación de su barco al trazar la posición de las estrellas (pág. 40)

atomic bomb a weapon that receives its explosive power from the splitting of atoms (p. 828)
bomba atómica arma cuyo poder explosivo es generado por la división de átomos (pág. 828)

Axis Powers the coalition of nations in World War II that included Germany, Italy, and Japan (p. 806)
potencias del Eje coalición de naciones de la Segunda Guerra Mundial formada por Alemania, Italia y Japón (pág. 806)

B

baby boom a sharp increase in the number of American births during the 1950s and 1960s (p. 858)
boom de la natalidad gran aumento en la cantidad de nacimientos en Estados Unidos durante las décadas de 1950 y 1960 (pág. 858)

Bacon's Rebellion (1676) an atttack led by Nathaniel Bacon against American Indians and the colonial government in Virginia (p. 74)
Rebelión de Bacon (1676) ataque encabezado por Nathaniel Bacon contra los indígenas norteamericanos y el gobierno colonial en Virginia (pág. 74)

Bank of the United States a national bank chartered by Congress in 1791 to provide security for the U.S. economy (p. 242)
Banco de los Estados Unidos banco nacional formado por el Congreso en 1791 para dar seguridad a la economía de Estados Unidos (pág. 242)

Bataan Death March a forced march of American and Filipino soldiers captured by the Japanese along the Bataan Penninsula (p. 820)
marcha de la muerte de Bataán marcha forzada en la península de Bataán de soldados estadounidenses y filipinos capturados por los japoneses (pág. 820)

Battle of Antietam (1862) a Union victory in the Civil War that marked the bloodiest single-day battle in U.S. military history (p. 519)
batalla de Antietam (1862) victoria del ejército de la Unión durante la Guerra Civil en la batalla de un solo día más sangrienta de la historia militar de Estados Unidos (pág. 519)

Battle of Bunker Hill (1775) a Revolutionary War battle in Boston that demonstrated that the colonists could fight well against the British army (p. 115)
batalla de Bunker Hill (1775) batalla de la Guerra de Independencia estadounidense en Boston; en ésta se demostró que los colonos podían luchar bien contra el ejército británico (pág. 115)

Battle of El Alamein (1942) a turning point in World War II, in which Allied forces defeated the Afrika Korps of Germany (p. 816)
batalla del El Alamein (1942) momento decisivo en la Segunda Guerra Mundial, en el que las fuerzas aliadas derrotaron al *Afrika Korps* de Alemania (pág. 816)

Battle of Fallen Timbers (1794) a battle between U.S. troops and an American Indian confederation that ended Indian efforts to halt white settlement in the Northwest Territory (p. 247)
batalla de Fallen Timbers (1794) batalla entre las tropas estadounidenses y una confederación de indígenas norteamericanos que puso fin a los intentos de los indígenas para detener la emigración de personas de raza blanca al Territorio del Noroeste (pág. 247)

Battle of Gettysburg (1863) a Union Civil War victory that turned the tide against the Confederates at Gettysburg, Pennsylvania (p. 537)
batalla de Gettysburg (1863) victoria del ejército de la Unión durante la Guerra Civil que cambió el curso de la guerra en contra de los confederados en Gettysburg, Pensilvania (pág. 537)

Battle of Lake Erie (1813) U.S. victory in the War of 1812, led by Oliver Hazard Perry; broke Britain's control of Lake Erie (p. 285)
batalla del lago Erie (1813) victoria en la Guerra de 1812 en la que el ejército estadounidense, comandado por Oliver Hazard Perry, puso fin al control británico del lago Erie (pág. 285)

Battle of Leyte Gulf (1944) the largest naval battle in history, during which the American fleet destroyed most of the Japanese fleet (p. 822)
batalla del golfo de Leyte (1944) la mayor batalla naval de la historia, durante la cual la flota estadounidense destruyó la mayor parte de la flota japonesa (pág. 822)

Battle of Midway (1942) battle of World War II that ended the Japanese advance in the Pacific (p. 821)
batalla de Midway (1942) batalla de la Segunda Guerra Mundial que puso fin al avance de los japoneses en el Pacífico (pág. 821)

Battle of New Orleans (1815) the greatest U.S. victory in the War of 1812; actually took place two weeks after a peace treaty had been signed ending the war (p. 286)
batalla de Nueva Orleáns (1815) la mayor victoria del ejército estadounidense en la Guerra de 1812; tuvo lugar dos semanas después de la firma de un tratado de paz en el que se declaraba el final de la guerra (pág. 286)

Battle of San Jacinto (1836) the final battle of the Texas Revolution; resulted in the defeat of the Mexican army and independence for Texas (p. 352)
batalla de San Jacinto (1836) batalla final de la Revolución Texana en la que el ejército mexicano fue derrotado y Texas obtuvo su independencia (pág. 352)

Battle of Saratoga (1777) a Revolutionary War battle in New York that resulted in a major defeat of British troops; marked the Patriots' greatest victory up to that point in the war (p. 130)
batalla de Saratoga (1777) batalla de la Guerra de Independencia estadounidense que tuvo lugar en Nueva York y en la que las fuerzas británicas sufrieron una de sus mayores derrotas; los patriotas obtuvieron su mayor victoria hasta ese momento (pág. 130)

Battle of Shiloh (1862) a Civil War battle in Tennessee in which the Union army gained greater control over the Mississippi River valley (p. 523)
batalla de Shiloh (1862) batalla de la Guerra Civil en Tennessee en la que el ejército de la Unión adquirió mayor control sobre el valle del río Mississippi (pág. 523)

Battle of Stalingrad (1942–1943) a major turning point in World War II; Soviet forces defeated Nazi forces after which the Nazis never recovered (p. 817)
batalla de Stalingrado (1942–1943) momento decisivo de la Segunda Guerra Mundial; las fuerzas soviéticas vencieron a las fuerzas nazis, que nunca más se recuperaron (pág. 817)

Battle of the Bulge (1944–1945) the last German advance of World War II, which was stopped by Allied forces (p. 826)
batalla del Bulge (1944–1945) último avance alemán de la Segunda Guerra Mundial, que fue detenido por las fuerzas aliadas (pág. 826)

Battle of the Coral Sea (1942) the first strategic defeat of the Japanese Imperial Navy by American forces during World War II (p. 821)
batalla del mar del Coral (1942) primera derrota estratégica de la armada imperial japonesa ante las fuerzas estadounidenses en la Segunda Guerra Mundial (pág. 821)

Battle of the Little Big Horn (1876) "Custer's Last Stand"; battle between U.S. soldiers, led by George Armstrong Custer, and Sioux warriors, led by Crazy Horse and Sitting Bull, that resulted in the worst defeat for the U.S. Army in the West (p. 596)
batalla de Little Big Horn (1876) última batalla del general Custer; esta batalla entre las tropas de George Armstrong Custer y los guerreros siux al mando de Caballo Loco y Toro Sentado produjo la mayor derrota del ejército estadounidense en el Oeste (pág. 596)

Battle of Tippecanoe (1811) U.S. victory over an Indian confederation that wanted to stop white settlement in the Northwest Territory; increased tensions between Great Britain and the United States (p. 282)
batalla de Tippecanoe (1811) victoria del ejército estadounidense sobre la confederación indígena que intentaba evitar el establecimiento de poblaciones de blancos en el Territorio del Noroeste; esta batalla aumentó las hostilidades entre Gran Bretaña y Estados Unidos (pág. 282)

Battle of Trenton (1776) a Revolutionary War battle in New Jersey in which Patriot forces captured more than 900 Hessian troops (p. 129)
batalla de Trenton (1776) batalla de la Guerra de Independencia estadounidense que tuvo lugar en Nueva Jersey; en esta batalla las fuerzas de los patriotas capturaron a más de 900 soldados hessianos (pág. 129)

Battle of Yorktown (1781) the last major battle of the Revolutionary War; site of British general Charles Cornwallis's surrender to the Patriots in Virginia (p. 137)
batalla de Yorktown (1781) la última batalla importante de la Guerra de Independencia estadounidense; lugar donde se rindió el general británico Charles Cornwallis ante los patriotas en Virginia (pág. 137)

Bear Flag Revolt (1846) a revolt against Mexico by American settlers in California who declared the territory an independent republic (p. 358)
Revuelta de Bear Flag (1846) rebelión iniciada por colonos estadounidenses en contra de México para declarar al territorio de California una república independiente (pág. 358)

beats young people, many of whom were writers and artists, who discussed their dissatisfaction with the American society of the 1950s (p. 861)
beatniks jóvenes, en su mayoría escritores y artistas, que debatían acerca de su descontento con la sociedad estadounidense de la década de 1950 (pág. 861)

benevolent society an aid organization formed by immigrant communities (p. 639)
sociedad de beneficencia organización de ayuda formada por comunidades de inmigrantes (pág. 639)

Berbers a group of people from northern Africa (p. 16)
bereberes grupo de habitantes del norte de África (pág. 16)

Berlin Wall a barrier of concrete and barbed wire between Communist East Berlin and West Berlin (p. 896)
Muro de Berlín barrera de concreto y alambre de púas que separaba la Berlín oriental comunista de la Berlín occidental (pág. 896)

Bering Land Bridge a strip of land connecting Alaska with Russia that emerged from underwater around 38,000 BC (p. 6)
Puente de Tierra de Bering franja de tierra que conecta Alaska con Rusia y que surgió del agua alrededor del año 38,000 a.C. (pág. 6)

Bessemer process a process developed in the 1850s that led to faster, cheaper steel production (p. 615)
proceso de Bessemer proceso de producción de acero más económico y rápido, desarrollado en la década de 1850 (pág. 615)

Bill of Rights the first 10 amendments to the Constitution; ratified in 1791 (p. 173)
Declaración de Derechos primeras 10 enmiendas a la Constitución; aprobada en 1791 (pág. 173)

Black Codes laws passed in the southern states during Reconstruction that greatly limited the freedom and rights of African Americans (p. 558)

Códigos Negros decretos aprobados en los estados sureños en la época de la Reconstrucción que limitaron en gran medida la libertad y los derechos de los afroamericanos (pág. 558)

Black Death a series of plagues that killed about 25 million people in Europe starting in 1347 (p. 25)
Peste Negra serie de plagas que mataron a unos 25 millones de personas en Europa a partir de 1347 (pág. 25)

Black Power a social movement that called for African American power and independence (p. 880)
Black Power (Poder Negro) movimiento social que exigía el poder y la independencia de los afroamericanos (pág. 880)

Black Tuesday October 29, 1929, one of the largest U.S. stock market drops (p. 779)
martes negro 29 de octubre de 1929, una de las mayores caídas de la bolsa de valores de Estados Unidos (pág. 779)

bond a certificate that represents money the government has borrowed from private citizens (p. 238)
bono certificado que representa dinero que el gobierno toma prestado de los ciudadanos (pág. 238)

Bonus Army a group of World War I veterans that demanded their bonus payments early (p. 781)
Bonus Army grupo de veteranos de la Primera Guerra Mundial que exigía el pago de sus bonos por adelantado (pág. 781)

boomtown a Western community that grew quickly because of the mining boom and often disappeared when the boom ended (p. 588)
pueblo de rápido crecimiento comunidad del Oeste que se desarrolló con gran rapidez debido a la fiebre del oro, pero que desapareció cuando la fiebre terminó (pág. 588)

border states Delaware, Kentucky, Maryland, and Missouri; slave states that lay between the North and the South and did not join the Confederacy during the Civil War (p. 512)
estados fronterizos Delaware, Kentucky, Maryland y Missouri; estados esclavistas ubicados entre el Norte y el Sur y que no se unieron a la Confederación durante la Guerra Civil (pág. 512)

Boston Massacre (1770) an incident in which British soldiers fired into a crowd of colonists, killing five people (p. 101)
masacre de Boston (1770) incidente en el que los soldados británicos le dispararon a una multitud de colonos, dando muerte a cinco personas (pág. 101)

Boston Tea Party (1773) a protest against the Tea Act in which a group of colonists boarded British tea ships and dumped more than 340 chests of tea into Boston Harbor (p. 102)
Motín del Té de Boston (1773) protesta en contra de la Ley del Té en la que un grupo de colonos abordó barcos británicos que transportaban té y arrojó al mar alrededor de 340 baúles de té en el puerto de Boston (pág. 102)

Boxer Rebellion (1900) a siege of a foreign settlement in Beijing by Chinese nationalists who were angry at foreign involvement in China (p. 695)
rebelión de los boxers (1900) asedio a un asentamiento extranjero en Beijing por parte de un grupo de nacionalistas chinos que estaban enojados por la participación extranjera en China (pág. 695)

brinkmanship the Cold War foreign policy designed to "get to the verge without getting into the war" (p. 856)
política arriesgada política exterior durante la Guerra Fría diseñada para "llegar al borde de la guerra sin llegar a la guerra" (pág. 856)

Brown* v. *Board of Education (1954) Supreme Court decision that ended segregation in public schools (p. 871)
Brown* contra la *Junta Educativa (1954) decisión de la Corte Suprema que puso fin a la segregación en las escuelas públicas (pág. 871)

buffalo soldiers African American soldiers who served in the cavalry during the wars for the west (p. 596)
soldados búfalo soldados afroamericanos que sirvieron en la caballería durante las guerras del oeste (pág. 596)

Bureau of Indian Affairs a government agency created in the 1800s to oversee federal policy toward Native Americans (p. 332)
Oficina de Asuntos Indígenas agencia creada por el gobierno en el siglo XIX para supervisar las políticas federales en cuanto a los indígenas norteamericanos (pág. 332)

business cycle the rhythym in which an economy expands and contracts its production (p. 780)
ciclo económico ritmo al que la producción de una economía se expande y se contrae (pág. 780)

buying on margin the process of purchasing stock with credit, hoping to sell at a high enough price to pay the loan and make a profit (p. 778)
compra a crédito proceso de comprar acciones con préstamos, con la esperanza de venderlas a un precio suficientemente alto para pagar el préstamo y obtener una ganancia (pág. 778)

C

Californios Spanish colonists in California in the 1800s (p. 357)
californios colonos españoles que vivían en California en el siglo XIX (pág. 357)

Camp David Accords (1978) an agreement between the heads of Israel and Egypt that began a process for peace in the Middle East (p. 935)
Acuerdos de Camp David (1978) acuerdo entre los líderes de Israel y Egipto que dio inicio a un proceso de paz en el Medio Oriente (pág. 935)

capitalism an economic system in which private businesses run most industries (p. 674)
capitalismo sistema económico en el que las empresas privadas controlan la mayoría de las industrias (pág. 674)

caravels ships that used triangular sails to sail against the wind, and had rudders to improve steering (p. 40)
carabelas barcos con velas triangulares usadas para navegar contra el viento y que tenían timones para mejorar la dirección (pág. 40)

cattle drive a long journey on which cowboys herded cattle to northern markets or better grazing lands (p. 589)
arreo de ganado viaje largo en el que los vaqueros arreaban ganado para llevarlo a los mercados del Norte o a mejores pastos (pág. 589)

Cattle Kingdom an area of the Great Plains on which many ranchers raised cattle in the late 1800s (p. 589)
Reino del Ganado área de las Grandes Planicies en la que muchos rancheros criaban ganado a finales de siglo XIX (pág. 589)

Central Powers the coalition of nations in World War I that included the German, Austrio-Hungary, and Ottoman empires (p. 721)
Potencias Centrales coalición de naciones de la Primera Guerra Mundial formada por los imperios alemán, austrohúngaro y otomano (pág. 721)

charter an official document that gives a person the right to establish a colony (p. 54)
carta de constitución documento oficial que da a una persona el derecho de establecer una colonia (pág. 54)

checks and balances a system established by the Constitution that prevents any branch of government from becoming too powerful (p. 167)
equilibrio de poderes sistema establecido por la Constitución para evitar que cualquier poder del gobierno adquiera demasiada autoridad (pág. 167)

Chinese Exclusion Act (1882) a law passed by Congress that banned Chinese from immigrating to the United States for 10 years (p. 641)
Ley de Exclusión de Chinos (1882) ley aprobada por el Congreso que prohibió la inmigración de chinos a Estados Unidos por 10 años (pág. 641)

Chisholm Trail a trail that ran from San Antonio, Texas, to Abilene, Kansas, established by Jesse Chisholm in the late 1860s for cattle drives (p. 589)
Camino de Chisholm camino creado por Jesse Chisholm a finales de la década de 1860 que iba desde San Antonio, Texas hasta Abilene, Kansas, para arreos de ganado (pág. 589)

circumnavigate to travel all the way around the globe (p. 44)
circunnavegar darle la vuelta al planeta (pág. 44)

Civil Rights Act of 1866 a law that gave African Americans legal rights equal to those of white Americans (p. 560)
Ley de Derechos Civiles de 1866 ley que dio a los afroamericanos los mismos derechos legales que tenían los estadounidenses blancos (pág. 560)

Civil Rights Act of 1964 a law that ended discrimination based on race or gender (p. 879)
Ley de Derechos Civiles de 1964 ley que puso fin a la discriminación en base a la raza o al sexo (pág. 879)

Clermont the first full-sized U.S. commercial steamboat; developed by Robert Fulton and tested in 1807 (p. 397)
Clermont primer barco comercial de vapor de gran tamaño, diseñado por Robert Fulton y probado en 1807 (pág. 397)

Cold War a period of hostility between Western powers and Communist powers (p. 846)
Guerra Fría período de hostilidades entre las potencias de Occidente y las potencias comunistas (pág. 846)

collective bargaining a technique used by labor unions in which workers act collectively to change working conditions or wages (p. 626)
negociación colectiva método empleado por los sindicatos en el que los trabajadores actúan colectivamente para cambiar las condiciones laborales o los salarios (pág. 626)

Columbian Exchange the transfer of plants, animals, and diseases between the Americas and Europe, Asia, and Africa (p. 45)
intercambio colombino intercambio de plantas, animales y enfermedades entre las Américas y Europa, Asia y África (pág. 45)

Committees of Correspondence committees created by the Massachusetts House of Representatives in the 1760s to help towns and colonies share information about resisting British laws (p. 99)
comités de correspondencia comités creados por la Cámara de Representantes de Massachusetts en la década de 1760 para que los pueblos y colonias compartieran información sobra la resistencia a las leyes británicas (pág. 99)

common-school movement a social reform effort that began in the mid-1800s and promoted the idea of having all children educated in a common place regardless of social class or background (p. 450)
movimiento de escuelas comunes reforma social iniciada a mediados del siglo XIX para fomentar la idea de que todos los niños debían recibir educación en un mismo lugar sin importar su origen o clase social (pág. 450)

Common Sense (1776) a pamphlet written by Thomas Paine that criticized monarchies and convinced many American colonists of the need to break away from Britain (p. 118)
Sentido común (1776) folleto escrito por Thomas Paine en el que criticaba a las monarquías y convenció a muchos colonos norteamericanos de la necesidad de independizarse de Gran Bretaña (pág. 118)

Communists people who believe in communism, or the political system in which all resources are shared equally (p. 731)
comunistas personas que creen en el comunismo, es decir, el sistema político en el que los recursos se distribuyen a todos por igual (pág. 731)

Compromise of 1850 Henry Clay's proposed agreement that allowed California to enter the Union as a free state and divided the rest of the Mexican Cession into two territories where slavery would be decided by popular sovereignty (p. 479)
Compromiso de 1850 acuerdo propuesto por Henry Clay en que se permitía a California entrar en la Unión como estado libre y se proponía la división del resto del territorio de la Cesión Mexicana en dos partes donde la esclavitud sería reglamentada por soberanía popular (pág. 479)

Compromise of 1877 an agreement to settle the disputed presidential election of 1876; Democrats agreed to accept Republican Rutherford B. Hayes as president in return for the removal of federal troops from the South (p. 567)
Compromiso de 1877 acuerdo en el que se resolvieron las disputadas elecciones presidenciales de 1876; los demócratas aceptaron al republicano Rutherford B. Hayes como presidente a cambio del retiro de las tropas federales del Sur (pág. 567)

Comstock Lode Nevada gold and silver mine discovered by Henry Comstock in 1859 (p. 587)
veta de Comstock mina de oro y plata descubierta en Nevada por Henry Comstock en 1859 (pág. 587)

Confederate States of America the nation formed by the southern states when they seceded from the Union; also known as the Confederacy (p.497)
Estados Confederados de América nación formada por los estados del Sur cuando se separaron de la Unión; también conocida como Confederación (pág. 497)

Congress of Industrial Organizations (CIO) a union that organized workers according to industry, not by skill (p. 788)
Congreso de Organizaciones Industriales (CIO, por sus siglas en inglés) sindicato que organizó a los trabajadores según la industria y no el nivel de especialización (pag. 788)

conquistador a Spanish soldier and explorer who led military expeditions in the Americas and captured land for Spain (p. 46)
conquistador soldado y explorador español que encabezó expediciones militares en América y capturó territorios en nombre de España (pág. 46)

conservation the planned management of natural resources to prevent their destruction (p. 681)
conservación administración planificada de los recursos naturales para evitar su destrucción (pág. 681)

constitution a set of basic principles that determines the powers and duties of a government (p. 153)
constitución conjunto de principios básicos que determina los poderes y las obligaciones de un gobierno (pág. 153)

Constitutional Convention (1787) a meeting held in Philadelphia at which delegates from the states wrote the Constitution (p. 164)
Convención Constitucional (1787) reunión en Filadelfia en la que delegados de los estados redactaron la Constitución (pág. 164)

Constitutional Union Party a political party formed in 1860 by a group of northerners and southerners who supported the Union, its laws, and the Constitution (p. 495)
Partido Constitucional por la Unión partido político formado en 1860 por habitantes del Norte y del Sur en apoyo de la Unión, sus leyes y la Constitución (pág. 495)

containment a foreign policy that attempts to stop the spread of communism without ending it in the countries in which it already exists (p. 847)
contención política exterior que intenta detener el avance del comunismo sin eliminarlo en los países en los que ya existe (pág. 847)

Continental Army the army created by the Second Continental Congress in 1775 to defend the American colonies from Britain (p. 114)
Ejército Continental ejército creado por el Segundo Congreso Continental en 1775 para defender a las colonias norteamericanas del dominio británico (pág. 114)

contraband an escaped slave who joined the Union army during the Civil War (p. 531)
contrabando esclavo que escapó y se unió al ejército de la Unión durante la Guerra Civil (pág. 531)

Convention of 1818 an agreement between the United States and Great Britain that settled fishing rights and established new North American borders (p. 298)
Convención de 1818 acuerdo entre Estados Unidos y Gran Bretaña para definir los derechos de pesca y establecer las nuevas fronteras norteamericanas (pág. 298)

Copperheads a group of northern Democrats who opposed abolition and sympathized with the South during the Civil War (p. 532)
copperheads grupo de demócratas del Norte que se oponían a la abolición de la esclavitud y simpatizaban con las creencias sureñas durante la Guerra Civil (pág. 532)

corporation a business that sells portions of ownership called stock shares (p. 619)
corporación compañía que vende algunas partes en forma de acciones (pág. 619)

cotton belt a region stretching from South Carolina to east Texas where most U.S. cotton was produced during the mid-1800s (p. 416)
región algodonera zona que se extendía desde Carolina del Sur hasta el este de Texas, en la que se producía la mayor parte del algodón cosechado en Estados Unidos a mediados del siglo XIX (pág. 416)

cotton diplomacy Confederate efforts to use the importance of southern cotton to Britain's textile industry to persuade the British to support the Confederacy in the Civil War (p. 513)
diplomacia del algodón esfuerzos de la Confederación por aprovechar la importancia del algodón del Sur en la industria textil británica para convencer a Gran Bretaña de apoyar a la Confederación en la Guerra Civil (pág. 513)

cotton gin a machine invented by Eli Whitney in 1793 to remove seeds from short-staple cotton; revolutionized the cotton industry (p. 415)
desmotadora de algodón máquina inventada por Eli Whitney en 1793 para separar las fibras de algodón de las semillas; revolucionó la industria del algodón (pág. 415)

Cuban missile crisis a threat to national security that occurred when the Soviet Union placed nuclear missiles in Cuba (p. 896)
crisis de los misiles de Cuba amenaza a la seguridad nacional que ocurrió cuando la Unión Soviética colocó misiles nucleares en Cuba (pág. 896)

culture the common values and traditions of a society, such as language, government, and family relationships (p. 7)
cultura valores y tradiciones comunes de una sociedad, como el lenguaje, la forma de gobierno y las relaciones familiares (pág. 7)

Cumberland Road the first federal road project, construction of which began in 1815; ran from Cumberland, Maryland, to present-day Wheeling, West Virginia (p. 303)
camino de Cumberland primer proyecto federal de construcción de carreteras, iniciado en 1815 para crear un camino entre Cumberland, Maryland y el poblado que actualmente lleva el nombre de Wheeling, en Virginia Occidental (pág. 303)

D

Dawes General Allotment Act (1887) legislation passed by Congress that split up Indian reservation lands among individual Indians and promised them citizenship (p. 598)
Ley de Adjudicación General de Dawes (1887) ley aprobada por el Congreso que dividía el terreno de las reservas indígenas entre sus habitantes y les prometía la ciudadanía (pág. 598)

D-Day (1944) an invasion of Nazi-occupied France by Allied forces (p. 819)
día D (1944) invasión de las fuerzas aliadas en Francia, ocupada por los nazis (pág. 819)

Declaration of Independence (1776) the document written to declare the colonies free from British rule (p. 119)
Declaración de Independencia (1776) documento redactado para declarar la independencia de las colonias del dominio británico (pág. 119)

Declaration of Sentiments (1848) a statement written and signed by women's rights supporters at the Seneca Falls Convention; detailed their beliefs about social injustice against women (p. 464)
Declaración de Sentimientos (1848) declaración redactada y firmada por partidarios de los derechos de la mujer durante la Convención de Seneca Falls; se describía con detalle su punto de vista sobre las injusticias sociales que afectaban a las mujeres (pág. 464)

deficit the amount by which a government's spending exceeds its revenue (p. 938)
déficit cantidad en la que los gastos del gobierno superan sus ingresos (pág. 938)

deflation a decrease in money supply and overall lower prices (p. 604)
deflación reducción de la disponibilidad del dinero y baja general en los precios (pág. 604)

democracy a government in which people rule themselves (p. 23)
democracia gobierno en el que el pueblo se gobierna a sí mismo (pág. 23)

Democratic Party a political party formed by supporters of Andrew Jackson after the presidential election of 1824 (p. 323)
Partido Demócrata partido político formado por partidarios de Andrew Jackson después de las elecciones presidenciales de 1824 (pág. 323)

Democratic-Republican Party a political party founded in the 1790s by Thomas Jefferson, James Madison, and other leaders who wanted to preserve the power of the state governments and promote agriculture (p. 250)

Partido Demócrata Republicano partido político formado en la década de 1790 por Thomas Jefferson, James Madison y otros líderes políticos para preservar el poder de los gobiernos estatales y promover la agricultura (pág. 250)

department store giant retail shop (p. 645)
tiendas por departamentos grandes comercios de venta al público (pág. 645)

deport to send an immigrant back to his or her country of origin (p. 222)
deportar enviar a un inmigrante de regreso a su país de origen (pág. 222)

depression a steep drop in economic activity combined with rising unemployment (p. 161)
depresión bajón considerable en la actividad económica, combinado con un alza en el desempleo (pág. 161)

détente a period of closer diplomatic relations between the United States and the Communist powers of China and the Soviet Union (p. 928)
distensión período de relaciones diplomáticas más estrechas entre Estados Unidos y las potencias comunistas de China y la Unión Soviética (pág. 928)

Disabled in Action (DIA) a group organized to promote the interests of people with disabilities (p. 885)
Discapacitados en Acción (DIA, por sus siglas en inglés) grupo organizado para promover los intereses de personas con discapacidades (pág. 885)

domino theory the idea that Communism would spread rapidly throughout Southeast Asia (p. 898)
teoría del efecto dominó idea de que el comunismo se extendería rápidamente por el sureste de Asia (pág. 898)

Donner party a group of western travelers who were stranded in the Sierra Nevada during the winter of 1846-47; only 45 of the party's 87 members survived (p. 365)
grupo Donner grupo de viajeros del Oeste perdidos en la Sierra Nevada durante el invierno de 1846-47; sólo 45 de los 87 viajeros sobrevivieron (pág. 365)

double jeopardy the act of trying a person twice for the same crime (p. 218)
doble riesgo acto de juzgar a una persona dos veces por el mismo delito (pág. 218)

doves opponents of the Vietnam War (p. 904)
palomas opositores a la guerra de Vietnam (pág. 904)

draft a system of required service in the armed forces (p. 223)
conscripción sistema de servicio obligatorio en las fuerzas armadas (pág. 223)

dry farming a method of farming used by Plains farmers in the 1890s that shifted focus from water-dependent crops to more hardy crops (p. 601)
agricultura de secano método de cultivo que usaban los agricultores de las Planicies en la década de 1890 que provocó un cambio de los cultivos que dependían del agua a otros más resistentes (pág. 601)

due process the fair application of the law (p. 218)
debido proceso aplicación justa de la ley (pág. 218)

Dust Bowl an area of the United States that suffered a severe drought during the 1930s (p. 790)
Dust Bowl área de Estados Unidos que sufrió una grave sequía en la década de 1930 (pág. 790)

E

Eighteenth Amendment (1919) a constitutional amendment that outlawed the production and sale of alcoholic beverages in the United States; repealed in 1933 (p. 676)
Decimoctava Enmienda (1919) enmienda constitucional que prohibió la producción y venta de bebidas alcohólicas en Estados Unidos; revocada en 1933 (pág. 676)

electoral college a group of people selected from each of the states to cast votes in presidential elections (p. 234)
colegio electoral grupo de personas seleccionado en cada estado para votar en las elecciones presidenciales (pág. 234)

emancipation freeing of the slaves (p. 529)
emancipación liberación de los esclavos (pág. 529)

Emancipation Proclamation (1862) an order issued by President Abraham Lincoln freeing the slaves in areas rebelling against the Union; took effect January 1, 1863 (p. 529)
Proclamación de Emancipación (1862) orden emitida por el presidente Abraham Lincoln para liberar a los esclavos en las áreas que se rebelaban contra la Unión; entró en vigor el primero de enero de 1863 (pág. 529)

embargo the banning of trade with a country (p. 279)
embargo prohibición del comercio con un país (pág. 279)

Embargo Act (1807) a law that prohibited American merchants from trading with other countries (p. 279)
Ley de Embargo (1807) ley que prohibía a los comerciantes norteamericanos comerciar con otros países (pág. 279)

eminent domain the government's power to take personal property to benefit the public (p. 218)
derecho de expropiación poder otorgado al gobierno para tomar propiedades personales en beneficio del público (pág. 218)

empresarios agents who were contracted by the Mexican republic to bring settlers to Texas in the early 1800s (p. 350)
empresarios agentes contratados por la República Mexicana para traer pobladores a Texas a principios del siglo XIX (pág. 350)

encomienda system a system in Spanish America that gave settlers the right to tax local Indians or to demand their labor in exchange for protecting them and converting them to Christianity (p. 50)
sistema de encomienda sistema adoptado en la América española que permitía a los colonos cobrar impuestos a los indígenas o exigirles trabajo a cambio de su protección y de convertirlos al cristianismo (pág. 50)

English Bill of Rights (1689) a shift of political power from the British monarchy to Parliament (p. 91)
Declaración de Derechos inglesa (1689) cambio del poder político de la monarquía británica al Parlamento inglés (pág. 91)

Enlightenment the Age of Reason; movement that began in Europe in the 1700s as people began examining the natural world, society, and government (p. 95)
Ilustración Era de la Razón; movimiento iniciado en Europa en el siglo XVIII cuando las personas empezaron a examinar la naturaleza, la sociedad y el gobierno (pág. 95)

environment the climate and landscape that surrounds living things (p. 7)
medio ambiente clima y paisaje donde habitan seres vivos (pág. 7)

Equal Rights Amendment (ERA) a proposed amendment to the Constitution that would provide equal rights to women (p. 883)
Enmienda por la Igualdad de Derechos (ERA, por sus siglas en inglés) enmienda constitucional propuesta que otorgaría la igualdad de derechos a la mujer (pág. 833)

Era of Good Feelings a period of peace, pride, and progress for the United States from 1815 to 1825 (p. 303)
Era de los Buenos Sentimientos período de paz, orgullo y progreso en Estados Unidos de 1815 a 1825 (pág. 303)

Erie Canal the canal that runs from Albany to Buffalo, New York; completed in 1825 (p. 303)
canal de Erie canal que va de Albany a Buffalo, Nueva York; completado en 1825 (pág. 303)

escalation increased involvment in the Vietnam War (p. 902)
escalada mayor participación en la guerra de Vietnam (pág. 902)

executive branch the division of the federal government that includes the president and the administrative departments; enforces the nation's laws (p. 167)
poder ejecutivo división del gobierno federal que incluye al presidente y a los departamentos administrativos; hace cumplir las leyes de la nación (pág. 167)

executive orders nonlegislative directives issued by the U.S. president in certain circumstances; executive orders have the force of congressional law (p. 185)
órdenes ejecutivas órdenes no legislativas dictadas por el presidente de Estados Unidos en circunstancias específicas; tienen la misma validez que las leyes del Congreso (pág. 185)

Exodusters African Americans who settled western lands in the late 1800s (p. 601)
Exodusters afroamericanos que se establecieron en el Oeste a finales del siglo XIX (pág. 601)

expatriates citizens who leave their country to live elsewhere (p. 768)
expatriados ciudadanos que abandonan su país para vivir en otro lugar (pág. 768)

F

fascism a political system in which the state or government is seen as more important than the individual (p. 804)
fascismo sistema político en el que se considera que el estado o gobierno es más importante que las personas (pág. 804)

factor a crop broker who managed the trade between southern planters and their customers (p. 417)
agente agrícola persona que administraba el comercio entre las plantaciones del Sur y sus clientes (pág. 417)

Fair Deal President Truman's legislative plan for the nation that included antilynching laws (p. 850)
Fair Deal plan legislativo para la nación propuesto por el presidente Truman que incluía leyes en contra de los linchamientos (pág. 850)

federal system a system that divided powers between the states and the federal government (p. 182)
sistema federal sistema en el que se distribuye el poder entre los estados y el gobierno federal (pág. 182)

federalism U.S. system of government in which power is distributed between a central government and individual states (p. 167)
federalismo sistema de gobierno de Estados Unidos en el que el poder se divide entre una autoridad central y estados individuales (pág. 167)

Federalist Papers a series of essays that defended and explained the Constitution and tried to reassure Americans that the states would not be overpowered by the proposed national government (p. 171)
Federalist Papers serie de ensayos que defendían y explicaban la Constitución para convencer a los estadounidenses de que el gobierno nacional propuesto no tendría más poder que los estados (pág. 171)

Federalist Party a political party created in the 1790s and influenced by Alexander Hamilton that wanted to strengthen the federal government and promote industry and trade (p. 250)
Partido Federalista partido político creado en la década de 1790 e influenciado por las ideas de Alexander Hamilton para fortalecer al gobierno federal y fomentar la industria y el comercio (pág. 250)

Federalists people who supported ratification of the Constitution (p. 170)
federalistas personas que apoyaban la ratificación de la Constitución (pág. 170)

Fifteenth Amendment (1870) a constitutional amendment that gave African American men the right to vote (p. 563)
Decimoquinta Enmienda (1870) enmienda constitucional que daba a los hombres afroamericanos el derecho al voto (pág. 563)

54th Massachusetts Infantry African American Civil War regiment that captured Fort Wagner in South Carolina (p. 531)
54to Batallón de Infantería de Massachusetts regimiento afroamericano de la Guerra Civil que tomó el fuerte Wagner en Carolina del Sur (pág. 531)

fireside chats radio programs in which Franklin Roosevelt explained his plan for recovery from the Great Depression (p. 785)
charlas junto a la chimenea programas de radio en los cuales Franklin Roosevelt explicaba su plan para que el país se recuperara de la Gran Depresión (pág. 785)

First Battle of Bull Run (1861) the first major battle of the Civil War, resulting in a Confederate victory; showed that the Civil War would not be won easily (p. 517)
primera batalla de Bull Run (1861) primera batalla importante de la Guerra Civil, en la cual ganó el ejército confederado; demostró que la guerra no se ganaría fácilmente (pág. 517)

First Continental Congress (1774) a meeting of colonial delegates in Philadelphia to decide how to respond to the closing of Boston Harbor, increased taxes, and abuses of authority by the British government; delegates petitioned King George III, listing the freedoms they believed colonists should enjoy (p. 112)
Primer Congreso Continental (1774) reunión de delegados de las colonias en Filadelfia para decidir cómo responder al cierre del puerto de Boston, al alza de impuestos y a los abusos de la autoridad por parte del gobierno británico; los delegados hicieron peticiones al rey Jorge III, enumerando los derechos que consideraban justos para los colonos (pág. 112)

flappers young women who challenged traditional ideas of womanhood in the 1920s (p. 759)
flappers mujeres jóvenes que desafiaron las ideas tradicionales sobre la condición de la mujer en la década de 1920 (pág. 759)

folktale a story that often provides a moral lesson (p. 427)
cuento folclórico narración que con frecuencia ofrece una moraleja (pág. 427)

Fort Sumter a federal outpost in Charleston, South Carolina, that was attacked by the Confederates in April 1861, sparking the Civil War (p. 511)
fuerte Sumter puesto de avanzada federal en Charleston, Carolina del Sur, cuyo ataque por parte de los confederados en abril de 1861 dio origen a la Guerra Civil (pág. 511)

forty-niner a gold-seeker who moved to California during the gold rush (p. 365)
del cuarenta y nueve buscador de oro que se mudó a California durante la fiebre del oro (pág. 365)

Fourteenth Amendment (1866) a constitutional amendment giving full rights of citizenship to all people born or naturalized in the United States, except for American Indians (p. 561)
Decimocuarta Enmienda (1866) enmienda constitucional que otorgaba derechos totales de ciudadanía a todas las personas nacidas en Estados Unidos o naturalizadas estadounidenses, con excepción de los indígenas americanos (pág. 561)

Freedmen's Bureau an agency established by Congress in 1865 to help poor people throughout the South (p. 556)
Oficina de los Libertos oficina creada por el Congreso en 1865 para ayudar a los pobres del Sur del país (pág. 556)

Freedom Rides a series of integrated bus rides through the South (p. 877)
Viajes de la Libertad serie de viajes en autobús por el Sur en los que se integraban las razas (pág. 877)

Freeport Doctrine (1858) a statement made by Stephen Douglas during the Lincoln-Douglas debates that pointed out how people could use popular sovereignty to determine if their state or territory should permit slavery (p. 492)
Doctrina de Freeport (1858) declaración hecha por Stephen Douglas durante los debates Lincoln-Douglas que señalaba que el pueblo podía usar la soberanía popular para decidir si su estado o territorio debía permitir la esclavitud (pág. 492)

Free-Soil Party a political party formed in 1848 by antislavery northerners who left the Whig and Democratic parties because neither addressed the slavery issue (p. 477)
Partido Tierra Libre partido político formado en 1848 por abolicionistas de los estados del Norte que habían abandonado el Partido Whig y el Partido Demócrata porque ninguno de los dos partidos tenía una postura sobre la esclavitud (pág. 477)

French Revolution French rebellion that began in 1789 in which the French people overthrew the monarchy and made their country a republic (p. 243)
Revolución Francesa rebelión francesa iniciada en 1789 en la que la población francesa derrocó a la monarquía y convirtió el país en una república (pág. 243)

frontier an undeveloped area (p. 586)
frontera área que no está siendo utilizada por el ser humano (pág. 586)

Fugitive Slave Act (1850) a law that made it a crime to help runaway slaves; allowed for the arrest of escaped slaves in areas where slavery was illegal, and required their return to slaveholders (p. 479)
Ley de Esclavos Fugitivos (1850) ley que hacía que ayudar a un esclavo a escapar de su amo fuera un delito; permitía la captura de esclavos fugitivos en zonas donde la esclavitud era ilegal para devolverlos a sus dueños (pág. 479)

fundamentalism a religious belief characterized by a literal interpretation of the Bible (p. 762)
fundamentalismo creencia religiosa caracterizada por una interpretación literal de la Biblia (pág. 762)

G

Gadsden Purchase (1853) U.S. purchase of land from Mexico that included the southern parts of presentday Arizona and New Mexico (p. 361)
Compra de Gadsden (1853) compra por parte del gobierno de Estados Unidos de territorio mexicano que incluía la región ocupada actualmente por el sur de Arizona y Nuevo México (pág. 361)

genocide the complete destruction of a racial or ethnic minority (p. 827)
genocidio destrucción total de una minoría racial o étnica (pág. 827)

Gettysburg Address (1863) a speech given by Abraham Lincoln in which he praised the bravery of Union soldiers and renewed his commitment to winning the Civil War (p. 540)
Discurso de Gettysburg (1863) discurso de Abraham Lincoln en el que alababa la valentía de las tropas de la Unión y renovaba su compromiso de triunfar en la Guerra Civil (pág. 540)

Ghost Dance a religious movement among Native Americans that spread across the Plains in the 1880s (p. 598)
Danza de los Espíritus movimiento religioso de los indígenas norteamericanos que se extendió por la región de las Planicies en la década de 1880 (pág. 598)

GI Bill of Rights (1944) a law that offered veterans money for school, houses, farms, and businesses (p. 848)
Declaración de Derechos de los Soldados (1944) ley que ofrecía a los veteranos de guerra dinero para su educación, vivienda, granjas y negocios (pág. 848)

Gibbons* v. *Ogden (1824) a Supreme Court ruling that reinforced the federal government's authority over the states (p. 397)
Gibbons* contra *Ogden (1824) decisión de la Corte Suprema que reforzó la autoridad del gobierno federal sobre los estados (pág. 397)

globalization the process in which the United States is becoming more interdependent with other nations (p. 960)
globalización proceso por el cual Estados Unidos empieza a tener más interdependencia con otras naciones (pág. 960)

global warming an environmental crisis in which the average temperature of the Earth is rising due to pollution (p. 962)
calentamiento global crisis del medio ambiente por la cual está aumentando la temperatura promedio de la Tierra debido a la contaminación (pág. 962)

Great Awakening a religious movement that became widespread in the American colonies in the 1730s and 1740s (p. 94)
Gran Despertar movimiento religioso que tuvo gran popularidad en las colonias norteamericanas en las décadas de 1730 y 1740 (pág. 94)

Great Compromise (1787) an agreement worked out at the Constitutional Convention establishing that a state's population would determine representation in the lower house of the legislature, while each state would have equal representation in the upper house of the legislature (p. 165)
Gran Compromiso (1787) acuerdo redactado durante la Convención Constitucional en el que se establece que la población de un estado debe determinar su representación en la cámara baja de la asamblea legislativa y que cada estado debe tener igual representación en la cámara alta de la asamblea. (pág. 165)

Great Depression a severe economic crisis that lasted for the entire decade of the 1930s (p. 780)
Gran Depresión grave crisis económica que duró toda la década de 1930 (pág. 780)

Great Migration a period of African American movement from the South to cities in the North (p. 763)
Gran Migración período en que los afroamericanos del Sur se fueron a ciudades del Norte (pág. 763)

Great Society President Lyndon Johnson's legislative plan that included civil rights laws (p. 880)
Gran Sociedad plan legislativo del presidente Lyndon Johnson que incluía leyes a favor de los derechos civiles (pág. 880)

H

habeas corpus the constitutional protection against unlawful imprisonment (p. 532)
hábeas corpus protección constitucional contra el encarcelamiento ilegal (pág. 532)

hajj a pilgrimage to Mecca made by devout Muslims (p. 18)
hajj peregrinación a La Meca realizada por los musulmanes devotos (pág. 18)

Harlem Renaissance a period of artistic achievement during the 1920s (p. 768)
Renacimiento de Harlem período de logros artísticos durante la década de 1920 (pág. 768)

Hartford Convention (1815) a meeting of Federalists at Hartford, Connecticut, to protest the War of 1812 (p. 287)
Convención de Hartford (1815) reunión de federalistas en Hartford, Connecticut, para protestar por la Guerra de 1812 (pág. 287)

hawks supporters of the Vietnam War (p. 904)
halcones partidarios de la guerra de Vietnam (pág. 904)

Haymarket Riot a riot that broke out at Haymarket Square in Chicago over the deaths of two strikers (p. 626)
Revuelta de Haymarket revuelta que se originó en la Plaza Haymarket de Chicago por la muerte de dos huelguistas (pág. 626)

hippies young people who rebelled against the mainstream culture of the 1960s (p. 909)
hippies jóvenes que se rebelaron contra la cultura convencional en la década de 1960 (pág. 909)

Ho Chi Minh Trail a series of jungle paths that allowed Communist forces to travel from North Vietnam to South Vietnam (p. 902)
Camino de Ho Chi Minh serie de caminos por la selva que permitía a las fuerzas comunistas ir desde Vietnam del Norte hacia Vietnam del Sur (pág. 902)

Holocaust a program of mass murder in which the Nazis tried to kill all Jews (p. 827)
Holocausto programa de asesinato en masa ideado por los nazis para exterminar a todos los judíos (pág. 827)

Homestead Act (1862) a law passed by Congress to encourage settlement in the West by giving government-owned land to small farmers (p. 600)
Ley de Heredad (1862) ley aprobada por el Congreso para fomentar la colonización del Oeste mediante la cesión de tierras del gobierno a pequeños agricultores (pág. 600)

Homestead strike (1892) a labor-union strike at Andrew Carnegie's Homestead Steel factory in Pennsylvania that erupted in violence between strikers and private detectives (p. 627)
huelga de Homestead (1892) huelga sindical en la fábrica de acero Homestead de Andrew Carnegie en Pensilvania, que produjo violencia entre huelguistas y detectives privados (pág. 627)

horizontal integration owning all the businesses in a certain field (p. 621)
integración horizontal posesión de todas las empresas en un campo específico (pág. 621)

Hudson River school a group of American artists in the mid-1800s whose paintings focused on the American landscape (p. 310)
Escuela del Río Hudson grupo de artistas estadounidenses de mediados del siglo XIX que pintaban diversos paisajes del territorio estadounidense (pág. 310)

Hull House a settlement house founded by Jane Addams and Ellen Gates Starr in 1889 (p. 648)
Casa Hull casa de asistencia a la comunidad fundada por Jane Addams y Ellen Gates Starr en 1889 (pág. 648)

human rights the basic rights of all people (p. 935)
derechos humanos derechos fundamentales de todas las personas (pág. 935)

hunter-gatherer a person who hunts animals and gathers wild plants to provide for his or her needs (p. 6)
cazador y recolector persona que caza animales y recolecta plantas para satisfacer sus necesidades (pág. 6)

hydrogen bomb a thermonuclear weapon that gets its power from splitting a hydrogen atom (p. 856)
bomba de hidrógeno arma termonuclear cuya potencia es generada por la división de un átomo de hidrógeno (pág. 856)

ENGLISH AND SPANISH GLOSSARY

I

immigrant a person who moves to another country after leaving his or her homeland (p. 78)
inmigrante persona que abandona su país para establecerse en un país diferente (pág. 78)

immune having a natural resistance to disease (p. 58)
inmune la condición de tener resistencia natural contra la enfermedad (pág. 58)

impeach to bring charges against a public official (p. 184)
someter a juicio político presentar cargos en contra de un funcionario público (pág. 184)

impeachment the process used by a legislative body to bring charges of wrongdoing against a public official (p. 562)
juicio político proceso por el cual un cuerpo legislativo presenta cargos en contra de un funcionario público (pág. 562)

imperialism the practice of extending a nation's power by gaining territories for a colonial empire (p. 692)
imperialismo práctica en la que una nación amplía su poder adquiriendo territorios para un imperio colonial (pág. 692)

impressment the practice of forcing people to serve in the army or navy; led to increased tensions between Great Britain and the United States in the early 1800s (p. 279)
leva práctica que obligaba a las personas a servir en el ejército o la marina; aumentó las fricciones entre Gran Bretaña y Estados Unidos a principios del siglo XIX (pág. 279)

indentured servant a colonist who received free passage to North America in exchange for working without pay for a certain number of years (p. 74)
sirviente por contrato colono que recibía un pasaje gratuito a América del Norte a cambio de trabajar sin salario por varios años (pág. 74)

Indian Removal Act (1830) a congressional act that authorized the removal of Native Americans who lived east of the Mississippi River (p. 332)
Ley de Expulsión de Indígenas (1830) ley del Congreso que autorizaba la expulsión de los indígenas norteamericanos que vivían al este del río Mississippi (pág. 332)

Indian Territory an area covering most of present-day Oklahoma to which most Native Americans in the Southeast were forced to move in the 1830s (p. 332)
Territorio Indígena área que abarcaba la mayor parte del actual estado de Oklahoma a la que la mayoría de las tribus indígenas del sureste fueron obligadas a trasladarse durante la década de 1830 (pág. 332)

indict to formally accuse (p. 218)
acusar presentar cargos formales en contra de alguien (pág. 218)

Industrial Revolution a period of rapid growth in the use of machines in manufacturing and production that began in the mid-1700s (p. 385)
Revolución Industrial período de rápido desarrollo debido al uso de maquinaria en la fabricación y producción; comenzó a mediados del siglo XVIII (pág. 385)

Industrial Workers of the World (IWW) a union founded in 1905 by socialists and union leaders that included workers not welcomed in the AFL (p. 674)
Trabajadores Industriales del Mundo (IWW, por sus siglas en inglés) sindicato fundado en 1905 por socialistas y líderes sindicales que incluía a los trabajadores que no admitía la Federación Americana del Trabajo (pág. 674)

inflation increased prices for goods and services combined with the reduced value of money (p. 161)
inflación subida en los precios de los bienes al mismo tiempo que se reduce al valor del dinero (pág. 161)

Information Revolution an increase in the ability to share information between people and locations brought about by the Internet (p. 961)
Revolución de la Información aumento de la capacidad de compartir información entre personas y lugares producido por Internet (pág. 961)

initiative a method of allowing voters to propose a new law if enough signatures are collected on a petition (p. 666)
iniciativa método que permite a los votantes proponer una nueva ley si consiguen suficientes firmas para una petición (pág. 666)

interchangeable parts a process developed by Eli Whitney in the 1790s that called for making each part of a machine exactly the same (p. 387)
piezas intercambiables proceso desarrollado por Eli Whitney en la década de 1790 para que todas las piezas de una máquina fueran exactamente iguales (pág. 387)

interest group a group of people who share common interests for political action (p. 224)
grupo de interés grupo de personas que comparten intereses comunes en iniciativas políticas (pág. 224)

Internet a global system of computers that allows people across the world to communicate (p. 961)
Internet sistema global de computadoras que permite la comunicación entre personas de todo el mundo (pág. 961)

internment the imprisonment of Japanese Americans in special camps during World War II (p. 813)
internamiento encarcelamiento de japoneses-americanos en campos especiales durante la Segunda Guerra Mundial (pág. 813)

interstate commerce trade between two or more states (p. 160)
comercio interestatal intercambio comercial entre dos o más estados (pág. 160)

Intolerable Acts (1774) laws passed by Parliament to punish the colonists for the Boston Tea Party and to tighten government control of the colonies (p. 102)
Leyes Intolerables (1774) serie de leyes aprobadas por el Parlamento para castigar a los colonos que participaron en el Motín del Té de Boston y para aumentar su control sobre las colonias (pág. 102)

Iran-Contra affair a scandal during the Reagan administration in which government officials were accused of selling weapons to Iran and passing the profits to a revolutionary group known as the Contras (p. 939)
asunto Irán-Contras escándalo durante el gobierno de Reagan en el cual funcionarios del gobierno fueron acusados de vender armas a Irán y de entregar las ganancias a un grupo revolucionario conocido como los contras (pág. 939)

Iran hostage crisis a crisis in which Americans were taken hostage by militants in Iran and held for over a year (p. 936)
crisis de los rehenes de Irán crisis en la cual varios estadounidenses fueron tomados como rehenes por militantes iraníes durante más de un año (pág. 936)

ironclad a warship that is heavily armored with iron (p. 520)
acorazado buque de guerra fuertemente protegido con hierro (pág. 520)

Iroquois League a political confederation of five northeastern Native American nations of the Seneca, Oneida, Mohawk, Cayuga, and Onondaga that made decisions concerning war and peace (p. 14)
Liga de Iroqueses confederación política formada por cinco naciones indígenas del noreste de Estados Unidos (los senecas, los oneidas, los mohawks, los cayugas y los onondagas) para tomar decisiones relacionadas con asuntos de guerra y paz (pág. 14)

island-hopping the strategy used by U.S. forces in the Pacific during World War II that involved taking only strategically important islands (p. 822)
saltar de isla en isla estrategia de las fuerzas de Estados Unidos en el Pacífico durante la Segunda Guerra Mundial que consistía en tomar sólo las islas importantes desde el punto de vista estratégico (pág. 822)

isolationism a national policy of avoiding involvement in other countries' affairs (p. 693)
aislacionismo política nacional de evitar involucrarse en los asuntos de otras naciones (pág. 693)

J

Jacksonian Democracy an expansion of voting rights during the popular Andrew Jackson administration (p. 323)
democracia jacksoniana ampliación del derecho al voto durante el popular gobierno del presidente Andrew Jackson (pág. 323)

Jamestown the first colony in the United States; set up in 1607 along the James River in Virginia (p. 72)
Jamestown primera colonia en territorio estadounidense; fundada en 1607 a orillas del río James en Virginia (pág. 72)

Jay's Treaty (1794) an agreement negotiated by John Jay to work out problems between Britain and the United States over northwestern lands, British seizure of U.S. ships, and U.S. debts owed to the British (p. 245)
Tratado de Jay (1794) acuerdo negociado por John Jay para resolver los problemas entre Gran Bretaña y Estados Unidos por los territorios del noroeste, la confiscación británica de barcos estadounidenses, y las deudas que los estadounidenses les debían a los británicos (pág. 245)

Jazz Age a name for the decade of the 1920s based on the popularity of jazz music (p. 767)
Era del Jazz nombre que se le dio a la década de 1920 por la popularidad de la música de jazz (pág. 767)

Jim Crow law a law that enforced segregation in the southern states (p. 568)
ley de Jim Crow ley que imponía la segregación en los estados del Sur (pág. 568)

John Brown's raid (1859) an incident in which abolitionist John Brown and 21 other men captured a federal arsenal in Harpers Ferry, Virginia, in hope of starting a slave rebellion (p. 493)
ataque de John Brown (1859) incidente en el que el abolicionista John Brown y otros 21 hombres capturaron un arsenal federal en Harpers Ferry, Virginia, con la esperanza de iniciar una rebelión de esclavos (pág. 493)

joint-stock company a business formed by a group of people who jointly make an investment and share in the profits and losses (p. 27)
sociedad por acciones negocio formado por un grupo de personas que hacen una inversión juntos y comparten las ganancias y las pérdidas (pág. 27)

judicial branch the division of the federal government that is made up of the national courts; interprets laws, punishes criminals, and settles disputes between states (p. 167)
poder judicial división del gobierno federal formada por las cortes nacionales; interpreta las leyes, castiga a los delincuentes y resuelve las disputas entre estados (pág. 167)

judicial review the Supreme Court's power to declare acts of Congress unconstitutional (p. 270)
recurso de inconstitucionalidad (revision judicial) poder de la Corte Suprema para declarar inconstitucionales las leyes del Congreso (pág. 270)

Judiciary Act of 1789 legislation passed by Congress that created the federal court system (p. 236)
Ley de Judicatura de 1789 ley aprobada por el Congreso para crear el sistema federal de cortes (pág. 236)

K

kamikaze Japanese pilots who flew suicide missions during World War II (p. 822)
kamikaze piloto japonés que volaba en misiones suicidas durante la Segunda Guerra Mundial (pág. 822)

Kansas-Nebraska Act (1854) a law that allowed voters in Kansas and Nebraska to choose whether to allow slavery (p. 485)
Ley de Kansas y Nebraska (1854) ley que permitía a los votantes de Kansas y Nebraska decidir si permitían la esclavitud (pág. 485)

Kellogg-Briand Pact an agreement between nations proposing peaceful solutions to conflicts, signed after World War I (p. 754)
Pacto Kellogg-Briand acuerdo firmado entre naciones luego de la Primera Guerra Mundial que proponía soluciones pacíficas a los conflictos (pág. 754)

Kentucky and Virginia Resolutions (1798–1799) Republican documents that argued that the Alien and Sedition Acts were unconstitutional (p. 253)
Resoluciones de Kentucky y Virginia (1798–1799) documentos republicanos que argumentaban que las Leyes de No Intervención Extranjera y Sedición eran inconstitucionales (pág. 253)

Kitchen Cabinet President Andrew Jackson's group of informal advisers; so called because they often met in the White House kitchen (p. 324)
gabinete de la cocina grupo informal de consejeros del presidente Andrew Jackson; llamado así porque solían reunirse en la cocina de la Casa Blanca (pág. 324)

kivas underground ceremonial chambers at the center of Anasazi communities (p. 11)
kivas cámaras ceremoniales subterráneas en el centro de las comunidades anasazi (pág. 11)

knights warriors who fought on horseback in return for land from nobles (p. 24)
caballeros guerreros que luchaban a caballo a cambio de tierras de los nobles (pág. 24)

Knights of Labor secret society that became the first truly national labor union in the United States (p. 625)
Caballeros del Trabajo sociedad secreta que se convirtió en el primer sindicato verdaderamente nacional en Estados Unidos (pág. 625)

Know-Nothing Party a political organization founded in 1849 by nativists who supported measures making it difficult for foreigners to become citizens and to hold office (p. 440)
Partido de los Ignorantes organización política fundada en 1849 por un grupo de nativistas; apoyaba medidas que dificultaban que los extranjeros obtuvieran la ciudadanía y que tuvieran cargos públicos (pág. 440)

Ku Klux Klan a secret society created by white southerners in 1866 that used terror and violence to keep African Americans from obtaining their civil rights (p. 566)
Ku Klux Klan sociedad secreta creada en 1866 por blancos del Sur que usaba el terror y la violencia para impedir que los afroamericanos obtuvieran derechos civiles (pág. 566)

L

Land Ordinance of 1785 legislation passed by Congress authorizing surveys and the division of public lands in the western region of the country (p. 155)
Ordenanza de Territorios de 1785 legislación aprobada por el Congreso en la que se autorizaban las mediciones de terreno y la división de territorios públicos en el oeste del país (pág. 155)

League of Nations a coalition of governments designed to find peaceful solutions to disagreements, proposed by Woodrow Wilson (p. 737)
Liga de las Naciones coalición de gobiernos propuesta por Woodrow Wilson y diseñada para buscar soluciones pacíficas a los desacuerdos (pág. 737)

legislative branch the division of the government that proposes bills and passes them into laws (p. 167)
poder legislativo división del gobierno que propone proyectos de ley y los aprueba para convertirlos en leyes (pág. 167)

Lend-Lease Act (1941) a law giving Franklin Roosevelt the power to sell, transfer, exchange, or lease military equipment to any country to help it defend itself against the Axis powers (p. 808)

Ley de Préstamo y Arriendo (1941) ley que dio a Franklin Roosevelt el poder de vender, transferir, intercambiar o arrendar equipo militar a cualquier país para la defensa contra las potencias del Eje (pág. 808)

Lewis and Clark expedition an expedition led by Meriwether Lewis and William Clark that began in 1804 to explore the Louisiana Purchase (p. 275)
expedición de Lewis y Clark expedición encabezada por Meriwether Lewis y William Clark que empezó en 1804 para explorar la Compra de Luisiana (pág. 275)

Liberty bonds loans to the government that aided its ability to prepare for World War I (p. 727)
bonos de la Libertad préstamos hechos al gobierno que le permitieron prepararse para la Primera Guerra Mundial (pág. 727)

Lincoln-Douglas debates a series of debates between Republican Abraham Lincoln and Democrat Stephen Douglas during the 1858 U.S. Senate campaign in Illinois (p. 491)
debates Lincoln-Douglas serie de debates entre el republicano Abraham Lincoln y el demócrata Stephen Douglas durante la campaña de 1858 para el Senado estadounidense en Illinois (pág. 491)

Line of Demarcation boundary between Spanish and Portuguese territories in the New World (p. 44)
Línea de Demarcación límite entre los territorios españoles y portugueses en el Nuevo Mundo (pág. 44)

Little Rock Nine a group of nine African American students who began the integration of the Little Rock, Arkansas, public school system (p. 871)
los nueve de Little Rock grupo de nueve estudiantes afroamericanos que empezaron la integración del sistema de escuelas públicas de Little Rock, Arkansas (pág. 871)

Long Walk (1864) a 300-mile march made by Navajo captives to a reservation in Bosque Redondo, New Mexico, that led to the deaths of hundreds of Navajo (p. 597)
Larga Marcha (1864) caminata de 300 millas que hizo un grupo de prisioneros navajos hasta una reserva indígena en Bosque Redondo, Nuevo México, en la que murieron cientos de ellos (pág. 597)

loose construction a way of interpreting the Constitution that allows the federal government to take actions that the Constitution does not specifically forbid it from taking (p. 242)
interpretación flexible interpretación de la Constitución que permite al gobierno federal tomar acciones que la Constitución no prohíbe de manera específica (pág. 242)

Lost Generation the generation of young people who fought in World War I and eventually became disillusioned with the promise of American society (p. 768)
generación perdida generación de jóvenes que lucharon en la Primera Guerra Mundial y terminaron desilusionados con las promesas de la sociedad estadounidense (pág. 768)

Louisiana Purchase (1803) the purchase of French land between the Mississippi River and the Rocky Mountains that doubled the size of the United States (p. 274)
Compra de Luisiana (1803) adquisición del territorio francés localizado entre el río Mississippi y las montañas Rocallosas que duplicó el tamaño de Estados Unidos (pág. 274)

Lowell system the use of waterpowered textile mills that employed young, unmarried women in the 1800s (p. 392)
sistema de Lowell uso de molinos de agua en la industria textil, dando empleo a muchas mujeres jóvenes solteras en el siglo XIX (pág. 392)

Loyalists colonists who sided with Britain in the American Revolution (p. 119)
leales colonos que apoyaron la causa británica durante la Guerra de Independencia estadounidense (pág. 119)

Lusitania a passenger ship bombed by Germany (p. 726)
Lusitania barco de pasajeros bombardeado por Alemania (pág. 726)

M

Magna Carta (1215) a charter of liberties agreed to by King John of England, it made the king obey the same laws as citizens (p. 152)
Carta Magna (1215) carta de libertades firmada por el rey Juan de Inglaterra que decía que el rey debía obedecer las mismas leyes que los ciudadanos (pág. 152)

majority rule the idea that policies are decided by the greatest number of people (p. 216)
gobierno de la mayoría idea de que las políticas se adoptan según lo que decida el mayor número de personas (pág. 216)

Manhattan Project the U.S. effort to build an atomic bomb (p. 828)
Proyecto Manhattan plan de Estados Unidos de fabricar una bomba atómica (pág. 828)

manifest destiny a belief shared by many Americans in the mid-1800s that the United States should expand across the continent to the Pacific Ocean (p. 354)
destino manifiesto creencia de muchos ciudadanos estadounidenses a mediados del siglo XIX de que Estados Unidos debía expandirse por todo el continente hasta el océano Pacífico (pág. 354)

Marbury* v. *Madison (1803) U.S. Supreme Court case that established the principle of judicial review (p. 270)
Marbury* contra *Madison (1803) caso de la Corte Suprema de Estados Unidos que estableció recurso de inconstitucionalidad (pág. 270)

March on Washington a huge demonstration organized by Martin Luther King Jr. to protest racial discrimination (p. 878)
Marcha en Washington manifestación enorme organizada por Martin Luther King, Jr. en protesta por la discriminación racial (p. 878)

Marshall Plan the idea that the U.S. could help rebuild wartorn Europe with loans and other economic aid (p. 847)
Plan Marshall idea de que Estados Unidos podía contribuir con préstamos y otros tipos de ayuda económica a la reconstrucción de la Europa devastada por la guerra (pág. 847)

Massacre at Wounded Knee (1890) the U.S. Army's killing of approximately 150 Sioux at Wounded Knee Creek in South Dakota; ended U.S-Indian wars on the Plains (p. 597)
masacre de Wounded Knee (1890) matanza de aproximadamente 150 indios siux en Wounded Knee Creek, Dakota del Sur; dio por terminadas las guerras entre estadounidenses e indígenas en las Planicies (pág. 597)

mass culture leisure and cultural activities shared by many people (p. 644)
cultura de masas actividades culturales y del tiempo libre que les gustan a muchas personas (pág. 644)

mass production the efficient production of large numbers of identical goods (p. 387)
producción en masa producción eficiente de grandes cantidades de productos idénticos (pág. 387)

mass transit public transportation (p. 644)
transporte colectivo transporte público (pág. 644)

matrilineal related to ancestry traced through the maternal, or mother's, line (p. 14)
materno basado en linaje seguido por línea materna, o de la madre (pág. 14)

Mayflower Compact (1620) a document written by the Pilgrims establishing themselves as a political society and setting guidelines for self-government (p. 79)
Pacto del Mayflower (1620) documento redactado por los peregrinos en el que se establecían como sociedad política y establecían principios para gobernarse a sí mismos (pág. 79)

McCulloch* v. *Maryland (1819) U.S. Supreme Court case that declared the Second Bank of the United States was constitutional and that Maryland could not interfere with it (p. 330)
McCulloch* contra *Maryland (1819) caso de la Corte Suprema de Estados Unidos que declaraba que el Segundo Banco de la Nación era constitucional y que Maryland no podía intervenir en sus operaciones (pág. 330)

mercenaries hired foreign soldiers (p. 128)
mercenarios soldados extranjeros a sueldo (pág. 128)

Mexican Revolution a revolution led by Francisco Madero in 1910 that eventually forced the Mexican dictator Díaz to resign (p. 708)
Revolución Mexicana revolución iniciada en 1910 por Francisco Madero, que finalmente obligó al dictador mexicano Díaz a renunciar (pág. 708)

middle class the social and economic level between the wealthy and the poor (p. 440)
clase media nivel social y económico ubicado entre la clase rica y la clase pobre (pág. 440)

Middle Passage a voyage that brought enslaved Africans across the Atlantic Ocean to North America and the West Indies (p. 59)
Viaje Intermedio viaje a través del océano Atlántico para transportar esclavos africanos a América del Norte y a las Antillas (pág. 59)

migration the movement of people from one region to another (p. 6)
migración movimiento de personas de una región a otra (pág. 6)

militarism an increase in the importance of the military of a country (p. 721)
militarismo aumento de la importancia del ejército de un país (pág. 721)

minutemen American colonial militia members ready to fight at a minute's notice (p. 114)
minutemen milicanos norteamericanos en la época colonial que estaban preparados para combatir en cualquier momento si la situación lo requería (pág. 114)

Missouri Compromise (1820) an agreement proposed by Henry Clay that allowed Missouri to enter the Union as a slave state and Maine to enter as a free state and outlawed slavery in any territories or states north of 36°30´ latitude (p. 305)
Compromiso de Missouri (1820) acuerdo propuesto por Henry Clay en el que se aceptaba a Missouri en la Unión como estado esclavista y a Maine como estado libre, además de prohibir la esclavitud en los territorios o estados al norte del paralelo 36°30´ (pág. 305)

mobilize to prepare for war (p. 721)
mobilizarse prepararse para la guerra (pág. 721)

Model T Henry Ford's automobile designed with the average American in mind (p. 755)
modelo T automóvil de Henry Ford diseñado para el estadounidense promedio (pág. 755)

monopoly a complete control over the entire supply of goods or a service in a particular market (p. 622)
monopolio control absoluto de toda la oferta de bienes o de un servicio en un mercado en particular (pág. 622)

Monroe Doctrine (1823) President James Monroe's statement forbidding further colonization in the Americas and declaring that any attempt by a foreign country to colonize would be considered an act of hostility (p. 300)
Doctrina Monroe (1823) declaración hecha por el presidente James Monroe en la que se prohibía la colonización adicional de las Américas y se declaraba que cualquier intento de colonización por parte de otro país se consideraría un acto hostil (pág. 300)

Montgomery bus boycott a boycott of the Montgomery, Alabama, public bus system to protest its policy of segregation (p. 873)
boicot a los autobuses de Montgomery boicot al sistema público de autobuses de Montgomery, Alabama, en protesta por su política de segregación (pág. 873)

Mormon a member of the Church of Jesus Christ of Latter-day Saints (p. 349)
mormón miembro de la Iglesia de Jesucristo de los Santos de los Últimos Días (pág. 349)

Morrill Act (1862) a federal law passed by Congress that gave land to western states to encourage them to build colleges (p. 600)
Ley de Morrill (1862) ley federal aprobada por el Congreso que otorgaba tierras a los estados del Oeste para fomentar la construcción de universidades (pág. 600)

Morse code a system developed by Alfred Lewis Vail for the telegraph that used a certain combination of dots and dashes to represent each letter of the alphabet (p. 403)
clave Morse sistema desarrollado por Alfred Lewis Vail para el telégrafo en el que una combinación de puntos y rayas representa cada letra del alfabeto (pág. 403)

mosques buildings used for Muslim prayer (p. 19)
mezquitas casas de oración musulmanas (pág. 19)

mountain men men hired by eastern companies to trap animals for fur in the Rocky Mountains and other western regions of the United States (p. 346)
montañeses hombres contratados por compañías del este para atrapar animales y obtener sus pieles en las montañas Rocallosas y en otras regiones del oeste de Estados Unidos (pág. 346)

moving assembly line an innovation of Henry Ford's that dramatically reduced the cost of production (p. 755)
cadena de montaje móvil innovación de Henry Ford que redujo significativamente el costo de producción (pág. 755)

muckrakers a term coined for journalists who "raked up" and exposed corruption and problems of society (p. 664)
muckrakers término acuñado para nombrar a los periodistas que se dedicaban a investigar y exponer la corrupción y los problemas de la sociedad (pág. 664)

N

National American Woman Suffrage Association (NAWSA) an organization founded by Elizabeth Cady Stanton and Susan B. Anthony in 1890 to obtain women's right to vote (p. 676)
Asociación Nacional Americana para el Sufragio Femenino (NAWSA, por sus siglas en inglés) organización fundada en 1890 por Elizabeth Cady Stanton y Susan B. Anthony para obtener el derecho al voto de las mujeres (pág. 676)

National Association for the Advancement of Colored People (NAACP) an organization founded in 1909 by W. E. B. Du Bois and other reformers to bring attention to racial inequality (p. 678)
Asociación Nacional para el Progreso de la Gente de Color (NAACP, por sus siglas en inglés) organización fundada en 1909 por W. E. B. Du Bois y otros reformadores para llamar la atención sobre la desigualdad racial (pág. 678)

national debt the total amount of money owed by a country to its lenders (p. 238)
deuda nacional cantidad total de dinero que un país debe a quienes se lo prestaron (pág. 238)

National Grange a social and educational organization for farmers (p. 603)
National Grange organización social y educativa para los agricultores (pág. 603)

nationalism a sense of pride and devotion to a nation (p. 302)
nacionalismo sentimiento de orgullo y lealtad a una nación (pág. 302)

National Organization for Women (NOW) a group that organized to promote the interests of women (p. 883
Organización Nacional de la Mujer (NOW, por sus siglas en inglés) grupo organizado para promover l intereses de la mujer (pág. 883)

National War Labor Board a government agency organized to help settle disputes between work and employers in war industries (p. 729)
Junta Nacional del Trabajo en Tiempos de Gu agencia del gobierno destinada a resolver c entre trabajadores y empleadores en las ir relacionadas con la guerra (pág. 729)

nativists U.S. citizens who opposed immigration because they were suspicious of immigrants and feared losing jobs to them (p. 440)
nativistas ciudadanos estadounidenses que se oponían a la inmigración porque sospechaban de los inmigrantes y temían que se apropiaran de sus empleos (pág. 440)

Nat Turner's Rebellion (1831) a rebellion in which Nat Turner led a group of slaves in Virginia in an unsuccessful attempt to overthrow and kill planter families (p. 428)
Rebelión de Nat Turner (1831) rebelión de un grupo de esclavos encabezados por Nat Turner en Virginia en un intento frustrado de derrocar y asesinar familias que eran dueñas de plantaciones (pág. 428)

naturalized citizen a person born in another country who has been granted citizenship in the United States (p. 222)
ciudadano naturalizado persona nacida en otro país que ha obtenido la ciudadanía estadounidense (pág. 222)

Nazis the National Socialist Party of Germany, headed by Adolf Hitler (p. 805)
nazis Partido Nacional Socialista de Alemania, liderado por Adolf Hitler (pág. 805)

Neutrality Proclamation (1793) a statement made by President George Washington that the United States would not side with any of the nations at war in Europe following the French Revolution (p. 244)
Proclamación de Neutralidad (1793) declaración en la que el presidente George Washington anunció que Estados Unidos no sería aliado de ninguna de las naciones europeas en guerra después de la Revolución Francesa (pág. 244)

New Deal Franklin Roosevelt's legislative plan to end the Great Depression that included dramatic reforms of government agencies and powers (p. 784)
***New Deal* (Nuveo Trato)** plan legislativo de Franklin Roosevelt para poner fin a la Gran Depresión; incluía profundas reformas en las agencias y poderes del gobierno (pág. 784)

new immigrant a term often used for an immigrant who arrived in the United States beginning in the 1880s (p. 636)
nuevo inmigrante término empleado a menudo para referirse a los inmigrantes que llegaron a Estados Unidos a partir de la década de 1880 (pág. 636)

New Jersey Plan a proposal to create a unicameral legislature with equal representation of states rather than representation by population; rejected at the Constitutional Convention (p. 165)
lan de Nueva Jersey propuesta para la creación un gobierno de una cámara con la misma esentación para cada estado sin importar año de su población; fue rechazada en la ción Constitucional (pág. 165)

Nineteenth Amendment (1920) a constitutional amendment that gave women the vote (p. 677)
Decimonovena Enmienda (1920) enmienda constitucional que dio a la mujer el derecho al voto (pág. 677)

nominating conventions a meeting at which a political party selects its presidential and vice presidential candidate; first held in the 1820s (p. 323)
convenciones de nominación reunión en la que un partido político elige a sus candidatos a la presidencia y la vicepresidencia; se realizaron por primera vez en la década de 1820 (pág. 323)

Non-Intercourse Act (1809) a law that replaced the Embargo Act and restored trade with all nations except Britain, France, and their colonies (p. 280)
Ley de No Interacción (1809) ley que reemplazaba a la Ley de Embargo, restableciendo el comercio con todas las naciones, excepto Gran Bretaña, Francia y sus colonias (pág. 280)

North American Free Trade Agreement (NAFTA) a treaty that eliminated trade barriers between Canada, the United States, and Mexico (p. 952)
Tratado de Libre Comercio de América del Norte (TLCAN o NAFTA) tratado que eliminó las barreras comerciales entre Canadá, Estados Unidos y México (pág. 952)

North Atlantic Treaty Organization (NATO) an alliance of Western powers (p. 848)
Organización del Tratado del Atlántico Norte (OTAN) alianza de potencias occidentales (pág. 848)

Northwest Ordinance of 1787 legislation passed by Congress to establish a political structure for the Northwest Territory and create a system for the admission of new states (p. 155)
Ordenanza del Noroeste de 1787 legislación aprobada por el Congreso para establecer una estructura política en el Territorio del Noroeste y crear un proceso de admisión de nuevos estados (pág. 155)

Northwest Passage a nonexistent path through North America that early explorers searched for that would allow ships to sail from the Atlantic to the Pacific Ocean (p. 54)
Paso del Noroeste ruta inexistente buscada por muchos exploradores a lo largo de América del Norte para cruzar en barco del océano Atlántico al océano Pacífico (pág. 54)

Northwest Territory lands including present-day Illinois, Indiana, Michigan, Ohio, and Wisconsin; organized by the Northwest Ordinance of 1787 (p. 155)
Territorio del Noroeste región que incluía los actuales estados de Illinois, Indiana, Michigan, Ohio y Wisconsin; creado por la Ordenanza del Noroeste de 1787 (pág. 155)

nullification crisis a dispute led by John C. Calhoun that said that states could ignore federal laws if they believed those laws violated the Constitution (p. 328)
crisis de anulación controversia iniciada por John C. Calhoun que decía que los estados no tenían que hacer caso a las leyes federales si consideraban que desobedecían la Constitución (pág. 328)

Nuremberg trials the war crimes trials of Nazi leaders (p. 845)
juicios de Nuremberg juicios de los crímenes de guerra de los líderes Nazis (pág. 845)

O

old immigrant a term often used for an immigrant who arrived in the United States before the 1880s (p. 636)
antiguo inmigrante término empleado con frecuencia para referirse a los inmigrantes que llegaron a Estados Unidos antes de la década de 1880 (pág. 636)

Open Door Policy a policy established by the United States in 1899 to promote equal access for all nations to trade in China (p. 695)
política de puertas abiertas política establecida por Estados Unidos en 1899 para promover el acceso igualitario de todas las naciones al comercio con China (pág. 695)

Operation Desert Storm the military effort to free Kuwait from Saddam Hussein's invasion (p. 951)
Operación Tormenta del Desierto acción militar para liberar a Kuwait de la invasión de Saddam Hussein (pág. 951)

Oregon Trail a 2,000-mile trail stretching through the Great Plains from western Missouri to the Oregon Territory (p. 348)
Camino de Oregón ruta de 2,000 millas que cruzaba las Grandes Planicies desde el oeste de Missouri hasta el Territorio de Oregón (pág. 348)

Organization of Petroleum Exporting Countries (OPEC) an alliance of oil rich countries that coordinates oil policies (p. 927)
Organización de Países Exportadores de Petróleo (OPEP) alianza de países ricos en petróleo que coordina las políticas petroleras (pág. 927)

ozone layer a level of the Earth's atmosphere that is being depleted by pollution (p. 962)
capa de ozono nivel de la atmósfera de la Tierra que se está desgastando debido a la contaminación (pág. 962)

P

Paleo-Indians the first Americans who crossed from Asia into North America sometime between 38,000 and 10,000 BC (p. 6)
paleoindígenas primeros habitantes de América que cruzaron de Asia a América del Norte entre 38,000 y 10,000 a. C. (pág. 6)

Panama Canal an artificial waterway across the Isthmus of Panama; completed by the United States in 1914 (p. 705)
canal de Panamá canal artificial que atraviesa el istmo de Panamá; Estados Unidos completó su construcción en 1914 (pág. 705)

Panic of 1837 a financial crisis in the United States that led to an economic depression (p. 331)
Pánico de 1837 crisis financiera en Estados Unidos que provocó una depresión económica (pág. 331)

pardon freedom from punishment (pp. 185, 931)
indulto liberación de un castigo (págs. 185, 931)

patent an exclusive right to make or sell an invention (p. 616)
patente derecho exclusivo para fabricar o vender un invento (pág. 616)

Patriots American colonists who fought for independence from Great Britain during the Revolutionary War (p. 113)
patriotas colonos norteamericanos que lucharon para independizarse de Gran Bretaña durante la Guerra de Independencia estadounidense (pág. 113)

Peace Corps a nonmilitary aid program introduced by John Kennedy (p. 894)
Cuerpos de Paz programa de ayuda no militar introducido por John Kennedy (pág. 894)

Pearl Harbor a harbor in Hawaii that serves as the base of the U.S. Pacific fleet and was bombed in 1941 by Japan (p. 808)
Pearl Harbor puerto de Hawai que es la base de la flota del Pacífico de Estados Unidos; fue bombardeado por Japón en 1941 (pág. 808)

Pentagon the headquarters of the U.S. military, located outside of Washington, D.C. (p. 956)
Pentágono sede central del ejército de Estados Unidos, ubicado en las afueras de Washington, D.C. (pág. 956)

petition to make a formal request of the government (p. 217)
peticionar hacer una solicitud formal al gobierno (pág. 217)

Pickett's Charge (1863) a failed Confederate attack during the Civil War led by General George Pickett at the Battle of Gettysburg (p. 539)
ataque de Pickett (1863) ataque fallido del ejército confederado, al mando del general George Pickett, en la batalla de Gettysburg durante la Guerra Civil (pág. 539)

Pilgrim a member of a Puritan Separatist sect that left England in the early 1600s to settle in the Americas (p. 78)
peregrino miembro de una secta separatista puritana que se fue de Inglaterra a principios del siglo XVII para establecerse en América (pág. 78)

Pinckney's Treaty (1795) an agreement between the United States and Spain that changed Florida's border and made it easier for American ships to use the port of New Orleans (p. 245)
Tratado de Pinckney (1795) acuerdo entre Estados Unidos y España que modificó los límites de Florida y facilitó a los barcos estadounidenses el uso del puerto de Nueva Orleáns (pág. 245)

placer miner a person who mines for gold by using pans or other devices to wash gold nuggets out of loose rock and gravel (p. 366)
buscador de oro con batea persona que busca oro con bateas u otros aparatos similares para lavar las pepitas de oro y separarlas de las piedras y la gravilla (pág. 366)

plantation a large farm that usually specialized in growing one kind of crop for profit (p. 50)
plantación gran finca que por lo general se especializaba en un cultivo específico para obtener ganancias (pág. 50)

planter a large-scale farmer who held more than 20 slaves (p. 416)
hacendado agricultor a gran escala que tenía más de 20 esclavos (pág. 416)

Platt Amendment a part of the Cuban constitution drafted under the supervision of the United States that limited Cuba's right to make treaties, gave the U.S. the right to intervene in Cuban affairs, and required Cuba to sell or lease land to the U.S (p. 701)
Enmienda Platt parte de la constitución cubana redactada bajo la supervisión de Estados Unidos que limitaba el derecho de Cuba a firmar tratados, le daba a Estados Unidos el derecho de intervenir en los asuntos cubanos y le exigía a Cuba vender o arrendar tierras a Estados Unidos (pág. 701)

Plessy* v. *Ferguson (1896) U.S. Supreme Court case that established the "separate-but-equal" doctrine for public facilities (p. 569)
Plessy contra Ferguson (1896) caso en el que la Corte Suprema de Estados Unidos estableció la doctrina de "separados pero iguales" en los lugares públicos (pág. 569)

political action committee (PAC) an organization that collects money to distribute to candidates who support the same issues as the contributors (p. 224)
comité de acción política (PAC, por sus siglas en inglés) organización que recolecta dinero para distribuirlo a los candidatos que apoyen los mismos asuntos que los contribuyentes (pág. 224)

political machine a powerful organization that influenced city and county politics in the late 1800s (p. 662)
maquinaria política organización poderosa que influía en la política municipal y del condado a finales del siglo XIX (pág. 662)

political party a group of people who organize to help elect government officials and influence government policies (p. 250)
partido político grupo de personas que se organiza para facilitar la elección de los funcionarios del gobierno e influye en las políticas del gobierno (pág. 250)

poll tax a special tax that a person had to pay in order to vote (p. 568)
impuesto electoral impuesto especial que tenía que pagar una persona para poder votar (pág. 568)

Pony Express a system of messengers that carried mail between relay stations on a route 2,000-miles long in 1860 and 1861 (p. 590)
Pony Express sistema de mensajeros que llevaban el correo entre estaciones de relevo a lo largo de una ruta de 2,000 millas en 1860 y 1861 (pág. 590)

popular sovereignty the idea that political authority belongs to the people (p. 167, 476)
soberanía popular idea de que la autoridad política pertenece al pueblo (pág. 167, 476)

Populist Party a political party formed in 1892 that supported free coinage of silver, work reforms, immigration restrictions, and government ownership of railroads and telegraph and telephone systems (p. 604)
Partido Populista partido político formado en 1892 que apoyaba la libre producción de monedas de plata, reformas laborales y restricciones de la inmigración, además de asignar al gobierno la propiedad de los sistemas ferroviario, telegráfico y telefónico (pág. 604)

Pottawatomie Massacre (1856) an incident in which abolitionist John Brown and seven other men murdered pro-slavery Kansans (p. 487)
masacre de Pottawatomie (1856) incidente en el que el abolicionista John Brown y siete hombres más asesinaron a habitantes esclavistas de Kansas (pág. 487)

precedent an action or decision that later serves as an example (p. 235)
precedente acción o decisión que más tarde sirve de ejemplo (pág. 235)

privateer a private ship authorized by a nation to attack its enemies (p. 244)
corsario barco privado autorizado por una nación para atacar a sus enemigos (pág. 244)

Progressives a group of reformers who worked to improve social and political problems in the late 1800s (p. 664)
progresistas grupo de reformistas que trabajaron para resolver problemas sociales y políticos a finales del siglo XIX (pág. 664)

Progressive Party a short-lived political party that attempted to institute social reforms (p. 682)
Partido Progresista partido político de poca duración que intentó establecer reformas sociales (pág. 682)

prospect to search for gold (p. 366)
prospectar buscar oro (pág. 366)

Protestant Reformation a religious movement begun by Martin Luther and others in 1517 to reform the Catholic Church (p. 53)
Reforma Protestante movimiento religioso iniciado por Martín Lutero y otros en 1517 para reformar la Iglesia católica (pág. 53)

Protestants reformers who protested certain practices of the Catholic Church (p. 53)
protestantes reformistas que protestaban por ciertas prácticas de la Iglesia católica (pág. 53)

pueblos above ground houses made of a heavy clay called adobe that were built by Native Americans of the southwestern United States (p. 11)
pueblos casas de arcilla gruesa, llamada adobe, construidas más arriba de la superficie por indígenas del suroeste de Estados Unidos (pág. 11)

Pullman strike (1894) a railroad strike that ended when President Grover Cleveland sent in federal troops (p. 627)
huelga de Pullman (1894) huelga del ferrocarril que terminó cuando el presidente Grover Cleveland envió a tropas federales (pág. 627)

Pure Food and Drug Act (1906) a law that set regulatory standards for industries involved in preparing food (p. 681)
Ley de Alimentos y Medicamentos Puros (1906) ley que estableció normas regulatorias para las industrias de preparación de productos alimenticios (pág. 681)

Puritans Protestants who wanted to reform the Church of England (p. 78)
puritanos protestantes que querían reformar la Iglesia anglicana (pág. 78)

Q

Quakers Society of Friends; Protestant sect founded in 1640s in England whose members believed that salvation was available to all people (p. 86)
cuáqueros Sociedad de Amigos; secta protestante fundada en la década de 1640 en Inglaterra cuyos miembros creían que la salvación estaba al alcance de todos (pág. 86)

R

Radical Republicans members of Congress who felt that southern states needed to make great social changes before they could be readmitted to the Union (p. 559)
republicanos radicales miembros del Congreso convencidos de que los estados del Sur necesitaban hacer grandes cambios sociales antes de volver a ser admitidos en la Unión (pág. 559)

ratification an official approval (p. 154)
ratificación aprobación formal (pág. 154)

realpolitik a foreign policy in which U.S. interests are put over ethical or principled concerns (p. 928)
realpolitik política exterior según la cual los intereses de Estados Unidos están por encima de los asuntos éticos o de principios (pág. 928)

reason clear and ordered thinking; Greek philosopher Aristotle believed it was the basis of a good life (p. 22)
razón ideas claras y ordenadas; el filósofo griego Aristóteles pensaba que la razón era la base de una vida buena (pág. 22)

recall a vote to remove an official from office (p. 666)
destitución votación para sacar a un funcionario de su cargo (pág. 666)

Reconstruction (1865–1877) the period following the Civil War during which the U.S. government worked to reunite the nation and to rebuild the southern states (p. 552)
Reconstrucción (1865–1877) período posterior a la Guerra Civil en el que el gobierno de Estados Unidos trabajó por reunificar de la nación y reconstruir los estados del Sur (pág. 552)

Reconstruction Acts (1867–1868) the laws that put the southern states under U.S. military control and required them to draft new constitutions upholding the Fourteenth Amendment (p. 561)
Leyes de Reconstrucción (1867–1868) leyes que declaraban a los estados del Sur territorio sujeto al control militar estadounidense y los obligaban a reformar sus constituciones de manera que defendieran la Decimocuarta Enmienda (pág. 561)

Redcoats British soldiers who fought against the colonists in the American Revolution; so called because of their bright red uniforms (p. 114)
casacas rojas soldados británicos que lucharon contra los colonos en la Guerra de Independencia estadounidense, llamados así por el color rojo fuerte de sus uniformes (pág. 114)

Red Scare a widespread fear of communism and Communists (p. 760)
Terror Rojo miedo ampliamente difundido al comunismo y los comunistas (pág. 760)

referendum a procedure that allows voters to approve or reject a law already proposed or passed by government (p. 666)
referéndum proceso que permite a los votantes aprobar o rechazar una ley previamente propuesta o aprobada por el gobierno (pág. 666)

Republican Party a political party formed in the 1850s to stop the spread of slavery in the West (p. 488)
Partido Republicano partido político formado en la década de 1850 para detener la expansión de la esclavitud en el Oeste (pág. 488)

reparations financial payments by the loser of a war (p. 737)
indemnizaciones compensación económica pagada por el bando que es vencido en la guerra (pág. 737)

reservations federal lands set aside for American Indians (p. 595)
reservas territorios federales reservados para los indígenas norteamericanos (pág. 595)

Rhode Island system a system developed by Samuel Slater in the mid-1800s in which whole families were hired as textile workers and factory work was divided into simple tasks (p. 391)
sistema de Rhode Island sistema desarrollado por Samuel Slater a mediados del siglo XIX mediante el cual se contrataba a familias completas para trabajar en la industria textil y en el que el trabajo de las fábricas estaba dividido en tareas sencillas (pág. 391)

Roosevelt Corollary (1904) Theodore Roosevelt's addition to the Monroe Doctrine warning nations in the Americas that if they didn't pay their debts, the United States would get involved (p. 707)
Corolario de Roosevelt (1904) agregado del presidente Theodore Roosevelt a la Doctrina Monroe advirtiendo a las naciones de América que si no pagaban sus deudas, el gobierno de Estados Unidos intervendría (pág. 707)

Rush-Bagot Agreement (1817) an agreement that limited naval power on the Great Lakes for both the United States and British Canada (p. 298)
Acuerdo de Rush-Bagot (1817) acuerdo que limitaba el poder naval de Estados Unidos y la Canadá británica en los Grandes Lagos (pág. 298)

S

sanctions economic restrictions placed on a country in an attempt to change its policy decisions (p. 935)
sanciones restricciones económicas aplicadas a un país en un intento de cambiar sus políticas (pág. 935)

Santa Fe Trail an important trade trail west from Independence, Missouri, to Santa Fe, New Mexico (p. 349)
Camino de Santa Fe importante ruta comercial que va desde Independence, Missouri, hasta Santa Fe, Nuevo México (pág. 349)

Scopes trial a trial in which John Scopes was accused of teaching evolution illegally (p. 762)
juicio de Scopes juicio en el cual John Scopes fue acusado de enseñar ilegalmente la teoría de la evolución (pág. 762)

search-and-destroy missions the strategy used in the Vietnam War in which enemy targets were located and attacked (p. 903)
misiones de búsqueda y destrucción estrategia de localización y ataque de objetivos enemigos usada en la guerra de Vietnam (pág. 903)

search warrant a judge's order authorizing the search of a person's home or property to look for evidence of a crime (p. 218)
orden de registro orden de un juez que permite registrar el hogar y las pertenencias de una persona en busca de pruebas de un delito (pág. 218)

secede to formally withdraw from the Union (p. 478)
separarse salirse formalmente de la Unión (pág. 478)

Second Battle of Bull Run (1862) a Civil War battle in which the Confederate army forced most of the Union army out of Virginia (p. 518)
segunda batalla de Bull Run (1862) batalla de la Guerra Civil en la que el ejército confederado obligó a gran parte del ejército de la Unión a abandonar Virginia (pág. 518)

Second Continental Congress (1775) a meeting of colonial delegates in Philadelphia to decide how to react to fighting at Lexington and Concord (p. 114)
Segundo Congreso Continental (1775) reunión de delegados coloniales en Filadelfia para decidir cómo reaccionar ante la lucha en Lexington y Concord (pág. 114)

Second Great Awakening a period of religious evangelism that began in the 1790s and became widespread in the United States by the 1830s (p. 448)
Segundo Gran Despertar período de evangelización religiosa iniciado en la década de 1790 que se extendió por Estados Unidos para la década de 1830 (pág. 448)

Second Industrial Revolution a period of rapid growth in manufacturing and industry in the late 1800s (p. 615)
Segunda Revolución Industrial período de gran crecimiento en la manufactura y en la industria a finales del siglo XIX (pág. 615)

sectionalism a devotion to the interests of one geographic region over the interests of the country as a whole (p. 304, 477)
regionalismo lealtad a los intereses de una región geográfica más que a los del país entero (págs 304, 477)

segregation the forced separation of people of different races in public places (p. 568)
segregación separación obligada de personas de diferentes razas en lugares públicos (pág. 568)

Selective Service Act (1917) a law that allowed the president to draft soldiers in times of war (p. 727)
Ley de Servicio Selectivo (1917) ley que permitía al presidente reclutar soldados en épocas de guerra (pág. 727)

Seneca Falls Convention (1848) the first national women's rights convention at which the Declaration of Sentiments was written (p. 464)
Convención de Seneca Falls (1848) primera convención nacional a favor de los derechos de la mujer, en la cual se redactó la Declaración de Sentimientos (pág. 464)

service economy an economy in which most jobs involve providing services instead of producing goods (p. 960)
economía de servicios economía en la cual la mayoría de los trabajos consisten en ofrecer un servicio en lugar de producir bienes (pág. 960)

settlement houses neighborhood centers staffed by professionals and volunteers for education, recreation, and social activities in poor areas (p. 648)
organizaciones de servicio a la comunidad centros comunitarios atendidos por profesionales y voluntarios para ofrecer educación, recreación y actividades sociales en zonas pobres (pág. 648)

Seven Days' Battles (1862) a series of Civil War battles in which Confederate army successes forced the Union army to retreat from Richmond, Virginia, the Confederate capital (p. 518)
batallas de los Siete Días (1862) serie de batallas de la Guerra Civil en las que las victorias del ejército confederado obligaron a las tropas de la Unión a retirarse de Richmond, Virginia, la capital confederada (pág. 518)

Seventeenth Amendment (1913) a constitutional amendment allowing American voters to directly elect U.S. senators (p. 666)
Decimoséptima Enmienda (1913) enmienda constitucional que permite a los votantes estadounidenses elegir directamente a los senadores de Estados Unidos (pág. 666)

sharecropping a system used on southern farms after the Civil War in which farmers worked land owned by someone else in return for a small portion of the crops (p. 569)
cultivo de aparceros sistema usado en las granjas sureñas después de la Guerra Civil en el que los agricultores trabajaban las tierras de otra persona a cambio de una pequeña porción de la cosecha (pág. 569)

Shays's Rebellion (1786-87) an uprising of Massachusetts's farmers, led by Daniel Shays, to protest high taxes, heavy debt, and farm foreclosures (p. 161)
Rebelión de Shays (1786-87) rebelión de agricultores de Massachusetts, encabezados por Daniel Shays, para protestar por los altos impuestos, las grandes deudas y el embargo de las granjas (pág. 161)

Sherman Antitrust Act (1890) a law that made it illegal to create monopolies or trusts that restrained free trade (p. 622)
Ley Antimonopolio de Sherman (1890) ley que prohibía la creación de monopolios o consorcios que restringieran el libre comercio (pág. 622)

Siege of Vicksburg (1863) the Union army's six-week blockade of Vicksburg that led the city to surrender during the Civil War (p. 524)
Sitio de Vicksburg (1863) bloqueo de seis semanas realizado por el ejército de la Unión en Vicksburg para forzar la rendición de esa ciudad durante la Guerra Civil (pág. 524)

sit-down strike a strike in which workers stay at their work stations so that strikebreakers cannot replace them (p. 788)
huelga de brazos caídos huelga en la cual los trabajadores permanecen en el lugar de trabajo para que los rompehuelgas no los puedan reemplazar (pág. 788)

sit-in a form of protest in which African Americans sat at segregated lunch counters and requested service (p. 874)
sentada forma de protesta de los afroamericanos; se sentaban en los comedores que practicaban la segregación racial y pedían que les sirvieran (pág. 874)

Sixteenth Amendment (1913) an amendment to the Constitution that allows personal income to be taxed (p. 683)
Decimosexta Enmienda (1913) enmienda constitucional que permite los impuestos sobre los ingresos personales (pág. 683)

slave codes laws passed in the colonies to control slaves (p. 77)
códigos de esclavos leyes aprobadas por las colonias para controlar a los esclavos (pág. 77)

social Darwinism a view of society based on Charles Darwin's scientific theory of natural selection (p. 621)
darwinismo social visión de la sociedad basada en la teoría científica de la selección natural de Charles Darwin (pág. 621)

socialism economic system in which the government owns and operates a country's means of production (p. 674)
socialismo sistema económico en el que el gobierno controla y maneja los medios de producción de un país (pág. 674)

sodbusters the name given to Plains farmers who worked hard to break up the region's tough sod (p. 601)
sodbusters nombre dado a los agricultores de las Planicies que se esforzaron mucho para trabajar el duro terreno de la región (pág. 601)

Social Security Act (1935) a law that instituted the pension plan Social Security (p. 787)
Ley del Seguro Social (1935) ley que estableció el plan de pensiones del Seguro Social (pág. 787)

Spanish Armada a large Spanish fleet defeated by England in 1588 (p. 53)
Armada española gran flota española derrotada por las tropas de Inglaterra en 1588 (pág. 53)

speculator an investor who buys items at low prices in hope that their values will rise (p. 239)
especulador inversionista que compra artículos a precios bajos con la esperanza de que su valor aumente (pág. 239)

sphere of influence an area where foreign countries control trade or natural resources of another nation or area (p. 695)
esfera de influencia nación o lugar cuyos recursos naturales y comercio son controlados por otro país (pág. 695)

spirituals emotional Christian songs sung by enslaved people in the South that mixed African and European elements and usually expressed slaves' religious beliefs (p. 427)
espirituales canciones religiosas emotivas cantadas por los esclavos del Sur que combinaban elementos de origen africano y europeo y solían expresar sus creencias religiosas (pág. 427)

spoils system a politicians' practice of giving government jobs to his or her supporters (p. 324)
tráfico de influencias práctica de los políticos de ofrecer empleos a las personas que los apoyan (pág. 324)

Sputnik the first artificial satellite, launched by the Soviet Union in 1957 (p. 856)
Sputnik primer satélite artificial, lanzado por la Unión Soviética en 1957 (pág. 856)

stagflation a term describing a slowing economy mixed with high unemployment (p. 927)
estagflación término que describe una economía que disminuye su ritmo, acompañado de un desempleo alto (pág. 927)

stalemate a situation in which neither side can win a victory (p. 723)
punto muerto situación en la cual ninguna de las partes puede alcanzar la victoria (pág. 723)

Stamp Act of 1765 a law passed by Parliament that raised tax money by requiring colonists to pay for an official stamp whenever they bought paper items such as newspapers, licenses, and legal documents (p. 100)
Ley del Sello de 1765 ley aprobada por el Parlamento para recaudar impuestos en la que se obligaba a los colonos a pagar un sello oficial cada vez que compraran artículos de papel, como periódicos, licencias y documentos legales (pág. 100)

staple crop a crop that is continuously in demand (p. 87)
cultivo básico cultivo de demanda constante (pág. 87)

states' rights doctrine the belief that the power of the states should be greater than the power of the federal government (p. 328)
doctrina de los derechos estatales creencia de que el poder de los estados debe ser mayor que el del gobierno federal (pág. 328)

steerage the area on a ship in the lower levels where the steering mechanisms were located and where cramped quarters were provided for people who could only afford cheap passage (p. 637)
tercera clase nivel inferior un barco en el que se encontraban los mecanismos del timón y se ofrecían habitaciones reducidas para las personas que sólo podían comprar un pasaje barato (pág. 637)

Strategic Arms Limitation Talks (SALT) negotiations between the United States and the Soviet Union designed to limit nuclear weapons (p. 928)
Tratados de Limitación de Armas Estratégicas (SALT, por sus siglas en inglés) negociaciones entre Estados Unidos y la Unión Soviética diseñadas para limitar el número de armas nucleares (pág. 928)

strict construction a way of interpreting the Constitution that allows the federal government to take only those actions the Constitution specifically says it can take (p. 242)
interpretación estricta interpretación de la Constitución que sólo permite al gobierno federal hacer las acciones mencionadas específicamente en ella (pág. 242)

strike the refusal of workers to perform their jobs until employers meet their demands (p. 394)
huelga negativa de los empleados a trabajar hasta que sus empleadores satisfagan sus demandas (pág. 394)

Student Nonviolent Coordinating Committee (SNCC) a group organized to promote civil rights for African Americans through nonviolent protests (p. 874)
Comité Coordinador Estudiantil No Violento (SNCC, por sus siglas en inglés) grupo organizado para promover los derechos civiles de los afroamericanos con protestas no violentas (pág. 874)

Students for a Democratic Society (SDS) a group organized to protest U.S. involvement in the Vietnam War (p. 908)
Estudiantes por una Sociedad Democrática (SDS, por sus siglas en inglés) grupo organizado para protestar por la participación de Estados Unidos en la guerra de Vietnam (pág. 908)

suburb a neighborhood outside of a downtown area (p. 644)
suburbio vecindario en las afueras de una ciudad (pág. 644)

suffrage voting rights (p. 153)
sufragio derecho al voto (pág. 153)

Sun Belt the southern area of the United States from Florida to California that experienced an increase in population during the 1970s (p. 858)
Sun Belt área del sur de Estados Unidos, desde Florida hasta California, en la que hubo un aumento de la población durante la década de 1970 (pág. 858)

supply-side economics economic theory that focuses on influencing the supply of labor and goods; it usually involves sharp tax cuts (p. 938)
economía de la oferta teoría económica que pretende influenciar la oferta de mano de obra y de bienes; por lo general, implica grandes reducciones de impuestos (pág. 938)

sweatshops hot, stuffy workshops in which workers prepare materials for low wages (p. 640)
fábricas explotadoras talleres calurosos y con el aire cargado en los cuales los trabajadores preparan materiales por salarios reducidos (pág. 640)

T

talkie a film that includes sound (p. 766)
película sonora película que incluye sonido (pág. 766)

tariff a tax on imports or exports (p. 159)
arancel impuesto pagado por las importaciones o exportaciones (pág. 159)

Tariff of Abominations (1828) the nickname given to a tariff by southerners who opposed it (p. 327)
Arancel de Abominaciones (1828) sobrenombre dado a un arancel por los habitantes del Sur que se oponían a éste (pág. 327)

Tea Act (1773) a law passed by Parliament allowing the British East India Company to sell its low-cost tea directly to the colonies, undermining colonial tea merchants; led to the Boston Tea Party (p. 102)
Ley del Té (1773) ley aprobada por el Parlamento británico que le permitía a la British East India Company vender té a bajo costo a las colonias directamente, afectando a los comerciantes de té coloniales; dio origen al Motín del Té de Boston (pág. 102)

Teapot Dome scandal a scandal under the Harding adminstration in which government officials were accused of taking bribes to allow oil to be mined from federal lands (p. 753)
escándalo de Teapot Dome escándalo durante el gobierno de Harding en el que se acusó a funcionarios del gobierno de aceptar sobornos para permitir que se usaran tierras federales para extraer petróleo (pág. 753)

technology the tools used to produce goods or to do work (p. 387)
tecnología herramientas utilizadas para producir bienes o realizar un trabajo (pág. 387)

teepees cone-shaped shelters made of buffalo skins used by Native Americans in the Plains region (p. 14)
tipis viviendas en forma de cono hechas de piel de búfalo que usaban los indígenas norteamericanos en la región de las Planicies (pág. 14)

telegraph a machine perfected by Samuel F. B. Morse in 1832 that uses pulses of electric current to send messages across long distances through wires (p. 402)
telégrafo máquina perfeccionada por Samuel F. B. Morse en 1832 que emplea impulsos eléctricos transmitidos por cables para enviar mensajes a grandes distancias (pág. 402)

Teller Amendment (1898) a congressional resolution stating that the U.S. had no interest in taking control of Cuba (p. 698)
Enmienda Teller (1898) resolución del Congreso en la que Estados Unidos declaró que no tenía intención de tomar el control de Cuba (pág. 698)

temperance movement a social reform effort begun in the mid-1800s to encourage people to drink less alcohol (p. 449)
movimiento de abstinencia movimiento de reforma social iniciado a mediados del siglo XIX para promover el que las personas bebieran menos alcohol (pág. 449)

tenements poorly built, overcrowded housing where many immigrants lived (p. 442)
casas de vecindad viviendas mal construidas y llenas de gente donde vivían muchos inmigrantes (pág. 442)

Tennessee Valley Authority (TVA) a governmental agency designed to bring jobs and electricity to rural areas of the Tennessee River valley (p. 785)
Autoridad del Valle del Tennessee (TVA, por sus siglas en inglés) agencia del gobierno destinada a proveer empleos y energía eléctrica a las áreas rurales del valle del río Tennessee (pág. 785)

Ten Percent Plan President Abraham Lincoln's plan for Reconstruction; once 10 percent of voters in a former Confederate state took a U.S. loyalty oath, they could form a new state government and be readmitted to the Union (p. 553)
Plan del Diez por Ciento plan de Reconstrucción del presidente Abraham Lincoln; si el 10 por ciento de los votantes de un estado que había sido confederado juraba lealtad a la nación, podían formar un nuevo gobierno y ser readmitidos en la Unión (pág. 553)

terrorism the systematic use of fear or terror to gain goals (p. 953)
terrorismo uso sistemático del miedo o el terror para alcanzar objetivos (pág. 953)

Tet Offensive (1968) a series of attacks by Vietcong forces that proved to many Americans the Vietnam War was not being won (p. 904)
ofensiva del Tet (1968) serie de ataques de las fuerzas del Vietcong que demostró a muchos estadounidenses que no estaban ganando la guerra de Vietnam (pág. 904)

textile cloth (p. 385)
textil tela (pág. 385)

Thirteenth Amendment (1865) a constitutional amendment that outlawed slavery (p. 554)
Decimotercera Enmienda (1865) enmienda constitucional que prohibió la esclavitud (pág. 554)

38th Parallel the boundary between North and South Korea before the Korean War (p. 852)
paralelo 38 límite entre Corea del Sur y Corea del Norte antes de la Guerra de Corea (pág. 852)

Three-Fifths Compromise (1787) an agreement worked out at the Constitutional Convention stating that only three-fifths of the slaves in a state would count when determining a state's population for representation in the lower house of Congress (p. 166)
Compromiso de las Tres Quintas Partes (1787) acuerdo negociado durante la Convención Constitucional en el que se estableció que solamente tres quintas de los esclavos en un estado contarían para al determinar la representación de ese estado en la cámara baja del Congreso (pág. 166)

Toleration Act of 1649 a Maryland law that made restricting the religious rights of Christians a crime; the first law guaranteeing religious freedom to be passed in America (p. 75)
Ley de Tolerancia de 1649 ley de Maryland que calificaba como delito la restricción de los derechos religiosos de los cristianos; fue la primera ley que garantizó la libertad religiosa en América (pág. 75)

Tonkin Gulf Resolution (1964) gave President Johnson the power to send combat troops to Vietnam (p. 902)
Resolución del Golfo de Tonkin (1964) otorgó al presidente Johnson la autoridad de enviar tropas de combate a Vietnam (pág. 902)

totalitarianism a form of government in which every aspect of citizen's lives are controlled by the government (p. 804)
totalitarismo forma de gobierno en la cual todos los aspectos de la vida de los ciudadanos están bajo el control del gobierno (pág. 804)

total war a type of war in which an army destroys its opponent's ability to fight by targeting civilian and economic as well as military resources (p. 542)
guerra total tipo de guerra en la que un ejército destruye la capacidad de lucha de su oponente mediante ataques a la población civil y a la economía así como a los recursos militares (pág. 542)

totems images of ancestors or animal spirits; often carved onto tall, wooden poles by Native American peoples of the Pacific Northwest (p. 12)
tótems imágenes de antepasados o espíritus de animales; a menudo talladas en altos troncos de madera por los indígenas americanos de la costa noroeste del Pacífico (pág. 12)

town meeting a political meeting at which people make decisions on local issues; used primarily in New England (p. 91)
reunión del pueblo reunión política en la que las personas toman decisiones sobre temas locales; se usan principalmente en Nueva Inglaterra (pág. 91)

trade unions workers' organizations that try to improve working conditions (p. 394)
sindicatos organizaciones de trabajadores que intentan mejorar sus condiciones laborales (pág. 394)

Trail of Tears (1838-39) an 800-mile forced march made by the Cherokee from their homeland in Georgia to Indian Territory; resulted in the deaths of almost one fourth of the Cherokee people (p. 334)
Ruta de las Lágrimas (1838-39) marcha forzada de 800 millas que hicieron los cheroquíes desde su territorio natal en Georgia hasta el Territorio Indígena, y en la que perdió la vida casi una cuarta parte del pueblo cheroquí (pág. 334)

transcendentalism the idea that people could rise above the material things in life; a popular movement among New England writers and thinkers in the mid-1800s (p. 443)
trascendentalismo creencia de que las personas podían prescindir de los objetos materiales en la vida; movimiento popular entre los escritores y pensadores de Nueva Inglaterra a mediados del siglo XIX (pág. 443)

transcontinental railroad a railroad system that crossed the continental United States; construction began in 1863 (p. 590)
tren transcontinental línea ferroviaria que cruzaba Estados Unidos de un extremo a otro; su construcción se inició en 1863 (pág. 590)

Transportation Revolution the rapid growth in the speed and convenience of transportation (p. 396)
Revolución del Transporte rápido desarrollo de la velocidad y comodidad de los medios de transporte (pág. 396)

Treaty of Fort Jackson (1814) a treaty signed after the U.S. victory at the Battle of Horseshoe Bend; the Creek were forced to give up 23 million acres of their land (p. 286)
Tratado del Fuerte Jackson (1814) tratado que se firmó tras la victoria de Estados Unidos en la batalla de Horseshoe Bend; los indígenas creek se vieron obligados a ceder 23 millones de acres de su territorio (pág. 286)

Treaty of Fort Laramie (1851) a treaty signed in Wyoming by the United States and northern Plains nations (p. 594)
Tratado del Fuerte Laramie (1851) tratado firmado en Wyoming por Estados Unidos y las naciones indígenas de las Planicies del norte (pág. 594)

Treaty of Ghent (1814) a treaty signed by the United States and Britain ending the War of 1812 (p. 287)
Tratado de Gante (1814) tratado firmado por Estados Unidos y Gran Bretaña para dar fin a la Guerra de 1812 (pág. 287)

Treaty of Greenville (1795) an agreement between Native American confederation leaders and the U.S. government that gave the United States Indian lands in the Northwest Territory and guaranteed that U.S. citizens could safely travel through the region (p. 247)
Tratado de Greenville (1795) acuerdo entre los líderes de la confederación de indígenas norteamericanos y el gobierno estadounidense que otorgó a Estados Unidos tierras indígenas en el Territorio del Noroeste y garantizó la seguridad a los ciudadanos estadounidenses que viajaran por la región (pág. 247)

Treaty of Guadalupe Hidalgo (1848) a treaty that ended the Mexican-American War and gave the United States much of Mexico's northern territory (p. 361)
Tratado de Guadalupe Hidalgo (1848) tratado que daba por terminada la Guerra contra México y daba a Estados Unidos gran parte del norte del territorio mexicano (pág. 361)

Treaty of Medicine Lodge (1867) an agreement between the U.S. government and southern Plains Indians in which the Indians agreed to move onto reservations (p. 595)
Tratado de Medicine Lodge (1867) acuerdo entre el gobierno de Estados Unidos y los indígenas de las Planicies del sur en el que los indígenas aceptaron irse a las reservas (pág. 595)

Treaty of Paris of 1783 a peace agreement that officially ended the Revolutionary War and established British recognition of the independence of the United States (p. 139)
Tratado de París de 1783 acuerdo de paz que oficialmente dio por terminada la Guerra de Independencia estadounidense y en el que Gran Bretaña reconocía la independencia de Estados Unidos (pág. 139)

Treaty of Tordesillas (1494) a treaty between Spain and Portugal that moved the Line of Demarcation (p. 44)
Tratado de Tordesillas (1494) tratado entre España y Portugal que modificó la Línea de Demarcación (pág. 44)

Treaty of Versailles (1919) brought an end to World War I, but was never ratified by the United States (p. 738)
Tratado de Versalles (1919) puso fin a la Primera Guerra Mundial, pero Estados Unidos nunca lo ratificó (pág. 738)

Tredegar Iron Works a large iron factory that operated in Richmond, Virginia, in the early to mid-1800s (p. 419)
Tredegar Iron Works gran fábrica de acero que operaba a mediados del siglo XIX en Richmond, Virginia (pág. 419)

trench warfare a new kind of warfare in World War I that involved troops digging and fighting from deep trenches (p. 722)
guerra de trincheras nuevo tipo de guerra utilizado en la Primera Guerra Mundial en el cual las tropas cavaban trincheras profundas y luchaban desde ellas (pág. 722)

Triangle Shirtwaist Fire a factory fire that killed 146 workers trapped in the building; led to new safety standard laws (p. 673)
incendio de Triangle Shirtwaist incendio de una fábrica en el que murieron 146 trabajadores atrapados en el edificio; este suceso obligó a crear nuevas leyes de seguridad (pág. 673)

triangular trade trading networks in which goods and slaves moved among England, the American colonies, and Africa (p. 93)
comercio triangular redes comerciales en las que los bienes y los esclavos se intercambiaban entre Inglaterra, las colonias americanas y África (pág. 93)

Truman Doctrine a policy attempting to contain the spread of communism, beginning with military aid to the monarchies of Turkey and Greece (p. 847)
Doctrina Truman política que intentaba contener el avance del comunismo, ofreciendo inicialmente ayuda militar a las monarquías de Turquía y Grecia (pág. 847)

trust a number of companies legally grouped under a single board of directors (p. 621)
consorcio varias compañías agrupadas legalmente bajo el mando de una sola junta directiva (pág. 621)

Tuskegee Airmen a group of African American pilots who flew missions in World War I; they were the first African American military pilots (p. 812)
Aviadores de Tuskegee grupo de pilotos afroamericanos que volaron en misiones de la Primera Guerra Mundial; fueron los primeros pilotos afroamericanos del ejército (pág. 812)

Twenty-first Amendment (1933) an amendment to the Constitution that ended Prohibition (p. 761)
Vigésimoprimera Enmienda (1933) enmienda constitucional que puso fin a la Ley Seca (pág. 761)

Twenty-sixth Amendment (1971) an amendment to the Constitution that lowered the voting age to 18 (p. 911)
Vigésimosexta Enmienda (1971) enmienda constitucional que redujo la edad mínima para votar a 18 años (pág. 911)

U

U-boats German submarines or "untersee boats" (p. 724)
U-boats submarinos alemanes o "barcos untersee" (pág. 724)

Uncle Tom's Cabin (1852) an antislavery novel written by Harriet Beecher Stowe that showed northerners the violent reality of slavery and drew many people to the abolitionists' cause (p. 481)
La cabaña del tío Tom (1852) novela abolicionista escrita por Harriet Beecher Stowe que mostró a los habitantes del norte del país la violenta realidad de la esclavitud e hizo que muchos se unieran a la causa abolicionista (pág. 481)

Underground Railroad a network of people who helped thousands of enslaved people escape to the North by providing transportation and hiding places (p. 456)
Tren Clandestino red de personas que ayudó a miles de esclavos a escapar al Norte ofreciéndoles transporte y lugares para esconderse (pág. 456)

United Farm Workers a group organized to promote the interests of migrant farm workers, it eventually led to the Chicano movement (p. 882)
Trabajadores Agrícolas Unidos grupo organizado para promover los intereses de los trabajadores agrícolas migratorios; con el tiempo, dio origen al movimiento chicano (pág. 882)

United Nations an alliance of nations that attempts to end disputes between countries peacefully (p. 846)
Naciones Unidas alianza de naciones que intenta resolver de manera pacífica las disputas entre los países (pág. 846)

USS *Constitution* a large warship (p. 278)
USS *Constitution* gran buque de guerra (pág. 278)

urban renewal a governmental program that attempted to rid innercities of slums and replace them with low- and middle-income housing (p. 859)
renovación urbana programa gubernamental que intentó eliminar las barriadas de los centros urbanos y reemplazarlos con viviendas para personas de recursos bajos y medios (pág. 859)

utopian communities places where people worked to establish a perfect society; such communities were popular in the United States during the late 1700s and early to mid-1800s (p. 444)
comunidades utópicas lugares en los que un grupo de personas trabajaba para establecer una sociedad perfecta; se popularizaron en Estados Unidos a finales del siglo XVIII y principios y mediados del XIX (pág. 444)

V

vaqueros Mexican cowboys in the West who tended cattle and horses (p. 357)
vaqueros arrieros mexicanos que vivían en el Oeste y se ganaban la vida ocupándose del ganado y los caballos (pág. 357)

vertical integration the business practice of owning all of the businesses involved in each step of a manufacturing process (p. 620)
integración vertical práctica empresarial de poseer todas las empresas que participan en cada paso de un proceso de manufactura (pág. 620)

veto to cancel a law (p. 184)
vetar cancelar una ley (pág. 184)

Vietcong the South Vietnam forces that were supported by North Vietnamese Communists (p. 899)
Vietcong fuerzas de Vietnam del Sur apoyadas por los comunistas de Vietnam del Norte (pág. 899)

Vietnamization a policy introduced in an attempt to leave the Vietnam War, in which Vietnamese forces would take over the fighting (p. 910)
vietnamización política introducida en un intento de salir de la guerra de Vietnam, según la cual las fuerzas vietnamitas se harían cargo de la lucha (pág. 910)

Vietnam Veterans Memorial a war memorial in Washington, D.C., dedicated to the veterans of Vietnam (p. 913)
Monumento a los Veteranos de Vietnam monumento conmemorativo de la guerra en Washington, D.C. dedicado a los veteranos de Vietnam (pág. 913)

Virginia Plan (1787) the plan for government proposed at the Constitutional Convention in which the national government would have supreme power and a legislative branch would have two houses with representation determined by state population (p. 164)
Plan de Virginia (1787) plan de gobierno propuesto en la Convención Constitucional por el que el gobierno nacional tendría poder supremo y habría un poder legislativo con dos cámaras en las que la representación de cada estado sería determinada por su población (pág. 164)

Virginia Statute for Religious Freedom (1786) a document that gave people in Virginia freedom of worship and prohibited tax money from being used to fund churches (p. 153)
Estatuto de Virginia para la Libertad Religiosa (1786) documento que reconocía a los habitantes de Virginia la libertad de culto y prohibía utilizar los impuestos para financiar iglesias (pág. 153)

Voting Rights Act of 1965 provided new powers to the federal government to protect African Americans' voting rights (p. 879)
Ley de Derecho al Voto de 1965 dio nueva autoridad al gobierno federal para proteger el derecho al voto de los afroamericanos (pág. 879)

W

War Hawks members of Congress who wanted to declare war against Britain after the Battle of Tippecanoe (p. 282)
halcones de guerra miembros del Congreso que querían declarar la guerra a Gran Bretaña tras la batalla de Tippecanoe (pág. 282)

War Powers Act (1973) a law that requires a president to get Congressional approval before sending troops into combat (p. 913)
Ley de Poderes de Guerra (1973) ley que requiere la aprobación del Congreso para que el presidente pueda enviar tropas a la guerra (pág. 913)

War Production Board a government agency set up to oversee production of war materials during World War II (p. 810)
Junta de Producción de Guerra agencia creada por el gobierno para supervisar la producción de materiales de guerra durante la Segunda Guerra Mundial (pág. 810)

Watergate a scandal in which President Nixon resigned over accusations of illegal activity (p. 929)
Watergate escándalo que provocó la renuncia del presidente Nixon por acusaciones de actividades ilegales (pág. 929)

weapons of mass destruction chemical, biological, or nuclear weapons that can kill thousands (p. 957)
armas de destrucción masiva armas químicas, biológicas o nucleares que pueden matar a miles de personas (pág. 957)

Whig Party a political party formed in 1834 by opponents of Andrew Jackson and who supported a strong legislature (p. 330)
Partido Whig partido político formado en 1834 por oponentes de Andrew Jackson que apoyaba una asamblea legislativa con mucha autoridad (pág. 330)

Whiskey Rebellion (1794) a protest of small farmers in Pennsylvania against new taxes on whiskey (p. 247)
Rebelión del Whisky (1794) protesta de pequeños agricultores de Pensilvania contra los nuevos impuestos sobre el whisky (pág. 247)

Wilderness Campaign (1864) a series of battles between Union and Confederate forces in northern and central Virginia that delayed the Union capture of Richmond (p. 540)
Campaña de Wilderness (1864) serie de batallas entre la Unión y los confederados en el norte y el centro de Virginia que retrasaron la captura de Richmond por parte de la Unión (pág. 540)

Wilmot Proviso (1846) a proposal to outlaw slavery in the territory added to the United States by the Mexican Cession; passed in the House of Representatives but was defeated in the Senate (p. 476)
Condición de Wilmot (1846) propuesta de prohibir la esclavitud en el territorio anexado a Estados Unidos por la Cesión Mexicana; aprobada por la Cámara de Representantes, pero rechazada por el Senado (pág. 476)

Worcester v. _Georgia_ (1832) the Supreme Court ruling that stated that the Cherokee nation was a distinct territory over which only the federal government had authority; ignored by both President Andrew Jackson and the state of Georgia (p. 334)
Worcester contra Georgia (1832) decisión de la Corte Suprema que establecía que la nación cheroquí era un territorio distinto sobre el que sólo el gobierno federal tenía autoridad; fue ignorada por el presidente Andrew Jackson y por el estado de Georgia (pág. 334)

World Trade Center a complex of several office buildings that were attacked by terrorists (p. 956)
World Trade Center complejo de varios edificios de oficinas que fue atacado por terroristas (pág. 956)

X

XYZ affair (1797) an incident in which French agents attempted to get a bribe and loans from U.S. diplomats in exchange for an agreement that French privateers would no longer attack American ships; it led to an undeclared naval war between the two countries (p. 252)
asunto XYZ (1797) incidente en el que funcionarios franceses intentaron obtener sobornos y préstamos de diplomáticos estadounidenses a cambio de un acuerdo por el cual sus corsarios no atacarían más a los barcos estadounidenses; provocó una guerra no declarada entre las fuerzas navales de ambas naciones (pág. 252)

Y

Yalta Conference a meeting between the leaders of the Allied powers that resulted in a plan for peace after World War II (p. 844)
Conferencia de Yalta reunión de los líderes de las fuerzas aliadas que produjo un plan de paz despúes de la Segunda Guerra Mundial (pág. 844)

yellow journalism the reporting of exaggerated stories in newspapers to increase sales (p. 697)
prensa amarillista publicación de noticias exageradas en los periódicos para aumentar las ventas (pág. 697)

yeomen owners of small farms (p. 422)
pequeños terratenientes dueños de granjas pequeñas (pág. 422)

Z

Zimmermann note a telegram from Germany to Mexico offering Mexico a return of territory in exchange for declaring war on the United States (p. 726)
telegrama Zimmermann telegrama de Alemania a México en el cual se ofrecía a México una devolución de territorios si le declaraba la guerra a Estados Unidos (pág. 726)

zoot-suit riots a series of riots during which Mexican Americans were attacked by whites (p. 813)
disturbios _zoot-suit_ serie de disturbios durante los cuales personas de raza blanca atacaron a mexicano-americanos (pág. 813)

Index

KEY TO INDEX

c = chart	*p* = photo
f = feature	*R* = Reference
m = map	

A

INDEX

B

INDEX

C

D

E

INDEX

F

G

H

I

INDEX

J

M

INDEX

N

Q

R

INDEX

T

U

INDEX

X

Y

Z